COMEDK

13 Years'

SOLVED PAPERS

2024-2012

5 Mock Tests

for 2025 Exam

COMEDK

13 Years'
SOLVED PAPERS
2024-2012

5 Mock Tests
for 2025 Exam

Authors
Sagar, Vikas, SN Sharma

arihant
SUCCESS AND NOTHING LESS

arihant
SUCCESS AND NOTHING LESS

ARIHANT PRAKASHAN (Series), MEERUT

卐 **Administrative & Production Offices**

Regd. Office
'Ramchhaya' 4577/15, Agarwal Road, Darya Ganj, New Delhi -110002
Tele: 011- 47630600, 43518550

卐 **Head Office**
Kalindi, TP Nagar, Meerut (UP) - 250002
Tel: 0121-7156203, 7156204

卐 **Sales & Support Offices**
Agra, Ahmedabad, Bengaluru, Bareilly, Chennai, Delhi, Guwahati, Hyderabad, Jaipur, Jhansi, Kolkata, Lucknow, Nagpur & Pune.

卐 **PRICE** ₹565.00

卐 **PO No :** TXT-XX-XXXXXXX-X-XX

Published by Arihant Publications (India) Ltd.

For further information about the books published by Arihant, log on to www.arihantbooks.com or e-mail at info@arihantbooks.com

Follow us on

PREFACE

Whenever a student decides to prepare for any examination his/her first and foremost curiosity is to know about the type of questions that are expected in the exam. This becomes more important in the context of competitive examinations where there is neck-to-neck competition.

We feel great pleasure in presenting before you this book containing Error Free Solutions of previous years' **COMEDK** Entrance Exams. Going through this book, you will get an exact idea of the questions generally asked in COMEDK.

We have made maximum efforts to provide correct solutions to the best of our knowledge and opinion. Solutions are not just sketchy–rather, have been drafted in a manner that the students will surely be able to solve some other related problems too. In this way, the students shall be able to judge the extent upto which they have been able to comprehend the methods.

Along with past exams solutions, the book also has **5 Mock Tests** framed exactly on latest pattern & trend of COMEDK. These Mock Tests will help you to assess your preparation level before the exam.

We hope, these sets of papers along with error free solutions would be highly beneficial to the students. We would be grateful if any discrepancy or mistake in the questions or answers is brought to our notice so that these could be rectified in subsequent editions.

Publisher

CONTENTS

SOLVED PAPERS

MOCK TESTS

COMEDK

Solved Paper 2024

Instructions

- There are 180 questions in all. The number of questions in each section is as given below.

Sections	No. of Questions
Section I : Physics	1-60
Section II : Chemistry	61-120
Section III : Mathematics	121-180

- All the questions are Multiple Choice Questions having four options out of which **ONLY ONE** is correct.
- Candidates will be awarded 1 mark for each correct answer. There will be no negative marking for incorrect answer.

PHYSICS

1. The acceleration of a train between two stations is shown in the figure. The maximum speed of the train is

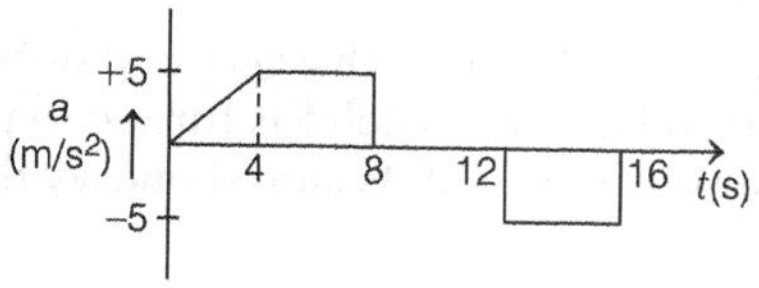

a. 60 m/s   *b.* 30 m/s
c. 120 m/s   *d.* 90 m/s

2. A hydraulic automobile lift is designed to lift cars with a maximum mass of 3000 kg. The area of cross-section of the piston carrying the board is 425 cm^2. What maximum pressure would smaller piston have to bear?

a. 5.2×10^4 Pa
b. 4.2×10^5 Pa
c. 6.92×10^4 Pa
d. 5.92×10^5 Pa

3. An electric bulb is rated at 220 V and 100 W. Power consumed by bulb when operated at 110 V will be

a. 50 W   *b.* 75 W
c. 100 W   *d.* 25 W

4. Calculate the radius of the second Bohr's orbit of electron of hydrogen atom.

a. 3.68 Å   *b.* 2.12 Å
c. 4.77 Å   *d.* 2.68 Å

5. The radius of curvature of the curved surface of a plano-convex lens is 60 cm. If refractive index of the material of prism is 1.6, then focal length of the lens is

a. 100 cm   *b.* 80 cm
c. 60 cm   *d.* 120 cm

6. In a helium ion, if potential energy of electron in ground state is assumed to be zero, then its energy in first excited state is equal to

a. 13.6 eV   *b.* 27.2 eV
c. 54.4 eV   *d.* 95.2 eV

7. Electromagnetic waves travel in a medium with a speed of 2×10^8 ms^{-1}. The relative permeability of the medium is 1. The value of relative permittivity of medium is

a. 1.95   *b.* 7.21   *c.* 3.36   *d.* 2.25

8. Which of the following does not change during refraction of light?

a. Velocity   *b.* Wavelength
c. Frequency   *d.* Intensity

9. In forward biasing of a *p-n* junction,

a. electrons move from lower to higher energy level
b. electrons move from higher to lower energy level
c. holes in valence band move from higher energy level to lower energy level
d. None of the above

10. Two diodes of silicon and germanium are connected in series as shown below. The current flowing through the circuit will be around

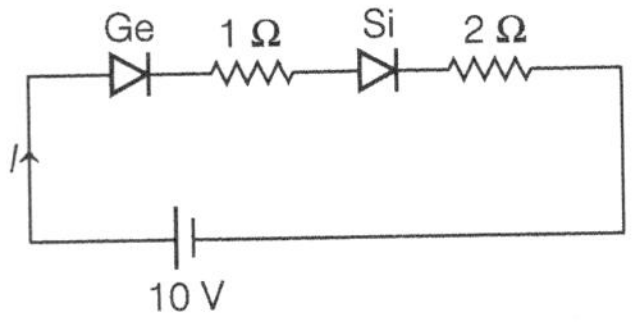

a. 0 *b.* 3 A
c. 4 A *d.* 3.5 A

11. A 5.80 μF parallel plate air capacitor has a plate separation of 5 mm and is charged to a potential difference of 400 V. The energy density in the region between the plates is

a. $2.83 \times 10^{-2}\ \text{J/m}^3$ *b.* $2.83\ \text{J/m}^3$
c. $2.83 \times 10^{-4}\ \text{J/m}^3$ *d.* $2.83 \times 10^{6}\ \text{J/m}^3$

12. A charge q is enclosed by an imaginary Gaussian surface.

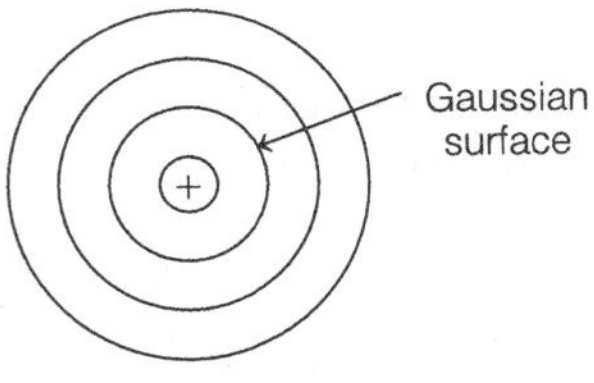

If the radius of Gaussian surface is increasing at a rate $\frac{dr}{dt} = \alpha$, then flux linked with surface is

a. increasing at a rate, $\frac{d\phi}{dt} = \alpha$
b. decreasing at a rate, $\frac{d\phi}{dt} = -\alpha$
c. decreasing at a rate, $\frac{d\phi}{dt} = \frac{1}{k}$
d. $\frac{q}{\varepsilon_0}$

13. A circular ring of radius r is placed in a homogeneous magnetic field perpendicular to the plane of the ring. The field B changes with time according to the equation $B = Kt$, where K is a constant and t is the time. The electric field in the ring is

a. $\frac{Kr}{4}$ *b.* $\frac{Kr}{3}$
c. $\frac{Kr}{2}$ *d.* $\frac{K}{2r}$

14. O is the centre of an equilateral triangle ABC. F_1, F_2 and F_3 are three forces acting along the sides AB, BC and AC as shown in figure.

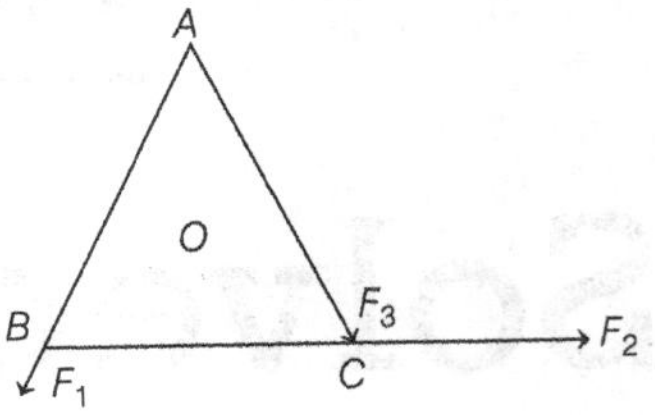

What should be the magnitude of F_3, so that the total torque about O is zero?

a. $\frac{(F_1 + F_2)}{2}$ *b.* $(F_1 - F_2)$
c. $(F_1 + F_2)$ *d.* $2(F_1 + F_2)$

15. The heat generated in a wire depends on the resistance, current and time. If the error in measuring the above are 1%, 2% and 1%, respectively, the maximum error in measuring the heat is

a. 8% *b.* 6%
c. 18% *d.* 12%

16. A thin copper wire of length L increases in length by 1%, when heated from temperature T_1 to T_2. What is the percentage change in area when a thin copper plate having dimensions $(10L \times 2L)$ is heated from T_1 to T_2?

a. 2% *b.* 20%
c. 10% *d.* 40%

17. A capacitor of 2 μF is charged as shown in the figure. When the switch S is turned to position 2, the percentage of its stored energy dissipated is

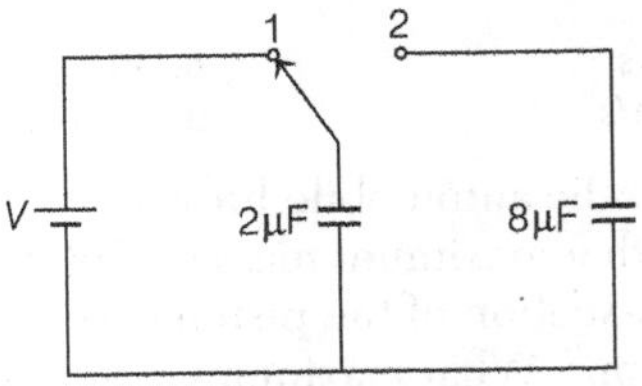

a. 40% *b.* 60%
c. 80% *d.* 90%

18. A battery of emf 12V and negligible resistance is connected across the diagonally opposite corners of a cubical network consisting of 12 resistors each of resistance 2 Ω. The equivalent resistance of the network is

a. $\frac{1}{2}\ \Omega$ *b.* $\frac{4}{3}\ \Omega$
c. $\frac{1}{4}\ \Omega$ *d.* $\frac{5}{3}\ \Omega$

19. Choose the valid field pattern for both electric field as well as magnetic field.

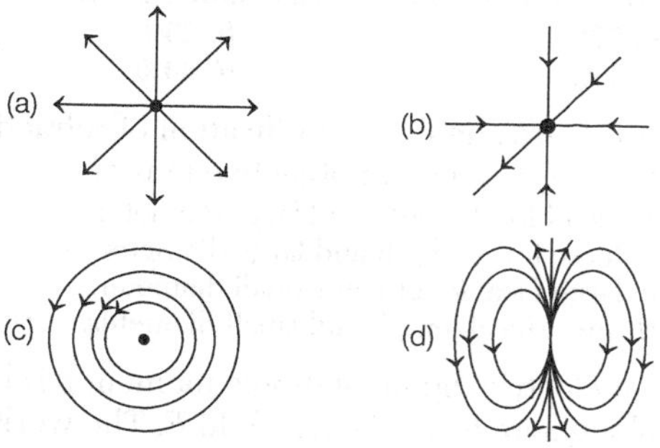

20. When a beam of 10.6 eV photons of intensity 2.0 W/m^2 falls on a platinum surface of area $1.0 \times 10^{-4} \text{m}^2$ and work function 5.6 eV. 0.53% of the incident photons eject photoelectrons. The number of photoelectrons emitted per second is

a. 6.25×10^{11} *b.* 4.25×10^{10}
c. 6.25×10^{10} *d.* 4.25×10^{11}

21. In an experiment to determine the period of a simple pendulum of length 100 cm, it is attached to different spherical bobs have uniform mass distribution. If the relative difference in the periods is found to be 5×10^{-4} s, the difference in radii $|r_1 - r_2|$ is best given by

a. 10^{-2} m *b.* 10^{-3} m *c.* 10^{-1} m *d.* 10^{-4} m

22. Three equal charges are placed on the three corners of a square. If the force between q_1 and q_2 is F_{12} and that between q_1 and q_3 is F_{13}, then the ratio of magnitudes $\left(\frac{F_{13}}{F_{12}}\right)$ is

a. $\frac{1}{2}$ *b.* $\frac{2}{3}$ *c.* $\frac{1}{\sqrt{2}}$ *d.* $\frac{1}{3}$

23. Four charges each with charge $+q$ are placed at the four corners of a square of side l, a charge $\frac{-q}{4}$ is at centre of the square. Force on the charge at the centre due to other charges is

a. $\frac{Kq^2}{l^2}$ *b.* $K\frac{\sqrt{2}q^2}{l^2}$ *c.* zero *d.* $K\frac{2\sqrt{2}q^2}{l^2}$

24. Two unlike charges of the same magnitude Q are placed at a distance d. The intensity of the electric field at the middle point is the line joining the two charges is

a. zero *b.* $\frac{8Q}{4\pi\varepsilon_0 d^2}$
c. $\frac{6Q}{4\pi\varepsilon_0 d^2}$ *d.* $\frac{4Q}{4\pi\varepsilon_0 d^2}$

25. 100 g of ice at 0°C is mixed with 100 g of water at 80°C. The final temperature of the mixture is (Given, latent heat of fusion of ice, L_f = 80 cal/g and specific heat capacity of water, S_{water} = 1 cal/g °C)

a. 0°C b. 20°C
c. 40°C *d.* 60°C

26. The molar heat capacity in a process of a diatomic gas if it does a work of $\frac{Q}{4}$, when a heat of Q is supplied to it is

a. $\frac{2}{5}R$ *b.* $\frac{5}{2}R$
c. $\frac{10}{3}R$ *d.* $\frac{6}{7}R$

27. An elevator cable is to have a maximum stress of $7 \times 10^7 \text{N/m}^2$ to allow for appropriate safety factors. Its maximum upward acceleration is 1.5 m/s^2. If the cable has to support the total weight of 2000 kg of a loaded elevator, the area of cross-section of the cable should be

a. 3.22 cm² *b.* 2.38 cm²
c. 0.32 cm² *d.* 8.23 cm²

28. If no external force acts on particle, then which of the following statement is incorrect about particle?

a. Particle may be at rest.
b. Particle moves with uniform velocity on linear path.
c. Particle moves with uniform speed on circle.
d. None of the above

29. Which of the following statement(s) is/are correct?

a. Displacing a vector parallel to itself leaves the vector unchanged.
b. Three equal vectors cannot add upto zero.
c. If $|\mathbf{A} + \mathbf{B}| \neq |\mathbf{A} - \mathbf{B}|$, they are perpendicular vectors.
d. Both *b.* and *c.*

30. Which of the given substances A, B and C have more specific heat?

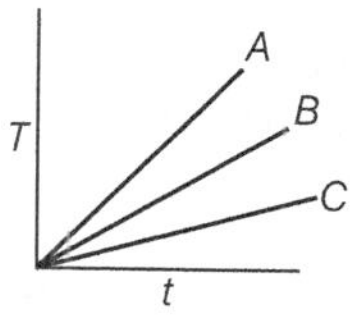

a. A *b.* B
c. C *d.* Both *a.* and *b.*

31. If the coefficient of volume expansion of brass is 6×10^{-5} °C^{-1}, then fractional change in its density for a 60°C rise in temperature will be

a. 2×10^{-6} *b.* 10^{-6}
c. 3.6×10^{-5} *d.* -3.6×10^{-3}

32. A particle of mass 1 kg is kept on the surface of a uniform sphere of mass 20 kg and radius 1.0 m. The work to be done against the gravitational force between them to take the particle away from the sphere is

a. 0.5×10^{-9} J
b. 1.334×10^{-9} J
c. 2.532×10^{-9} J
d. zero

33. The escape velocity is 11.2 km/s. If a body is to be projected in a direction making an angle 60° to the vertical, then the escape velocity is

a. $11.2 \times \sqrt{2}$ km/s
b. $\frac{11.2}{\sqrt{2}}$ km/s
c. $11.2\sqrt{3}$ km/s
d. 11.2 km/s

34. A block slides on rough horizontal surface with a velocity of 20 m/s. It comes to rest after travelling a distance of 80 m. The coefficient of kinetic friction between block and surface is (Take, $g = 10\ \text{m/s}^2$)

a. 0.20
b. 0.25
c. 0.125
d. 0.05

35. Two point masses 1 kg and 4 kg are separated by a distance of 10 cm. The gravitational potential energy of the two point masses is

a. -16.58×10^{-10} J
b. -20.45×10^{-10} J
c. -26.68×10^{-10} J
d. -35.65×10^{-10} J

36. Let I_A and I_B be moments of inertia of a body about two axes A and B, respectively. The axis A passes through the centre of mass of the body but B does not, then

a. $I_A < I_B$
b. $I_A < I_B$, whether the axes are parallel or not parallel
c. if the axes are parallel $I_A < I_B$
d. if the axes are not parallel $I_A \geq I_B$

37. A thermally insulated rigid container contains an ideal gas heated by a filament of resistance 100 Ω through a current of 1 A for 5 min, then change in internal energy is

a. 0 kJ
b. 10 kJ
c. 20 kJ
d. 30 kJ

38. The resistor of resistance R is connected to 25 V supply and heat produced in it is 25 Js^{-1}. The value of R is

a. 225 Ω
b. 1 Ω
c. 25 Ω
d. 50 Ω

39. An electron is moving along positive X-axis. To get it moving on an anti-clockwise circular path in X-Y-plane, a magnetic field is applied

a. along positive Y-axis
b. along positive Z-axis
c. along negative Y-axis
d. along negative Z-axis

40. If the length of a wire is increased by 20% by stretching it, then its resistance is increased to

a. 22%
b. 33%
c. 55%
d. 44%

41. For large angular magnification of refracting telescope, it has an objective lens of

a. small focal length and large diameter.
b. large focal length and large diameter.
c. large focal length and small diameter.
d. small focal length and small diameter.

42. An electric dipole of dipole moment p is lying along a uniform electric field E. The work done in rotating the dipole from 60° to 90° from the direction of electric field, is

a. $\frac{2}{3}pE$
b. $\frac{3pE}{2}$
c. pE
d. $\frac{pE}{2}$

43. A light of wavelength 5000 Å and frequency 20^{14} Hz is travelling in a medium. The refractive index of the medium is

a. 5
b. 3
c. 2.5
d. 3.8

44. Magnetic field in a region is changing at a constant rate. As a result, an induced electric field appears in the region which give rise to an emf. Induced electric field lines are

a. open curves
b. closed loops
c. can be open or closed depending on magnetic field
d. no field lines are produced

45. An electric dipole is placed at an angle of 60° with an electric field intensity 10^4 N/C. If experiences a torque equal to $4\sqrt{3}$N-m. The charge on the dipole, if the dipole length is 1 cm, is

a. 60 mC
b. 80 mC
c. 20 mC
d. 10 mC

46. The displacement-time graph of a moving particle is shown below

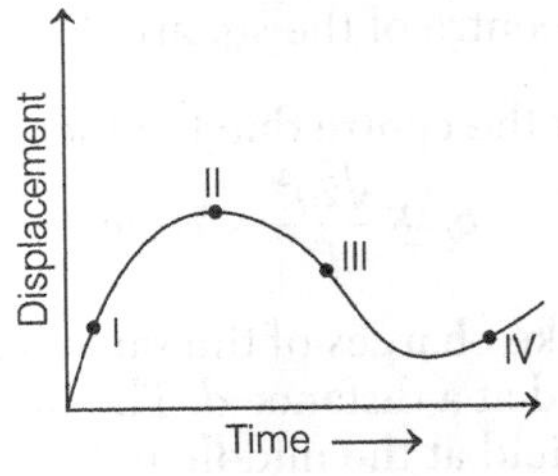

The instantaneous velocity of the particle is negative at the point

a. IV
b. I
c. II
d. III

47. In a plane electromagnetic wave, the electric field oscillates sinusoidally at a frequency of 2×10^{10} Hz and amplitude 48 V/m. The wavelength of the wave is

a. 24×10^{-10} m *b.* 1.5×10^{-2} m
c. 4.16×10^{8} m *d.* 3×10^{8} m

48. When an alternating voltage source $V = 100 \sin\left(100\pi t + \frac{\pi}{6}\right)$ is applied to a pure capacitor of 1 μF, then the instantaneous value of current through capacitor is

a. $0.01\,\pi \sin\left(100\pi t + \frac{\pi}{3}\right)$

b. $0.01\,\pi \sin\left(100\pi t + \frac{\pi}{6}\right)$

c. $0.04\,\pi \sin\left(100\pi t + \frac{\pi}{3}\right)$

d. $0.04\,\pi \sin\left(100\pi t + \frac{\pi}{6}\right)$

49. For a cell, V-I graph is given below.

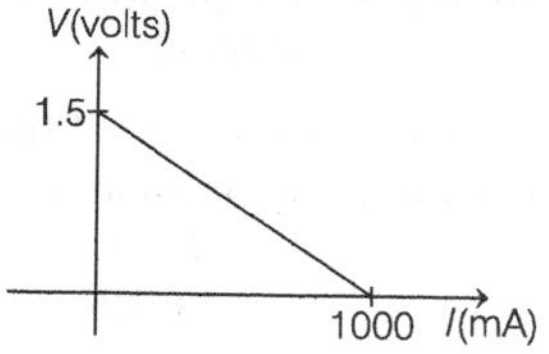

Which of the following options gives correct value of emf of cell and its internal resistance?

a. 1.5 V, 1.0 Ω *b.* 1.5 V, 2.0 Ω
c. 1.0 V, 1.5 Ω *d.* 1.5 V, 1.5 Ω

50. The minimum radial distance between first orbit and second orbit in He^+ ion, if the de-Broglie wavelength of an electron in first orbit is λ, will be

a. 2λ *b.* $\frac{2\lambda}{\pi}$
c. $\frac{\lambda}{2\pi}$ *d.* $\frac{\lambda}{4\pi}$

51. The drift velocity of free electrons in a conducting wire is the order of 10^{-4} m/s. Yet, the bulb glows very quickly after the switch is put ON because

a. the random speed of electrons is very high of order of 10^{6} m/s
b. the electrons transfer their energy very quickly through collisions
c. electric field is set-up in the wire with a speed of light producing a current through each cross-section, almost instantaneously
d. the random speed of electrons is very low of order of 10^{-6} m/s

52. A step down transformer is used to reduce the main supply of 220 V to 10 V. If the primary draws 5 A and secondary 88 A current, calculate the efficiency of the transformer.

a. 40% *b.* 60%
c. 80% *d.* 45%

53. Output of an AC source is $V = 100 \sin 100\pi t \cos 100\,\pi t$. Which of these are correct?

a. Peak voltage of source is 100 V
b. Peak voltage of source is $50\sqrt{2}$ V
c. Peak voltage of source is 50 V
d. Frequency of the source is 50 Hz

54. The current drawn from the battery by the network of resistors as shown in the figure is

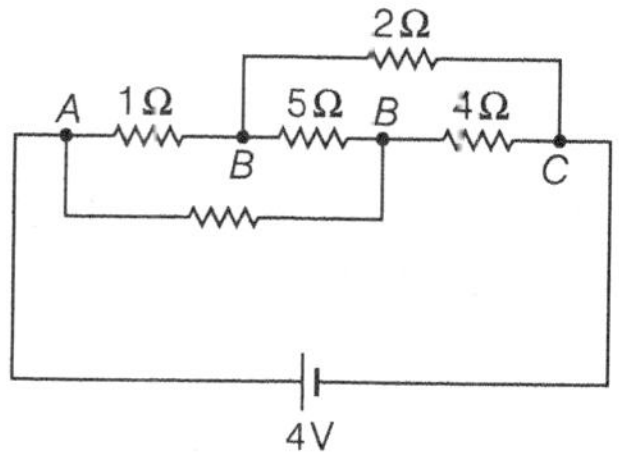

a. 1 A *b.* 2 A
c. 0.5 A *d.* 0 A

55. A closed loop lying in the XY-plane carries a current. If a uniform magnetic field **B** is present in the region, the force acting on the loop will be zero, if **B** is in

a. the x-direction
b. the y-direction
c. the z-direction
d. Any of the above directions

56. If an equiconvex lens is made of number of layers of different refractive index for a given wavelength as shown in the figure, then number of images formed for an object kept in front is

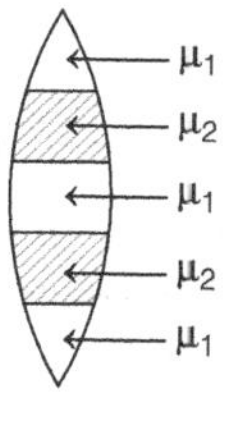

a. only 1 *b.* 2
c. 2.5 *d.* 5

57. The thickness of a metallic plate is 0.4 cm. The temperature between its two surfaces is 20°C. The quantity of heat flowing per second is 50 cal from 5 cm^2 area. In CGS system, the coefficient of thermal conductivity will be

a. 0.4 *b.* 0.6
c. 0.2 *d.* 0.5

58. In a resonance column experiment, the first resonance is obtained, when the level of the water in tube is 20 cm from the open end. Resonance will also be obtained when the water level is at a distance of

a. 40 cm from the open end
b. 60 cm from the open end
c. 80 cm from the open end
d. 90 cm from the open end

59. A piece of marble is projected from Earth's surface with velocity of $19.6\sqrt{2}$ m/s at 45°. After 2 s, its velocity makes an angle α with horizontal, where α is

a. 45° *b.* 30°
c. 60° *d.* 0°

60. In Young's double slit experiment, the separation between two slits is 0.3×10^{-3} m. When light beam is passed through the two slits, then interference pattern is observed on the screen 1.5 m away. If the first violet and red fringes are formed 2.0 mm and 3.5 mm away from the central white fringe, then the difference in wavelength of red and violet light is $x \times 10^{-9}$ m. The value of x is

a. 100 *b.* 300
c. 400 *d.* 500

CHEMISTRY

61. In the following given reaction the molecule/compound 'S' is

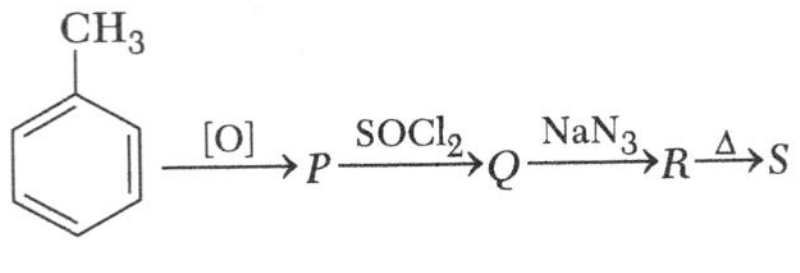

a. primary amine
b. an amide
c. phenyl isocyanate
d. chain hydrocarbon

62. 1.12 mL of gas is produced at STP by the action of 4.12 mg of alcohol, ROH, methyl magnesium iodide. The molecular mass of alcohol is

a. 16.0 g/mol *b.* 41.2 g/mol
c. 82.4 g/mol *d.* 156 g/mol

63. An aqueous KCl solution of density 1.20 g/mL has a molality of 6.60 mol/kg. The molarity of solution in mol/L is .... (Nearest integer)

[Molar mass of KCl = 74.5]

a. 5 *b.* 7
c. 3 *d.* 8

64. The product X in the following reaction is

$$R—C\equiv N \xrightarrow[\text{(ii) } H_2O]{\text{(i) AlH}(i\text{–Bu})_2} X$$

a. R—CHO
b. RCOOH
c. RCH_2NH_2
d. $RCONH_2$

65. Which of the following compounds on reaction with NaOH and Na_2O_2 gives yellow colour?

a. $Zn(OH)_2$ *b.* $Al(OH)_3$
c. $Cr(OH)_3$ *d.* $CaCO_3$

66. A dilute solution of sulphuric acid is electrolysed using a current of 0.20 A for 4 hours to produce hydrogen and oxygen gas. The total volume of gas produced at STP is .... cm^3 [Nearest integer]

[Given, Faraday constant $F = 96500$ C/mol at STP molar volume of an ideal gas is 22.7 L/mol]

a. 512 *b.* 516
c. 530 *d.* 508

67. Which of the following will not form a Schiff's base on reaction with *p*-nitrobenzaldehyde?

(a) 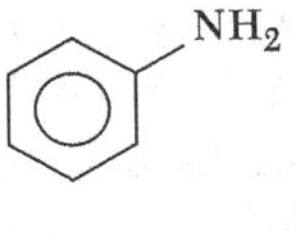

(b) 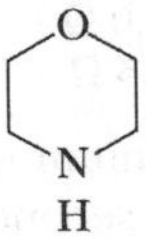

(c) 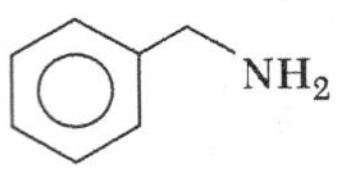

(d) 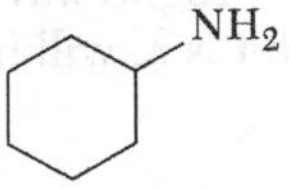

68. Which of the following pair of solutions can we expect to be isotonic at the same temperature?

a. 0.1 M NaCl and 0.1 M Na_2SO_4
b. 0.1 M Na_2SO_4 and 0.1 M $Ca(NO_3)_2$
c. 0.1 M urea and 0.1 M NaCl
d. 0.1 M urea and 0.2 M $MgCl_2$

69. Observe the given below reaction.

$$\text{Aqueous } CuSO_4 \xrightarrow{\text{Excess } aq \text{ KCN}} A \xrightarrow{H_2S} B$$

A, B respectively are

a. $K_3[Cu(CN)_4]$, no precipitate
b. $K_2[Cu(CN)_4]$, no precipitate
c. $K_4[Cu(CN)_6]$, white ppt.
d. $K_2[Cu(CN)_4]$, black precipitate

70. The equivalent weight of potassium permanganate in acid solution is
a. 158 *b.* 31.6
c. 52.16 *d.* 79

71. Formation of alkanes by action of Zn on alkyl halides is called
a. Frankland reaction
b. Cannizzaro reaction
c. Wurtz reaction
d. Kolbe's reaction

72. From the given aqueous solutions below, arrange them in the order of their increasing boiling points.
(i) 10^{-4} M NaCl (ii) 10^{-3} M urea
(iii) 10^{-3} M $MgCl_2$ (iv) 10^{-3} M NaCl
a. (ii) < (i) = (iii) < (iv) *b.* (i) < (ii) < (iii) < (iv)
c. (i) < (ii) < (iv) <(iii) *d.* (iv) < (iii) < (ii) = (i)

73. In the given reaction below, the coefficient of SO_2 is

$$IO_3^- + SO_2 + 4H_2O \longrightarrow I_2 + SO_4^{2-} + 8H^+$$

a. 3 *b.* 4
c. 5 *d.* 6

74. 3 Faraday of electricity is passed through three electrolytic cells connected in series containing Ag^+, Ca^{2+} and Al^{+3} ions respectively. The molar ratio in which the 3 metal ions are liberated at the electrodes is
a. 3 : 2 : 1 *b.* 1 : 2 : 3
c. 6 : 3 : 2 *d.* 4 : 4 : 2

75. In a closed vessel, 5 moles of $A_2(g)$ and 7 moles of $B_2(g)$ are reacted in following manner.

$$A_2(g) + 3B_2(g) \longrightarrow 2AB_3(g)$$

What is the total number of moles of the gases present in the container at the end of the reaction?
a. $\frac{22}{3}$ *b.* $\frac{5}{3}$ *c.* $\frac{11}{3}$ *d.* $\frac{8}{3}$

76. Which of the following statements is/are true about the diagonal relationship of Be and Al?
(i) Both react with NaOH to liberate hydrogen.
(ii) Their oxides are basic.
(iii) They are made passive by nitric acid.
(iv) Their carbides give acetylene on treatment with water.
a. Only (i) *b.* (i) and (iii)
c. (ii) and (iv) *d.* (i), (ii), (iii)

77. The instantaneous rate of disappearance of MnO_4^- ion in the following reaction is 2.28×10^{-3} M/s.

$$2MnO_4^- + 10I^- + 16H^+ \longrightarrow 2Mn^{2+} + 5I_2 + 8H_2O$$

The rate of appearance of I_2 is $(x) \times 10^{-3}$ M/s. The value of x is .... [Nearest integer]
a. 7 *b.* 6 *c.* 8 *d.* 5

78. How many grams of potassium dichromate are required to oxidise 20.0 g of Fe^{2+} in $FeSO_4$ to Fe^{3+} if the reaction carried out in an acidic medium? Molar mass of $K_2Cr_2O_7$ and $FeSO_4$ are 294 and 152 respectively.
a. 6.5 g *b.* 5.5 g
c. 3.5 g *d.* 4.5 g

79. At 300 K, one mole of ideal gas in thermal contact with surrounding expands isothermally from 1.0 L to 2.0 L against a constant pressure of 3.0 atm. In this process the change in entropy of surrounding (ΔS_{surr}) in J/K.
(1 L atm = 101.3 J)
a. 6.763 *b.* 1.013
c. – 1.013 *d.* – 6.673

80. Which of the following acid is a vitamin?
a. Aspartic acid *b.* Ascorbic acid
c. Adipic acid *d.* Saccharic acid

81. An aromatic compound (A) is heated with another compound (B) in presence of alcoholic KOH to give a bad smelling compound with molecular formula C_6H_5NC. The compound (B) can be prepared by heating compound (C) with Cl_2 and slake lime. The compound *C.* is
a. $C_6H_5NH_2$ *b.* C_2H_5OH
c. $CHCl_3$ *d.* CH_3OCH_3

82. The segment of DNA which acts as the instruction manual for the synthesis of the protein is
a. ribose *b.* gene
c. nucleoside *d.* nucleotide

83. *p*-toluene sulphonic acid on fusion with solid KOH at 573 K followed by treatment with dilute HCl gives
a. *p*-cresol *b.* toluene
c. benzoic acid *d.* benzene 1, 4-diol

84. In $SOCl_2$ the Cl—S—Cl and Cl—S—O bond angle are
a. 130° and 115° *b.* 106° and 96°
c. 107° and 108° *d.* 96° and 106°

85. A sample of 0.50 g of an organic compound was treated according to Kjeldahl's method. The ammonia evolved was absorbed in 50 mL of 0.5 M H_2SO_4. The residual acid required 60 mL of 0.5 M solution of NaOH for neutralisation. The percentage of nitrogen in the compound is
a. 25 *b.* 30 *c.* 28 *d.* 56

86. $Cu(s) + Sn^{2+}(0.01\ M) \longrightarrow Cu^{2+}\ (0.1\ M) + Sn(s)$

The gibbs free energy change for above mention reaction at NTP is $x \times 10^{-1}$ kJ/mol. The value of x is .... [Nearest integer]

[Given $E^{\circ}_{Cu^{2+}/Cu} = 0.34\ V$, $E^{\circ}_{Sn^{2+}/Sn} = -0.14\ V$

$F = 96500$ C/mol]

a. 983 *b.* 883
c. 1083 *d.* 863

87. The pH at which an acid indicator with $K_{\alpha} = 1 \times 10^{-5}$ changes colour when the indicator concentration is 1×10^{-3} M is

a. 4 *b.* 5
c. 6 *d.* 3

88. A substance X decomposes in solution following the first order kinetics. Flask I contains 1 L of 1 M solution of X and flask II contain 100 mL of 0.6 M solution. After 8 hours, the concentration, of X in flask I becomes 0.25 M.

The time required for concentration to become 0.3 M in flask II is ....

a. 6 hrs *b.* 5 hrs
c. 4 hrs *d.* 2 hrs

89. Which of the following species has lowest ionisation enthalpy?

a. O *b.* O_2
c. O_2^+ *d.* O_2^-

90. A compound with fruity smell is obtained when

a. Acetic acid is treated with ethyl alcohol in presence of few drop of H_2SO_4.
b. Acetyl chloride is reacted with ethyl alcohol in presence of pyridine.
c. Acetic anhydride is reacted with ethyl alcohol.
d. All of the above

91. N_2O_5 decomposes to NO_2 and O_2 and follow first order kinetics. After 50 minutes, the pressure inside the vessel increases from 50 mm Hg to 87.5 mm Hg. The pressure of the gaseous mixture after 100 minutes at constant temperature will be .... mm of Hg. [Nearest integer]

a. 108 *b.* 107
c. 106 *d.* 109

92. Which amino acid has phenolic OH group as its backbone?

a. Glycine *b.* Leucine
c. Serine *d.* Tyrosine

93. Light of wavelength λ shines on a metal surface with intensity x and the metal emits Y electrons per second of average energy Z. What will happen to Y and Z if x is doubled?

a. Y will be doubled, Z will become half.
b. Y will be remains same, Z will be doubled.
c. Both will doubled.
d. Y will be doubled, Z will remains same.

94. The compound A formed in the reaction is

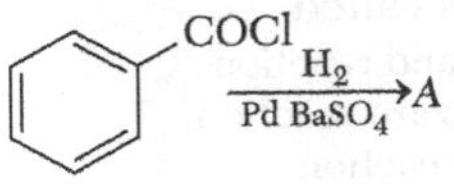

a. C_6H_5CHO *b.* C_6H_5OH
c. $C_6H_5COCH_3$ *d.* C_6H_5Cl

95. Name of the gas that can readily decolourise acidified $KMnO_4$ solution is

a. CO_2 *b.* SO_2
c. NO_2 *d.* P_2O_5

96. Nitrogen forms five stable oxides with oxygen of the formula N_2O, NO, N_2O_3, N_2O_4 and N_2O_5. The formation of these oxides explains fully the

a. law of definite proportion.
b. law of partial pressure.
c. law of multiple proportion.
d. law of reciprocal proportion.

97. The product Y in given reaction is

$$CH_3CH_2COOH \xrightarrow[\text{Red P}]{Cl_2} X \xrightarrow{\text{alc. KOH}} Y$$

a. CH_3CH_2COCl
b. CH_3CH_2CHO
c. $CH_2 = CHCOOH$
d. $ClCH_2CH_2COOH$

98. The enolic form of butanone contains

a. 12 σ bonds, 1 π bond and 2 lone pairs of electrons.
b. 11 σ bonds, 1 π bond and 2 lone pairs of electrons.
c. 12 σ bonds, 1 π bond and 1 lone pairs of electrons.
d. 13 σ bonds, 1 π bond and 1 lone pairs of electrons.

99. Aldol condensation gives methyl vinyl ketone between which two compound given below?

a. Formaldehyde and acetone.
b. Formaldehyde and acetaldehyde.
c. Two molecules of acetone.
d. Two molecule of acetaldehyde.

100. One mole of an ideal gas for which $C_V = \frac{3}{2}R$ is heated reversibly at constant pressure of 1 atm from 25°C to 100°C. ΔH will be

a. 372.56 cal *b.* 3.72 cal
c. 37256 cal *d.* 37.2 cal

101. The maximum number of electrons which can be held by subshell with azimuthal quantum number 'l' in an atom is given by

a. $2(l + 1)$
b. $2(2l + 1)$
c. $2l$
d. $2(2l + 2)$

102. The halide which will not react with C_6H_6 in presence of anhydrous $AlCl_3$ is
a. $CH_3CHClCH_3$ *b.* $C_6H_5CH_2Cl$
c. C_6H_5Cl *d.* $CH_3CH_2CH_2Cl$

103. Presence of peroxides in old stocks of ethers can be tested by first treating them with Fe^{2+} ions and then adding an aqueous solution of
a. KCNS *b.* $HgCl_2$
c. $SnCl_2$ *d.* KI

104. The ionisation energy of hydrogen atom is 13.6 eV. The ionisation energy of Li^{2+} ion will be
a. 54.4 eV *b.* 40.8 eV
c. 27.2 eV *d.* 122.4 eV

105. Given the bond enthalpies of N ≡ N is 946 kJ/mol. H—H is 435 kJ/mol, N—N is 159 kJ/mol and N—H is 389 kJ/mol, heat of formation of hydrazine in the gas phase (in kJ/mol) is
a. 101 *b.* 404
c. 798 *d.* 1268

106. In the equilibrium, $2NH_3 \rightleftharpoons N_2 + 3H_2$, 6 mol of NH_3 is taken in 10 L flask. If concentration of N_2 at equilibrium is x, then concentration of NH_3 at equilibrium is
a. $0.6 - x$ *b.* $0.6 - 2x$
c. $0.6 - \frac{x}{2}$ *d.* $0.6 - \frac{x}{3}$

107. Correct order of polarising power is
a. $Cs^+ < K^+ < Mg^{2+} < Al^{3+}$
b. $K^+ < Cs^+ < Mg^{2+} < Al^{3+}$
c. $Mg^{2+} < Al^{3+} < K^+ < Cs^+$
d. $Mg^{2+} < Al^{3+} < Cs^+ < K^+$

108. Total number of isomeric xylenes or dichlorobenzenes or cresols is
a. 2 *b.* 3
c. 4 *d.* 5

109. Which of the following molecules have three bond pairs but different shape?
(i) BCl_3 (ii) H_2S
(iii) PH_3 (iv) AsF_5
a. (i) and (ii) *b.* (ii) and (iii)
c. (i) and (iii) *d.* (iii) and (iv)

110. Given are the following molecules.
H_3PO_2, H_3PO_3, H_3PO_4, $H_4P_2O_7$
Which of the above oxoacids results into two series of salt?
a. H_3PO_2 *b.* H_3PO_3
c. H_3PO_4 *d.* $H_4P_2O_7$

111. The species having tetrahedral shape is
a. $[PdCl_4]^{2-}$ *b.* $[Ni(CN)_4]^{2-}$
c. $[Pd(CN)_4]^{2-}$ *d.* $[NiCl_4]^{2-}$

112. The magnetic moment of a divalent ion in aqueous solution if the atomic number of metal is 25 will be
a. 5.92 BM *b.* 1.73 BM
c. 3.87 MM *d.* 4.90 BM

113. The oxidation number of oxygen in CO_3 and Na_2O_2 is
a. 3, 2 *b.* 1, 0
c. 0, 1 *d.* – 0.33, – 1

114. In the reaction given below, identify *B*.

$$CH_2 = CHCl \xrightarrow{Cl_2} A \xrightarrow[363\ K]{Ca(OH)_2} B$$

a. 1, 1, 2-trichloroethane
b. 1, 1-dichloroethene
c. 1, 2-dichloroethene
d. chloroethylene

115. The equilibrium constant of given reaction is 100.

$$N_2(g) + 2O_2(g) \rightleftharpoons 2NO_2\ (gas)$$

What is the equilibrium constant for the reaction given below?

$$NO_2(g) \rightleftharpoons \frac{1}{2}N_2(g) + O_2(g)$$

a. 10 *b.* 1
c. 0.1 *d.* 0.01

116. Which one of the following is most stable?
a. $CH_3CH_2^-$
b. $HC \equiv C^-$
c. CH_3^-
d. $(CH_3)_3C^-$

117. Which of the following compounds will show geometric isomerism?
a. Cyclohexane
b. 2-hexene
c. 3-hexyne
d. 1, 1-diphenylethylene

118. When a colourless gas is passed through bromine water only decolourisation take place. The gas is
a. SO_2 *b.* HBr
c. HCl *d.* H_2S

119. *n*-pentane and isopentane can be distinguished by
a. Br_2 *b.* C_3
c. conc. H_2SO_4 *d.* $KMnO_4$

120. Which among the following given reagent is widely used for detection of sulphide ion?
a. 1-nitroso-2-naphthol
b. Potassium ferricyanide
c. Disodium hydrogen phosphate
d. Sodium nitroprusside

MATHEMATICS

121. The value of $2\log_{2}^{3} \cdot 3\log_{3}^{2}$ is

a. 2 *b.* 3
c. 6 *d.* 4

122. The slope of the tangent to the curve, $y = x^3 - 3x^2 y$ at (1, 1) is

a. $\frac{1}{3}$ *b.* -3
c. $\frac{-1}{3}$ *d.* 3

123. The value of $\lim_{x \to 0} \frac{\sin 3x + e^{2x} - 1}{x}$ is equal to

a. 2 *b.* 3
c. 5 *d.* 1

124. The radius and centre of circle which equation is $3x^2 + 3y^2 + 6x + 12y + 5 = 0$ is

a. $(-3, -4), \sqrt{20}$ *b.* $(3, 4), \sqrt{20}$
c. $(-1, -2), 5\sqrt{\frac{2}{3}}$ *d.* $(1, 2), 5\sqrt{\frac{2}{3}}$

125. Find the approximate value of function $f(x) = x^3 - 5x + 10$ at $x = 3.001$.

a. 31.023 *b.* 22.007
c. 31.23 *d.* 22.07

126. The length of y-intercept of the circle $x^2 + y^2 - 6x + 4y + 3 = 0$ is

a. 2 *b.* $2\sqrt{2}$
c. $2\sqrt{7}$ *d.* $2\sqrt{6}$

127. Let $f(x) = 5 + (2x - 3)^{\frac{4}{3}}$, then the minimum value of $f(x)$ is

a. 5 *b.* 6
c. 7 *d.* 4

128. If $f(x) = \begin{cases} x^2 + 1 & x < 0 \\ x^3 - a & 0 \le x < 1 \\ 2b - x & x \ge 1 \end{cases}$ and it is continuous $\forall x \in R$, then

a. $a = 1$ and $b = -1$
b. $a = 1$ and $b = 1$
c. $a = -1$ and $b = \frac{3}{2}$
d. $a = -1$ and $b = \frac{-3}{2}$

129. The value of $\lim_{x \to 0} \left(\frac{2 + x}{2 - x}\right)^{\frac{1}{x}}$ is

a. e *b.* e^2
c. $e^{\frac{1}{2}}$ *d.* $e^{\frac{-1}{2}}$

130. If $c_1 \equiv x^2 + y^2 - 2x + 4y + 5 = 0$ and $c_2 \equiv x^2 + y^2 - x + 2 = 0$ are two circles. Then the point (1, 0) lies

a. Inside c_1 only
b. Inside c_1 and c_2
c. Inside c_2 only
d. Outside c_1 and c_2

131. If four digit number is formed using the digit 0, 1, 2, 3 with no repetition. Then the probability that the number is both even and divisible by 3 is

a. $\frac{6}{18}$ *b.* $\frac{5}{18}$
c. $\frac{11}{18}$ *d.* $\frac{7}{18}$

132. The maximum value of $x + y$ subjected to $2x + 3y \le 12$, $xy \ge 0$

a. 4 *b.* 6
c. 8 *d.* 10

133. The number of common tangent to the circle $x^2 + y^2 = 9$ and $x^2 + y^2 - 6x - 8y + 21 = 0$

a. 0 *b.* 1
c. 3 *d.* 4

134. If $A = \begin{bmatrix} 3 & 4 \\ 1 & 2 \end{bmatrix}$, then A^{-1} equal to

a. $\begin{bmatrix} 3 & -4 \\ -1 & 2 \end{bmatrix}$ *b.* $\begin{bmatrix} \frac{3}{2} & -2 \\ \frac{-1}{2} & 1 \end{bmatrix}$
c. $\begin{bmatrix} 2 & -4 \\ -1 & 3 \end{bmatrix}$ *d.* $\begin{bmatrix} 1 & -2 \\ \frac{-1}{2} & \frac{3}{2} \end{bmatrix}$

135. The approximate value of $(0.026)^{\frac{1}{3}}$ is

a. $\frac{7}{27}$ *b.* $\frac{8}{27}$ *c.* $\frac{5}{27}$ *d.* $\frac{4}{27}$

136. $\int \frac{9^x}{\sqrt{1 - 81^x}} dx$ is equal to

a. $\sin^{-1}(9^x) + c$ *b.* $\ln^9 \sin^{-1}(9^x) + c$
c. $\sin^{-1}(81^x) + c$ *d.* $\frac{1}{\ln 9} \sin^{-1}(9^x) + c$

137. The angle between the vectors $a = 2\hat{i} + \hat{j} + \hat{k}$ and $b = \hat{i} - 2\hat{j} + \hat{k}$ is

a. $\sin^{-1}\left(\frac{1}{6}\right)$ *b.* $\cos^{-1}\left(\frac{1}{6}\right)$
c. $\sin^{-1}\left(\frac{1}{\sqrt{6}}\right)$ *d.* $\cos^{-1}\left(\frac{1}{\sqrt{6}}\right)$

138. The argument of $\frac{4+3i}{4-3i}$ is

a. $\tan^{-1}\left(\frac{7}{24}\right)$ *b.* $-\tan^{-1}\left(\frac{7}{24}\right)$

c. $\tan^{-1}\left(\frac{24}{7}\right)$ *d.* $\tan^{-1}\left(\frac{-24}{7}\right)$

139. The feasible region for the inequations $x + y \le 4$, $2x + y \le 5$, $x, y \ge 0$ is

(a) 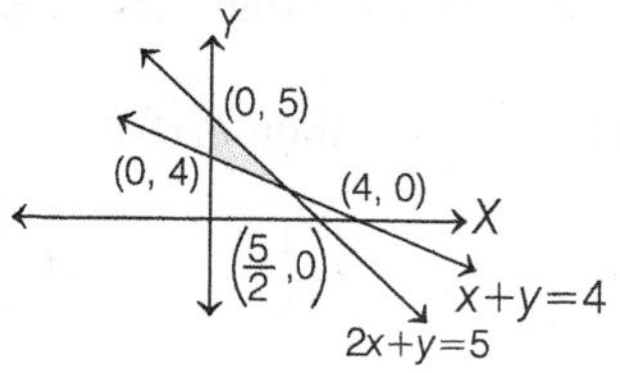

(b) 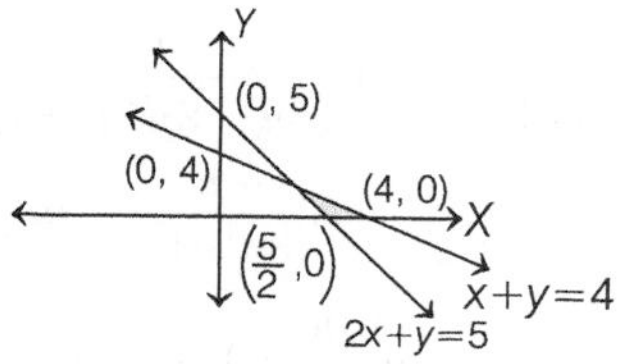

(c) 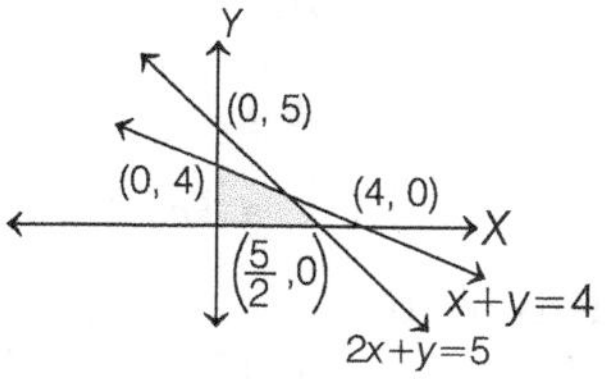

(d) 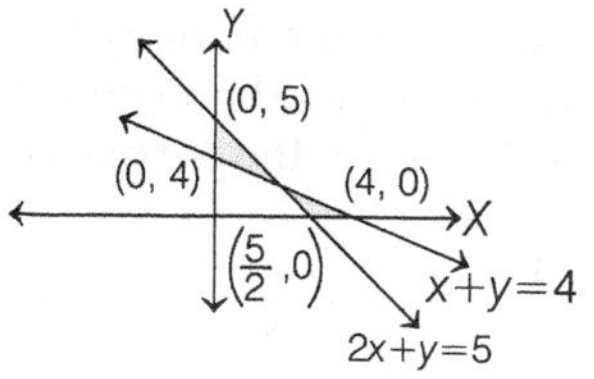

140. If $a = \hat{i} - \hat{j} + \hat{k}$, $b = 2\hat{i} - \hat{j} + \hat{k}$ and $c = \hat{i} - \hat{k}$, then the unit vector in the direction of $a - b + c$ is

a. $\frac{\hat{i}-\hat{j}}{\sqrt{2}}$ *b.* $\pm\hat{k}$

c. $\frac{\hat{j}-\hat{k}}{\sqrt{2}}$ *d.* $\frac{\hat{i}+\hat{j}-\hat{k}}{\sqrt{3}}$

141. The angle between the lines $\frac{x-2}{3} = \frac{y-1}{1} = \frac{z+3}{-1}$ and $\frac{x+1}{2} = \frac{y-1}{-1} = \frac{z}{2}$ is

a. $\cos^{-1}\left(\frac{3}{\sqrt{11}}\right)$ *b.* $\sin^{-1}\left(\frac{3}{\sqrt{11}}\right)$

c. $\cos^{-1}\left(\frac{1}{\sqrt{11}}\right)$ *d.* $\sin^{-1}\left(\frac{1}{\sqrt{11}}\right)$

142. The total number of terms in $(x-y)^{20} + (x+y)^{20}$ is

a. 10 *b.* 20

c. 21 *d.* 11

143. If the lines $\frac{x+4}{3} = \frac{y-2}{a} = \frac{z}{2}$ and $\frac{x}{2} = \frac{y-3}{4} = \frac{z-1}{1}$ are perpendicular, then the value of a is

a. 2 *b.* -2

c. 3 *d.* -3

144. The value of $\int \frac{1}{1-\cos 4x}\,dx$ is

a. $\frac{\cot 2x + c}{2}$ *b.* $\frac{-\cot 2x + c}{4}$

c. $2\cot 2x + c$ *d.* $\frac{-\cot 2x + c}{2}$

145. Middle term of the expansion $\left(x^2 + \frac{1}{x^2} + 2\right)^n$ is

a. ${}^{2n}C_n$ *b.* ${}^{2n}C_{n+1}$

c. ${}^{4n}C_n$ *d.* ${}^{4n}C_{n+1}$

146. If $A = \begin{bmatrix} x-2 & x+2 \\ -2 & 1 \end{bmatrix}$ is a singular matrix, then possible value of x is

a. 2 *b.* -2

c. $\frac{3}{2}$ *d.* $\frac{-3}{2}$

147. The distance between the point (1, 2) from the line $3x + 4y = 6$ measured parallel to the line $3x - 4y = 5$.

a. $\sqrt{5}$ *b.* $\frac{\sqrt{5}}{3}$

c. $\frac{3}{5}$ *d.* $\frac{5}{3}$

148. The expression $\frac{\sin\theta - 2\sin^3\theta}{2\cos^3\theta - \cos\theta}$ is equal to

a. $\cot\theta$ *b.* $\tan\theta$

c. $\sec\theta\tan\theta$ *d.* $\tan\theta\sin\theta$

149. The number of solution of $\cos^2 x = 3 - 3\sin x$ $\forall x \in [0, 2\pi]$ is

a. 0 *b.* 1

c. 2 *d.* 3

150. If the equation of pair of lines $y = m_1 x$ and $y = m_2 x$ can be written as $(y - m_1 x)(y - m_2 x) = 0$. Then the equation of pair of the angle bisector of the lines $5x^2 + 2xy + 3y^2 = 0$ is

a. $x^2 - 4xy - y^2 = 0$ *b.* $x^2 - 2xy - y^2 = 0$

c. $x^2 - 8xy - y^2 = 0$ *d.* $x^2 - 6xy - y^2 = 0$

151. If a n-sided polygon has total 54 diagonal then the value of n is

a. 10 *b.* 11 *c.* 12 *d.* 13

152. The line $\frac{x-1}{2}=\frac{y}{1}=\frac{z+1}{1}$ is parallel to the plane

a. $2x+y+z=2$
b. $2x-y+z=2$
c. $x-y+2z=2$
d. $x-y-z=3$

153. If ${}^{10}C_x = {}^{10}C_4$ then the value of x is

a. 6 only
b. 4 only
c. both 4 and 6
d. 5 and 6

154. The coefficient of x^{24} in the expansion of $(1-x^5)^{10}$ is

a. 0 *b.* ${}^{10}C_5$ *c.* ${}^{10}C_4$ *d.* 110

155. If A is a matrix of order 3 such that $|A|=5$, then the value $|\text{adj } A|$ is

a. 5 *b.* 25 *c.* 125 *d.* 625

156. The coefficient of x^6 in the expansion of $(1+x^2+2x)^{10}$ is

a. ${}^{10}C_6$
b. ${}^{10}C_3$
c. ${}^{10}C_5$
d. ${}^{20}C_6$

157. The solution of differential equation

$$\frac{dy}{dx}-\frac{\cos^2 y}{\sqrt{1-x^2}}=0$$

a. $y=\sin^{-1}x+C$
b. $\sec y=\sin^{-1}x+C$
c. $\tan y=\sin^{-1}x+C$
d. None of these

158. The value of $\int e^{x^5}\cdot x^4 dx$ is

a. $e^{x^5}+C$
b. $5e^{x^5}+C$
c. $\frac{e^{x^5}}{5}+C$
d. None of these

159. Evaluate $i^{2024}+i^{2025}+i^{2026}+i^{2027}$ (where $i=\sqrt{-1}$)

a. 1 *b.* 0 *c.* -1 *d.* $-i$

160. If $(1+i)^{200}=2^{98}(a+ib)$ then the value of $a+b$ is

a. 2
b. 4
c. 6
d. 8

161. If the vectors $\mathbf{a}=\hat{\mathbf{i}}+2\hat{\mathbf{j}}-\hat{\mathbf{k}}$, $\mathbf{b}=\hat{\mathbf{i}}-2\hat{\mathbf{j}}+\lambda\hat{\mathbf{k}}$ and $\mathbf{c}=\hat{\mathbf{i}}+\hat{\mathbf{j}}+\hat{\mathbf{k}}$ are coplanar, then the value of λ is

a. 4
b. 5
c. 6
d. 7

162. Out of 10 given point, 3 are collinear. How many different straight line can be drawn by joining any 2 points from those 10 points?

a. 40
b. 36
c. 42
d. 43

163. The value of $\sin 18° + \cos 36°$ is equal to

a. $\sqrt{5}$ *b.* $\frac{\sqrt{5}}{2}$ *c.* $2\sqrt{5}$ *d.* $\frac{\sqrt{5}-1}{4}$

164. The slope of line which makes an Angle 60° with the line $x+y=2$ is

a. $2\pm\sqrt{3}$ *b.* $\sqrt{2}\pm 1$ *c.* $\frac{1}{3}, -3$ *d.* $-\frac{1}{2}, 2$

165. If the x and y intercept are 2 and 3 in positive direction then the slope of that line is

a. $\frac{2}{3}$ *b.* $\frac{3}{2}$ *c.* $\frac{-2}{3}$ *d.* $\frac{-3}{2}$

166. If A and B are events, such that $P(A)=\frac{1}{4}$, $P\left(\frac{A}{B}\right)=\frac{1}{2}$ and $P\left(\frac{B}{A}\right)=\frac{2}{3}$ then $P(B)$ is

a. $\frac{1}{3}$ *b.* $\frac{2}{3}$ *c.* $\frac{1}{2}$ *d.* $\frac{1}{6}$

167. The value of

$$\frac{1}{1\cdot 4}+\frac{1}{4\cdot 7}+\frac{1}{7\cdot 10}+\ldots+\frac{1}{(3n-2)(3n+1)} \text{ is}$$

a. $\frac{n}{3n+1}$ *b.* $\frac{n}{3n+2}$ *c.* $\frac{-n}{3n+1}$ *d.* $\frac{-n}{3n+2}$

168. The general solution of $\frac{dy}{dx}=1+x+y+xy$

a. $y=ke^{x+\frac{x^2}{2}}-1$
b. $ke^{x-\frac{x^2}{2}}+1$
c. $ke^{1+\frac{x^2}{2}}-1$
d. $ke^{1-\frac{x^2}{2}}+1$

169. $(2^{4n}-1)$ is divisible by

a. 8 *b.* 7 *c.* 15 *d.* 16

170. Three vertices are chosen randomly from the 10 vertices of a regular 10 sided polygon. The probability that they form the vertices of an isosceles triangle is

a. $\frac{4}{7}$ *b.* $\frac{3}{7}$ *c.* $\frac{4}{8}$ *d.* $\frac{3}{8}$

171. If the sum of 4th and 7th term of an AP is 31 and sum of first two term is 7 then find the 10th term of AP is

a. 20
b. 29
c. 33
d. 28

172. If $n(A)=2$ and $n(B)=3$ then number of relation from set A to the set B is

a. 9
b. 32
c. 64
d. 128

173. A number n is choosen at random from $S=\{1, 2, 3, \ldots, 100\}$. Let $A=\{n\in S: n \text{ is a perfect square}\}$, $B=\{n\in S: n \text{ is odd number}\}$ and $C=\{n\in S: n \text{ is a even prime number}\}$ then, correct order of their probability is

a. $P(A)<P(B)<P(C)$
b. $P(A)>P(B)>P(C)$
c. $P(B)>P(A)>P(C)$
d. $P(A)>P(C)<P(B)$

174. If $f(x)+2f(1-x)=x \;\forall\; x \in R$, then $f(x)$ is equal to

a. $2-3x$
b. $\frac{1}{2}(2-3x)$
c. $\frac{1}{3}(2-3x)$
d. $\frac{1}{3}(2x-3)$

175. $\sum_{k=1}^{20} k\,k!$ is equal to

a. $21!$
b. $20!-1$
c. $21!-1$
d. $20!-1$

176. For a torch has 10 batteries are available out of which 4 are dead. If 3 batteries are selected without replacement and tested, then the probability that all 3 are dead is

a. $\frac{1}{30}$
b. $\frac{1}{4}$
c. $\frac{1}{15}$
d. $\frac{1}{10}$

177. The differential equation of all the $2-d$ lines are

a. $\frac{dy}{dx}=0$
b. $\frac{dy}{dx}=1$
c. $\frac{d^2y}{dx^2}=0$
d. $\frac{d^2y}{dx^2}=1$

178. If $A=\{4, 5, 9\}$ and $B=\{1, 2, 4, 6\}$, then $(A\cup B)\cap(B-A)$ is

a. $\{1, 2\}$
b. $\{1, 2, 6\}$
c. $\{1, 2, 4\}$
d. $\{1, 2, 4, 6\}$

179. A six digit number is formed by using 1, 2, 3, 4, 5, 6 with no repetition. Then the probability that number 1 and 3 always come together.

a. $\frac{1}{2}$
b. $\frac{1}{3}$
c. $\frac{2}{3}$
d. $\frac{1}{4}$

180. The maximum value of $Z=5x-y$, subject to constraint $x\ge 0, y\ge 0, x+y\le 6, 2x+y\le 10$ is

a. 28
b. 31
c. 22
d. 25

ANSWERS

Physics

1.	(b)	2.	(c)	3.	(d)	4.	(b)	5.	(a)	6.	(d)	7.	(d)	8.	(c)	9.	(b)	10.	(b)
11.	(c)	12.	(d)	13.	(c)	14.	(c)	15.	(b)	16.	(a)	17.	(c)	18.	(d)	19.	(c)	20.	(a)
21.	(b)	22.	(a)	23.	(c)	24.	(b)	25.	(a)	26.	(c)	27.	(a)	28.	(c)	29.	(a)	30.	(c)
31.	(d)	32.	(b)	33.	(d)	34.	(b)	35.	(c)	36.	(c)	37.	(d)	38.	(c)	39.	(b)	40.	(d)
41.	(b)	42.	(d)	43.	(b)	44.	(a)	45.	(b)	46.	(d)	47.	(b)	48.	(a)	49.	(d)	50.	(c)
51.	(c)	52.	(c)	53.	(c)	54.	(b)	55.	(d)	56.	(b)	57.	(c)	58.	(b)	59.	(d)	60.	(b)

Chemistry

61.	(c)	62.	(c)	63.	(a)	64.	(a)	65.	(c)	66.	(d)	67.	(b)	68.	(b)	69.	(a)	70.	(b)
71.	(a)	72.	(c)	73.	(c)	74.	(c)	75.	(a)	76.	(b)	77.	(b)	78.	(a)	79.	(c)	80.	(b)
81.	(b)	82.	(b)	83.	(a)	84.	(d)	85.	(d)	86.	(a)	87.	(b)	88.	(c)	89.	(d)	90.	(d)
91.	(c)	92.	(d)	93.	(d)	94.	(a)	95.	(b)	96.	(c)	97.	(c)	98.	(a)	99.	(a)	100.	(a)
101.	(b)	102.	(c)	103.	(a)	104.	(d)	105.	(a)	106.	(b)	107.	(a)	108.	(b)	109.	(c)	110.	(b)
111.	(d)	112.	(a)	113.	(d)	114.	(b)	115.	(c)	116.	(b)	117.	(b)	118.	(a)	119.	(d)	120.	(d)

Mathematics

121.	(c)	122.	(d)	123.	(c)	124.	(c)	125.	(d)	126.	(a)	127.	(a)	128.	(c)	129.	(a)	130.	(d)
131.	(c)	132.	(b)	133.	(c)	134.	(d)	135.	(b)	136.	(d)	137.	(b)	138.	(c)	139.	(c)	140.	(b)
141.	(c)	142.	(d)	143.	(b)	144.	(b)	145.	(a)	146.	(d)	147.	(d)	148.	(b)	149.	(b)	150.	(b)
151.	(c)	152.	(d)	153.	(c)	154.	(a)	155.	(b)	156.	(d)	157.	(c)	158.	(c)	159.	(b)	160.	(b)
161.	(d)	162.	(d)	163.	(b)	164.	(a)	165.	(d)	166.	(b)	167.	(a)	168.	(a)	169.	(c)	170.	(d)
171.	(b)	172.	(c)	173.	(c)	174.	(c)	175.	(c)	176.	(a)	177.	(c)	178.	(b)	179.	(b)	180.	(c)

HINTS & SOLUTIONS

Physics

1. *(b)* v_{max} = Maximum positive area of a-t graph
= area between 0 and 8 s

Area of triangle + Area of rectangle $= \frac{1}{2} \times 4 \times 5 + 4 \times 5$

$= 30$ m/s

2. *(c)* The maximum force, which the bigger piston can bear,

$$F = 30000 \text{ kgf} = 3000 \times 9.8 \text{ N}$$

Area of piston,

$$A = 425 \text{ cm}^2 = 425 \times 10^{-4} \text{ m}^2$$

$\therefore$ Maximum pressure on the bigger piston,

$$p = \frac{F}{A} = \frac{300 \times 9.8}{425 \times 10^{-4}} = 6.92 \times 10^4 \text{ Pa}$$

Since, the liquid transmits pressure equally, therefore the maximum pressure the shaller piston can bear is 6.92×10^4 Pa.

3. *(d)* $P_{\text{rated}} = \frac{V^2_{\text{rated}}}{R}$ or $R = \frac{(220)^2}{100}$

Now, power consumed

$$= \frac{V^2}{R} = \frac{(110)^2 \times 100}{(220)^2} = 25 \text{ W}$$

4. *(b)* Radius of the nth Bohr's orbit of the hydrogen atom is given by

$$r_n = \frac{4\pi\varepsilon_0 n^2 h^2}{4\pi^2 me^2}$$

$$r_2 = \frac{4\pi \times 8.85 \times 10^{-12} \times (2)^2 \times (6.625 \times 10^{-24})^2}{4\pi^2 \times 9.1 \times 10^{-31} \times (1.6 \times 10^{-19})^2}$$

$$= \frac{8.85 \times 10^{-12} \times 4 \times (6.625 \times 10^{-34})^2}{\pi \times 9.1 \times 10^{-31} \times (1.6 \times 10^{-19})^2}$$

$$= 2.123 \times 10^{-10} \text{ m}$$

$$= 2.12 \text{ Å}$$

5. *(a)* Given, refractive index of plano convex lens, $\mu = 1.6$

Radius of curvature, $R_1 = 60$ cm

By lens Maker's formula, focal length is given by

$$\frac{1}{f} = (\mu - 1)\left(\frac{1}{R_1} - \frac{1}{R_2}\right)$$

$$= (1.6 - 1)\left(\frac{1}{60} - \frac{1}{\infty}\right) \quad [\because R_2 = \infty]$$

$$= \frac{0.6}{60} = \frac{0.1}{10}$$

$$\Rightarrow \quad \frac{1}{f} = 0.01$$

$$\Rightarrow \quad f = \frac{1}{0.01} = 100 \text{ cm}$$

6. *(d)* Potential energy of a He^+ ion in ground state is

$$U_1 = 2E_1 = 2\left(-13.6\frac{Z^2}{n^2}\right)$$

$\because \quad n = 1$ and $Z = 2$

$\Rightarrow \quad U_1 = -108.8$ eV

But PE in ground state is given zero. So, we have to increase PE (and total energy) by 108.8 eV.

Hence, for given He^+ ion, energy of first excited state ($n = 2$) will be

$$E(n = 2) = -13.6\frac{Z^2}{n^2} + 108.8$$

$$= -13.6 \times \frac{4}{4} + 108.8$$

$$= 95.2 \text{ eV}$$

7. *(d)* Given, $v = 2 \times 10^8 \text{ ms}^{-1}$ and $\mu_r = 1$

The speed of EM waves in a medium is given by

$$v = \frac{1}{\sqrt{\mu\varepsilon}} \quad \text{...(i)}$$

where, μ and ε are absolute permeability and absolute perimittivity of the medium.

Now, $\mu = \mu_0 \mu_r$ and $\varepsilon = \varepsilon_0 \varepsilon_r$

$\therefore$ Eq. (i) becomes

$$v = \frac{1}{\sqrt{\mu_0 \mu_r \varepsilon_0 \varepsilon_r}} = \frac{1}{\sqrt{\mu_0 \varepsilon_0}} \times \frac{1}{\mu_r \varepsilon_r}$$

$$v = \frac{c}{\sqrt{\mu_r \varepsilon_r}}$$

$$\varepsilon_r = \frac{c^2}{v^2 \mu_r} = \frac{(3 \times 10^8)^2}{(2 \times 10^8)^2 \times 1} = 2.25$$

8. *(c)* When a ray of light travels from one medium to another medium, it deviates from its original path. This phenomenon of light is called refraction of light. In refraction, velocity, wavelength and intensity of light are changed while frequency of light remains same.

9. *(b)* When a p-n junction is connected in forward bias, an electric field exists which causes electrons to move from n to p-side (forward current).

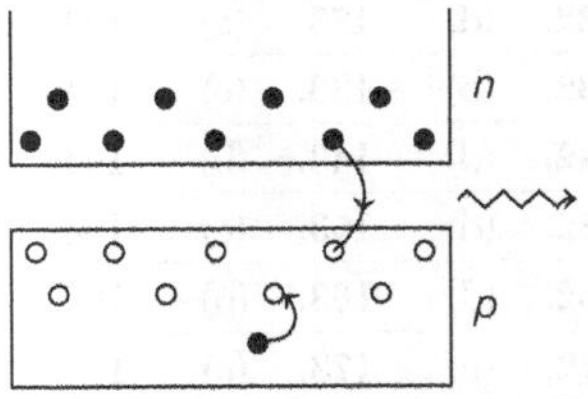

As electrons are in conduction band and holes are in valence band, thus electrons move from higher to lower energy levels.

10. *(b)* We know that, barrier potential of Ge, $V_{B_1} = 0.3$ V and barrier potential of Si, $V_{B_2} = 0.7$ V

Redrawing the given figure as

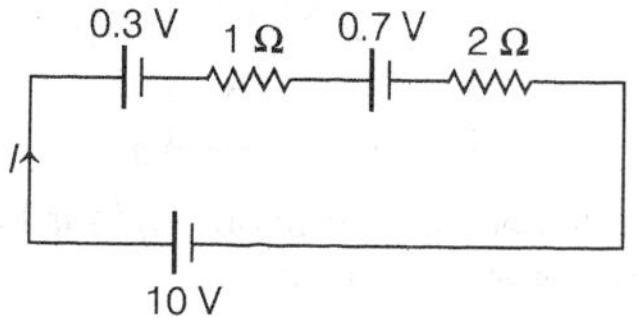

Applying KVL, we get

$$10 - 0.3 - I \times 1 - 0.7 - 2 \times I = 0$$

$$\Rightarrow \quad 3I = 9 \Rightarrow I = 3 \text{ A}$$

11. *(c)* The energy density in the region between the plates is given by

$$u = \frac{1}{2}\varepsilon_0 E^2$$

$$= \frac{1}{2}\varepsilon_0\left(\frac{V}{d}\right)^2 \qquad \left(\because E = \frac{V}{d}\right)$$

$$\Rightarrow \quad u = \frac{1}{2} \times 8.85 \times 10^{-12} \times \left(\frac{400}{5 \times 10^{-3}}\right)^2$$

$$= 283.2 \times 10^{-12} \times 10^6$$

$$= 283.2 \times 10^{-6}$$

$$= 2.83 \times 10^{-4} \text{ J/m}^3$$

12. *(d)* Electric flux coming out from a surface does not depend on its surface area. It depends only on charge enclosed by surface.

As, flux, $\phi = \dfrac{q}{\varepsilon_0}$

13. *(c)* $B = kt$

According to Maxwell's is equation, (Faraday's law of electro magnetic induction)

$$\oint \mathbf{E} \cdot d\mathbf{l} = \frac{-d\phi_B}{dt}$$

or $$E \cdot 2\pi r = \frac{d}{dt}(BA)$$

$$= \frac{d}{dt}(kt \times \pi r^2) \qquad \{\therefore A = \pi r^2\}$$

$$\Rightarrow \quad E \cdot 2\pi r = k\pi r^2$$

$$\Rightarrow \quad E = \frac{k\pi r^2}{2\pi r} = \frac{kr}{2}$$

14. *(c)* For total torque about O to be zero,

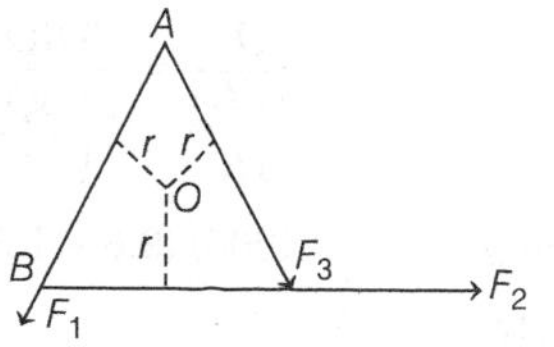

$$F_1 r + F_2 r - F_3 r = 0$$

$$\Rightarrow \quad F_3 = F_1 + F_2$$

15. *(b)* $H = i^2 R t$

$\therefore$ % error in H = 2 (% error in i) + (% error in R) + (% error in t)

$$= 2(2)\% + 1\% + 1\% = 6\%$$

16. *(a)* $A = 10L \times 2L = 20L^2$

$$\frac{\Delta A}{A} \times 100 = 2\frac{\Delta L}{L} \times 100 = 2 \times 1 = 2\%$$

17. *(c)* Consider the given figure,

When the switch S is connected to point 1, then initial energy stored in the capacitor can be given as

$$= \frac{1}{2}(2\mu\text{F}) \times V^2$$

When the switch S is connected to point 2, energy dissipated on connection across 8 μF will be

$$= \frac{1}{2}\left(\frac{C_1 C_2}{C_1 + C_1}\right), V^2 = \frac{1}{2} \times \frac{2\,\mu\text{F} \times 8\,\mu\text{F}}{10\,\mu\text{F}} \times V^2$$

$$= \frac{1}{2} \times (1.6\,\mu\text{F}) \times V^2$$

Therefore, % loss of energy

$$= \frac{1.6}{2} \times 100 = 80\%$$

18. *(d)* In a closed loop, say $ABCC'EA$ and apply Kirchhoff's second rule, $-IR - \left(\dfrac{I}{2}\right)R - IR + \varepsilon = 0$

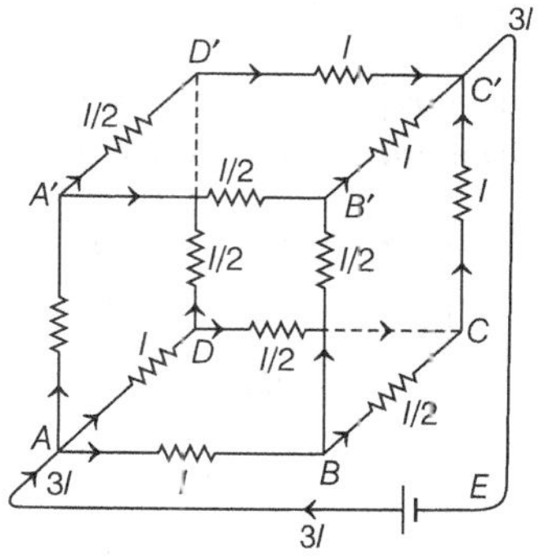

where, R is the resistance of each edge and ε the emf of battery.

Thus, $\varepsilon = \dfrac{5}{2}IR$

The equivalent resistance R_{eq} of the network is

$$R_{eq} = \frac{\varepsilon}{3I} = \frac{5}{6}R = \frac{5}{6} \times 2 = \frac{5}{3}\,\Omega$$

19. *(c)* Correct answer is (c), because induced electric field lines (produced by change in magnetic field) and magnetic field lines form closed loops.

20. *(a)* Energy of incident photons,

$$E_1 = 10.6 \text{ eV} = 10.6 \times 1.6 \times 10^{-19} \text{ J}$$

$$= 16.96 \times 10^{-19} \text{ J}$$

Energy incident per unit area per unit time (intensity) = 2 J

$\therefore$ Number of photons incident on unit area in unit time

$$= \frac{2}{16.96 \times 10^{-19}}$$

$$= 1.18 \times 10^{18}$$

Therefore, number of photons incident per unit time on given area.

$(1.0 \times 10^{-4}\ \text{m}^2)$

$$= (1.18 \times 10^{18})(1.0 \times 10^{-4})$$

$$= 1.18 \times 10^{14}$$

But only 0.53% of incident, photons emit photoelectrons.

$\therefore$ Number of photoelectrons emitted per second,

$$n = \left(\frac{0.53}{100}\right)(1.18 \times 10^{14})$$

$$n = 6.25 \times 10^{11}$$

21. *(b)* Given, $\Delta T = 5 \times 10^{-4}$ s

We know that,

$$T = 2\pi\sqrt{\frac{l}{g}}$$

$$\Rightarrow \quad T \propto \sqrt{l}$$

$$\therefore \quad \Delta T = \frac{1}{2}\Delta l$$

$$\Rightarrow \quad 5 \times 10^{-4} = \frac{|r_1 - r_2|}{2}$$

$$\Rightarrow \quad |r_1 - r_2| = 2 \times 5 \times 10^{-4} = 10^{-3}\ \text{m}$$

22. *(a)* The given situation is shown in the figure.

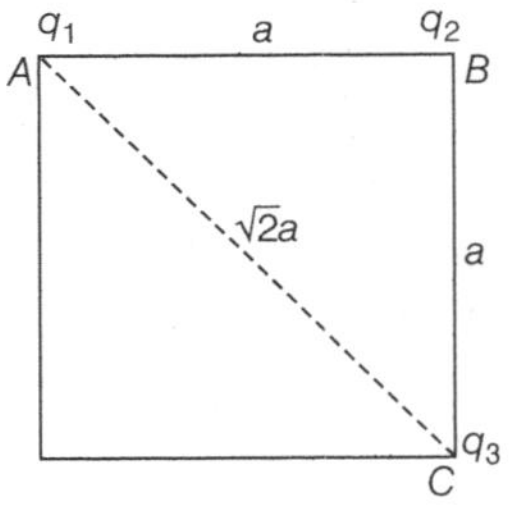

$$|q_1| = |q_2| = |q_3| = q$$

$$\therefore \quad F_{12} = \frac{kq_1q_2}{AB^2} = \frac{kq \cdot q}{a^2}$$

$$F_{12} = \frac{kq^2}{a^2}$$

$$F_{13} = \frac{k \cdot q_1 q_3}{AC^2} = \frac{k \cdot q \cdot q}{(\sqrt{2}a)^2}$$

$$[\because AC = \sqrt{AB^2 + BC^2} = \sqrt{a^2 + a^2} = \sqrt{2}a]$$

$$= \frac{kq^2}{2a^2}$$

$$\therefore \quad \frac{F_{13}}{F_{12}} = \frac{\frac{kq^2}{2a^2}}{\frac{kq^2}{a^2}} = \frac{1}{2}$$

23. *(c)*

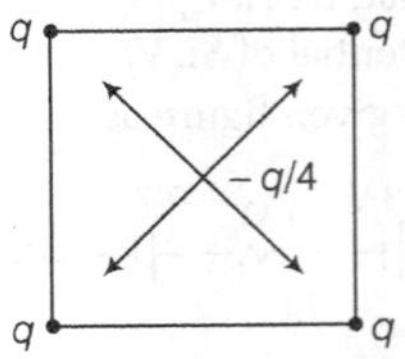

Force due to each q charge on $-q/4$ is balanced by diagonally opposite charge.

$$F_{\text{net}} = 0$$

24. *(b)* The magnitude of electric field due to charge at point A is

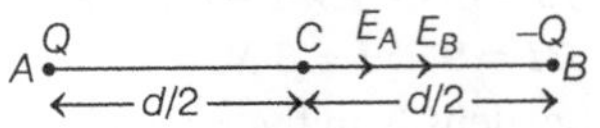

$$E_A = |\mathbf{E}| = \frac{1}{4\pi\varepsilon_0} \cdot \frac{Q}{\left(\frac{d}{2}\right)^2} = \frac{1}{4\pi\varepsilon_0} \cdot \frac{4Q}{d^2}$$

Similarly, $E_B = |\mathbf{E}| = \dfrac{1}{4\pi\varepsilon_0} \cdot \dfrac{Q}{\left(\frac{d}{2}\right)^2} = \dfrac{1}{4\pi\varepsilon_0} \cdot \dfrac{4Q}{d^2}$

From figure, it is clear that E_A and E_B are in same direction, hence.

Net electric field,

$$E = E_A + E_B = 2|\mathbf{E}| = 2 \cdot \frac{1}{4\pi\varepsilon_0} \cdot \frac{4Q}{d^2}$$

$$E = \frac{1}{4\pi\varepsilon_0} \cdot \frac{8Q}{d^2}$$

25. *(a)* Let the final temperature of mixture be T°C.

From principle of calorimetry,

Heat given by 100 g of water = Heat taken by 100 g of ice

$$m_1 S_{\text{water}}(\Delta T_1) = m_2 L_f + m_2 S_{\text{water}} \Delta T_2$$

Substituting the given values, we get

$$100 \times 1 \times (80 - T) = 100 \times 80 + 100 \times 1 \times (T - 0)$$

$$\Rightarrow \quad 80 - T = 80 + T$$

$$\Rightarrow \quad 2T = 0 \Rightarrow T = 0°\text{C}$$

26. *(c)* $dU = C_V\, dT = \left(\dfrac{5}{2}R\right) dT$ or $dT = \dfrac{2(dU)}{5R}$

From first law of thermodynamics,

$$dU = dQ - dW = Q - \frac{Q}{4} = \frac{3Q}{4}$$

Now, molar heat capacity,

$$C = \frac{dQ}{dT} = \frac{Q}{\frac{2(dU)}{5R}} = \frac{5RQ}{2\left(\frac{3Q}{4}\right)} = \frac{10}{3}R$$

27. *(a)* $T_{\text{max}} = m(g + a) = (2000)(9.8 + 1.5) = 22600$ N

Maximum stress $= \dfrac{T_{\text{max}}}{\text{Area}}$

$$\therefore \text{Area} = \frac{T_{\text{max}}}{\text{Maximum stress}} = \frac{22600}{7 \times 10^7}$$

$$= 3.22 \times 10^{-4}\ \text{m}^2 = 3.22\ \text{cm}^2$$

28. *(c)* The statement given in option (c) is incorrect and it can be corrected as,
When particle moves in a circle even with uniform or constant speed, it faces an external force towards its centre called centripetal force.

29. *(a)* Three equal vectors can add upto zero when each of them is inclined at 120° with the other.
If $|\mathbf{A}+\mathbf{B}|=|\mathbf{A}-\mathbf{B}|$, they are inclined at 90° as shown below.

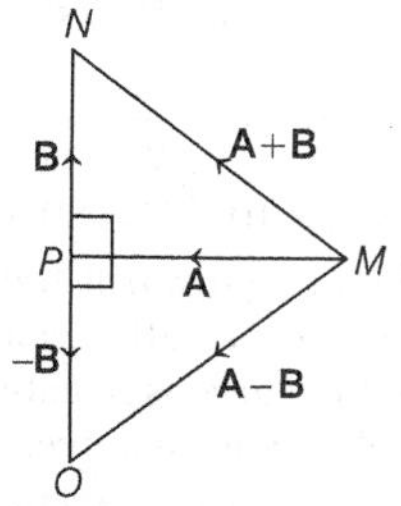

In this figure, length of MN is equal to length of MO.
So, $|\mathbf{A}+\mathbf{B}|=|\mathbf{A}-\mathbf{B}|$.
Thus, the statement given in option (a) is correct, rest are incorrect.

30. *(c)* Substances having more specific heat take longer time to get heated to a higher temperature and longer time to get cooled.

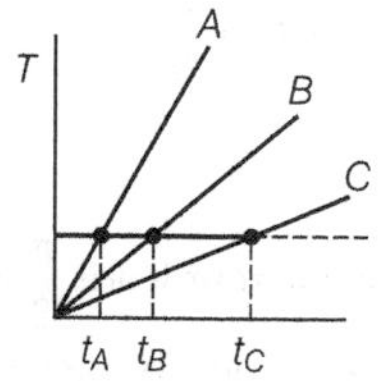

If we draw a line parallel to the time axis, then it cuts the given graphs at three different points.
Corresponding points on the time axes shows that,

$$t_C > t_B > t_A$$
$$\Rightarrow \quad c_C > c_B > c_A$$

31. *(d)* Density at temperature T is given by

$$\rho = \rho_0(1-\alpha\Delta T)$$
$$\rho = \rho_0 - \rho_0 \alpha \Delta T$$
$$\Rightarrow \frac{\rho-\rho_0}{\rho_0} = -\alpha\Delta T$$

∴ Fractional change in density,

$$\frac{\Delta\rho}{\rho_0} = -\alpha\Delta T = -6\times10^{-5}\times 60$$
$$\frac{\Delta\rho}{\rho_0} = -3.6\times10^{-3}$$

Note Negative sign indicates that density decreases with rise in temperature.

32. *(b)* Potential at the surface of earth,

$$V = -\frac{GM}{R}$$
$$= -\frac{6.67\times10^{-11}\times 20}{1}$$
$$= -1.334\times10^{-9}\text{ J/K}$$

i.e., 1.334×10^{-9} J work is done to bring a mass of 1 kg from infinity to the surface of sphere. Hence, the same amount of work will have to be done to take the particle away from the surface of sphere.

$$\therefore W = 1.334\times10^{-9}\text{ J}$$

33. *(d)* Escape velocity does not depend on the angle of projection, hence escape velocity remains same.

34. *(b)* Friction force, $F = \mu N$

and acceleration, $a = \frac{-F}{m} = -\frac{\mu mg}{m}$

$$a = -\mu g = -10\mu$$

Using third equation of motion,

$$v^2 = u^2 + 2as$$
or $$0^2 = (20)^2 + 2(-10\mu)80$$
or $$\mu = \frac{(20)^2}{2\times10\times80} = \frac{1}{4}$$
or $$\mu = 0.25$$

35. *(c)* Given, $m_1 = 1$ kg, $m_2 = 4$ kg
$r = 10\text{ cm} = 10\times10^{-2}$ m
∴ Gravitational potential energy,

$$U = -\frac{Gm_1m_2}{r} = \frac{-6.67\times10^{-11}\times1\times4}{10\times10^{-2}}$$
$$= -26.68\times10^{-10}\text{ J}$$

36. *(c)* I_{CM} is less than I about any other axis not passing through centre of mass but only when two axes are parallel.

$$\Rightarrow \quad I_B = I_A + I_A r^2$$

where, r is the distance between parallel axes.

$$\therefore \quad I_A < I_B$$

37. *(d)* Volume of the ideal gas is constant, so $W = 0$.
Using first law of thermodynamics,

$$\Delta Q = \Delta U \Rightarrow \Delta U = i^2Rt$$
$$= 1^2\times100\times5\times60$$
$$= 30\times10^3 = 30\text{ kJ}$$

38. *(c)* Given, $\frac{H}{t} = 25\text{J/s} = 25\text{ W}$

$$V = 25\text{ V}$$

We know that,

$$H = \frac{V^2}{R}t$$
$$\Rightarrow \frac{H}{t} = \frac{V^2}{R}$$
$$\Rightarrow 25 = \frac{25^2}{R}$$
$$\Rightarrow R = \frac{25^2}{25} = 25\ \Omega$$

39. *(b)* For the particle to move along anti-clockwise path, force should be along $\hat{j}$ y-direction.

Since, velocity is along $\hat{i}$,

Hence, $F_m = -e(\mathbf{v}\times\mathbf{B})$

In terms of unit vectors,

$$\hat{j} = -(\hat{i}\times\hat{p})$$

$$\Rightarrow \quad \hat{j} = \hat{p}\times\hat{i}$$

Clearly, $\hat{p} = \hat{k}$

Hence, magnetic field is applied along positive Z-axis.

40. *(d)* Given $l_1 = l$, $A_1 = A$

$$l_2 = l\left(1+\frac{20}{100}\right) = \frac{6l}{5},\ A_2 = A'$$

We have, $A_1 l_1 = A_2 l_2$

$$Al = A'\frac{6l}{5} \Rightarrow A' = \frac{5A}{6}$$

$$\therefore \quad \frac{R_2}{R_1} = \frac{\frac{\rho l_2}{A_2}}{\frac{\rho l_1}{A_1}} = \frac{l_2}{l_1}\cdot\frac{A_1}{A_2} = \frac{\frac{6l}{5}}{l}\cdot\frac{A}{\frac{5A}{6}} = \frac{36}{25}$$

Increase in the resistance,

$$\left(\frac{R_2}{R_1}-1\right)\times 100 = \left(\frac{36}{25}-1\right)\times 100 = 44\%$$

41. *(b)* Angular magnification of astronomical refracting telescope in normal adjustment is given as

$$m = \frac{f_0}{f_e}$$

where, f_0 and f_e are focal lengths of objective and eyepiece.

Hence, for large angular magnification of refracting telescope, it has an objective lens of large focal length and large diameter.

42. *(d)* Given, $\theta_1 = 60°$, $\theta_2 = 90°$

Work done in rotating a dipole from θ_1 to θ_2 in electric field is given as

$$W = pE(\cos\theta_1 - \cos\theta_2)$$

$$= pE(\cos 60° - \cos 90°)$$

$$= pE\left(\frac{1}{2}-0\right) = \frac{pE}{2}$$

43. *(b)* Given, frequency of light wave in medium $\nu = 2\times 10^{14}$ Hz

Wavelength, $\lambda = 5000\ \text{Å} = 5\times 10^{-7}$m

Refractive index of material is given as,

$$\mu = \frac{\text{velocity of light in air } (c)}{\text{velocity of light in medium } (v)} = \frac{c}{v}$$

$$= \frac{c}{\nu\lambda} \qquad [\because v = \nu\lambda]$$

$$= \frac{3\times 10^8}{2\times 10^{14}\times 5\times 10^{-7}}$$

$$\Rightarrow \quad \mu = 3$$

44. *(a)* Induced electric field lines are open loops. It emerges from positive charge and going to infinity and it enters into negative charge coming from infinity.

45. *(b)* Given, $E = 10^4$ N/C, $\tau = 4\sqrt{3}$ N-m, $\theta = 60°$

Dipole length, $2l = 1$ cm $= 10^{-2}$ m

We know that, torque on dipole,

$$\tau = pE\sin\theta$$

$$\Rightarrow \quad \tau = 2qlE\sin\theta \qquad [\because p = 2ql]$$

$$\Rightarrow \quad 4\sqrt{3} = 10^{-2}\cdot q\cdot 10^4\cdot\sin 60°$$

$$\Rightarrow \quad 4\sqrt{3} = 10^2\cdot q\cdot\frac{\sqrt{3}}{2}$$

$$\Rightarrow \quad q = 8\times 10^{-2}\ \text{C} = 80\times 10^{-3}\ \text{C} = 80\ \text{mC}$$

46. *(d)* The curve bending towards time axis represents decreasing velocity or negative velocity. So, at point III, the slope of the curve is negative. At this point, instantaneous velocity is negative.

47. *(b)* Here, speed of electromagnetic wave in vacuum/air, $c = 3\times 10^8$ m/s

Frequency, $f = 2\times 10^{10}$ Hz

As we know, wavelength,

$$\lambda = \frac{c}{f} = \frac{3\times 10^8}{2\times 10^{10}}$$

$$= 1.5\times 10^{-2}\ \text{m}$$

48. *(a)* $V = 100\sin\left(100\pi t + \frac{\pi}{6}\right)$

$$\therefore \quad \phi_1 = \frac{\pi}{6}$$

Since, alternating current leads $\frac{\pi}{2}$ angle from alternating voltage in purely capacitive circuit, hence phase angle of alternating current,

$$\phi_2 = \frac{\pi}{2} - \phi_1 = \frac{\pi}{2} - \frac{\pi}{6} = \frac{\pi}{3}$$

$\therefore$ Instantaneous value of alternative current,

$$i = i_0\sin(100\pi t + \phi_2)$$

$$= V_0\omega C\sin\left(100\pi t + \frac{\pi}{3}\right)$$

$$= 100\times 100\pi\times 1\times 10^{-6}\sin\left(100\pi t + \frac{\pi}{3}\right)$$

$$= 0.01\pi\sin\left(100\pi t + \frac{\pi}{3}\right)$$

49. *(d)* From graph, $V = 1.5$ V at $I = 0$

$\therefore$ EMF of cell $= 1.5$ V

At $V = 0$, $I = 1000$ mA $= 1$ A

Now using, $E - V = Ir$

We have, $1.5 - 0 = 1\times r$

$$\Rightarrow \quad r = 1.5\ \Omega$$

50. *(c)* By de-Broglie hypothesis,

$$2\pi r_n = n\lambda$$

For first orbit, $n = 1$, $r = r_1$, then

$2\pi r_1 = \lambda$ or $r_1 = \dfrac{\lambda}{2\pi}$

For second orbit, $n = 2$, $r = r_2$, then

$$2\pi r_2 = 2\lambda$$

or $$r_2 = \frac{2\lambda}{2\pi}$$

Minimum radial distance between first orbit and second orbit is

$$r_2 - r_1 = \frac{2\lambda}{2\pi} - \frac{\lambda}{2\pi}$$

$$\Rightarrow \quad r_2 - r_1 = \frac{\lambda}{2\pi}$$

51. *(c)* When electric field is applied, the random motion of all free electrons converted into uni-directional within very short duration of time of order 10^{-9} s. Which in turn sets up on electric field instantaneously. Thus, a current through each cross-section is produced almost instantaneously.
Hence, the bulb glows very quickly.

52. *(c)* $e_p = 220$ V, $e_s = 10$ V, $I_p = 5$ A and $I_s = 88$ A
Input power, $P_i = e_P \times I_P = 220 \times 5 = 1100$ W
Output power, $P_o = e_s \times I_s = 10 \times 88 = 880$ W
Efficiency, $\eta = \dfrac{P_0}{P_i} = \dfrac{880}{1100} = 0.8$ or 80%

53. *(c)* The given output voltage can be written as
$V = 100 \sin 100\pi t \cos 100\pi t$

$$= 50 \times 2 \sin 100\pi t \cos 100\pi t$$
$$= 50 \sin 2(100\pi t) \quad [\because 2\sin A \cos A = \sin 2A]$$
$$= 50 \sin 200\pi t$$

$\therefore$ Peak voltage of given AC source,

$$V_0 = 50 \text{ V}$$

$\therefore$ Angular frequency,

$$w = 2\pi f = 200\pi$$

$$\Rightarrow \quad f = \frac{200\pi}{2\pi} = 100 \text{ Hz}$$

54. *(b)* The given circuit is equivalent to given below,

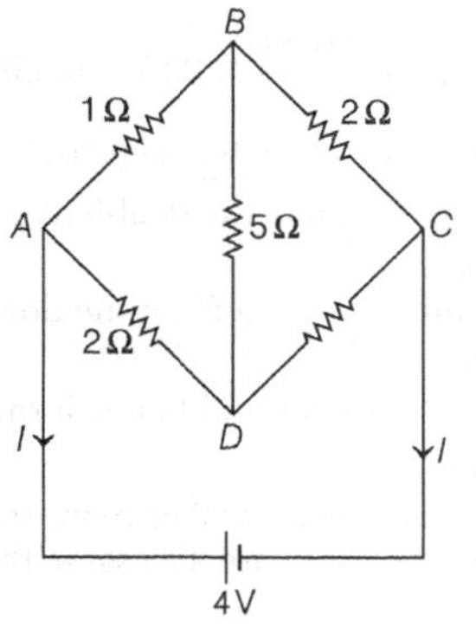

Now, $\dfrac{1\,\Omega}{2\,\Omega} = \dfrac{2\,\Omega}{4\,\Omega}$

i.e., $\dfrac{P}{Q} = \dfrac{R}{S}$

The given circuit is a balanced Wheatstone bridge. The resistance of 5 Ω in arm *BD* is ineffective.
$\therefore$ Now circuit can be drawn as

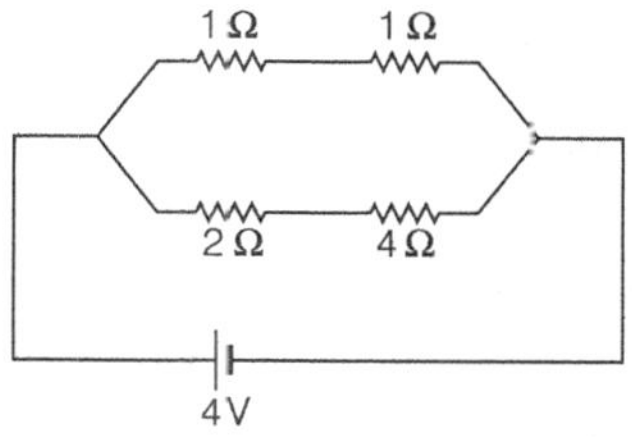

$\therefore$ Equivalent resistance,

$$R' = (1 + 2)||(2 + 4)$$
$$= 3 || 6 = \frac{3 \times 6}{3 + 6} = 2\,\Omega$$

$\therefore$ Current drawn from the battery,

$$I = \frac{V}{R'} = \frac{4}{2} = 2 \text{ A}$$

55. *(d)* When a closed current carrying loop of any shape placed in any uniform magnetic field in any direction, then it experiences no force.

56. *(b)* Given materials of μ_1 and μ_2 refractive indices are used to form lens. So, corresponding to these, there are two focal lengths of lens. Thus, the number of images formed will be 2.

57. *(c)* $$\frac{Q}{t} = \frac{KA(\Delta\theta)}{l}$$

$$\Rightarrow \quad 50 = \frac{5 \times 20K}{0.4}$$

$$\Rightarrow \quad K = \frac{1}{5} = 0.2$$

58. *(b)* Given, $\dfrac{\lambda}{4} = 20$ cm

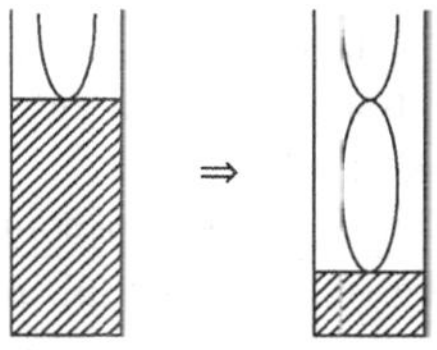

Next resonance will be obtained at $\dfrac{3\lambda}{4} = 60$ cm

59. *(d)* $u_x = 19.6$ m/s and $u_y = 19.6$ m/s. After 2 s, vertical component of velocity v_y will become zero. So, particle is at its highest point.

60. *(b)* In a Young's double slit experiment for interference pattern, the position of bright fringe is given by

$$y_n = \frac{n\lambda D}{d}$$

Here, $D = 1.5$ m

$d = 0.3 \times 10^{-3}$ m

and $n = 1;\ \lambda = \dfrac{y_n d}{D}$

For first violet, $y_n = 2\,\text{mm} = 2 \times 10^{-3}$ m

$\therefore \lambda_{\text{violet}} = 2 \times 10^{-3}\dfrac{d}{D}$

For first red,

$y_n = 3.5\ \text{mm} = 3.5 \times 10^{-3}$ m

$\lambda_{\text{red}} = 3.5 \times 10^{-3}\dfrac{d}{D}$

The difference in wavelengths of red and violet light is

$$\Delta\lambda = \lambda_{\text{red}} - \lambda_{\text{violet}}$$
$$= 3.5 \times 10^{-3}\frac{d}{D} - 2 \times 10^{-3}\frac{d}{D}$$
$$= \frac{d}{D}(1.5) \times 10^{-3}$$
$$= \frac{0.3 \times 10^{-3}}{1.5} \times 1.5 \times 10^{-3}$$
$$= 0.3 \times 10^{-6} = 0.3 \times 10^{-6} \times 10^{3} \times 10^{-3}$$
$$= 300 \times 10^{-9}$$
$$= x \times 10^{-9}\ \text{m} \qquad \text{(given)} \therefore x = 300$$

Chemistry

61. *(c)* The complete reaction is as follows.

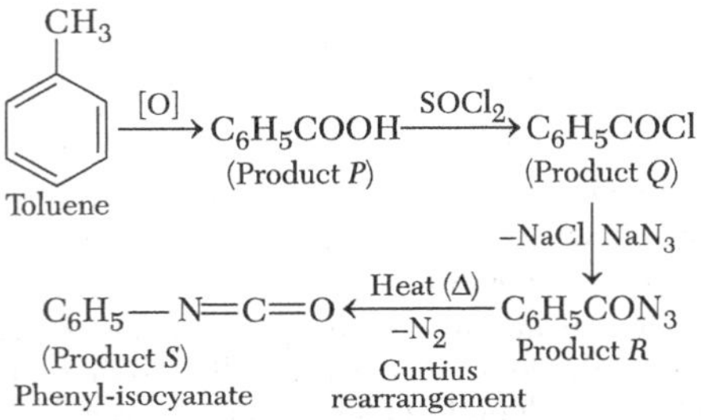

62. *(c)* The complete reaction involved is,

$$ROH + CH_3MgI \longrightarrow \underset{1\ \text{mole}}{CH_4} + Mg(OH)I$$

$= 22400$ mL

1.12 mL is obtained from $\dfrac{4.12}{1.12} \times 22400$ mg

$= 82.4$ g

$\therefore$ Molecular mass of alcohol $= 82.4$ g

63. *(a)* Given,

Density of KCl solution = 1.20 g/mL

Molality of solution = 6.60 mol/kg

Molar mass of KCl = 74.5

$$\text{Molality} = \frac{6.60\ \text{mol}}{\text{kg}} = \frac{6.60\ \text{mol solute}}{1000\ \text{g solvant}}$$

Mass of solution $= 6.6 \times 74.5 + 1000$

$= 1491.7$ g

$$\text{Volume of solution} = \frac{\text{Mass}}{\text{Density}} = \frac{1491.7}{1.20}$$

$$\text{So, molarity} = \frac{6.60 \times 1.2}{1491.7} \times 1000$$

$M = 5.3$ mol/L

Nearest integer = 5 mol/L

64. *(a)* Due to bulky isobutyl group, $AlH(i\text{—}Bu)_2$ reduces cyanides only to CH $=$ NH which upon subsequent hydrolysis with H_2O gives aldehyde.

$$R\text{—}C\equiv N \xrightarrow{AlH(i\text{-}Bu)_2} RCH = NH \xrightarrow[-NH_3]{H_2O} \underset{(X)}{R\text{—}CHO}$$

65. *(c)* Yellow colour is obtained due to the formation of CrO_4^{2-} (chromate) ion when $Cr(OH)_3$ is oxidised by Na_2O_2 in basic medium.

The complete reaction is as follows,

$$Cr(OH)_3 + NaOH + Na_2O_2 \longrightarrow Na_2CrO_4 + 2H_2O$$

66. *(d)* At anode

$$2H_2O \longrightarrow O_2(g) + 4H^+ + 4e^-$$

At cathode

$$2H_2O + 2e^- \longrightarrow H_2(g) + 2OH^-$$

$$\text{Now number of gram equivalent} = \frac{\text{Current} \times \text{Time}}{\text{Faraday constant}}$$
$$= \frac{0.2 \times 4 \times 60 \times 60}{96500} = 0.0298$$
$$V_{O_2} = \frac{0.0298}{4} \times 22.7 = 0.1693$$
$$V_{H_2} = \frac{0.0298}{2} \times 22.7 = 0.3387$$
$$V_{\text{Total}} = V_{O_2} + V_{H_2} = 0.5077 = 508\,\text{mL or CC}$$

67. *(b)* Only 1° amines react with aldehydes to form Schiff's base.

Only morpholine being a 2° amine does not form a Schiff's base.

All other are 1° amines and hence form Schiff's base.

68. *(b)* $\pi = iCRT$

When, i, C, T are same for 2 or more solution then their osmotic pressure are also same that are known as isotonic.

(a) $NaCl \longrightarrow Na^+ + Cl^- \Rightarrow i = 2$

$Na_2SO_4 \longrightarrow 2Na^+ + SO_4^{-2}$

$\Rightarrow \quad i = 3$

(i) is different, so not an isotonic

(b) $Ca(NO_3)_2 \longrightarrow Ca^{+2} + 2NO_3^- \ [i = 3]$
$Na_2SO_4 \longrightarrow 2Na^+ + SO_4^{-2} [i = 3]$
(i) is same, so this pair is an isotonic.
(c) Urea $i = 1$ non electrolyte
NaCl, $i = 2[Na^+ + Cl^-]$
(i) is different, so not an isotonic
(d) Urea $i = 1$
$MgCl_2 \ i = 3[Mg^{2+} + 2Cl^-]$
(i) is different, so not an isotonic

69. *(a)* The complete reaction is as follow.

$$2CuSO_4 + 10KCN \longrightarrow \underset{(A)}{2K_3[Cu(CN)_4]} + 2K_2SO_4 + (CN)_2$$
$$\downarrow H_2S$$
$$\text{No precipitate}(B)$$

As CN^- is a strong ligand, the complex formed is highly stable and does not dissociate to give Cu^+ ions. However, no precipitate of CuS is formed when H_2S gas is passes through solution.

70. *(b)* In acidic medium, $KMnO_4$ reacts as follows,

$$2KMnO_4 + 3H_2SO_4 \longrightarrow K_2SO_4 + 2MnSO_4 + 3H_2O + 5(O)$$

Or

$$MnO_4^- + 8H^+ + 5e^- \longrightarrow Mn^{2+} + 4H_2O$$

$\therefore$ equivalent weight of $KMnO_4 = \frac{M}{5}$

$$= \frac{158}{5} = 31.6$$

71. *(a)* Formation of alkanes by action of Zn on alkyl halides is called as Frankland reaction.

72. *(c)* (i) 10^{-4} M NaCl

$$NaCl \longrightarrow Na^+ + Cl^-$$
$$\pi = iCRT \ [i = 2]$$
$$\pi = 2 \times 10^{-4} RT$$

(ii) 10^{-3} M urea

$$\pi = 1 \times 10^{-3} RT \ [i = 1]$$

(iii) 10^{-3} M $MgCl_2$

$$MgCl_2 \longrightarrow Mg^{+2} + 2Cl^-$$
$$\pi = 3 \times 10^{-3} \ RT \ [i = 3]$$

(iv) 10^{-3} M NaCl

$$\pi = 2 \times 10^{-3} RT \qquad [i = 2]$$

Then the correct increasing order is
(i) < (ii) < (iv) < (iii).

73. *(c)* Writing the complete balance equation.

$$2IO_3^- + 5SO_2 + 4H_2O \longrightarrow I_2 + SO_4^{2-} + 8H^+$$

Hence, coefficient of SO_2 is 5.

74. *(c)*

$$Ag^+ + e^- \longrightarrow Ag$$
$$Ca^{+2} + 2e^- \longrightarrow Ca$$
$$Al^{+3} + 3e^- \longrightarrow Al$$

For 1 mol of Ag^+, Ca^{+2} and Al^{+3}, 1 mol of e^-, 2 mol of e^- and 3 mol of e^- are required respectively.

For 3-faraday $\rightarrow 1 \times 3$; $\rightarrow 2 \times 3$ mole electron; $\rightarrow 3 \times 3$

For 1 mole e^- = 1 Faraday $\longrightarrow$ 1 mole of Ag^+

For 1 mole e^- = 1 Faraday $\longrightarrow \frac{1}{2}$ mole of Ca^{+2}

For 1 mole e^- = 1 Faraday $\longrightarrow \frac{1}{3}$ mole of Al^{+3}

So, for 3 Faraday $\longrightarrow 1 \times 3, \frac{1}{2} \times 3, \frac{1}{3} \times 3$

$$= 3 : \frac{3}{2} : 1 \text{ or } 6 : 3 : 2$$

75. *(a)*

	A_2	+	$3B_2$	$\longrightarrow$	$2AB_3$
Initial	5 moles		7 moles		0 moles

Thus 1 mole of A_2 react with 3 mole of B_2

$\therefore$ 7 moles of B_2 will react with $A_2 = \frac{7}{3}$ moles

A_2 left $= 5 - \frac{7}{3} = \frac{8}{3}$ moles

1 mole of A_2 produces 2 moles of AB_3

$\therefore \frac{7}{3}$ moles of A_2 will produce $AB_3 = \frac{7}{3} \times 2 = \frac{14}{3}$ moles

$\therefore$ Total moles of gases in vessel $= \frac{8}{3}$ moles of $A_2 + \frac{14}{3}$ moles of $AB_3 = \frac{22}{3}$ moles

76. *(b)* Statement given in (i) and (iii) are correct, while in (ii) and (iv) are incorrect.

BeO and Al_2O_3 are amphoteric. These react with acid as well as alkalines to given corrosponding salts.

$$BeO + 2HCl \longrightarrow BeCl_2 + H_2O$$
$$BeO + 2NaOH \longrightarrow Na_2BeO_2 + H_2O$$
$$Al_2O_3 + 6HCl \longrightarrow 2AlCl_3 + 3H_2O$$
$$Al_2O_3 + 2NaOH \longrightarrow 2NaAlO_2 + H_2O$$

Be_2C and Al_4C_3 give methane on treatment with water.

$$Be_2C + 4H_2O \longrightarrow 2Be(OH)_2 + CH_4$$
$$Al_4C_3 + 12H_2O \longrightarrow 4\,Al\,(OH)_3 + 3CH_4$$

77. *(b)* Given,

Rate of disappearance $= \frac{-d[MnO_4^-]}{dt}$

$$= 2.28 \times 10^{-3} \text{ M/s}$$

From the reaction,

$$-\frac{1}{2}\frac{d[MnO_4^-]}{dt} = \frac{1}{2}[2.28 \times 10^{-3}] \qquad \text{...(i)}$$

$$-\frac{1}{2}\frac{d[MnO_4^-]}{dt} = \frac{1}{5}\frac{dI_2}{dt}$$

$$-\frac{5}{2}\frac{d[MnO_4^-]}{dt} = \frac{dI_2}{dt} \qquad \text{...(ii)}$$

Substituting the value of Eq. (i) in (ii)

$$+\frac{5}{2}\times 2.28\times 10^{-3}=\frac{dI_2}{dt}$$

$$=5.7\times 10^{-3}\ \text{M/s}$$

Nearest integer value $= 6\times 10^{-3}$M/s

78. *(a)* Number of moles of $FeSO_4 = \frac{20\ \text{g}}{152\ \text{g mol}^{-1}}$

$= 0.132$ mole

The balance ionic equation of redox reaction is

$$Cr_2O_7^{2-} + 6Fe^{2+} + 14H^+ \longrightarrow 2Cr^{3+} + 6Fe^{3+} + 7H_2O$$

6 moles of Fe^{2+} = 1 mole of $K_2Cr_2O_7$

$\therefore 0.132$ mole of $Fe^{2+} = \frac{1}{6}\times 0.132$

$= 0.022$ moles of $K_2Cr_2O_7$

Mass of $K_2Cr_2O_7$ in 0.02 moles

$= 0.022\times 294 = 6.5$ g

79. *(c)* $\Delta S_{surrounding} = \frac{q_{surrounding}}{T} = \frac{-q_{system}}{T} = \frac{W_{system}}{T}$

(For isothermal process, $\Delta U = 0, \because q = -W$)

$W_{system} = -P_{ext}(V_f - V_i)$

$= -3(2-1) = -3$ L atm

$\therefore \Delta S_{surrounding} = \frac{-3}{300}$ L atm $= -0.01$ Latm

$= -0.01\times 101.3$ J $= -1.013$ J

80. *(b)* Vitamin C is also called as ascorbic acid.

81. *(b)* The complete reaction involved are,

$$\underset{(A)}{C_6H_5NH_2} + CHCl_2 \xrightarrow{\text{Alc. KOH}} C_6H_5NC$$

$$\underset{(C)}{CH_3CH_2OH} \xrightarrow[-2HCl]{+Cl_2} [CH_3CHO] \xrightarrow[-3HCl]{3Cl_2} \underset{\text{Chloral}}{CCl_3\cdot CHO} \xrightarrow{Ca(OH)_2} \underset{(B)}{CHCl_3}$$

82. *(b)* Gene acts as the instruction manual for the synthesis of protein.

83. *(a)* The complete reaction involved is as follows,

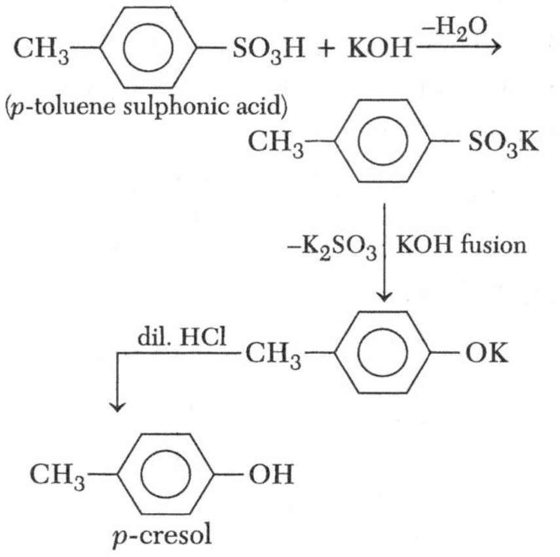

84. *(d)* $SOCl_2$ has one S = 0 double bond and two S—Cl single bond.

Hybridisation of S $= \frac{1}{2}[6+2-0+0] = 4$

Thus, S is sp^3. Since, $SOCl_2$ has only three sigma bond, therefore it has one lone pair of electrons on S atom and hence its shape is pyramidal and the bond angle are less than 109.5° due to repulsion between lone pairs.

Further, since π-electrons of the S = O bonds are more polarised, therefore, they repel the bond pair of S—Cl bond.

Thus, making Cl—S—O bond larger than Cl—S—Cl bond angle.

85. *(d)* Volume of acid taken = 50 mL of 0.5 MH_2SO_4

= 25 mL of 1 M H_2SO_4

Volume of alkali used for neutralisation of excess acid.

= 60 mL of 0.5 M NaOH = 30 mL of 1 M NaOH

Now 1 mole of H_2SO_4 neutralises 2 moles of NaOH,

(i.e, $H_2SO_4 + 2NaOH \longrightarrow Na_2SO_4 + H_2O$)

$\therefore$ 30 mL of 1 M NaOH = 15 mL of 1 M H_2SO_4

$\therefore$ Volume of acid used by NH_3 = 25 − 15 = 10 mL

$$\text{Now \% N} = \frac{1.4\times M\times B\times V}{\text{Mass of the substance taken}}$$

$$= \frac{1.4\times 1\times 2\times 10}{0.5} = 56\ \text{g}$$

86. *(a)* Given,

$$Cu(s) + Sn^{2+}(0.01\ M) \longrightarrow Cu^{2+}(0.1\ M) + Sn(s)$$

$$E^\circ_{cell} = E^\circ_{cathode} - E^\circ_{anode}$$

$$= -0.14 - (0.34) = -0.48\ V$$

$$E_{cell} = E^\circ_{cell} - \frac{0.059}{n}\log\frac{[Cu^{2+}]}{[Sn^{2+}]}\ [n=2]$$

$$= -0.48 - \frac{0.059}{2}\log\frac{[0.1]}{0.01}$$

$$= -0.48 - 0.0290\log[10] = -0.5095\ V$$

Gibb's free energy,

$$\Delta G = -nFE_{cell}$$

$$= +2(96500)\times 0.5095$$

$$= 98.33\times 10^3\ \text{J/mol}$$

or 983×10^{-1} kJ/mol

Hence, the value of x is 983.

87. *(b)* An acid indicator is a weak acid. It dissociates

$$\underset{\text{Colour } A}{HIn} \rightleftharpoons H^+ + \underset{\text{Colour } B}{In^-}$$

$$K_{In} = \frac{[H^+][In^-]}{[HIn]}$$

The indicator HIn will show a colour change at mid point, i.e. the point at which $[In^-] = [HIn]$

Hence, $K_{In} = [H^+] = 10^{-5}$

or $\quad pH = 5$

88. *(c)* Flask I

$$1M \xrightarrow[t=t_{1/2}=4\text{ hrs}]{} 0.25\text{ M} \xrightarrow[t=t_{1/2}=4\text{ hrs}]{} 0.25\text{ M}$$

total time t=8 hrs

$\therefore \quad t_{1/2} = 4$ hrs.

Flask II

$$0.6\text{ M} \xrightarrow[t_{1/2}\,=\,4\text{ hrs}]{} 0.3\text{ M}$$

A first order reaction is independent of the initial concentration of the reactant.

Hence, the time required is 4 hours.

89. *(d)* During addition of electron to O_2 to form O_2^-, the additional π-molecular electron is added to the less stable antibonding orbital.

Therefore, it is easier to remove an electron from O_2^- ion to form a neutral O_2 molecule.

Thus ionisation enthalpy of O_2^- is lowest.

90. *(d)* Acetic acid, acetyl chloride and acetic anhydride all react with ethyl alcohol to form ethyl acetate which has fruity smell.

$$\underset{\text{Acetic acid}}{CH_3COOH} + CH_3CH_2OH \longrightarrow \underset{\text{Ethyl acetate}}{CH_3COOC_2H_5} + H_2O$$

91. *(c)*

	N_2O_5	$\rightleftharpoons 2NO_2$	$+\frac{1}{2}O_2$
A $t=0$	50 mm Hg	0	0
At $t=50$ mm	$50-p_1$	$2p_1$	$\frac{p_1}{2}$

Total pressure at $t=50$ min is

$$50 - p_1 + 2p_1 + \frac{p_1}{2} = 87.5 \text{ mm Hg}$$

$$p_1 = \frac{37.5}{1.5} = 25 \text{ mm Hg}$$

Since, $t=50$ minutes is the half life period for reaction.

Thus $t=100$ min is equal to 2 half lives.

	N_2O_5	$\rightleftharpoons 2NO_2$	$+\frac{1}{2}O_2$
$t=100$ min	$50-p_2$	$2p_2$	$\frac{p_2}{2}$

$$\therefore \quad 50 - p_2 = \frac{25}{2} \qquad \text{(At 2}^{\text{nd}}\text{ half life)}$$

$$p_2 = 37.5 \text{ mm Hg}$$

Total pressure at $t = 100$ min $\Rightarrow 50 - p_2 + 2p_2 + \frac{p_2}{2}$

$$= 50 + 1.5p_2 \Rightarrow 50 + 1.5 \times 37.5$$

$$= 106.25 \text{ mm Hg}$$

Hence, nearest integer will be 106.

92. *(d)* Tyrosine has phenolic OH group.

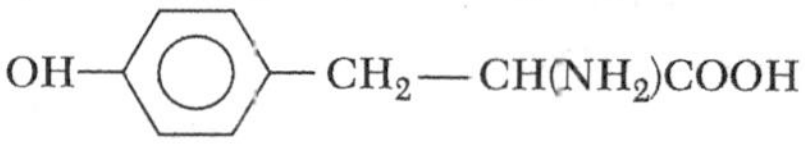

93. *(d)* When intensity is doubled, number of electron emitted per second is also doubled but average energy of photoelectron emitted remains same. Thus, Y will be doubled, Z will remain same.

94. *(a)* The complete reaction is as follows,

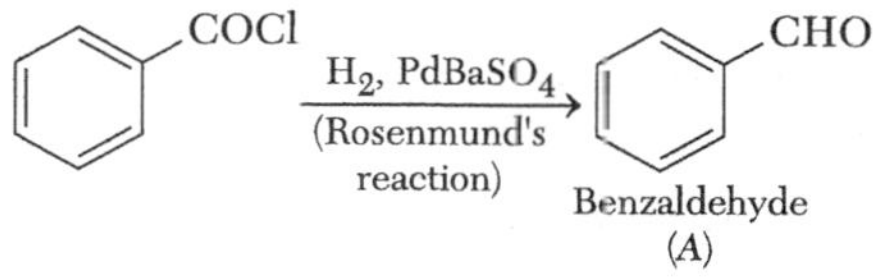

95. *(b)* Sulphur dioxide is the gas that can readily decolourised acidified $KMnO_4$ solution.

The complete reaction is as follows,

$$\underset{\text{Purple colour}}{2KMnO_4} + 5SO_2 + 2H_2O \longrightarrow K_2SO_4 + \underset{\text{Colourless}}{2MnSO_4} + 2H_2SO_4$$

96. *(c)* The weight of oxygen which combine with the fixed weight of nitrogen (= 28 g) in N_2O, NO, N_2O_3, N_2O_4 and N_2O_5 are 16, 32, 48, 64, 80 g respectively. They are in the ratio 1 : 2 : 3 : 4 : 5. This proves the law of multiple proportion.

97. *(c)* The complete reaction is as follows.

$$CH_3CH_2COOH \xrightarrow[\text{H.V.Z reaction}]{Cl_2,\ \text{red P}} \underset{\text{Product}}{\underset{(X)}{CH_3—\underset{\displaystyle Cl}{\underset{|}{CH}}—COOH}}$$

$$\underset{\text{(Product }Y)}{CH_2{=}CH—COOH} \xleftarrow[\text{dehydrochlorination reaction}]{\text{Alk. KOH}} (X)$$

98. *(a)*

$$\underset{\text{Keto form}}{CH_3—CH_2—\overset{\displaystyle O}{\overset{||}{C}}—CH_3} \rightleftharpoons \underset{\text{Enolic form}}{CH_3—CH_2—\overset{\displaystyle \ddot{O}—H}{\overset{|}{C}}{=}CH_2}$$

i.e enolic form of butane is

$$H—\overset{\displaystyle H}{\underset{\displaystyle H}{C}}—\overset{\displaystyle H}{\underset{\displaystyle H}{C}}—\overset{\displaystyle \ddot{O}H}{C}{=}\overset{\displaystyle H}{C}—H$$

12σ bond, 1 π bond and 2 lone pairs.

99. *(a)* Aldol condensation gives methyl vinyl ketone when formaldehyde react with acetone.

The complete reaction is as follows,

COMEDK 2024

$$\underset{\text{Formaldehyde}}{CH_2{=}O} + \underset{\text{Acetone}}{CH_3COCH_3} \xrightarrow[\text{Aldol condensation}]{\text{Dil NaOH}} HOCH_2—CH_2COCH_2$$

$$\xrightarrow[(-H_2O)]{\text{Dehydration}} \underset{\text{Methyl vinyl ketone}}{CH_2{=}CH—COCH_3}$$

100. *(a)* We know that,

$$C_P = C_V + R$$

$$C_P = \frac{3}{2}R + R = \frac{5}{2}R$$

At constant pressure, heat absorb by one mole of gas (q_p)

$$= nC_p\Delta T = 1 \times \frac{5}{2}[100 - 25]R$$

$$= 1 \times \frac{5}{2} \times 1.987 \times 75$$

$$q_p = 372.56 \text{ cal}$$

101. *(b)* Number of orbitals in subshell with azimuthal quantum number $l = -l$ to $+l$ including orbitals $= 2l + 1$

$\therefore$ Each orbital can have maximum 2 electron, therefore maximum electron present

$$= 2(2l + 1)$$

102. *(c)* Aryl halides being less reactive do not under goes Friedel-craft reaction with benzene.

$$C_6H_6 + C_6H_5Cl \xrightarrow{AlCl_3} \text{No reaction}$$

103. *(a)* Peroxides, if present, in old stocks of ethers oxidise Fe^{2+} to Fe^{3+} ions which then combines with KCNS to form blood red colouration due to formation of ferric sulphocyanide.

$$Fe^{2+} \xrightarrow{\text{Peroxide}} Fe^{3+}$$

$$Fe^{3+} + 3KCNS \longrightarrow Fe(CNS)_3 + 3K^+$$

104. *(d)* For hydrogen like particle, energy of nth-orbital is given as,

$$E_n = -\frac{2\pi^2 mZe^4}{n^2h^2} \text{ or } -\frac{KZ^2}{n^2}$$

where $K = \dfrac{2\pi^2 me^4}{h^2}$

Ionisation energy, IE = Energy at infinity – Energy at $n = 1$

$$IE = 0 - \left[-\frac{KZ^2}{1^2}\right] = KZ^2$$

For H, $Z = 1$

$\therefore$ IE $= K = 13$ eV

For Li^{2+}, $Z = 3$, IE $= K \times 9 = 122.4$ eV

105. *(a)* The reaction to form hydrazine is as follows

$$N_2(g) + 2H—H(g) \longrightarrow N_2H_4(g)$$

$N{\equiv}N + 2H—H \longrightarrow$ 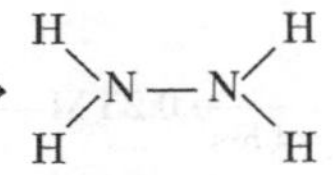

$$\Delta_r H° = \Delta_f H°(N_2H_4) = \Sigma BE\text{ (reactant)} - \Sigma BE\text{ (product)}$$

$$= [B.E\ (N{\equiv}N + 2\ B.E.(H—H)] - [BE\ (N—N) + 4(BE)(N—H)]$$

$$= [946 + 2(435)] - [159 + 4 \times 389]$$

$$= 101 \text{ kJ/mol}$$

106. *(b)*

	$2NH_3$	$\rightleftharpoons$	N_2	+	$3H_2$
Initial concentration	$\frac{6}{10}$ mol/L = 0.6 mol/L		0		0
Concentration at equilibrium	$0.6 - 2x$		x		$3x$

When x moles of N_2 are formed, $3x$ moles of H_2 will formed and $2x$ moles of NH_3 would react (according to balance equation).

107. *(a)* Polarising power is determined by charge/size ratio. Higher charge and smaller size gives more polarising power.

Thus, the correct order is

$$Cs^+ < K^+ < Mg^{2+} < Al^{3+}$$

108. *(b)* All the three are disubstituted benzenes, i.e., xylenes has two CH_3 groups, dichlorobenzenes has two Cl atoms and cresol has one CH_3 and one OH group.

Therefore, each one has three isomers i.e, *o*-(1, 2), *m*-(1, 3) and *p*-(1, 4).

109. *(c)* Both BCl_3 and PH_3 has 3 bond pairs each but PH_3 also has one lone pair of electron on P.

Therefore BCl_3 is triangular planar whereas PH_3 has trigonal pyramidal shape.

110. *(b)* Phosphorous acid (H_3PO_3) is a diprotic acid. It form two series of salt such as NaH_2PO_3 and Na_2HPO_3 but, none of the type Na_3PO_3 with NaOH.

Structure of H_3PO_3

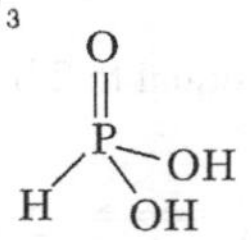

111. *(d)* The complex in which size of transition metal is small and ligand is weak field, has tetrahedral shape and sp^3 hybridisation.

$$Ni^{2+} = [Ar]\ 3d^8, 4s^0$$

$$[NiCl_4]^{2-} = [Ar]\ 3d^8$$

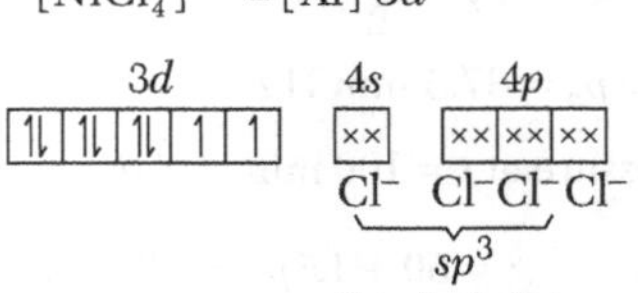

Tetrahedral shape

112. *(a)* Atomic number, $(z) = 25$ for Mn
electronic configuration of Mn $= [Ar]\ 3d^5 4s^2$
electronic configuration of $Mn^{2+} = [Ar]\ 3d^5$
Thus, $Mn^{2+}(aq)$ has 5 unpaired electrons.
Magnetic moment is given by the formula.

$$\mu_s = \sqrt{n(n+2\_} = \sqrt{5(5+2)} = \sqrt{35} \text{ B.M.}$$
$$= 5.92 \text{ B.M.}$$

113. *(d)* Let oxidation number of oxygen $= x$
O.N. of oxygen in $CO_3 = 1 + 3x = 0$

$$\therefore \quad x = \frac{-1}{3} \text{ or } -0.33$$

Oxidation number of oxygen in Na_2O_2

$$= 2 \times 1 + 2x = 0$$
$$\therefore \quad x = -1$$

114. *(b)* The complete reaction is as follows,

$$CH_2{=}CHCl \xrightarrow{Cl_2} \underset{(A)}{ClCH_2{-}CHCl_2}$$
$$\xrightarrow[363K-HCl]{Ca(OH)_2} \underset{\substack{1,\,1\text{-dichloroethene}\\(B)}}{CH_2 = CCl_2}$$

During dehydrohalogination of (*A*), the more acidic hydrogen (i.e. $CHCl_2$) is eliminated.

115. *(c)* $N_2 + 2O_2 \rightleftharpoons 2NO_2;\ k = 100$ ...(i)
To find equilibrium constant of

$$NO_2(g) \rightleftharpoons \frac{1}{2}N_2(g) + O_2(g) \quad ...(ii)$$

If we divide eq (i) by 2 and taking the reverse we will obtain equation (ii).

$$\text{Required } k = \sqrt{\frac{1}{100}} = \frac{1}{10} = 0.1$$
$$k = 0.1$$

116. *(b)* Due to greater electronegativity of *sp*-hybridised carbon, − ve charge on $HC \equiv C^-$ is most stable. The stability of other carbanions decreases as the + *I* effect of the alkyl groups increases. Thus, $(CH_3)_3C^-$ is the least stable.

117. *(b)* 2-hexene shows geometrical isomerism since each carbon of the doubles bond has twc different substituent [CH_3, H] and [H, $CH_2CH_2CH_3$]. 3-hexyne being linear does not show geometrical isomerism. Cyclohexane, (*cis*-isomer) however, due to angle strain cannot get converted into the *trans*-isomers.

118. *(a)* Bromine water is an oxidising agent. It oxidises SO_2 to SO_3 and itself get reduced to colourless HBr.

$$\underset{\text{Orange red}}{Br_2} + H_2O \longrightarrow \underset{\text{Colourless}}{2HBr} + [O]$$
$$\underset{\text{Colourless}}{SO_2} + [O] \longrightarrow SO_3$$
$$H_2O + SO_3 \longrightarrow H_2SO_4$$

H_2S is also oxidised by bromine water but in this case, decolourisation is also accompanied by formation of sulphur.

$$H_2S + [O] \longrightarrow H_2O + S$$

119. *(d)* $KMnO_4$ oxidises 3° H of isopentane to 3°—OH group. As a result, pink violet colour of $KMnO_4$ get discharged.
In constants, 1° or 2°H of *n*-pentane does not get oxidised to the corresponding OH group and hence colour of $KMnO_4$ is not discharged.

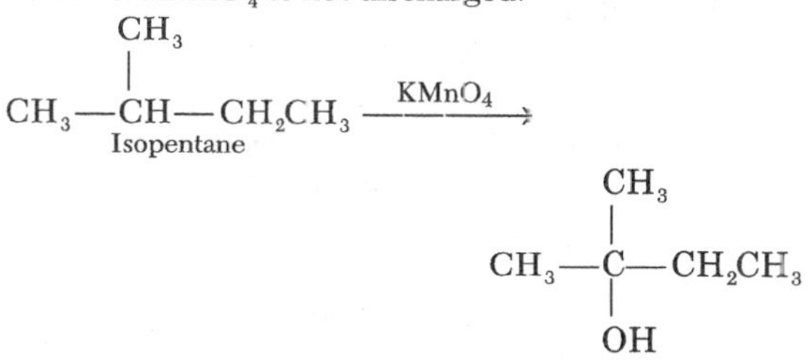

120. *(d)* The sulphide ion S^{2-} react with sodium nitroprusside to give a dark purple complex.
The complete reaction is as follows,

$$S^{2-} + \underset{\text{Sodium nitroprusside}}{Na_2[Fe(CN)_5NO]} \longrightarrow \underset{\text{Dark purple complex}}{Na_2[Fe(CN)_5NOS]^-}$$

Mathematics

121. *(c)*

$$2^{\log_2 3} . 3^{\log_3 2}$$
$$= 3^{\log_2 2} . 2^{\log_3 3} \quad [\because a \log_b c = c \log_b a]$$
$$= 3 \cdot 2 \quad [\because \log_a a = 1]$$
$$= 6$$

122. *(d)* We have, $y = x^3 - 3x^2y$ ...(i)
Differentiate Eq. (i) w.r.t. *x*

$$\therefore \quad \frac{dy}{dx} = 3x^2 - 3\left(2xy - x^2\frac{dy}{dx}\right)$$
$$\frac{dy}{dx} = 3x^2 - 6xy + 3x^2\frac{dy}{dx}$$
$$\frac{dy}{dx} - 3x^2\frac{dy}{dx} = 3x^2 - 6xy$$
$$\frac{dy}{dx}(1 - 3x^2) = 3x^2 - 6xy$$
$$\frac{dy}{dx} = \frac{3x^2 - 6xy}{1 - 3x^2}$$

Put $x = 1$ and $y = 1$

$$\therefore \quad \left[\frac{dy}{dx}\right]_{(1,1)} = \frac{3-6}{1-2}$$
$$\left[\frac{dy}{dx}\right]_{(1,1)} = 3$$

123. *(c)* $\lim_{x \to 0} \dfrac{\sin 3x + e^{2x} - 1}{x}$

Put $x = 0 \Rightarrow \dfrac{\sin 0 + e^0 - 1}{0} \left(\dfrac{0}{0}\right)$

Using L'hospital's rule we can differentiate both Numerator and denominator separately

$\therefore \lim_{x \to 0} \dfrac{3\cos 3x + 2e^{2x}}{1}$

Now put $x = 0$

$$= \frac{3\cos 0 + 2e^0}{1} = 3 + 2 = 5$$

124. *(c)* If equation of circle is $x^2 + y^2 + 2gx + 2fg + c = 0$

Then, centre $= (-g, -f)$

Radius $= \sqrt{g^2 + f^2 - c}$

$\Rightarrow x^2 + y^2 + 2x + 4y + \dfrac{5}{3} = 0$

$\therefore$ Centre $= (-g, -f) = (-1, -2)$

$\therefore$ Radius $= \sqrt{1^2 + 2^2 - \dfrac{5}{3}} = \sqrt{5 - \dfrac{5}{3}} = 5\sqrt{\dfrac{2}{3}}$

125. *(d)* We can write 3.001 as $x = 3$ and $\Delta x = 0.001$ and use the relation

$$f(x + \Delta x) \approx f(x) + \Delta x f'(x)$$
$$f'(x) = 3x^2 - 5$$

Now, $f(3 + 0.001) \approx f(3) + (0.001)(f'(5))$

$$\approx 27 - 15 + 10 + 0.001(75 - 5)$$
$$\approx 27 - 5 + \frac{70}{1000}$$
$$\approx 22 + 0.07 \approx 22.07$$

126. *(a)* General equation of circle is

$x^2 + y^2 + 2gx + 2fy + c = 0$

On comparing with given equation

$x^2 + y^2 - 6x + 4y + 3 = 0$, we get

$$g = -3$$
$$f = 2$$
$$c = 3$$

y-intercept $= 2\sqrt{f^2 - c}$

$$= 2\sqrt{4 - 3} = 2\sqrt{1} = 2$$

127. *(a)* We have,

$$f(x) = 5 + (2x - 3)^{\frac{4}{3}}$$

Differentiate w.r.t. x

$$f'(x) = 0 + \frac{4}{3}(2x - 3)^{\frac{1}{3}} \times 2$$

$$f'(x) = \frac{8}{3}(2x - 3)^{\frac{1}{3}}$$

$$f'(x) = \frac{8}{3}(2x - 3)^{\frac{1}{3}} = 0$$

$$2x - 3 = 0$$

$$x = \frac{3}{2}$$

Hence, $f\left(\dfrac{3}{2}\right) = 5 + \left(2\left(\dfrac{3}{2}\right) - 3\right)^{\frac{4}{3}}$

$$f\left(\frac{3}{2}\right) = 5$$

128. *(c)* If $f(x)$ is continuous, then

$\therefore \quad f(0^-) = f(0^+)$

$$0 + 1 = 0 - a$$
$$-1 = a$$

$\therefore \quad f(1^-) = f(1^+)$

$$1 - a = 2b - 1$$
$$2 = 2b - 1$$
$$\frac{3}{2} = b$$

129. *(a)* Put $x = 0$

$$\left(\frac{2+0}{2-0}\right)^{\frac{1}{0}} = 1^\infty$$

$\therefore \quad e^{\lim_{x \to 0}\left(\frac{2+x}{2-x} - 1\right) \times \frac{1}{x}}$

$$\left[\because \lim_{x \to 0} [f(x)]^{g(x)} = e^{\lim_{x \to 0} g(x)[f(x) - 1]}\right]$$

$$= e^{\lim_{x \to 0}\left[\frac{2 + x - 2 + x}{x(2 - x)}\right]} e^{\lim_{x \to 0} \frac{2}{2 - x}}$$

Put $x = 0$,

$$e^{\frac{2}{2}} = e^1$$

130. *(d)* $c_1(1, 0) = 1^2 + 0^2 - 2(1) + 4(0) + 5$

$$= 1 - 2 + 5 = 4 > 0$$

$\therefore (1, 0)$ lies outside of c_1

$$c_2(1, 0) = 1^2 + 0^2 - 1 + 2$$
$$= 1 - 1 + 2 = 2 > 0$$

$\therefore (1, 0)$ lies outside of c_2

131. *(c)* Total four digit number formed whose last digit is $0 = 6$.

Total four digit number formed whose last digit is $2 = 5$

There is no repetition hence every number is divisible by 3.

Maximum number of four digit formed using these digits = 18

$\therefore$ Required probability $= \dfrac{6 + 5}{18} = \dfrac{11}{18}$

132. *(b)* Let $Z = x + y$

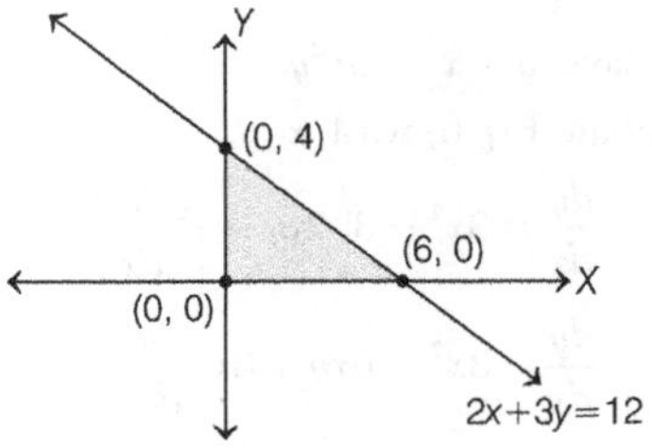

$Z(0, 0) = 0$
$Z(6, 0) = 6$
$Z(0, 4) = 4$

$\therefore$ Maximum value of Z is 6.

133. *(c)* If equation of circle is $x^2 + y^2 + 2gx + 2fy + c = 0$

Then, centre $\equiv (-g, -f)$

radius $= \sqrt{g^2 + f^2 - c}$

$\Rightarrow$ Centre of first circle $\equiv (0, 0)$

radius of first circle $\equiv 3$

$\Rightarrow$ Centre of second circle $\equiv (3, 4)$

radius of second circle $\equiv \sqrt{9 + 16 - 21} = 2$

$\because$ Distance between centres of circle (c_1c_2)

$= \sqrt{3^2 + 4^2} = 5$

$\therefore$ Sum of radius $(r_1 + r_2) = 5$

$c_1c_2 = r_1 + r_2$ (circle touches externally)

$\therefore$ Number of common tangent = 3

134. *(d)* We have, $A = \begin{bmatrix} 3 & 4 \\ 1 & 2 \end{bmatrix}$

$\therefore |A| = 3 \times 2 - 1 \times 4 = 6 - 4 = 2$

$\Rightarrow \text{adj} A = \begin{bmatrix} 2 & -4 \\ -1 & 3 \end{bmatrix}$

$\left[\text{If } A = \begin{bmatrix} a & b \\ c & d \end{bmatrix}, \text{ then adj} A = \begin{bmatrix} d & -b \\ -c & a \end{bmatrix}\right]$

Hence, $A^{-1} = \dfrac{1}{|A|} \text{adj} A$

$$A^{-1} = \frac{1}{2}\begin{bmatrix} 2 & -4 \\ -1 & 3 \end{bmatrix} = \begin{bmatrix} 1 & -2 \\ -\frac{1}{2} & \frac{3}{2} \end{bmatrix}$$

135. *(b)* Let $f(x) = x^{\frac{1}{3}}$ and $x = 0.027$

$\Delta x = -0.001$

Now use, $f(x + \Delta x) = f(x) + \Delta x f'(x)$

$\therefore f'(x) = \dfrac{1}{3(x)^{\frac{2}{3}}}$

Now, $f(0.027) \simeq f(0.027) - (0.001) \times \dfrac{1}{3(0.027)^{\frac{2}{3}}}$

$$\approx (0.3) - \frac{1}{1000} \times \frac{1}{3 \times (0.3)^2}$$

$$\approx 0.3 - \frac{1}{1000} \times \frac{100}{27} \approx \frac{3}{10} - \frac{1}{270}$$

$$\approx \frac{80}{270} \approx \frac{8}{27}$$

136. *(d)* Let $9^x = t$

Differentiate both side w.r.t. x

$9^x \ln 9 dx = dt$

$\Rightarrow \quad 9^x dx = \dfrac{dt}{\ln 9}$

Now, $\displaystyle\int \frac{9^x}{\sqrt{1 - 9^{2x}}} dx = \frac{1}{\ln 9} \int \frac{dt}{\sqrt{1 - t^2}}$

$$= \frac{1}{\ln 9} \sin^{-1}(t) + c \quad \left[\because \int \frac{1}{\sqrt{1 - t^2}} dt = \sin^{-1} t\right]$$

$$= \frac{1}{\ln 9} \sin^{-1}(9^x) + c$$

137. *(b)* We have, $a = 2\hat{i} + \hat{j} + \hat{k}$

$b = \hat{i} - 2\hat{j} + \hat{k}$

$\therefore \quad |a| = \sqrt{4 + 1 + 1} = \sqrt{6}$

$\therefore \quad |b| = \sqrt{1 + 4 + 1} = \sqrt{6}$

$\therefore \quad a \cdot b = 2 \times 1 + 1 \times (-2) + 1 \times 1$

$a \cdot b = 2 - 2 + 1 = 1$

$$\cos \theta = \frac{a \cdot b}{|a||b|} = \frac{1}{\sqrt{6}\sqrt{6}}$$

$$\theta = \cos^{-1}\left(\frac{1}{6}\right)$$

138. *(c)* We have, $\dfrac{4 + 3i}{4 - 3i}$

$\therefore$ Multiply and divide above equation by '$4 + 3i$'

$$\Rightarrow \quad \frac{4 + 3i}{4 - 3i} \times \frac{4 + 3i}{4 + 3i} = \frac{16 + 12i + 12i + 9i^2}{16 - 9i^2}$$

$$= \frac{16 + 24i - 9}{16 + 9} \quad [\because i^2 = -1]$$

$$= \frac{7}{25} + \frac{24}{25} i$$

$\therefore$ Argument of complex number is $\tan^{-1}\left(\dfrac{\frac{24}{25}}{\frac{7}{25}}\right)$

$\left[\because \arg(x + iy) = \tan^{-1}\left(\dfrac{y}{x}\right)\right]$

$$= \tan^{-1}\left(\frac{24}{7}\right)$$

139. *(c)* The given inequation are $x + y \le 4$ and $2x + y \le 5$, $xy \ge 0$ mean shaded part must lie in first quadrant or below both the line. Hence required region is

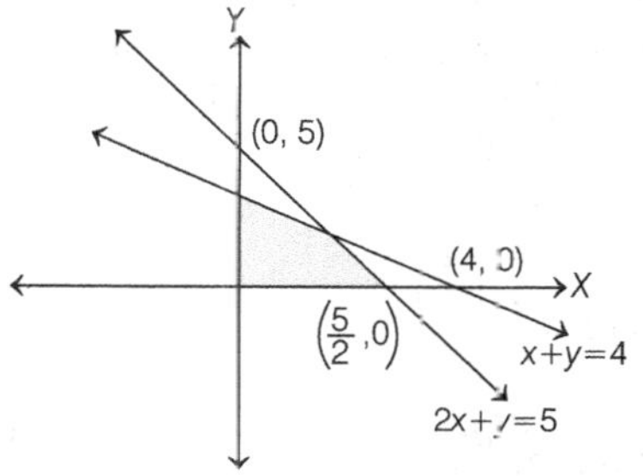

140. *(b)* We have $a = \hat{i} - \hat{j} + \hat{k}$,

$$b = 2\hat{i} - \hat{j} + \hat{k}$$
$$c = \hat{i} - \hat{k}$$

$\therefore$ Vector along $a - b + c = \lambda(a - b + c)$

$$= \lambda(\hat{i} - \hat{j} + \hat{k} - 2\hat{i} + \hat{j} - \hat{k} + \hat{i} - \hat{k})$$
$$= \lambda(-\hat{k}) = -\lambda\hat{k}$$

$\therefore$ Unit vector along $a - b + c = \pm\left(\dfrac{a - b + c}{|a - b + c|}\right)$

$$= \pm\left(\frac{-\lambda\hat{k}}{\lambda}\right) = \pm\hat{k}$$

141. *(c)* Let, $L_1 \equiv \dfrac{x - 2}{3} = \dfrac{y - 1}{1} = \dfrac{z + 3}{-1}$

$\therefore$ Direction ratio of $L_1(l_1, m_1, n_1) = (3, 1, -1)$

$$L_2 \equiv \frac{x + 1}{2} = \frac{y - 1}{-1} = \frac{z - 0}{2}$$

$\therefore$ Direction ratio of $L_2(l_2, m_2, n_2) = (2, -1, 2)$

Angle between L_1 and L_2

$$= \cos\theta = \frac{l_1l_2 + m_1m_2 + n_1n_2}{\sqrt{l_1^2 + m_1^2 + n_1^2}\sqrt{l_2^2 + m_2^2 + n_2^2}}$$

$$\cos\theta = \frac{6 - 1 - 2}{\sqrt{9 + 1 + 1}\sqrt{4 + 1 + 4}} = \frac{3}{3\sqrt{11}} = \frac{1}{\sqrt{11}}$$

$$\theta = \cos^{-1}\left(\frac{1}{\sqrt{11}}\right)$$

142. *(d)* By using binomial expansion

$$(x + y)^{20} = {}^{20}C_0x^{20} + {}^{20}C_1x^{19}y + {}^{20}C_2x^{18}y^2 + \ldots + {}^{20}C_{20}y^{20} \ldots \text{(i)}$$

and $(x - y)^{20} = {}^{20}C_0x^{20} - {}^{20}C_1x^{19}y + {}^{20}C_2x^{18}y^2 - \ldots + {}^{20}C_{20}y^{20} \ldots \text{(ii)}$

Add both the Eqs. (i) and (ii),

$$(x + y)^{20} + (x - y)^{20} = 2[{}^{20}C_0x^{20} + {}^{20}C_2x^{18}y^2 + \ldots + {}^{20}C_{20}y^{20}]$$

$\therefore$ Total number of terms = 11

143. *(b)* Let $L_1 \equiv \dfrac{x + 4}{3} = \dfrac{y - 2}{a} = \dfrac{z}{2}$

$\therefore$ Direction ratio of $L_1(l_1, m_1, n_1) = (3, a, 2)$

$$L_2 \equiv \frac{x}{2} = \frac{y - 3}{4} = \frac{z - 1}{1}$$

$\therefore$ Direction ratio of $L_2(l_2, m_2, n_2) = (2, 4, 1)$

If given lines are perpendicular, then

$$l_1l_2 + m_1m_2 + n_1n_2 = 0$$
$$\Rightarrow \quad 3 \times 2 + 4 \times a + 2 \times 1 = 0$$
$$\Rightarrow \quad 4a + 8 = 0$$
$$\Rightarrow \quad a = -2$$

144. *(b)* Let $I = \displaystyle\int \frac{1}{1 - \cos 4x}\,dx$

$$I = \int \frac{1}{2\sin^2 2x}\,dx \quad [\because 1 - \cos 2\theta = 2\sin^2\theta]$$

$$I = \frac{1}{2}\int \operatorname{cosec}^2 2x\,dx$$

$$I = \frac{1}{2} \times \left[\frac{-\cot 2x}{2}\right] + c$$

$[\because \int \operatorname{cosec}^2\theta = -\cot\theta + c]$

$$I = \frac{-1}{4}\cot 2x + c$$

145. *(a)* We have, $\left(x^2 + \dfrac{1}{x^2} + 2\right)^n = \left(x + \dfrac{1}{x}\right)^{2n}$

Coefficient of middle term of $(x + y)^n$, if n is even $= {}^nC_{n/2}$

$\Rightarrow$ Coefficient of middle term of $\left(x + \dfrac{1}{x}\right)^{2n}$

$$= {}^{2n}C_{\frac{2n}{2}} = {}^{2n}C_n$$

146. *(d)* $|A| = 0$ $\quad$ [$\because$ matrix is singular]

$$\Rightarrow |A| = (x - 2) \times 1 - (-2)(x + 2) = 0$$
$$\Rightarrow \quad x - 2 + 2x + 4 = 0 \Rightarrow 3x + 2 = 0$$
$$\Rightarrow \quad x = -\frac{3}{2}$$

147. *(d)* Perpendicular distance of point (1, 2) to the line $3x + 4y = 6$ is

$$= \left|\frac{3 \times 1 + 4 \times 2 - 6}{\sqrt{9 + 16}}\right| = \frac{5}{5} = 1$$

$\therefore$ Slope of line $3x - 4y = 5$ is $\dfrac{3}{4}$.

$$\Rightarrow \quad \tan\theta = \frac{3}{4}$$
$$\therefore \quad \sin\theta = \frac{3}{5}$$

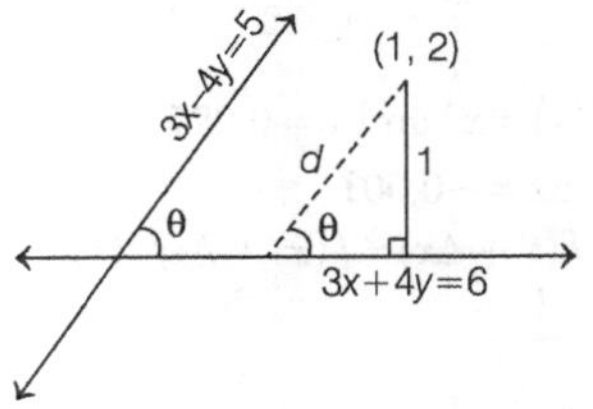

From above figure $\sin\theta = \dfrac{1}{d}$

$$\Rightarrow \quad \frac{3}{5} = \frac{1}{d}$$
$$\Rightarrow \quad d = \frac{5}{3}$$

148. *(b)* Let $t = \dfrac{\sin\theta - 2\sin^3\theta}{2\cos^3\theta - \cos\theta}$

$$t = \frac{\sin\theta\,[1 - 2\sin^2\theta]}{\cos\theta\,[2\cos^2\theta - 1]} \quad \left[\because \tan\theta = \frac{\sin\theta}{\cos\theta}\right]$$

$$t = \tan\theta\left[\frac{1 - 2(1 - \cos^2\theta)}{2\cos^2\theta - 1}\right] \quad [\because \sin^2\theta = 1 - \cos^2\theta]$$

$$t = \tan\theta\left[\frac{2\cos^2\theta - 1}{2\cos^2\theta - 1}\right]$$

$$t = \tan\theta$$

149. *(b)* We have, $\cos^2 x = 3 - 3\sin x$

$1 - \sin^2 x = 3 - 3\sin x$

$\sin^2 x - 3\sin x + 2 = 0$

$(\sin x - 1)(\sin x - 2) = 0$

$\therefore \quad \sin x - 2 = 0$

$\sin x = 2$ has no solution

$\therefore \sin x = 1$ has one solution which is $x = \frac{\pi}{2}$

150. *(b)* If $L \equiv ax^2 + by^2 + 2hxy = 0$

Then equation of pair of angle bisector is $\frac{x^2 - y^2}{a - b} = \frac{xy}{h}$

$\therefore$ Equation of pair of angle bisector of $5x^2 + 2xy + 3y^2 = 0$ is

$$\frac{x^2 - y^2}{5 - 3} = \frac{xy}{1}$$

$\Rightarrow \quad x^2 - y^2 = 2xy$

$\Rightarrow \quad x^2 - 2xy - y^2 = 0$

151. *(c)* $\because$ Number of diagonal in n-sided polygon

$$= \frac{n(n-3)}{2}$$

$\Rightarrow \quad \frac{n(n-3)}{2} = 54$

$n^2 - 3n = 108$

$n^2 - 3n - 108 = 0$

$\therefore \quad n = 12$ or $n = -9$

n is number of side, so it cannot be negative.

152. *(d)* Direction ratio's of given line $\equiv (2, 1, 1)$

From option (d), direction ratio's of plane $\equiv (1, -1, -1)$

$\therefore 2 \times 1 + 1(-1) + 1(-1)$ $[l_1 l_2 + m_1 m_2 + n_1 n_2 = 0$ if line and plane are parallel$]$

$2 - 1 - 1 = 0$

153. *(c)* $\because {}^nC_x = {}^nC_y$ (when $x = y$ or $x + y = n$)

$\Rightarrow \quad x = 4$ or $x + 4 = 10$

$\Rightarrow \quad x = 4$ or $x = 6$

154. *(a)* $\because$ General term of $(x + y)^n = {}^nC_r (x)^{n-r} (y)^r$

$\Rightarrow \quad T_{r+1} = {}^{10}C_r (1)^{10-r} (-x^5)^r = {}^{10}C_r (-1)^r (x)^{5r}$

$\therefore \quad 5r = 24 \Rightarrow r = 4.8$

$\therefore$ r cannot be in fraction means no such terms are possible.

$\therefore$ Coefficient of $x^{24} = 0$

155. *(b)* $|\text{adj } A| = |A|^{n-1}$, where n is order

$|\text{adj} A| = (5)^{3-1}$

$|\text{adj } A| = 25$

156. *(d)* We have, $(1 + x^2 + 2x)^{10} = [(1 + x)^2]^{10} = (1 + x)^{20}$

$\therefore$ General term of $(x + y)^n = {}^nC_r (x)^{n-r} (y)^r$

$\Rightarrow \quad T_{r+1} = {}^{20}C_r (1)^{20-r} (x)^r = {}^{20}C_r (x)^r$

To find coefficient of x^6 we need to put $r = 6$

$\therefore$ Coefficient of $x^6 = {}^{20}C_6$

157. *(c)* We have, $\frac{dy}{dx} = \frac{\cos^2 y}{\sqrt{1 - x^2}}$

$$\frac{dy}{\cos^2 y} = \frac{dx}{\sqrt{1 - x^2}}$$

$$\sec^2 y \, dy = \frac{1}{\sqrt{1 - x^2}} dx$$

$\therefore$ Integrate both sides,

$$\int \sec^2 y \, dy = \int \frac{1}{1 - x^2} dz$$

$\Rightarrow \quad \tan y = \sin^{-1} x + C \quad \left[\because \int \frac{dx}{\sqrt{1 - x^2}} = \sin^{-1} x + C\right]$

158. *(c)* Let $x^5 = t$

Differentiate both sides w.r.t. x,

$5x^4 dx = dt$

$x^4 dx = \frac{dt}{5}$

$$\int e^{x^5} x^4 dx = \int e^t \frac{dt}{5}$$

$$= \frac{1}{5} \int e^t dt \quad \left[\because \int e^t dt = e^t + C\right]$$

$$= \frac{1}{5} e^t + C = \frac{1}{5} e^{x^5} + C$$

159. *(b)* We have, $i^{2024} + i^{2025} + i^{2026} + i^{2027}$

$= i^{4 \times (506)} + i^{4 \times 506 + 1} + i^{4 \times 506 + 2} + 6^{4 \times 506 + 3}$ $\quad [\because i^{4n} = 1]$

$= 1 + i + i^2 + i^3$ $\quad [\because i^2 = -1]$

$= 1 + i - 1 - i = 0$

160. *(b)* We have, $(1 + i)^{200}$

Multiply and divide by $\sqrt{2}$

$$\left[\sqrt{2}\left(\frac{1}{\sqrt{2}} + \frac{i}{\sqrt{2}}\right)\right]^{200} = \sqrt{2}^{200} \left(\frac{1}{\sqrt{2}} + \frac{i}{\sqrt{2}}\right)^{200}$$

$$= 2^{100} \left(\cos \frac{\pi}{4} + i \sin \frac{\pi}{4}\right)^{200}$$

$$= 2^{100} \left[\cos 200 \frac{\pi}{4} + i \sin 200 \frac{\pi}{4}\right] = 2^{100} [1 + 0] = 2^{100}$$

$\Rightarrow \quad (1 + i)^{200} = 2^{100} = 2^{98}(a + ib)$

$2^2 = a + ib$

$4 + i0 = a + ib$

On comparing $a = 4, b = 0$

$\therefore \quad a + b = 4$

161. *(d)* Given, vector a, b and c are coplanar

$$\therefore \quad \begin{vmatrix} 1 & 2 & -1 \\ 1 & -2 & \lambda \\ 1 & 1 & 1 \end{vmatrix} = 0$$

$1(-2 - \lambda) - 2(1 - \lambda) - 1(1 + 2) = 0$

$-2 - \lambda - 2 + 2\lambda - 3 = 0$

$\lambda - 7 = 0$

$\lambda = 7$

162. *(d)* If there are m points in which n points are collinear $(m \geq n)$ then number of different straight line are ${}^mC_2 - {}^nC_2 + 1$

$$\Rightarrow {}^{10}C_2 - {}^3C_2 + 1 = \frac{10 \times 9}{2} - 3 + 1 = 45 - 3 + 1 = 43$$

163. *(b)* We have, $\sin 18° + \cos 36°$

$$= \frac{\sqrt{5}-1}{4} + \frac{\sqrt{5}+1}{4} \quad \left[\because \sin 18° = \frac{\sqrt{5}-1}{4} \text{ and } \cos 36° = \frac{\sqrt{5}+1}{4}\right]$$

$$= \frac{\sqrt{5}}{4} + \frac{\sqrt{5}}{4} - \frac{1}{4} + \frac{1}{4} = \frac{\sqrt{5}}{2}$$

164. *(a)*

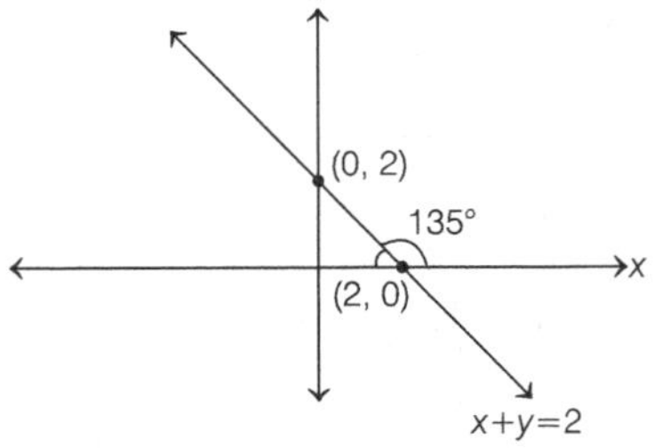

$\therefore$ The line which make 60° to given line has slope 135° + 60° or 135°– 60° (from the above figure)

$$\Rightarrow \quad m_1 = \tan(135° + 60°)$$
$$m_1 = \tan(195°)$$
$$m_1 = \tan(15°) = 2 - \sqrt{3}$$
$$\Rightarrow \quad m_2 = \tan(135° - 60°)$$
$$m_2 = \tan(75°) = 2 + \sqrt{3}$$

165. *(d)*

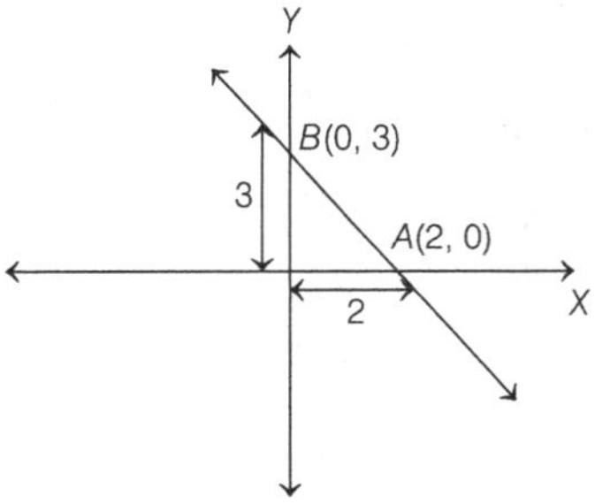

$\therefore$ From the above figure line passes through (2, 0) and (0, 3)

$$\Rightarrow \text{Slope} = \frac{3-0}{0-2} = \frac{-3}{2} \quad \left[\because \text{Slope} = \frac{y_2 - y_1}{x_2 - x_1}\right]$$

166. *(b)* Given, $P(A) = \frac{1}{4}, P\left(\frac{A}{B}\right) = \frac{1}{2}$ and $P\left(\frac{B}{A}\right) = \frac{2}{3}$

We know that, $P\left(\frac{E_1}{E_2}\right) = \frac{P(E_1 \cap E_2)}{P(E_2)}$

$$\Rightarrow \quad P\left(\frac{B}{A}\right) = \frac{P(A \cap B)}{P(A)}$$

$$\Rightarrow \quad \frac{2}{3} \times \frac{1}{4} = P(A \cap B) \Rightarrow \frac{1}{6} = P(A \cap B)$$

$$\Rightarrow \quad P\left(\frac{A}{B}\right) = \frac{P(A \cap B)}{P(B)}$$

$$P(B) = \frac{1}{6} \times \frac{4}{1}$$

$$P(B) = \frac{2}{3}$$

167. *(a)* $\frac{1}{1\cdot 4} + \frac{1}{4\cdot 7} + \frac{1}{7\cdot 10} + \ldots + \frac{1}{(3n-2)(3n+1)}$

$$= \frac{1}{3}\left[\frac{4-1}{1\cdot 4} + \frac{7-4}{4\cdot 7} + \frac{10-7}{7\cdot 10} + \ldots + \frac{(3n+1)-(3n-2)}{(3n-2)(3n+1)}\right]$$

$$= \frac{1}{3}\left[\frac{4}{1\cdot 4} - \frac{1}{1\cdot 4} + \frac{7}{4\cdot 7} - \frac{4}{4\cdot 7} + \frac{10}{7\cdot 10} - \frac{7}{7\cdot 10} + \ldots + \frac{1}{3n-2} - \frac{1}{3n+1}\right]$$

$$= \frac{1}{3}\left[\frac{1}{1} - \frac{1}{4} + \frac{1}{4} - \frac{1}{7} + \frac{1}{7} - \frac{1}{10} + \ldots + \frac{1}{3n-2} - \frac{1}{3n+1}\right]$$

$$= \frac{1}{3}\left[1 - \frac{1}{3n+1}\right] = \frac{3n}{3(3n+1)} = \frac{n}{3n+1}$$

168. *(a)* We have, $\frac{dy}{dx} = 1 + x + y(1+x)$

$$\frac{dy}{dx} = (1+x)(1+y)$$

$$\frac{dy}{1+y} = (1+x)dx$$

$\therefore$ Integrate both sides,

$$\int \frac{dy}{1+y} = \int (1+x)dx$$

$$\ln(1+y) = x + \frac{x^2}{2} + C \quad \left[\because \int \frac{1}{t}dt = \ln t + C\right]$$

$$1 + y = e^{x + \frac{x^2}{2}} \times e^C$$

$$y = ke^{x + \frac{x^2}{2}} - 1 \quad [\because e^c = k \text{ (Constant)}]$$

169. *(c)* We have, $2^{4n} - 1 = 16^n - 1$

$\therefore \; a^n - 1$ is divisible by $a - 1$

$\Rightarrow 16^n - 1$ is divisible by $16 - 1 = 15$

170. *(d)* Number of triangle formed $= {}^{10}C_3$

Number of isosceles triangle $= 10\left(\frac{10-1}{2}\right)$

$$= 5 \times 9 = 45$$

So, required probability $= \frac{45}{{}^{10}C_3}$

$$= \frac{45 \times 3 \times 2}{10 \times 9 \times 8} = \frac{3}{8}$$

171. *(b)* Let a be the first term and d is the common difference also a_n be the nth term.

$\therefore \quad a_4 + a_7 = 31$

$a + 3d + a + 6d = 31 \quad [\because a_n = a + (n-1)d]$

$2a + 9d = 31 \quad$ ...(i)

$\therefore \quad a_1 + a_2 = 7$

$a + a + d = 7$

$2a + d = 7 \quad$ ...(ii)

Subtract Eq. (ii) from Eq. (i), we get

$\Rightarrow \quad 2a + 9d - 2a - d = 31 - 7$

$8d = 24$

$d = 3$

$\therefore \quad 2a + 3 = 7$

$a = 2$

$\therefore \quad a_{10} = a + 9d$

$= 2 + 27 = 29$

172. *(c)* If $n(A) = p$ and $n(B) = q$

Then number of relation from set (A) to set (B) is 2^{pq}.

$\Rightarrow$ Number of relation $= 2^{2\times 3}$

$= 2^6 = 64$

173. *(c)* Total number of outcomes = 100

Total number of perfect square = 10

Total odd number = 50

Total number of even prime number = 1

$P(A) = \frac{10}{100} = \frac{1}{10} = 0.1$

$P(B) = \frac{50}{100} = \frac{1}{2} = 0.5$

$P(C) = \frac{1}{100} = 0.01$

$\therefore \quad P(B) > P(A) > P(C)$

174. *(c)* We have, $f(x) + 2f(1-x) = x \quad$ ...(i)

Now, replace x by $1 - x$

$\therefore f(1-x) + 2f(1-(1-x)) = 1 - x$

$f(1-x) + 2f(x) = 1 - x \quad$ ...(ii)

Multiply by 2 to the Eq. (ii) and subtract from Eq. (i),

$2f(1-x) + 4f(x) - f(x) - 2f(1-x) = 2 - 2x - x$

$\Rightarrow \quad 3f(x) = 2 - 3x$

$\Rightarrow \quad f(x) = \frac{1}{3}(2 - 3x)$

175. *(c)* We have, $\sum_{k=1}^{20} k\, k!$

$\sum_{k=1}^{20} k\, k! = \sum_{k=1}^{20} (k+1-1)k! = \sum_{k=1}^{20} [(k+1)k! - k!]$

$= \sum_{k=1}^{20} (k+1)! - \sum_{k=1}^{20} k! \quad [\because (n+1)n! = (n+1)!]$

$= 2! - 1! + 3! - 2! + 21! - 3! + \ldots + 21! - 20!$

$= 21! - 1$

176. *(a)* Total number of batteries are 10

Number of dead batteries is 4

$\therefore$ Probability (all three dead) $= \frac{4}{10} \times \frac{3}{9} \times \frac{2}{8} = \frac{1}{30}$

177. *(c)* $\because$ General equation of $2-d$ line is $ax + by = 1$

$a + b\frac{dy}{dx} = 0$

$0 + b\frac{d^2y}{dx^2} = 0$

$\frac{d^2y}{dx^2} = 0$

178. *(b)* We have, $A = \{4, 5, 9\}$

$B = \{1, 2, 4, 6\} \Rightarrow B - A = \{1, 2, 6\}$

$\Rightarrow \quad A \cup B = \{1, 2, 4, 5, 6, 9\}$

$\therefore \quad (A \cup B) \cap (B - A) = \{1, 2, 6\}$

179. *(b)* Total number formed using this number $= 6!$

Total number formed when 1, 3 are together $= 5! \times 2$

So, required probability $= \frac{2 \times 5!}{6!} = \frac{2 \times 5!}{6 \times 5!} = \frac{1}{3}$

180. *(c)*

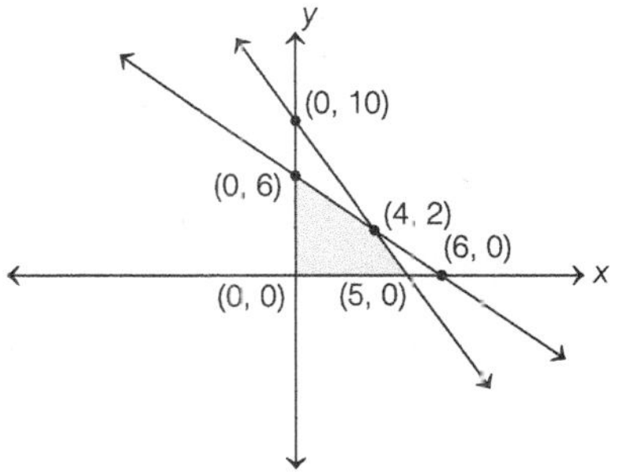

$z = 5x + y$

$z(0, 0) = 0$

$z(0, 6) = 0 + 6 = 6$

$z(5, 0) = 25 + 0 = 25$ (Maximum)

$z(4, 2) = 20 + 2 = 22$

COMEDK

Solved Paper 2023

Instructions

- There are 180 questions in all. The number of questions in each section is as given below.

Sections	No. of Questions
Section I : Physics	1-60
Section II : Chemistry	61-120
Section III : Mathematics	121-180

- All the questions are Multiple Choice Questions having four options out of which **ONLY ONE** is correct.
  Candidates will be awarded 1 mark for each correct answer. There will be no negative
- marking for incorrect answer.

PHYSICS

1. The mean energy per molecule for a diatomic gas is

a. $\frac{5k_BT}{N}$ *b.* $\frac{5k_BT}{2N}$ *c.* $\frac{5k_BT}{2}$ *d.* $\frac{3k_BT}{2}$

2. The phase difference between displacement and velocity of a particle in simple harmonic motion is

a. π rad *b.* $3\pi/2$ rad
c. zero *d.* $\pi/2$ rad

3. The mass density of a nucleus varies with mass number A as

a. Å *b.* A^2 *c.* $\frac{1}{A}$ *d.* $\ln A$

4. A capacitor of capacity 2 μF is charged upto a potential 14 V and then connected in parallel to an uncharged capacitor of capacity 5 μF. The final potential difference across each capacitor will be

a. 6 V *b.* 4 V *c.* 8 V *d.* 14 V

5. The ratio of amplitude of magnetic field to the amplitude of electric field of an electromagnetic wave propagating in vacuum is

a. reciprocal of speed of light in vacuum
b. the speed of light in vacuum
c. proportional to frequency of the electromagnetic wave
d. inversely proportional to the frequency of the electromagnetic wave

6. A particle is projected at an angle 30° with horizontal having kinetic energy K. The kinetic energy of the particle at highest point is.

a. $\frac{1}{2}K$ *b.* $\frac{3}{4}K$ *c.* $\frac{3}{8}K$ *d.* $\frac{5}{8}K$

7. An air bubble in water $\left(\mu = \frac{4}{3}\right)$ is shown in figure. The apparent depth of the image of the bubble in plane mirror viewed by observer is.

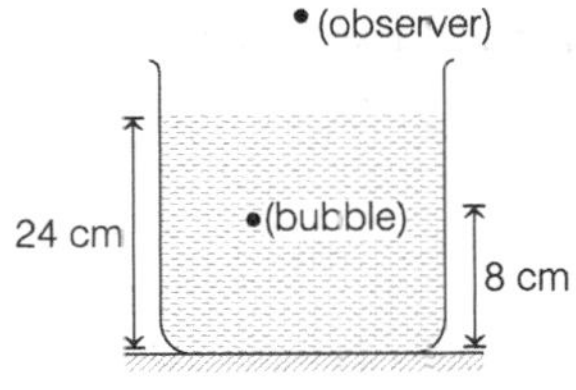

a. 16 cm *b.* 18 cm *c.* 24 cm *d.* 12 cm

COMEDK 2023

8. A TV tower has a height 72 m. The maximum distance upto which TV transmission can be received is (Take, radius of the earth as 6.4×10^6 m)

a. 27.52 km **b.** 34.25 km **c.** 30.35 km **d.** 25.12 km

9. A transistor is connected in CE configuration. The collector supply is 10V and the voltage drop across a resistor of 1000 Ω in the collector circuit is 0.5V. If the current gain factor is 0.96, then the base current is

a. 25 μ A **b.** 20.8 μ A **c.** 22.5 μ A **d.** 15μ A

10. One end of the string of length l is connected to a particle of mass m and the other end is connected to a small peg on a smooth horizontal table. If the particle moves in circle with speed v, the net force on the particle (directed towards centre) will be (T represents the tension in the string)

a. T **b.** $T + \frac{mv^2}{l}$ **c.** $T - \frac{mv^2}{l}$ **d.** zero

11. A thin circular ring of mass M and radius R rotates about an axis through its centre and perpendicular to its plane, with a constant angular velocity ω. Four small spheres each of mass m (negligible radius) are kept gently to the opposite ends of two mutually perpendicular diameters of the ring. The new angular velocity of the ring will be

a. $\left(\frac{M+4m}{M}\right)\omega$ **b.** $\frac{M}{4m}\omega$

c. $\left(\frac{M}{M+4m}\right)\omega$ **d.** $\left(\frac{M}{M-4m}\right)\omega$

12. Two wire of same material having radius in ratio 2 : 1 and lengths in ratio 1 : 2. If same force is applied on them, then ratio of their change in length will be

a. 1 : 1 **b.** 1 : 2 **c.** 1 : 4 **d.** 1 : 8

13. In the figure, pendulum bob on left side is pulled a side to a height h from its initial position. After it is released it collides with the right pendulum bob at rest, which is of same mass. After the collision, the two bobs stick together and rise to a height

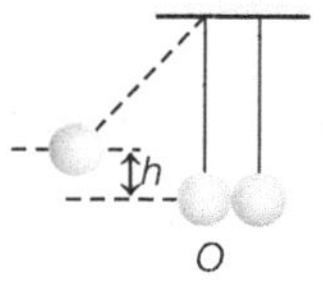

a. $\frac{3h}{4}$ **b.** $\frac{2h}{3}$ **c.** $\frac{h}{2}$ **d.** $\frac{h}{4}$

14. A gas is taken through the cycle $A \rightarrow B \rightarrow C \rightarrow A$, as shown in figure. What is the net work done by the gas?

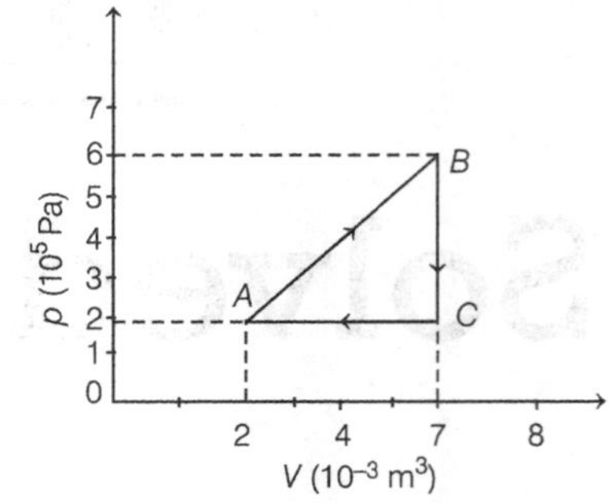

a. 2000 J **b.** 1000 J **c.** Zero **d.** – 2000 J

15. The gases carbon monoxide (CO) and nitrogen at the same temperature have kinetic energies E_1 and E_2, respectively. Then,

a. $E_1 = E_2$ **b.** $E_1 > E_2$

c. $E_1 < E_2$ **d.** None of these

16. Two wires are made of the same material and have the same volume. The first wire has cross-sectional area A and the second wire has cross-sectional area $3A$. If the length of the first wire is increased by Δl on applying a force F, how much force is needed to stretch the second wire by the same amount?

a. $4F$ **b.** $6F$ **c.** $9F$ **d.** F

17. Starting from the centre of the earth having radius R, the variation of g (acceleration due to gravity) is shown by

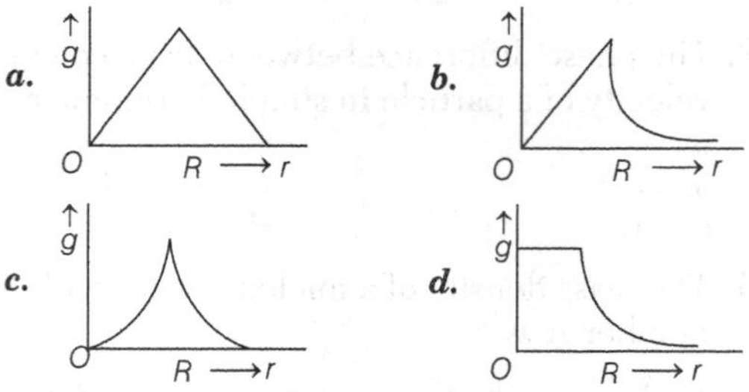

18. A long spring, when stretched by a distance x, has potential energy U. On increasing the stretching to nx, the potential energy of the spring will be

a. $\frac{U}{n}$ **b.** nU **c.** n^2U **d.** $\frac{U}{n^2}$

19. With what velocity should an observer approach a stationary sound source, so that the apparent frequency of sound should appear double the actual frequency?

a. $v/2$ **b.** $3v$

c. $2v$ **d.** v

20. A dielectric of dielectric constant K is introduced such that half of its area of a capacitor of capacitance C is occupied by it. The new capacity is

a. $2C$ *b.* $\frac{C}{2}$ *c.* $\frac{(1+K)C}{2}$ *d.* $2C(1+K)$

21. Two very long straight parallel wires carry currents i and $2i$ in opposite directions. The distance between the wires is r. At a certain instant of time a point charge q is at a point equidistant from the two wires in the plane of the wires. Its instantaneous velocity v is perpendicular to this plane. The magnitude of the force due to the magnetic field acting on the charge at this instant is

a. zero *b.* $\frac{3\mu_0}{2\pi}\frac{iqv}{r}$

c. $\frac{\mu_0}{\pi}\frac{iqv}{r}$ *d.* $\frac{\mu_0}{2\pi}\frac{iqv}{r}$

22. The magnetic flux linked with a coil satisfies the relation $\phi = (4t^2 + 6t + 9)$ Wb, where t is time in second. The emf induced in the coil at $t = 2$ s is

a. 22 V *b.* 18 V *c.* 16 V *d.* 40 V

23. The instantaneous values of alternating current and voltages in a circuit given as

$i = \frac{1}{\sqrt{2}} \sin(100\pi t)$ amp,

$e = \frac{1}{\sqrt{2}} \sin(100\pi t + \pi/3)$ volt

The average power (in watts) consumed in the circuit is

a. $\frac{1}{4}$ *b.* $\frac{\sqrt{3}}{4}$ *c.* $\frac{1}{2}$ *d.* $\frac{1}{8}$

24. A car is moving towards a high cliff. The car driver sounds a horn of frequency f. The reflected sound heard by the driver has a frequency $2f$. If v be the velocity of sound, then the velocity of the car in the same velocity units, will be

a. $\frac{v}{\sqrt{2}}$ *b.* $\frac{v}{3}$ *c.* $\frac{v}{4}$ *d.* $\frac{v}{2}$

25. If escape velocity on earth surface is 11.1 kmh^{-1}, then find the escape velocity on moon surface. If mass of moon is $\frac{1}{81}$ times of mass of earth and radius of moon is $\frac{1}{4}$ times radius of earth.

a. 2.46 kmh^{-1} *b.* 3.46 kmh^{-1}

c. 4.4 kmh^{-1} *d.* None of these

26. An ideal gas goes from state A to state B *via* three different processes as indicated in the p-V diagram.

If Q_1, Q_2 and Q_3 indicate the heat absorbed by the three processes and $\Delta U_1, \Delta U_2$ and ΔU_3 indicate the change in internal energy along the three processes respectively, then

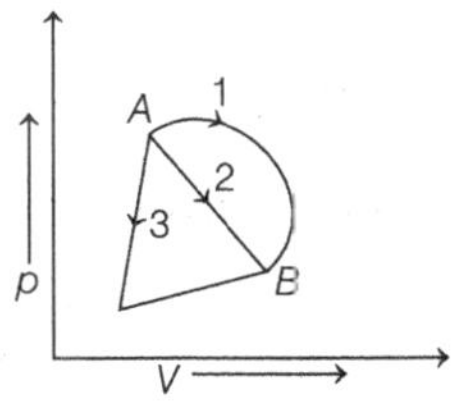

a. $Q_1 > Q_2 > Q_3$ and $\Delta U_1 = \Delta U_2 = \Delta U_3$

b. $Q_3 > Q_2 > Q_1$ and $\Delta U_1 = \Delta U_2 = \Delta U_3$

c. $Q_1 = Q_2 = Q_3$ and $\Delta U_1 > \Delta U_2 > \Delta U_3$

d. $Q_3 > Q_2 > Q_1$ and $\Delta U_1 > \Delta U_2 > \Delta U_3$

27. In the series L-C-R circuit shown, the impedance is

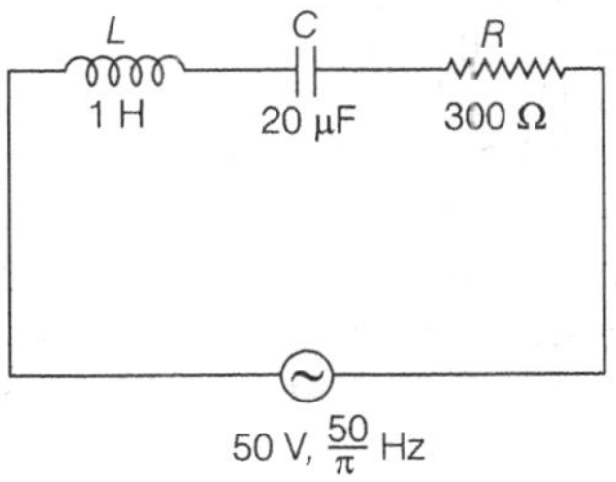

a. 200 Ω *b.* 100 Ω

c. 300 Ω *d.* 500 Ω

28. In Young's double slit interference experiment, using two coherent waves of different amplitudes, the intensities ratio between bright and dark fringes is 3. Then, the value of the ratio of the amplitudes of the wave that arrive there is

a. $\left(\frac{\sqrt{3}+1}{\sqrt{3}-1}\right)$ *b.* $\left(\frac{\sqrt{3}-1}{\sqrt{3}+1}\right)$

c. $\sqrt{3} : 1$ *d.* $1 : \sqrt{3}$

29. The wavelength of the first line of Lyman series for H- atom is equal to that of the second line of Balmer series for a H-like ion. The atomic number Z of H-like ion is

a. 4 *b.* 1

c. 2 *d.* 3

30. If 150 J of heat is added to a system and the work done by the system is 110 J, then change in internal energy will be

a. 40 J *b.* 110 J *c.* 150 J *d.* 260 J

31. In the figure below, the capacitance of each capacitor is 3 μF. The effective capacitance between A and B is

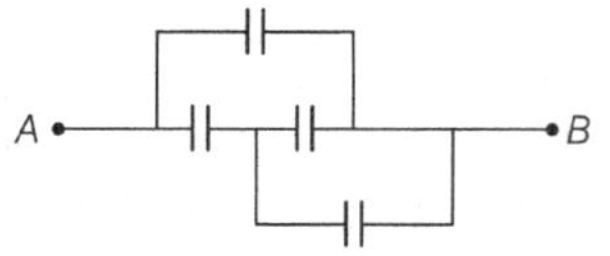

a. $\frac{3}{4}$ μF *b.* 3 μF *c.* 6 μF *d.* 5 μF

32. The first emission of hydrogen atomic spectrum in Lyman series appears at a wavelength of

a. $\frac{3R}{4}\ \text{cm}^{-1}$ *b.* $\frac{4}{3R}$ cm *c.* $\frac{7R}{144}\ \text{cm}^{-1}$ *d.* $\frac{400}{9R}$ cm

33. In Young's double slit experiment, the ratio of maximum and minimum intensities in the fringe system is 9 : 1. The ratio of amplitudes of coherent sources is

a. 9 : 1 *b.* 3 : 1 *c.* 2 : 1 *d.* 1 : 1

34. In the case of an inductor

a. voltage lags the current by $\pi/2$
b. voltage leads the current by $\pi/2$
c. voltage leads the current by $\pi/3$
d. voltage leads the current by $\pi/4$

35. The height vertically above the earth's surface at which the acceleration due to gravity becomes 1% of its value at the surface is

a. $8R$ *b.* $9R$
c. $10R$ *d.* $20R$

36. If C be the capacitance and V be the electric potential, then the dimensional formula of CV^2 is

a. $[ML^2T^{-2}A^0]$ *b.* $[MLT^{-2}A^{-1}]$
c. $[M^0LT^{-2}A^0]$ *d.* $[ML^{-3}TA]$

37. Which logic gate is represented by the following combination of logic gates?

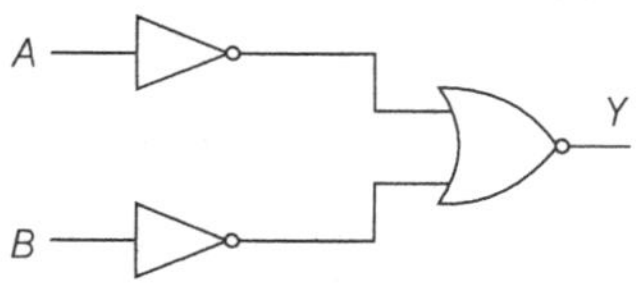

a. OR *b.* NAND *c.* AND *d.* NOR

38. An LED is constructed from a p-n junction diode using GaAsP. The energy gap is 1.9 eV. The wavelength of the light emitted will be equal to

(a) 10.4×10^{-26} m *b.* 654 nm
(c) 654 Å *d.* 654×10^{-11} m

39. A body is projected vertically upwards. The times corresponding to height h while ascending and while descending are t_1 and t_2, respectively. Then, the velocity of projection will be (take, g as acceleration due to gravity)

a. $\frac{g\sqrt{t_1t_2}}{2}$ *b.* $\frac{g(t_1+t_2)}{2}$
c. $g\sqrt{t_1t_2}$ *d.* $g\frac{t_1t_2}{(t_1+t_2)}$

40. When a certain metal surface is illuminated with light of frequency ν, the stopping potential for photoelectric current is V_0. When the same surface is illuminated by light of frequency $\frac{\nu}{2}$, the stopping potential is $\frac{V_0}{4}$. The threshold frequency for photoelectric emission is

a. $\frac{\nu}{6}$ *b.* $\frac{\nu}{3}$ *c.* $\frac{2\nu}{3}$ *d.* $\frac{4\nu}{3}$

41. A fish in water (refractive index n) looks at a bird vertically above in the air. If y is the height of the bird and x is the depth of the fish from the surface, then the distance of the bird as estimated by the fish is

a. $x + y\left(1 - \frac{1}{n}\right)$ *b.* $x + ny$
c. $x + y\left(1 + \frac{1}{n}\right)$ *d.* $y + x\left(1 - \frac{1}{n}\right)$

42. A car starts from rest and accelerates uniformly to a speed of 180 kmh^{-1} in 10 s. The distance covered by the car in this time interval is

a. 500 m *b.* 250 m *c.* 100 m *d.* 200 m

43. A plane electromagnetic wave of frequency 20 MHz travels through a space along x-direction. If the electric field vector at a certain point in space is 6 Vm^{-1}, then what is the magnetic field vector at that point?

a. 2×10^{-8} T *b.* $\frac{1}{2} \times 10^{-8}$ T
c. 2 T *d.* $\frac{1}{2}$ T

44. The sides of a parallelogram are represented by vectors $\mathbf{p} = 5\hat{\mathbf{i}} - 4\hat{\mathbf{j}} + 3\hat{\mathbf{k}}$ and $\mathbf{q} = 3\hat{\mathbf{i}} + 2\hat{\mathbf{j}} - \hat{\mathbf{k}}$. Then, the area of the parallelogram is

a. $\sqrt{684}$ sq units *b.* $\sqrt{72}$ sq units
c. 171 sq units *d.* 72 sq units

45. If θ_1 and θ_2 be the apparent angles of dip observed in two vertical planes at right angles to each other, then the true angle of dip θ is given by

a. $\cot^2\theta = \cot^2\theta_1 + \cot^2\theta_2$
b. $\tan^2\theta = \tan^2\theta_1 + \tan^2\theta_2$
c. $\cot^2\theta = \cot^2\theta_1 - \cot^2\theta_2$
d. $\tan^2\theta = \tan^2\theta_1 - \tan^2\theta_2$

46. Let K_1 be the maximum kinetic energy of photoelectrons emitted by light of wavelength λ_1 and K_2 corresponding to wavelength λ_2. If $\lambda_1 = 2\lambda_2$, then

a. $2K_1 = K_2$ *b.* $K_1 = 2K_2$
c. $K_1 < K_2/2$ *d.* $K_1 > 2K_2$

47. A ball is projected horizontally with a velocity of 5 ms^{-1} from the top of a building 19.6 m high. How long will the ball take to hit the ground?

a. $\sqrt{2}$ s *b.* 2 s
c. $\sqrt{3}$ s *d.* 3 s

48. A galvanometer having a resistance of 8 Ω is shunted by a wire of resistance 2 Ω. If the total current is 1 A, the part of it passing through the shunt will be

a. 0.25 A *b.* 0.8 A
c. 0.2 A *d.* 0.5 A

49. In the diagram shown below, m_1 and m_2 are the masses of two particles and x_1 and x_2 are their respective distances from the origin O.

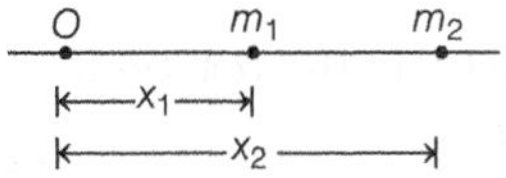

The centre of mass of the system is

a. $\frac{m_1x_2 + m_2x_2}{m_1 + m_2}$ *b.* $\frac{m_1 + m_2}{2}$
c. $\frac{m_1x_1 + m_2x_2}{m_1 + m_2}$ *d.* $\frac{m_1m_2 + x_1x_2}{m_1 + m_2}$

50. A block of wood floats in water with $(4/5)$ th of its volume submerged. If the same block just floats in a liquid, the density of the liquid is (in kgm^{-3})

a. 1250 *b.* 600
c. 400 *d.* 800

51. A balloon with mass m is descending down with an acceleration a (where, $a < g$). How much mass should be removed from it so that it starts moving up with an acceleration a?

a. $\frac{2ma}{g+a}$ *b.* $\frac{2ma}{g-a}$ *c.* $\frac{ma}{g+a}$ *d.* $\frac{ma}{g-a}$

52. A straight wire of length 2 m carries a current of 10 A. If this wire is placed in uniform magnetic field of 0.15 T making an angle of 45° with the magnetic field, the applied force on the wire will be

a. 1.5 N *b.* 3 N *c.* $3\sqrt{2}$ N *d.* $3/\sqrt{2}$ N

53 Two slabs are of the thicknesses d_1 and d_2. Their thermal conductivities are K_1 and K_2, respectively. They are in series. The free ends of the combination of these two slabs are kept at temperatures θ_1 and θ_2. Assume $\theta_1 > \theta_2$. The temperature θ of their common junction is

a. $\frac{K_1\theta_1 + K_2\theta_2}{\theta_1 + \theta_2}$ *b.* $\frac{K_1\theta_1 d_1 + K_2\theta_2 d_2}{K_1d_2 + K_2d_1}$
c. $\frac{K_1\theta_1 d_2 + K_2\theta_2 d_1}{K_1d_2 + K_2d_1}$ *d.* $\frac{K_1\theta_1 + K_2\theta_2}{K_1 + K_2}$

54. A square wire of each side l carries a current I. The magnetic field at the mid-point of the square

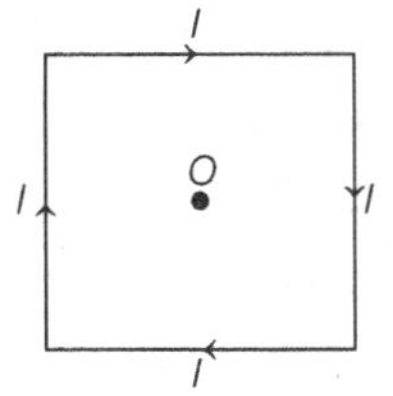

a. $4\sqrt{2}\frac{\mu_0}{4\pi}\frac{I}{l}$ *b.* $8\sqrt{2}\frac{\mu_0}{4\pi}\frac{I}{l}$
c. $16\sqrt{2}\frac{\mu_0}{4\pi}\frac{I}{l}$ *d.* $32\sqrt{2}\frac{\mu_0}{4\pi}\frac{I}{l}$

55. A cylinder of radius r and of thermal conductivity K_1 is surrounded by a cylindrical shell of inner radius r and outer radius $2r$ made of a material of thermal conductivity K_2. The effective thermal conductivity of the system is

a. $\frac{1}{3}(K_1 + 2K_2)$ *b.* $\frac{1}{2}(2K_1 + 3K_2)$
c. $\frac{1}{3}(3K_2 + 2K_1)$ *d.* $\frac{1}{4}(K_1 + 3K_2)$

56 The speeds of air-flow on the upper and lower surfaces of a wing of an aeroplane are v_1 and v_2, respectively. If A is the cross-sectional area of the wing and ρ is the density of air, then the upward lift is

a. $\frac{1}{2}\rho A(v_1 - v_2)$
b. $\frac{1}{2}\rho A(v_1 + v_2)$
c. $\frac{1}{2}\rho A(v_1^2 - v_2^2)$
d. $\frac{1}{2}\rho A(v_1^2 + v_2^2)$

57. Two cells with the same emf E and different internal resistances r_1 and r_2 are connected in series to an external resistance R. If the potential difference across the first cell is zero then value of R.

a. $\sqrt{r_1 r_2}$ ***b.*** $r_1 + r_2$ ***c.*** $r_1 - r_2$ ***d.*** $\frac{r_1 + r_2}{2}$

58 A string vibrates with a frequency of 200 Hz. When its length is doubled and tension is altered, it begins to vibrate with a frequency of 300 Hz. The ratio of the new tension to the original tension is

a. 9 : 1 ***b.*** 1 : 9 ***c.*** 3 : 1 ***d.*** 1 : 3

59. When 10^{19} electrons are removed from a neutral metal plate, the electric charge on it is

a. – 1.6 C ***b.*** + 1.6 C
c. 10^{+19} C ***d.*** 10^{-19} C

60. In an electrical circuit R, L, C and AC voltage source are all connected in series. When L is removed from the circuit, the phase difference between the voltage and the current in the circuit is $\pi/3$. If instead C is removed from the circuit, the phase difference is again $\pi/3$. The power factor of the circuit is

a. 1/2 ***b.*** $1\sqrt{2}$
c. 1 ***d.*** $\frac{\sqrt{3}}{2}$

CHEMISTRY

61. Which of the following hexoses will form the same osazone when treated with excess phenyl hydrazine?

a. D-glucose, D-fructose and D-galactose
b. D-glucose, D-fructose and D-mannose
c. D-glucose, D-mannose and D-galactose
d. D-fructose, D-mannose and D-galactose

62. Product of the following reaction is

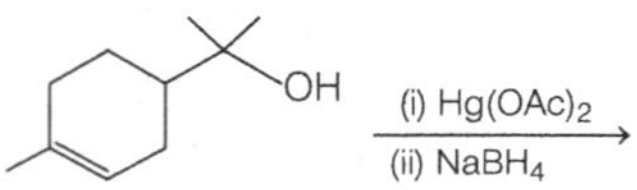

(a) 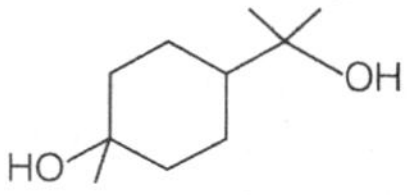

(b) 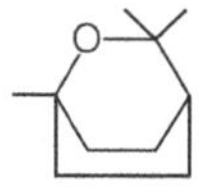

(c) 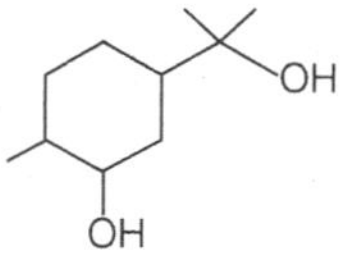

(d) 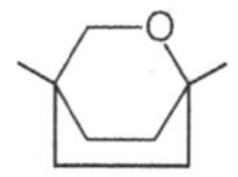

63. Which one of the following is an example of step growth polymerisation?

a. Teflon ***b.*** Neoprene
c. Nylon 6, 6 ***d.*** Buna-S.

64. Acetophenone when reacted with a base, C_2H_5ONa, yields a stable compound which has the structure

(a) 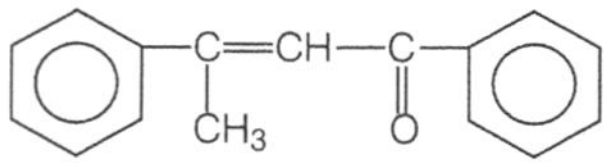

(b) 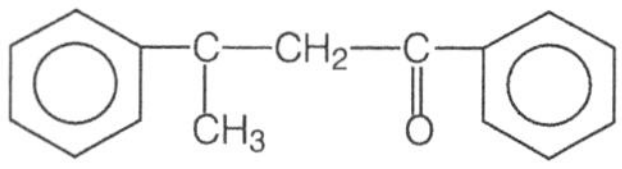

(c) 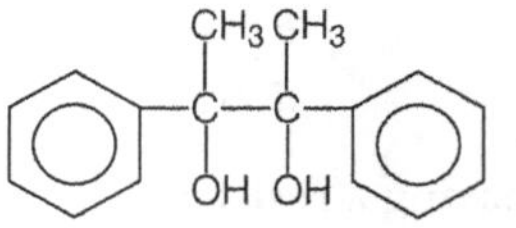

(d) 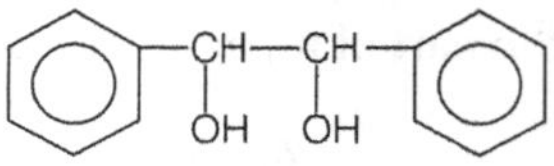

65. Gabriel's synthesis is used frequency for the preparation of which of the following?

a. 1° amines ***b.*** 1° alcohols
c. 3° amines ***d.*** 3° alcohols

66. The product P in the reaction,

a. 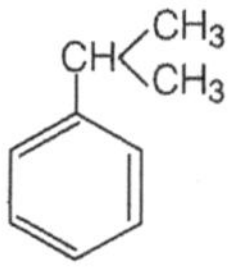

b. 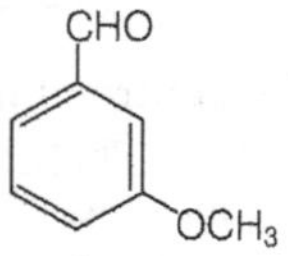

c. 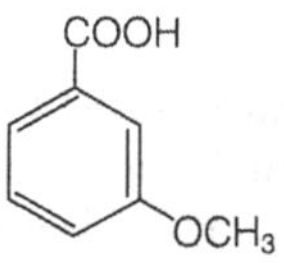

d. 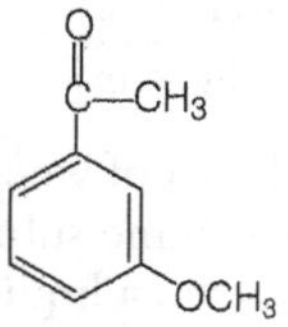

67. Pick out the incorrect statement(s) from the following.

1. Glucose exists in two different crystalline forms, α-D-glucose and β-D-glucose.
2. α-D-glucose and β-D-glucose are anomers.
3. α-D-glucose and β-D-glucose are enantiomers.

4. Cellulose is a straight chain polysaccharide made of only β-D-glucose units.

5. Starch is a mixture of amylase and amylopectin, both contain unbranched chain of α-D-glucose units.

a. 1 and 2 only *b.* 2 and 3 only
c. 3 and 4 only *d.* 3 and 5 only

68. A drug that is antipyretic as well as analgesic is
a. chloroquine
b. penicilline
c. paracetamol
d. chloropromazine hydrochloride

69. Ozone in stratosphere is depleted by
a. C_7F_{16} *b.* CF_2Cl_2
c. $C_6H_6Cl_2$ *d.* CF_3Cl

70. Which of the following is incorrect?
a. Primary alcohols are very easily oxidised to aldehydes, which are oxidised to acids with same number of C-atoms.
b. Secondary alcohols are very easily oxidised to ketones, which are oxidised to acids with same number of C-atoms.
c. Secondary alcohols are easily oxidised to ketones, which are oxidised to acids with lesser number of C-atoms.
d. Secondary and tertiary alcohols on oxidation form acids with lesser number of C-atoms.

71. Rank the following compounds in order of increasing basicity.

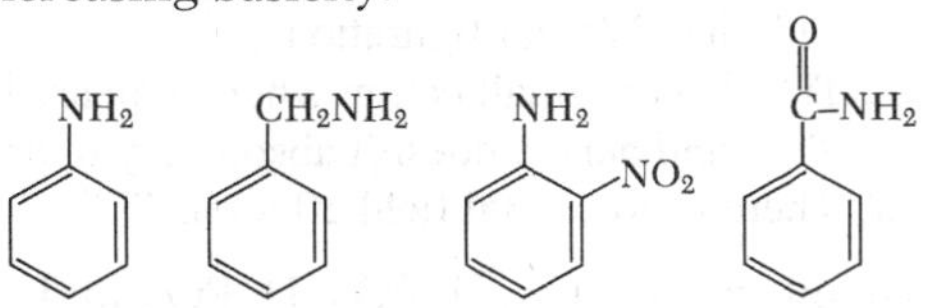

1 2 3 4

a. $4 < 2 < 1 < 3$ *b.* $4 < 1 < 3 < 2$
c. $4 < 3 < 1 < 2$ *d.* $2 < 1 < 3 < 4$

72. Ammoniacal silver nitrate forms a white precipitate easily with
a. $CH_3C\equiv CH$ *b.* $CH_3C\equiv CCH_3$
c. $CH_3CH=CH_2$ *d.* $CH_2=CH_2$

73. Which defect leads to decrease in the density of crystal?
a. Schottky *b.* F-centre
c. Frenkel *d.* Interstitial

74. Consider the following equilibrium,

$$2No(g) \rightleftharpoons N_2 + O_2; K_{C_1} = 2.4 \times 10^{20}$$

$$No(g) + \frac{1}{2}Br_2(g) \rightleftharpoons NoBr(g); K_{C_2} = 1.4$$

Calculate K_C for the reaction,

$$\frac{1}{2}N_2(g) + \frac{1}{2}O_2(g) + \frac{1}{2}Br_2(g) \rightleftharpoons NOBr(g)$$

a. 8.96×10^{-11}
b. 9.48×10^{-9}
c. 8.08×10^{-12}
d. 8.96×10^{11}

75. Which of the following is incorrect regarding Henry's law?
a. Gas reacts with solvent chemically.
b. Pressure and concentrations are not too high.
c. Temperature is not too low.
d. Gas does not change its molecular state in solution i.e., neither dissociates nor associates.

76. *t*-butyl chloride prefeably undergo hydrolysis by
a. S_N1 mechanism
b. S_N1 mechanism
c. any of (a) and (b)
d. None of the above

77. Which of the following is not true?
a. Enthalpy change in negative for adsorption of a gas on solid.
b. Increase in temperature favours adsorption.
c. Adsorption is a surface phenomena.
d. Entropy change is negative.

78. Which of these represents the correct order of decreasing bond order?
a. $C_2^{2-} > O_2^{2+} > O_2^- > He_2^{2+}$
b. $O_2^- > O_2^+ > He_2^+ > C_2^{2-}$
c. $He_2^+ > O_2^- > C_2^{2-} > O_2^+$
d. $He_2^+ > O_2^{2-} > O_2^+ > O_2^-$

79. In a 0.2 M aqueous solution, lactic acid is 6.9% dissociated. The value of dissociation constant is
a. 1.2×10^{-4} *b.* 9.5×10^{-4}
c. 6.5×10^{-4} *d.* 3.6×10^{-2}

80. Pick up the correct statement.
a. Dipole moment of ammonia is due to orbital dipole and resultant diapole in same direction.
b. O_2, H_2 shown bond diapole due to polarisation.
c. Dipole moment is scalar quantity.
d. In BF_3 bond dicopoles are zero but dipole moment is higher.

81. Total number of σ and π bonds in ethene molecule is
a. 1 σ and 2π bonds
b. 5 σ and 1π bonds
c. 5 σ and 2π bonds
d. 3 σ and 1π bonds

82. A buffer solution has equal volumes of 0.1 M NH_4OH and 0.01 M NH_4Cl. The pK_b of the base is 5. The pH is
a. 10 *b.* 9 *c.* 4 *d.* 7

83. Oil of winter green is

a. 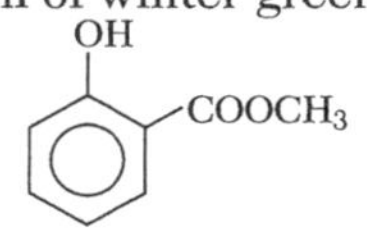
b. 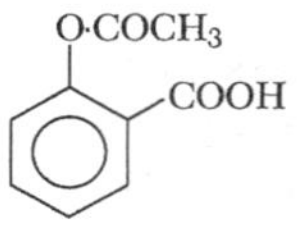
c. 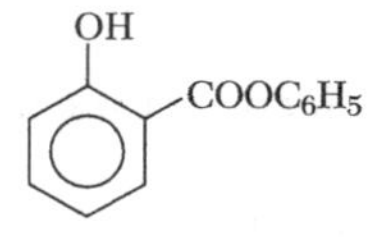
d. 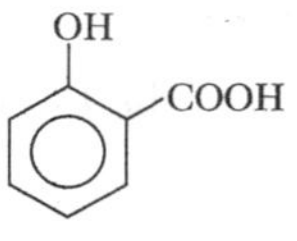

84. Assuming no change in volume, the time required to obtain solution of pH = 4 by electrolysis of 100 mL of 0.1 M NaOH (using current 0.5 A) will be

a. 1.93 s
b. 2.63 s
c. 1.80 s
d. 4.26 s

85. In a normal spinel type structure, the oxide ions are arranged in ccp, whereas 1/8 tetrahedral holes are occupied by Zn^{2+} ions and 50% of octahedral holes are occupied by Fe^{3+} ions. The formula of compound is

a. $ZnFe_2O_4$
b. $ZnFe_2O_3$
c. $ZnFe_2O_2$
d. $Zn_2Fe_2O_4$

86. Which of the following compounds would not be expected to decarboxylate when heated?

a. 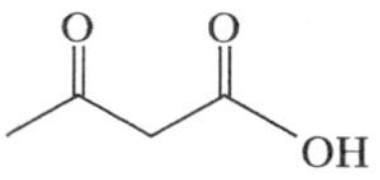
b. 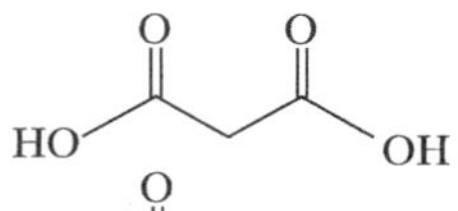
c. 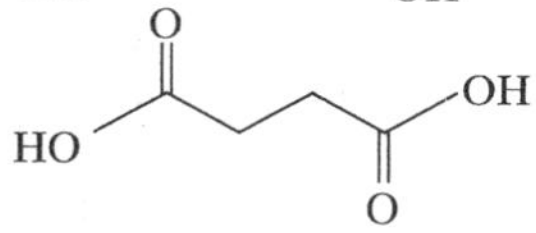
d. 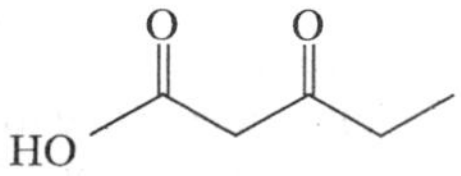

87. Which of these molecules have non-bonding electron pairs on the cental atom?

I : SF_4 ; II : ICl_3 ; III : SO_2

a. II only
b. I and II only
c. I and III only
d. I, II and III

88. For a cell reaction,

$A(s) + B^{2+}(aq) \longrightarrow A^{2+}(aq) + B(s)$; the standard emf of the cell is 0.295 V at 25°C. The equilibrium constant at 25°C will be

a. 1×10^{10}
b. 10
c. 2.95×10^{-2}
d. 2.95×10^{-10}

89. Which of the following shows negative deviation from Raoult's law?

a. Benzene-acetone
b. Benzene-chloroform
c. Benzene-ethanol
d. Benzene-carbon tetrachloride

90. 5 g of non-volatile water soluble compound *X* is dissolved in 100 g of water. The elevation in boiling point is found to be 0.25. The molecular mass of compound *X* is

a. 35 g
b. 40 g
c. 20 g
d. 60 g

91. The correct decreasing order of negative electron gain enthalpy for C, Ca, Al, F and O is

a. F > O > C > Al > Ca
b. Ca > Al > O > F > C
c. Al > F > Ca > C > O
d. F > C > O > Ca > Al

92. 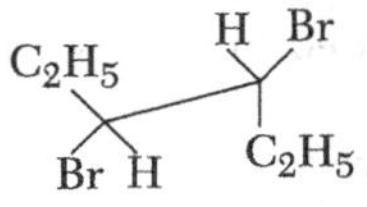 and 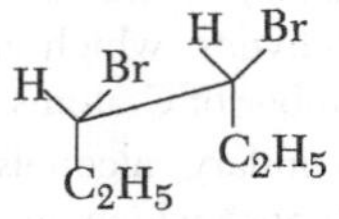

(I) (II)

I and II are

a. identical
b. a pair of conformers
c. a pair of geometrical isomers
d. a pair of optical isomers

93. Ti^{2+} is purple while Ti^{4+} is colourless because

a. Ti^{2+} has $3d^2$ configuration
b. Ti^{4+} has $3d^2$ configuration
c. Ti^{2+} is very small cation when compared to Ti^{2+} and hence, doesn't absorb any radiation
d. There is no crystal field effect in Ti^{4+}

94. Given are H_3PO_2, H_3PO_3, H_3PO_4 and $H_4P_2O_7$. Which of the above oxacids results into two series of salts?

a. H_3PO_2
b. H_3PO_3
c. H_3PO_4
d. $H_4P_2O_7$

95. In Friedal-Crafts alkylation reaction of phenol with chloromethane, the product formed will be

a. *p*-cresol only
b. *m*-cresol only
c. mixture of *o*-and *p*-cresol
d. *o*-cresol only

96. Which among the following is diamagnetic?

a. $[Ni(CN)_4]^{2-}$
b. $[Co(F_6)]^{3-}$
c. $[NiCl_4]^{2-}$
d. $[Fe(CN)_6]^{3-}$

97. NaCl has face centred structure with edge length equal to 361 pm. The radius is

a. 127.6 pm
b. 64 pm
c. 180.5 pm
d. 160.5 pm

98. Which one of the following is an important component of chlorophyll?

a. Mn *b.* Mg *c.* Fe *d.* Zn

99. The order of acidic strength of boron trihalides is

a. $BI_3 < BBr_3 < BCl_3 < BF_3$
b. $BF_3 < BCl_3 < BBr_3 < BI_3$
c. $BBr_3 < BCl_3 < BF_3 < BI_3$
d. $BCl_3 < BBr_3 < BI_3 < BF_3$

100. A volatile compound is formed by carbon monoxide and

a. Cu *b.* Al *c.* Ni *d.* Si

101. The complex $[PtCl_2(en)_2]^{2+}$ ion shows

a. structural isomerism
b. geometrical isomerism only
c. optical isomerism only
d. geometrical and optical isomerism

102. 15g of $CaCO_3$ completely reacts with

a. 6.95 g of HCl *b.* 10.95 g of HCl
c. 11.95 of HCl *d.* 1.15 g of HCl

103. The behaviour of real gas approaches ideal behaviour at

a. low temperature, low pressure
b. low pressure, high temperature
c. high pressure, low temperature
d. high temperature, high pressure

104. Bohr's radius of 2nd orbit of Be^{3+} is equal to that of

a. 4th orbit of hydrogen
b. 2nd orbit of He^+
c. 3 rd obit of Li^{2+}
d. 1st orbit of hydrogen

105. How much faster would a reaction proceed at 25°C than at 0°C if the activation energy is 65 kJ?

a. 4 times *b.* 6 times
c. 12 times *d.* 11 times

106. The blue colouration obtained from the Lassaigne's test of nitrogen is due to the formation of

a. $Fe_4[Fe(CN)_6]_3$ *b.* $Fe_2[Fe(CN)_6]_5$
c. $K_2[Fe(CN)_6]_5$ *d.* $K_4[Fe(CN)_6]_3$

107. The ion that is isoelectronic with CO is

a. O_2^+ *b.* CN^-
c. O_2^- *d.* N_2^+

108. At 300 K, the half-life period of a gaseous reaction at an initial pressure of 40 kPa is 350s. When pressure is 20 kPa, the half-life period is 175s. What is the order of the reaction?

a. Three *b.* Two *c.* One *d.* Zero

109. If 2 moles of $C_6H_6(g)$ are completely burnt 4100 kJ of heat is liberated. If $\Delta H°$ for $CO_2(g)$ and $H_2O(l)$ are –410 and – 285 kJ per mole respectively then the heat of formation of $C_2H_6(g)$ is

a. –116 kJ *b.* –375 kJ *c.* –775 kJ *d.* –885 kJ

110. Abnormal colligative properties are observed only when the dissolved non-volatile solute in a given dilute solution

a. is a non-electrolyte
b. offers an intense colour
c. associates and dissociates
d. offers no colour

111. Aqueous $CuSO_4$ changes its colour from sky blue to deep blue on addition of NH_3 because

a. Cu^{2+} forms hydrate
b. Cu^{2+} changes to Cu^+
c. $[Cu(H_2O)_4]^{2+}$ is labile complex and changes to $[Cu(NH_3)_4]^{2+}$ as NH_3 is stronger ligand than H_2O
d. Cu^+ changes to Cu^{2+}

112.

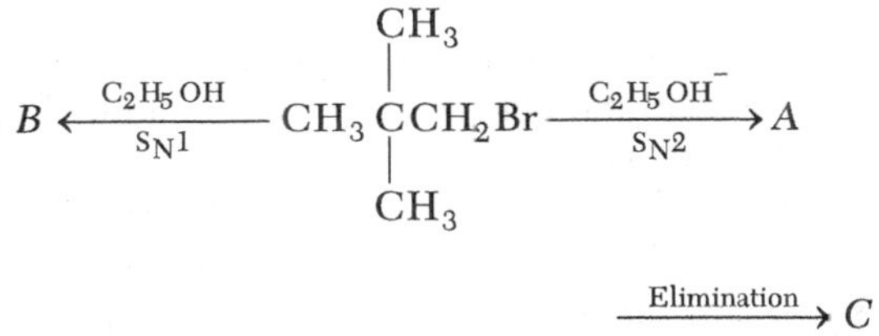

Identify *A*, *B* and *C*.

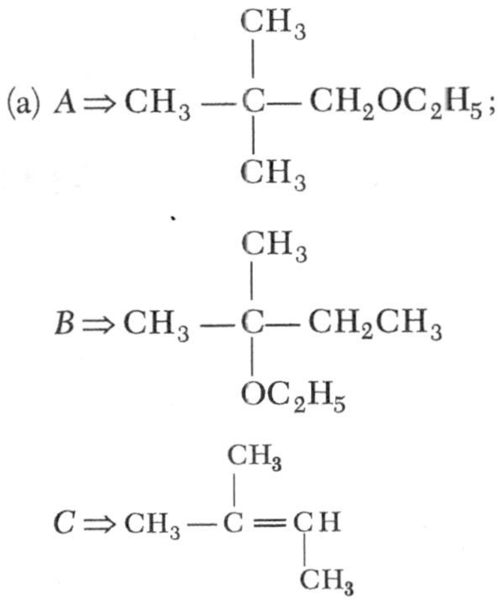

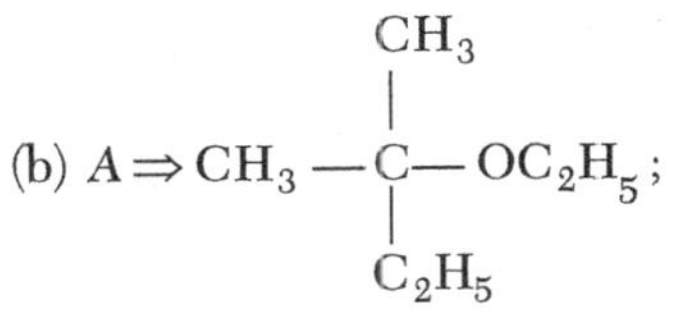

$B \Rightarrow CH_3 - \underset{\underset{OC_2H_5}{|}}{C} - CH_3$;

(c) $C \Rightarrow CH_3 - \overset{\overset{CH_3}{|}}{C} - CH{=}Cl$

(d) $A \Rightarrow CH_3 - \overset{\overset{CH_3}{|}}{\underset{\underset{CH_3}{|}}{C}} - O - CH_3$

$B \Rightarrow CH_3 - \underset{\underset{OC_2H_5}{|}}{C} - C_2H_5$;

$C \Rightarrow CH_2 - \overset{\overset{CH_3}{|}}{C} - CH_2CH_3$

113. Decomposition of hydrogen peroxide can be prevented by adding

a. urea *b.* MnO_2
c. oxalic acid *d.* NaOH

114. For a reaction, $2A + B \longrightarrow$ products,

If concentration of B is kept constant and concentration of A is doubled then rate of reaction is

a. doubled *b.* quadrupled
c. halfed *d.* remain same

115. For an adiabatic change in a system, the condition which is applicable is

a. $q = 0$ *b.* $w = 0$
c. $q = -w$ *d.* $q = w$

116. In dilute alkaline solution MnO_4^- changes to

a. MnO_2 *b.* MnO_4^{-} *c.* MnO *d.* Mn_2O_3

117. Which of the following complex show optical isomerism?

(i) *cis*-$[COCl(en)_2(NH_3)]^{2+}$
(ii) *cis*-$[CrCl_2(ox)_2]^{3-}$
(iii) *cis*-$[CO(en)_2Cl_2]Cl$
(iv) *cis*-$[CO(NH_3)_4Cl_2]^+$

a. (i), (ii), (iii) *b.* (i), (ii)
c. (i), (iv) *d.* (i), (ii), (iv)

118.

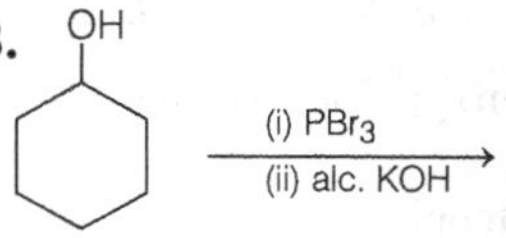

a. 

b. 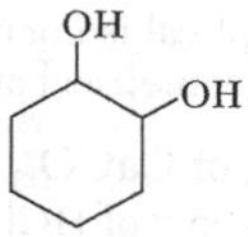

c. 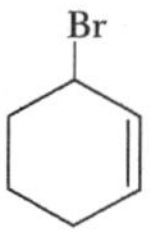

d. 

119. The ratio of average velocity of a gas molecule to the root mean square velocity at a particular temperature is

a. 1 : 1.81 *b.* 1.81 :1 *c.* 2. : 1.81 *d.* 1.81 : 2

120. Mohr's salt has the formula

a. $FeSO_4 \cdot 7H_2O$
b. $FeSO_4(NH_4)_2SO_4 \cdot 6H_2O$
c. $Fe(SO_4)_3(NH_4)_2SO_4 \cdot 6H_2O$
d. $MgSO_4 \cdot 7H_2O$

MATHEMATICS

121. The value of $a^{\log_b c} - c^{\log_b a}$, where $a, b, c > 0$ but $a, b, c \neq 1$, is

a. a *b.* b *c.* c *d.* 0

122. The slope of the tangent to the curve, $y = x^2 - xy$ at $\left(1, \frac{1}{2}\right)$ is

a. $\frac{4}{3}$ *b.* $\frac{2}{3}$ *c.* $\frac{3}{4}$ *d.* $\frac{3}{2}$

123. The value of $\lim_{x \to 0} \frac{e^{ax} - e^{bx}}{2x}$ is equal to

a. $\frac{a+b}{2}$ *b.* $\frac{a-b}{2}$ *c.* $\frac{e^{ab}}{2}$ *d.* 0

124. The points of intersection of circles $(x+1)^2 + y^2 = 4$ and $(x-1)^2 + y^2 = 9$ are $(a, \pm b)$, then (a, b) equals to

a. $\left(1.25, \frac{3}{4}\sqrt{7}\right)$ *b.* $\left(-1.25, \frac{3}{4}\sqrt{7}\right)$
c. $(-1, 2)$ *d.* $(1, 3)$

125. The approximate value of $f(5.001)$, where $f(x) = x^3 - 7x^2 + 10$

a. -39.995 *b.* -38.995 *c.* -37.335 *d.* -40.995

126. The circle $x^2 + y^2 + 3x - y + 2 = 0$ cuts an intercept on X-axis of length

a. 3 *b.* 4 *c.* 2 *d.* 1

127. Let $f(x) = a + (x-4)^{\frac{4}{9}}$, then minima of $f(x)$ is

a. 4 *b.* a
c. a-4 *d.* None of these

128. If $f(x) = \begin{cases} 2\sin x & ; -\pi \le x \le \frac{-\pi}{2} \\ a\sin x + b & ; -\frac{\pi}{2} < x < \frac{\pi}{2} \\ \cos x & ; \frac{\pi}{2} \le x \le \pi \end{cases}$ and it is continuous on $[-\pi, \pi]$, then

a. $a = 1$ and $b = 1$
b. $a = -1$ and $b = -1$
c. $a = -1$ and $b = 1$
d. $a = 1$ and $b = -1$

129. The value of $\lim_{x \to \infty} \left(\frac{x^2 - 2x + 1}{x^2 - 4x + 2} \right)^{2x}$ is

a. e^2 *b.* e^4
c. e *d.* e^{16}

130. $S \equiv x^2 + y^2 - 2x - 4y - 4 = 0$ and $S' \equiv x^2 + y^2 - 4x - 2y - 16 = 0$ are two circles, the point $(-2, -1)$ lies

a. inside S' only *b.* inside S only
c. inside S and S' *d.* outside S and S'

131. A number n is chosen at random from $s = \{1, 2, 3, \ldots, 50\}$. Let $A = \{n \in s : n$ is a square $\}$, $B = \{n \in s : n$ is a prime$\}$ and $C = \{n \in s : n$ is a square$\}$. Then, correct order of their probabilities is

a. $p(A) < p(B) < p(C)$ *b.* $p(A) > p(B) > p(C)$
c. $p(B) < p(A) < p(C)$ *d.* $p(A) > p(c) > p(B)$

132. The feasible region for the inequations $x + 2y \ge 4$, $2x + y \le 6$, $x, y \ge 0$ is

a.

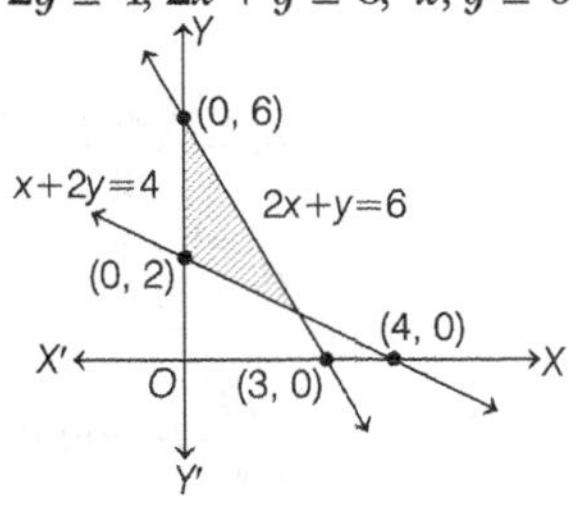

b.

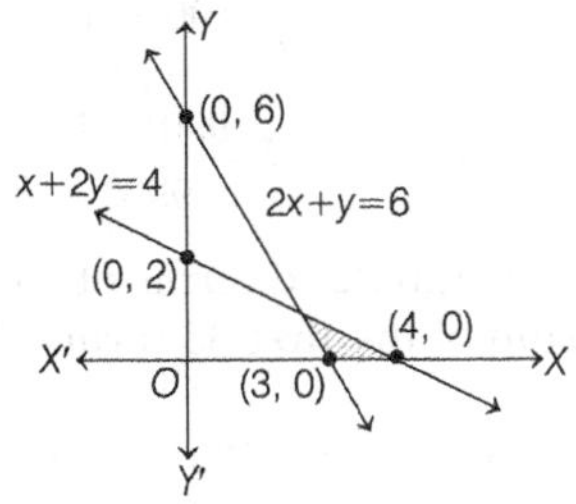

c.

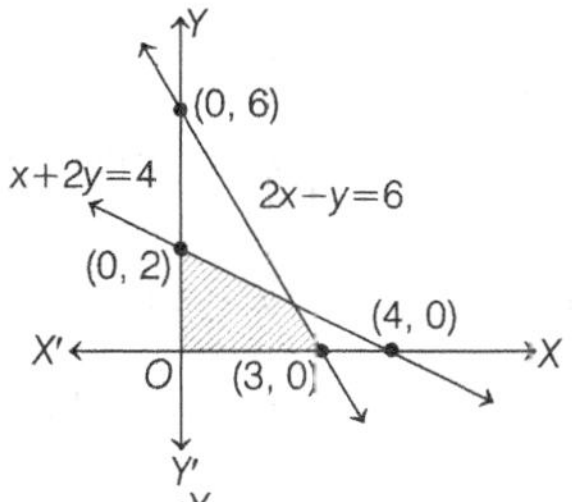

d.

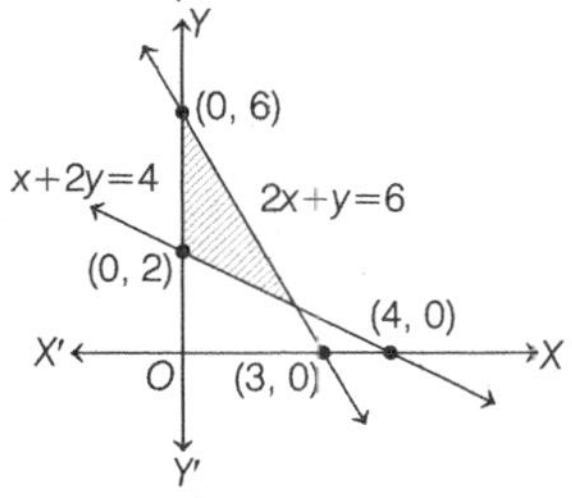

133. The maximum value of $Z = 10x + 16y$, subject to constraints $x \ge 0$, $y \ge 0$, $x + y \le 12$, $2x + y \le 20$ is

a. 144 *b.* 192 *c.* 120 *d.* 240

134. If $A = \begin{bmatrix} 2 & 2 \\ 3 & 4 \end{bmatrix}$, then A^{-1} equals to

a. $\begin{bmatrix} 2 & 1 \\ -3/2 & -1 \end{bmatrix}$ *b.* $\begin{bmatrix} 2 & -1 \\ -3/2 & 1 \end{bmatrix}$
c. $\begin{bmatrix} -2 & 1 \\ 3/2 & -1 \end{bmatrix}$ *d.* $\begin{bmatrix} -2 & -1 \\ 3/2 & 1 \end{bmatrix}$

135. If A is a matrix of order 4 such that $A\,(\text{adj } A) = 10\,I$, then $|\text{adj } A|$ is equal to

a. 10 *b.* 100
c. 1000 *d.* 10000

136. If $A = \begin{bmatrix} k+1 & 2 \\ 4 & k-1 \end{bmatrix}$ is a singular matrix, then possible values of k are

a. ± 1 *b.* ± 2
c. ± 3 *d.* ± 4

137. The angle between the vectors $\mathbf{a} = \hat{\mathbf{i}} + 2\hat{\mathbf{j}} + 2\hat{\mathbf{k}}$ and $\mathbf{b} = \hat{\mathbf{i}} + 2\hat{\mathbf{j}} - 2\hat{\mathbf{k}}$ is

a. $\sin^{-1}(1/9)$ *b.* $\cos^{-1}(8/9)$
c. $\sin^{-1}(8/9)$ *d.* $\cos^{-1}(1/9)$

138. If the vectors $\mathbf{a} = 2\hat{\mathbf{i}} - 3\hat{\mathbf{j}} + 4\hat{\mathbf{k}}$, $\mathbf{b} = \hat{\mathbf{i}} + 2\hat{\mathbf{j}} - \hat{\mathbf{k}}$ and $\mathbf{c} = m\hat{\mathbf{i}} - \hat{\mathbf{j}} + 2\hat{\mathbf{k}}$ are coplanar, then the value of m is

a. $\frac{5}{8}$ *b.* $\frac{8}{5}$ *c.* $\frac{-7}{4}$ *d.* $\frac{2}{3}$

139. The maximum value of $Z = 12x + 13y$, subject to constraints $x \ge 0$, $y \ge 0$, $x + y \le 5$ and $3x + y \le 9$ is

a. 63 *b.* 65 *c.* 60 *d.* 117

140. $\mathbf{a} = 2\hat{\mathbf{i}} + \hat{\mathbf{j}} - \hat{\mathbf{k}}$, $\mathbf{b} = \hat{\mathbf{i}} - \hat{\mathbf{j}}$ and $\mathbf{c} = 5\hat{\mathbf{i}} - \hat{\mathbf{j}} + \hat{\mathbf{k}}$, then unit vector parallel to $\mathbf{a} + \mathbf{b} - \mathbf{c}$ but in opposite direction is

a. $\frac{1}{3}(2\hat{\mathbf{i}} - \hat{\mathbf{j}} + 2\hat{\mathbf{k}})$ *b.* $\frac{1}{2}(2\hat{\mathbf{i}} - \hat{\mathbf{j}} + 2\hat{\mathbf{k}})$
c. $\frac{1}{3}(2\hat{\mathbf{i}} - \hat{\mathbf{j}} - 2\hat{\mathbf{k}})$ *d.* None of these

141. The place $x - 2y + z = 0$ is parallel to the line

a. $\frac{x-3}{4} = \frac{y-4}{5} = \frac{z-3}{6}$ *b.* $\frac{x-2}{1} = \frac{y-2}{-2} = \frac{z-3}{1}$
c. $\frac{x-2}{2} = \frac{y-3}{3} = \frac{z-4}{4}$ *d.* $\frac{x-4}{3} = \frac{y-5}{4} = \frac{z-6}{3}$

142. $\int \frac{x\,dx}{2(1+x)^{3/2}}$ is equal to

a. $\frac{2+x}{\sqrt{1+x}} + C$ *b.* $\frac{2+x}{x\sqrt{1+x}} + C$
c. $\frac{x}{\sqrt{1+x}} + C$ *d.* $-\frac{x}{\sqrt{1+x}} + C$

143. $\int \frac{4^x}{\sqrt{1-16^x}} dx$ is equal to

a. $(\log 4) \sin^{-1} 4^x + C$ *b.* $\frac{1}{4}\sin^{-1}(4^x) + C$
c. $\frac{1}{\log 4}\sin^{-1} 4^x + C$ *d.* $4\log 4 \sin^{-1} 4 + C$

144. $\int_{-\pi/2}^{\pi/2} \sin^2 x\,dx$ is equal to

a. 0 *b.* π *c.* $\frac{\pi}{2}$ *d.* $\frac{\pi}{4}$

145. The lines $\frac{x-1}{2} = \frac{y-4}{4} = \frac{z-2}{3}$ and $\frac{1-x}{1} = \frac{y-2}{5} = \frac{3-z}{a}$ are perpendicular to each other, then a equals to

a. −6 *b.* 6 *c.* $\frac{22}{3}$ *d.* $-\frac{22}{3}$

146. If two lines $L_1 : \frac{x-1}{2} = \frac{y+1}{3} = \frac{z-1}{4}$ and $L_2 : \frac{x-3}{1} = \frac{y-k}{2} = z$ intersect at a point, then $2k$ is equal to

a. 9 *b.* $\frac{1}{2}$ *c.* $\frac{9}{2}$ *d.* 1

147. A five-digits number is formed by using the digits 1, 2, 3, 4, 5 with no repetition. The probability that the numbers 1 and 5 are always together, is

a. $\frac{2}{5}$ *b.* $\frac{1}{5}$ *c.* $\frac{3}{5}$ *d.* $\frac{1}{4}$

148. If a number n is chosen at random from the set $\{11, 12, 13, \ldots\ldots, 30\}$. Then, the probability that n is neither divisible by 3 nor divisible by 5, is

a. $\frac{7}{20}$ *b.* $\frac{9}{20}$ *c.* $\frac{11}{20}$ *d.* $\frac{13}{20}$

149. Three vertices are chosen randomly from the nine vertices of a regular 9-sided polygon. The probability that they form the vertices of an isosceles triangle, is

a. $\frac{4}{7}$ *b.* $\frac{3}{7}$ *c.* $\frac{2}{7}$ *d.* $\frac{5}{7}$

150. If A, B and C are mutually exclusive and exhaustive events of a random experiment such that $P(B) = \frac{3}{2}P(A)$ and $P(C) = \frac{1}{2}P(B)$, then $P(A \cup C)$ equals to

a. $\frac{10}{13}$ *b.* $\frac{3}{13}$ *c.* $\frac{6}{13}$ *d.* $\frac{7}{13}$

151. Using mathematical induction, the numbers a_ns are defined by $a_0 = 1$, $a_{n+1} = 3n^2 + n + a_n$, $(n \geq 0)$. Then, a_n is equal to

a. $n^3 + n^2 + 1$ *b.* $n^3 - n^2 + 1$
c. $n^3 - n^2$ *d.* $n^3 + n^2$

152. If $49^n + 16^n + k$ is divisible by 64 for $n \in N$, then the least negative integral value of k is

a. −1 *b.* −2 *c.* −3 *d.* −4

153. $2^{3n} - 7n - 1$ is divisible by

a. 64 *b.* 36 *c.* 49 *d.* 25

154. The sum of n terms of the series, $\frac{4}{3} + \frac{10}{9} + \frac{28}{27} + \ldots$ is

a. $\frac{3^n(2n+1)+1}{2(3^n)}$ *b.* $\frac{3^n(2n+1)-1}{2(3^n)}$
c. $\frac{3^n n - 1}{2(3^n)}$ *d.* $\frac{3^n - 1}{2}$

155. The value of $\frac{1}{2!} + \frac{2}{3!} + \ldots + \frac{99}{100!}$ is equal to

a. $\frac{100!-1}{100!}$ *b.* $\frac{100!+1}{100!}$
c. $\frac{999!-1}{999!}$ *d.* $\frac{999!+1}{999!}$

156. If the sum of 12th and 22nd terms of an AP is 100, then the sum of the first 33 terms of an AP is

a. 1700 *b.* 1650 *c.* 3300 *d.* 3500

COMEDK 2023

157. The differential equation of all non-vertical lines in a plane is

a. $\frac{d^2y}{dx^2}=0$ **b.** $\frac{d^2x}{dy^2}=0$ **c.** $\frac{dy}{dx}=0$ **d.** $\frac{dx}{dy}=0$

158. The general solution of $\left(\frac{dy}{dx}\right)^2=1-x^2-y^2+x^2y^2$ is

a. $2\sin^{-1}y=x\sqrt{1-x^2}+\sin^{-1}x+C$

b. $\cos^{-1}y=x\cos^{-1}x$

c. $\sin^{-1}y=\frac{1}{2}\sin^{-1}x+C$

d. $2\sin^{-1}y=x\sqrt{1-y^2}+C$

159. The solution of the differential equation $\left(\frac{dy}{dx}\right)\tan y=\sin(x+y)+\sin(x-y)$ is

a. $\sec x=-2\sec y+C$ **b.** $\sec y=2\cos y+C$
c. $\sec y=-2\cos x+C$ **d.** $\sec x=-2\cos y+C$

160. Find ${}^nC_{21}$, if ${}^nC_{10}={}^nC_{12}$

a. 1 **b.** 21
c. 22 **d.** 2

161. In a trial, the probability of success is twice the probability of failure. In six trials, the probability of at most two failure will be

a. $\frac{600}{729}$ **b.** $\frac{500}{729}$ **c.** $\frac{400}{729}$ **d.** $\frac{496}{729}$

162. If $\cos A=m\cos B$ and $\cot\left(\frac{A+B}{2}\right)=\lambda\tan\left(\frac{B-A}{2}\right)$, then λ is equal to

a. $\frac{m}{m-1}$ **b.** $\frac{m+1}{m}$
c. $\frac{m+1}{m-1}$ **d.** None of these

163. The expression $\frac{2\tan A}{1-\cot A}+\frac{2\cot A}{1-\tan A}$ can be written as

a. $\sin 2A+\cos 2A$ **b.** $2\sec A\operatorname{cosec}A+2$
c. $\tan 2A+\cot 2A$ **d.** $\sec 2A+\operatorname{cosec}2A$

164. The general solution of $2\cos 4x+\sin^2 2x=0$ is

a. $x=\frac{n\pi}{2}\pm\sin^{-1}\left(\frac{1}{5}\right)$

b. $x=\frac{n\pi}{4}+\frac{(-1)^n}{4}\sin^{-1}\left(\pm\frac{2\sqrt{2}}{3}\right)$

c. $x=\frac{n\pi}{2}\pm\cos^{-1}\left(\frac{1}{5}\right)$

d. $x=\frac{n\pi}{4}+\frac{(-1)^n}{4}\cos^{-1}\left(\frac{1}{5}\right)$

165. If $2f(x^2)+3f\left(\frac{1}{x^2}\right)=x^2-1,\ \forall\, x\in R-\{0\}$, then $f(x^8)$ is equal to

a. $\frac{(1-x^8)(2x^8+3)}{5x^8}$ **b.** $\frac{(1+x^8)(2x^8-3)}{5x^8}$
c. $\frac{(1-x^8)(2x^8-3)}{5x^8}$ **d.** None of these

166. If $A=\{a,b,c\}$, $B=\{b,c,d\}$ and $C=\{a,d,c\}$, then $(A-B)\times(B\cap C)$ is equal to

a. $\{(a,c),(a,d)\}$ **b.** $\{(a,b),(c,d)\}$
c. $\{(c,a),(d,a)\}$ **d.** $\{(a,c),(a,d),(b,d)\}$

167. If $n(A)=p$ and $n(B)=q$, then the numbers of relations from the set A to the set B is

a. 2^{p+q} **b.** 2^{pq} **c.** $p+q$ **d.** pq

168. If $z=\sqrt{3}+i$, then the argument of z^2e^{z-i} is equal to

a. $e^{\pi/3}$ **b.** $\frac{\pi}{3}$ **c.** $\frac{\pi}{6}$ **d.** $e^{\pi/6}$

169. If $i=\sqrt{-1}$ and n is a positive integer, then $i^n+i^{n+1}+i^{n+2}+i^{n+3}$ is equal to

a. 1 **b.** i **c.** i^n **d.** 0

170. If $\left(\frac{3}{2}+i\frac{\sqrt{3}}{2}\right)^{50}=3^{25}(x+iy)$, where x and y are real, then the ordered pair $(2x,2y)$ is

a. $(-6,0)$ **b.** $(0,6)$
c. $(0,-6)$ **d.** $(1,\sqrt{3})$

171. There are 10 points in a plane out of which 4 points are collinear. How many straight lines can be drawn by joining any two of them?

a. 39 **b.** 40 **c.** 45 **d.** 21

172. The total number of numbers greater than 1000 but less than 4000 that can be formed using 0, 2, 3, 4 (using repetition allowed) are

a. 125 **b.** 105 **c.** 128 **d.** 625

173. A polygon of n sides has 105 diagonals, then n is equal to

a. 20 **b.** 21 **c.** 15 **d.** -14

174. Let the equation of pair of lines $y=m_1x$ and $y=m_2x$ can be written as $(y-m_1x)(y-m_2x)=0$. Then, the equation of the pair of the angle bisector of the line $3y^2-5xy-2x^2=0$ is

a. $x^2+5xy-y^2=0$

b. $x^2-5xy+y^2=0$

c. $x^2-xy+y^2=0$

d. $x^2+xy-y^2=0$

175. The distance of the point (3, 4) from the line $3x + 2y + 7 = 0$ measured along the line parallel to $y - 2x + 7 = 0$ is equal to

a. $\frac{24\sqrt{5}}{7}$ *b.* $3\sqrt{5}$

c. $\frac{23\sqrt{5}}{7}$ *d.* $4\sqrt{5}$

176. The slope of lines which makes an angle 60° with the line $y - 3x + 18 = 0$

a. $\frac{3\sqrt{3}-3}{1+3\sqrt{3}}, \frac{3\sqrt{3}-3}{1+3\sqrt{3}}$

b. $\frac{3-\sqrt{3}}{1+3\sqrt{3}}, \frac{3+\sqrt{3}}{1-3\sqrt{3}}$

c. $\frac{3}{1+\sqrt{3}}, \frac{3}{1-\sqrt{3}}$

d. $\frac{\sqrt{3}-1}{3}, \frac{\sqrt{3}+1}{3}$

177. 3 and 5 are intercepts of a line $L = 0$, then the distance of $L = 0$ from (3, 7) is

a. $\sqrt{31}$ *b.* $\sqrt{34}$ *c.* $\frac{21}{\sqrt{34}}$ *d.* $\frac{\sqrt{34}}{31}$

178. The total number of terms in the expansion of $(x+y)^{60} + (x-y)^{60}$ is

a. 60 *b.* 61
c. 30 *d.* 31

179. The coefficient of x^{29} in the expansion of $(1 - 3x + 3x^2 - x^3)^{15}$ is

a. ${}^{45}C_{29}$ *b.* ${}^{45}C_{28}$
c. $-{}^{45}C_{16}$ *d.* ${}^{45}C_{30}$

180. In the expansion of $(1 + 3x + 3x^2 + x^3)^{2n}$, the term which has greatest binomial coefficient, is

a. $(3n)$ th term *b.* $(3n+1)$ th term
c. $(3n-1)$ th term *d.* $(3n+2)$ th term

ANSWERS

Physics

1.	(c)	2.	(d)	3.	(a)	4.	(b)	5.	(a)	6.	(b)	7.	(c)	8.	(c)	9.	(b)	10.	(a)
11.	(c)	12.	(d)	13.	(d)	14.	(b)	15.	(a)	16.	(c)	17.	(b)	18.	(c)	19.	(d)	20.	(c)
21.	(a)	22.	(a)	23.	(d)	24.	(b)	25.	(a)	26.	(a)	27.	(d)	28.	(a)	29.	(c)	30.	(a)
31.	(d)	32.	(b)	33.	(c)	34.	(b)	35.	(b)	36.	(a)	37.	(c)	38.	(b)	39.	(b)	40.	(b)
41.	(b)	42.	(b)	43.	(a)	44.	(a)	45.	(a)	46.	(c)	47.	(b)	48.	(b)	49.	(c)	50.	(d)
51.	(a)	52.	(d)	53.	(c)	54.	(b)	55.	(d)	56.	(c)	57.	(c)	58.	(a)	59.	(b)	60.	(c)

Chemistry

61.	(b)	62.	(b)	63.	(c)	64.	(a)	65.	(a)	66.	(d)	67.	(d)	68.	(c)	69.	(b)	70.	(b)
71.	(c)	72.	(a)	73.	(a)	74.	(a)	75.	(a)	76.	(a)	77.	(b)	78.	(a)	79.	(b)	80.	(a)
81.	(b)	82.	(a)	83.	(a)	84.	(a)	85.	(a)	86.	(c)	87.	(d)	88.	(a)	89.	(b)	90.	(c)
91.	(a)	92.	(b)	93.	(a)	94.	(b)	95.	(c)	96.	(a)	97.	(a)	98.	(b)	99.	(b)	100.	(c)
101.	(d)	102.	(b)	103.	(b)	104.	(d)	105.	(d)	106.	(a)	107.	(b)	108.	(d)	109.	(b)	110.	(c)
111.	(c)	112.	(a)	113.	(a)	114.	(b)	115.	(a)	116.	(b)	117.	(a)	118.	(a)	119.	(a)	120.	(b)

Mathematics

121.	(d)	122.	(c)	123.	(b)	124.	(b)	125.	(a)	126.	(d)	127.	(b)	128.	(d)	129.	(b)	130.	(a)
131.	(b)	132.	(a)	133.	(b)	134.	(b)	135.	(c)	136.	(c)	137.	(d)	138.	(b)	139.	(b)	140.	(a)
141.	(a)	142.	(a)	143.	(c)	144.	(c)	145.	(b)	146.	(a)	147.	(a)	148.	(c)	149.	(b)	150.	(d)
151.	(b)	152.	(a)	153.	(c)	154.	(b)	155.	(a)	156.	(b)	157.	(a)	158.	(a)	159.	(c)	160.	(c)
161.	(d)	162.	(c)	163.	(b)	164.	(b)	165.	(a)	166.	(a)	167.	(b)	168.	(b)	169.	(d)	170.	(d)
171.	(b)	172.	(c)	173.	(c)	174.	(d)	175.	(a)	176.	(b)	177.	(c)	178.	(d)	179.	(c)	180.	(b)

HINTS & SOLUTIONS

Physics

1. *(c)* For an ideal gas, mean kinetic energy per molecule

$$= \frac{f}{2} k_B T$$

For diatomic gas, degree of freedom,

$$f = 5$$

$\therefore$ K.E per molecule $= \frac{5k_BT}{2}$

2. *(d)* The displacement of a particle executing SHM is $x = A\sin \omega t$

$\therefore$ Velocity, $v = \frac{dx}{dt} = A\omega \cos \omega t$

$\therefore v = A\,\omega \sin\left(\omega t + \frac{\pi}{2}\right)$

$\therefore$ Phase difference, $\Delta\phi = \left(\omega t + \frac{\pi}{2}\right) - \omega t = \frac{\pi}{2}$ rad.

3. *(a)* As, the mass density of a nucleus is constant

$\therefore$ Mass density, $= \frac{3m}{4\pi R_0^3}$

4. *(b)* When two capacitors are connected then their common potential difference is

$$V = \frac{C_1V_1 + C_2V_2}{C_1 + C_2}$$

Given, $C_1 = 2\,\mu\text{F}, V_1 = 14\,\text{V}, C_2 = 5\,\mu\text{F}, V_2 = 0\,\text{V}$

$$\therefore \quad V = \frac{2\times 14 + 5\times 0}{2+5} = 4\,\text{V}$$

5. *(a)* For an electromagnetic wave,

Speed of electromagnetic wave, $c = \frac{E_0}{B_0}$

$\therefore \frac{B_0}{E_0} = \frac{1}{c}$ = reciprocal of speed

6. *(b)* Initial kinetic energy is

$$K = \frac{1}{2}mv^2 \quad \ldots \text{(i)}$$

Final kinetic energy is

$$K' = \frac{1}{2}mv^2 = \frac{1}{2}m(u\cos 30°)^2 \quad [\because v = u\cos 30°]$$

$$= \frac{3}{4}\left(\frac{1}{2}mu^2\right) = \frac{3}{4}K \quad \text{[From Eq. (i)]}$$

7. *(c)* The refractive index of water,

$$\mu = \frac{4}{3}$$

The real depth of image of bubble from the surface of water,

$$d = 24 + 8 = 32\,\text{cm}$$

$\therefore$ Apparent depth of the image of bubble is

$$d' = \frac{d}{\mu} = \frac{32}{4/3} = 24\,\text{cm}$$

8. *(c)* The height of TV tower, $h = 72\,\text{m}$

The maximum distance upto which transmission can be received,

$$d = \sqrt{2Rh} = \sqrt{2\times 6.4\times 10^6 \times 72} = 30.35\,\text{km}$$

9. *(b)* Current gain factor, $\alpha = 0.96$

$R = 1000\Omega$, Voltage drop across collector resistor $= 0.5\,\text{V}$

$$\therefore \quad \beta = \frac{\alpha}{1-\alpha} = \frac{0.96}{1-0.96} = 24$$

$\therefore$Collector current,

$$i_c = \frac{\text{Voltage drop across collector resistor}}{R}$$

$$= \frac{0.5}{1000} = 0.5\times 10^{-3}\,\text{A}$$

The base current, $i_b = \frac{i_c}{\beta} = \frac{0.5\times 10^{-3}}{24} = 20.8\ \mu\text{A}$

10. *(a)* Consider the string of length l connected to a particle as shown in the figure

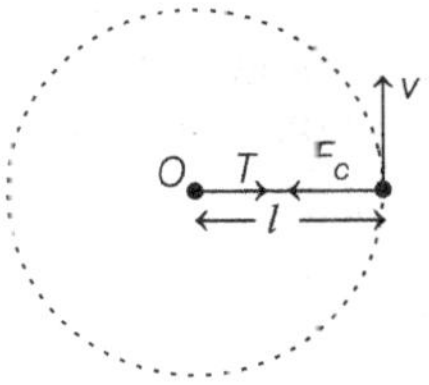

Speed of the particle is v. As, the particle is in uniform circular motion, the net force on the particle must be equal to centripetal force which is provided by the tension (T).

$\therefore$ Net force = Centripetal force = Tension in string

$$\Rightarrow \quad \frac{mv^2}{l} = T$$

11 *(c)* According to conservation of angular momentum,

$$I\omega = \text{constant}$$

i.e. we can write,

$$I_1\omega_1 = I_2\omega_2$$

or $\quad MR^2\omega = (M + 4m)R^2\,\omega_2 \quad (\because \omega_1 = \omega)$

or $\quad \omega_2 = \left(\frac{M}{M+4m}\right)\omega$

12. *(d)* Given, ratio of radius of two wires,

$$\frac{r_1}{r_2} = \frac{2}{1}$$

and ratio in their lengths,

$$\frac{l_1}{l_2} = \frac{1}{2}$$

When same force is applied on them, then ratio change in their lengths,

$$\frac{\Delta l_1}{\Delta l_2} = ?$$

We known that, Young's modulus,

$$Y = \frac{Fl}{A\Delta l} \Rightarrow \Delta l = \frac{Fl}{AY}$$

$$\Delta l \propto \frac{l}{A}$$

$$\therefore \quad \frac{\Delta l_1}{\Delta l_2} = \frac{l_1 / A_1}{l_2 / A_2} = \frac{l_1 A_2}{l_2 A_2}$$

$$\Rightarrow \quad \frac{\Delta l_1}{\Delta l_2} = \frac{l_1 / A_1}{r_2^2 / r_1^2} = \frac{1}{2} \cdot \left(\frac{1}{2}\right)^2 = \frac{1}{8}$$

13. *(d)* When bob A strikes to the bob B, then

$$mu = (m + m)v'$$

$$\Rightarrow \quad v' = \frac{u}{2} \quad \text{...(i)}$$

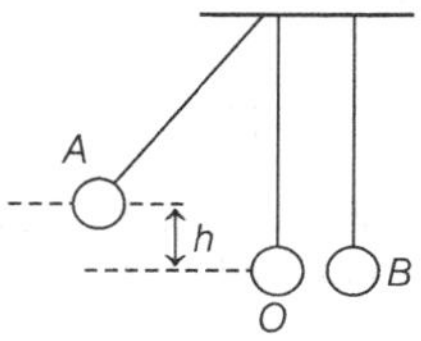

The potential energy of A at height h gets converted into kinetic energy of this mass, at point O, i.e.

$$mgh = \frac{1}{2} mu^2$$

$$\Rightarrow \quad u = \sqrt{2gh} \quad \text{[From Eq. (i)]}$$

$$\therefore \quad v' = \frac{\sqrt{2gh}}{2} = \sqrt{\frac{gh}{2}}$$

Let the combined mass moves to a height h', then total mass $= 2m$

Then, $2mgh' = \frac{1}{2}(2m)v'^2$

$$\Rightarrow \quad gh' = \frac{gh}{4} \Rightarrow h' = \frac{h}{4}$$

14. *(b)* Net work done by the gas = Area enclosed in p-V curve, i.e. area of ΔABC.

$$W_{net} = \frac{1}{2} \times 5 \times 10^{-3} \times 4 \times 10^5 \text{ J} = 10^3 \text{ J} = 1000 \text{ J}$$

15. *(a)* The gases carbon monoxide (CO) and nitrogen (N_2) are diatomic, so both have equal kinetic energy $\frac{5}{2}KT$, i.e.

$$E_1 = E_2$$

16. *(c)* According to the question,

For wire 1 : Area of cross-section $= A_1$,

Force applied $= F_1$

and increase in length $= \Delta l$.

From the relation of Young's modulus of elasticity,

$$Y = \frac{Fl}{A\Delta l}$$

Substituting the values for wire 1 in the above relation, we get

$$\Rightarrow \quad Y_1 = \frac{F_1 l_1}{A_1 \Delta l} \quad \text{...(i)}$$

For wire 2 : Area of cross-section $= A_2$

Force applied $= F_2$

increase in length $= \Delta l$

$$\text{Similarly, } Y_2 = \frac{F_2 l_2}{A_2 \Delta l} \quad \text{...(ii)}$$

$\because$ Volume, $V = Al$ or $l = \frac{V}{A}$

Substituting the value of l in Eqs. (i) and (ii), we get

$$Y_1 = \frac{F_1 V}{A_1^2 \Delta l} \quad \text{and} \quad Y_2 = \frac{F_2 V}{A_2^2 \Delta l}$$

As it is given that the wires are made up of same material,

i.e. $\quad Y_1 = Y_2$

$$\Rightarrow \quad \frac{F_1 V}{A_1^2 \Delta l} = \frac{F_2 V}{A_2^2 \Delta l} \Rightarrow \frac{F_1}{F_2} = \frac{A_1^2}{A_2^2} = \frac{A^2}{9A^2} = \frac{1}{9}$$

$(\because \; A_1 = A \text{ and } A_2 = 3A)$

or $\quad F_2 = 9F_1 = 9F \quad$ (given, $F_1 = F$)

17. *(b)* Acceleration due to gravity at a depth d below the surface of the earth is given by

$$g_{depth} = g_{surface}\left(1 - \frac{d}{R}\right)$$

$$= g_{surface}\left[\frac{R-d}{R}\right] = d_{surface}\left(\frac{r}{R}\right)$$

Also, for a point at height h above surface,

$$g_{height} = g_{surface}\left[\frac{R^2}{(R+h)^2}\right]$$

Therefore, we can say that value of g increases from centre to maximum at the surface and then decreases as depicted in graph (b).

18. *(c)* Potential energy of the spring,

$$U = \frac{1}{2}kx^2 \quad \text{...(i)}$$

and $\quad U' = \frac{1}{2}k(nx)^2 \Rightarrow U' = n^2 \frac{1}{2}kx^2$

$$\Rightarrow \quad U' = n^2 U \quad \text{[From Eq. (i)]}$$

19. *(d)* By using $v' = v\left[\frac{v - v_0}{v - v_s}\right]$

$$\Rightarrow \quad 2v = v\left[\frac{v - v_0}{v - 0}\right]$$

$$\Rightarrow \quad v_0 = -v$$

Negative sign indicates that observer is moving opposite to the direction of velocity of sound.

20 *(c)* The dielectric is introduced such that half of its area is occupied by it.

In the given case, the two capacitors are in parallel.

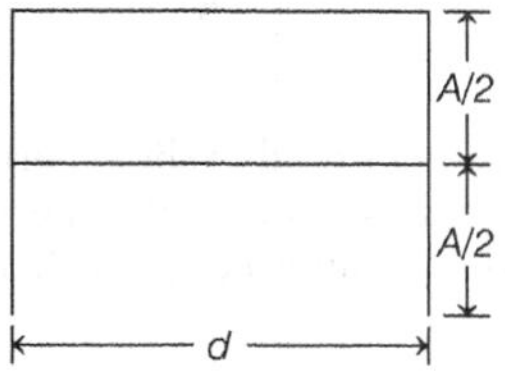

$\therefore \quad C' = C_1 + C_2$

But $\quad C_1 = \dfrac{A\varepsilon_0}{2d}$ and $C_2 = \dfrac{KA\varepsilon_0}{2d}$

Thus, $\quad C' = \dfrac{A\varepsilon_0}{2d} + \dfrac{KA\varepsilon_0}{2d} \Rightarrow C' = \dfrac{C}{2}(1 + K)$

21. *(a)* The magnetic field induction at P due to currents through both the wires is

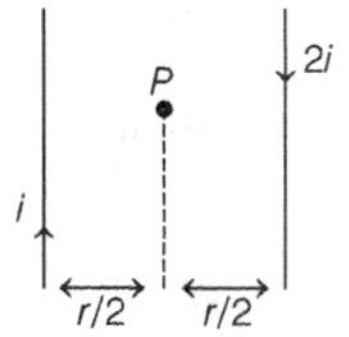

$$B = \frac{\mu_0}{4\pi}\frac{2i}{(r/2)} + \frac{\mu_0}{4\pi}\frac{2(2i)}{(r/2)} = \frac{\mu_0}{4\pi}\cdot\frac{12i}{r}$$

acting perpendicular to plane of wire inwards. Now, B and v are acting in the same direction, i.e. $\theta = 0°$

Force on charged particle is

$F = qvB\sin\theta = qvB \times 0 = 0.$

22. *(a)* Given, $\phi = (4t^2 + 6t + 9)$ Wb and $t = 2$ s

We know that, $|\varepsilon| = \left|\dfrac{d\phi}{dt}\right|$

Here, $\left|\dfrac{d\phi}{dt}\right| = |8t + 6| \Rightarrow \left(\dfrac{d\phi}{dt}\right)_{t=2} = 8 \times 2 + 6$

Induced emf in the coil = 22 V

23. *(d)* Given,

$$i = \frac{1}{\sqrt{2}}\sin(100\pi t) \text{ amp}$$

and $\quad e = \dfrac{1}{\sqrt{2}}\sin(100\pi t + \pi/3)$ volt

$\Rightarrow \quad i_0 = \dfrac{1}{\sqrt{2}}$ and $e_0 = \dfrac{1}{\sqrt{2}}$

We know that, average power,

$$P_{av} = V_{rms} \times i_{rms}\cos\phi = \frac{1}{2} \times \frac{1}{2} \times \cos 60°$$

$$(\because i_{rms} = i_0/\sqrt{2} \text{ and } V_{rms} = V_0/\sqrt{2})$$

$$= \frac{1}{2} \times \frac{1}{2} \times \frac{1}{2} = \frac{1}{8} \text{ W}$$

24. *(b)* When the sound is reflected from the cliff, it approaches the driver of the car. Therefore, the driver acts as an observer and both the source (car) and observer are moving.

Hence, apparent frequency heard by the observer (driver) is given by

$$f' = f\left(\frac{v + v_o}{v - v_s}\right) \quad \ldots(i)$$

where, $\quad v_s$ = velocity of sound

and $\quad v_o$ = velocity of the car

Thus, Eq. (i) becomes

$$2f = f\left(\frac{v + v_o}{v - v_o}\right)$$

$$\Rightarrow 2v - 2v_o = v + v_o \Rightarrow 3v_o = v \Rightarrow v_o = \frac{v}{3}$$

25. *(a)* Given, Escape velocity on the surface of the earth is given by

i.e. $\quad v_e = \sqrt{2gR_e}$

$$v_e = \sqrt{\frac{2GM_e}{R_e}} \quad \ldots(i)$$

Mass of the moon, $M_m = \dfrac{M_e}{81}$

Radius of the moon, $R_m = \dfrac{R_e}{4}$

$\therefore$ Escape velocity on the surface of the moon

$$v_m = \sqrt{\frac{2G\,M_m}{R_m}} = \sqrt{\frac{2G\left(\frac{Me}{81}\right)}{\frac{R_e}{4}}} = \frac{2\sqrt{2}}{9}\sqrt{\frac{GM_e}{R_e}}$$

From Eq. (i),

$$= \frac{2}{9}\sqrt{\frac{2GM_e}{R_e}} = \frac{2}{9}v_e$$

Escape velocity $v_e = 11.1$ km/h

$$= \frac{2}{9} \times 11.1 = 2.46 \text{km h}^{-1}$$

26. *(a)* For all processes 1, 2 and 3

Change in internal energy, i.e.

$$\Delta U = U_B - U_A$$

$\therefore \Delta U_1 = \Delta U_2 = \Delta U_3 \Rightarrow Q = \Delta U + \Delta W$

Now, ΔW = work done by the gas, i.e. area under p-V curve.

As, area (1) > area (2) > area (3)

$\therefore \quad \Delta W_1 > \Delta W_2 > \Delta W_3$

$\therefore \quad Q_1 > Q_2 > Q_3$

27. *(d)* Here, $L = 1$ H, $C = 20\,\mu$F, $R = 300\,\Omega$

$$X_L = 2\pi fL = 2\pi\left(\frac{50}{\pi}\right) \times 1 = 100\ \Omega$$

$$X_C = \frac{1}{2\pi fC} = \frac{1}{2\pi\left(\frac{50}{\pi}\right)20 \times 10^{-6}} = 500\ \Omega$$

Impedance, $Z = \sqrt{R^2 + (X_C - X_L)^2}$
$$= \sqrt{(300)^2 + (400)^2} = 500\ \Omega$$

28. (*a*) Here, $\dfrac{I_{bright}}{I_{dark}} = \dfrac{I_{max}}{I_{min}} = 3$ (given)

$$\Rightarrow \quad \frac{(a_1 + a_2)^2}{(a_1 - a_2)^2} = \frac{3}{1} \Rightarrow \frac{a_1 + a_2}{a_1 - a_2} = \sqrt{3}$$

$$\Rightarrow \quad a_1 + a_2 = \sqrt{3}(a_1 - a_2) \Rightarrow \frac{a_1}{a_2} = \left(\frac{\sqrt{3}+1}{\sqrt{3}-1}\right)$$

29. (*c*) Lyman series of H-atom, we can write

$$\frac{hc}{\lambda} = Rhc\left(\frac{1}{1^2} - \frac{1}{2^2}\right)$$

where, symbols have their usual meaning and for second line of Balmer series of H-like ion

$$\frac{hc}{\lambda} = Z^2 Rhc\left(\frac{1}{2^2} - \frac{1}{4^2}\right).$$

Therefore, $\left(\dfrac{1}{1^2} - \dfrac{1}{2^2}\right) = Z^2\left(\dfrac{1}{4} - \dfrac{1}{16}\right)$

$$\left(1 - \frac{1}{4}\right) = Z^2\left(\frac{1}{4} - \frac{1}{16}\right)$$

$$\Rightarrow \quad Z = 2.19 \simeq 2$$

The approximately value of Z will be 2.

30. (*a*) From the first law of thermodynamics, if an amount of heat Q is given to a system, a part of it is used in increasing the internal energy ΔU of the system and the rest in doing work W by the system.

$$\therefore \quad Q = \Delta U + W$$

$$\Rightarrow \quad \Delta U = Q - W \Rightarrow \Delta U = 150 - 110$$
$$= 40\ \text{J}$$

31. (*d*) From figure,

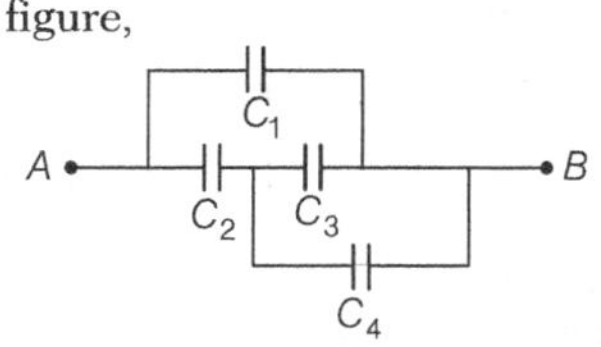

$C_1 = C_2 = C_3 = C_4 = 3\ \mu\text{F}$ (given)

$\because C_4$ and C_3 are in parallel, i.e.

$$C_{eq} = C_4 + C_3 = (3 + 3)\ \mu\text{F} = 6\mu\text{F}$$

Now arrangement of capacitors will be as follows

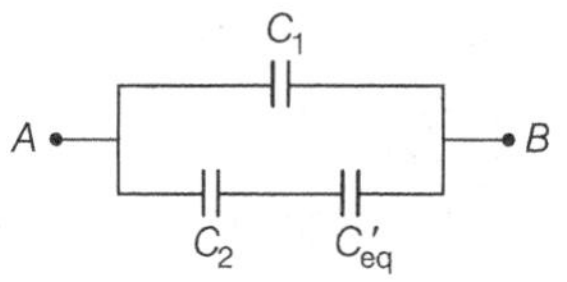

$\because C_1$ is in parallel with the series combination of C_2 and C'_{eq}.

$\therefore C''_{eq}$ between A and B

$$= \frac{(C_2 \times C'_{eq})}{C_2 + C'_{eq}} + C_1 \Rightarrow \left(\frac{3 \times 6}{3 + 6}\right) + 3 = 5\ \mu\text{F}$$

32. (*b*) We know that, $\dfrac{1}{\lambda} = R\left(\dfrac{1}{n_1^2} - \dfrac{1}{n_2^2}\right)$

$$\Rightarrow \quad \frac{1}{\lambda} = R\left(\frac{1}{1_1^2} - \frac{1}{2^2}\right) = \frac{3R}{4} \Rightarrow \lambda = \frac{4}{3R}\ \text{cm}$$

33. (*c*) Assume, Young's double slit experiment, amplitudes corresponding to the sources S_1 and S_2 be a_1 and a_2 and intensities be I_1 and I_2 respectively.

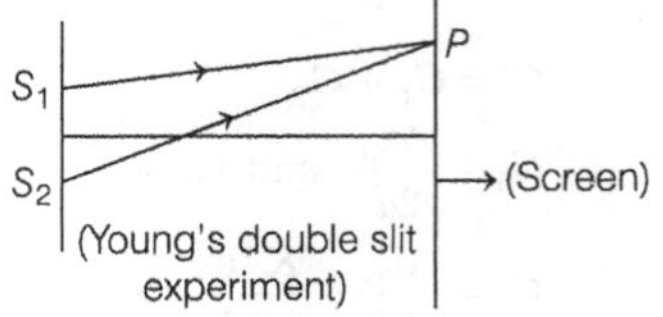

So, $I_{max} \propto a^2_{max}$ and $I_{min} \propto a^2_{min}$

$$\Rightarrow \quad \frac{I_{max}}{I_{min}} = \left(\frac{a_{max}}{a_{min}}\right)^2 = \left(\frac{a_1 + a_2}{a_1 - a_2}\right)^2$$

According to given question,

$$\frac{I_{max}}{I_{min}} = \frac{9}{1}$$

$$\Rightarrow \quad 9 = \left(\frac{a_1/a_2 + 1}{a_1/a_2 - 1}\right)^2$$

$$\Rightarrow \quad (3)^2 = \left(\frac{a_1/a_2 + 1}{a_1/a_2 - 1}\right)^2 \quad \text{(given)}$$

$$\Rightarrow \quad 3 = \frac{a_1/a_2 + 1}{a_1/a_2 - 1} \Rightarrow 3 = \frac{\left(\frac{a_1 + a_2}{a_2}\right)}{\left(\frac{a_1 - a_2}{a_2}\right)} \Rightarrow 3 = \frac{a_1 + a_2}{a_1 - a_2}$$

$$\Rightarrow \quad 3(a_1 - a_2) = a_1 + a_2 \Rightarrow 3a_1 - 3a_2 = a_1 + a_2$$

$$\Rightarrow \quad 2a_1 = 4a_2 \Rightarrow \frac{a_1}{a_2} = \frac{4}{2} \Rightarrow a_1 : a_2 = 2 : 1$$

34. (*b*) In case of an inductor, voltage leads the current by phase difference of $\dfrac{\pi}{2}$.

35. (*b*) Acceleration due to gravity at a height h from the earth's surface,

$$g' = \frac{GM}{(R + h)^2}$$

Given, $g' = 1\%$ of $g = \dfrac{g}{100}$

$$\Rightarrow \quad \frac{g}{100} = \frac{GM}{(R + h)^2}$$

$$\frac{(R + h)^2}{100} = \frac{GM}{g} \quad \text{or} \quad \frac{(R + h)^2}{100} = R^2 \quad \left(\because g = \frac{GM}{R^2}\right)$$

or $R + h = 10R$

$$h = 9R$$

where, R is the radius of the earth.

36. *(a)* We know that energy, $E = \frac{1}{2} CV^2$

Dimensions of CV^2 = Dimensions of energy, E

$$= [ML^2T^{-2}A^0]$$

37. *(c)* The output,

$Y = \overline{\overline{A} + \overline{B}} = \overline{\overline{A}} \cdot \overline{\overline{B}} = A \cdot B$

This is the boolean expression for AND gate.

38. *(b)* The energy of light of wavelength λ is given by

$$E = h\nu = \frac{hc}{\lambda}$$

$$\Rightarrow \quad \lambda = \frac{hc}{E} \quad \text{...(i)}$$

Here, h = Planck's constant $= 6.63 \times 10^{-34}$ J-s

c = speed of light $= 3 \times 10^8$ m/s

E = energy gap = 1.9 eV

$= 1.9 \times 1.6 \times 10^{-19}$ J

Substituting the given values in Eq. (i), we get

$$\Rightarrow \lambda = \frac{6.63 \times 10^{-34} \times 3 \times 10^8}{1.9 \times 1.6 \times 10^{-19}} = 6.54 \times 10^{-7} \text{ m}$$

$$\approx 654 \text{ nm}$$

Thus, the wavelength of light emitted from LED will be 654 nm.

39. *(b)* Let v be initial velocity of vertical projection and t be the time taken by the body to reach a height h from ground.

Here, $u = u, a = -g, s = h, t = t$

Using, $s = ut + \frac{1}{2} at^2$, we have

$$h = ut + \frac{1}{2}(-g)\, t^2$$

or $\quad gt^2 - 2ut + 2h = 0$

$$\therefore \quad t = \frac{2u \pm \sqrt{4u^2 - 4g \times 2h}}{2g} = \frac{u \pm \sqrt{u^2 - 2gh}}{g}$$

It means t has two values, i.e.

$$t_1 = \frac{u + \sqrt{u^2 - 2gh}}{g} \Rightarrow t_2 = \frac{u - \sqrt{u^2 - 2gh}}{g}$$

$$t_1 + t_2 = \frac{2u}{g} \text{ or } u = \frac{g(t_1 + t_2)}{2}$$

40 *(b)* We know that,

$$eV_0 = h\nu - \phi_0$$

where, V_0 = stopping potential

and ν = frequency of light.

Case I $eV_0 = h\nu - \phi_0 \quad \text{...(i)}$

Case II $\frac{eV_0}{4} = \frac{h\nu}{2} - \phi_0$

$$\Rightarrow \quad eV_0 = 2h\nu - 4\phi_0 \quad \text{...(ii)}$$

From Eqs. (i) and (ii), we get

$$h\nu - \phi_0 = 2h\nu - 4\phi_0$$

$$\Rightarrow \quad h\nu = 3\phi_0 \Rightarrow h\nu = 3h\nu_0 \quad (\because \phi_0 = h\nu_0)$$

$$\Rightarrow \quad \nu_0 = \frac{h\nu}{3h} \Rightarrow \nu_0 = \frac{\nu}{3}$$

41. *(b)* When object is in rarer medium and observer is in denser medium, then normal shift,

$$d = (n-1)h$$

where, h = real depth = y

Now, apparent depth or the apparent height of the bird from the surface of the water $= y + (n-1)y = ny$. The total distance of the bird as estimated by fish is $x + ny$.

42. *(b)* Speed of car, $v = 180 \text{ kmh}^{-1} = 50 \text{ ms}^{-1}$ and time, $t = 10$ s

$\therefore$ Acceleration of the car,

$$a = \frac{v-u}{t} = \frac{50-0}{10} = 5 \text{ ms}^{-2}$$

Thus, the distance covered by the car,

$$s = \frac{1}{2}at^2 = \frac{1}{2} \times 5 \times (10)^2 = 250 \text{ m}$$

43. *(a)* Magnetic field,

$$B = \frac{E}{c}, \text{ where } c = 3 \times 10^8 \text{ m/s.}$$

$$B = \frac{6}{3 \times 10^8} = 2 \times 10^{-8} \text{ T}$$

44. *(a)* Area of a parallelogram $= |\mathbf{a} \times \mathbf{b}|$

where, **a** and **b** are sides of parallelogram.

Given, $\mathbf{a} = \mathbf{p} = 5\hat{\mathbf{i}} - 4\hat{\mathbf{j}} + 3\hat{\mathbf{k}}$

and $\mathbf{b} = \mathbf{q} = 3\hat{\mathbf{i}} + 2\hat{\mathbf{j}} - \hat{\mathbf{k}}$

$$\therefore \quad \mathbf{a} \times \mathbf{b} = \begin{vmatrix} \hat{\mathbf{i}} & \hat{\mathbf{j}} & \hat{\mathbf{k}} \\ 5 & -4 & 3 \\ 3 & 2 & -1 \end{vmatrix}$$

$$\Rightarrow \quad \mathbf{a} \times \mathbf{b} = \hat{\mathbf{i}}(4-6) - \hat{\mathbf{j}}(-5-9) + \hat{\mathbf{k}}(10+12)$$

$$\Rightarrow \quad \mathbf{a} \times \mathbf{b} = -2\hat{\mathbf{i}} + 14\hat{\mathbf{j}} + 22\hat{\mathbf{k}}$$

Thus, $|\mathbf{a} \times \mathbf{b}| = \sqrt{(2)^2 + (14)^2 + (22)^2} = \sqrt{684}$ sq units

45. *(a)* Let the B_H and B_V be the horizontal and vertical component of the earth's magnetic field B.

$$\tan\theta = \frac{B_V}{B_H} \Rightarrow \cot\theta = \frac{B_H}{B_V} \quad \text{...(i)}$$

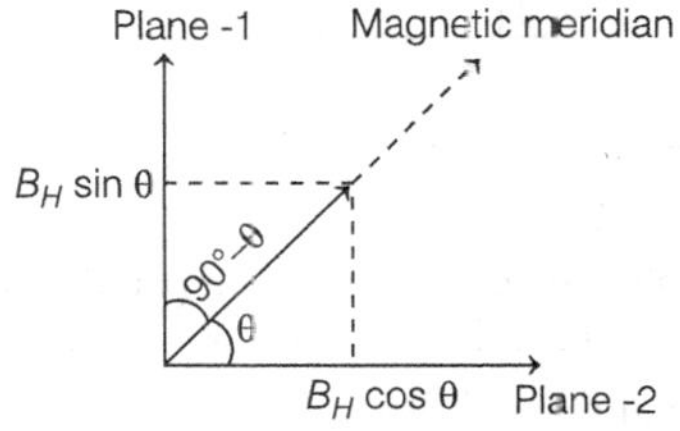

Let plane-1 and 2 be mutually perpendicular planes making angle θ and $(90^\circ - \theta)$ with magnetic meridian. The vertical component of the earth's magnetic field remain same in two plane but effective horizontal components in the two planes is given by

$$B_1 = B_H \cos\theta \quad \text{...(ii)}$$

and $$B_2 = B_H \sin\theta \quad \text{...(iii)}$$

Then, $\tan\theta_1 = \dfrac{B_V}{B_1} = \dfrac{B_V}{B_H \cos\theta}$

$$\cot\theta_1 = \frac{B_H \cos\theta}{B_V} \quad \text{...(iv)}$$

Similarly, $\Rightarrow \tan\theta_2 = \dfrac{B_V}{B_2} = \dfrac{B_V}{B_H \sin\theta}$

$$\Rightarrow \cot\theta_2 = \frac{B_H \sin\theta}{B_V} \quad \text{...(v)}$$

From Eqs. (iv) and (v), we get

$$\Rightarrow \cot^2\theta_1 + \cot^2\theta_2 = \frac{B_H^2 \cos^2\theta}{B_V^2} + \frac{B_H^2 \sin^2\theta}{B_V^2}$$

$$\Rightarrow \cot^2\theta_1 + \cot^2\theta_2 = \frac{B_H^2}{B_V^2}(\cos^2\theta + \sin^2\theta)$$

$$\Rightarrow \cot^2\theta_1 + \cot^2\theta_2 = \cot^2\theta$$

46. *(c)* Here, $K_1 = \dfrac{hc}{\lambda_1} - W$ ...(i)

and $K_2 = \dfrac{hc}{\lambda_2} - W$ ...(ii)

Substituting $\lambda_1 = 2\lambda_2$ in Eq. (i), we get

$$K_1 = \frac{hc}{2\lambda_2} - W$$

$$\Rightarrow K_1 = \frac{1}{2}\left(\frac{hc}{\lambda_2}\right) - W = \frac{1}{2}(K_2 + W) - W$$

$$K_1 = \frac{K_2}{2} - \frac{W}{2}$$

$$\Rightarrow K_1 < \frac{K_2}{2}$$

47. *(b)* The time taken to hit the ground is given by

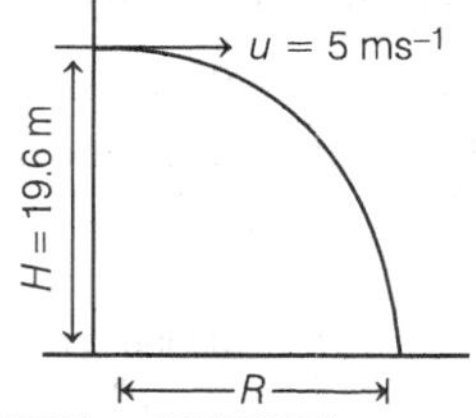

$$T = \sqrt{\frac{2H}{g}} = \sqrt{\frac{2 \times 19.6}{9.8}} = 2\,\text{s}$$

48. *(b)* Let total current through the parallel combination be I, the current through the galvanometer be I_g and the current through the shunt be $I - I_g$.

The shunted galvanometer is shown in the figure.

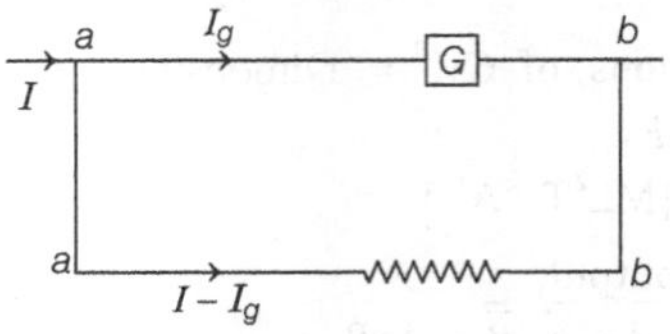

The potential difference, $V_{ab} = (V_a - V_b)$ is the same for both paths, so $I_g G = (I - I_g)S$

$$\Rightarrow I_g(G + S) = IS \Rightarrow \frac{I_g}{I} = \frac{S}{S + G}$$

The fraction of current passing through shunt

$$= \frac{I - I_g}{I} = 1 - \frac{I_g}{I} = 1 - \frac{S}{S+G} = \frac{G}{S+G}$$

$$= \frac{8}{2+8} = \frac{8}{10} = 0.8\ \text{A}$$

49. *(c)* The centre of mass of the system is given by

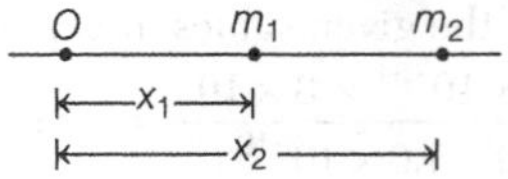

$$x = \frac{m_1 x_1 + m_2 x_2}{m_1 + m_2}$$

50. *(d)* Applying Archimedes' principle, submerged part = replaced water

$$\Rightarrow \frac{4}{5} h \rho_w g = h \times \rho_l \times g$$

where, ρ_w = density of water

and ρ_l = density of the liquid.

$$\therefore \rho_l = \frac{4}{5} \times \rho_w = \frac{4}{5} \times 1000$$

$$\Rightarrow \rho_l = 800\ \text{kgm}^{-3}$$

51. *(a)* When the balloon is descending down with an acceleration a,

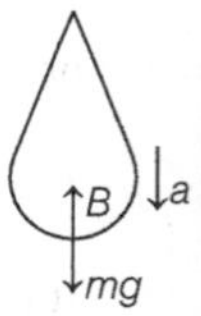

$$mg - B = ma \quad \text{...(i)}$$

where, B = buoyant force.

Here, we should assume that while removing some mass the volume of balloon and hence buoyant force will not change.

Let the new mass of the balloon is m',

so

$$B - m'g = m'a \quad \text{...(ii)}$$

On solving Eqs. (i) and (ii), we get

$$mg - m'g = ma + m'a$$

$$\Rightarrow m(g - a) = m'(g + a) \Rightarrow m' = \frac{m(g-a)}{g+a}$$

So, mass removed, $\Delta m = m - m'$

$$= m\left[1 - \frac{(g-a)}{(g+a)}\right] = m\left[\frac{g + a - g + a}{g + a}\right] = \frac{2ma}{g+a}$$

52. *(d)* Given, $i = 10$ A, $B = 0.15$ T,

$\theta = 45^\circ$ and $l = 2$ m

Here, $F = ilB\sin\theta = 10 \times 2 \times 0.15 \sin 45^\circ = \frac{3}{\sqrt{2}}$ N

53. *(c)* For first slab,

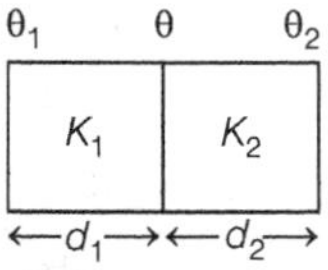

Heat current, $H_1 = \frac{K_1(\theta_1 - \theta)A}{d_1}$

For second slab,

Heat current, $H_2 = \frac{K_2(\theta - \theta_2)A}{d_2}$

As slabs are in series, $H_1 = H_2$

$$\therefore \quad \frac{K_1(\theta_1 - \theta)A}{d_1} = \frac{K_2(\theta - \theta_2)A}{d_2}$$

$$\Rightarrow \quad \theta = \frac{K_1\theta_1 d_2 + K_2\theta_2 d_1}{K_2 d_1 + K_1 d_2}$$

54. *(b)* $B = 4\left[\frac{\mu_0}{4\pi}\cdot\frac{I}{a}(\sin\phi_1 + \sin\phi_2)\right]$

Here, $a = \frac{l}{2}$ and $\phi_1 = \phi_2 = 45^\circ$

$$B = 4 \times \frac{\mu_0}{4\pi}\frac{I}{(l/2)}\left[\frac{1}{\sqrt{2}} + \frac{1}{\sqrt{2}}\right]$$

$$\therefore \quad B = \frac{16}{\sqrt{2}}\left[\frac{\mu_0}{4\pi}\frac{I}{l}\right] = 8\sqrt{2}\left(\frac{\mu_0}{4\pi}\cdot\frac{I}{l}\right)$$

55. *(d)* Both the cylinders are in parallel, for the heat flow from one end as shown

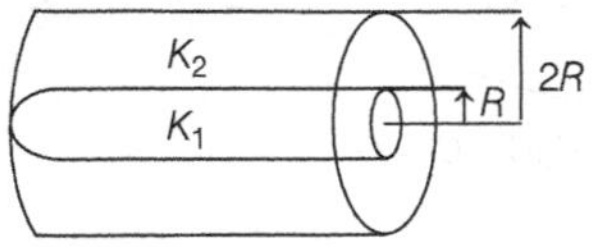

So, $K_{eq} = \frac{K_1A_1 + K_2A_2}{A_1 + A_2}$

where, A_1 = area of cross-section of inner cylinder $= \pi R^2$

and A_2 = area of cross-section of cylindrical shell $= \pi\{(2R)^2 - (R)^2\} = 3\pi R^2$

$$\Rightarrow \quad K_{eq} = \frac{K_1(\pi R^2) + K_2(3\pi R^2)}{\pi R^2 + 3\pi R^2} = \frac{1}{4}(K_1 + 3K_2)$$

56. *(c)* Due to the specific shape of wings, when the aeroplane runs, air passes at higher speed over it as compared to its lower surface. This difference of air speeds above and below the wings, in accordance with Bernoulli's principle, creates a pressure difference, due to which an upward force called 'dynamic lift' acts on the plate.

$\therefore$ Upward lift = pressure difference × area of the wings $[\because F = p \times A]$

From Bernoulli's equation,

$$p_1 + \frac{1}{2}\rho v_1^2 = p_2 + \frac{1}{2}\rho v_2^2$$

$$\because \quad p_2 - p_1 = \frac{1}{2}\rho(v_1^2 - v_2^2)$$

Hence, upward lift $= \frac{1}{2}\rho A(v_1^2 - v_2^2)$

57. *(c)* Here are two batteries with emf E each and the internal resistances r_1 and r_2, respectively.

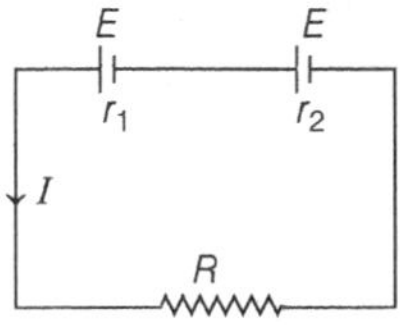

We have $I(R + r_1 + r_2) = 2E$

Current in the circuit, $I = \frac{2E}{R + r_1 + r_2}$ ...(i)

Now, the potential difference across the first cell would be equal to $V = E - Ir_1$. From the question, $V = 0$, there

$$E = Ir_1 = \frac{2Er_1}{R + r_1 + r_2} \quad \text{[From Eq. (i)]}$$

where, $R + r_1 + r_2 = 2r_1$

Hence, $R = r_1 - r_2$.

58. *(a)* Given,

$\nu_1 = 200$ Hz, $\nu_2 = 300$ Hz,

$l_1 = l$ and $l_2 = 2l$

$$\nu = \frac{1}{2l}\sqrt{\frac{T}{m}} \Rightarrow \nu \propto \frac{\sqrt{T}}{l} \Rightarrow \sqrt{T} \propto v \cdot l$$

$$\Rightarrow \quad \frac{T_2}{T_1} = \left[\frac{\nu_2}{\nu_1}\right]^2\left[\frac{l_2}{l_1}\right]^2 = \left[\frac{300}{200}\right]^2\left[\frac{2l}{l}\right]^2 = \frac{9}{1}$$

59. *(b)* Charge, $q = ne$

$$\Rightarrow \quad q = 10^{19} \times 1.6 \times 10^{-19} = 1.6 \text{ C}$$

60. *(c)* Here, phase difference

$$\tan\phi = \frac{X_L - X_C}{R} \Rightarrow \tan\frac{\pi}{3} = \frac{X_L - X_C}{R}$$

When L is removed, $\tan\frac{\pi}{3} = \frac{X_C}{R} = \sqrt{3}$

$\therefore \quad X_C = \sqrt{3}R$ ...(i)

Similarly, when C is removed

$$\tan\frac{\pi}{3} = \frac{X_L}{R} = \sqrt{3}$$

$\Rightarrow \quad X_L = \sqrt{3}R$

$\Rightarrow \quad X_C = X_L$ ...(ii) [from Eq. (i)]

Now, $\tan\phi = 0$

$\Rightarrow \quad \phi = 0^\circ$

$\therefore$ Power factor, $\cos\phi = \cos 0^\circ = 1$

Chemistry

61. *(b)* D-glucose, D-fructose and D-mannose form the same osazone treated with excess phenyl hydrazine because they differ only Ist and 2nd carbon atoms which are transformed to the same form.

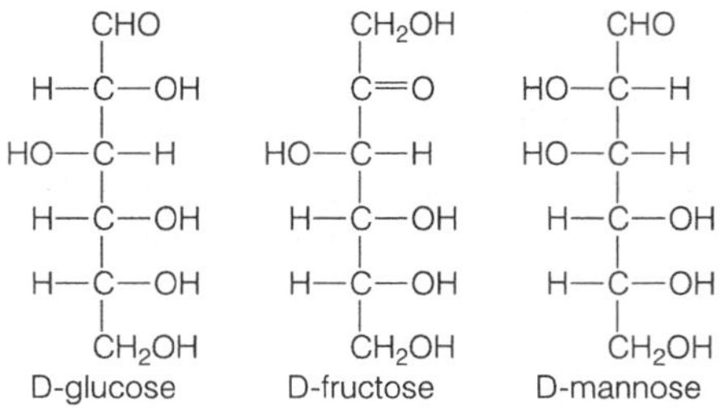

They form same osazone

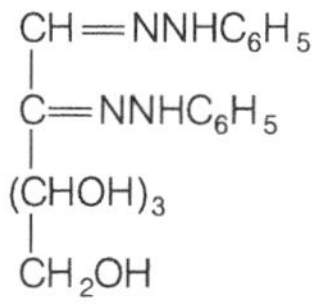

62. *(b)* Addition of OH at most substituted side of the ene and final product is formed by loss of H_2O resulting in the formation of ring.

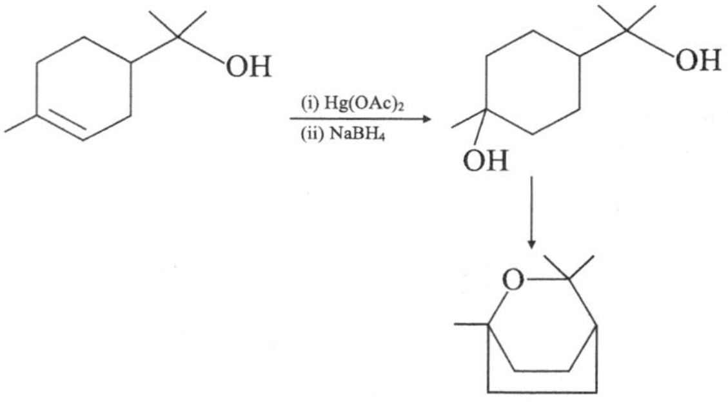

63. *(c)* Nylon 6, 6 is an example of step growth polymerisation. As monomers adipic acid and hexamethylenediamine are bifunctional and form bond with the loss of simple molecules. The dimer formed also contains two functional groups, thus undergoes a series of condensation reaction in a stepwise manner.

64. *(a)* Aldehydes or ketones with α-H atom, in presence of dilute base, undergoes aldol condensation to give β-hydroxy aldehyde or ketone. On heating, aldol eliminate water molecule to form α,β-unsaturated compounds.

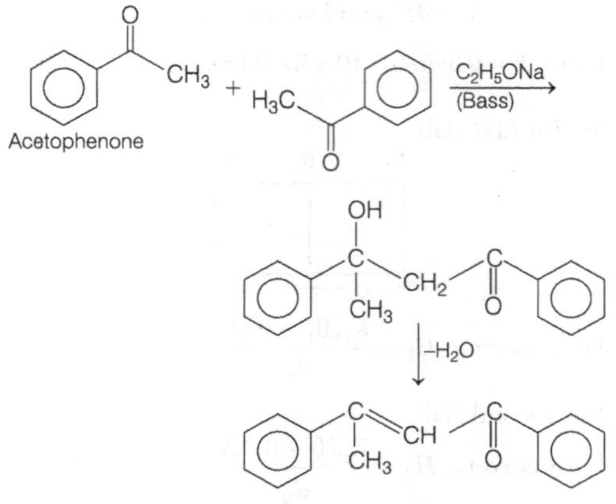

65. *(a)* Gabriel,s synthesis is used for the preparation of 1° amines.

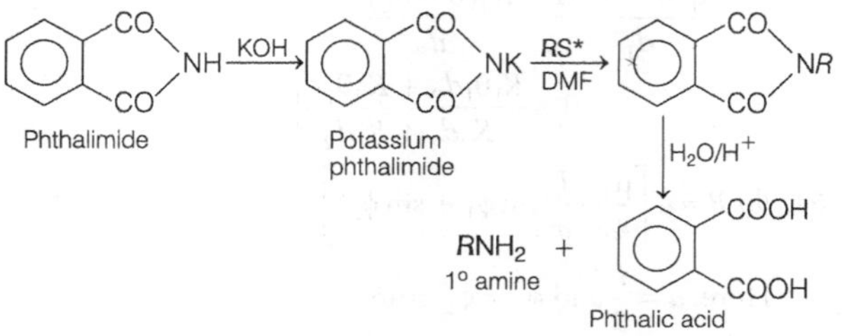

66. *(d)*

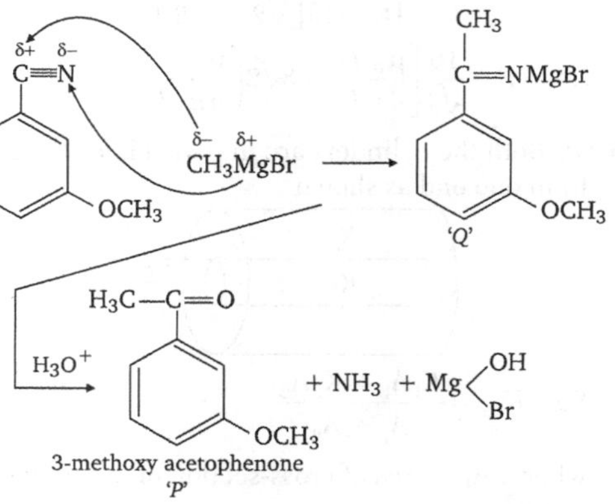

67. *(d)* α-D-glucose and β-glucose, differ in the orientation of —H and —OH groups are first carbon atom. Such isomers are called anomers.

Starch is a mixture of amylase and amylopectin but amylase is a straight chain polymer while amylopectin is a branched chain polymer of α-D-glucose.

68. *(c)* Analgesic drugs are used in relieving pain while antipyretic drugs are used to control fever. Paracetamol is widely used as an antipyretics as well as analgesics.

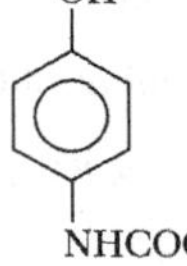

Paracetamol

69. *(b)* Ozone depletion is caused by a number of pollutants like chlorofluoro carbons (CF_2Cl_2) nitrogen oxides, CCl_4 etc.

70. *(b)* Primary alcohols are easily oxidised to aldehydes and then to acid, both containing the same number of carbon atoms, while secondary alcohols are easily oxidised to ketones with same number of carbon atoms, but ketone oxidised to carboxylic acid containing lesser number of carbon atoms than original alcohol.

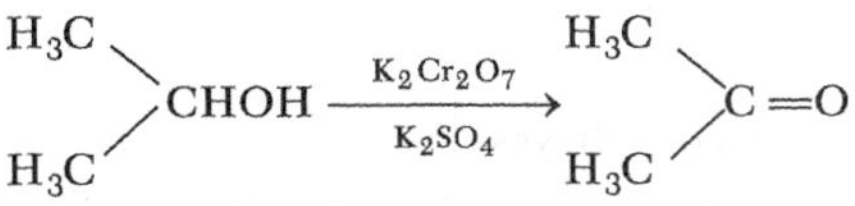

Isopropyl alcohol　　　　Acetone

$$\xrightarrow{[O]} \underset{\text{Acetic acid}}{CH_3COOH} + CO_2 + H_2O$$

Thus all alcohols on oxidation finally give acids but acids obtained from 2° and 3° alcohols contain less C-atom.

71. *(c)* As, EDG on benzene increase the basicity and EWG decrease thus when (EWG) is directly attached to benzene nucleus it is, least basic strength.

(1) aromatic amine

(2) aliphatic —CH_2NH_2, thus maximum basic strength

(3) aromatic but —NO_2 group is (EWG) decreasing electron density at N-atom

(4) $-\overset{\overset{\large O}{\|}}{C}$ directly attached hence, least basic strength

$4 < 3 < 1 < 2$

72. *(a)* In general, C_2H_2 and all 1-alkynes given white precipitate with ammoniacal silver nitrate.

Thus, in this question, propyne-1 ($CH_3C \equiv CH$) will give white precipitate with ammoniacal silver nitrate.

$$\underset{\text{Propyne-1}}{CH_3C \equiv CH} + NH_4OH + AgNO_3 \longrightarrow \underset{\text{White ppt.}}{CH_3C \equiv CAg} + NH_4NO_3 + H_2O$$

73. *(a)* Due to the presence of vacant lattice sites in Schottky defect, there is decrease in density of crystal.

74. *(a)* For, $2NO(g) \rightleftharpoons N_2 + O_2$

$$K_{C_1} = \frac{[N_2][O_2]}{[NO]^2} = 2.4 \times 10^{20}$$

For, $NO(g) + \frac{1}{2}Br_2(g) \rightleftharpoons NOBr(g)$

$$K_{C_2} = \frac{[NOBr]}{[NO][Br_2]^{1/2}} = 1.4$$

and $$K_C = \frac{[NOBr]}{[N_2]^{1/2}[O_2]^{1/2}[Br_2]^{1/2}}$$

or $$K_C = \sqrt{\frac{1}{K_{C_1}}} \times K_{C_2} = \sqrt{\frac{1}{2.4 \times 10^{20}}} \times 1.4$$

$$K_C = 8.96 \times 10^{-11}$$

75. *(a)* Most of the gases obey Henry's law when gases do not react with solvent chemically.

76. *(a)* Tertiary halide perferentially undergo S_N1 substitution as they can give stable carbocation.

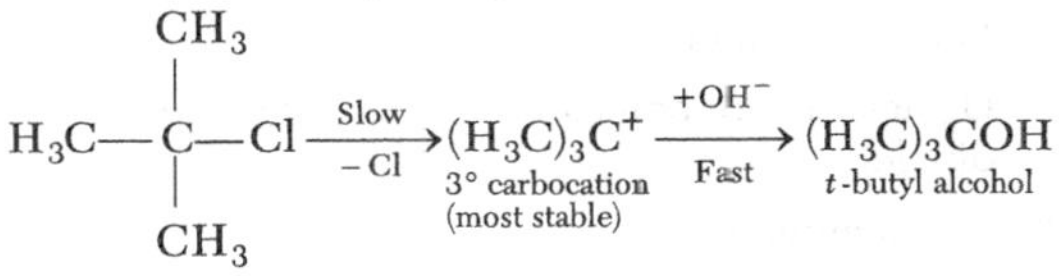

77. *(b)* Adsorption is a surface phenomena that involves equillibrium between two opposing processes adsorption and desorption.

Gas + Solid $\rightleftharpoons$ Gas adsorbed on solid + Heat

As adsorption is exothermic thus according to Le-Chatelier's principle it will decrease with increase in temperature.

78. *(a)* $He_2^+ : \sigma 1s^2, \sigma 1s^1$

$$BO = \frac{1}{2}(N_b - N_a) = \frac{1}{2}(2-1) = \frac{1}{2} = 0.5$$

$C_2^{2-} : \sigma 1s^2, \sigma^* 1s^2, \sigma 2s^2, \sigma^* 2s^2, (\pi 2p_x^2 \approx \pi 2p_y^2), \sigma 2p_z^2$

$$BO = \frac{1}{2}(10-4) = \frac{6}{2} = 3.0$$

$O_2^+ = \sigma 1s^2, \sigma^* 1s^2, \sigma 2s^2, \sigma^* 2s^2 \sigma 2p_z^2 (\pi 2p_x^2 \approx \pi 2p_y^2), \pi^* 2p_x^1$

$$BO = \frac{1}{2}(10-5) = \frac{5}{2} = 2.5$$

$O_2^- = \sigma 1s^2, \sigma^* 1s^2, \sigma 2s^2, \sigma^* 2s^2, \sigma 2p_z^2 (\pi 2p_x^2 \approx \pi 2p_y^2), (\pi^* 2p_x^2 \approx \pi^* 2p_y^1)$

$$BO = \frac{1}{2}(10-7) = \frac{3}{2} = 1.5$$

Thus, the correct order of decreasing bond order is

$C_2^{2-} > O_2^+ > O_2^- > He_2^+$

COMEDK 2023

79. *(b)* Given, $\alpha = 6.9\%$

$\therefore$ Degree of dissociation, $\alpha = \frac{6.9}{100}$

$\therefore \quad \alpha = 0.069$

According to ostwald's dilution law,

$$K_a = \alpha^2 C = (0.069)^2 \times 0.2$$

$$K_a = 9.5 \times 10^{-4}$$

80. *(a)* Option (a) is the correct option.

In ammonia,

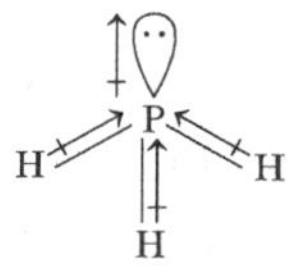

As, nitrogen is more electronegative than hydrogen, the resultant dipole moment adds up in the same direction.

Dipole moment is a vector quantity.

O_2 and H_2 are homoatomic molecules thus, show no dipole.

81. *(b)* In ethene,

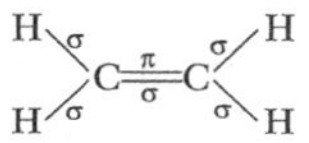

5 σ-bond and 1 π-bond.

82. *(a)* $pOH = pK_b + \log\frac{[\text{Salt}]}{[\text{Base}]}$

$$= 5 + \log\frac{0.01}{0.01} = 5 + \log\frac{1}{10} = 5 + (-1) = 4$$

$$pH = 14 - pOH = 14 - 4 = 10$$

83. *(a)*

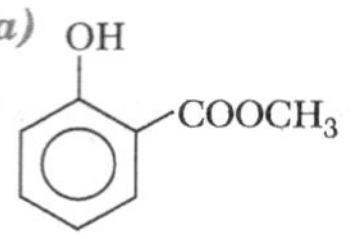

Methyl salicylate is known as oil of winter green. It is the methyl ester of salicyclic acid.

It is colourless, viscous liquid with a sweet, fruity odour.

84. *(a)* $[H^+] = 10^{-4}$ M

No. of moles of NaOH in100 mL solution

$$= \frac{MV}{1000} = \frac{10^{-4} \times 100}{1000} = 10^{-5}$$

Mass of NaOH in solution $= 10^{-5} \times 40 = 4 \times 10^{-4}$ g

By Faraday's law,

$$W = \frac{ItE}{96500}$$

or $4 \times 10^{-4} = \frac{0.5 \times t \times 40}{96500}$

$$t = \frac{4 \times 10^{-4} \times 96500}{0.5 \times 40} = 1.93 \text{ s}$$

85. *(a)* In one unit cell, number of $O^{2-} = 4$

The number of $Zn^{2+} = \frac{1}{8} \times 8 = 1$

The number of $Fe^{3+} = \frac{1}{2} \times 4 = 2$

$\therefore$ Molecular formula of given spinel structure is $ZnFe_2O_4$.

86. *(c)* *Gem* dicarboxylic acid like 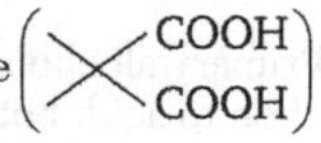 or an acid having a keto group at β-position is decarboxylated on heating.

(a) 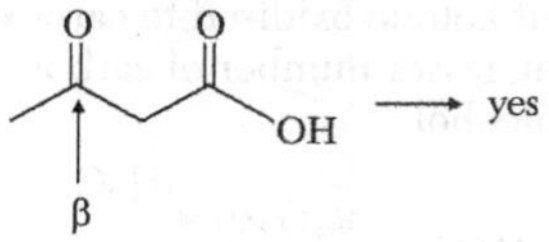

(b) yes (c) no (d) yes

87. *(d)*

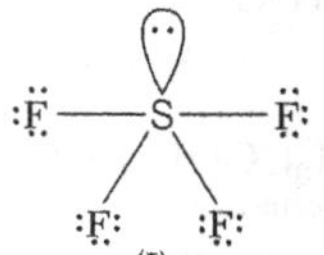

(I)

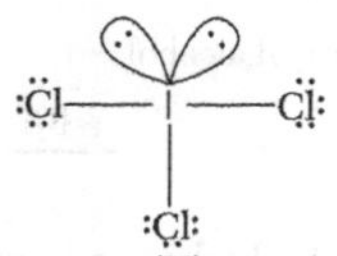

(II)

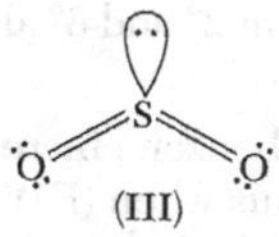

(III)

(I), (II) and (III) all of them have non-bonding electron (lone pair) on the central atom.

88. *(a)* For this given reaction, $n = 2$. At 25°C,

$$\therefore \quad K = \text{antilog}\left[\frac{nE^\circ}{0.059}\right] = \text{antilog}\left[\frac{2 \times (-0.295)}{0.059}\right]$$

$$K = 1 \times 10^{10}$$

89. *(b)* Negative deviation from Raoult's law are noticed when solvent-solvent and solute-solute interactions are weaker than solute-solvent intractions. In such solutions, the mixing of two components leads to the strengthening of intermolecular attractions and thus results in lesser values of vapour pressure of solution. $\therefore$ Benzene-chloroform mixtures shows negative deviation.

90. *(c)* The elevation in boiling point is,

$$\Delta T_b = \frac{1000 k_b \times w_2}{M_2 \times w_1(\text{in}(g))} \Rightarrow M_2 = \frac{1000 \times k_b \times 5}{0.25 \times 100}$$

$$\Rightarrow M_2 = 20 \text{ g}$$

91. *(a)* Electron gain enthalpy becomes less negative as we move down in a group white it becomes more negative along the period.

$\therefore$Correct order is

F > O > C > Al > Ca

92. *(b)* I and II are staggered and eclipsed conformers.

93. *(a)* Ti(22) = [Ar] $4s^2$ $3d^2$ 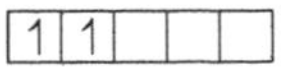

$Ti^{2+} = [Ar]\,3d^2$

$Ti^{4+} = [Ar]\,3d^0$

Ti^{2+} has two unpaired electrons in $3d$ orbital and hence d-d transition is possible due to absorption of light in visible region whereas Ti^{4+} is diamagnetic hence colourless.

94. *(b)* Phosphorus acid (H_3PO_3) is a diprotic acid. If forms two series of salts such as NaH_2PO_3 and Na_2HPO_3 but none of the type $NaPO_3$ with NaOH. Its structure is as

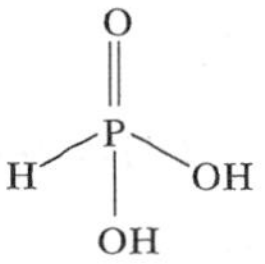

95. *(c)* The reaction is reprerseded as

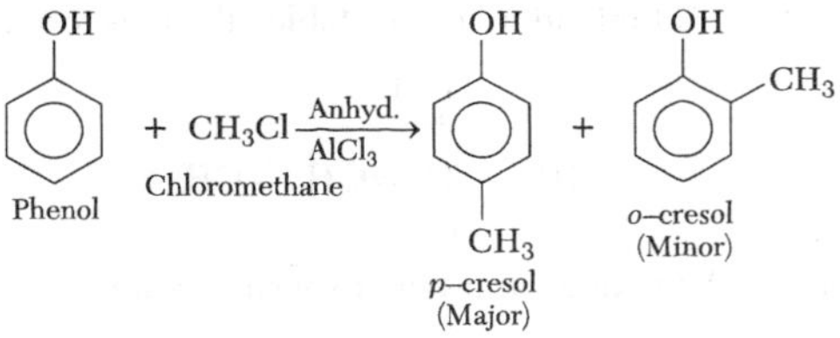

96. *(a)* In $[Ni(CN)_4]^{2-}$ CN^- is strong field ligand and causes pairing of electrons.

$\therefore Ni^{2+} = 3d^8$

$[Ni(CN)_4]^{2-}$

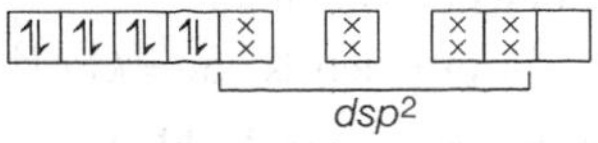

As, all the electrons are paired, hence, it is diamagnetic.

97. *(a)* For fcc lattice,

$$a\sqrt{2} = 4r$$

$$\therefore r = \frac{\sqrt{2}}{4}a \Rightarrow r = \frac{1.414 \times 361}{4} \Rightarrow r = 127.6 \text{ pm}$$

98. *(b)* Magnesium is an important structural component of chlorophyll molecules. It is present in the tetraphyrrole ring of chlorophyll in its centre.

99. *(b)* Boron trihalides are Lewis acids. The back bonding determines its acidic strength, more is the π-back bonding, less is the acidity. Thus, due to better overlapping of orbitals it promotes better π-back bonding, hence BF_3 is least acidic in nature. Thus, order of acidic strength is $BF_3 < BCl_3 < BBr_3 < BI_3$.

100. *(c)* Nickel on heating in a steam of carbon monoxide forms a volatile complex nickel tetracarbonyl.

$$Ni + 4CO \xrightarrow{330\text{-}350\text{ K}} [Ni(CO)_4].$$

101. *(d)* $[PtCl_2(en)_2]^{2+}$ shows both geometrical and optical isomerism as the complex forms *cis* and *trans* isomers. *trans*-isomer doesn t show optical isomerism since it is symmetrical but *cis*-isomer shows optical isomerism as it is unsymmetrical.

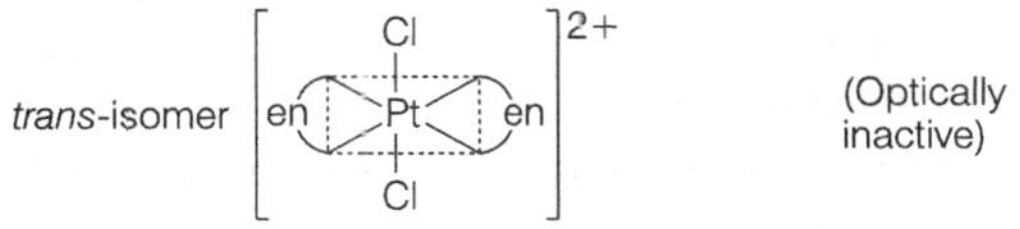

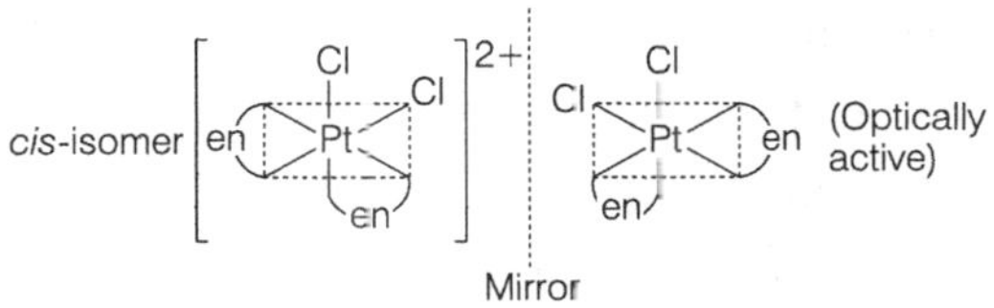

(Non-superimposable mirror image)

102. *(b)* The balanced equation the reaction is

$$\underset{100\text{ g}}{CaCO_3} + \underset{73\text{ g}}{2HCl} \longrightarrow CaCl_2 + H_2O + CO_2$$

100g of $CaCO_3$ completely reacts with 73g of HCl

So, 15 g of $CaCO_3$ will react with $= \frac{73}{100} \times 15$ g of HCl

$= 10.95$ g of HCl.

103. *(b)* Real gases obey the gas laws and approaches ideal behaviour at low pressure and high temperature.

104. *(d)* Bohr radius for nth orbit $= 0.53\,\text{Å} \times \frac{n^2}{Z}$

where, Z = atomic number

$\therefore$Bohr radius of 2nd orbit of

$$Be^{3+} = \frac{0.53 \times (2)^3}{4} = 0.53\,\text{Å}$$

For option (d) Bohr radius of 1st orbit of

$$H = \frac{0.53 \times (1)^3}{1} = 0.53\,\text{Å}$$

Hence, Bohr's radius of 2nd orbit of Be^{3+} is equal to that of first orbit of hydrogen.

105. *(d)* We known,

$$2.303 \log \frac{k_2}{k_1} = \frac{E_a}{R}\left[\frac{T_2 - T_1}{T_1 T_2}\right]$$

$$\therefore 2.303 \log \frac{k_2}{k_1} = \frac{65 \times 10^3}{8.314}\left[\frac{25}{298 \times 273}\right]$$

$$\frac{k_2}{k} = 11.5.$$

$\therefore$ The reaction would proceed 11 times faster.

106. *(a)* The blue colouration is due to the formation of $Fe_4[Fe(CN)_6]_3$ (ferriferrocyanide).

$$Fe(OH)_2 + 6NaCN \longrightarrow \underset{\text{Sodium ferrocyanide}}{Na_4[Fe(CN)_6]} + 2NaOH$$

$$3Na_4[Fe(CN)_6] + 2Fe_2(SO_4)_3 \longrightarrow \underset{\substack{\text{Ferric ferrocyanide}\\ \text{(Prussian blue)}}}{Fe_4[Fe(CN)_6]_3} + 6Na_2SO_4$$

107. *(b)* CN^- is isoelectronic to CO as they have same number of electrons.

Number of electrons in the given species is as follows,

$CO = 6 + 8 = 14$

$O_2^- = 16 + 1 = 17$

$N_2^+ = 14 - 1 = 13$

$O_2^+ = 16 - 1 = 15$

$CN^- = 6 + 7 + 1 = 14$

108. *(d)* We know that

$$\frac{(t_{1/2})_1}{(t_{1/2})_2} = \left(\frac{p_2}{p_1}\right)^{n-1}$$

where, n is the order of reaction and $t_{1/2}$ is half-life.

$$\frac{350}{175} = \left(\frac{20}{40}\right)^{n-1}$$

or $$2 = \left(\frac{1}{2}\right)^{n-1}$$

$\Rightarrow$ $$n - 1 = -1$$

$$n = 0$$

$\therefore$ It is a zero order reaction.

109. *(b)* $2C_2H_6(g) + 7O_2(g) \longrightarrow 4CO_2(g) + 6H_2O(l)$; $\Delta H = -4100$ kJ

Let, $\Delta H_f^\circ (C_2H_6) = x$,

$$\Delta H = \Sigma H_f^\circ{}_{(\text{products})} - \Sigma H_f^\circ{}_{(\text{reactants})}$$

$$-4100 = [4(-410) + 6(-285)] - [2x + 0]$$

$$x = -375 \text{ kJ}$$

110. *(c)* As the colligative properties depend only upon the number of particles of solute, so if the non-volatile solute dissociates or associates in the solution, the value of colligative properties deviates i.e., abnormal colligative properties are obtained.

111. *(c)* As, H_2O is a weak field ligand and thus $[Cu(H_2O)_4]^{2+}$ absorbs red light in visible spectrum. But the colour appears blue because $[Cu(H_2O)_4]^{2+}$ is a labile complex and changes to $[Cu(NH_3)_4]^{2+}$, where NH_3 is strong field ligand thus absorbs yellow light of visible spectrum and impart blue colour.

112. *(a)* For S_N1 reaction, the stable carbocation formation leads to stable product thus, there is 1, 2-methyl shift.

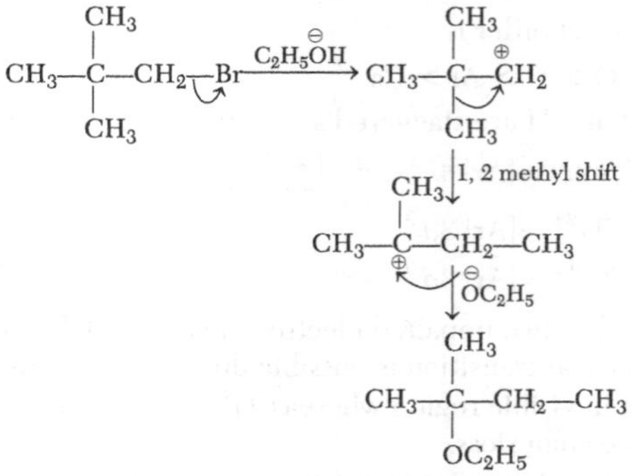

(B)

- For S_N2 reaction, direct attack occurs, thus no rearrangement occurs in the reaction.

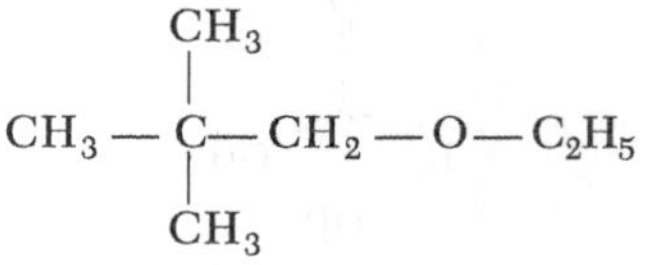

(A)

- For elimination, more stable alkene is formed.

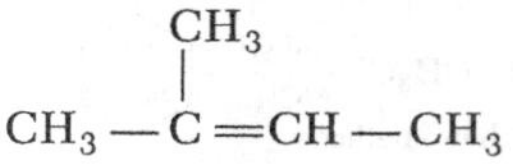

(C)

113. *(a)* H_2O_2 decompose on exposure to light

$$2H_2O_2 \longrightarrow 2H_2O + O_2$$

Thus, its decomposition can be prevented by adding urea as a stabiliser.

$$CO(NH_2)_2 + H_2O_2 \longrightarrow \underset{\text{Urea peroxide}}{CO(NH_2)_2 \cdot H_2O_2}$$

114. *(b)* The rate of reaction for

$2A + B \longrightarrow$ products is rate $= k[A]^2[B]$

If concentration of A is doubled,

Rate$' = [2A]^2[B] = 4k[A]^2[B]$

Rate$' = 4$ Rate.

115. *(a)* There is no heat exchange between the system and the surrounding for adiabatic change.

$\therefore$ $$q = 0$$

116. *(b)* In strong base,

$$4MnO_4^- + 4OH^- \longrightarrow 4MnO_4^{2-} + O_2 + 2H_2O$$

117. *(a)* Octahedral complex having general formula $[M(AA)_2a_2]^{n\pm}$ or $[M(AA)_2ab]^{n\pm}$, shows optical isomersim.

cis-$[Co(NH_3)_4Cl_2]^+$ does not show optical isomerism due to symmetry, while other three complexes show optical isomerism.

118. *(a)*

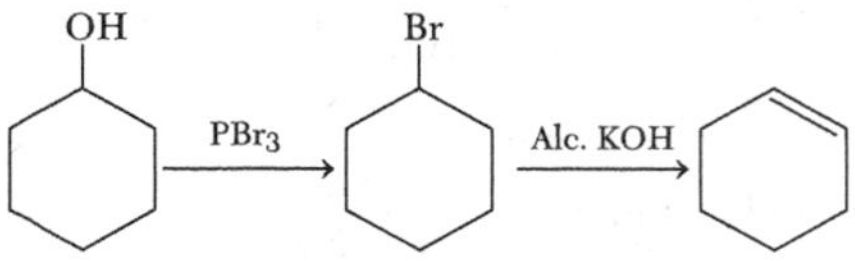

119. *(a)* The expression for root mean square velocity is

$$(\mu_{rms}) = \sqrt{\frac{3RT}{M}},$$

and for average speed, $(\mu_{avg}) = \sqrt{\frac{8RT}{\pi M}}$

For a particular gas, at particular temperature M and T are constant.

$$\therefore \quad \frac{\mu_{avg}}{\mu_{rms}} = \sqrt{\frac{8RT}{\pi M}} : \sqrt{\frac{3RT}{M}}$$

$$= \sqrt{2.54} : \sqrt{3}$$

$$= 1 : 1.81$$

120. *(b)* When $FeSO_4 . 7H_2O$ reacts with $(NH_4)_2SO_4$, it forms a double salt known as ferrous ammonium sulphate $(FeSO_4(NH_4)_2SO_4 \cdot 6H_2O)$ or Mohr's salt.

Mathematics

121. *(d)* Let $y = C^{\log_b a}$

$$\Rightarrow \quad \log_C y = \log_b a$$

$$\Rightarrow \quad \frac{\log y}{\log c} = \frac{\log a}{\log b} \qquad \left[\because \log_a b = \frac{\log b}{\log a}\right]$$

$$\Rightarrow \quad \frac{\log y}{\log a} = \frac{\log c}{\log b} \Rightarrow \log_a y = \log_b c$$

$$\Rightarrow \quad y = a^{\log_b c} \qquad [\because \log_a x = y \Rightarrow a^y = x]$$

$$\therefore \quad a^{\log_b c} - c^{\log_b a} = a^{\log_b c} - a^{\log_b c}$$

$$= 0$$

122. *(c)* Given curve, $y = x^2 - xy$.

On differentiating the equation, $y = x^2 - xy$ w.r.t. x, we get $\frac{dy}{dx} = 2x - \left(x\frac{dy}{dx} + y\right)$

$$\Rightarrow \quad (1 + x)\frac{dy}{dx} = 2x - y \Rightarrow \frac{dy}{dx} = \frac{2x - y}{1 + x}$$

$$\Rightarrow \quad \left(\frac{dy}{dx}\right)_{(1, 1/2)} = \frac{2(1) - \left(\frac{1}{2}\right)}{1 + (1)} = \frac{3/2}{2} = \frac{3}{4}$$

123. *(b)* $\lim_{x \to 0} \frac{e^{ax} - e^{bx}}{2x}$

$$= \lim_{x \to 0} \frac{\left(1 + ax + \frac{(ax)^2}{2!} + \frac{(ax)^3}{3!} + \ldots\right) - \left(1 + bx + \frac{(bx)^2}{2!} + \frac{(bx)^3}{3!}\right)}{2x}$$

$$= \lim_{x \to 0} \frac{x\left[(a - b) + \left(\frac{a^2x}{2!} + \frac{a^3x^2}{3!} + \ldots\right) + \left(\frac{b^2x}{2!} + \frac{b^3x^2}{3!} + \ldots\right)\right]}{2x}$$

$$= \frac{1}{2}[(a - b) + (0 + 0 + \ldots) + (0 + 0 + \ldots)]$$

$$= \frac{a - b}{2}$$

124. *(b)* Given, $(x + 1)^2 + y^2 = 4$ ...(i)

and $(x - 1)^2 + y^2 = 9$ ...(ii)

On subtracting Eq. (ii) from Eq. (i), we get

$$(x + 1)^2 - (x - 1)^2 = 4 - 9$$

$$\Rightarrow (x^2 + 2x + 1) - (x^2 - 2x + 1) = -5$$

$$\Rightarrow \quad 4x = -5$$

$$\Rightarrow \quad x = -1.25$$

On putting, $x = -1.25$ into Eq. (i), we get

$$(-0.25)^2 + y^2 = 4$$

$$\Rightarrow \quad y^2 = 3.9375 \Rightarrow y = \pm\sqrt{3.9375}$$

$$\Rightarrow \quad y = \pm\frac{3}{4}\sqrt{7}$$

$$\therefore \quad a = -1.25 \text{ and } b = \frac{3}{4}\sqrt{7}$$

$$\therefore \quad (a, b) = \left(-1.25, \frac{3}{4}\sqrt{7}\right)$$

125. *(a)* First, break the number 5.001 as $x = 5$ and $\Delta x = 0.001$ and use the relation

$$f(x + \Delta x) \approx f(x) + \Delta x f'(x)$$

consider $f(x) = x^3 - 7x^2 + 10 \Rightarrow f'(x) = 3x^2 - 14x$

Therefore,

$$f(x + \Delta x) \approx (x^3 - 7x^2 + 10) + \Delta x(3x^2 - 14x)$$

$$\Rightarrow f(5.001) \approx (5^3 - 7(5)^2 + 10) + (0.001)(3(5)^2 - 14(5))$$

$$= (125 - 175 + 10) + (0.001)(75 - 70)$$

$$= -40 + (0.001)(5) = -40 + 0.005 = -39.995$$

126. *(d)* Given equation of circle is $x^2 + y^2 + 3x - y + 2 = 0$.
On comparing this equation with
$x^2 + y^2 + 2gx + 2fy + c = 0$, we get
$g = \frac{3}{2}, f = -\frac{1}{2}$ and $c = 2$
Now, the length of intercept on X-axis $= 2\sqrt{g^2 - c}$
$$= 2\sqrt{\left(\frac{3}{2}\right)^2 - 2} = 2\sqrt{\frac{9}{4} - 2} = 2\sqrt{\frac{1}{4}} = 2\left(\frac{1}{2}\right) = 1$$

127. *(b)* $\because f(x) = a + (x-4)^{4/9}$
$\therefore \quad f'(x) = 0 + \frac{4}{9}(x-4)^{-5/9}$
Clearly, at $x = 4$, $f'(x)$ is not defined
Hence, $x = 4$ is the point of extremum.
$\because \quad f(4) = a + (4-4)^{4/9} = a$
$\therefore$ The minimum value of $f(x)$ is a.

128. *(d)* At, $x = \frac{\pi}{2}$
LHL $= \lim_{x \to \pi/2^-} (a \sin x + b) = a + b$
RHL $= \lim_{x \to \pi/2^+} (\cos x) = 0$
Since, $f(x)$ is continuous at $x = \pi/2$
$\therefore \quad a + b = 0 \quad \ldots$(i)
At, $x = -\frac{\pi}{2}$
LHL $= \lim_{x \to -\pi/2^-} (2\sin x) = -2$
RHL $= \lim_{x \to -\pi/2^+} (a \sin x + b) = -a + b$
Since, $f(x)$ is continuous at $x = -\pi/2$
$\therefore \quad -a + b = -2 \quad \ldots$(ii)
On solving Eqs. (i) and (ii), we get
$a = 1$ and $b = -1$

129. *(b)* Let $L = \lim_{x \to \infty}\left(\frac{x^2 - 2x + 1}{x^2 - 4x + 2}\right)^{2x}$
$$\Rightarrow \ln L = \lim_{x \to \infty}\left[2x \ln\left(\frac{x^2 - 2x + 1}{x^2 - 4x + 2}\right)\right]$$
$$\Rightarrow \ln L = \lim_{x \to \infty}\left[2x \ln\left(1 + \frac{2x - 1}{x^2 - 4x + 2}\right)\right]$$
$$\Rightarrow \ln L = \lim_{x \to \infty}\left[2x\left(\frac{2x-1}{x^2 - 4x + 2} - \frac{\left(\frac{2x-1}{x^2-4x+2}\right)^2}{2} + \frac{\left(\frac{2x-1}{x^2-4x+2}\right)^3}{3} \ldots\right)\right]$$
$$\Rightarrow \ln L = \left(\lim_{x \to \infty}\frac{2x(2x-1)}{x^2 - 4x + 2}\right) - 0 + 0 \ldots$$
$$\Rightarrow \ln L = \lim_{x \to \infty}\frac{4x^2\left(1 - \frac{1}{2x}\right)}{x^2\left(1 - \frac{4}{x} + \frac{2}{x}\right)}$$
$$\ln L = \frac{4(1-0)}{(1 - 0 + 0)}$$
$$\Rightarrow \ln L = 4$$
$$\Rightarrow L = e^4$$

130. *(a)* $S(-2, -1) = (-2)^2 + (-1)^2 - 2(-2) - 4(-1) - 4$
$= 4 + 1 + 4 + 4 - 4 = 9 > 0$
$\therefore$ $(-2, -1)$ lies outside of S
$S'(-2, -1) = (-2)^2 + (-1)^2 - 4(-2) - 2(-1) - 16$
$= 4 + 1 + 8 + 2 - 16 = -1 < 0$
$\therefore$ $(-2, -1)$ lies inside of S'
Thus, $(-2, -1)$ lies inside S' only.

131. *(b)* Given, $S = \{1, 2, 3 \ldots, 50\}$
$A + \{n \in S : n + \frac{50}{n} > 27\}$
$= \{n \in S : n^2 - 27n + 50 > 0\}$
$= \{n \in S : (n - 25)(n - 2) > 0\}$
$= \{n \in S : n < 2 \text{ or } n > 25\}$
$= \{1, 26, 27, 28, \ldots, 50\}$
$\Rightarrow n(A) = 26$
$B = \{n \in S : n \text{ is prime}\}$
$= \{2, 3, 5, 7, 11, 13, 17, 19, 23, 29, 31, 37, 41, 43, 47\}$
$\Rightarrow n(B) = 15$
$C = \{n \in S : n \text{ is a square}\} = \{1, 4, 9, 16, 25, 36, 49\}$
$\Rightarrow n(C) = 7$
$\therefore \quad p(A) = \frac{n(A)}{n(S)} = \frac{26}{50},$
$\Rightarrow \quad p(B) = \frac{n(B)}{n(S)} = \frac{15}{50},$
$p(C) = \frac{n(C)}{n(S)} = \frac{7}{50}$
$\therefore \quad p(A) > p(B) > p(C)$

132. *(a)* The given inequations are $x + 2y \geq 4$, $2x + y \leq 6$, $x, y \leq 0$.
According to the inequtions $x, y \geq 0$, the feasible region be the first quadrant (including positive X and positive Y-axis). According to the inequation $x + 2y \geq 4$, the feasible region be the region above or on the line $x + 2y = 4$.
According to the inequation $2x + y \leq 6$, the feasible region be the region below or on the line $2x + y = 6$.
Now, the common feasible region will be the required feasible region.
Thus, option (a) is correct.

133. *(b)* Given, constraints are

$x \geq 0, y \geq 0, x + y \leq 12, 2x + y \leq 20$

The feasible region is $OABCO$.

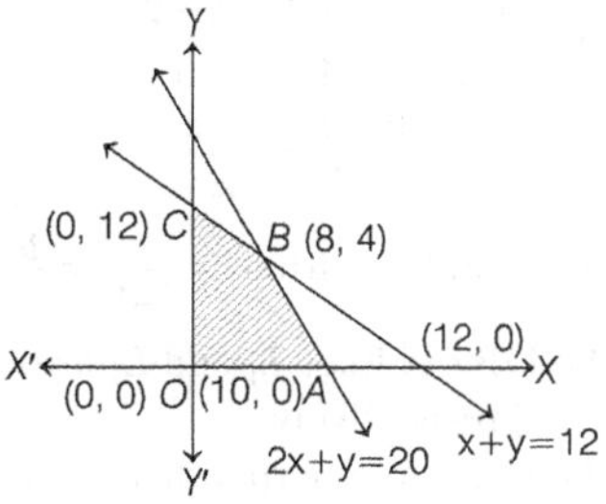

$\because Z = 10x + 16y$

At, $O(0, 0)$, $Z = 10(0) + 16(0) = 0$

At, $A(10, 0)$, $Z = 10(10) + 16(0) = 100$

At, $B(8, 4)$ $Z = 10(8) + 16(4) = 144$

At, $C(0, 12)$, $Z = 10(0) + 16(12) = 192$

Hence, the maximum value of Z is 192.

134. *(b)* Given, $A = \begin{bmatrix} 2 & 2 \\ 3 & 4 \end{bmatrix}$

$\therefore \quad |A| = \begin{vmatrix} 2 & 2 \\ 3 & 4 \end{vmatrix} = 2 \times 4 - 3 \times 2 = 8 - 6 = 2$

Now, $A_{11} = 4$, $A_{12} = -3$, $A_{21} = -2$ and $A_{22} = 2$

$\therefore \quad adj_A = \begin{bmatrix} 4 & -3 \\ -2 & 2 \end{bmatrix}^T = \begin{bmatrix} 4 & -2 \\ -3 & 2 \end{bmatrix}$

$A^{-1} = \frac{1}{|A|} adj\, A = \frac{1}{2}\begin{bmatrix} 4 & -2 \\ -3 & 2 \end{bmatrix}$

$= \begin{bmatrix} 2 & -1 \\ -3/2 & 1 \end{bmatrix}$

135. *(c)* Given, $A(\text{adj} A) = 10I$

We know that $A(\text{adj} A) = |A| I$

$\therefore \quad 10I = |A| I$

$\Rightarrow \quad |A| = 10$

We know that $|\text{adj}A| = |A|^{n-1}$, where n is order of A

$\therefore |\text{adj } A| = |A|^{4-1} = 10^3 = 1000$

136. *(c)* Given, $A = \begin{bmatrix} k+1 & 2 \\ 4 & k-1 \end{bmatrix}$ is a singular matrix.

$\therefore \quad |A| = 0$

$\Rightarrow \quad \begin{vmatrix} k+1 & 2 \\ 4 & k-1 \end{vmatrix} = 0$

$\Rightarrow \quad (k+1)(k-1) - 4 \times 2 = 0$

$\Rightarrow \quad k^2 - 1 - 8 = 0$

$\Rightarrow \quad k^2 - 9 = 0$

$\Rightarrow \quad k^2 = 9$

$\Rightarrow \quad k = \pm 3$

137. *(d)* We have, $\mathbf{a} = \hat{\mathbf{i}} + 2\hat{\mathbf{j}} + 2\hat{\mathbf{k}}$ and $\mathbf{b} = \hat{\mathbf{i}} + 2\hat{\mathbf{j}} - 2\hat{\mathbf{k}}$

Clearly, $|\mathbf{a}| = \sqrt{1 + 4 + 4} = \sqrt{9} = 3$

and $\quad |\mathbf{b}| = \sqrt{1 + 4 + 4} = \sqrt{9} = 3$

$\because \quad \mathbf{a} \cdot \mathbf{b} = |a||b| \cos\theta$

$\Rightarrow \quad \cos\theta = \frac{1 \cdot 1 + 2 \cdot 2 + 2 \cdot (-2)}{3 \times 3}$

$\Rightarrow \quad \cos\theta = \frac{1 + 4 - 4}{9} \Rightarrow \cos\theta = \frac{1}{9}$

$\therefore \quad \theta = \cos^{-1}\left(\frac{1}{9}\right)$

138. *(b)* Since, vectors **a**, **b** and **c** are coplanar

$\therefore [\mathbf{a}\ \mathbf{b}\ \mathbf{c}] = 0 \Rightarrow \mathbf{a} \cdot (\mathbf{b} \times \mathbf{c}) = 0$

Now, $\mathbf{b} \times \mathbf{c} = \begin{vmatrix} \hat{\mathbf{i}} & \hat{\mathbf{j}} & \hat{\mathbf{k}} \\ 1 & 2 & -1 \\ m & -1 & 2 \end{vmatrix}$

$= \hat{\mathbf{i}}(4 - 1) - \hat{\mathbf{j}}(2 + m) + \hat{\mathbf{k}}(-1 - 2m)$

$= 3\hat{\mathbf{i}} - (2 + m)\hat{\mathbf{j}} - (1 + 2m)\hat{\mathbf{k}}$

and

$\mathbf{a} \cdot (\mathbf{b} \times \mathbf{c}) = (2\hat{\mathbf{i}} - 3\hat{\mathbf{j}} + 4\hat{\mathbf{k}}) \cdot (3\hat{\mathbf{i}} - (2 + m)\hat{\mathbf{j}} - (1 + 2m)\hat{\mathbf{k}})$

$= 2(3) + 3(2 + m) - 4(1 + 2m)$

$= 6 + 6 + 3m - 4 - 8m = 8 - 5m$

$\because \quad \mathbf{a} \cdot (\mathbf{b} \times \mathbf{c}) = 0$

$\therefore \quad 8 - 5m = 0 \Rightarrow m = \frac{8}{5}$

139. *(b)* Given constraints are $x \geq 0$, $y \geq 0$, $x + y \leq 5$ and $3x + y \leq 9$ and $z = 12x + 13y$

The feasible region is $OABCO$.

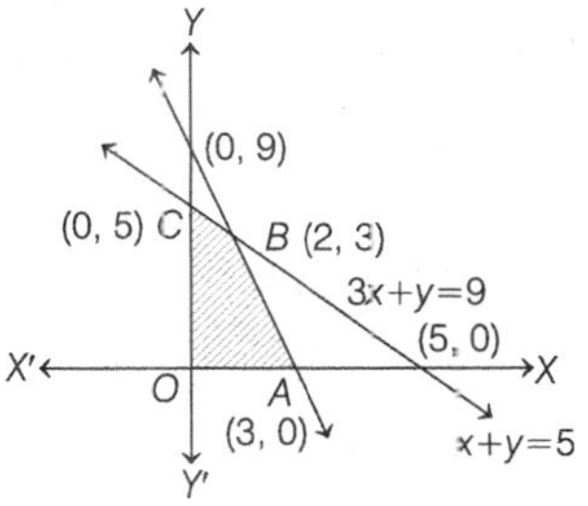

$\because \quad Z = 12x + 13y$

At, $O(0, 0)$, $Z = 12(0) + 13(0) = 0$

At, $A(3, 0)$, $Z = 12(3) + 13(0) = 36$

At, $B(2, 3)$, $Z = 12(2) + 13(3) = 63$

At, $C(0, 5)$, $Z = 12(0) + 13(5) = 65$

Here, maximum value of Z is 65.

140. *(a)* Given, $\mathbf{a} = 2\hat{\mathbf{i}} + \hat{\mathbf{j}} - \hat{\mathbf{k}}$, $\mathbf{b} = \hat{\mathbf{i}} - \hat{\mathbf{j}}$ and $\mathbf{c} = 5\hat{\mathbf{i}} - \hat{\mathbf{j}} + \hat{\mathbf{k}}$

$\therefore \mathbf{a} + \mathbf{b} - \mathbf{c} = (2 + 1 - 5)\hat{\mathbf{i}} + (1 - 1 + 1)\hat{\mathbf{j}} + (-1 + 0 - 1)\hat{\mathbf{k}}$

$= -2\hat{\mathbf{i}} + \hat{\mathbf{j}} - 2\hat{\mathbf{k}} = -(2\hat{\mathbf{i}} - \hat{\mathbf{j}} + 2\hat{\mathbf{k}})$

Now, the unit vector in the direction of $\mathbf{a} + \mathbf{b} - \mathbf{c}$ be

$\frac{-(2\hat{\mathbf{i}} - \hat{\mathbf{j}} + 2\hat{\mathbf{k}})}{\sqrt{2^2 + (-1)^2 + 2^2}} = -\frac{1}{3}(2\hat{\mathbf{i}} - \hat{\mathbf{j}} + 2\hat{\mathbf{k}})$

$\therefore$ The required unit vector be $\frac{1}{3}(2\hat{\mathbf{i}} - \hat{\mathbf{j}} + 2\hat{\mathbf{k}})$.

141. *(a)* Consider the equation of line given in option (a). The DR's of this line or (4, 5, 6).

We know that if the line $\frac{x-x_0}{a_1}=\frac{y-y_0}{b_1}=\frac{z-z_0}{c_1}$ is parallel to the plane $a_2x+b_2y+c_2z+d=0$, then $a_1a_2+b_1b_2+c_1c_2=0$, that is the normal to the plane is perpendicular to the line.

Here, the vector $\hat{\mathbf{i}}-2\hat{\mathbf{j}}+\hat{\mathbf{k}}$ is normal to the plane $x-2y+z=0$

and $4(1)+5(-2)+6(1)=4-10+6=10-10=0$

So, option (a) is correct.

142. *(a)* Let $I=\int\frac{x\,dx}{2(1+x)^{3/2}}$

On putting, $1+x=t$, we get $dx=dt$

$$\therefore\quad I=\int\frac{(t-1)\,dt}{2t^{3/2}}=\frac{1}{2}[\int t^{-1/2}dt-\int t^{-3/2}dt]$$

$$=\frac{1}{2}\left[\frac{t^{1/2}}{1/2}-\frac{t^{-1/2}}{-1/2}\right]+C$$

$$=\frac{1}{2}\times 2\left[\sqrt{t}+\frac{1}{\sqrt{t}}\right]+C$$

$$=\frac{t+1}{\sqrt{t}}+C=\frac{x+2}{\sqrt{1+x}}+C$$

143. *(c)* Let $I=\int\frac{4^x}{\sqrt{1-16^x}}dx$

$$=\int\frac{4^x}{\sqrt{1-(4^x)^2}}dx$$

On putting, $4^x=t$, we get $4^x\log 4dx=dt$

$$\Rightarrow\quad 4^x\,dx=\frac{dt}{\log 4}$$

$$\therefore\quad I=\frac{1}{\log 4}\int\frac{dt}{\sqrt{1-t^2}}$$

$$=\frac{1}{\log 4}\sin^{-1}t+C$$

$$=\frac{1}{\log 4}\sin^{-1}4^x+C$$

144. *(c)* Let $f(x)=\sin^2 x$

Now, $f(-x)=\sin^2(-x)=(\sin(-x))^2$

$$=(-\sin x)^2=\sin^2 x=f(x)$$

So, f is an even function

$$\therefore\int_{-\pi/2}^{\pi/2}\sin^2 x=2\int_0^{\pi/2}\sin^2 x\,dx$$

$$\left[\because\int_{-a}^{a}f(x)dx=2\int_0^a f(x)\,dx,\text{ if } f \text{ is even}\right]$$

$$=2\int_0^{\frac{\pi}{2}}\frac{1-\cos 2x}{2}dx=\left[x-\frac{\sin 2x}{2}\right]_0^{\pi/2}$$

$$=\left(\frac{\pi}{2}-\frac{\sin 2\times\pi/2}{2}\right)-\left(0-\frac{\sin(2\times 0)}{2}\right)$$

$$=\left(\frac{\pi}{2}-0\right)-(0-0)=\frac{\pi}{2}$$

145. *(b)* Let $L_1:\frac{x-1}{2}=\frac{y-4}{4}=\frac{z-2}{3}$

and $L_2=\frac{1-x}{1}=\frac{y-2}{5}=\frac{3-z}{a}$

the line L_2 can be written as $\frac{x-1}{-1}=\frac{y-2}{5}=\frac{z-3}{-a}$

Now, the DR's of lines L_1 and L_2 are (2, 4, 3) and $(-1, 5, -a)$ respectively.

Since, L_1 and L_2 are perpendicular to each other.

$\therefore\ 2(-1)+4)(5)+3(-a)=0$

$$\Rightarrow\quad -2+20-3a=0$$

$$\Rightarrow\quad -3a=-18\Rightarrow a=6$$

146. *(a)* Let $\frac{x-1}{2}=\frac{y+1}{3}=\frac{z-1}{4}=\lambda$

Now, any point P that lies on the lines L_1 has the form $(1+2\lambda,\ -1+3\lambda, 1+4\lambda)$.

Now, on putting $x=1+2\lambda$, $y=-1+3\lambda$ and $z=1+4\lambda$ into the equation of lines L_2, we get

$$\frac{1+2\lambda-3}{1}=\frac{-1+3\lambda-k}{2}=1+4\lambda$$

$$\Rightarrow\quad\frac{1+2\lambda-3}{1}=1+4\lambda$$

$$\Rightarrow\quad -2\lambda=3\Rightarrow\lambda=\frac{-3}{2}$$

and
$$\frac{-1+3\lambda-k}{2}=1+4\lambda$$

$$\Rightarrow\quad -1+3\lambda-k=2+8\lambda$$

$$\Rightarrow\quad -5\lambda=3+k$$

$$\Rightarrow\quad -5\left(-\frac{3}{2}\right)=3+k\qquad[\because\lambda=-3/2]$$

$$\Rightarrow\quad k=\frac{15}{2}-3$$

$$\Rightarrow\quad k=\frac{9}{2}$$

$$\Rightarrow\quad 2k=9$$

147. *(a)* The total number of possible five-digit numbers $=5!$

The total number of possible five-digit numbers in which 1 and 5 are always together $=2\times 4!$

$\therefore$Required probability $=\frac{2\times 4!}{5!}=\frac{2\times 4!}{5\times 4!}=\frac{2}{5}$

148. *(c)* Here, number which are divisible by either 3 or 5 are 12, 15, 18, 20, 21, 24, 27, 30.

$\therefore$Total numbers = 9

P (number either divisible by 3 or 5) $=\frac{9}{20}$

P (number neither divisible by 3 nor 5)

$=1-P$ (number either divisible by 3 or 5)

$$=1-\frac{9}{20}=\frac{11}{20}$$

149. *(b)* Number of triangles formed = $^9C_3$

Number of isosceles triangles $= 9 \times \left(\frac{9-1}{2}\right)$

$= 9 \times 4 = 36$

So, required probability

$$= \frac{36}{^9C_3} = \frac{36}{\frac{9!}{3!(9-3)!}} = \frac{36 \times 3 \times 2 \times 6!}{9 \times 8 \times 7 \times 6!} = \frac{3}{7}$$

150. *(d)* Given, $P(B) = \frac{3}{2}P(A)$ and $P(C) = \frac{1}{2}P(B)$

Since, A, B and C are mutually exclusive and exhaustive events.

$\therefore \quad P(A) + P(B) + P(C) = 1$

$\Rightarrow \quad P(A) + \frac{3}{2}P(A) + \frac{1}{2} \times \frac{3}{2}P(A) = 1$

$\Rightarrow \quad P(A)\left(1 + \frac{3}{2} + \frac{3}{4}\right) = 1$

$\Rightarrow \quad P(A)\left(\frac{13}{4}\right) = 1 \Rightarrow P(A) = \frac{4}{13}$

$\therefore \quad P(C) = \frac{1}{2} \times \frac{3}{2}P(A) = \frac{3}{4} \times \frac{4}{13} = \frac{3}{13}$

Also, A, B and C are mutually exclusive.

$\therefore P(A \cap B) = P(B \cap C) = P(C \cap A) = 0$

Now, $P(A \cup C) = P(A) + P(C) - P(A \cap C)$

$= \frac{4}{13} + \frac{3}{13} - 0 = \frac{7}{13}$

151. *(b)* Given, $a_0 = 1$, $a_{n+1} = 3n^2 + n + a_n$

$\Rightarrow \quad a_1 = 3(0)^2 + (0) + a_0 = 0 + 0 + 1 = 1$

$\Rightarrow \quad a_2 = 3(1)^2 + (1)\ a_1 = 3 + 1 + 1 = 5$

From option (b),

Let $P(n) = n^3 - n^2 + 1$

$P(0) = (0)^3 - (0)^2 + 1 = 1 = a_0$

$P(1) = (1)^3 - (1)^2 + 1 = 1 - 1 + 1 = a_1$

$P(2) = (2)^3 - (2)^2 + 1 = 8 - 4 + 1 = 5 = a_2$

Thus, $a_n = n^3 - n^2 + 1$

152. *(a)* Let $P(n) = 49^n + 16^n + k$

For $n = 1$, we get

$P(1) = 49^{(1)} + 16^{(1)} + k = 65 + k$

As $P(1)$ is divisible by 64, we take

$k = -1$

$\therefore \quad P(1) = 65 - 1 = 64$, which is divisible by 64.

Thus, the least negative integral value of k be -1.

153. *(c)* Let $P(n) = 2^{3n} - 7n - 1$

$\Rightarrow \quad P(1) = 2^{3(1)} - 7(1) - 1 = 8 - 8 = 0$

$\Rightarrow \quad P(2) = 2^{3(2)} - 7(2) - 1 = 64 - 15 = 49$

$P(1)$ and $P(2)$ are divisible by 49.

Let $P(k) = 2^{3k} - 7k - 1 = 49t$, where t is an integer

Now,

$P(k+1) = 2^{3(k+1)} - 7(k+1) - 1 = 2^{3k} \cdot 2^3 - 7k - 7 - 1$

$= 8(2^{3k} - 7k - 1) + 49k$

$= 8(49t) + 49k$

$= 49\,(8t + k)$, where $8t + k$ is an integer

Thus, $2^{3n} - 7n - 1$ is divisible by 49.

154. *(b)* Given series is

$\frac{4}{3} + \frac{10}{9} + \frac{28}{27} + \ldots$

The sum of the given series upto n-terms

$\frac{4}{3} + \frac{10}{9} + \frac{28}{27} + \ldots$ upto n-terms

$= \left(1 + \frac{1}{3}\right) + \left(1 + \frac{1}{9}\right) + \left(1 + \frac{1}{27}\right) + \ldots$ upto n-terms

$= (1 + 1 + 1 + \ldots$ upto n-terms$)$
$+ \left(\frac{1}{3} + \frac{1}{3^2} + \frac{1}{3^3} + \ldots \text{ upto } n\text{-terms}\right)$

$$= n + \frac{1}{3}\left(\frac{1 - \frac{1}{3^n}}{1 - \frac{1}{3}}\right) = n + \frac{(3^n - 1)}{2(3^n)} = \frac{3^n(2n+1) - 1}{2(3^n)}$$

155. *(a)* Given, $\frac{1}{2!} + \frac{2}{3!} + \ldots + \frac{99}{100!}$

$= \frac{2-1}{2!} + \frac{3-1}{3!} + \frac{4-1}{4!} + \ldots + \frac{100-1}{100!}$

$= \left(\frac{1}{1!} - \frac{1}{2!}\right) + \left(\frac{1}{2!} - \frac{1}{3!}\right) + \left(\frac{1}{3!} - \frac{1}{4!}\right) + \ldots + \left(\frac{1}{99!} - \frac{1}{100!}\right)$

$= 1 - \frac{1}{100!} = \frac{100! - 1}{100!}$

156. *(b)* Here, $T_{12} = a + 11d$ and $T_{22} = a + 21d$

Since, $100 = T_{12} + T_{22}$

$\therefore \quad 100 = a + 11d + a + 21d$

$\Rightarrow a + 16d = 50 \quad \ldots(i)$

Now, $S_{33} = \frac{33}{2}[2a + (33-1)d]$

$= 33(a + 16d) = 33 \times 50$ [From Eq. (i)]

$= 1650$

Thus, required sum be 1650.

157. *(a)* The general equation of all non-vertical lines in a plane is $ax + by = 1$, where $b \neq 0$.

On differentiating both sides w.r.t. x, we get

$$a + b\frac{dy}{dx} = 0$$

Again, differentiating w.r.t x, we get

$$b\frac{d^2y}{dx^2}$$

$\Rightarrow \quad \frac{d^2y}{dx^2} = 0 \quad [\because b \neq 0]$

COMEDK 2023

158. *(a)* Given, $\left(\frac{dy}{dx}\right)^2 = 1 - x^2 - y^2 + x^2y^2$

$$\Rightarrow \left(\frac{dy}{dx}\right)^2 = (1-y^2) - x^2(1-y^2) = (1-x^2)(1-y^2)$$

$$\therefore \frac{dy}{dx} = \sqrt{(1-x^2)(1-y^2)}$$

$$\Rightarrow \frac{dy}{\sqrt{1-y^2}} = \sqrt{1-x^2}\,dx$$

On integrating both sides, we get

$$\int \frac{dy}{\sqrt{1-y^2}} = \int \sqrt{1-x^2}\,dx$$

$$\Rightarrow \sin^{-1} y = \frac{x}{2}\sqrt{1-x^2} + \frac{1}{2}\sin^{-1} x + \frac{C}{2}$$

$$\Rightarrow 2\sin^{-1} y = x\sqrt{1-x^2} + \sin^{-1} x + C$$

159. *(c)* Given, differential equation is

$$\left(\frac{dy}{dx}\right)\tan y = \sin(x+y) + \sin(x-y)$$

$$\Rightarrow \left(\frac{dy}{dx}\right)\tan y = 2\sin\left(\frac{x+y+x-y}{2}\right)\cos\left(\frac{x+y-x+y}{2}\right)$$

$$\Rightarrow \left(\frac{dy}{dx}\right)\frac{\sin y}{\cos y} = 2\sin x\cos y$$

$$\Rightarrow \frac{\sin y}{\cos^2 y}\,dy = 2\sin x\,dx$$

On integration both sides, we get

$$\int \frac{\sin y}{\cos^2 y}\,dy = \int 2\sin x\,dx$$

$$\Rightarrow -\frac{(\cos y)^{-2+1}}{(-2+1)} = -2\cos x + C$$

$$\Rightarrow \frac{1}{\cos y} = -2\cos x + C \Rightarrow \sec y = -2\cos x + C$$

160. *(c)* We know that if ${}^nC_x = {}^nC_y$, then either $x = y$ or $x + y = n$

Since, ${}^nC_{10} = {}^nC_{12}$

$\therefore \quad 10 + 12 = n$

$\Rightarrow \quad n = 22$

Now, ${}^nC_{21} = {}^{22}C_{21}$

$$= \frac{22!}{(22-21)!\,21!} = \frac{22!}{1!\,21!} = \frac{22\times 21!}{1\times 21!} = 22$$

161. *(d)* Let the probability of failure and success be p and q, respectively.

Let X represents the number of failure

According to the question, $q = 2p$

$\because \quad p + q = 1$ and $q = 2p$

$\therefore \quad p = \frac{1}{3}$ and $q = \frac{2}{3}$

Now, required probability $= P(X \le 2)$

$$= P(X=0) + P(X=1) + P(X=2)$$

$$= {}^6C_0p^0q^6 + {}^6C_1p^1q^5 + {}^6C_2p^2q^4$$

$$= \left(\frac{2}{3}\right)^6 + 6\left(\frac{1}{3}\right)^1\left(\frac{2}{3}\right)^5 + 15\left(\frac{1}{3}\right)^2\left(\frac{2}{3}\right)^4$$

$$= \frac{1}{729}(64 + 192 + 240) = \frac{496}{729}$$

162. *(c)* Given, $\cos A = m\cos B \Rightarrow \frac{\cos A}{\cos B} = m$

On applying componendo and dividendo rule, we get

$$\frac{\cos A + \cos B}{\cos A - \cos B} = \frac{m+1}{m-1}$$

$$\Rightarrow \frac{2\cos\left(\frac{A+B}{2}\right)\cos\left(\frac{A-B}{2}\right)}{2\sin\left(\frac{A+B}{2}\right)\sin\left(\frac{B-A}{2}\right)} = \frac{m+1}{m-1}$$

$$\Rightarrow \frac{\cot\left(\frac{A+B}{2}\right)}{\tan\left(\frac{B-A}{2}\right)} = \frac{m+1}{m-1}$$

$$\Rightarrow \cot\left(\frac{A+B}{2}\right) = \left(\frac{m+1}{m-1}\right)\tan\left(\frac{B-A}{2}\right)$$

$$\therefore \lambda = \frac{m+1}{m-1}$$

163. *(b)* Given, $\frac{2\tan A}{1-\cot A} + \frac{2\cot A}{1-\tan A}$

$$= \frac{\frac{2\sin A}{\cos A}}{1 - \frac{\cos A}{\sin A}} + \frac{\frac{2\cos A}{\sin A}}{1 - \frac{\sin A}{\cos A}}$$

$$= \left(\frac{\sin A}{\cos A}\right)\left(\frac{2\sin A}{\sin A - \cos A}\right) + \left(\frac{\cos A}{\sin A}\right)\left(\frac{2\cos A}{\cos A - \sin A}\right)$$

$$= \frac{2}{\sin A - \cos A}\left[\frac{\sin^2 A}{\cos A} - \frac{\cos^2 A}{\sin A}\right]$$

$$= \frac{2}{\sin A - \cos A}\left[\frac{\sin^3 A - \cos^3 A}{\sin A\cos A}\right]$$

$$= \frac{2(\sin A - \cos A)(\sin^2 A + \cos^2 A + \sin A\cos A)}{(\sin A - \cos A)(\sin A\cos A)}$$

$$= 2\left(\frac{1}{\sin A\cos A} + 1\right)$$

$$= 2(\sec A\,\text{cosec} A + 1) = 2\sec A\,\text{cosec} A + 2$$

164. *(b)* Given, $2\cos 4x + \sin^2 2x = 0$

$$\Rightarrow 2\cos 4x + \left(\frac{1-\cos 4x}{2}\right) = 0$$

$$\Rightarrow 3\cos 4x + 1 = 0$$

$\Rightarrow \quad \cos 4x = -\frac{1}{3}$

$\Rightarrow \quad \sin 4x = \pm\frac{2\sqrt{2}}{3}$

$\Rightarrow \quad 4x = n\pi + (-1)^n \sin^{-1}\left(\pm\frac{2\sqrt{2}}{3}\right)$

$\Rightarrow \quad x = \frac{n\pi}{4} + \frac{(-1)^n}{4}\sin^{-1}\left(\pm\frac{2\sqrt{2}}{3}\right)$

165. *(a)* Given, $2f(x^2) + 3f\left(\frac{1}{x^2}\right) = x^2 - 1$ ...(i)

Replacing x by $\frac{1}{x}$, we get

$2f\left(\frac{1}{x^2}\right) + 3f(x^2) = \frac{1}{x^2} - 1$ ...(ii)

On multiplying Eq. (i) by 2, Eq. (ii) by 3 and then subtracting Eq. (i) from Eq. (ii), we get

$5f(x^2) = 3\left(\frac{1}{x^2} - 1\right) - 2(x^2 - 1)$

$\Rightarrow \quad 5f(x^2) = \frac{3}{x^2} - 2x^2 - 1$

$\Rightarrow \quad f(x^2) = \frac{1}{5}\left(\frac{3}{x^2} - 2x^2 - 1\right)$

$\Rightarrow \quad f(x^2) = \frac{1}{5x^2}(3 - 2x^4 - x^2)$

$\Rightarrow \quad f(x^2) = \frac{(2x^2 + 3)(1 - x^2)}{5x^2}$

$\therefore \quad f(x^8) = \frac{(1 - x^8)(2x^8 + 3)}{5x^8}$

166. *(a)* Given, $A = \{a, b\ c\}$, $B = \{b, c, d\}$ and $C = \{a, d, c\}$

Now, $A - B = \{a, b, c\} - \{b, c, d\} = \{a\}$

and $B \cap C = \{b, c, d\} \cap \{a, d, c\} = \{c, d\}$

$\therefore (A - B) \times (B \cap C) = \{a\} \times \{c, d\} = \{(a, c), (a, d)\}$

167. *(b)* Given, $n(A) = p$ and $n(B) = q$

$\therefore n(A \times B) = pq$

The number of relations from a set A to a set B is same as the total number of subset of the set $A \times B$.

We know that if $n(A) = k$, then $n(P(A)) = 2^k$

Now, the total number of subset of $A \times B$ be 2^{pq}

$\therefore$Then number of relations from the set A to the set B is 2^{pq}.

168. *(b)* Given, $Z = \sqrt{3} + i$

$\therefore \arg(z^2 e^{z-i}) = \arg[(\sqrt{3} + i)^2 e^{\sqrt{3}+i) - i}]$

$= \arg[(2 + 2\sqrt{3}i)e^{\sqrt{3}}]$

$= \arg[2e^{\sqrt{3}}(1 + \sqrt{3}i)]$

$= \arg[(1 + \sqrt{3}i)]$

$= \tan^{-1}\left(\frac{\sqrt{3}}{1}\right) = \tan^{-1}\left(\tan\frac{\pi}{3}\right) = \frac{\pi}{3}$

169. *(d)* Given, $i^n + i^{n+1} + i^{n+2} + i^{n+3} = i^n(1 + i + i^2 + i^3)$

$= i^n(1 + i + (-1) + (i^2)i)$

$= i^n(1 + i + (-1) + (-1)i)$

$= i^n[(1 + i) - (1 + i)] = i^n(0) = 0$

170. *(d)* We have, $\left(\frac{3}{2} + i\frac{\sqrt{3}}{2}\right)^{50} = 3^{25}(x + iy)$

$\Rightarrow \quad (\sqrt{3})^{50}\left(\frac{\sqrt{3}}{2} + i\frac{1}{2}\right)^{50} = 3^{25}(x + iy)$

$\Rightarrow \quad 3^{25}\left[-i\left(-\frac{1}{2} + i\frac{\sqrt{3}}{2}\right)\right]^{50} = 3^{25}(x + iy)$

$\Rightarrow \quad (-i)^{50}\omega^{50} = x + iy$

$\Rightarrow \quad (i^4)^{12} \cdot i^2 \cdot (\omega^3)^{16} \cdot \omega^2 = x + iy$

$\Rightarrow \quad (1)^{12} \cdot (-1) \cdot (1)^{16} \cdot \left(-\frac{1}{2} - i\frac{\sqrt{3}}{2}\right) = x + iy$

$\Rightarrow \quad \frac{1}{2} + i\frac{\sqrt{3}}{2} = x + iy$

$\Rightarrow \quad 1 + i\sqrt{3} = 2x + i(2y)$

$\therefore \quad (2x, 2y) = (1, \sqrt{3})$

171. *(b)* From 10 given points, ${}^{10}C_2$ straight lines can be drawn.

But 4 points are collinear, using 4 points, ${}^4C_2$ straight lines can be drawn.

From 4 collinear points, 1 straight line can be drawn.

So, total number of straight lines $= {}^{10}C_2 - {}^4C_2 + 1$

$= \frac{10!}{8!\,2!} - \frac{4!}{2!\,2!} + 1$

$= 45 - 6 + 1 = 40$

172. *(c)* Since, numbers should be greater than 1000 but less than 4000.

$\therefore$The first digit must be either 2 or 3.

It is clear that required numbers must be 4 digit numbers.

Now, there are four choices (0, 2, 3, 4), for each unit, ten and hundred place digit.

Thus, total number $= {}^2C_1 \times 4 \times 4 \times 4$

$= 2 \times 4 \times 4 \times 4 = 128$

173. *(c)* $\because$ The total number of lines joining any two points of the polygon is given by ${}^nC_2$

So, ${}^nC_2 = 105$

$\Rightarrow \quad \frac{n(n-1)}{2} = 105$

$\Rightarrow \quad n^2 - n = 210$

$\Rightarrow \quad n^2 - n - 210 = 0$

$\Rightarrow \quad n^2 - 15n + 14n - 210 = 0$

$\Rightarrow \quad n(n - 15) + 14(n - 15) = 0$

$\Rightarrow \quad (n-15)(n+14)=0$

either $n-15=0$ or $n+14=0$

$\Rightarrow \quad n=15$ or -14

$\because$ Number of sides cannot be negative

$\therefore \quad n=15$

174. *(d)* $\because$ Equation of angles of bisector of pair of straight line, $ax^2+2bxy+by^2$ is

$$\frac{x^2-y^2}{a-b}=\frac{xy}{h}$$

$\therefore$ For, $3y^2-5xy-2x^2=0$

$$a=3, b=-2, h=-5$$

So, equation of angle bisector is

$$\frac{x^2-y^2}{3-(-2)}=\frac{xy}{-5}$$

$$\Rightarrow \frac{x^2-y^2}{5}=\frac{xy}{-5} \Rightarrow x^2-y^2+xy=0$$

175. *(a)*

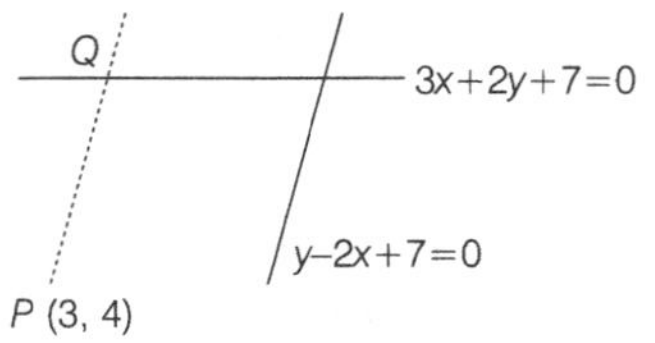

The slope of the line, $y-2x+7=0$

$\Rightarrow \quad y=2x-7$

Slope $\quad (m)=2$

$\therefore$ Slope of $PQ=m_{PQ}=2$

Equation of PQ,

$$(y-4)=2(x-3)$$

$\Rightarrow \quad y=2x-2 \quad \ldots$(i)

and $3x+2y+7=0 \quad \ldots$(ii)

On putting, the value of y in Eq. (ii), we get

$$3x+2(2x-2)+7=0$$

$$\Rightarrow \quad 7x=-3 \Rightarrow x=-\frac{3}{7}$$

Then, $y=2\times\left(-\frac{3}{7}\right)-2=-\frac{20}{7}$

So, coordinates of $Q=\left(-\frac{3}{7}, \frac{-20}{7}\right)$

Thus, distance

$$PQ=\sqrt{\left(3-\left(\frac{-3}{7}\right)^2\right)+\left(4-\left(-\frac{20}{7}\right)\right)^2}=\frac{24\sqrt{5}}{7}$$

176. *(b)* Slope of the line,

$y-3x+18=0$

$\Rightarrow y=3x-18 \Rightarrow$ Slope $(m_1)=3$

and angle $(\theta)=60°$

so, $\tan 60°=\left|\frac{m_1-m_2}{1+m_1m_2}\right|$

$$\Rightarrow \quad \sqrt{3}=\left|\frac{3-m_2}{1+3m_2}\right|$$

$$\Rightarrow \quad \frac{3-m_2}{1+3m_2}=\pm\sqrt{3}$$

Either, $\frac{3-m_2}{1+3m_2}=\sqrt{3}$ or $\frac{3-m_2}{1+3m_2}=-\sqrt{3}$

$\Rightarrow \quad 3-m_2=\sqrt{3}+3\sqrt{3}m_2$

or $\quad 3-m_2=-\sqrt{3}-3\sqrt{3}m_2$

$\Rightarrow \quad m_2(1+3\sqrt{3})=3-\sqrt{3}$

or $\quad m_2(1-3\sqrt{3})=3+\sqrt{3}$

$\Rightarrow \quad m_2=\frac{3-\sqrt{3}}{1+3\sqrt{3}}$ or $m_2=\frac{3+\sqrt{3}}{1-3\sqrt{3}}$

$\therefore \quad m_2=\frac{3-\sqrt{3}}{1+3\sqrt{3}}, \frac{3+\sqrt{3}}{1-3\sqrt{3}}$

177. *(c)* If 3 and 5 are intercepts of a line $L=0$, then

x-intercept $=a=3$

y-intercept $=b=5$

Equation of line is

$$\frac{x}{3}+\frac{y}{5}=1 \Rightarrow \quad 5x+3y-15=0$$

$\therefore$ Required distance

$$=\left|\frac{5(3)+3(7)-15}{\sqrt{5^2+3^2}}\right|=\frac{21}{\sqrt{34}}$$

178. *(d)* $(x+y)^{60}={}^{60}C_0x^{60}-{}^{60}C_1x^{59}y+\ldots..$

$$+{}^{60}C_{60}y^{60} \ldots\text{(i)}$$

$(x-y)^{60}={}^{60}C_0x^{60}+{}^{60}C_1x^{59}y+\ldots+{}^{60}C_{60}y^{60} \quad \ldots$(ii)

By adding Eq. (i) and Eq. (ii)

$$(x+y)^{60}+(x-y)^{60}$$

$$=\underbrace{2({}^{60}C_0x^6+{}^{60}C_2x^{58}y^2+\ldots+{}^{60}C_{60}y^{60})}_{31 \text{ terms}}$$

Hence, the expansion of $(x+y)^{60}+(x-y)^{60}$ has 31 terms.

179. *(c)* $(1-3x+3x^2-x^3)^{15}=[(1-x)^3]^{15}$

$=(1-x)^{45}$

So, $T_{r+1}={}^{45}C_r(1)^{45-r}(-x)^r$

For coefficient of x^{29}, put $r=29$

Then, $T_{30}={}^{45}C_{29}(1)^{45-29}(-x)^{29}=-{}^{45}C_{29}x^{29}$

Hence, coefficient of $x^{29}=-{}^{45}C_{29}$

and $-{}^{45}C_{29}=-{}^{45}C_{16}$

180. *(b)* $\because$ Middle term has greatest binomial coefficient.

In the expansion of $(1+3x+3x^2+x^3)^{2n}$

$=((1+x)^3)^{2n}=(1+x)^{6n}$

$\because$ $6n$ is even

So, middle term of $(1+x)^{6n}=T_{\left(\frac{6n}{2}+1\right)}$

$=T_{(3n+1)}=(3n+1)$ th term.

COMEDK

Solved Paper 2022

Instructions

- There are 180 questions in all. The number of questions in each section is as given below.

Sections	No. of Questions
Section I : Physics	1-60
Section II : Chemistry	61-120
Section III : Mathematics	121-180

- All the questions are Multiple Choice Questions having four options out of which **ONLY ONE** is correct.
- Candidates will be awarded 1 mark for each correct answer. There will be no negative marking for incorrect answer.
- Time allotted to complete this paper is 3 hrs.

COMEDK 2022

PHYSICS

1. During the phenomenon of resonance
a. the amplitude of oscillation becomes large
b. the frequency of oscillation becomes large
c. the time period of oscillation becomes large
d. All of the above

2. If the earth were to spin faster, acceleration due to gravity at the poles
a. increases
b. decreases
c. remains the same
d. depends on how fast it spins

3. Maximum amplitude of message signal in amplitude modulation is 20 cm. If the amplitude of carrier wave is 40 cm, then modulation index of modulated wave is
a. 1 *b.* 0.5 *c.* 0.25 *d.* 2

4. If heat engine is filled at temperature 27°C and heat of 100 k cal is taken from source at temperature 677°C. Work done (in J) is
a. 0.28×10^6 *b.* 2.8×10^6
c. 28×10^6 *d.* 0.028×10^6

5. During α-decay, atomic mass of parent nuclei is
a. decreased by 2 units
b. increased by 2 units
c. decreased by 4 units
d. increased by 4 units

6. A point object is placed on the optic axis of a convex lens of focal length f at a distance of $2f$ to the left of it. The diameter of the lens is d. An eye is placed at a distance of $3f$ to the right of the lens and a distance h below the optic axis. The maximum value of h to see the image is
a. d *b.* $\frac{d}{2}$
c. $\frac{d}{3}$ *d.* $\frac{d}{4}$

7. For CE transistor amplifier, the audio signal voltage across the collector resistance of 4 kΩ is 5 V. If the current amplification factor of the transistor is 100 and base resistance is 2 kΩ, then input signal voltage is
a. 75 mV *b.* 25 mV
c. 20 mV *d.* 50 mV

8. From the following p-V diagram, an ideal gas undergoing a change of state from A to B. Four different processes I, II, III and IV as shown in the figure may lead to same change of state.

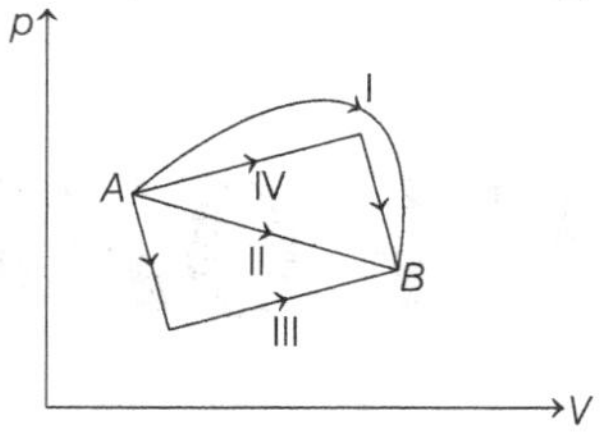

a. Work done is maximum in case I

b. Change in internal energy is same in all the four cases

c. Change in internal energy is same in IV and III cases, but not in I and II

d. Work done is minimum in case II

9. A copper and a steel wire of same diameter are connected end to end. A deforming force F_1 is applied to the wire which causes an elongation of 1 cm. The two wires will have

a. the same stress *b.* different stress
c. the same strain *d.* different strain

10. If kinetic energy of a body is increased by 300%, then percentage change in momentum will be

a. 100% *b.* 150% *c.* 265% *d.* 73.2%

11. Which of the following diagram represents the variation of the electric field with distance r from the centre of a uniformly charged non-conducting sphere of radius R?

a.

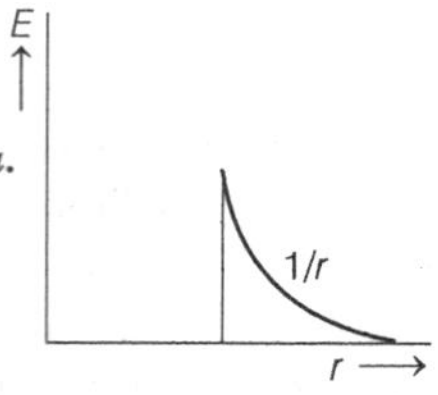

b.

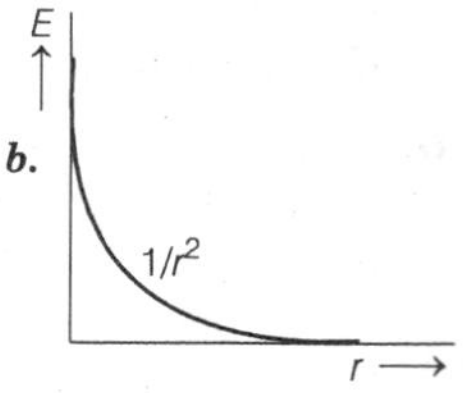

c.

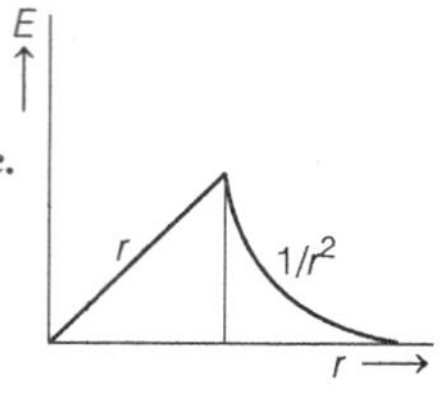

d.

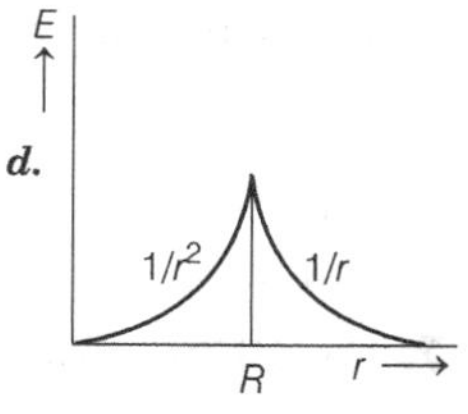

12. A DC ammeter and a hot wire ammeter are connected to a circuit in series. When a direct current is passed through circuit, the DC ammeter shows 6 A. When AC current flows through circuit, what is the average readings in DC ammeter and the AC ammeter, if DC and AC currents flow simultaneously through the circuit?

a. DC = 6 A, AC = 10 A *b.* DC = 3 A, AC = 5 A
c. DC = 5 A, AC = 8 A *d.* DC = 2 A, AC = 3 A

13. A bullet of mass m hits a mass M and gets embedded in it. If the block rises to a height h as a result of this collision, the velocity of the bullet before collision is

a. $v = \sqrt{2gh}$ *b.* $v = \sqrt{2gh}\left[1 + \left(\frac{m}{M}\right)\right]$

c. $v = \sqrt{2gh}\left(1 + \sqrt{\frac{M}{m}}\right)$ *d.* $v = \sqrt{2gh}\left[1 - \left(\frac{m}{M}\right)\right]$

14. A particle of mass m is moving in a horizontal circle of radius r under a centripetal force given by $\left(\frac{-K}{r^2}\right)$, where K is a constant. Then

a. the total energy of the particle is $\left(\frac{-K}{2r}\right)$

b. the kinetic energy of the particle is $\left(\frac{K}{r}\right)$

c. the potential energy of the particle is $\left(\frac{K}{2r}\right)$

d. the kinetic energy of the particle is $\left(\frac{-K}{r}\right)$

15. The height at which the acceleration due to gravity becomes $\frac{g}{16}$ (where, g = acceleration due to gravity on the surface of the earth) in terms of R is, if R is the radius of earth.

a. $2R$ *b.* $3R$
c. $\sqrt{2}R$ *d.* $\sqrt{3}R$

16. Which of the following series spectrum of hydrogen atom lies in ultraviolet region?

a. Paschen series *b.* Brackett series
c. Pfund series *d.* Lyman series

17. Speed of electromagnetic wave in a medium having relative permittivity ε_r and relative permeability μ_r is (speed of light in air, $c = 3 \times 10^8$ m/s)

a. $\frac{1}{\sqrt{\mu_r \varepsilon_r}}$ *b.* $\frac{c}{\sqrt{\mu_r \varepsilon_r}}$ *c.* $c\sqrt{\frac{\mu_r}{\varepsilon_r}}$ *d.* $\frac{c}{\mu_r \varepsilon_r}$

18. The wavelength of the second line of Balmer series is 486.4 nm. What is the wavelength of the first line of Lyman series?

a. 78.8 nm *b.* 121.6 nm
c. 418.2 nm *d.* 610.5 nm

19. A bat emitting an ultrasonic wave of frequency 4.5×10^4 Hz at speed of 6 m/s between two parallel walls. The two frequencies heard by the bat will be

a. 4.67×10^4 Hz, 4.34×10^4 Hz
b. 4.34×10^4 Hz, 4.67×10^4 Hz
c. 4.5×10^4 Hz, 5.4×10^4 Hz
d. 4.67×10^3 Hz, 4.34×10^4 Hz

20. A disc of moment of inertia 4 kg -m^2 revolving with 16 rad/s is placed on another disc of moment of inertia 8 Kg-m^2 revolving 4 rad/s. The angular frequency of composite disc

a. 4 rad/s *b.* $\frac{3}{16}$ rad/s *c.* 8 rad/s *d.* $\frac{16}{3}$ rad/s

21. An electric current I enters and leaves a uniform circular wire of radius r through diametrically opposite points. A charged particle q moves along the axis of circular wire passes through its centre with speed v. The magnetic force on the particle when it passes through the centre has a magnitude

a. $\frac{qv\mu_0 I}{2\pi r}$ *b.* $qv\frac{\mu_0 I}{\pi r}$ *c.* $\frac{qv\mu_0 I}{r}$ *d.* 0

22. Television frequencies are of the order of 100 MHz, while radio frequencies are of the order of 1 MHz. Using these as typical frequencies, the ratio of the emf generated in a loop antenna by a television wave to that generated by a radio wave, if both have equal electric field intensities.

a. 1 *b.* 10 *c.* 100 *d.* 66.6

23. A particle is performing simple harmonic motion. Equation of its motion is $x = 5\sin\left(4t - \frac{\pi}{6}\right)$, x being the displacement from mean position. Velocity (in ms^{-1}) of the particle at the instant when its displacement is 3, will be

a. $\frac{2\pi}{3}$ *b.* $\frac{5\pi}{6}$ *c.* 20 *d.* 16

24. A raft of density 600 g/m^3 and mass 120 kg floats in water. How much weight can be put on the raft to make it just sink?

a. 120 kg *b.* 200 kg *c.* 40 kg *d.* 80 kg

25. The displacement x of a particle in a straight line motion is given by $x = 1 - t - t^2$. The correct representation of the motion is

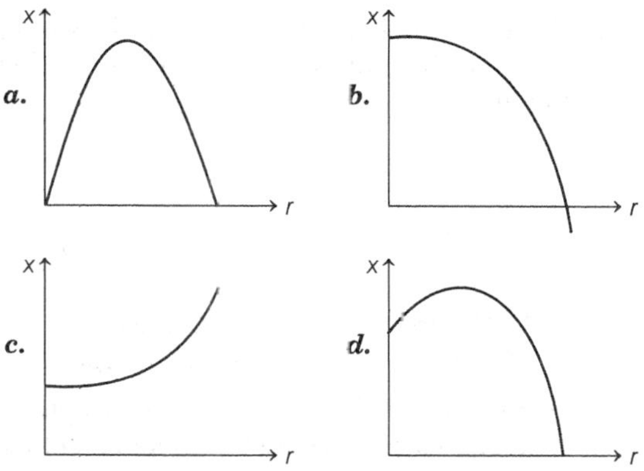

26. A galvanometer having a resistance of 4 Ω is shunted by a wire of resistance 2 Ω. If the total current is 1.5 A, the current passing through shunt is

a. 1.25 A *b.* 1 A *c.* 0.75 A *d.* 0.5 A

27. In Young's double slit experiment, the two slits are separated by 0.2 mm and they are 1 m from the screen. The wavelength of the light used is 500 nm. The distance between 6th maxima and 10th minima on the screen is closest to

a. 12 mm *b.* 10 mm *c.* 14 mm *d.* 8 mm

28. A series L-C-R circuit is connected to an AC source of 220 V and 50 Hz shown in figure. If the readings of the three voltmeters V_1, V_2 and V_3 are 65 V, 415 V and 204 V respectively, the value of inductance and capacitance will be

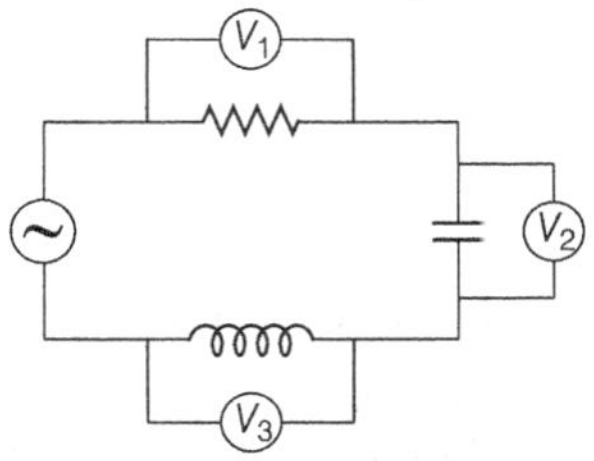

a. 2.0 H, 5 μF *b.* 1.0 H, 5 μF
c. 4.0 H, 6 μF *d.* 1.0 H, 2 μF

29. A regular hexagon of side m which is a wire of length 24 m is coiled on that hexagon. If current in hexagon is I, then the magnetic moment,

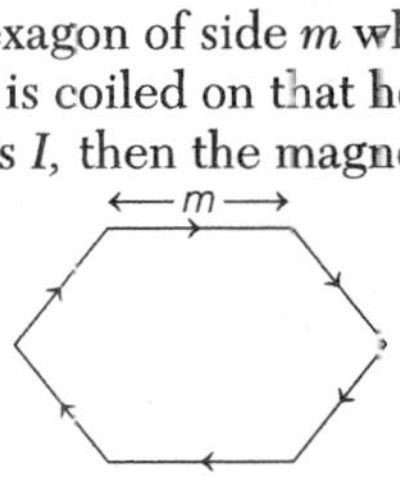

a. $6\sqrt{3}\, Im^2$ *b.* $3\sqrt{3}\, Im^2$ *c.* $\frac{3\sqrt{3}}{2} Im^2$ *d.* $6\, Im^2$

30. Which of the following gate give the similar output as the output of circuit diagram shown in the figure?

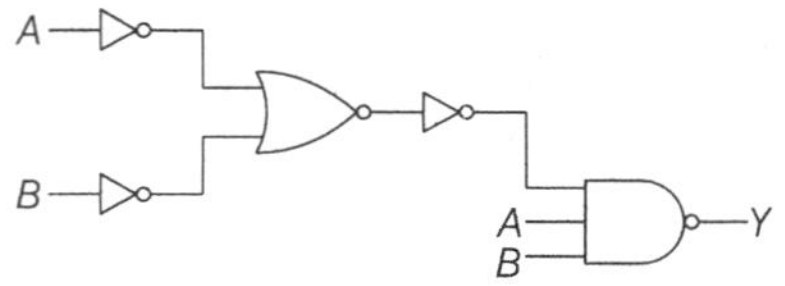

a. AND gate *b.* OR gate
c. NOR gate *d.* NAND gate

31. Water is poured in a tank through a cylindrical tube of area of cross-section A and ejecting water at a constant speed 4 m/s. The tank contains a hole of area $\frac{A}{2}$ at bottom. Level of water in the tank will not go up beyond

a. 5.6 m *b.* 4.8 m *c.* 3.2 m *d.* 1.8 m

32. If R and C denote resistance and capacitance of a material, then the dimension of CR will be :

a. $[ML^0T]$ *b.* $[M^0L^0T]$ *c.* $[M^0L^0T^2]$ *d.* $[M^2L^0T]$

33. An ideal gas is taken through the cycle $A \rightarrow B \rightarrow C \rightarrow A$, as shown in the figure. If the net heat supplied to the gas in the cycle is 5 J, the work done by the gas in the process $C \rightarrow A$ is,

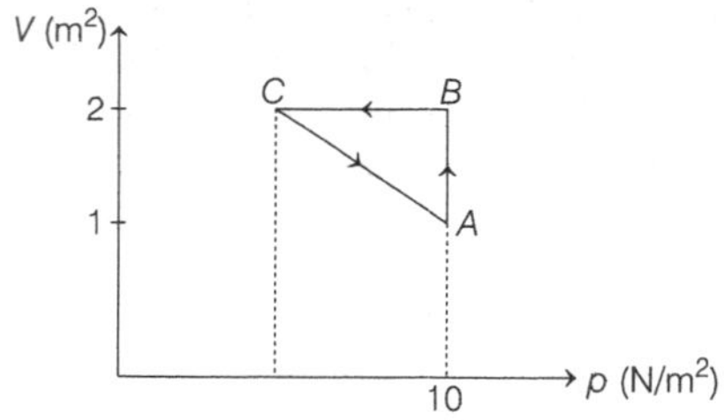

a. – 5 J *b.* – 10 J *c.* – 15 J *d.* – 20 J

34. From a circular disc of radius R, a square is cut out with a radius as its diagonal. The centre of mass of remaining portion is at a distance (from the centre)

a. $\frac{R}{(4\pi - 2)}$ *b.* $\frac{R}{2\pi}$ *c.* $\frac{R}{\pi - 2}$ *d.* $\frac{R}{2\pi - 2}$

35. A bar magnet of length 6 cm, is placed in the magnetic meridian with N pole, pointing towards the geographical north. Two neutral points, separated by a distance of 8 cm are obtained on the equitorial axis of the magnet. If $B_H = 1.2 \times 10^{-5}$ T. Then the pole strength of the magnet is

a. 0.75 A-m^2 *b.* 0.25 A-m^2
c. 0.50 A-m^2 *d.* 1.50 A-m^2

36. A force F applied on the wire of radius r and length L and change in the length of the wire is l. If the same force F is applied on the wire of the same material and radius $4r$ and length $4l$, then change in length of the other wire is,

a. $\frac{l}{4}$ *b.* $2l$
c. $\frac{l}{2}$ *d.* $4l$

37. A 30 mW laser beam has a cross-sectional area of 15 mm^2. The magnitude of the maximum electric field in this electromagnetic wave is given by $\begin{bmatrix} \text{Permittivity of space, } \varepsilon_0 = 9 \times 10^{-12} \\ \text{Speed of light, } c = 3 \times 10^8 \text{ m/s} \end{bmatrix}$

a. 1.22 kV/m *b.* 12 kV/m
c. 10 kV/m *d.* 201 kV/m

38. The average kinetic energy of a molecule in air at room temperature of 20°C

a. 6×10^{-22} J *b.* 7.06×10^{-21} J
c. 6.07×10^{-21} J *d.* 6.70×10^{-21} J

39. Two guns P and Q can fire bullets at speeds 2 km/s and 4 km/s, respectively. From a point on a horizontal ground, they are fired in all possible directions. The ratio of maximum or areas covered by the bullets fired by the two guns, on the ground is

a. 1 : 2 *b.* 1 : 4
c. 1 : 8 *d.* 1: 16

40. A cell of emf $2V$ is connected with a load of resistance 1.5 Ω. The power delivered by the cell to the load is maximum, then power transferred to the load is

a. 0.33 W *b.* 2.67 W
c. 1.33 W *d.* 3.25 W

41. A plane glass mirror of thickness 3 cm of material of $\mu = \frac{3}{2}$ is silvered on the black surface. When a point object is placed 9 cm from the front surface of the mirror, then the position of the brightest image from the front surface is

a. 9 cm *b.* 11 cm
c. 12 cm *d.* 13 cm

42. Ultraviolet light of wavelength 99 mm falls on a metal plate of work function 1.0 eV. If the mass of the electron is 9.1×10^{-31} kg, the wavelength of the fastest photoelectron emitted is

a. 0.63 nm *b.* 0.66 nm
c. 0.33 nm *d.* 0.36 nm

43. In Young's double slit experiment, the fringe width is found to be 0.4 mm. If the whole apparatus is immersed in a liquid of refractive index $\frac{4}{3}$ without changing geometrical arrangement, the new fringe width will be

a. 0.45 mm *b.* 0.4 mm *c.* 0.53 mm *d.* 0.30 mm

44. There are two identical containers C_1 and C_2 containing to identical gases. Gas in C_1 is reduced to half of its original volume adiabatically, while the gas in container C_2 is also reduced to half of its initial volume isothermally. Find the ratio of final pressure in these containers. (γ be the adiabatic constant).

a. 2 : 1 *b.* 1 : 2 *c.* $2^{\gamma} : 1$ *d.* $2^{\gamma-1} : 1$

45. If K_1 and K_2 are maximum kinetic energies of photoelectrons emitted when lights of wavelengths λ_1 and λ_2, respectively incident on a metallic surface and $\lambda_1 = 3\lambda_2$, then

a. $K_1 > \left(\frac{K_2}{3}\right)$ *b.* $K_1 < \left(\frac{K_2}{3}\right)$

c. $K_1 = 2K_2$ *d.* $K_2 = 2K_1$

46. A car is moving with a speed of 54 km/h. If after 3 s, the driver applies brakes and it stops, then how much distance is covered by the car before coming to rest?

a. 22.5 m *b.* 20 m *c.* 25 m *d.* 45.2 m

47. A source of sound emits sound waves at frequency f_0. It is moving towards an observer with fixed speed v_s ($v_s < v$, where v is the speed of sound in air.) If the observers were to move towards the source with speed v_0, one of the following two graphs (*A* and *B*) will give the correct variation of the frequency f heard by the observer as v_0 is changed.

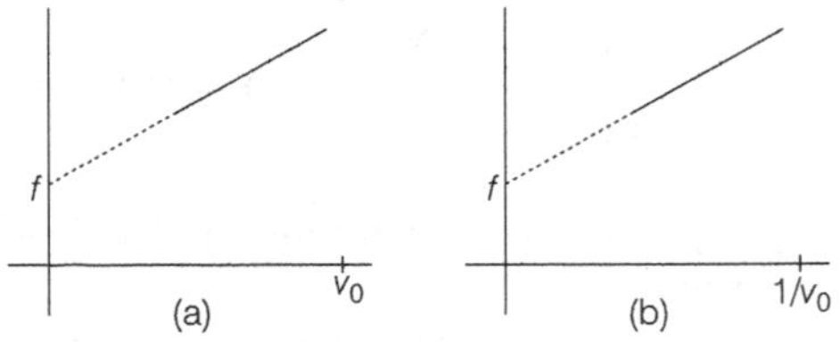

The variation of f with v_0 is given correctly by

a. graph *A* with slope $= \frac{f_0}{(v + v_s)}$

b. graph *B* with slope $= \frac{f_0}{(v - v_s)}$

c. graph *A* with slope $= \frac{f_0}{(v - v_s)}$

d. graph *B* with slope $= \frac{f_0}{(v + v_s)}$

48. In which mode of transmission, the heat waves travel along straight line with the speed of light?

a. Thermal radiation *b.* Forced convection

c. Natural convection *d.* Thermal conduction

49. The escape velocity of a projectile on the earth's surface is 11.2 km/s. A body is projected out with thrice this speed. The speed of the body far away from the earth will be

a. 22.4 km/s *b.* 31.7 km/s

c. 33.6 km/s *d.* None of these

50. Consider a compound slab consisting of two different materials having equal lengths, thickness and thermal conductivities K and $2K$ respectively. The equivalent thermal conductivity of the slab is

a. $\sqrt{2}K$ *b.* $3K$ *c.* $\frac{4}{3}K$ *d.* $\frac{2}{3}K$

51. A circular coil of 20 turns and radius 10 cm is placed in a uniform magnetic field of 0.10 T normal to the plane of the coil. If the current in the coil is 5 A, then the average force on each electron in the coil due to the magnetic field is

a. 2.5×10^{-25} N *b.* 4.5×10^{-25} N

c. 5×10^{-25} N *d.* 5.5×10^{-25} N

52. With what minimum acceleration can a fireman slide down a rope while breaking strength of the rope is $\frac{2}{3}$ of the weight?

a. $\frac{2}{3}g$ *b.* g *c.* $\frac{1}{3}g$ *d.* zero

53. The string of length 2 m is fixed at both ends. If the string vibrates in its fourth normal mode with a frequency of 500 Hz, then the waves would travel on it with a velocity of

a. 125 m/s *b.* 250 m/s

c. 500 m/s *d.* 1000 m/s

54. An alternating voltage = 200 sin 100*t* is applied to a series combination of $R = 30\,\Omega$ and an inductor of 400 mH. The power factor of the circuit is,

a. 0.01 *b.* 0.6 *c.* 0.05 *d.* 0.042

55. In the network shown in figure, the equivalent capacitance between points P and Q is

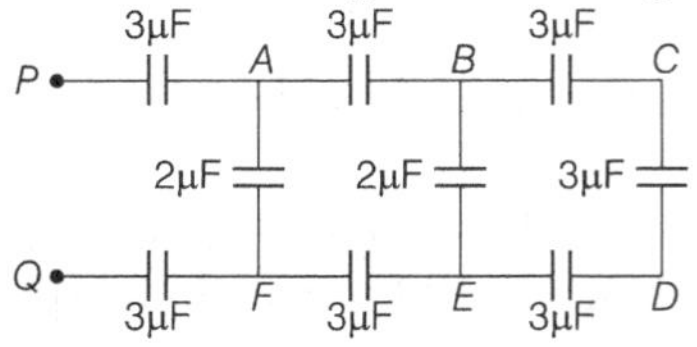

a. 1 μF *b.* 2 μF *c.* 3 μF *d.* 4 μF

56. The resultant of two forces acting at an angle of 120° is 10 kg-W and is perpendicular to one of the forces. That force is

a. $\frac{10}{\sqrt{3}}$ kg-W *b.* 10 kg-W

c. $20\sqrt{3}$ kg-W *d.* $10\sqrt{3}$ kg-W

57. Choose the incorrect statements.

a. Silicon is used in the fabrication of LED.

b. LED works on the principle of electroluminescence.

c. LED is a power efficient device.

d. LED is fabricated with direct band gap semiconductor.

58. Charge on electron is

a. 3.2×10^{-19} C *b.* 1.6×10^{-19} C

c. -1.6×10^{-19} C *d.* -3.2×10^{-19} C

59. Two charged spheres of −20 μC and 60 μC are kept at a certain distance. They are touched and kept again at the same distance. What is the ratio of force experienced before and after?

a. 1 : 3 *b.* 3 : 1 *c.* 2 : 1 *d.* 1 : 2

60. The AC voltage across a resistance can be measured using a

a. hot wire voltmeter

b. moving coil galvanometer

c. potential coil galvanometer

d. moving magnet galvanometer

CHEMISTRY

61. .... is unstable at cooking temperature, whereas the control of sweetness of food is difficult while using ....

a. Alitame and aspartame

b. Aspartame and sucralose

c. Aspartame and alitame

d. Alitame and sucralose

62. The chemical formula of Lucas reagent is

a. Anhy. $ZnCl_2/HCl$ *b.* $C_6H_5SO_2Cl$

c. NaOH + CaO *d.* HNO_2

63. Give the correct order of acidity of

a. $HClO_4 < HClO_3 < HClO_2 < HClO$

b. $HClO < HClO_2 < HClO_3 < HClO_4$

c. $HClO_4 < HClO_2 < HClO < HClO_3$

d. $HClO < HClO_3 < HClO_2 < HClO_4$

64. The process of aggregation of colloidal particles into an insoluble precipitate by the addition of suitable electrolyte is called

a. coagulation

b. diffusion

c. peptisation

d. electrolysis

65. Alkyl halides undergoing S_N2 reaction do inverse

a. racemic mixture

b. retention of configuration

c. formation of carbocation

d. inversion of configuration

66. X and Y in the following reactions are

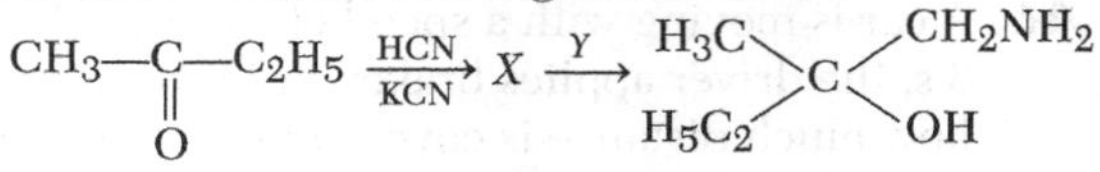

a. $X =$ 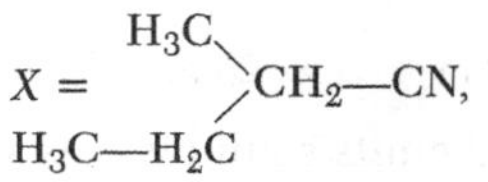

, $Y = NaBH_4$

b. $X =$ 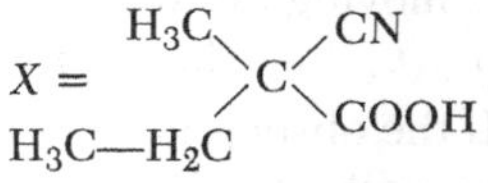

, $Y = CH_3NH_2$

c. $X =$ 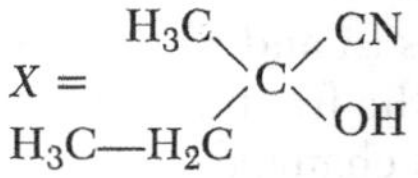

, $Y = LiAlH_4$

d. $X =$ 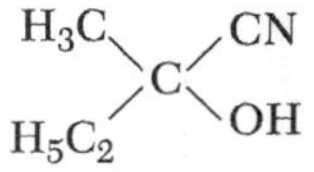

, $Y = CH_3NH_2$

67. Doping of silicon (Si) with indium (In) leads to the formation of

a. n-type semiconductor *b.* metal

c. p-type semiconductor *d.* insulator

68. For the reaction, $H_2(g) + I_2(g) \rightleftharpoons 2HI(g)$ the position of equilibrium can be shifted to the right by

a. addition of HI

b. addition of both I_2 and HI

c. increasing temperature

d. addition of I_2

69. Which of the following are not path functions?

I. $H-TS$ II. W

II. q IV. $q+W$

a. I and III   *b.* I, II, IV

c. II, III and IV   *d.* I and IV

70. The system that forms maximum boiling azeotropes is

a. acetone-chloroform   *b.* ethyl alcohol-water

c. benzene-toluene   *d.* CS_2 + acetone

71. $KMnO_4$ acts as an oxidising agent in acidic medium. The number of moles of $KMnO_4$ that will be required to react with one mole of oxalate ions (to form CO_2) in acidic solution is

a. $\frac{2}{5}$ *b.* $\frac{5}{2}$

c. 5   *d.* $\frac{5}{4}$

72. What can be A and B in the following reaction?

$$CH_3CH{=}CH_2 \xrightarrow{A} CH_3CH_2CH_2Br \xrightarrow{B} CH_3CH_2CH_2OH$$

	A	B
a.	HBr	alc. KOH
b.	HBr, Peroxide	alc. KOH
c.	HBr, Peroxide	*aq.* KOH, Δ
d.	HBr	*aq.* KOH, Δ

73. Which of the following is a false statement?

a. Methoxymethane has higher boiling point than ethanol.

b. Alcohols are more soluble is water than hydrocarbons of comparable molecular mass.

c. *ortho*-and *para*-nitrophenols are more acidic than phenols.

d. Phenol is more acidic than alcohol.

74. Which of the following molecules does not exhibit dipole moment?

(i) CCl_4 (ii) CO_2

(iii) NH_3 (iv) $CHCl_3$

(v) H_2O (vi) $CH_3—O—CH_3$

a. (ii), (v), (iv)   *b.* (i), (iii), (vi)

c. (i), (ii)   *d.* (iii), (iv), (vi)

75. Which of the following is highly basic?

a. Diphenylamine   *b.* Benzylamine

c. Aniline   *d.* Triphenylamine

76. The relation between work done in reversible and irreversible process is

a. $W_{irr} > W_{rev}$ *b.* $W_{irr} < W_{rev}$

c. $W_{irr} = W_{rev}$ *d.* $W_{irr} \neq W_{rev}$

77. What is the function platelets?

a. It binds to oxygen

b. It binds to carbon dioxide

c. It forms cyanide in body

d. It leads to coagulation of blood

78. The monosaccharides of maltose is

a. α-D-glucose and α-D-glucose

b. β-D-glucose and α-D-glucose

c. α-D-glucose and α-D-fructose

d. α-D-glucose and β-D-fructose

79. Which of the following does not affect solubility of a gas in liquid?

a. Nature of gas and liquid

b. Pressure

c. Concentration

d. Temperature

80. Which of the following statement is incorrect for H_2O_2 structure?

a. It has an open book structure.

b. Its dihedral angle is 180°.

c. It O—O bond length is 145.8 and O—H is 98.8.

d. Angle between both planes is 90.2.

81. A newly prepared radioactive nuclide has a decay constant of 6.93 s^{-1}. What is the half-life of the nuclide?

a. 0.1 s   *b.* 0.2 s

c. 0.3 s   *d.* 0.4 s

82. Which of the following show both Frenkel and Schottky defect?

a. ZnS   *b.* AgBr

c. NaCl   *d.* AgCl

83. The essential amino acid are

(i) Leucine   (ii) Glutamic acid

(iii) Asparagine   (iv) Valine

correct option is

a. (i), (ii)   *b.* (ii), (iii)

c. (iii), (iv)   *d.* (i), (iv)

84. Increasing order of bond order of oxygen and its ions is

a. $O_2 < O_2^+ < O_2^{2-} < O_2^-$

b. $O_2^- < O_2^{2-} < O_2^+ < O_2$

c. $O_2^+ < O_2 < O_2^- < O_2^{2-}$

d. $O_2^{2-} < O_2^- < O_2 < O_2^+$

85. Minimum number of nodes are present in
a. 2*s* *b.* 3*s* *c.* 4*s* *d.* 5*s*

86. pH of 10^{-3}M solution of KOH is
a. 7.01 *b.* 2 *c.* 11 *d.* 9

87. Barbiturates are used to treat
a. fatigue *b.* hallucinations
c. allergies *d.* depression

88. Which of the product is not possible in Wurtz reaction?
a. Methane *b.* Ethane *c.* Propane *d.* Butane

89. The colour of CrO_4^{2-} changes to $Cr_2O_7^{2-}$ is
a. yellow to orange *b.* orange to yellow
c. yellow to blue *d.* orange to blue

90. On treatment of glucose with bromine water the product formed is
a. saccharic acid *b.* gluconic acid
c. glutamic acid *d.* acetic acid

91. Which among the following forms minimum boiling azeotropes?
(i) Heptane + Octane
(ii) Water + Nitric acid
(iii) Ethanol + Water
(iv) Acetone + Carbon dioxide
a. (i), (ii), (iv) *b.* (i), (ii) only
c. (i), (iii), (iv) *d.* (iv) only

92. Which of the following statement is incorrect about activation energy?
a. Higher the activation energy slower is the rate of reaction.
b. Catalyst decreases the activation energy.
c. SI unit of activation energy is J/mol/K^{-1}.
d. Activation energy depends upon the rate of reaction.

93. The P—O bond order in PO_4^{3-} is
a. 1 *b.* 1.5 *c.* 1.45 *d.* 1.25

94. $O_2^-, F^-, Mg^{2+}, Al^{3+}, O_2, F_2$. How many of the species given above isoelectronic?
a. 4 *b.* 2 *c.* 3 *d.* 5

95. How many atoms are present in hcp per unit cell?
a. 4 *b.* 2 *c.* 1 *d.* 6

96. The equilibrium constant, K_C for $3C_2H_2(g) \rightleftharpoons C_6H_6(g)$ is 4 L^2mol^{-2}. If the equilibrium concentration of benzene is 0.5 mol^{-1} than what is the value of concentration of ethylene?
a. 0.05 mol/L *b.* 0.5 mol/L
c. 0.25 mol/L *d.* 0.025 mol/L

97. Which of the following artificial sweeteners can be used in soft drinks only?
a. Alitame *b.* Aspartame
c. Sucralose *d.* Saccharine

98. Identify the product formed in the given reaction.

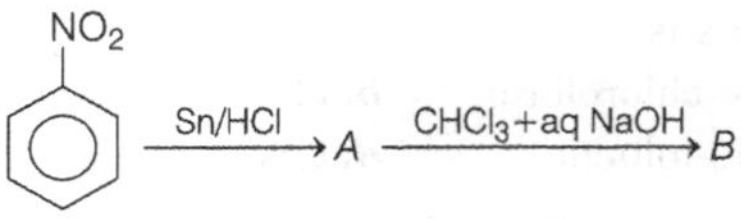

A B

a.

b.

c.

d.

99. Which of the following gas readily de-colourises the acidified $KMnO_4$ solution?
a. CO_2 *b.* SO_2
c. P_2O_5 *d.* NO_2

100. What is the molecular mass of *X* if the rate of diffusion of methane is twice that of *X*.
a. 32.0 *b.* 64
c. 40 *d.* 80

101. Which of the following is used to prepare the inner lining of a blast furnance?
a. Graphite bricks *b.* Silica bricks
c. Fire clay bricks *d.* basic bricks

102. What will be the emf of the following cell at 25°C?
$Fe/Fe^{2+}(0.001\ M)||H^+\ (0.01\ M)|H_2(g)$ (1 Bar) | Pt (*s*)
$E^\circ_{(Fe^{2+}/Fe)} = -0.44\ V$; $E^\circ_{(H^+/H_2)} = 0.00\ V$
a. 0.44 V *b.* –0.44 V
c. 0.41 V *d.* –0.41 V

103. Which of the following vitamin is responsible for beri-beri disease?
a. A *b.* B_1
c. K *d.* D

104. Find the product formed for the given reaction.

$$C_6H_5CHO + H_3C—CH_2—CHO \xrightarrow{\text{Dil. NaOH}/\Delta}$$

a. $C_2H_5—CH=\underset{CH_3}{\underset{|}{C}}—CHO$

b. $C_6H_5—CH_2CH_2CH_2CHO$

c. $C_6H_5—CH_2—\underset{CH_3}{\underset{|}{C}}—CHO$

d. $C_6H_5CH=\underset{CH_3}{\underset{|}{C}}—CHO$

105. In which of the following changes, entropy decreases?

a. Rusting of iron

b. Melting of ice

c. Vaporisation of camphor

d. Crystallisation of sucrose from solution

106. Which of the following is added to soaps to impart antiseptic properties?

a. Iodine *b.* Furacine

c. Bithional *d.* Terpineol

107. Which among the following will not liberate nitrogen on reaction with nitrous acid?

a. dimethylamine *b.* 2-aminopropane

c. ethylamine *d.* methylamine

108. The complex which does not show optical isomerism is

a. *cis* - $[Co(en)_2Cl_2]Cl$

b. *cis* - $[CrCl_2(ox)_2]^{3-}$

c. *cis* - $[CoCl(en)_2(NH_3)]^{2+}$

d. *cis* - $[Co(NH_3)_4Cl_2]^+$

109. What will be the density of N_2 gas at 230°C and 3 atm pressure? ($R = 0.082$ L atm K^{-1} mol^{-1})

a. 3.41 g/mL *b.* 2.03 g/mL

c. 4.30 g/mL *d.* 0.27 g/mL

110. The solution which have lowest freezing point is

a. 0.2 M K_2SO_4 *b.* 0.2 M KCl

c. 0.2 M $NaNO_3$ *d.* 0.2 M $MgSO_4$

111. Calculate the molar conductance of 0.025 M aqueous solution of calcium chloride at 25°C. The specific conductance of calcium chloride is 12.04×10^{-2} Sm^{-1}

a. 4.816×10^{-5} Sm^2 mol^{-1}

b. 3.816×10^{-5} Sm^2 mol^{-1}

c. 381.6×10^{-5} Sm^2 mol^{-1}

d. 481.6×10^{-5} Sm^2 mol^{-1}

112. For the reaction $2N_2O_5 \longrightarrow 4NO_2 + O_2$.

If inital pressure is 100 atm and rate constant k is 3.38×10^{-5} s^{-1}. After 20 min the final pressure of N_2O_5 will be

a. 96 atm *b.* 50 atm

c. 70 atm *d.* 60 atm

113. The difference between heat capacity at constant pressure and heat capacity at constant volume is

a. R *b.* $\frac{R}{T}$

c. $\frac{R}{V}$ *d.* 1

114. Which of the following gas is responsible for acid rain?

a. Sulphur dioxide and nitrous oxide

b. Sulphur dioxide and carbon monoxide

c. Sulphur dioxide and carbon dioxide

d. Sulphur dioxide and nitrogen oxide

115. Which of the following compound does not exists?

a. NCl_3 *b.* NCl_5

c. $SbCl_3$ *d.* NI_3

116. The major product in the given reaction is

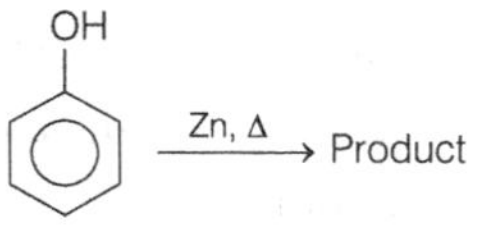

a. toluene

b. *p*-methyl toluene

c. benzene

d. *o*-methyl benzene

117. The spectrum of He^+ is similar to

a. H *b.* Li^+

c. Na *d.* He^+

118. The Paschen series of hydrogen spectrum lies in which region?

a. UV region *b.* IR region

c. Visible region *d.* Microwave region

119. The oxidation state of nickel in $[Ni(CO_4)]$ is

a. 1 *b.* 2

c. 3 *d.* 0

120. The correct condition for physical adsorption is

a. High T and high p

b. High T and low p

c. Low T and high p

d. T and p do not affect

MATHEMATICS

121. The value of $3^{\log_4 5} - 5^{\log_4 3}$ is

a. 0 *b.* 1 *c.* 2 *d.* 4

122. If the tangent to the curve $xy + ax + by = 0$ at $(1, 1)$ is inclined at an angle $\tan^{-1} 2$ with X-axis, then

a. $a = 1, b = 2$ *b.* $a = 1, b = -2$
c. $a = -1, b = 2$ *d.* $a = -1, b = -2$

123. If $\lim\limits_{x \to 0} \dfrac{(1 + a^3) + 8e^{1/x}}{1 + (1 - b^3)e^{1/x}} = 2$, then

a. $a = 1, b = 2$ *b.* $a = 1, b = -3^{1/3}$
c. $a = 2, b = 3^{1/3}$ *d.* None of these

124. If two circles $(x - 1)^2 + (y - 3)^2 = r^2$ and $x^2 + y^2 - 8x + 2y + 8 = 0$ intersect in two distinct points, then

a. $2 < r < 8$ *b.* $r < 2$ *c.* $r = 2$ *d.* $r > 2$

125. The approximate value of $(0.007)^{1/3}$ is

a. $\dfrac{21}{120}$ *b.* $\dfrac{23}{120}$ *c.* $\dfrac{29}{120}$ *d.* $\dfrac{31}{120}$

126. The circle $x^2 + y^2 + 4x - 7y + 12 = 0$ cuts an intercept on Y-axis of length

a. 3 *b.* 4 *c.* 7 *d.* 1

127. Let $f(x) = a - (x - 3)^{8/9}$, then maxima of $f(x)$ is

a. 3 *b.* $a - 3$ *c.* a *d.* None

128. If the derivative of the function $f(x) = \begin{cases} bx^2 + ax + 4; & x \geq -1 \\ ax^2 + b; & x < -1 \end{cases}$ is everywhere continuous, then

a. $a = 2, b = 3$ *b.* $a = 3, b = 2$
c. $a = -2, b = -3$ *d.* $a = -3, b = -2$

129. If $\lim\limits_{x \to \infty} \left(1 + \dfrac{a}{x} + \dfrac{b}{x^2}\right)^{2x} = e^2$, then

a. $a = 1, b = 2$ *b.* $a = 2, b = 1$
c. $a = 1, b \in R$ *d.* None of these

130. $S \equiv x^2 + y^2 + 2x + 3y + 1 = 0$ and $S' \equiv x^2 + y^2 + 4x + 3y + 2 = 0$ are two circles. The point $(-3, -2)$ lies

a. inside S' only *b.* inside S only
c. inside S and S' *d.* outside S and S'

131. The probability of choosing randomly a number c from the set $\{1, 2, 3, \ldots 9\}$ such that the quadratic equation $x^2 + 4x + c = 0$ has real roots, is

a. $\dfrac{1}{9}$ *b.* $\dfrac{2}{9}$ *c.* $\dfrac{3}{9}$ *d.* $\dfrac{4}{9}$

132. Shade the feasible region for the inequations $6x + 4y \leq 120$, $3x + 10y \leq 180$, $x, y \geq 0$ in a rough figure.

a.

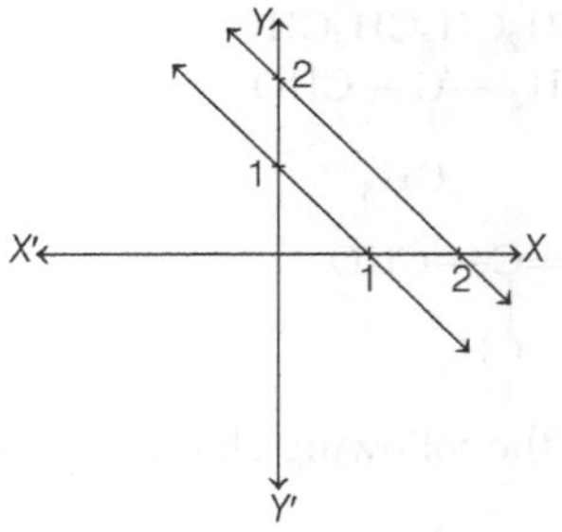

b.

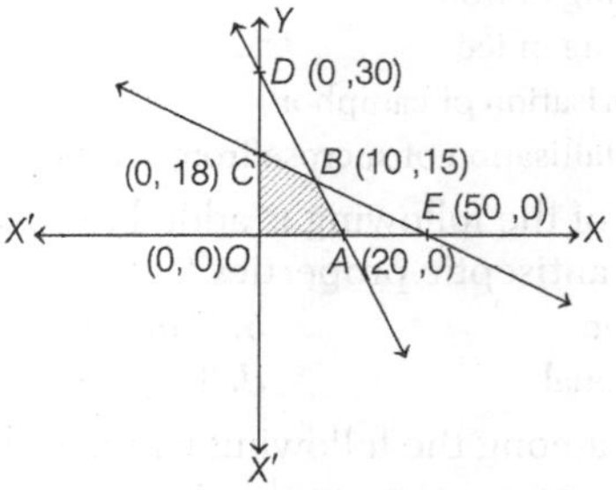

c.

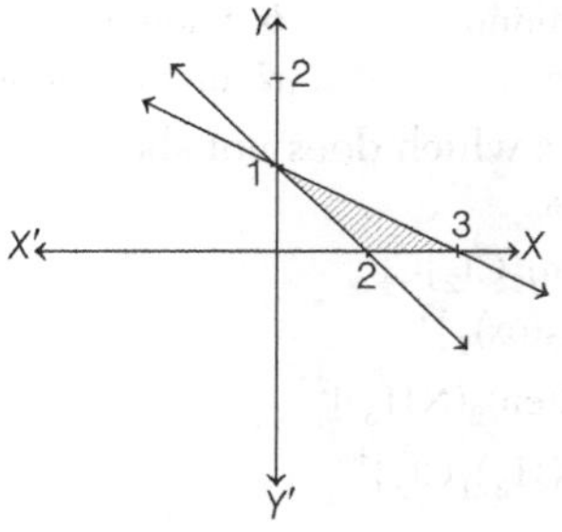

d.

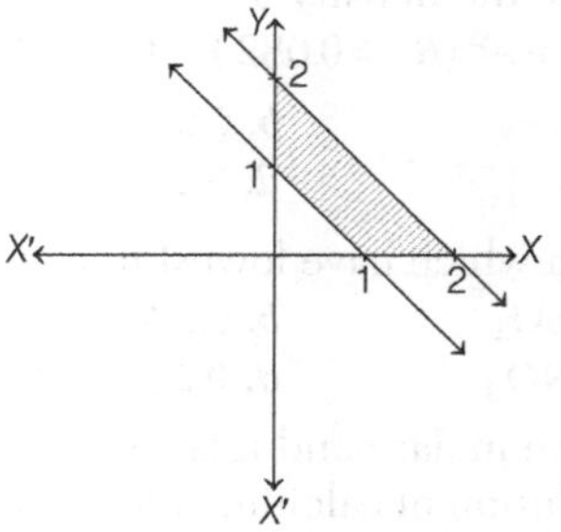

133. The maximum of Z is where, $Z = 4x + 2y$ subject to constraints $4x + 2y \geq 46$, $x + 3y \leq 24$ and $x, y \geq 0$ is

a. 46 *b.* 96
c. 52 *d.* None of these

134. If for any 2×2 square matrix A,

$A(adj\ A) = \begin{bmatrix} 8 & 0 \\ 0 & 8 \end{bmatrix}$, then find the value of det (A).

a. 6 *b.* 7 *c.* 8 *d.* 5

135. If $A = \begin{bmatrix} a & 0 & 0 \\ 0 & a & 0 \\ 0 & 0 & a \end{bmatrix}$, then $|A||adj\ A|$ is equal to

a. a^{3n} *b.* a^{-3n} *c.* $-a^{3n}$ *d.* $2a^{3n}$

136. If $A = \begin{bmatrix} 2-k & 2 \\ 1 & 3-k \end{bmatrix}$ is a singular matrix, then the value of $5k - k^2$ is

a. 0 *b.* 6 *c.* –6 *d.* 4

137. If θ be the angle between the vectors $\mathbf{a} = 2\hat{i} + 2\hat{j} - \hat{k}$ and $\mathbf{b} = 6\hat{i} - 3\hat{j} + 2\hat{k}$, then

a. $\cos\theta = \frac{4}{21}$ *b.* $\cos\theta = \frac{3}{19}$

c. $\cos\theta = \frac{2}{19}$ *d.* $\cos\theta = \frac{5}{21}$

138. If x, y and z are non-zero real numbers and $\mathbf{a} = x\hat{i} + 2\hat{j}$, $\mathbf{b} = y\hat{j} + 3\hat{k}$ and $\mathbf{c} = x\hat{i} + y\hat{j} + z\hat{k}$ are such that $\mathbf{a} \times \mathbf{b} = z\hat{i} - 3\hat{j} + \hat{k}$, then $[\mathbf{a}\,\mathbf{b}\,\mathbf{c}]$ is equal to

a. 3 *b.* 10 *c.* 9 *d.* 6

139. Maximum value of $z = 12x + 3y$, subject to constraints $x \geq 0$, $y \geq 0$, $x + y \leq 5$ and $3x + y \leq 9$ is

a. 15 *b.* 36 *c.* 60 *d.* 40

140. If $\mathbf{p} = \hat{i} + \hat{j}$, $\mathbf{q} = 4\hat{k} - \hat{j}$ and $\mathbf{r} = \hat{i} + \hat{k}$, then the unit vector in the direction of $3\mathbf{p} + \mathbf{q} - 2\mathbf{r}$ is

a. $\frac{1}{3}(\hat{i} + 2\hat{j} + 2\hat{k})$ *b.* $\frac{1}{3}(\hat{i} - 2\hat{j} - 2\hat{k})$

c. $\frac{1}{3}(\hat{i} - 2\hat{j} + 2\hat{k})$ *d.* $\hat{i} + 2\hat{j} + 2\hat{k}$

141. The line $\frac{x-3}{4} = \frac{y-4}{5} = \frac{z-5}{6}$ is parallel to the plane

a. $3x + 4y + 5z = 7$ *b.* $x + y + z = 2$

c. $x - 2y + z = 0$ *d.* $2x + 3y + 4z = 0$

142. $\int \frac{1}{x\sqrt{ax - x^2}}\,dx$ is

a. $\frac{-3}{a}\sqrt{\frac{a-x}{x}} + C$ *b.* $-\frac{2}{a}\sqrt{\frac{x}{a-x}} + C$

c. $\frac{-2}{a}\sqrt{\frac{a-x}{x}} + C$ *d.* None of these

143. $\int \frac{3^x}{\sqrt{1-9^x}}\,dx$ is equal to

a. $(\log 3)\sin^{-1} 3^x + C$ *b.* $\frac{1}{3}\sin^{-1}(3^x) + C$

c. $\frac{1}{\log 3}\sin^{-1} 3^x + C$ *d.* $3\log 3 \sin^{-1} 3^x + C$

144. $\int_{-\frac{\pi}{2}}^{\frac{\pi}{2}} \cos x\,dx$

a. 2 *b.* 0 *c.* –1 *d.* 5

145. The angle between the lines $\frac{x+4}{3} = \frac{y-1}{5} = \frac{z+3}{4}$ and $\frac{x+1}{1} = \frac{y-4}{1} = \frac{z-5}{2}$ is

a. 30° *b.* $\cos^{-1}\left(\frac{3}{2\sqrt{2}}\right)$

c. $\cos^{-1}\left(\frac{8}{5\sqrt{3}}\right)$ *d.* None of these

146. The point of intersection of the lines $\frac{x-1}{1} = \frac{y-1}{2} = \frac{z-2}{3}$ and $\frac{x-5}{2} = \frac{y-2}{1} = z$ is

a. (1, –2, 0) *b.* (3, 1, 0)

c. (–2, –5, –7) *d.* None of these

147. Five persons A, B, C, D and E are in queue of a shop. The Probability that A and B are always together is

a. $\frac{2}{5}$ *b.* $\frac{1}{4}$ *c.* $\frac{3}{5}$ *d.* $\frac{2}{3}$

148. If the probability for A to fail in an examination is 0.2 and that for B is 0.3, then the probability that either A or B fail is

a. 0.38 *b.* 0.44

c. 0.50 *d.* 0.94

149. Three vertices are chosen randomly from the seven vertices of a regular 7-sided polygon. The probability that they form the vertices of an isosceles triangle is

a. $\frac{1}{7}$ *b.* $\frac{1}{3}$ *c.* $\frac{3}{7}$ *d.* $\frac{3}{5}$

150. If A, B and C are three mutually exclusive and exhaustive events such that $P(A) = 2P(B) = 3P(C)$. What is $P(B)$?

a. $\frac{6}{11}$ *b.* $\frac{6}{22}$ *c.* $\frac{1}{6}$ *d.* $\frac{1}{3}$

151. If $U_{n+1} = 3U_n - 2U_{n-1}$ and $U_0 = 2$, $U_1 = 3$, then U_n is equal to

a. $1 - 2^n$ *b.* $2^n + 1$ *c.* $2^n - 1$ *d.* $2^n + 2$

152. If $4^n + 15n + P$ is divisible by 9 for all $n \in N$, then the least negative integral value of P is

a. -1 *b.* -2 *c.* -3 *d.* -4

153. $(2^{3n} - 1)$ is divisible by

a. 6 *b.* 7 *c.* 8 *d.* 9

154. If $S = \frac{2^2 - 1}{2} + \frac{3^2 - 2}{6} + \frac{4^2 - 3}{12} + \ldots$ upto 10 terms, then S is equal to

a. $\frac{120}{11}$ *b.* $\frac{13}{11}$ *c.* $\frac{110}{11}$ *d.* $\frac{19}{11}$

155. $\sum_{n=1}^{m} n \cdot n!$ is equal to

a. $m! - 1$ *b.* $(m-1)! - 1$
c. $(m+1)! - 1$ *d.* $m!(m-1)!$

156. The first and fifth terms of an A.P. are –14 and 2 respectively and the sum of its n terms is 40. The value of n is

a. 8 *b.* 12 *c.* 10 *d.* 13

157. The solution of the differential equation $\frac{d^2y}{dx^2} = 0$ represents

a. all circles in a plane
b. all straight lines in a plane
c. all parabolas in a plane
d. all ellipses in a plane

158. The solution of the differential equation $\frac{dy}{dx} + \sqrt{\frac{1-y^2}{1-x^2}} = 0$ is

a. $\cos^{-1} x + \cos^{-1} y = c$ *b.* $\sin^{-1} x + \sin^{-1} y = c$
c. $\cosh^{-1} x + \cosh^{-1} y = c$ *d.* $\sinh^{-1} x + \sinh^{-1} y = c$

159. The solution of the differential equation $x\frac{dy}{dx} = \cot y$ is

a. $y \cos x = c$ *b.* $x \cos y = c$
c. $\log(x \cos y) = c$ *d.* $\log(y \cos x) = c$

160. If ${}^nC_3 = 220$, then $n = ?$

a. 11 *b.* 12 *c.* 10 *d.* 9

161. A multiple choice examination has 5 questions. Each question has three alternative answers of which exactly one is correct. The probability that a student will get 4 or more correct answer just by guessing, is

a. $\frac{13}{3^5}$ *b.* $\frac{11}{3^5}$ *c.* $\frac{10}{3^5}$ *d.* $\frac{17}{3^5}$

162. If $\sin A + \sin B = a$ and $\cos A + \cos B = b$, then $\cos(A + B)$ equals?

a. $\frac{a^2 + b^2}{b^2 - a^2}$ *b.* $\frac{2ab}{a^2 + b^2}$ *c.* $\frac{b^2 - a^2}{a^2 + b^2}$ *d.* $\frac{a^2 - b^2}{a^2 + b^2}$

163. What is $\frac{\cos\theta}{1 - \tan\theta} + \frac{\sin\theta}{1 - \cot\theta}$ equal to?

a. $\sin\theta - \cos\theta$ *b.* $2\sin\theta$
c. $\sin\theta + \cos\theta$ *d.* $2\cos\theta$

164. Find the general solution of $\sin 2x + \cos x = 0$.

a. $(n \pm 1)\frac{\pi}{2}$

b. $n\pi \pm \frac{\pi}{2}$

c. $n\pi + (-1)^n \frac{7\pi}{6}$ or $(2n \pm 1)\frac{\pi}{2}$

d. None of the above

165. If $f(x) + 2f(1-x) = x^2 + 5$ $\forall$ real values of x, then $f(x)$ is given by

a. $x^2 - 5$ *b.* 2
c. $\frac{(x-2)^2 + 3}{3}$ *d.* None of these

166. If $A = \{3, 5, 7\}$ and $B = \{1, 2, 3, 5\}$, then $A \times B \cap B \times A$ is equal to

a. $\{(3, 3), (5, 3), (2, 7), (7, 2)\}$
b. $\{(3, 3), (3, 5), (5, 3), (5, 5)\}$
c. $\{(3, 3), (5, 5)\}$
d. $\{(3, 5), (5, 5), (5, 3)\}$

167. Total number of elements in the power set of A containing 17 elements is

a. 2^{17+1} *b.* 2^{17-1} *c.* $17^2 - 1$ *d.* 2^{17}

168. The argument of $\frac{1 - i\sqrt{3}}{1 + i\sqrt{3}}$ is

a. $\frac{\pi}{3}$ *b.* $\frac{2\pi}{3}$ *c.* $\frac{4\pi}{3}$ *d.* $\frac{-2\pi}{3}$

169. Evaluate $\left[i^{22} + \left(\frac{1}{i}\right)^{25}\right]^3$

a. $4(i-1)$ *b.* $2 - 7i$ *c.* $i - 1$ *d.* $2(1-i)$

170. $(i + \sqrt{3})^{100} + (i - \sqrt{3})^{100} + 2^{100}$ is equal to

a. 0 *b.* 1 *c.* –1 *d.* 2^{101}

171. There are 12 points in a plane out of which 3 points are collinear. How many straight lines can be drawn by joining any two of them?

a. 60 *b.* 64 *c.* 72 *d.* 84

173. A regular polygon of n sides has 170 diagonals, then n is equal to

a. -20 b. -17 c. 24 d. 20

174. Let the equation of the pair of lines $y = px$ and $y = qx$ can be written as $(y - px)(y - qx) = 0$. Then the equation of the pair of the angle bisectors of the line $x^2 - 4xy - 5y^2 = 0$ is

a. $x^2 - 3xy + y^2 = 0$ b. $x^2 + 4xy - y^2 = 0$

c. $x^2 + 3xy - y^2 = 0$ d. $x^2 - 3xy - y^2 = 0$

175. The distance of the point (1, 2) from the line $x + y + 2 = 0$ measured along the line parallel to $2x - y = 5$ is equal to

a. $\frac{125}{3}$ b. $\frac{125}{\sqrt{3}}$

c. $\frac{5\sqrt{5}}{3}$ d. $\frac{5\sqrt{3}}{3}$

176. The slope of lines which makes an angle 45° with the line $2x - y = -7$

a. $\frac{1}{3}, -3$ b. $-1, 1$ c. $3, \frac{-1}{3}$ d. $1, \frac{1}{3}$

177. If 2 and 3 are intercepts of a line $L = 0$, then the distance of $L \equiv 0$ from the origin is

a. $\frac{5}{\sqrt{13}}$ b. $\frac{\sqrt{13}}{6}$ c. $\frac{6}{\sqrt{13}}$ d. 1

178. The total number of terms in the expansion of $(x + y)^{100} + (x - y)^{100}$ is

a. 49 b. 50 c. 51 d. 99

179. The coefficient of x^{20} in the expansion of $(1 + 3x + 3x^2 + x^3)^{20}$ is

a. ${}^{60}C_{40}$ b. ${}^{30}C_{20}$

c. ${}^{15}C_2$ d. None of these

180. In the expansion of $(1 - 3x + 3x^2 - x^3)^{2n}$, the middle term is

a. $(n + 1)$ th term b. $(2n + 1)$ th term

c. $(3n + 1)$ th term d. None of these

COMEDK 2022

ANSWERS

Physics

1. (a)	2. (c)	3. (b)	4. (a)	5. (c)	6. (d)	7. (b)	8. (a,b)	9. (a,d)	10. (a)
11. (c)	12. (a)	13. (c)	14. (a)	15. (b)	16. (d)	17. (b)	18. (b)	19. (a)	20. (c)
21. (d)	22. (c)	23. (d)	24. (d)	25. (b)	26. (b)	27. (d)	28. (b)	29. (a)	30. (a)
31. (c)	32. (b)	33. (a)	34. (a)	35. (b)	36. (a)	37. (a)	38. (c)	39. (d)	40. (a)
41. (d)	42. (d)	43. (d)	44. (d)	45. (b)	46. (a)	47. (c)	48. (a)	49. (b)	50. (c)
51. (c)	52. (c)	53. (c)	54. (b)	55. (a)	56. (a)	57. (a)	58. (c)	59. (b)	60. (b)

Chemistry

61. (c)	62. (a)	63. (b)	64. (a)	65. (d)	66. (c)	67. (c)	68. (d)	69. (d)	70. (a)
71. (a)	72. (c)	73. (a)	74. (c)	75. (b)	76. (b)	77. (d)	78. (a)	79. (c)	80. (b)
81. (a)	82. (b)	83. (d)	84. (d)	85. (a)	86. (c)	87. (d)	88. (a)	89. (a)	90. (b)
91. (c)	92. (c)	93. (d)	94. (a)	95. (d)	96. (b)	97. (b)	98. (b)	99. (b)	100. (b)
101. (c)	102. (c)	103. (b)	104. (d)	105. (d)	106. (c)	107. (a)	108. (d)	109. (b)	110. (a)
111. (d)	112. (a)	113. (a)	114. (d)	115. (b)	116. (c)	117. (a)	118. (b)	119. (d)	120. (c)

Mathematics

121. (a)	122. (b)	123. (b)	124. (a)	125. (b)	126. (d)	127. (c)	128. (a)	129. (c)	130. (a)
131. (d)	132. (b)	133. (b)	134. (c)	135. (a)	136. (d)	137. (a)	138. (c)	139. (b)	140. (a)
141. (c)	142. (c)	143. (c)	144. (a)	145. (c)	146. (d)	147. (a)	148. (b)	149. (d)	150. (b)
151. (b)	152. (a)	153. (b)	154. (a)	155. (c)	156. (c)	157. (b)	158. (b)	159. (b)	160. (b)
161. (b)	162. (c)	163. (c)	164. (c)	165. (c)	166. (b)	167. (d)	168. (d)	169. (d)	170. (a)
171. (b)	172. (b)	173. (d)	174. (c)	175. (c)	176. (a)	177. (c)	178. (c)	179. (a)	180. (c)

HINTS & SOLUTIONS

Physics

1. *(a)* During the phenomenon of resonance, the amplitude of oscillation becomes large.

2. *(c)* The variation of g with angular velocity ω is given by

$$g' = g - R\omega^2$$

If earth were to spin faster, that is angular velocity increases, then except at poles, the weight of bodies will decrease at all places.

3. *(b)* Given, $A_m = 20$ cm

$$A_C = 40 \text{ cm}$$

$\therefore$ Modulation index,

$$\mu = \frac{A_m}{A_c} = \frac{20}{40} = 0.5$$

4. *(a)* Given, $T_2 = 27°\text{C} = 300$ K

$$T_1 = 677°\text{C} = 950 \text{ K}$$

$$\eta = \frac{W}{Q_1} = \frac{Q_1 - Q_2}{Q_1}$$

$$= 1 - \frac{Q_2}{Q_1} = 1 - \frac{T_2}{T_1}$$

$$\therefore \quad \eta = 1 - \frac{300}{950} = \frac{13}{19}$$

$$\therefore \quad W = \eta Q_1 = 100 \times 10^3 \times \frac{13}{19} \text{ cal}$$

Also, 4.2 J = 1 cal

$$\therefore \quad W = 100 \times 10^3 \times \frac{13}{19} \times 4.2$$

$$\Rightarrow \quad W = 2.87 \times 10^5 = 0.28 \times 10^6 \text{ J}$$

5. *(c)* During α-decay, atomic mass of parent nuclei is decreased by 4 units while atomic number is decreased by 2 units.

6. *(d)* From two similar triangles,

$$\frac{h}{\frac{d}{2}} = \frac{f}{2f}$$

$$h = \frac{d}{4}$$

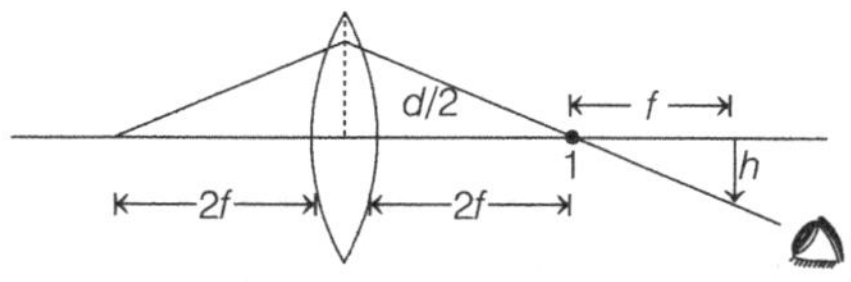

7. *(b)* Given, collector resistance $= R_{out} = 4$ kΩ

$$\beta = 100$$

$$R_{in} = 2 \text{ k}\Omega$$

$$V_{out} = 5 \text{ V}$$

$\therefore$ Voltage amplification,

$$A_V = \beta \frac{R_{out}}{R_{in}} = \frac{V_{out}}{V_{in}}$$

$$\because \quad V_{in} = \frac{V_{out} \times R_{in}}{\beta \times R_{out}}$$

$$= \frac{5 \times 2 \times 10^3}{100 \times 4 \times 10^3}$$

$$= \frac{1}{40} = 25 \text{ mV}$$

8. *(a, b)* As work done = area under p-V curve, work done is maximum in case I

Change in internal energy is independent of the path from A to B. Therefore, in all cases change in internal energy is same.

9. *(a, d)* As Young's modulus Y for two wires is different, hence strain is different but stress is same as equal force F on each wire having same diameter and area of cross-section act on both wires.

10. *(a)* As,

$$K = \frac{1}{2} mv^2$$

$$\Rightarrow \quad K = \frac{1}{2m} p^2$$

$$\Rightarrow \quad p^2 = 2mK$$

$$\Rightarrow \quad p = \sqrt{2mK}$$

Suppose, p_1 is the momentum of the body and K_1 = kinetic energy of the body initially. As the kinetic enery of the body is increased by 300%, new kinetic energy of the body = $K_1 + 3K_1$

Hence, percentage change in momentum

$$= \frac{p_2 - p_1}{p_1} \times 100$$

$$= \frac{\sqrt{2mK_2} - \sqrt{2mK_1}}{\sqrt{2mK_1}} \times 100$$

$$= \frac{\sqrt{2m}\sqrt{K_2} - \sqrt{K_1}}{\sqrt{2m}\sqrt{K_1}} \times 100$$

$$= \frac{\sqrt{K_1 + 3K_1} - \sqrt{K_1}}{\sqrt{K_1}} \times 100$$

$$= \frac{\sqrt{4K_1} - \sqrt{K_1}}{\sqrt{K_1}} \times 100 = 100\%$$

11. *(c)* The electric field intensity at a point lying outside the sphere (non-conducting) is

$$E = \frac{1}{4\pi\varepsilon_0} \cdot \frac{q}{r^2}$$

$$\Rightarrow \quad E \propto \frac{1}{r^2} \quad \ldots\text{(i)}$$

The electric field intensity at the sphere $(r = R)$,

$$E = \frac{1}{4\pi\varepsilon_0} \frac{q}{R^2}$$

$$\Rightarrow \quad E \propto \frac{1}{R^2}$$

where, R being the radius of sphere.

The electric field intensity inside the sphere is

$$E = \frac{1}{4\pi\varepsilon_0} \cdot \frac{qr}{R^3}$$

$$\Rightarrow \quad E \propto r$$

At the centre of sphere, $E = 0$

Hence, option *(c)* is correct representation.

12. *(a)* Resultant current is superposition of two currents, i.e. I (instantaneous total current)

$$= 6 + I_0 \sin \omega t$$

DC ammeter will read average value

$$= \overline{6 + I_0 \sin \omega t}$$

$$= 6 \text{ A} \qquad (\because \overline{I_0 \sin \omega t} = 0)$$

AC ammeter will read average value

$$= \sqrt{\overline{(6 + I_0 \sin^2 \omega t)^2}}$$

$$= \sqrt{36 + 12 I_0 \sin \omega t + I_0^2 \sin^2 \omega t} \qquad (\because \overline{I_0 \sin \omega t} = 0)$$

Since, $\overline{\sin^2 \omega t} = \frac{1}{2}$ and $I_{rms} = 8 = \frac{I_0}{\sqrt{2}}$

$$\therefore \text{ AC reading} = \sqrt{36 + \frac{I_0^2}{2}} = \sqrt{36 + 64}$$

$$= 10 \text{ A}$$

13. *(c)* Let the velocity of the bullet before collision be v, then according to law of conservation of linear momentum,

$$mv = (m + M)v' \qquad \ldots \text{(i)}$$

As the mass m of the bullet gets embedded in the wall, hence velocity of bullet + target just after collision will be same,

$$\frac{1}{2}(M + m)v'^2 = (m + M)gh$$

$$\Rightarrow \quad v' = \sqrt{2gh}$$

Putting the value of v' in Eq. (i), we get

$$\Rightarrow \quad v = \sqrt{2gh}\, \frac{(m + M)}{m} = \sqrt{2gh}\left(1 + \frac{M}{m}\right)$$

14. *(a)* The potential energy is given by

$$U = \int F \cdot dr = \int \frac{K}{r^2}\, dr = K \int r^{-2}\, dr$$

$$= K\left[\frac{r^{-1}}{-1}\right] = \frac{-K}{r}$$

The kinetic energy is given by

$$K = \frac{1}{2} mv^2 = \frac{1}{2}\left(\frac{K}{r}\right) \qquad \left[\because \frac{mv^2}{r} = \frac{K}{r^2}\right]$$

Total energy, $E = U + K$

$$= \frac{-K}{r} + \frac{K}{2r} = \frac{-K}{2r}$$

15. *(b)* As, acceleration due to gravity at height h,

$$g' = \frac{GM}{(R + h)^2},$$

$$\Rightarrow \quad \frac{g}{16} = \frac{GM}{R^2}\left(\frac{R^2}{(R + h)^2}\right) = g\frac{R^2}{(R + h)^2} \qquad \left(\because g' = \frac{g}{16}\right)$$

$$\Rightarrow \quad \frac{1}{4} = \frac{R}{R + h} \Rightarrow h = 3R$$

16. *(d)* Lyman series lies in the ultraviolet region whereas Paschen, Brackett and Pfund series lie in the infrared region.

17. *(b)* Speed of EM wave in medium is given as

$$v = \frac{c}{\sqrt{\mu_r \varepsilon_r}}$$

18. *(b)* Wavelength in Balmer series for hydrogen are given by

$$\frac{1}{\lambda} = R_H\left(\frac{1}{2^2} - \frac{1}{n^2}\right)$$

$$= R_H\left(\frac{1}{4} - \frac{1}{n^2}\right), n = 3, 4, 5, \ldots$$

The second line in Balmer series corresponds to $n = 4$

Hence, $\frac{1}{\lambda_2} = R_H\left(\frac{1}{4} - \frac{1}{16}\right) = \frac{3R_H}{16}$

or, $\lambda_2 = \frac{16}{3R_H}$

The wavelength of the first line $(n = 2)$ in Lyman series is

$$\frac{1}{\lambda_1} = R_H\left(1 - \frac{1}{2^2}\right) = R_H\left(1 - \frac{1}{4}\right) = \frac{3R_H}{4}$$

or, $\quad \lambda_1 = \frac{4}{3R_H}$

$$\therefore \quad \frac{\lambda_1}{\lambda_2} = \frac{4}{3R_H} \times \frac{3R_H}{16} = \frac{1}{4}$$

$$\Rightarrow \quad \lambda_1 = \frac{\lambda_2}{4} = \frac{486.4}{4} = 121.6 \text{ nm}$$

19. *(a)*

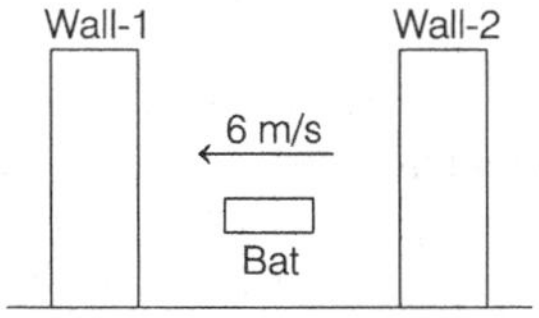

Frequency received by bat after reflection from wall-1,

$$f_1 = f\left[\frac{v + u}{v - u}\right] = 4.5 \times 10^4 \left[\frac{330 + 6}{330 - 6}\right]$$

Given, $\quad f = 4.5 \times 10^4$ Hz

$$\Rightarrow \quad f_1 = 4.67 \times 10^4 \text{ Hz}$$

Frequency received by bat after reflection from wall-2

$$f_2 = f\left[\frac{v-u}{v+u}\right]$$

$$= 4.5 \times 10^4 \left[\frac{330-6}{300+6}\right]$$

$$= 4.34 \times 10^4 \text{ Hz}$$

20. *(c)* Given that, moment of inertia of disc, $I_1 = 4 \text{ kg-m}^2$

$$I_2 = 8 \text{ kg-m}^2$$

Angular velocities of discs,

$$\omega_1 = 16 \text{ rad/s}$$

$$\omega_2 = 4 \text{ rad/s}$$

From angular momentum conservation principle,

$$I_1\omega_1 + I_2\omega_2 = (I_1 + I_2)\omega$$

$$\Rightarrow \quad 4 \times 16 + 8 \times 4 = (4+8)\,\omega$$

$$\Rightarrow \quad 64 + 32 = 12\omega$$

$$\Rightarrow \quad \omega = \frac{96}{12} = 8 \text{ rad/s}$$

21. *(d)* Force on a moving charged particle in uniform magnetic field,

$$F = Bqv \sin\theta \qquad \ldots\text{(i)}$$

Since, charge particle moves along the axis of circular current carrying loop, therefore, $\theta = 0°$ or $180°$.

When $\theta = 0°$, $F = Bqv \sin 0°$ [from Eq. (i)]

$$F = 0$$

When $\theta = 180°$, $F = Bqv \sin 180°$

$$F = 0$$

22. *(c)* As we know that, emf induced $e = \dfrac{d\phi_B}{dt}$

or $\quad e = \dfrac{dB}{dt}$ (When area is constant $\phi_B \propto B$)

Now for television wave, $e_1 = \dfrac{d}{dt}(B)$

$$= \frac{d}{dt}(B_0 \sin(2\pi f_1 t + \phi))$$

$$e_1 = B_0 2\pi f_1 \cos(2\pi f_1 t + \phi)$$

For radiowave, $e_2 = \dfrac{d}{dt}(B)$

$$= \frac{d}{dt}(B_0 \sin(2\pi f_2 t + \phi))$$

$$= B_0\, 2\pi f_2 \cos(2\pi f_2 + \phi)$$

The ratio of emf induced

$$= \frac{e_1}{e_2} = \frac{B_0\, 2\pi f_1 \cos(2\pi f_1 t + \phi)}{B_0\, 2\pi f_2 \cos(2\pi f_2 t + \phi)}$$

Since, $f_1 = 100$ MHz, $f_2 = 1$ MHz

and $\cos(2\pi f_1 t + \phi) = \cos(2\pi f_2 t + \phi) = \cos\phi$

(For complete cycle)

We get, $\dfrac{e_1}{e_2} = \dfrac{100}{1} = 100$

23. *(d)* According to the question,

$$x = 5 \sin\left(4t - \frac{\pi}{6}\right)$$

When $x = 3$,

$$\Rightarrow \quad \frac{3}{5} = \sin\left(4t - \frac{\pi}{6}\right)$$

$$\Rightarrow \quad 4t - \frac{\pi}{6} = 37°$$

Hence, velocity $= \dfrac{dx}{dt} = 5 \times 4 \cos\left(4t - \dfrac{\pi}{6}\right)$

$$= 5 \times 4 \times \cos 37°$$

$$= 16 \text{ ms}^{-1} \qquad \left(\because \cos 37° = \frac{4}{5}\right)$$

24. *(d)* Volume of wood $= \dfrac{\text{Mass}}{\text{Density}}$

$$= \frac{120}{600} = 0.2 \text{ m}^3$$

Weight of displaced water,

$$vdg = 0.2 \times 1000 \times 10 = 2000 \text{ N}$$

$$Mg = v\,dg$$

$$\Rightarrow \quad (120 + m)\,g = 2000$$

$$\Rightarrow \quad m = 80 \text{ kg}$$

25. *(b)* If we differentiate the equation of motion, $x = 1 - t - t^2$ w.r.t. time, we get velocity.

$$v = \frac{dx}{dt} = -1 - 2t$$

Comparing with $v = u + at$, we have $u = -1 \text{ ms}^{-1}$ and $a = -2 \text{ ms}^{-2}$

At $t = 0$, $x = 1$ m. Then, u and a both are negative.

Hence, x-coordinate of particle will go on decreasing.

26. *(b)* From figure,

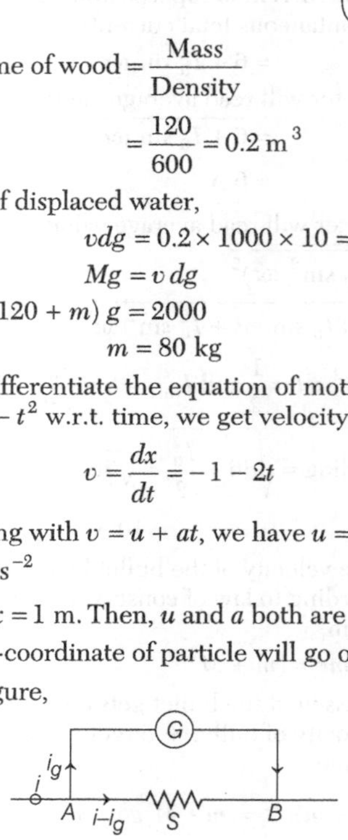

Shunt current $= i - i_g$

galvanometer current $= i_g$

$$i = \text{total current}$$

$$\therefore \quad i = 1.5 \text{ A}$$

By KVL,

$$i_g - G = (i - i_g)\,S$$

Putting $G = 4\Omega$ and $S = 2\Omega$ and $i = 1.5$ A

$$\therefore \quad i_g \times 4 = (1.5 - i_g) \times 2$$

$$4i_g = 3 - 2i_g$$

$$6i_g = 3 \Rightarrow i_g = 0.5 \text{ A}$$

$\therefore$ Current passing through shunt $= i - i_g$

$$= 1.5 - 0.5 = 1 \text{ A}$$

27. *(d)* Given, $d = 0.2\text{ mm} = 2\times 10^{-4}$ m

$D = 1$ m, $\lambda = 500$ nm $= 5\times 10^{-7}$ m

The distance between 6th maxima and 10th minima is given as

$$\Delta x = (x_{10})_{\text{dark}} - (x_6)_{\text{bright}}$$
$$= \frac{(2\times 10 - 1)D\lambda}{2d} - \frac{6D\lambda}{d}$$
$$= \frac{D\lambda}{d}\left[\frac{19}{2} - 6\right)$$
$$= \frac{1\times 5\times 10^{-7}}{2\times 10^{-4}}\left[\frac{7}{2}\right] = \frac{35}{4}\times 10^{-3}\text{ m}$$
$$= 8.75\times 10^{-3}\text{ m}$$
$$= 8.75\text{ mm}$$

Hence, 8 mm is closest to 8 mm.

28. *(b)* As $V = I_{\text{rms}}R$

$$I_{\text{rms}} = \frac{V_R}{R} = \frac{65}{100} = 0.65\text{ A}$$
$$V_L = I_{\text{rms}}\times X_L$$
$$X_L = \frac{V_L}{I_{\text{rms}}} = \frac{204}{0.65} = 313.85\ \Omega$$
$$X_L = \omega L = 2\pi f L$$

or $$L = \frac{X_L}{2\pi f}$$

$$L = \frac{313.85}{2\times\pi\times 50} = 1.0\text{ H}$$
$$X_C = \frac{V_C}{I_{\text{rms}}} = \frac{415}{0.65} = 638.46\ \Omega$$
$$X_C = \frac{1}{\omega C} = \frac{1}{2\pi f C}$$
$$C = \frac{1}{2\times\pi\times 50\times 638.46}$$
$$= 5\times 10^{-6} = 5\ \mu\text{F}$$

29. *(a)* Let number of turns of the regular hexagon $= n$

Now, $n\times 6m = 24m$

$\therefore \quad n = 4$

Magnetic moment, $M = nIA = 4IA$

$\therefore$ Area of hexagon

$$= \frac{1}{2}m^2\sin^2 60^\circ + m\cdot 2m\sin 60^\circ + \frac{1}{2}m^2\sin 120^\circ$$
$$= \frac{\sqrt{3}}{4}m^2 + \sqrt{3}m^2 + \frac{\sqrt{3}m^2}{4}$$
$$= \frac{6\sqrt{3}m^2}{4} = \frac{3\sqrt{3}m^2}{2}$$

Hence, magnetic moment $= 4I\left(\frac{3\sqrt{3}m^2}{2}\right)$

$$= 6\sqrt{3}Im^2$$

30. *(a)* From the given circuit diagram, output Y is given as

$$Y = (\overline{\overline{A} + \overline{B}})\,AB$$
$$= (\overline{\overline{A}}\cdot\overline{\overline{B}})\,AB \qquad [\text{By De morgan's law, } \overline{A+B} = \overline{A}\cdot\overline{B}]$$
$$= (AB)(AB) \qquad [\because A\cdot A = A]$$
$$= AB$$

= output of AND gate.

31. *(c)* According to fluid dynamics, for maximum level of water in tank,

$$A_1 v_1 = A_2 v_2$$

Given, $A_1 = A$,

velocity, $v_1 = 4\text{ ms}^{-1}$

area of hole $A_2 = \frac{A}{2}$

$$\Rightarrow \quad A\times 4 = \frac{A}{2}\times\sqrt{2gh}$$
$$\Rightarrow \quad 16 = \frac{2gh}{4}$$
$$\Rightarrow \quad h = \frac{16\times 4}{2\times 10} = 3.2\text{ m}$$

32. *(b)* The capacitance of a conductor is defined as the ratio of the charge given to the rise in the potential of the conductor.

$$C = \frac{q}{V} = \frac{q^2}{W} \qquad \left(V = \frac{W}{q}\right)$$
$$C = \frac{\text{ampere}^2\text{- second}^2}{\text{kg}^2\text{- metre}^2\text{ second}^{-2}}$$

Hence, dimensionally $[M^{-1}L^{-2}T^4A^2]$

From Ohm's law, $V = IR$,

Hence, $R = \frac{V}{I} = \frac{\text{Volt}}{\text{Ampere}} = \frac{W}{q}\times\frac{t}{q}$

$$R = \frac{F\times s\times t}{q^2} = \text{kg}\,\frac{\text{m}}{\text{s}^2}\times\frac{\text{m}\times\text{s}}{\text{A}^2\times\text{s}^2}$$
$$= \text{kg m}^2\text{ s}^{-3}\text{A}^{-2}$$

Dimensionally, $R = [ML^2T^{-3}A^{-2}]$

Hence, $CR = [M^{-1}L^{-2}T^4A^2][ML^2T^{-3}A^{-2}]$

$$= [M^0L^0T]$$

33. *(a)* Net work done by a gas,

$$\Delta W_{AB} = p\cdot\Delta V = 10\times(2-1) = 10\text{ J}$$
$$\Delta W_{BC} = 0 \qquad (\text{as } V = \text{constant})$$

From first law of thermodynamics

we have, $\Delta Q = \Delta W + \Delta U$

$$\Delta U = 0 \qquad (\text{process } ABCA \text{ is cyclic})$$

Therefore, $\Delta Q = \Delta W_{AB} + \Delta W_{BC} + \Delta W_{CA}$

$$\therefore \quad \Delta W_{CA} = (\Delta Q - W_{AB} - W_{BC})$$
$$= (5 - 10 - 0)\text{ J} = -5\text{ J}$$

34. *(a)*

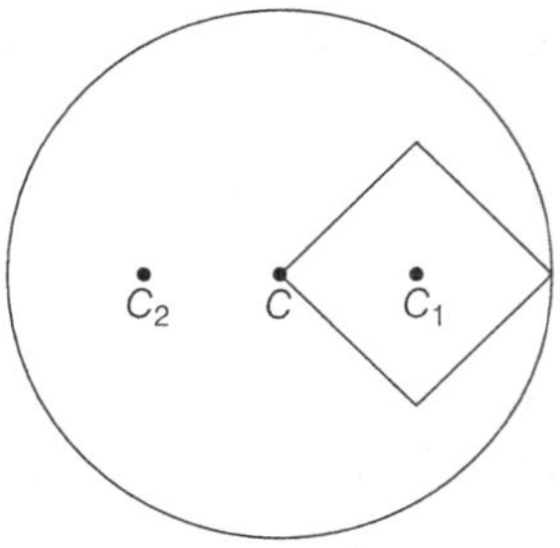

Radius of the circular disc $= R$

Suppose, centre of mass of remaining portion is at a distance C_2 from the centre C.

Now, $A_1\,(CC_1) = A_2(CC_2)$

For square, $(\text{side})^2 + (\text{side})^2 = (\text{radius})^2$

$$2\,(\text{side})^2 = R^2$$

$$(\text{side})^2 = \frac{R^2}{2}$$

$$\text{side} = \frac{R}{\sqrt{2}}$$

Now, $A_1(CC_1) = A_2(CC_2)$

$$\therefore \quad CC_2 = \frac{A_1}{A_2}(CC_1)$$

A_1 = area of the square $= \left(\frac{R}{\sqrt{2}}\right)^2$

A_2 = area of the remaining part of the circle

$$= \pi R^2 - \left(\frac{R}{\sqrt{2}}\right)^2$$

$$CC_2 = \frac{\left(\frac{R}{\sqrt{2}}\right)^2}{\pi R^2 - \left(\frac{R}{\sqrt{2}}\right)^2}\left(\frac{R}{2}\right)$$

$$= \frac{R^2}{2\left(\pi R^2 - \frac{R^2}{2}\right)} \cdot \frac{R}{2}$$

$$= \frac{R^2}{2\pi R^2 - R^2} \cdot \frac{R}{2}$$

$$= \frac{R \cdot R \cdot R}{R^2(2\pi - 1)\,2} = \frac{R}{4\pi - 2}$$

35. *(b)* At neutral point

$$B = B_H$$

$$\Rightarrow \quad \frac{\mu_0}{4\pi} \times \frac{M}{(r^2 + l^2)^{3/2}} = B_H$$

$$\Rightarrow \quad 10^{-7} \times \frac{m \times 2l}{(r^2 + l^2)^{3/2}} = 1.2 \times 10^{-5}$$

$$\Rightarrow \quad 10^{-7} \times \frac{m \times 2 \times 3 \times 10^{-2}}{[(4 \times 10^{-2})^2 + (3 \times 10^{-2})^2]^{3/2}} = 1.2 \times 10^{-5}$$

$$\Rightarrow \quad \frac{6m \times 10^{-4}}{[(5 \times 10^{-2})^2]^{3/2}} = 1.2$$

$$\Rightarrow \quad \frac{6m \times 10^{-4}}{125 \times 10^{-6}} = 1.2$$

$$\Rightarrow \quad m = \frac{1.2 \times 125 \times 10^{-2}}{6}$$

$$= 0.25 \text{ A-m}^2$$

36. *(a)* As per formula, the Young's modulus, $Y = \frac{\text{Stress}}{\text{Strain}}$

$$= \frac{\frac{F}{A}}{\frac{\Delta l}{l}}$$

$$\Rightarrow \quad F = \frac{YA\Delta l}{l}$$

In first case, $Y = \dfrac{\frac{F}{A_1}}{\frac{l_1}{L}}$

$$\Rightarrow \quad F = \frac{Yl_1A_1}{L} \quad \ldots\text{(i)}$$

Similarly, for the second case,

$$F = \frac{Yl_2A_2}{\Delta l} \quad \ldots\text{(ii)}$$

From Eqs. (i) and (ii), we get

$$\frac{Yl_1A_1}{L} = \frac{Yl_2A_2}{4L}$$

As Y is same, as the same material is taken, $l_1A_1 = \dfrac{l_2A_2}{4}$

$$l_1\pi r^2 = \frac{l_2}{4}\pi(4r)^2$$

$$l_1 = \frac{l_2}{4} \cdot \frac{16r^2}{r^2} = 4l_2 \Rightarrow l_2 = \frac{l_1}{4}$$

Here, $l_1 = l,\ l_2 = \dfrac{l}{4}$

37. *(a)* Given, power of laser beam,

$$P = 30 \text{ mW} = 30 \times 10^{-3} \text{ W}$$

Area of cross section, $A = 15 \text{ mm}^2 = 15 \times 10^{-6} \text{ m}^2$

Permittivity of free space, $\varepsilon_0 = 9 \times 10^{-12}$ SI unit

Speed of light, $c = 3 \times 10^8$ m/s

Intensity of electromagnetic wave is given by

$$I = \frac{1}{2} nc\varepsilon_0 E^2$$

where, n is refractive index for air, $n = 1$

$$I = \frac{1}{2} c \cdot \varepsilon_0 E^2 \quad \ldots\text{(i)}$$

$$I = \frac{P}{A} \quad \ldots\text{(ii)}$$

From Eqs. (i) and (ii), we get

$$\frac{1}{2}c\varepsilon_0E^2 = \frac{P}{A}$$

$$E^2 = \frac{2P}{Ac\varepsilon_0}$$

$$E = \sqrt{\frac{2\times 30\times 10^{-3}}{15\times 10^{-6}\times 3\times 10^{8}\times 9\times 10^{-12}}}$$

$$= 1.22\times 10^{3}\ \text{V/m} = 1.22\ \text{kV/m}$$

38. *(c)* The average molecular kinetic energy is expressed as

$$\overline{K} = \frac{1}{2}mv^2 = \frac{3}{2}kT$$

Given, $T = 20°C = 20 + 273 = 293$ K

$k = 1.38\times 10^{-23}$ J/K = Boltzmann's constant

Substituting all the values, we get

$$\overline{K} = \frac{3}{2}\times 1.38\times 10^{-23}\times 293$$

$$= 6.07\times 10^{-21}\ \text{J}$$

39. *(d)* As for the projectile motion, horizontal range,

$$R = \frac{u^2\sin 2\theta}{g}$$

$\because$ Maximum range $= u^2/g$

$\because$ $A = \pi R^2$

$\therefore$ $A \propto R^2$

i.e., $A \propto u^4$

$$\therefore\ \frac{A_1}{A_2} = \frac{u_1^4}{u_2^4} = \left(\frac{2}{4}\right)^4 = \left(\frac{1}{2}\right)^4 = \frac{1}{16}$$

40. *(a)* Given, emf of cell, $E = 2$ V

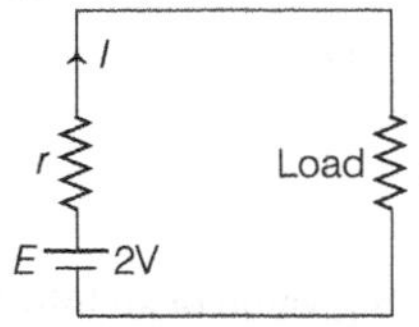

Load resistance, $R_L = 1.5\ \Omega$

Current flowing the circuit is

$$I = \frac{E}{R+r}$$

Power transferred to the load, R,

$$P = I^2R = \left(\frac{E}{R+r}\right)^2\cdot R = \frac{E^2R}{(R+r)^2}$$

Power P will be maximum, if

$$dP/dR = 0$$

$$\Rightarrow\ \frac{d}{dR}\frac{E^2R}{(R+r)^2} = 0$$

$$\Rightarrow\ \frac{E^2(R+r)^2 - E^2\cdot R\cdot 2(R+r)}{(R+r)^3} = 0$$

$$\Rightarrow\ E^2(R+r)[R+r-2R] = 0$$

$$\Rightarrow\ E^2(R+r)(r-R) = 0$$

$$\Rightarrow\ r - R = 0$$

$$\Rightarrow\ r = R$$

$\therefore$ Maximum power, $P = \frac{E^2R}{(R+r)^2} = \frac{E^2R}{(R+R)^2} = \frac{E^2}{4R}$

$$\Rightarrow\ P = \frac{2^2}{4\times 1.5} = \frac{1}{3} = 0.33\ \text{W}$$

41. *(d)* A thick glass mirror produces a number of images. There is an apparent shift of actual silvered surface towards the unsilvered face.

Effective distance of the reflecting surface from unsilvered face $= \frac{d}{\mu}$

$$= \frac{3}{3/2}\ \text{cm} = 2\ \text{cm}$$

Distance of point object from effective reflecting surface = 9 cm + 2 cm = 11 cm

Distance of image from point object

= 11 cm + 11 cm = 22 cm

Distance of image from unsilvered face

= (22 − 9) cm = 13 cm

42. *(d)* Given $K_{max} = h\nu - W_0$

$$= \frac{(6.6\times 10^{-34})\times(3\times 10^{8})}{99\times 10^{-9}} - 1.0\times 1.6\times 10^{-19}$$

$$= 2\times 10^{-18} - 1.6\times 10^{-19}$$

$$= 1.84\times 10^{-18}\ \text{J}$$

Now, $\lambda = \frac{h}{\sqrt{2mK_{max}}}$

$$= \frac{6.6\times 10^{-34}}{\sqrt{2\times(9.1\times 10^{-31})\times 1.84\times 10^{-18}}}$$

$$= 0.36\times 10^{-9}\ \text{m} = 0.36\ \text{nm}$$

43. *(d)* If fringe widths of air and water are β_{air} and β_{water} respectively, then fringe width, $\beta_{water} = \frac{\beta_{air}}{\mu}$

Given, $\mu = \frac{4}{3}$, $\beta_{air} = 0.4$

Hence, $\beta_{water} = \frac{0.4}{4/3} = 0.3$ mm

44. *(d)* Since, container are identical, so initial volume and pressure will be same for identical gases.

For container C_1,

$$p_1V_1^{\gamma} = p_2V_2^2 \qquad \text{(adiabatic)}$$

$$p_2 = \left(\frac{V_1}{V_2}\right)^{\gamma} p_1 = \left(\frac{V_1}{V_1/2}\right)^{\gamma} p_1 = 2^{\gamma} p_1 \quad \ldots\text{(i)}$$

For container C_2,

$$p_1V_1 = p_2'V_2 \text{ (isothermal)}$$

$$p_2' = \left(\frac{V_1}{V_2}\right) p_1 = \left(\frac{V_1}{V_1/2}\right) p_1 = 2p_1 \quad \ldots\text{(ii)}$$

From Eqs. (i) and (ii), we get

$$\frac{p_2}{p_2'} = \frac{2^{\gamma} p_1}{2p_1} = 2^{\gamma - 1} : 1$$

45. *(b)* Let W_0 be the work function of the metal, then kinetic energy of photoelectrons emitted when light of wavelength λ_1 is incident will be

$$K_1 = \frac{hc}{\lambda_1} - W_0$$

Similarly, $$K_2 = \frac{hc}{\lambda_2} - W_0$$

Now, $$K_1 - K_2 = \frac{hc}{\lambda_1} - \frac{hc}{\lambda_2} = hc\left[\frac{1}{\lambda_1} - \frac{1}{\lambda_2}\right]$$

$$= hc\left[\frac{1}{3\lambda_2} - \frac{1}{\lambda_2}\right]$$

$$K_1 - K_2 = \frac{-2hc}{3\lambda_2} = \frac{-2}{3}(K_2 + W_0)$$

$$\Rightarrow \quad K_1 = K_2 - \frac{2}{3}K_2 - \frac{2}{3}W_0$$

$$= \frac{K_2}{3} - \frac{2}{3}W_0 \Rightarrow K_1 < \frac{K_2}{3}$$

46. *(a)* Given, speed of car, $u = 54 \text{ km/h} = 54 \times \frac{5}{18}$

$$= 15 \text{ m/s}$$

Since, car stops in 3 s on applying brakes, so acceleration can be calculated from first equation of motion,

$$v = u + at \Rightarrow 0 = 15 + a(3)$$

$$\Rightarrow \quad a = -\frac{15}{3} = -5 \text{ ms}^{-2}$$

Using second equation of motion,

$$s = ut + \frac{1}{2}at^2$$

$$= 15 \times 3 + \frac{1}{2} \times (-5) \times (3)^2$$

$$= 45 - 22.5 = 22.5 \text{ m}$$

47. *(c)* According to Doppler's effect, the apparent frequency of sound when both source and observer are moving towards each other

$$\Rightarrow \quad f = \frac{(v + v_0) f_0}{(v - v_0)}$$

$$\Rightarrow \quad f = \left(\frac{v}{v - v_s}\right) f_0 + \left(\frac{v_0}{v - v_s}\right) f_0$$

$$\Rightarrow \quad f = \left(\frac{f_0}{v - v_s}\right) v_0 + \left(\frac{f_0}{v - v_s}\right) v$$

Equation of straight line, $y = mx + c$ which is equation of straight line making an intercept c on Y-axis,

Slope of the graph $= \frac{f_0}{v - v_s}$ and intercept $= \frac{vf_0}{v - v_s}$

This condition is represented in graph A plotted between f and v_0.

Hence, option (c) is correct.

48. *(a)* The energy emitted by a body, in the form of radiation on account of its temperature, is called thermal radiation. These radiations are heat radiations and travel along straight lines with speed of light.

49. *(b)* By the law of conservation of energy,

$$(U + K)_{\text{surface}} = (U + K)_{\infty}$$

$$\Rightarrow \quad \frac{-GM}{R} + \frac{1}{2}m(3v_e)^2 = 0 + \frac{1}{2}mv^2$$

$$\Rightarrow \quad -\frac{GM}{R} + \frac{9v_e^2}{2} = \frac{1}{2}v^2$$

Since, $v_e^2 = \frac{2GM}{R}$

$$\therefore \quad \frac{-v_e^2}{2} + \frac{9v_e^2}{2} = \frac{1}{2}v^2$$

$$\Rightarrow \quad v^2 = 8v_e^2$$

$$v = 2\sqrt{2}v_e = 2\sqrt{2} \times 11.2 = 31.7 \text{ km/s}$$

50. *(c)* Equivalent thermal conductivity of the compound slab,

$$K_{\text{eq}} = \frac{l_1 + l_2}{\frac{l_1}{K_1} + \frac{l_2}{K_2}} = \frac{l + l}{\frac{l}{K} + \frac{l}{2K}} = \frac{2l}{\frac{3l}{2K}} = \frac{4K}{3}$$

51. *(c)* Magnetic Lorenz force acting on each electron,

$$F = evB \quad \ldots\text{(i)}$$

As, current, $i = neAv$

$$ev = \frac{i}{nA}$$

Therefore, substituting value of ev into Eq. (i),

$$F = \frac{i}{nA}B$$

Given, $i = 5$ A, $n = 20$ turns, $B = 0.1$ T

$$F = evB = \frac{iB}{nA} = \frac{5 \times 0.1}{10^{29} \times 10^{-5}} = 5 \times 10^{-25} \text{ N}$$

52. *(c)* If a man slides down with some acceleration, then its apparent weight decreases. For critical condition, rope can bear only $\frac{2}{3}$ of his weight. If a is the minimum acceleration, then tension in the rope

$$= m(g - a) = \text{breaking strength}$$

$$\Rightarrow \quad m(g - a) = \frac{2}{3}mg$$

$$\Rightarrow \quad a = g - \frac{2g}{3} = \frac{g}{3}$$

53. *(c)* In general, nth mode of a string fixed at ends has frequency,

$$\nu = \frac{nv}{2l}$$

where, $n = 1, 2, 3, \ldots$

where, v is the velocity of wave and l is the length of string.

In fourth normal mode, $n = 4$

$$v = \frac{4\nu}{2l}$$

Given, $\nu = 500$ Hz, $l = 2$ m

Hence, $500 = \frac{4\nu}{2 \times 2}$

or $v = \frac{500 \times 4}{4} = 500$ m/s

54. *(b)* As we know,

$$\text{power factor} = \frac{R}{Z} = \frac{R}{\sqrt{R^2 + \omega L^2}}$$

Given $\omega = 100$, $L = 400$ mH

$$= \frac{30}{\sqrt{(30)^2 + (100 \times 400 \times 10^{-3})^2}}$$

$$= \frac{30}{\sqrt{900 + 160000 \times 10^{-3 \times 2}}}$$

$$= \frac{30}{50} = 0.6$$

55. *(a)* The given network can be simplified as shown in following figure

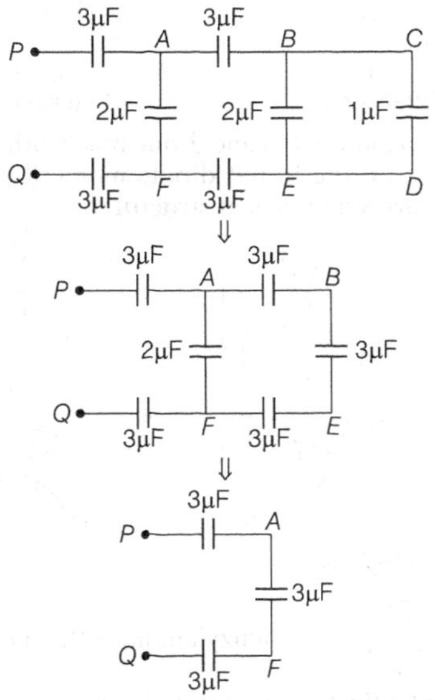

The equivalent capacitance between P and Q is given by

$$\frac{1}{C_{eq}} = \frac{1}{3} + \frac{1}{3} + \frac{1}{3} = 1\ \mu\text{F}$$

$$C_{eq} = 1\ \mu\text{F}$$

56. *(a)* From the diagram we get,

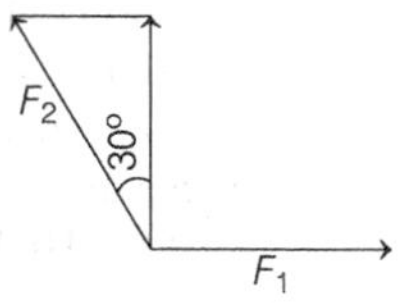

$$\tan 30° = \frac{1}{\sqrt{3}} = \frac{x}{10}$$

$$\Rightarrow \quad x = \frac{10}{\sqrt{3}}$$

57. *(a)* The most commonly used material in LEDs is gallium arsenide.

58. *(c)* Charge on electron is negative and its magnitude is 1.6×10^{-19} C

59. *(b)* Given, $q_1 = -20\ \mu\text{C} = -2 \times 10^{-5}$ C

$$q_2 = 60\ \mu\text{C} = 6 \times 10^{-5}\ \text{C}$$

Force of attraction between the both charges, kept at a certain distance r,

$$F_1 = \frac{Kq_1q_2}{r^2} = \frac{K \times 2 \times 10^{-5} \times 6 \times 10^{-5}}{r^2} = \frac{12 \times 10^{-10}\ K}{r^2}$$

When both charges are touched, then new charge on both spheres,

$$q_1' = q_2' = \frac{q_1 + q_2}{2} = \frac{-20 + 60}{2} = 20\ \mu\text{C}$$

$$= 2 \times 10^{-5}\ \text{C}$$

$\therefore$ Force between the two spheres,

$$F_2 = \frac{Kq_1' \cdot q_2'}{r^2} = \frac{K \cdot 2 \times 10^{-5} \times 2 \times 10^{-5}}{r^2} = \frac{4 \times 10^{-10}}{r^2} K$$

$$\therefore \quad \frac{F_1}{F_2} = \frac{\frac{12 \times 10^{-10}\ K}{r^2}}{\frac{4 \times 10^{-10}}{r^2}} = \frac{12}{4} = \frac{3}{1}$$

$\therefore \quad F_1 : F_2 = 3 : 1$

60. *(b)* An AC voltage across a resistance can be measured by using a moving coil galvanometer. It can be used as a voltmeter by inserting a resistor in series with it. It responds only to direct current. Hence, it requires a rectifier, so that coil deflects only in one direction.

Chemistry

61. *(c)* Use of **aspartame** is limited to cold foods because it is unstable at cooking temperature.

Alitame is more stable than aspartame but the control of sweetness of food is difficult while using it.

62. *(a)* Lucas reagent : Anhyd. $ZnCl_2$ / HCl.

It is used to differentiate 1°, 2° and 3° alcohols.

63. *(b)* Acidic strength of oxo-acids containing the same halogen are in the order :

$$HCl < HClO_2 < HClO_3 < HClO_4$$

This is because ClO_4^- is the most stable due to dispersal of negative charge on four D-atoms (O being more electromagnetic than Cl).

64. *(a)* **Coagulation** The process of aggregation of colloidal particles into an insoluble precipitate by the addition of suitable electrolyte.

Diffusion The process of movement of molecules from a region of higher concentration to a region of lower concentration.

Peptisation The process of converting a precipitate into colloidal sol by shaking it with dispersion medium in the presence of small amount of electrolyte.

Electrolysis The process by which electric current is passed through a substance to effect a chemical change.

65. *(d)* S_N2 mechanism

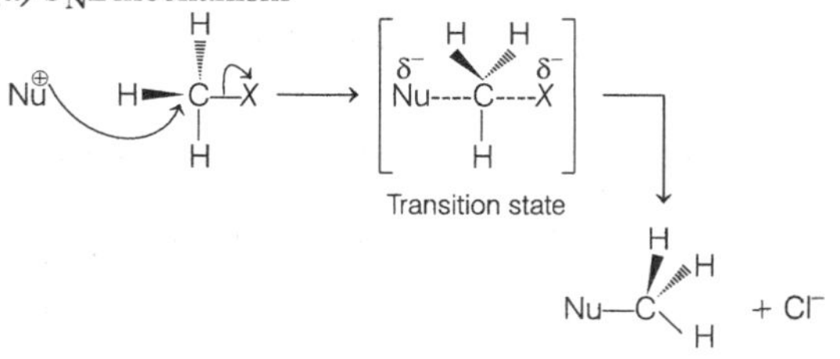

Inversion of configuration takes place. There is no carbocation formation.

66. *(c)*

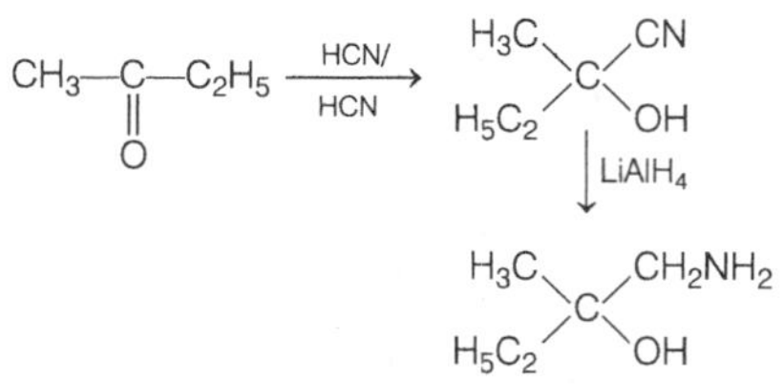

67. *(c)* Doping Si with In or B leads to the formation of *p*-type semiconductors.

In *p*-type semiconductors, trivalent impurities are used for doping, whereas, in *n*-type semiconductors, pentavalent impurities are used for doping.

68. *(d)* According to Le-Chatelier's principle when concentration of reactant increases, the equilibrium shifts in favour of forward reaction.

69. *(d)* Thermodynamic parameters which depend only on the initial and final states of system are called **state functions,** such as enthalpy ($H = q + W$), Gibb's free energy ($G = H - TS$).

Whereas, thermodynamic parameters which depend on the path by which the process is performed and not on initial and final states, are called path functions, such as work done (W), heat (q) etc.

70. *(a)* When the non-ideal binary solution shows the negative deviation, it is known as a maximum boiling azeotrope e.g. acetone-chloroform. Rest all three options show positive deviation from Raoult's law.

71. *(a)*

$$MnO_4^- + 8H^+ + 5e^- \longrightarrow Mn^{2+} + 4H_2O\,] \times 2$$

$$C_2O_4^{2-} \longrightarrow CO_2 + 2e^-] \times 5$$

$$2MnO_4^- + 5C_2O_4^{2-} + 16H^+ \longrightarrow 2Mn^{2+} + 10CO_2 + 8H_2O$$

5 moles of $C_2O_4^{2-}$ need 2 moles of $KMnO_4$.

1 mole of $C_2O_4^{2-}$ would need $= \frac{2}{5}$ mole of $KMnO_4$.

72. *(c)* $CH_3CH = CH_2 \xrightarrow[\text{Anti-Markownikoff addition}]{\text{HBr, Peroxide}} CH_3CH_2CH_2Br \xrightarrow[\text{Hydrolysis}]{\Delta,\ aq\ KOH} CH_3CH_2CH_2OH$ (Propanol)

73. *(a)* Ethanol undergoes intermolecular H-bonding due to the presence of a hydrogen attached to a electronegative oxygen atom. Hence, ethanol exists as associated molecules and a large amount of energy is required to break these H-bonds. Therefore, the boiling point of ethanol is higher than that of methoxy methane which does not form H-bonds.

74. *(c)*

Dipole moments cancel out reach other in CCl_4 and CO_2 resulting in net dipole moment as zero because these are symmetrical structures.

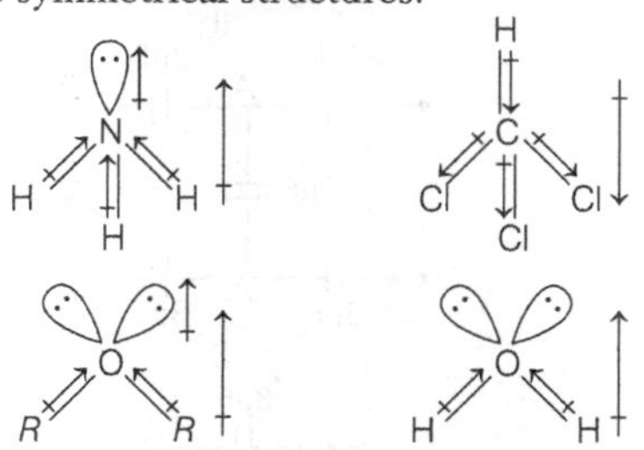

75. *(b)*

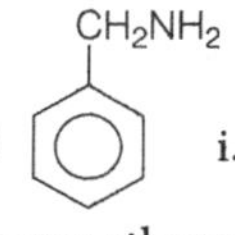

i.e. benzylamine is the most basic among other given options because lone pairs of N are available for donation.

whereas lone pair of N in aniline, diphenylamine and triphenyl amine are delocalised over the benzene ring, hence are not available for donation, making them weaker bases.

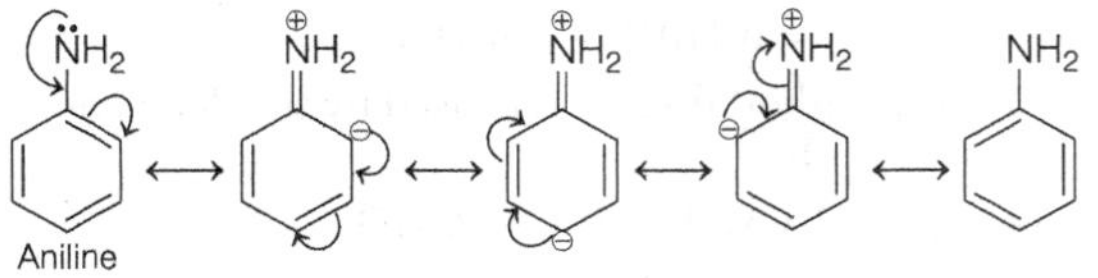

Aniline

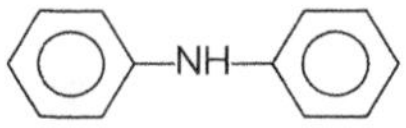

Diphenylamine

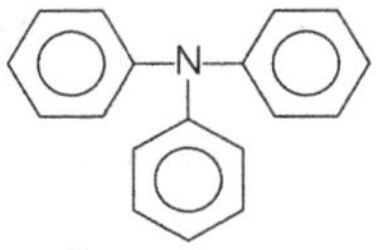

Triphenyl amine

76. *(b)* All natural processes are generally irreversible and net work done in an irreversible process is some what less than in reversible process.

77. *(d)* Platelets are pieces of very large cells in bone marrow. They help in forming blood clots to stop bleeding and wounds heal.

78. *(a)* Hydrolysis of maltose yields two moles of α-D-glucose in which C-1 of one glucose linked to C-4 of another glucose.

79. *(c)* The solubility of any gas in a particular liquid is the volume of gas that can be dissolved in unit volume of liquid. It only depend upon pressure, temperature and nature of gas and liquid.

80. *(b)* H_2O_2 has open book structure with O—O spins. Its dihedral angle is 111°.

81. *(a)* Radioactive nuclide follow first order kinetics

$$t_{1/2} = \frac{0.693}{\lambda} = \frac{0.693}{6.93} = 0.1 \text{ s}$$

82. *(b)* ZnS and AgCl show Frenkel defect. NaCl show Schottky defect but AgBr show both defect.

83. *(d)* The essential amino acids are histidine, isoleucine, leucine, lysine, methionine, phenylalanine, threonine, tryptophan and valine.

84. *(d)* According to MOT, bond order is given by the formula, BO $= \frac{N_b - N_a}{2}$ where N_a, N_b are the number of electrons in antibonding and bonding molecular orbital respectively.

Bond order for $O_2 = \frac{10-6}{2} = 2$

$$O_2^- = \frac{10-7}{2} = 1.5$$

$$O_2^+ = \frac{10-5}{2} = 2.5$$

$$O_2^{2-} = \frac{10-8}{2} = 1$$

85. *(a)* Total number of nodes is given by $(n-1)$

$$2s = (2-1) = 1$$
$$3s = (3-1) = 2$$
$$4s = (4-1) = 3$$
$$5s = (5-1) = 4$$

86. *(c)* As KOH is a base.

$$pOH = -\log[OH^-]$$
$$pOH = -\log[10^{-3}] = 3$$
$$pH + pOH = 14$$
$$p_H = 14 - 3 = 11$$

87. *(d)* Barbiturates are the depressants drug used to treat depression.

88. *(a)* Wurtz reaction is kind of reaction in which there is a formation of simple higher alkane from alkyl halides. Minimum two carbon chains should be present to form alkane in this reaction. So, methane cannot be formed.

89. *(a)* The CrO_4^{2-} (yellow) exist in acidic medium with pH = 6 and changes to orange in basic medium as $Cr_2O_7^{2-}$ with pH = 8.

90. *(b)* Bromine acts as mild oxidising agent and oxidation of glucose with bromine water form gluconic acid. This show presence of aldehyde group in glucose.

91. *(c)* Those azeotropes which boils at a temperature lower than boiling point of each component forms the minimum boiling azeotrope.

e.g. Heptane + octane, ethanol + water, acetone + carbon dioxide

92. *(c)* The incorrect statement about activation energy is option (c) because the SI unit of activation energy is J/mol or kJ/mol or kcal/mol.

93. *(d)* The structure of PO_4^{3-} is

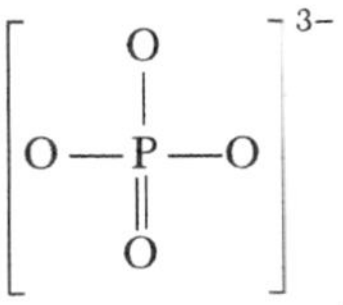

$$\text{Bond order} = \frac{\text{Number of bonds}}{\text{Number of resonating structure}} = \frac{5}{4} = 1.25$$

94. *(a)* Those species which have same number of electrons are called isoelectronic species.

O_2^-, F^-, Mg^{2+}, Al^{3+} have 10 electrons. Hence, 4 isoelectronic species are present.

95. *(d)* The hcp (hexagonal close packing) has a coordination number of 12 and contains 6 atoms per unit cell.

96. *(b)* $3C_2H_2(g) \rightleftharpoons C_6H_6(g)$

$$K_C = \frac{[C_6H_6]}{[C_2H_2]^3} = \frac{0.5}{[C_2H_2]^3}$$

$$4 = \frac{0.5}{[C_2H_2]^3}$$

$$[C_2H_2] = \sqrt[3]{\frac{0.5}{4}} = \frac{1}{2}$$

$$[C_2H_2] = 0.5 \text{ mol L}^{-1}$$

Therefore, the concentration of ethylene is 0.5 mol/L.

97. *(b)* Aspartame is used in soft drinks. It is an artificial sweetening agent which is unstable at higher temperatures. It is a compound formed from aspartic acid and phenyl alanine. It is 100 times as sweet as cane sugar.

98. *(b)* Complete reaction of the given reaction is as follows.

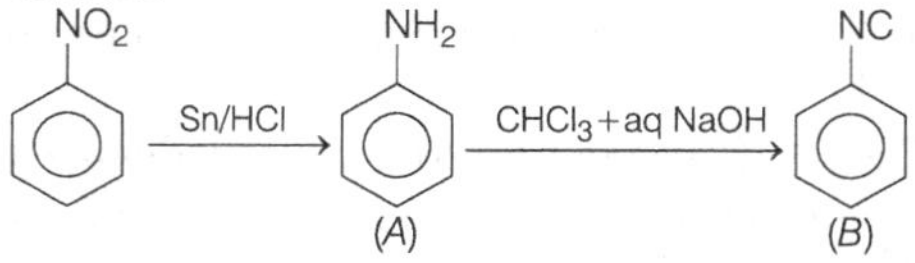

99. *(b)* Sulphur dioxide gas readily decolourises the purple colour of acidifide $KMnO_4$ solution. In this case, $KMnO_4$ acts as an oxidising agent and sulphur dioxide gas acts as a reducing agent.

100. *(b)* Let, the rate of diffusion of gas X, $r_1 = b$. Therefore, rate of diffusion of methane, $r_2 = 2b$

According to Graham's law of diffusion,

$$\left(\frac{r_1}{r_2}\right) = \left(\sqrt{\frac{M_2}{M_1}}\right)$$

M_1 = molecular mass of gas X

M_2 = molecular mass of methane = 16 g

$$\therefore \quad \frac{b}{2b} = \sqrt{\frac{16}{M_2}}$$

$$\Rightarrow \quad \left(\frac{1}{4}\right) = \frac{16}{M_2}$$

$$\Rightarrow \quad M_2 = 64\text{ g}$$

Therefore, molecular mass of X is 64 g.

101. *(c)* Fire clay bricks is used to prepare the inner lining of a blast furnance. It is highly refractory in nature and does not melt, even at huge temperature. Its main components are silica and alumina.

102. *(c)* For the given cell representation, the cell reaction will be,

$$Fe(s) + 2H^+(aq) \longrightarrow Fe^{2+}(aq) + H_2(g)$$

The standard emf of the cell will be,

$$E^\circ_{cell} = E^\circ_{H^+/H_2} - E^\circ_{Fe^{2+}/Fe}$$

$$= 0 - (-0.44) = 0.44 \text{ V}$$

The Nernst equation for the cell reaction at 25°C,

$$E_{cell} = E^\circ_{cell} - \frac{0.0591}{n}\log\frac{[Fe^{2+}]}{[H^+]}$$

$$= 0.44 - \frac{0.0591}{2}\log\frac{[0.001]}{[0.01]^2}$$

$$= 0.44 - 0.02955(\log 10)$$

$$= 0.44 - 0.02955\ (1)$$

$$= 0.41045 \text{ V} = 0.41 \text{ V}$$

103. *(b)* Beri-beri disease is caused by the deficiency of vitamin B_1.

104. *(d)* $C_6H_5CHO + H_2C(CH_3){-}CHO \xrightarrow{\text{Dil. NaOH}/\Delta} C_6H_5{-}CH{=}C(CH_3){-}CHO$

2-methyl-3-phenyl prop-2-en-1-al

105. *(d)* Among the given options, entropy decreases during the crystallisation of sucrose from solution. It is because entropy is a measure of randomness and during the process of crystallisation liquid state changes into solid state. Hence, entropy decreases.

106. *(c)* Bithional is an antiseptic which is widely used in medicinal soaps, so that soaps can impart antiseptic properties.

107. *(a)* Only aliphatic primary amines can react with nitrous acid to produce alcohol, water and nitrogen gas.

$$\underset{\text{1-amine}}{R{-}NH_2} + HONO \xrightarrow{273\text{–}278\text{K}} \underset{\text{Alcohol}}{R{-}OH} + N_2 + H_2O$$

So, dimethylamine which is a secondary amine cannot liberate N_2 with HONO.

108. *(d)* Octahedral complex of general formula $[M(AA)_2a_2]^{n\pm}$ shows optical isomerism. *cis*-$[Co(NH_3)_4Cl_2]^+$ does not show optical isomerism due to symmetry, while other three complexes show optical isomerism.

109. *(b)* We know, $pV = nRT$

$$\text{or } pV = \frac{W}{M}RT \quad \left[\text{Here, } n = \frac{\text{Weight of gas taken } (W)}{\text{Molar mass of gas } (M)}\right]$$

$$\text{or } p = \frac{W}{VM}RT$$

$$\text{or } p = \frac{dRT}{M} \quad \left[\text{Here, density}(d) = \frac{\text{Mass}}{\text{Volume}}\right]$$

$$\therefore \quad d = \frac{pM}{RT} = \frac{3 \times 28}{0.082 \times 503} = \frac{84}{41.246} = 2.03 \text{ g/mL}$$

110. *(a)* Higher the value of van't Hoff factor (i), higher will be depression in freezing point and lower will be the freezing point of solution.

So, 'i' value, 0.2M K_2SO_4 = 3

0.2M KCl = 2

0.2M $NaNO_3$ = 2

0.2M $MgSO_4$ = 2

Hence, 0.2 M K_2SO_4 will have lowest freezing point.

111. *(d)* Molar conductance = λ_m

$$\lambda_m = \frac{\kappa \times 10^{-3}}{M} \text{ mol}^{-1}\text{m}^3$$

$$= \frac{(12.04 \times 10^{-2} \text{ Sm}^{-1}) \times 10^{-3} (\text{mol}^{-1}\text{m}^3)}{0.025}$$

$$= 481.6 \times 10^{-5} \text{ Sm}^2 \text{ mol}^{-1}$$

112. *(a)* $2N_2O_5 \longrightarrow 4NO_2 + O_2$

Initial	p_0	0	0
Final	$p_0 - 2x$	$4x$	x

$$k = \frac{2.303}{t} \log \frac{p_0}{p_t}$$

$$3.38 \times 10^{-5} = \frac{2.303}{20 \times 60} \log \frac{100}{p_t}$$

$$0.0176 = \log \frac{100}{p_t}$$

$$p_t = 96 \text{ atm}$$

113. *(a)* Heat capacity at constant.
Pressure = C_p
Heat capacity at constant volume = C_V
As we all know,

$$C_p - C_V = R$$

114. *(d)* Among the given options, sulphur dioxide and nitrogen oxides are responsible for acid rain. It is because sulphur dioxide and nitrogen oxide reacts with water to give sulphuric acid and nitric acid respectively.

115. *(b)* N belongs to second period as it has no *d*-orbital. So, five pairs of bonding electrons around nitrogen is not possible. As a result NCl_5 does not exist.

116. *(c)* Phenol is converted to benzene on heating with zinc dust.

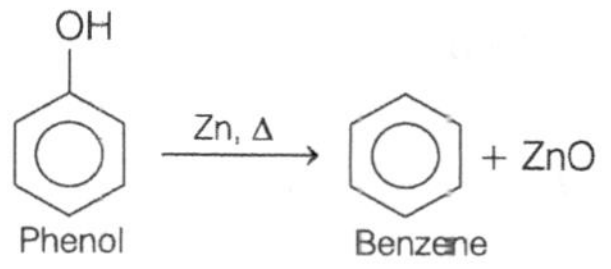

Hence, benzene is the major product.

117. *(a)* As He^+ and H contain same number of electron. So, they show same type of spectra.

118. *(b)* Paschen series of atomic spectrum of hydrogen gas lies in infrared region.

119. *(d)* $[Ni(CO_4)]$

$$x + 4(0) = 0$$

$$x = 0$$

Therefore, oxidation state of Ni is zero.

120. *(c)* Low temperature and high pressure favours physical adsorption because van der Waals' forces of attraction will increase.

Mathematics

121. *(a)* We have,

$$3^{\log_4 5} - 5^{\log_4 3} = 3^{\log_4 5} - 3^{\log_4 5} = 0$$

122. *(b)* Given curve, $xy + ax + by = 0$ ...(i)

(1, 1) lie on curve (i)

$\therefore \quad 1 + a + b = 0$ ...(ii)

From Eq. (i),

$$x \frac{dy}{dx} + y \cdot 1 + a + b \frac{dy}{dx} = 0$$

$$\Rightarrow \quad \frac{dy}{dx} = \frac{-(a+y)}{(b+x)}$$

$$\therefore \quad \left(\frac{dy}{dx}\right)_{(1,1)} = -\frac{(a+1)}{b+1} = 2 \quad (\because m = \tan\theta)$$

$$\therefore \quad \frac{-(-b)}{b+1} = 2 \quad \text{[from Eq. (ii)]}$$

$$\Rightarrow \quad b = 2b + 2$$

$$\therefore \quad b = -2$$

From Eq. (ii), $a = 1$

Hence, $a = 1, b = -2$

123. *(b)* Divide and multiply by $e^{1/x}$, then

$$\lim_{x \to 0} \frac{(1 + a^3) e^{-1/x} + 8}{e^{-1/x} + (1 - b^3)} = 2$$

$$\Rightarrow \quad \frac{0 + 8}{0 + 1 - b^3} = 2 \Rightarrow 1 - b^3 = 4 \Rightarrow b^3 = -3$$

$$\Rightarrow \quad b = -3^{1/3}$$

Then, $a \in R$.

124. *(a)* Centres and radii of the given circles are $C_1(1, 3)$, $r_1 = r$ and $C_2(4, -1)$, $r_2 = 3$ respectively. Since, circles intersect in two distinct points, then

$$|r_1 - r_2| < C_1C_2 < r_1 + r_2$$

$$\Rightarrow \quad |r - 3| < 5 < r + 3 \quad \text{...(i)}$$

From last two relations, $r > 2$

From first two relations,

$$|r - 3| < 5$$

$$\Rightarrow \quad -5 < r - 3 < 5$$

$$\Rightarrow \quad -2 < r < 8 \quad \text{...(ii)}$$

$\therefore$ From Eq. (i) and Eq. (ii), we get

$$2 < r < 8$$

125. *(b)* Let $\delta(x) = x^{\frac{1}{3}}$

Now, $f(x + \delta x) - f(x) = f'(x)\,\delta(x) = \dfrac{\delta x}{3x^{2/3}}$

We may write $0.007 = 0.008 - 0.001$

Taking $x = 0.008$ and $\delta x = -0.001$

We have,

$$f(0.007) - f(0.008) = \frac{-0.001}{3(0.008)^{2/3}}$$

or $$f(0.007) - f(0.008) = \frac{-1}{120}$$

$\therefore$ $$f(0.007) = f(0.008) - \frac{1}{120} = 0.2 - \frac{1}{120}$$

$\Rightarrow$ $$(0.007)^{1/3} = \frac{23}{120}$$

126. *(d)* Intercept on Y-axis $= 2\sqrt{f^2 - c}$

$$= 2\sqrt{\frac{49}{4} - 12} = 1$$

127. *(c)* $\because f(x) = a - (x - 3)^{8/9}$

$\therefore\ f'(x) = 0 - \dfrac{8}{9}(x - 3)^{-1/9}$

At $x = 3$, $f'(x)$ is not defined.

Hence, $x = 3$ is the point of extremum.

Hence, maximum value of $f(x) = a$ at $x = 3$

128. *(a)* We have,

$$f(x) = \begin{cases} ax^2 + b\,; & x < -1 \\ bx^2 + ax + 4\,; & x \ge -1 \end{cases}$$

$\therefore$ $$f'(x) = \begin{cases} 2ax\,, & x < -1 \\ 2bx + a\,, & x \ge -1 \end{cases}$$

$\because f(x)$ is differentiable at $x = -1$

$\therefore$It is continuous at $x = -1$ and hence

$$\lim_{(x \to -1^-)} f(x) = \lim_{x \to -1^+} f(x)$$

$\Rightarrow$ $a + b = b - a + 4$

$\Rightarrow$ $a = 2$

and also, $\displaystyle\lim_{(x \to -1^-)} f'(x) = \lim_{x \to -1^+} f'(x)$

$\Rightarrow$ $-2a = -2b + a$

$\Rightarrow$ $3a = 2b \Rightarrow b = 3$ $\quad (\because a = 2)$

Hence, $a = 2,, b = 3$

129. *(c)* $\displaystyle\lim_{x \to \infty}\left(1 + \frac{a}{x} + \frac{b}{x^2}\right)^{2x} = e^2$

$\Rightarrow \displaystyle\lim_{x \to \infty}\left(1 + \frac{(ax + b)}{x^2}\right)^{2x} = e^2$ $\quad$ ...(i)

$\displaystyle\lim_{x \to \infty}\frac{ax + b}{x^2}$ must be equal to zero.

$\Rightarrow$ $$\lim_{x \to \infty}\frac{ax + b}{x^2} = 0$$

$\Rightarrow$ $$\lim_{x \to \infty}\left(\frac{a}{x} + \frac{b}{x^2}\right) = 0$$

$\therefore a$ and $b \in R$

From Eq. (i), $\displaystyle\lim_{e^{x \to \infty}}\left(1 + \frac{ax + b}{x^2} - 1\right)2x = e^2$

$\Rightarrow$ $$\lim_{e^{x \to \infty}}\frac{2(ax + b)}{x} = e^2$$

$\therefore$ $$e^{2a} = e^2$$

$\Rightarrow$ $a = 1$ and $b \in R$

130. *(a)* $S(-3, -2) = 9 + 4 - 6 - 6 + 1 = 2 > 0$

$\therefore(-3, -2)$ outside of S

and $S'(-3, -2) = 9 + 4 - 12 - 6 + 2 = -3 < 0$

$\therefore(-3, -2)$ inside of S'.

131. *(d)* $x^2 + 4x + c = 0$

For real roots, $D = b^2 - 4ac \ge 0$

$16 - 4c \ge 0$

So, $c = 1, 2, 3, 4$ will satisfy the above inequality.

$\therefore$Required probability $= \dfrac{4}{9}$

132. *(b)* Given constraints are

$6x + 4y \le 120$

$3x + 10y \le 180,\ x, y \ge 0$

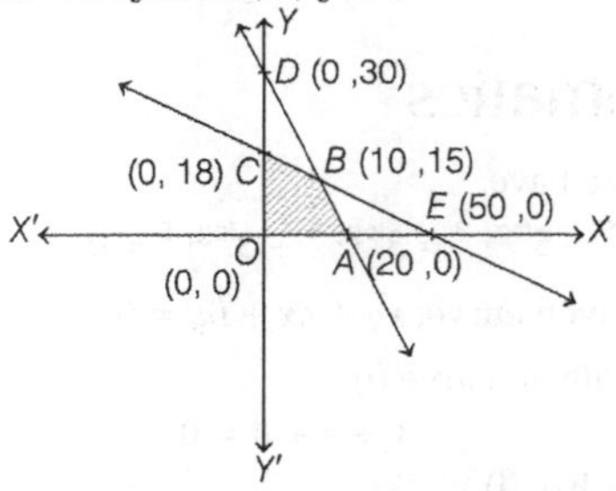

Here, $OABCO$ is the required feasible region whose corner points are O, A, B and C.

133. *(b)* Feasible region $ABCA$ and $Z = 4x + 2y$

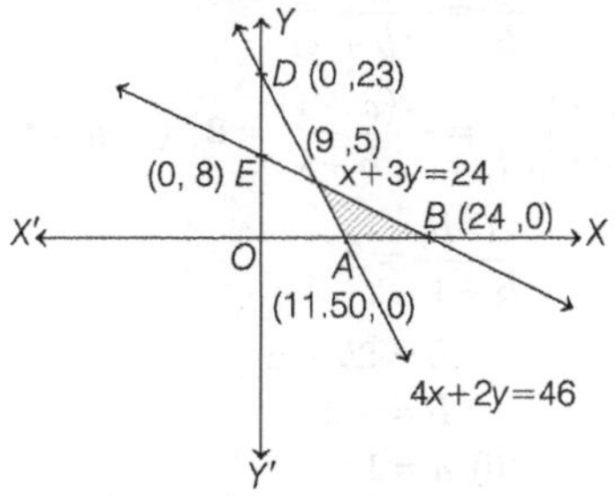

At point $C(9, 5)$, $Z = 4 \times 9 + 2 \times 5 = 46$

At point $A(11.5, 0)$, $Z = 4 \times 11.5 + 2 \times 0 = 46$

At point $B(24, 0)$, $Z = 4 \times 24 + 0 = 96$

Hence, maximum value of Z is 96.

134. *(c)* Given, $A(adj\ A) = \begin{bmatrix} 8 & 0 \\ 0 & 8 \end{bmatrix}$,

By using property $A(adj\ A) = |A| I_n$

$\Rightarrow \quad |A| I_n = \begin{bmatrix} 8 & 0 \\ 0 & 8 \end{bmatrix}$

$\Rightarrow \quad |A| I_n = 8\begin{bmatrix} 1 & 0 \\ 0 & 1 \end{bmatrix} \Rightarrow |A| = 8$

135. *(a)* Given, $A = \begin{bmatrix} a & 0 & 0 \\ 0 & a & 0 \\ 0 & 0 & a \end{bmatrix}$

Now, $|A| = a^3$

$\therefore |A||adj\ A| = |A||A|^{n-1} = |A|^n = (a^3)^n = a^{3n}$

136. *(d)* Given, $A = \begin{bmatrix} 2-k & 2 \\ 1 & 3-k \end{bmatrix}$

Since, the Matrix A is singular

$\therefore \quad |A| = 0$

$\Rightarrow \quad \begin{vmatrix} 2-k & 2 \\ 1 & 3-k \end{vmatrix} = 0$

$\Rightarrow \quad (2-k)(3-k) - 2 = 0$

$\Rightarrow \quad 6 - 5k + k^2 - 2 = 0$

$\Rightarrow \quad 4 - 5k + k^2 = 0$

$\Rightarrow \quad 5k - k^2 = 4$

137. *(a)* $\cos\theta = \dfrac{\mathbf{a}\cdot\mathbf{b}}{|\mathbf{a}||\mathbf{b}|}$

$= \dfrac{(2\hat{i} + 2\hat{j} - \hat{k})\cdot(6\hat{i} - 3\hat{j} + 2\hat{k})}{\sqrt{2^2 + 2^2 + (-1)^2}\sqrt{6^2 + (-3)^2 + 2^2}}$

$= \dfrac{12 - 6 - 2}{\sqrt{4 + 4 + 1}\sqrt{36 + 9 + 4}} = \dfrac{4}{21}$

138. *(c)* Given; $\mathbf{a} = x\hat{i} + 2\hat{j}$, $\mathbf{b} = y\hat{j} + 3\hat{k}$ and $\mathbf{c} = x\hat{i} + y\hat{j} + z\hat{k}$

Now, $\mathbf{a} \times \mathbf{b} = \begin{vmatrix} \hat{i} & \hat{j} & \hat{k} \\ x & 2 & 0 \\ 0 & y & 3 \end{vmatrix}$

$= \hat{i}(6 - 0) - \hat{j}(3x - 0) + \hat{k}(xy - 0)$

$= 6\hat{i} - 3x\hat{j} + xy\hat{k}$

$= 6\hat{i} - 3x\hat{j} + xy\hat{k} = z\hat{i} - 3\hat{j} + \hat{k}$

On equating the coefficients of $\hat{i}$, $\hat{j}$ and $\hat{k}$, we get

$z = 6, x = 1$ and $xy = 1$

$\because \quad xy = 1 \Rightarrow y = 1$

$\Rightarrow \quad \mathbf{a} = \hat{i} + 2\hat{j}, \mathbf{b} = \hat{j} + 3\hat{k}$

and $\quad \mathbf{c} = \hat{i} + \hat{j} + 6\hat{k}$

$\therefore \quad [\mathbf{a}\ \mathbf{b}\ \mathbf{c}] = \begin{vmatrix} 1 & 2 & 0 \\ 0 & 1 & 3 \\ 1 & 1 & 6 \end{vmatrix}$

$[\mathbf{a}\ \mathbf{b}\ \mathbf{c}] = 1(6 - 3) - 2(0 - 3) + 0 = 3 + 6 = 9$

139. *(b)* Given, constraints are $x \ge 0, y \ge 0, x + y \le 5$ and $3x + y \le 9$ and $z = 12x + 3y$

Here, feasible region is $OABCO$.

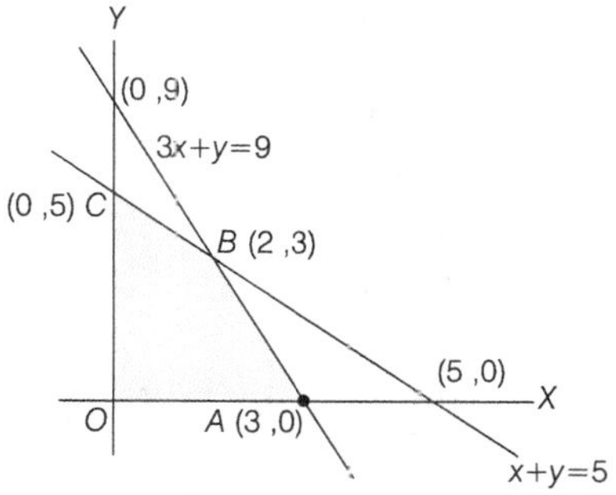

At point $O(0, 0)$, $z = 12(0) + 3(0) = 0$

At point $A(3, 0)$, $z = 12(3) + 3(0) = 36$

At point $B(2, 3)$, $z = 12(2) + 3(3) = 33$

At point $C(0, 5)$, $z = 12(0) + 3(5) = 15$

Hence, maximum value of z is 36.

140. *(a)* $3\mathbf{p} + \mathbf{q} - 2\mathbf{r}$

$= 3(\hat{i} + \hat{j}) + (4\hat{k} - \hat{j}) - 2(\hat{i} + \hat{k})$

$= \hat{i} + 2\hat{j} + 2\hat{k}$

$\therefore$ Unit vector in the direction of

$3\mathbf{p} + \mathbf{q} - 2\mathbf{r} = \dfrac{1}{3}(\hat{i} + 2\hat{j} + 2\hat{k})$

141. *(c)* Given equation of line is

$\dfrac{x-3}{4} = \dfrac{y-4}{5} = \dfrac{z-5}{6}$

So, DR's of line are (4, 5, 6)

Since, line is parallel to the plane, therefore the normal to plane is perpendicular to the line.

$\therefore \quad a_1a_2 + b_1b_2 + c_1c_2 = 0$

Consider the plane is

$x - 2y + z = 0$

Here, $a_2 = 1, b_2 = -2, c_2 = 1$

So, $a_1a_2 + b_1b_2 + c_1c_2$

$= (4 \times 1) + (5 \times -2) + (6 \times 1) = 4 - 10 + 6$

$= 10 - 10 = 0$

Hence, required plane is

$x - 2y + z = 0$

So, option (c) is correct.

142. *(c)* Let $I = \displaystyle\int \frac{1}{x\sqrt{ax - x^2}}\,dx$

Putting $x = \dfrac{a}{t}$

$\Rightarrow \quad dx = \dfrac{-a}{t^2}\,dt$

$\therefore \quad I = \displaystyle\int \frac{1}{\frac{a}{t}\sqrt{a\cdot\frac{a}{t} - \frac{a^2}{t^2}}} \times -\frac{a}{t^2}\,dt$

$$= \int \frac{-t}{t^2\sqrt{\frac{a^2}{t} - \frac{a^2}{t^2}}}\,dt$$

$$= \int \frac{-1}{at\sqrt{\frac{1}{t}-\frac{1}{t^2}}}\,dt$$

$$= \frac{-1}{a}\int \frac{1}{\sqrt{\frac{t^2}{t}-\frac{t^2}{t^2}}}\,dt$$

$$= \frac{-1}{a}\int\frac{1}{\sqrt{t-1}}\,dt = \frac{-1}{a}\int (t-1)^{-1/2}\,dt$$

$$= \frac{-1}{a}\frac{(t-1)^{1/2}}{1/2}+C = \frac{-2}{a}\left(\frac{a}{x}-1\right)^{1/2}+C$$

$$I = \frac{-2}{a}\sqrt{\frac{a-x}{x}}+C$$

Option (c) is correct.

143. *(c)* We have,

$$I = \int \frac{3^x}{\sqrt{1-9^x}}\,dx = \int \frac{3^x}{\sqrt{1-(3^x)^2}}\,dx$$

Putting $3^x = t$

$\Rightarrow \quad 3^x \log 3\, dx = dt$

$\Rightarrow \quad 3^x\, dx = \frac{1}{\log 3}\,dt$

$\therefore \quad I = \frac{1}{\log 3}\int \frac{1}{\sqrt{1-t^2}}\,dt$

$$= \frac{1}{\log 3}\sin^{-1} t + C$$

$$= \frac{1}{\log 3}\sin^{-1}(3^x) + C$$

Option (c) is correct.

144. *(a)* Here $f(x) = \cos x$

$$f(-x) = \cos(-x) = \cos x = f(x)$$

So, f is even function.

$\therefore \quad \int_{-\frac{\pi}{2}}^{\frac{\pi}{2}} \cos x\, dx = 2\int_0^{\frac{\pi}{2}} \cos x\, dx$

$$\left[\because \int_{-a}^{a} f(x)\,dx = 2\int_0^a f(x)\,dx, \text{ if } f \text{ is even}\right]$$

$$= 2[\sin x]_0^{\pi/2}$$

$$= 2\left[\sin\frac{\pi}{2} - \sin 0\right] = 2[1-0] = 2$$

145. *(c)* The angle between two lines $\frac{x-x_1}{a_1} = \frac{y-y_1}{b_1} = \frac{z-z_1}{c_1}$ and $\frac{x-x_2}{a_2} = \frac{y-y_2}{b_2} = \frac{z-z_2}{c_2}$ is given by

$$\cos\theta = \frac{a_1a_2 + b_1b_2 + c_1c_2}{\sqrt{a_1^2+b_1^2+c_1^2}\sqrt{a_2^2+b_2^2+c_2^2}}$$

$$= \frac{3\times 1 + 5\times 1 + 4\times 2}{\sqrt{3^2+5^2+4^2}\sqrt{1^2+1^2+2^2}}$$

$$= \frac{16}{\sqrt{50}\sqrt{6}} = \frac{16}{\sqrt{300}}$$

$\Rightarrow \quad \cos\theta = \frac{16}{10\sqrt{3}}$

$\Rightarrow \quad \cos\theta = \frac{8}{5\sqrt{3}}$

$\Rightarrow \quad \theta = \cos^{-1}\left(\frac{8}{5\sqrt{3}}\right)$

So, option (c) is correct.

146. *(d)* Given lines are

$$\frac{x-1}{1} = \frac{y-1}{2} = \frac{z-2}{3} = \lambda \text{ (let)}$$

$\Rightarrow \quad x = \lambda + 1,\ y = 2\lambda + 1,\ z = 3\lambda + 2$

and $\frac{x-5}{2} = \frac{y-2}{1} = z = \mu$ (let)

$\Rightarrow x = 2\mu + 5,\ y = \mu + 2,\ z = \mu$

For point of intersection, we have

$\lambda + 1 = 2\mu + 5$ and $2\lambda + 1 = \mu + 2$ and $3\lambda + 2 = \mu$

$\lambda - 2\mu = 4 \quad \ldots$(i)

and $\quad 2\lambda - \mu = 1 \quad \ldots$(ii)

and $\quad 3\lambda - \mu = -2 \quad \ldots$(iii)

On solving Eqs. (ii) and (iii), we get

$$2\lambda - \mu = 1$$
$$3\lambda - \mu = -2$$
$$- \quad + \quad +$$
$$-\lambda = 3$$

$\Rightarrow \quad \lambda = -3$

So, $\quad \mu = -7$

Now, put $\lambda = -3$ and $\mu = -7$ in Eq. (i), we get

$$-3 + 14 = 11 \neq 4$$

Hence, the lines do not intersect.

Hence, option (d) is correct.

147. *(a)* Given, 5 persons are in a queue of a shop. A and B itself can arrange in two ways therefore number of arrangement for A and $B = 2! = 2$

So, probability that A and B are always together

$$= \frac{2!\times 4!}{5!} = \frac{2\times 4!}{5\times 4!} = \frac{2}{5}$$

Option (a) is correct.

148. *(b)* $P(\overline{A}) = 0.2,\ P(\overline{B}) = 0.3$

$\therefore P(A) = 0.8,\ P(B) = 0.7$

$\therefore$ Required probability

$$= P(\overline{A})P(\overline{B}) + P(\overline{A})P(\overline{B}) + P(\overline{A})P(\overline{B})$$

$$= 0.2\times 0.7 + 0.8\times 0.3 + 0.2\times 0.3$$

$$= 0.44$$

149. *(d)* Number of triangles formed = $^7C_3$

Number of isosceles triangles = $7 \times 3 = 21$

So, probability $= \dfrac{21}{^7C_3} = \dfrac{21}{\dfrac{7!}{3!(7-3)!}}$

$= \dfrac{21 \times 3! \times 4!}{7 \times 6 \times 5 \times 4!} = \dfrac{3}{5}$

Option (d) is correct.

150. *(b)* Given that *A*, *B* and *C* are three mutually exclusive events

$\Rightarrow \quad P(A) = 2P(B) = 3P(C)$

$P(A \cup B \cup C) = P(A) + P(B) + P(C)$

$= 2P(B) + P(B) + \dfrac{2}{3}P(B)$

$= \dfrac{11}{3}P(B)$

$\because P(A \cup B \cup C) = 1$

$\Rightarrow \quad \dfrac{11}{3}P(B) = 1 \Rightarrow P(B) = \dfrac{3}{11}$

$\Rightarrow \quad P(B) = \dfrac{6}{22}$

Option (b) is correct.

151. *(b)* $\because U_{n+1} = 3U_n - 2U_{n-1}$ ...(i)

Step I Given, $U_1 = 3 = 2 + 1 = 2^1 + 1$, which is true for $n = 1$, put $n = 1$ in Eq. (i),

Then $\quad U_{1+1} = 3U_1 - 2U_{1-1}$

$\Rightarrow \quad U_2 = 3U_1 - 2U_0$

$= 3 \times 3 - 2 \times 2 = 5 = 2^2 + 1$

Which is true for $n = 2$.

$\therefore$ The result are true for $n = 1$ and $n = 2$.

Step II Assume it is true for $n = k$, then it is also true for $n = k - 1$

Then, $\quad U_k = 2^k + 1$ ...(ii)

and $\quad U_{k-1} = 2^{k-1} + 1$ ...(iii)

Step III On putting $n = k$ in Eq. (i), we get

$U_{k+1} = 3U_k - 2U_{k-1}$

$= 3(2^k + 1) - 2(2^{k-1} + 1)$ [From Eqs. (ii) and (iii)]

$= 3 \cdot 2^k + 3 - 2 \cdot 2^{k-1} - 2$

$= 3 \cdot 2^k + 3 - 2^k - 2$

$= (3-1)2^k + 1$

$= 2 \cdot 2^k + 1 = 2^{k+1} + 1$

This shows that the result is ture for $n = k + 1$. Hence by the principle of mathematical induction the result is true for all $n \in N$.

152. *(a)* We have, $P(n) = 4^n + 15n + P$

For $n = 1$, $P(1) = 4 + 15 + P = 19 + P$ is divisible by 9.

Thus, *P* should be –1.

Since, $19 - 1 = 18$ is divisible by 9.

153. *(b)* For $n = 1$, $2^{3n} - 1$ has value $2^3 - 1 = 7$

For $n = 2$, $2^{3n} - 1$ has value $2^6 - 1 = 63 = 7 \times 9$

which is divisible by 7 not by 6 or 8 or 9.

Hence, option (b) is correct.

154. *(a)* We know, $T_n = \dfrac{(n+1)^2 - n}{n(n+1)}$

$= 1 + \left(\dfrac{1}{n} - \dfrac{1}{n+1}\right)$

$\therefore \quad S_{10} = 10 + \left(1 - \dfrac{1}{11}\right) = \dfrac{120}{11}$

155. *(c)* We have, $n \cdot n!$

$= (n + 1 - 1) \cdot n!$

$= (n+1)! - n!$

$= V(n) - V(n-1)$

$\Rightarrow \sum_{n=1}^{m} n\,(n!) = V(m) - V(0) = (m+1)! - 1$

156. *(c)* We have,

$a = -14$ and $a + 4d = 2$

$\Rightarrow \quad -14 + 4d = 2 \Rightarrow 4d = 14 + 2$

$\Rightarrow \quad 4d = 16$

$\therefore \quad d = 4$

Now, $\quad S_n = \dfrac{n}{2}[2a + (n-1)d]$

$\Rightarrow \quad 40 = \dfrac{n}{2}[-28 + (n-1)4]$

$\Rightarrow \quad n^2 - 8n - 20 = 0$

$\Rightarrow \quad (n-10)(n+2) = 0$

$\Rightarrow \quad n = 10$

157. *(b)* Given, differential equation is $\dfrac{d^2y}{dx^2} = 0$

On integrating, we get

$\dfrac{dy}{dx} = c$, where *c* is a constant

$\Rightarrow dy = c\,dx$

Again integrating,

$\Rightarrow \quad \int dy = c\int dx$

$\Rightarrow \quad y = cx + d$, where *d* is a constant.

$\therefore$ The solution of differential equation represents all straight lines in a plane.

158. *(b)* Given, $\dfrac{dy}{dx} + \dfrac{\sqrt{1-y^2}}{\sqrt{1-x^2}} = 0$

$\Rightarrow \quad \dfrac{dy}{\sqrt{1-y^2}} + \dfrac{dx}{\sqrt{1-x^2}} = 0$

On integrating, we get

$\Rightarrow \quad \int \dfrac{dy}{\sqrt{1-y^2}} + \int \dfrac{dx}{\sqrt{1-x^2}} = 0$

$\Rightarrow \quad \sin^{-1} y - \sin^{-1} x = c$

159. *(b)* Given, $x\dfrac{dy}{dx} = \cot y$

$\Rightarrow \quad \tan y\, dy = \dfrac{dx}{x}$

On integrating, we get

$\Rightarrow \quad \int \tan y\, dy = \int \dfrac{dx}{x}$

$\Rightarrow \quad \log \sec y = \log x + \log c_1$

$\Rightarrow \quad \log \sec y = \log x \cdot c_1$

$\Rightarrow \quad \sec y = x \cdot c_1$

$\Rightarrow \quad x \cos y = c,$

where $c = \dfrac{1}{c_1}$

160. *(b)* We have, ${}^nC_3 = 220$

$\Rightarrow \quad \dfrac{n(n-1)(n-2)}{6} = 220$

$\Rightarrow \quad n(n-1)(n-2) = 1320$

$\Rightarrow \quad n = 12 \qquad [\because 12 \times 11 \times 10 = 1320]$

161. *(b)* Total number of questions, $n = 5$

Probability of correct answer, $p = \dfrac{1}{3}$

Probability of incorrect answer, $q = \dfrac{2}{3}$

Required probability $= P(x \geq 4)$

$= p(x = 4) + p(x = 5)$

$= {}^5C_4 \times \left(\dfrac{1}{3}\right)^4 \times \left(\dfrac{2}{3}\right)^1 + {}^5C_5 \left(\dfrac{1}{3}\right)^5 \times \left(\dfrac{2}{3}\right)^0$

$= \dfrac{10}{3^5} + \dfrac{1}{3^5} = \dfrac{11}{3^5}$

162. *(c)* Given, $\sin A + \sin B = a \qquad \ldots(i)$

$\cos A + \cos B = b \qquad \ldots(ii)$

Dividing Eq. (i) by Eq. (ii), we get

$\dfrac{\sin A + \sin B}{\cos A + \cos B} = \dfrac{a}{b}$

$\Rightarrow \quad \dfrac{2 \sin\left(\dfrac{A+B}{2}\right) \cos\left(\dfrac{A-B}{2}\right)}{2 \cos\left(\dfrac{A+B}{2}\right) \cos\left(\dfrac{A-B}{2}\right)} = \dfrac{a}{b}$

$\Rightarrow \quad \tan \dfrac{A+B}{2} = \dfrac{a}{b} \qquad \ldots(iii)$

Now, $\quad \cos(A+B) = \dfrac{1 - \tan^2\left(\dfrac{A+B}{2}\right)}{1 + \tan^2\left(\dfrac{A-B}{2}\right)}$

$\left(\because \text{using } \cos\theta = \dfrac{1 - \tan^2\dfrac{\theta}{2}}{1 + \tan^2\dfrac{\theta}{2}}\right)$

$\Rightarrow \quad \cos(A+B) = \dfrac{1 - \dfrac{a^2}{b^2}}{1 + \dfrac{a^2}{b^2}} \qquad$ [Using Eq. (iii)]

$\therefore \quad \cos(A+B) = \dfrac{b^2 - a^2}{b^2 + a^2}$

163. *(c)* $\dfrac{\cos\theta}{1 - \tan\theta} + \dfrac{\sin\theta}{1 - \cot\theta} = \dfrac{\cos\theta}{1 - \dfrac{\sin\theta}{\cos\theta}} + \dfrac{\sin\theta}{1 - \dfrac{\cos\theta}{\sin\theta}}$

$= \dfrac{\cos^2\theta}{\cos\theta - \sin\theta} + \dfrac{\sin^2\theta}{\sin\theta - \cos\theta}$

$= \dfrac{\cos^2\theta}{\cos\theta - \sin\theta} - \dfrac{\sin^2\theta}{\cos\theta - \sin\theta}$

$= \dfrac{\cos^2\theta - \sin^2\theta}{\cos\theta - \sin\theta}$

$= \dfrac{(\cos\theta + \sin\theta)(\cos\theta - \sin\theta)}{(\cos\theta - \sin\theta)}$

[Using identity $a^2 - b^2 = (a+b)(a-b)$]

$= \sin\theta + \cos\theta$

164. (c) $\sin 2x + \cos x = 0$

$\Rightarrow \quad 2 \sin x \cos x + \cos x = 0$

$\Rightarrow \quad \cos x(2 \sin x + 1) = 0$

$\Rightarrow \quad \cos x = 0$ or $2 \sin x + 1 = 0$

$\Rightarrow \quad \cos x = \cos \dfrac{\pi}{2} \Rightarrow x = n\pi \pm \dfrac{\pi}{2}, n \in z$

or $\quad \sin x = -\dfrac{1}{2} = -\sin\left(\dfrac{\pi}{6}\right)$

$= \sin\left(\pi + \dfrac{\pi}{6}\right)$

$\Rightarrow \quad \sin x = \sin\left(\dfrac{7\pi}{6}\right)$

$\therefore \quad x = n\pi + (-1)^n \dfrac{7\pi}{6}, n \in Z$

165. *(c)* Given, $f(x) + 2f(1-x) = x^2 + 5 \qquad \ldots(i)$

Replace $x \to 1 - x$

$\therefore \quad f(1-x) + 2f(x) = (1-x)^2 + 5 \qquad \ldots(ii)$

Multiplying Eq. (ii) by 2 and subtracting Eq. (i) from it

$\Rightarrow \quad 2f(1-x) + 4f(x) - f(x) - 2f(1-x)$

$= 2(1-x)^2 + (5 \times 2) - x^2 - 5$

$\Rightarrow 3f(x) = 2(x^2 - 2x + 1) - x^2 + 5 = x^2 - 4x + 7$

$\therefore f(x) = \dfrac{(x-2)^2 + 3}{3}$

166. *(b)* $A \times B = \{(3, 1), (3, 2), (3, 3), (3, 5), (5, 1), (5, 2), (5, 3), (5, 5), (7, 1), (7, 2), (7, 3), (7, 5)\}$

$B \times A = \{(1, 3), (1, 5), (1, 7), (2, 3), (2, 5) (2, 7), (3, 3), (3, 5), (3, 7), (5, 3), (5, 5), (5, 7)\}$

$\therefore A \times B \cap B \times A = \{(3, 3), (3, 5), (5, 3), (5, 5)\}$

167. *(d)* For a given set A with n elements, number of elements in power set $P(A)$ is 2^n.

Here, $n = 17$

$\therefore$ Power set contains 2^{17} elements.

168. *(d)* $\frac{1-i\sqrt{3}}{1+i\sqrt{3}} = \frac{1-i\sqrt{3}}{1+i\sqrt{3}} \times \frac{1-i\sqrt{3}}{1-i\sqrt{3}} = \frac{(1-i\sqrt{3})^2}{4}$

[Using identity $(a+b)(a-b) = a^2 - b^2$]

$= \frac{1-2\sqrt{3}i-3}{4} = \frac{-2-2\sqrt{3}i}{4}$

$= \frac{-1}{2} - \frac{\sqrt{3}}{2}i$

$\therefore arg\left(\frac{-1}{2} - \frac{\sqrt{3}}{2}i\right) = -(\pi - \tan^{-1}\sqrt{3}) = \frac{-2\pi}{3}$

169. *(d)* $\left[i^{22} + \left(\frac{1}{i}\right)^{25}\right]^3 = \left[(i^2)^{11} + \frac{1}{(i^2)^{12} i}\right]^3$

$= \left[(-1)^{11} + \frac{1}{i}\right]^3 = \left(-1 + \frac{1}{i}\right)^3 \quad [\because i^2 = -1]$

$= (-1)^3 + \left(\frac{1}{i}\right)^3 + 3(-1)\left(\frac{1}{i}\right)\left(-1 + \frac{1}{i}\right)$

[Using $(a+b)^3 = a^3 + b^3 + 3ab(a+b)$]

$= -1 + \frac{1}{i^2 i} - \frac{3}{i}\left(-1 + \frac{1}{i}\right)$

$= -1 - \frac{1}{i} + \frac{3}{i} - \frac{3}{i^2}$

$= -1 + \frac{2}{i} + 3 \quad (\because i^2 = -1)$

$= 2 + \frac{2i}{i \times i} = 2 - 2i = 2(1-i)$

170. *(a)* $(i+\sqrt{3})^{100} = 1 \times (i+\sqrt{3})^{100} = i^{100}(i+\sqrt{3})^{100}$

(As $i^{4m} = 1$, where $m = 25 \therefore i^{100} = 1$)

$= (i^2 + i\sqrt{3})^{100} = (-1+i\sqrt{3})^{100} = (2\omega)^{100}$

Similarly, $(i-\sqrt{3})^{100} = (-1-\sqrt{3})^{100} = (2\omega^2)^{100}$

$\therefore (i+\sqrt{3})^{100} + (i-\sqrt{3})^{100} + 2^{100}$

$= (2\omega)^{100} + (2\omega^2)^{100} + 2^{100}$

$= 2^{100}(\omega^{100} + \omega^{200} + 1)$

$= 2^{100}(0) = 0$

$\therefore (i+\sqrt{3})^{100} + (i-\sqrt{3})^{100} + 2^{100} = 0$

171. *(b)* From 12 given points ${}^{12}C_2$ straight lines can be drawn.

But 3 points are collinear, using 3 points ${}^{3}C_2$ straight lines can be drawn.

So, total straight lines without the straight line using three points = ${}^{12}C_2 - {}^{3}C_2$

From 3 collinear points 1 straight line can be drawn

So, total number of straight lines = ${}^{12}C_2 - {}^{3}C_2 + 1$

$= \frac{12!}{2! \times 10!} - \frac{3!}{2! \times 1!} + 1$

$= \frac{12 \times 11 \times 10!}{2 \times 1 \times 10!} - \frac{3 \times 2!}{2! \times 1} + 1$

$= 66 - 3 + 1 = 64$

172. *(b)* Total number formed by using 5 digits $= \frac{5!}{2!}$

$= \frac{5 \times 4 \times 3 \times 2!}{2!} = 60$

For number greater than 50,000, digit 2 cannot come at first place.

Hence, number formed in which 2 is at the first place

$= \frac{4!}{2!} = \frac{4 \times 3 \times 2!}{2!} = 12$

Hence, total number formed greater than 50000

$= 60 - 12 = 48$

173. *(d)* A polygon of n sides has number of diagonals = 170

$\Rightarrow \quad \frac{n(n-3)}{2} = 170$

$\Rightarrow \quad n^2 - 3n = 340$

$\Rightarrow \quad n^2 - 3n - 340 = 0$

$\Rightarrow \quad n^2 - 20n + 17n - 340 = 0$

$\Rightarrow \quad n(n-20) + 17(n-20) = 0$

$\Rightarrow \quad (n-20)(n+17) = 0$

$\Rightarrow \quad n - 20 = 0$ or $n + 17 = 0$

$n = 20$ or $n = -17$ [it is not possible]

So, $n = 20$

174. *(c)* Equation of angle of equation of pair of straight line $ax^2 + 2hxy + by^2$ is

$$\frac{x^2 - y^2}{a-b} = \frac{xy}{h}$$

For $x^2 - 4xy - 5y^2 = 0$

$a = 1, h = -2, b = -5$

So, equation of angle bisector is

$$\frac{x^2 - y^2}{1-(-5)} = \frac{xy}{-2}$$

$\Rightarrow \quad x^2 - y^2 = -3xy$

$\Rightarrow \quad x^2 + 3xy - y^2 = 0$

175. *(c)* We have to find, PQ

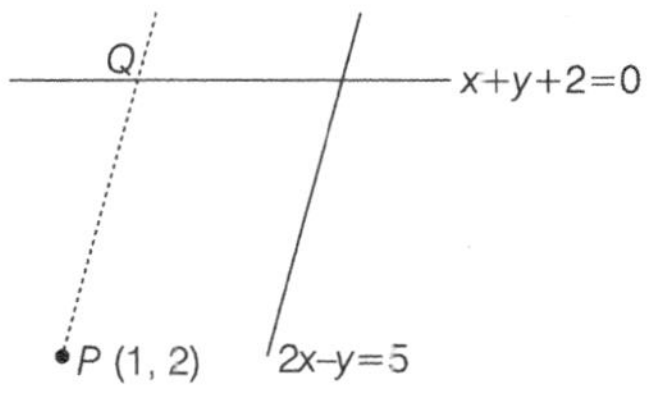

The slope of the line $2x - y = 5$

$\Rightarrow \quad y = 2x - 5$

On comparing with $y = mx + c$, we get

$m = 2$

Also, slope of PQ, $m_{PQ} = 2$

Eq. of PQ, $(y - 2) = 2(x - 1)$

$\Rightarrow \quad y - 2 = 2x - 2$

$\Rightarrow \quad y = 2x$

So, from $x + y + 2 = 0 \Rightarrow x + 2x + 2 = 0$

$\Rightarrow \quad 3x + 2 = 0 \Rightarrow x = -\dfrac{2}{3}$

$y = 2 \times \dfrac{-2}{3} = \dfrac{-4}{3}$

$\therefore$ The point Q is $\left(\dfrac{-2}{3}, \dfrac{-4}{3}\right)$.

and $\quad P = (1, 2)$

Distance, $PQ = \sqrt{\left(\dfrac{-2}{3} - 1\right)^2 + \left(\dfrac{-4}{3} - 2\right)^2}$

$= \sqrt{\left(\dfrac{-5}{3}\right)^2 + \left(\dfrac{-10}{3}\right)^2}$

$= \sqrt{\dfrac{25}{9} + \dfrac{100}{9}} = \sqrt{\dfrac{125}{9}} = \dfrac{\sqrt{125}}{3} = \dfrac{5\sqrt{5}}{3}$

176. *(a)* We have, $\theta = \dfrac{\pi}{4}$

Given, line is $2x - y = -7$

$y = 2x + 7$

Here, slope $m_1 = 2$

The required line makes an angle 45° with this line

So, $\tan 45° = \left|\dfrac{2 - m_2}{1 + 2m_2}\right|$

$\Rightarrow \quad 1 = \left|\dfrac{2 - m_2}{1 + 2m_2}\right|$

$\Rightarrow 1 + 2m_2 = 2 - m_2$ or $1 + 2m_2 = -(2 - m_2)$

$2m_2 + m_2 = 2 - 1$ or $1 + 2m_2 = -2 + m_2$

$\Rightarrow \quad 3m_2 = 1 \quad \Rightarrow 2m_2 - m_2 = -2 - 1$

$\therefore m_2 = \dfrac{1}{3}, \; m_2 = -3$

177. *(c)* If 2, 3 are intercepts of a line $L = 0$, then

x-intercept $= 2 = a$

y-intercept $= 3 = b$

Equation of line is $\dfrac{x}{a} + \dfrac{y}{b} = 1$

$\Rightarrow \quad \dfrac{x}{2} + \dfrac{y}{3} = 1$

$\Rightarrow \quad 3x + 2y - 6 = 0$

$\therefore$ Required distance from origin is given by

$= \left|\dfrac{3(0) + 2(0) - 6}{\sqrt{3^2 + 2^2}}\right| = \dfrac{|-6|}{\sqrt{13}} = \dfrac{6}{\sqrt{13}}$

$\therefore$ Distance $= \dfrac{6}{\sqrt{13}}$ units

178. *(c)* The expansion $(x + y)^{100} + (x - y)^{100}$ has $\left(\dfrac{100}{2} + 1\right) = 51$ terms

179. *(a)* Given expansion is $(1 + 3x + 3x^2 + x^3)^{20}$

$= ((1 + x)^3)^{20}$

$= (1 + x)^{60} \quad \ldots(\text{i})$

In the expansion of $(a + b)^n$, $(r + 1)$th term is given by

$t_{r+1} = {}^nC_r a^r \cdot b^{n-r}$

or $\quad t_{r+1} = {}^nC_r a^{n-r} \cdot b^r$

$\therefore$ 21st term in Eq. (i) will contain the coefficient of x^{20} and it is given by

$t_{21} = {}^{60}C_{20}\, x^{20}, 1^{40} = {}^{60}C_{20}\, x^{20}$

$\therefore$ Coefficient of x^{20} in $(1 + x)^{60}$ is ${}^{60}C_{20}$ or ${}^{60}C_{40}$.

180. *(c)* Given expansion is $(1 - 3x + 3x^2 - x^3)^{2n}$

$= [(1 - x)^3]^{2n}$

$= (1 - x)^{6n}$

$\therefore$ Middle term $= \dfrac{6n + 2}{2}$th term [here, $6n$ is even]

$= (3n + 1)$th term

COMEDK

Solved Paper 2021

Instructions

- There are 180 questions in all. The number of questions in each section is as given below.

Sections	No. of Questions
Section I : Physics	1–60
Section II : Chemistry	61–120
Section III : Mathematics	121–180

- All the questions are Multiple Choice Questions having four options out of which **ONLY ONE** is correct.
- Candidates will be awarded 1 mark for each correct answer. There will be no negative marking for incorrect answer.
- Time allotted to complete this paper is 3 hrs.

PHYSICS

1. The Lyman series of a hydrogen atom belongs in which category

a. ultraviolet region *b.* infrared region
c. visible region *d.* None of these

2. Insulators can be charged by which of the following process?

a. Induction *b.* Diverging
c. Friction *d.* Heating

3. In an adiabatic process with the ratio of two specific heat, $\gamma = \frac{3}{2}$, pressure is increased by $\frac{2}{3}\%$, then decrease in the volume will be

a. $\frac{4}{9}\%$ *b.* $\frac{2}{3}\%$ *c.* 4% *d.* $\frac{9}{4}\%$

4. Two converging lenses of focal length 20 cm and 40 cm are placed in contact. The effective power of the combination is

a. 5.25 D *b.* 7.25 D *c.* 2.75 D *d.* 7.5 D

5. The formula of capacitative reactance is

a. $2\pi fC$ *b.* $\frac{fC}{2\pi}$
c. $\frac{C}{2\pi f}$ *d.* $\frac{1}{2\pi fC}$

6. Which graph shows the correct v - x graph of a freely falling body ?

a.
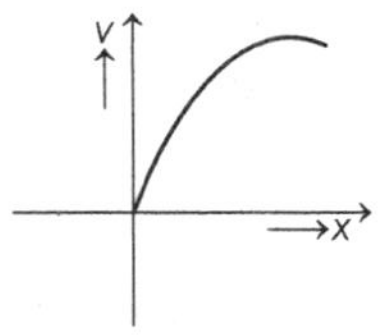

b.
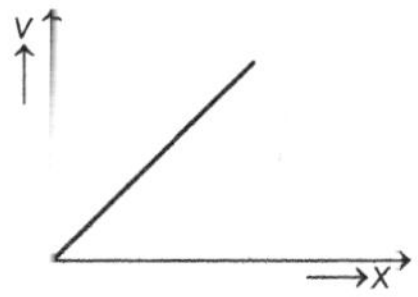

c.
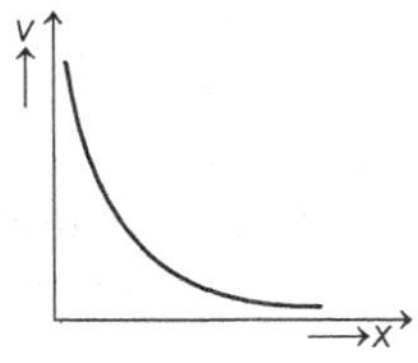

d.
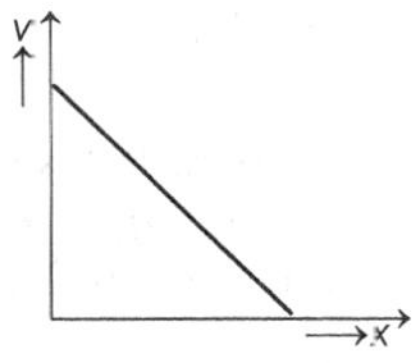

7. The displacement x of a particle varies with time t, $x = ae^{-pt} + be^{qt}$, where a, b, p and q are positive constant. The velocity of the particle will

a. go on increasing forever
b. be independent of p and q
c. drop to zero when $p = q$
d. go on decreasing with time

8. Which of the following quantity represents the dimensions of momentum?

a. Impulse *b.* Pressure
c. Viscosity *d.* Power

9. The angle of projection with the horizontal in terms of maximum height attained and horizontal range is given by

a. $\tan^{-1}\left(\frac{2H}{3R}\right)$ *b.* $\tan^{-1}\left(\frac{4R}{3H}\right)$
c. $\tan^{-1}\left(\frac{4H}{R}\right)$ *d.* $\tan^{-1}\left(\frac{R}{H}\right)$

10. For the same resonant frequency, if L is changed from L to $\frac{L}{3}$, then capacitance should change from C to

a. $\frac{C}{3}$ *b.* $3C$
c. $\frac{2}{3}C$ *d.* $2C$

11. The velocity of the proton is one-fourth the velocity of the electron. What is the ratio of the de-Broglie wavelength of an electron to that of a proton?

a. 1 *b.* $\frac{1}{2}$ *c.* $\frac{1}{3}$ *d.* $\frac{1}{4}$

12. For an ideal gas, coefficient of volume expansion is given by

a. $\frac{1}{p}$ *b.* $\frac{1}{pV}$
c. $\frac{1}{R}$ *d.* $\frac{1}{T}$

13. Which of the following is not a green house gas?

a. CH_4 *b.* CO_2
c. O_3 *d.* H_2O

14. Two particles of masses $m_1 = m$, $m_2 = 2m$ and charges $q_1 = q$, $q_2 = 2q$ entered into uniform magnetic field. Find F_1/F_2 (force ratio).

a. $\frac{1}{2}$ *b.* 1 *c.* $\frac{1}{3}$ *d.* 2

15. Work done in moving a charge of 25C is 50 J. Calculate potential difference, between two points.

a. 0.5 V *b.* 1 V
c. 2 V *d.* 2.5 V

16. The correct arrangement in increasing order of wavelength of X-rays, UV rays, microwave is

a. microwave, X-rays, UV rays
b. UV rays, X- rays, microwave
c. X-rays, UV rays, microwave
d. microwave, UV rays, X-rays

17. What is the electric field near infinite plane sheet of charge density σ ?

a. $\frac{\sigma}{2\varepsilon_0}$ *b.* $\frac{\sigma A}{2\varepsilon_0}$
c. $\frac{\sigma}{2\varepsilon_0 A}$ *d.* $\frac{\sigma}{\varepsilon_0}$

18. Which of the following waves are used to treatment of muscles ache?

a. Ultraviolet *b.* Infrared
c. Microwave *d.* X-rays

19. Find the logic gate, when both the inputs are high but the output is low and *vice-versa*.

a. AND *b.* OR
c. NAND *d.* NOR

20. What is the minimum band-gap of the LED diode?

a. 1.5 eV *b.* 1.7 eV
c. 1.8 eV *d.* 0.8 eV

21. The displacement of a wave is given by

$$y = 20\cos(\omega t + 4z)$$

The amplitude of the given wave is

a. 10 *b.* 20
c. $20\sqrt{2}$ *d.* $10\sqrt{2}$

22. If frequencies are $(\nu - 1)$ and $(\nu + 2)$, then find the value of beats.

a. 2 *b.* 1
c. 3 *d.* 4

23. The function $y = \log \omega t$ can represent

a. a periodic function *b.* non-periodic function
c. oscillatory function *d.* circulatory motion

24. Two spring of force constant k_1 and k_2 are configured as the figure given below

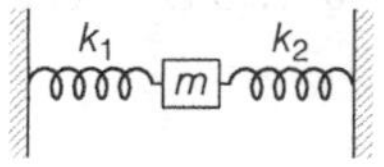

The angular frequency of this configuration is

a. $\frac{k_1 + k_2}{m}$ b. $\sqrt{\frac{k_1 + k_2}{m}}$

c. $\sqrt{\frac{k_1}{k_2 m}}$ d. $\frac{k_2 m}{k_1}$

25. The resistance of a wire is R ohm. If it is melted and stretched to n times its original length, its new resistance will be

a. nR b. $\frac{R}{n}$

c. $n^2 R$ d. $\frac{R}{n^2}$

26. An unpolarised beam of intensity I_0 is incident on a pair of nicols making an angle of 60° with each other. The intensity of light emerging from the pair is

a. I_0 b. $\frac{I_0}{4}$

c. $\frac{I_0}{2}$ d. $\frac{I_0}{8}$

27. The collision of the molecules of an ideal gas is taken as

a. elastic b. inelastic

c. partially elastic d. partially inelastic

28. The average energy associated with a monoatomic molecule is

a. $K_B T$ b. $\frac{1}{2} K_B T$

c. $\frac{3}{2} K_B T$ d. $2K_B T$

29. For the given electrical arrangement, what is the value of current I?

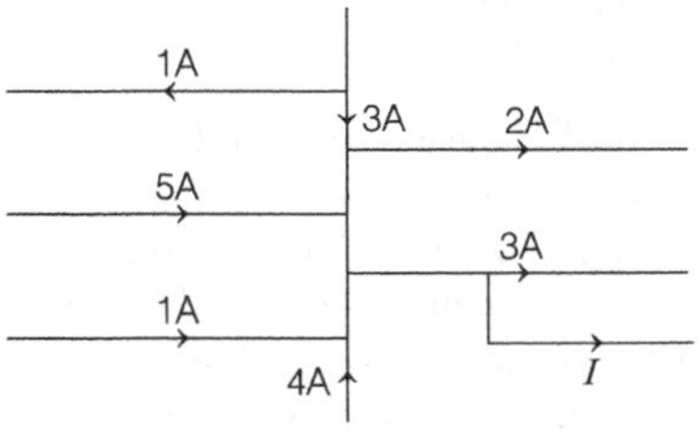

a. 6A b. 5A c. 7A d. 8A

30. If an electron in hydrogen atom jumps from an orbit of level $n = 3$ to an orbit at level $n = 2$, emitted radiation has a frequency of (R = Rydberg's constant and c = velocity of light)

a. $\frac{3Rc}{27}$ b. $\frac{Rc}{25}$

c. $\frac{8Rc}{9}$ d. $\frac{5Rc}{36}$

31. Within the elastic limit, the corresponding stress is known as

a. tensile strength b. yield strength

c. elastic fatigue d. yield point

32. A wire is stretched to double of its length. The strain is

a. 1 b. 2

c. 3 d. 4

33. Kepler's second law of planetary motion corresponds to

a. conservation of energy

b. conservation of angular momentum

c. conservation of linear momentum

d. conservation of mass

34. A constant potential energy of a satellite is given as

$$PE = r(KE)$$

where, PE = potential energy

and KE = kinetic energy.

The value of r will be

a. -1 b. -2

c. $\frac{-1}{2}$ d. $\frac{-3}{2}$

35. A long solenoid has 20 turns cm^{-1}. The current necessary to produce a magnetic field of 20 mT inside the solenoid is approximately

a. 1 A b. 2A

c. 4A d. 8A

36. A constant current flows from A to B as shown in the figure. What is the direction of current in the circle?

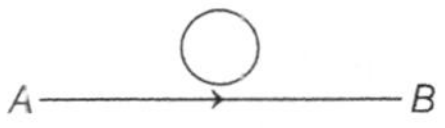

a. Clockwise

b. Anti-clockwise

c. Straight line

d. None of the above

37. According to Pascal's law, pressure in a fluid at rest is the same at all points, if

a. they are at the same plane

b. they are at the same height

c. they are along same line

d. Both (a) and (b)

38. The surface tension of a liquid at its boiling point

a. becomes zero

b. becomes infinity

c. is equal to the value at room temperature

d. is half of the value at room temperature

39. Centre of mass of the given system of particles will be at

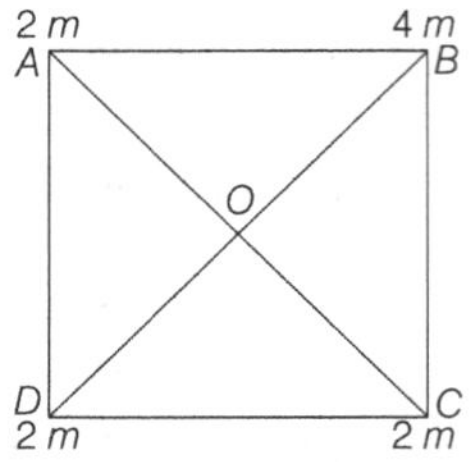

a. OA *b.* OB *c.* OC *d.* OD

40. Newton's second law of rotational motion of a system particles having angular momentum L is given by

a. $\frac{dp}{dt} = \tau_{ext}$ *b.* $\frac{dL}{dt} = \tau_{int}$

c. $\frac{dL}{dt} = \tau_{ext}$ *d.* $\frac{dL}{dt} = \tau_{int} + \tau_{ext}$

41. The motion of a particle of mass m is described by $y = ut + gt^2$. The force acting on the particle will be

a. zero *b.* 4 mg *c.* 3 mg *d.* 2 mg

42. When a car of mass m is moving with speed v along a circle of radius r on a level road, the centripetal force is provided by f, where f denotes

($\mu_s \rightarrow$ coefficient of friction, $N \rightarrow$ normal reaction)

a. $\frac{mv^2}{r} = f \leq \mu_s N$ *b.* $f < \mu_s = \frac{mv^2}{r}$

c. $f = \mu_s N = \frac{mv^2}{r}$ *d.* $f = \mu_k N = \frac{mv^2}{r}$

43. Ba-122 has half-life of 2 min. Experiment has to be done using Ba-122 and it takes 10 min to set up the experiment. It initially 80 g at Ba-122 was taken, how much Ba was left when experiment was started ?

a. 2.5 g *b.* 5 g *c.* 10 g *d.* 20 g

44. When the speed of light becomes $\frac{2}{3}$ of its present value, then the energy released in a given atomic explosion would

a. decrease by a factor $\frac{2}{3}$

b. decrease by a factor $\frac{4}{9}$

c. decrease by a factor $\frac{5}{9}$

d. decrease by a factor $\frac{\sqrt{5}}{9}$

45. What should be the value of self-inductance of an inductor that should be connected to 220 V 50 Hz supply, so that a maximum current of 0.9 A flows through it?

a. 11 H *b.* 2 H

c. 1.1 H *d.* 5 H

46. The magnifying power of a telescope is 9. When it is adjusted for parallel rays, the distance between the objective and eyepiece is 20 cm. The focal length of lenses are

a. 10 cm, 10 cm *b.* 15 cm, 5 cm

c. 18 cm, 2 cm *d.* 11 cm, 9 cm

47. Two masses of 1g and 9g are moving with equal kinetic energy. The ratio of magnitude of their momentum is

a. 3 : 1 *b.* 1 : 3

c. 1 : 2 *d.* 2 : 1

48. When two bodies collide with each other such that their kinetic energy remains constant. Their collision is said to be

a. elastic

b. inelastic

c. Both (a) and (b)

d. None of the above

49. In detector, output circuit consists of $R = 10\ k\Omega$ and $C = 100\ pF$. The frequency of carrier signal which it can detect is

a. >> 1 MHz *b.* 0.1 kHz

c. >> 1 GHz *d.* 10^3 Hz

50. For motion under central forces, which quantity will be conserved ?

a. Kinetic energy

b. Mechanical energy

c. Potential energy

d. None of the above

51. Which of the following statement is incorrect?

a. Classical Physics deals with macroscopic phenomena and includes subject like mechanics, electrodynamics, optics and thermodynamics.

b. All Physics and also mathematics is based on assumptions each of which is variously called hypothesis or axiom or postulate etc.

c. A hypothesis is a supposition with assuming that is true.

d. An axiom is a self-evident truth, while a model is a theory proposed to explain observed phenomena.

52. If impedance is $\sqrt{3}$ times of resistance, then find phase difference.

a. Zero *b.* 30°

c. 60° *d.* Data is incomplete

53. A bar magnet is oscillating in the earth's magnetic field with a period T. What happens to its period and motion, if its mass is quadrupled?

a. Motion remains simple harmonic with time period $4T$.

b. Motion remains simple harmonic with time period nearly constant.

c. Motion remains simple harmonic and time period becomes $T/2$.

d. Motion remains simple harmonic with time period $2T$.

54. The relative permeability of iron is 6000. Its magnetic susceptibility is

a. 5999 *b.* 6001

c. 6000×10^{-7} *d.* 6000×10^{7}

55. Which of the following technique is not used for measuring small time intervals?

a. Electronic oscillator

b. Decay of elementary particles

c. Atomic clock

d. Spring oscillator

56. The relative errors in the measurement of two lengths $1.02 \text{ cm} \pm 0.01 \text{ cm}$ and $9.89 \text{ cm} \pm 0.01 \text{ cm}$ is

a. ±1% and ±0.1 %

b. ± 1% and ± 0.2%

c. ± 1% and ± 1%

d. 0.1% and ± 1%

57. In Young's double slit experiment with sodium vapour lamp of wavelength 589 nm and slit 0.589 mm apart, the half angular width of the central maxima is

a. $\sin^{-1}(0.01)$ *b.* $\sin^{-1}(0.0001)$

c. $\sin^{-1}(0.001)$ *d.* $\sin^{-1}(0.1)$

58. From the figure describing photoelectric effect, we may infer correctly that

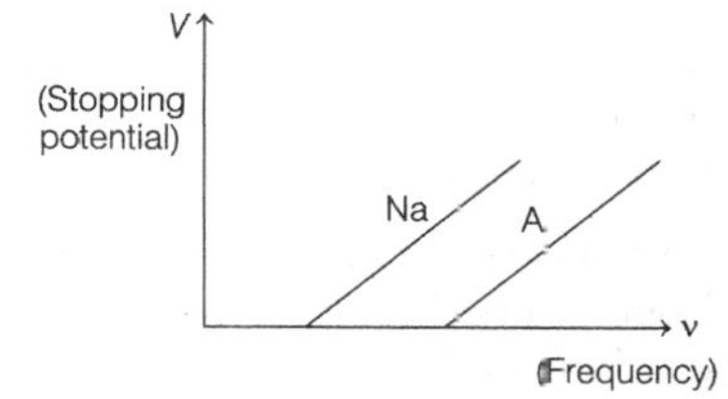

a. Na and Al both have the same threshold frequency

b. Maximum kinetic energy for both the metals depends linearly on the frequency

c. the stopping potential are different for Na and Al for the same change in frequency

d. Al is better photosensitive material than Na

59. Carnot cycle of an engine is given below

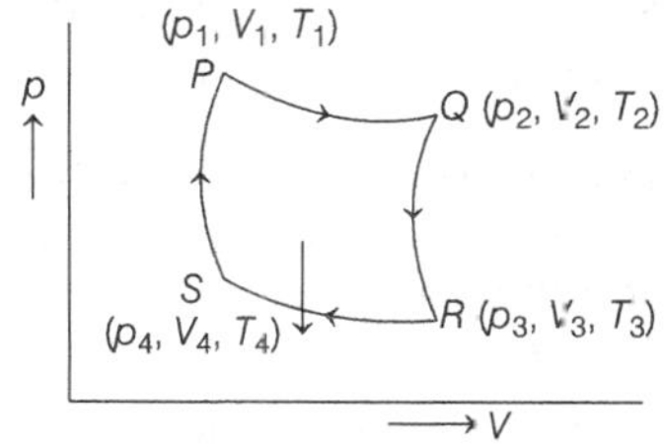

Total work done by the gas in one cycle is

a. $\mu RT_2 \log \frac{V_2}{V_1} - \mu RT_1 \log \frac{V_3}{V_4}$

b. $\mu RT_1 \log \frac{V_2}{V_1} - \mu RT_2 \log \frac{V_3}{V_4}$

c. $\mu RT_1 \log \frac{V_2}{V_1} + \mu RT_2 \log \frac{V_3}{V_4}$

d. Zero

60. An optical fibre communication system works on a wavelength of $1.3\,\mu\text{m}$. The number of subscribers it can feed, if a channel requires 20 kHz are

a. 2.3×10^{10} *b.* 1.15×10^{10}

c. 1×10^{5} *d.* None of these

CHEMISTRY

61. When the expansion of a gas occurs in vaccum and at constant volume, then

a. $\Delta U = qV$ *b.* $\Delta U = qp$

c. $\Delta H = qV$ *d.* $\Delta H = qp$

62. Carbon monoxide is poisonous to human beings because

a. it binds 300 times more strongly to haemoglobin than oxygen.

b. it doesn't bind to haemoglobin

c. it forms cyanide in body.

d. it leads to coagulation of blood.

63. Which one of the following sets of monosaccharides forms sucrose?

a. α-D-galactopyranose and α-D-glucopyranose

b. α-D-glucopyranose and β-D-fructofuranose

c. β-D-glucopyranose and α-D-fructofuranose

d. α-D-glucopyranose and β-D-fructopyranose

64. Under which of the following condition, the gases does not follow Henry's law?

a. When gases are placed under high temperature.

b. When the molecules of the system are in equilibrium state.

c. When gases are placed under extremely high pressure.
d. All of the above

65. An aqueous solution of X on addition of hydrogen peroxide in ice cold conditions gives blue colour to the ethereal layer. Then, X can be
a. acidified potassium chromate
b. alkaline potassium dichromate
c. acidified potassium manganate
d. acidified potassium permanganate

66. Determine the specific rate constant of the reaction. If the half-life period of a first order reaction is 1402 s.
a. $4.94 \times 10^{-3}\ s^{-1}$ b. $0.49 \times 10^{-3}\ s^{-1}$
c. $0.49 \times 10^{-4}\ s^{-1}$ d. $4.94 \times 10^{-5}\ s^{-1}$

67. Sodium metal crystallises in a body centred cubic lattice with a unit cell edge of 4.29Å. The radius of sodium atom is
a. 1.86 Å b. 3.22 Å c. 5.72 Å d. 0.93 Å

68. Which of the following amino acid ($NH_2CHRCOOH$) contains polar R group?
a. Alanine b. Valine
c. Glycine d. Glutamine

69. Find the correct order of C—O bond length among CO, CO_3^{2-}, CO_2.
a. $CO_2 < CO_3^{2-} < CO$ b. $CO < CO_3^{2-} < CO_2$
c. $CO_3^{2-} < CO_2 < CO$ d. $CO < CO_2 < CO_3^{2-}$

70. The total number of nodes are given by
a. $(n+1)$ b. $(n-l-1)$
c. $(n-1)$ d. $(n-l+1)$

71. In the equilibrium, $AB \rightleftharpoons A + B$, if the equilibrium concentration of A is double, then equilibrium concentration of B will be
a. half b. twice c. $\frac{1}{4}$th d. $\frac{1}{8}$th

72. Which of the following is used as a drug to reduce fever?
a. Antibiotic b. Antipyretic
c. Analgesic d. Tranquiliser

73. The reaction

$ArN_2^+Cl^- \xrightarrow{Cu/HCl} ArCl + N_2 + CuCl$ is called as
a. Sandmeyer reaction b. Gattermann reaction
c. Claisen reaction d. Carbylamine reaction

74. In 3d-transition series, which one has the least melting point?
a. V b. Zn c. Mn d. Cu

75. Among the following enzymes, which one is involved in the given below catalytic reaction?

$C_6H_{12}O_6(aq) \longrightarrow 2C_2H_5OH(aq) + 2CO_2(g)$
a. Maltase b. Urease
c. Zymase d. Invertase

76. Which of the following is correct mixture of azeotrope?
a. Chlorobenzene + bromobenzene
b. $C_2H_5Br + C_2H_5Cl$
c. $C_6H_{14} + C_7H_{16}$
d. $CCl_4 + CHCl_3$

77. Rate constant (K) of a reaction has least value at
a. high T and high E_a b. high T and low E_a
c. low T and low E_a d. low T and high E_a

78. Arrange stability of the given carbon cation in decreasing order

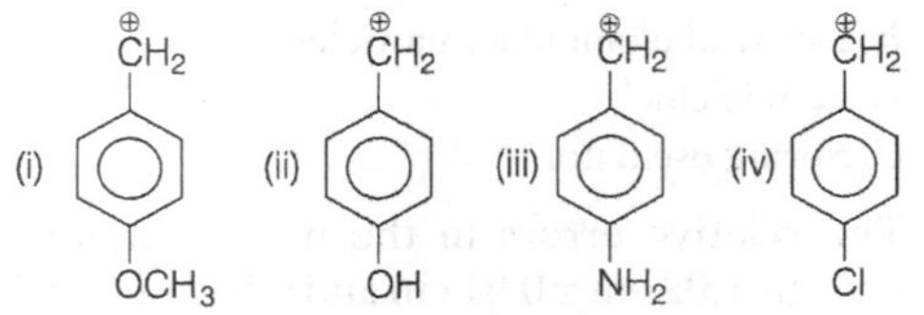

a. (iii) > (ii) > (i) > (iv) b. (i) > (ii) > (iii) > (iv)
c. (iii) > (i) > (ii) > (iv) d. (ii) > (iii) > (i) > (iv)

79. Which of the following pairs of ions in iso-electronic and iso-structural?
a. CO_3^{2-}, NO_3^- b. SO_3^{2-}, NO_3^-
c. ClO_3^-, CO_3^{2-} d. SO_3^{2-}, CO_3^{2-}

80. How much part of any corner atom actually belongs to a particular unit cell?
a. $\frac{1}{4}$th b. $\frac{1}{6}$th c. $\frac{1}{8}$th d. $\frac{1}{10}$th

81. For the equilibrium,

$2NOCl(g) \rightleftharpoons 2NO(g) + Cl_2(g)$,

the value of the equilibrium constant, K_C is 3.75×10^{-6} at 1069 K. The value of K_p for the reaction at this temperature will be
a. 0.133 b. 1.242
c. 0.033 d. 0.00033

82. Arrange the following artificial Sweetening agents in order of increasing sweetness.

Aspartame, Saccharin, Sucralose, Alitame
a. Alitame > Saccharin > Sucralose > Aspartame
b. Aspartame > Alitame > Saccharin > Sucralose
c. Alitame > Sucralose > Saccharin > Aspartame
d. Sucralose > Aspartame > Alitame > Saccharin

83. Coupling reaction is an example of
a. nucleophilic addition reaction.
b. nucleophilic substitution reaction.
c. electrophilic substitution reaction.
d. electrophilic addition reaction.

84. The oxidation number of Cr in CrO_5 which has the following structure, is

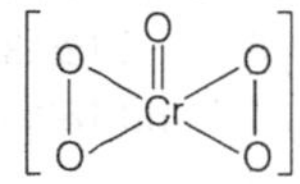

a. +4 *b.* +5
c. +3 *d.* +6

85. Identify the pair of gases that have equal rates of diffusion
a. CO, NO *b.* N_2O, CO
c. N_2O, CO_2 *d.* CO_2, NO_2

86. The reducing agent which is used to reduce iron oxide in blast furnace is
a. CO *b.* coke
c. silica *d.* lime

87. Given that molar conductances for $Ba(OH)_2$, $BaCl_2$ and NH_4Cl are 523.28, 280.0 and 129.8 $\Omega^{-1}cm^2\ mol^{-1}$ respectively. What is the molar conductivity ($\Omega^{-1}cm^2mol^{-1}$) of NH_4OH?
a. 502.88 *b.* 251.44
c. 1005.76 *d.* 209.42

88. Xerophthalmia disease causes by which deficiency of vitamin?
a. Vitamin-A *b.* Vitamin-C
c. Vitamin-B *d.* Vitamin-B_6

89. Find the final product for the reaction

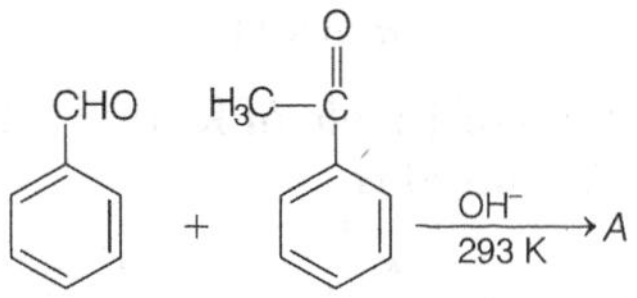

a. 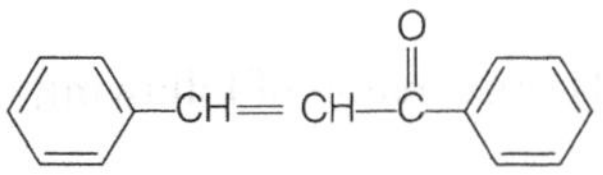

b. 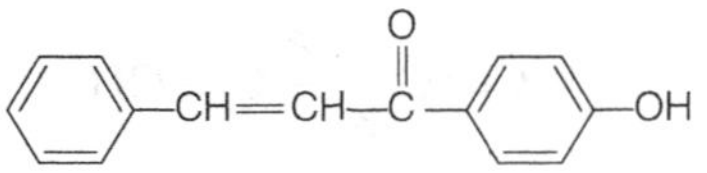

c. 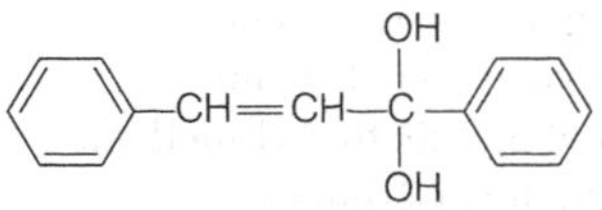

d. 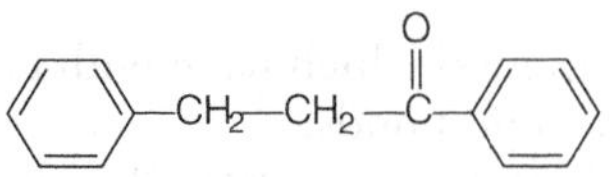

90. The melting of ice
a. is the phase transformation
b. takes place at constant pressure and temperature
c. takes place at 373 K
d. Both (a) and (b)

91. Which of the following options represent the correct composition of dettol?
a. Chloroxylenol and terpineol
b. Chloroxylenol and furacine
c. Terpineol and iodine
d. Iodine and furacine

92. The chemical formula of Hinsberg's reagent is
a. HNO_2 *b.* NaOH + CaO
c. $C_6H_5SO_2Cl$ *d.* CH_3CONH_2

93. The increasing order of atomic radii of the following group 13 elements is
a. Al < Ga < In < Tl *b.* Ga < Al < In < Tl
c. Al < In < Tl < Ga *d.* Al < Ga < Tl < In

94. Which of the following colloids resemble to the true solutions?
a. Macromolecular colloids
b. Micelles
c. Micromolecular colloids
d. Lyophobic colloids

95. The hydrocarbon that cannot be prepared effectively by Wurtz reaction

a. 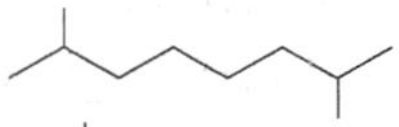

b. 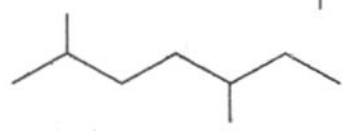

c. 

d. 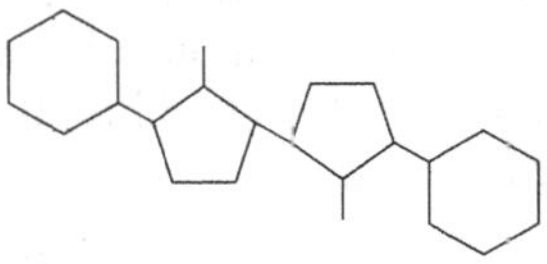

96. Reaction 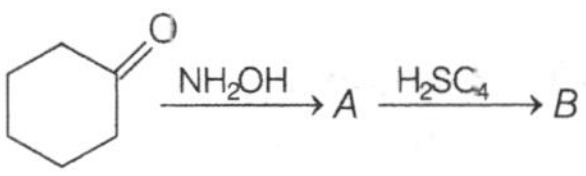

find the product *B*.

a. 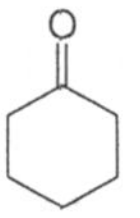
b. 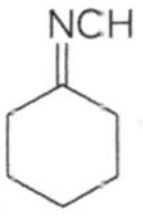
c. 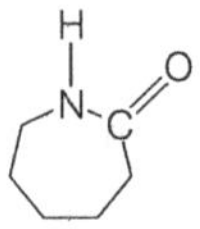
d. 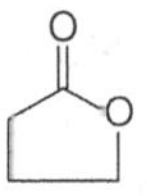

97. Why, ketones and carboxylic acids have higher boiling point as compared to aldehydes?
a. Due to —CHO group
b. Due to Fazan's rule
c. Due to inter molecular hydrogen bonding
d. Due to intramolecular hydrogen bonding

98. The vacant space in bcc lattice cell is
a. 26% *b.* 48%
c. 23% *d.* 32%

99. In the chemical reaction,
$N_2 + 3H_2 \rightleftharpoons 2NH_3$ at equilibrium point.
a. equal volumes of N_2 and H_2 are reacting.
b. equal manes of N_2 and H_2 are reacting.
c. the reaction has stopped.
d. the same amount of ammonia is formed, as it is decomposed into N_2 and H_2.

100. The change in the energy of system if 500 cal of heat energy are added to a system and system does 350 cal of work on the surroundings will be
a. −150 cal *b.* +150 cal
c. +850 cal *d.* −850 cal

101. Which of the following is not an antacid?
a. Aluminium hydroxide *b.* Cimetidine
c. Phenelzine *d.* Ranitidine

102. Which of the following is most stable?
a. $CH_2N_2^+X^-$ *b.* $C_6H_5N_2^+X^-$
c. $CH_3CH_2N_2^+X^-$ *d.* $C_6H_5CH_2N_2^+X^-$

103. Which type of ligand is EDTA?
a. Monodentate *b.* Hexadentate
c. Bidentate *d.* Tridentate

104. The density of a gas *A* is thrice that of a gas *B* at the same temperature. The molecular weight of gas *B* is twice that of *A*. What will be the ratio of pressure acting on *B* and *A*?
a. $\frac{1}{4}$ *b.* $\frac{7}{8}$ *c.* $\frac{2}{5}$ *d.* $\frac{1}{6}$

105. Which of the following is correct order of their increasing boiling points?
a. 10^{-4} M NaCl > 10^{-3}M $MgCl_2$ > 10^{-2} M NaCl > 10^{-4}M urea.
b. 10^{-2} M NaCl > 10^{-3}M $MgCl_2$ > 10^{-4} M NaCl > 10^{-4}M urea.
c. 10^{-4} M urea > 10^{-4}M NaCl > 10^{-3} M $MgCl_2$ > 10^{-2}M NaCl.
d. 10^{-2} M NaCl > 10^{-3} M $MgCl_2$ > 10^{-4} M NaCl > 10^{-4}M urea.

106. The specific conductivity of a solution containing 1.0 g of anhydrous $BaCl_2$ in 200 cm^3 of the solution has been found to be 0.0058 Scm^{-1}. The molar and equivalent conductivity of the solution respectively are
a. 120.83 S cm^2 eq^{-1} and 241.67 S cm^2 eq^{-1}
b. 150.5 S cm^2 eq^{-1} and 289.7 S cm^2 eq^{-1}
c. 241.6 S cm^2 mol^{-1} and 120.83 S cm^2 eq^{-1}
d. 248.6 S cm^2 mol^{-1} and 180.3 S cm^2 eq^{-1}

107. For the reaction $2N_2O_5 \longrightarrow 4NO_2 + O_2$, rate constant *k* is 4.48×10^{-5} s^{-1} and the initial pressure is 600 atm. After 10 min, determine the final pressure of N_2O_5.
a. 590 atm *b.* 490 atm
c. 588 atm *d.* 580 atm

108. Calculate the difference between C_p and C_V for 10 moles of an ideal gas
a. 83.14 J/K *b.* 8.314 J/K
c. 831.4 J/K *d.* 0.831 J/K

109. Which of the following particulate matter is emitted from vehicles?
a. Co *b.* Pb *c.* Sn *d.* Se

110. Arrange the hydrides of group 15 in correct decreasing order of reducing nature.
a. $NH_3 < PH_3 < AsH_3 < SbH_3 < BiH_3$
b. $NH_3 > PH_3 > AsH_3 > SbH_3 > BiH_3$
c. $PH_3 < AsH_3 < SbH_3 < BiH_3 < NH_3$
d. $BiH_3 > SbH_3 > AsH_3 > PH_3 > NH_3$

111. What would be the molarity of one litre solution of 22.2 g of $CaCl_2$?
a. 0.2 M *b.* 0.4 M
c. 0.6 M *d.* 0.8 M

112. For decolourisation of 1 mole of $KMnO_4$, the moles of H_2O_2 required is
a. $\frac{1}{2}$ *b.* $\frac{3}{2}$ *c.* $\frac{5}{2}$ *d.* $\frac{7}{2}$

113. What is the IUPAC name of following compound?

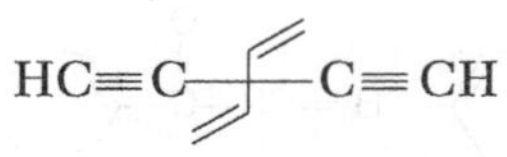

a. 3, 3-diethynylpenta-1, 4-diene
b. 3, 3-diethynylpenta-1, 4-diyne
c. 3, 3-diethenyl-3, 3-diethynyl-methane
d. 3-ethyl-3-ethylpent-1-en-4-yne

114. Find the compound which have both polar and non-polar covalent bonds.
a. HCN *b.* H_2O_2 *c.* NH_4Cl *d.* CH_4

115. What is the product formed when benzene react with CO and HCl in presence of anhydrous $AlCl_3$?

a. 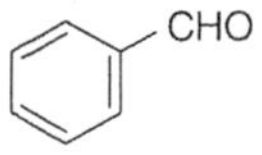

b. 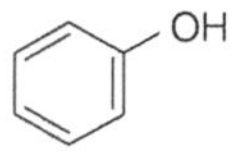

c. 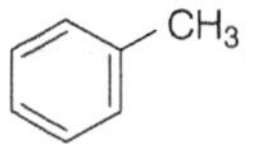

d. 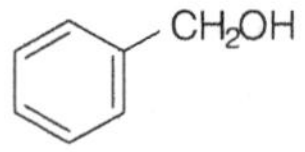

116. Which of the following series of transitions in the spectrum of hydrogen atom fall in visible region?

a. Balmer series *b.* Paschen series
c. Brackett series *d.* Lyman series

117. The value of $\Delta G°$ for the phosphorylation of glucose in glycolysis is 13.8 kJ/mol. The value of K_C at 298 K is

a. 7.72×10^{-4} *b.* 5.62×10^{-4}
c. 4.81×10^{-3} *d.* 3.81×10^{-3}

118. The Lyman series of hydrogen spectrum lies in which region

a. Infrared region
b. Visible region
c. Ultraviolet region
d. X-ray region

119. The correct IUPAC name of the coordination compound $K_3[Fe(CN)_5NO]$ is

a. potassium pentacyanonitrosylferrate (II)
b. potassium pentacyanonitro-N-ferrate (III)
c. potassium nitritopentacyanoferrate (IV)
d. potassium nitritopentacyanoiron (II)

120. Which of the following conditions are favourable for chemisorption?

a. Low temperature and high pressure
b. High temperature and low pressure
c. High temperature and high pressure
d. Low temperature and low pressure

MATHEMATICS

121. Shade the feasible region for the inequations $x + y \geq 2$, $2x + 3y \leq 6$, $x \geq 0$, $y \geq 0$ in a rough figure.

a. 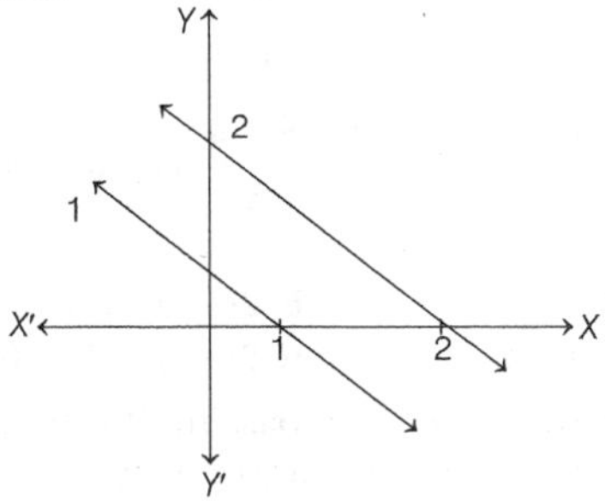

b. 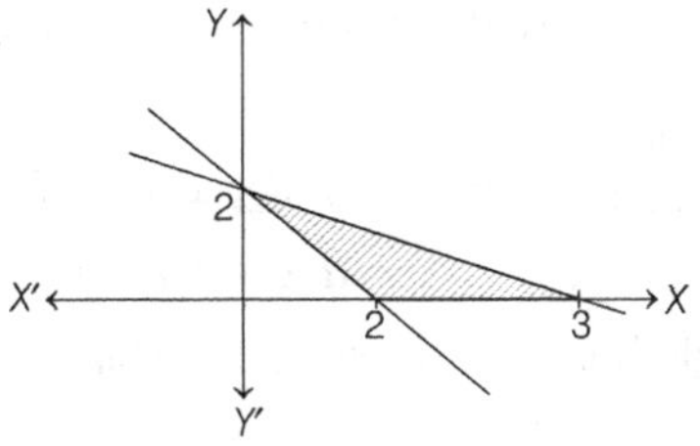

c. 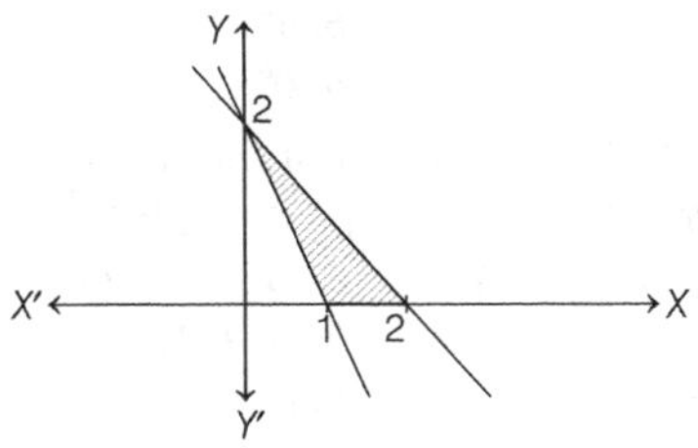

(d) None of the above

122. The maximum value of $x + y$ subject to $2x + 3y \leq 6$, $x \geq 0$, $y \geq 0$ is

a. 5 *b.* 4 *c.* 6 *d.* 3

123. Write the solution of the following LPP
Maximise $Z = x + y$
Subject to $3x + 4y \leq 12$, $x \geq 0$, $y \geq 0$.
Which point the value of Z is maximum?

a. (0, 4) *b.* (4, 0) *c.* (6, 0) *d.* (0, 6)

124. The vector that must be added to $\hat{i} - 3\hat{j} + 2\hat{k}$ and $3\hat{i} + 6\hat{j} - 7\hat{k}$ so resultant vector is a unit vector along the X - axis is

a. $4\hat{i} + 2\hat{j} + 5\hat{k}$ *b.* $-4\hat{i} + 2\hat{j} + 5\hat{k}$
c. $3\hat{i} + 4\hat{j} + 5\hat{k}$ *d.* Null vector

125. If $|\mathbf{a}| = 8$, $|\mathbf{b}| = 3$ and $|\mathbf{a} \times \mathbf{b}| = 12$, then find the angle between **a** and **b**.

a. $\frac{\pi}{3}$ *b.* $\frac{\pi}{6}$
c. $\frac{\pi}{4}$ *d.* None of these

126. If for $\mathbf{a} = 2\hat{i} + 3\hat{j} + \hat{k}$, $\mathbf{b} = \hat{i} - 2\hat{j} + \hat{k}$ and $\mathbf{c} = -3\hat{i} + \hat{j} + 2\hat{k}$, then find $[\mathbf{a}\ \mathbf{b}\ \mathbf{c}]$.

a. −15 *b.* −10 *c.* −30 *d.* −5

127. If for any 2×2 square matrix A,

$$A\,(\text{adj } A) = \begin{bmatrix} 8 & 0 \\ 0 & 8 \end{bmatrix},$$ then the value of det (A).

a. 6 *b.* 5 *c.* 7 *d.* 8

128. If matrix $A = \begin{bmatrix} 2 & -2 \\ -2 & 2 \end{bmatrix}$ and $A^2 = pA$, then the value of p is

a. 6 *b.* −4 *c.* 4 *d.* 8

129. If $A\,(\text{adj } A) = \begin{bmatrix} -2 & 0 & 0 \\ 0 & -2 & 0 \\ 0 & 0 & -2 \end{bmatrix}$, then $|\text{adj } A|$ equals

a. −2 *b.* −4 *c.* 4 *d.* 8

130. The coefficients a, b and c of the quadratic equation, $ax^2 + bx + c = 0$ are obtained by throwing a dice three times. The probability that this equation has equal roots is

a. $\frac{1}{72}$ *b.* $\frac{5}{216}$

c. $\frac{1}{36}$ *d.* $\frac{1}{54}$

131. $8^{3\log_8 5}$ is equal to

a. $\log_8 25$ *b.* 120

c. 125 *d.* $\log_8 15$

132. The equation of normal to the curve $y = (1+x)^y + \sin^{-1}(\sin^2 x)$ at $x = 0$ is

a. $x + y = 1$ *b.* $x - y = 1$

c. $x + y = -1$ *d.* $x - y = -1$

133. If $L = \lim\limits_{x \to 0} \dfrac{a - \sqrt{a^2 - x^2} - \dfrac{x^2}{4}}{x^4}$, $a > 0$. If L is finite, then

a. $a = 2$ *b.* $a = 1$

c. $a = \frac{1}{3}$ *d.* None of these

134. What will be the equation of circle whose centre is (1, 2) and touches X - axis?

a. $x^2 + y^2 - 2x - 4y + 1 = 0$

b. $x^2 - y^2 + 2x + 4y + 1 = 0$

c. $x^2 + y^2 + 2x - 4y - 1 = 0$

d. $x^2 + y^2 + 2x + 4y - 1 = 0$

135. The approximate value of $f(5.001)$, where $f(x) = x^3 - 7x^2 + 15$ is

a. −34.995 *b.* −33.995 *c.* −33.335 *d.* −35.995

136. Find the centre and radius of the circle given by the equation $2x^2 + 2y^2 + 3x + 4y + \frac{9}{8} = 0$.

a. 1 *b.* −1 *c.* 2 *d.* −2

137. Find the maximum value of $f(x) = \dfrac{1}{4x^2 + 2x + 1}$.

a. $\frac{3}{4}$ *b.* $\frac{4}{3}$

c. $\frac{1}{3}$ *d.* None of these

138. If $f(x) = \begin{cases} ax + 3, & x \le 2 \\ a^2 x - 1 & x > 2 \end{cases}$, then the values of a for which f is continuous for all x are

a. 1 and −2 *b.* 1 and 2

c. −1 and 2 *d.* −1 and −2

139. The value of $\lim\limits_{x \to 0} \left(\dfrac{a^x + b^x + c^x}{3} \right)^{2/x}$, $(a, b, c > 0)$ is

a. $(abc)^3$ *b.* abc

c. $(abc)^{1/3}$ *d.* None of these

140. What will be the equation of the circle whose centre is (1, 2) and which passes through the point (4, 6)?

a. $x^2 + y^2 - 2x - 4y - 20 = 0$

b. $x^2 + y^2 + 2x + 4y - 20 = 0$

c. $x^2 - y^2 - 2x - 4y + 20 = 0$

d. $x^2 - y^2 + 2x - 4y - 20 = 0$

141. The line $\dfrac{x-2}{3} = \dfrac{y-3}{4} = \dfrac{z-4}{5}$ is parallel to the plane

a. $3x + 4y + 5z = 7$ *b.* $2x + 3y + 4z = 0$

c. $x + y - z = 2$ *d.* $2x + y - 2z = 0$

142. The equation of a plane passing through the line of intersection of the planes $x + 2y + 3z = 2$, $x - y + z = 3$ and at a distance $\frac{2}{\sqrt{3}}$ from the point (3, 1, −1) is

a. $5x - 11y + z = 17$ *b.* $\sqrt{2}x + y = 3\sqrt{2} - 1$

c. $x + y + z = \sqrt{3}$ *d.* $x - \sqrt{2}y = 1 - \sqrt{2}$

143. The angle between the lines $2x = 3y = -z$ and $6x = -y = -4z$ is

a. 30° *b.* 45°

c. 90° *d.* 0°

144. The point of intersection of the lines $\dfrac{x-1}{2} = \dfrac{y-2}{3} = \dfrac{z-3}{4}$ and $\dfrac{x-4}{5} = \dfrac{y-1}{2} = z$ is

a. (0, 0, 0) *b.* (1, 1, 1)

c. (−1, −1, −1) *d.* (1, 2, 3)

145. $\int \frac{2^x}{\sqrt{1-4^x}} dx$ is equal to

a. $(\log 2)\sin^{-1} 2^x + C$ b. $\frac{1}{2}\sin^{-1} 2^x + C$

c. $\frac{1}{\log 2}\sin^{-1} 2^x + C$ d. $2\log 2 \sin^{-1} 2^x + C$

146. $\int_{-\pi/2}^{\pi/2} \sin x dx$

a. 2 b. 3 c. 0 d. 5

147. Integral of $\int \frac{dx}{x^2[1+x^4]^{3/4}}$.

a. $-4(x^{1/4}+1)^{1/4}+C$ b. $4(x^{1/4}+1)^{1/4}+C$

c. $4(x^4+1)^{1/4}+C$ d. None of these

148. Three of the six vertices of a regular hexagon are chosen at random. The probability that the triangle with three vertices is equilateral equals

a. $\frac{1}{2}$ b. $\frac{1}{5}$ c. $\frac{1}{10}$ d. $\frac{1}{20}$

149. Five persons A, B, C, D and E are in queue of a shop. The probability that A and E are always together, is

a. $\frac{1}{4}$ b. $\frac{2}{3}$ c. $\frac{2}{5}$ d. $\frac{3}{5}$

150. If A, B and C are mutually exclusive and exhaustive events of a random experiment such that $P(B) = \frac{3}{2} P(A)$ and $P(C) = \frac{1}{2} P(B)$, then $P(A \cup C)$ equals

a. $\frac{10}{13}$ b. $\frac{3}{13}$

c. $\frac{6}{13}$ d. $\frac{7}{13}$

151. A student answers a multiple choice question with 5 alternatives, of which exactly one is correct. The probability that he knows the correct answer is $p, 0 < p < 1$. If he does not know the correct answer, he randomly ticks one answer. Given that he has answered the question correctly, the probability that he did not tick the answer randomly, is

a. $\frac{3p}{4p+3}$ b. $\frac{5p}{3p+2}$

c. $\frac{5p}{4p+1}$ d. $\frac{4p}{3p+1}$

152. If x and y are acute angles, such that $\cos x + \cos y = \frac{3}{2}$ and $\sin x + \sin y = \frac{3}{4}$, then $\sin(x+y)$ equals

a. $\frac{2}{5}$ b. $\frac{3}{4}$

c. $\frac{3}{5}$ d. $\frac{4}{5}$

153. The expression $\frac{\tan A}{1-\cot A} + \frac{\cot A}{1-\tan A}$ can be written as

a. $\sin A \cos A + 1$

b. $\sec A \operatorname{cosec} A + 1$

c. $\tan A + \cot A$

d. $\sec A + \operatorname{cosec} A$

154. If $\sin 2x = 4\cos x$, then x is equal to

a. $\frac{n\pi}{2} \pm \frac{\pi}{4}, n \in Z$ b. no value

c. $n\pi + (-1)^n \frac{\pi}{4}, n \in Z$ d. $2n\pi \pm \frac{\pi}{2}, n \in Z$

155. If $f(x)$ satisfies the relation $2f(x) + f(1-x) = x^2$ for all real x, then $f(x)$ is

a. $\frac{x^2+2x-1}{6}$ b. $\frac{x^2+2x-1}{3}$

c. $\frac{x^2+4x-1}{3}$ d. $\frac{x^2+4x-1}{6}$

156. If $A = \{1, 2, 5, 6\}$ and $B = \{1, 2, 3\}$, then $(A \times B) \cap (B \times A)$ is equal to

a. $\{(1, 1), (2, 1), (6, 1), (3, 2)\}$

b. $\{(1, 1), (1, 2), (2, 1), (2, 2)\}$

c. $\{(1, 1), (2, 2)\}$

d. $\{(1, 1), (1, 2), (2, 5), (2, 6)\}$

157. Total number of elements in the power set of A containing 15 elements is

a. 2^{15} b. 15^2

c. 2^{15-1} d. $2^{15}-1$

158. What is the argument of the complex number $\frac{(1+i)(2+i)}{3-i}$, where $i = \sqrt{-1}$?

a. 0 b. $\frac{\pi}{4}$ c. $-\frac{\pi}{4}$ d. $\frac{\pi}{2}$

159. Evaluate $\left[i^{18} + \left(\frac{1}{i}\right)^{25}\right]^3$.

a. $2(1-i)$ b. $7(i-1)$

c. $2-7i$ d. $8i+4$

160. If $(\sqrt{3}+i)^{100} = 2^{99}(a+ib)$, then a^2+b^2 is equal to

a. $\sqrt{2}$ b. 4

c. $\sqrt{3}$ d. None of these

COMEDK 2021

161. Using mathematical induction, the numbers a_n's are defined by $a_0 = 1$, $a_{n+1} = 3n^2 + n + a_n$, $(n \geq 0)$. Then, a_n is equal to

a. $n^3 + n^2 + 1$ **b.** $n^3 - n^2 + 1$
c. $n^3 - n^2$ **d.** $n^3 + n^2$

162. If $49^n + 16n + P$ is divisible by 64 for all $n \in N$, then the least negative integral value of P is

a. –2 **b.** –3
c. –4 **d.** –1

163. $2^{3n} - 7n - 1$ is divisible by

a. 64 **b.** 36 **c.** 49 **d.** 25

164. The solution of the differential equation

$\sec^2 x \tan y \, dx + \sec^2 y \tan x \, dy = 0$ is

a. $\tan y \cdot \tan x = C$ **b.** $\frac{\tan y}{\tan x} = C$
c. $\frac{\tan^2 x}{\tan y} = C$ **d.** None of these

165. The solution of the differential equation

$$y \frac{dy}{dx} = x\left[\frac{y^2}{x^2} + \frac{\phi\left(\frac{y^2}{x^2}\right)}{\phi'\left(\frac{y^2}{x^2}\right)}\right] \text{ is}$$

(where, C is a constant)

a. $\phi\left(\frac{y^2}{x^2}\right) = Cx$ **b.** $x\phi\left(\frac{y^2}{x^2}\right) = C$
c. $\phi\left(\frac{y^2}{x^2}\right) = Cx^2$ **d.** $x^2\phi\left(\frac{y^2}{x^2}\right) = C$

166. The solution of the differential equation

$(1 + y^2) + (x - e^{\tan^{-1} y}) \frac{dy}{dx} = 0$ is

a. $2xe^{\tan^{-1} y} = e^{2\tan^{-1} y} + C$
b. $xe^{\tan^{-1} y} = \tan^{-1} y + C$
c. $xe^{2\tan^{-1} y} = e^{\tan^{-1} y} + C$
d. $(x - 2) = Ce^{-\tan^{-1} y}$

167. The value of $1 \cdot 1! + 2 \cdot 2! + 3 \cdot 3! + \quad + n \cdot n!$ is

a. $(n + 1)!$ **b.** $(n + 1)! + 1$
c. $(n + 1)! - 1$ **d.** None of these

168. The sum of the series $(1 + 2) + (1 + 2 + 2^2) + (1 + 2 + 2^2 + 2^3) + \quad$ upto n terms is

a. $2^{n+2} - n - 4$ **b.** $2(2^n - 1) - n$
c. $2^{n+1} - n$ **d.** $2^{n+1} - 1$

169. If a, b, c are in AP, $b - a, c - b$ and a are in GP, then $a : b : c$ is

a. 1 : 2 : 3 **b.** 1 : 3 : 5
c. 2 : 3 : 4 **d.** 1 : 2 : 4

170. The number of triangles which can be formed by using the vertices of a regular polygon of $(n + 3)$ sides is 220. Then, n is equal to

a. 8 **b.** 9
c. 10 **d.** 11

171. Out of 8 given points, 3 are collinear. How many different straight lines can be drawn by joining any two points from those 8 points?

a. 26 **b.** 28
c. 27 **d.** 25

172. How many numbers greater than 40000 can be formed from the digits 2, 4, 5, 5, 7 ?

a. 12 **b.** 24
c. 36 **d.** 48

173. If a polygon of n sides has 275 diagonals, then n is equal to

a. 25 **b.** 35
c. 20 **d.** 15

174. If two pairs of lines $x^2 - 2mxy - y^2 = 0$ and $x^2 - 2nxy - y^2 = 0$ are such that one of them represents the bisector of the angles between the other, then

a. $mn = 1$ **b.** $m + n = mn$
c. $mn = -1$ **d.** $m - n = mn$

175. The distance of the point (1, 2) from the line $x + y + 5 = 0$ measured along the line parallel to $3x - y = 7$ is equal to

a. $4\sqrt{10}$ **b.** 40
c. $\sqrt{40}$ **d.** $10\sqrt{2}$

176. The slopes of the lines, which make an angle 45° with the line $3x - y = -5$, are

a. 1, – 1 **b.** $\frac{1}{2}$, – 1
c. 1, $\frac{1}{2}$ **d.** – 2, $\frac{1}{2}$

177. If 3 and 4 are intercepts of a line $L \equiv 0$, then the distance of $L \equiv 0$ from the origin is

a. 5 units **b.** 12 units
c. $\frac{5}{12}$ unit **d.** $\frac{12}{5}$ units

178. Number of terms in the binomial expansion of $(x + a)^{53} + (x - a)^{53}$ is

a. 25 **b.** 26
c. 27 **d.** 26.5

COMEDK 2021

179. The coefficient of x^{10} in the expansion of $1+(1+x)+\ldots+(1+x)^{20}$ is

a. $^{19}C_9$ *b.* $^{20}C_{10}$

c. $^{21}C_{11}$ *d.* $^{22}C_{12}$

180. Middle term in the expansion of $\left(x^2+\frac{1}{x^2}+2\right)^n$ is

a. $\frac{n!}{(n!)^2}$ *b.* $\frac{(2n)!}{(n!)^2}$

c. $\frac{(2n-1)!}{n!}$ *d.* $\frac{(2n)!}{n!}$

ANSWERS

Physics

1. (a)	2. (c)	3. (a)	4. (d)	5. (d)	6. (a)	7. (a)	8. (a)	9. (c)	10. (b)
11. (d)	12. (d)	13. (d)	14. (a)	15. (c)	16. (c)	17. (a)	18. (b)	19. (c)	20. (c)
21. (b)	22. (a)	23. (b)	24. (b)	25. (c)	26. (d)	27. (a)	28. (c)	29. (d)	30. (d)
31. (d)	32. (a)	33. (b)	34. (b)	35. (d)	36. (d)	37. (b)	38. (a)	39. (b)	40. (c)
41. (d)	42. (a)	43. (a)	44. (c)	45. (d)	46. (c)	47. (b)	48. (a)	49. (a)	50. (b)
51. (c)	52. (c)	53. (d)	54. (a)	55. (d)	56. (a)	57. (c)	58. (b)	59. (b)	60. (b)

Chemistry

61. (a)	62. (a)	63. (b)	64. (c)	65. (a)	66. (b)	67. (a)	68. (d)	69. (d)	70. (c)
71. (a)	72. (b)	73. (b)	74. (b)	75. (c)	76. (d)	77. (d)	78. (a)	79. (a)	80. (c)
81. (d)	82. (c)	83. (c)	84. (d)	85. (c)	86. (a)	87. (b)	88. (a)	89. (a)	90. (d)
91. (a)	92. (c)	93. (b)	94. (a)	95. (b)	96. (c)	97. (a)	98. (d)	99. (d)	100. (b)
101. (c)	102. (b)	103. (b)	104. (d)	105. (b)	106. (c)	107. (c)	108. (a)	109. (b)	110. (d)
111. (a)	112. (c)	113. (a)	114. (b)	115. (a)	116. (a)	117. (d)	118. (c)	119. (b)	120. (c)

Mathematics

121. (b)	122. (d)	123. (b)	124. (*)	125. (b)	126. (c)	127. (d)	128. (c)	129. (c)	230. (b)
131. (c)	132. (a)	133. (a)	134. (a)	135. (a)	136. (a)	137. (b)	138. (c)	139. (d)	140. (a)
141. (d)	142. (a)	143. (c)	144. (c)	145. (c)	146. (c)	147. (d)	148. (c)	149. (c)	150. (d)
151. (c)	152. (d)	153. (b)	154. (d)	155. (b)	156. (b)	157. (a)	158. (d)	159. (a)	160. (b)
161. (b)	162. (d)	163. (c)	164. (a)	165. (c)	166. (a)	167. (c)	168. (a)	169. (a)	170. (b)
171. (a)	172. (d)	173. (a)	174. (c)	175. (c)	176. (d)	177. (d)	178. (c)	179. (c)	180. (b)

Note (*) None of the option is correct.

HINTS & SOLUTIONS

Physics

1. *(a)* Lyman series of a hydrogen atom belongs to the ultraviolet region of electromagnetic spectrum.

2. *(c)* Insulator can be charged by rubbing or friction with another body. For example, or rubbing a glass rod with the silk gets negatively charged while the glass rod gets positively charged.

3. *(a)* In an adiabatic process,

$$pV^{\gamma} = \text{constant}\,(k)$$

where p is pressure, V is volume and γ is the ratio of the specific heats.

Given, $$\frac{C_p}{C_V} = \gamma = \frac{3}{2}$$

Since, for adiabatic process $pV^{\gamma} = k$

$$\Rightarrow \quad pV^{3/2} = k \Rightarrow \log p + \frac{3}{2}\log V = \log k$$

$$\therefore \quad \frac{\Delta p}{p} + \frac{3}{2}\frac{\Delta V}{V} = 0$$

$$\Rightarrow \quad \frac{\Delta V}{V} \times 100 = -\frac{2}{3}\left(\frac{\Delta p}{p} \times 100\right) = -\frac{2}{3} \times \frac{2}{3} = -\frac{4}{9}\,\%$$

Negative sign implies that volume decreases by $\frac{4}{9}\%$.

4. *(d)* Given, $f_1 = 20$ cm, $f_2 = 40$ cm

Since, power $P = \frac{1}{f} \Rightarrow P_1 = \frac{1}{f_1} = \frac{100}{20} = 5$ D

and $P_2 = \frac{1}{f_2} = \frac{100}{40} = 2.5$ D

Effective power, $P = P_1 + P_2 = 5 + 2.5 = 7.5$ D

5. *(d)* The reactance of a capacitor of capacitance C connected to a AC source of frequency f is given by

$$X_C = \frac{1}{\omega C} = \frac{1}{2\pi f C}$$

6. *(a)* For a freely falling body, $v^2 - u^2 = 2gx \quad (\because u = 0)$

Therefore, $v^2 = 2gx$ or $x = \frac{v^2}{2g}$

Thus, graph will be a parabola, symmetric along +ve X-axis

7. *(a)* Given, $x = ae^{-pt} + be^{qt}$

$$\Rightarrow \quad v = \frac{dx}{dt} = -pae^{-pt} + qbe^{qt}$$

and $$a = \frac{dv}{dt} = p^2ae^{-pt} + q^2be^{qt}$$

Acceleration is positive, so velocity goes on increasing with time.

8. *(a)* As we know that, Impulse = Force × Time

$$= [\text{MLT}^{-2}] \times [\text{T}]$$
$$= [\text{ML}^1\text{T}^{-1}]$$

Momentum = Mass × Velocity

$$p = mv$$
$$[p] = [m] \times [v] = [\text{M}]\,[\text{LT}^{-1}] = [\text{ML}^1\text{T}^{-1}]$$

Thus, dimension of impulse represent dimensions of momentum.

9. *(c)* As we know that, maximum height,

$$H = \frac{u^2 \sin^2\theta}{2g} \quad \ldots(\text{i})$$

Horizontal range, $$R = \frac{u^2 \sin 2\theta}{g} \quad \ldots(\text{ii})$$

Dividing Eq. (i) by Eq. (ii), we get

$$\frac{H}{R} = \frac{\tan\theta}{4} \Rightarrow \theta = \tan^{-1}\left(\frac{4H}{R}\right)$$

10. *(b)* The resonant frequency of a LC circuit is given by

$$f = \frac{1}{2\pi\sqrt{LC}}$$

when $L' = \frac{L}{3}$, as per question,

$$f' = f \Rightarrow \frac{1}{2\pi\sqrt{L'C'}} = \frac{1}{2\pi\sqrt{LC}}$$

$$\Rightarrow \quad LC = L'C' \Rightarrow C' = \frac{LC}{L'} = \frac{LC}{L/3} = 3C$$

11. *(d)* The de-Broglie wavelength is given by

$$\lambda = \frac{h}{p} = \frac{h}{mv}$$

$$\Rightarrow \quad \frac{\lambda_e}{\lambda_p} = \frac{\frac{h}{mv_e}}{\frac{h}{mv_p}} = \frac{v_p}{v_e} = \frac{\frac{v_e}{4}}{v_e} = \frac{1}{4} \quad \left(\because v_p = \frac{1}{4} \times v_e\right)$$

12. *(d)* For an ideal gas coefficient of volume expansion can be deduced as

According to ideal gas equation,

$$pV = nRT \quad \ldots(\text{i})$$

at constant pressure, $p\Delta V = nR\Delta T \quad \ldots(\text{ii})$

Dividing Eq (ii) by Eq. (i), we get

$$\frac{\Delta V}{V} = \frac{\Delta T}{T} \quad \ldots(\text{iii})$$

But $$\frac{\Delta V}{V} = \alpha \Delta T \quad \ldots(\text{iv})$$

$\therefore$ From Eqs. (iii) and (iv), we get

For ideal gas $\alpha = \frac{1}{T}$

So, for an ideal gas, coefficient of volume expansion is given by $\frac{1}{T}$.

13. *(d)* Green house gases are CO_2, CH_4, N_2O, CF_xCl_x and O_3. Thus, H_2O is not a greenhouse gas.

14. *(a)* Force on a charge particle moving in a uniform magnetic field at angle θ is given by

$$F = qvB\sin\theta \Rightarrow F \propto q$$

Hence, $q_1 = q$ and $q_2 = 2q$

$$\therefore \quad \frac{F_1}{F_2} = \frac{q_1}{q_2} = \frac{q}{2q} = \frac{1}{2}$$

15. *(c)* Given, $W = 50$ J and $q = 25$ C

$$\text{Potential difference, } V = \frac{\text{Work done }(W)}{\text{Charge }(q)}$$

$$\Rightarrow \quad V = \frac{50}{25} = 2\text{ V}$$

16. *(c)* The increasing order of frequency is Microwave < UV Rays ≤ X-rays
The frequency is the inverse of wavelength. So, the order of increasing wavelength is
X-rays < UV rays < Microwave

17. *(a)* For an infinite plane sheet as shown below

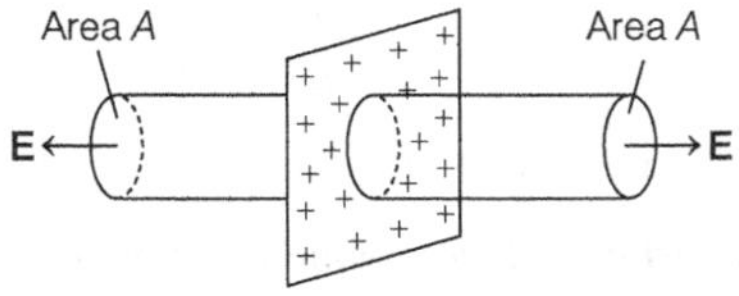

As, the lines of force are parallel to the currect surface of cylinder, the flux passing through the curved surface is zero. The flux through the plane-end faces of the cylinder is $\phi_E = EA + EA = 2EA$
By Gauss's law,

$$\phi_E = \int E \cdot ds = \frac{q}{\varepsilon_0} \Rightarrow 2EA = \frac{\sigma A}{\varepsilon_0} \Rightarrow E = \frac{\sigma}{2\varepsilon_0}$$

18. *(b)* Infrared rays are used for the treatment of muscles ache. Due to their heating properties they are used in infrared therapy.

19. *(c)* The output of gate is given by

$$Y = \overline{A \cdot B}$$

It is a NAND gate output and its truth table is given by

A	B	Y
0	0	1
0	1	1
1	0	1
1	1	0

20. *(c)* LED is a light emitting diode Which emits light in the spectral range of visible light is the range of wavelengths 0.4 μm to 0.7 μm. The energy corressponding to these wavelength is from 1.8 eV to 3 eV. Hence, for the fabrication of LED in the visible range, the minimum band gap energy should be 1.8 eV.
It convert electrical energy into light energy.

21. *(b)* Given, $y = 20\cos(\omega t + 4z)$

On comparing if with general equation,

$$y = A\cos(kx + \omega t)$$

we get, $A = 20$
Therefore, amplitude of the wave is 20.

22. *(a)* Given, frequencies, $\nu_1 = \nu - 1$ and $\nu_2 = \nu + 1$

$$\text{Beats} = \text{Difference in frequencies}$$
$$= (\nu + 1) - (\nu - 1) = 2$$

23. *(b)* $y = \log \omega t$ is a monotonically increasing function. It cannot repeat its value, therefore it is a non-periodic function.

24. *(b)* The equation of motion of this system about mean position is given by

$$F = k_1x + k_2x$$

$$\Rightarrow \quad m\frac{d^2x}{dt^2} = k_1x + k_2x \Rightarrow \frac{d^2x}{dt^2} = x\left(\frac{k_1 + k_2}{m}\right)$$

$$\because \quad a = \frac{d^2x}{dt^2} = \omega^2 x$$

$$\therefore \quad \omega^2 = \frac{k_1 + k_2}{m} \quad \text{or} \quad \omega = \sqrt{\frac{k_1 + k_2}{m}}$$

25. *(c)* Volume of material remain same after stretching.
As volume remains same,

$$A_1l_1 = A_2l_2$$

Here, $l_2 = nl_1$

$$\Rightarrow \quad A_2 = \frac{A_1l_1}{l_2} = \frac{A_1}{n}$$

Resistance of wire after stretching,

$$R_2 = \frac{\rho l_2}{A_2} = \rho\frac{nl_1}{A_1/n} = n^2\rho\frac{l_1}{R_1} = n^2R \quad \left(\because R = \rho\frac{l_1}{A_1}\right)$$

26. *(d)* Since, the incidence light beam is unpolarised, the intensity of light on being transmitted through first nicol polaroid, will become

$$I = \frac{I_0}{2}$$

So, according to law of Malus, intensity on passing through second nicol will be

$$I' = I\cos^2\theta = \frac{I_0}{2}\cos^2 60° = \frac{I_0}{2} \times \left(\frac{1}{2}\right)^2 = \frac{I_0}{8}$$

27. *(a)* The collision of the molecules of an ideal gas is taken as elastic.

28. *(c)* The average energy associated with a particle of a monoatomic gas is $\frac{3}{2}K_BT$.

29. *(d)* According to Kirchhoff's first law, redrawing the circuit, we get

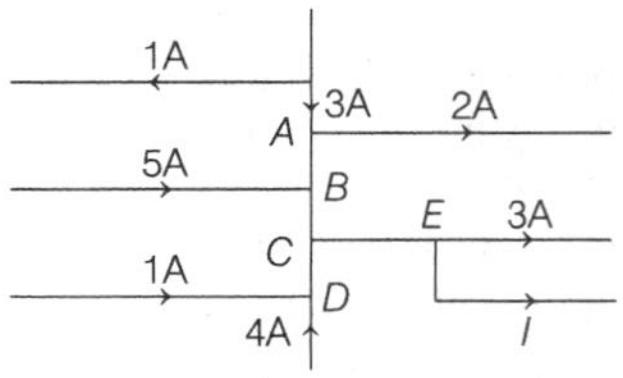

Current at $A = 3 - 2 = 1\text{A}$

Current at $B = 1 + 5 = 6\text{A}$

Current at $D = 1 + 4 = 5\text{A}$

Current at $C = 6 + 5 = 11\text{A}$

$\therefore \quad I = 11 - 3 = 8\text{A}$

30. *(d)* When an electron jumps from orbit n_i to n_f, then the frequency of emitted photon is

$$\nu = cR\left(\frac{1}{n_f^2} - \frac{1}{n_i^2}\right)$$

Here, $n_i = 3$, $n_f = 2$

$$\Rightarrow \quad \nu = cR\left[\frac{1}{(2)^2} - \frac{1}{(3)^2}\right] = \frac{5Rc}{36}$$

31. *(d)* The graph of stress *versus* strain is given below

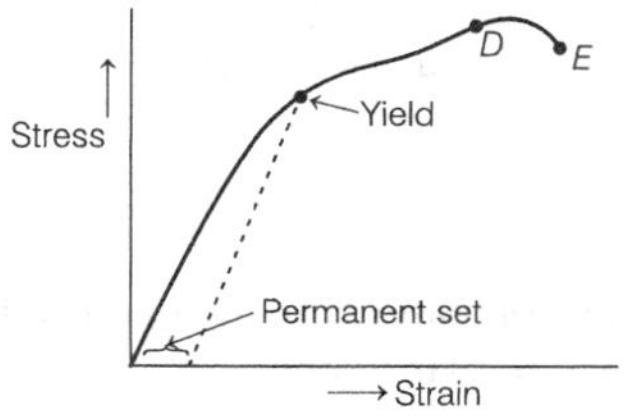

From the graph it is clear that within the elastic limit, the corresponding stress refers to yield point.

32. *(a)* If a wire is stretched to double its length, then

$$\text{Strain} = \frac{\text{Change in length}}{\text{Actual length}} = \frac{2L - L}{L} = 1$$

33. *(b)* From Kepler's second law of planetary motion,

$$\frac{dL}{dt} = \frac{L}{2m}$$

Thus, angular momentum remains conserved.

34. *(b)* As we know that, PE of satellite revolving at height h from the surface of the earth.

$$= -\frac{GM_e m}{R_e + h}$$

$$\text{KE of satellite,} = \frac{1}{2}\frac{GM_e m}{(R_e + h)}$$

Therefore, PE = −2KE

$\therefore \quad r = -2$

35. *(d)* Given, $n = 20\text{cm}^{-1} = 2000\text{m}^{-1}$

$$B = 20\text{mT} = 20 \times 10^{-3}\text{T}$$

Using, $B = \mu_0 nI$

$$20 \times 10^{-3} = 4\pi \times 10^{-7} \times 2000 \times I$$

$$\Rightarrow \quad I = \frac{20 \times 10^{-3}}{4\pi \times 10^{-7} \times 2000} = 8\,\text{A}$$

36. *(d)* The magnetic field through the circle is constant as current through the straight wire is constant. So,

$$\frac{d\phi_B}{dt} = 0$$

$$\text{As,} \quad E = \frac{d\phi_B}{dt} = 0 \quad \therefore \quad I = \frac{E}{R} = 0$$

Here, no current is flowing in circle.

37. *(b)* Pressure at a point inside a liquid is given by

$$p = \frac{F}{A} = \rho hg$$

Therefore, at same height, pressure in a fluid at rest will be the same.

38. *(a)* The interatomic forces decreases or becomes very weak at the boiling point of a liquid. Therefore, surface tension becomes zero.

39. *(b)* If all the masses will remain same, then centre of mass will lie at the centre O. But as the mass at B is $4m$, so the centre of mass of the system will shift towards B. So centre of mass will be on line OB.

40. *(c)* The external torque changes the angular momentum, therefore the second law in rotational motion is given by,

$$\tau_{\text{ext}} = \frac{dL}{dt}$$

41. *(d)* Given, $y = ut + gt^2$

Comparing with equation of motion $y = ut + \frac{1}{2}at^2$

we get, $a = 2g$

$\therefore$ Force $= m \times a = m \times 2g = 2mg$

42. *(a)* The centripetal force is balanced by the normal reaction exerted i.e. $mv^2 / r \le \mu_s N$

where, μ_s is the coefficient of friction.

$$\therefore \quad \frac{mv^2}{r} = f \le \mu_s N$$

43. *(a)* Given, $n = 2$ min to 10 min = 5 half-lives and $N_0 = 80$ g

$$\text{We know,} \quad \frac{N}{N_0} = \left(\frac{1}{2}\right)^n$$

$$\Rightarrow \quad N = \frac{N_0}{2^n} = \left(\frac{80}{2^5}\right) = \frac{80}{32} = 2.5\text{ g}$$

44. *(c)* Energy released in the nuclear process is

$$E = mc^2 - mc^2\left(\frac{2}{3}\right)^2 = \left(1 - \frac{4}{9}\right)mc^2 = \frac{5}{9}mc^2$$

Hence, energy released decrease by a factor of $\frac{5}{9}$.

45. *(d)* Given $|e| = 220$ V, $di = 0.9$ A, $\nu = 50$ Hz

As $\nu = \frac{1}{t} \Rightarrow t = \frac{1}{\nu} = \frac{1}{50}$

Since, $|e| = L\frac{di}{dt} \Rightarrow 220 = L \times \frac{0.9}{1/50}$

$\Rightarrow L = \frac{220}{0.9 \times 50} = 4.88\text{H} \simeq 5\text{H}$

46. *(c)* Given $M = \frac{f_o}{f_e} = 9 \Rightarrow f_o = 9f_e$

Also, $f_o + f_e = 20$

$\Rightarrow 9f_e + f_e = 20 \Rightarrow f_e = 2\text{ cm}$

$\therefore f_o = 9 \times 2 = 18\text{ cm}$

47. *(b)* Given that, $\frac{1}{2}m_1v_1^2 = \frac{1}{2}m_2v_2^2$

$\Rightarrow \frac{1}{2} \times 1 \times v_1^2 = \frac{1}{2} \times 9 \times v_2^2 \Rightarrow v_1^2 = 9v_2^2 \Rightarrow v_1 = 3v_2$

Now, momentum $p = mv$

Therefore, $\frac{m_1v_1}{m_2v_2} = \frac{1 \times v_1}{9 \times v_2} = \frac{3v_2}{9v_2} = \frac{1}{3}$

48. *(a)* When kinetic energy is conserved in a collision, then the collision is said to be elastic.

49. *(a)* Given, $R = 10\text{k}\Omega = 10^4\Omega$

$C = 100\text{pF} = 100 \times 10^{-12}\text{F}$

Time constant of RC circuit,

$\tau = RC = 10^4 \times 100 \times 10^{-12} = 10^{-6}$ s

For demodulation $\frac{1}{f_C} << RC \Rightarrow f_C >> \frac{1}{RC}$

or $f_C >> \frac{1}{10^{-6}} = 10^6$ Hz

$\therefore f_C >> 1$ MHz

50. *(b)* For motion under central forces, the total mechanical energy i.e. the sum of kinetic energy and potential energy of a body is constant. The familiar example is the free fall of an object under gravity.

51. *(c)* The statement given in the option (c) is incorrect, it can be corrected as

A hypothesis is a supposition without assuming that it is true.

52. *(c)* Using relation, $\tan\theta = \frac{X_L - X_C}{R}$

$\Rightarrow \theta = \tan^{-1}\left(\frac{X_L - X_C}{R}\right) = \tan^{-1}\left(\frac{Z}{R}\right)$

Here, $Z = \sqrt{3}R$

$\Rightarrow \theta = \tan^{-1}\left(\frac{\sqrt{3}R}{R}\right) = \tan^{-1}(\sqrt{3}) = 60°$

53. *(d)* Time period of simple harmonic motion,

$$T = 2\pi\sqrt{\left|\frac{\theta}{\alpha}\right|} = 2\pi\sqrt{\frac{I}{mH}}$$

$\Rightarrow T \propto \sqrt{I} \Rightarrow T \propto \sqrt{m}$ $\left[\because I = \frac{ml^2}{12}\right]$

$\frac{T_1}{T_2} = \sqrt{\frac{m_1}{m_2}} = \sqrt{\frac{m}{4m}} = \frac{1}{2}$

$\Rightarrow T_2 = 2T_1 = 2T$ $[\because T_1 = T]$

So, motion remains simple harmonic with time period $2T$.

54. *(a)* Given, $\mu_r = 6000$

As we know, $\mu_r = 1 + X_m$

$\Rightarrow X_m = \mu_r - 1 = 6000 - 1 = 5999$

55. *(d)* Since, frequency of spring oscillator is smallest among all the given options, hence small time interval cannot be measured with spring oscillator.

56. *(a)* The error in measurement of length 1.02 cm is ±0.01 cm and error in measurement of length 9.89 cm is ±0.01 cm.

$\therefore$The relative error is 1.02 cm

$= \left[\pm\frac{0.01}{1.02} \times 100\%\right] = \pm 0.98\% = \pm 1\%$

Similarly, the relative error in 9.89 cm

$= \left[\pm\frac{0.01}{9.89} \times 100\%\right] = \pm 0.1\%$

Therefore, relative errors in measurement of two masses are ±1% and ±0.1%.

57. *(c)* Given, $\lambda = 589\text{ nm} = 589 \times 10^{-9}$ m

$d = 0.589\text{ mm} = 0.589 \times 10^{-3}$ m

In Young's double slit experiment, half angular width of central maxima is

$\sin\theta = \frac{\lambda}{d} = \frac{589 \times 10^{-9}}{0.589 \times 10^{-3}} = 10^{-3} \Rightarrow \theta = \sin^{-1}(0.001)$

58. *(b)* The graph between stopping potential and frequency is a straight line, so stopping potential and hence maximum kinetic energy of the photoelectrons depends linearly on the frequency.

59. *(b)* Total work done by the gas

$W_{\text{Total}} = W_{A\to B} + W_{B\to C} + W_{C\to D} + W_{D\to A}$

Work done in isothermal process by ideal gas

$W_{A\to B} = \mu RT_1 \log\frac{V_2}{V_1}$ ...(i)

Work done in adiabatic process by ideal gas

$W_{B\to C} = \frac{\mu R(T_1 - T_2)}{r - 1}$ ...(ii)

Work done in isothermal process by ideal gas,

$W_{C\to D} = -\mu RT_2 \log\frac{V_3}{V_4}$ ...(iii)

Work done in adiabatic process, by ideal gas

$W_{D\to A} = \frac{-\mu R(T_1 - T_2)}{r - 1}$ ...(iv)

Adding Eqs. (i), (ii), (iii) and (iv) we get

$$W_{\text{Total}} = \mu RT_1 \log\frac{V_2}{V_1} - \mu RT_2 \log\frac{V_3}{V_4}$$

60. *(b)* Given, $\lambda = 1.3 \mu m = 1.3 \times 10^{-6}$ m

Bandwidth of channel, BW = 20 kHz = 20×10^3 Hz

Optical source frequency,

$$f = \frac{c}{\lambda} = \frac{3 \times 10^8}{1.3 \times 10^{-6}}$$
$$= 2.3 \times 10^{14} \text{ Hz}$$

$\therefore$ Number of channels, $n = \dfrac{f}{\text{BW}} = \dfrac{2.3 \times 10^{14}}{20 \times 10^3}$

$$= 1.15 \times 10^{10}$$

Chemistry

61. *(a)* As we know that,

$$\Delta U = q - p_{\text{ext}} \Delta V$$

Now, if a process of expansion of a gas occurs in vaccum and at constant volume, then

$$\Delta U = qV \qquad (\because \Delta V = 0, p_{\text{ext}} = 0)$$

62. *(a)* Carbon monoxide binds with haemoglobin to form carboxy haemoglobin, which is about 300 times more stable than the oxygen haemoglobin complex.

63. *(b)* Sucrose is formed by the condensation of α-D-glucopyranose and β-D-fructofuranose.

64. *(c)* Henry's law does not hold true when the gases are placed under extremely high pressure. It is one of the limitations of Henry's law.

65. *(a)* Both chromate and dichromate radicals on reaction with acidified H_2O_2 give blue solution which turns green on standing. In the presence of organic solvents such as diethyl ether, amyl alcohol or pyridine, permanent blue colour obtained.

$$K_2Cr_2O_4 + H_2SO_4 + H_2O_2 \xrightarrow{\text{Ether}} CrO_5 + K_2SO_4 + 3H_2O$$

$$K_2Cr_2O_7 + 4H_2SO_4 + 4H_2O_2 \xrightarrow{\text{Ether}} \underset{\text{(Blue colour)}}{2CrO_5} + K_2SO_4 + 5H_2O$$

66. *(b)* We know,

specific rate constant, $k = \dfrac{0.693}{t_{1/2}}$

$$\therefore \quad k = \frac{0.693}{1402} \Rightarrow k = 0.49 \times 10^{-3} \text{ s}^{-1}$$

67. *(a)* Given, $a = 4.29$Å

$$r = \frac{\sqrt{3}}{4} \times a = \frac{\sqrt{3}}{4} \times 4.29 \text{ Å} = 1.86\text{Å}$$

68. *(d)* Glutamine contains polar *R* group as amide group is present in the side chain of glutamine.

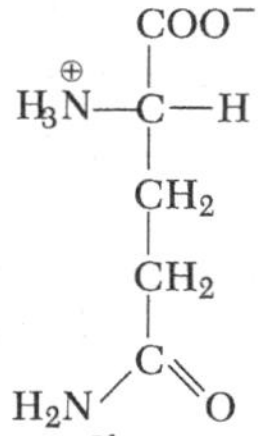

Glutamine

69. *(d)* A multiple bond is always shorter bond the corresponding single bond. The C-atom in CO_3^{2-} is sp^2-hybridised.

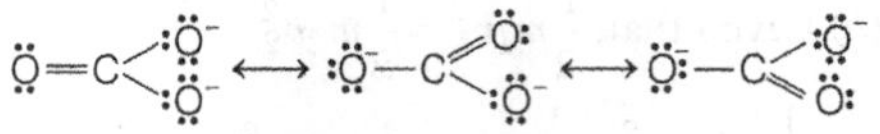

CO_2 is *sp*-hybridised with bond length of carbon oxygen is 122 pm.

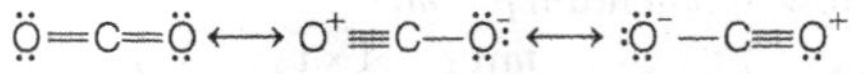

The C-atom in CO is *sp*-hybridised with C—O bond length 110 pm.

$$^{+}C \equiv O^{-}$$

So, the correct order of bond length is

$$CO < CO_2 < CO_3^{2-}.$$

70. *(c)* The total number of nodes are given by $(n-1)$, i.e. sum of angular nodes l and radial nodes $(n-l-1)$.

71. *(a)* $AB \rightleftharpoons A + B$

or $\quad K = \dfrac{[A][B]}{[AB]}$

if concentration of *A* is doubled, the equilibrium concentration of *B* becomes half to maintain *K* constant.

72. *(b)* Antipyretics are used to reduce fever. Antibiotics are used to treat bacterial infection. Analgesic are pain reliever and tranquilisers are used to treat mental illness.

73. *(b)* The given reaction is Gattermann reaction. In this reaction, chlorine or bromine can be introduced in the benzene ring by treating the diazonium salt solution with corresponding halogen acid in the presence of copper powder.

74. *(b)* The melting point of *d*-block elements is due to the presence of unpaired electrons in the last *d*-orbital or *s*-orbital. So, the element which has all the electrons in pairs will have the least melting point.

- Vanadium (V) with atomic number 23.
  [Ar] $3d^3 4s^2$ has 3 unpaired electrons.
- Zinc (Zn) with atomic number (30).
  [Ar] $3d^{10} 4s^2$ has zero unpaired electron.
- Manganese (Mn) with atomic number 25.
  [Ar] $3d^5 4s^2$ has five unpaired electrons.
- Copper (Cu) with atomic number 29.
  [Ar] $3d^{10} 4s^1$ has one unpaired electron.

Therefore zinc has least melting point.

75. *(c)* The zymase enzyme is involved in the catalytic reaction of glucose into ethyl alcohol and carbon dioxide.

$$\underset{\text{Glucose}}{C_6H_{12}O_6(aq)} \xrightarrow{\text{Zymase}} \underset{\text{Ethyl alcohol}}{2C_2H_5OH(aq)} + \underset{\text{Carbon dioxide}}{2CO_2(g)}$$

76. *(d)* Among the given mixture, only CCl_4 and $CHCl_3$ form non-ideal solution, thus they form azeotropic mixture as only non-ideal solutions form azeotropic mixture.

77. *(d)* k varies with temperature as given by Arrhenius equation.

$$k = Ae^{-E_a/RT} \Rightarrow k \propto T \text{ and } k \propto \frac{1}{E_a}$$

$\therefore$ k has least value at low T and high E_a.

78. *(a)* The correct decreasing order of the stabilities of given carbocations is

(iii) > (ii) > (i) > (iv)

Because electron releasing effect stabilises the carbocation. Electron releasing order is

$$NH_2 > OH > OCH_3 > Cl.$$

79. *(a)* In ClO_3^-, total number of electrons = 42

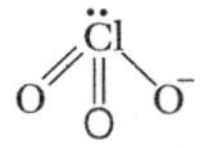

Pyramidal shape

In CO_3^{2-}, total number of electrons = 32

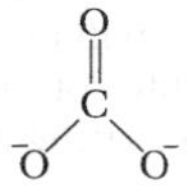

Trigonal planar shape

In NO_3^-, total number of electrons = 32

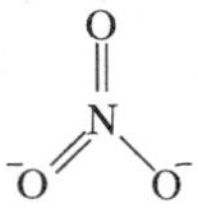

Trigonal planar shape

In SO_3^{2-}, total number of electrons = 42

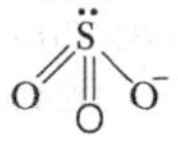

Pyramidal shape

So, the option (a) is correct.

80. *(c)* Only $\frac{1}{8}$th of an atom or molecule or ion actually belongs to a particular unit cell.

81. *(d)* We know that, $K_p = K_C(RT)^{\Delta n_g}$

for the given reaction,

$$\Delta n_g = (2+1) - 2 = 1$$

$$K_p = 3.75 \times 10^{-6}(0.0831 \times 1069) = 0.00033$$

82. *(c)*

Artificial Sweetener	Sweetness value in comparison to cane sugar
Aspartame	100
Saccharin	550
Sucralose	600
Alitame	2000

83. *(c)* Coupling reaction is an example of electrophilic substitution reaction.

84. *(d)* In the structure of CrO_5, it has O-atoms as peroxide which have oxidation number = – 1 and one O as oxide (double bonded O) atom with oxidation number = –2

Let the oxidation number of Cr be x.

Then, $x + 4 \times (-1) + 1 \times (-2) = 0$

or $x = +6$

$\therefore$ The oxidation number of Cr in CrO_5 is +6.

85. *(c)* At constant pressure and temperature, the rate of diffusion or effusion of gas is inversely proportional to the square root of its density.

Rate of diffusion $\propto \frac{1}{\sqrt{d}}$

$$\frac{r_1}{r_2} = \sqrt{\frac{d_2}{d_1}} = \sqrt{\frac{M_2}{M_1}}$$

$r_1 = r_2$ only when $M_1 = M_2$

Hence, N_2O and CO_2 have equal rate of diffusion due to equal molecular weight.

86. *(a)* Carbon monoxide (CO) is the reducing agent which reduces iron oxide (Fe_2O_3) to iron in the blast furnace.

$$Fe_2O_3 + 3CO \longrightarrow 2Fe + 3CO_2\uparrow$$

87. *(b)* $\mu^{\infty}_{Ba(OH)_2} = \lambda^{\infty}_{Ba^{2+}} + 2\lambda^{\infty}_{OH^-} = 523.28$ ...(i)

$\mu^{\infty}_{BaCl_2} = \lambda^{\infty}_{Ba^{2+}} + 2\lambda^{\infty}_{Cl^-} = 280.00$ ...(ii)

$\mu^{\infty}_{NH_4Cl} = \lambda^{\infty}_{NH_4^+} + \lambda^{\infty}_{Cl^-} = 129.80$ ...(iii)

$\mu^{\infty}_{NH_4OH} = \lambda^{\infty}_{NH_4^+} + \lambda^{\infty}_{OH^-}$

Eq. (iii) + $\frac{\text{Eq. (i)}}{2} - \frac{\text{Eq. (ii)}}{2}$ will gives

$$\Rightarrow \lambda^{\infty}_{NH_4^+} + \lambda^{\infty}_{OH^-} = \lambda^{\infty}_{NH_4OH} = \frac{502.88}{2}$$

$$= 251.44\ \Omega^{-1}cm^2\ mol^{-1}.$$

88. *(a)* Xerophthalmia disease is type of (hardening of cornea of eye) disease. It is caused by deficiency of vitamin-A.

89. *(a)* The final product from this reaction is

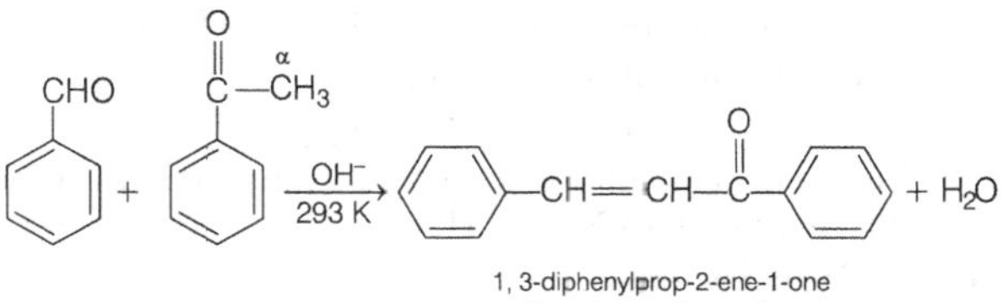

1, 3-diphenylprop-2-ene-1-one
(Benzalacetophenone)

So the correct option is (a).

90. *(d)* Phase transformation involve the energy changes e.g., ice requires heat for melting. Normally this melting takes place at constant pressure and during phase change, temperature remains constant (at 273 K).

91. *(a)* Dettol is a mixture of chloroxylenol and terpineol.

92. *(c)* The chemical formula of Hinsberg's reagent is $C_6H_5SO_2Cl$.

93. *(b)* The increasing order of atomic radii of group-13 elements is

Ga (135 pm) < Al (143 pm) < In (167 pm) < Tl (170 pm)

On moving down the group the atomic radii increases. However due to poor shielding of nuclear charge by 3*d*-electron.

$$\underset{(135\text{ pm})}{r_{Ga}} < \underset{(143\text{ pm})}{r_{Al}}$$

The electrons in the outermost shell of Ga experience more force of attraction towards nucleus than Al which decreases atomic radius.

94. *(a)* Macromolecular colloids are quite stable and resemble to the true solutions in many respects.

95. *(b)* Wurtz reaction is used to prepare symmetrical alkanes having even number of carbon atoms. Option (b) contains an alkane with odd number of carbon atoms. Thus, it can be prepared by Wurtz reactions.

96. *(c)*

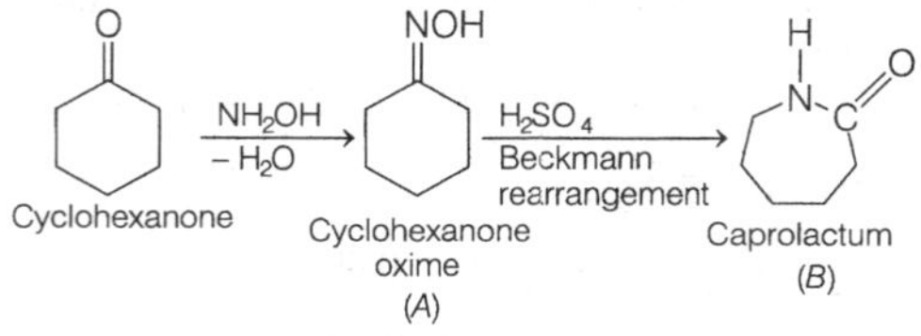

97. *(a)* Due to intermolecular hydrogen bonding, ketones and carboxylic acids have higher boiling point as compare to aldehyde.

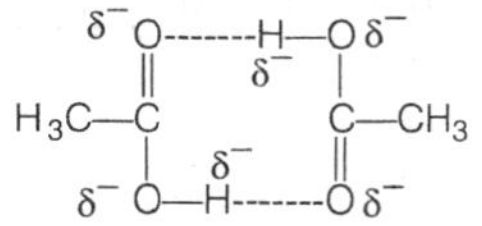

Hydrogen bonding in carboxylic acid

98. *(d)* In case of bcc lattice cell,

packing efficiency = 68%

∴ Percent vacant space = 100 − 68 = 32%

99. *(d)* Since, at equilibrium,

rate of forward reaction = rate of backward reaction.

Therefore, in the chemical reaction,

$$N_2 + 3H_2 \rightleftharpoons 2NH_3$$

the same amount of ammonia is formed, as it is decomposed into N_2 and H_2.

100. *(b)* Heat absorbed,

$$q = 500 \text{ cal}$$

Work done by the system, $W = -350$ cal

According to the first law of thermodynamics,

$\Delta E = q + W = 500 + (-350) = +150$ cal.

101. *(c)* Phenelzine is used to treat panic attacks.

102. *(b)* $C_6H_5N_2^+X^-$ is most stable due to resonance.

103. *(b)* EDTA is a hexadentate ligand because it has six binding sites i.e. it has six donor atoms per ligand.

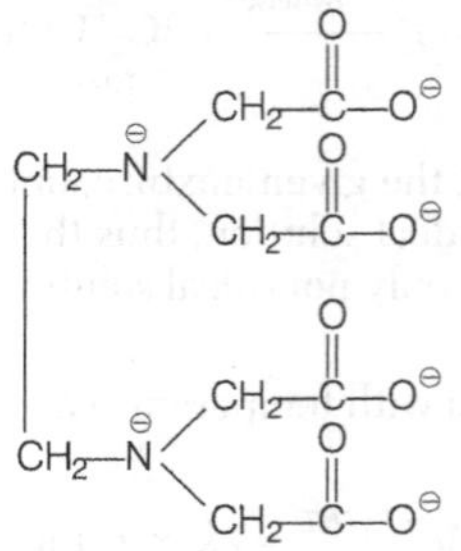

104. *(d)* $\dfrac{d}{p} = \dfrac{M}{RT}$

Let density of gas *B* be *d*.

∴ Density of gas $A = 3d$

and let molecular weight of *A* be *M*.

∵ Molecular weight of $B = 2M$.

Since, *R* is a gas constant and *T* is same for both gases, so,

$$p_A = \frac{d_A RT}{M_A} \text{ and } p_B = \frac{d_B RT}{M_B}$$

$$\frac{p_B}{p_A} = \frac{d_B}{d_A} \times \frac{M_A}{M_B} = \frac{d}{3d} \times \frac{M}{2M} = \frac{1}{6}$$

105. *(b)* More the value of *i*, more will be the elevation in boiling point. Also, more dilute solution has low boiling point. Hence, the increasing order of boiling points is

$$\underset{(i=2)}{10^{-2}\text{ M NaCl}} > \underset{(i=3)}{10^{-3}\text{ M MgCl}_2} > \underset{(i=2)}{10^{-4}\text{ M NaCl}} > \underset{(i=1)}{10^{-4}\text{ M urea}}.$$

106. *(c)* Molarity of $BaCl_2 = \dfrac{1 \times 1000}{208 \times 200} = 0.024$ M

Also, normality of $BaCl_2 = 0.024 \times 2 = 0.048$ N

$(\because N = M \times V \cdot f)$

$$\lambda_m = \frac{\kappa \times 1000}{M} = \frac{0.0058 \times 1000}{0.024}$$

$$= 241.678 \text{ S cm}^2 \text{ mol}^{-1}$$

Also, $\lambda_{eq.} = \dfrac{\kappa \times 1000}{N} = \dfrac{0.0058 \times 1000}{0.048}$

$$= 120.83 \text{ S cm}^2 \text{eq}^{-1}.$$

107. *(c)* $2N_2O_5 \longrightarrow 4NO_2 + O_2$

∵ The above reaction is first order.

so, $$k = \frac{2.303}{t} \log \frac{P_0}{P_t}$$

Put the values

$$4.48 \times 10^{-5} = \frac{2.303}{10 \times 60} \log \frac{600}{P_t}$$

$$\log \frac{600}{P_t} = 0.01167$$

$$\frac{600}{P_t} = \text{antilog}\,(0.01167)$$

$$\frac{600}{P_t} = 1.02$$

$$P_t = \frac{600}{1.02} \Rightarrow 588 \text{ atm}$$

108. *(a)* As we know that, $C_p - C_V = nR$

where, n = number of moles of gas

$$R = 8.314\,\text{J}/\text{Kmol}^{-1}$$

$$C_p - C_V = 10 \times 8.314 = 83.14 \text{ J/K}$$

109. *(b)* Use of lead (Pb) in petrol causes emission of lead by vehicles.

110. *(d)* Trihydrides of group 15 elements are given on the basis of reducing character as follows :

$BiH_3 > SbH_3 > AsH_3 > PH_3 > NH_3$

The reducing character increases down the group because the bond strength of E-H bond decreases. As the size of element E down the group increases and thus, the bond dissociation energy decreases. This facilitates the dissociation of hydrogen atoms and hence, down the group, the reducing character increase.

111. *(a)* Given, mass of solute = 22.2 g

Volume of solution = 1 L

∴ Molarity

$$(M) = \frac{\text{mass of solute (in g)}}{\text{mol. weight of solute} \times \text{Volume of solution (in L)}}$$

$$= \frac{22.2\text{ g}}{111 \text{ g mol}^{-1} \times 1 \text{ L}}$$

$[\because \text{Mol. weight of } CaCl_2 = 111 \text{ g mol}^{-1}]$

$$= 0.2 \text{ mol L}^{-1} = 0.2 \text{ M}$$

112. *(c)* The reaction for decolourisation of 1 mole of $KMnO_4$ by H_2O_2 are given as follow:

$$2KMnO_4 + 3H_2SO_4 \longrightarrow K_2SO_4 + 2MnSO_4 + 3H_2O + 5[O]$$

$$5H_2O_2 + 5[O] \longrightarrow 5H_2O + 5O_2$$

The overall reaction is

$$2KMnO_4 + 3H_2SO_4 + 5H_2O_2 \longrightarrow K_2SO_4 + 2MnSO_4 + 8H_2O + 5O_2$$

As 2 moles of $KMnO_4$ require H_2O_2 = 5 moles

$\therefore$ 1 mole of $KMnO_4$ require $H_2O_2 = \frac{5}{2} = 2.5$ moles

113. *(a)* The correct IUPAC name of given molecule is 3, 3-diethynylpenta-1, 4-diene.

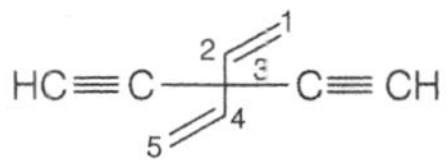

114. *(b)* In case of H_2O_2, O—O bond is non-polar and O—H bond is polar.

So, the option (b) is correct.

115. *(a)* This is a named reaction known as Gattermann-koch reaction.

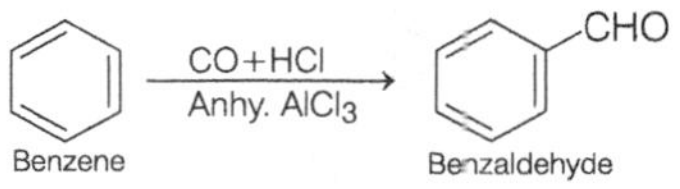

116. *(a)* Balmer series of transitions in the spectrum of hydrogen atom fall in visible region. Lyman series fall in ultraviolet, while Paschen, Brackett and Pfund fall in infrared region.

117. *(d)* Given, $\Delta G° = 13.8$ kJ/mol $= 13.8 \times 10^3$ J/mol

$$\because \quad \Delta G° = -RT \ln K_C$$

$$13800 = -8.314 \times 298 \ln K_C$$

$$\therefore \quad K_C = 3.81 \times 10^{-3}$$

118. *(c)* Lyman series is a hydrogen spectral series of transitions and result in ultraviolet emission lines of the hydrogen atom as electron goes from $n \geq 2$ to $n = 1$ (where n is the principal quantum number) the lowest energy level of electron. Hence, it lies in ultraviolet region.

119. *(b)* $K_3[Fe(CN)_5NO]$

$(CN)_5$ = pentacyano

(NO) = nitro-N

So, IUPAC name of given compound is potassium pentacyanonitro-N-ferrate (III).

120. *(c)* Chemisorption occurs at very high temperature and high pressure as it involves chemical reaction between adsorbate and adsorbent molecules and involves high activation energy to start the reaction which requires high pressure and temperature.

Mathematics

121. *(b)* Consider the given inequation as $2x + 3y = 6$.

Table for equation $2x + 3y = 6$ or $y = \frac{6 - 2x}{3}$ is

x	0	3
y	2	0

On putting (0, 0) in the inequality $2x + 3y \leq 6$, we get

$0 \leq 6$ which is true

Consider $x + y = 2$

x	0	2
y	2	0

$\Rightarrow$ Feasible region will be towards origin

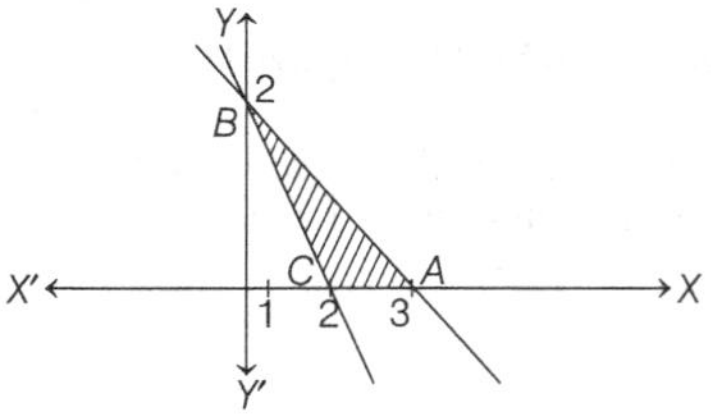

122. *(d)* Let $Z = x + y$

Given, constraints are $2x + 3y \leq 6, x \geq 0, y \geq 0$.
These constraints consider as equation $2x + 3y = 6$

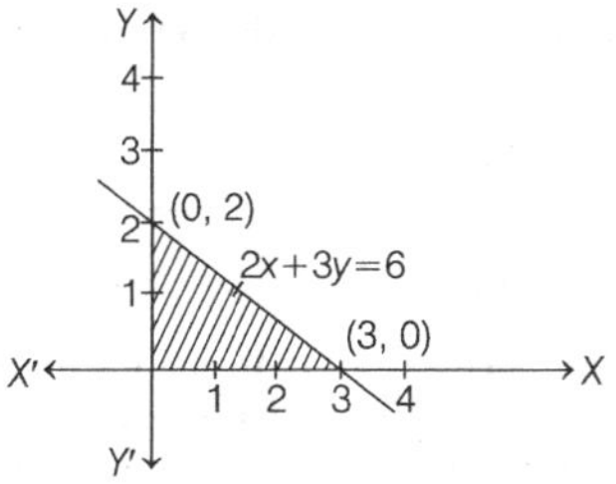

This equation intersect X and Y-axes at $A(3, 0)$ and $B(0, 2)$. On putting (0, 0) in the inequality $2x + 3y \leq 6$, we get $2 \times 0 + 3 \times 0 \leq 6 \Rightarrow 0 \leq 6$ (which is true). So, the feasible region is towards the origin.

$\therefore$ The corner points of a feasible region are $O(0, 0)$, $A(3, 0)$ and $B(0, 2)$.

The value of Z on these corner points are given below

Corner points	Value of Z ($Z = x + y$)
$O(0, 0)$	$Z = 0 + 0 = 0$
$A(3, 0)$	$Z = 3 + 0 = 3$ (maximum)
$B(0, 2)$	$Z = 0 + 2 = 2$

Hence, maximum value of Z is 3.

123. *(b)* The corner points of the feasible region are $O(0, 0)$, $A(4, 0)$ and $B(0, 3)$.

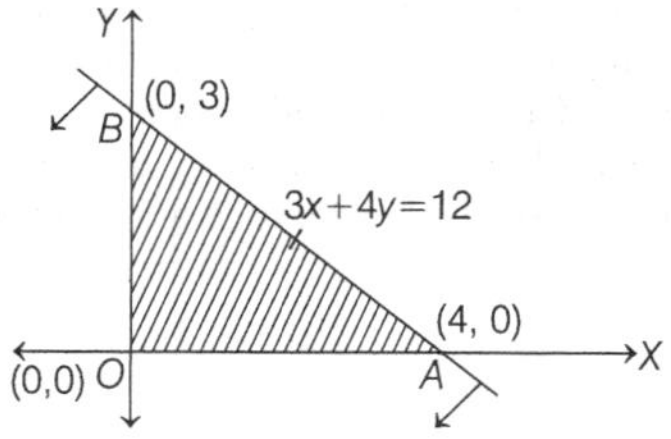

The value of Z on these corner points are given below

Corner points	Value of Z ($Z = x + y$)
$O(0, 0)$	$Z = 0 + 0 = 0$
$A(4, 0)$	$Z = 4 + 0 = 4$ (maximum)
$B(0, 3)$	$Z = 0 + 3 = 3$

Hence, Z(max) is 4 at point $x = 4$ and $y = 0$.

124. *(*)* Let the vector be $x\hat{i} + y\hat{j} + z\hat{k}$

Since, unit vector along X-axis is $\mathbf{i}$

$$\mathbf{i} = \mathbf{V}_1 + \mathbf{V}_2 + \mathbf{V}_3$$

$$\mathbf{i} = \hat{i} - 3\hat{j} + 2\hat{k} + 3\hat{i} + 6\hat{j} - 7\hat{k} + x\hat{i} + y\hat{j} + z\hat{k}$$

$$\mathbf{i} + 0\hat{j} + 0\hat{k} = (4 + x)\hat{i} + (3 + y)\hat{j} + (z - 5)\hat{k}$$

$\Rightarrow x + 4 = 1 \Rightarrow x = -3$

$\Rightarrow y + 3 = 0 \Rightarrow y = -3 \quad \Rightarrow z - 5 = 0 \rightarrow z = 5$

The vector $-3\hat{i} - 3\hat{j} + 5\hat{k}$.

125. *(b)* Given, $|\mathbf{a}| = 8, |\mathbf{b}| = 3$ and $|\mathbf{a} \times \mathbf{b}| = 12$

We know that, $\sin\theta = \dfrac{|\mathbf{a} \times \mathbf{b}|}{|\mathbf{a}||\mathbf{b}|}$

$$\Rightarrow \quad \sin\theta = \frac{12}{8 \times 3} = \frac{1}{2} \Rightarrow \sin\theta = \sin\frac{\pi}{6}$$

$$\Rightarrow \quad \theta = \frac{\pi}{6} \qquad \left[\sin\frac{\pi}{6} = \frac{1}{2}\right]$$

Hence, angle between $\mathbf{a}$ and $\mathbf{b}$ is $\frac{\pi}{6}$.

126. *(c)* Given, $\mathbf{a} = 2\hat{i} + 3\hat{j} + \hat{k}, \mathbf{b} = \hat{i} - 2\hat{j} + \hat{k}$

and $\quad \mathbf{c} = -3\hat{i} + \hat{j} + 2\hat{k}$

We know that, $[\mathbf{a\ b\ c}] = \begin{vmatrix} a_1 & a_2 & a_3 \\ b_1 & b_2 & b_3 \\ c_1 & c_2 & c_3 \end{vmatrix}$

$$\therefore \quad [\mathbf{a\ b\ c}] = \begin{vmatrix} 2 & 3 & 1 \\ 1 & -2 & 1 \\ -3 & 1 & 2 \end{vmatrix}$$

$$= 2(-4 - 1) - 3(2 + 3) + 1(1 - 6)$$
$$= -10 - 15 - 5 = -30$$

127. *(d)* Let $A = \begin{bmatrix} a & b \\ c & d \end{bmatrix} \Rightarrow \text{adj}(A) = \begin{bmatrix} d & -b \\ -c & a \end{bmatrix}$

Now, $A(\text{Adj } A) = \begin{bmatrix} a & b \\ c & d \end{bmatrix} \times \begin{bmatrix} d & -b \\ -c & a \end{bmatrix}$

$$\Rightarrow \begin{bmatrix} 8 & 0 \\ 0 & 8 \end{bmatrix} = \begin{bmatrix} a & b \\ c & d \end{bmatrix} \times \begin{bmatrix} d & -b \\ -c & a \end{bmatrix} = \begin{bmatrix} ad - bc & 0 \\ 0 & ad - bc \end{bmatrix}$$

$\Rightarrow \quad ad - bc = 8, -ab + ab = 0, dc - dc = 0$

$\Rightarrow \quad -bc + ad = 8$

$$\det(A) = \begin{vmatrix} a & b \\ c & d \end{vmatrix} = ad - bc = 8$$

128. *(c)* Given, $A = \begin{bmatrix} 2 & -2 \\ -2 & 2 \end{bmatrix} \Rightarrow A^2 = \begin{bmatrix} 2 & -2 \\ -2 & 2 \end{bmatrix}\begin{bmatrix} 2 & -2 \\ -2 & 2 \end{bmatrix}$

$$= \begin{bmatrix} 4 + 4 & -4 - 4 \\ -4 - 4 & 4 + 4 \end{bmatrix} = \begin{bmatrix} 8 & -8 \\ -8 & 8 \end{bmatrix}$$

Given that, $\quad A^2 = pA$

$$\Rightarrow \begin{bmatrix} 8 & -8 \\ -8 & 8 \end{bmatrix} = p\begin{bmatrix} 2 & -2 \\ -2 & 2 \end{bmatrix} \Rightarrow \begin{bmatrix} 8 & -8 \\ -8 & 8 \end{bmatrix} = \begin{bmatrix} 2p & -2p \\ -2p & 2p \end{bmatrix}$$

Now, $\quad 2p = 8 \Rightarrow p = 4$

129. *(c)* $A(\text{adj } A) = \begin{bmatrix} -2 & 0 & 0 \\ 0 & -2 & 0 \\ 0 & 0 & -2 \end{bmatrix} = -2I$

$$A(\text{adj}A) = |A| I \Rightarrow -2I = |A| I$$
$$|A| = -2$$
$$\Rightarrow \quad |\text{adj } A| = |A|^{n-1}, n = 3$$
$$\Rightarrow \quad |\text{adj } A| = |A|^{3-1} = |A|^2$$
$$\Rightarrow \quad |\text{adj } A| = (-2)^2 = 4$$

130. *(b)* Given, $ax^2 + bx + c = 0$

For equal roots $D = 0 \Rightarrow b^2 = 4ac \Rightarrow b^2 = 4ac$

In **Case I** : $ac = 1$

$$(a, b, c) = (1, 2, 1)$$

Case II : $ac = 4$

$(a, b, c) = (1, 4, 4)$ or $(4, 4, 1)$ or $(2, 4, 2)$

Case III : $ac = 9$

$$(a, b, c) = (3, 6, 3)$$

Required probability $= \dfrac{5}{216}$

131. *(c)* $8^{3\log_8 5} \Rightarrow 8^{\log_8 5^3} = (5)^3 \qquad [a^{\log_a x} = x]$

$$= 5 \times 5 \times 5 = 125$$

132. *(a)* Given curve is $y = (1 + x)^y + \sin^{-1}(\sin^2 x)$

On differentiating both sides w.r.t. x,

$$\frac{dy}{dx} = (1 + x)^y \left[\frac{y}{1 + x} + \log(1 + x)\frac{dy}{dx}\right] + \frac{2\sin x \cos x}{\sqrt{1 - \sin^4 x}}$$

$$\left(\frac{dy}{dx}\right)_{at(0, 1)} = +1 \qquad [\text{at } x = 0, y = 1]$$

$\Rightarrow$ Slope of normal at $(x = 0) = -1$

Hence, equation of the normal at $(0, 1)$ is $x + y = 1$

133. *(a)* Given, $L = \lim\limits_{x \to 0} \dfrac{a - \sqrt{a^2 - x^2} - \dfrac{x^2}{4}}{x^4} \qquad \left[\dfrac{0}{0} \text{ form}\right]$

$$= \lim_{x \to 0} \frac{0 - \dfrac{(0 - 2x)}{2\sqrt{a^2 - x^2}} - \dfrac{2x}{4}}{4x^3} \qquad [\text{by using } L' \text{ hospital rule}]$$

$$= \lim_{x \to 0} \frac{x\left(\dfrac{1}{\sqrt{a^2 - x^2}} - \dfrac{1}{2}\right)}{4x^3} = \lim_{x \to 0} \frac{\dfrac{1}{\sqrt{a^2 - x^2}} - \dfrac{1}{2}}{4x^2}$$

$$\left(\frac{\dfrac{1}{a} - \dfrac{1}{2}}{0} \text{ form}\right)$$

For limit to be exist $\Rightarrow \dfrac{1}{a} - \dfrac{1}{2} = 0 \Rightarrow a = 2$.

134. *(a)* Given, centre $(h, k) = (1, 2)$

and circle touches on X axis.

$\therefore$ Radius $(r) = y$ coordinate of centre $= 2$

So, equation of circle is

$(x - 1)^2 + (y - 2)^2 = 2^2 \qquad [\because (x - h)^2 + (y - k)^2 = r^2]$

$\Rightarrow x^2 - 2x + 1 + y^2 - 4y + 4 = 4$

$$[\because (a - b)^2 = a^2 + b^2 - 2ab]$$

$$\Rightarrow \quad x^2 + y^2 - 2x - 4y + 1 = 0$$

135. *(a)* First, break the number 5.001 as $x = 5$ and $\Delta x = 0.001$ and use the relation

$$f(x + \Delta x) = f(x) + \Delta x\, f'(x)$$

Consider, $\quad f(x) = x^3 - 7x^2 + 15$

$\Rightarrow \quad f'(x) = 3x^2 - 14x$

Let $\quad x = 5$ and $\Delta x = 0.001$

Also, $\quad f(x + \Delta x) \approx f(x) + \Delta x\, f'(x)$

Therefore,

$$f(x + \Delta x) \approx (x^3 - 7x^2 + 15) + \Delta x\,(3x^2 - 14x)$$

$$\Rightarrow \quad f(5.001) \approx (5^3 - 7 \times 5^2 + 15) + (3 \times 5^2 - 14 \times 5)(0.001)$$

$$[\text{as } x = 5, \Delta x = 0.001]$$

$= (125 - 175 + 15) + (75 - 70)(0.001)$

$= -35 + (5)(0.001) = -35 + 0.005 = -34.995$

136. *(a)* Given equation is

$$2x^2 + 2y^2 + 3x + 4y + \frac{9}{8} = 0.$$

On dividing both sides by 2, we get

$$x^2 + y^2 + \frac{3}{2}x + 2y + \frac{9}{16} = 0 \qquad \ldots(\text{i})$$

From Eq. (i), we have coefficient of $x = \dfrac{3}{2}$

and coefficient of $y = 2$

$$\therefore \quad \alpha = \frac{-1}{2}\left(\frac{3}{2}\right) = -\frac{3}{4} \text{ and } \beta = \frac{-1}{2}(2) = -1$$

Hence, centre $= \left(-\dfrac{3}{4}, -1\right)$

From Eq. (i), we have constant term $= \dfrac{9}{16}$

$$\therefore \text{ Radius} = \sqrt{\left(\frac{-3}{4}\right)^2 + (-1)^2 - \frac{9}{16}} = \sqrt{\frac{9}{16} + 1 - \frac{9}{16}} = 1$$

137. *(b)* For maximum value of $f(x) = \dfrac{1}{4x^2 + 2x + 1}$

$4x^2 + 2x + 1$ must be minimum.

For minimum values of $4x^2 + 2x + 1$,

$$4x^2 + 2x + 1 = 4x^2 + 2x + \frac{1}{4} + \frac{3}{4} = \left(2x + \frac{1}{2}\right)^2 + \frac{3}{4}$$

So, $4x^2 + 2x + 1$ becomes minimum when $2x + \frac{1}{2} = 0$

Then, minimum value of $4x^2 + 2x + 1$ becomes $\frac{3}{4}$.

Hence, the maximum value of $f(x) = \frac{1}{3/4} = \frac{4}{3}$

138. *(c)* Given, $f(x) = \begin{cases} ax + 3, & x \le 2 \\ a^2x - 1, & x > 2 \end{cases}$

Continuity at $x = 2$,

$$\text{LHL} = \lim_{x \to 2^-} f(x) = \lim_{x \to 2} (ax + 3) = 2a + 3$$

$$\text{RHL} = \lim_{x \to 2^+} f(x) = \lim_{x \to 2} (a^2x - 1) = 2a^2 - 1$$

Since, $f(x)$ is continuous for all values of x.

$\therefore$ LHL = RHL

$\Rightarrow$ $2a + 3 = 2a^2 - 1 \Rightarrow 2a^2 - 2a - 4 = 0$

$\Rightarrow$ $a^2 - a - 2 = 0 \Rightarrow a^2 - 2a + a - 2 = 0$

$\Rightarrow$ $a(a - 2) + 1(a - 2) = 0 \Rightarrow (a + 1)(a - 2) = 0$

$\therefore$ $a = -1, 2$

139. *(d)* Let $y = \lim_{x \to 0} \left(\frac{a^x + b^x + c^x}{3} \right)^{2/x}$

$\Rightarrow \log y = \lim_{x \to 0} \frac{2}{x} \log \left(\frac{a^x + b^x + c^x}{3} \right)$

$\Rightarrow \log y = \lim_{x \to 0} \frac{2\log(a^x + b^x + c^x) - \log 3}{x} \left(\frac{0}{0} \text{ form} \right)$

$\Rightarrow$ $\log y = \log(abc)^{2/3}$

[using L' Hospital's rule]

$\therefore$ $y = (abc)^{2/3}$

140. *(a)* Coordinates of centre of given circle is (1, 2) and it passes through the point (4, 6) the radius of the required circle is equal to the distance from the centre to a point on a circle.

$\therefore$ Radius of circle $= \sqrt{(1-4)^2 + (2-6)^2} = \sqrt{9 + 16} = 5$

Hence, the required equation of the circle is

$$(x - 1)^2 + (y - 2)^2 = (5)^2$$

$$x^2 + y^2 - 2x - 4y - 20 = 0$$

141. *(d)* We know that, any line is parallel to the plane, then normal to the plane is perpendicular to the line.

Given, line is $\frac{x-2}{3} = \frac{y-3}{4} = \frac{z-4}{5}$

So, DR's of line are $\langle 3, 4, 5 \rangle$.

Let us consider the equation of plane be

$2x + y - 2z = 0$ [from the given options]

Hence, DR's of a plane are $\langle 2, 1, -2 \rangle$.

Now, $3 \times 2 + 4 \times 1 + 5 \times (-2) = 6 + 4 - 10$
$= 10 - 10 = 0$

Option (d) is correct.

142. *(a)* Equation of plane passing through intersection of two planes

$$x + 2y + 3z = 2 \text{ and } x - y + z = 3$$

$\Rightarrow$ $(x + 2y + 3z - 2) + \lambda(x - y + z - 3) = 0$

$\Rightarrow (1 + \lambda)x + (2 - \lambda)y + (3 + \lambda)z - (2 + 3\lambda) = 0$

whose distance from $(3, 1, -1)$ is $\frac{2}{\sqrt{3}}$.

$\therefore \frac{|3(1 + \lambda) + 1 \cdot (2 - \lambda) - 1(3 + \lambda) - (2 + 3\lambda)|}{\sqrt{(1 + \lambda)^2 + (2 - \lambda)^2 + (3 + \lambda)^2}} = \frac{2}{\sqrt{3}}$

$\Rightarrow \lambda = -\frac{7}{2}$

Hence, equation of plane is $5x - 11y + z - 17 = 0$.

143. *(c)* The given lines can be rewritten as $\frac{x}{3} = \frac{y}{2} = \frac{z}{-6}$

and $\frac{x}{2} = \frac{y}{-12} = \frac{z}{-3}$

$\therefore$ Angle between the lines is

$$\theta = \cos^{-1} \left(\frac{3 \times 2 + 2(-12) - 6(-3)}{\sqrt{3^2 + 2^2 + (-6)^2} \sqrt{(2)^2 + (-12)^2 + (-3)^2}} \right)$$

$= 0$

$\Rightarrow$ $\theta = 90°$

144. *(c)* Given lines are

$$\frac{x-1}{2} = \frac{y-2}{3} = \frac{z-3}{4} = r \quad \text{[say]} \ldots\text{(i)}$$

and $\frac{x-4}{5} = \frac{y-1}{2} = z$ ...(ii)

Any point on the line (i) is $(2r + 1, 3r + 2, 4r + 3)$.

If they intersect, then this point satisfies the second line, we get

$$\frac{2r + 1 - 4}{5} = \frac{3r + 2 - 1}{2} = 4r + 3$$

$\Rightarrow$ $\frac{2r - 3}{5} = \frac{3r + 1}{2} \Rightarrow r = -1$

Hence, the required point is $(-1, -1, -1)$.

145. *(c)* Let $I = \int \frac{2^x}{\sqrt{1 - 4^x}} dx = \int \frac{2^x}{\sqrt{1 - (2^x)^2}} dx$

Putting $2^x = t \Rightarrow 2^x \cdot \log 2 dx = dt$

$\Rightarrow$ $2^x dx = \frac{dt}{\log 2}$

$\therefore$ $I = \frac{1}{\log 2} \int \frac{dt}{\sqrt{1 - t^2}} = \frac{1}{\log 2} \sin^{-1}(t) + C$

$= \frac{1}{\log 2} \sin^{-1}(2^x) + C$

146. *(c)* $\int_{-\pi/2}^{\pi/2} \sin x \, dx = \int_{-\pi/2}^{0} \sin x \, dx + \int_0^{\pi/2} \sin x \, dx$

$= -[\cos x]_{-\pi/2}^{0} - [\cos x]_0^{\pi/2} = (-1 - 0) - (0 - 1) = 0$

COMEDK 2021

147. *(d)* Let $I = \int \frac{dx}{x^2[1+x^4]^{\frac{3}{4}}} = \int \frac{dx}{x^2\left(x^4\left(\frac{1}{x^4}+1\right)\right)^{3/4}}$

[taking x^4 common from denominator]

$$\Rightarrow \int \frac{dx}{x^5\left(\frac{1}{x^4}+1\right)^{3/4}}$$

Let $\left(\frac{1}{x^4}+1\right) = t^4 \Rightarrow \frac{-4dx}{x^5} = 4t^3dt \Rightarrow \frac{dx}{x^5} = -t^3dt$

$$\therefore I = \int \frac{-t^3dt}{t^3} = -t + C = -\left(\frac{1}{x^4}+1\right)^{1/4} + C$$

148. *(c)* In a regular hexagon, there are two equilateral triangles are possible.

$$\therefore \text{ Required probability} = \frac{2}{^6C_3} = \frac{2}{\frac{6\times5\times4}{3\times2}} = \frac{2}{20} = \frac{1}{10}$$

149. *(c)* Total number of ways $= 5!$

and favourable number of ways $= 2\cdot 4!$

$$\therefore \text{ Required probability} = \frac{2\cdot 4!}{5!} = \frac{2}{5}$$

150. *(d)* Given, $P(B) = \frac{3}{2}P(A)$ and $P(C) = \frac{1}{2}P(B)$

Since, A, B and C are exclusive events.

$$\therefore \quad P(A) + P(B) + P(C) = 1$$

$$\Rightarrow \quad P(A) + \frac{3}{2}P(A) + \frac{1}{2}\times\frac{3}{2}P(A) = 1$$

$$\Rightarrow \quad P(A)\left(1 + \frac{3}{2} + \frac{3}{4}\right) = 1$$

$$\Rightarrow \quad \frac{13}{4}P(A) = 1 \Rightarrow P(A) = \frac{4}{13}$$

$$\Rightarrow \quad P(C) = \frac{1}{2}\times\frac{3}{2}P(A) = \frac{3}{4}\times\frac{4}{13} = \frac{3}{13}$$

Also, A, B and C are mutually exclusive.

$$\therefore \quad P(A\cap B) = P(B\cap C) = P(C\cap A) = 0$$

$$\Rightarrow \quad P(A\cup C) = P(A) + P(C) - 0 = \frac{4}{13} + \frac{3}{13} = \frac{7}{13}$$

151. *(c)* Let E_1 = Student does not know the answer

E_2 = Student knows the answer

and E = Student answer correctly

$$\therefore \quad P(E_1) = 1 - p \Rightarrow P(E_2) = p$$

$$\Rightarrow \quad P\left(\frac{E}{E_2}\right) = 1 \text{ and } P\left(\frac{E}{E_1}\right) = \frac{1}{5}$$

Note that, the probability that student did not know the answer randomly = The probability that student know the answer.

$$\therefore \quad P\left(\frac{E_2}{E}\right) = \frac{P(E_2)P\left(\frac{E}{E_2}\right)}{P(E_1)\,P\left(\frac{E}{E_1}\right) + P(E_2)\,P\left(\frac{E}{E_2}\right)}$$

$$= \frac{p(1)}{(1-p)\frac{1}{5} + p(1)} = \frac{p}{\frac{1-p+5p}{5}} = \frac{5p}{1+4p}$$

152. *(d)* Given, $\cos x + \cos y = \frac{3}{2}$

$$\Rightarrow \quad 2\cos\left(\frac{x+y}{2}\right)\cos\left(\frac{x-y}{2}\right) = \frac{3}{2} \quad \ldots(i)$$

and $\qquad \sin x + \sin y = \frac{3}{4}$

$$\Rightarrow \quad 2\sin\left(\frac{x+y}{2}\right)\cos\left(\frac{x-y}{2}\right) = \frac{3}{4} \quad \ldots(ii)$$

On dividing Eq. (i) by Eq. (ii), we get

$$\frac{2\sin\left(\frac{x+y}{2}\right)\cos\left(\frac{x-y}{2}\right)}{2\cos\left(\frac{x+y}{2}\right)\cos\left(\frac{x-y}{2}\right)} = \frac{3/4}{3/2} \Rightarrow \tan\left(\frac{x+y}{2}\right) = \frac{1}{2}$$

$$\therefore \quad \sin(x+y) = \frac{2\tan\left(\frac{x+y}{2}\right)}{1+\tan^2\left(\frac{x+y}{2}\right)} = \frac{2\times\frac{1}{2}}{1+\left(\frac{1}{2}\right)^2}$$

$$= \frac{4}{4+1} = \frac{4}{5}$$

153. *(b)* $\frac{\tan A}{1-\cot A} + \frac{\cot A}{1-\tan A} = \frac{\sin A}{\cos A}\times\frac{\sin A}{\sin A - \cos A} + \frac{\cos A}{\sin A}\times\frac{\cos A}{\cos A - \sin A}$

$$= \frac{1}{\sin A - \cos A}\left\{\frac{\sin^3 A - \cos^3 A}{\cos A\sin A}\right\}$$

$$= \frac{\sin^2 A + \cos^2 A + \sin A\cos A}{\cos A\sin A} = \sec A\,\text{cosec} A + 1$$

154. *(d)* We have, $\sin 2x = 4\cos x \Rightarrow 2\sin x\cos x = 4\cos x$

$$\Rightarrow \quad \cos x(\sin x - 2) = 0 \Rightarrow \cos x = 0 \quad [\because \sin x \neq 2]$$

$$\Rightarrow \quad \cos x = 0 = \cos\pi/2 \Rightarrow x = 2n\pi \pm \frac{\pi}{2}, n\in Z$$

155. *(b)* Given, $2f(x) + f(1-x) = x^2 \quad \ldots(i)$

Replacing x by $(1-x)$, we get

$$2f(1-x) + f(x) = (1-x)^2$$

$$\Rightarrow \quad 2f(1-x) + f(x) = 1 + x^2 - 2x \quad \ldots(ii)$$

Multiplying Eq. (i) by 2 and subtracting Eq. (ii) from Eq. (i), we get

$$3f(x) = x^2 + 2x - 1 \Rightarrow f(x) = \frac{x^2+2x-1}{3}$$

156. *(b)* Given, $A = \{1, 2, 5, 6\}$ and $B = \{1, 2, 3\}$

$A\times B = \{(1, 1), (1, 2), (1, 3), (2, 1), (2, 2), (2, 3), (5, 1), (5, 2), (5, 3), (6, 1), (6, 2), (6, 3)\}$

$B\times A = \{(1, 1), (1, 2), (1, 5), (1, 6), (2, 1), (2, 2), (2, 5), (2, 6), (3, 1), (3, 2), (3, 5), (3, 6)\}$

$\therefore (A\times B)\cap(B\times A) = \{(1, 1), (1, 2), (2, 1), (2, 2)\}$

157. *(a)* If a set A has n elements, then its power set will contain 2^n elements.

$\therefore$ Total number of elements is in power set of $A = 2^{15}$

158. *(d)* Let $z = \frac{(1+i)(2+i)}{(3-i)} = \frac{2+3i+i^2}{3-i} = \frac{2+3i-1}{3-i}$ $[\because i^2 = -1]$

$$= \frac{1+3i}{3-i} \times \frac{3+i}{3+i} = \frac{3+10i+3i^2}{9-i^2}$$

$$= \frac{3+10i-3}{9+1} = \frac{10i}{10} = i \quad [\because i^2 = -1]$$

$\therefore \quad z = 0 + i \cdot 1$

So, $\arg(z) = \tan^{-1}\left(\frac{1}{0}\right) = \tan^{-1}(\infty) = \frac{\pi}{2}$

159. *(a)* We have, $\left[i^{18} + \left(\frac{1}{i}\right)^{25}\right]^3 \quad \{i^{18} = i^{16+2} = 1 \cdot i^2 = -1\}$

$$= [-1 + (-i)^{25}]^3 = [-1 - i]^3 = -[1+i]^3$$

$$= -[1 + 3i - 3 - i] = -[-2 + 2i] = 2(1 - i)$$

160. *(b)* $(\sqrt{3} + i)^{100} = 2^{99}(a + ib) \Rightarrow (-2i\omega)^{100} = 2^{99}(a + ib)$

$$\left[\because \omega = -\frac{1+\sqrt{3}i}{2},\ i\omega = -\frac{i-\sqrt{3}}{2}\right.$$

$$, \quad -2i\omega = i + \sqrt{3} \text{ and } \omega^{100} = \omega^{99}\omega = 1 \cdot \omega = \omega]$$

$$\Rightarrow \quad 2^{100}\omega = 2^{99}(a + ib)$$

$$\Rightarrow 2\left\{\frac{-1-\sqrt{3}i}{2}\right\} = a + ib \quad \Rightarrow a = -1 \text{ and } b = \sqrt{3}$$

$$\therefore \quad a^2 + b^2 = (-1)^2 + (\sqrt{3})^2 = 4$$

161. *(b)* Given, $a_0 = 1$, $a_{n+1} = 3n^2 + n + a_n$

Put $n = 0 \Rightarrow a_1 = 3(0) + 0 + a_0 = 1$

$\Rightarrow \quad a_2 = 3(1)^2 + 1 + a_1 = 3 + 1 + 1 = 5$

From option (b),

Let $\quad P(n) = n^3 - n^2 + 1$

$\therefore \quad P(0) = 0 - 0 + 1 = 1 = a_0$

$\quad P(1) = 1^3 - 1^2 + 1 = 1 = a_1$

and $\quad P(2) = (2)^3 - (2)^2 + 1 = 5 = a_2$

162. *(d)* Put $n = 1$ in $49^n + 16n + P$, then

$$(49)^1 + 16(1) + P = 49 + 16 + P = 65 + P$$

So, here if $P = -1$

Then, the given expression is divisible by 64.

163. *(c)* Let $P(n) = 2^{3n} - 7n - 1 \Rightarrow P(1) = 0,\ P(2) = 49$

$P(1)$ and $P(2)$ are divisible by 49.

Let $\quad P(k) = 2^{3k} - 7k - 1 = 49I$

$$P(k+1) = 2^{3k+3} - 7k - 8 = 8(49I + 7k + 1) - 7k - 8$$

$$= 49(8I) + 49k = 49\lambda$$

where, $\lambda = 8I + k$, which is an integer.

164. *(a)* Given, $\frac{\sec^2 x}{\tan x}\,dx = -\frac{\sec^2 y}{\tan y}\,dy$

$$\Rightarrow \int \frac{\sec^2 x}{\tan x}\,dx = -\int \frac{\sec^2 y}{\tan y}\,dy$$

Put $\quad \tan x = u \Rightarrow \sec^2 x\,dx = du$

and $\quad \tan y = v \Rightarrow \sec^2 y\,dy = dv$

$$\therefore \quad \int \frac{du}{u} = -\int \frac{dv}{v}$$

$$\Rightarrow \log u = -\log v + \log C \Rightarrow uv = C \Rightarrow \tan x \cdot \tan y = C$$

165. *(c)* Given differential equation can be rewritten as

$$\frac{dy}{dx} = \frac{y}{x} + \frac{x\,\phi\left(\frac{y^2}{x^2}\right)}{y\,\phi'\left(\frac{y^2}{x^2}\right)}$$

Put $\quad y = vx \Rightarrow \frac{dy}{dx} = v + x\frac{dv}{dx}$

Given equation becomes,

$$v + x\frac{dv}{dx} = \frac{vx}{x} + \frac{x\,\phi\left(\frac{v^2x^2}{x^2}\right)}{vx\,\phi'\left(\frac{v^2x^2}{x^2}\right)}$$

$$\Rightarrow \quad x\frac{dv}{dx} = \frac{\phi(v^2)}{v\,\phi'(v^2)} \Rightarrow \frac{v\,\phi'(v^2)}{\phi(v^2)}\,dv = \frac{dx}{x}$$

On integrating both sides, we get

$$\frac{1}{2}\log\phi(v^2) = \log x + \log C_1 \Rightarrow \log\phi(v^2) = 2\log x\,C_1$$

$$\Rightarrow \phi(v^2) = (xC_1)^2 \Rightarrow \phi\left(\frac{y^2}{x^2}\right) = x^2C_1^2 \Rightarrow \phi\left(\frac{y^2}{x^2}\right) = x^2C$$

$[\text{put } C_1^2 = C]$

166. *(a)* Given differential equation is

$$(1 + y^2) + (x - e^{\tan^{-1} y})\frac{dy}{dx} = 0$$

$$\Rightarrow \quad (1 + y^2)\frac{dx}{dy} = -x + e^{\tan^{-1} y}$$

$$\Rightarrow \quad \frac{dx}{dy} + \frac{x}{1+y^2} = \frac{e^{\tan^{-1} y}}{1+y^2}$$

which is a linear differential equation.

Here, $P = \frac{1}{1+y^2}$, $Q = \frac{e^{\tan^{-1} y}}{1+y^2}$ and

$$\therefore \quad \text{IF} = e^{\int P\,dy} = e^{\int \frac{1}{1+y^2}dy} = e^{\tan^{-1} y}$$

Hence, required solution is $x \cdot \text{IF} = \int Q \cdot \text{IF}\,dy + C$

$$\Rightarrow \quad x\,e^{\tan^{-1} y} = \int\left(\frac{e^{\tan^{-1} y}}{1+y^2} \cdot e^{\tan^{-1} y}\right)dy + \frac{C}{2}$$

COMEDK 2021

$\Rightarrow \quad x\,e^{\tan^{-1}y} = \dfrac{e^{2\tan^{-1}y}}{2} + \dfrac{C}{2}$

$\Rightarrow \quad 2x\,e^{\tan^{-1}y} = e^{2\tan^{-1}y} + C$

167. *(c)* We have, $1\cdot 1! + 2\cdot 2! + 3\cdot 3! + \cdots + n\cdot n!$

$= \sum_{r=1}^{n} r\cdot(r!) = \sum_{r=1}^{n}[(r+1)\,r! - r!] = \sum_{r=1}^{n}[(r+1)! - r!]$

$= (2! - 1!) + (3! - 2!) + \cdots + [(n+1)! - n!]$

$= (n+1)! - 1! = (n+1)! - 1$

168. *(a)* Here, $T_n = 1 + 2 + 2^2 + 2^3 + \cdots + 2^n$

$= \dfrac{1(2^{n+1} - 1)}{2-1} = 2^{n+1} - 1$

$\therefore \; \Sigma T_n = \Sigma(2^{n+1} - 1) = \Sigma 2^{n+1} - \Sigma 1$

$= (2^2 + 2^3 + \cdots + 2^{n+1}) - n = 2(2 + 2^2 + \cdots + 2^n) - n$

$= \dfrac{4(2^n - 1)}{2-1} - n = 2^{n+2} - n - 4$

169. *(a)* Given, $2b = a + c$ and $(c-b)^2 = (b-a)a$

$\therefore \quad (b-a)^2 = (b-a)a$

$\Rightarrow \; b = 2a \;\Rightarrow\; c = 3a \;\Rightarrow\; a:b:c = 1:2:3$

170. *(b)* Number of triangles $= {}^{n+3}C_3 = 220$

$\Rightarrow \quad \dfrac{(n+3)!}{3!\,n!} = 220$

$\Rightarrow \; (n+1)(n+2)(n+3) = 1320 = 12 \times 10 \times 11$

$= (9+1)(9+2)(9+3)$

$\therefore \quad n = 9$

171. *(a)* Required number of straight lines

$= {}^8C_2 - {}^3C_2 + 1 = 26$

172. *(d)* Total numbers formed by using given 5 digits $= \dfrac{5!}{2!}$

For number greater than 40000, digit 2 cannot come at first place.

Hence, numbers formed in which 2 is at the first place $= \dfrac{4!}{2!}$

$\therefore$Total numbers formed greater than 40000 $= \dfrac{5!}{2!} - \dfrac{4!}{2!}$

$= 60 - 12 = 48$

173. *(a)* A polygon of n sides has number of diagonals

$= \dfrac{n(n-3)}{2} = 275$ [given]

$\Rightarrow \quad n^2 - 3n - 550 = 0 \;\Rightarrow\; (n-25)(n+22) = 0$

$\therefore \quad n = 25 \quad [\because n \neq -22]$

174. *(c)* Bisector of the angles between the lines $x^2 - 2mxy - y^2 = 0$ is

$\dfrac{x^2 - y^2}{xy} = \dfrac{[1-(-1)]}{-m} = \dfrac{2}{-m} \;\Rightarrow\; mx^2 + 2xy - my^2 = 0$

But it is also represented by $x^2 - 2nxy - y^2 = 0$.

$\therefore \quad \dfrac{m}{1} = \dfrac{2}{-2n} \;\Rightarrow\; mn = -1$

175. *(c)* Let equation of line parallel to $3x - y = 7$ be $3x - y = \lambda$.

Since, it passes through (1, 2).

$\therefore \quad 3 - 2 = \lambda \;\Rightarrow\; \lambda = 1$

Now, line is $3x - y = 1$.

Since, the point of intersection of $x + y + 5 = 0$ and $3x - y = 1$ is $(-1, -4)$.

So, distance between (1, 2) and $(-1, -4)$

$= \sqrt{\{1-(-1)\}^2 + \{2-(-4)\}^2}$

$= \sqrt{(2)^2 + (6)^2} = \sqrt{4 + 36} = \sqrt{40}$

176. *(d)* Let m be the required slope.

$\therefore \quad \left|\dfrac{m-3}{1+3m}\right| = 1 \;\Rightarrow\; \dfrac{m-3}{1+3m} = \pm 1$

$\Rightarrow \quad m - 3 = 1 + 3m$ and $m - 3 = -1 - 3m$

$\Rightarrow \quad m = -2$ and $m = \dfrac{1}{2}$

177. *(d)* Equation of line is $\dfrac{x}{3} + \dfrac{y}{4} = 1 \;\Rightarrow\; 4x + 3y - 12 = 0$

Now, distance from origin $= \left|\dfrac{4\times 0 + 3\times 0 - 12}{\sqrt{3^2 + 4^2}}\right| = \dfrac{12}{5}$ units

178. *(c)* Let $f(x) = (x+a)^{53} + (x-a)^{53}$

Here $n = 53$, which is odd.

$\therefore$ Total number of terms $= \dfrac{n+1}{2} = \dfrac{53+1}{2} = \dfrac{54}{2} = 27$

179. *(c)* The given series is in GP. Hence, its sum

$S = \dfrac{1\{(1+x)^{20+1} - 1\}}{(1+x) - 1} \quad [\because a = 1, r = 1 + x]$

$= \dfrac{(1+x)^{21} - 1}{x}$

Therefore, the required coefficient of x^{10} in the expansion of $\dfrac{(1+x)^{21} - 1}{x}$

= Coefficient of x^{11} in the expansion of $(1+x)^{21} - 1$

$= {}^{21}C_{11}$

180. *(b)* The given expression is

$$\left(x^2 + \frac{1}{x^2} + 2\right)^n = \left[\left(x + \frac{1}{x}\right)^2\right]^n = \left(x + \frac{1}{x}\right)^{2n}$$

The binomial contains $(2n+1)$ terms in its expansion.

$\therefore$The middle terms is T_{n+1}.

$T_{n+1} = {}^{2n}C_n\,(x)^{2n-n}\left(\dfrac{1}{x}\right)^n = {}^{2n}C_n = \dfrac{(2n)!}{(2n-n)!\,n!} = \dfrac{(2n)!}{(n!)^2}$

COMEDK

Solved Paper 2020

Instructions

- There are 180 questions in all. The number of questions in each section is as given below.

Sections	No. of Questions
Section I : Physics	1-60
Section II : Chemistry	61-120
Section III : Mathematics	121-180

- All the questions are Multiple Choice Questions having four options out of which **ONLY ONE** is correct.
- Candidates will be awarded 1 mark for each correct answer. There will be no negative marking for incorrect answer.
- Time allotted to complete this paper is 3 hrs.

PHYSICS

1. Light of frequency 10^{15} Hz falls on a metal surface of work function 2.5 eV. The stopping potential of photoelectrons (in V) is

a. 1.6 *b.* 2.5 *c.* 4.1 *d.* 6.6

2. A proton accelerated through a potential V has de-Broglie wavelength λ. Then, the de-Broglie wavelength of an α-particle, when accelerated through the same potential V is

a. $\frac{\lambda}{2}$ *b.* $\frac{\lambda}{\sqrt{2}}$ *c.* $\frac{\lambda}{2\sqrt{2}}$ *d.* $\frac{\lambda}{8}$

3. Consider a thin spherical shell of radius R consisting of uniform surface charge density s. The electric field at a point of distance x from its centre and outside the shell is

a. inversely proportional to s

b. directly proportional to x^2

c. directly proportional to R

d. inversely proportional to x^2

4. An electron of an atom transits from n_1 to n_2. In which of the following maximum frequency of photon will be emitted?

a. $n_1 = 1$ to $n_2 = 2$

b. $n_1 = 2$ to $n_2 = 1$

c. $n_1 = 2$ to $n_2 = 6$

d. $n_1 = 6$ to $n_2 = 2$

5. Two protons are kept at a separation of 40 Å. F_n is the nuclear force and F_e is the electrostatic force between them. Then,

a. $F_n << F_e$

b. $F_n \approx F_e$

c. $F_n >> F_e$

d. $F_n = F_e$

6. Two radioactive materials X_1 and X_2 have decay constant 5λ and λ, respectively. If initially they have the same number of nuclei, then the ratio of the number of nuclei of X_1 to that X_2 will be $1/e$ after a time

a. $1/4\lambda$ *b.* e/λ

c. λ *d.* $\frac{1}{2}\lambda$

7. The Poisson's ratio of a material is 0.1. If the longitudinal strain of a rod of this material is 10^{-3}, then the percentage change in the volume of the rod will be

a. 0.008% *b.* 0.08%

c. 0.8% *d.* 8%

8. A satellite can be in a geostationary orbit around a planet if it is at a distance R from the centre of the planet. If the planet starts rotating about its axis with double the angular velocity, then to make the satellite geostationary, its orbital radius should be

a. $2R$ *b.* $\frac{R}{2}$ *c.* $\frac{R}{2^{1/3}}$ *d.* $\frac{R}{4^{1/3}}$

9. When a *p-n* junction diode is connected in forward bias, its barrier potential

a. decreases and less current flows in the circuit
b. decreases and more current flows in the circuit
c. increases and more current flows in the circuit
d. decreases and no current flows in the circuit

10. Ground waves have wavelength

a. less than that of sky waves
b. greater than that of sky waves
c. less than that of space waves
d. equal to that of space waves

11. A ball floats on the surface of water in a container exposed to the atmosphere. When the container is covered and the air is partially removed, then the ball

a. rises
b. gets immersed more in water
c. remains immersed at its former depth
d. may rise or sink

12. A frame made of metallic wire enclosing a surface area A is covered with a soap film. If the area of the frame of metallic wire is reduced by 50%, then the energy of the soap film will be changed by

a. 100% *b.* 75%
c. 50% *d.* 25%

13. A compound slab is made of two parallel plates of copper and brass of the same thickness and having thermal conductivities in the ratio 4 : 1. The free face of copper is at 0°C. The temperature of the interface is 20°C. What is the temperature of the free face of brass?

a. 0°C *b.* 20°C
c. 40°C *d.* 100°C

14. 1 mm^3 of a gas is compressed at 1 atmospheric pressure and temperature 27°C to 627°C. What is the final pressure under adiabatic condition? (γ for the gas = 1.5)

a. $27 \times 10^5\text{ N/m}^2$ *b.* $80 \times 10^5\text{ N/m}^2$
c. $36 \times 10^5\text{ N/m}^2$ *d.* $56 \times 10^5\text{ N/m}^2$

15. If sink is at a temperature of – 39°C and source at 0°C, then efficiency will be

a. 39.4% *b.* 14.2%
c. 35.2% *d.* 45.5%

16. Which of the following laws of Physics is valid across all domains of nature?

a. Newton's law of motion
b. Conservation of momentum
c. Conservation of energy
d. All of the above

17. A particle of mass m is moving in a horizontal circle of radius R under a centripetal force equal to $-\frac{A}{R^2}$ (A = constant). The total energy of the particle is

a. $\frac{A}{R}$ *b.* $-\frac{A}{R}$
c. $\frac{A}{2R}$ *d.* $-\frac{A}{2R}$

18. A force of 20 N is applied on a body of mass 5 kg resting on a horizontal plane. The body gains a kinetic energy of 10 J after it moves a distance 2 m. The frictional force is

a. 10 N *b.* 15 N
c. 20 N *d.* 30 N

19. A body under the action of a force $\mathbf{F} = 6\hat{\mathbf{i}} - 8\hat{\mathbf{j}} + 10\hat{\mathbf{k}}$, acquires an acceleration of 1 m/s^2. The mass of this body must be

a. 10 kg *b.* 20 kg
c. $10\sqrt{2}$ kg *d.* $2\sqrt{10}$ kg

20. A body of mass 1000 kg is moving horizontally with a velocity 50 m/s. A mass of 250 kg is added. Find the final velocity.

a. 40 m/s *b.* 20 m/s
c. $30\sqrt{2}$ m/s *d.* 50 m/s

21. Equal volumes of two gases, having their densities in the ratio of 1 : 16 exert equal pressures on the walls of two containers. The ratio of their rms velocities $\left(\frac{c_1}{c_2}\right)$

a. 1 : 8 *b.* 8 : 1
c. 1 : 4 *d.* 4 : 1

22. A gaseous mixture consists of 16 g of helium and 16 g of oxygen. The ratio C_p / C_V of the mixture is

a. 1.4 *b.* 1.54
c. 1.59 *d.* 1.62

23. A particle executes a linear SHM with an amplitude of 4 cm. At the mean position the velocity of the particle is 10 cm/s. What is the displacement of the particle when its speed becomes 5 cm/s?

a. $2(\sqrt{3})$ cm *b.* $2(\sqrt{5})$ cm
c. $\sqrt{5}$ cm *d.* $\sqrt{3}$ cm

24. The equation of a progressive wave can be given by $y = 15\sin(660\pi t - 0.02\pi x)$ cm. The frequency of the wave is

a. 330 Hz *b.* 342 Hz
c. 365 Hz *d.* 660 Hz

25. A source of sound gives 5 beats per second, when sounded with another source of frequency $100\ s^{-1}$. The second harmonic of the source, together with a source of frequency $205\ s^{-1}$ gives 5 beats per second. What is frequency of the source?

a. $95\ s^{-1}$ *b.* $105\ s^{-1}$
c. $100\ s^{-1}$ *d.* $205\ s^{-1}$

26. A charge of 0.8 C is divided into two charges Q_1 and Q_2. These are kept at a separation of 30 cm. The force on Q_1 is maximum when

a. $Q_1 = Q_2 = 0.4$ C
b. $Q_1 \approx 0.8$ C, Q_2 negligible
c. Q_1 negligible, $Q_2 \approx 0.8$ C
d. $Q_1 = 0.2$ C, $Q_2 = 0.6$ C

27. An electric dipole has a pair of equal and opposite point charges q and $-q$ separated by a distance $2x$. The axis of the dipole is defined as

a. direction from positive charge to negative charge
b. direction from negative charge to positive charge
c. perpendicular to the line joining the two charges drawn at the centre and pointing upward direction
d. perpendicular to the line joining the two charges at the centre and pointing downward direction

28. An electric dipole is placed in a uniform electric field with the dipole axis making an angle θ with the direction of the electric field. The orientation of the dipole for stable equilibrium is

a. $\frac{\pi}{6}$ *b.* $\frac{\pi}{3}$ *c.* 0 *d.* $\frac{\pi}{2}$

29. Two point charges $A = +3$ nC and $B = +1$ nC are placed 5 cm apart in air. The work done to move charge B towards A by 1 cm is

a. 2.0×10^{-7} J *b.* 1.35×10^{-7} J
c. 2.7×10^{-7} J *d.* 1.21×10^{-7} J

30. The potential energies associated with four orientations of an electric dipole in an electric field are

(i) $-5U_0$ (ii) $-7U_0$
(iii) $3U_0$ (iv) $5U_0$

where U_0 is positive. Rank the orientations according to the angle between the electric dipole moment **p** and electric field **E**, greatest first

a. (i), (ii), (iii), (iv) *b.* (ii), (iii), (i), (iv)
c. (iv), (iii), (i), (ii) *d.* (iv), (i), (iii), (ii)

31. Suppose refractive index μ is given as $\mu = A + \frac{B}{\lambda^2}$, where A and B are constants and λ is wavelength, then dimensions of B are same as that of

a. wavelength *b.* volume
c. pressure *d.* area

32. If voltage $V = (200 \pm 8)$ V and current $I = (20 \pm 0.5)$ A, then the percentage error in resistance R is

a. 5.2% *b.* 25% *c.* 3% *d.* 6.5%

33. A body is projected vertically upwards. The times corresponding to height h, while ascending and while descending are t_1 and t_2, respectively. Then, the velocity of projection is (g is acceleration due to gravity)

a. $\frac{g\sqrt{t_1 t_2}}{2}$ *b.* $\frac{g(t_1 + t_2)}{2}$
c. $g\sqrt{t_1 t_2}$ *d.* $\frac{g t_1 t_2}{t_1 + t_2}$

34. A particle shows distance-time curve as given in this figure. The maximum instantaneous velocity of the particle is around the point

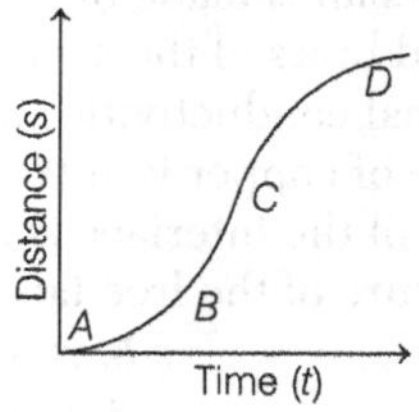

a. D *b.* A *c.* B *d.* C

35. A fluid is in streamline flow across a horizontal pipe of variable area of cross-section. For this which of the following statements is correct?

a. Velocity of fluid is maximum at narrowest part.
b. Pressure of the fluid is maximum at widest part.
c. Both (a) and (b)
d. Neither (a) nor (b)

36. Two capacitors C_1 and C_2 are charged to 120 V and 200 V, respectively. When they are connected in parallel, it is found that potential on each one of them is zero. Therefore,

a. $5C_1 = 3C_2$ *b.* $3C_1 = 5C_2$
c. $3C_1 + 5C_2 = 0$ *d.* $9C_1 = 4C_2$

37. Point out the right statements about the validity of Kirchhoff's junction rule,

a. it is based on conservation of charge.
b. outgoing currents add up and are equal to incoming currents at a junction.
c. bending or reorienting the wire does not change the validity of Kirchhoff's junction rule.
d. All of the above

38. Four particles each of the mass m are placed at the corners of a square of side length l. The radius of gyration of the system about an axis perpendicular to the square and passing through its centre is

a. $\frac{l}{\sqrt{2}}$ *b.* $\frac{l}{2}$ *c.* l *d.* $\sqrt{2}l$

39. A steel wire of length 4.7 m and cross-sectional area 3.0×10^{-5} m^2 stretches by the same amount as a copper wire of length 3.5 m and cross-sectional area of 4.0×10^{-5} m^2 under a given load. What is the ratio of Young's modulus of steel to that of copper?

a. 1.8 : 1 *b.* 2.8 : 1 *c.* 3.8 : 1 *d.* 4.8 : 1

40. The masses of 200 g and 300 g are attached to the 20 cm and 70 cm marks of a light meter rod, respectively. The moment of inertia of the system about an axis passing through 50 cm mark is

a. 0.15 kg m^2 *b.* 0.036 kg m^2
c. 0.3 kg m^2 *d.* Zero

41. Two spherical bodies of masses M and $5M$ and radii R and $2R$ are released in free space with initial separation between their centres equal to 12 R. If they attract each other due to gravitational force only, then the distance covered by the smaller body before collision is

a. 2.5 R *b.* 4.5 R *c.* 7.5 R *d.* 1.5 R

42. If $P = Q = R = 10\,\Omega$ and $S = 20\,\Omega$, then what resistance should be joined with S to balance the Wheatstone's network?

a. Join a resistance of 10 Ω in series with S
b. Join a resistance of 10 Ω in parallel with S
c. Join a resistance of 20 Ω in parallel with S
d. Join a resistance of 20 Ω in series with S

43. To the potentiometer wire of length L and 10 Ω resistance, a battery of emf 2.5 V and a resistance R are connected in series. If a potential difference of 1 V is balanced across $L/2$ length, the value of R in Ω will be

a. 1 *b.* 1.5
c. 2 *d.* 2.5

44. An electron moves with speed of 2×10^5 m/s along the positive x-direction in a magnetic field $\mathbf{B} = (\hat{\mathbf{i}} - 4\hat{\mathbf{j}} - 3\hat{\mathbf{k}})$ T. The magnitude of the force (in N) experienced by the electron is

a. 1.18×10^{-13} *b.* 1.28×10^{-13}
c. 1.6×10^{-13} *d.* 1.72×10^{-13}

45. A horizontal overhead power line carries a current of 90 A in East to West direction. What is the magnitude and direction of the magnetic field due to the current, 1.5 m below the line?

a. 1.2×10^{-5} T, towards South
b. 1.2×10^{-5} T, towards North
c. 1.2×10^{-5} T, towards East
d. 1.2×10^{-5} T, towards West

46. A moving coil galvanometer has 28 turns and area of coil is 4×10^{-2} m^2. If the magnetic field is 0.2 T, then to increase the sensitivity by 25% without changing area and field, the number of turns should be changed to

a. 24 *b.* 35
c. 60 *d.* 54

47. The intensity of magnetic field due to an isolated pole of strength m_p at a point distant r from it will be

a. m_p/r^2 *b.* $m_p r^2$
c. r^2/m_p *d.* m_p/r

48. The particle that cannot be accelerated by a cyclotron is

a. proton *b.* α-particle
c. electron *d.* deuteron nucleus

49. The angle which the total magnetic field of earth makes with the surface of the earth is called

a. declination *b.* magnetic meridian
c. geographic meridian *d.* inclination

50. The angle of dip of at a place where horizontal and vertical components of earth's magnetic field are equal is

a. 45° *b.* 30° *c.* 0° *d.* 60°

COMEDK 2020

51. A coil of wire of a certain radius has 100 turns and a self inductance of 15 mH. The self inductance of a second similar coil of 500 turns will be

a. 75 mH *b.* 375 mH
c. 15 mH *d.* None of the above

52. A coil of 100 turns carries a current of 5 mA and creates a magnetic flux of 10^{-5} Wb. The inductance is

a. 0.2 mH *b.* 2.0 mH
c. 0.02 mH *d.* None of these

53. In step-up transformer, relation between number of turns in primary (N_P) and number of turns in secondary (N_S) coils is

a. N_S is greater than N_P
b. N_P is greater than N_S
c. N_S is equal to N_P
d. $N_P = 2N_S$

54. For a series *L-C-R* circuit at resonance, which statement is not true?

a. Wattless current is zero.
b. Power factor is zero.
c. Peak energy stored by a capacitor = peak energy stored by an inductor.
d. Average power = apparent power.

55. Which of the following has/have zero average value in a plane electromagnetic wave?

a. Electric field
b. Magnetic field
c. Both (a) and (c)
d. Magnetic energy

56. A convex lens is made of 3 layers of glass of 3 different materials as in the figure.

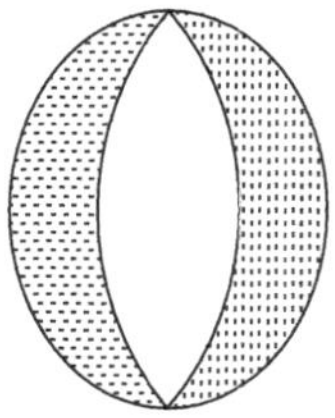

A point object is placed on its axis. The number of images of the object are

a. 3 *b.* 4
c. 1 *d.* 2

57. A ray of light suffers minimum deviation in equilateral prism *P*. Additional prisms *Q* and *R* of identical shape and of same material as that of *P* are now combined as shown in figure. The ray will now suffer

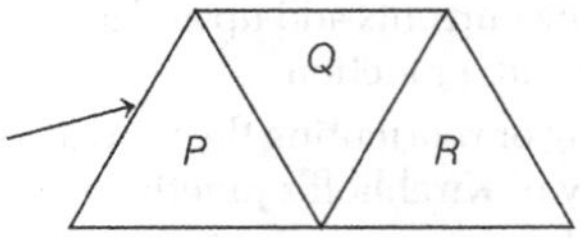

a. greater deviation
b. no deviation
c. same deviation as before
d. total internal reflection

58. Two identical light waves, propagating in the same direction, have a phase difference δ. After they superpose the intensity of the resulting wave will be proportional to

a. $\cos\delta$ *b.* $\cos(\delta/2)$
c. $\cos^2(\delta/2)$ *d.* $\cos^2\delta$

59. A plastic sheet (refractive index = 1.6) covers one slit of a double slit arrangement for the Young's experiment. When the double slit is illuminated by monochromatic light (wavelength = 5867 Å), the centre of the screen appears dark rather than bright. The minimum thickness of the plastic sheet to be used for this to happen is

a. 3300 Å *b.* 6600 Å
c. 2062 Å *d.* 5500 Å

60. A particle starts moving from point (2, 10, 1). Displacement for the particle is $8\hat{i} - 2\hat{j} + \hat{k}$. The final coordinates of the particle is

a. (10, 8, 2) *b.* (8, 10, 2)
c. (2, 10, 8) *d.* (8, 2, 10)

COMEDK 2020

CHEMISTRY

61. During the extraction of gold the following reactions take place

$Au + CN^- + H_2O \xrightarrow{O_2} [X]$

$[X] + Zn \longrightarrow [Y] + Au$

X and Y are respectively

a. $[Au(CN)_2]^-$ and $[Zn(CN)_4]^{2-}$
b. $[Au(CN)_4]^{3-}$ and $[Zn(CN)_4]^{2-}$
c. $[Au(CN)_4]^{2-}$ and $[Zn(CN)_4]^{2-}$
d. $[Au(CN)_2]^-$ and $[Zn(CN)_6]^{4-}$

62. The number of gram molecules of chlorine in 6.02×10^{25} hydrogen chloride molecules is

a. 5 *b.* 50
c. 100 *d.* 10

63. Graphite is a soft solid lubricant extremely difficult to melt. The reason for this anomalous behaviour is that, graphite

a. has molecules of variable molecular masses like polymers.
b. has carbon atoms arranged in large plates of rings of strongly bound carbon atoms with weak interplate bonds.
c. is a non-crystalline substance.
d. is an allotropic form of carbon.

64. Paracetamol is a/an

a. antimalarial
b. antipyretic
c. analgesic
d. Both (b) and (c)

65. Which one of the following has maximum number of atoms of oxygen?

a. 2 g of water
b. 2 g of sulphur dioxide
c. 2 g of carbon dioxide
d. 2 g of carbon monoxide

66. Which one of the following shows functional isomerism?

a. CH_2Cl_2 *b.* C_2H_5OH
c. C_3H_6 *d.* C_2H_4

67. In the ionic equation,
$BiO_3^- + 6H^+ + xe^- \longrightarrow Bi^{3+} + 3H_2O$,
the value of x is

a. 3 *b.* 4
c. 2 *d.* 6

68. Molarity of a given orthophosphoric acid solution is 3M. It's normality is

a. 1 N *b.* 3 N
c. 0.3 N *d.* 9 N

69. Acidified sodium fusion extract on addition of ferric chloride solution gives blood red colouration which confirms the presence of

a. S *b.* N
c. N and S *d.* S and Cl

70. A body of mass 10 mg is moving with a velocity of 100 ms^{-1}. The wavelength of de-Broglie wave associated with it would be
($h = 6.63 \times 10^{-34}$ Js)

a. 6.63×10^{-37} m
b. 6.63×10^{-31} m
c. 6.63×10^{-34} m
d. 6.63×10^{-35} m

71. Mg^{2+} is isoelectronic with

a. Ca^{2+} *b.* Na^+
c. Zn^{2+} *d.* Cu^{2+}

72. Gram molecular volume of oxygen at STP is

a. 11200 cm^3 *b.* 22400 cm^3
c. 5600 cm^3 *d.* 3200 cm^3

73. Presence of halogen in organic compounds can be detected using

a. Beilstien's test *b.* Kjeldahl test
c. Duma's test *d.* Liebig's test

74. The electronic configuration of Cr^{3+} is

a. [Ar] $3d^5 4s^1$ *b.* [Ar] $3d^2 4s^1$
c. [Ar] $3d^3 4s^0$ *d.* [Ar] $3d^4 4s^2$

75. The mass of a metal, with equivalent mass 31.75, which would combine with 8 g of oxygen is

a. 31.75 *b.* 3.175 *c.* 8 *d.* 1

76. Benzene reacts with chlorine in sunlight to give a final product

a. C_6H_5Cl *b.* C_6Cl_6
c. $C_6H_6Cl_6$ *d.* CCl_4

77. In the periodic table metals usually used as catalysts belong to

a. s-block *b.* p-block
c. d-block *d.* f-block

78. Dalton's law of partial pressures is applicable to which one of the following systems?

a. $CO + H_2$ *b.* $H_2 + Cl_2$
c. $NO + O_2$ *d.* $NH_3 + HCl$

79. The general formula of a cycloalkene is

a. C_nH_{2n+2} *b.* C_nH_{2n-2}
c. C_nH_{2n} *d.* C_nH_n

80. In acetylene molecule, between the carbon atoms there are

a. three σ-bonds
b. two σ and one π-bonds
c. one σ and two π -bonds
d. three π-bonds

81. Denatured alcohol is

a. rectified spirit
b. undistilled ethanol
c. rectified spirit + methanol + naphtha
d. ethanol + methanol

82. During the formation of a chemical bond

a. energy decreases
b. energy increases
c. energy of the system does not change
d. electron-electron repulsion becomes more than the nucleus-electron attraction

83. One mole of oxygen at 273 K and one mole of sulphur dioxide at 546 K are taken in two separate containers, then

a. kinetic energy of O_2 > kinetic energy of SO_2
b. kinetic energy of O_2 < kinetic energy of SO_2
c. kinetic energy of both are equal
d. None of the above

84. + *I*-effect is shown by

a. $-NO_2$ *b.* $-Cl$
c. $-Br$ *d.* $-CH_3$

85. Formation of coloured solution is possible, when metal ion in the compound contains

a. paired electrons
b. unpaired electrons
c. lone pair of electrons
d. None of the above

86. Which of the following is an intensive property?

a. Temperature
b. Surface tension
c. Viscosity
d. All of the above

87. Hofmann's bromamide reaction is to convert

a. amine to amide *b.* amide to amine
c. alcohol to acid *d.* acid to alcohol

88. IUPAC name of $Na_3[Co(NO_2)_6]$ is

a. sodium cobaltonitrite
b. sodium hexanitrito cobaltate (III)
c. sodium hexanitro cobaltate (III)
d. sodium hexanitrito cobaltate (II)

89. Thermodynamic standard conditions of temperature and pressure are

a. 0°C and 1 atm *b.* 273 K and 101.3 kPa
c. 298 K and 1 atm *d.* 0°C and 101.3 kPa

90. How many chiral carbon atoms are present in 2, 3, 4-trichloropentane ?

a. 3 *b.* 2 *c.* 1 *d.* 4

91. The number of unidentate ligands in the complex ion is called

a. EAN *b.* coordination number
c. primary valency *d.* oxidation number

92. $2SO_2(g) + O_2(g) \xrightleftharpoons{V_2O_5}$ is an example for

a. irreversible reaction
b. heterogeneous catalysis
c. homogeneous catalysis
d. neutralisation reaction

93. The amino acid which is not optically active is

a. glycine *b.* alanine
c. serine *d.* lactic acid

94. For a stable molecule the value of bond order must be

a. negative
b. positive
c. zero
d. there is no relationship between stability and bond order

95. Which one of the following is a second order reaction?

a. $CH_3COOCH_3 + NaOH \longrightarrow CH_3COONa + H_2O$
b. $H_2 + Cl_2 \xrightarrow{\text{Sunlight}} 2HCl$
c. $NH_4NO_3 \longrightarrow N_2 + 3H_2O$
d. $H_2 + Br_2 \longrightarrow 2HBr$

96. According to Baeyer's strain theory which is highly stable?

a. cyclohexane *b.* cycloheptane
c. cyclopentane *d.* cyclobutane

97. The number of antibonding electron pairs in O_2^{2-} molecular ion on the basis of molecular orbital theory is

[Atomic number of O is 18]

a. 2 *b.* 3 *c.* 4 *d.* 5

98. Hydroxyl ion concentration of 1M HCl is
a. 1×10^{-14} mol dm^{-3} *b.* 1×10^{-1} mol dm^{-3}
c. 1×10^{-13} mol dm^{-3} *d.* 1×10^{1} mol dm^{-3}

99. Geometrical isomerism is shown by
a. $>C-C<$ *b.* $-C\equiv C-$
c. $>C=C<$ *d.* None of these

100. The oxidation state of iron in $K_4[Fe(CN)_6]$ is,
a. 2 *b.* 3
c. 4 *d.* 1

101. In which of the following process, a maximum increase in entropy is observed?
a. dissolution of salt in water
b. condensation of water
c. sublimation of naphthalene
d. melting of ice

102. Decomposition of benzene diazonium chloride by using Cu_2Cl_2/HCl to form chlorobenzene is
a. Cannizarro's reaction
b. Kolbe's reaction
c. Sandmeyer's reaction
d. Raschig's reaction

103. Which complex cannot ionise in solution?
a. $[Pt(NH_3)_6]Cl_4$ *b.* $K_2[Pt(F_6)]$
c. $K_4[Fe(CN)_6]$ *d.* $[CoCl_3(NH_3)_3]$

104. Considering the reaction,
$C(s)+O_2(g)\longrightarrow CO_2(g)+393.5$ kJ
The signs of ΔH, ΔS and ΔG respectively are
a. −, +, − *b.* −, −, −
c. −, +, + *d.* +, −, −

105. The product formed when hydroxylamine condenses with a carbonyl compound is called
a. hydrazone *b.* hydrazine
c. oxime *d.* hydrazide

106. Which of the following forms a colourless solution in aqueous medium?
a. Ti^{3+} *b.* Sc^{3+}
c. V^{3+} *d.* Cr^{3+}

107. When a sulphur sol is evaporated, sulphur is obtained. On mixing with water, sulphur sol is not formed. The sol is
a. hydrophilic *b.* hydrophobic
c. reversible *d.* lyophilic

108. An alkyl halide reacts with alcoholic ammonia in a sealed tube, the product formed will be
a. a primary amine *b.* a secondary amine
c. a tertiary amine *d.* a mixture of all the three

109. When conc. H_2SO_4 is heated with P_2O_5, the acid is converted into
a. sulphur
b. sulphur dioxide
c. sulphur trioxide
d. a mixture of sulphur dioxide and sulphur trioxide

110. Entropy of the universe is
a. continuously increasing *b.* continuously decreasing
c. zero *d.* constant

111. Which of the following salts on being dissolved in water gives pH > 7 at 25°C ?
a. NH_4CN *b.* NH_4Cl *c.* KNO_3 *d.* KCN

112. The reagent used in Clemmenson's reduction is
a. alc. KOH *b.* *aq.* KOH
c. Zn-Hg/ conc. HCl *d.* conc. H_2SO_4

113. When KBr is dissolved in water, K^+ ions are
a. oxidised *b.* reduced
c. hydrolysed *d.* hydrated

114. The noble gas mixture is cooled in a coconut bulb at 173 K. The gases that are not adsorbed are
a. He and Ne *b.* Ar and Kr
c. He and Xe *d.* Ne and Xe

115. The volume of 10N and 4N HCl required to make 1 litre of 7N HCl are
a. 0.75 litre of 10N HCl and 0.25 litre of 4N HCl
b. 0.80 litre of 10 N HCl and 0.20 litre of 4N HCl
c. 0.60 litre of 10 N HCl and 0.40 litre of 4N HCl
d. 0.50 litre of 10 N HCl and 0.50 litre of 4N HCl

116. A metal present in insulin is
a. copper *b.* iron
c. zinc *d.* aluminium

117. Carbon forms two oxides which have different compositions. The equivalent mass of which remains constant?
a. Carbon
b. Oxygen
c. Neither carbon nor oxygen
d. Both carbon and oxygen

118. Maximum number of molecules of CH_3I that can react with a molecule of CH_3NH_2 are
a. 1 *b.* 2 *c.* 4 *d.* 3

119. Ellingham diagram represents a graph of
a. ΔG *vs* T *b.* ΔG° *vs* T
c. ΔS *vs* p *d.* ΔG *vs* T

120. Identify the ore not containing iron
a. chalcopyrites *b.* carnallite
c. siderite *d.* limonite

MATHEMATICS

121. $7^{2\log_7 5}$ is equal to

a. 5 *b.* $\log_7 35$

c. $\log_7 25$ *d.* 25

122. In the group $(G \otimes_{15})$, where $G = \{3, 6, 9, 12\}$, $\otimes_{15}$ is multiplication modulo 15, the identity element is

a. 6 *b.* 3

c. 9 *d.* 12

123. A group $(G\ *)$ has 10 elements. The minimum number of elements of G, which are their own inverses is

a. 1 *b.* 2

c. 0 *d.* 9

124. If **a** and **b** are vectors such that $|\mathbf{a} \times \mathbf{b}| = |\mathbf{a} - \mathbf{b}|$, then the angle between **a** and **b** is

a. 60° *b.* 120°

c. 30° *d.* 90°

125. $\dfrac{3x^2 + 1}{x^2 - 6x + 8}$ is equal to

a. $\dfrac{49}{2(x-4)} - \dfrac{13}{2(x-2)}$ *b.* $3 + \dfrac{49}{2(x-4)} - \dfrac{13}{2(x-2)}$

c. $\dfrac{49}{2(x-4)} + \dfrac{13}{2(x-2)}$ *d.* $\dfrac{-49}{2(x-4)} + \dfrac{13}{2(x-2)}$

126. If $\mathbf{a} = 2\hat{\mathbf{i}} + 3\hat{\mathbf{j}} - \hat{\mathbf{k}}$, $\mathbf{b} = \hat{\mathbf{i}} + 2\hat{\mathbf{j}} - 5\hat{\mathbf{k}}$, $\mathbf{c} = 3\hat{\mathbf{i}} + 5\hat{\mathbf{j}} - \hat{\mathbf{k}}$, then a vector perpendicular to **a** and in the plane containing **b** and **c** is

a. $17\hat{\mathbf{i}} + 21\hat{\mathbf{j}} - 123\hat{\mathbf{k}}$ *b.* $-17\hat{\mathbf{i}} + 21\hat{\mathbf{j}} - 97\hat{\mathbf{k}}$

c. $-17\hat{\mathbf{i}} - 21\hat{\mathbf{j}} - 97\hat{\mathbf{k}}$ *d.* $-17\hat{\mathbf{i}} - 21\hat{\mathbf{j}} + 97\hat{\mathbf{k}}$

127. **OA** and **BO** are two vectors of magnitudes 5 and 6 respectively. If $\angle BOA = 60°$, then $\mathbf{OA} \cdot \mathbf{OB}$ is equal to

a. 15 *b.* 0

c. $15\sqrt{3}$ *d.* -15

128. A vector perpendicular to the plane containing the points $A(1, -1, 2)$, $B(2, 0, -1)$, $C(0, 2, 1)$ is

a. $8\hat{\mathbf{i}} + 4\hat{\mathbf{j}} + 4\hat{\mathbf{k}}$ *b.* $4\hat{\mathbf{i}} + 8\hat{\mathbf{j}} - 4\hat{\mathbf{k}}$

c. $\hat{\mathbf{i}} + \hat{\mathbf{j}} - \hat{\mathbf{k}}$ *d.* $3\hat{\mathbf{i}} + \hat{\mathbf{j}} + 2\hat{\mathbf{k}}$

129. $\dfrac{1}{2\cdot 5} + \dfrac{1}{5\cdot 8} + \dfrac{1}{8\cdot 11} + \ldots \dfrac{1}{(3n-1)(3n+2)} =$

a. $\dfrac{n}{6n+3}$ *b.* $\dfrac{n}{6n-4}$

c. $\dfrac{n+1}{6n+4}$ *d.* $\dfrac{n}{6n+4}$

130. The ninth term of the expansion $\left(3x - \dfrac{1}{2x}\right)^8$ is

a. $\dfrac{-1}{512x^9}$ *b.* $\dfrac{1}{512x^9}$

c. $\dfrac{1}{256\cdot x^8}$ *d.* $\dfrac{-1}{256\cdot x^8}$

131. If $A = \begin{bmatrix} 1 & -1 & 1 \\ 2 & 1 & -3 \\ 1 & 1 & 1 \end{bmatrix}$, $10B = \begin{bmatrix} 4 & 2 & 2 \\ -5 & 0 & \alpha \\ 1 & -2 & 3 \end{bmatrix}$ and B is the inverse of A, then the value of α is

a. 0 *b.* 2

c. 4 *d.* 5

132. If $A = \begin{bmatrix} 0 & x & 16 \\ x & 5 & 7 \\ 0 & 9 & x \end{bmatrix}$ is singular, then the possible values of x are

a. 0, 1, −1 *b.* 0, +12, −12

c. 0, 5, −5 *d.* 0, 4, −4

133. If $A = \begin{bmatrix} 1 & -2 & 2 \\ 0 & 2 & -3 \\ 3 & -2 & 4 \end{bmatrix}$, then $A \cdot \text{adj}(A)$ is equal to

a. $\begin{bmatrix} 5 & 0 & 0 \\ 0 & 5 & 0 \\ 0 & 0 & 5 \end{bmatrix}$ *b.* $\begin{bmatrix} 5 & 1 & 1 \\ 1 & 5 & 1 \\ 1 & 1 & 5 \end{bmatrix}$

c. $\begin{bmatrix} 0 & 0 & 0 \\ 0 & 0 & 0 \\ 0 & 0 & 0 \end{bmatrix}$ *d.* $\begin{bmatrix} 8 & 0 & 0 \\ 0 & 8 & 0 \\ 0 & 0 & 8 \end{bmatrix}$

134. If $f : R \to R$ is defined by $f(x) = |x|$, then

a. $f^{-1}(x) = \dfrac{1}{|x|}$

b. $f^{-1}(x) = -x$

c. $f^{-1}(x) = \dfrac{1}{x}$

d. The function $f^{-1}(x)$ does not exist.

135. The value of $\begin{vmatrix} x & p & q \\ p & x & q \\ p & q & x \end{vmatrix}$ is

a. $(x-p)(x-q)(x+p+q)$

b. $x(x-p)(x-q)$

c. $pq(x-p)(x-q)$

d. $(p-q)(x-q)(x-p)$

136. The number of common tangents to the circles $x^2 + y^2 = 4$ and $x^2 + y^2 - 6x - 8y - 24 = 0$ is,

a. 4 *b.* 3 *c.* 1 *d.* 2

137. If $3x + y + k = 0$ is a tangent to the circle $x^2 + y^2 = 10$, the values of k are

a. ± 5 *b.* ± 7 *c.* ± 9 *d.* ± 10

138. The negation of the proposition "If 2 is prime, then 3 is odd" is

a. 2 is prime and 3 is not odd.
b. If 2 is not prime then 3 is not odd.
c. If 2 is not prime then 3 is odd.
d. 2 is not prime and 3 is odd.

139. The equation to two circles which touch the Y-axis at (0, 3) and make an intercept of 8 units on X-axis are

a. $x^2 + y^2 \pm 6x - 10y + 9 = 0$
b. $x^2 + y^2 \pm 10x - 6y + 9 = 0$
c. $x^2 + y^2 + 10x \pm 6y + 9 = 0$
d. $x^2 + y^2 - 8x \pm 10y + 9 = 0$

140. The orthocentre of the triangle with vertices $A(0, 0)$, $B(0, 3/2)$, $C(-5, 0)$ is

a. $(-5/2, 3/4)$ *b.* (5/2, 3/4)
c. (0, 0) *d.* $(-5, 3/2)$

141. $x^2 + y^2 - 6x - 6y + 4 = 0$,
$x^2 + y^2 - 2x - 4y + 3 = 0$,
$x^2 + y^2 + 2kx + 2y + 1 = 0$. If the Radical centre of the above three circles exists, then which of the following cannot be the value of k?

a. 1 *b.* 2
c. 4 *d.* 5

142. If the circles $x^2 + y^2 - 2x - 2y - 7 = 0$ and $x^2 + y^2 + 4x + 2y + k = 0$ cut orthogonally, then the length of the common chord of the circles is

a. 2 *b.* $12/\sqrt{13}$
c. 8 *d.* 5

143. The coordinates of the foot of the perpendicular drawn from the point (3, 4) on the line $2x + y - 7 = 0$ is

a. (1, 5) *b.* $\left(\frac{9}{5}, \frac{17}{5}\right)$
c. $(1, -5)$ *d.* $(-5, 1)$

144. The area enclosed by the pair of lines $xy = 0$, the line $x - 4 = 0$ and $y + 5 = 0$ is

a. 10 sq units *b.* 20 sq units
c. 0 sq units *d.* $\frac{5}{4}$ sq units

145. If the area of the auxillary circle of the ellipse $\frac{x^2}{a^2} + \frac{y^2}{b^2} = 1 (a > b)$ is twice the area of the ellipse, then the eccentricity of the ellipse is

a. $\frac{\sqrt{3}}{2}$ *b.* $\frac{1}{\sqrt{2}}$ *c.* $\frac{1}{2}$ *d.* $\frac{1}{\sqrt{3}}$

146. A graph G has m vertices of odd degree and 'n' vertices of even degree. Then which of the following statements is necessarily true?

a. $m + n$ is an even number
b. $m + n$ is an odd number
c. $m + 1$ is an odd number
d. $n + 1$ is an even number

147. If p is any point on the ellipse $\frac{x^2}{36} + \frac{y^2}{16} = 1$, and S and S' are the foci, then $PS + PS' =$

a. 8 *b.* 4
c. 12 *d.* 10

148. The value of $\sin\left[2\cos^{-1}\frac{\sqrt{5}}{3}\right]$ is

a. $\frac{2\sqrt{5}}{3}$ *b.* $\frac{\sqrt{5}}{3}$ *c.* $\frac{2\sqrt{5}}{9}$ *d.* $\frac{4\sqrt{5}}{9}$

149. If $\frac{x^2}{36} - \frac{y^2}{k^2} = 1$ is a hyperbola, then which of the following statements can be true?

a. (3, 1) lies on the hyperbola.
b. (– 3, 1) lies on the hyperbola.
c. (5, 2) lies on the hyperbola.
d. (10, 4) lies on the hyperbola.

150. The focus of the parabola is

a. $\left(\frac{1}{3}, \frac{-3}{2}\right)$ *b.* $\left(\frac{-1}{3}, \frac{3}{2}\right)$
c. $\left(\frac{1}{3}, \frac{-1}{2}\right)$ *d.* $\left(\frac{1}{3}, \frac{3}{2}\right)$

151. The solution of $\tan^{-1} x + 2\,\text{co:}^{-1} x = \frac{2\pi}{3}$ is

a. $\frac{1}{\sqrt{3}}$ *b.* $-\frac{1}{\sqrt{3}}$
c. $\sqrt{3}$ *d.* $-\sqrt{3}$

152. $\sin^2 17.5° + \sin^2 72.5°$ is equal to

a. $\tan^2 45°$ *b.* $\cos^2 90°$
c. $\sin^2 45°$ *d.* $\cos^2 30°$

153. The conjugate of the complex number $\frac{(1+i)^2}{1-i}$ is

a. $1 + i$ *b.* $1 - i$ *c.* $-1 - i$ *d.* $-1 + i$

154. ABC is a triangle with $\angle A = 30°$ and $BC = 10$ cm. The area of the circum circle of the triangle is

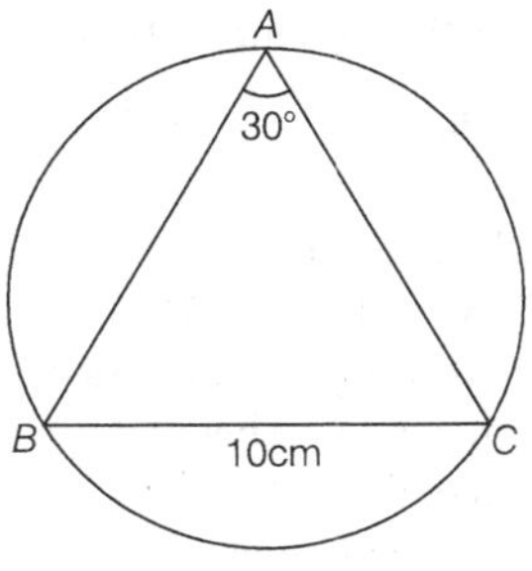

a. 5 sq cm *b.* 100π sq cm
c. $\frac{100\pi}{3}$ sq cm *d.* 25 sq cm

155. If $\sin 3\theta = \sin\theta$, how many solutions exist such that $-2\pi < \theta < 2\pi$?

a. 9 *b.* 8 *c.* 7 *d.* 5

156. The imaginary part of i^i is

a. 1 *b.* 0
c. -1 *d.* 2

157. The amplitude of $(1+i)^5$ is

a. $\frac{-3\pi}{4}$ *b.* $\frac{3\pi}{4}$
c. $\frac{5\pi}{4}$ *d.* $\frac{-5\pi}{4}$

158. ABC is a triangle, G is the centroid, D is the mid-point of BC. If $A = (2, 3)$ and $G = (7, 5)$, then the point D is

a. $\left(\frac{19}{2}, 6\right)$ *b.* $\left(\frac{9}{2}, 4\right)$
c. $\left(8, \frac{13}{2}\right)$ *d.* $\left(\frac{11}{2}, \frac{11}{2}\right)$

159. $\lim_{x \to 1} \frac{\tan(x^2 - 1)}{x - 1}$ is equal to

a. $\frac{1}{2}$ *b.* 2
c. $\frac{-1}{2}$ *d.* -2

160. If $y = 2^{\log x}$, then $\frac{dy}{dx}$ is

a. $2^{\log x} \cdot \log 2$ *b.* $\frac{2^{\log x}}{\log 2}$
c. $\frac{2^{\log x} \log 2}{x}$ *d.* $\frac{2^{\log x}}{x}$

161. If $\sec^{-1}\left(\frac{1+x}{1-y}\right) = a$, then $\frac{dy}{dx}$ is

a. $\frac{y+1}{x-1}$ *b.* $\frac{y-1}{x+1}$
c. $\frac{x-1}{y+1}$ *d.* $\frac{x-1}{y-1}$

162. If $y = \cos^2 \frac{3x}{2} - \sin^2 \frac{3x}{2}$, then $\frac{d^2y}{dx^2}$ is

a. $9y$ *b.* $-3\sqrt{1-y^2}$
c. $3\sqrt{1-y^2}$ *d.* $-9y$

163. If the function $f(x) = \begin{cases} \frac{1-\cos x}{x^2}, & \text{for } x \neq 0 \\ k, & \text{for } x = 0 \end{cases}$ is continuous at $x = 0$, then the value of k is

a. 0 *b.* 1
c. -1 *d.* 1/2

164. If $1, \omega, \omega^2$ are the cube roots of unity, then $(1+\omega)(1+\omega^2)(1+\omega^4)(1+\omega^8)$ is equal to

a. 0 *b.* 1 *c.* ω *d.* ω^2

165. If $x^x = y^y$, then $\frac{dy}{dx}$ is

a. $-\frac{x}{y}$ *b.* $-\frac{y}{x}$
c. $\frac{1+\log x}{1+\log y}$ *d.* $1 + \log\left(\frac{x}{y}\right)$

166. The point on the curve $y^2 = x$, the tangent at which makes an angle 45° with X-axis is

a. (1/2, 1/4) *b.* (1/4, 1/2)
c. (1/2, 1/2) *d.* $(1/2, -1/2)$

167. The length of the subtangent to the curve $x^2y^2 = a^4$ at $(-a, a)$ is

a. $2a$ *b.* $a/2$ *c.* $a/3$ *d.* a

168. The number of positive divisors of 252 is

a. 5 *b.* 9 *c.* 10 *d.* 18

169. The remainder obtained when 5^{124} is divided by 124 is

a. 0 *b.* 5 *c.* 1 *d.* 2

170. Which of the following is not a group with respect to the given operation?

a. The set of odd integers under addition.
b. The set of even integers under addition.
c. $\{1, -1\}$ under multiplication.
d. $\{0\}$ under addition.

171. The range in which $y = -x^2 + 6x - 3$ is increasing, is

a. $x > 3$ *b.* $x < 3$
c. $5 < x < 6$ *d.* $7 < x < 8$

172. The value of the integral $\int_0^{\pi/2} (\sin^{100} x - \cos^{100} x)\, dx$ is

a. $\frac{100!}{(100)^{100}}$ *b.* $\frac{1}{100}$
c. 0 *d.* $\frac{\pi}{100}$

173. *OA* and *OB* are two roads enclosing an angle of 120°. *X* and *Y* start from *O* at the same time. *X* travels along *OA* with a speed of 4 km/h and *Y* travels along *OB* with a speed of 3 km/h. The rate at which the shortest distance between *X* and *Y* is increasing after 1 hour is

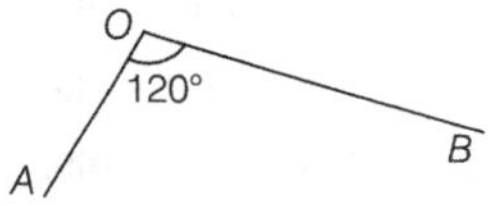

a. 37 km/h *b.* $\sqrt{37}$ km/h
c. $\sqrt{13}$ km/h *d.* 13 km/h

174. If $k\int_0^1 x \cdot f(3x)\, dx = \int_0^3 t \cdot f(t)\, dt$, then the value of k is

a. 3 *b.* 9 *c.* 1/3 *d.* 1/9

175. The value of $\int \frac{1}{1+\cos 8x}\, dx$ is

a. $\frac{\tan 8x}{8} + C$ *b.* $\frac{\tan 2x}{8} + C$
c. $\frac{\tan 4x}{8} + C$ *d.* $\frac{\tan 4x}{4} + C$

176. The value of $\int e^x (x^5 + 5x^4 + 1) \cdot dx$ is

a. $e^x \cdot x^5 + e^x + C$ *b.* $e^x \cdot x^5$
c. $5x^4 \cdot e^x$ *d.* $e^{x+1} \cdot x^5 + C$

177. The value of $\int \frac{x^2+1}{x^2-1}\, dx$ is

a. $\log\left(\frac{x+1}{x-1}\right) + C$ *b.* $\log\left(\frac{x-1}{x+1}\right) + C$
c. $\log(x^2 - 1) + C$ *d.* $x + \log\left(\frac{x-1}{x+1}\right) + C$

178. The area bounded by the curve $x = 4 - y^2$ and the *Y*-axis is

a. 32 sq units *b.* 16 sq units
c. $\frac{16}{3}$ sq units *d.* $\frac{32}{3}$ sq units

179. The differential equation of the family of straight lines whose slope is equal to y-intercept is

a. $(x+1)\frac{dy}{dx} + y = 0$
b. $(x+1)\frac{dy}{dx} - y = 0$
c. $\frac{dy}{dx} = \frac{x+1}{y+1}$
d. $\frac{dy}{dx} = \frac{x-1}{y-1}$

180. The order and degree of the differential equation $\left[1 + \left(\frac{dy}{dx}\right)^5\right]^{\frac{1}{3}} = \frac{d^2y}{dx^2}$ are respectively

a. 2, 1 *b.* 1, 5
c. 2, 3 *d.* 2, 5

ANSWERS

Physics

1. (a)	2. (c)	3. (d)	4. (b)	5. (c)	6. (a)	7. (b)	8. (d)	9. (b)	10. (b)
11. (b)	12. (c)	13. (d)	14. (a)	15. (b)	16. (c)	17. (d)	18. (b)	19. (c)	20. (a)
21. (d)	22. (d)	23. (a)	24. (a)	25. (b)	26. (a)	27. (b)	28. (c)	29. (b)	30. (c)
31. (d)	32. (d)	33. (b)	34. (d)	35. (c)	36. (b)	37. (d)	38. (a)	39. (a)	40. (b)
41. (c)	42. (c)	43. (d)	44. (c)	45. (a)	46. (b)	47. (*)	48. (c)	49. (d)	50. (a)
51. (b)	52. (d)	53. (a)	54. (b)	55. (c)	56. (c)	57. (c)	58. (c)	59. (d)	60. (a)

Chemistry

61. (a)	62. (b)	63. (b)	64. (d)	65. (a)	66. (b)	67. (c)	68. (d)	69. (c)	70. (c)
71. (b)	72. (b)	73. (a)	74. (c)	75. (a)	76. (c)	77. (c)	78. (a)	79. (b)	80. (c)
81. (d)	82. (a)	83. (b)	84. (d)	85. (b)	86. (d)	87. (b)	88. (c)	89. (a)	90. (b)
91. (b)	92. (b)	93. (a)	94. (b)	95. (a)	96. (c)	97. (c)	98. (a)	99. (c)	100. (a)
101. (c)	102. (c)	103. (d)	104. (a)	105. (c)	106. (b)	107. (b)	108. (d)	109. (c)	110. (a)
111. (d)	112. (c)	113. (d)	114. (a)	115. (d)	116. (c)	117. (b)	118. (d)	119. (b)	120. (b)

Mathematics

121. (d)	122. (a)	123. (a)	124. (d)	125. (b)	126. (c)	127. (a)	128. (a)	129. (d)	230. (c)
131. (d)	132. (b)	133. (d)	134. (d)	135. (a)	136. (c)	137. (d)	138. (a)	139. (b)	140. (a)
141. (d)	142. (b)	143. (b)	144. (b)	145. (a)	146. (a)	147. (c)	148. (d)	149. (d)	150. (*)
151. (c)	152. (a)	153. (c)	154. (b)	155. (a)	156. (b)	157. (a)	158. (a)	159. (b)	160. (c)
161. (b)	162. (d)	163. (d)	164. (b)	165. (c)	166. (b)	167. (d)	168. (d)	169. (b)	170. (a)
171. (b)	172. (c)	173. (b)	174. (b)	175. (c)	176. (a)	177. (d)	178. (d)	179. (b)	180. (c)

Note (*) None of the option is correct.

HINTS & SOLUTIONS

Physics

1. *(a)* Frequency of incident light,

$$\nu = 10^{15} \text{ Hz}$$

Work function, $\phi_0 = 2.5$ eV

Energy of incident photon,

$$E = h\nu$$
$$= 6.62 \times 10^{-34} \times 10^{15}$$
$$= 6.62 \times 10^{-19} \text{ J}$$
$$= \frac{6.62 \times 10^{-19}}{1.6 \times 10^{-19}} \text{ eV}$$
$$= 4.1 \text{ eV}$$

According to Einstein's photoelectric equation,

$$K_{max} = h\nu - \phi_0$$
$$\Rightarrow \quad eV_0 = h\nu - \phi_0$$
$$\Rightarrow \quad eV_0 = 4.1\, eV - 2.5\, eV$$
$$\Rightarrow \quad eV_0 = 1.6 eV$$
$$\Rightarrow \quad V_0 = 1.6 \text{ V}$$

2. *(c)* When a charged particle of charge q is accelerated through a potential V, then de-Broglie wavelength is given as

$$\lambda = \frac{h}{\sqrt{2mqV}}$$
$$\Rightarrow \quad \lambda \propto \frac{1}{\sqrt{mq}}$$
$$\Rightarrow \quad \frac{\lambda_\alpha}{\lambda_p} = \sqrt{\frac{m_p}{m_\alpha}} \cdot \sqrt{\frac{q_p}{q_\alpha}}$$
$$\Rightarrow \quad \frac{\lambda_\alpha}{\lambda} = \sqrt{\frac{m_p}{4m_p}} \sqrt{\frac{q_p}{2q_p}} \quad \left[\because m_\alpha = 4m_p \text{ and } q_\alpha = 2q_p\right]$$
$$\Rightarrow \quad \frac{\lambda_\alpha}{\lambda} = \frac{1}{\sqrt{8}}$$
$$\Rightarrow \quad \lambda_\alpha = \frac{\lambda}{2\sqrt{2}}$$

3. *(d)* Electric field due to thin spherical shell at a distance x outside from the centre is given as

$$E = \frac{1}{4\pi\varepsilon_0} \cdot \frac{Q}{x^2} \quad \ldots \text{(i)}$$

where, $Q = s \cdot A$

$$= s \times 4\pi R^2$$

$\therefore$ From Eq. (i), we get

$$E = \frac{1}{4\pi\varepsilon_0} \cdot \frac{s \times 4\pi R^2}{x^2} = \frac{sR^2}{\varepsilon_0 x^2}$$
$$\therefore \quad E \propto \frac{1}{x^2}$$

4. *(b)* For emission of energy, electron of H-atom must fall from higher energy state to lower energy state. Hence, options (a) and (c) are not possible.

In option (b), $n_1 = 2$, $n_2 = 1$

$\therefore$ Energy of emitted photon is given as

$$E' = -13.6\, Z^2\left(\frac{1}{n_1^2} - \frac{1}{n_2^2}\right)$$
$$\Rightarrow \quad h\nu' = -13.6Z^2\left(\frac{1}{2^2} - \frac{1}{1^2}\right)$$
$$\nu' = \frac{13.6Z^2}{h} \times \frac{3}{4} \quad \ldots \text{(i)}$$

In option (c), $n_1 = 2$, $n_2 = 6$, hence energy of emitted photon is given as

$$E'' = -13.6\, Z^2\left(\frac{1}{6^2} - \frac{1}{2^2}\right)$$
$$\Rightarrow \quad h\nu'' = 13.6Z^2 \times \frac{8}{36}$$
$$\Rightarrow \quad \nu'' = \frac{13.6Z^2}{h} \times \frac{8}{36} \quad \ldots \text{(ii)}$$

Hence, from Eqs. (i) and (ii), we get

$$\nu' > \nu''$$

5. *(c)* Nuclear force F_n are attractive in nature. As in the given case, the two protons are kept at a separation of 40 Å (short range), hence in this range, nuclear force F_n is much greater than the electrostatic force F_e.

i.e. $\quad F_n >> F_e$

6. *(a)* Decays constants of radioactive materials X_1 and X_2 is given as $\lambda_1 = 5\lambda$ and $\lambda_2 = \lambda$

If N_0 be the initial number of nuclei in both radioactive materials, then according to radioactive decay law,

$$N_{X_1} = N_0 e^{-\lambda_1 t}$$

and

$$N_{X_2} = N_0 e^{-\lambda_2 t}$$
$$\therefore \quad \frac{N_{X_1}}{N_{X_2}} = \frac{N_0 e^{-\lambda_1 t}}{N_0 e^{-\lambda_2 t}}$$

$$\frac{1}{e} = e^{(-\lambda_1 + \lambda_2)t} \quad \left[\text{Given, } \frac{N_{X_1}}{N_{X_2}} = \frac{1}{e}\right]$$

$$\Rightarrow \quad e^{-1} = e^{-(\lambda_1 - \lambda_2)t}$$

$$\Rightarrow \quad (\lambda_1 - \lambda_2)t = 1$$

$$\Rightarrow \quad t = \frac{1}{\lambda_1 - \lambda_2}$$

$$= \frac{1}{5\lambda - \lambda} = \frac{1}{4\lambda}$$

7. *(b)* If α and β be the longitudinal strain and lateral strain respectively, then

$$\alpha = \frac{l_2 - l_1}{l_1} = 10^{-3} = 0.001$$

$$\Rightarrow \quad \frac{l_2}{l_1} = 1.001 \quad \ldots \text{(i)}$$

Poisson's ratio, $\sigma = \dfrac{\text{Lateral strain}}{\text{Longitudinal strain}}$

$$= \frac{\beta}{\alpha}$$

$$\Rightarrow \quad \beta = \sigma\alpha = 0.1 \times 10^{-3} = 10^{-4}$$

But, $\beta = \dfrac{r_1 - r_2}{r_1}$

$$\therefore \quad \frac{r_1 - r_2}{r_1} = 10^{-4} = 0.0001$$

$$\Rightarrow \quad \frac{r_2}{r_1} = 0.9999 \quad \ldots \text{(ii)}$$

Hence, percentage increase in volume

$$= \frac{V_2 - V_1}{V_1} \times 100$$

$$= \frac{\pi r_2^2 l_2 - \pi r_1^2 l_1}{\pi r_1^2 l_1} \times 100$$

$$= \left[\left(\frac{r_2}{r_1}\right)^2 \left(\frac{l_2}{l_1}\right)^2 - 1\right] \times 100$$

$$= [(0.9999)^2 \times (1.0001)^2 - 1] \times 100$$

$$= 0.0008 \times 100 = 0.08\%$$

8. *(d)* We know that, angular velocity,

$$\omega = \frac{2\pi}{T}$$

$$\Rightarrow \quad T = \frac{2\pi}{\omega}$$

$$\Rightarrow \quad \frac{T_2}{T_1} = \frac{\omega_1}{\omega_2}$$

$$= \frac{\omega_1}{2\omega_1} \quad [\because \omega_2 = 2\omega_1]$$

$$\Rightarrow \quad \frac{T_2}{T_1} = \frac{1}{2}$$

$$\Rightarrow \quad T_2 = \frac{T_1}{2} \quad \ldots \text{(i)}$$

According to Kepler's law,

$$T^2 \propto R^3$$

$$\Rightarrow \quad R \propto T^{2/3}$$

$$\Rightarrow \quad \frac{R_2}{R_1} = \left(\frac{T_2}{T_1}\right)^{2/3}$$

$$= \left(\frac{T_1/2}{T}\right)^{2/3}$$

$$= \left(\frac{1}{2}\right)^{2/3}$$

$$R_2 = \frac{R_1}{2^{2/3}}$$

$$= \frac{R}{4^{1/3}}$$

9. *(b)* When a p-n junction diode is connected in forward bias, then its potential barrier decreases because more number of charge carriers (electrons in n-side and holes in p-side) move through the junction. Due to increase of drifting of charge carriers, electric current is increased.

10. *(b)* Wavelength of ground waves have frequency greater than the wavelength of sky waves and space waves both.

11. *(b)* In the given situation, the weight of the ball is supported by the buoyant force of water and buoyant force due to air. As the density of air becomes less, the buoyant force due to the air becomes less. Therefore, to compensate a greater buoyant force due to water is required which is achieved by a greater immersion of ball into the water.

12. *(c)* Given, initial surface area, $A_1 = A$

Final surface area, $A_2 = A_1 - 50\%$ of A

$$A_2 = A - 50\% \text{ of } A = A - \frac{A}{2} = \frac{A}{2}$$

Initial surface energy, $E_1 = T \cdot 2A = 2TA$ ... (i)

Final surface energy, E_2 = Surface tension × Surface area

$$\Rightarrow \quad E_2 = T \times 2(A_1 - A_2)$$

$$= T \times 2\left(A - \frac{A}{2}\right)$$

$$= T \times 2 \times \frac{A}{2}$$

$$\Rightarrow \quad E_2 = TA$$

∴ Percentage change in the energy of soap film

$$= \frac{E_1 - E_2}{E_1} \times 100$$

$$= \frac{2TA - TA}{2TA} \times 100$$

$$= 50\%$$

13. *(d)* Given, $K_{copper} : K_{brass} = 4:1$

$$\Rightarrow \quad \frac{K_{copper}}{K_{brass}} = \frac{4}{1}$$

Let the temperature of the free surface of brass = θ

Rate of flow of heat will be equal in both the plates as connected in series.

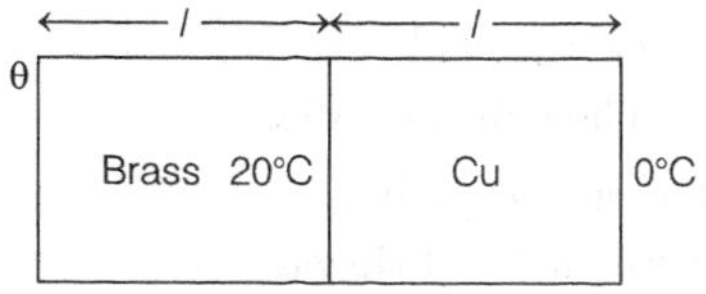

i.e. $H = K_{brass} \dfrac{A(\theta - 20)}{l} = K_{copper} \dfrac{A(20-0)}{l}$

$$\Rightarrow \quad \frac{\theta - 20}{20} = \frac{K_{copper}}{K_{brass}} = \frac{4}{1}$$

$$\Rightarrow \quad \theta - 20 = 80$$

$$\theta = 100°C$$

14. *(a)* Given, $V_1 = 1\ mm^3$

$$= 10^{-9}\ m^3$$

$$p_1 = 1\ atm$$

$$= 1 \times 10^5\ N/m^2$$

$$T_1 = 27 + 273$$

$$= 300\ K$$

$$T_2 = 627 + 273$$

$$= 900\ K$$

Under adiabatic condition,

$$p_1^{1-\gamma} T_1^{\gamma} = p_2^{1-\gamma} T_2^{\gamma}$$

$$\Rightarrow \quad \left(\frac{p_2}{p_1}\right)^{1-\gamma} = \left(\frac{T_1}{T_2}\right)^{\gamma}$$

$$\Rightarrow \quad \left(\frac{p_2}{p_1}\right)^{1-1.5} = \left(\frac{300}{900}\right)^{1.5}$$

$$\Rightarrow \quad \left(\frac{p_2}{p_1}\right)^{-0.5} = \left(\frac{1}{3}\right)^{1.5}$$

$$\Rightarrow \quad \left(\frac{p_1}{p_2}\right)^{0.5} = \left(\frac{1}{3}\right)^{1.5}$$

$$\Rightarrow \quad \frac{p_1}{p_2} = \left(\frac{1}{3}\right)^{\frac{1.5}{0.5}} = \left(\frac{1}{3}\right)^{3} = \frac{1}{27}$$

$$\Rightarrow \quad p_2 = 27\,p_1 = 27 \times 1 \times 10^5$$

$$= 27 \times 10^5\ N/m^2$$

15. *(b)* Given, temperature of sink,

$$T_2 = -39°C$$

$$= (273 - 39)\ K$$

$$= 234\ K$$

Temperature of source,

$$T_1 = 0°C$$

$$= (273 + 0)\ K$$

$$= 273\ K$$

∴ Efficiency, $\eta = 1 - \dfrac{T_2}{T_1}$

$$= 1 - \frac{234}{273}$$

$$= \frac{39}{273}$$

$$= 0.142$$

$$= 14.2\%$$

16. *(c)* Law of conservation of energy is valid across all domains of nature. In the universe, all kinds of violent phenomenon occur all the time. Yet the total energy of the universe is remains conserved.

17. *(d)* Given, centripetal force, $F = -\dfrac{A}{R^2}$

∴ Potential energy, $U = -\dfrac{dF}{dR}$

$$= -\frac{d}{dR}\left(-\frac{A}{R^2}\right)$$

$$= -\frac{A}{R}$$

In circular motion, centripetal force is responsible for the motion of object.

$$\therefore \quad \frac{mv^2}{R} = \frac{A}{R^2}$$

$$\Rightarrow \quad mv^2 = \frac{A}{R}$$

$$\Rightarrow \quad \frac{1}{2}mv^2 = \frac{A}{2R}$$

∴ Kinetic energy, $K = \dfrac{1}{2}mv^2 = \dfrac{A}{2R}$

∴ Total energy $= U + K$

$$= -\frac{A}{R} + \frac{A}{2R} = -\frac{A}{2R}$$

18. *(b)* Given, force $F = 20$ N

$$m = 5 \text{ kg}$$

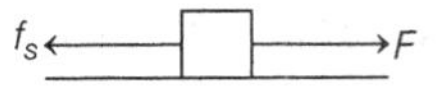

Net force on the body,

$$F_{net} = F - f_s \quad \text{[where, } f_s = \text{friction]}$$

$\therefore$ Work done by displacing 2 m is given as

$$W = F_{net} \times \text{displacement}$$
$$= (F - f_s)2$$
$$= (20 - f_s)2$$
$$\Rightarrow \quad W = 40 - 2f_s$$

According to work-energy theorem,

Work done = gain in kinetic energy

$$\Rightarrow \quad 40 - 2f_s = 10$$
$$\Rightarrow \quad 2f_s = 40 - 10 = 30$$
$$\Rightarrow \quad f_s = \frac{30}{2}$$
$$= 15 \text{ N}$$

19. *(c)* Given, $\mathbf{F} = 6\hat{\mathbf{i}} - 8\hat{\mathbf{j}} + 10\hat{\mathbf{k}}$

$$a = 1 \text{ m/s}^2$$
$$|\mathbf{F}| = \sqrt{6^2 + (-8)^2 + 10^2}$$
$$= \sqrt{200}$$
$$\Rightarrow \quad |\mathbf{F}| = 10\sqrt{2} \text{ N}$$
$$\Rightarrow \quad ma = 10\sqrt{2} \quad [\because F = ma]$$
$$\Rightarrow \quad m = \frac{10\sqrt{2}}{a}$$
$$= \frac{10\sqrt{2}}{1}$$
$$= 10\sqrt{2} \text{ kg}$$

20. *(a)* Mass of the body, $m = 1000$ kg

$$v = 50 \text{ m/s}$$

After adding 250 kg, new mass of the body,

$$m' = m + 250$$
$$= 1000 + 250$$
$$= 1250 \text{ kg}$$

If v' be the final velocity of the body, then by conservation of linear momentum,

$$mv = m'v'$$
$$\Rightarrow 1000 \times 50 = 1250 \times v'$$
$$\Rightarrow \quad v' = \frac{1000 \times 50}{1250}$$
$$= 40 \text{ m/s}$$

21. *(d)* Densities ratio of two gases,

$$\rho_1 : \rho_2 = 1 : 16$$
$$\Rightarrow \quad \frac{\rho_1}{\rho_2} = \frac{1}{16}$$

Since, pressure of both gases are equal.

$$\therefore \quad p_1 = p_2$$
$$\frac{1}{3}\rho_1 c_1^2 = \frac{1}{2}\rho_2 c_2^2$$
$$\Rightarrow \quad \frac{c_1^2}{c_2^2} = \frac{\rho_2}{\rho_1} = \frac{16}{1}$$
$$= \left(\frac{4}{1}\right)^2$$
$$\Rightarrow \quad \frac{c_1}{c_2} = \frac{4}{1}$$
$$\Rightarrow \quad c_1 : c_2 = 4 : 1$$

22. *(d)* Mass of helium, $m_1 = 16$ g

Mass of oxygen, $m_2 = 16$ g

$\therefore$ Number of moles of He gas,

$$n_1 = \frac{m_1}{4} = \frac{16}{4} = 4$$

Number of moles of O_2 gas,

$$n_2 = \frac{m_2}{32} = \frac{16}{32} = \frac{1}{2}$$

We know that for the mixture,

$$C_V = \frac{n_1 C_{V_1} + n_2 C_{V_2}}{n_1 + n_2}, \text{ where } C_V = \frac{fR}{2}$$

$$\text{and } C_p = \frac{n_1 C_{p_1} + n_2 C_{p_2}}{n_1 + n_2}, \text{ where } C_p = \left(\frac{f}{2} + 1\right)R$$

For He gas, $f = 3$, $n_1 = 4$

For O_2 gas, $f = 5$, $n_2 = \frac{1}{2}$

$$\therefore \quad \frac{C_p}{C_V} = \frac{n_1 C_{p_1} + n_2 C_{p_2}}{n_1 C_{V_1} + n_2 C_{V_2}}$$
$$= \frac{4 \times \left(\frac{3}{2} + 1\right)R + \frac{1}{2}\left(\frac{5}{2} + 1\right)R}{4 \times \frac{3}{2}R + \frac{1}{2} \times \frac{5}{2}R}$$
$$= \frac{\left(4 \times \frac{5}{2}R\right) + \left(\frac{1}{2} \times \frac{7}{2}R\right)}{\left(4 \times \frac{3}{2}R\right) + \left(\frac{1}{2} \times \frac{5}{2}R\right)} = \frac{47}{29}$$
$$= 1.62$$

23. *(a)* Amplitude of the particle is SHM,

$$A = 4 \text{ cm}$$

At mean position velocity,

$$v_{max} = 10 \text{ cm/s}$$
$$\Rightarrow \quad A\omega = 10$$

$$\Rightarrow \quad \omega = \frac{10}{A}$$

$$= \frac{10}{4} = 2.5 \text{ rad/s}$$

Again when $v = 5$ cm/s, then displacement, $x = ?$

We know that,

$$v = \omega\sqrt{A^2 - x^2}$$

$$\Rightarrow \quad 5 = 2.5\sqrt{4^2 - x^2}$$

$$\Rightarrow \quad 2 = \sqrt{A^2 - x^2}$$

$$\Rightarrow \quad 4 = A^2 - x^2$$

$$\Rightarrow \quad 4 = 4^2 - x^2$$

$$\Rightarrow \quad x^2 = 16 - 4 = 12$$

$$\therefore \quad x = \sqrt{12} = 2\sqrt{3} \text{ cm}$$

24. *(a)* Given, equation of progressive wave,

$$y = 15\sin(660\pi t - 0.02\,\pi x)$$

Comparing this equation with standard equation of progressive wave as $y = A\sin\left(\frac{2\pi}{T}.t - \frac{2\pi}{\lambda}.x\right)$

We get,

$$\frac{2\pi}{T} = 660\pi$$

$$\Rightarrow \quad T = \frac{2\pi}{660\pi}$$

$$\Rightarrow \quad T = \frac{1}{330}$$

$\therefore$ Frequency of the wave,

$$\nu = \frac{1}{T}$$

$$= \frac{1}{1/330} = 330 \text{ Hz}$$

25. *(b)* Let the frequency of the sound is f.

In first case, $f = 100 \pm 5$

$= 105$ Hz or 95 Hz

The frequency of second harmonic $= 2f$

According to second case,

$2f = 200 \pm 10$

$= 210$ Hz or 190 Hz

If 5 beats are produced with frequency 105 Hz, then frequency of second harmonic will be 210 Hz.

i.e. $\quad 2f = 210$

$$\Rightarrow \quad f = 105 \text{ Hz}$$

$$= 105 \text{ s}^{-1}$$

26. *(a)* Given, $Q_1 + Q_2 = 0.8\,\text{C}$

$$r = 30 \text{ cm} = 0.3 \text{ m}$$

$\therefore$ According to Coulomb's law

$$F = k\frac{Q_1Q_2}{r^2}$$

$$\Rightarrow \quad F = k\frac{Q_1(0.8 - Q_1)}{r^2}$$

The force on Q_1 will be maximum if

$$\frac{dF}{dQ_1} = 0$$

$$\Rightarrow \quad \frac{d}{dQ}\,k\frac{Q_1(0.8 - Q_1)}{r^2} = 0$$

$$0.8 - 2Q_1 = 0$$

$$\Rightarrow \quad Q_1 = 0.4 \text{ C}$$

$$\therefore \quad Q_2 = 0.8 - Q_1$$

$$= 0.8 - 0.4 = 0.4 \text{ C}$$

27. *(b)* The axis of the electric dipole is directed along the direction of dipole moment and the direction of electric dipole moment is taken from negative charge to positive charge.

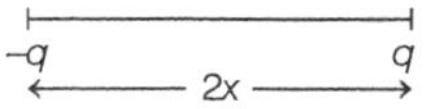

28. *(c)* The orientation of the dipole for the stable equilibrium, $\theta = 0°$.

29. *(b)* The given situation is shown below

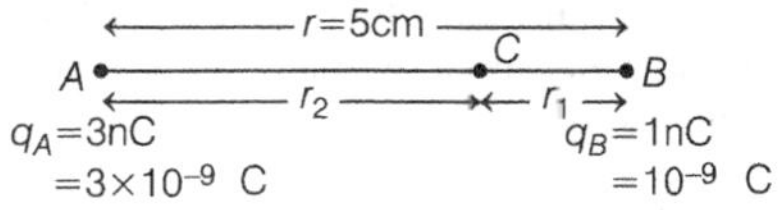

$$r_1 = 1 \text{ cm}$$

$$= 1 \times 10^{-2} \text{ m}$$

$$r_2 = 5 - 1$$

$$= 4 \text{ cm}$$

$$= 4 \times 10^{-2} \text{ m}$$

Required work done = Changes in potential energy

$$= k\,q_Aq_B\left[\frac{1}{r_2} - \frac{1}{r_1}\right]$$

$$= 9 \times 10^9 \times 3 \times 10^{-9} \times 10^{-9}\left[\frac{1}{4 \times 10^{-2}} - \frac{1}{1 \times 10^{-2}}\right]$$

$$= 1.35 \times 10^{-7} \text{ J}$$

30. *(c)* We know that, potential energy of electric dipole,

$$U = -\mathbf{p}\cdot\mathbf{E} = -pE\cos\theta$$

When, $90 < \theta < 180$, then $\cos\theta$ is negative.

As θ increases, $\cos\theta$ decreases.

$$\therefore \quad \theta_{(iv)} > \theta_{(iii)}$$

When $0° < \theta \leq 90°$, then $\cos\theta$ is positive.

Also, when θ increases, then $\cos\theta$ decreases.

$\therefore$ Hence, $\theta_{(i)} > \theta_{(ii)}$

Therefore, $\theta_{(iv)} > \theta_{(iii)} > \theta_{(i)} > \theta_{(ii)}$.

31. *(d)* Refractive index, $\mu = A + \dfrac{B}{\lambda^2}$

According to principle of homogeneity,

Dimension of $\dfrac{B}{\lambda^2}$ = Dimension of μ

$$\Rightarrow \quad [B] = [\mu][\lambda^2] = [M^0L^0T^0][L^2] = [L^2] = \text{Dimension of area}$$

32. *(d)* Voltage, $V = (200 \pm 8)$ V

Current, $I = (20 \pm 0.5)$ A

$\therefore$ Resistance, $R = \dfrac{V}{I} = \dfrac{200}{20} = 10\,\Omega$

Taking maximum error condition,

$$\frac{\Delta R}{R} = \frac{\Delta V}{V} + \frac{\Delta I}{I} = \frac{8}{200} + \frac{0.5}{20} = \frac{13}{200}$$

$$\Rightarrow \quad \frac{\Delta R}{R} \times 100 = \frac{13}{200} \times 100 = \frac{13}{2}\% = 6.5\%$$

33. *(b)* Let u be the initial velocity of vertical projection and t be the time taken by the body to reach at height h from the ground.

$\therefore$ Using equation, $h = ut + \dfrac{1}{2}at^2$

Here, $u = u$, $a = -g$

$$\therefore \quad h = ut - \frac{1}{2}gt^2$$

$$\Rightarrow \quad gt^2 - 2ut + 2h = 0$$

$$\therefore \quad t = \frac{2u \pm \sqrt{4u^2 - 4g \times 2h}}{2g} = \frac{u \pm \sqrt{u^2 - 2gh}}{g}$$

It means t has two values, t_1 and t_2. Where, t_1 is time taken by the body in reaching maximum height and t_2 be the time taken by the body in reaching ground from maximum height.

$$\therefore \quad t_1 = \frac{u + \sqrt{u^2 - 2gh}}{g}$$

and $$t_2 = \frac{u - \sqrt{u^2 - 2gh}}{g}$$

$$\therefore \quad t_1 + t_2 = \frac{2u}{g} \quad \text{or} \quad u = \frac{g(t_1 + t_2)}{2}$$

34. *(d)* Slope of distance-time graph gives the velocity of the particle. Since at the point C, slope of the curve is maximum, hence maximum instantaneous velocity of particle occurs at point C.

35. *(c)* According to the equation of continuity,

$$Av = \text{constant}$$

Therefore, velocity of the fluid is minimum at the widest part and maximum at the narrowest part of the horizontal pipe.

Again, according to Bernoulli's principle for horizontal pipe,

$$p + \frac{1}{2}\rho v^2 = \text{constant}$$

Hence, p is more, v is less and *vice-versa*.

Therefore, when a fluid is flowing through the horizontal pipe of variable area of cross-section, then velocity is maximum at the narrowest part of the pipe and pressure is maximum at the widest part of the pipe.

36. *(b)* Given, $V_1 = 120$ V, $V_2 = 200$ V

Since, potential on each capacitor is zero when they are connected in parallel. Hence, charge on each capacitor must be equal with unlike polarities together.

i.e. $$q_1 = q_2$$

$$\Rightarrow \quad C_1V_1 = C_2V_2$$

$$\Rightarrow \quad C_1 \times 120 = C_2 \times 200$$

$$\Rightarrow \quad 3C_1 = 5C_2$$

37. *(d)* According to Kirchhoff's junction rule,

$$\Sigma I = 0$$

i.e. sum of total incoming currents = sum of total outgoing currents.

Hence, it is based on the law of conservation of charges. Hence, all the statements are correct.

38. *(a)* The given situation is shown in figure.

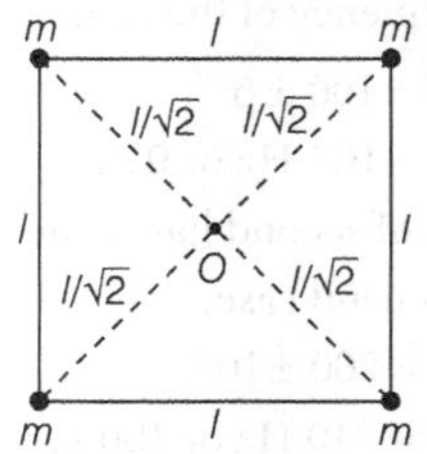

Moment of inertia of the systems about an axis perpendicular to the square and passing through the centre is given as

$$I = m\left(\frac{l}{\sqrt{2}}\right)^2 + m\left(\frac{l}{\sqrt{2}}\right)^2 + m\left(\frac{l}{\sqrt{2}}\right)^2 + m\left(\frac{l}{\sqrt{2}}\right)^2$$

$$= 4\frac{ml^2}{2} = 2ml^2 \quad \ldots \text{(i)}$$

If k be the radius of gyration, then

$$I = 4mk^2 \quad \text{... (ii)}$$

$\therefore$ From Eqs. (i) and (ii), we have

$$2ml^2 = 4mk^2$$

$$\Rightarrow \quad k = \frac{l}{\sqrt{2}}$$

39. *(a)* Given, for steel wire,

Area, $A_1 = 3 \times 10^{-5}\ \text{m}^2$

Length, $L_1 = 4.7\ \text{m}$

For copper wire,

$$A_2 = 4 \times 10^{-5}\ \text{m}^2,\ L_2 = 3.5\ \text{m}$$

If Y_1 and Y_2 be the Young's modulus for the material steel wire and copper wire respectively, then

$$\frac{Y_1}{Y_2} = \frac{\frac{F_1 L_1}{A_1 \Delta l}}{\frac{F_2 L_2}{A_2 \Delta l}}$$

$$\Rightarrow \quad \frac{Y_1}{Y_2} = \frac{L_1 A_2}{L_2 A_1} \quad [\because F_1 = F_2]$$

$$= \frac{4.7 \times 4 \times 10^{-5}}{3.5 \times 3 \times 10^{-5}} = 1.8$$

$$\Rightarrow \quad Y_1 : Y_2 = 1.8 : 1$$

40. *(b)* Given, $m_1 = 200\ \text{g} = 0.2\ \text{kg}$

$m_2 = 300\ \text{g} = 0.3\ \text{kg}$

$l_1 = 50 - 20 = 30\ \text{cm}$

$$\Rightarrow \quad l_1 = 0.3\ \text{m}$$

$l_2 = 70 - 50 = 20\ \text{cm} = 0.2\ \text{m}$

$\therefore$ Moment of inertia of the system about an axis passing through 50 cm mark (i.e. mid-point)

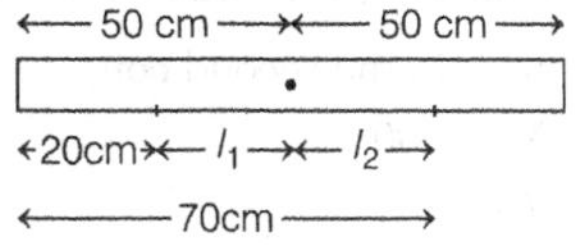

$$I = m_1 l_1^2 + m_2 l_2^2$$

$$= 0.2 \times (0.3)^2 + 0.3 \times (0.2)^2$$

$$= 0.036\ \text{kg m}^2$$

41. *(c)* The given situation is shown below.

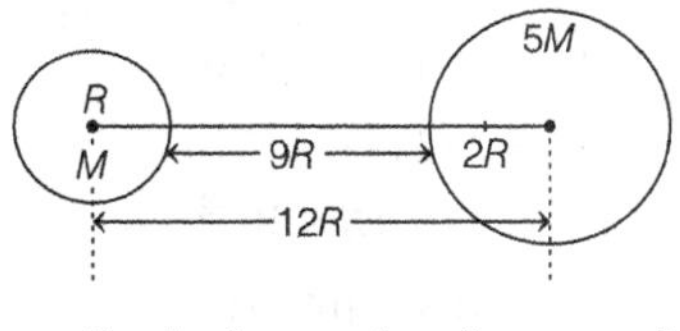

Let the smaller body travels a distance x before collision due to gravitation attraction.

Hence, $Mx = 5M(9R - x)$

$$\Rightarrow \quad x = 5(9R - x)$$

$$\Rightarrow \quad x = 45R - 5x$$

$$\Rightarrow \quad 6x = 45R$$

$$\Rightarrow \quad x = \frac{45}{6}R = \frac{15}{2}R = 7.5R$$

42. *(c)* The given Wheatstone bridge circuit is shown below.

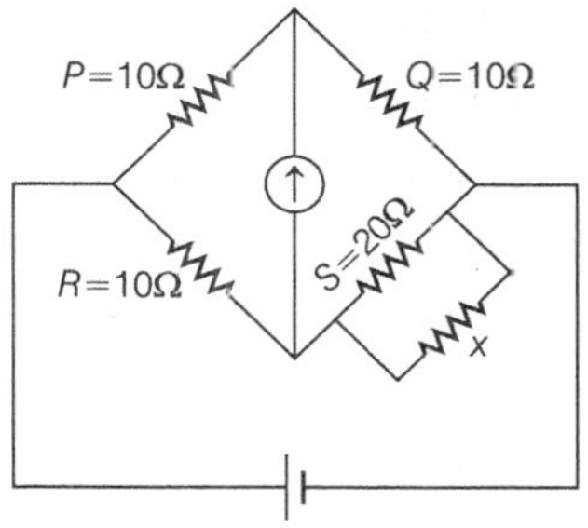

Wheatstone is balanced only when

$$\frac{P}{Q} = \frac{R}{S}$$

Thus, the value of resistance S should be 10 Ω. But it is given to 20 Ω.

Hence, to decrease its value upto 10 Ω, suppose x Ω resistance is connected parallel to it

$$\therefore \quad \frac{1}{10} = \frac{1}{20} + \frac{1}{x}$$

$$\Rightarrow \quad \frac{1}{x} = \frac{1}{10} - \frac{1}{20} = \frac{1}{20}$$

$$\Rightarrow \quad x = 20\ \Omega$$

43. *(d)* The given situation is shown below.

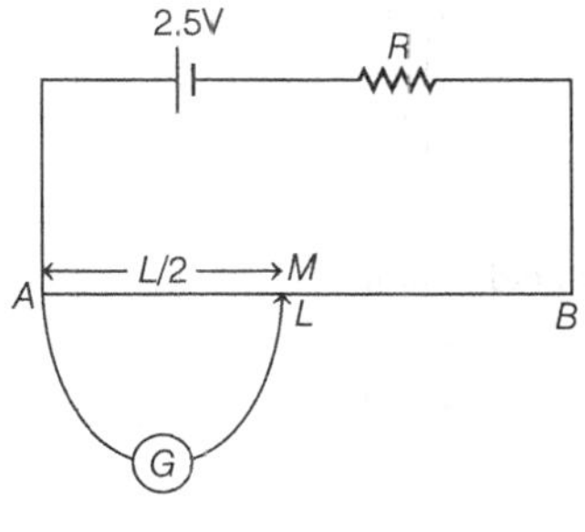

Resistance of potentiometer wire, $R_P = 10\ \Omega$

Emf, $E = 2.5\ \text{V}$

Total resistance, $R' = R_P + R = (10 + R)\ \Omega$

Current through potentiometer wire,

$$I = \frac{E}{R_P} = \frac{2.5}{10 + R}$$

Since, potential difference across length $AL = \frac{L}{2}$,

$$V = I\left(\frac{R_P}{2}\right)$$

$$\Rightarrow \quad 1 = \frac{25}{10+R} \times \frac{10}{2}$$

$$\Rightarrow \quad 10 + R = 125$$

$$\Rightarrow \quad R = 25\ \Omega$$

44. *(c)* Given,

$$\mathbf{v} = 2 \times 10^5 \hat{\mathbf{i}}\ \text{m/s}$$

$$\mathbf{B} = (\hat{\mathbf{i}} - 4\hat{\mathbf{j}} - 3\hat{\mathbf{k}})\ \text{T}$$

Charge on electron, $q = 1.6 \times 10^{-19}$ C

$\therefore$ Force, $\mathbf{F} = q(\mathbf{v} \times \mathbf{B})$

$$= 1.6 \times 10^{-19} [(2 \times 10^5 \hat{\mathbf{i}}) \times (\hat{\mathbf{i}} - 4\hat{\mathbf{j}} - 3\hat{\mathbf{k}})]$$

$$= 1.6 \times 10^{-19} \begin{vmatrix} \hat{\mathbf{i}} & \hat{\mathbf{j}} & \hat{\mathbf{k}} \\ 2 \times 10^5 & 0 & 0 \\ 1 & -4 & -3 \end{vmatrix}$$

$$\mathbf{F} = 1.6 \times 10^{-19} (6 \times 10^5\ \hat{\mathbf{j}} - 8 \times 10^5 \hat{\mathbf{k}})$$

$$= 9.6 \times 10^{-14}\ \hat{\mathbf{j}} - 12.8 \times 10^{-14}\ \hat{\mathbf{k}}$$

$$\Rightarrow \quad |\mathbf{F}| = \sqrt{(9.6 \times 10^{-14})^2 + (-12.8 \times 10^{-14})^2}$$

$$= 10^{-14} \sqrt{(9.6)^2 + (12.8)^2}$$

$$= 16 \times 10^{-14}\ \text{N}$$

$$= 1.6 \times 10^{-13}\ \text{N}$$

45. *(a)* The given situation is shown below

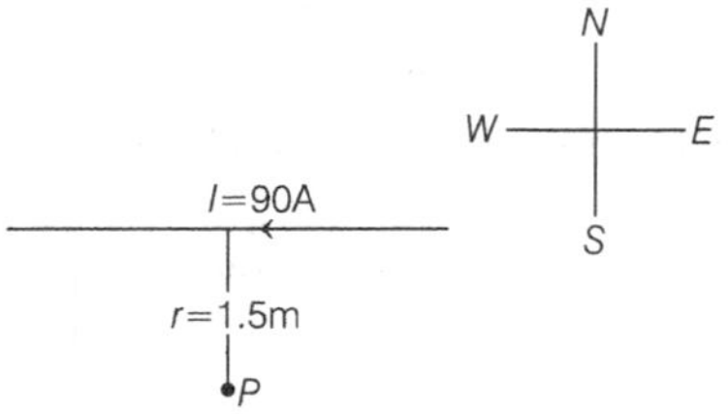

Magnetic field at point P,

$$B = \frac{\mu_0}{2\pi} \cdot \frac{I}{r}$$

$$= 2 \times 10^{-7} \times \frac{90}{1.5}$$

$$= 1.2 \times 10^{-5}\ \text{T (South)}$$

46. *(b)* Given, number of turns in moving coil galvanometer, $N_i = 28$

Initial sensitivity, $S_i = S$

Final sensitivity, $S_f = S_i + 25\%$ of S_i

$$= S + 25\% \text{ of } S$$

$$= S + \frac{S}{4} = \frac{5S}{4}$$

Since, sensitivity of moving coil galvanometer is given as

$$S = \frac{NAB}{K}$$

$\Rightarrow \quad S \propto N$ [A, B and K are constant]

$$\Rightarrow \quad \frac{S_f}{S_i} = \frac{N_f}{N_i}$$

$$\Rightarrow \quad \frac{\frac{5S}{4}}{S} = \frac{N_f}{28}$$

$$\Rightarrow \quad N_f = \frac{28 \times 5}{4} = 35$$

47. *(*)* The intensity of magnetic field due to isolated pole of strength m_p at a point distance r from it is given as

$$B = \frac{\mu_0}{4\pi} \cdot \frac{m_p}{r^2}$$

Hence, no option is correct.

48. *(c)* Light particle (like electron) cannot be accelerated by a cyclotron because due its small mass, a small increase in its energy makes the electrons move with a very high speed. As a result of it, the electrons go quickly out of step with oscillation electric field.

49. *(d)* The angle which the total magnetic field of earth makes with the surface of the earth is called inclination or angle of dip.

50. *(a)* Given, $B_H = B_V$

If δ be the angle of dip, then

$$\tan\delta = \frac{B_V}{B_H} = \frac{B_V}{B_V} = 1$$

$$= \tan 45°$$

$$\Rightarrow \quad \delta = 45°$$

51. *(b)* Given, number of turns in the first coil, $N_1 = 100$

Its self-inductance, $L_1 = 15$ mH $= 1.5 \times 10^{-2}$ H

Number of turns in the second coil,

$$N_2 = 500$$

$$\therefore \quad L_2 = ?$$

We know that, self inductance of the coil is given by

$$L = \frac{\mu_0 \pi N^2 R}{2}$$

$$\Rightarrow \quad L \propto N^2$$

$$\therefore \quad \frac{L_2}{L_1} = \left(\frac{N_2}{N_1}\right)^2 = \left(\frac{500}{100}\right)^2 = 25$$

$$\Rightarrow \quad L_2 = 25\, L_1$$

$$= 25 \times 1.5 \times 10^{-2}$$

$$= 37.5 \times 10^{-2}\ \text{H}$$

$$= 375 \times 10^{-3}\ \text{H} = 375\ \text{mH}$$

52. *(d)* Given, number of turns, $N = 100$

Current, $I = 5 \text{ mA} = 5 \times 10^{-3}$ A

Magnetic flux, $\phi = 10^{-5}$ Wb

Inductance, $L = ?$

We know that,

$$N\phi = LI$$

$$\Rightarrow \quad L = \frac{N\phi}{I} = \frac{100 \times 10^{-5}}{5 \times 10^{-3}}$$

$$= 20 \times 10^{-2} \text{ H} = 0.2 \text{ H}$$

53. *(a)* In step-up transformer, number of turns in secondary coil is greater than the number of turns in the primary coil.

i.e. $N_S > N_P$

54. *(b)* In L-C-R series resonance circuit,

$$X_L = X_C$$

$\therefore$ Impedance, $Z = \sqrt{R^2 + (X_L - X_C)^2} = \sqrt{R^2 + 0^2}$

$$\Rightarrow \quad Z = R$$

$\therefore$ Power factor, $\cos\phi = \frac{R}{Z} = \frac{R}{R} = 1$

Which is not zero.

Since, circuit behaves like a resistive circuit. So, power loss occurs always in this circuits.

i.e. wattless current is zero.

55. *(c)* Both magnet and electric fields have zero average value in a plane electromagnetic wave.

56. *(c)* From the given diagram, we see that lenses L_1 and L_3 are identical but contribute opposite sense, hence their combined effect of making image is ineffective.

Hence, only lens L_2 forms the image.

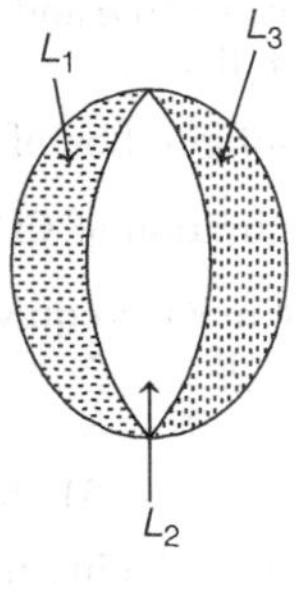

57. *(c)* The complete ray diagram for the given combination of prisms is shown below.

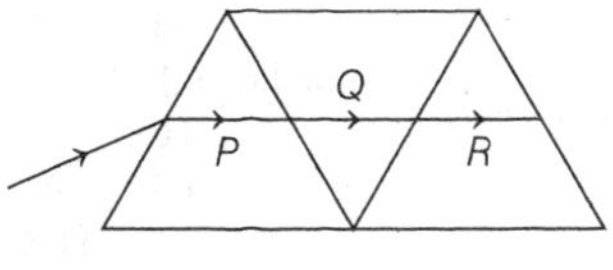

Since, ray of light incident on prism P suffers minimum deviation, hence it becomes parallel to the base of prism P. As prism Q and R are of identical shape and of same material as that of prism P, therefore, the ray continues to be parallel to base of prisms Q and R. Hence, the ray will now suffer same deviation as before.

58. *(c)* Phase difference between the two identical waves $= \delta$

For identical wave,

$$a_1 = a_2 = a$$

After superposition, intensity of resultant wave

$$I \propto (\text{Amplitude})^2$$

$$\propto A^2$$

$$\propto (a_1^2 + a_2^2 + 2a_1a_2 \cos\delta)$$

$$\propto (a^2 + a^2 + 2a^2 \cos\delta)$$

$$\propto 2a^2(1 + \cos\delta)$$

$$\propto 2a^2 \cdot \left(2\cos^2\frac{\delta}{2}\right)$$

$$\propto 4a^2 \cos^2\left(\frac{\delta}{2}\right)$$

$$\Rightarrow \quad I \propto \cos^2\left(\frac{\delta}{2}\right)$$

59. *(d)* Given, wavelength of monochromatic light, $\lambda = 5867$ Å

Refractive index, $\mu = 1.6$

Let t be the thickness of the plastic.

Since, the centre of the screen appears dark when plastic sheet is introduced, hence path difference,

$$\mu t = \frac{\lambda}{2} \text{ or } \frac{3\lambda}{2}$$

when, $\mu t = \frac{3\lambda}{2}$

$$\Rightarrow \quad t = \frac{3\lambda}{2\mu} = \frac{3 \times 5867}{2 \times 1.6} = 5500 \text{ Å}$$

60. *(a)* Position vector of starting point (2, 10, 1) of particle is given as

$$\mathbf{r}_1 = 2\hat{\mathbf{i}} + 10\hat{\mathbf{j}} + \hat{\mathbf{k}}$$

If final co-ordinate of the particle be (x, y, z), then its position vector

$$\mathbf{r}_2 = x\hat{\mathbf{i}} + y\hat{\mathbf{j}} + z\hat{\mathbf{k}}$$

$\therefore$ Displacement, $\Delta\mathbf{r} = \mathbf{r}_2 - \mathbf{r}_1$

$$8\hat{\mathbf{i}} - 2\hat{\mathbf{j}} + \hat{\mathbf{k}} = x\hat{\mathbf{i}} + y\hat{\mathbf{j}} + z\hat{\mathbf{k}} - (2\hat{\mathbf{i}} + 10\hat{\mathbf{j}} + \hat{\mathbf{k}})$$

$$\Rightarrow \quad 8\hat{\mathbf{i}} - 2\hat{\mathbf{j}} + \hat{\mathbf{k}} = (x-2)\hat{\mathbf{i}} + (y-10)\hat{\mathbf{j}} + (z-1)\hat{\mathbf{k}}$$

Comparing the coefficients of $\hat{\mathbf{i}}, \hat{\mathbf{j}}$ and $\hat{\mathbf{k}}$, we get

$$x - 2 = 8, \; y - 10 = -2, \; z - 1 = 1$$

$$\Rightarrow \quad x = 10, \; y = 8, \; z = 2$$

$\therefore$ Final co-ordinate $= (10, 8, 2)$

Chemistry

61. *(a)* During the extraction of gold, following reactions take place

$$\underset{\text{Impure gold}}{4Au(s)} + 8CN^-(aq) + 2H_2O(aq) \xrightarrow{O_2} \underset{(X)}{4[Au(CN)_2]^-} + 4OH^-(aq)$$

$$\underset{(X)}{2[Au(CN)_2]^-} + Zn(s) \longrightarrow \underset{(Y)}{[Zn(CN)_4]^{2-}(aq)} + \underset{\text{Pure gold}}{2Au(s)}$$

One chlorine molecule contains 2 chlorine atoms and one HCl molecule contains 1 chlorine atom.

62. *(b)* Number of gram molecules of chlorine in HCl

$$= \frac{\text{number of molecules of HCl}}{N_A \times 2}$$

$$= \frac{6.02 \times 10^{25}}{6.02 \times 10^{23} \times 2}$$

$$= \frac{100}{2} = 50$$

63. *(b)* Graphite is a soft solid lubricant extremely difficult to melt. The reason for this anomalous behaviour is that graphite has carbon atoms arranged in large plates of rings of strongly bound carbon atoms with weak interplate bonds.

64. *(d)* Paracetamol is an analgesic and antipyretic drug. It is used in medication for treatment of fever, mild to moderate pain.

65. *(a)* 2g of water has maximum number of molecules as its molecular mass is minimum among the given compounds.

Number of O-atoms in $H_2O = \frac{2}{18}N_A = \frac{1}{9}N_A$

Number of O-atoms in $SO_2 = \frac{2}{64}N_A = \frac{1}{32}N_A$

Number of O-atoms in $CO_2 = \frac{2}{44} \times 2N_A = \frac{1}{11}N_A$

Number of O-atoms in $CO = \frac{2}{28}N_A = \frac{1}{14}N_A$

66. *(b)* C_2H_5OH (alcohol) shows functional group isomerism. It's isomers are

$$\underset{\text{Alcohol}}{C_2H_5OH}, \qquad \underset{\text{Ether}}{CH_3—O—CH_3}$$

67. *(c)* For the following reaction,

$$BiO_3^- + 6H^+ + xe^- \longrightarrow Bi^{3+} + 3H_2O$$

On balancing charge on both sides

$$-1 + 6 + x(-1) = 3 + 3 \times 0$$

$\therefore \quad x = 2$

68. *(d)* For orthophosphoric acid solution,

Molarity = 3 M, n-factor = 3

$\therefore$ Normality = n-factor × molarity

$= 3 \times 3$

$= 9$ N

69. *(c)* Acidified sodium fusion extract on addition of ferric chloride solution gives blood red colouration, which confirms the presence of N and S.

$$Na + C + N + S \longrightarrow NaCNS \text{ (Sodium thiocyanate)}$$

$$Fe^{3+} + 3CNS^- \longrightarrow \underset{\text{Red ppt.}}{Fe(CNS)_3}$$

70. *(c)* $m = 10$ mg, $v = 100\ ms^{-1}$, $\lambda = ?$

de-Broglie wavelength, $\lambda = \frac{h}{mv}$

$$= \frac{6.63 \times 10^{-34}}{10 \times 10^{-3} \times 100}$$

$$= 6.63 \times 10^{-34}\ m$$

71. *(b)* Number of electrons in Mg = 12

Number of electrons in $Mg^{2+} = 10$

Number of electrons in $Na^+ = 10$

$\therefore Mg^{2+}$ is isoelectronic with Na^+.

72. *(b)* Gram molecular volume of oxygen at STP is 22400 cm^3.

i.e. volume of 1 mole of oxygen molecule

$$= \frac{22400}{1} = 22400\ cm^3.$$

73. *(a)* Presence of halogen in organic compounds can be detected using Beilstien's test. In this test, an organic compound react with copper wire, when they are heated in a flame and produce a brilliant, long lasting green flame.

74. *(c)* Electronic configuration of Cr = [Ar] $3d^5 4s^1$

Electronic configuration of Cr^{3+} = [Ar] $3d^3 4s^0$

75. *(a)* Equivalent of metal = equivalent of oxygen

$$\frac{w}{31.75} = \frac{8}{8}$$

$\therefore \quad w = 31.75$ g

76. *(c)* Benzene reacts with chlorine in sunlight to give a final product gammaxene.

$$C_6H_6 + 3Cl_2 \xrightarrow{\text{Sunlight}}$$

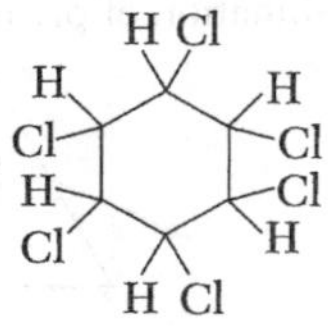

$C_6H_6Cl_6$
(Gammaxene)

77. *(c)* In the periodic table metals usually used as catalyst belong to *d*-block as they have variable oxidation state.

78. *(a)* Dalton's law is applicable to mixture of gases, when they are non-reacting, so that the total pressure of all gases is equal to the sum of the partial pressure of each gas. CO and H_2 are non-reacting gases.

$$\therefore \quad p_T = p_{CO} + p_{H_2}$$

79. *(b)* The general formula of cycloalkene is C_nH_{2n-2}.

80. *(c)* In acetylene, between carbon atoms, there are one σ and two π-bonds i.e.

Acetylene

81. *(d)* Denaturated alcohol is ethanol + methanol. Ethanol is made unfit for drinking by adding poisonous substance such as methanol. It is called denaturation.

82. *(a)* During the formation of a chemical bond energy of system decreases with the release of energy. This result in stability of bond formed.

83. *(b)* O_2 is diatomic and degree of freedom is 5.

$$\therefore \text{ Kinetic energy of } O_2 = \frac{5}{2} \times k \times T$$

$$= \frac{5}{2} \times 273 \times k$$

SO_2 is triatomic and degree of freedom is 7.

$$\therefore \text{ Kinetic energy of } SO_2 = \frac{7}{2} \times 546 \times k$$

$\therefore$ So, kinetic energy of SO_2 is more than that of O_2 i.e.

$$SO_2 > O_2$$

84. *(d)* + *I*-effect is shown by $—CH_3$ group.

While, $—NO_2$, —Br and —Cl shows –*I*-effect.

85. *(b)* Formation of coloured solution is possible, when metal ion in the compound contains unpaired electrons due to transition of electrons in excited state.

86. *(d)* Temperature, surface tension and viscosity are intensive properties. They are independent of the quantity of matter.

87. *(b)* Hofmann's bromamide reaction is used to convert amide to amine.

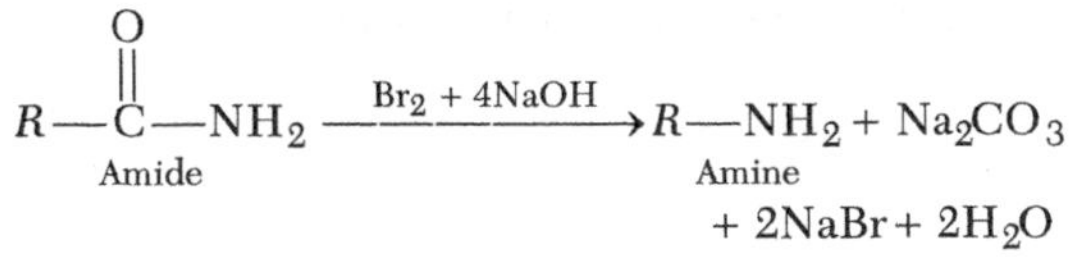

88. *(c)* IUPAC name of $Na_3[Co(NO_2)_6]$ is sodium hexanitro cobaltate (III).

89. *(a)* Thermodynamic standard condition of temperature and pressure is 273 K (0°C) and 1 atm (760 mm Hg).

90. *(b)* The structure of 2, 3, 4-trichloropentane is

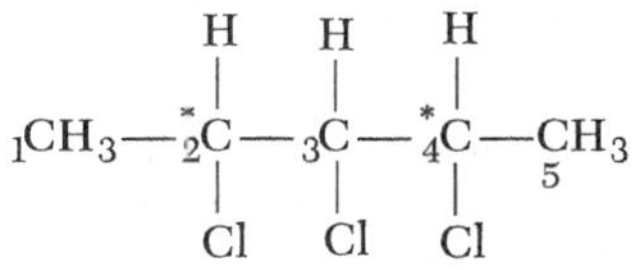

Carbon 2 and 4 are chiral carbons as all the groups are different.

$\therefore$ Two chiral carbons are present in 2,3-4-trichloropentane.

91. *(b)* The number of unidentate ligands in the complex ion is called coordination number. Coordination is the number of lone pair of electron shared by ligands with central metal atom.

If all the ligand are unidentate, then number of ligand is equal to coordination number.

92. *(b)* The reaction, $2SO_2(g) + O_2(g) \xrightleftharpoons{V_2O_5}$ is an example of heterogeneous catalysis as the reactant and catalyst are not present in same phase.

93. *(a)* The amino acid which is not optically active is glycine.

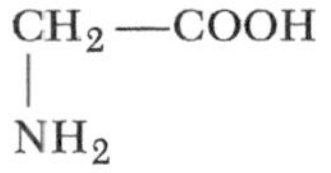

94. *(b)* For a stable molecule the value of bond order must be positive.

$\because$ Stability is directly proportional to bond order.

95. *(a)* The second order reaction is

$$\underset{\text{Methyl ethanoate}}{CH_3COOCH_3} + NaOH \longrightarrow \underset{\substack{\text{Sodium salt of}\\\text{carboxylic acid}}}{CH_3COONa} + H_2O$$

96. *(c)* According to Baeyer's strain theory, cyclopentane is highly stable as, it has lowest angle strain. The desired angle for sp^3 hybridised carbon in cyclopentane should be 109°28′ and the actual angle is 108°. Thus the angle strain is minimum.

97. *(c)* Configuration of $O_2^{2-} = \sigma 1s^2, \sigma^* 1s^2, \sigma 2s^2, \sigma^* 2s^2, \sigma 2p_z^2, \pi 2p_x^2 \approx \pi 2p_y^2, \pi^* 2p_x^2 \approx \pi^* 2p_y^2$.

$\therefore$ Number of antibonding electron pairs is four.

98. *(a)* For 1 M HCl,

$$[H^+] = 1 = 10^0$$

$$[H^+][OH^-] = 10^{-14}$$

$$[OH^-] = 10^{-14} \text{ mol dm}^{-3}.$$

99. *(c)* Geometrical isomerism is shown by alkene with different group attached to carbon i.e.

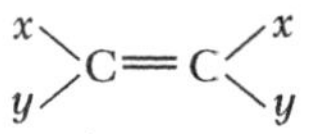

where, $x \neq y$

100. *(a)* Oxidation state of iron (x) in $K_4[Fe(CN)_6]$ is

$$4 + x + 6 \times (-1) = 0$$
$$x = 2$$

101. *(c)* During sublimation of naphthalene, phase changes from solid to gaseous state. Hence, the randomness of the particles increases drastically.

$\therefore$ It has maximum increase in entropy.

102. *(c)* Decomposition of benzene diazonium chloride by using Cu_2Cl_2 / HCl to form chlorobenzene is called Sandmeyer reaction.

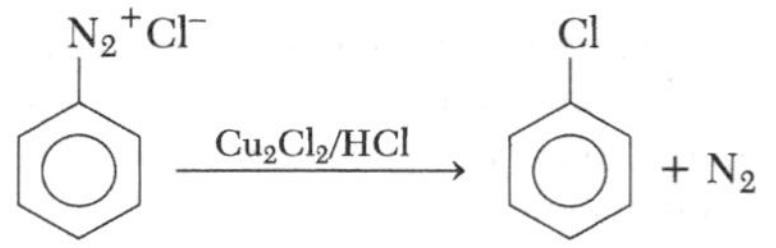

Benzene diazonium chloride   Chloro benzene

103. *(d)* The complex $[CoCl_3(NH_3)_3]$ cannot ionise in the solution as there is no primary valency in this compound and all the ions are within the coordination entity.

104. *(a)* The reaction $C(s) + O_2(g) \longrightarrow CO_2(g) + 393.5$ kJ is a combustion reaction.

For combustion reaction. ΔH and ΔG are negative but ΔS is positive.

105. *(c)* The product formed, when hydroxylamine condenses with a carbonyl compound is called oxime.

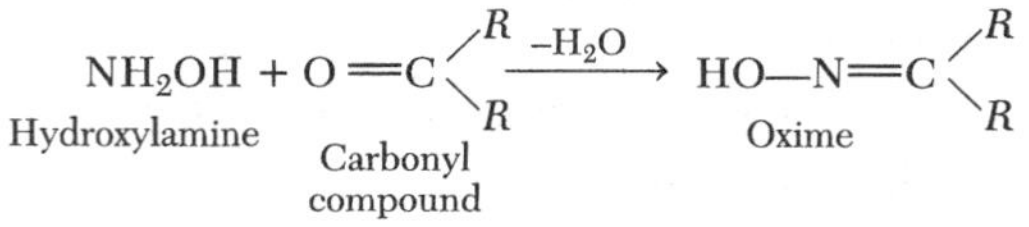

106. *(b)* The electronic configuration of Sc is

$1s^2 2s^2 2p^6 3s^2 3p^6 3d^1 4s^2$

Electronic configuration of Sc^{3+} is $1s^2 2s^2 2p^6 3s^2 3p^6$.

So, Sc^{3+} is colourless due to the absence of unpaired electrons in d-orbital.

107. *(b)* When a sulphur sol is evaporated, sulphur is obtained. On mixing with water, sulphur sol is not formed.

The sol is hydrophobic. Hydrophobic sols are irreversible in nature.

There is a little affinity between the dispersed phase and the dispersion medium.

108. *(d)* When an alkyl halide reacts with alcoholic ammonia in a sealed tube, the product formed will be mixture of primary, secondary and tertiary amine.

109. *(c)* When conc. H_2SO_4 is heated with P_2O_5, the acid is converted into sulphur trioxide.

$$H_2SO_4 + P_2O_5 \longrightarrow SO_3 + 2HPO_3$$

110. *(a)* According to second law of thermodynamics, entropy of the universe is continuously increasing.

111. *(d)* KCN is a salt of strong base (KOH) and weak acid (HCN).

$$KCN + H_2O \rightleftharpoons \underset{\text{Strong base}}{KOH} + \underset{\text{Weak acid}}{HCN}$$

$\therefore$ pH of the solution is greater than 7 at 25°C.

112. *(c)* The reagent used in Clemmenson's reduction is Zn - Hg / conc. HCl. It is used for reduction of carbonyl group to alkanes.

113. *(d)* When KBr is dissolved in water, K^+ ions are hydrated due to ionic nature. KBr is soluble in water due to hydration of K^+ ion by H_2O molecule.

114. *(a)* When the mixture of noble gas is cooled in coconut bulb at 173K, the gases that are not absorbed are He and Ne. As they have low critical temperature.

115. *(d)* Let the volume of 10 N HCl used is x litre.

$\therefore$ The volume of 4N HCl used is $(1 - x)$ litre.

$$\therefore \quad 7 = \frac{10 \times x + 4 \times (10 - x)}{1}$$

$$\therefore \quad x = 0.5 \text{ L}$$

$\therefore$ Volume of 10 N HCl and 4 N HCl used is 0.5 L each.

116. *(c)* The metal present in insulin is zinc.

117. *(b)* The equivalent mass of oxygen in CO and CO_2 remains constant. While, that of carbon changes as it have different oxidation state in different compound.

118. *(d)* Maximum number of molecules of CH_3I, that can react with CH_3NH_2 is 3. The reaction is as follows :

$$CH_3{-}NH_2 \xrightarrow{CH_3I} (CH_3)_2NH \xrightarrow{CH_3I} (CH_3)_3N \xrightarrow{CH_3I} \underset{\text{Tetramethyl ammonium iodide}}{(CH_3)_4\overset{+}{N}\overset{-}{I}}$$

119. *(b)* Ellingham diagram represent a graph of ΔG° *vs* T. It shows the temperature dependence of the stability of compound.

120. *(b)* The ore not containing iron is carnallite. It's formula is $KCl \cdot MgCl_2 \cdot 6H_2O$.

Mathematics

121. *(d)* We have,

$$7^{2\log_7 5}$$

$$= 7^{\log_7 5^2} \quad [\because m\log a = \log a^m]$$

$$= 5^2 \quad [\because a^{\log_a b} = b]$$

$$= 25$$

122. *(a)* The composition table is

$\otimes_{15}$	3	6	9	12
3	9	3	12	6
6	3	6	9	12
9	12	9	6	3
12	6	12	3	9

From the table 6 is the identity element.

123. *(a)* Since, identity element is its own inverse.

So, minimum number of element is 1.

124. *(d)* We have,

$$|\mathbf{a} + \mathbf{b}| = |\mathbf{a} - \mathbf{b}|$$

$$\Rightarrow |\mathbf{a} + \mathbf{b}|^2 = |\mathbf{a} - \mathbf{b}|^2$$

$$\Rightarrow (\mathbf{a} + \mathbf{b})\cdot(\mathbf{a} + \mathbf{b}) = (\mathbf{a} - \mathbf{b})\cdot(\mathbf{a} - \mathbf{b})$$

$$\Rightarrow |\mathbf{a}|^2 + |\mathbf{b}|^2 + 2\mathbf{a}\cdot\mathbf{b} = |\mathbf{a}|^2 + |\mathbf{b}|^2 - 2\mathbf{a}\cdot\mathbf{b}$$

$$\Rightarrow 4\mathbf{a}\cdot\mathbf{b} = 0$$

$$\Rightarrow \mathbf{a}\cdot\mathbf{b} = 0$$

$$\Rightarrow \mathbf{a} \perp \mathbf{b}$$

So, angle between **a** and **b** is 90°.

125. *(b)* We have,

$$\frac{3x^2 + 1}{x^2 - 6x + 8} = 3 + \frac{18x - 23}{x^2 - 6x + 8}$$

$$= 3 + \frac{18x - 23}{(x - 4)(x - 2)}$$

Again, let $\frac{18x - 23}{(x - 4)(x - 2)} = \frac{A}{x - 4} + \frac{B}{x - 2}$

$$\Rightarrow 18x - 23 = A(x - 2) + B(x - 4)$$

Put $x = 4$, we get

$$72 - 23 = 2A \Rightarrow A = \frac{49}{2}$$

Put $x = 2$, we get

$$36 - 23 = -2B$$

$$\Rightarrow B = \frac{-13}{2}$$

So, $\frac{3x^2 + 1}{x^2 - 6x + 8} = 3 + \frac{49}{2(x - 4)} - \frac{13}{2(x - 2)}$

126. *(c)* We know that, any vector perpendicular to **a** and in the plane containing **b** and **c** is **a** × (**b**× **c**).

$$\text{Now, } \mathbf{b} \times \mathbf{c} = \begin{vmatrix} \mathbf{i} & \mathbf{j} & \mathbf{k} \\ 1 & 2 & -5 \\ 3 & 5 & -1 \end{vmatrix} = 23\mathbf{i} - 14\mathbf{j} - \mathbf{k}$$

$$\text{Again, } \mathbf{a} \times (\mathbf{b} \times \mathbf{c}) = \begin{vmatrix} \mathbf{i} & \mathbf{j} & \mathbf{k} \\ 2 & 3 & -1 \\ 23 & -14 & -1 \end{vmatrix}$$

$$= -17\mathbf{i} - 21\mathbf{j} - 97\mathbf{k}$$

which is required vector.

127. *(a)* We have,

$|\mathbf{OA}| = 5, |\mathbf{OB}| = 6, \angle \mathbf{BOA} = 60°$

Now, $\mathbf{OA}\cdot\mathbf{OB} = |\mathbf{OA}|\,|\mathbf{OB}| \cos(\angle BOA)$

$$= 5 \times 6 \cos 60° = 5 \times 6 \times \frac{1}{2} = 15$$

128. *(a)* We have,

$A(1, -1, 2)$, $B(2, 0, -1)$ and $C(0, 2, 1)$

$$\therefore \quad \mathbf{AB} = (2 - 1)\mathbf{i} + (0 - (-1))\mathbf{j} + (-1 - 2)\mathbf{k}$$

$$= \mathbf{i} + \mathbf{j} - 3\mathbf{k}$$

and $\mathbf{AC} = (0 - 1)\mathbf{i} + (2 - (-1))\mathbf{j} + (1 - 2)\mathbf{k}$

$$= -\mathbf{i} + 3\mathbf{j} - \mathbf{k}$$

Now, required vector = **AB** × **AC**

$$= \begin{vmatrix} \mathbf{i} & \mathbf{j} & \mathbf{k} \\ 1 & 1 & -3 \\ -1 & 3 & -1 \end{vmatrix}$$

$$= 8\mathbf{i} + 4\mathbf{j} + 4\mathbf{k}$$

129. *(d)* Let $S_n = \frac{1}{2\times 5} + \frac{1}{5 \times 8} + \frac{1}{8\times 11} + \dots + \frac{1}{(3n - 1)(3n + 2)}$

$$= \frac{1}{3}\left[\frac{3}{2\times 5} + \frac{3}{5 \times 8} + \frac{3}{8\times 11} + \dots + \frac{3}{(3n - 1)(3n + 2)}\right]$$

$$= \frac{1}{3}\left[\frac{5 - 2}{2\times 5} + \frac{8 - 5}{5 \times 8} + \frac{11 - 8}{8\times 11} + \dots + \frac{(3n + 2) - (3n - 1)}{(3n - 1)(3n + 2)}\right]$$

$$= \frac{1}{3}\left[\frac{1}{2} - \frac{1}{5} + \frac{1}{5} - \frac{1}{8} + \frac{1}{8} - \frac{1}{11} + \dots + \frac{1}{3n - 1} - \frac{1}{3n + 2}\right]$$

$$= \frac{1}{3}\left[\frac{1}{2} - \frac{1}{3n + 2}\right] = \frac{1}{3}\left[\frac{3n + 2 - 2}{2(3n + 2)}\right]$$

$$= \frac{n}{2(3n + 2)} = \frac{n}{6n + 4}$$

130. (c) $T_9 = T_{8+1}$

$$= {}^8C_8(3x)^{8-8}\left(\frac{-1}{2x}\right)^8$$

$$= {}^8C_8(3x)^0\left(\frac{-1}{2x}\right)^8$$

$$= 1 \times 1 \times \frac{1}{2^8x^8} = \frac{1}{256x^8}$$

131. (d) We have,

$$A = \begin{bmatrix} 1 & -1 & 1 \\ 2 & 1 & -3 \\ 1 & 1 & 1 \end{bmatrix} \text{ and } B = \frac{1}{10}\begin{bmatrix} 4 & 2 & 2 \\ -5 & 0 & \alpha \\ 1 & -2 & 3 \end{bmatrix}$$

Since, B is inverse of A, then

$AB = I$

$$\Rightarrow \frac{1}{10}\begin{bmatrix} 1 & -1 & 1 \\ 2 & 1 & -3 \\ 1 & 1 & 1 \end{bmatrix}\begin{bmatrix} 4 & 2 & 2 \\ -5 & 0 & \alpha \\ 1 & -2 & 3 \end{bmatrix} = \begin{bmatrix} 1 & 0 & 0 \\ 0 & 1 & 0 \\ 0 & 0 & 1 \end{bmatrix}$$

$$\Rightarrow \frac{1}{10}\begin{bmatrix} 10 & 0 & 5-\alpha \\ 0 & 10 & \alpha-5 \\ 0 & 0 & 5+\alpha \end{bmatrix} = \begin{bmatrix} 1 & 0 & 0 \\ 0 & 1 & 0 \\ 0 & 0 & 1 \end{bmatrix}$$

$$\Rightarrow \begin{bmatrix} 10 & 0 & 5-\alpha \\ 0 & 10 & \alpha-5 \\ 0 & 0 & 5+\alpha \end{bmatrix} = \begin{bmatrix} 10 & 0 & 0 \\ 0 & 10 & 0 \\ 0 & 0 & 10 \end{bmatrix}$$

$\therefore 5 - \alpha = 0$ or $\alpha - 5 = 0$ or $5 + \alpha = 10$

$\Rightarrow \quad \alpha = 5$

132. (b) Since, A is singular matrix, then

$$|A| = 0$$

$$\begin{vmatrix} 0 & x & 16 \\ x & 5 & 7 \\ 0 & 9 & x \end{vmatrix} = 0$$

$\Rightarrow -x[x^2 - 144] = 0 \quad \Rightarrow \quad x = 0, \pm 12$

133. (d) We have,

$$A = \begin{bmatrix} 1 & -2 & 2 \\ 0 & 2 & -3 \\ 3 & -2 & 4 \end{bmatrix}$$

$$\therefore \quad |A| = \begin{bmatrix} 1 & -2 & 2 \\ 0 & 2 & -3 \\ 3 & -2 & 4 \end{bmatrix}$$

$$= 1[8-6] + 3[6-4] = 2 + 6 = 8$$

Now, we know that

$$A\cdot(\text{adj}A) = 8I = \begin{bmatrix} 8 & 0 & 0 \\ 0 & 8 & 0 \\ 0 & 0 & 8 \end{bmatrix}$$

134. (d) Since, $f(x) = |x|$ is neither one-one nor onto, so $f(x)$ is not invertible.

$\therefore f^{-1}(x)$ does not exist.

135. (a) We have,

$$\begin{bmatrix} x & p & q \\ p & x & q \\ p & q & x \end{bmatrix}$$

Applying $C_1 \to C_1 + C_2 + C_3$, we get

$$\begin{vmatrix} x+p+q & p & q \\ x+p+q & x & q \\ x+p+q & q & x \end{vmatrix}$$

Taking common $(x + p + q)$ from C_1, we get

$$(x+p+q)\begin{vmatrix} 1 & p & q \\ 1 & x & q \\ 1 & q & x \end{vmatrix}$$

Applying $R_1 \to R_1 - R_2$, $R_2 \to R_2 - R_3$, we get

$$(x+p+q)\begin{vmatrix} 0 & p-x & 0 \\ 0 & x-q & q-x \\ 1 & q & x \end{vmatrix}$$

$$= (x+p+q)\cdot 1\,[(p-x)(q-x) - 0]$$

$$= (x-p)(x-q)(x+p+q)$$

136. (c) We have,

Equation of circle is $x^2 + y^2 = 4$. Its centre is $C_1(0, 0)$ and radius (r_1) is 2.

Equation of another circle is

$$x^2 + y^2 - 6x - 8y - 24 = 0$$

i.e. $(x-3)^2 + (y-4)^2 = (7)^2$. Its centre is $C_2(3, 4)$ and radius (r_2) is 7.

Now, $C_1C_2 = \sqrt{(3-0)^2 + (4-0)^2} = 5$

and $|r_1 - r_2| = |2 - 7| = 5$

$\therefore \quad C_1C_2 = |r_1 - r_2|$

So, both circles touch each other internally.

Hence, number of common tangents is 1.

137. (d) We have, $3x + y + k = 0$ is tangent to the circle $x^2 + y^2 = 10$.

So, distance of line $3x + y + k = 0$ from centre of the circle will be equal to the radius of circle.

$$\therefore \quad \left|\frac{3(0) + (0) + K}{\sqrt{(3)^2 + (1)^2}}\right| = \sqrt{10}$$

$$\Rightarrow \quad \frac{K}{\sqrt{10}} = \pm\sqrt{10} \quad \Rightarrow K = \pm 10$$

138. (a) Negation of $\sim(p \to q) = p \wedge \sim q$

So, negation of given statement is

If 2 is prime and 3 is not odd.

139. *(b)*

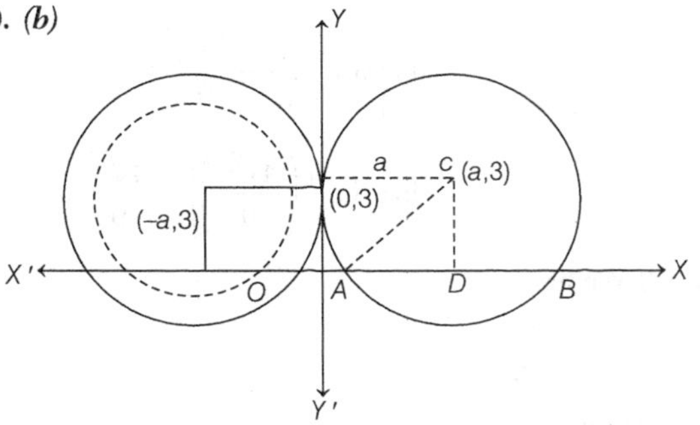

Equation of circle will be

$$(x \pm a)^2 + (y - 3)^2 = a^2 \quad \dots(i)$$

Now, in ΔACD,

$$AC^2 = AD^2 + CD^2$$

$$\Rightarrow \quad a^2 = (4)^2 + (3)^2$$

$$\left[\because AC = a,\ AD = \frac{1}{2} AB = 4,\ CD = 3\right]$$

$$\Rightarrow \quad a^2 = 25 \ \Rightarrow a = 5$$

So, equation of circles will be

$$(x \pm 5)^2 + (y - 3)^2 = 5^2$$

$$\Rightarrow x^2 \pm 10x + 25 + y^2 - 6y + 9 = 25$$

$$\Rightarrow \quad x^2 + y^2 \pm 10x - 6y + 9 = 0$$

140. *(a)* The triangle formed with vertices $A(0, 0)$, $B\left(0, \frac{3}{2}\right)$ and $C(-5, 0)$ is a right-angled triangle at A. So, BC is hypotenuse.

So, orthocentre of ΔABC is mid-point of BC.

$$\therefore \text{Orthocentre} = \left(\frac{0-5}{2}, \frac{\frac{3}{2}+0}{2}\right) = \left(\frac{-5}{2}, \frac{3}{4}\right)$$

141. *(d)* Let

$$S_1 : x^2 + y^2 - 6x - 6y + 4 = 0$$

$$S_2 : x^2 + y^2 - 2x - 4y + 3 = 0$$

$$S_3 : x^2 + y^2 + 2kx + 2y + 1 = 0$$

Now, radical cnetre of S_1 and S_2 is given by

$$S_1 - S_2 = 0$$

$$\Rightarrow \quad -4x - 2y + 1 = 0$$

$$\Rightarrow \quad 4x + 2y - 1 = 0 \quad \dots(i)$$

Radical centre of S_2 and S_3 is given by

$$S_2 - S_3 = 0$$

$$-2(1 + k)x - 6y + 2 = 0$$

$$(1 + k)x + 3y - 1 = 0 \quad \dots(ii)$$

Now, Eq. (ii) becomes, if

$$k = 1 : 2x + 3y - 1 = 0$$

$$k = 2 : 3x + 3y - 1 = 0$$

$$k = 4 : 5x + 3y - 1 = 0$$

$$k = 5 : 6x + 3y - 1 = 0$$

Now, only $6x + 3y - 1 = 0$ is parallel to $4x + 2y - 1 = 0$

So, for this radical centre does not exists.

So, $k \neq 5$

142. *(b)* We have,

$$S_1 : x^2 + y^2 - 2x - 2y - 7 = 0$$

$$S_2 : x^2 + y^2 + 4x + 2y + k = 0$$

Since, S_1 and S_2 cut orthogonally, then

$$2g_1g_2 + 2f_1f_2 = c_1 + c_2$$

$$\Rightarrow \quad 2(-1)(2) + 2(-1)(1) = -7 + k$$

$$\Rightarrow \quad -4 - 2 = -7 + k$$

$$\Rightarrow \quad k' = 1$$

Now, let r_1 and r_2 be the radius of S_1 and S_2, respectively. Then,

$$r_1 = \sqrt{(-1)^2 + (-1)^2 - (-7)} = 3$$

$$r_2 = \sqrt{(2)^2 + (1)^2 - 1} = 2$$

Now, length of common chord

$$= \frac{2r_1r_2}{\sqrt{r_1^2 + r_2^2}}$$

$$= \frac{2 \times 3 \times 2}{\sqrt{(3)^2 + (2)^2}} = \frac{12}{\sqrt{13}}$$

143. *(b)*

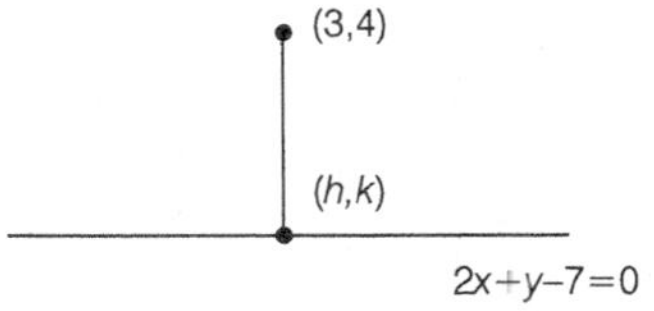

Let (h, k) be the coordinate of foot of perpendicular.

Now, slope of line $2x + y - 7 = 0$ is $\left(\frac{-2}{1}\right)$, i.e. -2.

So, slope of perpendicular line.

$$= \frac{-1}{(-2)} = \frac{1}{2}$$

$\therefore$ Equation of perpendicular line is given by

$$y - 4 = \frac{1}{2}(x - 3)$$

$$\Rightarrow \quad 2y - 8 = x - 3$$

$$\Rightarrow \quad x - 2y + 5 = 0$$

On solving $2x + y - 7 = 0$ and $x - 2y + 5 = 0$,

we get $x = \frac{9}{5}$ and $y = \frac{17}{5}$

So, $(h, k) = \left(\frac{9}{5}, \frac{17}{5}\right)$

144. *(b)* We have,

$$xy = 0, x - 4 = 0, y + 5 = 0$$

$$\Rightarrow \quad x = 0, y = 0, x = 4, y = -5$$

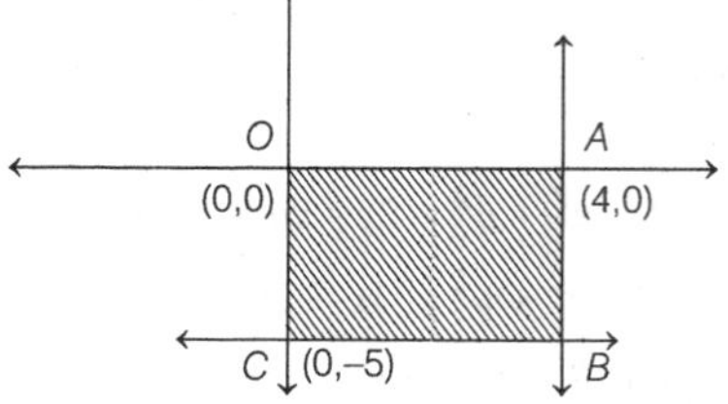

So, area enclosed = Area of rectangle $OABC$

$$= AB \times BC$$
$$= 5 \times 4$$
$$= 20 \text{ sq units}$$

145. *(a)* Equation of ellipse is $\frac{x^2}{a^2} + \frac{y^2}{b^2} = 1$

Then, equation of auxillary circle will be

$$x^2 + y^2 = a^2 \quad (a > b)$$

Now, it is given that

Area of auxillary circle = 2 × Area of ellipse

$$\Rightarrow \quad \pi a^2 = 2 \times \pi ab$$

$$\Rightarrow \quad a = 2b$$

Now, eccentricity of the ellipse,

$$e = \sqrt{1 - \frac{b^2}{a^2}} = \sqrt{1 - \frac{b^2}{(2b)^2}}$$

$$= \sqrt{1 - \frac{b^2}{4b^2}} = \sqrt{1 - \frac{1}{4}} = \frac{\sqrt{3}}{2}$$

146. *(a)* Since, the number of vertices of odd degree is always even and number of even degree is always even.

So, $m + n$ is an even number.

147. *(c)* We have, equation of ellipse is

$$\frac{x^2}{36} + \frac{y^2}{16} = 1 \Rightarrow \frac{x^2}{(6)^2} + \frac{y^2}{(4)^2} = 1$$

$$\therefore \quad a = 6, b = 4$$

Now, $PS + PS' = 2a = 2 \times 6 = 12$

148. *(d)* We have,

$$\sin\left(2\cos^{-1}\frac{\sqrt{5}}{3}\right) = \sin\left\{\cos^{-1}\left(2 \times \left(\frac{\sqrt{5}}{3}\right)^2 - 1\right)\right\}$$

$$= \sin\left\{\cos^{-1}\left(\frac{10}{9} - 1\right)\right\}$$

$$= \sin\left(\cos^{-1}\frac{1}{9}\right)$$

$$= \sin\left\{\sin^{-1}\sqrt{1 - \left(\frac{1}{9}\right)^2}\right\}$$

$$= \sin\left\{\sin^{-1}\left(\frac{4\sqrt{5}}{9}\right)\right\} = \frac{4\sqrt{5}}{9}$$

149. *(d)* We have,

$$\frac{x^2}{36} - \frac{y^2}{k^2} = 1$$

Option (a) (3, 1)

$$\frac{9}{36} - \frac{1}{k^2} = 1$$

$$\Rightarrow \quad \frac{1}{k^2} = \frac{-27}{36} \Rightarrow k^2 = \frac{-36}{27}$$

which is not possible.

Option (b) (– 3, 1)

$$\frac{9}{36} - \frac{1}{k^2} = 1 \Rightarrow k^2 = \frac{-36}{27}$$

which is not possible.

Option (c) (5, 2)

$$\frac{25}{36} - \frac{4}{k^2} = 1$$

$$\frac{4}{k^2} = \frac{-11}{36}$$

$$k^2 = \frac{-144}{11}$$

which is not possible.

Option (d) (10, 4)

$$\frac{100}{36} - \frac{16}{k^2} = 1 \Rightarrow \frac{16}{k^2} = \frac{64}{36}$$

$\Rightarrow k^2 = 9$, which is possible.

150. *(*)* Because information is not sufficient.

151. *(c)* We have,

$$\tan^{-1}x + 2\cot^{-1}x = \frac{2\pi}{3}$$

$$\Rightarrow \quad \tan^{-1}x + \cot^{-1}x + \cot^{-1}x = \frac{2\pi}{3}$$

$$\Rightarrow \quad \frac{\pi}{2} + \cot^{-1}x = \frac{2\pi}{3}$$

$$\Rightarrow \quad \cot^{-1}x = \frac{\pi}{6}$$

$$\Rightarrow \quad x = \cot\frac{\pi}{6} = \sqrt{3}$$

152. *(a)* We have,

$$\sin^2 17.5° + \sin^2 72.5° = \sin^2 17.5° + \cos^2(90° - 72.5°)$$

$$= \sin^2 17.5° + \cos^2 17.5° = 1 = \tan^2 45°$$

153. *(c)* Let $Z = \frac{(1+i)^2}{1-i} = \frac{1+i^2+2i}{1-i} = \frac{2i}{1-i} \times \frac{1+i}{1+i}$

$$= \frac{2i+2i^2}{1-i^2} = \frac{2i-2}{1+1} = \frac{2i-2}{2} = -1+i$$

$\therefore \quad \overline{Z} = -1-i$

154. *(b)*

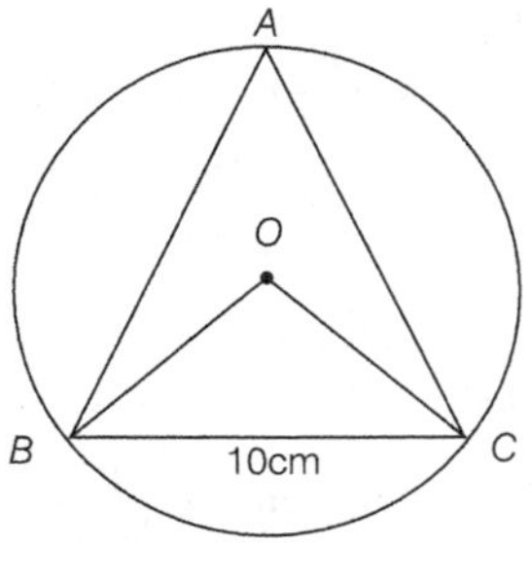

We know that,

$\angle BOC = 2\angle BAC = 2 \times 30° = 60°$

Since, $OB = OC$

$\therefore \ \angle OBC = \angle OCB = \frac{1}{2}(180° - \angle BOC) = 60°$

So, ΔBOC is an equilateral triangle.

$\therefore \quad OB = BC = 10$ cm

Therefore, area of circumcircle $= \pi(OB)^2 = \pi(10)^2$

$= 100\,\pi$ sq cm

155. *(a)* We have,

$$\sin 3\theta = \sin\theta$$

$\Rightarrow \quad 3\sin\theta - 4\sin^3\theta = \sin\theta$

$\Rightarrow \quad 4\sin^3\theta - 2\sin\theta = 0$

$\Rightarrow \quad 2\sin\theta(2\sin^2\theta - 1) = 0$

$\Rightarrow \quad \sin\theta = 0$ or $\sin\theta = \pm\frac{1}{\sqrt{2}}$

If $\sin\theta = 0$ and if $\sin\theta = \pm\frac{1}{\sqrt{2}}$

$\theta = 0, \pi, -\pi$

$\Rightarrow \ \theta = \frac{\pi}{4}, \frac{3\pi}{4}, \frac{-5\pi}{4}, \frac{-7\pi}{4}, \frac{-\pi}{4}, \frac{-3\pi}{4}, \frac{5\pi}{4}, \frac{7\pi}{4}$

$\therefore$There are nine solutions.

156. *(b)* We have,

$$e^{ix} = \cos x + i\sin x$$

Put $x = \frac{\pi}{2}$

$\Rightarrow \quad e^{i\frac{\pi}{2}} = \cos\frac{\pi}{2} + i\sin\frac{\pi}{2}$

$\Rightarrow \quad e^{i\frac{\pi}{2}} = i \Rightarrow e^{i^2\frac{\pi}{2}} = (i)^i \Rightarrow i^i = e^{-\frac{\pi}{2}}$

$\therefore$Imaginary part of i^i is zero.

157. *(a)* Let $Z = (1+i)^5$

$= [(1+i)^2]^2\,[1+i]$

$= [1+i^2+2i]^2[1+i] = (2i)^2(1+i)$

$= -4(1+i) = -4-4i$

Let θ be amplitude of z. Then,

$$\theta = \tan^{-1}\left|\frac{-4}{-4}\right| - \pi = \tan^{-1}(1) - \pi$$

$$= \frac{\pi}{4} - \pi = \frac{-3\pi}{4}$$

158. *(a)* We know that, centroid divides median in the ratio 2 : 1.

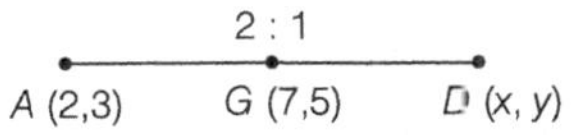

$$(7,5) = \left(\frac{2x+2}{2+1}, \frac{2y+3}{2+1}\right)$$

$$(7,5) = \left(\frac{2x+2}{3}, \frac{2y+3}{3}\right)$$

$\therefore \quad \frac{2x+2}{3} = 7$ and $\frac{2y+3}{3} = 5$

$\Rightarrow \quad x = \frac{19}{2}$ and $y = 6$

$\therefore \ D$ is $\left(\frac{19}{2}, 6\right)$.

159. *(b)* We have,

$$\lim_{x\to 1} \frac{\tan(x^2-1)}{x-1}$$

$= \lim_{x\to 1} \frac{\sec^2(x^2-1)\cdot 2x}{1}$ [using L' Hospital Rule]

$= 2\sec^2 0 = 2$

160. *(c)* We have,

$$y = 2^{\log x}$$

$\therefore \quad \frac{dy}{dx} = 2^{\log x}\cdot\log 2\cdot\frac{d}{dx}(\log x) = \frac{2^{\log x}\log 2}{x}$

161. *(b)* We have,

$$\sec^{-1}\left(\frac{1+x}{1-y}\right) = a \Rightarrow \frac{1+x}{1-y} = \sec a$$

$\Rightarrow \quad \dfrac{1(1-y) - (1+x)\left(-\frac{dy}{dx}\right)}{(1-y)^2} = 0$

$\Rightarrow \quad 1 - y + (1+x)\frac{dy}{dx} = 0 \Rightarrow \frac{dy}{dx} = \frac{y-1}{x+1}$

162. *(d)* We have,

$$y = \cos^2\frac{3x}{2} - \sin^2\frac{3x}{2} \Rightarrow y = \cos 3x$$

$\Rightarrow \quad \frac{dy}{dx} = -\sin 3x \cdot 3 = -3\sin 3x$

and $\quad \frac{d^2y}{dx^2} = -3\cos 3x \cdot 3 = -9\cos 3x = -9y$

163. *(d)* We have,

$$f(x) = \begin{cases} \frac{1-\cos x}{x^2}, & x \neq 0 \\ k, & x = 0 \end{cases}$$

Since, $f(x)$ is continuous at $x = 0$, then

$$f(0) = \lim_{x \to 0} f(x) \Rightarrow k = \lim_{x \to 0} \frac{1-\cos x}{x^2}$$

$$\Rightarrow \quad k = \lim_{x \to 0} \frac{\sin x}{2x} \quad \text{[using L' Hospital Rule]}$$

$$\Rightarrow \quad k = \frac{1}{2}$$

164. *(b)* We have,

$(1+\omega)(1+\omega^2)(1+\omega^4)(1+\omega^8)$

$= (1+\omega)(1+\omega^2)(1+\omega)(1+\omega^2)$

$[\because \omega^4 = \omega^3 \cdot \omega = \omega \text{ and } \omega^8 = (\omega^3)^2 \cdot \omega^2 = \omega^2]$

$= ((1+\omega)(1+\omega^2))^2 = (1+\omega+\omega^2+\omega^3)^2$

$= (\omega^3)^2 \quad [\because 1+\omega+\omega^2 = 0]$

$= (1)^2 = 1 \quad [\because \omega^3 = 1]$

165. *(c)* We have,

$$x^x = y^y \Rightarrow x\log x = y\log y$$

$$\Rightarrow \quad 1 \cdot \log x + \frac{x}{x} = y' \log y + \frac{y}{y} y'$$

$$\Rightarrow \quad \log x + 1 = y'(\log y + 1)$$

$$\Rightarrow \quad \frac{dy}{dx} = \frac{1+\log x}{1+\log y}$$

166. *(b)* We have,

$$y^2 = x$$

$$\Rightarrow \quad 2y\frac{dy}{dx} = 1 \Rightarrow \frac{dy}{dx} = \frac{1}{2y}$$

Let the required point be (x_1, y_1). So, slope of tangent $= \left.\frac{dy}{dx}\right|_{(x_1, y_1)}$

$$\Rightarrow \quad m = \frac{1}{2y_1} \quad \ldots(i)$$

Since, tangent makes 45° with X-axis, so

$$m = \tan 45° = 1 \quad \ldots(ii)$$

From Eqs. (i) and (ii), we have

$$\frac{1}{2y_1} = 1 \Rightarrow y_1 = \frac{1}{2}$$

Again, (x_1, y_1) lies on th curve $y^2 = x$. So,

$$y_1^2 = x_1 \Rightarrow x_1 = \left(\frac{1}{2}\right)^2 = \frac{1}{4}$$

So, required point is $\left(\frac{1}{4}, \frac{1}{2}\right)$.

167. *(d)* We have,

$$x^2y^2 = a^4 \Rightarrow 2xy^2 + x^2(2yy') = 0$$

$$\Rightarrow \quad y' = \frac{-2xy^2}{2x^2y} = \frac{-y}{x}$$

$$\therefore \quad \left.\frac{dy}{dx}\right|_{(-a,\, a)} = \frac{-a}{-a} = 1$$

Now, length of subtangent $= \left|\frac{y}{dy/dx}\right| = \left|\frac{a}{1}\right| = a$

168. *(d)* We have,

$$252 = 2^2 \times 3^2 \times 7^1$$

$\therefore$ Number of positive divisors of

$$252 = (2+1)(2+1)(1+1) = 3 \times 3 \times 2 = 18$$

169. *(b)* We have,

$$5^{124} = (5^3)^{41} \cdot 5$$

Now, $5^3 = 1 \cdot (\text{mod } 124)$

$(5^3)^{41} = 1 \cdot (\text{mod } 124)$

$(5^3)^{41} \cdot 5 = 1 \times 5 \ (\text{mod } 124) = 5 \ (\text{mod } 124)$

So, the remainder obtained when 5^{124} is divided by 124 is 5.

170. *(a)* **Option** (a) Since, sum of two odd integers is an even integer. Closure property does not hold.

So, it is not a group.

Option (b) Since, sum of two even integers is an even integer.

So, it is a group.

Option (c) $1 \times (-1) = -1$, which belongs to given set.

So, it is a group.

Option (d) $0 + 0 = 0$, which belongs to given set.

So, it is a group.

171. *(b)* We have,

$$y = -x^2 + 6x - 3 \Rightarrow \frac{dy}{dx} = -2x + 6$$

Now, for increasing.

$$\frac{dy}{dx} > 0 \Rightarrow -2x + 6 > 0$$

$$\Rightarrow \quad 2x < 6 \Rightarrow x < 3$$

So, for $x < 3$, $f(x)$ is increasing.

172. (c) Let $I = \int_0^{\pi/2} (\sin^{100} x - \cos^{100} x)\, dx$ ...(i)

$\Rightarrow \quad I = \int_0^{\pi/2} \left(\sin^{100}\left(\frac{\pi}{2} - x\right) - \cos^{100}\left(\frac{\pi}{2} - x\right)\right) dx$

$[\because \int_0^a f(x)\, dx = \int_0^a f(a-x)\, dx]$

$\Rightarrow \quad I = \int_0^{\pi/2} (\cos^{100} x - \sin^{100} x)\, dx$ ...(ii)

On adding Eqs. (i) and (iii), we get

$2I = 0 \Rightarrow I = 0$

173. (b) After time t hour distance covered by X and Y are $4t$ and $3t$ respectively.

Now, shortest distance between X and Y after time t hour is given by

$$AB^2 = OA^2 + OB^2 - 2OA \cdot OB \cos\theta$$
$$= (4t)^2 + (3t)^2 - 2 \times 4t \times 3t \cos 120°$$
$$= 16t^2 + 9t^2 - 24t^2 \times \left(\frac{-1}{2}\right)$$
$$= 16t^2 + 9t^2 + 12t^2 = 37t^2$$

$\Rightarrow \quad AB = \sqrt{37}t$

Now, $\frac{d(AB)}{dt} = \sqrt{37}$

$\therefore$ Rate at which the shortest distance between x and y is increasing is $\sqrt{37}$ km/h.

174. (b) Let $I = \int_0^3 t f(t)$

Put $t = 3x \Rightarrow dt = 3\,dx$

When $t = 0 \Rightarrow x = 0$

and $t = 3 \Rightarrow x = 1$

$\therefore \quad I = \int_0^1 3x f(3x)\,(3\,dx)$

$= 9\int_0^1 x f(3x)\, dx$

$= k\int_0^1 x f(3x)\, dx$

$\therefore \quad k = 9$

175. (c) Let $I = \int \frac{1}{1 + \cos 8x}\, dx$

$= \int \frac{1}{2\cos^2 4x}\, dx = \frac{1}{2}\int \sec^2 4x\, dx$

$= \frac{1}{2}\left(\frac{\tan 4x}{4}\right) + C = \frac{1}{8}\tan 4x + C$

176. (a) Let $I = \int e^x (x^5 + 5x^4 + 1)\, dx$

$= \int \underset{\text{II}}{e^x} \underset{\text{I}}{(x^5 + 1)}\, dx + \int e^x (5x^4)\, dx$

$= (x^5 + 1)\int e^x\, dx - \int\left[\left(\int e^x dx\right)\frac{d}{dx}(x^5 + 1)\right] dx + \int e^x (5x^4)\, dx$

$= (x^5 + 1)e^x - \int e^x (5x^4)\, dx + \int e^x (5x^4)\, dx$

$= (x^5 + 1)e^x + C = e^x \cdot x^5 + e^x + C$

177. (d) Let $I = \int \frac{x^2 + 1}{x^2 - 1}\, dx = \int \frac{x^2 - 1 + 2}{x^2 - 1}\, dx$

$= \int \left(1 + \frac{2}{x^2 - 1}\right) dx = x + 2 \times \frac{1}{2}\log\left|\frac{x - 1}{x + 1}\right| + C$

$= x + \log\left|\frac{x-1}{x+1}\right| + C$

178. (d) We have,

$x = 4 - y^2 \Rightarrow y^2 = -(x - 4)$

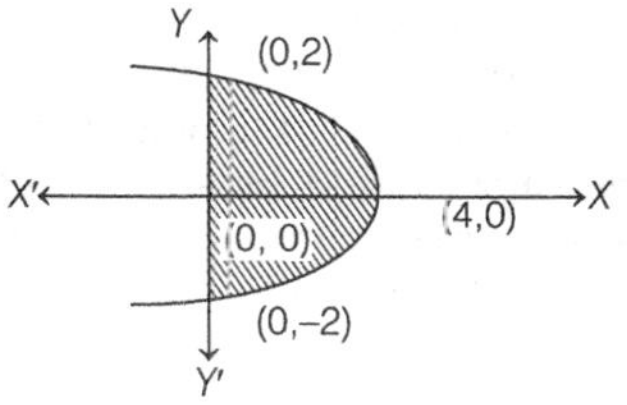

Required area $= 2\int_0^4 y\, dx = 2\int_0^4 \sqrt{4 - x}\, dx$

$= 2\left[\frac{-(4 - x)^{3/2}}{3/2}\right]_0^4$

$= \frac{-4}{3}[(4-4)^{3/2} - (4-0)^{3/2}]$

$= \frac{-4}{3}(-8) = \frac{32}{3}$ sq units

179. (b) We have, equation of line is

$y = mx + C$

But $m = C$ (given)

$\therefore \quad y = Cx + C$

Now, $\frac{dy}{dx} = C$

$\therefore \quad y = \frac{dy}{dx}(x + 1) \Rightarrow (x + 1)\frac{dy}{dx} - y = 0$

which is required differential equation.

180. (c) We have,

$$\left[1 + \left(\frac{dy}{dx}\right)^5\right]^{1/3} = \frac{d^2y}{dx^2} \Rightarrow \left(\frac{d^2y}{dx^2}\right)^3 = 1 + \left(\frac{dy}{dx}\right)^5$$

$\therefore$ Order = 2 and degree = 3

COMEDK

Solved Paper 2019

Instructions

- There are 180 questions in all. The number of questions in each section is as given below.

Sections	No. of Questions
Section I : Physics	1-60
Section II : Chemistry	61-120
Section III : Mathematics	121-180

- All the questions are Multiple Choice Questions having four options out of which **ONLY ONE** is correct.
- Candidates will be awarded 1 mark for each correct answer. There will be no negative marking for incorrect answer.
- Time allotted to complete this paper is 3 hrs.

PHYSICS

1. A thin plano-convex lens acts like a concave mirror of focal length 0.2 m when silvered from its plane surface. The refractive index of the material of the lens is 1.5. The radius of curvature of the convex surface of the lens will be

a. 0.4 m *b.* 0.2 m
c. 0.1 m *d.* 0.75 m

2. The physical quantity having the same dimensions as Planck's constant h is

a. Boltzmann constant
b. force
c. linear momentum
d. angular momentum

3. A balloon is rising vertically up with a velocity of 29 ms^{-1}. A stone is dropped from it and it reaches the ground in 10 s. The height of the balloon when the stone was dropped from it is ($g = 9.8\ ms^{-2}$)

a. 100 m *b.* 200 m
c. 400 m *d.* 150 m

4. A thread is tied slightly loose to a wire frame as in figure and the frame is dipped into a soap solution and taken out. The frame is completely covered with the film. When the portion A is punctured with a pin, the thread

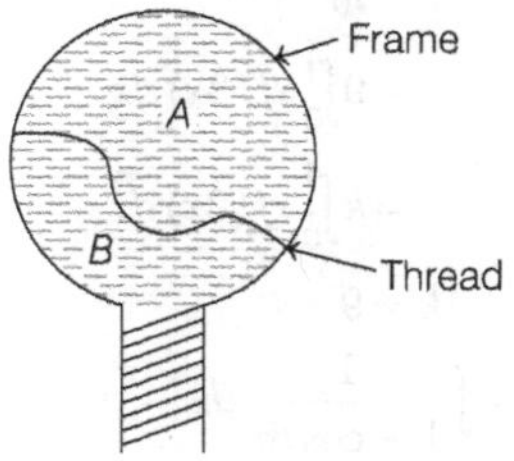

a. becomes concave towards A
b. becomes convex towards A
c. remains in the initial position
d. Either (a) or (b) depending on the size of A w.r.t. B

5. Oxygen is 16 times heavier than hydrogen. Equal volumes of hydrogen and oxygen are mixed. The ratio of speed of sound in the mixture to that in hydrogen is

a. $\sqrt{1/8}$ *b.* $\sqrt{\frac{32}{17}}$ *c.* $\sqrt{8}$ *d.* $\sqrt{\frac{2}{17}}$

6. When light is incident on a diffraction grating, the zero order principal maximum will be

a. one of the component colours
b. absent
c. spectrum of the colours
d. white

7. H-polaroid is prepared by

a. stretching polyvinyl alcohol and then heated with dehydrating agent
b. stretching polyvinyl alcohol and then impregnating with iodine
c. orienting herapathite crystal in the same direction in nitrocellulose
d. by using thin tourmaline crystals

8. SI unit of permittivity is

a. $C^2m^2N^{-1}$ *b.* $C^{-1}m^2N^{-2}$
c. $C^2m^2N^2$ *d.* $C^2m^{-2}N^{-1}$

9. A spherical drop of capacitance $1\mu F$ is broken into eight drops of equal radius. Then, the capacitance of each small drop is

a. $\frac{1}{8}\mu F$ *b.* $8\mu F$
c. $\frac{1}{2}\mu F$ *d.* $\frac{1}{4}\mu F$

10. Two equal forces (p each) act at a point inclined to each other at an angle of 120°. The magnitude of their resultant is

a. p *b.* $2p$
c. $p/2$ *d.* $p/4$

11. If two waves of the same frequency and amplitude respectively on superposition produce a resultant disturbance of the same amplitude the waves differ in phase by

a. $\pi/3$ *b.* $2\pi/3$
c. π *d.* zero

12. A man, standing between two cliffs, claps his hands and starts hearing a series of echoes at intervals of one second. If the speed of sound in air is 340 ms^{-1}, then the distance between the cliffs, is

a. 340 m *b.* 1620 m
c. 680 m *d.* 1700 m

13. A beam of light of wavelength 600 nm from a distant source falls on a single slit 1 mm wide and the resulting diffraction pattern is observed on a screen 2 m away. The distance between the first dark fringes on either side of the central bright fringe is

a. 1.2 mm *b.* 1.2 cm
c. 2.4 cm *d.* 2.4 mm

14. Specific rotation of sugar solution is 0.01 SI units. 200 kgm^{-3} of impure sugar solution is taken in a polarimeter tube of length 0.25 m and an optical rotation of 0.4 rad is observed. The percentage of purity of sugar in the sample is

a. 80% *b.* 89%
c. 11% *d.* 20%

15. An electron is accelerated through a potential difference of 45.5 V. The velocity acquired by it (in ms^{-1}) is

a. 4×10^6 *b.* 4×10^4
c. 10^6 *d.* zero

16. When a body is earth connected, electrons from the earth flow into the body. This means, the body is

a. uncharged *b.* charged positively
c. charged negatively *d.* an insulator

17. Effective capacitance between A and B in the figure shown is (all capacitances are in μF)

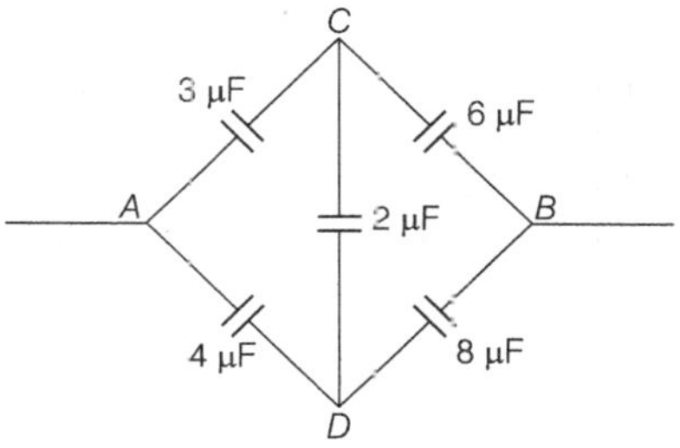

a. $21\mu F$ *b.* $23\mu F$
c. $\frac{3}{14}\mu F$ *d.* $\frac{14}{3}\mu F$

18. Which state of triply ionised Beryllium (Be^{+++}) has the same orbital radius as that of the ground state of hydrogen ?

a. $n = 1$ *b.* $n = 2$
c. $n = 3$ *d.* $n = 4$

19. If M is the atomic mass and A is the mass number, packing fraction is given by

a. $\frac{A}{M - A}$ *b.* $\frac{A - M}{A}$
c. $\frac{M}{M - A}$ *d.* $\frac{M - A}{A}$

20. A count rate meter shows a count of 240 per min from a given radioactive source. One hour later the meter shows a count rate of 30 per min. The half-life of the source is

a. 20 min *b.* 30 min
c. 80 min *d.* 120 min

21. The refractive index of a particular material is 1.67 for blue light, 1.65 for yellow light and 1.63 for red light. The dispersive power of the material is

a. 0.0615 *b.* 0.024 *c.* 0.031 *d.* 1.60

22. An ideal gas heat engine operates in a Carnot's cycle between 227°C and 127°C. It absorbs 6×10^4 J at high temperature. The amount of heat converted into work is

a. 4.8×10^4 J *b.* 3.5×10^4 J
c. 1.6×10^4 J *d.* 1.2×10^4 J

23. Which one of the following graphs represents the behaviour of an ideal gas?

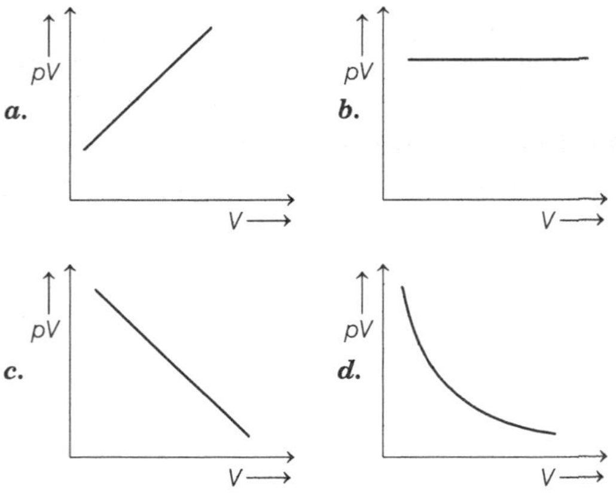

24. Rainbow is formed due to

a. refraction
b. dispersion and total internal reflection
c. total internal reflection
d. scattering

25. A beam of parallel rays is brought to a focus by a plano-convex lens. A thin concave lens of the same focal length is joined to the first lens. The effect of this is

a. the focal point shifts away from the lens by a small distance
b. the focus remains undisturbed
c. the focus shifts to infinity
d. the focal point shifts towards the lens by a small distance

26. Two conductors of the same material have their diameters in the ratio 1 : 2 and their lengths in the ratio 2 : 1. If the temperature difference between their ends is the same, then the ratio of amounts of heat conducted per second through them will be

a. 8 : 1 *b.* 1 : 8 *c.* 4 : 1 *d.* 1 : 4

27. Blowing air with open mouth is an example of

a. isothermal process
b. adiabatic process
c. isobaric process
d. isochoric process

28. Sound waves in air are always longitudinal because

a. air is a mixture of several gases
b. density of air is very small
c. of the inherent characteristics of sound waves in air
d. air does not have a modulus of rigidity

29. In Young's double slit experiment, if monochromatic light used is replaced by white light, then

a. all bright fringes become white
b. all bright fringes have colours between violet and red
c. no fringes are observed
d. only central fringe is white, all other fringes are coloured

30. In a Young's double slit experiment, the separation between the two slits is 0.9 mm and the fringes are observed 1m away. If it produces the second dark fringe at a distance of 1 mm from the central fringe, the wavelength of the monochromatic source of light used is

a. 500 nm *b.* 600 nm
c. 450 nm *d.* 400 nm

31. An uncharged sphere of metal is placed inside a charged parallel plate capacitor. The lines of force will look like

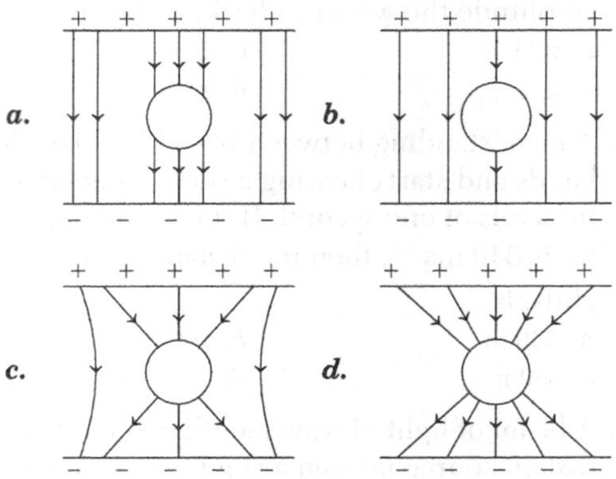

32. A wire has a resistance of 6Ω. It is cut into two parts and both half values are connected in parallel. The new resistance is

a. 12 Ω *b.* 1.5 Ω
c. 3 Ω *d.* 6 Ω

33. A current flows in a conductor from East to West. The direction of the magnetic field at a point above the conductor is

a. towards North *b.* towards South
c. towards East *d.* towards West

34. A bar magnet is equivalent to

a. solenoid carrying current
b. circular coil carrying current
c. torroid carrying current
d. straight conductor carrying current

35. Excitation energy of a hydrogen like ion in its first excitation state is 40.8 eV. Energy needed to remove the electron from the ion in ground state is

a. 54.4 eV *b.* 13.6 eV
c. 40.8 eV *d.* 27.2 eV

36. Threshold wavelength for photoelectric emission from a metal surface is 5200 Å. Photoelectrons will be emitted when this surface is illuminated with monochromatic radiation from

a. 50 W IR-lamp *b.* 10 W IR-lamp
c. 1 W IR-lamp *d.* 50 W UV-lamp

37. The emitter-base junction of a transistor is ……… biased, while the collector-base junction is …… biased.

a. reverse, forward *b.* reverse, reverse
c. forward, forward *d.* forward, reverse

38. In a forward biased *p-n* junction diode, the potential barrier in the depletion region is of the form

a.
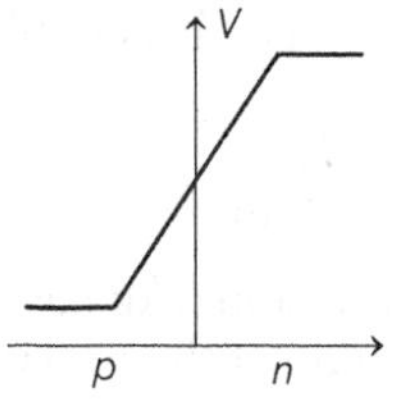

b.
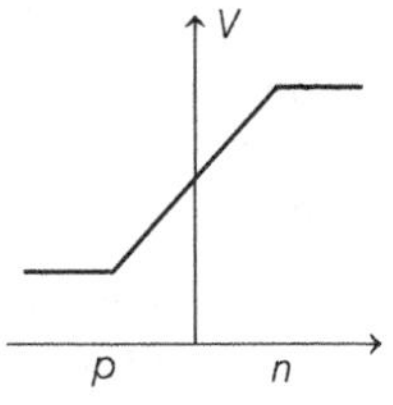

c.
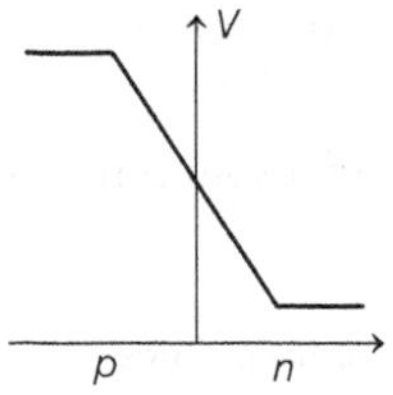

d.
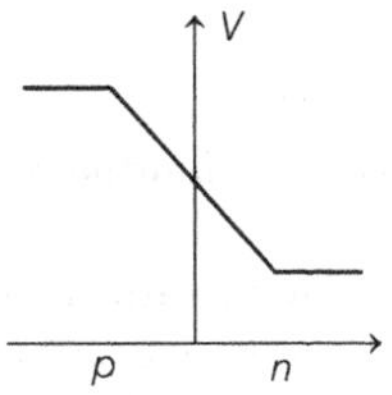

39. A cylinder of radius r and length l is placed in an uniform electric field E parallel to the axis of the cylinder. The total flux for the surface of the cylinder is given by

a. $\pi r^2 E$ *b.* $(\pi r^2 + \pi l^2)E$
c. Zero *d.* $2\pi r^2 E$

40. Two electric bulbs A and B are rated as 60 W and 100 W. They are connected in parallel to the same source. Then,

a. Both draw the same current
b. A draws more current than B
c. B draws more current than A
d. currents drawn are in the ratio of their resistances

41. Three long straight wires A, B and C are carrying currents as shown in figure. Then, the resultant force on B is directed

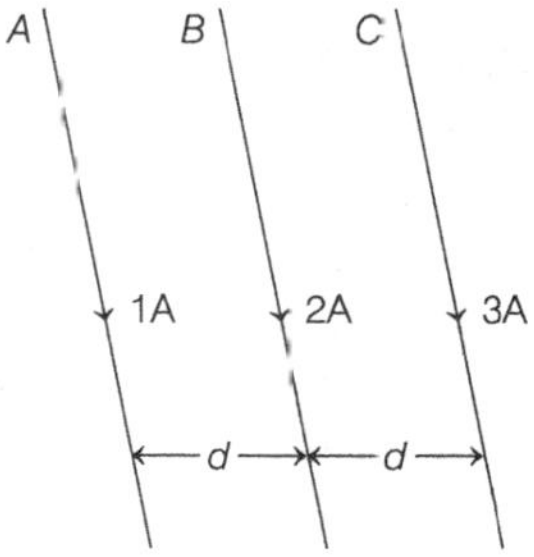

a. towards A
b. towards C
c. perpendicular to the plane of paper and outward
d. perpendicular to the plane of paper and inward

42. Curie-Weiss law is obeyed by iron at a temperature

a. below Curie temperature
b. above Curie temperature
c. at Curie temperature only
d. at all temperatures

43. The dimensional formula for inductance is

a. $[ML^2T^{-1}A^{-2}]$ *b.* $[ML^2T^{-2}A^{-1}]$
c. $[ML^2T^{-2}A^{-2}]$ *d.* $[ML^2TA^{-2}]$

44. A magnet NS is suspended from a spring and while it oscillates, the magnet moves in and out of the coil C. The coil is connected to a galvanometer G. Then, as the magnet oscillates,

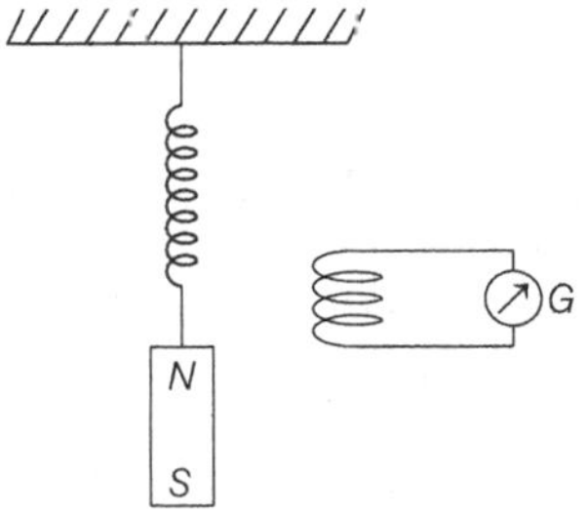

a. G shows deflection to the left and right with constant amplitude
b. G shows deflection on one side
c. G shows no deflection
d. G shows deflection to the left and right but the amplitude steadily decreases

45. The maximum current that can be measured by a galvanometer of resistance 40 Ω is 10 mA. It is converted into a voltmeter that can read upto 50 V. The resistance to be connected in series with the galvanometer (in ohm) is

a. 5040 *b.* 4960 *c.* 2010 *d.* 4050

46. An unknown resistance R_1 is connected in series with a resistance of 10 Ω. This combination is connected to one gap of a meter bridge, while a resistance R_2 is connected in the other gap. The balance point is at 50 cm. Now, when the 10 Ω resistance is removed the balance point shifts to 40 cm. The value of R_1 (in ohm) is

a. 60 *b.* 40 *c.* 20 *d.* 10

47. In the circuit shown, the internal resistance of the cell is negligible. The steady state current in the 2 Ω resistor is

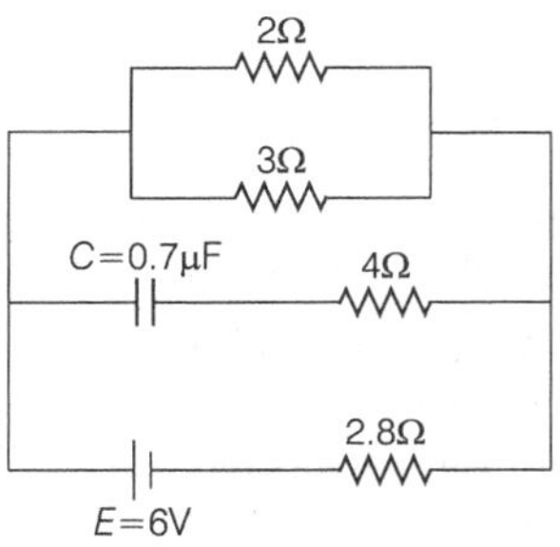

a. 0.9A *b.* 1.5 A
c. 0.6 A *d.* 1.2 A

48. A rectangular coil of 300 turns has an average area of 25 cm × 10 cm. The coil rotates with a speed of 50 cps in a uniform magnetic field of strength 4×10^{-2} T about an axis perpendicular to the field. The peak value of the induced emf (in volt) is

a. 3π *b.* 30π
c. 300π *d.* 3000π

49. In a *L-C-R* circuit the potential difference between the terminals of the inductance is 60 V, between the terminals of the capacitor is 30 V and that between the terminals of resistance is 40 V. The supply voltage will be equal to

a. 50 V *b.* 70 V
c. 130 V *d.* 10 V

50. A vertical circular coil of radius 0.1 m and having 10 turns carries a steady current. When the plane of the coil is normal to the magnetic meridian, a neutral point is observed at the centre of the coil. If $B_H = 0.314 \times 10^{-4}$ T, then the current in the coil is

a. 2 A *b.* 1 A
c. 0.5 A *d.* 0.25 A

51. The spectrum obtained from the chromosphere of the sun at the time of total solar eclipse is

a. continuous emission spectrum
b. line absorption spectrum
c. line emission spectrum
d. band absorption spectrum

52. Heavy water is

a. water, in which soap does not lather
b. compound of heavy oxygen and heavy hydrogen
c. compound of deuterium and oxygen
d. water at 4°C

53. The nuclear reactor at Kaiga is a

a. breeder reactor
b. power reactor
c. research reactor
d. fusion reactor

54. When a body moves in a circular path, no work is done by the force since

a. there is no displacement
b. there is no net force
c. force and displacement are perpendicular to each other
d. the force is always away from the centre

55. A bullet moving with a speed of 100 ms^{-1} can just penetrate two planks of equal thickness. Then, the number of such planks penetrated by the same bullet when the speed is doubled will be

a. 4 *b.* 8
c. 6 *d.* 10

56. Two bodies of masses 1 kg and 2 kg have equal momentum. Then, the ratio of their kinetic energies is

a. 1 : 3 *b.* 1 : 1
c. 2 : 1 *d.* 3 : 1

57. The loudness and pitch of a sound note depends on

a. intensity and frequency
b. frequency and number of harmonics
c. intensity and velocity
d. frequency and velocity

58. Absorption co-efficient of an open window is

a. Zero *b.* 0.5
c. 1 *d.* 0.25

59. In Melde's experiment in the transverse mode, the frequency of the tuning fork and the frequency of the waves in the string are in the ratio

a. 1 : 1 *b.* 1 : 2 *c.* 2 : 1 *d.* 4 : 1

60. The difference between the apparent frequency of a source of sound as perceived by the observer during its approach and recession is 2% of the frequency of the source. If the speed of sound in air is 300 ms^{-1}, then the velocity of the source is

a. 6 ms^{-1} *b.* 3 ms^{-1}
c. 1.5 ms^{-1} *d.* 12 ms^{-1}

CHEMISTRY

61. Ozone in stratosphere is depleted by

a. CF_2Cl_2 *b.* C_7F_{16} *c.* $C_6H_6Cl_2$ *d.* C_6F_6

62. Which one of the following is an unsaturated fatty acid?

a. Palmitic acid *b.* Lauric acid
c. Linolenic acid *d.* Myristic acid

63. When chlorine is passed through boiling toluene, we get

a. *o*-chloro toluene
b. *p*-chlorotoluene
c. mixture of *o* and *p*-chlorotoluene
d. benzyl chloride

64. The standard temperature used in thermo chemical calculations is

a. 273 K *b.* 298 K *c.* 297 K *d.* 303 K

65. Which of the following is an intensive property?

a. Enthalpy *b.* Entropy
c. Density *d.* Mass

66. Schiff's reagent contains

a. rochelle salt *b.* resorcinol
c. rosaniline *d.* α-naphthol

67. The formula of chromyl chloride is

a. CrCl *b.* $CrCl_3$ *c.* $CrOCl_2$ *d.* CrO_2Cl_2

68. Horn silver is

a. oxide ore *b.* sulphide ore
c. halide ore *d.* carbonate ore

69. Tetrahedral structure is formed by

a. sp^2-hybridisation *b.* sp^3-hybridisation
c. dsp^3-hybridisation *d.* d^2sp^3-hybridisation

70. NO^+ ligand is

a. nitronium *b.* nitrosyl
c. nitrosonium *d.* nitro

71. Cationic complex is

a. hexa amino platinum chloride
b. potassium ferro cyanide
c. sodium argento cyanide
d. nickel carbonyl

72. $2p_x$ atomic orbital undergoes linear combination with

a. $2p_y$ orbital
b. $2p_x$ orbital
c. Both $2p_y$ and $2p_z$ orbitals
d. $2p_z$ orbital

73. In a first order reaction, molar concentration of a reactant decreases from 0.1 to 0.01 in 100 s. The rate constant of the reaction is

a. 2.3030 *b.* 0.02303
c. 0.2303 *d.* 0.002303

74. In which one of the following equilibria, pressure has no effect

a. $PCl_5 \rightleftharpoons PCl_3 + Cl_2$
b. $2NH_3 \rightleftharpoons N_2 + 3H_2$
c. $2SO_2 + O_2 \rightleftharpoons 2SO_3$
d. $N_2 + O_2 \rightleftharpoons 2NO$

75. Conductivity of a solution is not affected by

a. addition of water
b. process of heating
c. addition of acetic acid
d. addition of ethanol

76. The lowering in vapour pressure is maximum for

a. 0.1 M urea
b. 0.1 M NaCl
c. 0.1 M $MgCl_2$
d. 0.1 M $K_4[Fe(CN)_6]$

77. Bromo ethane and isopropyl chloride with metallic sodium in ether forms

a. pentane *b.* 2-methyl butane
c. 3-methyl butane *d.* 2,3-dimethyl butane

78. To dry ammonia gas the drying agent used is

a. conc. H_2SO_4 *b.* P_2O_5
c. soda lime *d.* anhydrous $CaCl_2$

79. The metal hydroxide which is soluble in excess of ammonium hydroxide is

a. $Fe(OH)_2$ *b.* $Fe(OH)_3$
c. $Cu(OH)_2$ *d.* $Al(OH)_3$

80. Potassium dichromate can be converted to potassium chromate by adding
a. KOH *b.* conc. H_2SO_4
c. NH_4OH *d.* acetic acid

81. 0.5 g of an acid is neutralised by 40 cc of 0.125 N NaOH. The equivalent mass of the acid is
a. 50 *b.* 100 *c.* 40 *d.* 80

82. 5 L of NaOH solution of pH 12 contains
a. 200 g *b.* 0.2 g
c. 20 g *d.* 2g

83. 50 cc of oxalic acid is oxidised by 25 cc of 0.20 N $KMnO_4$. The mass of oxalic acid present in 500 cc of the solution is
a. 3.15 g *b.* 31.5 g *c.* 6.3 g *d.* 63 g

84. Pure water is neutral because
a. pH = 7
b. litmus has no effect
c. it is free from dissolved salts
d. pH = 0

85. In the titration of mohr salt against $KMnO_4$, the indicator used is
a. diphenyl amine *b.* $KMnO_4$
c. phenolphthalein *d.* methyl orange

86. The relationship between half-life of a reaction and the order of reaction is
a. $t_{\frac{1}{2}} \propto \frac{1}{a^{(n+1)}}$ *b.* $t_{\frac{1}{2}} \propto \frac{1}{a^{(n+2)}}$
c. $t_{\frac{1}{2}} \propto \frac{1}{a^{n}}$ *d.* $t_{\frac{1}{2}} \propto \frac{1}{a^{(n-1)}}$

87. 6g of urea is dissolved in 90g of water. Relative lowering of vapour pressure is
a. 0.02 *b.* 0.2 *c.* 0.002 *d.* 0.04

88. 6.84g of sucrose is dissolved in 200g of water. The molality of the solution is
a. 0.2 M *b.* 0.3 M *c.* 0.1 M *d.* 0.02 M

89. When common salt is added of a saturated solution of soap is precipitated. This is based on the principle of
a. common ion effect
b. principle of solubility product
c. adsorption from solution
d. peptisation

90. Highest osmotic pressure is shown by a solution of
a. 0.1 M aluminium sulphate
b. 0.1 M potassium nitrate
c. 0.1 M magnesium chloride
d. 0.1 M barium chloride

91. 50% of first order reaction is completed in 30 min. The velocity constant of the reaction is
a. 0.231 *b.* 2.31 *c.* 0.00231 *d.* 0.0231

92. The ebullioscopic constant is the elevation in boiling point produced by
a. 1 molar solution *b.* 1 molal solution
c. 1 N solution *d.* 10% solution

93. The mass of glucose to be dissolved in 50g of water to get 0.3 molal solution is
a. 27g *b.* 0.27 g *c.* 2.7 g *d.* 5.4 g

94. 25 mL of 0.08 N Mohr salt solution is oxidised by 20 mL of $K_2Cr_2O_7$ in acid medium. The mass of Mohr's salt present in 500 cc is
a. 3.96 g *b.* 19.6 g
c. 39.6 g *d.* 39.2 g

95. A reaction is spontaneous at all temperature, when
a. ΔH is –ve and ΔS is + ve
b. ΔH is + ve and ΔS is – ve
c. Both ΔH and ΔS are – ve
d. Both ΔH and ΔS are + ve

96. The coordination number of sodium chloride is
a. 4 *b.* 8 *c.* 6 *d.* 12

97. Conjugate acid of NH_2^- is
a. NH_3 *b.* NH_4^+
c. N *d.* NH_2^+

98. Highest molar conductivity is given by
a. 0.005 M NaCl *b.* 0.1 M NaCl
c. 0.05 M NaCl *d.* 0.01 M NaCl

99. In the detection of III group basic radicals NH_4OH is added after NH_4Cl to
a. increase in the ionisation of NH_4OH
b. increase in the ionisation of salt solution
c. decrease in the ionisation of salt solution
d. decrease in the ionisation of NH_4OH

100. Just before attaining the chemical equilibrium
a. rate of forward reaction decreases and rate of backward reaction increases
b. rate of forward reaction increases and rate of backward reaction decreases
c. no change in the rates of forward and backward reactions.
d. rate of forward reaction equals the rate backward reaction.

101. Which one of the following shows highest magnetic moment?
a. Fe^{2+} *b.* Co^{2+}
c. Cr^{3+} *d.* Ni^{2+}

COMEDK 2019

102. In 3rd series as we move from scandium to zinc the paramagnetism
a. increases
b. decreases
c. first increases to a maximum and then decreases
d. first decreases to a minimum and then increases

103. The number of unpaired electrons in Fe^{3+} is
a. 2 *b.* 3
c. 4 *d.* 5

104. The IUPAC name of $K_4[Fe(CN)_6]$ is
a. potassium ferri cyanide
b. potassium ferro cyanide
c. potassium hexa cyano ferrate (II)
d. potassium hexa cyano ferrate (III)

105. The adsorption of an inert gases on activated charcoal increase with
a. decrease of pressure
b. increase of temperature
c. decrease of atomic mass
d. decrease of temperature

106. Electrolysis of brine gives a mixture of
a. H_2, Na, Cl_2 *b.* Cl_2, H_2, NaOH
c. H_2, O_2, NaOH *d.* O_2, Cl_2, NaOH

107. Sucrose is a non-reducing sugar due to
a. 1-2 linkage *b.* 1-4 linkage
c. 1-5 linkage *d.* 1-6 linkage

108. Sulphur containing amino acid is
a. alanine *b.* proline
c. tyrosine *d.* cysteine

109. Lysine is
a. neutral amino acid
b. acidic amino acid
c. basic amino acid
d. heterocyclic amino acid

110. In the Molisch reagent, the substance used is
a. β-naphthol in alcohol
b. α-naphthol in alcohol
c. Resorcinal in alcohol
d. Resonance in water

111. In benzene, each carbon atom undergoes
a. *sp* hybridisation
b. sp^2 hybridisation
c. sp^3 hybridisation
d. dsp^2 hybridisation

112. When vapours of isopropyl alcohol is passed over heated copper, we get acetone. It is an example for
a. dehydration *b.* dehalogenation
c. dehydrohalogenation *d.* dehydrogenation

113. The IUPAC name of $CH_3-\underset{}{\overset{CH_3}{\overset{|}{N}}}-CH_3$ is
a. trimethyl amine
b. 2-methyl ethanamine
c. N, N-dimethyl methanamine
d. trimethyl ammonia

114. When benzaldehyde is condensed with acetic anhydride in presence of fused sodium acetate, we get
a. crotonic acid *b.* cinnamic acid
c. aspartic acid *d.* salicylic acid

115. When a mixture of calcium benzoate and calcium formate is dry distilled, we get
a. formaldehyde *b.* acetaldehyde
c. benzaldehyde *d.* salicylaldehyde

116. Which one of the following is strongly basic?
a. Dimethyl amine *b.* Methyl amine
c. Ammonia *d.* Aniline

117. Which one of the following is bi-functional compound?
a. Formic acid *b.* Acetic acid
c. Benzoic acid *d.* Cinnamic acid

118. When phenol is treated with chloromethane in presence of $AlCl_3$ we get
a. *o*-cresol
b. *m*-cresol
c. *p*-cresol
d. mixture of *o* and *p*-cresol

119. In the synthesis of ammonia
$N_2 + 3H_2 \rightleftharpoons 2NH_3$
a. $K_p = K_C RT$ *b.* $K_p = K_C$
c. $K_p = K_C(RT)^{-2}$ *d.* $K_p = K_C(RT)^{-1}$

120. When the same amount of electricity is passed through solutions of silver nitrate and copper sulphate, 0.4 g copper is deposited. The amount of silver deposited is
a. 1.35 g *b.* 2.7 g
c. 5.1 g *d.* 5.4 g

MATHEMATICS

121. A variable line $\frac{x}{a}+\frac{y}{b}=1$ is such that $a+b=4$. The locus of the mid-point of the portion of the line intercepted between the axes is

a. $x+y=4$ *b.* $x+y=8$
c. $x+y=1$ *d.* $x+y=2$

122. The point $(5,-7)$ lies outside the circle

a. $x^2+y^2-8x=0$
b. $x^2+y^2-5x+7y=0$
c. $x^2+y^2-5x+7y-1=0$
d. $x^2+y^2-8x+7y-2=0$

123. If the circle $x^2+y^2=9$ and $x^2+y^2+2\alpha x+2y+1=0$ touch each other internally, then $\alpha=$

a. $\pm\frac{4}{3}$ *b.* 1
c. $\frac{4}{3}$ *d.* $\frac{-4}{3}$

124. The locus of the mid-points of the line joining the focus and point on the parabola $y^2=4ax$ is a parabola with the equation of directrix as

a. $x+a=0$ *b.* $2x+a=0$
c. $x=0$ *d.* $x=\frac{a}{2}$

125. The tangents drawn at the extremities of a focal chord of the parabola $y^2=16x$

a. intersect on $x=0$
b. intersect on the line $x+4=0$
c. intersect at an angle of 60°
d. intersect at an angle of 45°

126. On the set Z, of all integers * is defined by $a*b=a+b-5$. If $2*(x*3)=5$, then $x=$

a. 0   *b.* 3
c. 5   *d.* 10

127. Which of the following is false?

a. Addition is commutative in N.
b. Multiplication is associative in N.
c. If $a*b=a^b$ for all $a,b\in N$, then $*$ is commutative in N.
d. Addition is associative in N.

128. If $\mathbf{a}\hat{\mathbf{i}}=\mathbf{a}(\hat{\mathbf{i}}+\hat{\mathbf{j}})=\mathbf{a}(\hat{\mathbf{i}}+\hat{\mathbf{j}}+\hat{\mathbf{k}})=1$, then $\mathbf{a}=$

a. $\hat{\mathbf{i}}+\hat{\mathbf{j}}$ *b.* $\hat{\mathbf{i}}-\hat{\mathbf{k}}$
c. $\hat{\mathbf{i}}$ *d.* $\hat{\mathbf{i}}+\hat{\mathbf{j}}-\hat{\mathbf{k}}$

129. If $\mathbf{a}$ and $\mathbf{b}$ are unit vectors and $|\mathbf{a}+\mathbf{b}|=1$, then $|\mathbf{a}-\mathbf{b}|$ is equal to

a. $\sqrt{2}$ *b.* 1
c. $\sqrt{5}$ *d.* $\sqrt{3}$

130. The projection of $\mathbf{a}=3\hat{\mathbf{i}}-\hat{\mathbf{j}}+5\hat{\mathbf{k}}$ on $\mathbf{b}=2\hat{\mathbf{i}}+3\hat{\mathbf{j}}+\hat{\mathbf{k}}$ is

a. $\frac{8}{\sqrt{35}}$ *b.* $\frac{8}{\sqrt{39}}$
c. $\frac{8}{\sqrt{14}}$ *d.* $\sqrt{14}$

131. If $f:R\to R$ is defined by $f(x)=x^3$, then $f^{-1}(8)=$

a. $\{2\}$ *b.* $\{2,2\omega,2\omega^2\}$
c. $\{2,-2\}$ *d.* $\{2,2\}$

132. R is a relation on N given by $R=\{(x,y)\mid 4x+3y=20\}$. Which of the following belongs of R?

a. $(-4,12)$ *b.* $(5,0)$
c. $(3,4)$ *d.* $(2,4)$

133. If $\log_{10}7=0.8451$, then the position of the first significant figure of 7^{-20} is

a. 16   *b.* 17
c. 20   *d.* 15

134. $\frac{1}{2\cdot5}+\frac{1}{5\cdot8}+\frac{1}{8\cdot11}+\ldots$ upto n terms is equal to

a. $\frac{n}{4n+6}$ *b.* $\frac{1}{4n+4}$
c. $\frac{n}{6n+4}$ *d.* $\frac{n}{3n+7}$

135. The ten's digit in $1!+4!+7!+10!+12!+13!+15!+16!+17!$ is divisible by

a. 4   *b.* 3!   *c.* 5   *d.* 7

136. The equation $\frac{x^2}{2-\lambda}-\frac{y^2}{\lambda-5}-1=0$ represents an ellipse if

a. $\lambda>5$ *b.* $\lambda<2$
c. $2<\lambda<5$ *d.* $2>\lambda>5$

137. The equation to the normal to the hyperbola $\frac{x^2}{16}-\frac{y^2}{9}=1$ at $(-4,0)$ is

a. $2x-3y=1$ *b.* $x=0$
c. $x=1$ *d.* $y=0$

COMEDK 2019

138. The converse of the contrapositive of the conditional $p \to \sim q$ is

a. $p \to q$ **b.** $\sim p \to \sim q$
c. $\sim q \to p$ **d.** $\sim p \to q$

139. The perimeter of a certain sector of a circle is equal to the length of the arc of the semicircle. Then, the angle at the centre of the sector in radians is

a. $\pi - 2$ **b.** $\pi + 2$
c. $\frac{\pi}{3}$ **d.** $\frac{2\pi}{3}$

140. The value of $\tan 67\frac{1^\circ}{2} + \cot 67\frac{1^\circ}{2}$ is

a. $\sqrt{2}$ **b.** $3\sqrt{2}$
c. $2\sqrt{2}$ **d.** $2 - \sqrt{2}$

141. If e_1 and e_2 are the eccentricities of a hyperbola $3x^2 - 3y^2 = 25$ and its conjugate, then

a. $e_1^2 + e_2^2 = 2$ **b.** $e_1^2 + e_2^2 = 4$
c. $e_1 + e_2 = 4$ **d.** $e_1 + e_2 = \sqrt{2}$

142. If p and q are prime numbers satisfying the condition $p^2 - 2q^2 = 1$, then the value of $p^2 + 2q^2$ is

a. 5 **b.** 15
c. 16 **d.** 17

143. If $A(\text{adj } A) = 5I$, where I is the identity matrix of order 3, then $|\text{adj } A|$ is equal to

a. 125 **b.** 25
c. 5 **d.** 10

144. The number of solutions for the equation $\sin 2x + \cos 4x = 2$ is

a. 0 **b.** 1
c. 2 **d.** Infinite

145. $\int e^x \cdot x^5 \, dx$ is

a. $e^x[x^5 + 5x^4 + 20x^3 + 60x^2 + 120x + 120] + C$
b. $e^x[x^5 - 5x^4 - 20x^3 - 60x^2 - 120x - 120] + C$
c. $e^x[x^5 - 5x^4 + 20x^3 - 60x^2 + 120x - 120] + C$
d. $e^x[x^5 + 5x^4 + 20x^3 - 60x^2 - 120x + 120] + C$

146. If $f(x)$ is an even function and $f'(x)$ exists, then $f'(e) + f'(-e)$ is

a. > 0 **b.** 0
c. ≥ 0 **d.** < 0

147. If α is a complex number satisfying the equation $\alpha^2 + \alpha + 1 = 0$, then α^{31} is equal to

a. α **b.** α^2
c. 1 **d.** i

148. The derivative of $\sin(x^3)$ w.r.t. $\cos(x^3)$ is

a. $-\tan(x^3)$ **b.** $\tan(x^3)$
c. $-\cot(x^3)$ **d.** $\cot(x^3)$

149. A unit vector perpendicular to both the vectors $\hat{i} + \hat{j}$ and $\hat{j} + \hat{k}$ is

a. $\frac{-\hat{i} - \hat{j} + \hat{k}}{\sqrt{3}}$ **b.** $\frac{\hat{i} + \hat{j} - \hat{k}}{3}$
c. $\frac{\hat{i} + \hat{j} + \hat{k}}{\sqrt{3}}$ **d.** $\frac{\hat{i} - \hat{j} + \hat{k}}{\sqrt{3}}$

150. If $A = \begin{vmatrix} a_1 & b_1 & c_1 \\ a_2 & b_2 & c_2 \\ a_3 & b_3 & c_3 \end{vmatrix}$ and $B = \begin{vmatrix} c_1 & c_2 & c_3 \\ a_1 & a_2 & a_3 \\ b_1 & b_2 & b_3 \end{vmatrix}$ then

a. $A = -B$ **b.** $A = B$
c. $B = 0$ **d.** $B = A^2$

151. The locus of a point which moves such that the sum of its distances from two fixed points is a constant is

a. a circle **b.** a parabola
c. an ellipse **d.** a hyperbola

152. The centroid of the ΔABC, where $A \equiv (2, 3)$, $B \equiv (8, 10)$ and $C \equiv (5, 5)$ is

a. (5, 6) **b.** (6, 5) **c.** (6, 6) **d.** (15, 18)

153. If $3x^2 + xy - y^2 - 3x + 6y + k = 0$ represents a pair of lines, then $k =$

a. 0 **b.** 9 **c.** 1 **d.** -9

154. The equation of the smallest circle passing through the points (2, 2) and (3, 3) is

a. $x^2 + y^2 + 5x + 5y + 12 = 0$
b. $x^2 + y^2 - 5x - 5y + 12 = 0$
c. $x^2 + y^2 + 5x - 5y + 12 = 0$
d. $x^2 + y^2 - 5x + 5y - 12 = 0$

155. The characteristic roots of the matrix $\begin{bmatrix} 1 & 0 & 0 \\ 2 & 3 & 0 \\ 4 & 5 & 6 \end{bmatrix}$ are

a. 1, 3, 6 **b.** 1, 2, 4
c. 4, 5, 6 **d.** 2, 4, 6

156. If $A = \begin{bmatrix} 1 & 2 \\ 3 & 4 \end{bmatrix}$, then $A^{-1} =$

a. $\frac{-1}{2}\begin{bmatrix} 4 & -2 \\ -3 & 1 \end{bmatrix}$ **b.** $\frac{1}{2}\begin{bmatrix} 4 & -2 \\ -3 & 1 \end{bmatrix}$
c. $\begin{bmatrix} -2 & 4 \\ 1 & 3 \end{bmatrix}$ **d.** $\begin{bmatrix} 2 & 4 \\ 1 & 3 \end{bmatrix}$

157. The set $\{-1, 0, 1\}$ is not a multiplicative group because of the failure of

a. Closure law *b.* Associative law
c. Identity law *d.* Inverse law

158. The angle of elevation of the top of a TV tower from three points A, B and C in a straight line through the foot of the tower are α, 2α and 3α respectively. If $AB = a$, then height of the tower is

a. $a\tan\alpha$ *b.* $a\sin\alpha$ *c.* $a\sin 2\alpha$ *d.* $a\sin 3\alpha$

159. The angles A, B and C of a ΔABC are in A.P. If $b : c = \sqrt{3} : \sqrt{2}$, then the angle A is

a. 30° *b.* 15° *c.* 75° *d.* 45°

160. $\sin\left(2\sin^{-1}\sqrt{\frac{63}{65}}\right)$ is equal to

a. $\frac{2\sqrt{126}}{65}$ *b.* $\frac{4\sqrt{65}}{65}$ *c.* $\frac{8\sqrt{63}}{65}$ *d.* $\frac{\sqrt{63}}{65}$

161. The general solution of $|\sin x| = \cos x$ is (when $n \in Z$) given by

a. $n\pi + \frac{\pi}{4}$ *b.* $2n\pi \pm \frac{\pi}{4}$
c. $n\pi \pm \frac{\pi}{4}$ *d.* $n\pi - \frac{\pi}{4}$

162. The real root of the equation $x^3 - 6x + 9 = 0$ is

a. -6 *b.* -9 *c.* 6 *d.* -3

163. The digit in the unit's place of 5^{834} is

a. 0 *b.* 1 *c.* 3 *d.* 5

164. The remainder when $3^{100} \times 2^{50}$ is divided by 5 is

a. 1 *b.* 2 *c.* 3 *d.* 4

165. $\int \frac{\sin x \cos x}{\sqrt{1-\sin^4 x}}\,dx =$

a. $\frac{1}{2}\sin^{-1}(\sin^2 x) + C$ *b.* $\frac{1}{2}\cos^{-1}(\sin^2 x) + C$
c. $\tan^{-1}(\sin^2 x) + C$ *d.* $\tan^{-1}(2\sin x) + C$

166. The value of $\int_{-2}^{2}(ax^3 + bx + c)\,dx$ depends on the

a. value of b *b.* value of c
c. value of a *d.* value of a and b

167. The area of the region bounded by $y = 2x - x^2$ and the X-axis is

a. $\frac{8}{3}$ sq units *b.* $\frac{4}{3}$ sq units
c. $\frac{7}{3}$ sq units *d.* $\frac{2}{3}$ sq units

168. The differential equation $y\frac{dy}{dx} + x = c$ represents

a. a family of hyperbolas.
b. a family of circles whose centres are on the Y-axis.
c. a family of parabolas.
d. a family of circles whose centres are on the X-axis.

169. If $f(x^5) = 5x^3$, then $f'(x) =$

a. $\frac{3}{\sqrt[5]{x^2}}$ *b.* $\frac{3}{\sqrt[5]{x}}$
c. $\frac{3}{x}$ *d.* $\sqrt[5]{x}$

170. $f(x) = 2a - x$ in $-a < x < a$

$= 3x - 2a$ in $a \geq x$

Then which of the following is true?

a. $f(x)$ is discontinuous at $x = a$
b. $f(x)$ is not differentiable at x
c. $f(x)$ is differentiable at all $x \geq a$
d. $f(x)$ is continuous at all $x < a$

171. The maximum area of a rectangle that can be inscribed in a circle of radius 2 units is (in square units)

a. 4 *b.* 8π
c. 8 *d.* 5

172. If Z is a complex number such that $Z = -\overline{Z}$, then

a. Z is purely real.
b. Z is purely imaginary.
c. Z is any complex number.
d. Real part of Z is the same as its imaginary part.

173. The value of $\sum_{K=1}^{6}\left[\sin\frac{2K\pi}{7} - i\cos\frac{2K\pi}{7}\right]$ is

a. i *b.* 0
c. $-i$ *d.* -1

174. $\lim_{x\to\infty} x\sin\left(\frac{2}{x}\right)$ is equal to

a. ∞ *b.* 0
c. 2 *d.* $\frac{1}{2}$

175. A stone is thrown vertically upwards and the height x ft. reached by the stone in t sec is given by $x = 80t - 16t^2$. The stone reaches the maximum height in

a. 2 sec *b.* 2.5 sec
c. 3 sec *d.* 1.5 sec

176. The maximum value of $\frac{\log x}{x}$ in $(2, \infty)$ is

a. 1 *b.* $\frac{2}{e}$ *c.* e *d.* $\frac{1}{e}$

177. If $f(x) = be^{ax} + ae^{bx}$, then $f''(0) =$

a. 0 b. $2ab$

c. $ab(a+b)$ d. ab

178. If $\sqrt{\dfrac{1+\cos A}{1-\cos A}} = \dfrac{x}{y}$, then the value of $\tan A =$

a. $\dfrac{x^2+y^2}{x^2-y^2}$ b. $\dfrac{2xy}{x^2+y^2}$

c. $\dfrac{2xy}{x^2-y^2}$ d. $\dfrac{2xy}{y^2-x^2}$

179. $\int \dfrac{\sec x}{\sec x + \tan x}\, dx =$

a. $\tan x - \sec x + C$ b. $\log(1+\sin x) + C$

c. $\sec x + \tan x + C$ d. $\log \sin x + \log \cos x + C$

180. If $\int f(x)\,dx = g(x)$, then $\int f(x)\, g(x)\, dx =$

a. $\dfrac{1}{2} f^2(x)$ b. $\dfrac{1}{2} g^2(x)$

c. $\dfrac{1}{2} [g'(x)]^2$ d. $f'(x)\, g(x)$

ANSWERS

Physics

1. (c)	2. (d)	3. (b)	4. (a)	5. (d)	6. (d)	7. (b)	8. (d)	9. (c)	10. (a)
11. (b)	12. (a)	13. (d)	14. (a)	15. (a)	16. (b)	17. (d)	18. (b)	19. (d)	20. (a)
21. (a)	22. (d)	23. (b)	24. (b)	25. (c)	26. (b)	27. (c)	28. (d)	29. (d)	30. (b)
31. (c)	32. (b)	33. (a)	34. (a)	35. (a)	36. (d)	37. (d)	38. (a)	39. (c)	40. (c)
41. (b)	42. (b)	43. (c)	44. (d)	45. (b)	46. (c)	47. (a)	48. (a)	49. (a)	50. (c)
51. (c)	52. (c)	53. (b)	54. (c)	55. (b)	56. (c)	57. (a)	58. (c)	59. (a)	60. (b)

Chemistry

61. (a)	62. (c)	63. (c)	64. (b)	65. (c)	66. (c)	67. (d)	68. (c)	69. (b)	70. (c)
71. (a)	72. (b)	73. (b)	74. (d)	75. (d)	76. (d)	77. (b)	78. (c)	79. (c)	80. (a)
81. (b)	82. (d)	83. (a)	84. (a)	85. (b)	86. (d)	87. (a)	88. (c)	89. (a)	90. (a)
91. (d)	92. (b)	93. (c)	94. (*)	95. (a)	96. (c)	97. (a)	98. (a)	99. (d)	100. (a)
101. (a)	102. (c)	103. (d)	104. (c)	105. (d)	106. (b)	107. (a)	108. (d)	109. (c)	110. (b)
111. (b)	112. (d)	113. (c)	114. (b)	115. (c)	116. (a)	117. (c)	118. (d)	119. (c)	120. (a)

Mathematics

121. (d)	122. (a)	123. (c)	124. (c)	125. (b)	126. (d)	127. (c)	128. (c)	129. (d)	130. (c)
131. (a)	132. (d)	133. (b)	134. (c)	135. (b)	136. (b)	137. (d)	138. (d)	139. (a)	140. (c)
141. (b)	142. (d)	143. (b)	144. (a)	145. (c)	146. (b)	147. (a)	148. (c)	149. (d)	150. (b)
151. (c)	152. (a)	153. (d)	154. (b)	155. (a)	156. (a)	157. (d)	158. (c)	159. (c)	160. (a)
161. (c)	162. (d)	163. (d)	164. (d)	165. (a)	166. (b)	167. (b)	168. (d)	169. (a)	170. (d)
171. (c)	172. (b)	173. (a)	174. (c)	175. (b)	176. (d)	177. (c)	178. (c)	179. (a)	180. (b)

Note (*) None of the option is correct.

HINTS & SOLUTIONS

Physics

1. *(c)* Resultant focal length (f) of the given combination is 0.2 m.

Refractive index of the material, $\mu = 1.5$

From the lens Maker formula, we get

$$\frac{1}{f} = (\mu - 1)\left(\frac{1}{R_1} - \frac{1}{R_2}\right)$$

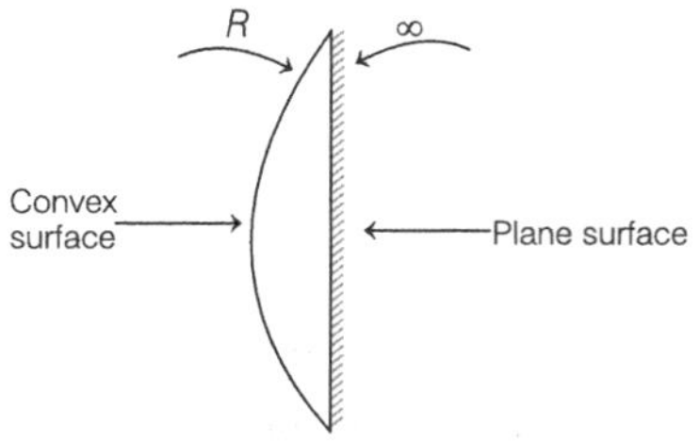

where, R_1 is the radius of curvature of convex surface and R_2 is the radius of curvature of plane surface ($R_2 = \infty$).

Hence,

$$\frac{1}{f} = (1.5 - 1)\left(\frac{1}{R_1} - \frac{1}{\infty}\right)$$

$$\Rightarrow \quad \frac{1}{0.2} = (0.5)\left(\frac{1}{R_1}\right)$$

$$\Rightarrow \quad R_1 = 0.5 \times 0.2 = 0.1 \text{ m}$$

2. *(d)* Dimensional formula of Planck's constant $= [M^1L^2T^{-1}]$

Similarly,

Boltzmann constant is given

$$K = \frac{\text{Energy}}{\text{Temperature}}$$

$\therefore$ The dimension of K is

$$= \frac{[ML^2T^{-2}]}{[K]} = [M^1L^2T^{-2}K^{-1}]$$

Dimensional formula of force is $[M^1L^1T^{-2}]$.

Dimensional formula of linear momentum is $[M^1L^1T^{-1}]$.

Dimensional formula of angular momentum is $[M^1L^2T^{-1}]$.

Hence, angular momentum and Planck's constant have same dimensional formula.

3. *(b)* Given, velocity of the balloon $= 29\text{ms}^{-1}$

When the stone is dropped, then the velocity of the stone

$$u = 29\text{ms}^{-1}$$

Time taken to reach the ground, $t = 10$ s

From the second equation of motion,

$$s = -ut + \frac{1}{2}gt^2$$

$$= -29 \times 10 + \frac{1}{2} \times 9.8 \times (10)^2$$

$$= -290 + 490 = 200 \text{ m}$$

4. *(a)* The potential energy due to surface tension is given by the formula $U = S \times A$

where, S is the surface tension and A is the area of film. Since after puncturing, the film will try to minimise its potential energy and hence the surface area. Thus, the thread will become concave towards A.

5. *(d)* The velocity of sound in a gas at a fixed temperature is given by

$$v = \sqrt{\frac{\gamma RT}{M}}$$

where, $\gamma = \left(\frac{C_p}{C_V}\right)$ is specific heat ratio and M is the molecular mass of the gas.

Let, velocity of sound in hydrogen, $v_1 = \sqrt{\frac{\gamma RT}{M_1}}$

Velocity of sound in oxygen, $v_2 = \sqrt{\frac{\gamma RT}{M_2}}$

Let, M_1 and M_2 be the molecular mass of hydrogen and oxygen respectively n_1 and n_2 be the moles of hydrogen and oxygen, respectively.

Molecular mass of the mixture,

$$M_{\text{mix}} = \frac{n_1M_1 + n_2M_2}{n_1 + n_2}$$

According to the question, $n_1 = n_2$ at given NTP.

$$M_2 = 16M \quad \text{(given)}$$

$$M_{\text{mix}} = \frac{M_1 + 16M_1}{2} = \frac{17M_1}{2}$$

Velocity of sound in mixture, $v_{\text{mix}} = \sqrt{\frac{\gamma RT}{M_{\text{mix}}}}$

$$\Rightarrow \quad v_{\text{mix}} = \sqrt{\frac{2\gamma RT}{17M_1}}$$

$\therefore$ The ratio of velocity of sound in mixture to that of hydrogen

$$\frac{v_1}{v_{\text{mix}}} = \frac{\sqrt{\frac{\gamma RT}{M_1}}}{\sqrt{\frac{\gamma 2RT}{17M_1}}}$$

$$\Rightarrow \quad \frac{v_{\text{mix}}}{v_1} = \sqrt{\frac{2}{17}}$$

6. *(d)* Zero order principal maximum contains all incoming wavelets in diffraction pattern, Hence, zero order principal maximum will be white.

7. *(b)* H-polaroid is one of the most common type of polaroid used today. It is prepared by stretching a thin sheet of polyvinyl alcohol and then impregnating it with iodine. In this process, the molecules get oriented in the direction of the applied strain and the material becomes dichronic. Each polaroid sheet is mounted between thin glass plate to provide mechanical support.

8. *(d)* From Coulomb's law, we know

$$F = \frac{1}{4\pi\varepsilon_0}\frac{q_1q_2}{r^2}$$

$$\Rightarrow \quad N = \frac{1}{\varepsilon_0}\frac{C^2}{m^2}$$

$$\Rightarrow \quad \varepsilon_0 = \frac{C^2}{m^2 N}$$

$$\Rightarrow \quad \varepsilon_0 = C^2 m^{-2} N^{-1}$$

9. *(c)* Given, capacitance of bigger drop = $1\mu F$

Let R be the radius of bigger drop and r be the radius of smaller drops.

According to the question, $\frac{4}{3}\pi R^3 = 8\times\frac{4}{3}\pi r^3$

$$\Rightarrow \quad R^3 = 8r^3$$

$$\Rightarrow \quad R = 2r$$

The capacitance of bigger drop ,

$$C = 4\pi\varepsilon_0 R$$

$$= 2\times 4\pi\varepsilon_0 r \quad (\because R = 2r)$$

Capacitance of smaller drop, $C' = 4\pi\varepsilon_0 r$

Thus, $$C' = \frac{C}{2}$$

Hence, $$C' = \frac{1}{2}\mu F$$

10. *(a)* The magnitude of the resultant force can be given by parallelogram's law of vector addition i.e.,

Resultant force = $\sqrt{p^2 + p^2 + 2p.p\cos\theta}$

$$\Rightarrow \quad F_{net} = \sqrt{2p^2 + 2p^2\times\cos(120^\circ)} \quad (\because \theta = 120^\circ)$$

$$= \sqrt{2p^2 + 2p^2\left(-\frac{1}{2}\right)}$$

$$= \sqrt{p^2}$$

$$= p$$

11. *(b)* Given that, amplitude and frequency of two waves are same.

Hence, resultant amplitude due to superposition of two waves with phase difference ϕ is given by

$$A^2 = A_1^2 + A_2^2 + 2A_1A_2\cos\phi$$

$$\Rightarrow A^2 = A^2 + A^2 + 2A^2\cos\phi \quad (\because A_1 = A_2 = A)$$

$$\Rightarrow A^2 = 2A^2 + 2A^2\cos\phi$$

$$\Rightarrow \quad \cos\phi = \frac{-1}{2}$$

$$\Rightarrow \quad \phi = \frac{2\pi}{3}$$

12. *(a)* Given, time interval between echoes = 1 s

Speed of sound in air, $v = 340\text{ms}^{-1}$

Let the distance between man and cliff be x.

Time taken by sound to hit cliff and return = $\frac{2x}{v}$

$$1 = \frac{2x}{v}$$

$$\Rightarrow \quad x = \frac{340}{2}\text{ m} = 170\text{ m}$$

Thus, distance between cliffs

$$= 170\times 2 = 340\text{ m}$$

13. *(d)* Given, wavelength of light beam,

$$\lambda = 600\text{ nm}$$

$$= 600\times 10^{-9}\text{ m}$$

Distance between slits, $d = 1\text{ mm} = 10^{-3}\text{ m}$

Distance between slits and screen, $D = 2\text{ m}$

Distance between first dark fringes from the central bright fringe, $2\beta = ?$

As we know, fringe width, $\beta = \frac{\lambda D}{d}$

$$= \frac{600\times 10^{-9}\times 2}{10^{-3}}$$

$$= 1.2\times 10^{-3}\text{ m}$$

Distance between first dark fringes on either side of central bright fringe $(2\beta) = 2\times\beta = 2\times 1.2\times 10^{-3}\text{ m}$

$$\Rightarrow \quad 2\beta = 2.4\text{ mm}$$

14. *(a)* Given, specific rotation of sugar solution,

$$\alpha = 0.01\text{ units}$$

Length of polarimeter tube, $l = 0.25$ m

Optical rotation, $\theta = 0.4$ rad

Concentration of solution, $c = ?$

As we know, specific rotation

$$= \frac{\text{Optical rotation}}{\text{Length of tube}\times\text{ Concentration of sol.}}$$

$$\alpha = \frac{\theta}{l\times c}$$

$$c = \frac{\theta}{l\times\alpha}$$

$$= \frac{0.4}{0.01\times 0.25}$$

$$= 160\text{kg}/\text{m}^3$$

Concentration of sugar solution = $200\text{kg}/\text{m}^{-3}$ (given)

Percentage impurity of sugar in the sample

$$= \frac{160}{200}\times 100\%$$

$$= 80\%$$

15. *(a)* Given, potential difference, $V = 45.5$ V

Velocity, $v = ?$

Energy acquired by the electron after getting accelerated through the potential difference V is eV, which is equal to its kinetic energy.

Hence, kinetic energy (KE) $= \frac{1}{2} m_e v^2 = eV$

[where, m_e = mass of electron]

$$\Rightarrow \quad v = \sqrt{\frac{2eV}{m_e}}$$

Substituting the given values, we get

$$\Rightarrow \quad v = \sqrt{\frac{2 \times 1.6 \times 10^{-19} \times 45.4}{9.11 \times 10^{-31}}}$$

$$= \sqrt{16 \times 10^{12}} = 4 \times 10^6 \text{ ms}^{-1}$$

16. *(b)* Earth is considered to be source of infinite charges having zero potential. When a body is connected to earth, it also acquires same potential as Earth i.e. zero. By this process excess charges flow through the body to the ground or the body acquires the opposite charges from the ground to make the body electrically neutral.

Thus, electrons flow from earth to the body to neutralise the positively charged body.

17. *(d)* The given combination is a balanced condition of Wheatstone bridge because potential at C and D points is same.

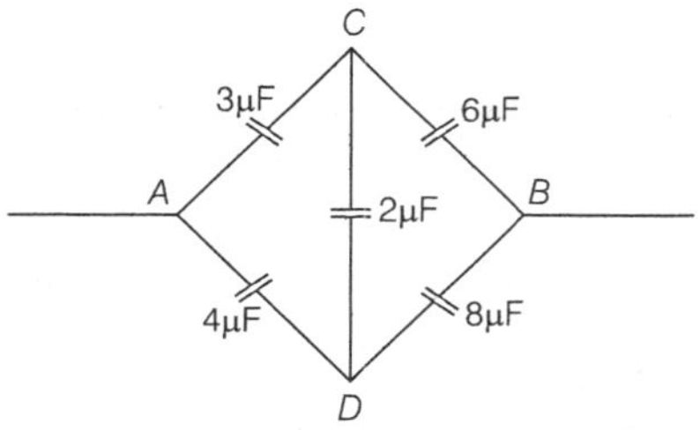

Hence, the 2μF capacitor can be neglected.

The equivalent circuit is given by the figure below

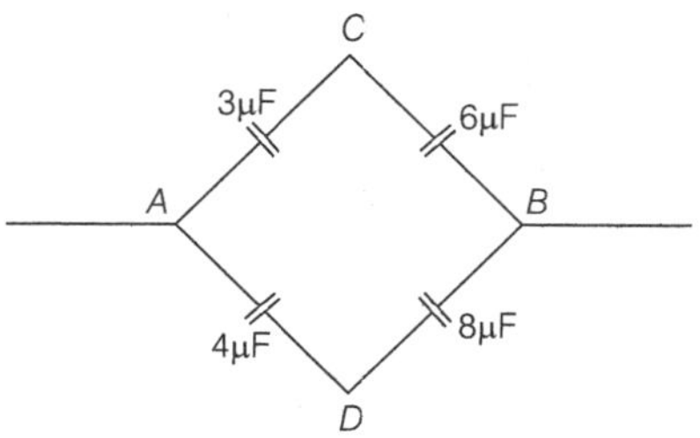

In the upper arm capacitors 3μF and 6μF are connected in series and similarly in lower arm capacitors 4μF and 8μF are connected in series . The equivalent capacitance is given by

$$\frac{1}{C_1} = \frac{1}{3} + \frac{1}{6} = \frac{2+1}{6} = \frac{3}{6}$$

$$\Rightarrow \quad C_1 = 2\mu\text{F}$$

and

$$\frac{1}{C_2} = \frac{1}{4} + \frac{1}{8} = \frac{2+1}{8} = \frac{3}{8}$$

$$\Rightarrow \quad C_2 = \frac{8}{3}\mu\text{F}$$

The reduced circuit with C_1 and C_2 capacitance is given as

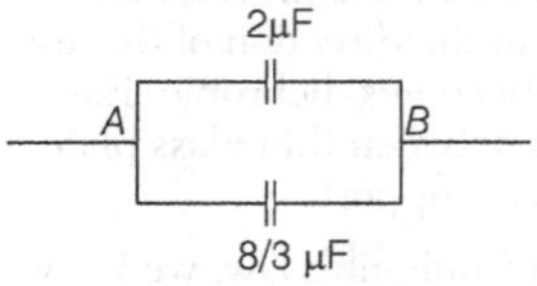

Now, C_1 and C_2 are connected in parallel combination. Hence, equivalent capacitance is given by

$$C_{eq} = C_1 + C_2$$

$$C_{eq} = 2 + \frac{8}{3} = \frac{14}{3}\mu\text{F}$$

18. *(b)* Radius of nth-orbit in hydrogen like atom is given by

$$r = \frac{n^2 h^2}{4\pi^2 mkZe^2}$$

i.e.,

$$r \propto \frac{n^2}{Z}$$

For hydrogen, Z = 1, $n = 1$ in ground state

$$\Rightarrow \quad \frac{n^2}{Z} = \frac{1^2}{1} = 1$$

For Beryllium (Be^{+++}), Z = 4 orbital is same

$$\therefore \quad \frac{n^2}{Z} = 1$$

$$\Rightarrow \quad n^2 = 1 \times Z \Rightarrow n^2 = 4$$

$$\Rightarrow \quad n = 2$$

Thus, the second level of triply ionised Be^{+++} has same radius as the ground state of hydrogen.

19. *(d)* Packing fraction is equal to the ratio of mass defect to total number of nucleons.

$$\text{i.e. PF} = \frac{\text{Mass defect}}{\text{No. of nucleons}} = \frac{M - A}{A}$$

20. *(a)* Let N be the amount of substance left, N_0 be the total amount of substance.

The amount of substance left after N half-life is given by

$$\frac{N}{N_0} = \frac{1}{2^n}$$

Hence,

$$\frac{30}{240} = \frac{1}{2^n}$$

(Since, decay rate proportional to amount of substance)

$$\Rightarrow \quad 2^n = 8 \Rightarrow n = 3$$

Number of half-life passed = 3

Time taken for the substance to decay from 240 count rate to 30 count rate = 1 h = 60 min

$$\text{Half-life} = \frac{\text{Total time}}{\text{Number of half - life}}$$

$$t_{1/2} = \frac{60}{3} = 20 \text{ min}$$

21. *(a)* Given, refractive index for blue light, $\mu_b = 1.67$
Refractive index for yellow light, $\mu_y = 1.65$
Refractive index for red light, $\mu_r = 1.63$
Dispersive power, $\omega = ?$
Dispersive power is the ratio of angular dispersion and mean deviation.
The formula of dispersive power is given as

$$\omega = \frac{\mu_b - \mu_r}{\mu_y - 1} = \frac{1.67 - 1.63}{1.65 - 1} = \frac{0.04}{0.65} = 0.0615$$

22. *(d)* Given, amount of heat absorbed, $Q = 6 \times 10^4$ J
Temperature of reservoir, $T_1 = 227° \text{ C} = 227 + 273 \text{ K} = 500 \text{ K}$
Temperature of sink, $T_2 = 127° \text{ C} = 127 + 273 \text{ K} = 400 \text{ K}$
Efficiency of Carnot engine, $\eta = 1 - \frac{T_2}{T_1} = 1 - \frac{400}{500} = \frac{1}{5}$
Work done by Carnot engine (W)
= Efficiency $(\eta) \times$ heat absorbed (Q) $\left[\eta = \frac{W}{Q}\right]$

$$W = \frac{1}{5} \times 6 \times 10^4 \text{ J} = 1.2 \times 10^4 \text{ J}$$

23. *(b)* According to Boyle's law, at constant temperature, the pV relation will be constant. The pV *versus* p or V graph will be a straight line parallel to X-axis.
Hence, the pV *versus* V graph is given by

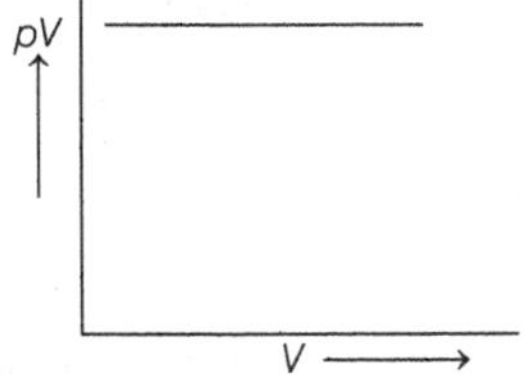

24. *(b)* Tiny water droplets suspended in air have greater density than air. The sunlight when changes medium, undergoes total internal reflection through these droplets thereby splitting in its component colours (since wavelength of each colour is different) and hence, results in rainbow formation.
Thus, dispersion and total internal reflection together results in rainbow formation.

25. *(c)* The combined focal length of plano-convex lens is

$$\frac{1}{f} = \frac{1}{f_1} + \frac{1}{f_2}$$

where, $f_1 = \infty$ for the plane surface and $f_2 = f$

$$\therefore \quad \frac{1}{f} = \frac{1}{\infty} + \frac{1}{f}$$

$$\Rightarrow \quad f = f$$

Now, when concave lens of same focal length is joined to first lens, then combined focal length

$$\frac{1}{F} = \frac{1}{F_1} + \frac{1}{F_2}$$

$$\Rightarrow \quad \frac{1}{F} = \frac{1}{f} - \frac{1}{f} \qquad (F_1 = f, F_2 = -f)$$

$$\Rightarrow \quad \frac{1}{F} = 0 \Rightarrow F = \infty$$

Thus, the image can be focused on infinity or focus shifts to infinity.

26. *(b)* Ratio of diameters, $\frac{d_1}{d_2} = \frac{1}{2}$
Ratio of lengths, $\frac{l_1}{l_2} = \frac{2}{1}$
The rate of heat conduction is given by the formula,

$$H = \frac{dQ}{dt} = k\frac{A}{l}\Delta T$$

where, dQ is the amount of heat transferred in dt time, k is coefficient of heat conduction for a particular material. Since, ΔT is same in both cases, the ratio is

$$\frac{H_1}{H_2} = \frac{A_1 l_2}{A_2 l_1}$$

$$\Rightarrow \quad \frac{H_1}{H_2} = \frac{d_1^2 l_2}{d_2^2 l_1} = \frac{1}{4} \times \frac{1}{2} \Rightarrow R = 1:8$$

27. *(c)* The pressure inside our body is usually equal to the atomospheric pressure. Since, our mouth is open when blowing air, it will have the same pressure as the atmosphere, Hence, blowing air with open mouth is an example of isobaric process.

28. *(d)* Air is a completely elastic medium, i.e. it does not have modulus of rigidity, therefore sound wave in air are always longitudinal.

29. *(d)* White light consists inumerable wavelengths. If monochromatic light is replaced by white light in Young's double slit experiment, then each wavelength form their separate interference pattern. The resultant effect of all these patterns is obtained on the screen.
The waves of all colours reach at mid-point with same or zero phase difference. Therefore, central fringe is white. As fringe width i.e. wavelength increases in order of colours denoted by VIBGYOR, therefore on either side of it some coloured fringes are obtained in reverse order of VIBGYOR. After this the fringes of many colours overlap at each point of the screen and so the screen appears uniformly illuminated.

30. *(b)* Given, separation between two slits,

$$d = 0.9 \text{ mm} = 0.9 \times 10^{-3} \text{ m}$$

Distance between slits and screen, $D = 1$ m

The distance between two consecutive dark or bright fringes is given as β (fringe width) and that between central fringe and first dark fringe on either side is $\frac{\beta}{2}$.

It is given that the spacing between second dark fringe and central fringe $= \beta + \frac{\beta}{2} = \frac{3\beta}{2}$

As we know, $\beta = \frac{\lambda D}{d}$

Hence, $\frac{3}{2} \times \frac{\lambda D}{d} = 1 \times 10^{-3}$ m

$$\Rightarrow \frac{3}{2} \times \lambda \times \frac{1}{0.9 \times 10^{-3}} = 1 \times 10^{-3} \text{ m}$$

$$\Rightarrow \lambda = \frac{2}{3} \times 10^{-3} \times \frac{0.9 \times 10^{-3}}{1} = 0.6 \times 10^{-6} \text{ m}$$

$\therefore$ Wavelength of monochromatic source of light,

$$\lambda = 600 \times 10^{-9} \text{ m} = 600 \text{ nm}$$

31. *(c)* When an uncharged sphere of metal is placed inside a charged parallel plate capacitor, charges of opposite polarity are induced on the surface of the sphere.

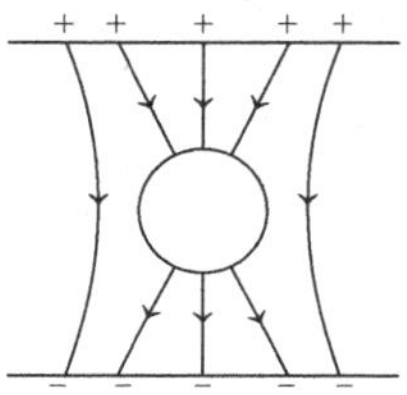

Negative charge would be induced on the upper surface of the sphere and similarly positive charge would be induced on lower surface of the sphere.

We know that, electric lines of force are always perpendicular to the surface and emerge from positive charge and enter into negative charge. Thus, the correct representation of the lines of force is given in the above figure.

32. *(b)* Given, resistance of the wire, $R = 6\Omega$

When it is cut in two equal parts, then resistance of the each part of wire is given by

$$r = \frac{R}{2} = 3\Omega \qquad (\because R \propto l)$$

Now, these new resistances are connected in parallel combination. The equivalent resistance is given by

$$\frac{1}{R_{eq}} = \frac{1}{r} + \frac{1}{r}$$

$$\Rightarrow \frac{1}{R_{eq}} = \frac{1}{3} + \frac{1}{3} = \frac{2}{3}$$

$$\Rightarrow R_{eq} = 1.5\,\Omega$$

33. *(a)* The direction of magnetic field in a current carrying straight wire is given by right hand thumb rule. If we point our thumb in a direction of East to West, the direction of magnetic field is found to be towards North, which is given by the curled fingers of our hand.

34. *(a)* Magnetic field lines of a bar magnet is equivalent to the magnetic field lines due to a solenoid.

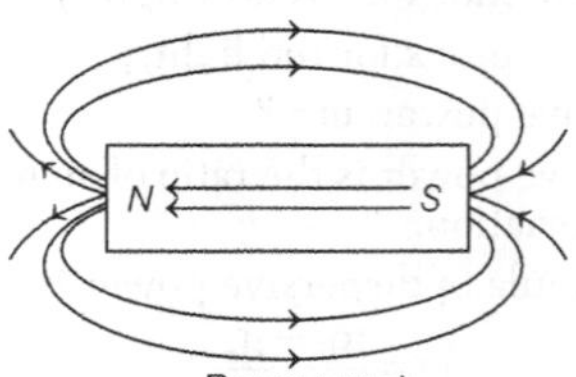

Bar magnet

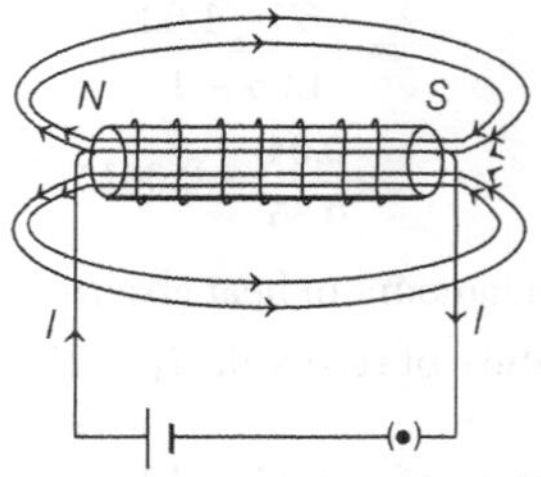

Hence, *A* bar magnet is equivalent to a solenoid carrying current.

35. *(a)* Excitation energy of hydrogen like ion in its first excitation state, $\Delta E = 40.8$eV

For the hydrogen like ion, energy in the ground state $(n = 1)$,

$$E = \frac{-13.6Z^2}{n^2} \text{eV} = -13.6Z^2\text{eV}$$

Energy in the first excited state, $E_2 = \frac{-13.6Z^2}{n^2} = \frac{-13.6Z^2}{4}$

Excitation energy, $\Delta E = E_2 - E_1$

$$= \left(\frac{-13.6Z^2}{4} + 13.6Z^2\right)\text{eV}$$

$$= (-3.4 + 13.6)Z^2\text{eV}$$

$$\Rightarrow 40.8\,\text{eV} = 10.2Z^2\text{eV}$$

$$\Rightarrow Z^2 = \frac{40.8}{10.2}$$

$$\Rightarrow Z^2 = 4$$

$$\Rightarrow Z = 2$$

Thus, energy of the electron in the ground state is given as $E_1 = -13.6Z^2$eV

$$\Rightarrow E_1 = -13.6(2)^2\text{ eV}$$

$$\Rightarrow E_1 = -54.4 \text{ eV}$$

Hence, the energy needed to remove the electron from the ion in ground state (ionisation energy)

$$= -(-54.4)\text{eV} = 54.4\text{eV}$$

36. *(d)* Threshold wavelength of the metal, $\lambda_0 = 5200\text{Å}$

$$= 5200 \times 10^{-10} \text{ m}$$

Frequency of the radiation, $\nu_0 = \frac{c}{\lambda}$

$$= \frac{3 \times 10^8}{5200 \times 10^{-10}}$$
$$= 0.57 \times 10^{15} \text{ Hz}$$
$$= 5.7 \times 10^{14} \text{ Hz}$$

The frequency of infrared radiation is lower than the threshold frequency of the metal. Hence, the surface of the metal is illuminated with monochromatic radiation which is greater than 5.7×10^{14} Hz.

The 50 W UV-lamp is suitable for this purpose.

37. *(d)* The emitter is always forward biased to enable the majority charge carriers to cross the emitter-base junction and collector-base function is in reverse biased to collect the charge carriers, so that current flows through the transistor.

Hence, the emitter-base junction of a transistor is forward biased, while collector-base junction is reverse biased.

38. *(a)* Potential across the *p-n* junction varies symmetrically linear, having *p*-side negative and *n*-side positive. In a forward biased *p-n* junction diode, the repulsion of holes and electrons takes place which decreases width of potential barrier by striking the combination of holes and electrons. The width of depletion region in forward biased is less than the reversed biased. Hence, the graph of the potential barrier in the depletion region is given by

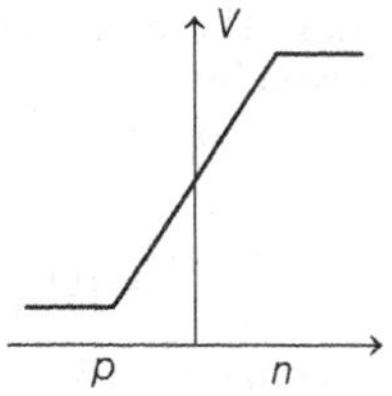

39. *(c)* The given diagram represents a cylinder placed in a uniform electric field.

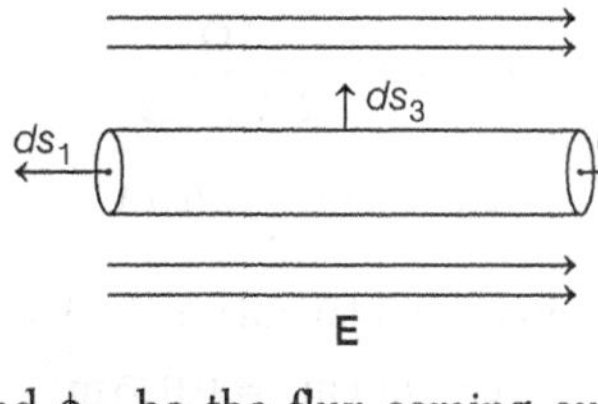

Let ϕ_1 and ϕ_2 be the flux coming out of a circular cross-sectional surface. ϕ_3 is flux through the curved surface. Since, normal to a curved surface is always 90° to electric field **E**, so

$\phi_3 = Eds_3 \cos\theta = Eds_3 \cos 90° = 0$

ϕ_1 and ϕ_2 are equal and opposite to each other, hence $\phi_1 + \phi_2 = 0$.

So, total flux through the surface of cylinder is zero.

40. *(c)* Given, power of bulb A, $P_A = 60$ W

Power of bulb B, $P_B = 100$ W

Since, both bulbs are connected to the same power source in parallel combination. Thus,

$$P_A = \frac{V^2}{R_A} = 60\text{W and } P_B = \frac{V^2}{R_B} = 100\text{ W}$$

$$R_A = \frac{V^2}{60}\Omega \text{ and } R_B = \frac{V^2}{100}\Omega$$

Current in bulb A, $I_A = \frac{\text{Potential}}{\text{Resistance}}$

$$\Rightarrow \quad I_A = \frac{V}{\frac{V^2}{60}} \Rightarrow I_A = \frac{60}{V}$$

Similarly, current in bulb B, $I_B = \frac{V}{\frac{V^2}{100}} = \frac{100}{V}$

It is clear that $I_B > I_A$.

41. *(b)* Magnetic field at any point due to a straight current carrying wire is given by

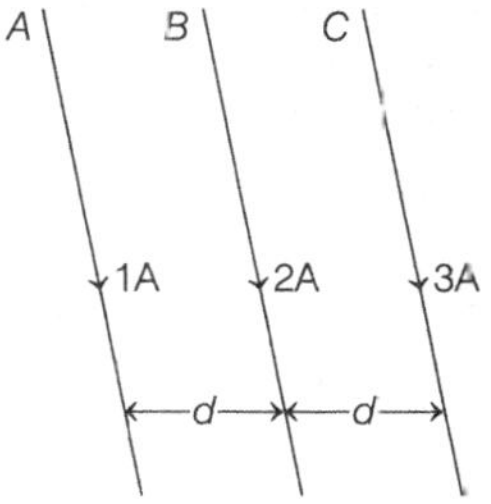

$$B = \frac{\mu_0 I}{2\pi d}$$

where, d is the distance of the point from the wire and I_1 is current flowing in the wire.

Force due to this magnetic field on current carrying wire is given by

$$F = BIL$$

where, L is the length of the wire.

∴ Force on wire B due to wire A, $F_A = BIL$

$$\Rightarrow \quad F_A = \frac{\mu_0 \times 1}{2\pi d} \times 2 \times L$$

Force on wire B due to wire C, $F_C = BIL$

$$\Rightarrow \quad F_C = \frac{\mu_0 \times 3}{2\pi d} \times 2 \times L$$

It is clear that $F_C > F_A$. Hence, net force is towards wire C.

42. *(b)* Ferromagnetic substances like iron, nickel and cobalt obey Curie-Weiss law above Curie temperature.

43. *(c)* EMF induced in circular coil of self-inductance L is given by $\varepsilon = -L\frac{dI}{dt}$

EMF is equal to the potential difference dimensionally.

Hence, $\varepsilon = V$

We know, $V = \frac{W}{q}$

Thus, dimensional formula of potential difference is given as

$$V = \frac{[M^1L^2T^{-2}]}{[AT]}$$
$$= [M^1L^2T^{-3}A^{-1}]$$

The self-inductance is given by, $L = V \times \frac{dt}{dI}$

Dimensional formula of self-inductance is given by,

$$L = [M^1L^2T^{-3}A^{-1}] \times \frac{[T]}{[A]}$$

Dimensional formula of self-inductance,
$$L = [M^1L^2T^{-2}A^{-2}]$$

44. *(d)* The magnet is attached to the spring. This magnet will execute simple harmonic motion. When a coil is placed in such a way that magnet moves in and out of the coil, an emf is induced in the coil which opposes the movement of magnet in the coil. Due to this induced emf galvanometer will show deflections to the left and right periodically.

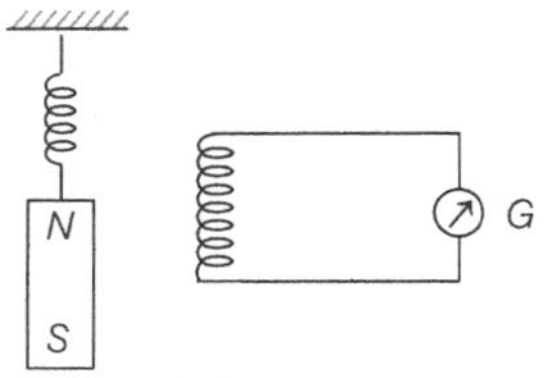

As the emf is induced in the coil eddy currents are also induced in the magnet, which lowers down the total magnetic strength of the magnet. Due to this reason, the magnetic flux linked with the coil decrease and hence amplitude of the deflections produced in the galvanometer also decreases.

45. *(b)* Given, resistance of the galvanometer, $G = 40\Omega$

Current in the galvanometer,

$$I_g = 10 \text{ m A} = 10 \times 10^{-3} \text{ A}$$

Maximum reading of voltmeter, $V = 50$ V

The galvanometer can be converted into voltmeter by connecting a shunt resistance (S) in the series.

Voltage in the voltmeter is given by

$$V = I_g(G + R)$$
$$\therefore \quad 50 = 10 \times 10^{-3}(40 + R)$$
$$\Rightarrow \quad 5000 = 40 + R$$
$$\Rightarrow \quad R = 4960\Omega$$

46. *(c)* R_1 is connected with 10Ω resistance. According to question, a balanced point is obtained at 50.

Thus, $\frac{R_1 + 10}{R_2} = \frac{50}{50}$

$$\Rightarrow \quad R_2 = R_1 + 10 \quad \ldots\text{(i)}$$

When 10Ω is removed the balanced point shifts to 40 cm.

Thus, $\frac{R_1}{R_2} = \frac{40}{60}$

$$\Rightarrow \quad R_2 = \frac{3}{2}R_1 \quad \ldots\text{(ii)}$$

From Eqs. (i) and (ii), we get

$$\frac{3}{2}R_1 = R_1 + 10$$
$$\Rightarrow \quad \frac{1}{2}R_1 = 10$$
$$\Rightarrow \quad R_1 = 20\Omega$$

47. *(a)* In the steady state analysis capacitor acts as an open circuit. Therefore, the equivalent circuit is given as

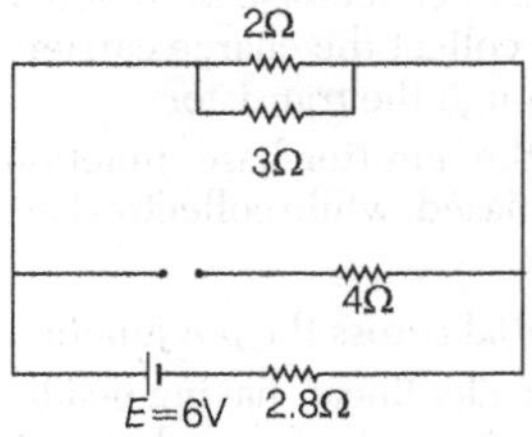

Thus, current in the 4Ω resistor is zero. 2Ω and 3Ω resistors are parallel to each other. Thus, the resistance in the upper branch is given by

$$R = \frac{2 \times 3}{2 + 3} = \frac{6}{5}\Omega$$

The upper branch resistor are connected to 2.8Ω resistor in series. Therefore, equivalent resistance in the circuit is given by

$$R_{eq} = 2.8 + \frac{6}{5}$$
$$= \frac{14.0 + 6}{5} = 4\Omega$$

Current, $I = \frac{\text{Voltage}}{\text{Resistance}} = \frac{6}{4} = 1.5$ A

Current in the 2Ω resistor is given by current division rule

i.e. $$I_{2\Omega} = I \times \frac{3\Omega}{2\Omega + 3\Omega}$$

$$\Rightarrow \quad I_{2\Omega} = 1.5 \times \frac{3}{5} = 0.9\text{A}$$

48. *(a)* Given, area of rectangular coil, $A = 25$ cm $\times 10$ cm

$$\Rightarrow \quad A = 250\text{cm}^2 = 0.025\,\text{m}^2$$

No. of turns in the coil, $N = 300$

Magnetic field strength, $B = 4 \times 10^{-2}$T

Peak voltage will be induced when the longer side of the coil moves perpendicular to the magnetic field.

$$\omega = 2\pi\nu = 2\pi \times 50 = 100\pi$$

Induced emf is given by

$$\varepsilon = NBA\omega$$
$$= 300 \times 40 \times 10^{-2} \times 0.025 \times 100\pi = 3\pi\,\text{V}$$

49. *(a)* The *L-C-R* circuit in series combination and phasor diagram is given below

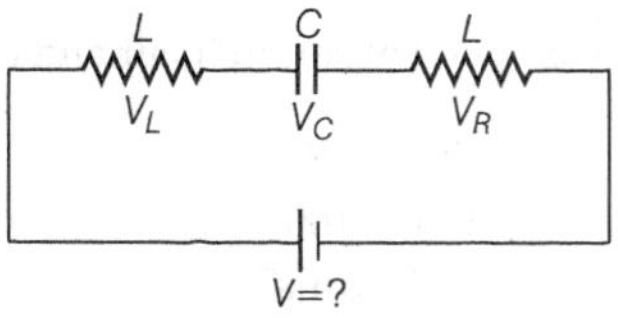

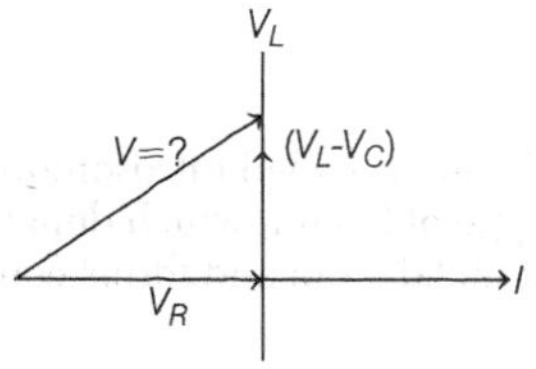

According to the question,
Potential difference across resistor, $V_R = 40$ V
Potential difference across inductor, $V_L = 60$ V
Potential difference across capacitor, $V_C = 30$ V
Magnitude of potential difference supplied is given by

$$V = \sqrt{V_R^2 + (V_L - V_C)^2} = \sqrt{40^2 + (60-30)^2}$$
$$= \sqrt{(40)^2 + (30)^2} = \sqrt{2500}$$
$$= 50 \text{ V}$$

50. *(c)* Given, radius of the coil = 0.1 m
No. of turns in the coil = 10
Horizontal component of magnetic field,

$$B_H = 0.314 \times 10^{-4} \text{ T}$$

The magnetic field at the centre of current carrying coil is given by the formula, $B = \dfrac{\mu_0 nI}{2R}$

According to question, magnetic field due to the coil obtains neutral point, in earth's magnetic field.
Hence, horizontal component of magnetic field,

$$B_H = \frac{\mu_0 nI}{2R}$$

Thus, $$I = \frac{2RB_H}{\mu_0 n}$$

$$\Rightarrow \quad I = \frac{2(0.1)(0.314 \times 10^{-4})}{10 \times 4 \times (3.142) \times 10^{-7}} = 0.5 \text{ A}$$

51. *(c)* The spectrum obtained from the chromosphere of the sun at the time of total is line emission spectrum. The spectrum obtained is of 5876Å wavelength from D_3 line in almost yellow colour.

52. *(c)* Heavy water is compound that contains heavy hydrogen or deuterium and oxygen. Heavy water is also called deuterium oxide D_2O.

53. *(b)* The nuclear reactor at Kaiga is a power reactor. The use of nuclear reactor for electricity and power generation classifies it as a power reactor.

54. *(c)* The work done by a force in moving a body is

$$W = \mathbf{F} \cdot \mathbf{s}$$

where, **s** is the displacement vector.

In circular path, the force is centripetal, thus always acting towards the centre along the radial direction.
However, the displacement is always along tangent to the circle at the instantaneous position of object. Hence, $\theta = 90°$

Thus, $$W = \mathbf{F} \cdot \mathbf{s} = Fs \cos 90° = 0$$

55. *(b)* Given, velocity of the bullet $v = 100 \text{ms}^{-1}$
Let, thickness of one plank, $t = s$
According to third equation of motion, we get

$$v^2 - u^2 = 2as$$
$$(0) - (100)^2 = 2 \times a \times (2s)$$

($\because$ two planks are penetrated)

$$\Rightarrow \quad -1000 = 4as \quad \ldots(i)$$

When velocity of bullet is doubled, $v = 200 \text{ms}^{-1}$
Applying third equation of motion again , we get

$$\Rightarrow \quad 0 - (200)^2 = 2 \times a \times (ns)$$

(where, n is number of planks)

$$-40000 = 2ans \quad \ldots(ii)$$

From Eqs. (i) and (ii), we get

$$\frac{-40000}{-10000} = \frac{2ans}{4as}$$
$$\Rightarrow \quad n = 8$$

Hence, 8 planks can be penetrated by the same bullet if speed is doubled.

56. *(c)* Let m_1 be the mass of 1st body , $m_1 = 1$ kg
m_2 be the mass of 2nd body, $m_2 = 2$ kg
The relation, between kinetic energy and momentum is given by

$$K = \frac{1}{2}mv^2 = \frac{p^2}{2m}$$

where, p is the momentum of the body. Since, momentum of both bodies are same.

Hence, $$\frac{k_1}{k_2} = \frac{p^2}{2m_1} \times \frac{2m_2}{p^2}$$
$$\frac{k_1}{k_2} = \frac{2}{1}$$

Thus, the ratio of their kinetic energies is 2 : 1.

57. *(a)* Pitch is dependent on the frequency of the source of sound whereas loudness depends upon the amplitude of sound wave.
Hence, the loudness and pitch of a sound note depends on intensity and frequency.

58. *(c)* Open windows and doors are considered to be perfect black body, hence absorption coefficient of an open window and door is 1.

59. *(a)* In Melde's experiment, the variation in frequency is created if the tension is increased in the string. Melde's showed that mechanical waves also undergo phenomenon of interference. To do this a resonance in tuning fork and frequency of standing waves was developed.
Hence, the frequency of the tuning fork and the frequency of the waves in the string are in the ratio 1 : 1.

60. *(b)* Given, speed of sound in air, $c = 300\text{ms}^{-1}$

Difference between apparent frequency during approach and apparent frequency during recession = 2%

Thus, frequency during approach – frequency during recession $= \frac{2}{100} \times f_0$

$$\Rightarrow \quad f_0\left(\frac{c+v}{c}\right) - f_0\left(\frac{c-v}{c}\right) = \frac{2}{100} f_0$$

where, c is speed of sound in air and v is the velocity of source.

$$\Rightarrow \quad \frac{2v}{300} = \frac{2}{100}$$

$$\Rightarrow \quad v = 3\text{ms}^{-1}$$

Chemistry

61. *(a)* Ozone in stratosphere is depleted by number of pollutants like CFC's (CF_2Cl_2), nitrogen oxide, CCl_4, Cl_2 etc.

62. *(c)* Linolenic acid is an unsaturated fatty acid. It is a carboxylic acid with 18- carbon chain having three double bond.

63. *(c)* When chlorine is passed through boiling toluene, mixture of *o* and *p*-chloro toluene is formed.

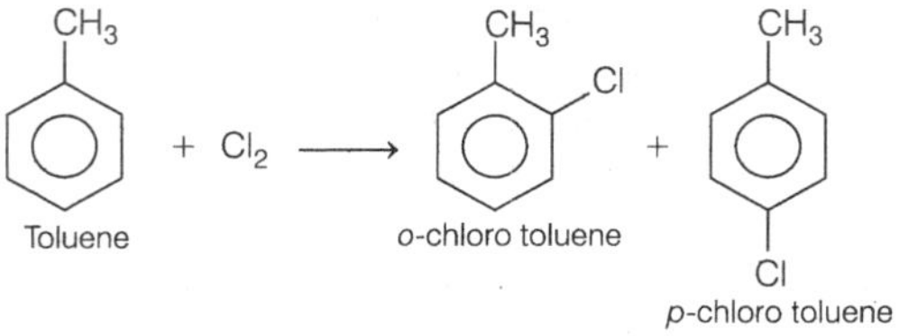

64. *(b)* The standard temperature used in thermo chemical calculation is 25° C or 298 K

$$K = T + 273 = 25 + 273 = 298\text{ K}$$

65. *(c)* Density is an intensive property. It is independent of the quantity of substance. While, enthalpy, entropy and mass are extensive properties.

66. *(c)* Schiff's reagent contains rosaniline ($C_{19}H_{18}N_3Cl$). It is used to check the presence of aldehyde in the given compound by giving purple or magneta colour.

67. *(d)* Chromyl chloride is inorganic compound with formula CrO_2Cl_2. It is reddish compound that is volatile at room temperature. It's structure is

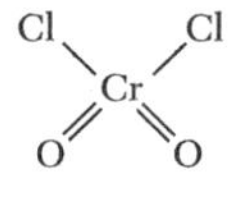

68. *(c)* Horn silver is a halide ore. The formula for horn silver is AgCl.

69. *(b)* Tetrahedral structure is formed by sp^3 hybridisation. Here, four sp^3-hybridised orbitals are arranged in tetrahedral structure.

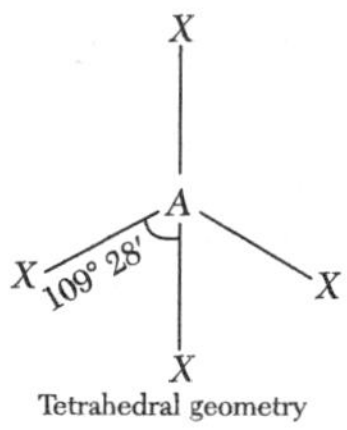

Tetrahedral geometry

70. *(c)* NO^+ ligand is called nitrosonium ligand. It is positive type of ligand, which donate pair of electrons to central metal atom and forms coordinate bond with them.

71. *(a)* A compound in which the complex ion carries positive charge is called cationic complex.

For hexaamino platinum chloride, chemical formula is $[Pt(NH_3)_6]Cl_4$.

$\therefore$ The complex ion $[Pt(NH_3)_6]^{4+}$ is positively charge.

72. *(b)* $2p_x$ atomic orbital undergoes linear combination with $2p_x$-orbital.

For linear combination, the combining orbitals should have same energy and same orientation of overlapping of p_x-orbital.

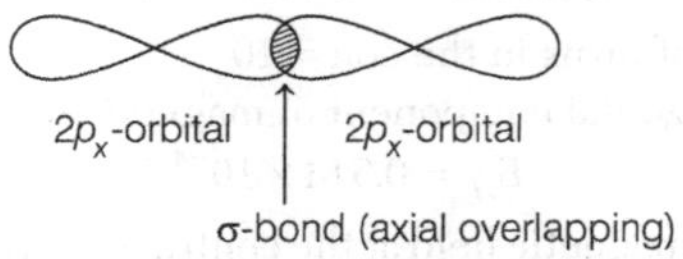

73. *(b)* $[A_0] = 0.1$

$$[A_t] = 0.01$$

$$t = 100\text{ s}$$

1st order reaction,

$$k = \frac{2.303}{t}\log\frac{[A_0]}{[A_t]}$$

$$= \frac{2.303}{100}\log\frac{0.1}{0.01} = 0.02303\text{ s}^{-1}$$

74. *(d)* When Δn_g i.e. difference in gaseous moles of product and reactant is zero, then pressure has no effect and it is equilibrium point for reaction.

$$N_2(g) + O_2(g) \rightleftharpoons 2NO(g)$$

$$\Delta n_g = 2 - (1 + 1) = 0$$

$\therefore$ Pressure has no effect for this reaction.

75. *(d)* Conductivity of a solution is not affected by addition of ethanol as it is a covalent compound and it do not dissociate into ions to change the number of ions in the solution.

76. *(d)* Lowering in vapour pressure is a colligative property so, the number of particle (i.e. ion) increase, which results in decrease of vapour pressure. The lowering in vapour pressure is maximum for 0.1M $K_4[Fe(CN)_6]$, as it dissociate into free ions i.e. four K^+ and one $[Fe(CN)_6]^-$.

77. *(b)* The given reaction takes place as follows :

$$\underset{\text{Bromoethane}}{CH_3—CH_2Br} + \underset{\substack{\text{Isopropyl chloride}\\ \text{(2-chloro propane)}}}{Cl—\overset{}{\underset{\substack{|\\ CH_3}}{CH}}— CH_3} \xrightarrow[\text{Na in ether}]{} \underset{\text{2-methyl butane}}{CH_3CH_2—\underset{\substack{|\\ CH_3}}{CH}—CH_3}$$

78. *(c)* NH_3 (ammonia) gas is dried by using sodalime, because NH_3 itself is basic in nature and only basic compound can be used to dry NH_3, while conc. H_2SO_4, anhy. $CaCl_2$ and P_2O_5 can not react with ammonia.

79. *(c)* Copper (II) hydroxide $[Cu(OH)_2]$ is amphoteric in nature and is soluble in excess of ammonium hydroxide.

$$\underset{\substack{\text{Copper (II)}\\ \text{hydroxide}}}{Cu(OH)_2} + \underset{\substack{\text{Ammonium}\\ \text{hydroxide}}}{4NH_4OH} \longrightarrow \underset{\substack{\text{Copper tetra ammine dihydroxide}\\ \text{(Soluble complex)}}}{[Cu(NH_3)_4](OH)_2} + 4H_2O$$

80. *(a)* Potassium dichromate $(K_2Cr_2O_7)$ can be converted into potassium chromate (K_2CrO_4) by adding potassium hydroxide (KOH).

$$\underset{\substack{\text{Potassium}\\ \text{dichromate}}}{K_2Cr_2O_7(aq)} + \underset{\substack{\text{Potassium}\\ \text{hydroxide}}}{2KOH} \longrightarrow \underset{\substack{\text{Potassium}\\ \text{chromate}}}{2K_2CrO_4} + H_2O$$

81. *(b)* Equivalent moles of NaOH = Equivalent moles of acid

$$N_1V_1 = \frac{\text{Weight}}{\text{Equivalent mass}}$$

$$40 \times 10^{-3} \times 0.125 = \frac{0.5}{\text{Equivalent mass}}$$

$\therefore$ Equivalent mass of acid = 100

82. *(d)* $M_1 = 5$ L and pH = 12

$$pOH = 14 - pH = 14 - 12 = 2$$
$$[OH^-] = 10^{-pOH} = 10^{-2}$$

$\therefore$ Moles of NaOH $= M_1V_1 = 5 \times 10^{-2}$ moles

$\therefore$ Mass of NaOH = moles × molar mass

$$= 5 \times 10^{-2} \times 40 = 2\,g$$

83. *(a)* Equivalent moles of oxalic acid = Equivalent moles of $KMnO_4$

$$= N_1V_1 = 25 \times 0.2 \times 10^{-3} = 5 \times 10^{-3} = 0.005$$

$$\frac{\text{Weight of oxalic acid}}{\text{Eq. weight of oxalic acid}} = 0.005$$

Weight of oxalic acid = 0.05 × 63 = 0.315 g

$\therefore$ 0.315 g in 50 cc of oxalic acid.

In 500cc solution, mass of oxalic acid is

$$= 0.315 \times \frac{500}{50} = 3.15\text{ g}$$

84. *(a)* Pure water is neutral as it has equal concentration of H^+ and OH^- ions. It has pH = 7.

85. *(b)* In the titration of Mohr's salt with $KMnO_4$, the indicator used is $KMnO_4$ itself. Because $KMnO_4$ is very intense purple in colour. When, the solution changes to pink, end point is noted.

$$\underset{\text{Dark purple}}{MnO_4^-} \xrightarrow[\text{Mohr's salt}]{\text{Reduction with}} \underset{\text{Pink}}{Mn^{2+}}$$

86. *(d)* The relationship between half-life of a reaction and order of reaction is

$$t_{1/2} \propto \frac{1}{a^{(n-1)}}$$

87. *(a)* $\dfrac{p^\circ - p_S}{p^\circ} = \dfrac{w_2M_1}{M_2w_1}$

Where, w_2 and M_2 are weight and molecular mass of solute.

M_1 and w_1 are molecular mass and weight of solvent.

$$\frac{\Delta p}{p^\circ} = \frac{6}{60} \times \frac{18}{90} = \frac{1}{50} = 0.02$$

88. *(c)* Molar mass of sucrose $(C_{12}H_{22}O_{11}) = 342$

$$\text{Molality} = \frac{\dfrac{\text{Weight of sucrose}}{\text{Molar mass of sucrose}}}{\text{Mass of solvent }(g)} \times 1000$$

$$= \frac{6.84 \times 1000}{342 \times 200} = 0.1\text{ M}$$

89. *(a)* NaCl on dissociation gives Na^+ and Cl^- ions as follows:

$$\underset{\text{Sodium chloride}}{NaCl(aq)} \longrightarrow \underset{\text{Common ions}}{Na^+} + Cl^-\text{ (ions)}$$

While, soap in the solution gives $RCOO^-$ and Na^+ ions as follows:

$$\underset{\text{Soap}}{R—CO\overset{-\ +}{ONa}(s)} \longrightarrow RCOO^- + Na^+$$

$\therefore$ Solubility of soap decrease due to common ion (Na^+) present in the solution due to Le-Chatelier's principle, reaction shifts towards the reactant side.

90. *(a)* Concentrations of ions in 0.1 M aluminium sulphate $[Al_2(SO_4)_3]$ is

$$= 0.1[2 \times (Al^{3+})\text{ions} + 3 \times (SO_4^{2-})\text{ions}]$$

$$= 0.1[2 \times 1 + 3 \times 1] = 0.1 \times 5 = 0.5\text{ M}$$

Concentrations of ions in 0.1 M potassium nitrate (KCl) is = 0.1 (1 mole of K^+ + 1 mole of Cl^-)

$$= 0.1 \times 2 = 0.2\text{ M}$$

Concentration of ions in 0.1 M magnesium chloride $(MgCl_2)$ is = 0.1 (1 mole of Mg^{2-} + 2 moles of Cl^-)

$$= 0.1 \times 3 = 0.3\text{ M}$$

Concentration of ions in 0.1 M barium chloride $(BaCl_2)$ is = 0.1 (1 mole of Ba^{2+} + 2 moles of Cl^-)

$$= 0.1 \times 3 = 0.3\text{ M}$$

$\therefore$ Order of concentration is

$$0.1\text{ M }Al_2(SO_4)_3 > 0.1\text{ M KCl} > 0.1\,MgCl_2 \approx 0.1\text{ M }BaCl_2$$

$\because$ Osmotic pressure is colligative property and, it depends on concentration of ions.

$\therefore$ Order of osmotic pressure is

$0.1\text{ M }(Al_2SO_4)_3 > 0.1\text{ M KCl} > 0.1\text{ M }MgCl_2 > 0.1\text{ M }BaCl_2$

91. *(d)* As reaction is completed 50% so, $t_{1/2} = 30$ min.

For first order reaction

$$k = \frac{0.693}{t_{1/2}} = \frac{0.693}{30} = 0.0231\text{min}^{-1}$$

92. *(b)* The ebullioscopic constant (K_b) is the elevation in boiling point produced by 1 molal solution

i.e. $\Delta T_b = K_b\, m$

When, $m = 1$

$K_b = \Delta T_b$

93. *(c)* Molecular mass of glucose = 180 g / mol

Mass of water = 50 g = 0.05 kg

$$\text{Molality }(m) = \frac{\text{Mass}}{\text{Molar mass} \times \text{mass of solvent (in kg)}}$$

$$0.3 = \frac{\text{Mass}}{160 \times 0.05}$$

Mass = 2.7 g

94. *(*)* The reaction of Mohr's salt and $K_2Cr_2O_7$ is as follow:

$$6Fe^{2+} + Cr_2O_7^{2-} + 14[H^+] \longrightarrow 6Fe^{3+} + 2Cr^{3+} + 7H_2O$$

n-factor of $Cr_2O_7^{2-}$ is 6 and n-factor of Fe^{2+} is 1.

As n-factor for Fe is 1 so,

Molarity = Normality Concentration of Mohr's salt = 0.08 M

Moles in 25 mL of 0.08 M Mohr's salt

$$= 0.08 \times \frac{25}{1000} = 0.002$$

$\therefore$ Moles in 500 cc of Mohr's salt

$$= 0.002 \times \frac{500}{25} = 0.04$$

Hence, mass of Mohr's salt in 500 cc

$= 0.04 \times 392 = 15.68$ g

95. *(a)* For a reaction to be spontaneous change in Gibbs free energy should be negative.

i.e. $\Delta G = \Delta H - T\Delta S < 0$

$= (-\text{ve}) - (+\text{ve}) = -\text{ve} - \text{ve} = -2\text{ve}$

$\Delta H < 0$ and $\Delta S > 0$

So, $\Delta H = -$ ve and $\Delta S = +$ve

96. *(c)* Sodium chloride is in simple closed cubic packing. Its coordination number is 6.

97. *(a)* Conjugate acid of NH_2^- is NH_3.

$$\underset{\text{Base}}{NH_2^-} + H^+ \longrightarrow \underset{\text{Conjugate acid}}{NH_3}$$

98. *(a)* Molar conductivity increases with decrease in concentration as the total volume, (V) of a solution containing one mole of electrolyte also increases.

$\therefore$ 0.005 M NaCl have highest molar conductivity.

99. *(d)* In the detection of III group, basic radicals NH_4OH is added after NH_4Cl to decrease the ionisation of NH_4OH due to common ion effect.

100. *(a)* Just before attaining chemical equilibrium rate of forward reaction decrease and rate of backward reaction increases.

As the concentration of product is slightly more than the equilibrium concentration.

101. *(a)* Atomic number of Fe (26) = $[Ar]3d^6 4s^2$

$Fe^{2+} = [Ar]3d^6 4s^0$

⇅	↑	↑	↑	↑

$3d^6$

Number of unpaired electrons = 4

For $Co^{2+} = [Ar]\ 3d^7$

Number of unpaired electrons = 3

It shows highest magnetic moment. As magnetic moment depends on number of unpaired electrons.

For $Cr^{3+} = [Ar]3d^3$

$\therefore$ Number of unpaired electrons = 3

For $Ni^+ = [Ar]3d^8$

$\therefore$ Number of unpaired electrons = 2

102. *(c)* In $3d$ series as we move from Sc to Zn paramagnetism first increases as number of unpaired electron increases . After the elements get half-filled the number of unpaired electron decreases as pairing take place.

$\therefore$ The number of unpaired electron, decreases thus, paramagnetism also decreases.

103. *(d)* Fe (26) = $[Ar]3d^6 4s^2$

$Fe^{3+}(23) = [Ar]3d^5\, 4s^0$

Fe^{3+} =

↑	↑	↑	↑	↑

$3d^5$

$\therefore$ Number of unpaired electrons = 5

104. *(c)* In $K_4[Fe(CN)_6]$,

Oxidation number of Fe $\Rightarrow 4 + x + 6 \times (-1) = 0$

$x = +2$

It's IUPAC name is potassium hexacyanoferrate (II).

105. *(d)* Adsorption of an inert gases on activated charcoal increases with decrease of temperature as it is an exothermic process. The adsorption of gas on solid surface is similar to condensation process, which is exothermic in nature.

106. *(b)* Brine is a solution of sodium chloride and water. On electrolysis, it gives chlorine (Cl_2), hydrogen (H_2) and sodium hydroxide (NaOH).

At cathode

$$2H^+(aq) + 2e^- \longrightarrow \underset{\text{Hydrogen}}{H_2}$$

$$2H_2O + 2e^- \longrightarrow H_2 + 2OH^-(aq)$$

At anode

$$2Cl^- \longrightarrow \underset{\text{Chlorine}}{Cl_2} + 2e^-$$

The hydroxide ion, with the unchanged sodium ion, forms NaOH.

$$Na^+ + OH^- \longrightarrow \underset{\text{Sodium hydroxide}}{NaOH}$$

107. *(a)* Sucrose is a non-reducing sugar due to 1, 2-glycosidic linkage between anomeric carbon atoms.

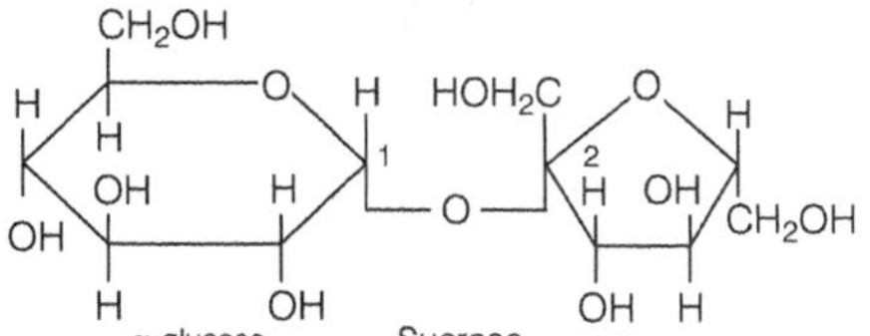

α-glucose Sucrose β-fructose

Therefore, there is no free aldehyde or ketone group (reducing of group) as they are involved in glycosidic linkage.

108. *(d)* Sulphur containing amino acid is cysteine. It's structure is

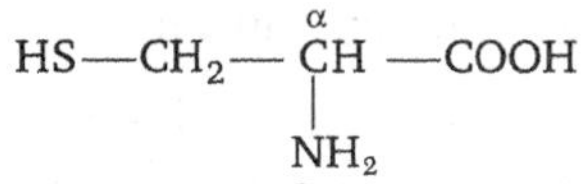

Cysteine

109. *(c)* Lysine is a basic amino acid as it contains more number of amino groups than carboxyl groups. It's structure is

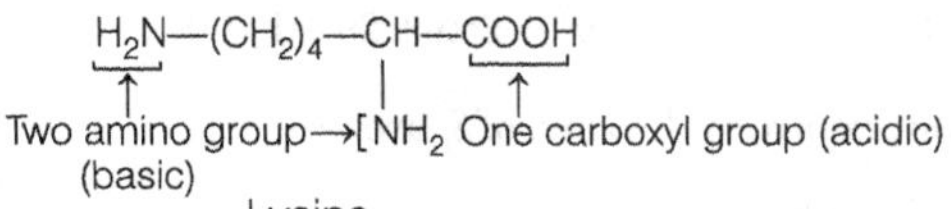

Lysine

110. *(b)* In Molisch's reagent substance used is α-napthol dissolved in ethanol. It gives positive test with carbohydrates, nucleic acids and glycoproteins by forming purple-coloured product.

111. *(b)* In benzene, each carbon have sp^2 hybridisation.

The structure of benzene is

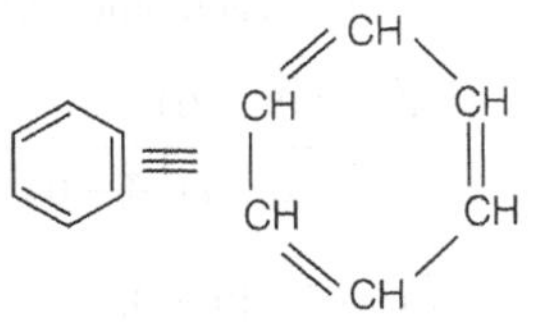

Each carbon have three σ-bonds.

$\therefore$ Hybridisation $= sp^2$

112. *(d)* Alcohols are oxidised by passing their vapours over heated copper. 2° alcohol (isopropyl alcohol) is oxidised to acetone i.e. it undergoes dehydrogenation as follows :

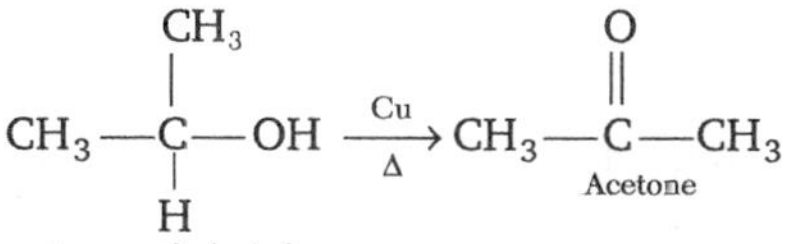

Isopropyl alcohol Acetone

113. *(c)* The IUPAC name of $CH_3—N(CH_3)—CH_3$ is N, N-dimethyl methanamine.

114. *(b)* The reaction of benzaldehyde with acetic anhydride in presence of fused sodium acetate gives cinnamic acid. This reaction is called Perkin condensation.

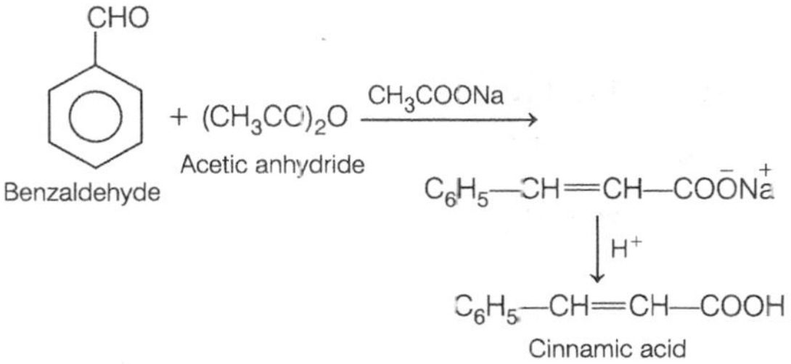

115. *(c)* When a mixture of calcium benzoate and calcium formate is dry distilled, we get benzaldehyde.

$$\underset{\text{Calcium benzoate}}{(Ph—COO)_2Ca} + \underset{\text{Calcium formate}}{(HCOO—)_2Ca} \xrightarrow[\text{Dry distillation}]{\Delta} \underset{\text{Benzaldehyde}}{2Ph—CHO} + 2CaCO_3$$

116. *(a)* Basic strength of amine increase with increases in strength of electron donating group. In dimethyl amine there are two methyl group with + *I*-effect and is most basic.

While, methyl amine has only one methyl group and ammonia has no methyl group.

In aniline due to resonance the lone pair of amines are delocalised and is least basic.

Basic strength order

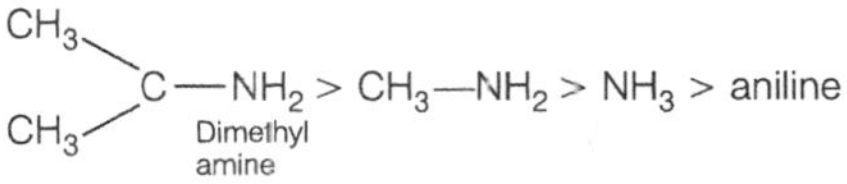

117. *(c)* Benzoic acid is bi-functional compound as it has two functional groups, carboxylic acid and aromatic ring.

Cinnamic acid is tri-functional compound as it has three functional groups, i.e., —COOH, C=C and aromatic ring.

Formic acid and acetic acid are mono-functional as they have one functional group i.e., (—COOH group).

118. *(d)* When phenol is treated with chloromethane in presence of $AlCl_3$ we get mixture of *o* and *p*-cresol. It is an example of Friedel-Craft's alkylation reaction.

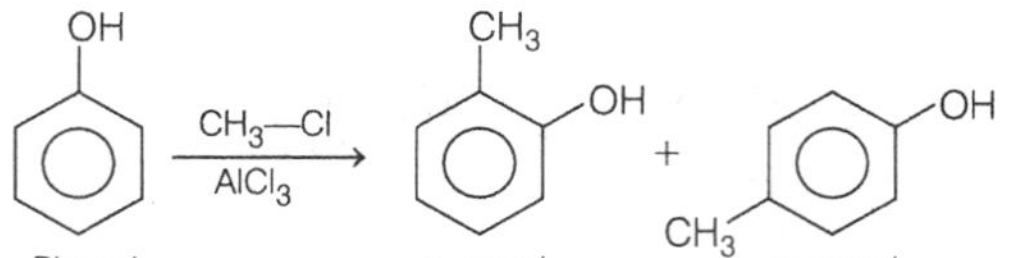

Phenol　　o-cresol　　p-cresol

119. *(c)* For the following reaction,

$$N_2(g) + 3H_2(g) \rightleftharpoons 2NH_3(g)$$

Δn = number of moles of product in gaseous state − number of moles of reactant in gaseous state

$$= 2 - (3+1) = -2$$

$$\because \quad K_p = K_C(RT)^{\Delta n}$$

$$\therefore \quad K_p = K_C(RT)^{-2}.$$

120. *(a)* According to Faraday's second law,

$$\frac{w_1}{E_1} = \frac{w_2}{E_2}$$

where, w and E are mass and equivalent weight respectively.

$$\frac{0.4}{\frac{63.5}{2}} = \frac{w_2}{108}$$

$$\therefore \quad w_2 = 1.35 \text{ g}$$

Mathematics

121. *(d)*

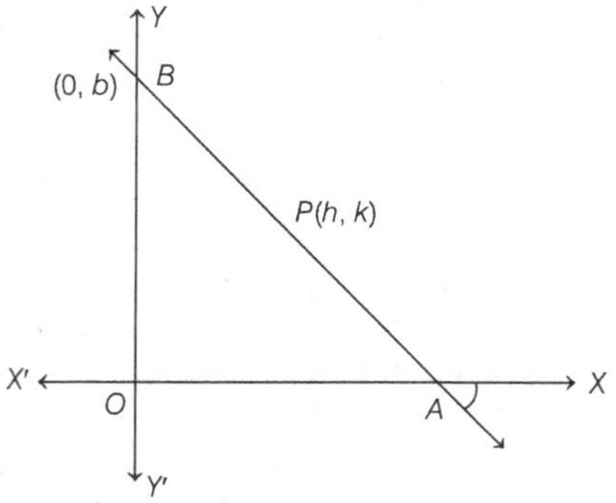

We have, equation of line $\frac{x}{a} + \frac{y}{b} = 1$.

Let $P(h, k)$ be the required point.

Now, coordinates A and B are $(a, 0)$ and $(0, b)$ respectively. Since, P is mid-point of AB.

Therefore,

$$(h, k) = \left(\frac{a+0}{2}, \frac{0+b}{2}\right)$$

$$\Rightarrow \quad h = \frac{a}{2} \text{ and } k = \frac{b}{2}$$

$$\Rightarrow \quad a = 2h \text{ and } b = 2k$$

Now, it is given that

$$a + b = 4$$

$$\Rightarrow \quad 2h + 2k = 4$$

$$\Rightarrow \quad h + k = 2$$

So, locus of P is $x + y = 2$

122. *(a)* Let $S_1: x^2 + y^2 - 8x = 0$

$$S_2: x^2 + y^2 - 5x + 7y = 0$$

$$S_3: x^2 + y^2 - 5x + 7y - 1 = 0$$

$$S_4: x^2 + y^2 - 8x + 7y - 2 = 0$$

Now, at $(5, -7)$

$$S_1 = 25 + 49 - 40 = 34 > 0$$

$$S_2 = 25 + 49 - 25 - 49 = 0$$

$$S_3 = 25 + 49 - 25 - 49 - 1 = -1 < 0$$

$$S_4 = 25 + 49 - 40 - 49 - 2 = -17 < 0$$

$\therefore (5, -7)$ lies outside the circle S_1.

123. *(c)* Let $\quad S_1: x^2 + y^2 = 9$

and $\quad S_2: x^2 + y^2 + 2\alpha x + 2y + 1 = 0$

Now, centre and radius of S_1 are

Centre $= C_1(0, 0)$

Radius $= 3$

Centre and radius of S_2 are

Centre $= C_2(-\alpha, -1)$

Radius $= \sqrt{(-\alpha)^2 + (-1)^2 - 1} = \alpha$

Since, S_1 and S_2 touch each other internally, then

$$C_1C_2 = |r_2 - r_1|$$

$$\Rightarrow \quad \sqrt{(-\alpha - 0)^2 + (-1 - 0)^2} = |\alpha - 3|$$

$$\Rightarrow \quad \sqrt{\alpha^2 + 1} = |\alpha - 3|$$

$$\Rightarrow \quad \alpha^2 + 1 = (\alpha - 3)^2$$

$$\Rightarrow \quad \alpha^2 + 1 = \alpha^2 - 6\alpha + 9$$

$$\Rightarrow \quad 6\alpha = 8 \Rightarrow \alpha = \frac{4}{3}$$

124. *(c)* Let the mid-point of any point $P(x_1, y_1)$ on parabola and focus $F(a, 0)$ be $Q(h, k)$.

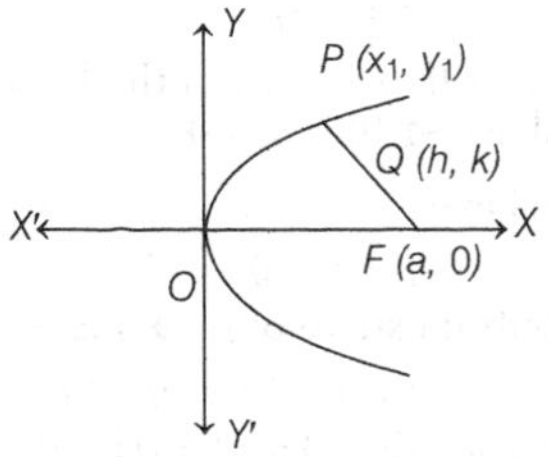

Then, $(h, k) = \left(\frac{x_1 + a}{2}, \frac{y_1 + 0}{2}\right)$

$\Rightarrow \quad h = \frac{x_1 + a}{2}$ and $k = \frac{y_1}{2}$

$\Rightarrow \quad x_1 = 2h - a$ and $y_1 = 2k$

Since, $P(x_1, y_1)$ lies on parabola $y^2 = 4ax$, then

$$(2k)^2 = 4a(2h - a)$$

$$4k^2 = 4a(2h - a)$$

$$k^2 = 2a\left(h - \frac{a}{2}\right)$$

$$\Rightarrow \quad y^2 = 2a\left(x - \frac{a}{2}\right)$$

Equation of its directrix is

$$x - \frac{a}{2} = \frac{-a}{2}$$

$$\Rightarrow \quad x = 0$$

125. *(b)* The tangent at the extremities of a focal chord of a parabola intersect at right angles on the directrix.
Now, equation of parabola is $y^2 = 16x$.
So, its directrix is $x = -4$ or $x + 4$.
So, tangent intersect on the line $x + 4 = 0$.

126. *(d)* We have,

$a * 3 = a + b - 5$

Now, $x * 3 = x + 3 - 5 = x - 2$

Again, $2 * (x * 3) = 5$

$\Rightarrow \quad 2 * (x - 2) = 5$

$\Rightarrow \quad 2 + x - 2 - 5 = 5$

$\Rightarrow \quad x = 10$

127. *(c)* (a) $a + b = b + a, \forall a, b \in N$.

So, addition is commutative in N.

(b) $(a \times b) \times c = a \times (b \times c), \forall a, b, c \in N$.

So, multiplication is associative in N.

(c) $a * b = a^b$ and $b * a = b^a$

$\therefore \quad a * b \neq b * a; \forall a, b \in N$

So, $*$ is commutative in N is false.

(d) $(a + b) + c = a + (b + c), \forall a, b$ and $c \in N$.

So, addition is associative in N.

128. *(c)* Let $\mathbf{a} = x\hat{\mathbf{i}} + y\hat{\mathbf{j}} + z\hat{\mathbf{k}}$

Now, $\mathbf{a} \cdot \hat{\mathbf{i}} = (x\hat{\mathbf{i}} + y\hat{\mathbf{j}} - z\hat{\mathbf{k}}) \cdot \hat{\mathbf{i}} = x$

$$\mathbf{a} \cdot (\hat{\mathbf{i}} + \hat{\mathbf{j}}) = (x\hat{\mathbf{i}} + y\hat{\mathbf{j}} + z\hat{\mathbf{k}}) \cdot (\hat{\mathbf{i}} + \hat{\mathbf{j}}) = x + y$$

and $\mathbf{a} \cdot (\hat{\mathbf{i}} + \hat{\mathbf{j}} + \hat{\mathbf{k}}) = (x\hat{\mathbf{i}} + y\hat{\mathbf{j}} + z\hat{\mathbf{k}}) \cdot (\hat{\mathbf{i}} + \hat{\mathbf{j}} + \hat{\mathbf{k}}) = x + y + z$

Now, according to the question,

$$\mathbf{a} \cdot \hat{\mathbf{i}} = \mathbf{a}(\hat{\mathbf{i}} + \hat{\mathbf{j}}) = \mathbf{a} \cdot (\hat{\mathbf{i}} + \hat{\mathbf{j}} + \hat{\mathbf{k}}) = 1$$

$\Rightarrow \quad x = x + y = x + y + z = 1$

$\Rightarrow \quad x = 1, y = 0, z = 0$

$\therefore \quad \mathbf{a} = \hat{\mathbf{i}}$

129. *(d)* We have

$$|\mathbf{a}| = |\mathbf{b}| = 1, |\mathbf{a} + \mathbf{b}| = 1$$

We know that,

$$|\mathbf{a} + \mathbf{b}|^2 + |\mathbf{a} - \mathbf{b}|^2 = 2(|\mathbf{a}|^2 + |\mathbf{b}|^2)$$

$\Rightarrow \quad (1)^2 + |\mathbf{a} - \mathbf{b}|^2 = 2((1)^2 + (1)^2)$

$\Rightarrow \quad 1 + |\mathbf{a} - \mathbf{b}|^2 = 4$

$\Rightarrow \quad |\mathbf{a} - \mathbf{b}| = \sqrt{3}$

130. *(c)* Projection of $\mathbf{a}$ on $\mathbf{b} = \frac{\mathbf{a} \cdot \mathbf{b}}{|\mathbf{b}|}$

$$= \frac{(3\hat{\mathbf{i}} - \hat{\mathbf{j}} + 5\hat{\mathbf{k}}) \cdot (2\hat{\mathbf{i}} + 3\hat{\mathbf{j}} + \hat{\mathbf{k}})}{|2\hat{\mathbf{i}} + 3\hat{\mathbf{j}} + \hat{\mathbf{k}}|}$$

$$= \frac{6 - 3 + 5}{\sqrt{4 + 9 + 1}} = \frac{8}{\sqrt{14}}$$

131. *(a)* Let $f^{-1}(8) = x$

$\Rightarrow \quad f(x) = 8$

$\Rightarrow \quad x^3 = 8$

$\Rightarrow \quad x = 2 \quad [\because x \in R]$

$\therefore \quad f^{-1}(8) = \{2\}$

132. *(d)* (a) When $x = -4$, then

$$4(-4) + 3y = 20 \Rightarrow y = 12$$

But $x = -4 \notin N$

$\therefore \quad (-4, 12) \notin R$

(b) When $x = 5$, then

$$4(5) + 3y = 20 \Rightarrow y = 0$$

$\therefore \quad (5, 0) \notin R$

(c) When $x = 3$, then

$$4(3) + 3y = 20 \Rightarrow y = \frac{8}{3}$$

$\therefore \quad (3, 4) \notin R$

(d) When $x = 2$, then

$$4(2) + 3y = 20 \Rightarrow y = 4$$

$\therefore \quad (2, 4) \in R$

133. *(b)* We have,

$\log_{10} 7 = 0.8451$

Let $\quad x = 7^{-20}$

$\Rightarrow \log x = -20 \log 7 = -20 \times 0.8451 = -16.902$

$\Rightarrow x = 10^{-16.902}$

Now, -16.902 lies between -16 and -17

So, position of first significant figure of 7^{-20} is 17.

134. *(c)* We have,

$$= \frac{1}{2\cdot5} + \frac{1}{5\cdot8} + \frac{1}{8\cdot11} + \ldots + \frac{1}{[(2+(n-1)3)][5+(n-1)3]}$$

$$= \frac{1}{2\cdot5} + \frac{1}{5\cdot8} + \frac{1}{8\cdot11} + \ldots + \frac{1}{(3n-1)(3n+2)}$$

$$= \frac{1}{3}\left[\frac{3}{2\cdot5} + \frac{3}{5\cdot8} + \frac{3}{8\cdot11} + \ldots + \frac{3}{(3n-1)(3n+2)}\right]$$

$$= \frac{1}{3}\left[\frac{5-2}{2\cdot5} + \frac{8-5}{5\cdot8} + \frac{11-8}{8\cdot11} + \ldots + \frac{(3n+2)-(3n-1)}{(3n-1)(3n+2)}\right]$$

$$= \frac{1}{3}\left[\frac{1}{2} - \frac{1}{5} + \frac{1}{5} - \frac{1}{8} + \frac{1}{8} - \frac{1}{11} + \ldots + \frac{1}{3n-1} - \frac{1}{3n+2}\right]$$

$$= \frac{1}{3}\left[\frac{1}{2} - \frac{1}{3n+2}\right] = \frac{1}{3}\left[\frac{3n+2-2}{2(3n+2)}\right] = \frac{n}{6n+4}$$

135. *(b)* We have,

$1! = 1, 4! = 24, 7! = 5040, 10! = 3628800,$
$11! = 39916800$

So, last two digit from $10!$ is always 00.

Now, $1! + 4! + 7! = 1 + 24 + 5040 = 5065$

So, ten's digit in given addition is 6 which is divisible by $3!$.

136. *(b)* We have,

$$\frac{x^2}{2-\lambda} - \frac{y^2}{\lambda-5} - 1 = 0$$

$$\Rightarrow \quad \frac{x^2}{2-\lambda} + \frac{y^2}{5-\lambda} = 1$$

It will represent an ellipse, when

$2-\lambda > 0$ and $5-\lambda > 0$

$\Rightarrow \quad \lambda < 2$ and $\lambda < 5$

$\Rightarrow \quad \lambda < 2$

137. *(d)* We have,

$$\frac{x^2}{16} - \frac{y^2}{9} = 1$$

Since, $(-4, 0)$ is vertex of the hyperbola, so equation of normal at $(-4, 0)$ is $y = 0$.

138. *(d)* We have,

$$p \to \sim q$$

The contrapositive of $p \to q$ is $\sim q \to \sim p$

and converse of $p \to q$ is $q \to p$.

$\therefore$ Contrapositive of $p \to \sim q$ is $\sim(\sim q) \to \sim p \equiv q \to \sim p$.

Converse of $q \to \sim p$ is $\sim p \to q$.

139. *(a)* It is given that,

Perimeter of sector = Length of arc of the semi-circles

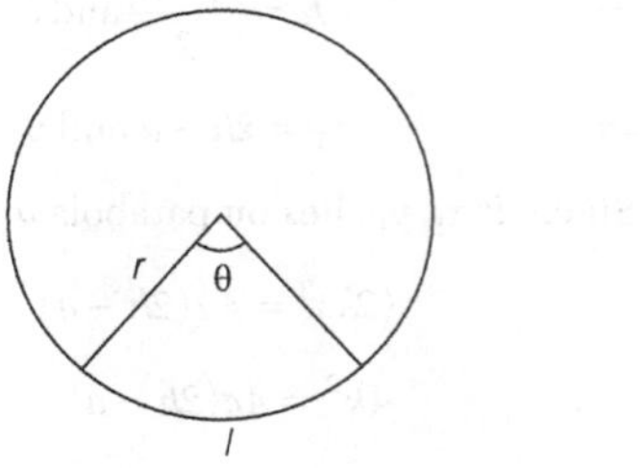

$\Rightarrow \quad 2r + l = \pi r$

$\Rightarrow \quad 2r + r\theta = \pi r \qquad [\because l = r\theta]$

$\Rightarrow \quad r(2+\theta) = \pi r$

$\Rightarrow \quad \theta = \pi - 2$

140. *(c)* We have,

$$\tan 67\frac{1}{2}^\circ + \cot 67\frac{1}{2}^\circ$$

$$= \frac{\sin 67\frac{1}{2}^\circ}{\cos 67\frac{1}{2}^\circ} + \frac{\cos 67\frac{1}{2}^\circ}{\sin 67\frac{1}{2}^\circ}$$

$$= \frac{\sin^2 67\frac{1}{2}^\circ + \cos^2 67\frac{1}{2}^\circ}{\cos 67\frac{1}{2}^\circ \sin 67\frac{1}{2}^\circ}$$

$$= \frac{2}{2\sin 67\frac{1}{2}^\circ \cos 67\frac{1}{2}^\circ}$$

$$= \frac{2}{\sin 135^\circ}$$

$$= \frac{2}{\sin(90^\circ+45^\circ)}$$

$$= \frac{2}{\cos 45^\circ} = 2 \times \sqrt{2} = 2\sqrt{2}$$

141. *(b)* We have, equation of hyperbola

$$3x^2 - 2y^2 = 25$$

$$\Rightarrow \quad \frac{x^2}{\left(\frac{5}{\sqrt{3}}\right)^2} - \frac{y^2}{\left(\frac{5}{\sqrt{2}}\right)^2} = 1$$

Equation of conjugate hyperbola is

$$\frac{y^2}{\left(\frac{5}{\sqrt{2}}\right)^2} - \frac{x^2}{\left(\frac{5}{\sqrt{3}}\right)^2} = 1$$

Now, eccentricity of hyperbola,

$$e_1 = \sqrt{1 + \frac{\left(\frac{5}{\sqrt{2}}\right)^2}{\left(\frac{5}{\sqrt{3}}\right)^2}}$$

$$= \sqrt{1 + \frac{3}{2}} = \sqrt{\frac{5}{2}}$$

and eccentricity of conjugate hyperbola,

$$e_2 = \sqrt{1 + \frac{\left(\frac{5}{\sqrt{3}}\right)^2}{\left(\frac{5}{\sqrt{2}}\right)^2}} = \sqrt{1 + \frac{2}{3}} = \sqrt{\frac{5}{3}}$$

Now, $e_1^2 + e_2^2 = \frac{5}{2} + \frac{5}{3} = \frac{25}{6} \simeq 4$

142. *(d)* We have,

$$p^2 - 2q^2 = 1$$

Let $p = 3,\ q = 2$

Then, $\quad p^2 - 2q^2$

$$= (3)^2 - 2(2)^2 = 9 - 8 = 1$$

$\therefore \quad p^2 - 2q^2 = 1$

Now, $p^2 + 2q^2 = (3)^2 + 2(2)^2$

$$= 9 + 8 = 17$$

143. *(b)* We have,

$$A(\text{adj}A) = 5I$$

$$\Rightarrow \quad |A(\text{adj}A)| = |5I|$$

$$\Rightarrow \quad |A||\text{adj}A| = 5^3|I| \qquad [\because |KB| = K^n|B|]$$

$$\Rightarrow \quad |A||A|^{3-1} = 125 \times I \qquad [\because |\text{adj}A| = |A|^{n-1}]$$

$$\Rightarrow \quad |A|^3 = 125$$

$$\Rightarrow \quad |A| = 5$$

Now, $|\text{adj}A| = |A|^{n-1}$

$$= |A|^2 \qquad [\because n = 3]$$

$$= (5)^2 = 25$$

144. *(a)* We have,

$$\sin 2x + \cos 4x = 2$$

$$\Rightarrow \quad \sin 2x + 1 - 2\sin^2 2x = 2$$

$$\Rightarrow \quad 2\sin^2 2x - \sin 2x + 1 = 0$$

Now, Discriminant $= b^2 - 4ac$

$$= (-1)^2 - 4(2)(1)$$

$$= 1 - 8 = -7$$

$$< 0$$

So, there is no real root of the given equation.

145. *(c)* Let $I = \int \underset{\text{II}}{e^x} \cdot \underset{\text{I}}{x^5}\, dx$

$$= x^5 \cdot e^x - \int e^x \cdot (5x^4)dx$$

$$= x^5 e^x - 5\int \underset{\text{II}}{e^x} \cdot \underset{\text{I}}{x^4}\, dx$$

$$= x^5 e^x - 5[x^4 \cdot e^x - \int e^x \cdot 4x^3 dx]$$

$$= x^5 e^x - 5x^4 e^x + 20\int \underset{\text{II}}{e^x} \cdot \underset{\text{I}}{x^3}\, dx$$

$$= x^5 e^x - 5x^4 e^x + 20[x^3 \cdot e^x - \int e^x \cdot 3x^2 dx]$$

$$= x^5 e^x - 5x^4 e^x + 20x^3 e^x - 60\int \underset{\text{II}}{e^x} \cdot \underset{\text{I}}{x^2}\, dx$$

$$= x^5 e^x - 5x^4 e^x + 20x^3 e^x - 60[x^2 \cdot e^x - \int e^x \cdot 2x\, dx]$$

$$= x^5 e^4 - 5x^4 e^x + 20x^3 e^x - 60x^2 e^x + 120\int e^x \cdot x\, dx$$

$$= x^5 e^x - 5x^4 e^x + 20x^3 e^x - 60x^2 e^x + 120\ [xe^x - \int e^x dx]$$

$$= x^5 e^x - 5x^4 e^x + 20x^3 e^x - 60x^2 e^x + 120xe^x - 120e^x + C$$

$$= e^x[x^5 - 5x^4 + 20x^3 - 60x^2 + 120x - 120] + C$$

146. *(b)* We have, $f(x)$ is an even function.

$$\therefore \quad f(-x) = f(x)$$

$$\Rightarrow \quad f'(-x)(-1) = f'(x)$$

$$\Rightarrow \quad f'(x) + f'(-x) = 0$$

$$\Rightarrow \quad f'(e) + f'(-e) = 0$$

147. *(a)* We have, $\alpha^2 + \alpha + 1 = 0$

$$\Rightarrow \quad \alpha = \omega \text{ or } \omega^2$$

Now, if $\alpha = \omega$, then

$$\alpha^{31} = \omega^{31} = (\omega^3)^{10} \cdot \omega = \omega = \alpha$$

and if $\alpha = \omega^2$, then

$$\alpha^{31} = (\omega^2)^{31} = \omega^{62} = (\omega^3)^{20} \cdot \omega^2 = \omega^2 = \alpha$$

$\therefore \quad \alpha^{31} = \alpha$

148. *(c)* Let $u = \sin(x^3)$

and $v = \cos(x^3)$

Then, $\frac{du}{dx} = \cos(x^3) \cdot (3x^2)$

and $\frac{dv}{dx} = -\sin(x^3)(3x^2)$

Now, $\frac{du}{dv} = \frac{\left(\frac{du}{dx}\right)}{\left(\frac{dv}{dx}\right)}$

$$= \frac{3x^2 \cos(x^3)}{-3x^2 \sin(x^3)} = -\cot(x^3)$$

149. *(d)* Let $\mathbf{a} = \hat{\mathbf{i}} + \hat{\mathbf{j}}$ and $\mathbf{b} = \hat{\mathbf{j}} + \hat{\mathbf{k}}$

Then, unit vector perpendicular to both **a** and **b** is $\frac{\mathbf{a} \times \mathbf{b}}{|\mathbf{a} \times \mathbf{b}|}$

Now, $\mathbf{a} \times \mathbf{b} = \begin{vmatrix} \hat{\mathbf{i}} & \hat{\mathbf{j}} & \hat{\mathbf{k}} \\ 1 & 1 & 0 \\ 0 & 1 & 1 \end{vmatrix} = \hat{\mathbf{i}} - \hat{\mathbf{j}} + \hat{\mathbf{k}}$

and $|\mathbf{a} \times \mathbf{b}| = \sqrt{(1)^2 + (-1)^2 + (1)^2} = \sqrt{3}$

Thus, required vector $= \frac{\hat{\mathbf{i}} - \hat{\mathbf{j}} + \hat{\mathbf{k}}}{\sqrt{3}}$

150. *(b)* We have,

$$A = \begin{vmatrix} a_1 & b_1 & c_1 \\ a_2 & b_2 & c_2 \\ a_3 & b_3 & c_3 \end{vmatrix}$$

$$= \begin{vmatrix} a_1 & a_2 & a_3 \\ b_1 & b_2 & b_3 \\ c_1 & c_2 & c_3 \end{vmatrix} \qquad [\because |A| = |A^T|]$$

$$= (-) \begin{vmatrix} b_1 & b_2 & b_3 \\ a_1 & a_2 & a_3 \\ c_1 & c_2 & c_3 \end{vmatrix} \qquad [R_1 \leftrightarrow R_2]$$

$$= (-)(-) \begin{vmatrix} c_1 & c_2 & c_3 \\ a_1 & a_2 & a_3 \\ b_1 & b_2 & b_3 \end{vmatrix} = \begin{vmatrix} c_1 & c_2 & c_3 \\ a_1 & a_2 & a_3 \\ b_1 & b_2 & b_2 \end{vmatrix} = B \quad [R_1 \leftrightarrow R_3]$$

151. *(c)* The locus of a point which moves such that the sum of its distances from the two fixed points is a constant is an ellipse.

152. *(a)* Centroid of $\Delta ABC = \left(\frac{2+8+5}{3}, \frac{3+10+5}{3}\right) = (5, 6)$

153. *(d)* If $3x^2 + xy - y^2 - 3x + 6y + k = 0$ represents a pair of lines, then

$$\begin{vmatrix} 3 & \frac{1}{2} & \frac{-3}{2} \\ \frac{1}{2} & -1 & 3 \\ \frac{-3}{2} & 3 & k \end{vmatrix} = 0$$

$$\Rightarrow 3(-k-9) - \frac{1}{2}\left(\frac{1}{2}k + \frac{9}{2}\right) - \frac{3}{2}\left(\frac{3}{2} - \frac{3}{2}\right) = 0$$

$$\Rightarrow \quad -3k - 27 - \frac{1}{4}k - \frac{9}{4} = 0$$

$$\Rightarrow \quad -\frac{13}{4}k - \frac{117}{4} = 0$$

$$k = -9$$

154. *(b)* (a) Put $x = 2, y = 2$, we have

$(2)^2 + (2)^2 + 5 \times 2 + 5 \times 2 + 12$

$= 4 + 4 + 10 + 10 + 12 = 40 \neq 0$

(b) Put $x = 2, \ y = 2$, we have

$(2)^2 + (2)^2 - 5 \times 2 - 5 \times 2 + 12$

$= 4 + 4 - 10 - 10 + 12 = 0$

Put $x = 3, y = 3$, we get

$(3)^2 + (3)^2 - 5 \times 3 - 5 \times 3 + 12$

$= 9 + 9 - 15 - 15 - 12 = 30 - 30 = 0$

So, both points satisfies the given equation.

(c) Put $x = 2, y = 2$, we get

$(2)^2 + (2)^2 + 5 \times 2 - 5 \times 2 + 12$

$= 4 + 4 + 10 - 10 + 12 = 20 \neq 0$

(d) Put $x = 2, y = 2$, we get

$(2)^2 + (2)^2 - 5 \times 2 + 5 \times 2 - 12$

$= 4 + 4 - 10 + 10 - 12 = -4 \neq 0$

155. *(a)* We have,

$$A = \begin{bmatrix} 1 & 0 & 0 \\ 2 & 3 & 0 \\ 4 & 5 & 6 \end{bmatrix}$$

which is a lower triangular matrix.

Since, characteristic roots of a lower triangular matrix are its diagonal elements.

So, charateristics roots of A are 1, 3, 6.

156. *(a)* If $A = \begin{bmatrix} a & b \\ c & d \end{bmatrix}$, then

$$A^{-1} = \frac{1}{|A|}\begin{bmatrix} d & -b \\ -c & a \end{bmatrix}$$

So, if $A = \begin{bmatrix} 1 & 2 \\ 3 & 4 \end{bmatrix}$, then

$$A^{-1} = \frac{1}{4-6}\begin{bmatrix} 4 & -2 \\ -3 & 1 \end{bmatrix}$$

$$= -\frac{1}{2}\begin{bmatrix} 4 & -2 \\ -3 & 1 \end{bmatrix}$$

157. *(d)* We have,

$A = \{-1, 0, 1\}$

Now, let e be the identity element.

Then, $a \times e = a \Rightarrow e = 1 \in A$

Again, a^{-1} be the inverse element.

Then, $a \times a^{-1} = e$

$\Rightarrow a \times a^{-1} = 1 \Rightarrow a^{-1} = \frac{1}{a}$

Now, for $a = 0$, $a^{-1} = \frac{1}{0} = \infty \notin A$

So, inverse law fails.

158. *(c)*

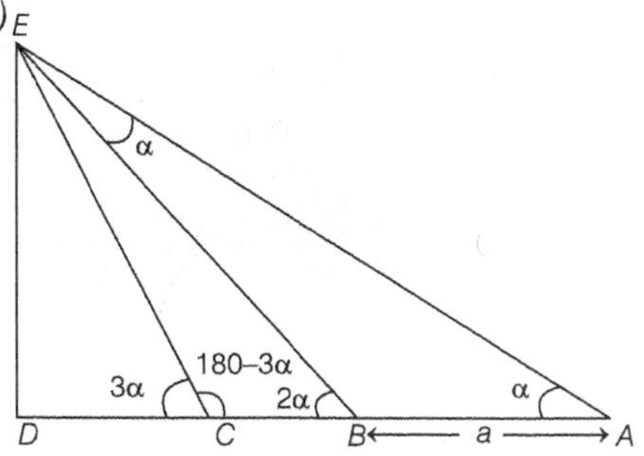

Let DE be the height of the tower.

Now, in ΔABE,

$\angle AEB = \angle EBC - \angle EAB$

$= 2\alpha - \alpha = \alpha$

$\therefore \angle AEB = \angle BAE$

$\Rightarrow BE = AB = a$

Now, $\angle ECB = 180° - \angle DCE = 180 - 3\alpha$

Now, in ΔBEC, $\frac{BE}{\sin(180 - 3\alpha)} = \frac{CE}{\sin 2\alpha}$

[using sine rule]

$\Rightarrow \frac{a}{\sin 3\alpha} = \frac{CE}{\sin 2\alpha}$

$\Rightarrow CE = \frac{a \sin 2\alpha}{\sin 3\alpha}$

In ΔEDC,

$\sin 3\alpha = \frac{DE}{CE}$

$\Rightarrow DE = CE \sin 3\alpha$

$= \frac{a \sin 2\alpha}{\sin 3\alpha} \times \sin 3\alpha = a \sin 2\alpha$

Hence, height of tower is $a \sin 2\alpha$.

159. *(c)* It is given that A, B, C are in AP.

$\therefore \quad 2B = A + C$

Now, $\quad A + B + C = 180°$

$\Rightarrow \quad B + 2B = 180°$

$\Rightarrow \quad B = 60°$

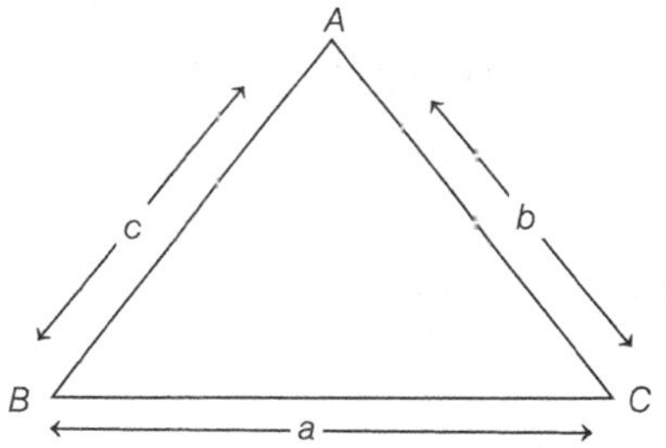

Now, using sine rule, we have

$\frac{b}{\sin B} = \frac{c}{\sin C}$

$\Rightarrow \sin C = \frac{c}{b} \sin B$

$= \frac{\sqrt{2}}{\sqrt{3}} \times \sin 60° \quad [\because b:c = \sqrt{3}:\sqrt{2}]$

$= \frac{\sqrt{2}}{\sqrt{3}} \times \frac{\sqrt{3}}{2} = \frac{1}{\sqrt{2}}$

$\therefore \quad c = 45°$

Now, $\quad A + B + C = 180°$

$\Rightarrow \quad A + 60° + 45° = 180°$

$\Rightarrow \quad A = 75°$

160. *(a)* We have,

$\sin\left(2\sin^{-1}\sqrt{\frac{63}{65}}\right)$

$= \sin\left\{\sin^{-1}\left(2\sqrt{\frac{63}{65}}\sqrt{1 - \left(\sqrt{\frac{63}{65}}\right)^2}\right)\right\}$

$[\because 2\sin^{-1} x = \sin^{-1} 2x\sqrt{1 - x^2}]$

$$= \sin\left\{\sin^{-1}\left(2\sqrt{\frac{63}{65}}\sqrt{1-\frac{63}{65}}\right)\right\}$$

$$= \sin\left\{\sin^{-1}\left(2\sqrt{\frac{63}{65}}\times\sqrt{\frac{2}{65}}\right)\right\} = \sin\left\{\sin^{-1}\frac{2\sqrt{126}}{65}\right\}$$

$$= \frac{2\sqrt{126}}{65} \qquad [\because \sin(\sin^{-1}x) = x]$$

161. *(c)* We have, $|\sin x| = \cos x$

$\Rightarrow \sin x = \pm\cos x$

$\Rightarrow \tan x = \pm 1$

$\Rightarrow \tan x = \tan\left(\pm\frac{\pi}{4}\right)$

$\Rightarrow x = n\pi \pm \frac{\pi}{4}$

162. *(d)* We have,

$$x^3 - 6x + 9 = 0$$

$\Rightarrow (x+3)(x^2-3x+3) = 0$

$\Rightarrow x + 3 = 0 \qquad [\because x^2 - 3x + 3 \neq 0, x \in R]$

$\Rightarrow x = -3$

163. *(d)* We know that,

$5^1 = 5$

$5^2 = 25$

$5^3 = 125$ and so on.

So, unit place is always 5.

So, unit's place of 5^{834} is 5.

164. *(d)* We have,

$3^2 = 4 \pmod 5$

$(3^2)^2 = 16 \pmod 5 = 1 \pmod 5$

$(3^4)^{25} = (1)^{25} \pmod 5$

$\Rightarrow 3^{100} = 1 \pmod 5$

Again, $2^2 = 4 \pmod 5$

$(2^2)^2 = 16 \pmod 5 = 1 \pmod 5$

$(2^4)^{12} = (1)^{12} \pmod 5 = 1 \pmod 5$

$2^{48} \cdot 2^2 = 4 \pmod 5$

$\therefore 3^{100} \times 2^{50} = 1 \times 4 \pmod 5 = 4 \pmod 5$

165. *(a)* Let $I = \int \frac{\sin x \cos x}{\sqrt{1-\sin^4 x}}dx$

Put $\sin^2 x = t \Rightarrow 2\sin x \cos x\, dx = dt$

$$\therefore \quad I = \frac{1}{2}\int\frac{dt}{\sqrt{1-t^2}}$$

$$= \frac{1}{2}\sin^{-1}t + C = \frac{1}{2}\sin^{-1}(\sin^2 x) + C$$

166. *(b)* Let $I = \int_{-2}^{2}(ax^3 + bx + c)dx \qquad \text{...(i)}$

$\Rightarrow I = \int_{-2}^{2}[(a(-2+2-x)^3 + b(-2+2-x) + c)]dx$

$$\left[\because \int_a^b f(x)dx = \int_a^b f(a+b-x)dx\right]$$

$= \int_{-2}^{2}(-ax^3 - bx + c)dx \qquad \text{...(ii)}$

On adding Eqs. (i) and (ii), we get

$$2I = \int_{-2}^{2} 2c\,dx$$

$$I = c(x)_{-2}^{2} = 4c$$

So, I depends on value of c.

167. *(b)* We have,

$y = 2x - x^2$

$\Rightarrow y = -(x^2 - 2x)$

$\Rightarrow y = -[(x-1)^2 - 1]$

$\Rightarrow y = -(x-1)^2 + 1$

$\Rightarrow (x-1)^2 = -(y-1)$

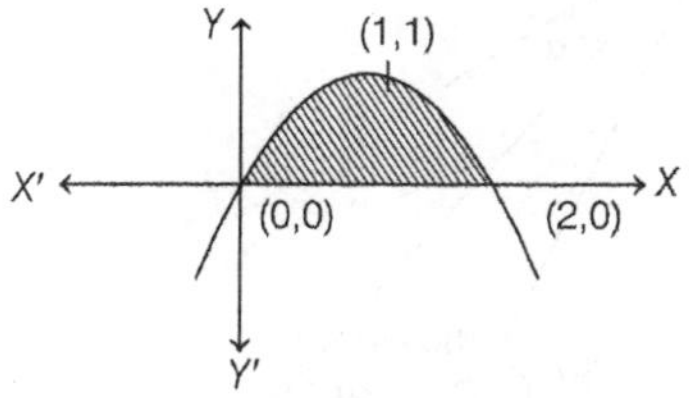

Required area $= \int_0^2 y\,dx$

$= \int_0^2 (2x - x^2)dx$

$= \left[x^2 - \frac{x^3}{3}\right]_0^2 = 4 - \frac{8}{3}$

$= \frac{4}{3}$ sq unit

168. *(d)* We have,

$$y\frac{dy}{dx} + x = c$$

$\Rightarrow y\frac{dy}{dx} = (c - x)$

$\Rightarrow y\,dy = (c-x)dx$

$$\Rightarrow \qquad y\,dy = -(x-c)dx$$

$$\Rightarrow \qquad \int y\,dy = -\int (x-c)dx$$

$$\Rightarrow \qquad \frac{y^2}{2} = -\frac{(x-c)^2}{2} + K$$

$$\Rightarrow \qquad (x-c)^2 + y^2 = 2K$$

which is a circle with centre $(c, 0)$ on the X-axis.

169. *(a)* We have,

$$f(x^5) = 5x^3$$

$$\Rightarrow \qquad f(x) = 5x^{3/5}$$

$$\Rightarrow \qquad f'(x) = 5 \times \frac{3}{5} x^{\frac{3}{5}-1} = 3x^{-\frac{2}{5}}$$

$$= \frac{3}{\sqrt[5]{x^2}}$$

170. *(d)* We have,

$$f(x) = \begin{cases} 2a - x, & -a < x < a \\ 3x - 2a, & x \geq a \end{cases}$$

At $x = a$

$\text{LHL} = \lim_{x \to a} (2a - x) = 2a - a = a$

$\text{RHL} = \lim_{x \to a} (3x - 2a) = 3a - 2a = a$

$f(a) = 3a - 2a = a$

$\because$ LHL = RHL = $f(a)$.

So, $f(x)$ is continuous at $x = a$.

Now, when $x < a, f(x) = 2a - x$,

which is continuous for all $x < a$.

Again, when $x > a$, $f(x) = 3x - 2a$, which is continuous for all $x > a$.

So, $f(x)$ is continuous for all x.

Now, at $x = a$

$$\text{LHD} = \lim_{x \to a} \frac{(2a - x) - a}{x - a}$$

$$= \lim_{x \to a} \frac{-(x-a)}{(x-a)} = -1$$

$$\text{and RHD} = \lim_{x \to a} \frac{(3x - 2a) - a}{x - a}$$

$$= \lim_{x \to a} \frac{3(x-a)}{x-a} = 3$$

$\therefore$ LHD $\neq$ RHD

So, $f(x)$ is not differentiable at $x = a$.

171. *(c)* The area of a rectangle that can be inscribed in a circle will have maximum area when it is a square.

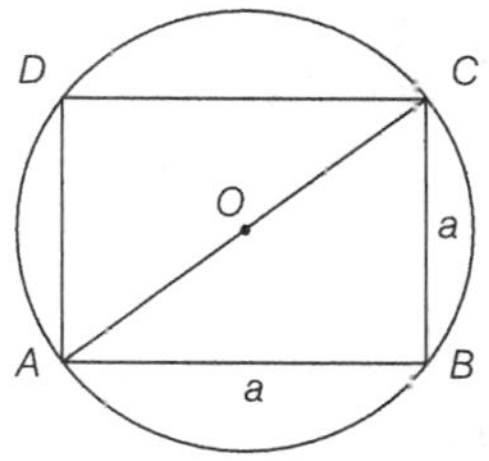

Let a be the side of square $ABCD$.

Then, $\qquad AB^2 + BC^2 = AC^2$

$$\Rightarrow \qquad a^2 + a^2 = (4)^2$$

$$\Rightarrow \qquad 2a^2 = 16$$

$$\Rightarrow \qquad a^2 = 8$$

$\therefore$ Area of square is 8 sq units.

172. *(b)* Let $Z = x + iy$

Then, $\overline{Z} = x - iy$

Now, it is given that

$$Z = -\overline{Z}$$

$$\Rightarrow \qquad x + iy = -(x - iy)$$

$$\Rightarrow \qquad x + iy = -x + iy$$

$$\Rightarrow \qquad 2x = 0$$

$$\Rightarrow \qquad x = 0$$

$\therefore Z$ is purely imaginary.

173. *(a)* We have,

$$\sum_{K=1}^{6} \left(\sin \frac{2K\pi}{7} - i \frac{\cos 2K\pi}{7} \right)$$

$$= -i \sum_{K=1}^{6} \left(\cos \frac{2K\pi}{7} + i \sin \frac{2K\pi}{7} \right)$$

$$= -i \sum_{K=1}^{6} e^{\frac{2K\pi}{7}}$$

$$= -i \left[e^{\frac{2\pi}{7}} + e^{\frac{4\pi}{7}} + e^{\frac{6\pi}{7}} + e^{\frac{8\pi}{7}} + e^{\frac{10\pi}{7}} + e^{\frac{12\pi}{7}} \right]$$

$$= -i \left[1 + e^{\frac{2\pi}{7}} + e^{\frac{4\pi}{7}} + e^{\frac{6\pi}{7}} + e^{\frac{8\pi}{7}} + e^{\frac{10\pi}{7}} + e^{\frac{12\pi}{7}} - 1 \right]$$

$= -i[0 - 1]$ [$\because$ Sum of all nth roots of unit is zero]

$= i$

174. *(c)* We have,

$$\lim_{x\to\infty} x\sin\left(\frac{2}{x}\right) = \lim_{x\to\infty} \frac{\sin\left(\frac{2}{x}\right)}{\left(\frac{2}{x}\right)} \times 2$$

Put $\frac{2}{x} = y$.

Then $x \to \infty$

$\Rightarrow \frac{2}{x} \to 0 \Rightarrow y \to 0$

$$\therefore \lim_{x\to\infty} \frac{\sin\left(\frac{2}{x}\right)}{\left(\frac{2}{x}\right)} \times 2$$

$$= \lim_{y\to 0} \frac{\sin y}{y} \times 2 = 1 \times 2 = 2$$

175. *(b)* We have,

$$x = 80t - 16t^2$$

$$\Rightarrow \frac{dx}{dt} = 80 - 32t$$

For maximum value of x,

$$\frac{dx}{dt} = 0$$

$$\Rightarrow 80 - 32t = 0 \Rightarrow t = \frac{80}{32} = 2.5$$

Again, $\frac{d^2x}{dt^2} = -32 < 0$

So, at $t = 2.5$ sec, x is maximum.

176. *(d)* We have,

$$f(x) = \frac{\log x}{x}$$

$$\Rightarrow f'(x) = \frac{\frac{1}{x} \times x - \log x \cdot 1}{x^2} = \frac{1 - \log x}{x^2}$$

For maxima or minima,

$$f'(x) = 0$$

$$\Rightarrow \frac{1 - \log x}{x^2} = 0$$

$$\Rightarrow \log x = 1$$

$$\Rightarrow x = e$$

Now, $f''(x) = \dfrac{-\frac{1}{x} \cdot x^2 - (1 - \log x) \cdot 2x}{x^4}$

$$= \frac{-x - 2x + 2x\log x}{x^4}$$

$$= \frac{-3x + 2x\log x}{x^4} = \frac{-3 + 2\log x}{x^3}$$

$$\therefore f''(e) = \frac{-3 + 2}{e^3} = \frac{-1}{e^3} < 0$$

Hence, $f(x)$ attains a local maxima at $x = e$.

$$\therefore f_{\max} = f(e) = \frac{\log e}{e} = \frac{1}{e}$$

177. *(c)* We have,

$$f(x) = be^{ax} + ae^{bx}$$

$$\Rightarrow f'(x) = abe^{ax} + abe^{bx}$$

$$\Rightarrow f''(x) = a^2be^{ax} + ab^2e^{bx}$$

$$\therefore f''(0) = a^2b + ab^2 = ab(a + b)$$

178. *(c)* We have,

$$\sqrt{\frac{1 + \cos A}{1 - \cos A}} = \frac{x}{y}$$

$$\Rightarrow \sqrt{\frac{2\cos^2\frac{A}{2}}{2\sin^2\frac{A}{2}}} = \frac{x}{y}$$

$$\Rightarrow \cot\frac{A}{2} = \frac{x}{y} \Rightarrow \tan\frac{A}{2} = \frac{y}{x}$$

Now, $\tan A = \dfrac{2\tan\frac{A}{2}}{1 - \tan^2\frac{A}{2}} = \dfrac{2\left(\frac{y}{x}\right)}{1 - \left(\frac{y}{x}\right)^2} = \dfrac{2xy}{x^2 - y^2}$

179. *(a)* Let $I = \int \frac{\sec x}{\sec x + \tan x} dx$

$$= \int \frac{1}{1 + \sin x} dx = \int \frac{1 - \sin x}{1 - \sin^2 x} dx$$

$$= \int \frac{1 - \sin x}{\cos^2 x} dx$$

$$= \int (\sec^2 x - \sec x \tan x) dx$$

$$= \tan x - \sec x + C$$

180. *(b)* We have,

$$\int f(x) dx = g(x)$$

$$\Rightarrow f(x) = g'(x)$$

Now, let $I = \int f(x) \cdot g(x) dx = \int g'(x) g(x) dx$

Put $g(x) = t$

$$\Rightarrow g'(x) dx = dt$$

$$\therefore I = \int t\, dt = \frac{t^2}{2} + C = \frac{1}{2}(g(x))^2 + C$$

COMEDK

Solved Paper 2018

Instructions

- There are 180 questions in all. The number of questions in each section is as given below.

Sections	No. of Questions
Section I : Physics	1-60
Section II : Chemistry	61-120
Section III : Mathematics	121-180

- All the questions are Multiple Choice Questions having four options out of which **ONLY ONE** is correct.
- Candidates will be awarded 1 mark for each correct answer. There will be no negative marking for incorrect answer.
- Time allotted to complete this paper is 3 hrs.

PHYSICS

1. A ray of light enters from a rarer to a denser medium. The angle of incidence is i. Then, the reflected and refracted rays are mutually perpendicular to each other. The critical angle for the pair of media is

a. $\sin^{-1}(\tan i)$

b. $\tan^{-1}(\sin i)$

c. $\sin^{-1}(\cot i)$

d. $\cos^{-1}(\tan i)$

2. A fish in water (refractive index n) looks at a bird vertically above in the air. If y is the height of the bird and x is the depth of the fish from the surface, then the distance of the bird as estimated by the fish is

a. $x + y\left(1 - \frac{1}{n}\right)$

b. $x + ny$

c. $x + y\left(1 + \frac{1}{n}\right)$

d. $y + x\left(1 - \frac{1}{n}\right)$

3. Figure shows a mixture of blue, green and red coloured rays incident normally on a right angled prism. The critical angles of the material of the prism for red, green and blue are 46°, 44° and 43°, respectively. The arrangement will separate

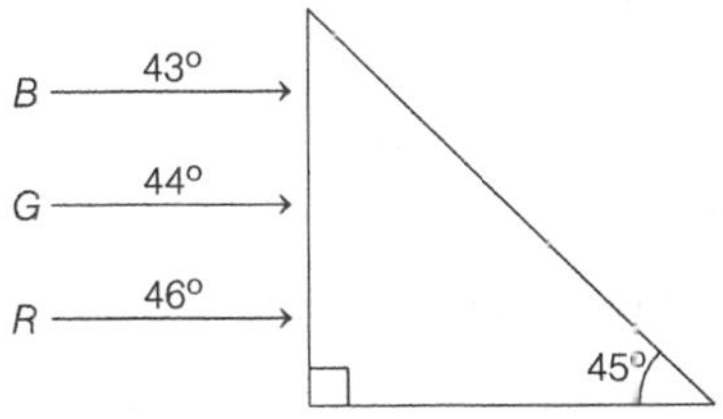

a. red colour from blue and green

b. blue colour from red and green

c. green colour from red and blue

d. All the three colours

4. A convex and a concave lens separated by distance d are then put in contact. The focal length of the combination

a. decreases

b. increases

c. becomes zero

d. remains the same

5. A convex lens is made of 3 layers of glass of 3 different materials as in the figure. A point object is placed on its axis. The number of images of the object are

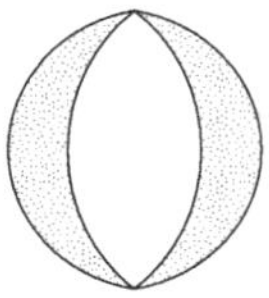

a. 1 *b.* 2
c. 3 *d.* 4

6. If μ_0 is permeability of free space and ε_0 is permittivity of free space, then the speed of light in vacuum is given by

a. $\sqrt{\mu_0 \varepsilon_0}$ *b.* $\sqrt{\mu_0 / \varepsilon_0}$
c. $\sqrt{\dfrac{1}{\mu_0 \varepsilon_0}}$ *d.* $\sqrt{\varepsilon_0 / \mu_0}$

7. In Young's double slit experiment, a third slit is made in between the double slits. Then,

a. intensity of fringes totally disappears
b. only bright light is observed on the screen
c. fringes of unequal width are formed
d. contrast between bright and dark fringes is reduced

8. The maximum number of possible interference maxima when slit separation is equal to 4 times the wavelength of light used in a double slit experiment is

a. ∞ *b.* 9
c. 8 *d.* 4

9. In a Fraunhofer diffraction experiment at a single slit using a light of wavelength 400 nm, the first minimum is formed at an angle of 30°. The direction θ of the first secondary maximum is given by

a. $\sin^{-1}(2/3)$ *b.* $\sin^{-1}(3/4)$
c. $\sin^{-1}(1/4)$ *d.* $\tan^{-1}(2/3)$

10. Maximum diffraction takes place in a given slit for

a. γ-rays *b.* ultraviolet light
c. infrared light *d.* radio waves

11. An unpolarised beam of intensity I_0 falls on a polaroid. The intensity of the emergent light is

a. $I_0 / 2$ *b.* I_0
c. $I_0 / 4$ *d.* Zero

12. Which of the following is a dichroic crystal?

a. Quartz *b.* Tourmaline
c. Mica *d.* Selenite

13. Two identical metal spheres charged with $+12\mu F$ and $-8\mu F$ are kept at certain distance in air. They are brought into contact and then kept at the same distance. The ratio of the magnitudes of electrostatic forces between them before and after contact is

a. 12 : 1 *b.* 8 : 1
c. 24 : 1 *d.* 4 : 1

14. A small conducting sphere of radius r is lying concentrically inside a bigger hollow conducting sphere of radius R. The bigger and smaller spheres are charged with Q and q $(Q > q)$ and are insulated from each other. The potential difference between the spheres will be

a. $\dfrac{1}{4\pi\varepsilon_0}\left(\dfrac{q}{r} - \dfrac{q}{R}\right)$ *b.* $\dfrac{1}{4\pi\varepsilon_0}\left(\dfrac{q}{R} - \dfrac{Q}{r}\right)$
c. $\dfrac{1}{4\pi\varepsilon_0}\left(\dfrac{q}{r} - \dfrac{Q}{R}\right)$ *d.* $\dfrac{1}{4\pi\varepsilon_0}\left(\dfrac{Q}{R} + \dfrac{q}{r}\right)$

15. The charges Q, $+q$ and $+q$ are placed at the vertices of an equilateral triangle of side l. If the net electrostatic potential energy of the system is zero, then Q is equal to

a. $-q/2$ *b.* $-q$
c. $+q/2$ *d.* Zero

16. How many $6\mu F$, 200 V condensers are needed to make a condenser of $18\mu F$, 600 V?

a. 9 *b.* 18
c. 3 *d.* 27

17. The total energy stored in the condenser system shown in the figure will be

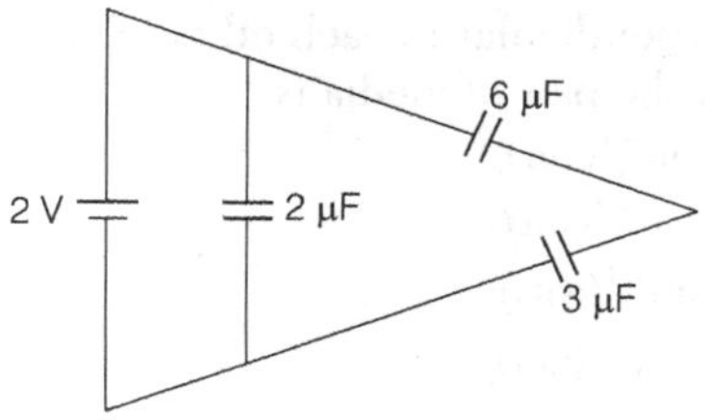

a. $2\mu J$ *b.* $4\mu J$
c. $8\mu J$ *d.* $16\mu J$

18. A metal wire is subjected to a constant potential difference. When the temperature of the metal wire increases, the drift velocity of the electron in it

a. increases, thermal velocity of the electron decreases
b. decreases, thermal velocity of the electron decreases
c. increases, thermal velocity of the electron increases
d. decreases, thermal velocity of the electron increases

19. The equivalent resistance between the points A and B will be (each resistance is $15\ \Omega$)

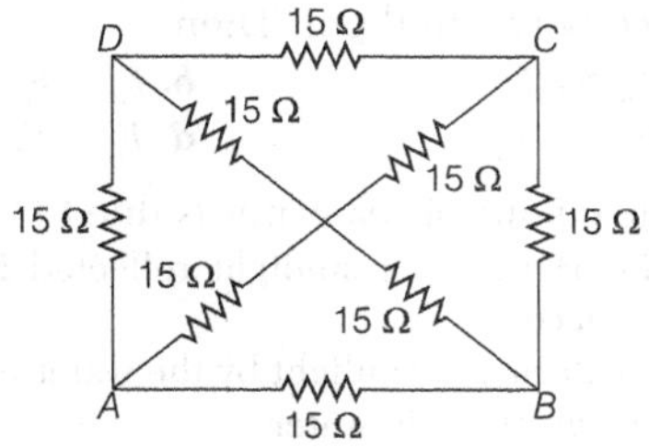

a. $30\ \Omega$ *b.* $8\ \Omega$
c. $10\ \Omega$ *d.* $40\ \Omega$

20. The terminals of a 18 V battery with an internal resistance of $1.5\ \Omega$ are connected to a circular wire of resistance $24\ \Omega$ at two points distant at one quarter of the circumference of a circular wire. The current through the bigger arc of the circle will be

a. 0.75 A *b.* 1.5 A
c. 2.25 A *d.* 3 A

21. The potential difference between A and B in the following figure is

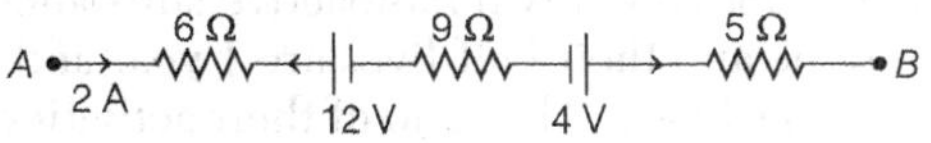

a. 32 V *b.* 48 V
c. 24 V *d.* 14 V

22. The magnetic field at the centre of a circular current carrying conductor of radius r is B_c. The magnetic field on its axis at a distance r from the centre is B_a. The value of $B_c : B_a$ will be

a. $1 : \sqrt{2}$ *b.* $1 : 2\sqrt{2}$
c. $2\sqrt{2} : 1$ *d.* $\sqrt{2} : 1$

23. Current I is flowing in a conductor shaped as shown in the figure. The radius of the curved part is r and the length of straight portion is very large. The value of the magnetic field at the centre O will be

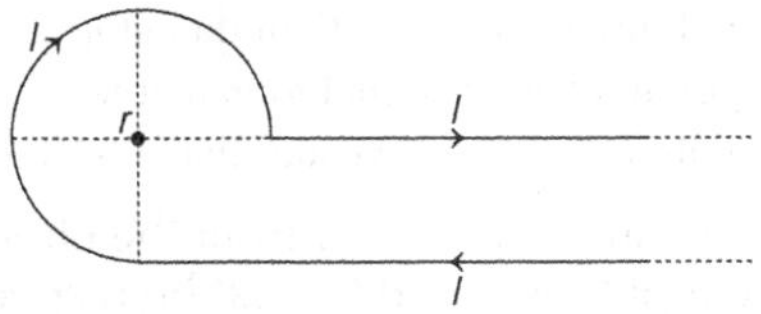

a. $\dfrac{\mu_0 I}{4\pi r}\left(\dfrac{3\pi}{2}+1\right)$ *b.* $\dfrac{\mu_0 I}{4\pi r}\left(\dfrac{3\pi}{2}-1\right)$

c. $\dfrac{\mu_0 I}{4\pi r}\left(\dfrac{\pi}{2}+1\right)$ *d.* $\dfrac{\mu_0 I}{4\pi r}\left(\dfrac{\pi}{2}-1\right)$

24. Two tangent galvanometers A and B are identical except in their number of turns. They are connected in series. On passing a current through them, deflections of 60° and 30° are produced. The ratio of the number of turns in A and B is

a. 1 : 3 *b.* 3 : 1
c. 1 : 2 *d.* 2 : 1

25. The resultant force on the current loop $PQRS$ due to a long current carrying conductor will be

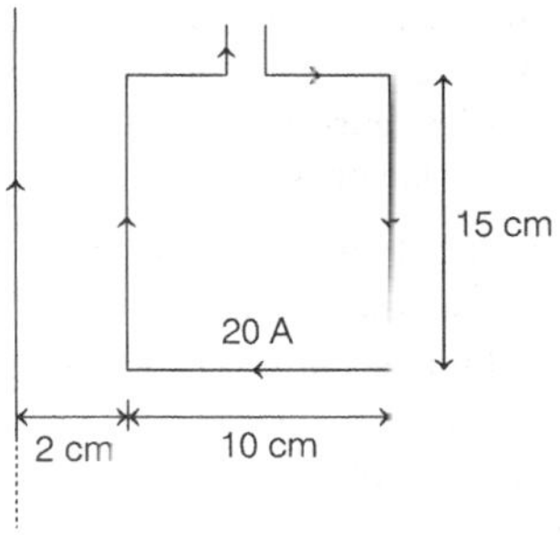

a. 10^{-4} N
b. 3.6×10^{-4} N
c. 1.8×10^{-4} N
d. 5×10^{-4} N

26. A certain current on passing through a galvanometer produces a deflection of 100 divisions. When a shunt of one ohm is connected, then the deflection reduces to 1 division. The galvanometer resistance is

a. $100\ \Omega$ *b.* $99\ \Omega$ *c.* $10\ \Omega$ *d.* $9.9\ \Omega$

27. Two similar circular loops carry equal currents in the same direction. On moving the coils further apart, the electric current will

a. increase in both
b. decrease in both
c. remain unaltered
d. increases in one and decreases in the second

28. The value of alternating emf E in the given circuit will be

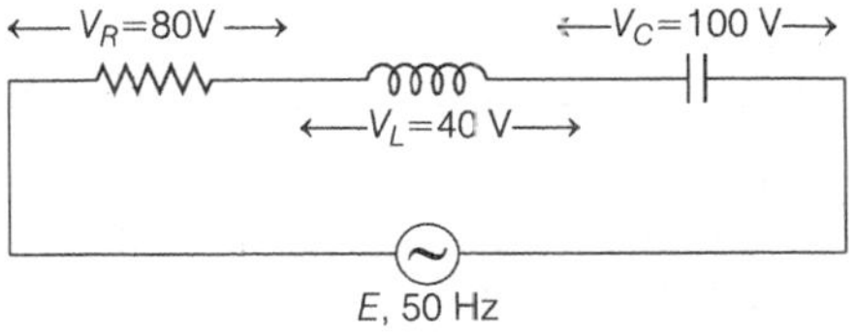

a. 220 V *b.* 140 V
c. 100 V *d.* 20 V

29. A current of 5 A is flowing at 220 V in the primary coil of a transformer. If the voltage produced in the secondary coil is 2200 V and 50% of power is lost, then the current in the secondary will be

a. 2.5 A *b.* 5 A
c. 0.25 A *d.* 0.5 A

30. For a series *L-C-R* circuit at resonance, the statement which is not true ?

a. Peak energy stored by a capacitor = peak energy stored by an inductor
b. Average power = Apparent power
c. Wattless current is zero.
d. Power factor is zero.

31. Solar spectrum is an example for

a. line emission spectrum
b. continuous emission spectrum
c. band absorption spectrum
d. line absorption spectrum

32. When a piece of metal is illuminated by a monochromatic light of wavelength λ, then stopping potential is 3V-s. When same surface is illuminated by light of wavelength 2λ, then stopping potential becomes V_s. The value of threshold wavelength for photoelectric emission will be

a. 4λ *b.* 8λ
c. $4/3\lambda$ *d.* 6λ

33. The maximum kinetic energy of emitted electrons in a photoelectric effect does not depend upon

a. wavelength *b.* frequency
c. intensity *d.* work-function

34. The ratio of minimum wavelength of Lyman and Balmer series will be

a. 1.25 *b.* 0.25
c. 5 *d.* 10

35. Hydrogen atom does not emit X-rays because

a. it contains only a single electron
b. energy levels in it are far apart
c. its size is very small
d. energy levels in it are very close to each other

36. If an electron and a proton have the same de-Broglie wavelength, then the kinetic energy of the electron is

a. Zero
b. less than that of a proton
c. more than that of a proton
d. equal to that of a proton

37. Two protons are kept at a separation of 40 Å. F_n is the nuclear force and F_e is the electrostatic force between them. Then,

a. $F_n >> F_e$ *b.* $F_n = F_e$
c. $F_n << F_e$ *d.* $F_n \simeq F_e$

38. Blue colour of sea water is due to

a. interference of sunlight reflected from the water surface
b. scattering of sunlight by the water molecules
c. image of sky in water
d. refraction of sunlight

39. The ratio of the nuclear radii of elements with mass numbers 216 and 125 is

a. 216 : 125 *b.* $\sqrt{216} : \sqrt{125}$
c. 6 : 5 *d.* None of these

40. On bombarding U^{235} by slow neutron, 200 MeV energy is released. If the power output of atomic reactor is 1.6 MW, then the rate of fission will be

a. 5×10^{22} / s *b.* 5×10^{16} / s
c. 8×10^{16} / s *d.* 20×10^{16} / s

41. The masses of two radioactive substances are same and their half-lives are 1 year and 2 years, respectively. The ratio of their activities after 6 years will be

a. 1 : 4 *b.* 1 : 2
c. 1 : 3 *d.* 1 : 6

42. ${}_{92}U^{235}$ undergoes successive disintegrations with the end product of ${}_{82}Pb^{203}$. The number of α and β particles emitted are

a. $\alpha = 6, \beta = 4$ *b.* $\alpha = 6, \beta = 0$
c. $\alpha = 8, \beta = 6$ *d.* $\alpha = 3, \beta = 3$

43. The most stable particle in Baryon group is

a. neutron *b.* omega-particle
c. proton *d.* lamda-particle

44. In an unbiased *p-n* junction

a. potential at *p* is more than that at *n*
b. potential at *p* is less than that at *n*
c. potential at *p* is equal to that at *n*
d. potential at *p* is + ve and that at *n* is – ve

45. To get an output $Y = 1$ from the circuit shown, the inputs *A*, *B* and *C* must be respectively

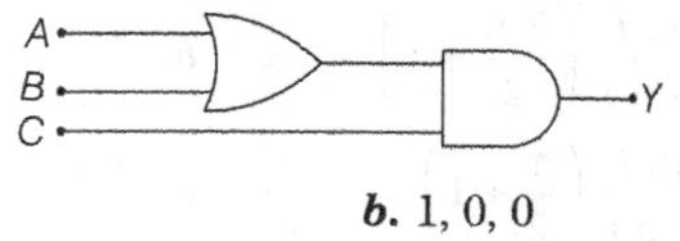

a. 0, 1, 0 *b.* 1, 0, 0
c. 1, 0, 1 *d.* 1, 1, 0

46. Dimensional formula for the universal gravitational constant G is

a. $[M^{-1}L^2T^{-2}]$ *b.* $[M^0L^0T^0]$
c. $[M^{-1}L^3T^{-2}]$ *d.* $[M^{-1}L^3T^{-1}]$

47. A body is projected vertically upwards. The times corresponding to height h, while ascending and descending are t_1 and t_2, respectively. Then, the velocity of projection is (g is acceleration due to gravity)

a. $g\sqrt{t_1t_2}$ *b.* $\frac{gt_1t_2}{t_1+t_2}$
c. $\frac{g\sqrt{t_1t_2}}{2}$ *d.* $\frac{g(t_1+t_2)}{2}$

48. A mass of 10 kg is suspended from a spring balance. It is pulled a side by a horizontal string, so that it makes an angle of 60° with the vertical. The new reading of the balance is

a. 20 kg-wt *b.* 10 kg-wt
c. $10\sqrt{3}$ kg-wt *d.* $20\sqrt{3}$ kg-wt

49. A body weight 50 g in air and 40 g in water. How much would it weight in a liquid of specific gravity 1.5?

a. 30 g *b.* 35 g
c. 65 g *d.* 45 g

50. A body of mass 4 kg is accelerated upon by a constant force, travels a distance of 5 m in the 1st second and a distance of 2 m in the 3rd second. The force acting on the body is

a. 2 N *b.* 4 N
c. 6 N *d.* 8 N

51. A simple pendulum is suspended from the ceiling of a lift. When the lift is at rest its time period is T. With what acceleration should the lift be accelerated upwards in order to reduce its period to $T/2$?
(g is acceleration due to gravity)

a. $2g$ *b.* $3g$
c. $4g$ *d.* g

52. If γ is the ratio of specific heats and R is the universal gas constant, then the molar specific heat at constant volume C_V is given by

a. γR *b.* $\frac{(\gamma-1)R}{\gamma}$
c. $\frac{R}{\gamma-1}$ *d.* $\frac{\gamma R}{\gamma-1}$

53. An ideal gas is taken via path $ABCA$ as shown in figure.

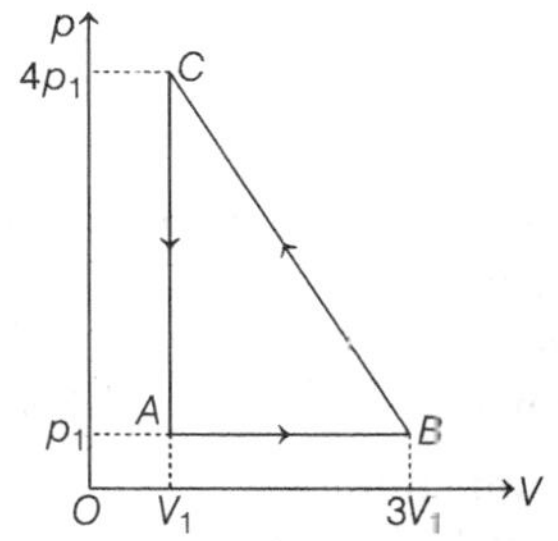

The network done in the whole cycle is

a. $3p_1V_1$ *b.* $-3p_1V_1$ *c.* $6p_1V_1$ *d.* Zero

54. In which of the processes, does the internal energy of the system remain constant?

a. Adiabatic *b.* Isochoric
c. Isobaric *d.* Isothermal

55. The coefficient of thermal conductivity of copper is 9 times that of steel. In the composite cylindrical bar shown in the figure, what will be the temperature at the junction of copper and steel?

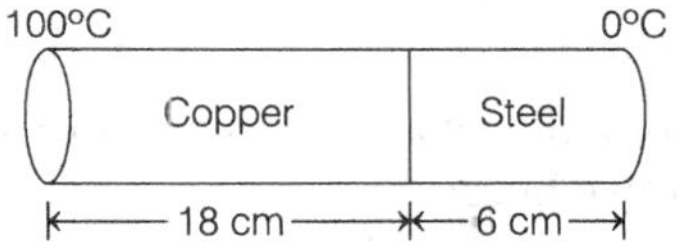

a. 75°C *b.* 67°C *c.* 25°C *d.* 33°C

56. The equation of a simple harmonic wave is given by $y = 6\sin 2\pi(2t - 0.1x)$, where x and y are in mm and t is in seconds. The phase difference between two particles 2 mm apart at any instant is

a. 18° *b.* 36° *c.* 54° *d.* 72°

57. With what velocity should an observer approach a stationary sound source, so that the apparent frequency of sound should appear double the actual frequency? (v is velocity of sound).

a. $v/2$ *b.* $3v$ *c.* $2v$ *d.* v

58. If a black body emits 0.5 J of energy per second when it is at 27°C, then the amount of energy emitted by it when it is at 627°C will be

a. 40.5 J *b.* 162 J *c.* 13.5 J *d.* 135 J

59. A string vibrates with a frequency of 200 Hz. When its length is doubled and tension is altered, it begins to vibrate with a frequency of 300 Hz. The ratio of the new tension to the original tension is

a. 9 : 1 *b.* 1 : 9 *c.* 3 : 1 *d.* 1 : 3

60. How many times more intense is a 60 dB sound than a 30 dB sound?

a. 1000 *b.* 2 *c.* 100 *d.* 4

CHEMISTRY

61. Which of the following is not an ore of magnesium?

a. Carnallite *b.* Dolomite
c. Calamine *d.* Sea water

62. The atomic numbers of Ni and Cu are 28 and 29 respectively. The electron configuration $1s^2 2s^2 2p^6 3s^2 3p^6 3d^{10}$ represents

a. Cu^+ *b.* Cu^{2+}
c. Ni^{2+} *d.* Ni

63. In the following, the element with the highest ionisation energy is

a. [Ne] $3s^2, 3p^1$ *b.* [Ne] $3s^2, 3p^3$
c. [Ne] $3s^2, 3p^2$ *d.* [Ne] $3s^2, 3p^4$

64. In the conversion of Br_2 to BrO_3^-, the oxidation number of Br changes from

a. zero to + 5 *b.* + 1 to + 5
c. zero to − 3 *d.* + 2 to + 5

65. Among the alkali metals caesium is the most reactive because

a. its incomplete shell is nearest to the nucleus
b. it has a single electron in the valence shell
c. it is the heaviest alkali metal
d. the outermost electron is more loosely bound than the outermost electron of the other alkali metals.

66. Which of the following represents the Lewis structure of N_2 molecule?

a.  *b.* 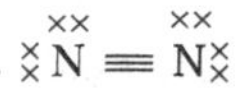
c. 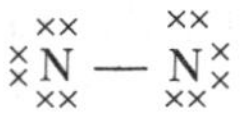 *d.* 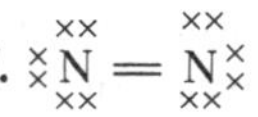

67. Hydrogen bond is strongest in

a. S—H ----- O *b.* O—H -----S
c. F—H ----- F *d.* O—H -----N

68. The decomposition of a certain mass of $CaCO_3$ gave 11.2 dm^3 of CO_2 gas at STP. The mass of KOH required to completely neutralise the gas is

a. 56 g *b.* 28 g
c. 42 g *d.* 20 g

69. The density of a gas is 1.964 g dm^{-3} at 273 K and 76 cm Hg. The gas is

a. CH_4 *b.* C_2H_6
c. CO_2 *d.* Xe

70. 0.06 mole of KNO_3 solid is added to 100 cm^3 of water at 298 K. The enthalpy of $KNO_3(aq)$ solution is 35.8 kJ mol^{-1}. After the solute is dissolved the temperature of the solution will be

a. 293 K *b.* 298 K *c.* 301 K *d.* 304 K

71. 4 moles each of SO_2 and O_2 gases are allowed to react to form SO_3 in a closed vessel. At equilibrium 25 % of O_2 is used up. The total number of moles of all the gases present at equilibrium is

a. 6.5 *b.* 7.0 *c.* 8.0 *d.* 2.0

72. An example for auto-catalysis is

a. oxidation of NO to NO_2
b. oxidation of SO_2 to SO_3
c. decomposition of $KClO_3$ to KCl and O_2
d. oxidation of oxalic acid by acidified $KMnO_4$

73. During the fusion of an organic compound with sodium metal, nitrogen of the compound is converted into

a. $NaNO_2$ *b.* $NaNH_2$
c. NaCN *d.* NaNC

74. Identify the product *Y* in the following reaction sequence

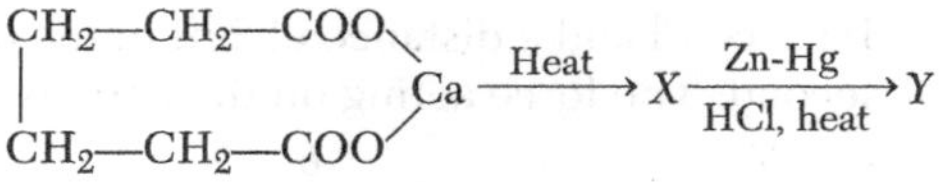

a. pentane *b.* cyclobutane
c. cyclopentane *d.* cyclopentanone

75. The reaction $C_2H_5ONa + C_2H_5I \longrightarrow C_2H_5OC_2H_5 + NaI$ is known as

a. Kolbe's synthesis
b. Wurtz's synthesis
c. Williamson's synthesis
d. Grignard's synthesis

76. ΔG° *vs T* plot in the Ellingham's diagram, slopes downwards for the reaction

a. $Mg + \frac{1}{2} O_2 \longrightarrow MgO$

b. $2Ag + \frac{1}{2} O_2 \longrightarrow Ag_2O$

c. $C + \frac{1}{2} O_2 \longrightarrow CO$

d. $CO + \frac{1}{2} O_2 \longrightarrow CO_2$

77. Which of the following reaction taking place in the blast furnace is endothermic ?

a. $CaCO_3 \longrightarrow CaO + CO_2$
b. $2C + O_2 \longrightarrow 2\,CO$
c. $C + O_2 \longrightarrow CO_2$
d. $Fe_2O_3 + 3CO \longrightarrow 2Fe + 3CO_2$

78. Liquor ammonia bottles are opened only after cooling. This is because

a. it is a mild explosive
b. it is a corrosive liquid
c. it is a lachrymatory
d. it generates high vapour pressure

79. The formation of $O_2^+[PtF_6]^-$ is basis for the formation of xenon fluorides. This is because

a. O_2 and Xe have comparable sizes
b. Both O_2 and Xe are gases
c. O_2 and Xe have comparable ionisation energies
d. O_2 and Xe have comparable electronegativities

80. The highest magnetic moment is shown by the transition metal ion with the configuration

a. $3d^2$ *b.* $3d^5$ *c.* $3d^7$ *d.* $3d^9$

81. A transition metal ion exists in its highest oxidation state. It is expected to behave as

a. a chelating agent
b. a central metal, in a coordination compound
c. an oxidising agent
d. a reducing agent

82. In which of the following complex ion, the central metal ion is in a state of sp^3d^2 hybridisation?

a. $[CoF_6]^{3-}$ *b.* $[Co(NH_3)_6]^{3+}$
c. $[Fe(CN)_6]^{3-}$ *d.* $[Cr(NH_3)_6]^{3+}$

83. Which of the following can participate in linkage isomerism?

a. NO_2 *b.* $H_2\ddot{N}CH_2CH_2\ddot{N}H_2$
c. H_2O *d.* $:NH_3$

84. Which of the following has the highest bond order?

a. N_2 *b.* O_2 *c.* He_2 *d.* H_2

85. Which of the following is diamagnetic?

a. H_2^+ *b.* O_2 *c.* Li_2 *d.* He_2^+

86. The concentration of a reactant X decreases from 0.1 M to 0.025 M in 40 min. If the reaction follows I order kinetics, the rate of the reaction when the concentration of X is 0.01 M will be

a. 1.73×10^{-4} M min^{-1} *b.* 3.47×10^{-4} M min^{-1}
c. 3.47×10^{-5} M min^{-1} *d.* 1.73×10^{-5} M min^{-1}

87. Chemical reactions with very high E_a values are generally

a. very fast *b.* very slow
c. moderately fast *d.* spontaneous

88. Which of the following does not conduct electricity?

a. Fused NaCl *b.* Solid NaCl
c. Brine solution *d.* Copper

89. When a quantity of electricity is passed through $CuSO_4$ solution, 0.16 g of copper gets deposited. If the same quantity of electricity is passed through acidulated water, then the volume of H_2 liberated at STP will be [Given, atomic weight of Cu = 64]

a. 4.0 cm^3 *b.* 56 cm^3 *c.* 604 cm^3 *d.* 8.0 cm^3

90. Solubility product of a salt AB is 1×10^{-8} M^2 in a solution in which the concentration of A^+ ions is 10^{-3} M. The salt will precipitate when the concentration of B^- ions is kept

a. between 10^{-8} M to 10^{-7} M
b. between 10^{-7} M to 10^{-6} M
c. $> 10^{-5}$ M
d. $< 10^{-8}$ M

91. Which one of the following condition will increase the voltage of the cell represented by the equation.

$Cu(s) + 2Ag^+(aq) \rightleftharpoons Cu^{2+}(aq) + 2Ag(s)$

a. increase in the dimensions of Cu electrode
b. increase in the dimensions of Ag electrode
c. increase in the concentration of Cu^{2+} ions
d. increase in the concentration of Ag^+ ions

92. The pH of 10^{-8} M HCl solution is

a. 8 *b.* more than 8
c. between 6 and 7 *d.* slightly more than 7

93. The mass of glucose that should be dissolved in 50 g of water in order to produce the same lowering of vapour pressure as is produced by dissolving 1g of urea in the same quantity of water is

a. 1 g *b.* 3 g *c.* 6 g *d.* 18 g

94. Osmotic pressure observed when benzoic acid is dissolved in benzene is less than that expected from theoretical considerations. This is because

a. benzoic acid is an organic solute
b. benzoic acid has higher molar mass than benzene
c. benzoic acid gets associated in benzene
d. benzoic acid gets dissociated in benzene

95. For a reaction to be spontaneous at all temperatures

a. ΔG and ΔH should be negative

b. ΔG and ΔH should be positive

c. $\Delta G = \Delta S = 0$

d. $\Delta H < \Delta G$

96. Which of the following electrolyte will have maximum flocculation value for $Fe(OH)_3$ sol.?

a. $NaCl$ *b.* Na_2S

c. $(NH_4)_3PO_4$ *d.* K_2SO_4

97. For a reversible reaction,

$$X(g) + 3Y(g) \rightleftharpoons 2Z(g)$$

$\Delta H = -40$ kJ the standard entropies of X, Y and Z are 60, 40 and 50 $JK^{-1}mol^{-1}$ respectively.

The temperature at which the above reaction attains equilibrium is about

a. 400 K *b.* 500 K

c. 273 K *d.* 373 K

98. The radii of Na^+ and Cl^- ions are 95 pm and 181 pm respectively. The edge length of NaCl unit cell is

a. 276 pm *b.* 138 pm

c. 552 pm *d.* 415 pm

99. Inductive effect involves

a. displacement of σ-electrons

b. delocalisation of π-electrons

c. delocalisation of σ-electrons

d. displacement of π-electrons

100. The basicity of aniline is less than that of cyclohexylamine. This is due to

a. + R-effect of $-NH_2$ group

b. − I-effect of $-NH_2$ group

c. − R-effect of $-NH_2$ group

d. hyperconjugation effect

101. Methyl bromide is converted into ethane by heating it in ether medium with

a. Al *b.* Zn

c. Na *d.* Cu

102. Which of the following compound is expected to be optically active?

a. $(CH_3)_2CHCHO$

b. $CH_3CH_2CH_2CHO$

c. $CH_3CH_2CHBrCHO$

d. $CH_3CH_2CBr_2CHO$

103. Which cycloalkane has the lowest heat of combustion per CH_2 group?

a. cyclopropane *b.* cyclobutane

c. cyclopentane *d.* cyclohexane

104. The catalyst used in the preparation of an alkyl chloride by the action of dry HCl on an alcohol is

a. anhydrous $AlCl_3$ *b.* $FeCl_3$

c. anhydrous $ZnCl_2$ *d.* Cu

105. In the reaction,

$R-X \xrightarrow[\text{KCN}]{\text{Alcoholic}} A \xrightarrow[\text{HCl}]{\text{Dilute}} B$, the product B is

a. alkyl chloride *b.* aldehyde

c. carboxylic acid *d.* ketone

106. Which of the following compound would not evolve CO_2 when treated with $NaHCO_3$ solution?

a. Salicylic acid *b.* Phenol

c. Benzoic acid *d.* 4-nitro benzoic acid

107. By heating phenol, with chloroform in alkali, it is converted into

a. salicylic acid *b.* salicylaldehyde

c. anisole *d.* phenyl benzoate

108. When a mixture of calcium benzoate and calcium acetate is dry distilled, the resulting compound is

a. acetophenone *b.* benzaldehyde

c. benzophenone *d.* acetaldehyde

109. Which of the following does not give benzoic acid on hydrolysis?

a. Phenyl cyanide *b.* Benzoyl chloride

c. Benzyl chloride *d.* Methyl benzoate

110. Which of the following would undergo Hofmann reaction to give a primary amine?

a. $R-\overset{\overset{\displaystyle O}{\|}}{C}-Cl$ *b.* $RCO\,NH\,CH_3$

c. $RCONH_2$ *d.* $RCOOR$

111. Glucose contains in addition to aldehyde group

a. one secondary OH and four primary OH groups

b. one primary OH and four secondary OH groups

c. two primary OH and three secondary OH groups

d. three primary OH and two secondary OH groups

112. A distinctive and characteristic functional group of fats is

a. a peptide group *b.* an ester group

c. an alcoholic group *d.* a ketonic group

113. At pH = 4 glycine exists as

a. $H_3\overset{+}{N}-CH_2-COO^-$

b. $H_3\overset{+}{N}-CH_2-COOH$

c. H_2N-CH_2-COOH

d. $H_2N-CH_2-COO^-$

114. Insulin regulates the metabolism of

a. minerals *b.* amino acids
c. glucose *d.* vitamins

115. The formula mass of Mohr's salt is 392 g. The iron present in it is oxidised by $KMnO_4$ in acid medium. The equivalent mass of Mohr's salt is

a. 392 *b.* 31.6
c. 278 *d.* 156

116. The brown ring test for nitrates depends on

a. the reduction of nitrate to nitric oxide
b. oxidation of nitric oxide to nitrogen dioxide
c. reduction of ferrous sulphate to iron
d. oxidising action of sulphuric acid

117. Acrolein test is positive for

a. polysaccharides *b.* proteins
c. oils and fats *d.* reducing sugars

118. An organic compound which produces a bluish green coloured flame on heating in presence of copper is

a. chlorobenzene *b.* benzaldehyde
c. aniline *d.* benzoic acid

119. For a reaction, $A + B \longrightarrow C + D$,
If the concentration of *A* is doubled without altering the concentration of *B*, the rate gets doubled. If the concentration of *B* is increased by nine times without altering the concentration of *A*, the rate gets tripled. The order of the reaction is

a. 2 *b.* 1 *c.* $\frac{3}{2}$ *d.* $\frac{4}{3}$

120. Which of the following solutions will exhibit highest boiling point?

a. 0.01 M $Na_2SO_4(aq)$ *b.* 0.01 M $KNO_3(aq)$
c. 0.015 M urea(aq) *d.* 0.015 M glucose(aq)

MATHEMATICS

121. If $\mathbf{u} = \mathbf{a} - \mathbf{b}$, $\mathbf{v} = \mathbf{a} + \mathbf{b}$, and $|\mathbf{a}| = |\mathbf{b}| = 2$, then $|\mathbf{u} \times \mathbf{v}|$ is

a. $2\sqrt{16 - (\mathbf{a} \cdot \mathbf{b})^2}$ *b.* $2\sqrt{4 - (\mathbf{a} \cdot \mathbf{b})^2}$
c. $\sqrt{16 - (\mathbf{a} \cdot \mathbf{b})^2}$ *d.* $\sqrt{4 - (\mathbf{a} \cdot \mathbf{b})^2}$

122. The volume of the tetrahedron formed by the points (1, 1, 1), (2, 1, 3) (3, 2, 2) and (3, 3, 4) in cubic units is

a. $\frac{5}{6}$ *b.* $\frac{6}{5}$
c. 5 *d.* $\frac{2}{3}$

123. Unit vector perpendicular to $\hat{\mathbf{i}} - 2\hat{\mathbf{j}} + 2\hat{\mathbf{k}}$ and lying in the plane containing $\hat{\mathbf{i}} + \hat{\mathbf{j}} - 2\hat{\mathbf{k}}$ and $-\hat{\mathbf{i}} + 2\hat{\mathbf{j}} + \hat{\mathbf{k}}$ is

a. $8\hat{\mathbf{i}} - 7\hat{\mathbf{j}} + 11\hat{\mathbf{k}}$ *b.* $8\hat{\mathbf{i}} + 7\hat{\mathbf{j}} - 11\hat{\mathbf{k}}$
c. $8\hat{\mathbf{i}} - 7\hat{\mathbf{j}} - 11\hat{\mathbf{k}}$ *d.* $\frac{1}{\sqrt{234}}(8\hat{\mathbf{i}} - 7\hat{\mathbf{j}} - 11\hat{\mathbf{k}})$

124. In the group $Q - \{1\}$ under the binary operation $*$ defined by $a * b = a + b + ab$ the inverse of 10 is

a. $\frac{1}{10}$ *b.* $\frac{11}{10}$ *c.* $\frac{-11}{10}$ *d.* $\frac{-10}{11}$

125. In the group {1, 2, 3, 4, 5, 6} under multiplication mod 7, $2^{-1} X_7^4 =$

a. 1 *b.* 4
c. 2 *d.* 3

126. The group (Z, +) has

a. exactly one sub-group
b. only two sub-groups
c. no sub-groups
d. infinitely many subgroups

127. If $3x \equiv 5 \pmod 7$, then

a. $x \equiv 2 \pmod 7$ *b.* $x \equiv 3 \pmod 7$
c. $x \equiv 4 \pmod 7$ *d.* None of these

128. The argument of the complex number

$$\sin\left(\frac{6\pi}{5}\right) + i\left(1 + \cos\frac{6\pi}{5}\right) \text{ is}$$

a. $\frac{\pi}{10}$ *b.* $\frac{5\pi}{6}$ *c.* $\frac{-\pi}{10}$ *d.* $\frac{2\pi}{5}$

129. The maximum value of $n < 101$, such that

$$1 + \sum_{k-1}^{n} i^k = 0 \text{ is}$$

a. 96 *b.* 97 *c.* 99 *d.* 100

130. The value of $(-1 + \sqrt{-3})^{62} + (-1 - \sqrt{-3})^{62}$ is

a. 2^{62} *b.* 2^{+3}
c. -2^{62} *d.* 0

131. All complex number z which satisfy the equation $\left|\frac{z - 6i}{z + 6i}\right| = 1$ lie on the

a. imginary axis *b.* real axis
c. neither of the axes *d.* None of the above

132. The value of $\sin[\cot^{-}\{\cos(\tan^{-1} x)\}]$ is

a. $\left(\sqrt{\frac{1+x^2}{2+x^2}}\right)$ *b.* $\left(\sqrt{\frac{2+x^2}{1+x^2}}\right)$

c. $\left(\sqrt{\frac{x^2-2}{x^2-1}}\right)$ *d.* $\left(\sqrt{\frac{x^2-1}{x^2-2}}\right)$

133. The value of $\alpha (\neq 0)$ for which the function $f(x) = 1 + \alpha x$ is the inverse of itself is

a. -2 *b.* 2

c. -1 *d.* 1

134. If x occurs is the expansion of $\left(x + \frac{1}{x}\right)^n$, then its coefficient is

a. $\frac{n!}{(r!)^1}$ *b.* $\frac{n!}{(r+1)!(r-1)!}$

c. $\frac{n!}{\left(\frac{n+r}{2}\right)!\left(\frac{n-r}{2}\right)!}$ *d.* $\frac{n!}{\left[\left(\frac{n}{2}\right)!\right]^2}$

135. If $\tan A - \tan B = x$ and $\cot B - \cot A = y$, then $\cot(A-B) =$

a. $\frac{1}{y} - \frac{1}{x}$ *b.* $\frac{1}{x} - \frac{1}{y}$

c. $\frac{1}{x} + \frac{1}{y}$ *d.* None of these

136. $\cos^2 \frac{\pi}{12} + \cos^2 \frac{\pi}{4} + \cos^2 \frac{5\pi}{12} =$

a. $\frac{3}{2}$ *b.* $\frac{3-\sqrt{3}}{2}$

c. $\frac{2}{3}$ *d.* $\frac{2}{3+\sqrt{3}}$

137. If $\sin\theta$, $\cos\theta$ and $\tan\theta$ are in GP, then $\cot^6\theta - \cot^2\theta$ is

a. 1 *b.* 1/2

c. 2 *d.* 3

138. If $\frac{3x^2 - 2x + 4}{(x-1)^6} = \frac{A_1}{x+1} + \frac{A_2}{(x+1)^2} + \frac{A_3}{(x+1)^3} + \frac{A_4}{(x+1)^4} + \frac{A_5}{(x+1)^5} + \frac{A_6}{(x+1)^6}$, then $(A_1 + A_2 + A_2 - A_4 - A_6) =$

a. (0, 0) *b.* (−8, −12)

c. (8, −12) *d.* (−8, 12)

139. If $\log_2(2^{x-1} + 6) + \log_2(4^{x-1}) = 5$, then $x =$

a. 4 *b.* 1

c. 3 *d.* 2

140. If a, b, c, and d are the roots of the equation $x^4 + 2x^3 + 3x^2 + 4x + 5 = 0$, then $1 + a^2 + b^2 + c^2 + d^2$ is equal to

a. -2 *b.* -1

c. 2 *d.* 1

141. If $c_0, c_1, c_2, \ldots, c_n$ are binomial coefficients of order n, then the value of $\frac{c_1}{2} + \frac{c_2}{4} + \frac{c_3}{6} + \ldots$

a. $\frac{2^n+1}{n-1}$ *b.* $\frac{2^n-1}{n+1}$

c. $\frac{2^n+1}{n-1}$ *d.* $\frac{2^n}{n+1}$

142. The value of $(0.2)^{\log_{\sqrt{5}}\left(\frac{1}{4}+\frac{1}{8}+\frac{1}{16}+\ldots\infty\right)}$ is

a. 4 *b.* $\frac{1}{4}$

c. 2 *d.* $\frac{1}{2}$

143. If $n(A) = n(B) = m$, then the number of possible bijection from A to B is

a. m *b.* m^2

c. $m!$ *d.* $2m$

144. $\sin^{-1}\left[x\sqrt{1-x} - \sqrt{x}\sqrt{1-x^2}\right] =$

a. $\sin^{-1} x - \sin^{-1}\sqrt{1-x^2}$

b. $\sin^{-1} x + \sin^{-1}\sqrt{1-x}$

c. $\sin^{-1} x - \sin^{1}\sqrt{x}$

d. $\sin^{-1} x + \sin^{-1}\sqrt{x}$

145. If $\tan\theta + \tan 4\theta + \tan 7\theta = \tan\theta \tan 4\theta \tan 7\theta$, then the general solution is

a. $\theta = \frac{n\pi}{4}$ *b.* $\theta = \frac{n\pi}{12}$

c. $\theta = \frac{n\pi}{6}$ *d.* None of these

146. If a circle with the point (−1, 1) as its center touches the straight line $x + 2y + 9 = 0$, then the coordinates of the points of contact is

a. (−3, 3) *b.* (−3, −3)

c. (0, 0) *d.* $\left(\frac{7}{3}, -\frac{17}{3}\right)$

147. If the circles $x^2 + y^2 + 2gx + 2fy = 0$ and $x^2 + y^2 + 2g'x + 2f'y = 0$ touch each other, then

a. $fg = f'g'$ *b.* $f'g = fg'$

c. $ff' = gg'$ *d.* None of these

COMEDK 2018

148. The number of common tangents to the circles $x^2+y^2=4$ and $x^2+y^2-4x+2y-4=0$ is

a. 1 b. 2 c. 3 d. 4

149. The length of the tangent drawn from any point on the circle $x^2+y^2-4x+6y-4=0$ to the circle $x^2+y^2-4x+6y=0$ is

a. 8 b. 4
c. 2 d. None of these

150. If the foci of the ellipse $\frac{x^2}{25}+\frac{y^2}{b^2}=1$ and the hyperbola $\frac{x^2}{144}-\frac{y^2}{81}=\frac{1}{25}$ coincide, then the value of b^2 is

a. 25 b. 9 c. 16 d. 4

151. The latusrectum of the ellipse is half the minor axis. Then, its eccentricity is

a. $\frac{1}{\sqrt{2}}$ b. $\frac{1}{\sqrt{3}}$
c. $\frac{\sqrt{3}}{2}$ d. None of these

152. The ends of the latusrectum of the parabola $x^2+10x-16y+25=0$ are

a. $(3, 4), (-13, 4)$ b. $(5, -8), (-5, 8)$
c. $(3, -4), (13, 4)$ d. $(-3, 4), (13, -4)$

153. Which of the following functions is differentiable at $x=0$?

a. $\cos(|x|)+|x|$ b. $\cos(|x|)-|x|$
c. $\sin(|x|)+|x|$ d. $\sin(|x|)-|x|$

154. If $x=a\left(\cos t+\log\tan\frac{t}{2}\right)$, $y=a\sin t$, then $\frac{dy}{dx}=$

a. $\tan t$ b. $\cot t$
c. $-\cot t$ d. $\tan t$

155. If $\begin{bmatrix}1 & -\tan\theta\\ \tan\theta & 1\end{bmatrix}\begin{bmatrix}1 & \tan\theta\\ -\tan\theta & 1\end{bmatrix}^{-1}=\begin{bmatrix}a & -b\\ b & a\end{bmatrix}$, then

a. $a=1=b$
b. $a=\cos 2\theta$, $b=\sin 2\theta$
c. $a=\sin 2\theta$, $b=\cos 2\theta$
d. $a=\cos\theta$, $b=\sin\theta$

156. If $A=\begin{bmatrix}1 & 2\\ 0 & 1\end{bmatrix}$, then A^n is

a. $\begin{bmatrix}1 & 2^n-2\\ 0 & 1\end{bmatrix}$ b. $\begin{bmatrix}1 & n^2\\ 0 & 1\end{bmatrix}$
c. $\begin{bmatrix}1 & 2n\\ 0 & 1\end{bmatrix}$ d. $\begin{bmatrix}1 & n^2\\ 1 & 1\end{bmatrix}$

157. If α, β, γ are the roots of the equation $x^3+px+q=0$, then the value of the determinant $\begin{vmatrix}\alpha & \beta & \gamma\\ \beta & \gamma & \alpha\\ \gamma & \alpha & \beta\end{vmatrix}$ is

a. q b. 0 c. p d. p^2-2q

158. The number of distinct real roots of $\begin{vmatrix}\sin x & \cos x & \cos x\\ \cos x & \sin x & \cos x\\ \cos x & \cos x & \sin x\end{vmatrix}$ in the interval $\left[\frac{-\pi}{4}, \frac{\pi}{4}\right]$ is

a. 0 b. 1 c. 2 d. 3

159. The sum of non-prime positive divisors of 450 is

a. 1209 b. 1299 c. 1199 d. 1099

160. The last digit of $\sum_{\substack{1<p<100\\ p\to \text{prime}}} p! - \sum_{n=1}^{50}(2n)!$ is

a. 2 b. 4 c. 6 d. 8

161. The interval I such that $\int_0^1 \frac{dx}{\sqrt{1+x^4}}\in I$ is given by

a. $\left[0, \frac{1}{\sqrt{2}}\right]$ b. $\left[\frac{1}{\sqrt{2}}, 1\right]$
c. $[\sqrt{2}, 2]$ d. $\left[\sqrt{2}, \frac{7}{4}\right]$

162. $\int_0^{\pi/2}\log(\tan x)\,dx=$

a. $\frac{\pi}{2}$ b. 0 c. 1 d. $\frac{\pi}{4}$

163. The value of $\int_{-2}^{2}(ax^3+bx+c)\,dx$ depends on the

a. value of b b. value of c
c. value of a d. values of a and b

164. The area of the region bound by the curves $y=x^2$ and $y=4x-x^2$ is

a. $\frac{16}{3}$ sq. units b. $\frac{8}{3}$ sq. units
c. $\frac{4}{3}$ sq. units d. $\frac{2}{3}$ sq. unit

165. The particular solution of $\frac{y}{x}\frac{dy}{dx}=\frac{1+y^2}{1+x^2}$, when $x=1$, $y=2$ is

a. $5(1+y^2)=2(1+x^2)$ b. $2(1+y^2)=5(1+x^2)$
c. $5(1+y^2)=(1+x^2)$ d. $(1+y^2)=2(1+x^2)$

166. The solution of the differential equation $\frac{dy}{dx} = (x+y)^2$ is

a. $\frac{1}{x+y} = c$ b. $\sin^{-1}(x+y) = x + c$

c. $\tan^{-1}(x+y) = c$ d. $\tan^{-1}(x+y) = x + c$

167. The maximum value of $\left(\frac{1}{x}\right)^{2x^2}$ is

a. $e^{1/e}$ b. $\sqrt{e}$

c. 1 d. e^2

168. Let x be a number which exceeds its square by the greatest possible quantity, then $x =$

a. 1/2 b. 1/4 c. 3/4 d. 1/3

169. The subtangent at $x = \pi/2$ on the curve $y = x \sin x$ is

a. 0 b. 1

c. $\pi/2$ d. None of these

170. The value of $\int \frac{10^{x/2}}{\sqrt{10^{-x} - 10^x}} dx$ is

a. $\frac{1}{\log_e 10} \sin^{-1}(10^x) + c$

b. $2\sqrt{10^{-x} + 10^x} + c$

c. $\frac{1}{\log_e 10} \sin h^{-1}(10^x) + c$

d. $\frac{-1}{\log_e 10} \sin h^{-1}(10^x) + c$

171. $\int e^x \left\{\frac{1 + \sin x \cos x}{\cos^2 x}\right\} dx =$

a. $e^x \cos x + c$ b. $e^x \sec x \tan x + c$

c. $e^x \tan x + c$ d. $e^x \cos^2 x - 1 + c$

172. $\int \frac{x^2 + 1}{x^4 + 1} dx$

a. $\frac{1}{\sqrt{2}} \log_e(x^2 + 1) + c$ b. $\frac{1}{\sqrt{2}} \tan^{-1}\left(\frac{x^2+1}{x\sqrt{2}}\right) + c$

c. $\frac{1}{\sqrt{2}} \tan^{-1}(x^2 - 1) + c$ d. $\frac{1}{\sqrt{2}} \tan^{-1}\left(\frac{x^2-1}{x\sqrt{2}}\right) + c$

173. The locus of the mid-point of the intercept of the line $x \cos\alpha + y \sin\alpha = p$ between the coordinate axes is

a. $x^{-2} + y^{-2} = 4p^{-2}$ b. $x^{-2} + y^{-2} = p^{-2}$

c. $x^2 + y^2 = 4p^{-2}$ d. $x^2 + y^2 = p^2$

174. If the line through $A = (4, -5)$ is inelined at an angle 45° with the positive direction of the X-axis, then the coordinates of the two points on opposite sides of A at a distance of $3\sqrt{2}$ units are

a. (7, 2), (1, 8) b. (7, 2), (1, –8)

c. (7, –2), (1, –8) d. (7, 2), (–1, 8)

175. If the line $px + qy = 0$ coincides with one of the lines given by $ax^2 + 2hxy + by^2 = 0$, then

a. $ap^2 + 2hpq + bq^2 = 0$ b. $aq^2 + 2hpq + bp^2 = 0$

c. $aq^2 - 2hpq + bp^2 = 0$ d. None of these

176. The function $f(x) = \left(\frac{\log_e(1+ax) - \log_e(1-bx)}{x}\right)$ is undefined at $x = 0$. The value which should be assigned to f at $x = 0$ so that it is continuous at $x = 0$ is

a. $\frac{a+b}{2}$ b. $a + b$ c. $\log_e(ab)$ d. $a - b$

177. $\lim_{n \to \infty} \frac{(1^2 + 2^2 + \ldots + n^2)\sqrt[n]{n}}{(n+1)(n+10)(n+100)} =$

a. 3 b. $\frac{1}{3}$ c. $\frac{2}{3}$ d. ∞

178. The number of triangles in a complete graph with 10 non-collinear vertices is

a. 360 b. 240 c. 120 d. 60

179. The angle between hands of a clock when the time is 4.25 AM is signed to

a. 17 1/2° b. 14 1/2°

c. 13 1/2° d. 12 1/2°

180. The point (5, – 7) lies outside the circle

a. $x^2 + y^2 - 8x = 0$

b. $x^2 + y^2 - 5x + 7y = 0$

c. $x^2 + y^2 - 5x + 7y - 1 = 0$

d. $x^2 + y^2 - 8x + 7y - 2 = 0$

COMEDK 2018

ANSWERS

Physics

1. (c)	2. (b)	3. (a)	4. (a)	5. (a)	6. (c)	7. (d)	8. (*)	9. (c)	10. (d)
11. (a)	12. (b)	13. (c)	14. (a)	15. (a)	16. (d)	17. (c)	18. (d)	19. (b)	20. (a)
21. (b)	22. (c)	23. (a)	24. (b)	25. (d)	26. (b)	27. (a)	28. (c)	29. (c)	30. (d)
31. (d)	32. (a)	33. (c)	34. (b)	35. (d)	36. (c)	37. (a)	38. (b)	39. (c)	40. (b)
41. (a)	42. (c)	43. (a)	44. (b)	45. (c)	46. (c)	47. (d)	48. (a)	49. (b)	50. (c)
51. (b)	52. (c)	53. (b)	54. (d)	55. (a)	56. (d)	57. (d)	58. (a)	59. (a)	60. (a)

Chemistry

61. (c)	62. (a)	63. (b)	64. (a)	65. (d)	66. (a)	67. (c)	68. (a)	69. (c)	70. (a)
71. (b)	72. (d)	73. (c)	74. (c)	75. (c)	76. (c)	77. (a)	78. (a)	79. (c)	80. (b)
81. (c)	82. (a)	83. (a)	84. (a)	85. (c)	86. (b)	87. (b)	88. (b)	89. (b)	90. (c)
91. (d)	92. (c)	93. (b)	94. (c)	95. (a)	96. (a)	97. (b)	98. (c)	99. (a)	100. (a)
101. (c)	102. (c)	103. (d)	104. (c)	105. (c)	106. (b)	107. (b)	108. (a)	109. (c)	110. (c)
111. (b)	112. (b)	113. (b)	114. (c)	115. (a)	116. (a)	117. (c)	118. (a)	119. (c)	120. (a)

Mathematics

121. (a)	122. (a)	123. (d)	124. (d)	125. (c)	126. (d)	127. (c)	128. (c)	129. (c)	130. (c)
131. (b)	132. (a)	133. (c)	134. (c)	135. (c)	136. (a)	137. (a)	138. (d)	139. (d)	140. (b)
141. (b)	142. (a)	143. (c)	144. (c)	145. (b)	146. (b)	147. (b)	148. (b)	149. (c)	150. (c)
151. (c)	152. (a)	153. (d)	154. (d)	155. (b)	156. (c)	157. (b)	158. (b)	159. (c)	160. (a)
161. (b)	162. (b)	163. (b)	164. (b)	165. (b)	166. (d)	167. (a)	168. (a)	169. (c)	170. (a)
171. (c)	172. (d)	173. (a)	174. (c)	175. (c)	176. (b)	177. (b)	178. (c)	179. (a)	180. (a)

Note (*) None of the option is correct.

HINTS & SOLUTIONS

Physics

1. *(c)* The angle of incidence $= i$

Let r be the angle of refraction.

According to given situation, reflected rays and refracted rays are perpendicular to each other.

i.e. $$i + r = 90^\circ \quad \ldots\text{(i)}$$

$\therefore$ According to Snell's law,

$$\mu = \frac{\sin i}{\sin r}$$

$$= \frac{\sin i}{\sin(90 - i)} \quad [\because \text{From Eq. (i)}]$$

$$= \frac{\sin i}{\cos i}$$

$$\mu = \tan i \quad \ldots\text{(ii)}$$

If i_C be the critical angle for the pair of media, then

$$\mu = \frac{1}{\sin i_C} \quad \ldots\text{(iii)}$$

From Eqs. (ii) and (iii), we get

$$\tan i = \frac{1}{\sin i_C}$$

$$\Rightarrow \quad \sin i_C = \cot i$$

$$\Rightarrow \quad i_C = \sin^{-1}(\cot i)$$

2. *(b)* Refractive index of water $= n$

Since, fish looks the bird from water (denser medium) to air (rarer medium).

Hence, normal shift $d = (n - 1)h$

But according to question, real depth $h = y$

$\therefore \quad d = (n-1)y \quad (\because \text{height of bird} = y)\ldots\text{(i)}$

The bird's height from the surface of the water is equal to the summation of the normal shift and height of the bird from the surface.

i.e. $$d' = y + d = y + (n-1)y \quad [\text{From Eq. (i)}]$$

$$d' = ny \quad \ldots\text{(ii)}$$

Total actual distance between bird and fish

$$= x + d' = x + ny$$

3. *(a)* The given situation is shown below

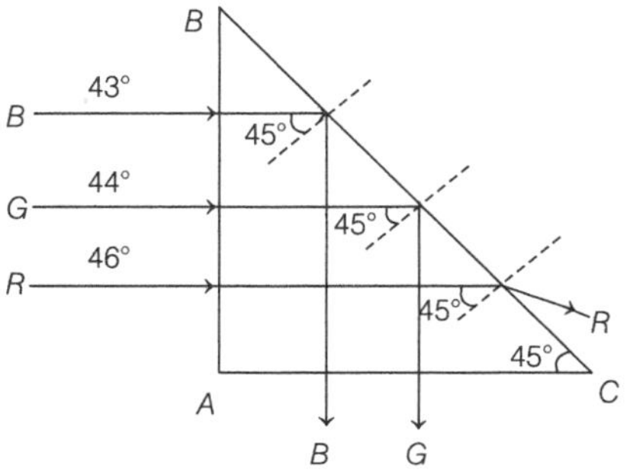

Since, critical angles for blue colour and green colour are less than angle of incidence, hence total internal reflection occurs for blue and green colours of light. Again, since critical angle for red colour is greater than angle of incidence hence red colour transmitted outside from surface BC.

4. *(a)* Let f_1 and f_2 are focal lengths of convex and concave lens respectively, when they are kept in contact co-axially, then focal length F of the combination is given as

$$\frac{1}{F} = \frac{1}{f_1} + \frac{1}{(-f_2)} \quad \left[\begin{array}{l}\text{Focal length of concave}\\ \text{lens is negative.}\end{array}\right]$$

$$\Rightarrow \quad \frac{1}{F} = \frac{f_2 - f_1}{f_1 f_2}$$

$$\Rightarrow \quad F = \frac{f_1 f_2}{f_2 - f_1} \quad \ldots\text{(i)}$$

When both lenses are kept at a distance d, then their combined focal length F' is given as

$$\frac{1}{F'} = \frac{1}{f_1} + \frac{1}{(-f_2)} - \frac{d}{f_1(-f_2)}$$

$$\Rightarrow \quad \frac{1}{F'} = \frac{1}{f_1} - \frac{1}{f_2} + \frac{d}{f_1 f_2}$$

$$\Rightarrow \quad \frac{1}{F'} = \frac{f_2 - f_1 + d}{f_1 f_2}$$

$$\Rightarrow \quad F' = \frac{f_1 f_2}{f_2 - f_1 + d} \quad \ldots\text{(ii)}$$

From Eqs. (i) and (ii), it is clear that $F' < F$

i.e. focal length of combination will decrease.

5. *(a)* Since, convex lens made of 3 layers of different materials have only one focal length. Thus, for a given object, there is only one image.

6. *(c)* Speed of light in terms of permittivity of free space ε_0 and permeability of free space μ_0 is given as

$$C = \frac{1}{\sqrt{\mu_0 \varepsilon_0}} = \sqrt{\frac{1}{\mu_0 \varepsilon_0}}$$

7. *(d)* When a third slit is made in between the double slits in YDSE, then contrast between bright and dark fringes is reduced. It is because in the case of double slits, light passes only two slits. Now, the same light is passing through the three slits which results in reducing the contrast of bright fringes as well as dark fringes.

8. *(*)* In double slit experiment, for possible interference maxima on the screen is given as

$$d \sin\theta = n\lambda$$

Given, slit width, $d = 4\lambda$

$$\therefore \quad 4\lambda \sin\theta = n\lambda$$

$$\Rightarrow \quad 4\sin\theta = n$$

Since, maximum value of $\sin\theta = 1$

$\therefore$ For maximum number of possible interference maxima,

$$4 \cdot 1 = n$$

$\Rightarrow \quad n = 4$

i.e., $\quad n = 0, 1, 2, 3$

$\therefore$ Maximum number of possible maxima will be 7

i.e. $0, \pm 1, \pm 2, \pm 3$

Hence, no option is correct.

9. *(c)* Given, wavelength of used light,

$$\lambda = 400 \text{ nm}$$

For minima in Fraunhofer diffraction,

$$d \sin\theta = n\lambda$$

For first minima $n = 1$, where $\theta = 30°$

$\therefore \quad d \sin 30° = 1 \times 400$

$\Rightarrow \quad d = 800$ nm

For maxima in diffraction,

$$d \sin\theta = (2n+1)\frac{\lambda}{2}$$

For first maxima $n = 0$

$\therefore \quad d \sin\theta = (0+1)\frac{\lambda}{2}$

$\Rightarrow \quad d \sin\theta = \frac{\lambda}{2}$

$\Rightarrow \quad 800 \sin\theta = \frac{400}{2}$

$\Rightarrow \quad \sin\theta = \frac{1}{4}$

$\Rightarrow \quad \theta = \sin^{-1}\left(\frac{1}{4}\right)$

10. *(d)* Greater is the wavelength of wave higher will be its degree of diffraction, since radiowave has maximum wavelength, hence maximum diffraction takes place in a given slit for radio waves.

11. *(a)* When an unpolarised beam of intensity I_0 falls on a polaroid, then after polarisation, the intensity of the emergent beam of light becomes $\frac{I_0}{2}$.

12. *(b)* Materials which have different absorption for perpendicular incident plane for light are called dichoric material crystal. Tourmaline is one example of such type of crystal.

13. *(c)* Given, $Q_1 = 12\mu\text{F} = 12 \times 10^{-6}\text{F}$

$$Q_2 = -8\mu\text{F} = -8 \times 10^{-6}\text{F}$$

Initial value of electrostatic force of attraction between both spheres,

$$F_1 = \frac{1}{4\pi\varepsilon_0}\frac{Q_1Q_2}{r^2} = \frac{1}{4\pi\varepsilon_0} \cdot \frac{12\times10^{-6}\times 8\times10^{-6}}{r^2}$$

$$F_1 = \frac{1}{4\pi\varepsilon_0}\frac{96\times10^{-12}}{r^2} \qquad \ldots\text{(i)}$$

When both charged spheres are kept in contact, then new charges on the spheres will be

$$Q_1' = Q_2' = \frac{Q_1+Q_2}{2} = \frac{12+(-8)}{2} = 2\mu\text{F} = 2\times10^{-6}\text{ F}$$

$\therefore$ Final value of electrostatic force between the spheres,

$$F_2 = \frac{1}{4\pi\varepsilon_0}\frac{Q_1' \times Q_2'}{r^2} = \frac{1}{4\pi\varepsilon_0} \cdot \frac{2\times10^{-6}\times 2\times10^{-6}}{r^2}$$

$$F_2 = \frac{1}{4\pi\varepsilon_0} \cdot \frac{4\times10^{-12}}{r^2} \qquad \ldots\text{(ii)}$$

From Eqs. (i) and (ii), we get

$$\therefore \quad \frac{F_1}{F_2} = \frac{\frac{1}{4\pi\varepsilon_0} \cdot \frac{96\times10^{-12}}{r^2}}{\frac{1}{4\pi\varepsilon_0} \cdot \frac{4\times10^{-12}}{r^2}}$$

$\Rightarrow \quad \frac{F_1}{F_2} = \frac{24}{1}$

$\Rightarrow \quad F_1 : F_2 = 24 : 1$

14. *(a)* According to given situation, potential at the surface of small conducting sphere of radius r,

$$V_r = \frac{kq}{r} + \frac{kQ}{R}$$

Potential at the surface of bigger conducting sphere of radius R,

$$V_R = \frac{kq}{R} + \frac{kQ}{R}$$

$\therefore$ Potential difference between the spheres is given as

$$V_r - V_R = \frac{kq}{r} + \frac{kQ}{R} - \frac{kq}{R} - \frac{kQ}{R} = \frac{kq}{r} - \frac{kq}{R} = k\left(\frac{q}{r} - \frac{q}{R}\right) = \frac{1}{4\pi\varepsilon_0}\left[\frac{q}{r} - \frac{q}{R}\right]$$

15. *(a)* The given situation is shown below

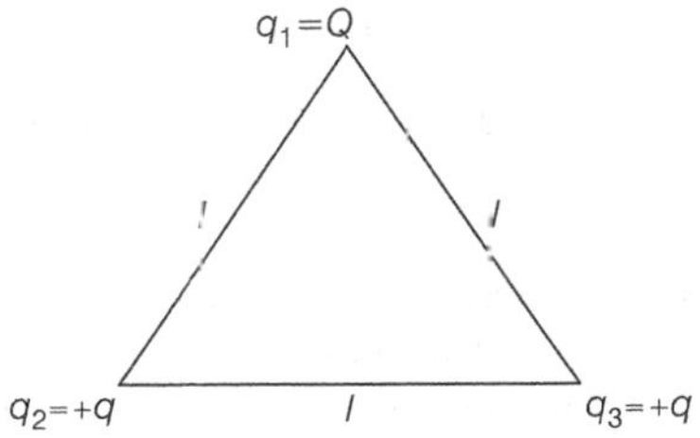

Net potential energy of the system = 0

i.e. $\quad U_{\text{net}} = 0$

$$\Rightarrow \quad \frac{1}{4\pi\varepsilon_0} \cdot \frac{q_1q_2}{l} + \frac{1}{4\pi\varepsilon_0} \cdot \frac{q_2q_3}{l} + \frac{1}{4\pi\varepsilon_0} \cdot \frac{q_3q_1}{l} = 0$$

$\Rightarrow \quad q_1q_2 + q_2q_3 + q_3q_1 = 0$

$\Rightarrow \quad Q.q + q.q + q.Q = 0$

$\Rightarrow \quad 2Qq + q^2 = 0$

$\Rightarrow \quad q(2Q + q) = 0$

Since, $\quad q \neq 0$

$\therefore \quad 2Q + q = 0$

$\Rightarrow \quad Q = \frac{-q}{2}$

16. *(d)* We know that, in series combination of capacitors, net potential difference is equal to sum of the individual potential difference of each capacitor

i.e., $V = V_1 + V_2 + V_3 \ldots\ldots \quad [V_1 = V_2 = V_3 = 200\,\text{V}]$

$\Rightarrow \quad 600 = n \times 200$

$\Rightarrow \quad n = 3$

So, there should be 3 capacitors in series to obtain the required potential difference. The equivalent capacitance of 3 capacitors in series is given as

$$\frac{1}{C_{\text{eq}}} = \frac{1}{6} + \frac{1}{6} + \frac{1}{6} = \frac{3}{6} = \frac{1}{2}$$

$\Rightarrow \quad C_{\text{eq}} = 2\mu\text{F}$

Now, we require 18 μF capacitance for this, we need 9 number of such capacitors in parallel.

$\therefore$ Total number of capacitors (condensers)

$= 9 \times 3 = 27$

17. *(c)* The given circuit diagram is redrawn as

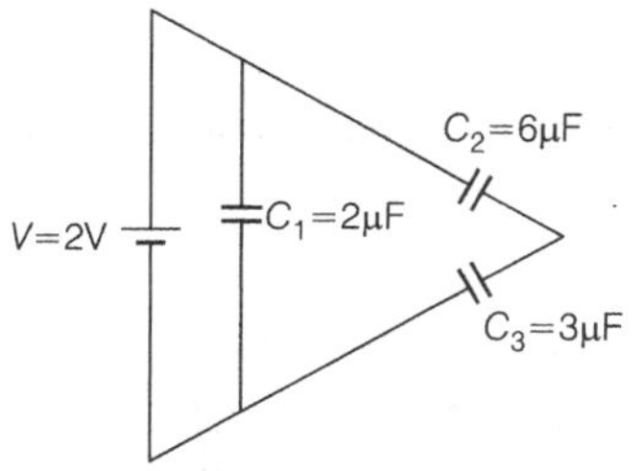

Equivalent capacitance is given as

$$C_{\text{eq}} = \frac{C_2C_3}{C_2 + C_3} + C_1 = \frac{6 \times 3}{6 + 3} + 2 = 4\mu\text{F}$$

$\therefore$ Total energy stored in the condenser system,

$$U = \frac{1}{2}C_{\text{eq}} \cdot V^2 = \frac{1}{2} \times 4 \times 10^{-6} \times 2^2$$

$$= 8 \times 10^{-6}\,\text{J} = 8\mu\text{J}$$

18. *(d)* Drift velocity of the electron is given as

$$v_d = \frac{eE\tau}{m}$$

where, e = charge on electron,

E = electric field,

τ = relaxation time

and m = mass of the electron.

Since, $\quad E = \frac{V}{l}$

$\therefore \quad v_d = \frac{eV\tau}{ml}$

Since, e, V, m and l are constant .

$\therefore \quad v_d \propto \tau$

On increasing the temperature of metal wire, relaxation time decreases, therefore drift velocity of electrons also decreases.

But on increasing temperature of metal wire, thermal velocity of electron increases.

19. *(b)* Redrawing the given circuit network as

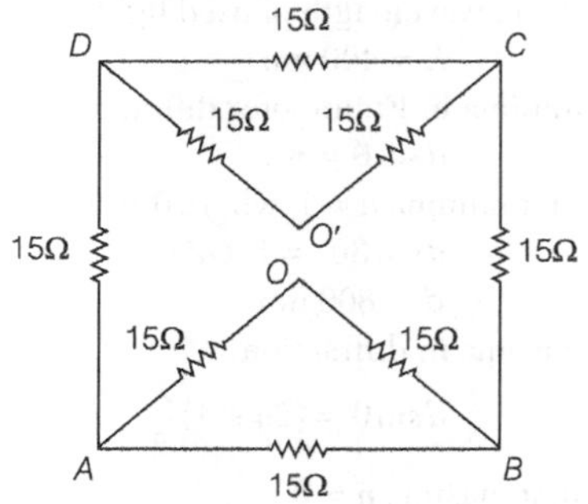

Equivalent resistance between points D and C,

$$R_{DC} = \frac{(15 + 15) \times 15}{(15 + 15) + 15} = \frac{30 \times 15}{45} = 10\,\Omega$$

Similarly, $\quad R_{AB} = R_{DC} = 10\Omega$

Now, circuit, diagram reduces as

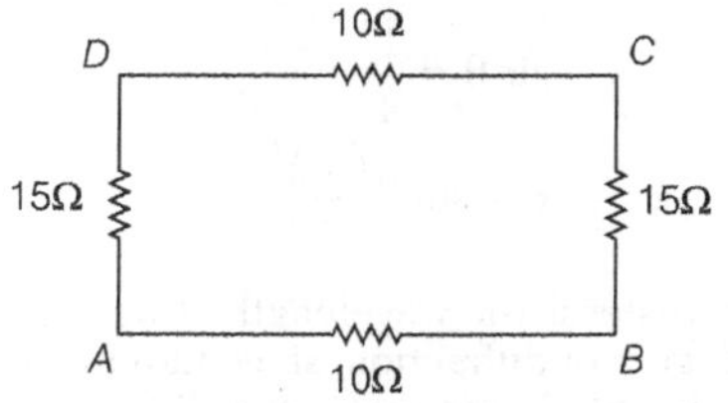

$\therefore$ Equivalent resistance between points A and B is given as

$$R_{AB} = (15 + 10 + 15)\,||\,10 = 40\,||\,10 = \frac{40 \times 10}{40 + 10}$$

$$= \frac{400}{50} = 8\Omega$$

20. *(a)* Since, the terminals of battery is connected at one quarter distance. Hence, ratio of lengths between two parts will be

$$\frac{l_1}{l_2} = \frac{1}{3}$$

$\Rightarrow \quad l_1 : l_2 = 1 : 3$

Since, $R \propto l$

$\therefore \quad R_1 : R_2 = 1 : 3$

$$R_1 = \frac{24}{1 + 3} = 6\Omega$$

$$R_2 = 24 \times \frac{3}{1 + 3} = 18\Omega$$

Since, potential difference across R_1 and R_2 is same, so they are connected in parallel.

$\therefore$ Equivalent resistance of R_1 and R_2,

$$R' = \frac{R_1 R_2}{R_1 + R_2}$$

$$= \frac{6 \times 18}{6 + 18} = 4.5\,\Omega$$

$\therefore$ Total resistance, $R_T = R' + r$

$$= 4.5 + 1.5 \qquad [\because r = 1.5\,\Omega]$$

$$= 6\,\Omega$$

Current, $I = \frac{V}{R_T} = \frac{18}{6} = 3\text{ A}$

According to current division rule, current through bigger arc (i.e. through R_2)

$$I_{R_2} = I.\frac{R_1}{R_1 + R_2} = 3 \times \frac{6}{6 + 18} = 0.75\text{ A}$$

21. *(b)*

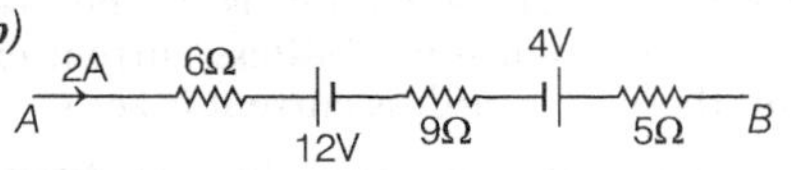

Applying Kirchhoff's voltage law, we get

$$-V_{AB} + 6 \times 2 + 12 + 9 \times 2 - 4 + 5 \times 2 = 0$$

$$\Rightarrow \quad -V_{AB} + 48 = 0$$

$$\Rightarrow \quad V_{AB} = 48\text{V}$$

22. *(c)* Magnetic field at the centre of circular carrying conductor,

$$B_c = \frac{\mu_0 I}{2r} \qquad \ldots\text{(i)}$$

Magnetic on the axis at a distance x from the centre is given as

$$B_{\text{axis}} = \frac{\mu_0 I r^2}{2(r^2 + x^2)^{3/2}}$$

Here , $x = r$

$$B_{\text{axis}} = \frac{\mu_0 I r^2}{2(r^2 + r^2)^{3/2}}$$

$$= \frac{\mu_0 I r^2}{2(2r^2)^{3/2}} = \frac{\mu_0 I r^2}{2 \cdot 2\sqrt{2} \cdot r^3}$$

$$B_{\text{axis}} = \frac{\mu_0 I}{4\sqrt{2}r}$$

$$B_{\text{axis}} = B_a = \frac{\mu_0 I}{4\sqrt{2}r}$$

$$\therefore \quad \frac{B_c}{B_a} = \frac{\mu_0 I / 2r}{\frac{\mu_0 I}{4\sqrt{2}r}} = \frac{4\sqrt{2}r}{2r} = 2\sqrt{2}$$

$$B_c : B_a = 2\sqrt{2} : 1$$

23. *(a)* The given current carrying conductor is shown below

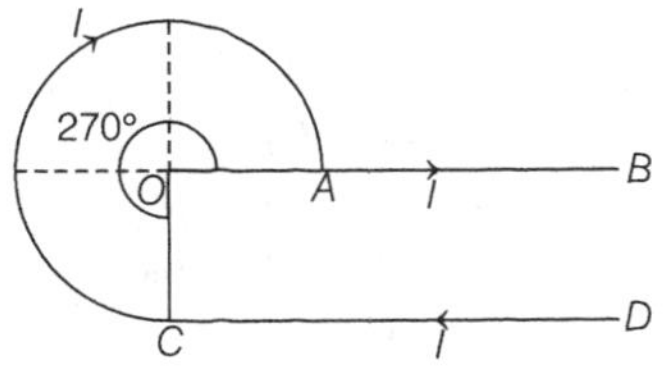

Magnetic field at the centre due to circular wire,

$$B_1 = \frac{\mu_0 I}{2r} \times \frac{270}{360} = \frac{\mu_0 I}{2r} \times \frac{3}{4}$$

$$B_1 = \frac{3\mu_0 I}{8r}$$

[in downward to the plane of paper]

Magnetic field at centre O due current carrying wire AB will be zero because point O lies along AB

$$\therefore \quad B_2 = 0$$

Magnetic field at O due to current carrying wire CD

$$B_3 = \frac{\mu_0 I}{4\pi r} \text{ (in downward to the plane of paper)}$$

$\therefore$ Net magnetic field at the centre,

$$B_{\text{net}} = B_1 + B_2 + B_3 = \frac{3\mu_0 I}{8r} + 0 + \frac{\mu_0 I}{4\pi r}$$

$$= \frac{\mu_0 I}{r}\left[\frac{3}{8} + \frac{1}{4\pi}\right] = \frac{\mu_0 I}{4\pi r}\left[\frac{3\pi}{2} + 1\right]$$

24. *(b)* Given, $\theta_A = 60°, \theta_B = 30°$

We know that, deflection in galvanometer θ and current I are related as

$$\tan\theta = KNI$$

where, K = constant,

N = number of turns in the coil of galvanometer

and I = current.

$$\therefore \quad \frac{\tan\theta_A}{\tan\theta_B} = \frac{N_A}{N_B}$$

$$\Rightarrow \quad \frac{\tan 60°}{\tan 30°} = \frac{N_A}{N_B}$$

$$\Rightarrow \quad \frac{\sqrt{3}}{\frac{1}{\sqrt{3}}} = \frac{N_A}{N_B}$$

$$\Rightarrow \quad \frac{3}{1} = \frac{N_A}{N_B}$$

$$\Rightarrow \quad N_A : N_B = 3 : 1$$

25. *(d)* $I_1 = 20\text{A}, I_2 = 20\text{A}$

$$r_1 = 2\text{ cm}$$

$$r_2 = (10 + 2)\text{ cm} = 12\text{ cm}$$

The given situation is shown in the figure.

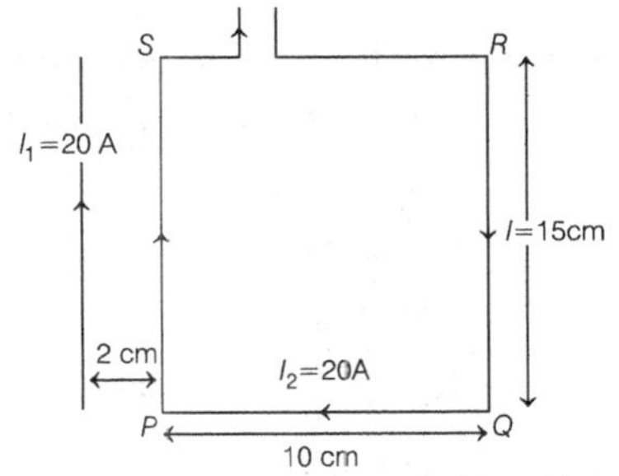

The forces on arm SR and PQ are equal in magnitude and opposite in direction and also having same line of action, hence they cancel to each other.

$\therefore$ Resultant force on the current loop *PQRS*,

$$F = F_{PS} - F_{QR}$$
$$= \frac{\mu_0}{2\pi}\cdot\frac{I_1 I_2 \times l}{r_1} - \frac{\mu_0}{2\pi}\cdot\frac{I_1 I_2 l}{r_2}$$
$$= \frac{\mu_0}{2\pi}\cdot I_1 I_2 l\left[\frac{1}{r_1} - \frac{1}{r_2}\right]$$
$$= 2\times 10^{-7} \times 20 \times 20 \times 15 \times 10^{-2}\left[\frac{1}{2\times 10^{-2}} - \frac{1}{12\times 10^{-2}}\right]$$
$$= 5 \times 10^{-4}\ \text{N}$$

26. *(b)* Given, shunt resistance, $R_S = 1\Omega$

Total current, $I = 100\text{A}$

Galvanometer current, $I_g = 1\text{A}$

We know that,

$$I_g = \frac{IR_S}{R_S + G}$$
$$\Rightarrow \quad 1 = \frac{100\times 1}{1+G}$$
$$\Rightarrow \quad 1 + G = 100$$
$$\Rightarrow \quad G = 99\Omega$$

27. *(a)* On moving the circular loops further apart, flux linked with loops will be reduced. Therefore, according to Lenz's law, current will increase in both circular loops to increase the linked flux.

28. *(c)* The given circuit diagram is *L-C-R*. series circuit, where

$$V_R = 80\text{ V}, V_C = 100\text{ V}$$
$$V_L = 40\text{V}$$

Since, $V_C > V_L$

Value of emf *E* is given as

$$E = \sqrt{V_R^2 + (V_C - V_L)^2}$$
$$= \sqrt{80^2 + (100-40)^2}$$
$$= \sqrt{6400 + 3600} = 100\text{ V}$$

29. *(c)* For a transformer,

$$I_P = 5\text{ A}, V_P = 220\text{ V}$$
$$V_S = 2200\text{V}$$

Power at primary side, $P_i = V_P I_P$

$$= 220\times 5 = 1100\text{ W}$$

Since, 50% power is lost, hence power at secondary side,

$$P_0 = 50\%\text{ of }P_i = \frac{50}{100}\times 1100$$
$$\Rightarrow \quad P_0 = 550\text{ W}$$
$$\Rightarrow \quad V_S I_S = 550$$
$$\Rightarrow \quad 2200\times I_S = 550$$
$$\Rightarrow \quad I_S = \frac{550}{2200} = \frac{1}{4} = 0.25\text{ A}$$

30. *(d)* In series *L-C-R* circuit,

$$X_L = X_C$$
$$\therefore \quad Z = \sqrt{R^2 + (X_L - X_C)^2}$$
$$= \sqrt{R^2 + 0^2}$$
$$Z = R$$

$\therefore$ Power factor $= \cos\phi$

$$= \frac{R}{Z} = \frac{R}{R} = 1$$

Hence, power factor is not zero.

Therefore option (d) is not correct.

In *L-C-R* series resonance circuit, peak energy stored by a capacitor is equal to peak energy stored by an inductor.

Average power, $P_{avg} = V_{rms} \times I_{rms} \times \cos 0°$

$$= V_{rms} \times I_{rms}$$
$$= \text{apparent power}$$

L-C-R series resonance circuit is purely resistive because $X_L = X_C$, hence no wattless current exists in this circuit therefore wattless current is zero.

31. *(d)* Solar spectrum is a line absorption spectrum which is also called as Fraunhofer line of missing wavelengths.

32. *(a)* According to first situation wavelength of incident radiation,

$$\lambda_1 = \lambda$$

Stopping potential, $V_{01} = 3V_S$

According to Einstein's photoelectric equation,

$$K_{max} = h\nu_1 - \phi$$
$$\Rightarrow \quad eV_{01} = \frac{hc}{\lambda_1} - \frac{hc}{\lambda_0}$$

[where, λ_0 = threshold wavelength.]

$$\Rightarrow \quad e\cdot 3V_s = hc\left(\frac{1}{\lambda} - \frac{1}{\lambda_0}\right)$$
$$\Rightarrow \quad 3V_s e = hc\left(\frac{1}{\lambda} - \frac{1}{\lambda_0}\right) \quad \ldots\text{(i)}$$

According to second situation, wavelength of incident radiation,

$$\lambda_2 = 2\lambda$$

Stopping potential, $V_{02} = V_S$

Again, Einstein's photelectric equation,

$$K_{max} = h\nu_2 - \phi$$
$$\Rightarrow \quad eV_{02} = hc\left(\frac{1}{\lambda_2} - \frac{1}{\lambda_0}\right)$$
$$\Rightarrow \quad eV_s = hc\left(\frac{1}{2\lambda} - \frac{1}{\lambda_0}\right) \quad \ldots\text{(ii)}$$

Dividing Eq. (i) by Eq (ii), we get

$$3 = \frac{\frac{1}{\lambda} - \frac{1}{\lambda_0}}{\frac{1}{2\lambda} - \frac{1}{\lambda_0}}$$
$$\Rightarrow \quad \frac{3}{2\lambda} - \frac{3}{\lambda_0} = \frac{1}{\lambda} - \frac{1}{\lambda_0}$$
$$\Rightarrow \quad \lambda_0 = 4\lambda$$

33. *(c)* According to Einstein's photoelectric equation maximum kinetic energy,

$$K_{max} = eV_0 = h\nu - \phi_0$$
$$= h(\nu - \nu_0) = hc\left(\frac{1}{\lambda} - \frac{1}{\lambda_0}\right)$$

Hence, in photoelectric effect, maximum kinetic energy of emitted photoelectrons depends on work function of metal surface, frequency and wavelength of incident radiation but does not depend on intensity of incident radiation.

34. *(b)* We know that, wavelength of hydrogen spectrum is given by

$$\frac{1}{\lambda} = R\left(\frac{1}{n_1^2} - \frac{1}{n_2^2}\right)$$

For minimum wavelength of Lyman series,

$$n_1 = 1 \text{ and } n_2 = \infty$$

$$\therefore \quad \frac{1}{(\lambda_L)_{min}} = R\left(\frac{1}{(1)^2} - \frac{1}{\infty}\right) = R$$

$$\Rightarrow \quad (\lambda_2)_{min} = \frac{1}{R}$$

For minimum wavelength of Balmer series,

$$n_1 = 2 \text{ and } n_2 = \infty$$

$$\therefore \quad \frac{1}{(\lambda_B)_{min}} = R\left(\frac{1}{2^2} - \frac{1}{\infty}\right)$$
$$= R\left(\frac{1}{4} - 0\right) = \frac{R}{4}$$

$$\Rightarrow \quad (\lambda_B)_{min} = \frac{4}{R}$$

$$\therefore \quad \frac{(\lambda_L)_{min}}{(\lambda_B)_{min}} = \frac{\frac{1}{R}}{\frac{4}{R}} = \frac{1}{4} = 0.25$$

35. *(d)* Hydrogen atom does not emit X-rays because its energy level are very close to each other. Hence, the transition of electron emits high energy radiations having short wavelength.

36. *(c)* Given, $\lambda_e = \lambda_p$ ...(i)

Since, de-Broglie wavelength,

$$\lambda = \frac{h}{mv} = \frac{h}{p} = \frac{h}{\sqrt{2mK}}$$

$$\Rightarrow \quad \lambda = \frac{h}{\sqrt{2mK}}$$

where, K is kinetic energy.

$$\therefore \quad \frac{\lambda_e}{\lambda_p} = \sqrt{\frac{m_p}{m_e}} \cdot \sqrt{\frac{K_p}{K_e}}$$

$$\Rightarrow \quad \frac{\lambda_e}{\lambda_e} = \sqrt{\frac{m_p}{m_e}} \cdot \sqrt{\frac{K_p}{K_e}} \quad \text{[From Eq. (i)]}$$

$$\Rightarrow \quad 1 = \sqrt{\frac{m_p}{m_e}} \cdot \sqrt{\frac{K_p}{K_e}}$$

$$\Rightarrow \quad \sqrt{\frac{K_e}{K_p}} = \sqrt{\frac{m_p}{m_e}}$$

Squaring both sides, we get

$$\frac{K_e}{K_p} = \frac{m_p}{m_e}$$

since $m_p > m_e$

$\therefore$ $K_e > K_p$

37. *(a)* Nuclear force between two protons at a separation of 40Å is much greater than electrostatic force between them.

i.e. $F_n >> F_e$

38. *(b)* Blue colour of water in the sea is due to scattering of light by water molecules. As blue colour of light has smaller wavelength, therefore scattering of blue colour of light is exceptionally large.

Therefore, blue colour of sea water is due to scattering of sunlight by the water molecules.

39. *(c)* Nuclear radius and mass number A are related with following relation,

$$R = R_0 A^{1/3}$$

$$\therefore \quad \frac{R_1}{R_2} = \left(\frac{A_1}{A_2}\right)^{1/3}$$

Given, $A_1 = 216$ and $A_2 = 125$

$$\therefore \quad \frac{R_1}{R_2} = \left(\frac{216}{125}\right)^{1/3}$$
$$= \left[\left(\frac{6}{5}\right)^3\right]^{1/3}$$
$$= \frac{6}{5}$$

$\therefore$ $R_1 : R_2 = 6 : 5$

40. *(b)* Given, output power, $P_o = 1.6$ MW

$$= 1.6 \times 10^6 \text{ W}$$

Energy released per fission,

$$E_1 = 200 \text{ MeV}$$
$$= 200 \times 10^6 \times 1.6 \times 10^{-19} \text{ J}$$
$$= 320 \times 10^{-13} \text{ J}$$
$$= 3.2 \times 10^{-11} \text{ J}$$

The rate of fission R is given as

$$R = \frac{P_0}{E_1}$$
$$= \frac{1.6 \times 10^6}{3.2 \times 10^{-11}}$$
$$= 0.5 \times 10^{17} = 5 \times 10^{16}\text{/s}$$

41. *(a)* Let initial masses of two radioactive substances be N_0.

If T_1 and T_2 be the half-lives of two radioactive substances,

Then, $T_1 = 1$ yr

$T_2 = 2$ yrs

Total time, $t = 6$ yrs

Hence, remaining mass of the first substances after $t = 6$ yrs

$$N_1 = N_0\left(\frac{1}{2}\right)^{\frac{t}{T_1}} = N_0\left(\frac{1}{2}\right)^{6/1} = \frac{N_0}{2^6}$$

$$\Rightarrow \quad N_1 = \frac{N_0}{64}$$

Similarly, remaining mass of the second substance after $t = 6$ yrs

$$N_2 = N_0\left(\frac{1}{2}\right)^{\frac{t}{T_2}} = N_0\left(\frac{1}{2}\right)^{6/2} = \frac{N_0}{8}$$

$$\Rightarrow \quad N_2 = \frac{N_0}{8}$$

$$\therefore \quad \frac{N_1}{N_2} = \frac{\frac{N_0}{64}}{\frac{N_0}{8}} = \frac{1}{8} \Rightarrow \frac{N_1}{N_2} = \frac{1}{8} \quad \ldots\text{(i)}$$

Since, activity, $A = \lambda N = \dfrac{0.693}{T} N$

$$\Rightarrow \quad A \propto \frac{N}{T}$$

$$\therefore \quad \frac{A_1}{A_2} = \frac{N_1 T_2}{N_2 T_1} = \frac{1}{8} \times \frac{2}{1} = \frac{1}{4}$$

$$\Rightarrow \quad A_1 : A_2 = 1 : 4$$

42. *(c)* When an α - particle emits from a radioactive nuclei, then its mass number is decreased by 4 unit and atomic number is decreased by 2 unit.

When a β-particle emits from a radioactive nuclei, then its mass number is unaffected, whereas atomic number is increased by one unit.

Here, initial nuclei = ${}_{92}U^{235}$

Final nuclei = ${}_{82}P^{203}$

Change in mass number = 235 − 203 = 32

Number of α-particle emitted = $\dfrac{32}{4} = 8$

$\therefore$ Number of emitted β-particles

$$= 8 \times 2 - (92 - 82) = 16 - 10 = 6$$

43. *(a)* Neutron is the most stable particle in the baryon group.

44. *(b)* An unbiased *p-n* junction is shown below.

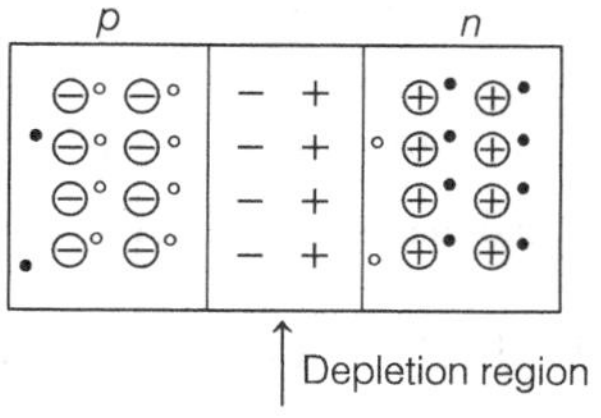

From the diagram, it is clear that in depletion region, *n*-side has immobile positive charge, whereas *p*-side has immobile negative charge.

Therefore, potential at *p* is less than that of *n*.

45. *(c)* The given logic diagram is shown as

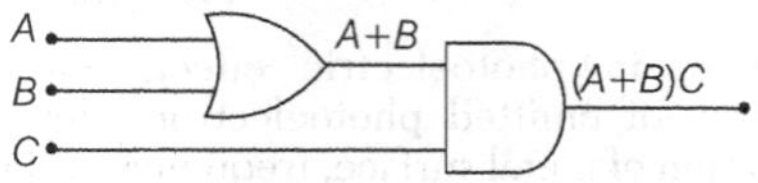

Output of logic gate is given as

$$Y = (A + B)C$$

In option (a), $A = 0$, $B = 1$, $C = 0$

$$\therefore \quad Y = (0 + 1)\cdot 0 = 0$$

In option (b), $A = 1$, $B = 0$, $C = 0$

$$\therefore \quad Y = (1 + 0)\cdot 0 = 0$$

In option (c), $A = 1$, $B = 0$, $C = 1$

$$\therefore \quad Y = (1 + 0)\cdot 1 = 1$$

In option (d), $A = 1$, $B = 1$, $C = 0$

$$\therefore \quad Y = (1 + 1)\cdot 0 = 0$$

Hence, to get an output $Y = 1$

$$A = 1, B = 0 \text{ and } C = 1$$

46. *(c)* According to Newton's law of gravitation,

$$F = \frac{G m_1 m_2}{r^2}$$

where, F = gravitational force between two bodies of masses m_1 and m_2,

r = distance between the two masses

and G = universal gravitational constant.

$$\therefore \quad G = \frac{Fr^2}{m_1 m_2}$$

$$\therefore \quad [G] = \frac{[F][r^2]}{[m_1][m_2]} = \frac{[MLT^{-2}][L^2]}{[M][M]} = [M^{-1}L^3T^{-2}]$$

47. *(d)* Let u be the initial vertical velocity of the body by which it is projected vertically upward.

If t be the time taken by the body to reach a height h from the point of projection, then using equation of vertical motion,

$$h = ut - \frac{1}{2}gt^2$$

$$\Rightarrow \quad gt^2 - 2ut + 2h = 0$$

$$\Rightarrow \quad t = \frac{2u \pm \sqrt{4u^2 - 4g \times 2h}}{2g} = \frac{u \pm \sqrt{u^2 - 2gh}}{g}$$

It means t has two values which is already given in question,

$$t_1 = \frac{u + \sqrt{u^2 - 2gh}}{g}$$

and $$t_2 = \frac{u - \sqrt{u^2 - 2gh}}{g}$$

$\therefore$ $$t_1 + t_2 = \frac{2u}{g}$$

$\Rightarrow$ $$u = \frac{g(t_1 + t_2)}{2}$$

48. *(a)* Given, mass suspended from spring balance, $m = 10$ kg

$$\theta = 60°$$

The given situation is shown below

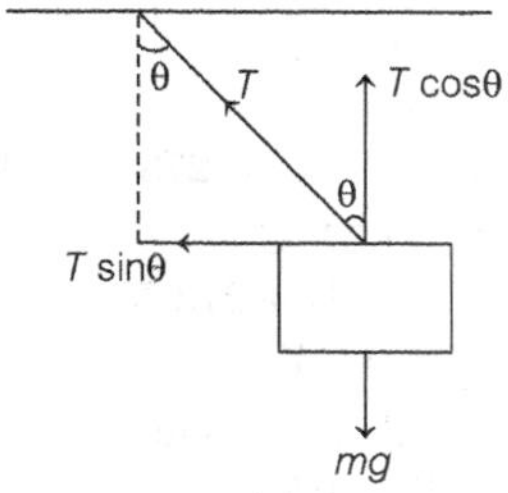

From the diagram, reading of spring balance,

$$F_s = T \quad \ldots(i)$$

Since, $T\cos\theta = mg$

$$T = \frac{mg}{\cos\theta} \quad \ldots(ii)$$

From Eqs. (i) and (ii) we get

$$F_s = \frac{mg}{\cos\theta} = \frac{mg}{\cos 60°}$$
$$= 2mg$$
$$= 2 \times 10 \times g$$
$$= 20 \text{ kg-wt}$$

49. *(b)* Weight of body in air,

$$m_1 = 50\text{g} = 5 \times 10^{-2} \text{ kg}$$

Weight of body in water,

$$m_2 = 40 \text{ g} = 4 \times 10^{-2} \text{ kg}$$

Buoyant force on the body,

$$F' = m_1 g - m_2 g$$
$$= g(m_1 - m_2)$$
$$= g(5 \times 10^{-2} - 4 \times 10^{-2})$$
$$F' = 10^{-2} g \text{ N} \quad \ldots(i)$$

But buoyant force is given as

$$F' = V\rho g$$

$\Rightarrow$ $$10^{-2}\text{g} = V\rho g \quad \text{[From Eq. (i)]}$$

$\Rightarrow$ $$10^{-2} = \rho V$$

$$10^{-2} = 10^3 \text{ V} \quad [\because \rho = 10^3 \text{ kg/m}^3]$$

$\Rightarrow$ $$V = 10^{-5} \text{m}^3$$

$\therefore$ Loss of weight in liquid $= \rho_l V g$

$$W' = 1.5\rho \times 10^{-5} \times 10 \quad [\because \rho_l = 1.5\rho]$$
$$= 1.5 \times 10^3 \times 10^{-5} \times 10$$
$$= 0.15 \text{ N}$$

$\therefore$ Loss of weight (in kg) $= \frac{w'}{g} = \frac{0.15}{10} = 0.015$ kg $= 15$g

$\therefore$ Weight of body in water $= 50 - 15 = 35$g

50. *(c)* We know that, displacement travelled by a moving body with constant acceleration a in *n*th second,

$$s_n = u + \frac{1}{2}a(2n - 1)$$

For first second, $n = 1$

$\therefore$ $$s_1 = u + \frac{1}{2}a(2 \times 1 - 1)$$

$$5 = u + \frac{a}{2} \quad \ldots(i) \; [\because s_1 = 5 \text{ m}]$$

For third second, $n = 3$

$\therefore$ $$s_3 = u + \frac{a}{2}(2 \times 3 - 1)$$

$$2 = u + \frac{5a}{2} \quad \ldots(ii) \; [\because s_3 = 2\text{m}]$$

Subtracting Eq. (i) from Eq. (ii), we get

$$-3 = 2a$$

$\Rightarrow$ $$a = \frac{-3}{2} \text{m / s}^2$$

Force acting on the body,

$$F = ma = 4 \times \left(\frac{-3}{2}\right) = -6 \text{ N}$$

Hence, force acting on the body in opposite direction of its motion will be 6N.

51. *(b)* Time-period of simple pendulum is given as

$$T = 2\pi\sqrt{\frac{l}{g}} \quad \ldots(i)$$

If a be the acceleration of the lift, so that time-period of simple pendulum is reduced to $T/2$.

i.e. $$T' = T/2$$

$\Rightarrow$ $$2\pi\sqrt{\frac{l}{g+a}} = \frac{1}{2} \times 2\pi\sqrt{\frac{l}{g}}$$

$\Rightarrow$ $$\frac{l}{g+a} = \frac{1}{4}.\frac{l}{g}$$

$\Rightarrow$ $$g + a = 4g$$

$\Rightarrow$ $$a = 3g$$

52. *(c)* According to Mayer's formula,

$$C_p - C_V = R$$

where, C_p = specific heat at constant pressure,
C_V = specific heat at constant volume
R = gas constant.

$\Rightarrow$ $$\frac{C_p}{C_V} - 1 = \frac{R}{C_V}$$

$\Rightarrow$ $$\gamma - 1 = \frac{R}{C_V}$$

$\Rightarrow$ $$C_V = \frac{R}{\gamma - 1}$$

53. *(b)* Net work done in cyclic process *ABCA*,

W_{net} = Area enclosed by path *ABCA*

$$= \frac{1}{2} \times (3V_1 - V_1)(4p_1 - p_1)$$

$$= \frac{1}{2} \times 2V_1 \times 3p_1 = 3p_1V_1$$

Since, cyclic process is taken in anti-clockwise direction, hence net work done will be negative.

$$W_{net} = -3p_1V_1$$

54. *(d)* In isothermal process, temperature remains constant, hence internal energy of the system remains constant in isothermal process.

55. *(a)* The given situation is shown below

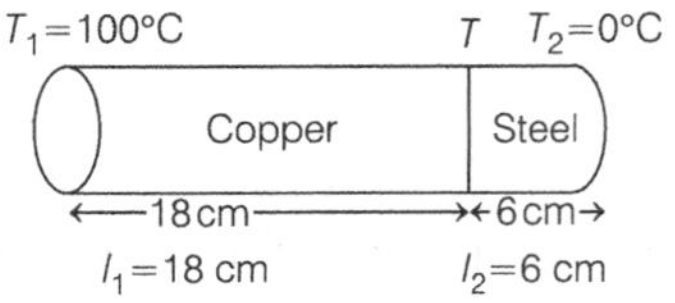

Thermal conductivity of copper

= 9× thermal conductivity of steel

$$K_c = 9K_s$$

Since, both bar are connected in series, hence heat current along the bar will be same.

i. e $$\frac{dQ}{dt} = \frac{K_cA(T_1 - T)}{l_1}$$

$$= \frac{K_sA(T - T_2)}{l_2}$$

$$\Rightarrow \frac{9K_SA(100 - T)}{18} = \frac{K_sA(T - 0)}{6}$$

$$\Rightarrow 3(100 - T) = T$$

$$300 - 3T = T$$

$$\Rightarrow 4T = 300$$

$$\Rightarrow T = 75°\text{C}$$

56. *(d)* Equation of simple harmonic wave is given as

$$y = 6\sin 2\pi(2t - 0.1x)$$

Path difference, $\Delta x = 2$ mm

Comparing with standard equation of wave,

$$y = A\sin(\omega t - kx)$$

$$= A\sin 2\pi\left(\nu t - \frac{k}{2\pi}\cdot x\right)$$

$$\frac{k}{2\pi} = 0.1$$

$$k = 0.2\pi$$

Wavelength, $\lambda = \frac{2\pi}{k} = \frac{2\pi}{0.2\pi} = 10$ mm

∴ We know that, phase difference,

$$\phi = \frac{2\pi}{\lambda} \times \text{path difference}(\Delta x)$$

$$= \frac{2\pi}{10} \times 2 = \frac{2\pi}{5} = \frac{2 \times 180}{5} = 72°$$

57. *(d)* Given, sound source is stationary, $v_S = 0$

Apparent frequency, $f' = 2f$

where, f is actual frequency of sound.

By using Doppler's effect,

$$f' = f\left(\frac{v + v_0}{v}\right)$$

[where, v is velocity of sound A.]

$$\Rightarrow 2f = f\left(\frac{v + v_0}{v}\right)$$

$$\Rightarrow 2v = v + v_0$$

$$\Rightarrow v = v_0$$

$$\Rightarrow v_0 = v$$

58. *(a)* Given, $T_1 = 27°\text{ C} = (273 + 27)\text{K} = 300\text{K}$

$$T_2 = 627°\text{ C} = (627 + 273)\text{K} = 900\text{ K}$$

Energy emitted per second

$$E_1 = 0.5\text{ J}$$

$$E_2 = ?$$

According to Stefan's Boltzmann law,

Energy radiated per unit area per second is given by

$$E = \sigma T^4$$

$$\Rightarrow \frac{E_2}{E_1} = \left(\frac{T_2}{T_1}\right)^4$$

$$= \left(\frac{900}{300}\right)^4 = 81$$

$$\Rightarrow E_2 = 81E_1 = 81 \times 0.5 = 40.5\text{ J}$$

59. *(a)* Given, $L_2 = 2L_1$, $f_1 = 200$ Hz, $f_2 = 300$ Hz

We know that, frequency of vibrating string is given as

$$f = \frac{1}{2L}\sqrt{\frac{T}{\mu}}$$

where, μ = mass per unit length of string

and L = length of the string.

$$\Rightarrow f \propto \frac{\sqrt{T}}{L}$$

$$\Rightarrow \frac{f_2}{f_1} = \sqrt{\frac{T_2}{T_1}}\cdot\frac{L_1}{L_2}$$

$$\Rightarrow \sqrt{\frac{T_2}{T_1}} = \frac{f_2L_2}{f_1L_1} = \frac{300}{200} \times \frac{2L_1}{L_1}$$

$$\sqrt{\frac{T_2}{T_1}} = 3$$

$$\Rightarrow \frac{T_2}{T_1} = 9$$

$$\therefore T_2 : T_1 = 9 : 1$$

60. *(a)* Loudness of sound is given as

$$L = 10\log_{10}\frac{I}{I_0}$$

So, we get $L_2 - L_1 = 10\log_{10}\frac{I_2}{I_1}$

here $L_1 = 30\text{dB}$, $L_2 = 60\text{dB}$

$$\therefore \quad 60 - 30 = 10\log_{10}\frac{I_2}{I_1}$$

$$\Rightarrow \quad 3 = \log_{10}\frac{I_2}{I_1}$$

$$\Rightarrow \quad \frac{I_2}{I_1} = 10^3 \Rightarrow I_2 = 1000I_1$$

Chemistry

61. *(c)* Carnallite : $KCl \cdot MgCl_2 \cdot 6H_2O$
Dolomite : $MgCO_3 \cdot CaCO_3$
Calamine : $ZnCO_3$
Sea water : ore of magneisum
$\therefore$ Calamine is not an ore of magnesium.

62. *(a)* Electronic configuration of Ni, Cu and their ions are

$Ni = 1s^2 2s^2 2p^6 3s^2 3p^6 3d^8 4s^2$

$Cu = 1s^2 2s^2 2p^6 3s^2 3p^6 3d^{10} 4s^1$

$Ni^{2+} = 1s^2 2s^2 2p^6 3s^2 3p^6 3d^8 4s^0$

$Cu^+ = 1s^2 2s^2 2p^6 3s^2 3p^6 3d^{10}\ 4s^0$

Electronic configuration represents Cu^+ ions.

63. *(b)* The element $[Ne]3s^2 3p^3$ have half-filled p-orbital.
As a result, it is more stable.
$\therefore$ The ionisation energy is highest for this element.

64. *(a)* The oxidation number of Br in Br_2 is zero.
The oxidation number of Br is BrO_3^-

$$x + 3\times(-2) = -1$$
$$x = -1 + 6$$
$$x = +5$$

65. *(d)* Among the alkali metals, caesium is most reactive because the outermost electron is more loosely bound than the outermost electron of other alkali metals.

66. *(a)* Electronic configuration of nitrogen is

$${}_7N = 1s^2 2s^2 2p^3 \text{ i.e. } 2, 5$$

In outer most shell, it has five electrons.
$\therefore$ It share 3 electrons to complete its octet as follows :

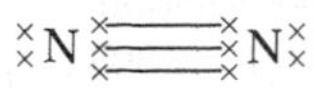

67. *(c)* Hydrogen bond is strongest in F—H --- F, as the electronegativity of fluorine is highest.

68. *(a)* Decomposition of $CaCO_3$ as follows:

$$\underset{\substack{100\text{ g} \\ 11.2\text{ dm}^3 \text{ or } (1/2\text{ mole})}}{CaCO_3} \xrightarrow{\Delta} CaO + \underset{\substack{44\text{ g} \\ 22\text{ g or } 1/2\text{ mole}}}{CO_2}$$

Neutralisation reaction of KOH and CO_2 as follows:

$$\underset{\substack{2\text{ moles} \\ 1\text{ mole}}}{2KOH} + \underset{\substack{1\text{ mole} \\ \frac{1}{2}\text{ mole}}}{CO_2} \xrightarrow{\Delta} K_2CO_3 + H_2O$$

1 mole of CO_2 reacts with 2 moles of KOH
1 / 2 mole of CO_2 reacts with 1 mole of KOH
$\therefore$ Mass of KOH $= 1\times 56.1 = 56.1\text{ g} \approx 56\text{ g}$

69. *(c)* $M = \frac{dRT}{p} = \frac{1.964\times 0.0821\times 273}{1}$

$\left[\because p = 76\text{ cm Hg} = 1\text{ atm}, \; d = 1.964\text{ g dm}^{-3}, \; R = 0.0821\text{ dm}^3\text{atm K}^{-1}\text{mol}^{-1}\right]$

$M = 44\text{ g / mol}$
$\therefore$ So, gas is CO_2.

70. *(a)* 0.06 mole KNO_3 added to 100 cm^3 of water at 298 K.

$$\Delta H = 35.8\text{ kJ/mol}$$
$$\Delta H = m\times C\times \Delta T$$

$\left[\Delta H \text{ for } 0.06\text{ mole} = 35.8\times 0.06 = 2.148\text{ kJ}, \; \text{Mass} = 100\text{ cm}^3 = 100\text{ g}\right]$

$$\therefore \quad 2.148 = 100\times 0.004184\text{ kJ}\times\Delta T$$
$$\Delta T = 5.133\text{ K}$$

It is an endothermic process as heat absorbed.
So, temperature will decrease.
$\therefore$ Final temperature

$$T = 298 - 5.133$$
$$T = 292.867\text{ K} \simeq 293\text{ K}$$

71. *(b)*

	$2SO_2$	$+ O_2$	$\rightleftharpoons$	$2SO_3$
Initially	4 moles	4 moles		0
At equili.	(4 − 2) = 2	(4 − 0.25 × 4) = 3		2

$\therefore$ Total moles at equilibrium $= 2 + 3 + 2 = 7$ moles.

72. *(d)* An example of auto-catalysis is oxidation of oxalic acid by acidified $KMnO_4$ solution.
In this reaction, one of the product (Mn^{2+}) formed act as a catalyst and speed up the reaction.

$$\underset{\text{Permagnate ion}}{2MnO_4^-} + 6H^+ + \underset{\text{Oxalic acid}}{5C_2H_2O_4} \longrightarrow \underset{\text{Auto-catalyst}}{2Mn^{2+}} + 8H_2O + 10CO_2$$

73. *(c)* When a nitrogeneous organic compound is fused with sodium, the nitrogen present in the compound is converted into sodium cyanide.
This reaction is also called Lassaigne's test.

74. *(c)* The complete reaction is as follows :

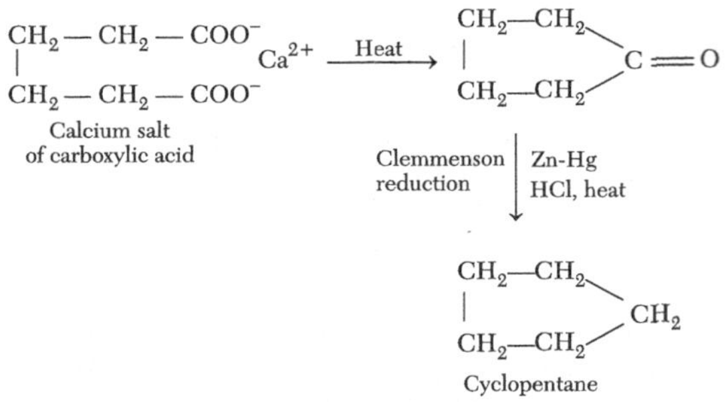

75. *(c)* Williamson ether synthesis is an organic reaction, forming an ether from alkyl halide and deprotonated alcohol i.e.

$$\underset{\text{Sodium ethoxide}}{C_2H_5ONa} + \underset{\text{Ethane iodide}}{C_2H_5I} \longrightarrow \underset{\text{Ethoxyethane (ester)}}{C_2H_5OC_2H_5} + NaI$$

76. *(c)* For the reaction, $C + \frac{1}{2}O_2 \longrightarrow CO$,

$\Delta G°$ *vs* T plot in the Ellingham's diagram slopes downwards.

As for this reaction $\Delta G°$ become more negative with increase in temperature.

77. *(a)* Decomposition of calcium carbonate to form calcium oxide and carbondioxide is endothermic reaction.

$$CaCO_3 \longrightarrow CaO + CO_2$$

78. *(a)* Liquor ammonia bottle is opened only after cooling because it is a mild explosive.

Note The concentrated ammonia solution in water results in liquor ammonia.

79. *(c)* The formation of $O_2^+[PtF_6]^-$ is the basis for the formation of xenon fluorides because O_2 and Xe have comparable ionisation energies.

80. *(b)* Magnetic moment of the element / ion is highest for configuration $3d^5$, | 1 | 1 | 1 | 1 | 1 | because number of unpaired electron is maximum i.e. five.

81. *(c)* If a transition metal ion exists in its highest oxidation state, then it behave as oxidising agent.

The oxidation number of metal can only decrease from its highest oxidation number i.e. it will undergoes reduction and oxidise other element.

82. *(a)* In $[CoF_6]^{3-}$, F^- is a weak ligand. It cannot pair up d-electrons and form outer orbital octahedral complex while NH_3 and CN^- are strong ligand.

In $[CoF_6]^{3-}$, outer orbital $4d$ is used in hybridisation. Thus, it is called outer orbital or high spin or spin free complex.

$Co = [Ar]\, 3d^7 4s^2$ and $Co^{3+} = [Ar]\, 3d^6$

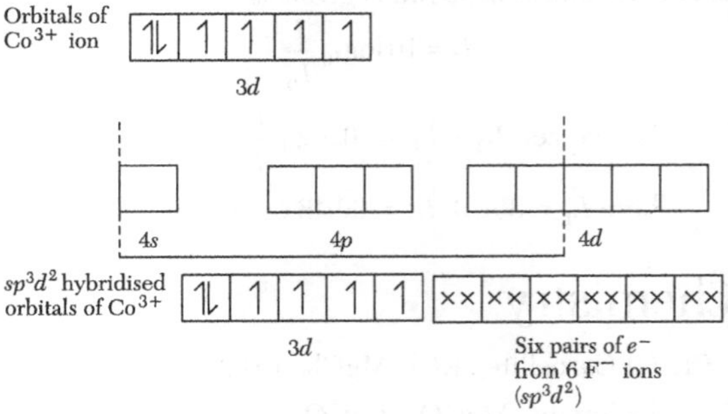

83. *(a)* Linkage isomerism can be shown by compound containing ambidentate ligand. In NO_2, NO_2 can bind either by N or by O.

e.g. $\underset{\text{Yellow}}{[Co(NH_3)_3(NO_2)]Cl_2}$ and $\underset{\text{Blue}}{[Co(NH_3)_3ONO]Cl_2}$

84. *(a)* N_2[14 electrons] =

$\sigma 1s^2, \sigma^* 1s^2, \sigma 2s^2, \sigma^* 2s^2, \pi 2p_x^2 = \pi 2p_y^2, \sigma 2p_z^2$

$$\text{Bond order} = \frac{N_b - N_a}{2} \quad \left[\begin{array}{l} N_b \text{ and } N_a \text{ are bonding and} \\ \text{anti bonding molecular} \\ \text{orbital } s\text{- electron} \end{array}\right]$$

$$= \frac{10 - 4}{2} = 3$$

$\therefore$ N_2 has highest bond order i.e. 3.

While O_2, He_2 and H_2 have 2, 0 and 1/2 bond order respectively.

85. *(c)* H_2^+ and He_2^+ contains odd number of electrons

$\therefore$ They are paramagnetic.

Among Li_2 and O_2

$Li_2(6) = \sigma 1s^2, \sigma^* 1s^2, \sigma 2s^2$

Li have no unpaired electron.

$\therefore$ It is diamagnetic

$O_2(18) = \sigma 1s^2, \sigma 1s^2, \sigma 2s^2, \sigma 2s^2\, \pi 2p_x^2 = \pi 2p_y^2$

$\sigma 2p_z^2, \pi^* 2p_x^1 = \pi^* 2p_y^1$

It has two unpaired electrons. So, it is paramagnetic.

86. *(b)* For 1st order reaction

$$k = \frac{2.303}{t}\log\frac{[R_0]}{[R]} = \frac{2.303}{40}\log\left[\frac{0.1}{0.025}\right]$$

$$= \frac{2.303}{40} \times \log 4 = 0.0347 \text{ min}^{-1}$$

Rate expression,

$r = k[A] = 0.0347 \times 0.01 = 3.47 \times 10^{-4}\ \text{M min}^{-1}$.

87. *(b)* According to Arrhenius equation

$$k = Ae^{\frac{-E_a}{RT}}$$

Here, k decreases with increase in E_a (activation energy).

Chemical reaction with very high E_a values are generally slow.

88. *(b)* Solid NaCl does not conduct electricity because the ions (Na^+ and Cl^-) are well arranged in the crystal structure and not free to move to conduct electricity.

89. *(b)* According to second law of Faraday,

$$\frac{w_1}{E_1}=\frac{w_2}{E_2}$$

$$\frac{0.16}{64}=\frac{w_2}{2}$$

$$w_2=\frac{0.16\times 2}{64}=\frac{0.01}{2}=0.005\text{ g}$$

$$\text{Volume of } H_2=\frac{0.005}{2}\times 22.400\text{ cm}^3=\frac{22.4}{4}=56\text{ cm}^3$$

90. *(c)* $K_{sp}=10^{-8}M^2$

$$K_{sp}=[A^+][B^-]$$

$$10^{-8}=(10^{-3})[B^-]$$

$$[B^-]=10^{-5}\text{ M}$$

$\therefore$ Salt will precipitate, when concentration of $[B^-]>10^{-5}$ M.

91. *(d)* According to Nernst equation,

$$E_{cell}=E^\circ_{cell}-\frac{0.0591}{n}\log\frac{[Cu^{+2}]}{[Ag^+]^2}$$

$\therefore$ The voltage of cell will increase with increase in concentration of Ag^+ ions.

92. *(c)* $pH=-\log[H^+]$

$$[H^+]=10^{-8}+10^{-7}=1.1\times 10^{-7}$$

$$pH=-\log(1.1\times 10^{-7})$$

$$pH=7-\log(1.1)$$

$\therefore$ It is between 6 and 7.

93. *(b)* Lowering in vapour pressure is directly proportional to moles of solute particles

$$(\Delta p)_{glucose}=(\Delta p)_{urea}$$

$$(\chi_B)_{glucose}=(\chi_B)_{urea}$$

i.e. $$\frac{W_B}{50}\times\frac{18}{180}=\frac{1\times 18}{50\times 60}$$

$$W_B=3\text{ g}$$

94. *(c)* Osmotic pressure is a colligative property. It depends upon the number of solute particles. Benzoic acid undergoes dimerisation.

$\therefore$ Number of particles reduces ($i<1$) Hence, osmotic pressure observed is less than the theoretical consideration.

95. *(a)* For a reaction to be spontaneous at all temperature ΔG should be negative. As we know $\Delta G=\Delta H-T\Delta S$

$$=-\text{ve}-T(+\text{ve})=-\text{ve}$$

$\therefore \Delta G$ and ΔH should be negative.

96. *(a)* Flocculation value $\propto\dfrac{1}{\text{Coagulating power}}$

Fe(OH) is a positively charged sol.

For coagulating $Fe(OH)_3$ negatively charged electrolyte is used and greater the value of –ve charge, coagulating power will be strong. Among given electrolyte, NaCl has lowest coagulating power. Hence, its flocculation value will be maximum.

97. *(b)* $\Delta H=-40\text{ kJ}=-40\times 10^3$ J

$$\Delta S=\Delta S_{Product}-\Delta S_{Reactant}$$

$$=2(50)-3(40)-60$$

$$=100-120-60=-80$$

$$\Delta G=\Delta H-T\Delta S$$

$$0=-40\times 10^3-T(-80)$$

$$T=\frac{40\times 10^3}{80}=500\text{ K}.$$

98. *(c)* NaCl forms fcc structure.

$\therefore$(Diagonal length)$^2=(\sqrt{2}a)^2=2(r^+)^2+2(r^-)^2$

Where, a = edge length, r^+ and r^- are radii of Na^+ and Cl^- ions.

$$a=2[(r^+)^2+(r^-)^2]=2(95+181)=2\times 276=552\text{pm}$$

99. *(a)* Inductive effect involves the displacement of σ-electrons from less electronegative element to more electronegative element in a compound.

100. *(a)* The basicity of aniline is less than that of cyclohexylamine because of + *R*-effect of NH_2 group in aniline.

101. *(c)* Methyl bromide is converted into ethane by heating, it is ether medium with Na.

$$\underset{\text{Methyl bromide}}{2CH_3—Br}+\underset{\text{Sodium}}{2Na}\longrightarrow \underset{\text{Ethane}}{CH_3—CH_3}+2NaBr$$

102. *(c)* The compound having chiral centre, $CH_3CH_2CHBrCHO$ is expected to be optically active.

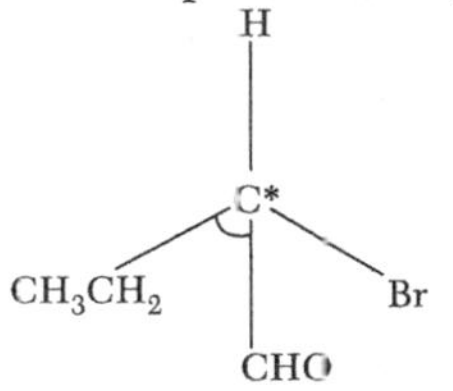

103. *(d)* Cyclohexane has the lowest heat of combustion per CH_2 group. As, stability increase upto 6 membered ring due to decrease in angular strain. Also heat of combustion is measure for chemical stability.

104. *(c)* The catalyst used in preparation of an alkyl chloride by action of dry HCl on alcohol is anhy. $ZnCl_2$. This process is also called Grove's process.

$$\underset{\text{Alcohol}}{ROH}+HCl\xrightarrow{\text{Anhy. }ZnCl_2}\underset{\text{Alkyl chloride}}{RCl}+H_2O$$

105. *(c)* The complete reaction is as follows :

$$\underset{\text{Alkyl halide}}{R—X}\xrightarrow{\text{Alc. KCN}}\underset{\text{Alkylcyanide}}{R—CN}\xrightarrow{\text{Dil. HCl}}\underset{\text{Carboxylic acid}}{R—COOH}$$

106. *(b)* Phenol does not decompose sodium bicarbonate ($NaHCO_3$) as it is a weaker acid than carbonic acid.
$\therefore CO_2$ gas is not evolved by phenol.

107. *(b)* Phenol on heating with chloroform in alkali get converted into salicylaldehyde.
This reaction is called Reimer-Tiemann reaction.

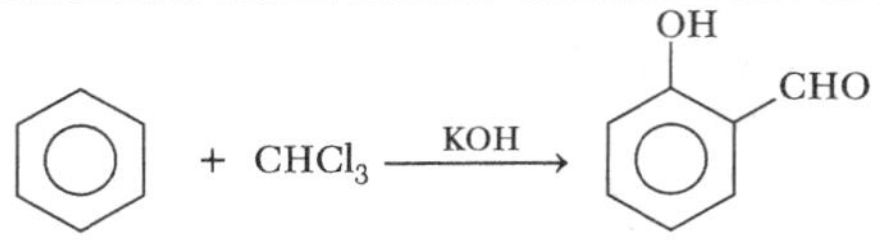

Phenol Salicylaldehyde

108. *(a)* When a mixture of calcium benzoate and calcium acetate is dry distilled, the resulting compound is acetophenone.

$$\underset{\text{Calcium benzoate}}{(C_6H_5COO)_2Ca} + \underset{\text{Calcium acetate}}{(CH_3COO)_2Ca} \xrightarrow[\Delta]{\text{Distillation}} \underset{\text{Acetophenone}}{2C_6H_5\overset{\overset{O}{\|}}{C}—CH_3} + 2CaCO_3$$

109. *(c)* Benzylchloride does not give benzoic acid on hydrolysis. It forms benzyl alcohol as major product.

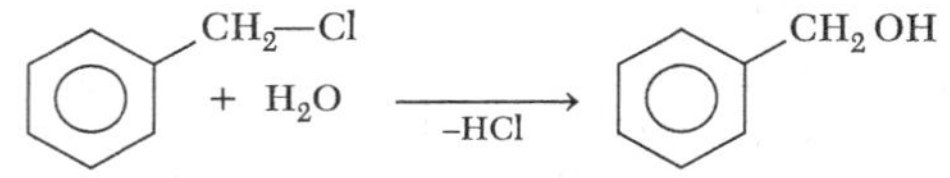

Benzyl chloride Benzyl alcohol

110. *(c)* In Hofmann bromamide reaction, primary amide reacts with bromine and sodium hydroxide to form isocyanate, which is hydrolysed to give primary amine (with one carbon less) along with decarboxylation.

$$\underset{\text{Primary amide}}{RCONH_2} + Br_2 + NaOH \longrightarrow R—N{=}C{=}O \xrightarrow[-CO_2]{H_2O} \underset{\text{Primary amine}}{RNH_2}$$

111. *(b)* Glucose contains in addition to aldehyde group on primary OH and four secondary OH groups.
The structure of glucose is

CHO ⟵ Aldehyde group
|
$(CHOH)_4$ ⟵ Four secondary OH group
|
CH_2OH ⟵ One primary OH group

112. *(b)* Fats are triglycerides which are triesters of fatty acid with glycerol. So, the characteristic feature of fats is an ester group.

113. *(b)* At pH = 4, glycine reacts with H^+ ion as

$$\underset{\text{Zwitter ion}}{H_3N^+—CH_2—COO^-} \xrightarrow{H^+} H_3N^+—CH_2—COOH$$

114. *(c)* Insulin regulate the metabolism of glucose (carbohydrates).

115. *(a)* The reaction between Mohr's salt and $KMnO_4$ is

$$2KMnO_4 + \underset{\text{Mohr's salt}}{10FeSO_4(NH_4)_2SO_4 \cdot 6H_2O} + 8H_2SO_4$$
$$\longrightarrow K_2SO_4 + 2MnSO_4 + 10(NH_4)_2SO_4 + 2Fe_2(SO_4)_3 + 8H_2O$$

Oxidation sate of Fe changes from + 2 to + 3.
$\therefore$ Equivalent weight of Mohr's salt

$$= \frac{\text{molecular weight}}{n\text{-factor}} = \frac{392}{1} = 392\text{ g}$$

116. *(a)* The brown ring is appeared due to formation of a brown complex between nitric oxide and Fe^{2+} ion. This nitric oxide is formed as a result of reduction of nitrate. Brown ring test for nitrates depends on reduction of nitrate to nitric oxide.

117. *(c)* Acrolein test is positive for oils and fats when fat is heated in presence of $KHSO_4$, the glycerol portion of molecule is dehydrated and form unsaturated aldehyde. $CH_2{=}CH—CHO$ (acrolein) a bad smelling compound.

118. *(a)* An organic compound which produces a bluish green flame, when heated in presence of copper is chlorobenzene. This is called Beilstein's test used to detect presence of halogen in an organic compound.

119. *(c)* Let rate expression, $r = k[A]^x[B]^y$ ...(i)

If, $[A_1] = [2A]$, then $r_1 = 2r$

$\therefore \quad x = 1$

If, $[B_2] = [9B]$, then $r_2 = 3r$

$\therefore \quad y = \frac{1}{2}$

Rate expression, $r = k[A][B]^{1/2}$ [By Eq. (i)]

$\therefore$ Order $= 1 + \frac{1}{2} = \frac{3}{2}$

120. *(a)* For, assume complete dissociation

For Na_2SO_4; $i = 3, m = 0.01$

$$\Delta T_b = iK_bm$$
$$\Delta T_b = 3 \times K_b \times 0.01 = 0.03\,K_b$$

For, 0.01 M KNO_3;

$$i = 2, m = 0.01$$
$$\Delta T_b = 2 \times K_b \times 0.01\,K_b = 0.02\,K_b$$

While, urea and glucose are non-electrolyte
They do not dissociate into ions highest boiling point is shown by 0.01 M Na_2SO_4 *(aq)* solution.

COMEDK 2018

Mathematics

121. *(a)* Given that, $\mathbf{u} = \mathbf{a} - \mathbf{b}, \mathbf{v} = \mathbf{a} + \mathbf{b}$

and $|\mathbf{a}| = |\mathbf{b}| = 2$

Now, $|\mathbf{u} \times \mathbf{v}| = |\mathbf{a} - \mathbf{b} \times \mathbf{a} + \mathbf{b}|$

$$= 2(\mathbf{a} \times \mathbf{b}) = 2|\mathbf{a}||\mathbf{b}|\sin\theta$$

$$= 2 \times 2 \times 2\sin\theta = 8\sin\theta = 8\sqrt{1-\cos^2\theta}$$

$$= 8\sqrt{1-\left(\frac{\mathbf{a}\cdot\mathbf{b}}{|\mathbf{a}||\mathbf{b}|}\right)^2}$$

$$= 8\sqrt{1-\left(\frac{\mathbf{a}\cdot\mathbf{b}}{4}\right)^2} = 8\sqrt{1-\left(\frac{\mathbf{a}\cdot\mathbf{b}}{16}\right)^2}$$

$$= \frac{8}{4}\sqrt{16-(\mathbf{a}\cdot\mathbf{b})^2} = 2\sqrt{16-(\mathbf{a}\cdot\mathbf{b})^2}$$

122. *(a)* Let $A(1, 1, 1), B(2, 1, 3), C(3, 2, 2)$ and $D(3, 3, 4)$.

So, $\mathbf{AB} = \hat{\mathbf{i}} + 2\hat{\mathbf{k}}$, $\mathbf{AC} = 2\hat{\mathbf{i}} + \hat{\mathbf{j}} + \hat{\mathbf{k}}$

and $\mathbf{AD} = 2\hat{\mathbf{i}} + 2\hat{\mathbf{j}} + 3\hat{\mathbf{k}}$

$$\text{Volume of tetrahedron} = \frac{1}{6}\begin{bmatrix} 1 & 0 & 2 \\ 2 & 1 & 1 \\ 2 & 2 & 3 \end{bmatrix}$$

$$= \frac{1}{6}|1(3-2) + 0(6-2) + 2(4-2)|$$

$$= \frac{1}{6}(1 + 0 + 4) = \frac{5}{6} \text{ cubic units}$$

123. *(d)* Let $\mathbf{a} = \hat{\mathbf{i}} - 2\hat{\mathbf{j}} + \hat{\mathbf{k}}$, $\mathbf{b} = \hat{\mathbf{i}} + \hat{\mathbf{j}} - 2\hat{\mathbf{k}}$ and $\mathbf{c} = -\hat{\mathbf{i}} + 2\hat{\mathbf{j}} + \hat{\mathbf{k}}$

$$\text{Now, } \mathbf{b} \times \mathbf{c} = \begin{vmatrix} \hat{\mathbf{i}} & \hat{\mathbf{j}} & \hat{\mathbf{k}} \\ 1 & 1 & -2 \\ -1 & 2 & 1 \end{vmatrix} = 5\hat{\mathbf{i}} + \hat{\mathbf{j}} + 3\hat{\mathbf{k}}$$

$$\text{Now, } \mathbf{a} \times (\mathbf{b} \times \mathbf{c}) = \begin{vmatrix} \hat{\mathbf{i}} & \hat{\mathbf{j}} & \hat{\mathbf{k}} \\ 1 & -2 & 2 \\ 5 & 1 & 3 \end{vmatrix} = -8\hat{\mathbf{i}} + 7\hat{\mathbf{j}} + 11\hat{\mathbf{k}}$$

Now, any vector perpendicular to **a** and lying in the plane containing $\hat{\mathbf{i}} + \hat{\mathbf{j}} - 2\hat{\mathbf{k}}$ and $-\hat{\mathbf{i}} + 2\hat{\mathbf{j}} + \hat{\mathbf{k}}$ is $\pm(\mathbf{a} \times (\mathbf{b} \times \mathbf{c}))$.

$$\therefore \text{Required unit vector} = \pm\frac{(-8\hat{\mathbf{i}} + 7\hat{\mathbf{j}} + 11\hat{\mathbf{k}})}{\sqrt{(-8)^2 + (7)^2 + (11)^2}}$$

$$= \pm\frac{(-8\hat{\mathbf{i}} + 7\hat{\mathbf{j}} + 11\hat{\mathbf{k}})}{\sqrt{234}}$$

124. *(d)* Let the inverse element of 10 be e, then

$$a * e = 0$$

Therefore, $10 * e = 10 + e + 10e = 0$

$$\Rightarrow \quad 10 + 11e = 0$$

$$\Rightarrow \quad 11e = -10$$

$$\Rightarrow \quad e = \frac{-10}{11}$$

125. *(c)* Under Multiplication Modulo 7, inverse of 2 is

$$2 \times 4 = 1 \pmod 7$$

Hence, $2^{-1} = 4$

Now, $2^{-1} \times 4 = 4 \times 4 = 16$

Now, $16 = 2 \times 7 + 2$

Hence dividing 16 by 7 gives a remainder 2,

Therefore, value of above multiplication mod is 2.

126. *(d)* The group $(z, +)$ has infinitely many subgroups.

127. *(c)* Given, $3x \equiv 5 \pmod 7$

$$\Rightarrow \quad 3x - 5 \equiv 0 \pmod 7 = \frac{7}{3x-5}$$

$$\Rightarrow \quad 3x - 5 = 7P, \text{ where } P \in Z$$

$$\Rightarrow \quad x \equiv 4 \pmod 7$$

128. *(c)* Let $z = \sin\left(\frac{6\pi}{5}\right) + i\cos\left(1 + \cos\frac{6\pi}{5}\right)$

Putting $\sin\frac{6\pi}{5} = r\cos\alpha$ ...(i)

and $1 + \cos\frac{6\pi}{5} = r\sin\alpha$ ...(ii)

On dividing Eq. (ii) by Eq. (i), we get

$$\tan\alpha = \frac{1+\cos\frac{6\pi}{5}}{\sin\left(\frac{6\pi}{5}\right)} = \frac{2\cos^2\frac{3\pi}{5}}{2\sin\frac{3\pi}{5}\cos\frac{3\pi}{5}}$$

$$= \cot\frac{3\pi}{5} = \tan\left(\frac{\pi}{2} - \frac{3\pi}{5}\right)$$

$$\tan\alpha = \tan\left(-\frac{\pi}{10}\right)$$

$\therefore$ Argument to z is $\alpha = -\frac{\pi}{10}$

129. *(c)* ***We have,***

$$\sum_{n=1}^{n} i^k = i + i^2 + i^3 + i^4 + i^5 + i^6 + i^7 + i^8 + i^9 + \ldots.$$

Now as, $i^4 = i^8 = i^{12} = \ldots i^{4n} = 1$

and $i + i^2 + i^3 + i^4 = 0$

$$\text{So, } \sum_{n=1}^{n} i^k = i + i^2 + i^3 + i^4 + i^5 + i^6 + \ldots i^7 + i^8 + i^9 + \ldots$$

$$= i + i^2 + i^3 + i^4 + (i + i^2 + i^3 + i^4) + (i + i^2 + i^3 + i^4) + \ldots$$

$$= 0 + 0 + 0 + \ldots$$

When we take $n = 99$ after 96th term, we will be left with $0 + i + i^2 + i^3 = -1$

So, for $n = 99$

$$\Rightarrow \quad 1 + \sum_{k=1}^{n} i^k = 0$$

130. *(c)* We have,

$$(-1 + \sqrt{-3})^{62} + (-1 - \sqrt{-3})^{62}$$

$$= 2^{62}\left[\left(\frac{-1+\sqrt{3}i}{2}\right)^{62} + \left(\frac{-1-\sqrt{3}i}{2}\right)^{62}\right]$$

$$= 2^{62}[\omega^{62} + \omega^{124}]$$

$$= 2^{62}[\omega + \omega^2]$$

$$= 2^{62}(-1) = -2^{62}$$

131. *(b)* We have,

$$\left|\frac{z-6i}{z+6i}\right| = 1$$

or $\quad |z - 6i| = |z + 6i|$

Let $\quad z = x + iy$

or $|x + iy - 6i| = |x + iy + 6i|$

$$|x + (y-6)i| = |x + (y+6)i|$$

$$\Rightarrow \sqrt{x^2 + (y-6)^2} = \sqrt{x^2 + (y+6)^2}$$

$$\Rightarrow \quad x^2 + (y-6)^2 = x^2 + (y+6)^2$$

$$\Rightarrow y^2 + 36 - 12y = y^2 + 36 + 12y$$

$$\Rightarrow \quad 24y = 0$$

$$\Rightarrow \quad y = 0$$

Hence, it is lie on the real axis.

132. *(a)* We have,

$$\sin[\cot^{-1}\{\cos(\tan^{-1}x)\}]$$

Now, $\cos(\tan^{-1}x) = \cos\left[\cos^{-1}\frac{1}{\sqrt{x^2+1}}\right]$

$$= \frac{1}{\sqrt{x^2+1}}$$

$[\because \cos(\cos^{-1}x) = x, \forall x \in [-1, 1]]$

So, $\cot^{-1}\left(\frac{1}{\sqrt{x^2+1}}\right) = \sin^{-1}\left(\frac{\sqrt{x^2+1}}{\sqrt{x^2+2}}\right)$

Thus, $\sin\left[\cot^{-1}\left(\frac{1}{\sqrt{x^2+1}}\right)\right] = \sin\left[\sin^{-1}\left(\frac{\sqrt{x^2+1}}{\sqrt{x^2+2}}\right)\right]$

$$= \frac{\sqrt{(x^2+1)}}{\sqrt{x^2+2}} \quad [\because \sin(\sin^{-1}x) = x, \forall x \in [-1, 1]$$

133. *(c)* Let $y = 1 + \alpha x \quad [f(x) = y]$

$$\Rightarrow \quad x = \frac{y-1}{\alpha}$$

$$\Rightarrow \quad f^{-1}(x) = \frac{x-1}{\alpha}$$

It is given that, $f(x) = f^{-1}(x)$

$$\Rightarrow \quad 1 + \alpha x = \frac{x-1}{\alpha}$$

$$\Rightarrow \quad \alpha + \alpha^2 x = x - 1$$

On compare the coefficients, we get

$$\alpha^2 = 1 \text{ and } \alpha = -1$$

$$\Rightarrow \quad \alpha = -1$$

134. *(c)* Let x^r occurs in the expansion of $\left(x + \frac{1}{x}\right)^n$

$$T_{r+1} = {}^nC_p x^{n-p}\left(\frac{1}{x}\right)^p$$

$$= {}^nC_p x^{n-p} x^{-p} = {}^nC_p x^{n-2p}$$

let $\quad n - 2p = r$

$$\Rightarrow \quad n - r = 2p \Rightarrow p = \frac{n-r}{2}$$

So, coefficient of $x^r = {}^nC_p = \frac{n!}{p!(n-p)!}$

$$= \frac{n!}{\left(\frac{n-r}{2}\right)!\left(n - \frac{n-r}{2}\right)!}$$

$$= \frac{n!}{\left(\frac{n-r}{2}\right)!\left(\frac{n+r}{2}\right)!}$$

135. *(c)* We have,

$$\tan A - \tan B = x$$

and $\cot B - \cot A = y$

$$\Rightarrow \quad \frac{1}{\tan B} - \frac{1}{\tan A} = y$$

$$\Rightarrow \quad \frac{\tan A - \tan B}{\tan A \tan B} = y$$

$$\Rightarrow \quad \tan A \tan B = \frac{x}{y}$$

$$\Rightarrow \quad \cot A \cot B = \frac{y}{x}$$

Now, $\cot(A - B) = \frac{1 + \cot A \cot B}{\cot B - \cot A}$

$$= \frac{1 + \frac{y}{x}}{y} = \frac{x+y}{xy} = \frac{1}{y} + \frac{1}{x}$$

136. *(a)* $\cos^2\frac{\pi}{12}+\cos^2\frac{\pi}{4}+\cos^2\frac{5\pi}{12}$

$=\cos^2\frac{\pi}{12}+\cos^2\frac{\pi}{4}+\cos^2\left(\frac{\pi}{2}-\frac{\pi}{12}\right)$

$=\cos^2\frac{\pi}{12}+\cos^2\frac{\pi}{4}+\sin^2\frac{\pi}{12}$

$=1+\cos^2\frac{\pi}{4}=1+\left(\frac{1}{\sqrt{2}}\right)^2=1+\frac{1}{2}=\frac{3}{2}$

137. *(a)* $\because \sin\theta, \cos\theta$ and $\tan\theta$ are in GP.

So, $\cos^2\theta=\sin\theta\cdot\tan\theta$

$\Rightarrow \cos^3\theta=\sin^2\theta$

$\Rightarrow \cot^3\theta=\frac{1}{\sin\theta}=\text{cosec}\,\theta$

Squaring both sides, we get

$\cot^6\theta=\text{cosec}^2\theta$

$\Rightarrow \cot^6\theta=1+\cot^2\theta$

$\Rightarrow \cot^6\theta-\cot^2\theta=1$

138. *(d)* We have,

$\frac{3x^2-2x+4}{(x-1)^6}=\frac{A_1}{x+1}+\frac{A_2}{(x+1)^2}+\frac{A_3}{(x+1)^3}$

$+\frac{A_4}{(x+1)^4}+\frac{A_5}{(x+1)^5}+\frac{A_6}{(x+1)^6}$ ...(i)

Now, put $x=0$ in Eq. (i), we get

$A_1+A_2+A_3+A_4+A_5+A_6=4$ ...(ii)

If $A_1+A_3+A_5=-8$

and $A_2+A_4+A_6=12$

satisfies the equation.

Hence, only option (i.e. –8, 12) satisfies the solution.

139. *(d)* We have,

$\log_2(2^{x-1}+6)+\log_2(4^{x-1})=5$

$\Rightarrow 2^{x-1}+6)(2^{2x-2})=2^5$

Let $y=2^{x-1}$

$\Rightarrow (y+6)y^2=2^5$

$\Rightarrow y^3+6y^2-32=0$

$\Rightarrow (y-2)(y^2+8y+16)=0$

So, $y=2$

$2^{x-1}=2^1$

On comparing both sides, we get

$x-1=1$

$x=2$

140. *(b)* As,

$(a+b+c+d)^2=a^2+b^2+c^2+a^2$

$+2(ab+bc+ad+bc+bd+cd)$

$\Rightarrow a^2+b^2+c^2+d^2=(a+b+c+d)^2$

$-2[ab+bc+ac+ad+bd+cd]$

Now, as a, b, c, d are the roots of the equation.

We have,

$a+b+c+d=\frac{-2}{1}=-2$

and $ab+ac+ad+bc+bd+cd=\frac{3}{1}=3$

We have, $1+a^2+b^2+c^2+d^2$

$=1+(-2)^2-2(3)$

$=1+4-6=-1$

141. *(b)* We have,

$c_1x+c_3x^3+c_5x^5+\ldots=\frac{1}{2}\{(1+x)^n-(1-x)^n\}$

$\Rightarrow \int_0^1(c_1x+c_3x^3+c_5x^5+\ldots)\,dx$

$=\frac{1}{2}\int_0^1(1+x)^n-(1-x)^n\,dx$

$\Rightarrow \frac{c_1}{2}+\frac{c_3}{4}+\frac{c_5}{6}+\ldots=\frac{2^n-1}{n+1}$

142. *(a)* $(0.2)^{\log_{\sqrt{5}}\left(\frac{1}{4}+\frac{1}{4.2}+\frac{1}{4}\left(\frac{1}{2}\right)^2+\ldots\infty\right)}$

$=(0.2)^{\log_{\sqrt{5}}\frac{1/4}{1-\frac{1}{2}}}$

$=(0.2)^{\log_{\sqrt{5}}\left(\frac{1}{2}\right)}$

$=\left(\frac{1}{5}\right)^{\log_{\sqrt{5}}\left(\frac{1}{2}\right)}=\left(\frac{1}{2}\right)^{2\log_5\frac{1}{5}}$

$=\frac{1}{2}^{-2\log_5 5}=\left(\frac{1}{2}\right)^{-2}$

$=(2^{-1})^{-2}=2^2=4$

143. *(c)* If set A and B has m elements, then the number of bijections from A to B is the total number of arrangements of n distinct items taken all at a time, i.e. $m!$.

144. *(c)* Let, $y=\sin^{-1}[x\sqrt{1-x}-\sqrt{x}\sqrt{1-x^2}]$

$=\sin^{-1}[x\sqrt{1-(\sqrt{x})^2}-\sqrt{x}\sqrt{1-x^2}]$

$=\sin^{-1}x-\sin^{-1}\sqrt{x}$

[Using $\sin^{-1}x-\sin^{-1}y=\sin^{-1}[x\sqrt{1-y^2}-y\sqrt{1-x^2}]$]

145. *(b)* We have,

$$\tan\theta + \tan 4\theta + \tan 7\theta = \tan\theta \tan 4\theta \tan 7\theta$$

$$\tan\theta + \tan 4\theta = \tan\theta \tan 4\theta \tan 7\theta - \tan 7\theta$$

$$\tan\theta + \tan 4\theta = -\tan 7\theta(1 - \tan\theta \tan 4\theta)$$

$$\frac{\tan\theta + \tan 4\theta}{1 - \tan\theta \tan 4\theta} = -\tan 7\theta$$

$$\tan(\theta + 4\theta) = -\tan 7\theta$$

$$\tan 5\theta = \tan(-7\theta)$$

$\therefore$ $$5\theta = -7\theta$$

$$12\theta = 0 \text{ or } 12\theta = n\pi$$

So, $$\theta = \frac{n\pi}{12}, \forall n \in I$$

146. *(b)* The normal to the tangent will pass through the centre. Also, the intersection of the normal and tangent will give the point of contact.

Hence, cosider the equation of tangent

$$y = -\frac{n}{2} - 45$$

Here, $$m = \frac{-1}{2}$$

Therefore, slope of the normal is 2.

Since, slope of normal and tangent are mutually perpendicular.

Therefore, equation of the normal at $(1, -1)$ is

$$\frac{y-1}{x+1} = 2 \text{ or } y - 1 = 2x + 2$$

$$\Rightarrow \quad 2x - y = -3$$

Therefore, we have two equations $2x - y = -3$ and $x + 2y + 9 = 0$

Solving these two equations give us $(x, y) = (-3, -3)$

Hence, point of contact is $(-3, -3)$.

147. *(b)* For given condition,

$$\frac{2g}{2g'} = \frac{2f}{2f'}$$

$$\Rightarrow \quad gf' = fg'$$

148. *(b)* Given, circles are $x^2 + y^2 = 4$ and $x^2 + y^2 - 4x + 2y - 4 = 0$

i.e. $$x^2 + y^2 = 4 \quad \ldots\text{(i)}$$

and $$(x-2)^2 - 4 + (y+1)^2 - 1 - 4 = 0$$

$$\Rightarrow x^2 + y^2 = 4 \text{ and } (x-2)^2 + (y+1)^2 = 9 \quad \ldots\text{(ii)}$$

Center and radius of circles (i) is

$$c_1 = (0, 0), r_1 = 2$$

and center and radii of circle (ii) is

$$c_2 = (2, -1), r_2 = 3$$

So, difference between c_1 and $c_2 = \sqrt{5}$

Now here,

$$1 = r_2 - r_1 < \sqrt{5} = c_1c_2 < 5 = r_1 + r_2$$

$$r_2 - r_1 < c_1c_2 < r_1 + r_2$$

Hence, there will be two common tangents.

149. *(c)* Length of tangent from $x^2 + y^2 + 2gx + 2fy + c_1 = 0$

To the circle $x^2 + y^2 + 2gx + 2fy + c_2 = 0$

is $\sqrt{c_2 - c_1}$

Here, $c_2 = 4$ and $c_1 = 0$

So, required length $= \sqrt{4-0} = \sqrt{4} = 2$

150. *(c)* Eccentricity for $\frac{x^2}{a^2} + \frac{y^2}{b^2} = 1$ is $b^2 = a^2(1 - e^2)$ and eccentricity for

$$\frac{x^2}{\frac{144}{25}} - \frac{y^2}{\frac{81}{25}} = 1 \text{ is}$$

$$e_1 = \frac{a_1^2 + b_1^2}{a_1^2}$$

So, $$e_1 = \sqrt{1 + \frac{81}{144}} = \frac{15}{12}$$

Again, foci $= a_1e_1 = \frac{12}{5} \times \frac{15}{12} = 3$

So, focus of hyperbola is $(3, 0) = (ae, 0)$

and focus of ellipse is $(ae, 0) = (5a, 0)$

As, this foci are same, so

$$5a = 3$$

$\therefore$ $$e = \frac{3}{5}$$

So, $$e^2 = 1 - \frac{b^2}{a^2} = 1 - \frac{b^2}{25}$$

$$\Rightarrow \quad \frac{b^2}{25} = 1 - e^2 = 1 - \frac{9}{25}$$

$$\Rightarrow \quad \frac{b^2}{25} = \frac{16}{25}$$

$$\Rightarrow \quad b^2 = 16$$

151. *(c)* Given that, $$\frac{2b^2}{a} = \frac{2b}{2}$$

$$a = 2b$$

Now, $$b^2 = a^2(1 - e^2)$$

$$b^2 = 4b^2(1 - e^2)$$

$$\frac{1}{4} = 1 - e^2$$

$\Rightarrow \quad e^2 = 1 - \frac{1}{4} = \frac{3}{4}$

$\Rightarrow \quad e = \sqrt{\frac{3}{4}} = \frac{\sqrt{3}}{2}$

152. *(a)* Given, equation of parabola is

$$x^2 + 10x - 16y + 25 = 0$$

It can be rewritten as

$$(x+5)^2 = 16y \quad \text{...(i)}$$

Here $a = 4$ and vertex $\equiv (-5, \ 0)$

and focus $\equiv (-5, 4)$

So, y-coordinate of ends of latusrectum will be 4.

Putting in equation, we have

$$(x+5)^2 = 16 \times 4 = 64$$

$\Rightarrow \quad x + 5 = \pm 8$

So, $\quad x = 3, -13$

Substituting x in Eq. (i), we get $y = 4, 4$

Hence, ends of latusrectum will be (3, 4) and (– 13, 4).

153. *(d)* (a) We have,

$$f(x) = \cos|x| + |x|$$

$$= \begin{cases} \cos(-x) + (-x), & x < 0 \\ \cos(x) + x, & x \geq 0 \end{cases}$$

$$= \begin{cases} \cos x - x, & x < 0 \\ \cos x + x, & x \geq 0 \end{cases}$$

$$\therefore f'(x) = \begin{cases} -\sin x - 1, & x < 0 \\ -\sin x + 1, & x \geq 0 \end{cases}$$

$\therefore f'(0^-) = -1$ and $f'(0^+) = 1$

$\Rightarrow \quad f'(0^-) \neq f'(0^+)$

So, it is not differentiable at $x = 0$.

(b) We have,

$$f(x) = \cos|x| - |x|$$

$$= \begin{cases} \cos(-x) - (-x), & x < 0 \\ \cos(x) - x, & x \geq 0 \end{cases}$$

$$= \begin{cases} \cos x + x, & x < 0 \\ \cos x - x, & x \geq 0 \end{cases}$$

$$\therefore f'(x) = \begin{cases} -\sin x + 1, & x < 0 \\ -\sin x - 1, & x \geq 0 \end{cases}$$

$\therefore f'(0^-) = 1$ and $f'(0^+) = -1$

$\Rightarrow \quad f'(0^-) \neq f'(0^+)$

So, it is not differentiable at $x = 0$.

(c) We have,

$$f(x) = \sin|x| + |x|$$

$$= \begin{cases} \sin(-x) + (-x), & x < 0 \\ \sin(+x) + (+x), & x \geq 0 \end{cases}$$

$$= \begin{cases} -\sin x - x, & x < 0 \\ \sin x + x, & x \geq 0 \end{cases}$$

$$\therefore \quad f'(x) = \begin{cases} -\cos x - 1, & x < 0 \\ \cos x + 1, & x \geq 0 \end{cases}$$

$\therefore \quad f'(0^-) = -1 - 1 = -2$

and $\quad f'(0^+) = 1 + 1 = 2 \Rightarrow f'(0^-) \neq f'(0^+)$

So, it is not differentiable at $x = 0$

(d) We have,

$$f(x) = \sin|x| - |x|$$

$$= \begin{cases} \sin(-x) - (-x), & x < 0 \\ \sin x - x, & x \geq 0 \end{cases}$$

$$= \begin{cases} -\sin x + x, & x < 0 \\ \sin x - x, & x \geq 0 \end{cases}$$

$$\therefore f'(x) = \begin{cases} -\cos x + 1, & x < 0 \\ \cos x - 1, & x \geq 0 \end{cases}$$

$\therefore f'(0^-) = -1 + 1 = -0$

and $f^1(0^+) = 1 - 1 = 0$

$\Rightarrow \quad f'(0^-) = f'(0^+)$

So, it is differentiable at $x = 0$.

154. *(d)* We have,

$$x = a\left(\cos t + \log \tan \frac{t}{2}\right)$$

Now, $\quad \frac{dx}{dt} = a\left\{-\sin t + \frac{1}{\tan \frac{t}{2}} \cdot \sec^2 \frac{t}{2} \cdot \frac{1}{2}\right\}$

$$= a\left\{-\sin t + \frac{1}{\sin t}\right\}$$

$$= a\left(\frac{1 - \sin^2 t}{\sin t}\right) = \frac{a\cos^2 t}{\sin t}$$

and $\quad y = a \sin t$

$$\frac{dy}{dt} = a\cos t$$

So, $\quad \frac{dy}{dx} = \frac{dy/dt}{dx/dt}$

$$= \frac{a(\cos t \sin t)}{a\cos^2 t} = \tan t$$

155. *(b)* We have,

$$\begin{bmatrix} 1 & \tan\theta \\ -\tan\theta & 1 \end{bmatrix}^{-1} = \frac{1}{1+\tan^2\theta}\begin{bmatrix} 1 & -\tan\theta \\ \tan\theta & 1 \end{bmatrix}$$

$$\left[\because \begin{bmatrix} a & b \\ c & d \end{bmatrix}^{-1} = \frac{1}{ad-bc}\begin{bmatrix} d & -b \\ -c & a \end{bmatrix}\right]$$

Now, $\begin{bmatrix} 1 & -\tan\theta \\ \tan\theta & 1 \end{bmatrix}\begin{bmatrix} 1 & \tan\theta \\ -\tan\theta & 1 \end{bmatrix}^{-1} = \begin{bmatrix} a & -b \\ b & a \end{bmatrix}$

$$\Rightarrow \begin{bmatrix} 1 & -\tan\theta \\ \tan\theta & 1 \end{bmatrix}\left(\frac{1}{1+\tan^2\theta}\right)\begin{bmatrix} 1 & -\tan\theta \\ \tan\theta & 1 \end{bmatrix} = \begin{bmatrix} a & -b \\ b & a \end{bmatrix}$$

$$\Rightarrow \frac{1}{1+\tan^2\theta}\begin{bmatrix} 1-\tan^2\theta & -2\tan\theta \\ 2\tan\theta & 1-\tan^2\theta \end{bmatrix} = \begin{bmatrix} a & -b \\ b & a \end{bmatrix}$$

$$\Rightarrow \begin{bmatrix} \cos 2\theta & -\sin 2\theta \\ \sin 2\theta & \cos 2\theta \end{bmatrix} = \begin{bmatrix} a & -b \\ b & a \end{bmatrix}$$

$\therefore \quad a = \cos 2\theta, b = \sin 2\theta$

156. *(c)* We have, $A = \begin{bmatrix} 1 & 2 \\ 0 & 1 \end{bmatrix}$

$$A^2 = \begin{bmatrix} 1 & 2 \\ 0 & 1 \end{bmatrix}\begin{bmatrix} 1 & 2 \\ 0 & 1 \end{bmatrix}$$

$$= \begin{bmatrix} 1+0 & 2+2 \\ 0+0 & 0+1 \end{bmatrix} = \begin{bmatrix} 1 & 4 \\ 0 & 1 \end{bmatrix}$$

$$A^3 = A^2 \times A\begin{bmatrix} 1 & 4 \\ 0 & 1 \end{bmatrix}\begin{bmatrix} 1 & 2 \\ 0 & 1 \end{bmatrix}$$

$$= \begin{bmatrix} 1+0 & 2+4 \\ 0+0 & 0+1 \end{bmatrix} = \begin{bmatrix} 1 & 6 \\ 0 & 1 \end{bmatrix}$$

$$= \begin{bmatrix} 1 & 2\times 3 \\ 0 & 1 \end{bmatrix}$$

$$A^n = \begin{bmatrix} 1 & 2n \\ 0 & 1 \end{bmatrix}$$

157. *(b)* We have, α, β and γ are roots of equation

$$x^3 + px + q = 0 \quad \ldots(i)$$

Here, $\alpha + \beta + \gamma = 0$

$\alpha\beta + \beta\gamma + \gamma\alpha = p$

$\alpha\beta\gamma = -q$

Applying $C_1 \to C_1 + C_2 + C_3$, we get

$$\begin{vmatrix} \alpha+\beta+\lambda & \beta & \gamma \\ \alpha+\beta+\lambda & \gamma & \alpha \\ \alpha+\beta+\lambda & \alpha & \beta \end{vmatrix} = (\alpha+\beta+\lambda)\begin{vmatrix} 1 & \beta & \gamma \\ 1 & \gamma & \alpha \\ 1 & \alpha & \beta \end{vmatrix}$$

Applying $R_2 \to R_2 - R_1$, $R_3 \to R_3 - R_1$, we get

$$(\alpha+\beta+\lambda)\begin{vmatrix} 1 & \beta & \gamma \\ 0 & \gamma-\beta & \alpha-\gamma \\ 0 & \alpha-\beta & \beta-\gamma \end{vmatrix}$$

$$= (\alpha+\beta+\lambda)[(\gamma-\beta)(\beta-\gamma) - (\alpha-\gamma)(\alpha-\beta)]$$

$$= 0 \times [(\gamma-\beta)(\beta-\gamma) - (\alpha-\gamma)(\alpha-\beta)] = 0$$

158. *(b)* $\begin{vmatrix} \sin x & \cos x & \cos x \\ \cos x & \sin x & \cos x \\ \cos x & \cos x & \sin x \end{vmatrix} = 0$

Applying $C_1 \to C_1 + C_2 + C_3$

$$\begin{vmatrix} 2\cos x + \sin x & \cos x & \cos x \\ 2\cos x + \sin x & \sin x & \cos x \\ 2\cos x + \sin x & \cos x & \sin x \end{vmatrix} = 0$$

$$\Rightarrow (2\cos x + \sin x)\begin{vmatrix} 1 & \cos x & \cos x \\ 1 & \sin x & \cos x \\ 1 & \cos x & \sin x \end{vmatrix} = 0$$

[Applying $R_2 \to R_2 - R_1$ and $R_3 \to R_3 - R_1$, we get

$$(2\cos x + \sin x)\begin{vmatrix} 1 & \cos x & \cos x \\ 0 & \sin x - \cos x & 0 \\ 0 & 0 & \sin x - \cos x \end{vmatrix} = 0$$

$\Rightarrow (2\cos x + \sin x)[1 \cdot (\sin - \cos x)^2] = 0$

$\Rightarrow (2\cos x + \sin x)(\sin x - \cos x)^2 = 0$

$\Rightarrow 2\cos x = -\sin x$ or $\sin x = \cos x$

$\Rightarrow \tan x = -2$ which is not possible as for

$-\frac{\pi}{4} \le x \le \frac{\pi}{4}$, we get $-1 \le \tan x \le 1$

or $\quad \tan x = 1$

So, $x = \frac{\pi}{4}$. Hence, only one real root exist.

159. *(c)* Prime factors of 450 is $2 \times 3 \times 3 \times 5 \times 5$.

Now, non-prime divisors will be combinations of these.

When two are multiplied,

$2 \times 3 = 6$, $2 \times 5 = 10$

$3 \times 3 = 9$, $3 \times 5 = 15$, $5 \times 5 = 25$

When three are multiplied,

$2 \times 3 \times 3 = 18$, $2 \times 3 \times 5 = 30$, $2 \times 5 \times 5 \times = 50$,
$3 \times 3 \times 5 = 45$, $3 \times 5 \times 5 = 75$

When four are multiplied,

$2 \times 3 \times 3 \times 5 = 90$, $2 \times 3 \times 5 \times 5 = 150$,

$3 \times 3 \times 5 \times 5 = 225$

When five are multiplied,

$2 \times 3 \times 3 \times 5 \times 5 = 450$

Also, 1 is also a non-prime divisor.

So, sum of divisors

$= 9 + 15 + 25 + 30 + 50 + 45 + 75 + 90$

$+150 + 225 + 450 + 1 = 1199$

160. *(a)* $\sum_{\substack{1<p<100 \\ p \to \text{prime}}} P! - \sum_{n=1}^{50} (2n!) = (2! + 3! + 5! + 7! + \ldots)$

$- (2! + 4! + 6! + \ldots)$

After $5!$ the number will have 0 at the one's place.

So, they will no effect the last digit of the total sum.

Now last digit of $(2! + 3!) = 2 + 6 = 8$

Last digit of $(2! + 4!) = 2 + 4 = 6$

Last digit of $\sum_{\substack{1<p<100 \\ p \to \text{prime}}} p! - \sum_{n=1}^{50} (2m!) = 8 - 6 = 2$

161. ***(b) Let*** $I = \int_0^1 \frac{1}{\sqrt{1+x^4}} dx$

We have, $0 \le x \le 1$

$0 \le x^4 \le 1$

$\Rightarrow \quad 1 \le 1 + x^4 \le 2$

$\Rightarrow \quad 1 \le \sqrt{1+x^4} \le \sqrt{2}$

$\Rightarrow \quad \frac{1}{\sqrt{2}} \le \frac{1}{\sqrt{1+x^4}} \le 1$

$\Rightarrow \quad \int_0^1 \frac{1}{\sqrt{2}} dx \int_0^1 \frac{1}{\sqrt{1+x^4}} dx \le \int_0^1 1\, dx$

$\Rightarrow \quad \frac{1}{\sqrt{2}} \le \int_0^1 \frac{1}{\sqrt{1+x^4}} dx \le 1$

$\therefore \quad I \in \left[\frac{1}{\sqrt{2}}, 1\right]$

162. *(b)* Let $\quad I = \int_0^{\pi/2} \log(\tan x) dx$

$\Rightarrow \quad I = \int_0^{\pi/2} \log \tan\left(\frac{\pi}{2} - x\right) dx$

$\Rightarrow \quad I = \int_0^{\pi/2} \log \cot x\, dx$

$\Rightarrow \quad I = \int_0^{\pi/2} \log \frac{1}{\tan x} dx$

$\Rightarrow \quad I = -\int_0^{\pi/2} \log \tan x\, dx$

$\Rightarrow \quad I = -I \Rightarrow 2I = 0 \quad \Rightarrow I = 0$

163. *(b)* Let $I = \int_{-2}^{2} (ax^3 + bx + c) dx$ ...(i)

$= \int_{-2}^{2} (a(-2 + 2 - x)^3 + b(-2 + 2)\, x + c) dx$

$\left[\because \int_a^b f(x) dx = \int_a^b f(a + b - x) dx\right]$

$\Rightarrow \quad I = \int_{-2}^{2} (-ax^3 - bx + c) dx$ ..(ii)

On adding Eqs. (i) and (ii), we get

$2I = \int_{-2}^{2} 2c\, dx$

$I = 4c$

So, value of I depends on the value of c.

164. *(b)* Given equation of curves are $y = x^2$ and

$y = 4x - x^2$

$y - 4 = -4 + 4x - x^2$

$y - 4 = -(x^2 - 4x + 4) = -(x - 2)^2$

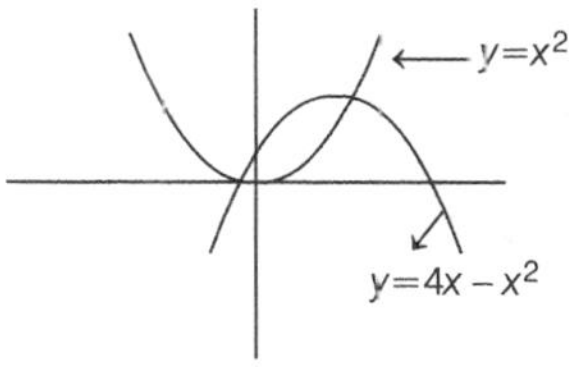

Now, required area $= \int_0^2 \{(4x - x^2) - x^2\}\, dx$

$= \int_0^2 \{(4x - 2x^2)\}\, dx$

$= \left[2x^2 - \frac{2}{3}x^3\right]_0^2$

$= \left[\left(8 - \frac{16}{3}\right) - 0\right]$

$= \frac{24 - 16}{3} = \frac{8}{3}$ sq. units

165. *(b)* We have, $\frac{y\, dy}{x\, dx} = \frac{1 + y^2}{1 + x^2}$

$\frac{y\, dy}{1 + y^2} = \frac{x\, dx}{1 + x^2}$

$\frac{2y\, dy}{1 + y^2} = \frac{2x\, dx}{1 + x^2}$

Integrating both sides, we get

$\int \frac{2y\, dy}{1 + y^2} = \int \frac{2x\, dx}{1 + x^2}$

$$\ln(1+y^2) = \ln(1+x^2) + \ln c$$
$$1+y^2 = c(1+x^2)$$

Now, $y = 2$ at $x = 1$

So, $5 = c(2)$

$2c = 5$

Therefore, $2(1+y^2) = 5(1+x^2)$

166. *(d)* We have,
$$\frac{dy}{dx} = (x+y)^2$$

Let $x + y = z$

$$\Rightarrow \frac{dy}{dx} + 1 = \frac{dz}{dx} \Rightarrow \frac{dy}{dx} = \frac{dz}{dx} - 1$$

Now, given equation becomes
$$\frac{dz}{dx} - 1 = z^2 \Rightarrow \frac{dz}{dx} = 1 + z^2$$
$$dx = \frac{dz}{1+z^2}$$

On integrating both sides, we get
$$\int dx = \int \frac{dz}{1+z^2}$$
$$\Rightarrow c + x = \tan^{-1}(z)$$
$$\Rightarrow \tan^{-1} z = x + c$$
$$\Rightarrow \tan^{-1}(x+y) = x + c$$

167. *(a)* Let $f(x) = \left(\frac{1}{x}\right)^{2x^2} = x^{-2x^2}$

$$\therefore \log f(x) = -2x^2 \log x$$
$$\Rightarrow \frac{1}{f(x)} f'(x) = -4x\log x - \frac{2x^2}{x}$$
$$\Rightarrow f'(x) = x^{-2x^2}\ [-4x\log x - 2x]$$

For maximum,
$$f'(x) = 0$$
$$\Rightarrow x^{-2x^2}[-4x\log x - 2x] = 0$$
$$\Rightarrow -4x\log x - 2x = 0$$
$$\Rightarrow \log x = -\frac{1}{2}$$
$$\Rightarrow x = e^{-\frac{1}{2}}$$

Again, $f''(x) = x^{-2x^2}\ [-4x\log x - 2x]^2$
$$+ x^{-2x^2}[-4\log x - 4 - 2]$$
$$\therefore f''(e^{-\frac{1}{2}}) < 0$$

So, $f(x)$ has maximum value at $x = e^{-\frac{1}{2}}$

$$\therefore f_{\max} = f(e^{-\frac{1}{2}}) = \left(\frac{1}{\frac{1}{\sqrt{e}}}\right)^{2\left(\frac{1}{\sqrt{e}}\right)^2} = (\sqrt{e})^{2\left(\frac{1}{e}\right)} = e^{1/e}$$

168. *(a)* Let the required numbers be x. Then,
$$f(x) = x - x^2$$
$$\Rightarrow f'(x) = 1 - 2x$$

For a local maxima or local minima, we must have
$$f'(x) = 0$$
$$\Rightarrow 1 - 2x = 0$$
$$\Rightarrow 2x = 1 \Rightarrow x = \frac{1}{2}$$

Now, $f''(x) = -2 < 0$

So, $x = \frac{1}{2}$ is point of local maxima.

Hence, required numbers is $\frac{1}{2}$.

169. *(c)* Given, curve is $y = x\sin x$ ...(i)

At $x = \frac{\pi}{2}$, we have $y = \frac{\pi}{2}$

Slope of the tangent at $x = \frac{\pi}{2}$

From Eq. (i), we get
$$\frac{dy}{dx} = \sin x + x\cos x$$
$$\Rightarrow \frac{dy}{dx} = 1 \text{ at } \frac{\pi}{2}$$

Now, equation of tangent will be
$$x - \frac{\pi}{2} = y - \frac{\pi}{2}$$
$$\Rightarrow x = y$$

This will intersect X-axis at (0, 0).

So, the subtangent will be $= \frac{\pi}{2} - 0 = \frac{\pi}{2}$

170. *(a)* Let $I = \int \frac{10^{x/2}}{\sqrt{10^{-x} - 10^x}} dx$

$$= \int \frac{10^{x/2}}{\sqrt{\frac{1}{10^x} - 10^x}} dx = \int \frac{10^{x/2} \cdot 10^{x/2}}{\sqrt{1-(10^x)^2}} dx$$
$$= \int \frac{10^x}{\sqrt{1-(10^x)^2}} dx$$

Put $10^x = t \Rightarrow 10^x \log 10\, dx = dt$

So, $I = \frac{1}{\log 10}\int \frac{dt}{\sqrt{1-t^2}}$

$= \frac{1}{\log 10}\sin^{-1}(t) + c = \frac{1}{\log 10}\sin^{-1}(10^x) + c$

171. *(c)* We have,

$\int e^x \left\{\frac{1+\sin x \cos x}{\cos^2 x}\right\} dx$

$= \int e^x \left\{\frac{1}{\cos^2 x} + \frac{\sin x \cos x}{\cos^2 x}\right\} dx$

$= \int e^x (\sec^2 + \tan x)\, dx = \int e^x \{f'(x) + f(x)\} dx$

[where $f(x) = \tan x$ and $f'(x) = \sec^2 x$]

$= e^x f(x) + c = e^x \tan x + c$

172. *(d)* We have, $\int \frac{x^2+1}{x^4+1} dx$

Divide numerator and denominator by x^2, we get

$$\int \frac{1+\frac{1}{x^2}}{x^2+\frac{1}{x^2}} dx = \int \frac{1+\frac{1}{x^2}}{x^2+\frac{1}{x^2}-2+2} dx$$

$$= \int \frac{1+\frac{1}{x^2}}{\left(x-\frac{1}{x}\right)^2+2} dx$$

Let $x - \frac{1}{x} = t$

$$\left(1+\frac{1}{x^2}\right)dx = dt = \int \frac{dx}{t^2+2}$$

$$= \frac{1}{\sqrt{2}}\tan^{-1}\left(\frac{t}{\sqrt{2}}\right) + c$$

$$= \frac{1}{\sqrt{2}}\tan^{-1}\left(\frac{x-\frac{1}{x}}{\sqrt{2}}\right) + c$$

$$= \frac{1}{\sqrt{2}}\tan^{-1}\left(\frac{x^2-1}{\sqrt{2}x}\right) + c$$

173. *(a)* Given, line segment is $x\cos\alpha + y\sin\alpha = p$

Therefore, it cuts the X-axis and Y-axis at points $(p\sec\alpha, 0)$ and $(0, p\,\text{cosec}\,\alpha)$.

Hence, the coordinate of the mid point are

$$\left(\frac{p\sec\alpha}{2}, \frac{p\,\text{cosec}\,\alpha}{2}\right)$$

Therefore, $x = \frac{p\sec\alpha}{2}$ and $y = \frac{p\,\text{cosec}\,\alpha}{2}$

or $\cos\alpha = \frac{p}{2x}$ and $\sin\alpha = \frac{p}{2y}$

$\because \quad \sin^2\alpha + \cos^2\alpha = 1$

$$\left(\frac{p}{2x}\right)^2 + \left(\frac{p}{2y}\right)^2 = 1$$

$$\Rightarrow \frac{p^2}{4x^2} + \frac{p^2}{4y^2} = 1 \Rightarrow \frac{1}{4x^2} + \frac{1}{4y^2} = \frac{1}{p^2}$$

$$\Rightarrow \frac{1}{x^2} + \frac{1}{y^2} = \frac{4}{p^2} \Rightarrow x^{-2} + y^{-2} = 4p^{-2}$$

174. *(c)* If the line is inclined at angle 45° with the positive direction of the X-axis i.e. the points are situated at angle $\theta = 45°$ from X-axis at a distance $r = 3\sqrt{2}$ from point (4, –5).

The two points can be given by

$(x_0 \pm r\cos\theta, y \pm r\sin\theta)$

The points are

$(4 + 3\sqrt{2}\cos 45°, -5 + 3\sqrt{2}\sin 45°)$

$= \left(4 + 3\sqrt{2}\frac{1}{\sqrt{2}}, -5 + 3\sqrt{2}\times\frac{1}{\sqrt{2}}\right) = (7, -2)$

and $(4 - 3\sqrt{2}\cos 45°, -5 - 3\sqrt{2}\sin 45°)$

$= \left(4 - 3\sqrt{2}\times\frac{1}{\sqrt{2}}, -5 - 3\sqrt{2}\times\frac{1}{\sqrt{2}}\right) = (1, -8)$

Thus, the points are $(1, -8)$ and $(7, -2)$.

175. *(c)* The equation $ax^2 + 2hxy + by^2 = 0$ can be rewritten as

$$a + \frac{2hy}{x} + b\left(\frac{y}{x}\right)^2 = 0 \quad ...(i)$$

Consider, $\quad px + qy = 0$

$$px = -qy \Rightarrow \frac{y}{x} = \frac{-p}{q}$$

Substituting in Eq. (i), we get

$$a + 2h\left(-\frac{p}{q}\right) + b\left(\frac{-p}{q}\right)^2 = 0 \Rightarrow a - \frac{2hp}{q} + b\frac{p^2}{q^2} = 0$$

$$\Rightarrow aq^2 - 2hpq + bp^2 = 0$$

176. *(b)* We have, $f(x) = \frac{\log_e(1+ax) - \log_e(1-bx)}{x}$

$$= \lim_{x\to 0}\frac{\log_e(1+ax) - \log_e(1-bx)}{x} \quad \left[\frac{0}{0}\text{ form}\right]$$

Applying L' Hospital rule,

$$\lim_{x\to 0}\frac{\frac{a}{1+ax} + \frac{b}{1-bx}}{1} = \frac{\frac{a}{1}+\frac{b}{1}}{1} = a + b$$

COMEDK 2018

177. *(b)* We have,

$$\lim_{n\to\infty} \frac{(1^2+2^2+\ldots+n^2)\sqrt[n]{n}}{(n+1)(n+10)(n+100)}$$

$$= \lim_{n\to\infty} \frac{n(n+1)(2n+n)}{6(n+1)(n+10)(n+100)} \left(\lim_{n\to\infty} \sqrt[n]{n}\right)$$

$$= \lim_{n\to\infty} \frac{2n^2+n}{6(n+10)(n+100)} \quad \ldots\text{(i)}$$

$$= \lim_{n\to\infty} \frac{2+\frac{1}{n}}{6\left(1+\frac{10}{n}\right)\left(1+\frac{100}{n}\right)}$$

$$= \frac{2+0}{6(1+0)(1+0)}$$

$$= \frac{2}{6} = \frac{1}{3}$$

178. *(c)* Consider that there are m collinear points out of total n points in a plane. To construct a triangle we require 3 non-collinear points.

Hence, the number of triangles will be ${}^nC_3 - {}^mC_3$.

Since, all the point in the above question are non-collinear, hence $n = 10$ and $m = 0$

Therefore, the total number of triangles are $= {}^{10}C_3$

$$= \frac{10\times9\times8}{3!} = \frac{90\times8}{6} = 15\times8 = 120$$

179. *(a)* Angle traced by the hour hand in 12 h = 360°

Anlge traced by it in 4 h 25 min, i.e.

$$4\frac{5}{12}\text{ h} = \frac{53}{12}\text{ h}$$

$$= \frac{360}{12}\times\frac{53}{12} = \frac{265}{2} = 132\frac{1^\circ}{2}$$

Angle traced by it in 25 min

$$= \frac{360^\circ}{60^\circ}\times 25 = 150^\circ$$

Now, required angle $= \left(150^\circ - 132\frac{1^\circ}{2}\right) = 17\frac{1^\circ}{2}$

180. *(a)* $x^2+y^2-8x=0$

$\Rightarrow\ 5^2+(-7)^2-8\times5$

$\Rightarrow\ 25+49-40=34$

$\Rightarrow\ 34>0$

Here, $34 > 0$, so the points $(5, -7)$ lies outside the circle.

COMEDK 2018

COMEDK

Solved Paper 2017

Instructions

- There are 180 questions in all. The number of questions in each section is as given below.

Sections	No. of Questions
Section I : Physics	1–60
Section II : Chemistry	61–120
Section III : Mathematics	121–180

- All the questions are Multiple Choice Questions having four options out of which **ONLY ONE** s correct.
- Candidates will be awarded 1 mark for each correct answer. There will be no negative marking for incorrect answer.
- Time allotted to complete this paper is 3 hrs.

PHYSICS

1. When a body falls in air, the resistance of air depends to a great extent on the shape of the body. Three different shapes are given

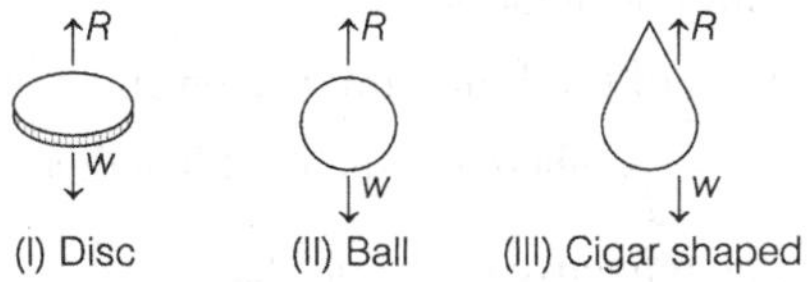

Identify the combination of air resistances which truly represents the physical situation. (The cross-sectional areas are the same.)

a. I < II < III ***b.*** II < III < I
c. III < II < I ***d.*** III < I < II

2. The adjacent figure is the part of a horizontally stretched net. Section AB is stretched with a force of 10 N.

The tensions in the sections BC and BF are

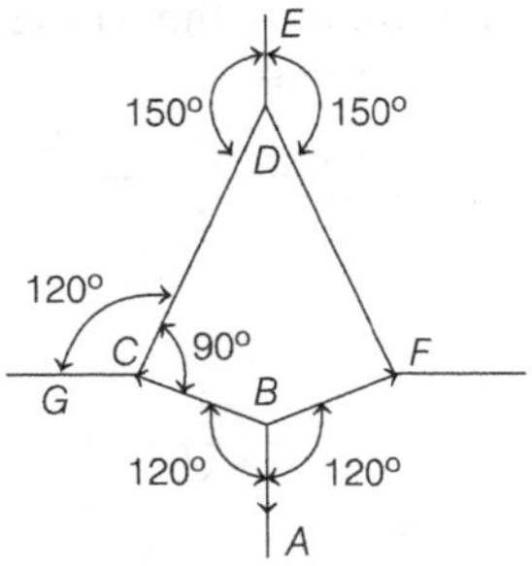

a. 10N, 11 N
b. 10 N, 6 N
c. 10 N, 10 N
d. Can't calculate due to insufficient data

3. Out of the following four dimensional quantities, which one qualifies to be called a dimensional constant?

a. Acceleration due to gravity
b. Surface tension of water
c. Weight of a standard kilogram mass
d. Velocity of light in vacuum

4. The relationship between the force F and position x of a body is as shown in the figure. The work done in displacing the body from $x = 1$ m to $x = 5$ m will be

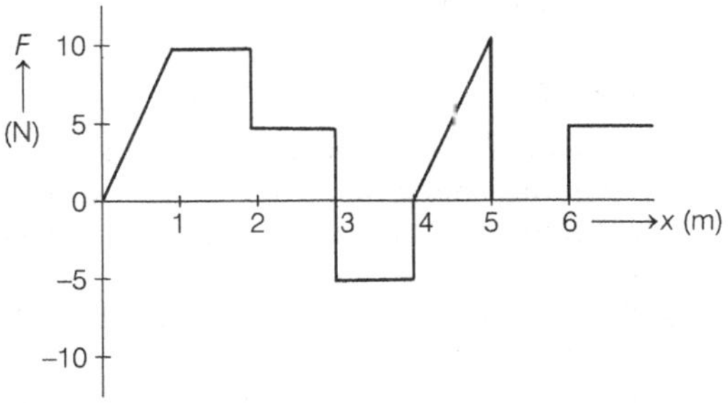

a. 30 J ***b.*** 15 J ***c.*** 25 J ***d.*** 20 J

5. From the top of a tower, two stones whose masses are in the ratio 1 : 2 are thrown - one straight up with an initial speed u and the second straight down with the same speed u. Then, neglecting air resistance

a. the heavier stone hits the ground with a higher speed
b. the lighter stone hits the ground with a higher speed
c. Both the stones will have the same speed when they hit the ground
d. the speed can't be determined with the given data

6. If M is the mass of the earth and R its radius, the ratio of the gravitational acceleration and the gravitational constant is

a. $\frac{R^2}{M}$ *b.* $\frac{M}{R^2}$ *c.* MR^2 *d.* $\frac{M}{R}$

7. A student unable to answer a question on Newton's laws of motion attempts to pull himself up by tugging on his hair. He will not succeed

a. as the force exerted is small
b. the frictional force, while gripping is small
c. Newton's law of inertia is not applicable to living beings
d. as the force applied is internal to the system

8. From the adjacent figure, the correct observation is

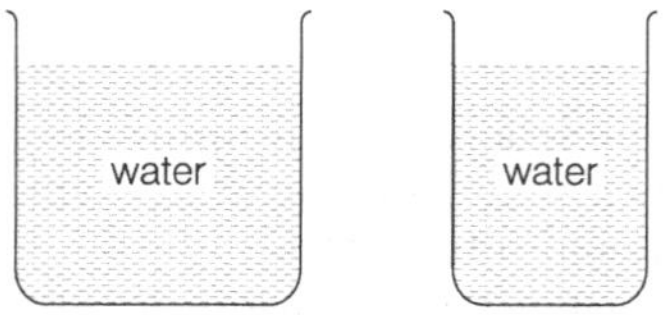

I II

a. the pressure on the bottom of tank (I) is greater than at the bottom of (II)
b. the pressure on the bottom of tank (I) is smaller than at the bottom of (II)
c. the pressure depend on the shape of the container
d. the pressure on the bottom of (I) and (II) is the same

9. Which one of the following is not a unit of Young's modulus?

a. Nm^{-1} *b.* Nm^{-2}
c. dyne cm^{-2} *d.* Mega pascal

10. A piece of blue glass heated to a high temperature and a piece of red glass at room temperature are taken inside a dimly lit room. Then

a. the blue piece will look blue and red will look as usual
b. red will look brighter red and blue will look ordinary blue
c. blue will shines like brighter red compared to the red piece
d. Both the pieces will look equally red

11. The wavelength of the radiation emitted by a body depends upon

a. the nature of the surface
b. the area of the surface
c. the temperature of the surface
d. All of the above

12. An ideal monoatomic gas is taken around the cycle $ABCDA$ as shown in the p-V diagram. The work done during the cycle is given by

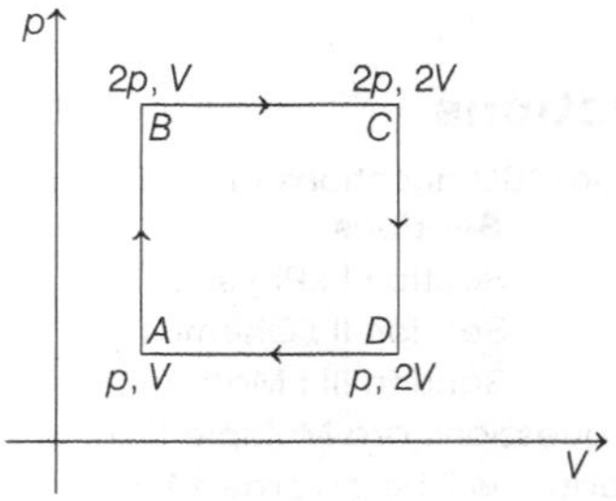

a. $\frac{1}{2}pV$ *b.* pV
c. $2pV$ *d.* $4pV$

13. Which mirror is to be used to obtain a parallel beam of light from a small lamp?

a. Plane mirror
b. Convex mirror
c. Concave mirror
d. Any one of the above

14. Which of the following is a wrong statement?

a. $D = \frac{1}{f}$, where f is the focal length and D is called the refractive power of a lens.
b. Power is called a dioptre when f is in metres.
c. Power is called a dioptre and does not depend on the system of unit used to measure f.
d. D is positive for convergent lens and negative for divergent lens.

15. Identify the wrong description of the below figures.

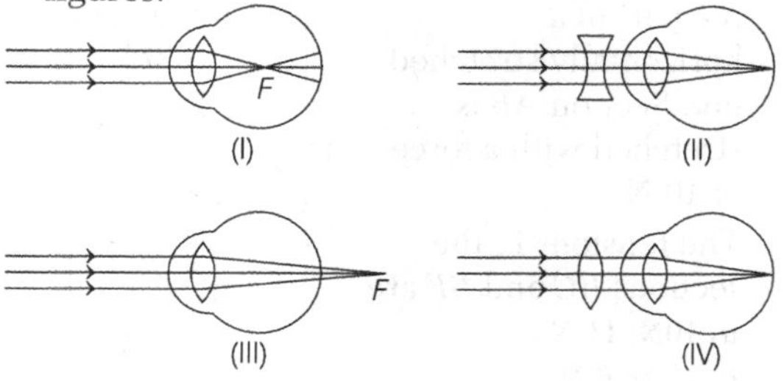

a. I represents far - sightedness
b. II correction for short-sightedness
c. III represents far - sightedness
d. IV correction for far - sightedness

16. Infrared radiation was discovered in 1800 by
a. William Wollaston *b.* William Herschel
c. Wilhelm Roentgen *d.* Thomas Young

17. A particle on the trough of a wave at any instant will come to the mean position after a time (T = time period)
a. $\frac{T}{2}$ *b.* $\frac{T}{4}$ *c.* T *d.* $2T$

18. The disc of a siren containing 60 holes rotates at a constant speed of 360 rpm. The emitted sound is in unison with a tuning-fork of frequency
a. 10 Hz *b.* 360 Hz
c. 216 kHz *d.* 6 Hz

19. The ratio of velocity of sound in hydrogen and oxygen at STP is
a. 16 : 1 *b.* 8 : 1
c. 4 : 1 *d.* 2 : 1

20. In an experiment with sonometer a tuning fork of frequency 256 Hz resonates with a length of 25 cm and another tuning fork resonates with a length of 16 cm. Tension of the string remaining constant the frequency of the second tuning fork is
a. 163.84 Hz *b.* 400 Hz
c. 320 Hz *d.* 204.8 Hz

21. The apparent frequency of a note is 200 Hz. When a listener is moving with a velocity of 40 ms^{-1} towards a stationary source. When he moves away from the same source with the same speed, the apparent frequency of the same note is 160 Hz. The velocity of sound in air (in m/s) is
a. 340 *b.* 330
c. 360 *d.* 320

22. The wave theory of light, in its original form, was first postulated by
a. Isaac Newton
b. Christian Huygens
c. Thomas Young
d. Augustin Jean Fresnel

23. If a liquid does not wet glass, its angle of contact is
a. zero *b.* acute
c. obtuse *d.* right angle

24. The magnitude of I in ampere unit is

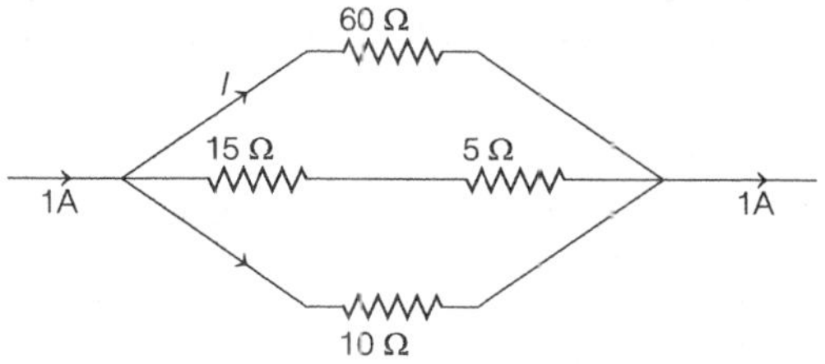

a. 0.1 *b.* 0.3
c. 0.6 *d.* None of these

25. Electron of mass m and charge q is travelling with a speed v along a circular path of radius r at right angles to a uniform magnetic field of intensity B. If the speed of the electron is doubled and the magnetic field is halved, then the resulting path would have a radius
a. $2r$ *b.* $4r$ *c.* $\frac{r}{4}$ *d.* $\frac{r}{2}$

26. If the potential difference across the internal resistance r_1 is equal to the emf E of the battery, then

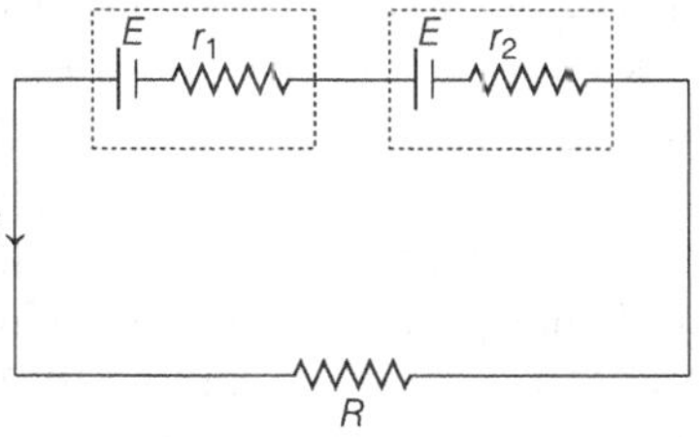

a. $R = r_1 + r_2$ *b.* $R = \frac{r_1}{r_2}$ *c.* $R = r_1 - r_2$ *d.* $R = \frac{r_2}{r_1}$

27. By using only two resistance coils-singly, in series, or in parallel-one should be able to obtain resistances of 3, 4, 12 and 16 ohms. The separate resistances of the coil are
a. 3 and 4 *b.* 4 and 12
c. 12 and 16 *d.* 16 and 3

28. The electrons in the beam of a television tube move horizontally from South to North. The vertical component of the earth's magnetic field points down. The electron is deflected towards
a. West *b.* no deflection
c. East *d.* North to South

29. A tangent galvanometer has a reduction factor of 1 A and it is placed with the plane of its coil perpendicular to the magnetic meridian. The deflection produced when a current of 1 A is passed through it is
a. 60° *b.* 45°
c. 30° *d.* None of these

30. In the given circuit, the voltmeter records 5 V. The resistance of the voltmeter (in ohms) is

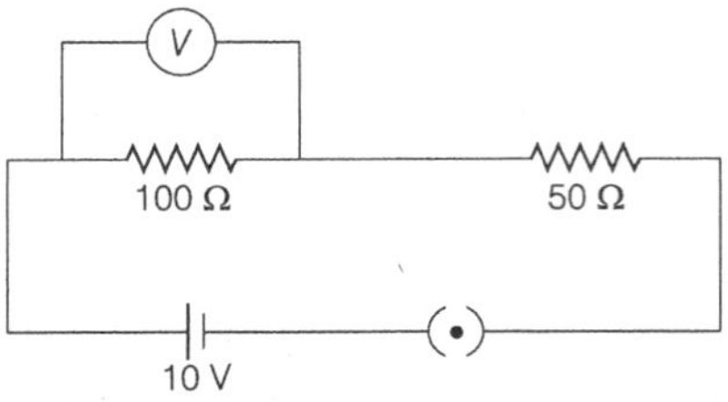

a. 200
b. 100
c. 10
d. 50

31. Three long, straight and parallel wires, carrying current, are arranged as shown in figure.

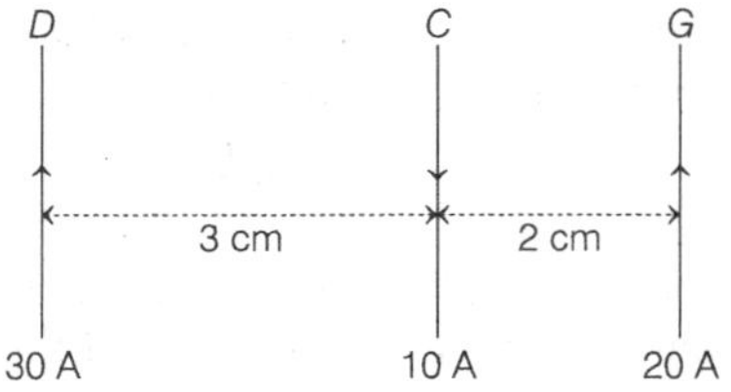

The force experienced by a 25 cm length of wire C is

a. 10^{-3} N
b. 2.5×10^{-3} N
c. Zero
d. 1.5×10^{-3} N

32. A 5.0 A current is setup in an external circuit by a 6.0 V storage battery for 6.0 min. The chemical energy of the battery is reduced by

a. 1.08×10^4 J
b. 1.08×10^4 V
c. 1.8×10^4 J
d. 1.8×10^4 V

33. The current in a simple series circuit is 5.0 A. When an additional resistance of 2.0 Ω is inserted, the current drops to 4.0 A. The original resistance of the circuit (in Ω) is

a. 1.25 *b.* 8 *c.* 10 *d.* 20

34. In the circuit given $E = 6.0$ V, $R_1 = 100\Omega$ $R_2 = R_3 = 50\Omega$ and $R_4 = 75\Omega$.
The equivalent resistance of the circuit (in Ω) is

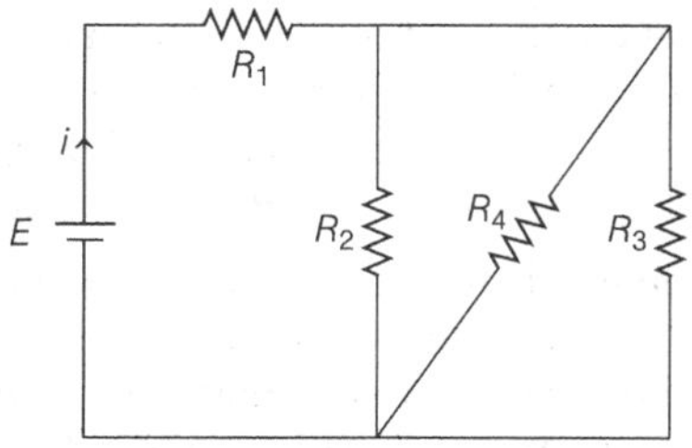

a. 11.875
b. 26.31
c. 118.75
d. None of these

35. Two resistances are connected in two gaps of a meterbridge. The balance point is 20 cm from the zero end. A resistance of 15 Ω is connected in series with the smaller of the two. The null point shifts to 40 cm. The value of the smaller resistance (in Ω) is

a. 3 *b.* 6 *c.* 9 *d.* 12

36. An electric field of 1500 V/m and a magnetic field of 0.40 Wb/m^2 act on a moving electron. The minimum uniform speed along a straight line the electron could have is

a. 1.6×10^{15} m/s
b. 6×10^{-16} m/s
c. 3.75×10^3 m/s
d. 3.75×10^2 m/s

37. In an ammeter 10% of main current is passing through the galvanometer. If the resistance of the galvanometer is G, then the shunt resistance (in Ω) is

a. $9G$ *b.* $\frac{G}{9}$ *c.* $90\,G$ *d.* $\frac{G}{90}$

38. Among the following properties describing diamagnetism identify the property that is wrongly stated.

I. Diamagnetic material do not have permanent magnetic moment.
II. Diamagnetism is explained in terms of electromagnetic induction.
III. Diamagnetic materials have a small positive susceptibility.
IV. The magnetic moment of individual electrons neutralise each other.

a. I *b.* II *c.* III *d.* IV

39. The induction coil works on the principle of

a. self-induction
b. mutual induction
c. Ampere's rule
d. Fleming's right hand rule

40. The square root of the product of inductance and capacitance has the dimension of

a. length
b. mass
c. time
d. no dimension

41. The electric flux for Gaussian surface A that enclose the charged particles in free space is (Given, $q_1 = -14$ nC, $q_2 = 78.85$ nC, $q_3 = -56$ nC)

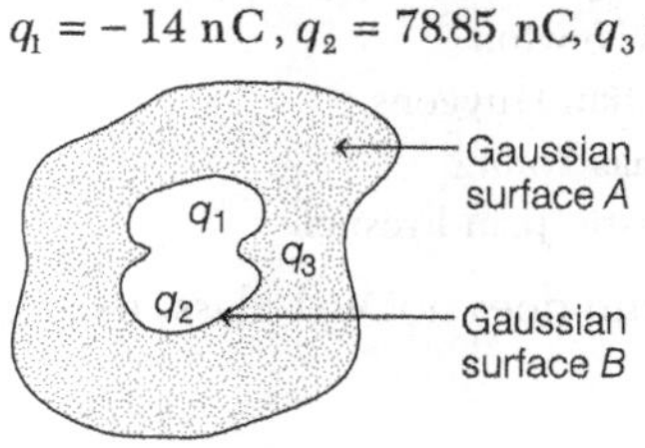

a. 10^3 N-m^{2}C^{-1}
b. 10^3CN^{-1}m^{-2}
c. 6.32×10^3N-m^{2}C^{-1}
d. 6.32×10^3CN^{-1}m^{-2}

42. Four metal conductors having different shapes a sphere, cylindrical, pear, lightning conductor are mounted on insulating stands and charged. The one which is best suited to retain the charges for a longer time is

a. 1 *b.* 2
c. 3 *d.* 4

43. The potential to which a conductor is raised, depends on

a. the amount of charge
b. geometry and size of the conductor
c. Both (a) and (b)
d. None of the above

44. The work done in carrying a charge q once round a circle of radius r with a charge Q at the centre is

a. $\dfrac{qQ}{4\pi\varepsilon_0 r}$ *b.* $\dfrac{qQ}{4\pi\varepsilon_0^2 r^2}$
c. $\dfrac{qQ}{4\pi\varepsilon_0 r^2}$ *d.* None of these

45. An air filled parallel plate condenser has a capacity of 2pF. The separation of the plates is doubled and the interspace between the plates is filled with wax. If the capacity is increased to 6pF, then the dielectric constant of wax is

a. 2 *b.* 3 *c.* 4 *d.* 6

46. Identify the wrong statement in the following. Coulomb's law correctly describes the electric force that

a. binds the electrons of an atom to its nucleus.
b. binds the protons and neutrons in the nucleus of an atom.
c. binds atoms together to form molecules.
d. binds atoms and molecules to form solids.

47. A single slit of width a is illuminated by violet light of wavelength 400 nm and the width of the diffraction pattern is measured as y. When half of the slit width is covered and illuminated by yellow light of wavelength 600 nm, the width of the diffraction pattern is

a. the pattern vanishes and the width is zero
b. $\dfrac{y}{3}$
c. $3y$
d. None of the above

48. At Kavalur in India, the astronomers using a telescope whose objective had a diameter of one metre started using a telescope of diameter 2.54 m. This resulted in

a. the increase in the resolving power by 2.54 times for the same λ
b. the increase in the limiting angle by 2.54 times for the same λ
c. decrease in the resolving power
d. no effect on the limiting angle

49. When unpolarised light beam is incident from air onto glass ($n = 1.5$) at the polarising angle

a. reflected beam is polarised 100 percent
b. reflected and refracted beams are partially polarised
c. the reason for (a) is that almost all the light is reflected
d. All of the above

50. Select the correct statement from the following.

a. Christian Huygens, a contemporary of Newton established the wave theory of light by assuming that light waves were transverse.
b. Maxwell provided the compelling theoretical evidence that light is a transverse wave.
c. Thomas Young experimentally proved the wave behaviour of light and Huygens assumption.
d. All three statements given above, correctly answers the question 'what is light'?

51. Two coherent light beams of intensity I and $4I$ are superposed. The maximum and minimum possible intensities in the resulting beam are

a. $9I$ and I *b.* $9I$ and $3I$
c. $5I$ and I *d.* $5I$ and $3I$

52. From the figure describing photoelectric effect we may infer correctly that

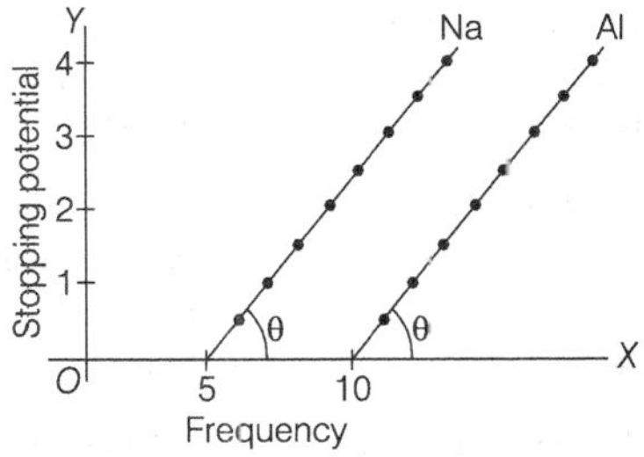

a. Na and Al both have the same threshold frequency
b. Maximum kinetic energy for both the metals depend linearly on the frequency
c. The stopping potentials are different for Na and Al for the same change in frequency
d. Al is a better photo sensitive material than Na

53. The electron in a hydrogen atom makes a transition from $n = n_1$ to $n = n_2$ state. The time period of the electron in the initial state n_1 is eight times that in the final state n_2. The possible values of n_1 and n_2 are

a. $n_1 = 8, n_2 = 1$ *b.* $n_1 = 4, n_2 = 2$
c. $n_1 = 2, n_2 = 4$ *d.* $n_1 = 1, n_2 = 8$

54. If the forward voltage in a diode is increased, then the width of the depletion region

a. increases *b.* decreases

c. fluctuates *d.* no change

55. Two nucleons are at a separation of one Fermi. Protons have a charge of $+1.6\times10^{-19}$ C. The net nuclear force between them is F_1, if both are neutrons, F_2 if both are protons and F_3 if one is proton and the other is neutron. Then,

a. $F_1 = F_2 > F_3$

b. $F_1 = F_2 = F_3$

c. $F_1 < F_2 < F_3$

d. $F_1 > F_2 > F_3$

56. The energy that should be added to an electron to reduce its de-Broglie wavelength from 1 nm to 0.5 nm is

a. four times the initial energy

b. equal to the initial energy

c. twice the initial energy

d. thrice the initial energy

57. Mean life of a radioactive sample is 100 s. Then, its half-life (in min) is

a. 0.693 *b.* 1

c. 10^{-4} *d.* 1.155

58. Consider two nuclei of the same radioactive nuclide. One of the nuclei was created in a supernova explosion 5 billion years ago. The other was created in a nuclear reactor 5 min ago. The probability of decay during the next time is

a. different for each nuclei

b. nuclei created in explosion decays first

c. nuclei created in the reactor decays first

d. independent of the time of creation

59. Bohr's atom model assumes

a. the nucleus is of infinite mass and is at rest

b. electrons in a quantised orbit will not radiate energy

c. mass of the electron remains constant

d. All of the above

60. Identify the property which is not characteristic for a semi-conductor.

a. At a very low temperatures it behaves like an insulator.

b. At higher temperatures two types of charge carriers will cause conductivity.

c. The charge carriers are electrons and holes in the valance band at higher temperatures.

d. The semiconductor is electrically neutral.

CHEMISTRY

61. The correct order in which the first ionisation potential increases is

a. Na, K, Be *b.* K, Na, Be

c. K, Be, Na *d.* Be, Na, K

62. 10 cm^3 of 0.1 N monobasic acid requires 15 cm^3 of sodium hydroxide solution whose normality is

a. 1.5 N *b.* 0.15 N

c. 0.066 N *d.* 0.66 N

63. The IUPAC name for tertiary butyl iodide is

a. 4-iodobutane

b. 2-iodobutane

c. 1-iodo, 3-methyl propane

d. 2-iodo, 2-methyl propane

64. When sulphur dioxide is passed in an acidified $K_2Cr_2O_7$ solution, the oxidation state of sulphur is changed from

a. + 4 to 0 *b.* + 4 to + 2

c. + 4 to + 6 *d.* + 6 to + 4

65. Mass of 0.1 mole of methane is

a. 1g *b.* 16 g *c.* 1.6 g *d.* 0.1 g

66. Methoxy methane and ethanol are

a. position isomers

b. chain isomers

c. functional isomers

d. optical isomers

67. When the azimuthal quantum number has the value of 2, the number of orbitals possible are

a. 7 *b.* 5

c. 3 *d.* 0

68. For the reaction,
$Fe_2O_3 + 3CO \longrightarrow 2Fe + 3CO_2$, the volume of carbon monoxide required to reduce one mole of ferric oxide is

a. 22.4 dm^3 *b.* 44.8 dm^3

c. 67.2 dm^3 *d.* 11.2 dm^3

69. The monomers of buna-S rubber are

a. vinyl chloride and sulphur

b. butadiene

c. styrene and butadiene

d. isoprene and butadiene

70. An element with atomic number 21 is a
a. halogen
b. representative element
c. transition element
d. alkali metal

71. The maximum number of hydrogen bonds that a molecule of water can have is
a. 1 *b.* 2 *c.* 3 *d.* 4

72. A gas deviates from ideal behaviour at a high pressure because its molecules
a. attract one another
b. show the Tyndall effect
c. have kinetic energy
d. are bound by covalent bonds

73. The reagent used to convert an alkyne to alkene is
a. Zn/HCl *b.* Sn/HCl
c. Zn-Hg / HCl *d.* Pd/H_2

74. When, compared to $\Delta G°$ for the formation of Al_2O_3, the $\Delta G°$ for the formation of Cr_2O_3 is
a. higher *b.* lower
c. same *d.* unpredicted

75. In order to increase the volume of a gas by 10%, the pressure of the gas should be
a. increased by 10% *b.* increased by 1%
c. decreased by 10% *d.* decreased by 1%

76. Catalytic dehydrogenation of a primary alcohol gives a/an
a. secondary alcohol *b.* aldehyde
c. ketone *d.* ester

77. Excess of PCl_5 reacts with conc.H_2SO_4 giving
a. chlorosulphonic acid *b.* thionyl chloride
c. sulphuryl chloride *d.* sulphurous acid

78. If one mole of ammonia and one mole of hydrogen chloride are mixed in a closed container to form ammonium chloride gas, then
a. $\Delta H > \Delta U$
b. $\Delta H = \Delta U$
c. $\Delta H < \Delta U$
d. there is no relationship

79. The compound on dehydrogenation gives a ketone. The original compound is
a. primary alcohol *b.* secondary alcohol
c. tertiary alcohol *d.* carboxylic acid

80. Which is the most easily liquefiable rare gas?
a. Xe *b.* Kr *c.* Ar *d.* Ne

81. Mesomeric effect involves delocalisation of
a. π-electrons *b.* σ-electrons
c. protons *d.* None of these

82. Which of the following has the maximum number of unpaired *d*-electrons?
a. Zn^{2+} *b.* Fe^{2+} *c.* Ni^{3+} *d.* Cu^{+}

83. One mole of which of the following has the highest entropy?
a. Liquid nitrogen *b.* Hydrogen gas
c. Mercury *d.* Diamond

84. Which of the following species does not exert a resonance effect?
a. $C_6H_5NH_2$ *b.* $C_6H_5\overset{+}{N}H_3$
c. C_6H_5OH *d.* C_6H_5Cl

85. A complex compound in which the oxidation number of a metal is zero, is
a. $K_4[Fe(CN)_6]$ *b.* $K_3[Fe(CN)_6]$
c. $[Ni(CO)_4]$ *d.* $[Pt(NH_3)_4]Cl_2$

86. Three moles of PCl_5, three moles of PCl_3 and two moles of Cl_2 are taken in a closed vessel. If at equilibrium the vessel has 1.5 moles of PCl_5, the number of moles of PCl_3 present in it is
a. 5 *b.* 3 *c.* 6 *d.* 4.5

87. How many optically active stereomers are possible for butan-2, 3-diol?
a. 1 *b.* 2 *c.* 3 *d.* 4

88. An octahedral complex is formed when hybrid orbitals of the following type are involved
a. sp^3 *b.* dsp^2
c. d^2sp^3 *d.* sp^2d^2

89. For the reaction,
$2HI(g) \rightleftharpoons H_2(g) + I_2(g); -Q$ kJ, the equilibrium constant depends upon
a. temperature *b.* pressure
c. catalyst *d.* volume

90. The angle strain in cyclobutane is
a. 24°44′ *b.* 29°16′
c. 19°22′ *d.* 9°44′

91. The number of nodal planes present in σ^*s-antibonding orbital is
a. 1 *b.* 2 *c.* 0 *d.* 3

92. Which of the following electrolytic solution has the least specific conductance?
a. 0.02 N *b.* 0.2 N
c. 2 N *d.* 0.002 N

93. The overlapping of orbitals in benzene is of the type
a. *sp-sp* *b.* *p-p*
c. sp^2-sp^2 *d.* sp^3-sp^3

94. The calculated bond order of superoxide ion (O_2^-) is

a. 2.5 *b.* 2
c. 1.5 *d.* 1

95. Which of the following can be measured by the Ostwald-Walker dynamic method?

a. Relative lowering of vapour pressure
b. Lowering of vapour pressure
c. Vapour pressure of the solvent
d. All of the above

96. *n*-propyl bromide on treating with alcoholic KOH produces

a. propane *b.* propene
c. propyne *d.* propanol

97. Mercury is a liquid metal because

a. it has a completely filled *s*-orbital
b. it has a small atomic size
c. it has a completely filled *d*-orbital that prevents *d*-*d* overlapping of orbitals
d. it has a completely filled *d*-orbital that causes *d*-*d* overlapping

98. A compound is formed by elements *A* and *B*. This crystallises in the cubic structure, where the *A* atoms are at the corners of the cube and *B* atoms are at the body centres.

a. AB *b.* A_6B
c. A_8B_4 *d.* AB_6

99. Anisole can be prepared by the action of methyl iodide on sodium phenate. The reaction is called

a. Wurtz's reaction *b.* Williamson's reaction
c. Fittig's reaction *d.* Etard's reaction

100. Malleability and ductility of metals can be accounted due to

a. the presence of electrostatic force
b. the crystalline structure in metal
c. the capacity of layers of metal ions to slide over the other
d. the interaction of electrons with metal ions in the lattice

101. An ionic compound is expected to have tetrahedral structure if r_+ / r_- lies in the range of

a. 0.414 to 0.732 *b.* 0.225 to 0.414
c. 0.155 to 0.225 *d.* 0.732 to 1

102. Among the following, which is least acidic?

a. phenol *b.* *o*-cresol
c. *p*-nitrophenol *d.* *p*-chlorophenol

103. A ligand can also be regarded as

a. Lewis acid *b.* Bronsted base
c. Lewis base *d.* Bronsted acid

104. The colour of sky is due to

a. transmission of light
b. wavelength of scattered light
c. absorption of light by atmospheric gases
d. All of the above

105. Which of the following organic compounds answers to both iodoform test and Fehling's test?

a. Ethanol *b.* Methanol
c. Ethanal *d.* Propanone

106. Helium is used in balloons in place of hydrogen because it is

a. incombustible
b. lighter than hydrogen
c. radioactive
d. more abundant than hydrogen

107. The basic principle of Cottnell's precipitator is

a. Le-Chatelier's principle
b. peptisation
c. neutralisation of charge on colloidal particles
d. scattering of light

108. When carbon monoxide is passed over solid caustic soda heated to 200°C, it forms

a. Na_2CO_3 *b.* $NaHCO_3$
c. $HCOONa$ *d.* CH_3COONa

109. $N_2 + 3H_2 \rightleftharpoons 2NH_3 + \text{Heat}$. What is the effect of the increase of temperature on the equilibrium of the reaction?

a. Equilibrium is shifted to the left
b. Equilibrium is shifted to the right
c. Equilibrium is unaltered
d. Reaction rate does not change

110. Hydrogen gas is not liberated when the following metal is added to dil. HCl

a. Ag *b.* Zn *c.* Mg *d.* Sn

111. Consider the Born-Haber cycle for the formation of an ionic compound, given below and identify the compound (Z) formed.

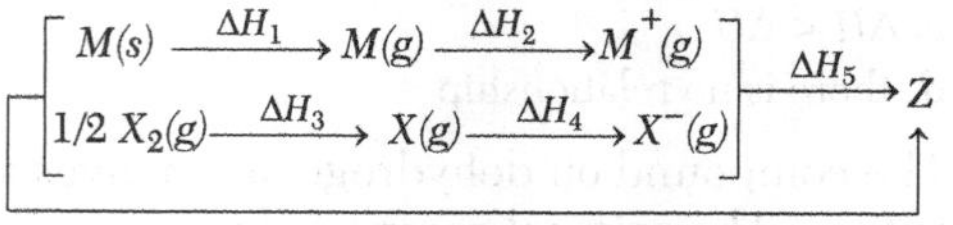

a. M^+X^- *b.* $M^-X^-(s)$ *c.* MX *d.* $M^+X^-(g)$

112. In the brown ring test, the brown colour of the ring is due to

a. ferrous nitrate
b. ferric nitrate
c. a mixture of NO and NO_2
d. nitrosoferrous sulphate

113. Amines behave as

a. Lewis acids
b. Lewis base
c. aprotic acid
d. neutral compound

114. Dalda is prepared from oils by

a. oxidation
b. reduction
c. hydrolysis
d. distillation

115. The chemical name of anisole is

a. ethanoic acid
b. methoxy benzene
c. propanone
d. acetone

116. The number of disulphide linkages present in insulin are

a. 1 *b.* 2 *c.* 3 *d.* 4

117. 80 g of oxygen contains as many atoms as in

a. 80 g of hydrogen
b. 1 g of hydrogen
c. 10 g of hydrogen
d. 5 g of hydrogen

118. Which metal has a greater tendency to form metal oxide?

a. Cr
b. Fe
c. Al
d. Ca

119. Identify the reaction that does not take place in a blast furnace.

a. $CaCO_3 \longrightarrow CaO + CO_2$
b. $CaO + SiO_2 \longrightarrow CaSiO_3$
c. $2Fe_2O_3 + 3C \longrightarrow 4Fe + 3CO_2$
d. $CO_2 + C \longrightarrow 2CO$

120. Waxes are esters of

a. glycerol
b. long chain alcohols
c. glycerol and fatty acid
d. long chain alcohols and long chain fatty acids

MATHEMATICS

121. Which of the following is an even function?

a. $\sqrt{x}$
b. $x^2 + \sin^2 x$
c. $\sin^3 x$
d. None of these

122. If $A = \{x : x^2 - x + 2 > 0\}$ and $B = \{x : x^2 - 4x + 3 \le 0\}$, then $A \cap B$ is

a. $[1, 3]$
b. $(-\infty, \infty)$
c. $(1, 3)$
d. $(-\infty, 1) \cup (3, \infty)$

123. If * be a binary operation on a set A and e be the identity element w.r.t. *, then $b \in A$ is said to be inverse of $a \in A$ w.r.t. *, if

a. $a * e = b * e$
b. $a = b$
c. $a * a = b * b$
d. $a * b = b * a = e$

124. If in a ΔABC, $\angle C = \frac{\pi}{2}$, then

$$\tan^{-1}\left(\frac{a}{b+c}\right) + \tan^{-1}\left(\frac{b}{c+a}\right) =$$

a. $\frac{\pi}{4}$
b. $\frac{\pi}{2}$
c. $\frac{\pi}{3}$
d. None of these

125. The sides a, b, c of a triangle are in AP. If

$$\cos\alpha = \frac{a}{b+c}, \cos\beta = \frac{b}{c+a}, \cos\gamma = \frac{c}{a+b}$$

then $\tan^2\frac{\alpha}{2} + \tan^2\frac{\gamma}{2} =$

a. 1 *b.* $\frac{1}{2}$ *c.* $\frac{1}{3}$ *d.* $\frac{2}{3}$

126. The value of $\cos(35° + A)\cos(35° - B) + \sin(35° + A)\sin(35° - B)$ is equal to

a. $\sin(A + B)$
b. $\sin(A - B)$
c. $\cos(A + B)$
d. $\cos(A - B)$

127. The value of $2\ \text{cosec}\ 2x + \text{cosec}\ x$ is equal to

a. $\tan x \cdot \sec(x/2)$
b. $\sec x \cdot \cot(x/2)$
c. $\sec x \cdot \tan(x/2)$
d. $\tan x \cdot \cot(x/2)$

128. The value of $\cot 2x \cot x - \cot 3x \cot 2x - \cot 3x \cot x$ is equal to

a. 3 *b.* 0 *c.* −1 *d.* 1

129. The value of $\cos\left(\frac{\pi}{4} - x\right)\cos\left(\frac{\pi}{4} - y\right) - \sin\left(\frac{\pi}{4} - x\right)\sin\left(\frac{\pi}{4} - y\right)$ is equal to

a. $\sin(x + y)$
b. $\sin(x - y)$
c. $\cos(x + y)$
d. $\cos(x - y)$

130. For all $n \in N$, $2 \cdot 4^{2n+1} + 3^{3n+1}$ is divisible by

a. 2
b. 9
c. 3
d. 11

131. The statement $P(n)$: '$1 \times 1! + 2 \times 2! + 3 \times 3! + \ldots + n \times n! = (n+1)! - 1$' is

a. true for all $n > 1$
b. not true for any n
c. true for all $n \in N$
d. None of these

132. If $z = re^{i\theta}$, then $|e^{iz}| =$

a. 1
b. $e^{2r\sin\theta}$
c. $e^{r\sin\theta}$
d. $e^{-r\sin\theta}$

COMEDK 2017

133. If $(\sqrt{5}+\sqrt{3}i)^{33}=2^{49}z$, then modulus of the complex number z is equal to

a. 1 *b.* $\sqrt{2}$
c. $2\sqrt{2}$ *d.* 4

134. The modulus of $[1-\cos\theta+i\sin\theta]^{-1}$ is

a. $\frac{1}{2}\text{cosec}\frac{\theta}{2}$ *b.* $\text{cosec}\frac{\theta}{2}$
c. $\frac{1}{2}\left|\text{cosec}\frac{\theta}{2}\right|$ *d.* $\left|\text{cosec}\frac{\theta}{2}\right|$

135. If a, b, c are real numbers and ω is a complex cube root of unity such that $a+b\omega+c\omega^2=0$, then

a. $b=-c$ *b.* $a=0, b=c$
c. $a=1, b=c$ *d.* $a=b=c$

136. If the cube roots of unity are $1, \omega, \omega^2$, then the roots of the equation $(x-1)^3+8=0$ are

a. $-1, -1, -1$
b. $-1, -1+2\omega. -1-2\omega^2$
c. $-1, 1+2\omega, 1+2\omega^2$
d. $-1, 1-2\omega, 1-2\omega^2$

137. Let α, β be the roots of the equation $ax^2+bx+c=0$. A root of the equation $a^3x^2+abcx+c^3=0$ is

a. $\alpha+\beta$ *b.* $\alpha^2+\beta$
c. $\alpha^2-\beta$ *d.* $\alpha^2\beta$

138. The sum of all 4-digit numbers that can be formed by using the digits 2, 4, 6,8 (repetition of digits is not allowed) is

a. 133320 *b.* 123330
c. 113230 *d.* 323430

139. In how many ways can 4 red, 3 yellow and 2 green discs be arranged in a row, if the discs of the same colour are indistinguishable?

a. 1200 *b.* 1220 *c.* 1240 *d.* 1260

140. Find the number of ways of choosing 4 face cards from a pack of 52 playing cards.

a. 495 *b.* 493
c. 490 *d.* 492

141. Given, the positive integers $r>1, n>2$ and the coefficients of $(3r)$th and $(r+2)$ th terms in the expansion of $(1+x)^{2n}$ are equal, then $n=$

a. $2r$ *b.* $2r-1$
c. $2r+1$ *d.* $3r$

142. Let the HM and GM of two positive numbers a and b be in the ratio 4 : 5, then $a:b$ is

a. 1 : 2 *b.* 2 : 3
c. 3 : 4 *d.* 1 : 4

143. If 2, 7, 9, 5 are subtracted respectively from four numbers forming a GP, the resulting numbers are in AP, then the smallest of the four numbers is

a. −24 *b.* 12 *c.* 6 *d.* 3

144. $\frac{1}{3!}+\frac{2}{5!}+\frac{3}{7!}+\ldots$ to ∞ is equal to

a. e *b.* $2e$ *c.* $\frac{1}{2e}$ *d.* $\frac{e}{2}$

145. Let PQR be a right angled isosceles triangle, right angled at $P(2, 1)$. If the equation of QR is $2x+y=3$, then the combined equation of the lines PQ and PR is

a. $3x^2-3y^2+8xy+20x+10y+25=0$
b. $3x^2-3y^2+8xy-20x-10y+25=0$
c. $3x^2-3y^2+8xy+10x+15y+20=0$
d. $3x^2-3y^2-8xy-10x-15y-20=0$

146. The sides of a triangle are $x=2$, $y+1=0$ and $x+2y=4$. Its circumcentre is

a. (4, 0) *b.* (2, −1)
c. (0, 4) *d.* (2, 3)

147. Find the coordinates of the foci and the length of the latusrectum of the hyperbola.

$$\frac{x^2}{9}-\frac{y^2}{16}=1$$

a. $(0, \pm 2), \frac{32}{3}$ *b.* $(0, \pm 5), \frac{32}{3}$
c. $(\pm 5, 0), \frac{32}{3}$ *d.* $(0, \pm 5), \frac{3}{32}$

148. The line $21x+5y=116$ is a tangent to the hyperbola $7x^2-5y^2=232$. Its point of contact is

a. (−6, −2) *b.* (6, 2)
c. (6, −2) *d.* (−6, 2)

149. Chords of the circle $x^2+y^2=r^2$ touch the hyperbola $\frac{x^2}{a^2}-\frac{y^2}{b^2}=1$. The locus of the mid-points of the chords is

a. $(x^2+y^2)^2=a^2x^2-b^2y^2$
b. $(x^2+y^2)^2=a^2x^2+b^2y^2$
c. $x^2+y^2=a^2x^2-b^2y^2$
d. $x^2+y^2=a^2x^2+b^2y^2$

150. If the latusrectum of a hyperbola subtends a right angle at the other focus, then its eccentricity is

a. $\sqrt{3}+1$ *b.* $\sqrt{2}+1$
c. $\sqrt{3}+\sqrt{2}$ *d.* 2

151. From the point (0, 1) two tangents are dawn to the hyperbola $2x^2 - y^2 = 1$. If θ is the angle between them, then $\tan\theta =$

a. $\frac{4}{3}$ *b.* $\frac{3}{4}$ *c.* $\frac{3}{2}$ *d.* $\frac{2}{3}$

152. Let (3, 4, – 1) and (–1, 2, 3) be the end points of a diameter of a sphere. Then, the radius of the sphere is equal to

a. 2 units *b.* 3 units *c.* 6 units *d.* 7 units

153. Differentiate $\cos^{-1}\left(\frac{1-x}{1+x}\right)$ w.r.t. x.

a. $\frac{1}{1+x}$ *b.* $\frac{1}{x(1+x)}$ *c.* $\frac{1}{(1+x)\sqrt{x}}$ *d.* $\frac{-1}{(1+x)\sqrt{x}}$

154. $f(x) = \left(\frac{5}{x} + 7\right)$, where $x \neq 0$ is decreasing for

a. $x \in R$ *b.* $x \in R - \{0\}$ *c.* $x \in R - \{1\}$ *d.* $x \in R - \{-1, 1\}$

155. Find the approximate value of $(15)^{\frac{1}{4}}$.

a. 1.9688 *b.* 0.9687 *c.* 2.0312 *d.* 0.1968

156. Find the point on the curve $y = x^2$, where the slope of the tangent is equal to the x coordinate of the point.

a. (1, 1) *b.* (–1, – 1) *c.* (1, 2) *d.* (0, 0)

157. Find the equations of the tangent and the normal to the curve $y = \frac{x^3}{4-x}$ at (2, 4).

a. $8x + y - 12 = 0; x + 8y + 34 = 0$
b. $8x - y - 12 = 0; x - 8y - 34 = 0$
c. $8x + 4y + 12 = 0, x - 8y + 34 = 0$
d. $8x - y - 12 = 0, x + 8y - 34 = 0$

158. If $y = \log_a x + \log_x a + \log_x x + \log_a a$, then $\frac{dy}{dx}$ is equal to

a. $\frac{1}{x} + x\log a$ *b.* $\frac{\log a}{x} + \frac{x}{\log a}$ *c.* $\frac{1}{x\log a} + x\log a$ *d.* $\frac{1}{x\log a} - \frac{\log a}{x(\log x)^2}$

159. Evaluate $\int \frac{1}{\sin x + \sqrt{3}\cos x}\,dx$.

a. $\log\left|\tan\left(\frac{x}{2}\right)\right| + C$
b. $-\frac{1}{2}\log\left|\tan\left(\frac{x}{2} + \frac{\pi}{6}\right)\right| + C$
c. $\frac{1}{2}\log\left|\tan\left(\frac{x}{2} + \frac{\pi}{6}\right)\right| + C$
d. None of the above

160. The value of $\int e^{2x}(2\sin 3x + 3\cos 3x)\,dx$ is

a. $e^{2x}\sin 3x + C$ *b.* $e^x \text{cosec}\, x + C$ *c.* $e^{2x} + C$ *d.* $e^{2x}(\sin 3x) + C$

161. Evaluate $\int_1^2 \frac{dx}{x^2}$.

a. $\frac{1}{2}$ *b.* 1 *c.* 2 *d.* –1

162. Evaluate $\int_0^{\pi/2} \frac{\cos x}{\left(\cos\frac{x}{2} + \sin\frac{x}{2}\right)^3}\,dx$.

a. $2 - \sqrt{2}$ *b.* $2 + \sqrt{2}$ *c.* $3 + \sqrt{3}$ *d.* $3 - \sqrt{3}$

163. To area bounded by the lines $|x| + |y| = 1$

a. 1 sq. unit *b.* 2 sq. units *c.* $2\sqrt{2}$ sq. units *d.* 4 sq. units

164. The value of $\int \frac{dx}{\sqrt{x} + \sqrt[3]{x}}$ is

a. $3\sqrt{x} + 3(\sqrt[3]{x}) - 6\sqrt[6]{x} + \log(\sqrt[6]{x} - 1) + C$
b. $2\sqrt{x} + 6(\sqrt[6]{x}) - 6\log(\sqrt[6]{x} + 1) + C$
c. $2\sqrt{x} - 3(\sqrt[3]{x}) + 6\sqrt[6]{x} - 6\log(\sqrt[6]{x} + 1) + C$
d. None of the above

165. If $\int_a^b \frac{x^n}{x^n + (16-x)^n}\,dx = 6$, then

a. $a = 4, b = 12, n \in R$ *b.* $a = 2, b = 14, n \in R$ *c.* $a = -4, b = 20, n \in R$ *d.* $a = 2, b = 8, n \in R$

166. $\int_{-\pi/4}^{\pi/4} \frac{dx}{1 + \cos 2x}$ is equal to

a. 1 *b.* 2 *c.* 3 *d.* 4

167. The differential equation of $y = ae^{bx+c}$ is

a. $y_2 = y_1 + y$ *b.* $y_2^2 = yy_1$ *c.* $y_1^2 = yy_2$ *d.* $y^2 = y_1y_2$

168. If $\mathbf{a} = \hat{\mathbf{i}} + \hat{\mathbf{j}} + 2\hat{\mathbf{k}}$ and $\mathbf{b} = 3\hat{\mathbf{i}} + 2\hat{\mathbf{j}} - \hat{\mathbf{k}}$, then find $(\mathbf{a} + 3\mathbf{b}) \cdot (2\mathbf{a} - \mathbf{b})$.

a. –15 *b.* 12 *c.* 13 *d.* – 10

169. The value of $[\mathbf{a}-\mathbf{b} \;\; \mathbf{b}-\mathbf{c} \;\; \mathbf{c}-\mathbf{a}]$, where $|\mathbf{a}|=1$, $|\mathbf{b}|=5\,|\mathbf{c}|=3$, is

a. 0 *b.* 1
c. 6 *d.* None of these

170. If $A=\begin{bmatrix}2 & -3\\5 & -7\end{bmatrix}$, then $A+A^{-1}=$

a. $\begin{bmatrix}1 & 0\\0 & 1\end{bmatrix}$ *b.* $\begin{bmatrix}-5 & 0\\0 & -5\end{bmatrix}$
c. $\begin{bmatrix}5 & 0\\0 & 5\end{bmatrix}$ *d.* $\begin{bmatrix}4 & 0\\0 & -5\end{bmatrix}$

171. If $A=\begin{bmatrix}\cos\theta & -\sin\theta & 0\\ \sin\theta & \cos\theta & 0\\ 0 & 0 & 1\end{bmatrix}$, then minor and cofactor of a_{32} are

a. 1, −1 *b.* 0, 1
c. −1, 0 *d.* 0, 0

172. An anti-aircraft gun can take a maximum of 4 shots at an enemy plane moving away from it. The probabilities of hitting the plane at the first, second, third and fourth shot are 0.4, 0.3, 0.2, 0.1 respectively. The probability that the gun hits the plane is

a. 0.6972 *b.* 0.6875
c. 0.64 *d.* 0.6976

173. The negation of the statement "If I become a teacher, then I will open a school", is

a. Neither I will become a teacher nor I will open a school.
b. I will not become a teacher or I will open a school.
c. I will become a teacher and I will not open a school.
d. Either I will not become a teacher or I will not open a school.

174. Maximize $Z=7x_1-3x_2$ subject to,

$x_1+2x_2\le 2,\ 2x_1+4x_2\ge 8,\ x_1\ge 0, x_2\ge 0.$

a. Unique solution
b. Unbounded solution
c. Infeasible solution
d. Infinite number of solutions

175. Find the transformed equation of the straight line $xy-x-y+1=0$, when the origin is shifted to the point (1, 1) after translation of axes.

a. $xy=5$ *b.* $xy=2$
c. $xy=0$ *d.* $xy=8$

176. If $\log_6 a+\log_6 b+\log_6 c=6$, where *a*, *b* and *c* are positive integers that form an increasing GP and $b-a$ is a square of an integer, then $a+b+c=$

a. 95 *b.* 99 *c.* 105 *d.* 111

177. A random variable *X* has the following probability distribution :

X	0	1	2	3
$P(X=x)$	0.5	0.2	0.18	0.12

Find the c.d.f. of *X*

a.

$X=x$	0	1	2	3
$F(x)$	0.12	0.18	0.2	0.5

b.

$X=x$	0	1	2	3
$F(x)$	0.5	0.88	1	0.7

c.

$X=x$	0	1	2	3
$F(x)$	0.5	0.7	0.88	1

d.

$X=x$	0	1	2	3
$F(x)$	1	0.5	0.88	0.7

178. From a lot of 20 items containing 4 defective items, 2 items are drawn at random. If *X* denotes the number of defective items, then find the mean of the probability distribution of *X*.

a. $\frac{3}{8}$ *b.* $\frac{1}{95}$ *c.* $\frac{2}{5}$ *d.* $\frac{28}{57}$

179. The total number of subsets of a finite set *A* has 56 more elements than the total number of subsets of another finite set *B*. What is the number of elements in the set *A*?

a. 5 *b.* 6
c. 7 *d.* 8

180. If $\log_4 2+\log_4 4+\log_4 x+\log_4 16=6$, then the value of *x* is

a. 64 *b.* 4 *c.* 8 *d.* 32

COMEDK 2017

ANSWERS

Physics

1.	(c)	**2.**	(c)	**3.**	(d)	**4.**	(b)	**5.**	(c)	**6.**	(b)	**7.**	(d)	**8.**	(d)	**9.**	(a)	**10.**	(c)
11.	(c)	**12.**	(b)	**13.**	(c)	**14.**	(c)	**15.**	(a)	**16.**	(b)	**17.**	(b)	**18.**	(b)	**19.**	(c)	**20.**	(b)
21.	(c)	**22.**	(b)	**23.**	(c)	**24.**	(a)	**25.**	(b)	**26.**	(c)	**27.**	(b)	**28.**	(a)	**29.**	(b)	**30.**	(b)
31.	(c)	**32.**	(a)	**33.**	(b)	**34.**	(c)	**35.**	(c)	**36.**	(c)	**37.**	(b)	**38.**	(c)	**39.**	(b)	**40.**	(c)
41.	(b)	**42.**	(a)	**43.**	(c)	**44.**	(d)	**45.**	(d)	**46.**	(b)	**47.**	(c)	**48.**	(a)	**49.**	(a)	**50.**	(b)
51.	(a)	**52.**	(b)	**53.**	(b)	**54.**	(b)	**55.**	(b)	**56.**	(d)	**57.**	(d)	**58.**	(d)	**59.**	(d)	**60.**	(a)

Chemistry

61.	(b)	**62.**	(c)	**63.**	(d)	**64.**	(c)	**65.**	(c)	**66.**	(c)	**67.**	(b)	**68.**	(c)	**69.**	(c)	**70.**	(c)
71.	(d)	**72.**	(a)	**73.**	(d)	**74.**	(b)	**75.**	(c)	**76.**	(b)	**77.**	(b)	**78.**	(c)	**79.**	(b)	**80.**	(a)
81.	(a)	**82.**	(b)	**83.**	(b)	**84.**	(b)	**85.**	(c)	**86.**	(d)	**87.**	(b)	**88.**	(c)	**89.**	(a)	**90.**	(d)
91.	(a)	**92.**	(d)	**93.**	(c)	**94.**	(c)	**95.**	(a)	**96.**	(b)	**97.**	(a)	**98.**	(a)	**99.**	(b)	**100.**	(c)
101.	(b)	**102.**	(b)	**103.**	(c)	**104.**	(b)	**105.**	(c)	**106.**	(a)	**107.**	(c)	**108.**	(c)	**109.**	(a)	**110.**	(a)
111.	(a)	**112.**	(d)	**113.**	(b)	**114.**	(b)	**115.**	(b)	**116.**	(c)	**117.**	(d)	**118.**	(d)	**119.**	(c)	**120.**	(d)

Mathematics

121.	(b)	**122.**	(a)	**123.**	(d)	**124.**	(a)	**125.**	(d)	**126.**	(c)	**127.**	(b)	**128.**	(d)	**129.**	(a)	**130.**	(d)
131.	(c)	**132.**	(d)	**133.**	(b)	**134.**	(c)	**135.**	(d)	**136.**	(d)	**137.**	(d)	**138.**	(a)	**139.**	(d)	**140.**	(a)
141.	(a)	**142.**	(d)	**143.**	(a)	**144.**	(c)	**145.**	(b)	**146.**	(a)	**147.**	(c)	**148.**	(c)	**149.**	(a)	**150.**	(b)
151.	(a)	**152.**	(b)	**153.**	(c)	**154.**	(b)	**155.**	(a)	**156.**	(d)	**157.**	(d)	**158.**	(d)	**159.**	(c)	**160.**	(a)
161.	(a)	**162.**	(a)	**163.**	(b)	**164.**	(c)	**165.**	(b)	**166.**	(a)	**167.**	(c)	**168.**	(a)	**169.**	(a)	**170.**	(b)
171.	(d)	**172.**	(d)	**173.**	(c)	**174.**	(c)	**175.**	(c)	**176.**	(d)	**177.**	(c)	**178.**	(c)	**179.**	(b)	**180.**	(d)

HINTS & SOLUTIONS

Physics

1. *(c)* The air resistance on an object depends on its area, normal to air flow.

Since, area normal to air flow is maximum in case of disc.

So, air resistance on it is maximum. The air flow in case of cigar shaped is streamlined, so air resistance is minimum.

Hence, the correct order is

$$\text{III} < \text{II} < \text{I}$$

2. *(c)* Let tension in section BC is T and in section BF is T_2, then according to Lami's theorem,

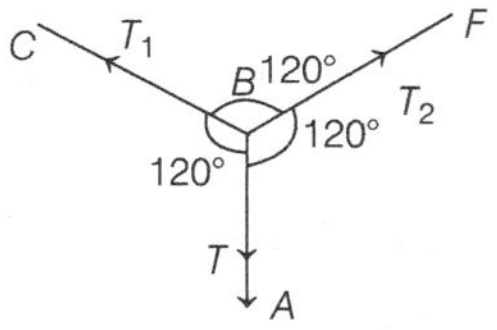

$$\frac{T_1}{\sin 120°} = \frac{T_2}{\sin 120°} = \frac{T}{\sin 120°}$$

$$\Rightarrow \quad T_1 = T_2 = T = 10 \text{ N}$$

3. *(d)* The velocity of light in vacuum is 3×10^8 m/s, which is a dimensional constant.

4. *(b)* The work done in a F-x graph is calculated by the area under the graph. The given graph can be shown as

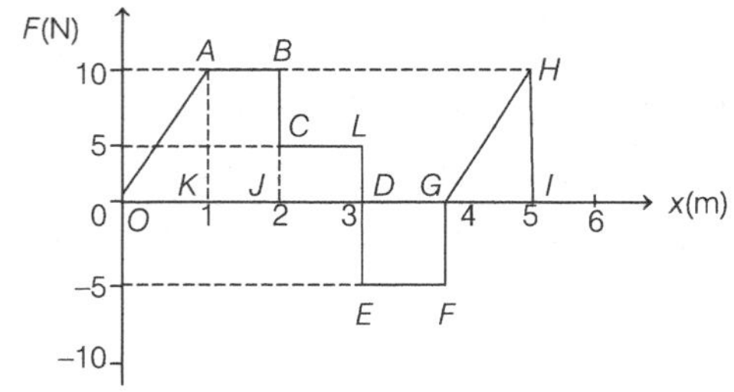

$\therefore$ Work done in displacing the object from $x = 1$ m to $x = 5$ m will be

$W =$ area under F-x graph

$=$ area $ABJK$ + area $CLDJ$ + area $DGFE$ + area GHI

$$= (10 \times 1) + (5 \times 1) + (-5 \times 1) + \left(\frac{1}{2} \times 1 \times 10\right)$$

$$= 10 + 5 - 5 + 5 = 15 \text{ J}$$

5. *(c)* The first stone move up to some height and then its velocity becomes zero. Now, it move downward and at the level of top of tower, it acquires the same initial velocity u and gravitational acceleration g in downward direction.

The second stone is moving with the same speed u and with downward acceleration g. So, both will have same final velocity when they reach the bottom and hit the ground.

6. *(b)* The gravitational acceleration on earth is given by

$$g = \frac{F}{m} = \frac{GMm}{R^2 \times m} = \frac{GM}{R^2}$$

$$\therefore \quad \frac{g}{G} = \frac{M}{R^2}$$

7. *(d)* According to Newton's law, the state of an object can be changed by applying external force on it.

In given case the force applied is internal, so he will not succeed.

8. *(d)* The pressure applied at the bottom of a container by a liquid column of height h is given by

$$p = h\rho g$$

Here, in two cases, the liquid used is same (water), so ρ is same. Also, the height of liquid column is same on both. So, the pressure applied at the bottom is same for both.

9. *(a)* Young's modulus, $Y = \dfrac{\text{Stress}}{\text{Strain}}$

Here, strain is a dimensionless quantity and stress is measured in SI unit of Nm^{-2}, dyne cm^{-2} or pascal.

So, the Young's modulus has the same unit as stress.

$\therefore \text{Nm}^{-1}$ is not a unit of Young's modulus.

10. *(c)* When blue glass is heated to a high temperature, it absorbs all radiations of higher wavelength except red. So, when it is taken inside a dimly lit room, it emits all radiations and hence looks brighter red compared to the red piece. This happens according to Kirchhoff's law of radiation.

11. *(c)* According to Wien's law, the wavelength of radiation emitted by a body is

$$\lambda \propto \frac{1}{T}$$

i.e., it depends on the temperature of the surface.

12. *(b)* Work done in a cyclic process is equal to the area enclosed by the cycle in p-V diagram.

$$\therefore \quad W = \text{Area } ABCD$$

$$= AB \times AD$$

$$= (2p - p) \times (2V - V) = p \times V = pV$$

13. *(c)* A concave mirror is of converging type as the light parallel to principal axis converges at its focus.

So, when a lamp is placed at its focus, the ray of light falling on it becomes parallel beam as shown below.

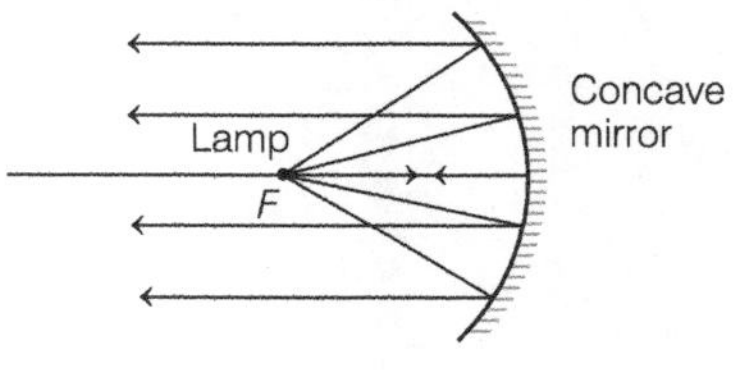

14. *(c)* The power of a lens is given by the reciprocal of its focal length,

$$P = \frac{1}{f}$$

When f is in metre, then power P is in dioptre. Thus, power depends on the system of unit used to measure f.

15. *(a)* In first figure, the parallel rays are converging at a point before the retina. So, the person is suffering from near-sightedness.

16. *(b)* Infrared radiation was discovered in 1800 by William Herschel.

17. *(b)* As total time period of a wave is T. The wave motion can be shown as

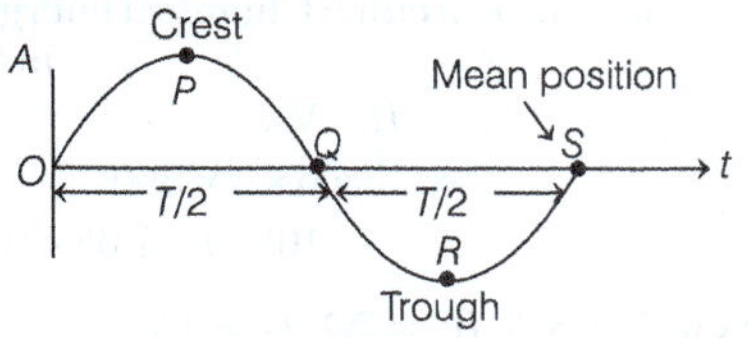

From figure, it can be seen that time taken by the particle to move from trough to its mean position i.e., from R to S is

$$T' = \frac{T/2}{2} = \frac{T}{4}$$

18. *(b)* The number of waves produced by the disc is equal to number of notes

i.e., $n = 60$

Speed of rotation, $v = 360$ rpm

$$= \frac{360}{60} = 6 \text{ rps}$$

$\therefore$ Frequency $= n \times v = 60 \times 6 = 360$ Hz

19. *(c)* The velocity of sound in a gas is given by

$$v = \sqrt{\frac{\gamma RT}{M}}$$

At STP, both gases are at same temperature and as they are diatomic, so their specific heat ratio (γ) is also same.

$$\therefore \quad \frac{v_H}{v_O} = \sqrt{\frac{M_O}{M_H}} = \sqrt{\frac{32}{2}} = 4 \text{ or } 4:1$$

20. *(b)* The wavelength of the sound is proportional to the length of wire. Also, the velocity of sound is same in both cases, so

$$v_1 = v_2$$

$$\Rightarrow \quad f_1\lambda_1 = f_2\lambda_2$$

$$\Rightarrow \quad 256 \times 25 = f_2 \times 16$$

$$\Rightarrow \quad f_2 = \frac{256 \times 25}{16} = 400 \text{ Hz}$$

21. *(c)* Let f_s be the frequency of source.

The apparent frequency heard when listener moves towards source is

$$f' = f_s\left(\frac{v_s + v_o}{v_s}\right)$$

$$\Rightarrow \quad 200 = f_s\left(\frac{v_s + 40}{v_s}\right) \quad \ldots\text{(i)}$$

The apparent frequency heard, when listener moves away from source is

$$f'' = f_s\left(\frac{v_s - v_o}{v_s}\right)$$

$$\Rightarrow \quad 160 = f_s\left(\frac{v_s - 40}{v_s}\right) \quad \ldots\text{(ii)}$$

Dividing Eq. (i) by Eq. (ii), we get

$$\frac{200}{160} = \frac{v_s + 40}{v_s - 40}$$

$$\Rightarrow \quad \frac{5}{4} = \frac{v_s + 40}{v_s - 40}$$

$$\Rightarrow \quad 5v_s - 200 = 4v_s + 160$$

$$\Rightarrow \quad v_s = 360 \text{ m/s}$$

22. *(b)* Christian Huygens believed that the light was made up of waves vibrating up and down perpendicular to the direction of propagation of wave. This is known as Huygens principle.

23. *(c)* If a liquid does not wet glass, it means that the liquid- liquid interaction (cohesion) is more than liquid - solid interaction (adhesion). So, the angle of contact is obtuse.

24. *(a)* Consider the diagram with current distribution as shown below.

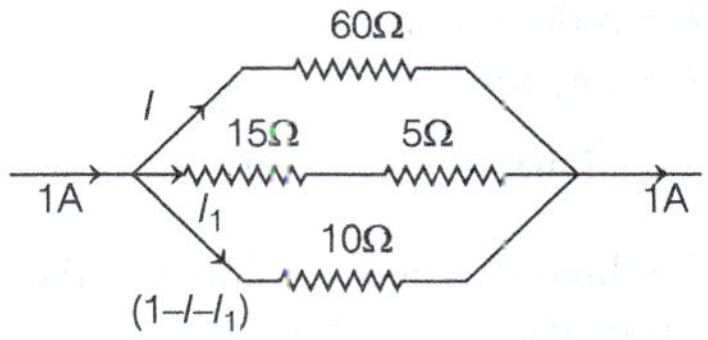

As voltage is same in parallel combination, so

$$60I = (15 + 5)I_1$$

$$60I = 20I_1 \text{ or } I_1 = 3I \quad \ldots\text{(i)}$$

Similarly, $(15 + 5)I_1 = 10(1 - I - I_1)$

$$\Rightarrow \quad 2I_1 = 1 - I - I_1$$

$$\Rightarrow \quad 3I_1 = 1 - I$$

$$\Rightarrow \quad 3(3I) = 1 - I \quad \text{[Using Eq. (i)]}$$

$$\Rightarrow \quad 10I = 1$$

$$\text{or} \quad I = \frac{1}{10} = 0.1\text{A}$$

25. *(b)* We know that, radius of charge particle of mass m having charge q moving with speed v in magnetic field perpendicular to it,

$$r = mv/Bq \quad \ldots\text{(i)}$$

For second case,

$$r' = \frac{mv'}{qB'} = \frac{m(2v)}{q\left(\frac{B}{2}\right)} \quad \left[\text{Since, } v' = 2v,\ B' = \frac{B}{2}\right]$$

$$= 4\frac{mv}{qB} = 4r \quad \text{[using Eq. (i)]}$$

COMEDK 2017

26. *(c)* Total emf of circuit, $E_T = E + E = 2E$

Total resistance of circuit, $R_T = r_1 + r_2 + R$

Current flowing through the circuit,

$$i = \frac{E_T}{R_T} = \frac{2E}{r_1 + r_2 + R} \quad \text{...(i)}$$

As per question $E = ir_1$

$$\Rightarrow \quad i = \frac{E}{r_1} \quad \text{...(ii)}$$

From Eqs. (i) and (ii), we get

$$\frac{E}{r_1} = \frac{2E}{r_1 + r_2 + R}$$

$$\Rightarrow \quad r_1 + r_2 + R = 2r_1$$

$$\Rightarrow \quad R = r_1 - r_2$$

27. *(b)* The maximum and minimum resistances are 16Ω and 3Ω that are obtained by series and parallel combination of resistances. From given option only 4Ω and 12Ω resistors satisfies this condition.

28. *(a)* According to Fleming's right hand rule, for current in South-North direction, magnetic field in inward direction, the force on the electrons will be to the left or in West side.

29. *(b)* The deflection in a tangent galvanometer is given by

$$\tan\theta = \frac{I}{K}$$

where, K = reduction factor

Here, $K = 1\text{A}, I = 1\text{A}$

$$\therefore \quad \tan\theta = \frac{1}{1} = 1 \Rightarrow \theta = 45°$$

30. *(b)* If R be the resistance of voltmeter, then the equivalent resistance of circuit is

$$R_{eq} = \frac{R \times 100}{100 + R} + 50$$

$$= \frac{150R + 5000}{R + 100}$$

Total current in circuit,

$$i = \frac{V}{R_{eq}} = \frac{10}{\frac{150R + 5000}{(R + 100)}}$$

$$= \frac{10(R + 100)}{150R + 5000}$$

Voltage across 100Ω resistor,

$$V = i\left(\frac{R \times 100}{R + 100}\right)$$

Given, $\quad V = 5\text{ V}$

$$\therefore \quad 5 = \frac{10(R + 100)}{150R + 5000} \times \frac{R \times 100}{R + 100}$$

$$= \frac{1000R}{150R + 5000}$$

$$\Rightarrow 750R + 25000 = 1000R$$

$$\Rightarrow \quad R = 100\Omega$$

31. *(c)* Force on 25 cm length of wire C due to wire D is

$$F_D = \frac{\mu_0}{4\pi}\frac{2I_1I_2}{r} \times l$$

$$= 10^{-7} \times \frac{30 \times 10 \times 2}{3 \times 10^{-2}} \times 25 \times 10^{-2}$$

$$= 5 \times 10^{-4}\text{ N, towards right}$$

Force of 25 cm length of wire C due to wire G is

$$F_G = 10^{-7} \times \frac{2 \times 20 \times 10}{2 \times 10^{-2}} \times 25 \times 10^{-2}$$

$$= 5 \times 10^{-4}\text{ N, towards left}$$

$\therefore$ Net force on wire $C = F_D - F_G = 0$

32. *(a)* Given, $I = 5\text{A}, V = 6\text{V}, t = 6\text{ min} = 6 \times 60 = 360\text{ s}$

Heat produced in a circuit = Chemical energy reduced in the battery

$$\Rightarrow \quad H = VIt$$

$$= 6 \times 5 \times 360$$

$$= 10800 = 1.08 \times 10^4\text{ J}$$

33. *(b)* Given, $I_1 = 5\text{ A}, R_2 = 2\Omega, I_2 = 4\text{A}$

Let initial resistance be R.

As voltage given is same in both cases, so

$$V_1 = V_2$$

$$\Rightarrow \quad I_1R = I_2R' = I_2(R + R_2)$$

$$\Rightarrow 5 \times R = 4 \times (R + 2) \Rightarrow R = 8\Omega$$

34. *(c)* Given, $R_1 = 100\Omega, R_2 = R_3 = 50\Omega, E = 6\text{V}, R_4 = 75\Omega$

As R_2, R_3 and R_4 are in parallel combination, so their equivalent resistance be

$$\frac{1}{R'} = \frac{1}{R_2} + \frac{1}{R_3} + \frac{1}{R_4}$$

$$= \frac{1}{50} + \frac{1}{50} + \frac{1}{75} = \frac{3 + 3 + 2}{150} = \frac{8}{150}$$

or $\quad R' = \frac{150}{8}\Omega$

Now, R' is in series with R_1, so

$$R_{net} = R_1 + R' = 100 + \frac{150}{8} = \frac{950}{8} = 118.75\Omega$$

35. *(c)* In first case, at balance point,

$$\frac{P}{Q} = \frac{l}{100 - l} = \frac{20}{100 - 20} = \frac{1}{4} \Rightarrow Q = 4P \quad \text{...(i)}$$

Let P be the smaller resistance, then in second case at balance point,

$$\frac{P + 15}{Q} = \frac{l'}{100 - l'} = \frac{40}{60} = \frac{2}{3}$$

$$\Rightarrow \quad \frac{P + 15}{4P} = \frac{2}{3} \quad \text{[Using Eq. (i)]}$$

$$\Rightarrow 3P + 45 = 8P \Rightarrow P = 9\Omega$$

36. *(c)* Given, electric field, $E = 1500\text{ V/m}$

Magnetic field, $B = 0.4\text{ Wb/m}^2$

Charge on electron, $q = e = 1.6 \times 10^{-19}\text{ C}$

For minimum uniform speed of electron along a straight line is a region, where electric field E and magnetic field B, both are present is given as

$$v = \frac{E}{B} \qquad \left[\because qE = Bqv \Rightarrow v = \frac{E}{B}\right]$$

$$= \frac{1500}{0.4}$$

$= 3750$ m/s

$= 3.75 \times 10^3$ m/s

37. *(b)* If I be the main current, then current passing through galvanometer,

$$I_g = 10\% \text{ of } I = \frac{I}{10}$$

Resistance of galvanometer, $R_g = G$

Shunt resistance, $R_S = \frac{I_g R_g}{I - I_g} = \frac{\frac{I}{10} \times G}{I - \frac{I}{10}} = \frac{G}{9}$

38. *(c)* Magnetic susceptibility of diamagnetic materials is small and negative.

Diamagnetic material do not have permanent magnetic moment because the magnetic moment of individual electrons neutralise each other due randomly oriented.

39. *(b)* The induction coil works on the principle of mutual induction. In the phenomena of mutual induction, an emf is induced across the secondary coil if the magnetic flux due to primary coil linked with the secondary coil changes.

40. *(c)* We know that, in L-C-R series resonant circuit, resonance frequency,

$$f = \frac{1}{2\pi\sqrt{LC}}$$

$$\Rightarrow \sqrt{LC} = \frac{1}{2\pi f}$$

$$\Rightarrow \sqrt{LC} = \frac{1}{\omega} \qquad [\omega = \text{angular frequency}]$$

$$\therefore \text{Dimension of } \sqrt{LC} = \frac{1}{\text{Dimension of } \omega}$$

$$\Rightarrow [\sqrt{LC}] = \frac{1}{[\omega]} = \frac{1}{[T^{-1}]} = [T]$$

Hence, square root of the product of inductance [L] and capacitance [C] has the dimension of time.

41. *(b)* Given, $q_1 = -14\,\text{nC} = -14 \times 10^{-9}$ C

$q_2 = 78.85\,\text{nC} = 78.85 \times 10^{-9}$ C

$q_3 = -56\,\text{nC} = -56 \times 10^{-9}$ C

According to Gauss's law

Net electric flux passing through closed surface A,

$$\phi_A = \frac{1}{\varepsilon_0}(\text{total charged enclosed by closed surface } A)$$

$$= \frac{1}{\varepsilon_0}(q_1 + q_2 + q_3)$$

$$= \frac{-14 \times 10^{-9} + 78.85 \times 10^{-9} - 56 \times 10^{-9}}{8.85 \times 10^{-12}}$$

$$= \frac{8.85}{8.85} \times 10^{-9+12} = 10^3 \text{CN}^{-1}\text{m}^{-2}$$

42. *(a)* In case of spherical metal conductor, the charges quickly spread over its entire surface uniformly because of which charges can stay for longer time on spherical conductor.

While in case of non-spherical surfaces, charge concentration is different at different points due to which the charges do not stay on the surfaces for longer time.

43. *(c)* When we give charge to a conductor, then its potential increases.

$$\text{Potential, } V = \frac{\text{Charge}(Q)}{\text{Capacitance}(C)}$$

$$\Rightarrow V = \frac{Q}{\varepsilon_0 \frac{A}{d}} \qquad \left[\because C = \frac{\varepsilon_0 A}{d}\right]$$

$$\Rightarrow V = \frac{Qd}{\varepsilon_0 A}$$

Hence, V also depends on d and A. Thus, potential of conductor depends on the amount of charge, area or geometry and size of the conductor.

44. *(d)* According to given situation of charges, electrostatic force works which is conservative in nature i.e., work done depends on initial and final position only. Here, initial and final position coincide, hence work done will be zero.

45. *(d)* Given, capacitance of air filled parallel plate capacitor,

$$C_0 = 2\text{pF}$$

$$\Rightarrow = 2 \times 10^{-12}\text{ F}$$

$$\Rightarrow \frac{\varepsilon_0 A}{d} = 2 \times 10^{-12}\text{ F} \qquad \text{...(i)}$$

When the separation between the plates is doubled, i.e., $d' = 2d$

And wax of dielectric constant k is filled between the plates of capacitor, then,

$$C' = 6\,\text{pF}$$

$$\frac{\varepsilon_0 kA}{d'} = 6 \times 10^{-12}\text{F}$$

$$\Rightarrow \frac{\varepsilon_0 kA}{2d} = 6 \times 10^{-12} \qquad [\because d' = 2d]$$

$$\Rightarrow \frac{\varepsilon_0 A}{d} \times \frac{k}{2} = 6 \times 10^{-12}$$

$$\Rightarrow 2 \times 10^{-12} \times \frac{k}{2} = 6 \times 10^{-12} \qquad [\text{from Eq. (i)}]$$

$$\Rightarrow k = 6$$

46. *(b)* According to Coulomb's law, electrostatic force acts only between two charge particles. Neutron is a neutral particle, therefore Coulomb's law is applicable only for protons.

47. *(c)* Given, In first case,

Wavelength of violet light,

$$\lambda_1 = 400 \text{ nm}$$

We know that, width of the diffraction pattern is given as

$$\beta = y = \frac{2D\lambda_1}{d}$$

$$\Rightarrow \quad y = \frac{2D\lambda_1}{d} = \frac{2D \times 400}{d}$$

$$y = \frac{800D}{d} \quad \text{....(i)}$$

In the second case,

$$\lambda_2 = 600 \text{ nm}, \ d' = \frac{d}{2}$$

$$\therefore \quad y' = \frac{2D\lambda'}{d'} = \frac{2D \times 600}{\frac{d}{2}}$$

$$= 2400\frac{D}{d} = 3 \times \frac{800D}{d}$$

$$= 3y \quad \text{[from Eq. (i)]}$$

48. *(a)* Diameter of objective,

$$D_1 = 1\text{m}, D_2 = 2.54 \text{ m}$$

Resolving power, $R_P = \dfrac{D}{1.22\lambda}$

Since, $R_P \propto D$ [For same value of λ]

$$\therefore \quad \frac{R_{P_1}}{R_{P_2}} = \frac{D_1}{D_2} = \frac{1}{2.54}$$

$$\Rightarrow \quad R_{P_2} = 2.54 \times R_{P_1}$$

49. *(a)* According to phenomena of polarisation by reflection, when unpolarised light beam is incident from air onto glass ($n = 1.5$) at the polarising angle (Brewster's angle), then reflected beam is polarised completely i.e. 100%.

50. *(b)* In Huygens principle, the wave theory was established by assuming that the waves were longitudinal. So, option (a) is not correct.

In Maxwell's theory of light, he stated that light is a transverse wave and conducted various experiments to prove so. Hence, option (b) is correct.

Thomas Young conducted his double slit experiment for determining fringe width and tried to prove the wave nature of light by providing that light undergoes interference which is a phenomenon showed by waves. He never proved the type of wave light is, i.e. transverse or longitudinal. Hence, option (c) is not correct.

These statements mostly highlight the wave nature of light.They do not comment on the particle nature of light or the dual nature of light established. Hence, they clearly do not answer the question "what is light" correctly. Hence, option (d) is not correct.

51. *(a)* Given, intensity of two coherent light beams,

$$I_1 = I \text{ and } I_2 = 4I$$

After superposition of two light beams,

$\therefore$ Maximum intensity,

$$I_{max} = (\sqrt{I_1} + \sqrt{I_2})^2$$
$$= I_1 + I_2 + 2\sqrt{I_1 I_2}$$
$$= I + 4I + 2\sqrt{I \cdot 4I} = 9I$$

Minimum intensity,

$$I_{min} = (\sqrt{I_1} - \sqrt{I_2})^2$$
$$= I_1 + I_2 - 2\sqrt{I_1 I_2}$$
$$= I + 4I - 2\sqrt{I \cdot 4I} = I$$

52. *(b)* According to given figure, the graph between stopping potential and frequency is a straight line, therefore stopping potential (V_0) and hence maximum kinetic energy ($K_{max} = eV_0$) of photoelectrons depends linearly on the frequency. Since, threshold frequency for Na is less than that of for Al, therefore work function for Na will be lesser than that of Al. Hence, Na is better photosensitive material than Al.

53. *(b)* Here, for hydrogen atom, Z = 1

We know that, time period of electron in nth orbit is given as

$$T_n \propto n^3$$

$$\therefore \quad \frac{T_{n_1}}{T_{n_2}} = \frac{n_1^3}{n_2^3}$$

Since, $T_{n_1} = 8T_{n_2}$

$$\therefore \quad \frac{8T_{n_2}}{T_{n_2}} = \frac{n_1^3}{n_2^3} \Rightarrow 2^3 = \left(\frac{n_1}{n_2}\right)^3$$

$$\Rightarrow \quad n_1 = 2n_2$$

Hence, this condition satisfies only in option (b).

i.e., $n_1 = 4$ and $n_2 = 2$

54. *(b)* When forward voltage in a diode is increased, then it opposes the potential barrier. Due to it, the potential barrier is considerably reduced and hence depletion region decreases.

55. *(b)* Since, nuclear force is independent of charge of the nucleons. Thus, nuclear force is same for any pair of two nucleons which are at same distance apart.

Therefore, $F_1 = F_2 = F_3$

56. *(d)* Given, initial value of de-Broglie wavelength,

$$\lambda_1 = 1 \text{ nm} = 1 \times 10^{-9} \text{ m}$$

Final value of de-Broglie wavelength,

$$\lambda_2 = 0.5 \text{ nm} = 0.5 \times 10^{-9} \text{m}$$

de-Broglie wavelength in terms of energy E is given as

$$\lambda = \frac{h}{\sqrt{2mE}}$$

$$\therefore \quad \lambda \propto \frac{1}{\sqrt{E}}$$

$$\Rightarrow \quad \frac{\lambda_1}{\lambda_2} = \sqrt{\frac{E_2}{E_1}}$$

where, E_1 and E_2 are initial and final energy,

$$\Rightarrow \quad \frac{1\times 10^{-9}}{0.5\times 10^{-9}} = \sqrt{\frac{E_2}{E_1}}$$

$$\Rightarrow \quad 2 = \sqrt{\frac{E_2}{E_1}}$$

$$\Rightarrow \quad E_2 = 4E_1$$

$\therefore$ Addition of energy $= E_2 - E_1 = 4E_1 - E_1 = 3E_1$
$=$ thrice the initial energy

57. *(d)* Given, mean life of radioactive sample,

$$\tau = 100 \text{ s} = \frac{100}{60} \text{ min} = \frac{5}{3} \text{ min}$$

We know that,

$$\tau = 1.44 T_{1/2}$$

$$\Rightarrow \quad T_{1/2} = \frac{\tau}{1.44} = \frac{5/3}{1.44} = \frac{5}{3\times 1.44} = 1.157 \text{ min}$$
$$\simeq 1.155 \text{ min}$$

58. *(d)* The decay's constant (λ) and half-life period of radioactive nuclei remains constant and independent of time of creation of radioactive nuclei.

Hence, the probability of decay during the next time is independent of the time of creation.

59. *(d)* Bohr assumed one of the postulates of Rutherford's atomic model. That is the mass of the nucleus is very large compared to that of the electrons and hence assumed to be infinite. Electrons in quantised orbit does not radiate energy. Mass of electron remains constant.

60. *(a)* A semiconductor acts like an insulator only at absolute temperature i.e. 0°K. It is because the free electrons in the valence band of semiconductor will not carry enough thermal energy to overcome the forbidden energy gap at absolute zero.

Hence, option (a) is not correct.

Chemistry

61. *(b)* The correct order in which first ionisation potential (IP) increases is K, Na, Be. On going down the group IP decreases while on going left to right IP increases.

62. *(c)* $V_1 = 10 \text{ cm}^3$

$V_2 = 15 \text{ cm}^3$

$N_1 = 0.1 \text{ N}$

$N_2 = ?$

$N_1V_1 = N_2V_2$

$$N_2 = \frac{0.1\times 10}{15} = 0.066 \text{ N}$$

63. *(d)* Tertiary butyl iodide is

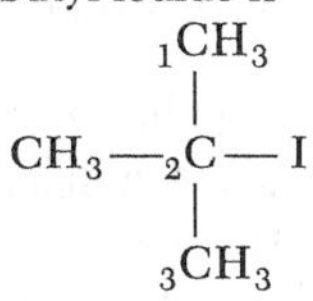

It's IUPAC name is 2-iodo-2-methyl propane.

64. *(c)* $3SO_2 + K_2Cr_2O_7 + H_2SO_4 \longrightarrow K_2SO_4 + Cr_2(SO_4)_3 + H_2O$

O.N. of S in SO_2 is

$x + 2(-2) = 0$

$\Rightarrow \quad x = +4$

O.N. of S in K_2SO_4 is

$2(1) + x + 2(-4) = 0$

$x = +6$

$\therefore$ O.N. changes from + 4 to + 6.

65. *(c)* Mass of 0.1 mole of methane = molar mass × no. of moles
$= 16 \times 0.1 = 1.6$ g

66. *(c)* Methoxy methane and ethanol are functional group isomer as one is ether and other is alcohol group.

CH_3—O—CH_3	CH_3—CH_2—OH
Functional group = ether	Functional group = alcohol
(Methoxy methane)	(Ethanol)

67. *(b)* The azimuthal quantum number has the value of 2 (i.e., $l = 2$) or (d-orbital).

$\therefore$ Magnetic quantum number (m) can be $= 2l + 1$
$= 2\times 2 + 1 = 5$

68. *(c)* For the following reaction,

$$\underset{\substack{\text{Ferric oxide}\\ \text{1 mole}}}{Fe_2O_3} + \underset{\substack{\text{Carbon monoxide}\\ \text{3 moles}}}{3CO} \longrightarrow \underset{\text{Iron}}{2Fe} + \underset{\text{Carbondioxide}}{3CO_2}$$

The volume of carbon monoxide require to reduce one mole of ferric oxide is

$$= 3\times 22.4 \text{ dm}^3 = 67.2 \text{ dm}^3$$

$\therefore$ Volume of CO required is 67.2 dm^3.

69. *(c)* The monomers of Buna-S rubber are styrene and butadiene.

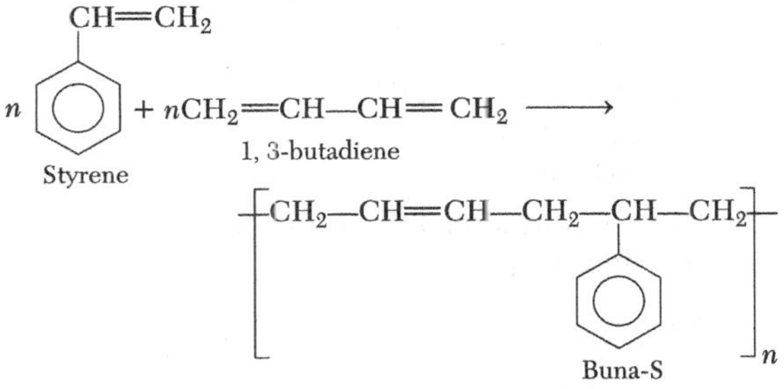

70. *(c)* Electronic configuration of element (21) is

$$1s^2 2s^2 2p^6 3s^2 3p^6 4s^2 3d^1$$

$\therefore$ It is a transition element as its last electron enters in d-orbital.

71. *(d)* The maximum number of hydrogen bonds that a molecule can have is 4.

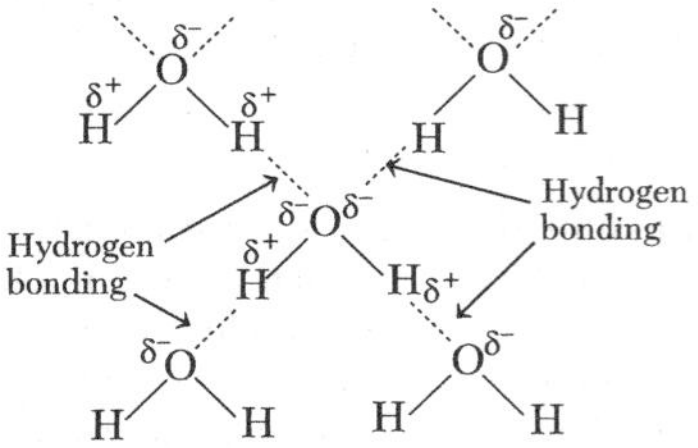

72. *(a)* A gas deviates from ideal behaviour at high pressure because its molecules attract one another as their intermolecular distance decreases.

73. *(d)* The reagent used to convert alkyne to alkene is Pd/H_2.

$$\underset{\text{Ethyne}}{CH\equiv CH} \xrightarrow[\text{Lindlar's catalyst}]{H_2/Pd} \underset{\text{Ethene}}{CH_2=CH_2}$$

74. *(b)* ΔG° for the formation of Al_2O_3 is higher than ΔG° for the formation of Cr_2O_3.

75. *(c)* According to ideal gas equation

$$pV = nRT$$

$$\therefore \quad V \propto \frac{1}{p}$$

$\therefore$ To increase the volume of gas by 10%, the pressure of gas should be decrease by 10%.

76. *(b)* Catalytic dehydration of a primary alcohol gives aldehyde i.e.,

$$\underset{\text{Primary alcohol}}{R—CH_2—OH} \xrightarrow[-H_2]{Cu,\ 300^\circ C} \underset{\text{Aldehyde}}{R—CHO}$$

77. *(b)* Excess of PCl_5 reacts with conc. H_2SO_4 to gives thionyl chloride (SO_2Cl_2), phosphorus oxychloride $(POCl_3)$ and HCl.

$$H_2SO_4 + 2PCl_5 \longrightarrow SO_2Cl_2 + 2POCl_3 + 2HCl$$

78. *(c)*
$$\underset{\text{Ammonical}}{NH_3(g)} + \underset{\text{Hydrogen chloride}}{HCl\,(g)} \longrightarrow \underset{\text{Ammonium chloride}}{NH_4Cl\,(g)}$$

$$\Delta n_g = n_P - n_R = 1 - 2 = -1$$

Also, $\Delta H = \Delta U + \Delta n_g RT$

$\therefore \quad \Delta H - \Delta U = -\text{ve} \qquad [\ \Delta n_g = -\text{ve}]$

$\therefore \quad \Delta H < \Delta U$

79. *(b)* Secondary alcohols gives ketones on dehydrogenation e.g.,

$$\underset{\text{Secondary alcohol}}{CH_3—\underset{\underset{OH}{|}}{CH}—CH_3} \xrightarrow[-H_2]{Cu/300^\circ C} \underset{\text{Ketone}}{CH_3—\underset{\underset{O}{||}}{C}—CH_3}$$

80. *(a)* Xenon has largest size and thus has high van der Waals' force of attraction. So, it is easily liquefiable rare gas.

81. *(a)* Mesomeric effect involves delocalisation of π-electrons. It can show + *M*-effect and –*M*-effect. The electron donating functional group shows + *M*-effect while electron withdrawing functional group shows –*M*-effect.

82. *(b)* The electronic configuration of

$Fe(26) = 1s^2 2s^2 2p^6 3s^2 3p^6 3d^6 4s^2$

$Fe^{2+} = 1s^2 2s^2 2p^6 3s^2 3p^6 3d^6 4s^0$

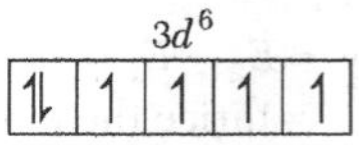

It has four unpaired electrons.

83. *(b)* The order of entropy is

$$S_{gas} > S_{liq} > S_{gas}$$

$\therefore$ One mole of hydrogen gas has the highest entropy.

84. *(b)* $C_6H_5\overset{+}{N}H_3$ does not exert a resonance effect because all the electron pairs of nitrogen are involved in bond formation.

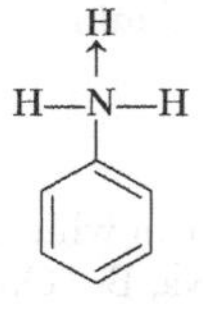

Hence, no lone pair is present on nitrogen for resonance.

85. *(c)* The oxidation number of Ni metal is zero in complex $Ni(CO)_4$. As CO is a neutral ligand i.e.,
$\Rightarrow Ni(CO)_4$

$$x + 4(0) = 0$$
$$x = 0$$

86. *(d)*

	PCl_3	+ Cl_2 ⇌	PCl_5
Initially	3 moles	2 moles	3 moles
At equilibrium	(3 + 1.5) moles		1.5 moles

$\therefore$ At equilibrium 1.5 moles of PCl_5 is converted into 4.5 moles of PCl_3.

$\therefore$ Total moles of PCl_3 at equilibrium is 4.5.

87. *(b)* The structure of butane-2, 3-diol is

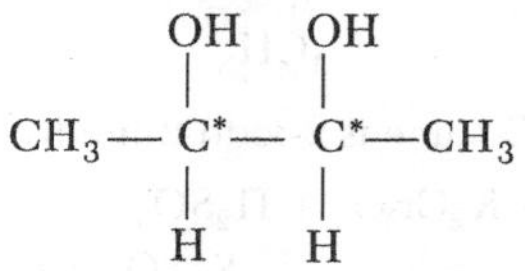

$\therefore$ It has three stereoisomers as follows:

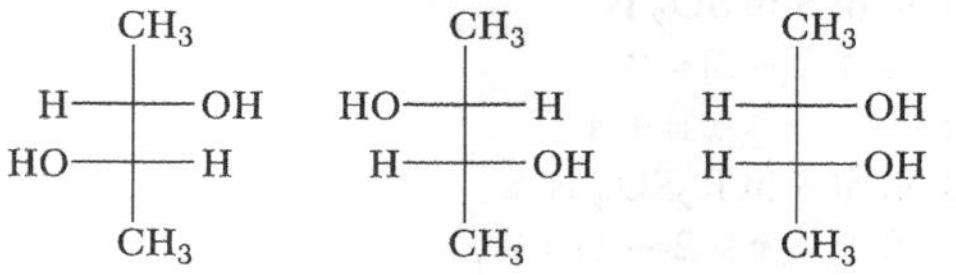

Optically active   *Meso* compound (optically inactive)

$\therefore$ It has two optically active isomers.

88. *(c)* An octahedral complex is formed when hybrid orbital of sp^3d^2 (outer orbital) or d^2sp^3 (inner orbital) types are involved.

89. *(a)* For the following reaction,

$$2HI(g) \rightleftharpoons H_2(g) + I_2(g);\ -Q\text{kJ}$$

$$\Delta n = (n_P)_g - (n_R)_g = (1 + 1) - 2 = 0$$

∴ Equilibrium constant (K_C) is independent of pressure and volume.

Heat is given in the reaction ($\Delta H = +$ ve)

∴According to Le-Chatelier's principle, on increasing temperature equilibrium shifts towards left hence, K_C decreases.

Catalyst only speeds up the reaction i.e., it help to achieves equilibrium faster without effecting the equilibrium point.

90. *(d)* The sp^3 hybridised carbon atom have bond angle of 109°28′ (tetrahedral angle). But in cyclobutane the bond angle is 90° due to square shape. Therefore,

$$\text{angle strain} = \frac{1}{2}(109°28' - 90°) = 9°44'$$

91. *(a)* The number of nodal planes in $\sigma^* s$-antibonding orbital is one. The σ^* orbital has nodal plane between nuclei and perpendicular to internuclear axis. As most of electron density is located away from the space between the nuclei, as a result of which there is a nodal plane between the nuclei.

92. *(d)* Specific conductance is least for 0.002 N electrolytic solution as it has least number of ions per unit volume of solution.

Specific conductance ∝ concentration of electrolyte.

93. *(c)* In benzene, the hybridisation of each carbon atom is sp^2.

∴ The overlapping in benzene is of sp^2-sp^2 type.

94. *(c)* The electronic configuration of O_2^- is

$$\sigma 1s^2 \sigma^* 1s^2 \sigma 2s^2 \sigma^* 2s^2 \sigma 2p_z^2 (\pi 2p_x^2 = \pi 2p_y^2)$$
$$(\pi^* 2p_x^2 = \pi^* 2p_y^1)$$

$$\therefore \text{Bond order} = \frac{10-7}{2} = 1.5$$

95. *(a)* Ostwald-Walker's method is used to measure the relative lowering in vapour pressure of the solution.

96. *(b)* n-propyl bromide on treating with alcoholic KOH undergoes elimination reaction to produce propene i.e.,

$$\underset{n\text{-propyl bromide}}{CH_3{-}CH_2{-}CH_2{-}Br} \xrightarrow{\text{Alc. KOH}} \underset{\text{Propene}}{CH_3{-}CH{=}CH_2} + HBr$$

97. *(a)* Mercury is a liquid metal because it has completely filled 6s-orbital. The inner f-orbital poorly screens nuclear charge that stabilise 6s-orbital. Thus, it is not possible to form any bond with other elements.

98. *(a)* A occupies corner of unit cell.

$$\therefore \text{Number of } A \text{ atoms} = 8 \times \frac{1}{8} = 1$$

B is at body centre.

∴Number of B atoms $= 1 \times 1 = 1$

The simplest formula of compound

$$A : B$$
$$1 : 1 = AB$$

99. *(b)* Anisole can be prepared by action of methyl iodide on sodium phenate. The reaction is called Williamson's reaction. It is used for preparation of simple or mixed ether.

$$C_6H_5OH + NaOH \xrightarrow[-H_2O]{} \underset{\text{Sodium phenoxide}}{C_6H_5ONa} \xrightarrow{CH_3I} \underset{\substack{\text{Anisole}\\ \text{(Ether)}}}{C_6H_5{-}O{-}CH_3}$$

100. *(c)* Malleability and ductility of metals can be accounted due to capacity of layers of metal ions to slide over the other.

101. *(b)* For tetrahedral structure radius range is 0.225 to 0.414.

102. *(b)* Acidic character of organic compound increases with increase in strength of electron withdrawing group and decreases with electron releasing group.

In o-cresol, methyl group show + I-effect. It increase the density of electron on oxygen atom after the release of H^+ ion. Hence, it decrease the acidic strength.

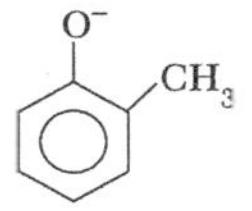

Stability decreases

103. *(c)* A ligand is an atom or group of atom which donates lone pair of electron to central metal ions in coordination compound. Also, Lewis base is the substance that donates a pair of electron. Hence, ligand can also be regarded as Lewis base.

104. *(b)* The colour of sky is due to wavelength of scattered light. This scattering of light take place by particles of much small size.

105. *(c)* Iodoform test is given by compounds having $\left(CH_3{-}\underset{\underset{O}{\|}}{C}{-}\right)$ functional group.

Acetaldehyde $\left(H{-}\underset{\underset{O}{\|}}{C}{-}CH_3\right)$, also contains this group.

It also gives Fehling's test as all aldehydes (—CHO) give Fehling's test.

∴Ethanal gives both the tests.

106. *(a)* Helium is used in balloons in place of hydrogen, because it is incombustible and inert in nature.

107. *(c)* The basic principle of Cottnell's precipitator is neutralisation of charge on colloidal particle by attracting them towards the wall of oppositively charged precipitator.

Thus, lose their charge and coagulate colloidal particle.

108. *(c)* When, carbon mono-oxide is passed over solid caustic soda heated to 200°C, it forms sodium formate.

$$\underset{\text{Carbon monoxide}}{CO} + \underset{\text{Caustic soda}}{NaOH} \longrightarrow \underset{\text{Sodium formate}}{HCOONa}$$

109. *(a)* The given reaction, $N_2 + 3H_2 \rightleftharpoons 2NH_3 + \text{Heat}$, is an exothermic reaction.

$\therefore$ According to Le-Chatelier's principle, on increase in temperature equilibrium is shifted to the left.

110. *(a)* The order of reactivity of given elements is

$$Ag < H < Zn < Sn < Mg$$

As, Ag is less reactive than hydrogen, it cannot replace hydrogen from HCl and H_2 gas is not liberated.

111. *(a)* The ionic compound formed is $M^+X^-(s)$ as the gaseous ions $[M^+(g)$ and $Cl^-(g)]$ combines in the crystal lattice which is in solid state.

112. *(d)* The brown ring is due to the formation of a brown complex between nitric oxide and Fe^{2+} ions.

$$NO_3^- + 3Fe^{2+} + 4H^+ \longrightarrow 3Fe^{3+} + NO + 2H_2O$$

or $$2HNO_3 + 2H_2SO_4 + 6FeSO_4 \longrightarrow \underset{\text{Brown colour complex or nitrosoferrous sulphate}}{[Fe(H_2O)_5NO]SO_4} + H_2O$$

113. *(b)* Amines behaves as Lewis base as if donates it lone pairs in the chemical reaction.

114. *(b)* Oils reacts with hydrogen in presence of metal catalyst to give saturated glycerides. Thus, vegetable ghee (Dalda) is obtained by hydrogenation (reduction) of oils.

115. *(b)* Anisole is 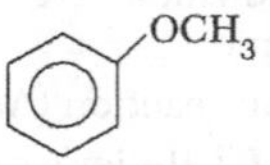

Its chemical name is methoxy benzene.

116. *(c)* The number of disulphide linkages present in insulin are three. Two linkages are between two polypeptide chains containing 21 and 30 amino acid residues. In addition, the smaller polypeptide chain (21 amino acids) has also an internal disulphide linkage.

117. *(d)* Number of atoms $= \dfrac{\text{mass}}{\text{molecular mass}} \times N_A$

Number of atoms is oxygen = product of atoms in hydrogen

$$\frac{80}{16} \times N_A = \frac{W}{1} \times N_A$$

$$\therefore \quad W = \frac{80}{16} = 5 \text{ g of hydrogen}$$

118. *(d)* Greater the stability of oxide, greater is the chance of its formation. Generally, ionic oxide are more stable, than covalent oxides and among the given metals only Ca form ionic oxide. Hence, Ca has greater tendency to form oxide.

119. *(c)* The reaction, $2Fe_2O_3 + 3C \longrightarrow 4Fe + 3CO_2$, do not occur in blast furnance. This reaction occurs at the end of the process.

120. *(d)* Wax is an ester of fatty acid and an alcohol. They are formed by combining one fatty acid with one fatty alcohol molecule.

$$\underset{\text{Fatty acid}}{RCOOH} + \underset{\text{Alcohol}}{R'OH} \longrightarrow \underset{\text{Wax (ester)}}{RCOOR'} + H_2O$$

Mathematics

121. *(b)* : Let $f(x) = x^2 + \sin^2 x$, then $f(-x) = f(x)$

Therefore, $f(x) = x^2 + \sin^2 x$ is an even functions.

122. *(a)* Here, $A = \{x : x^2 - x + 2 > 0\} = R$

$$\left(\because x^2 - x + 2 = x^2 - x + \frac{1}{4} + \frac{7}{4} = \left(x - \frac{1}{2}\right)^2 + \frac{7}{4} \geq \frac{7}{4}\right)$$

and $B = \{x : x^2 - 4x + 3 \leq 0\}$

$= \{x : (x-1)(x-3) \leq 0) = [1, 3]$

Hence, $A \cap B = R \cap [1, 3] = [1, 3]$

123. *(d)* : $b \in A$ is said to be an inverse of a w.r.t. operation $*$ if $a * b = b * a = e$. [by definition]

124. *(a)* Given, $\angle C = \dfrac{\pi}{2} \Rightarrow c^2 = a^2 + b^2$ {by pythagoras}

Now, $\tan^{-1}\left(\dfrac{a}{b+c}\right) + \tan^{-1}\left(\dfrac{b}{c+a}\right)$

$$= \tan^{-1}\left[\frac{\dfrac{a}{b+c} + \dfrac{b}{c+a}}{1 - \left(\dfrac{a}{b+c}\right)\left(\dfrac{b}{c+a}\right)}\right]$$

$$= \tan^{-1}\left(\frac{ac + a^2 + b^2 + bc}{bc + ba + c^2 + ca - ab}\right)$$

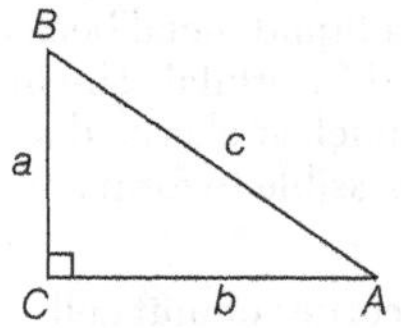

$$= \tan^{-1}\left(\frac{ac + c^2 + bc}{bc + c^2 + ca}\right)$$

$$= \tan^{-1}(1) = \frac{\pi}{4}$$

125. *(d)* $\frac{\cos\alpha}{1}=\frac{a}{b+c} \Rightarrow \frac{1}{\cos\alpha}=\frac{b+c}{a}$

By componendo and dividendo,we have

$$\frac{1-\cos\alpha}{1+\cos\alpha}=\frac{b+c-a}{b+c+a}$$

$$\Rightarrow \quad \tan^2\frac{\alpha}{2}=\frac{b+c-a}{3b} \quad \left\{\begin{array}{l}\because a, b, c \text{ are in A.P.}\\ \Rightarrow 2b=a+c\end{array}\right\}$$

$$\Rightarrow \quad \frac{1-\cos\gamma}{1+\cos\gamma}=\frac{a+b-c}{a+b-c}$$

$$\Rightarrow \quad \tan^2\frac{\gamma}{2}=\frac{a+b-c}{3b}$$

$$\therefore \quad \tan^2\frac{\alpha}{2}+\tan^2\frac{\gamma}{2}=\frac{2b}{3b}=\frac{2}{3}$$

126. *(c)* $\cos(35°+A)\cos(35°-B)$

$+\sin(35°+A)\sin(35°-B)$

$=\cos[(35°+A)-(35°-B)]$

$=\cos(A+B)$

127. *(b)* $2\operatorname{cosec} 2x+\operatorname{cosec} x$

$$=\frac{2}{\sin 2x}+\frac{1}{\sin x}=\frac{2}{2\sin x\cdot\cos x}+\frac{1}{\sin x}$$

$$=\frac{1}{\sin x}\left[\frac{1}{\cos x}+1\right]=\frac{1}{\sin x}\cdot\frac{(1+\cos x)}{\cos x}$$

$$=\frac{1}{\cos x}\cdot\frac{2\cos^2(x/2)}{2\cdot\sin(x/2)\cdot\cos(x/2)}$$

$$=\sec x.\frac{\cos(x/2)}{\sin(x/2)} \quad \left[\begin{array}{l}\because \cos 2x=2\cos^2 x-1\\ \sin 2x=2\sin x\cos x\end{array}\right]$$

$=\sec x\cdot\cot(x/2)$

128. *(d)* We have, $\cot 3x=\cot(2x+x)$

$$\Rightarrow \cot 3x=\frac{\cot 2x\cot x-1}{\cot 2x+\cot x}$$

$$\left\{\cot(A+B)=\frac{\cot A\cot B-1}{\cot A+\cot B}\right\}$$

$\Rightarrow \cot 3x\cot 2x+\cot 3x\cot x=\cot 2x\cot x-1$

$\Rightarrow \cot 2x\cot x-\cot 3x\cot 2x-\cot 3x\cot x=1$

129. *(a)* We have $\cos A\cos B-\sin A\sin B$

$$=\cos(A+B)=\cos\left[\left(\frac{\pi}{4}-x\right)+\left(\frac{\pi}{4}-y\right)\right]$$

where, $A=\frac{\pi}{4}-x$ and $B=\frac{\pi}{4}-y$

$$=\cos\left[\frac{\pi}{2}-(x+y)\right]=\sin(x+y)$$

130. *(d)* Let $P(n)=2\cdot4^{2n+1}+3^{3n+1}$

$P(1)\equiv128+81=209$, which is divisible by 11 only.

131. *(c)* $P(1)$: '$1\times1!=(1+1)!-1$' is true.

Let $P(k)$: "$1\times1!+2\times2!+3\times3!$
$+\ldots+k\times k!=(k+1)!-1$" is true.

Now, $P(k+1):1\times1!+2\times2!+\ldots$
$+k+k!+(k+1)\times(k+1)!$

$=(k+1)!-1+(k-1)(k+1)!$

$=(k+1)!+(k+1)\times(k+1)!-1$

$=(k+1)!(1+k+1)-1=(k+2)!-1$

i.e., $P(k)$ is true $\Rightarrow P(k+1)$ is true

132. *(d)* We have,

$z=re^{i\theta}=r(\cos\theta+i\sin\theta)$

$\therefore \; iz=ir(\cos\theta+i\sin\theta)$

$=ir\cos\theta+i^2r\sin\theta=-r\sin\theta+ir\cos\theta$

$|e^{iz}|=|e^{(-r\sin\theta+ir\cos\theta)}|$

$=|e^{-r\sin\theta}|.|ir\cos\theta|$

$$=e^{-r\sin\theta}\left[\sqrt{\cos^2(r\cos\theta)+\sin^2(r\cos\theta)}\right]$$

$=e^{-r\sin\theta}\times1=e^{-r\sin\theta}$

133. *(b)* We have, $(\sqrt{5}+\sqrt{3}i)^{33}=2^{49}z$

Taking modulus on both sides, we get

$2^{49}|z|=|\sqrt{5}+\sqrt{3}i)^{33}$

$\Rightarrow 2^{49}|z|=(\sqrt{5+3})^{33}=(\sqrt{8})^{33}=2^{33}2^{33/2}$

$$\Rightarrow \quad |z|=\frac{2^{33}2^{33/2}}{2^{49}}=2^{\frac{33}{2}-16}=2^{1/2}=\sqrt{2}$$

134. *(c)* $$\left|\frac{1}{1-\cos\theta+i\sin\theta}\right|=\frac{1}{|1-\cos\theta-i\sin\theta|}$$

$$=\frac{1}{\sqrt{(1-\cos\theta)^2+\sin^2\theta}}=\frac{1}{\sqrt{2-2\cos\theta}}$$

$$=\frac{1}{2|\sin(\theta/2)|}=\frac{1}{2}\left|\operatorname{cosec}\frac{\theta}{2}\right|$$

135. *(d)* We have, $a+b\omega+c\omega^2=0$

$$\Rightarrow \; a+b\left(-\frac{1}{2}+\frac{i\sqrt{3}}{2}\right)+c\left(-\frac{1}{2}-\frac{i\sqrt{3}}{2}\right)=0$$

$$\Rightarrow \; \left(a-\frac{b}{2}-\frac{c}{2}\right)+i\left(\frac{\sqrt{3}b}{2}-\frac{\sqrt{3}c}{2}\right)=0+0i$$

Real part $\Rightarrow a=\frac{b+c}{2}$.

Imaginary parts $\Rightarrow b=c$

$\therefore \quad a=b=c$

136. *(d)* We have,

$(x-1)^3=-8=(-2)^3$

$\therefore \quad x-1=-2,-2\omega,-2\omega^2$

$\Rightarrow \quad x=-1,1-2\omega,1-2\omega^2$

137. *(d)* We have, $a^3x^2+abcx+c^3=0$

$$\Rightarrow \; x^2+\frac{b}{a}.\frac{c}{a}x+\left(\frac{c}{a}\right)^3=0$$

$\Rightarrow \; x^2-(\alpha+\beta)\,\alpha\beta x+\alpha^3\beta^3=0$

$\Rightarrow \; x=\alpha^2\beta,\ \alpha\beta^2 \Rightarrow \alpha^2\beta$ is one of the root.

138. *(a)* There are $4! = 24$ numbers. Each digit occurring $3! = 6$ times, in the unit's, ten's, hundred's and thousand's places. We note that $(2+4+6+8) = 120$. Thus in the over all sum there will be 120 units, 120 tens, 120 hundreds and 120 thousands.

The required sum

$$= 120(1 + 10 + 10^2 + 10^3)$$
$$= 120 \times 1111 = 133320$$

139. *(d)* Total number of discs are $4 + 3 + 2 = 9$.

Out of 9 discs, 4 are of the first kind (red) 3 are of the second kind (yellow) and 2 are of the third kind (green).

Therefore, the number of arrangements

$$= \frac{9!}{4!3!2!} = 1260$$

140. *(a)* There are 12 face cards and 4 are to be selected, out of these 12 cards. This can be done in ${}^{12}C_4$ ways.

Therefore, the required number of $= \frac{12!}{4!8!} = 495$

141. *(a)* $\binom{2n}{3r-1} = \binom{2n}{r+1}$

$$\left\{\begin{matrix} {}^nC_x = {}^nC_y \Rightarrow x + y = n \\ \text{or } n - x = y \end{matrix}\right\}$$

$\Rightarrow \quad 2n = 3r - 1 + r + 1 \Rightarrow n = 2r$

142. *(d)* H.M. $= \frac{2ab}{a+b}$; G.M. $= \sqrt{ab}$,

Now, $\quad \frac{\text{H.M.}}{\text{G.M.}} = \frac{2\sqrt{ab}}{a+b} = \frac{4}{5}$

$\Rightarrow \quad 25ab = 4(a+b)^2$

$\Rightarrow \quad 4a^2 - 17ab + 4b^2 = 0$

$\Rightarrow \quad (4a - b)(a - 4b) = 0$

$\Rightarrow \quad 4a = b \Rightarrow a : b = 1 : 4$

143. *(a)* Let the numbers be a, ar, ar^2, ar^3.

$\Rightarrow \quad a - 2, ar - 7, ar^2 - 9$ are in A.P.

$\Rightarrow \quad a - 2 + ar^2 - 9 = 2(ar - 7)$

$\Rightarrow \quad a(r^2 + 1) - 11 = 2ar - 14$

$\Rightarrow \quad r^2 + 1 = 2r - \frac{3}{a} \quad \ldots \text{(i)}$

Further, $ar - 7 + ar^3 - 5 = 2(ar^2 - 9)$

$\Rightarrow \quad ar(r^2 + 1) - 12 = 2ar^2 - 18$

$\Rightarrow \quad r^2 + 1 = 2r - \frac{6}{ar} \quad \ldots \text{(ii)}$

Solving Eqs. (i) and (ii), we get $r = 2, a = -3$

The number are $-3, -6 -12, -24$

144. *(c)* nth term $= \frac{n}{(2n+1)!}$

$$= \frac{1}{2}\left[\frac{(2n+1)-1}{(2n+1)!}\right] = \frac{1}{2}\left[\frac{1}{(2n)!} - \frac{1}{(2n+1)!}\right]$$

$\therefore$ Sum of the series

$$= \frac{1}{2}\left[\frac{1}{2!} - \frac{1}{3!} + \frac{1}{4!} - \frac{1}{5!} + \frac{1}{6!} - \frac{1}{7!} + \ldots\right]$$
$$= \frac{1}{2}e^{-1} = \frac{1}{2e}$$

145. *(b)* Let m be the slope of PQ.

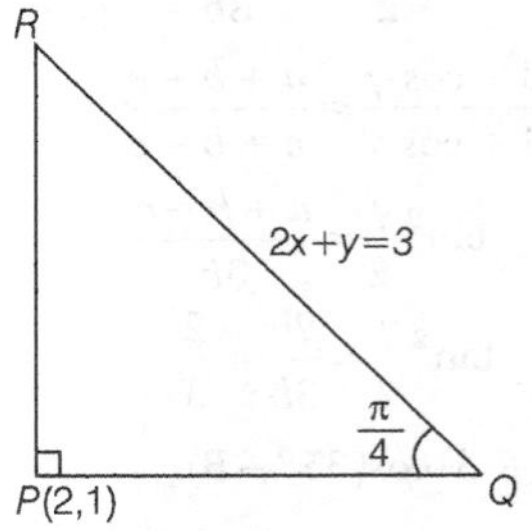

Slope of QR is -2.

$$\left|\frac{m+2}{1-2m}\right| = \tan\frac{\pi}{4} = 1$$

$\Rightarrow \quad m + 2 = \pm(1 - 2m) \Rightarrow m = 3, -\frac{1}{3}$

The lines PQ and PR are $\frac{y-1}{x-2} = 3, -\frac{1}{3}$

The combined equation is

$(3x - y - 5)(x + 3y - 5) = 0$

or $\quad 3x^2 - 3y^2 + 8xy - 20x - 10y + 25 = 0$

146. *(a)* The vertices are $(2, -1), (6, -1), (2, 1)$ forming a right angled triangle. Circumcentre is the mid-point of the hypotenuse,

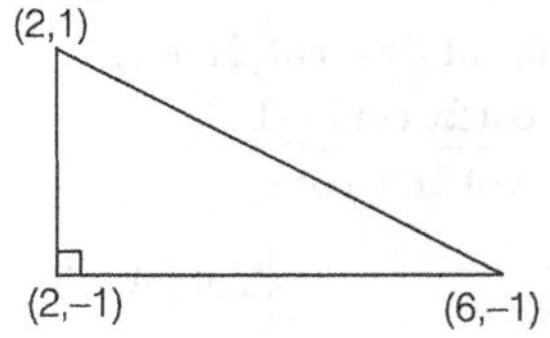

i.e., $\quad \left(\frac{6+2}{2}, \frac{1-1}{2}\right) = (4, 0)$

147. *(c)* We have, $a = 3, b = 4$ and

$$c = \sqrt{a^2 + b^2} = \sqrt{9 + 16} = 5$$

Therefore, the coordinates of the foci are $(\pm 5, 0)$.

Also, length of latusrectum $= \frac{2b^2}{a} = \frac{32}{3}$

148. *(c)* The line $21x + 5y = 116$ is a tangent to $7x^2 - 5y^2 = 232$. If $P(x_1, y_1)$ is the point of contact, then $S_1 = 0$.

$\Rightarrow 7x_1x - 5y_1y = 232$. It is same as $21x + 5y = 116$

$\therefore \quad \frac{7x_1}{21} = -\frac{5y_1}{5} = \frac{232}{116} = 2$

$\therefore \quad x_1 = 6, y_1 = -2$. So, P is $(6, -2)$.

149. *(a)* Let $P(x_1, y_1)$ be the mid-point of a chord of $x^2 + y^2 = r^2$.

Its equation is

$$S_1 = S_{11} \Rightarrow x_1 x + y_1 y = x_1^2 + y_1^2$$

or $y = \left(-\dfrac{x_1}{y_1}\right)x + \dfrac{x_1^2 + y_1^2}{y_1}$

The line $y = mx + c$ is a tangent to the hyperbola only if

$$c^2 = a^2m^2 - b^2$$

$\therefore \quad \dfrac{(x_1^2 + y_1^2)^2}{y_1^2} = \dfrac{a^2 x_1^2}{y_1^2} - b^2$

$\therefore$ The locus of P is

$$(x^2 + y^2)^2 = a^2x^2 - b^2y^2$$

150. *(b)* $\tan\dfrac{\pi}{4} = \dfrac{LS}{S_1S}$

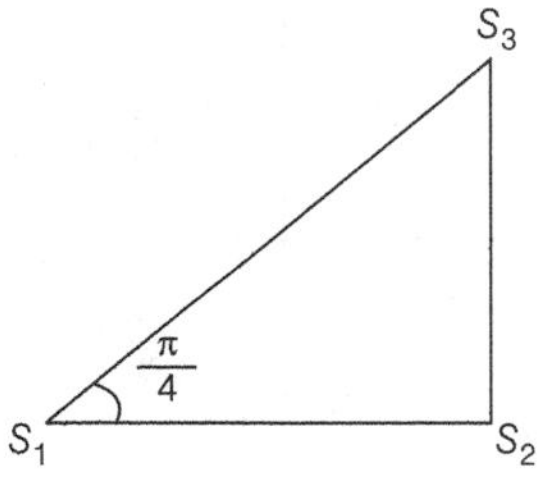

$$= \frac{a(e^2 - 1)}{2ae}$$

$\Rightarrow \quad 1 = \dfrac{e^2 - 1}{2e}$

$\Rightarrow \quad e^2 - 2e - 1 = 0$

Solving, $\quad e = \sqrt{2} + 1$

151. *(a)* Tangent with slope m is

$$y = mx \pm \sqrt{a^2m^2 - b^2}$$

It passes through (0, 1).

$\therefore \quad 1 = \sqrt{\dfrac{m^2}{2} - 1} \qquad \left[\text{Since, } a^2 = \dfrac{1}{2}, b^2 = 1\right]$

$\Rightarrow \quad 1 = \dfrac{m^2}{2} - 1$

$\Rightarrow \quad m = \pm 2$

$\Rightarrow \quad \tan\theta = \left|\dfrac{2-(-2)}{1-4}\right| = \dfrac{4}{3}$

152. *(b)* Let $P(3, 4, -1)$ and $Q(-1, 2, 3)$ be the end points of the diameter of a sphere.

$\therefore$ Length of diameter $= PQ$

$$= \sqrt{(-1-3)^2 + (2-4)^2 + (3+1)^2}$$

$$= \sqrt{16 + 4 + 16} = \sqrt{36} = 6 \text{ units}$$

$\therefore \quad$ Radius $= \dfrac{6}{2} = 3$ units

153. *(c)* Let $y = \cos^{-1}\left(\dfrac{1-x}{1+x}\right)$

Put $x = \tan^2\theta$

$\Rightarrow \theta = \tan^{-1}\sqrt{x}$

$\therefore \; y = \cos^{-1}\left(\dfrac{1 - \tan^2\theta}{1 + \tan^2\theta}\right)$

$$= \cos^{-1}(\cos 2\theta) = 2\theta = 2\tan^{-1}\sqrt{x}$$

$\therefore \quad \dfrac{dy}{dx} = 2\dfrac{d}{dx}(\tan^{-1}\sqrt{x})$

$$= 2 \times \frac{1}{1+x} \times \frac{1}{2\sqrt{x}} = \frac{1}{\sqrt{x}(1+x)}$$

154. *(b)* $f(x) = \left(\dfrac{5}{x} + 7\right)$

$\Rightarrow f'(x) = \dfrac{-5}{x^2} < 0$ for all

$x \in R$, where $x \neq 0$.

Hence, $f(x)$ is decreasing for $x \in R - \{0\}$.

155. *(a)* Let $f(x) = x^{1/4}$

$\Rightarrow \quad f'(x) = \dfrac{1}{4x^{3/4}}$

Now, $a + h = 15 = 16 - 1$, where

$a = 16, h = -1$

We know, $f(a + h) = f(a) + hf'(a)$

$\Rightarrow \; f(15) \approx f(16) - 1f'(16)$

$\Rightarrow (15)^{1/4} \approx (16)^{1/4} - \dfrac{1}{4(16)^{3/4}} \approx 2 - \dfrac{1}{32}$

$\Rightarrow (15)^{1/4} \approx 2 - 0.03125 \approx 1.9688$

156. *(d)* Let the required point be $P(x_1, y_1)$

The given curve is $y = x^2 \quad \ldots$ (i)

Differentiating Eq. (i) w.r.t. x, we get

$\dfrac{dy}{dx} = 2x \Rightarrow$ Slope of tangent at $P(x_1, y_1) = 2x$

But the slope of tangent at

$P(x_1, y_1) = x$-coordinate of P

$\Rightarrow \; 2x_1 = x_1 \Rightarrow 2x_1 - x_1 = 0$

$\Rightarrow \; x_1 = 0$

As $P(x_1, y_1)$ lies on the curve, we get

$y_1 = x_1^2 \Rightarrow y_1 = 0$

Hence, the required point is (0, 0).

157. *(d)* Given curve, $y = \dfrac{x^3}{4-x} \quad \ldots$(i)

is the given curve

Differentiating Eq. (i) w.r.t. x, we get

$$\frac{dy}{dx} = \frac{(4-x)(3x^2) - x^3(-1)}{(4-x)^2} = \frac{12x^2 - 2x^3}{(4-x)^2}$$

$\Rightarrow \left(\dfrac{dy}{dx}\right)_{x=2} = \dfrac{12(2)^2 - 2(2)^3}{(4-2)^2} = \dfrac{32}{4} = 8$

$\Rightarrow$ The slope of tangent at (2, 4) is 8.

$\therefore$ The equation of tangent is

$$y - 4 = 8(x - 2)$$

$$\Rightarrow \quad 8x - y - 12 = 0 \Rightarrow \text{slope} = \frac{-8}{-1} = 8$$

Now the slope of normal at $P(2, 4)$ is $\frac{-1}{8}$.

$\therefore$ The equation of normal is

$$y - 4 = \frac{-1}{8}(x - 2)$$

$$\Rightarrow \quad x + 8y - 34 = 0$$

158. *(d)* We have,

$$y = \log_a x + \frac{\log a}{\log x} + 1 + 1 \qquad [\because \log_x x = 1]$$

$$\Rightarrow \frac{dy}{dx} = \frac{1}{x}\log_a e - \log a\left(\frac{1}{\log x}\right)^2 \frac{1}{x} = \frac{1}{x \log a} - \frac{\log a}{x(\log x)^2}$$

159. *(c)* We have,

$$\int \frac{1}{\sin x + \sqrt{3}\cos x}\, dx = \frac{1}{2}\int \frac{dx}{\frac{1}{2}\sin x + \frac{\sqrt{3}}{2}\cos x}$$

$$= \frac{1}{2}\int \frac{1}{\sin\left(x + \frac{\pi}{3}\right)}\, dx = \frac{1}{2}\int \operatorname{cosec}\left(x + \frac{\pi}{3}\right) dx$$

$$= \frac{1}{2}\log\left|\tan\left(\frac{x}{2} + \frac{\pi}{6}\right)\right| + C$$

160. *(a)* $\int e^{2x}(2\sin 3x + 3\cos 3x)\, dx$

$$= 2\int e^{2x}\sin 3x\, dx + 3\int e^{2x}\cos 3x\, dx$$

$$= e^{2x}\sin 3x - 3\int e^{2x}\cos 3x\, dx + 3\int e^{2x}\cos 3x\, dx + C$$

$$= e^{2x}\sin 3x + C$$

161. *(a)* $\displaystyle\int_1^2 \frac{dx}{x^2} = \left[\left(\frac{-1}{x}\right)\right]_1^2 = \frac{1}{2}$

162. *(a)* We have,

$$I = \int_0^{\pi/2} \frac{\cos x}{\left(\cos\frac{x}{2} + \sin\frac{x}{2}\right)^3} dx = \int_0^{\pi/2} \frac{\cos^2\frac{x}{2} - \sin^2\frac{x}{2}}{\left(\cos\frac{x}{2} + \sin\frac{x}{2}\right)^3} dx$$

$$= \int_0^{\pi/2} \frac{\cos\frac{x}{2} - \sin\frac{x}{2}}{\left(\cos\frac{x}{2} + \sin\frac{x}{2}\right)^2} dx$$

Put $\cos\frac{x}{2} + \sin\frac{x}{2} = t$

$$\Rightarrow \frac{1}{2}\left(-\sin\frac{x}{2} + \cos\frac{x}{2}\right) dx = dt$$

Also, when $x = 0 \Rightarrow t = 1$

When $x = \frac{\pi}{2} \Rightarrow t = \sqrt{2}$

$$\therefore \quad I = \int_1^{\sqrt{2}} \frac{2dt}{t^2}$$

$$= 2\left[-\frac{1}{t}\right]_1^{\sqrt{2}} = 2\left[-\frac{1}{\sqrt{2}} + 1\right] = (2 - \sqrt{2})$$

163. *(b)* We have,

$x + y = 1 \ \forall\ x, y \geq 0$ ... (i)

$-x + y = 1 \ \forall\ x < 0, y \geq 0$ ... (ii)

$-x - y = 1 \ \forall\ x < 0, y < 0$ ... (iii)

$x - y = 1 \ \forall\ x \geq 0, y < 0$ ... (iv)

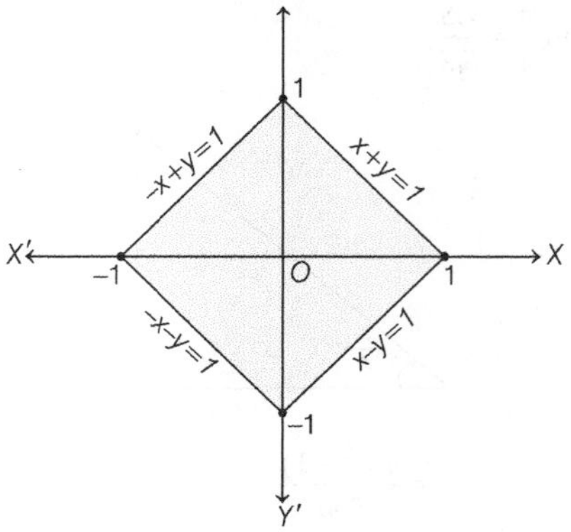

Required area is the area of shaded region

$$= 4\int_0^1 (1 - x)\, dx$$

$$= 4\left[x - \frac{x^2}{2}\right]_0^1 = 4 \times \frac{1}{2} = 2 \text{ sq. units}$$

164. *(c)* Let $I = \int \frac{dx}{\sqrt{x} + \sqrt[3]{x}}$

Put $x = t^6 \Rightarrow dx = 6t^5\, dt$

$$\therefore \quad I = \int \frac{6t^5}{t^3 + t^2}\, dt = 6\int \frac{t^3}{t+1}\, dt$$

$$= 6\int\left(t^2 - t + 1 - \frac{1}{t+1}\right) dt$$

$$= 2t^3 - 3t^2 + 6t - 6\log(t + 1) + C$$

$$= 2\sqrt{x} - 3(\sqrt[3]{x}) + 6(\sqrt[6]{x}) - 6\log(\sqrt[6]{x} + 1) + C$$

165. *(b)* $\displaystyle\int_a^b \frac{x^n}{x^n + (16 - x)^n}\, dx = 6$ ... (i)

Let $a + b = 16$, then

$$\int_a^b \frac{(16 - x)^n}{(16 - x)^n + x^n}\, dx = 6 \qquad \text{... (ii)}$$

Adding Eqs. (i) and (ii), we get

$$\int_a^b 1 \cdot dx = 12 \Rightarrow b - a = 12$$

Solving $a + b = 16$ and $b - a = 12$, we get

$$a = 2, b = 14, n \in R$$

166. *(a)* $f(x) = 1 + \cos 2x$ and

$$f(-x) = 1 + \cos(-2x) = 1 + \cos 2x = f(x)$$

$\Rightarrow \quad f(x) = f(-x)$

Hence, $f(x)$ is even function.

$$\Rightarrow \quad I = 2\int_0^{\pi/4} \frac{dx}{1 + \cos 2x}$$

$$= 2\int_0^{\pi/4} \frac{dx}{2\cos^2 x}$$

$$= 2\int_0^{\pi/4} \frac{1}{2}\sec^2 x \, dx$$

$$= [\tan x]_0^{\pi/4} = \left(\tan\frac{\pi}{4} - \tan 0\right) = 1$$

167. *(c)* We have, $y = ae^{bx + c}$ ... (i)

Differentiating Eq. (i) w.r.t. x, we get

$$y_1 = a(e^{bx + c})b = b(ae^{bx + c}) = by \quad \text{... (ii)}$$

Again differentiating Eq. (ii) w.r.t. x, we get

$$y_2 = by_1 \quad \text{...(ii)}$$

From Eq. (ii) and Eq. (i), we have

$$\Rightarrow \quad y \cdot y_2 = y_1^2$$

168. *(a)* Here, $\mathbf{a} + 3\mathbf{b} = \hat{\mathbf{i}} + \hat{\mathbf{j}} + 2\hat{\mathbf{k}} + 3(3\hat{\mathbf{i}} + 2\hat{\mathbf{j}} - \hat{\mathbf{k}})$

$$= 10\hat{\mathbf{i}} + 7\hat{\mathbf{j}} - \hat{\mathbf{k}}$$

and $2\mathbf{a} - \mathbf{b} = 2(\hat{\mathbf{i}} + \hat{\mathbf{j}} + 2\hat{\mathbf{k}}) - (3\hat{\mathbf{i}} + 2\hat{\mathbf{j}} - \hat{\mathbf{k}}) = -\hat{\mathbf{i}} + 5\hat{\mathbf{k}}$

$(\mathbf{a} + 3\mathbf{b}).(2\mathbf{a} - \mathbf{b}) = (10\hat{\mathbf{i}} + 7\hat{\mathbf{j}} - \hat{\mathbf{k}}).(-\hat{\mathbf{i}} + 5\hat{\mathbf{k}})$

$$= 10 \times (-1) + 7 \times 0 + -1 \times 5 = -15$$

169. *(a)* $[\mathbf{a} - \mathbf{b} \;\; \mathbf{b} - \mathbf{c} \;\; \mathbf{c} - \mathbf{a}] = (\mathbf{a} - \mathbf{b}) \cdot [(\mathbf{b} - \mathbf{c}) \times (\mathbf{c} - \mathbf{a})]$

$$= (\mathbf{a} - \mathbf{b}) \cdot [\mathbf{b} \times \mathbf{c} - \mathbf{b} \times \mathbf{a} - \mathbf{c} \times \mathbf{c} + \mathbf{c} \times \mathbf{a})]$$

$$= (\mathbf{a} - \mathbf{b}).[\mathbf{b} \times \mathbf{c} - \mathbf{b} \times \mathbf{a} + \mathbf{c} \times \mathbf{a}]$$

$$= \mathbf{a} \cdot (\mathbf{b} \times \mathbf{c}) - \mathbf{a} \cdot (\mathbf{b} \times \mathbf{a}) + \mathbf{a} \cdot (\mathbf{c} \times \mathbf{a}) - \mathbf{b}(\mathbf{b} \times \mathbf{c}) + \mathbf{b} \cdot (\mathbf{b} \times \mathbf{a}) - \mathbf{b}(\mathbf{c} \times \mathbf{a})$$

$$= [\mathbf{abc}] - [\mathbf{aba}] + [\mathbf{aca}] - [\mathbf{bbc}] + [\mathbf{bba}] - [\mathbf{bca}]$$

$$= [\mathbf{abc}] - [\mathbf{bca}] = 0 \qquad \{\because [\mathbf{abc}] = [\mathbf{bca}] = [\mathbf{cab}]\}$$

170. *(b)* $A = \begin{bmatrix} 2 & -3 \\ 5 & -7 \end{bmatrix}$

$\therefore \quad |A| = -14 + 15 = 1 \neq 0$

So, A^{-1} exists.

$$\therefore \quad \text{adj } A = \begin{bmatrix} -7 & 3 \\ -5 & 2 \end{bmatrix}$$

$$\Rightarrow \quad A^{-1} = \frac{1}{|A|}(\text{adj } A) = \begin{bmatrix} -7 & 3 \\ -5 & 2 \end{bmatrix}$$

$$\Rightarrow \quad A + A^{-1} = \begin{bmatrix} 2 & -3 \\ 5 & -7 \end{bmatrix} + \begin{bmatrix} -7 & 3 \\ -5 & 2 \end{bmatrix}$$

$$= \begin{bmatrix} -5 & 0 \\ 0 & -5 \end{bmatrix}$$

171. *(d)* We have,

$$A = \begin{bmatrix} \cos\theta & -\sin\theta & 0 \\ \sin\theta & \cos\theta & 0 \\ 0 & 0 & 1 \end{bmatrix}$$

$$\text{Minor of } a_{32} = \begin{vmatrix} \cos\theta & 0 \\ \sin\theta & 0 \end{vmatrix} = 0 - 0 = 0$$

and cofactor of $a_{32} = -$ Minor of $a_{32} = -0 = 0$

172. *(d)* The probability that the place does not hit is

$$P(\text{FFFF}) = (1 - 0.4)(1 - 0.3)(1 - 0.2)(1 - 0.1)$$

$$= (0.6)(0.7)(0.8)(0.9) = 0.3024$$

The probability of hitting is $1 - 0.3024 = 0.6976$

173. *(c)* The given statement is

"If I become a teacher, then I will open a school".

Negation of the given statements is

"I will become a teacher and I will not open a school".

($\because \sim(p \to q) = (p \wedge \sim q)$, where p is first statement and q is second statement.

174. *(c)* We have,

$$x_1 + 2x_2 = 2; \; 2x_1 + 4x_2 = 8$$

i.e., $$\frac{x_1}{2} + \frac{x_2}{1} = 1, \; \frac{x_1}{4} + \frac{x_2}{2} = 1$$

The constraint are shown by the graph

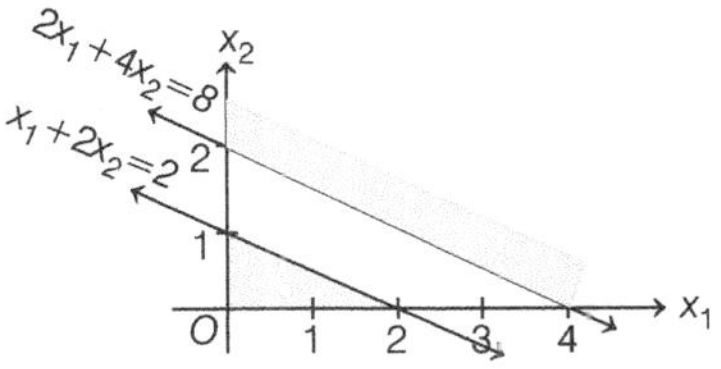

From the graph, we conclude that there is no feasible region, i.e. there is no unique solutions satisfying all the constraints.

175. *(c)* Let the coordinates of a point P changes from (x, y) to (x', y') in new coordinates axes where origin has the coordinates $h = 1$,

$$k = 1$$

Then, $\quad x = x' + 1, \; y = y' + 1.$

Substituting these values in the given equation of straight line

$$(x' + 1)(y' + 1) - (x' + 1) - (y' + 1) + 1 = 0$$

$$\Rightarrow x'y' + x' + y' + 1 - x' - 1 - y' - 1 + 1 = 0$$

$$\Rightarrow x'y' = 0$$

Therefore, the equation of straight line in the new system is $xy = 0$

176. *(d)* We have, $\log_6 abc = 6 \Rightarrow abc = 6^6$ ...(i)

Let $b = ar, c = ar^2$

Eq. (i), $a^3r^3 = 6^6 \Rightarrow b = ar = 36$

$b - a = 36 - a$ is square for $a = 35, 32, 27, 20, 11$

$c = \frac{b^2}{a} = \frac{36^2}{a}$ is an integer for $a = 27$

$\therefore$ $a = 27, b = 36, c = 48$

$\Rightarrow$ $a + b + c = 111$

177. *(c)* $F(x) = P(X < x)$

$F(0) = P(X \le 0) = 0.5$

$F(1) = P(X \le 1) = 0.5 + 0.2 = 0.7$

$F(2) = P(X \le 2) = 0.5 + 0.2 + 0.18 = 0.88$

$F(3) = P(X \le 3) = 0.5 + 0.2 + 0.18 + 0.12 = 1$

$\therefore$ The c.d.f. of X is

$X = x$	0	1	2	3
$F(x)$	0.5	0.7	0.88	1

178. *(c)* X can take values 0, 1, 2.

The probability distribution of X.

Since there are 16 items are perfect and 4 are defective. Given that two items are drawn randomly.

$\therefore$ P(no defective items are drawn) $= \frac{^{16}C_2}{^{20}C_2}$

$X = x$	0	1	2
$P(X = x)$	$\frac{^{16}C_2}{^{20}C_2} = \frac{12}{19}$	$\frac{^4C_1 \times ^{16}C_1}{^{20}C_2} = \frac{32}{95}$	$\frac{^4C_2}{^{20}C_2} = \frac{3}{95}$

179. *(b)* Let sets A and B have m and n elements, respectively.

Then, $2^m - 2^n = 56 \Rightarrow 2^n(2^{m-n} - 1) = 56$

$\Rightarrow$ $2^n(2^{m-n} - 1) = 8 \times 7$

$\Rightarrow$ $2^n(2^{m-n} - 1) = 2^3 \times 7$

One comparing both sides, we get

$2^n = 2^3$ and $2^{m-n} - 1 = 7$

$\Rightarrow$ $n = 3$ and $2^{m-n} = 8$

$\Rightarrow$ $2^{m-n} = 2^3$

$\Rightarrow$ $m - n = 3$

$\Rightarrow$ $m - 3 = 3$

$\Rightarrow$ $m = 6$

Hence, number of the elements is set A is 6.

180. *(d)* $\because \log_4 2 + \log_4 4 + \log_4 x + \log_4 16 = 6$

$\Rightarrow \log_4(2 \times 4 \times x \times 16) = 6$

$\Rightarrow$ $128x = 4^6$

$\therefore$ $x = \frac{4^3}{2} = 32$

COMEDK 2017

COMEDK

Solved Paper 2016

Instructions

- There are 180 questions in all. The number of questions in each section is as given below.

Sections	No. of Questions
Section I : Physics	1-60
Section II : Chemistry	61-120
Section III : Mathematics	121-180

- All the questions are Multiple Choice Questions having four options out of which **ONLY ONE** is correct.
- Candidates will be awarded 1 mark for each correct answer. There will be no negative marking for incorrect answer.
- Time allotted to complete this paper is 3 hrs.

PHYSICS

1. A simple pendulum has a period T inside a lift, when it is stationary. The lift is accelerated upwards with constant acceleration a. The period

a. decreases *b.* increases
c. remains same *d.* becomes infinite

2. 90 dB sound is x times more intense than 40 dB sound, then x is

a. 5 *b.* 50
c. 10^5 *d.* 500

3. A star is moving away from the earth with speed v. Change in wavelength $d\lambda$ observed on earth is

a. $\lambda v / c$ *b.* $\lambda v / (c + v)$
c. $\lambda c / (c + v)$ *d.* $\lambda c / v$

4. An open pipe emits a fundamental frequency n when it emits the 3rd harmonic, then the pipe can accommodate

a. 2 nodes, 2 anti-nodes
b. 3 nodes, 4 anti-nodes
c. 3 nodes, 3 anti-nodes
d. 1 node, 2 anti-nodes

5. In an adiabatic process,

a. temperature remains constant
b. pressure remains constant
c. volume remains constant
d. there is no transfer of heat

6. Carnot heat engine takes 300 J of heat from a source at 627°C and gives some part of it to sink at 27°C. Work done by engine in one cycle is

a. 200 J *b.* 300 J *c.* 150 J *d.* 120 J

7. 15/16th of a radioactive sample disintegrates in 2 h. Mean life of radioactive sample is approximately

a. 30 min *b.* 43 min
c. 21 min *d.* 15 min

8. Clear images of soft tissues can be well studied using

a. MRI *b.* X-rays
c. ultrasonics *d.* IR rays

9. Particles which are not composite and hence truly elementary are

a. mesons *b.* protons
c. neutrons *d.* leptons

10. A logic gate whose output will be in logic 0 state only, when all inputs are in logic 1 state is called
a. AND *b.* OR
c. NOR *d.* NAND

11. n-type and p-type semiconductors can be obtained by doping pure silicon, respectively with
a. arsenic, phosphorous
b. indium, aluminium
c. phosphorous, indium
d. aluminium, boron

12. In a CE amplifier, $\beta = 50$, $R_L = 4\,k\Omega$, $R_i = 500\,\Omega$. Power gain of the amplifier is
a. 2×10^4 *b.* 2×10^2
c. 2×10^3 *d.* 2×10^1

13. Electrons are excited from $n = 1$ to $n = 4$ state. During downward transitions, possible number of spectral lines observed in Balmer series is
a. 4 *b.* 3
c. 2 *d.* 1

14. IR region lies between
a. radiowaves and microwave regions
b. microwaves and visible
c. visible and UV region
d. UV rays and X-ray region

15. A proton and an alpha particle are subjected to same potential difference V. Their de-Broglie wavelengths λ_p, λ_α will be in the ratio
a. 2 : 1 *b.* $2\sqrt{2} : 1$
c. 1 : 1 *d.* 1 : 2

16. Raman shift depends on
a. incident wavelength
b. incident intensity
c. resolving power of the spectrograph used
d. molecular energy levels of the scatterer

17. $_6C^{14}$ and $_7N^{15}$ are the examples of
a. isotopes *b.* isobars
c. isotones *d.* mirror nuclei

18. In an interference experiment, intensity ratio at the bright to dark fringe is 9 : 1. Amplitudes of interfering waves are in the ratio
a. 3 : 1 *b.* 9 : 1
c. 2 : 1 *d.* 4 : 1

19. In Young's double slit experiment, 1st dark fringe occurs directly opposite to a slit. Wavelength of light used is
a. d^2 / D *b.* d / D
c. D^2 / d *d.* $2d^2 / D$

20. Newton's ring pattern in reflected system, viewed under white light consists of
a. equally spaced bright and dark bands with central dark spot
b. equally spaced bright and dark bands with central white spot
c. a few coloured rings with central dark spot
d. a few coloured rings with central white spot

21. It is difficult to observe diffraction in case of light waves, because
a. light waves can travel through vacuum
b. speed of light is more
c. light waves are transverse in nature
d. wavelength of light is small

22. A calcite crystal is placed over a dot on a paper sheet and the crystal is rotated. On viewing through the calcite or sees,
a. a single stationary dot
b. two stationary dots
c. two dots rotating about one another
d. one dot rotating about the other stationary dot sometimes coinciding with it

23. Critical angle of the medium is 45°. Polarising angle of incidence at the surface of the medium is
a. 45° *b.* 38°
c. 22.5° *d.* 54.7°

24. If only 2% of the main current is to be passed through a galvanometer of resistance G, then the resistance of shunt should be
a. $G/50$ *b.* $G/49$ *c.* $50\,G$ *d.* $49\,G$

25. A small current carrying loop of area A behaves like a tiny magnet of magnetic moment M. Current in the loop is
a. MA *b.* A / M *c.* A^2M *d.* M / A

26. Two concentric circular coils, each having 10 turns with radii 0.2 m and 0.4 m carry currents 0.2 A and 0.3 A respectively in opposite directions. Magnetic field at the centre is
a. $(2/3)\mu_0$ *b.* $(5/4)\mu_0$
c. $(1/4)\mu_0$ *d.* $(1/6)\mu_0$

27. Material of permanent magnet has
a. high retentivity and high coercivity
b. low retentivity and high coercivity
c. low retentivity and low coercivity
d. high retentivity and low coercivity

28. Power factor of a series L-C-R circuit is
a. R *b.* Z / R
c. R / Z *d.* RZ

29. An inductor 1H is connected across 220V, 50 Hz supply. Peak value of current is approximately

a. 0.5 A *b.* 0.7 A *c.* 1 A *d.* 1.4 A

30. Plane polarised light is passed through an analyser and the intensity of emerging light is reduced by 75%. Optical vibrations make an angle θ with the axis of analyser, then θ is

a. 60° *b.* 45° *c.* 30° *d.* 58°

31. A charge 10nC is situated in a medium of relative permittivity 10. The potential due to this charge at a distance of 0.1 m is

a. 900 V *b.* 90 V
c. 9 V *d.* 0.09 V

32. Dielectric constant of a metal is

a. zero *b.* infinite
c. finite *d.* unpredictable

33. Distance between the two point charges is increased by 20%. Force of interaction between the charges

a. increases by 10% *b.* decreases by 20%
c. decreases by 17% *d.* decreases by 31%

34. Potential energy of 2 charge 10 nC each separated by a distance of 0.09 m in air is

a. 10 μJ *b.* 1 mJ
c. 10 mJ *d.* 10 J

35. A metal plate of thickness $d/2$ is introduced in between the plates of a parallel plate air capacitor with plate separation of d, then capacity

a. decreases 2 times *b.* increases 2 times
c. remains same *d.* becomes zero

36. Specific resistance of a conductor material increases with

a. increase with area of cross-section
b. decrease in length
c. decrease in area of cross-section
d. increases with temperature

37. The resistance of mercury at 4.2 K is

a. infinity
b. greater than at lab temperature
c. same as that of lab temperature
d. almost zero

38. Temperature coefficient of resistance of platinum is 4×10^{-3} / K at 20°C. Temperature at which increase in resistance of platinum is 10% its value at 20°C is

a. 25°C *b.* 70°C
c. 45°C *d.* 100°C

39. Ideal voltmeter connected as shown reads

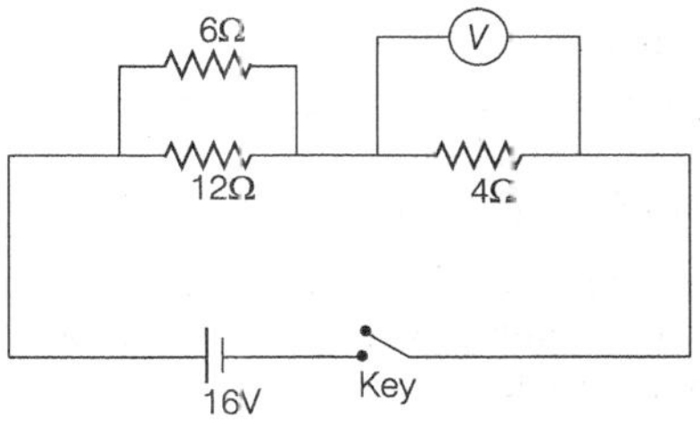

a. 16 V *b.* 12 V
c. 4 V *d.* 8 V

40. When a charged particle moves perpendicular to a uniform magnetic field, then

a. its momentum changes and total energy is same
b. Both momentum and its total energy remain the same
c. Both momentum and its total energy will change
d. total energy changes but momentum remains same

41. 0.04 m of glass contains the same number of waves as 0.05 m of water, when monochromatic light passes through them normally. Refractive index of water is 4/3. Refractive index of glass is

a. 5/3 *b.* 5/4 *c.* 5/2 *d.* 4/5

42. Critical angle will be maximum, when light travels from

a. glass to air *b.* glass to water
c. water to air *d.* diamond to air

43. A ray of light incident on one face of an equilateral prism at 60° enters and leaves the prism symmetrically. Refractive index of the prism material is

a. 1.5 *b.* 1.62 *c.* 1.73 *d.* 1.8

44. In the spectrum of visible light produced by a prism dispersion is

a. uniform throughout the spectrum
b. maximum in the middle decreases on either sides
c. maximum towards yellow
d. maximum towards violet

45. Convex lens of focal length f made of glass of refractive index 1.5 is immersed in water of refractive index 4/3. Focal length is

a. f *b.* greater than f
c. less than f *d.* $-f$

46. Two co-axial lenses of power + 4D and − 2D are placed in contact. The focal length of combination is

a. 0.5 m *b.* 0.25 m
c. 0.16 m *d.* − 0.5 m

47. Eddy currents are produced in a material, when it is

a. heated
b. placed in a time varying magnetic field
c. placed in an electric field
d. placed in a uniform magnetic field

48. Transformer works on 220 V and its efficiency is 80%. If output power is 8 kW, primary current is approximately

a. 35 A *b.* 18 A
c. 22 A *d.* 45 A

49. Quality factor of a series *L-C-R* circuit decreases from 3 to 2. Resonant frequency is 600 Hz. Change in bandwidth is

a. zero *b.* 100 Hz increase
c. 100 Hz decrease *d.* 300 Hz increase

50. A stone dropped from the top of the tower reaches ground in 4 s. Height of the tower is $(g = 10 \text{ m}/\text{s}^2)$

a. 20 m *b.* 40 m
c. 60 m *d.* 80 m

51. Liquid crystal phase which are more close to the solid than to liquid is

a. Nematic *b.* Smectic
c. Lyotropic *d.* Cholesteric

52. If the earth shrinks in its size (radius) mass remaining the same, the value of *g* on its surface will

a. increase *b.* decrease
c. remains same *d.* reduce to zero

53. Two rods of same area of cross-section and lengths and conductivities K_1 and K_2 are connected in series. Then in steady state, conductivity of the combination is

a. $(K_1 + K_2)/(K_1K_2)$
b. $2K_1K_2/(K_1 + K_2)$
c. $(K_1 + K_2)/2$
d. $K_1K_2/(K_1 + K_2)$

54. The square of the resultant of two equal forces acting at a point is equal to three times their product. Angle between them is

a. 30° *b.* 45°
c. 60° *d.* 90°

55. With the addition of impurities, surface tension of a liquid

a. increases
b. decreases
c. remains constant
d. may increase or decrease depending on impurities

56. Viscosity decreases with increase in temperature is the reason for

(i) hot water moving faster than cold water.
(ii) more viscous oils are used in motorcars during summer than in winter

a. Only (i) is correct *b.* Only (ii) correct
c. Both are correct *d.* Both are incorrect

57. Moment of momentum of an electron revolving in second Bohr orbit of hydrogen is

a. $2\pi h$ *b.* $h/2\pi$
c. h/π *d.* $2h/3\pi$

58. The existence of excitation and ionisation energies in an atom is an evidence for

a. stability of an atom
b. electrical neutrality of an atom
c. small size of the atom
d. stationary orbits in an atom

59. Work function of a photosensitive metal is 3 eV. The wavelength of incident radiations which can just eject photoelectrons from the metal is

a. 600 nm *b.* 510 nm
c. 414 nm *d.* 378 nm

60. Three identical capacitors are first connected in series and then in parallel. The ratio of effective capacitances in the two cases is

a. 9 : 1 *b.* 3 : 1
c. 1 : 3 *d.* 1 : 9

CHEMISTRY

61. A nitrogen containing organic compound gave an oily liquid on heating with bromine and potassium hydroxide solution. On shaking the product with acetic anhydride, an antipyretic drug was obtained. The reactions indicate that the starting compound is

a. acetamide *b.* nitrobenzene
c. aniline *d.* benzamide

62. The silver salt of a fatty acid on refluxing with an alkyl halide gives an

a. ether *b.* amine
c. acid *d.* ester

63. Pick out the one which does not belong to the family

a. ptyalin *b.* lipase
c. pepsin *d.* cellulose

64. Which of the following is wrongly matched?

a. Decomposition of H_2O_2–first order reaction.
b. Combination of H_2 and Br_2 to give HBr–zero order reaction.
c. Saponification of $CH_3COOC_2H_5$–second order reaction.
d. Hydrolysis of CH_3COOCH_3–pseudo unimolecular reaction.

65. The diameter of colloidal particle ranges from

a. 10^3 m to 10^{-3}m
b. 10^{-3} m to 10^{-6} m
c. 10^{-6} m to 10^{-9} m
d. 10^{-9} m to 10^{-12} m

66. The number of $2p$ electrons having spin quantum number $s = -1/2$ are

a. 2 *b.* 3 *c.* 6 *d.* 0

67. Pick out the alkane which differs from the other members of the group.

a. 2-methyl butane *b.* 2, 2-dimethyl butane
c. 2, 2-dimethyl propane *d.* Pentane

68. 56 g of nitrogen and 8 g of hydrogen gas are heated in a closed vessel. At equilibrium 34 g of ammonia are present. The equilibrium number of moles of nitrogen, hydrogen and ammonia are respectively

a. 1, 1, 2 *b.* 2, 1, 2
c. 1, 2, 2 *d.* 2, 2, 1

69. A process is taking place at constant temperature and pressure. Then,

a. $\Delta H = 0$ *b.* $\Delta S = 0$
c. $\Delta H = \Delta E$ *d.* $\Delta H = T\Delta S$

70. In a galvanic cell, the electrons flow from

a. anode to cathode through the external circuit.
b. cathode to anode through the external circuit.
c. anode to cathode through the solution.
d. cathode to anode through the solution.

71. On treating a mixture of two alkyl halides with sodium metal in dry ether, 2-methyl propane was obtained. The alkyl halides are

a. chloromethane and chloroethane
b. chloromethane and 1-chloropropane
c. 2-chloropropane and chloromethane
d. 2-chloropropane and chloroethane

72. Which of the following statements about benzyl chloride is incorrect?

a. It is a lachrymatory liquid and answers Beilstein's test.
b. It gives a white precipitate with alcoholic silver nitrate.
c. It is less reactive than alkyl halides.
d. It can be oxidised to benzaldehyde by boiling with copper nitrate solution.

73. The main product obtained when a solution of sodium carbonate reacts with mercuric chloride is

a. $HgCO_3$ *b.* $HgCO_3$, $Hg(OH)_2$
c. $Hg(OH)_2$ *d.* $HgCO_3$, HgO

74. In the electrothermal process, the compound displaced by silica from calcium phosphate is

a. phosphorus *b.* phosphorus pentoxide
c. calcium phosphide *d.* phosphine

75. The enthalpy of combustion of methane at 25°C is 890 kJ. The heat liberated when 3.2 g of methane is burnt in air is

a. – 890 kJ *b.* 178 kJ
c. 445 kJ *d.* 278 kJ

76. The pressure and temperature of 4 dm^3 of carbon dioxide gas are doubled. Then, the volume of carbon dioxide gas would be

a. 4 dm^3 *b.* 8 dm^3
c. 2 dm^3 *d.* 3 dm^3

77. 4 g of copper was dissolved in concentrated nitric acid. The copper nitrate solution on strong heating gave 5g of its oxide. The equivalent weight of copper is

a. 12 *b.* 20
c. 23 *d.* 32

78. In the manufacture of ammonia by the Haber's process,
$N_2(g) + 3H_2(g) \rightleftharpoons 2NH_3(g) + 92.3$ kJ, which of the following conditions is unfavourable?
a. Reducing the temperature
b. Removing ammonia as it is formed
c. Increasing the temperature
d. Increasing the pressure

79. The chemical equilibrium of a reversible reaction is not influenced by
a. concentration of the reactants
b. temperature
c. pressure
d. catalyst

80. Cumene process is the most important commercial method for the manufacture of phenol. Cumene is
a. vinyl benzene
b. propyl benzene
c. 1-methyl ethyl benzene
d. ethyl benzene

81. A solution contains 1.2046×10^{24} hydrochloric acid molecules in one dm^3 of the solution. The strength of the solution is
a. 4N *b.* 8N *c.* 6N *d.* 2N

82. Nuclear theory of the atom was put forward by
a. Neils Bohr *b.* J.J. Thomson
c. Rutherford *d.* Aston

83. In acetylene molecule, the two carbon atoms are linked by
a. three σ-bonds
b. three π-bonds
c. one σ-bond and two π-bonds
d. two σ-bonds and one π-bond

84. The enthalpy of the reaction,
$H_2(g) + 1/2\,O_2(g) \longrightarrow H_2O(g)$ is ΔH_1 and that of $H_2(g) + 1/2O_2(g) \longrightarrow H_2O(l)$ is ΔH_2. Then
a. $\Delta H_1 > \Delta H_2$ *b.* $\Delta H_1 = \Delta H_2$
c. $\Delta H_1 < \Delta H_2$ *d.* $\Delta H_1 + \Delta H_2 = 0$

85. A radioactive isotope decays at such a rate that after 192 minutes only $\frac{1}{16}$ of the original amount remains. The half-life of the radioactive isotope is
a. 12 min *b.* 24 min *c.* 32 min *d.* 48 min

86. The reagent which does not give acid chloride on treating with a carboxylic acid is
a. $SOCl_2$ *b.* PCl_3
c. PCl_5 *d.* Cl_2

87. Among the halogens, the one which is oxidised by nitric acid is
a. chlorine *b.* bromine
c. fluorine *d.* iodine

88. The metal which does not form ammonium nitrate by reaction with dilute nitric acid is
a. Pb *b.* Mg *c.* Al *d.* Fe

89. The elements with atomic numbers 9, 17, 35, 53, 85 are all
a. heavy metals *b.* light metals
c. noble gases *d.* halogens

90. In the electrolytic method of obtaining aluminium from purified bauxite, cryolite is added to the charge in order to
a. dissolve bauxite and render it conductor of electricity.
b. lower the melting point of bauxite.
c. minimise the heat loss due to radiation.
d. protect aluminium produced from oxygen.

91. Which of the following is not an amphoteric substance?
a. H_2O *b.* NH_3 *c.* HNO_3 *d.* HCO_3^-

92. When 50 cm^3 of 0.2 N H_2SO_4 is mixed with 50 cm^3 of 1N KOH, the heat liberated is
a. 573 kJ *b.* 573 J
c. 11.46 kJ *d.* 57.3 kJ

93. An artificial radioactive isotope gave $^{14}_{7}N$ after two successive β-particle emissions. The number of neutrons in the parent nucleus must be
a. 5 *b.* 7 *c.* 9 *d.* 14

94. Stainless steel does not rust because
a. nickel present in it, does not rust
b. iron forms a hard chemical compound with chromium present in it
c. chromium and nickel combine with iron
d. chromium forms an oxide layer and protects iron from rusting

95. Which of the following combinations can be used to synthesised ethanol?
a. CH_3MgI and $CH_3COOC_2H_5$
b. CH_3MgI and HCHO
c. CH_3MgI and CH_3COCH_3
d. CH_3MgI and C_2H_5OH

96. The reaction, $2SO_2(g) + O_2(g) \rightleftharpoons 2SO_3(g)$ is carried out in a 1 dm^3 vessel and 2 dm^3 vessel separately. The ratio of the reaction velocities will be
a. 4 : 1 *b.* 8 : 1 *c.* 1 : 8 *d.* 1 : 4

97. In a mixture of acetic acid and sodium acetate the ratio of concentrations of the salt to the acid is increased ten times. Then the pH of the solution

a. decreases ten fold *b.* increases ten fold
c. increases by one *d.* decreases by one

98. When a mixture of methane and oxygen is passed through heated molybdenum oxide, the main product formed is

a. methanol *b.* methanal
c. methanoic acid *d.* ethanal

99. Benzene can be obtained by heating either benzoic acid with *X* or phenol with *Y*. *X* and *Y* are respectively

a. zinc dust and sodium hydroxide
b. soda lime and copper
c. zinc dust and soda lime
d. soda lime and zinc dust

100. An organic compound is boiled with alcoholic potash. The product is cooled and acidified with HCl. A white solid separates out. The starting compound may be

a. ethyl acetate *b.* methyl acetate
c. ethyl benzoate *d.* ethyl formate

101. In qualitative analysis, in order to detect second group basic radical, H_2S gas is passed in the presence of dilute HCl to

a. decrease the dissociation of H_2S
b. increase the dissociation of salt solution
c. increase the dissociation of H_2S
d. decrease the dissociation of salt solution

102. Aluminium displaces hydrogen from dilute HCl, whereas silver does not. The emf of a cell prepared by combining Al / Al^{3+} and Ag / Ag^{+} is 2.46 V. The reduction potential of silver electrode is + 0.80 V. The reduction potential of aluminium electrode is

a. 3.26 V *b.* – 1.66V
c. + 1.66 V *d.* – 3.26 V

103. The first fraction obtained during the fractionation of petroleum is

a. gasoline *b.* diesel oil
c. hydrocarbon gases *d.* kerosene oil

104. Which of the following compounds gives trichloromethane on distilling with bleaching powder?

a. Ethanol *b.* Methanol
c. Methanal *d.* Phenol

105. Benzoin is

a. α-hydroxy aldehyde
b. α-hydroxy ketone
c. compound containing an aldehyde and a ketonic group
d. α, β- unsaturated acid

106. The velocity constant of a reaction at 290 K was found to be $3.2 \times 10^{-3} s^{-1}$. When the temperature is raised to 310 K, it will be about

a. 9.6×10^{-3} *b.* 1.28×10^{-2}
c. 6.4×10^{-3} *d.* 3.2×10^{-4}

107. Select the pK_a value of the strongest acid from the following.

a. 2.0 *b.* 4.5
c. 1.0 *d.* 3.0

108. Pick out the unsaturated fatty acid from the following

a. oleic acid *b.* palmitic acid
c. stearic acid *d.* lauric acid

109. Nylon is not a

a. copolymer *b.* homopolymer
c. condensation polymer *d.* polyamide

110. The coaltar fraction which contains phenol is

a. heavy oil *b.* light oil
c. middle oil *d.* green oil

111. The compounds *A* and *B* are mixed in equimolar proportion to form the products, $A + B \rightleftharpoons C + D$. At equilibrium, one-third of *A* and *B* are consumed. The equilibrium constant for the reaction is

a. 2.5 *b.* 0.25
c. 0.5 *d.* 4.0

112. In froth floatation process for the purification of ores, the particles of ore float because

a. they are insoluble
b. they bear electrostatic charge
c. their surface is not easily wetted by water
d. they are light

113. Which of the following statements about amorphous solids is incorrect?

a. There is no orderly arrangement of particles.
b. They are rigid and incompressible.
c. They melt over a range of temperature.
d. They are anisotropic.

114. Hydrogen diffuses six times faster than gas *A*. The molar mass of gas *A* is

a. 24 *b.* 36 *c.* 72 *d.* 6

115. Dulong and Petit's law is valid only for
a. gaseous elements *b.* solid elements
c. metals *d.* non-metals

116. Identify the gas which is readily adsorbed by activated charcoal
a. H_2 *b.* O_2
c. N_2 *d.* SO_2

117. If the distance between Na^+ and Cl^- ions in sodium chloride crystal is x pm, the length of the edge of the unit cell is
a. $\frac{x}{2}$ pm *b.* $2x$ pm
c. $4x$ pm *d.* $\frac{x}{4}$ pm

118. Which of the following statements is incorrect?
a. In $K_4[Fe(CN)_6]$ the ligand has satisfied both primary and secondary valencies of ferrous ion.
b. In $[Cu(NH_3)_4]SO_4$, the ligand has satisfied only the secondary valency of copper.
c. In $K_3[Fe(CN)_6]$, the ligand has satisfied only the secondary valency of ferric ion.
d. In $K_3[Fe(CN)_6]$, the ligand has satisfied both primary and secondary valencies of ferric ion.

119. 2-acetoxy benzoic acid is used as an
a. antiseptic
b. antipyretic
c. antimalarial
d. antidepressant

120. A nucleoside on hydrolysis gives
a. an aldopentose and a heterocyclic base
b. an aldopentose and orthophosphoric acid
c. a heterocyclic base and orthophosphoric acid
d. an aldopentose, a heterocyclic base and orthophosphoric acid

MATHEMATICS

121. If $A = \{a, b, c\}$, $B = \{b, c, d\}$ and $C = \{a, d, c\}$, then $(A - B) \times (B \cap C) =$
a. $\{(a, c), (a, d), (b, d)\}$
b. $\{(c, a), (d, a)\}$
c. $\{(a, b), (c, d)\}$
d. $\{(a, c), (a, d)\}$

122. The function $f : X \to Y$ defined by $f(x) = \sin x$ is one-one but not onto if X and Y are respectively, is equal to
a. $\left[\frac{-\pi}{2}, \frac{\pi}{2}\right]$ and $[-1, 1]$ *b.* $\left[0, \frac{\pi}{2}\right]$ and $[-, 1, 1]$
c. $[0, \pi]$ and $[0, 1]$ *d.* R and R

123. If $\log_4 2 + \log_4 4 + \log_4 16 + \log_4 x = 6$, then $x =$
a. 32 *b.* 8
c. 4 *d.* 64

124. If $S_n = \frac{1}{6 \cdot 11} + \frac{1}{11 \cdot 16} + \frac{1}{16 \cdot 21} + \ldots$ to n terms, then $6S_n =$
a. $\frac{1}{(5n + 6)}$ *b.* $\frac{(2n - 1)}{5n + 6}$
c. $\frac{n}{(5n + 6)}$ *d.* $\frac{5n - 4}{5n + 6}$

125. The remainder obtained when $(1!)^2 + (2!)^2 + (3!)^2 + \ldots + (100!)^2$ is divided by 10^2 is
a. 14 *b.* 17 *c.* 28 *d.* 27

126. If $(p \wedge \sim r) \to (\sim p \vee q)$ is false, then the truth values of p, q and r are respectively
a. T, F and T *b.* F, T and T
c. F, F and T *d.* T, F and F

127. If α, β and γ are the roots of the equation $x^3 - 8x + 8 = 0$, then $\Sigma\alpha^2$ and $\Sigma\frac{1}{\alpha\beta}$ are respectively is equal to
a. 16 and 0
b. – 16 and 0
c. 16 and 8
d. 0 and – 16

128. The gcd of 1080 and 675 is
a. 125 *b.* 225
c. 135 *d.* 145

129. If $a \mid (b + c)$ and $a \mid (b - c)$, where $a, b, c \in N$, then
a. $c^2 \equiv a^2 (\text{mod } b^2)$
b. $a^2 \equiv b^2 (\text{mod } c^2)$
c. $a^2 + c^2 = b^2$
d. $b^2 \equiv c^2 (\text{mod } a^2)$

130. If a, b and $c \in N$, which one of the following is not true?
a. $a \mid b$ and $a \mid c \Rightarrow a \mid b + c$
b. $a \mid b + c \Rightarrow a \mid b$ and $a \mid c$
c. $a \mid b$ and $b \mid c \Rightarrow a \mid c$
d. $a \mid b$ and $a \mid c \Rightarrow a \mid 3b + 2c$

131. If $2A + 3B = \begin{bmatrix} 2 & -1 & 4 \\ 3 & 2 & 5 \end{bmatrix}$ and $A + 2B = \begin{bmatrix} 5 & 0 & 3 \\ 1 & 6 & 2 \end{bmatrix}$, then $B =$

a. $\begin{bmatrix} 8 & 1 & 2 \\ 1 & 10 & 1 \end{bmatrix}$ *b.* $\begin{bmatrix} 8 & 1 & -2 \\ -1 & 10 & -1 \end{bmatrix}$

c. $\begin{bmatrix} 8 & 1 & 2 \\ -1 & 10 & -1 \end{bmatrix}$ *d.* $\begin{bmatrix} 8 & -1 & 2 \\ -1 & 10 & -1 \end{bmatrix}$

132. If $O(A) = 2 \times 3$, $O(B) = 3 \times 2$, and $O(C) = 3 \times 3$, which one of the following is not defined?

a. $C(A + B')$ *b.* $C(A + B')'$

c. BAC *d.* $CB + A'$

133. If $A = \begin{bmatrix} 1 & -3 \\ 2 & k \end{bmatrix}$ and $A^2 - 4A + 10I = A$, then $k =$

a. 1 or 4 *b.* 4 and not 1

c. – 4 *d.* 0

134. The value of $\begin{vmatrix} x+y & y+z & z+x \\ x & y & z \\ x-y & y-z & z-x \end{vmatrix} =$

a. 0

b. $(x + y + z)^3$

c. $2(x + y + z)^3$

d. $2(x + y + z)^2$

135. On the set Q of all rational numbers the operation * which is both associative and commutative is given by $a * b =$

a. $2a + 3b$ *b.* $ab + 1$

c. $a^2 + b^2$ *d.* $a + b + ab$

136. In the group $G = \{1, 5, 7, 11\}$ under multiplication modulo 12, the solution of $7^{-1} \times_{12} (x \times_{12} 11) = 5$ is $x =$

a. 11 *b.* 7 *c.* 1 *d.* 5

137. A subset of the additive group of real numbers which is not a sub group, is

a. $(Q, +)$ *b.* $(N, +)$

c. $(Z, +)$ *d.* $(\{0\}, +)$

138. If $\mathbf{p} = \hat{i} + \hat{j}$, $\mathbf{q} = 4\hat{k} - \hat{j}$ and $\mathbf{r} = \hat{i} + \hat{k}$, then the unit vector in tile direction of $3\mathbf{p} + \mathbf{q} - 2\mathbf{r}$ is

a. $\hat{i} + 2\hat{j} + 2\hat{k}$

b. $\frac{1}{3}(\hat{i} - 2\hat{j} + 2\hat{k})$

c. $\frac{1}{3}(\hat{i} - 2\hat{j} - 2\hat{k})$

d. $\frac{1}{3}(\hat{i} + 2\hat{j} + 2\hat{k})$

139. If **a** and **b** are the two vectors such that $|\mathbf{a}| = 3\sqrt{3}$, $|\mathbf{b}| = 4$ and $|\mathbf{a} + \mathbf{b}| = \sqrt{7}$, the angle between **a** and **b** is

a. 150° *b.* 30°

c. 60° *d.* 120°

140. If **a** is vector perpendicular to both **b** and **c**, then

a. $\mathbf{a} \cdot (\mathbf{b} \times \mathbf{c}) = 0$ *b.* $\mathbf{a} \times (\mathbf{b} \times \mathbf{c}) = 0$

c. $\mathbf{a} \times (\mathbf{b} + \mathbf{c}) = 0$ *d.* $\mathbf{a} + (\mathbf{b} + \mathbf{c}) = 0$

141. If the area of the parallelogram with **a** and **b** as two adjacent sides is 15 sq units, then the area of the parallelogram having $3\mathbf{a} + 2\mathbf{b}$ and $\mathbf{a} + 3\mathbf{b}$ as two adjacent sides in sq units is

a. 45 *b.* 75

c. 105 *d.* 120

142. The locus of the point which moves such that the ratio of its distances from two fixed points in the plane is always a constant $k(< 1)$ is

a. circle *b.* straight line

c. ellipse *d.* hyperbola

143. If the lines $x + 3y - 9 = 0$, $4x - by - 2 = 0$ and $2x - y - 4 = 0$ are concurrent, then $b =$

a. 0 *b.* 1 *c.* 5 *d.* – 5

144. The lines represented by $ax^2 + 2hxy + by^2 = 0$ are perpendicular to each other if

a. $h = 0$ *b.* $h^2 = ab$

c. $a + b = 0$ *d.* $h^2 = a + b$

145. The equation of the circle having $x - y - 2 = 0$ and $x - y + 2 = 0$ as two tangents and $x + y = 0$ as a diameter is

a. $x^2 + y^2 = 1$

b. $x^2 + y^2 = 2$

c. $x^2 + y^2 - 2x + 2y - 1 = 0$

d. $x^2 + y^2 + 2x - 2y + 1 = 0$

146. If the length of the tangent from any point on the circle $(x - 3)^2 + (y + 2)^2 = 5r^2$ to the circle $(x - 3)^2 + (y + 2)^2 = r^2$ is 16 units, then the area between the two circles in sq units is

a. 16π *b.* 8π

c. 4π *d.* 32π

147. The circles $ax^2 + ay^2 + 2g_1x + 2f_1y + c_1 = 0$ and $bx^2 + by^2 + 2g_2x + 2f_2y + c_2 = 0$ $(a \neq 0$ and $b \neq 0)$ cut orthogonally if

a. $g_1g_2 + f_1f_2 = c_1 + c_2$

b. $b\, g_1g_2 + a\, f_1f_2 = b\, c_1 + ac_2$

c. $g_1g_2 + f_1f_2 = b\, c_1 + a\, c_2$

d. $g_1g_2 + f_1f_2 = a\, c_1 + b\, c_2$

COMEDK 2016

148. The equation of the common tangent of the two touching circles, $y^2 + x^2 - 6x - 12y + 37 = 0$ and $x^2 + y^2 - 6y + 7 = 0$ is

a. $x + y + 5 = 0$ **b.** $x + y - 5 = 0$
c. $x - y + 5 = 0$ **d.** $x - y - 5 = 0$

149. The equation of the parabola with vertex at $(-1, 1)$ and focus $(2, 1)$ is

a. $y^2 - 2y - 12x + 13 = 0$
b. $y^2 - 2y - 12x + 11 = 0$
c. $x^2 + 2x - 12y + 13 = 0$
d. $y^2 - 2y - 12x - 11 = 0$

150. The equation of the line which is tangent to both the circle $x^2 + y^2 = 5$ and the parabola $y^2 = 40x$ is

a. $2x + y + 5 = 0$ **b.** $2x - y - 5 = 0$
c. $2x - y + 5 = 0$ **d.** $2x - y \pm 5 = 0$

151. $x = 4(1 + \cos\theta)$ and $y = 3(1 + \sin\theta)$ are the parametric equations of

a. $\frac{(x-4)^2}{16} + \frac{(y-3)^2}{9} = 1$
b. $\frac{(x-4)^2}{16} - \frac{(y-3)^2}{9} = 1$
c. $\frac{(x+4)^2}{16} + \frac{(y+3)^2}{9} = 1$
d. $\frac{(x-3)^2}{9} + \frac{(y-4)^2}{16} = 1$

152. If the distance between the foci and the distance between the directrices of the hyperbola $\frac{x^2}{a^2} - \frac{y^2}{b^2} = 1$ are in the ratio 3 : 2, then $a : b$ is

a. 2 : 1 **b.** 1 : 2
c. $\sqrt{3} : \sqrt{2}$ **d.** $\sqrt{2} : 1$

153. The ellipse $\frac{x^2}{25} + \frac{y^2}{16} = 1$ and the hyperbola $\frac{x^2}{25} - \frac{y^2}{16} = 1$ have in common

a. centre and vertices only
b. centre, foci and vertices
c. centre, foci and directrices
d. centre only

154. If $\sec\theta = m$ and $\tan\theta = n$, then

$\frac{1}{m}\left[(m+n) + \frac{1}{(m+n)}\right] =$

a. mn **b.** $2n$ **c.** $2m$ **d.** 2

155. The value of $\frac{\sin 85^\circ - \sin 15^\circ}{\cos 65^\circ} =$

a. 0 **b.** 1 **c.** -1 **d.** 2

156. From an aeroplane flying, vertically above a horizontal road, the angles of depression of two consecutive stones on the same side of the aeroplane are observed to be 30° and 60° respectively. The height at which the aeroplane is flying in km, is

a. 2 **b.** $\frac{2}{\sqrt{3}}$ **c.** $\frac{\sqrt{3}}{2}$ **d.** $\frac{4}{\sqrt{3}}$

157. If the angles of a triangle are in the ratio 3 : 4 : 5, then the sides are in the ratio

a. 3 : 4 : 5 **b.** $2 : \sqrt{3} : \sqrt{3} + 1$
c. $\sqrt{2} : \sqrt{6} : \sqrt{3} + 1$ **d.** $2 : \sqrt{6} : \sqrt{3} + 1$

158. If $\cos^{-1} x = \alpha, (0 < x < 1)$ and $\sin^{-1}(2x\sqrt{1-x^2}) + \sec^{-1}\left(\frac{1}{2x^2 - 1}\right) = \frac{2\pi}{3}$, then $\tan^{-1}(2x) =$

a. $\frac{\pi}{2}$ **b.** $\frac{\pi}{3}$ **c.** $\frac{\pi}{4}$ **d.** $\frac{\pi}{6}$

159. If $a > b > 0$, then the value of $\tan^{-1}\left(\frac{a}{b}\right) + \tan^{-1}\left(\frac{a+b}{a-b}\right)$ depends on

a. neither a nor b **b.** a and not b
c. b and not a **d.** both a and b

160. Which one of the following equations has no solution?

a. $\sqrt{3}\sin\theta - \cos\theta = 2$
b. $\cos\theta + \sin\theta = \sqrt{2}$
c. $\operatorname{cosec}\theta \cdot \sec\theta = 1$
d. $\operatorname{cosec}\theta - \sec\theta = \operatorname{cosec}\theta \cdot \sec\theta$

161. The complex number $\frac{(-\sqrt{3} + 3i)(1 - i)}{(3 + \sqrt{3}i)(i)(\sqrt{3} + \sqrt{3}i)}$, when represented in the Argand diagram lies

a. on the X-axis (Real axis)
b. on the Y-axis (Imaginary axis)
c. in the first quadrant
d. in the second quadrant

162. If $2x = -1 + \sqrt{3}i$, then the value of $(1 - x^2 + x)^6 - (1 - x + x^2)^6 =$

a. 0 **b.** 64 **c.** -64 **d.** 32

163. The modulus and amplitude of $(1 + i\sqrt{3})^8$ are respectively

a. 256 and $\frac{8\pi}{3}$ **b.** 2 and $\frac{2\pi}{3}$
c. 256 and $\frac{2\pi}{3}$ **d.** 256 and $\frac{\pi}{3}$

COMEDK 2016

164. The value of $\lim_{x \to 0} \frac{5^x - 5^{-x}}{2x} =$

a. 2log5 *b.* 1
c. 0 *d.* log5

165. Which one of the following is not true always?

a. If a function $f(x)$ is continuous at $x = a$, then $\lim_{x \to a} f(x)$ exists.
b. If $f(x)$ and $g(x)$ are differentiable at $x = a$, then $f(x) + g(x)$ is also differentiable at $x = a$.
c. If $f(x)$ is continuous at $x = a$, then it is differentiable at $x = a$.
d. If $f(x)$ is not continuous at $x = a$, then it is not differentiable at $x = a$.

166. If $y = 1 + \frac{1}{x} + \frac{1}{x^2} + \frac{1}{x^3} + \ldots \infty$ with $|x| > 1$, then $\frac{dy}{dx} =$

a. $\frac{-y^2}{x^2}$ *b.* $\frac{y^2}{x^2}$ *c.* x^2y^2 *d.* $\frac{x^2}{y^2}$

167. If $f(x)$ and $g(x)$ are two functions with $g(x) = x - \frac{1}{x}$ and $fog(x) = x^3 - \frac{1}{x^3}$, then $f'(x) =$

a. $3x^2 + \frac{3}{x^4}$ *b.* $1 + \frac{1}{x^2}$
c. $x^2 - \frac{1}{x^2}$ *d.* $3x^2 - 3$

168. The derivative of $a^{\sec x}$ w.r.t. $a^{\tan x} (a > 0)$ is

a. $a^{\sec x - \tan x}$ *b.* $\sin x a^{\sec x - \tan x}$
c. $\sin x a^{\tan x - \sec x}$ *d.* $\sec x \, a^{\sec x - \tan x}$

169. If $\sin(x + y) + \cos(x + y) = \log(x + y)$, then $\frac{d^2y}{dx^2} =$

a. 1 *b.* -1 *c.* 0 *d.* $\frac{-y}{x}$

170. If $f(x)$ is a function such that $f''(x) + f(x) = 0$ and $g(x) = [f(x)]^2 + [f'(x)]^2$ and $g(3) + 8$, then $g(8) =$

a. 8 *b.* 3
c. 0 *d.* 5

171. If the curve $y = 2x^3 + ax^2 + bx + c$ passes through the origin and the tangents drawn to it at $x = -1$ and $x = 2$ are parallel to the X-axis, then the values of a, b and c are respectively,

a. 3, -12 and 0 *b.* -3, 12 and 0
c. -3, -12 and 0 *d.* 12, -3 and 0

172. A circular sector of perimeter 60 m with maximum area is to be constructed, The radius of the circular arc in metre must be

a. 10 *b.* 15
c. 5 *d.* 20

173. The tangent and the normal drawn to the curve $y = x^2 - x + 4$ at $P(1, 4)$ cut the X-axis at A and B respectively. If the length of the subtangent drawn to the curve at P is equal to the length of the subnormal, then the area of the ΔPAB in square units is,

a. 16 *b.* 8 *c.* 32 *d.* 4

174. $\int \frac{(x^3 + 3x^2 + 3x + 1)}{(x + 1)^5} dx =$

a. $\tan^{-1} x + c$ *b.* $\log(x + 1) + c$
c. $\frac{1}{5} \log(x + 1) + c$ *d.* $-\frac{[illegible]}{(x - 1)} + c$

175. $\int \frac{\operatorname{cosec} x}{\cos^2\left(1 + \log \tan \frac{x}{2}\right)} dx =$

a. $-\tan[1 + \log \tan x / 2] + c$
b. $\sec^2[1 + \log \tan x / 2] + c$
c. $\tan[1 + \log \tan x / 2] + c$
d. $\sin^2[1 + \log \tan x / 2] + c$

176. $\int \frac{dx}{x\sqrt{x^6 - 16}}$

a. $\sec^{-1}\left(\frac{x^3}{4}\right) + c$ *b.* $\frac{1}{12} \sec^{-1}\left(\frac{x^3}{4}\right) + c$
c. $\cosh^{-1}\left(\frac{x^3}{4}\right) + c$ *d.* $\frac{1}{3} \sec^{-1}\left(\frac{x^3}{4}\right) + c$

177. If $I_1 = \int_0^{\pi/2} x \sin x \, dx$ and $I_2 = \int_0^{\pi/2} x \cos x \, dx$, then which one of the following is true?

a. $I_1 = I_2$ *b.* $I_1 + I_2 = 0$
c. $I_1 = \frac{\pi}{2} I_2$ *d.* $I_1 + I_2 = \frac{\pi}{2}$

178. If $f(x)$ is defined in $[-2, 2]$ by $f(x) = 4x^2 - 3x + 1$ and $g(x) = \frac{f(-x) - f(x)}{(x^2 + 3)}$, then $\int_{-2}^{2} g(x) \, dx =$

a. 24 *b.* 0 *c.* -48 *d.* 64

179. The area enclosed between the parabola $y = x^2 - x + 2$ and the line $y = x + 2$ in sq units =

a. $\frac{4}{3}$ *b.* $\frac{2}{3}$ *c.* $\frac{1}{3}$ *d.* $\frac{8}{3}$

180. The solution of the differential equation $e^{-x}(y + 1)\,dy + (\cos^2 x - \sin 2x)y\,(dx) = 0$ subjected to the condition that $y = 1$, when $x = 0$ is

a. $(y + 1) + e^x \cos^2 x = 2$
b. $y + \log y = e^x \cos^2 x$
c. $\log(y + 1) + e^x \cos^2 x = 1$
d. $y + \log y + e^x \cos^2 x = 2$

ANSWERS

Physics

1. (a)	**2.** (c)	**3.** (a)	**4.** (b)	**5.** (d)	**6.** (a)	**7.** (b)	**8.** (a)	**9.** (d)	**10.** (d)
11. (c)	**12.** (a)	**13.** (c)	**14.** (b)	**15.** (b)	**16.** (a)	**17.** (c)	**18.** (c)	**19.** (a)	**20.** (a)
21. (d)	**22.** (d)	**23.** (d)	**24.** (b)	**25.** (d)	**26.** (b)	**27.** (a)	**28.** (c)	**29.** (c)	**30.** (c)
31. (b)	**32.** (b)	**33.** (d)	**34.** (a)	**35.** (b)	**36.** (d)	**37.** (d)	**38.** (c)	**39.** (d)	**40.** (a)
41. (a)	**42.** (b)	**43.** (c)	**44.** (d)	**45.** (b)	**46.** (a)	**47.** (b)	**48.** (d)	**49.** (b)	**50.** (d)
51. (b)	**52.** (a)	**53.** (b)	**54.** (c)	**55.** (d)	**56.** (c)	**57.** (c)	**58.** (a)	**59.** (c)	**60.** (d)

Chemistry

61. (d)	**62.** (d)	**63.** (d)	**64.** (b)	**65.** (c)	**66.** (b)	**67.** (b)	**68.** (a)	**69.** (a)	**70.** (a)
71. (c)	**72.** (c)	**73.** (d)	**74.** (b)	**75.** (b)	**76.** (a)	**77.** (d)	**78.** (c)	**79.** (d)	**80.** (c)
81. (d)	**82.** (c)	**83.** (c)	**84.** (c)	**85.** (d)	**86.** (d)	**87.** (d)	**88.** (a)	**89.** (d)	**90.** (b)
91. (c)	**92.** (b)	**93.** (c)	**94.** (d)	**95.** (b)	**96.** (b)	**97.** (c)	**98.** (b)	**99.** (d)	**100.** (c)
101. (a)	**102.** (b)	**103.** (c)	**104.** (a)	**105.** (b)	**106.** (b)	**107.** (c)	**108.** (a)	**109.** (b)	**110.** (c)
111. (b)	**112.** (c)	**113.** (d)	**114.** (c)	**115.** (b)	**116.** (d)	**117.** (b)	**118.** (d)	**119.** (b)	**120.** (a)

Mathematics

121. (d)	**122.** (b)	**123.** (a)	**124.** (c)	**125.** (b)	**126.** (d)	**127.** (a)	**128.** (c)	**129.** (d)	**130.** (c)
131. (c)	**132.** (a)	**133.** (a)	**134.** (a)	**135.** (d)	**136.** (c)	**137.** (b)	**138.** (d)	**139.** (a)	**140.** (b)
141. (c)	**142.** (c)	**143.** (d)	**144.** (c)	**145.** (b)	**146.** (*)	**147.** (*)	**148.** (d)	**149.** (d)	**150.** (a)
151. (a)	**152.** (d)	**153.** (a)	**154.** (d)	**155.** (b)	**156.** (c)	**157.** (d)	**158.** (b)	**159.** (a)	**160.** (c)
161. (b)	**162.** (a)	**163.** (c)	**164.** (d)	**165.** (c)	**166.** (a)	**167.** (*)	**168.** (b)	**169.** (c)	**170.** (a)
171. (c)	**172.** (b)	**173.** (a)	**174.** (d)	**175.** (c)	**176.** (b)	**177.** (d)	**178.** (b)	**179.** (a)	**180.** (d)

Note (*) None of the option is correct.

HINTS & SOLUTIONS

Physics

1. *(a)* The time period of a pendulum is given by

$$T = \frac{1}{2\pi}\sqrt{\frac{l}{g}}$$

When a lift containing a simple pendulum is accelerated upwards with acceleration a, then its time period becomes

$$T' = \frac{1}{2\pi}\sqrt{\frac{l}{(g+a)}}$$

Clearly, $T' \angle T$

Hence, its time period decreases.

2. *(c)* The level of sound is given by

$$L = 10\log\left(\frac{I}{I_0}\right)\text{dB}$$

Let for 40 dB sound intensity be I and for 90dB sound intensity be I_x, then

$$40 = 10\log\left(\frac{I}{I_0}\right)$$

$$\Rightarrow \quad \log\left(\frac{I}{I_0}\right) = 4 \qquad \ldots\text{(i)}$$

and

$$90 = 10\log\left(\frac{I_x}{I_0}\right)$$

$$\Rightarrow \quad \log\left(\frac{I_x}{I_0}\right) = 9$$

Given, $I_x = xI$

$$\Rightarrow \quad \log\left(\frac{xI}{I_0}\right) = 9$$

or $\log x + \log\left(\frac{I}{I_0}\right) = 9$

$$\Rightarrow \quad \log x + 4 = 9 \qquad \text{[from Eq. (i)]}$$

$$\Rightarrow \quad \log x = 5 \Rightarrow x = 10^5$$

3. *(a)* The Doppler shift in wavelength of light from star is given by

$$d\lambda = \frac{\lambda v}{c}$$

4. *(b)* For third harmonic, $n = 3$. So, for an open pipe, the propagation of waves can be shown as

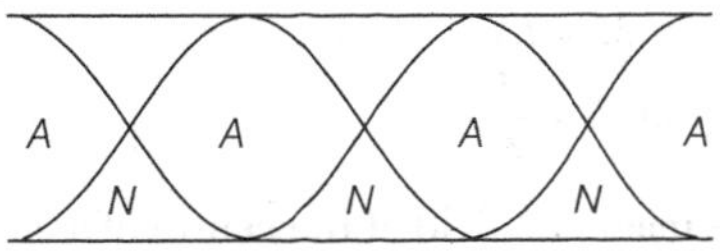

$\therefore$ Nodes = 3 and anti-nodes = 4

5. *(d)* In an adiabatic process, there is no transfer of heat takes place between a thermodynamic system and its surroundings.

6. *(a)* The efficiency of a Carnot engine is given by

$$\eta = 1 - \frac{T_2}{T_1}$$

Given, $T_1 = 627°\text{C} = 627 + 273 = 900\text{ K}$

and $T_2 = 27°\text{C} = 27 + 273 = 300\text{K}$

$$\Rightarrow \quad \eta = 1 - \frac{300}{900} = \frac{600}{900} = \frac{2}{3}$$

Also, $\eta = \frac{\text{Work done}}{\text{Heat taken}}$

$\Rightarrow$ Work done $= \eta \times$ Heat taken

$$= \frac{2}{3} \times 300 = 200\text{ J}$$

7. *(b)* The undecayed nuclei in a radioactive sample are given by

$$N = N_0\left(\frac{1}{2}\right)^{\frac{t}{t_{1/2}}}$$

Given, $N = N_0 - \frac{15}{16}N_0 = \frac{1}{16}N_0$, $t = 2\text{h}$

$$\Rightarrow \quad \frac{N_0}{16} = N_0\left(\frac{1}{2}\right)^{\frac{2}{t_{1/2}}}$$

$$\Rightarrow \quad \left(\frac{1}{2}\right)^{\frac{2}{t_{1/2}}} = \frac{1}{16} = \left(\frac{1}{2}\right)^4$$

$$\Rightarrow \quad \frac{2}{t_{t/2}} = 4 \Rightarrow t_{1/2} = \frac{1}{2}\text{h} = 30\text{ min}$$

$\therefore$ Mean life, $\tau = 1.44t_{1/2}$

$$= 1.44 \times 30 = 43.2\text{ min} \simeq 43\text{ min}$$

8. *(a)* MRI (magnetic resonance imaging) gives a detailed image of soft tissues like in brain.

9. *(d)* Of these leptons are truly elementary particles. While rest are composed of quarks, so they are composite particles.

10. *(d)* The output of NAND gate is as shown in the table below

Input		Output
A	B	Y
0	0	1
0	1	1
1	0	1
1	1	0

Thus, it will give logic 0 only when both inputs are in logic 1 state.

11. *(c)* n - type semiconductor has electrons as majority charge carriers. So, they are obtained by doping with pentavalent atoms like phosphorous, arsenic, etc.

p-type semiconductor has holes as majority charge carriers. So, they are obtained by doping with trivalent atoms like aluminium, boron, indium, etc.

12. *(a)* Given, current gain, $\beta = 50$

Input resistance, $R_i = 500\,\Omega$

Output resistance, $R_L = 4\,k\Omega = 4000\,\Omega$

Voltage gain = Current gain $\times \dfrac{R_L}{R_i}$

$$= 50 \times \frac{4000}{500} = 400$$

Power gain = Current gain × Voltage gain

$$= 50 \times 400 = 2 \times 10^4$$

13. *(c)* In Balmer series, the electrons moves to $n = 2$ state

So, possible transitions are $4 \to 2$, $3 \to 2$.

$\therefore$ Number of spectral lines are 2.

14. *(b)* The IR region lies between microwave and visible region of electromagnetic spectrum.

15. *(b)* The de-Broglie wavelength of a particle is given by

$$\lambda = \frac{h}{mv} = \frac{h}{p}$$

The momentum of proton,

$$p_p = \sqrt{2mE} = \sqrt{2meV}$$

Similarly, for α - particle,

$$p_\alpha = \sqrt{2 \times 4m \times 2e \times V} = \sqrt{16meV}$$

$$\therefore \quad \frac{\lambda_p}{\lambda_\alpha} = \frac{p_\alpha}{p_p} = \frac{\sqrt{16meV}}{\sqrt{2meV}} = \sqrt{8} = 2\sqrt{2} : 1$$

16. *(a)* Raman scattering is an inelastic scattering of a photon by molecules which are excited to higher vibrational or rotational energy level. Raman shift depends on the wavelength of incident radiation.

17. *(c)* In ${}_6C^{14}$, number of neutrons $= 14 - 6 = 8$

In ${}_7N^{15}$, number of neutrons $= 15 - 7 = 8$

These are the examples of isotones.

18. *(c)* Given, $\dfrac{I_{max}}{I_{min}} = \dfrac{9}{1}$

As we know,

$$\frac{I_{max}}{I_{min}} = \frac{(a_1 + a_2)^2}{(a_1 - a_2)^2} = \frac{9}{1}$$

$$\Rightarrow \quad \frac{a_1 + a_2}{a_1 - a_2} = \frac{3}{1}$$

$$\Rightarrow \quad a_1 + a_2 = 3a_1 - 3a_2$$

$$\Rightarrow \quad a_1 = 2a_2$$

or $$\frac{a_1}{a_2} = 2 : 1$$

19. *(a)* For dark fringe, path difference,

$$\Delta x = \left(n + \frac{1}{2}\right)\lambda$$

Also, $$\Delta x = \frac{dy}{D} \Rightarrow \frac{dy}{D} = \left(n + \frac{1}{2}\right)\lambda$$

For 1st dark fringe at directly opposite point of slit

$n = 0$, $y = \dfrac{d}{2}$

$$\Rightarrow \quad \frac{d\left(\frac{d}{2}\right)}{D} = \frac{\lambda}{2} \Rightarrow \lambda = \frac{d^2}{D}$$

20. *(a)* Newton's rings are fringes of equal thickness. These circular fringes were discovered by Newton, hence called Newton's rings. These rings are formed with equally spaced bright and dark band with central spot as dark.

21. *(d)* Diffraction pattern using light is difficult to observe in daily life because wavelength of light is very small.

22. *(d)* When a calcite crystal is placed over a dot on a piece of paper, one will observe two dots from above. If the crystal is rotated, then the dot produced by emergent ray will rotate around the stationary dot, which sometimes coincide with it.

23. *(d)* According to Brewster's law,

$$\Rightarrow \quad \mu = \tan i_p$$

At critical angle, $\mu = \dfrac{1}{\sin i_C} = \dfrac{1}{\sin 45^\circ}$

$$\Rightarrow \quad \mu = \sqrt{2}$$

$$\therefore \quad \sqrt{2} = \tan i_p$$

$$\Rightarrow \quad i_p = \tan^{-1}\sqrt{2} = 54.7^\circ$$

24. *(b)* For shunt resistance connected to galvanometer, current is given by

$$I_g = \left(\frac{S}{S+G}\right)I$$

$$\frac{2}{100}I = \left(\frac{S}{S+G}\right)I$$

$$\Rightarrow \quad S + G = 50S$$

or $$S = \frac{G}{49}$$

25. *(d)* Magnetic moment of a coil of area A carrying current I is given by

$$M = IA$$

$\Rightarrow$ Current, $I = \dfrac{M}{A}$

26. *(b)* The magnetic field at the centre of a circular coil carrying current I is given by

$$B = \frac{\mu_0 nI}{2R}$$

where, n = number of turns.

COMEDK 2016

For coil 1, $B_1 = \frac{\mu_0 \times 10 \times 0.2}{2 \times 0.2} = 5\mu_0$

For coil 2, $B_2 = \frac{\mu_0 \times 10 \times 0.3}{2 \times 0.4} = \frac{15}{4}\mu_0$

$\therefore$ Net magnetic field,

$$B = B_1 - B_2 = 5\mu_0 - \frac{15}{4}\mu_0 = \frac{5}{4}\mu_0$$

27. *(a)* Permanent magnet should have high retentivity to persist magnetism on removal of magnetic field. It should also have high coercivity, so that the magnetism is not lost by external magnetic field.

28. *(c)* The power factor is the cosine of phase angle between voltage and current. For L-C-R circuit, it is given by

$$\cos\phi = \frac{R}{Z}$$

where, Z = impedance of circuit.

29. *(c)* Given, $L = 1\text{ H}, V = 220\text{ V}, f = 50\text{ Hz}$

Peak value of current $I_0 = \frac{V_0}{X_L} = \frac{V_0}{\omega L}$

$$\Rightarrow I_0 = \frac{\sqrt{2}V}{2\pi fL} = \frac{\sqrt{2} \times 220}{2 \times \pi \times 50 \times 1} \simeq 1\text{ A}$$

30. *(c)* Let I_0 be the intensity of light incident on polariser. On passing through polariser, it gets reduced to $\frac{I_0}{2}$.

So, according to law of Malus,

$$I = \frac{I_0}{2}\cos^2\theta$$

Given, $I = \frac{75}{100} \times \frac{I_0}{2} = \frac{3I_0}{8}$

$$\therefore \quad \frac{3I_0}{8} = \frac{I_0}{2}\cos^2\theta \Rightarrow \cos\theta = \frac{\sqrt{3}}{2}$$

$$\Rightarrow \quad \theta = 30^\circ$$

31. *(b)* Potential due to a point charge at a distance r is given by

$$V = \frac{1}{4\pi\varepsilon_0\varepsilon_r} \times \frac{q}{r}$$

Given, $q = 10\text{ nC} = 10 \times 10^{-9}\text{ C}$,

$\varepsilon_r = 10, r = 0.1\text{ m}$

$$\Rightarrow V = \frac{9 \times 10^9 \times 10 \times 10^{-9}}{10 \times 0.1} = 90\text{ V}$$

32. *(b)* Permittivity of metal is very high, so its dielectric constant is infinite.

33. *(d)* Force between two point charges is given by

$$F = \frac{kq_1q_2}{r^2}$$

When $r' = r + 20\%$ of $r = 1.2r$, then

$$F' = \frac{kq_1q_2}{(1.2r)^2} = \frac{kq_1q_2}{1.44r^2} = \frac{F}{1.44}$$

Percentage decrease in force $= \frac{F - F'}{F} \times 100$

$$= \frac{F - \frac{F}{1.44}}{F} \times 100 = \frac{0.44}{1.44} \times 100 = 31\%$$

34. *(a)* Given $q_1 = q_2 = 10\text{ nC} = 10 \times 10^{-9}\text{C}$

$r = 0.09\text{ m}$

Potential energy of two point charges is given by

$$U = \frac{1}{4\pi\varepsilon_0} \times \frac{q_1q_2}{r}$$

$$= 9 \times 10^9 \times \frac{10 \times 10^{-9} \times 10 \times 10^{-9}}{0.09} = 10^{-5}\text{ J}$$

$$= 10\,\mu\text{J}$$

35. *(b)* Given, $t = \frac{d}{2}$

The capacitance is given by

$$C = \frac{\varepsilon_0 A}{d}$$

For dielectric medium between plates,

$$C' = \frac{\varepsilon_0 A}{d - t + \frac{t}{K}}$$

For metal, K = infinity

$$\Rightarrow \quad C' = \frac{\varepsilon_0 A}{d - \frac{d}{2}} = \frac{2\varepsilon_0 A}{d} = 2C$$

Hence, capacitance increases 2 times.

36. *(d)* The specific resistance is the property of material which does not depend on its geometry. It increases with increase in temperature.

37. *(d)* At 4.2 K, the resistance of mercury suddenly drops to zero and behaves as a super conductor at this temperature (called critical temperature).

38. *(c)* Given, $\alpha_r = 4 \times 10^{-3}\text{ / K}, T_1 = 20°\text{C}$

Final resistance, $R_2 = R + 10\%R = 1.1R$

We know that, $\Delta R = \alpha_r R \Delta T$

$$\Rightarrow \quad 1.1R - R = 4 \times 10^{-3} \times R \times (T_2 - 20)$$

$$\Rightarrow \quad 0.1 = 4 \times 10^{-3} \times (T_2 - 20)$$

$$\Rightarrow \quad T_2 = 25 + 20 = 45°\text{C}$$

39. *(d)* Here, 6Ω and 12Ω resistors are in parallel combination, so their equivalent resistance,

$$R_{eq} = \frac{6 \times 12}{6 + 12} = \frac{72}{18} = 4\Omega$$

Now, R_{eq} and 4Ω are in series, so total resistance,

$$R_t = 4 + 4 = 8\Omega$$

Emf of battery, $E = 16\text{ V}$

$\therefore$ Reading of voltmeter, $V' = \frac{4}{R_t} \times E = \frac{4 \times 16}{8} = 8\text{ V}$

40. *(a)* When a charged particle moves in a uniform magnetic field normally, then a magnetic force acts on it. Due to this force, it will move in a circular path.

At every point of circle, its velocity changes direction. So, its momentum also changes but the total energy will remain same.

41. *(a)* If n be the number of waves, then wavelength of light in glass, $\lambda_g = \frac{0.04}{n}$

and wavelength of light in water, $\lambda_w = \frac{0.05}{n}$

Speed of light in glass, $v_g = \lambda_g \times f = \frac{0.04f}{n}$

where, f = frequency of light.

Similarly, speed of light in water, $v_w = \lambda_w \times f = \frac{0.05f}{n}$

Relative refractive index

$$= \frac{\mu_w}{\mu_g} = \frac{v_g}{v_w} = \frac{0.04f}{n} \times \frac{n}{0.05f} = \frac{4}{5}$$

$$\Rightarrow \mu_g = \frac{5}{4} \times \mu_w = \frac{5}{4} \times \frac{4}{3} = \frac{5}{3}$$

42. *(b)* The critical angle between two media is given by

$$i_c = \sin^{-1}\left(\frac{\mu_1}{\mu_2}\right)$$

As we know that, $\mu_{air} = 1$, $\mu_{water} = 1.33$, $\mu_{glass} = 1.5$ and $\mu_{diamond} = 2.4$.

From given values, $\frac{\mu_1}{\mu_2}$ is maximum for water-glass interface. So, critical angle will also be maximum, when light travels from glass to water.

43. *(c)* Given, angle of prism, $A = 60°$

As, the ray of emergence is symmetrical to incident ray. So, the angle of minimum deviation, $D_m = 60°$.

$\therefore$ Refractive index of prism, $\mu = \frac{\sin\left(\frac{A + D_m}{2}\right)}{\sin\left(\frac{A}{2}\right)}$

$$= \frac{\sin\left(\frac{60° + 60°}{2}\right)}{\sin\left(\frac{60°}{2}\right)} = \frac{\sin 60°}{\sin 30°}$$

$$= \frac{\sqrt{3}}{2} \times \frac{2}{1} = \sqrt{3} = 1.73$$

44. *(d)* In the spectrum of visible light produced by a prism, the violet light have minimum wavelength. So, the dispersion will be maximum towards violet.

45. *(b)* Given, $\mu_g = 1.5$, $\mu_w = \frac{4}{3}$

From lens Maker's formula,

$$\frac{1}{f} = (\mu_g - 1)\left(\frac{1}{R_1} - \frac{1}{R_2}\right)$$

$$\Rightarrow \quad \frac{1}{R_1} - \frac{1}{R_2} = \frac{1}{f(\mu_g - 1)} \quad \ldots\text{(i)}$$

When lens is immersed in water, then

$$\frac{1}{f'} = \left(\frac{\mu_g}{\mu_w} - 1\right)\left(\frac{1}{R_1} - \frac{1}{R_2}\right)$$

$$= \left(\frac{\mu_g}{\mu_w} - 1\right)\frac{1}{f(\mu_g - 1)} \quad \text{[using Eq. (i)]}$$

$$\frac{f}{f'} = \left(\frac{1.5}{4/3} - 1\right) \times \frac{1}{(1.5 - 1)}$$

$$= \left(\frac{9}{8} - 1\right) \times 2 = \frac{1}{4}$$

$$\Rightarrow \quad f' = 4f \text{ or } f' > f$$

$\therefore$ The focal length of lens is greater than f in water.

46. *(a)* The focal length of combination of two lenses,

$$\frac{1}{f} = \frac{1}{f_1} + \frac{1}{f_2} = \frac{1}{(1/4)} + \frac{1}{(-1/2)} \quad \left(f = \frac{1}{P}\right)$$

$$= 4 - 2 = 2$$

$$\Rightarrow f = 0.5 \text{ m}$$

47. *(b)* Eddy currents are produced in a material, when it is placed in a time varying magnetic field. It is based on the Faraday's law of etectromagnetic induction.

48. *(d)* Given, $V_p = 220$ V, $\eta = 80\% = 0.8$

$$P_0 = 8 \text{ kW} = 8000 \text{ W}$$

Efficiency of transformer, $\eta = \frac{\text{Output power}}{\text{Input power}}$

$$\Rightarrow \quad \eta = \frac{P_o}{P_i} \Rightarrow 0.8 = \frac{8000}{P_i}$$

$$\Rightarrow \quad P_i = \frac{8000}{0.8} = 10000$$

$$\Rightarrow \quad V_p I_p = 10000$$

$$\text{or} \quad I_p = \frac{10000}{220} = 45.5 \text{ A} \simeq 45 \text{ A}$$

49. *(b)* Given, $f_0 = 600$ Hz, $Q_1 = 3$, $Q_2 = 2$

The bandwidth in *L-C-R* circuit,

$$\beta = \frac{f_0}{Q}$$

As, quality factor decreases, bandwidth increases. This increase in bandwidth is given by

$$\Delta\beta = \beta_2 - \beta_1 = \frac{f_0}{Q_2} - \frac{f_0}{Q_1} = f_0\left(\frac{1}{Q_2} - \frac{1}{Q_1}\right)$$

$$= 600\left(\frac{1}{2} - \frac{1}{3}\right) = 100 \text{ Hz}$$

50. *(d)* Given, $t = 4$ s, $u = 0$, $g = 10\text{ms}^{-2}$

Using equation of motion,

$$h = ut + \frac{1}{2}gt^2 = \frac{1}{2}gt^2 = \frac{1}{2} \times 10 \times (4)^2 = 80 \text{ m}$$

51. *(b)* In liquid crystal phases, there are 4 types of phases as Nematic, Smectic, Cholesteric and Discotic. Of these, Smectic phase is more close to solid than to liquid.

52. *(a)* The acceleration due to gravity at earth's surface is given by

$$g = \frac{GM}{R^2}$$

As, mass remains constant.

$$\Rightarrow \quad g \propto \frac{1}{R^2}$$

so, as the radius of earth decreases or the earth shrinks in size, the value of g increases.

53. *(b)* The thermal resistance of a rod is given by

$$R = \frac{l}{KA}$$

As, length and area of two rods are same, then in series combination,

$$R = R_1 + R_2$$

$$\Rightarrow \quad \frac{2l}{K_s A} = \frac{l}{K_1 A} + \frac{l}{K_2 A}$$

$$\Rightarrow \quad \frac{2}{K_s} = \frac{1}{K_1} + \frac{1}{K_2} = \frac{K_1 + K_2}{K_1 K_2}$$

$$\Rightarrow \quad K_s = \frac{2K_1 K_2}{K_1 + K_2}$$

54. *(c)* Let F_1 and F_2 be the two forces acting at a point, then their resultant,

$$F_R = \sqrt{F_1^2 + F_2^2 + 2F_1 F_2 \cos\theta}$$

Given, $\quad F_1 = F_2 = F$

$$\Rightarrow \quad F_R = \sqrt{2F^2 + 2F^2 \cos\theta}$$

$$\Rightarrow \quad F_R^2 = 2F^2(1 + \cos\theta) \quad \ldots\text{(i)}$$

As per question,

$$F_R^2 = 3F_1 F_2 = 3F^2$$

$$\Rightarrow \quad 2F^2(1 + \cos\theta) = 3F^2 \quad \text{[using Eq. (i)]}$$

$$\Rightarrow \quad 1 + \cos\theta = \frac{3}{2}$$

$$\Rightarrow \quad \cos\theta = \frac{1}{2} \text{ or } \theta = 60^\circ$$

55. *(d)* The addition of impurities in a liquid may increase or decrease the surface tension of liquid depending on the nature of impurities.

If the impurities are highly soluble in liquid, then it will increase the surface tension. But if it is less soluble in liquid, then it will decrease the surface tension of liquid.

56. *(c)* The viscosity decreases with increase in temperature. Due to this reason, the hot water moves faster than cold water. Since in summer temperature is high, so more viscous oils are used in motorcars.

57. *(c)* Moment of momentum of an electron in nth orbit is given by

$$L = \frac{nh}{2\pi}$$

For an electron in second Bohr orbit, $n = 2$

$$\therefore \quad L = \frac{2h}{2\pi} = \frac{h}{\pi}$$

58. *(a)* The excitation energy is the minimum energy required to excite an electron from ground state of atom to any of its excited state and ionisation energy is the amount energy needed to remove an electron from an atom.

So, lesser the excitation energy and more the ionisation energy, more the stability of atom.

59. *(c)* Given, work function, $\phi = 3$ eV

The wavelength of incident radiation is given by

$$\lambda = \frac{hc}{\phi} = \frac{1242}{\phi} = \frac{1242}{3} = 414 \text{ nm}$$

60. *(d)* The equivalent capacitance of three capacitors connected in series is given by

$$\frac{1}{C_s} = \frac{1}{C_1} + \frac{1}{C_2} + \frac{1}{C_3}$$

Given, $C_1 = C_2 = C_3 = C$

$$\frac{1}{C_s} = \frac{3}{C} \text{ or } C_s = \frac{C}{3}$$

Similarly, for parallel combination,

$$C_p = C + C + C = 3C$$

$\therefore$ Ratio of equivalent capacitance,

$$\frac{C_s}{C_p} = \frac{C/3}{3C} = \frac{1}{9} \text{ or } 1:9$$

COMEDK 2016

Chemistry

61. *(d)* An organic compound gives oily liquid on heating with bromine and potassium hydroxide solution. On shaking with acetic anhydride, an antipyretic drug acetanilide obtained is benzamide.

$$\underset{\text{Benzamide}}{C_6H_5\text{—}CONH_2} \xrightarrow{Br_2/KOH} C_6H_5NH_2 \xrightarrow{(CH_3CO)_2O} \underset{\text{Acetanilide}}{C_6H_5NHCOCH_3}$$

62. *(d)* Silver salt of fatty acid on refluxing with an alkyl halide gives an ester.

$$\underset{\text{Silver salt of fatty acid}}{CH_3COOAg} + \underset{\text{Alkyl halide}}{C_2H_5Br} \longrightarrow \underset{\text{Ester}}{CH_3COOC_2H_5} + AgBr$$

63. *(d)* Pepsin, ptyalin, lipase are all enzymes used for the breaking down of nutrients, while cellulose is a polysaccharide.

64. *(b)* Combination of H_2 and Br_2 to give HBr, is second order reaction.

$$H_2 + Br_2 \longrightarrow 2HBr$$

Rate law expression, $r = k[H_2][Br_2]$

$\therefore$ Order w.r.t. H_2 and Br_2 is one.

$\therefore$ Overall order $= 1 + 1 = 2$

65. *(c)* The diameter of colloidal particle ranges from 10^{-6} m to 10^{-9} m.

66. *(b)* The 2*p*-orbital has electronic configuration as follows

↑↓	↑↓	↑↓

$\therefore$ Three electrons are with $-1/2$ spin quantum number and other three electrons are with $+1/2$ spin quantum number.

67. *(b)* The molecular formula of 2-methyl butane, 2,2-dimethyl propane and pentane is same i.e. (C_5H_{12}). They are structural isomers.

68. *(a)* $\underset{\substack{1\text{ mole}\\(28\text{ g})}}{N_2} + \underset{\substack{3\text{ moles}\\(6\text{ g})}}{3H_2} \longrightarrow \underset{\substack{2\text{ moles}\\(34\text{ g})}}{2NH_3}$

$\therefore$ Mass of N_2 left $= 56 - 28 = 28$ g

$\therefore$ Moles of N_2 left $= \frac{28}{28} = 1$ mole

Mass of H_2 left $= 8 - 6 = 2$ g

$\therefore$ Moles of H_2 left $= \frac{2}{2} = 1$ mole

Moles of ammonia $= \frac{34}{17} = 2$ moles

69. *(a)* For constant pressure and temperature process, ΔH and $\Delta U = 0$

70. *(a)* In a galvanic cell, the electron flow from anode to cathode through the external circuit.

71. *(c)* The mixture of 2-chloropropane and chloromethane on treating with sodium metal in dry ether gives 2-methyl propane i.e.,

$$\underset{\text{2-chloropropane}}{CH_3\text{—}\overset{\overset{CH_3}{|}}{CH}\text{—}Cl} + \underset{\text{Chloromethane}}{Cl\text{—}CH_3} \xrightarrow[\text{Dry ether}]{2Na} \underset{\text{2-methylpropane}}{CH_3\text{—}\overset{\overset{CH_3}{|}}{CH}\text{—}CH_3} + 2NaCl$$

72. *(c)* Benzyl chloride is more reactive than alkyl halides as benzyl carbocation is stabilised by resonance. Hence, it easily gives nucleophilic substitution reaction.

73. *(d)* The main product obtained when sodium carbonate reacts with mercuric chloride is mercuric oxide.

$$HgCl_2 + Na_2CO_3 \longrightarrow HgO + CO_2 + 2NaCl \text{ or } HgCO_3 + 2NaCl$$

74. *(b)* In a electrothermal process, the compound displayed by silica from calcium phosphite is phosphorus pentoxide as follows:

$$2\,Ca_3(PO_4)_2 + 6\,SiO_2 \longrightarrow \underset{\text{(Slag)}}{6CaSiO_3} + P_4O_{10}$$

75. *(b)* $\underset{16\text{ g}}{CH_4} + \underset{64\text{ g}}{2O_2} \longrightarrow \underset{44\text{ g}}{CO_2} + \underset{36\text{ g}}{2H_2O}$; $\Delta H = 890$ kJ/mol

Heat liberated on combustion of 16 g CH_4 is 890 kJ.

$\therefore$ Heat liberation from 3.2 g methane

$$= \frac{3.2}{16} \times 890 = \frac{890}{5}$$

$$= 178 \text{ kJ}$$

76. *(a)* According to gas equation,

$$pV = nRT$$

$$\therefore \quad V = \frac{nRT}{p}$$

As both *p* and *T* are double, *V* remains constant i.e., 4 dm^3.

77. *(d)* Copper on reacting with conc.HNO_3 gives copper nitrate.

$$\underset{4\text{ g}}{Cu} + HNO_3\text{ (conc.)} \longrightarrow \underset{\text{Copper nitrate}}{Cu(NO_3)_2} + 2H_2O + 2NO_2$$

On strongly heating with copper nitrate, copper oxide is obtained.

$$2Cu(NO_3)_2 \longrightarrow \underset{\substack{\text{Copper oxide}\\(5\text{ g})}}{2CuO} + 4NO_2 + O_2$$

$\therefore$ Equivalent weight of Cu

$= $ Weight of copper $\times$ Equivalent weight of oxygen

$= 4 \times 8 = 32$

78. *(c)* For the following reaction,

$$N_2 + 3H_2 \rightleftharpoons 2NH_3 + 92.3 \text{ kJ}$$

(i) Reducing temperature is favourable as it is an exothermic process and shift equilibrium towards right.

(ii) Also on removing NH_3 equilibrium shift towards right according to Le-Chatelier's principle.

(iii) Δn_g is negative for the process. Increase in pressure, equilibrium towards right.

For an exothermic reaction, increasing temperature shifts the reaction to reactant side.

79. *(d)* The chemical equilibrium of a reversible reaction is not influenced by catalyst as it only increase the rate of reaction to achieve the equilibrium faster. The increase in rate of forward direction is equal to increase in rate of backward direction at equilibrium.

∴Equilibrium point is not shifted.

80. *(c)* The structure of cumene is

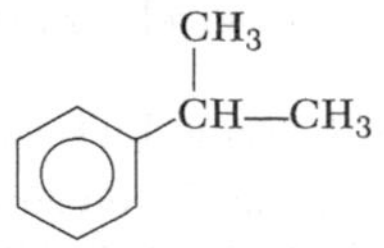

The IUPAC name is 1-methyl ethyl benzene.

81. *(d)* Moles of HCl $= \dfrac{1.2046 \times 10^{24}}{6.023 \times 10^{23}} = 2$

$$\therefore \text{Normality} = \frac{\text{moles of HCl}}{\text{volume of solution (L or dm}^3)} = \frac{2}{1} = 2\text{ N}$$

82. *(c)* Nuclear theory of atom was put forward by Rutherford. He discovered α and β-rays and projected the law of radioactive decay.

83. *(c)* In acetylene or ethyne molecule, the two carbon atoms are linked by one σ and two π-bonds.

84. *(c)* $H_2(g) + \frac{1}{2}O_2(g) \longrightarrow H_2O(g); \Delta H_1 = +\text{ ve}$

$H_2O(g) \longrightarrow H_2O(l) \quad ; \Delta H_3 = +\text{ ve}$

$H_2(g) + \frac{1}{2}O_2(g) \longrightarrow H_2O(l) \quad ; \Delta H_2 = \Delta H_1 + \Delta H_3$

$\therefore \Delta H_2 > \Delta H_1$

85. *(d)* For radioactive decay

$$t_{1/2} = \frac{0.693}{k}$$

For concentration to reduce to $\frac{1}{16}$ of original amount

$$t = t_{1/2} \times 4$$

$$\therefore \quad t_{1/2} = \frac{192}{4} = 48 \text{ min}$$

86. *(d)* The reagent, Cl_2 does not give acid chloride on heating with carboxylic acids, while other reagents give acid chloride.

R—COOH $\xrightarrow{PCl_5}$ R—COCl + $POCl_3$ + HCl

R—COOH $\xrightarrow{PCl_3}$ 3R—COCl + H_3PO_3

R—COOH $\xrightarrow{SOCl_2}$ R—COCl − SO_2↑ + HCl↑

87. *(d)* Reducing property of halogens increases from F to I.

∴I get oxidised by nitric acid.

$$\overset{0}{I_2} + 10\,HNO_3 \longrightarrow 2H\overset{+5}{I}O_3 + 10\,NO_2 + 4H_2O$$

Iodine, Nitric acid, Iodic acid

Oxidation (Iodine → Iodic acid)

88. *(a)* Lead form nitric oxide with dil. HNO_3. It does not form ammonium nitrate by reaction with dil. nitric acid.

$$3Pb + 8HNO_3 \longrightarrow 3Pb(NO_3)_2 + \underset{\text{Nitric oxide}}{2NO} + 4H_2O$$

89. *(d)* The elements with atomic number 9, 17, 35, 53 and 85 are all halogens, they have electronic configuration of ns^2np^5.

90. *(b)* In the electrolytic method of obtaining aluminium from purified bauxite, cryolite is added to the charge in order to lower the melting point of bauxite and brings conductivity.

91. *(c)* HNO_3 is not an amphoteric substance as, it behave only as acid. It can only donate H^+ ions. While, substance like HCO_3^-, H_2O, and NH_3 can act as both donor and acceptor to H^+ ions, so they are amphoteric in nature.

92. *(b)* Equivalent moles of H_2SO_4 and KOH undergoing neutralisation

$$= 50 \times 0.2 \times 10^{-3} = 0.01$$

∴Heat of neutralisation = 0.01 × 57.3 kJ = 573 J

93. *(c)*

$$\underset{\text{Parent nucleus}}{^{14}X_5} \longrightarrow {^{14}X_6} + {^{0}_{-1}e}$$

$$\downarrow$$

$$^{14}N_7 + {^{0}_{-1}e}$$

∴The number of neutrons in parent nucleus = 14 − 5 = 9

94. *(d)* Stainless steel does not rust because chromium forms an oxide layer and protects iron from rusting.

95. *(b)* Ethanol can be synthesised as follows:

$$CH_3MgI + \underset{\text{Formaldehyde}}{HCHO} \xrightarrow{H_2O} \underset{\text{Ethanol}}{CH_3\text{—}CH_2OH} + Mg(OH)I$$

96. *(b)* The rate law expression is, $r = k[SO_2]^2[O_2]$

As, volume increase 2 times, concentration reduces by $\frac{1}{2}$ times i.e., $[SO_2]_1 = [2SO_2]$ and $[O_2]_1 = [2O_2]$

$\therefore$ New rate, $r_1 = k[2SO_2]^2[2O_2]$

$\therefore$ $r_1 = 8r$

$\therefore$ $\frac{r_1}{r} = \frac{8}{1}$

97. *(c)* The pH of buffer solution is given as,

$$pH_1 = pK_a + \log \frac{[CH_3COONa]}{[CH_3COOH]} \quad \ldots(i)$$

Given, $[CH_3COONa]_2 / [CH_3COOH]_2$

$= 10[CH_3COONa]/[CH_3COOH]$

$pH_2 = pK_a + \log 10[CH_3COONa]/[CH_3COOH]$

$pH_2 = pK_a + \log[CH_3COONa]/[CH_3COOH] + \log 10$

$\therefore pH_2 = pH_1 + 1$ [From Eq. (i)]

98. *(b)* When mixture of methane and oxygen is passed through heated molybdenum oxide, the main product formed is methanal.

$$\underset{\text{Methane}}{CH_4} + O_2 \xrightarrow{\text{Mo-oxide}} \underset{\text{Methanal}}{HCHO} + H_2O$$

99. *(d)* Benzene can be obtained by heating benzoic acid with soda lime and phenol with zinc dust as follows:

$$\underset{\text{Benzoic acid}}{C_6H_5COOH} + \underset{\text{Soda lime }(X)}{2NaOH} \xrightarrow{\Delta} \underset{\text{Benzene}}{C_6H_6} + Na_2CO_3$$

$$\underset{\text{Phenol}}{C_6H_5—OH} + \underset{\substack{\text{Zinc dust}\\(Y)}}{Zn} \xrightarrow{\Delta} C_6H_6 + ZnO$$

100. *(c)* Ethyl benzoate is boiled with alc. potash to give ethyl alcohol and potassium benzoate.

$$\underset{\text{Ethyl benzoate}}{C_6H_5COOCH_2CH_3} \xrightarrow[H_2O]{\text{Alc. potash}} C_6H_5COOK + CH_3CH_2OH$$

Potassium benzoate is converted into benzoic acid, a white solid which separates out.

$$C_6H_5COOK + HCl \longrightarrow C_6H_5COOH + KCl$$

101. *(a)* On passing H_2S gas in presence of dil. HCl for qualitative analysis of second group due to common ion effect, lower concentration of sulphide ions is obtained. It is sufficient for the precipitation of second group cations in forms of their sulphides and hence their dissociation decreases.

102. *(b)* $E^\circ = E^\circ_{(Ag^+/Ag)} - E^\circ_{(Al^{3+}/Al)}$

$2.46 = 0.80 - E^\circ_{(Al^{3+}/Al)}$

$\therefore$ $E^\circ_{(Al^{3+}/Al)} = -1.66$ V

$\therefore$ Reduction potential $= -1.66$ V.

103. *(c)* The first fraction obtained during the fractionation of petroleum is hydrocarbon gases.

104. *(a)* Ethanol gives trichloromethane on distilling with bleaching powder.

(I) $Cl_2 + H_2O \longrightarrow 2HCl + [O]$

$$\underset{\text{Ethanol}}{CH_3CH_2OH} + [O] \longrightarrow CH_3CHO + H_2O$$

(II) $CH_3CHO + 3Cl_2 \longrightarrow CCl_3CHO + 3HCl$

(III) $CCl_3CHO + Ca(OH)_2 \longrightarrow \underset{\text{Trichloro methane}}{2CHCl_3} + (HCOO)_2Ca$

105. *(b)* Benzoin is a α-hydroxy ketone.

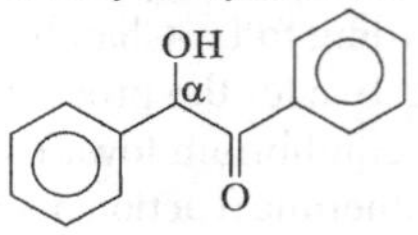

106. *(b)* For every 10K rise in temperature, rate of reaction double.

$\therefore$ From 298 K to 310 K, the reaction rate became $(2)^2$ times i.e., 4 times.

$\therefore$ $k = 3.2 \times 10^{-3}\ s^{-1} \times 4 = 1.28 \times 10^{-2} s^{-1}$

107. *(c)* The acidic strength of an acid increase with ionisation.

The value of pK_a is inversely proportional to ionisation constant (K_a).

$\therefore$ The acid with pK_a value 1.0 is strongest.

108. *(a)* Unsaturated fatty acids contains one or more double bond in their carbon chains.

Their general formula is $C_nH_{2n-2x}O_2$.

$\therefore$ Oleic acid $(C_{18}H_{34}O_2)$ is unsaturated fatty acid with one double bond.

109. *(b)* Nylon is not a homopolymer. It is a polymer of hexamethylenediamine and adipic acid.

110. *(c)* The coaltar fraction which contains phenol is called middle oil.

111. *(b)*

	A	+	B	$\rightleftharpoons$	C	+	D
Initially	1		1		0		0
at equilibrium	$\frac{2}{3}$		$\frac{2}{3}$		$\frac{1}{3}$		$\frac{1}{3}$

$\therefore$ Equilibrium constant $(K) = \frac{[C][D]}{[A][B]}$

$$= \frac{\frac{1}{3}\cdot\frac{1}{3}}{\frac{2}{3}\cdot\frac{2}{3}} = \frac{1}{4} = 0.25$$

112. *(c)* The particles of ore float because their surface is not easily wetted by water.

113. *(d)* Amorphous solids are isotropic in nature i.e., they shows same properties in all the directions.

114. *(c)* Rate of diffusion $\propto \frac{1}{\sqrt{\text{Molar mass}}}$

$\therefore$ $\frac{r_H}{r_A} = \sqrt{\frac{M_A}{M_H}}$

$\because$ $r_H = 6r_A$

$\therefore$ $6 = \sqrt{\frac{M_A}{2}}$

$\therefore$ $M_A = 72$

115. *(b)* Dulong and Petit's law is valid only for solid elements. According to this law, the product of atomic mass and specific heat of a solid element is approximately equal to 6.4 cal/mol.

116. *(d)* The gas which has greater critical temperature is readily adsorbed by activated charcoal.
The order of critical temperature is
$$H_2 < N_2 < O_2 < SO_2$$
$\therefore$ SO_2 gas is readily adsorbed by chorcoal.

117. *(b)* In fcc unit cell of NaCl, Na^+ ion is present at edge centre and Cl^- ion is present at corner.
$\therefore$ Edge length, $a = 2r^+ + 2r^-$
$$\therefore \quad a = 2(r^+ + r^-)$$
$$= 2x \qquad [\because x = r^+ + r^-]$$

118. *(d)* In $K_3[Fe(CN)_6]$, the ligand has satisfied both primary and secondary valencies of ferric ion. The + 3 charge of ferric ion is satisfied by negative charge on cyanide ion. The coordination sphere's secondary valency is satisfied by six cyanide ligands.

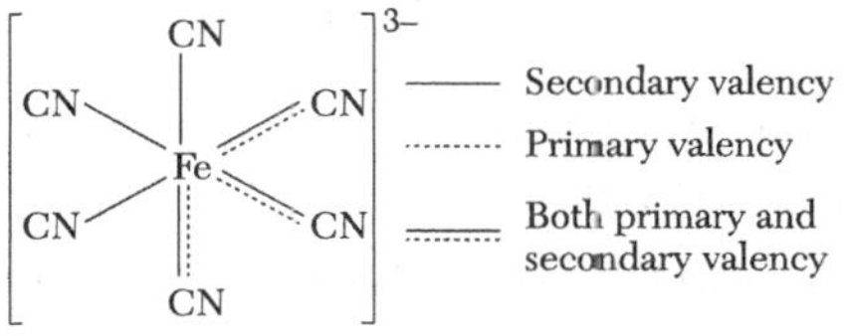

119. *(b)* 2-acetoxy benzoic acid is aspirin. It is used as an antipyretic to reduce body temperature.

120. *(a)* Nucleoside on hydrolysis gives an aldopentose and a heterocyclic base i.e. purine and pyrimidine.

Mathematics

121. *(d)* Given that, $A = \{a, b, c\}$, $B = \{b, c, d\}$
and $c = \{a, d, c\}$
Now, $A - B = \{a, b, c\} - \{b, c, d\} = \{a\}$
and $B \cap C = \{b, c, d\} \cap \{a, d, c\} = \{c, d\}$
$(A - B) \times (B \cap C) = \{a\} \times \{c, d\} = \{(a, c), (a, d)\}$

122. *(b)* We have,
$f : X \to Y$
X : domain and Y : codomain
In one-one function,
$$x_1 \neq x_2$$
$$f(x_1) \neq f(x_2)$$
In onto function,
Range = domain
$f(x) = \sin x$
So, if $X = \left[0, \frac{\pi}{2}\right]$ and $Y = [-1, 1]$
For each value of $x \in X$ and range $= [0, 1]$, there exists a unique value for $y \in Y$
Hence, function is one-one but not onto.

123. *(a)* We have,
$$\log_4 2 + \log_4 4 + \log_4 16 + \log_4 x = 6$$
$$\log_4 (2 \times 4 \times x \times 16) = 6$$
$$\log_4 (128x) = 6$$
$$\Rightarrow \quad 128x = 4^6$$
$$\Rightarrow \quad 128x = 64 \times 4^3$$
$$\Rightarrow \quad 2x = 4^3$$
$$\Rightarrow \quad x = \frac{64}{2} = 32$$

124. *(c)* We have,
$$S_n = \frac{1}{6 \cdot 11} + \frac{1}{11 \cdot 16} + \frac{1}{16 \cdot 21} + \dots + n \text{ terms}$$
$$= \frac{1}{5}\left(\frac{1}{6} - \frac{1}{11} + \frac{1}{11} - \frac{1}{16} + \dots \frac{1}{5n-1} - \frac{1}{5n+6}\right)$$
$$= \frac{1}{5}\left(\frac{1}{6} - \frac{1}{5n+6}\right)$$
$$= \frac{1}{5}\left[\frac{5n+6-6}{6(5n+6)}\right]$$
$$= \frac{1}{5}\left[\frac{5n}{6(5n+6)}\right]$$
$$\text{So, } 6S_n = \frac{n}{(5n+6)}$$

125. *(b)* Here, terms greater than $5!$, i.e.
$(5!)^2, (6!)^2, \dots, (100!)^2$ is divisible by 100.
$\therefore$ For terms
$(5!)^2, (6!)^2, \dots (100!)^2$ remainder is 0.
Now, consider $(1!)^2 + (2!)^2 + (3!)^2 + (4!)^2$
$$= 1 + 4 + 36 + 576$$
$$= 617$$
When, 617 is divided by 100, its remainder is 17.
So, required remainder is 17.

126. *(d)* Given that, $(p \wedge \sim r) \to (\sim p \vee q)$ is false
$\Rightarrow (p \wedge \sim r)$ is true and $(\sim p \vee q)$ is false
$\Rightarrow$ (p is true and $\sim r$ is true)
and ($\sim p$ is false and q is false)
$\Rightarrow p$ is true, r is false and q is false.

127. *(a)* Since, α, β and γ are the roots of the equation
$x^3 - 8x + 8 = 0$, then
$$\alpha + \beta + \gamma = 0, \ \alpha\beta + \beta\gamma + \gamma\alpha = -8,$$
$$\alpha\beta\gamma = -8 \qquad \dots \text{(i)}$$
Therefore, $(\alpha + \beta + \gamma)^2 = 0$
$$\Rightarrow \alpha^2 + \beta^2 + \gamma^2 + 2(\alpha\beta + \beta\gamma + \gamma\alpha) = 0$$

$\Rightarrow \alpha^2 + \beta^2 + \gamma^2 = -2(-8) = 16$

$\Sigma\alpha^2 = 16$

and $\dfrac{1}{\alpha\beta} + \dfrac{1}{\beta\gamma} + \dfrac{1}{\gamma\alpha} = \dfrac{\alpha+\beta+\gamma}{\alpha\beta\gamma} = \dfrac{0}{-8} = 0$

$\Sigma\dfrac{1}{\alpha\beta} = 0$

128. *(c)* $1080 = 2^3 \times 3^3 \times 5$ (prime factorization)

$675 = 3^3 \times 5^2$

So, Greatest Common divisor $= 3^3 \times 5 = 27 \times 5 = 135$

129. *(d)* $b \equiv c \pmod a$

So, $\dfrac{b+c}{a}$ and $\dfrac{b-c}{a} = \dfrac{(b+c)(b-c)}{a^2}$

$= \dfrac{b^2-c^2}{a^2}$ or $\dfrac{a^2}{b^2-c^2}$

Here, $b^2 \equiv c^2 (\text{mod } a^2)$

130. *(c)* By taking option (*c*),

$a \mid (b+c) \not\Rightarrow a \mid b$ and $a \mid c$

e.g. $6 \mid 18 \not\Rightarrow 6 \mid 1$ and $6 \mid 17$

131. *(c)* We have, $2A + 3B = \begin{bmatrix} 2 & -1 & 4 \\ 3 & 2 & 5 \end{bmatrix}$ ... (i)

and $A + 2B = \begin{bmatrix} 5 & 0 & 3 \\ 1 & 6 & 2 \end{bmatrix}$ ... (ii)

Multiply Eq. (ii) by 2, we get

$2A + 4B = \begin{bmatrix} 10 & 0 & 6 \\ 2 & 12 & 4 \end{bmatrix}$ ... (iii)

Now, subtracting Eq. (i) from Eq. (iii), we get

$$B = \begin{bmatrix} 10 & 0 & 6 \\ 2 & 12 & 4 \end{bmatrix} - \begin{bmatrix} 2 & -1 & 4 \\ 3 & 2 & 5 \end{bmatrix} = \begin{bmatrix} 8 & 1 & 2 \\ -1 & 10 & -1 \end{bmatrix}$$

132. *(a)* Given that,

$O(A) = 2 \times 3$, $O(B) = 3 \times 2$,

$O(C) = 3 \times 3$

$\Rightarrow O(A') = 3 \times 2$, $O(B') = 2 \times 3$

(a) $C(A + B')$

Now, $O(A + B') = 2 \times 3$

and $O(C) = 3 \times 3$

So, matrix $C(A + B')$ cannot be determined.

(b) $C(A + B')'$

$O(A + B') = 2 \times 3$

$\Rightarrow O(A + B')' = 3 \times 2$ and $O(C) = 3 \times 3$

Therefore, matrix $C(A + B')'$ can be determined.

(c) $O(BA) = 3 \times 3$ and $O(C) = 3 \times 3$

Therefore, matrix BAC can be determined.

(d) $CB + A'$

Now, order of CB = (order of C) (order of B)

= (order of C is 3×3) (order of B is 3×2)

= order of CB is 3×2

Since, $O(A') = 3 \times 2$

Therefore, matrix $CB + A'$ can be determined.

133. *(a)* We have, $A = \begin{bmatrix} 1 & -3 \\ 2 & k \end{bmatrix}$

Now, $A = \begin{bmatrix} 1 & -3 \\ 2 & k \end{bmatrix}\begin{bmatrix} 1 & -3 \\ 2 & k \end{bmatrix}$

$= \begin{bmatrix} 1-6 & -3-3k \\ 2+2k & -6+k^2 \end{bmatrix} = \begin{bmatrix} -5 & -3-3k \\ 2+2k & k^2-6 \end{bmatrix}$

Now, $A^2 - 4A + 10I = A$

$\Rightarrow \begin{bmatrix} -5 & -3-3k \\ 2+2k & k^2-6 \end{bmatrix} - 4\begin{bmatrix} 1 & -3 \\ 2 & k \end{bmatrix}$

$+ 10\begin{bmatrix} 1 & 0 \\ 0 & 1 \end{bmatrix} = \begin{bmatrix} 1 & -3 \\ 2 & k \end{bmatrix}$

$\Rightarrow \begin{bmatrix} -5-4+10 & -3-3k+12+0 \\ 2+2k-8+0 & k^2-6-4k+10 \end{bmatrix} = \begin{bmatrix} 1 & -3 \\ 2 & k \end{bmatrix}$

$\Rightarrow \begin{bmatrix} -1 & -3k+9 \\ 2k-6 & k^2-4k+4 \end{bmatrix} = \begin{bmatrix} 1 & -3 \\ 2 & k \end{bmatrix}$

On comparing both sides, we get

$k^2 - 4k + 4 = k$

$\Rightarrow k^2 - 5k + 4 = 0$

$\Rightarrow k^2 - 4k - k + 4 = 0$

$\Rightarrow k(k-4) - 1(k-4) = 0$

$\Rightarrow (k-4)(k-1) = 0$

$\Rightarrow k = 4, 1$

134. *(a)* $\begin{vmatrix} x+y & y+z & z+x \\ x & y & z \\ x-y & y-z & z-x \end{vmatrix}$

$= \begin{vmatrix} 2(x+y+z) & y+z & z+x \\ (x+y+z) & y & z \\ 0 & y-z & z-x \end{vmatrix}$

$[\because C_1 \to C_1 + C_2 + C_3]$

$= (x+y+z)\begin{vmatrix} 2 & y+z & z+x \\ 1 & y & z \\ 0 & y-z & z-x \end{vmatrix}$

$= (x+y+z)\begin{vmatrix} 2 & y+z & z+x \\ 0 & y-z & z-x \\ 0 & y-z & z-x \end{vmatrix}$

$[\because R_2 \to 2R_2 - R_1]$

$= (x+y+z) \times 0 = 0$

[$\because$ R_2 and R_3 are identical]

135. *(d)* If $a * b = b * a$, then the operation is commutative.

If $(a * b) * c = a * (b * c)$, then the operation is associative.

By option (d),

$a * b = a + b + ab$

$b * a = b + a + ba = a + b + ab$

Here, $a * b = b * a$, so the operation is commutative.

COMEDK 2016

$$(a*b)*c = (a+b+ab)*c$$
$$= (a+b+ab)+c+(a+b+ab)c$$
$$= a+b+ab+c+ac+bc+abc$$
$$= a+b+c+ab+ac+bc+abc$$
$$a*(b*c) = a*(b+c+bc)$$
$$= a+b+c+bc+a(b+c+bc)$$
$$= a+b+c+bc+ab+ac+abc$$

Here, $(a*b)*c = a*(b*c)$.

So, the operation is associative.

136. *(c)* Given that, $G = \{1, 5, 7, 11\}$ is a group under multiplication module 12.

$\because \quad 7^{-1} = 7 \quad [\because 7^{-1} \otimes_{12} 7 = 1]$

Now, $\quad 7^{-1} \otimes_{12} (x \otimes_{12} 11) = 5$

$\Rightarrow \quad 7 \otimes_{12} (11 \otimes_{12} x) = 5$

$\Rightarrow \quad (7 \otimes_{12} 11) \otimes_{12} x = 5$

$\{7 \otimes_{12} 11 = \text{remainder after dividing 77 from 12}\}$

$\Rightarrow \quad 5 \otimes_{12} x = 5$

$\Rightarrow \quad x = 1$

137. *(b)* In additive subgroup 'o' is the identity.

So, required set $(N, +)$ which is not a subgroup.

138. *(d)* We have, $\mathbf{p} = \hat{\mathbf{i}} + \hat{\mathbf{j}}$, $\mathbf{q} = 4\hat{\mathbf{k}} - \hat{\mathbf{j}}$ and $\mathbf{r} = \hat{\mathbf{i}} + \hat{\mathbf{k}}$

So, $3\mathbf{p} + \mathbf{q} - 2\mathbf{r} = 3\hat{\mathbf{i}} + 3\hat{\mathbf{j}} + 4\hat{\mathbf{k}} - \hat{\mathbf{j}} - 2\hat{\mathbf{i}} - 2\hat{\mathbf{k}}$

$= \hat{\mathbf{i}} + 2\hat{\mathbf{j}} + 2\hat{\mathbf{k}}$

Now, required unit vector $= \dfrac{\hat{\mathbf{i}} + 2\hat{\mathbf{j}} + 2\hat{\mathbf{k}}}{\sqrt{1+4+4}}$

$= \dfrac{1}{3}(\hat{\mathbf{i}} + 2\hat{\mathbf{j}} + 2\hat{\mathbf{k}})$

139. *(a)* We have, $|\mathbf{a}| = 3\sqrt{3}$, $|\mathbf{b}| = 4$ and $|\mathbf{a} + \mathbf{b}| = \sqrt{7}$

Now, $|\mathbf{a} + \mathbf{b}|^2 = |\mathbf{a}|^2 + |\mathbf{b}|^2 + 2|\mathbf{a}||\mathbf{b}| \cos\theta$

$\Rightarrow \quad (\sqrt{7})^2 = (3\sqrt{3})^2 + 16 + 2(3\sqrt{3})(4)\cos\theta$

$\Rightarrow \quad 7 = 27 + 16 + 24\sqrt{3}\cos\theta$

$\Rightarrow \quad 24\sqrt{3}\cos\theta = -36$

$\Rightarrow \quad \cos\theta = -\dfrac{36}{24\sqrt{3}}$

$\Rightarrow \quad \cos\theta = -\dfrac{\sqrt{3}}{2}$

$\Rightarrow \quad \theta = 150°$

140. *(b)* Given, **a** is perpendicular to **b** and **c**.

Thus, **a** is perpendicular to the plane of **b** and **c**.

Now, cross product of **b** and **c** will give a vector perpendicular to plane of **b** and **c**. This vector will be parallel to **a**.

Now, cross product of two parallel is zero vector.

Thus, $\mathbf{a} \times (\mathbf{b} \times \mathbf{c}) = 0$

141. *(c)* We know that, if **a** and **b** are two adjacent sides of a parallelogram, then

Area $= |\mathbf{a} \times \mathbf{b}| = 15$ (given) $\quad \dots$ (i)

If the sides are $(3\mathbf{a} + 2\mathbf{b})$ and $(\mathbf{a} + 3\mathbf{b})$

Then,area of parallelogram

$= 3|(3\mathbf{a} + 2\mathbf{b}) \times (\mathbf{a} + 3\mathbf{b})|$

$= |3\mathbf{a} \times \mathbf{a} + 9\mathbf{a} \times \mathbf{b} + 2\mathbf{b} \times \mathbf{a} + 6\mathbf{b} \times \mathbf{a}|$

$= |0 + 9\mathbf{a} \times \mathbf{b} - 2\mathbf{a} \times \mathbf{b} + 0|$

$= |7(\mathbf{a} \times \mathbf{b})|$

$= 7|\mathbf{a} \times \mathbf{b}|$

$= 7 \times 15 = 105$ sq units

142. *(c)* The locus of the point which such that the ratio of its distance from two fixed point in the plane is always a constant $k(k < 1)$ is an ellipse.

143. *(d)* Given lines are concurrent, then there coefficient determinant is zero.

So, $\begin{vmatrix} 1 & 3 & -9 \\ 4 & b & -2 \\ 2 & -1 & -4 \end{vmatrix} = 0$

$\Rightarrow 1(-4b - 2) - 3(-16 + 4) - 9(-4 - 2b) = 0$

$\Rightarrow -4b - 2 + 36 + 36 + 18b = 0$

$\Rightarrow 14b + 70 = 0$

$\Rightarrow b = -5$

144. *(c)* We know that the angle between the two lines $ax^2 + 2hxy + by^2 = 0$ is given by

$$\tan\theta = \left|\frac{2\sqrt{h^2 - ab}}{a + b}\right|$$

$\because \quad \theta = 90°$

$\therefore \quad a + b = 0$

145. *(b)* Since, the equation of tangents $x - y - 2 = 0$ and $x - y + 2 = 0$ are parallel.

Therefore, distance between them = Diameter of the circle

$= \left|\dfrac{2 - (-2)}{\sqrt{1^2 + 1^2}}\right|$

$= \dfrac{4}{\sqrt{2}} = 2\sqrt{2}$

Radius $= \dfrac{1}{2}(2\sqrt{2}) = \sqrt{2}$

Now, required equation of circle is

$(x - 0)^2 + (y - 0)^2 = (\sqrt{2})^2$

$x^2 + y^2 = 2$

146. *(*)* Let point $P(x_1, y_1)$ be any point on the circle, therefore it satisfy the circle

$(x_1 - 3)^2 + (y_1 + 2)^2 = 5r^2 \quad \dots$ (i)

The length of the tangent drawn from point $p(x_1, y_1)$ to the circle $(x - 3)^2 + (y + 2)^2 = r^2$ is

$\sqrt{(x_1 - 3)^2 + (y_1 + 2)^2 - r^2} = \sqrt{5r^2 - r^2}$

$= \sqrt{4r^2} = 2r$

$\Rightarrow \quad 2r = 16$

$\Rightarrow \quad r = 8$

So, area between two circles

$$= \pi(5r^2) - \pi r^2$$
$$= 5\pi r^2 - \pi r^2$$
$$= 4\pi r^2 = 4\pi \times 64$$
$$= 256\ \pi \text{ sq units}$$

147. *(*)* Given equation of circles are

$$ax^2 + ay^2 + 2g_1x + 2f_1y + c_1 = 0$$

and $bx^2 + by^2 + 2g_2x + 2f_2y + c_2 = 0$

It can be rewritten as,

$$x^2 + y^2 + \frac{2g_1}{a}x + \frac{2f_1}{a}y + \frac{c_1}{a} = 0$$

and $x^2 + y^2 + \frac{2g_2}{b}x + \frac{2f_2}{b}y + \frac{c_2}{b} = 0$

So, centres of circle $\left(-\frac{g_1}{a}, -\frac{f_1}{a}\right)$

and $\left(-\frac{g_2}{b}, -\frac{f_2}{b}\right)$ respectively.

We know that, if two circles cut orthogonally, then

$$2(g_1g_2 + f_1f_2) = c_1 + c_2$$

$$\Rightarrow 2\left(\frac{g_1g_2}{ab} + \frac{f_1f_2}{ab}\right) = \frac{c_1}{a} + \frac{c_2}{b}$$

$$2(g_1g_2 + f_1f_2) = bc_1 + ac_2$$

148. *(d)* Let

$$S_1 \equiv x^2 + y^2 - 6x - 12y + 37 = 0$$

and $S_2 \equiv x^2 + y^2 - 6y + 7 = 0$

The equation of common tangent of the two circles is $S_1 - S_2 = 0$

$$\Rightarrow x^2 + y^2 - 6x - 12y + 37 - (x^2 + y^2 - 6y + 7) = 0$$
$$\Rightarrow -6x + 6y + 30 = 0$$
$$\Rightarrow x - y - 5 = 0$$

149. *(d)* Given, vertex of the parabola $(h, k) = (-1, 1)$ and its focus is

$$(a + h, k) = (2, 1) \text{ or } a + h = 2 \Rightarrow a = 3$$

We know that as the y-coordinate of vertex and focus are same,therefore axis of parabola is parallel to X-axis. Thus, equation of parabola is

$$(y - k)^2 = 4a(x - h)$$
$$(y - 1)^2 = 4 \times 3(x + 1)$$
$$(y - 1)^2 = 12x + 12$$
$$y^2 + 1 - 2y = 12x + 12$$
$$y^2 - 12x - 2y - 11 = 0$$

150. *(a)* Let the equation of line by $y = mx + C$

Since, this is the tangent to the circle $x^2 + y^2 = 5$

So, $C = \pm a\sqrt{1 + m^2}$

$$= \pm\sqrt{5}\sqrt{1 + m^2} \quad \ldots \text{(i)}$$

Also, the above line is tangent to the parabola

$$y^2 = 40x$$

So, $c = \frac{a}{m} = \frac{10}{m} \quad \ldots \text{(ii)}$

By Eqs. (i) and (ii), we get

$$\frac{10}{m} = \pm\sqrt{5}\sqrt{1 + m^2}$$
$$m^4 + m^2 - 20 = 0$$
$$(m^2 + 5)(m^2 - 4) = 0$$
$$m^2 = 4\ (m^2 \neq -5)$$
$$m = \pm 2 \Rightarrow c = \pm 5$$

Here, $y = \pm 2x \pm 5$

151. *(a)* Given, $x = 4(1 + \cos\theta)$

and $y = 3(1 + \sin\theta)$

$$\Rightarrow \cos\theta = \frac{x}{4} - 1 = \frac{x - 4}{4}$$

and $\sin\theta = \frac{y}{3} - 1 = \frac{y - 3}{3}$

$$\because \sin^2\theta + \cos^2\theta = 1$$
$$\therefore \frac{(x - 4)^2}{16} + \frac{(y - 3)^2}{9} = 1$$

152. *(d)* Equation of hyperbola is

$$\frac{x^2}{a^2} - \frac{y^2}{b^2} = 1$$

Distance between foci $= 2ae$

and distance between directrices $= \frac{2a}{e}$

According to question,we have

$$\frac{2ae}{2a/e} = \frac{3}{2}$$
$$\Rightarrow e^2 = \frac{3}{2}$$
$$\because b^2 = a^2(e^2 - 1)$$
$$\Rightarrow \frac{b^2}{a^2} = \frac{3}{2} - 1 = \frac{1}{2}$$
$$\Rightarrow \frac{b}{a} = \frac{1}{\sqrt{2}}$$
$$\Rightarrow a : b = \sqrt{2} : 1$$

153. *(a)* Equation of ellipse is

$$\frac{x^2}{25} + \frac{y^2}{16} = 1,\ a > b$$

and equation of hyperbola is

$$\frac{x^2}{25} - \frac{y^2}{16} = 1,\ a > b$$

Let e and e' be the eccentricities of the ellipse and hyperbola.

So, $e = \sqrt{\frac{a^2 - b^2}{a^2}} = \sqrt{\frac{25 - 16}{25}} = \frac{3}{5}$

COMEDK 2016

and $e' = \sqrt{\dfrac{a^2 + b^2}{a^2}} = \sqrt{\dfrac{25 + 16}{25}} = \dfrac{\sqrt{41}}{5}$

(i) Centre of ellipse (0, 0) and centre of hyperbola is (0, 0)

(ii) Foci of ellipse are $(\pm ae, 0)$ or $(\pm 3, 0)$. Foci of hyperbola are $(\pm ae', o)$ or $(\pm\sqrt{41}, 0)$.

(iii) Direction of ellipse are

$$x = \pm \frac{a}{e} \Rightarrow x = \pm \frac{25}{3}$$

and directrices of hyperbola are $x = \pm \dfrac{a}{e}$

$$\Rightarrow \quad x = \pm \frac{25}{\sqrt{41}}$$

(iv) Vertices of ellipse are $(\pm a, 0)$ or $(\pm 5, 0)$. Vertices of hyperbola are $(\pm a, 0)$ or $(\pm 5, 0)$.

From the above discussions, their are common is centre and vertices.

154. *(d)* We have, $\sec\theta = m$ and $\tan\theta = n$

Now, $\dfrac{1}{m}\left[(m+n) + \dfrac{1}{(m+n)}\right]$

$$= \frac{1}{\sec\theta}\left[(\sec\theta + \tan\theta) + \frac{1}{(\sec\theta + \tan\theta)}\right]$$

$$= \frac{1}{\sec\theta}\left[\frac{(\sec\theta + \tan\theta)^2 + 1}{(\sec\theta + \tan\theta)}\right]$$

$$= \frac{1}{\sec\theta}\left[\frac{\sec^2\theta + \tan^2\theta + 2\sec\theta\tan\theta + 1}{(\sec\theta + \tan\theta)}\right]$$

$$= \frac{1}{\sec\theta}\left[\frac{\sec^2\theta + \sec^2\theta - 1 + 2\sec\theta + \tan\theta + 1}{\sec\theta + \tan\theta}\right]$$

$$= \frac{1}{\sec\theta}\left[\frac{2\sec^2\theta + 2\sec\theta\tan\theta}{\sec\theta + \tan\theta}\right]$$

$$= \frac{1}{\sec\theta}\left[\frac{2\sec\theta(\sec\theta + \tan\theta)}{(\sec\theta + \tan\theta)}\right]$$

$$= \frac{1}{\sec\theta}(2\sec\theta) = 2$$

155. *(b)* $\dfrac{\sin 85° - \sin 35°}{\cos 65°}$

$$= \frac{2\cos\left(\dfrac{85° + 35°}{2}\right)\sin\left(\dfrac{85° - 35°}{2}\right)}{\cos 65°}$$

$$= \frac{2\cos 60°\sin 25°}{\cos 65°}$$

$$= \frac{2 \times \frac{1}{2} \times \sin 25°}{\cos(90° - 25°)}$$

$$= \frac{\sin 25°}{\sin 25°} = 1$$

156. *(c)* Let the distance of two consecutive stones are $(x, x+1)$.

In ΔBCD, we have

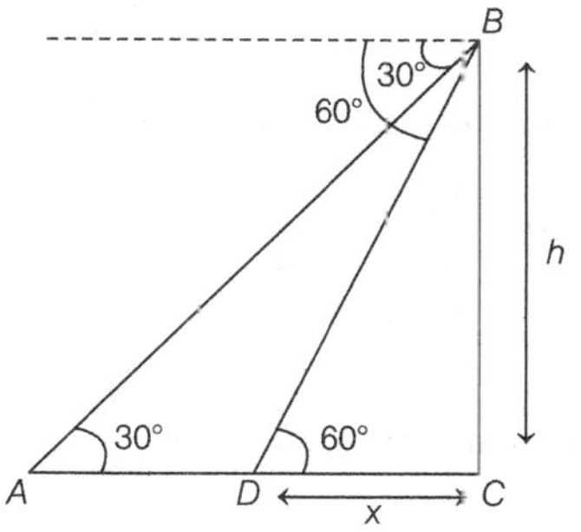

$$\tan 60° = \frac{h}{x}$$

$$\Rightarrow \quad x = \frac{h}{\sqrt{3}} \quad \ldots \text{(i)}$$

In ΔABC, we have

$$\tan 30° = \frac{h}{x+1}$$

$$\Rightarrow \quad \frac{1}{\sqrt{3}} = \frac{h}{x+1}$$

$$\Rightarrow \quad \frac{h}{\sqrt{3}} + 1 = \sqrt{3}h \quad \text{[by Eq. (i)]}$$

$$\Rightarrow \quad h\left(\sqrt{3} - \frac{1}{\sqrt{3}}\right) = 1$$

$$\Rightarrow \quad h \cdot \left(\frac{2}{\sqrt{3}}\right) = 1 \Rightarrow h = \frac{\sqrt{3}}{2}$$

157. *(d)* Let the angles of triangle are 3θ, 4θ, 5θ.

As we know that,

$$\angle A + \angle B + \angle C = 180°$$

$$\Rightarrow \quad 3\theta + 4\theta + 5\theta = 180°$$

$$\Rightarrow \quad 12\theta = 180° \Rightarrow \theta = 15°$$

So, angle are 45°, 60°, 75°.

Now, $\sin A = \sin 45° = \dfrac{1}{\sqrt{2}}$

$$\sin B = \sin 60° = \frac{\sqrt{3}}{2}$$

$$\sin C = \sin 75° = \frac{\sqrt{3}+1}{2\sqrt{2}}$$

So, $a : b : c = \sin A : \sin B : \sin C$

$$= \frac{1}{\sqrt{2}} : \frac{\sqrt{3}}{2} : \frac{\sqrt{3}+1}{2\sqrt{2}}$$

$$= 2 : \sqrt{6} : \sqrt{3} + 1$$

158. *(b)* Given that, $\cos^{-1} x = \alpha, (0 < x < 1)$ ... (i)

$$\Rightarrow \quad x = \cos\alpha$$

Thus, $\sin^{-1}(2x\sqrt{1-x^2}) + \sec^{-1}\left(\dfrac{1}{2x^2 - 1}\right) = \dfrac{2\pi}{3}$

COMEDK 2016

$$\Rightarrow \sin^{-1}(2\cos\alpha\sqrt{1-\cos^2\alpha}) + \sec^{-1}\left(\frac{1}{2\cos^2\alpha - 1}\right) = \frac{2\pi}{3}$$

$$\Rightarrow \sin^{-1}(\sin 2\alpha) + \sec^{-1}(\sec 2\alpha) = \frac{2\pi}{3}$$

$$\Rightarrow 2\alpha + 2\alpha = \frac{2\pi}{3} \Rightarrow \alpha = \frac{\pi}{6}$$

Now, $x = \cos\frac{\pi}{6} = \frac{\sqrt{3}}{2} \Rightarrow 2x = \sqrt{3}$

Therefore, $\tan^{-1}(2x) = \tan^{-1}\sqrt{3} = \frac{\pi}{3}$

159. *(a)* We have,

$$\tan^{-1}\left(\frac{a}{b}\right) + \tan^{-1}\left(\frac{a+b}{a-b}\right)$$

$$= \tan^{-1}\left[\frac{\frac{a}{b} + \frac{a+b}{a-b}}{1 - \left(\frac{a}{b}\right)\left(\frac{a+b}{a-b}\right)}\right]$$

$$= \tan^{-1}\left[\frac{\frac{a^2 - ab + ab + b^2}{b(a-b)}}{\frac{b(a-b) - a(a+b)}{b(a-b)}}\right]$$

$$= \tan^{-1}\left[\frac{a^2 + b^2}{ab - b^2 - a^2 - ab}\right]$$

$$= \tan^{-1}\left[\frac{a^2 + b^2}{-(a^2 + b^2)}\right] = \tan^{-1}(-1)$$

It does not depends neither a nor b.

160. *(c)* By option (c),

$\operatorname{cosec}\theta \cdot \sec\theta = 1$

$\sin\theta\cos\theta = 1$

$2\sin\theta\cos\theta = 2$

$\sin 2\theta = 2$

As we know that range of $\sin x$ is $[-1, 1]$.

Hence, this equation has no solution.

161. *(b)* Let $z = \dfrac{(-\sqrt{3} + 3i)(1-i)}{(3 + \sqrt{3}i)(i)(\sqrt{3} + \sqrt{3}i)}$

$$= \frac{\sqrt{3}(-1 + \sqrt{3}i)(1-i)}{(\sqrt{3})^2(\sqrt{3} + i)(1+i)(i)}$$

$$= \frac{(-1 + \sqrt{3}i)(1-i)}{\sqrt{3}(\sqrt{3}i + i^2)(1+i)} = \frac{(-1 + \sqrt{3}i)(1-i)}{\sqrt{3}(-1 + \sqrt{3}i)(1+i)}$$

$$= \frac{1-i}{(\sqrt{3})1+i} \times \frac{(1-i)}{(1-i)} = \frac{(1-i)^2}{(\sqrt{3})(1+1)}$$

$$= \frac{1 + i^2 - 2i}{2\sqrt{3}} = \frac{-2i}{2\sqrt{3}} = -\frac{i}{\sqrt{3}}$$

= Purely imaginary

162. *(a)* We have,

$$2x = -1 + \sqrt{3}i \Rightarrow x = \frac{-1 + \sqrt{3}i}{2} = \omega$$

So, $(1 - x^2 + x)^6 - (1 - x + x^2)^6$

$$= (1 - \omega^2 + \omega)^6 - (1 - \omega - \omega^2)^6$$

$$= (-2\omega^2)^6 - (-\omega - \omega)^6 = 2^6\omega^{12} - 2^6\omega^6$$

$$= 2^6 - 2^6 = 0 \qquad [\because \omega^3 = 1]$$

163. *(c)* Let $z = (1 + i\sqrt{3})^8$

$$= \left(2\left(\frac{1}{2} + \frac{\sqrt{3}}{2}i\right)\right)^8$$

$$= [2(\cos 60° + i\sin 60°)]^8 = (2^8 e^{i\pi/3})^8$$

$$= 2^8 . e^{\frac{8\pi}{3}i} = 2^8 . e^{\left(2\pi + \frac{2\pi}{3}\right)i} = 2^8 . e^{\frac{2\pi}{3}i}$$

So, modulus $= 2^8 = 256$

and amplitude $= \frac{2\pi}{3}$

164. *(d)* $\lim_{x \to 0} \dfrac{5^x - 5^{-x}}{2x} = \lim_{x \to 0} \dfrac{5^x \log 5 + 5^{-x}\log 5}{2}$

(Applying L' Hospital rule)

$$= \frac{\log 5 + \log 5}{2} = \log 5$$

165. *(c)* If a function $f(x$ is continuous at $x = a)$.

Then, it may or may not be differentiable at $x = a$.

166. *(a)* Given, $y = \dfrac{1}{x} + \dfrac{1}{x^2} + \dfrac{1}{x^3} + \ldots \infty$

This is an infinite GP with $a = 1$

and $r = \dfrac{1}{x}$

$\because \quad S_\infty = \dfrac{a}{1-r}$

$$y = \frac{1}{1 - \frac{1}{x}}$$

$$y = \frac{x}{x-1}$$

Now, $\dfrac{dy}{dx} = \dfrac{(x-1) - x}{(x-1)^2} = \dfrac{x - 1 - x}{(x-1)^2} = \dfrac{-1}{(x-1)^2}$

$$= -\frac{1}{\left(\frac{x^2}{y^2}\right)} = -\frac{y^2}{x^2}$$

167. *(*)* $f\{g(x)\} = x^3 - \dfrac{1}{x^3}$

$$f\left(x - \frac{1}{x}\right) = \left(x - \frac{1}{x}\right)\left(x^2 + \frac{1}{x^2} + 1\right)$$

$$= \left(x - \frac{1}{x}\right)\left\{\left(x - \frac{1}{x}\right)^2 + 2 + 1\right\}$$

$$f\left(x-\frac{1}{x}\right)=\left(x-\frac{1}{x}\right)\left\{\left(x-\frac{1}{x}\right)^2+3\right\}$$

Replace $x-\frac{1}{x}$ by x,

$$f(x)=(x)(x^2+3)=x^3+3x$$
$$f'(x)=3x^2+3$$

168. *(b)* Let $u=a^{\sec x} \Rightarrow v=a^{\tan x}$

$$\log u=\sec x \log a$$
$$\frac{du}{dx}=u\log a \sec x \tan x$$
$$=a^{\tan x}\log a \sec x \tan x$$

and $\log v=\tan x \log a$

$$\frac{dv}{dx}=v \log a \sec^2 x$$
$$=a^{\tan x}\log a \sec^2 x$$
$$\frac{du}{dv}=\frac{\left(\frac{du}{dx}\right)}{\frac{dv}{dx}}=\frac{a^{\sec x}\log a \sec x \tan x}{a^{\tan x}\log a \sec^2 x}$$
$$=\frac{a^{\sec x}\sin x}{a^{\tan x}}=\sin x\, a^{\sec x-\tan x}$$

169. *(c)* Given that, $\sin(x+y)+\cos(x+y)=\log(x+y)$

On differentiating w.r.t. x,

$$\cos(x+y)\cdot\left(1+\frac{dy}{dx}\right)-\sin(x+y)\left(1+\frac{dy}{dx}\right)$$
$$=\frac{1}{(x+y)}\left(1+\frac{dy}{dx}\right)$$
$$\Rightarrow \left(1+\frac{dy}{dx}\right)\left\{\cos(x+y)-\sin(x+y)-\frac{1}{(x+y)}\right\}=0$$
$$\Rightarrow \quad 1+\frac{dy}{dx}=0$$

Again differentiating w.r.t. 'x'

$$0+\frac{d^2y}{dx^2}=0 \Rightarrow \frac{d^2y}{dx^2}=0$$

170. *(a)* We have,

$$g(x)=[f(x)]^2+[f'(x)]^2$$

Differentiate the function $g(x)$

$$g'(x)=2f(x)f'(x)+2f'(x)f''(x)$$

Use chain rule,

$$2f'(x)[f(x)+f''(x)]=2f'(x)(0)=0$$

Hence, $g(x)$ is *a* constant function

$\Rightarrow$ $g(x)=c$, constant

But, $g(3)=8$, so $g(x)=8$

For all real x.

Hence, $g(8)=8$

171. *(c)* $y=2x^3+ax^2+bx+c$ ... (i)

Since, it passes through (0, 0),

$$0=2(0)+a(0)+b(0)+c$$
$$c=0 \quad \text{... (ii)}$$
$$\frac{dy}{dx}=6x^2+2ax+b$$

Since, tangents at $x=-1$ and $x=2$ are parallel to X-axis.

$$\therefore \quad \frac{dy}{dx}=0$$

At $x=-1$

$$6(-1)^2+2a(-1)+b=0$$
$$6-2a+b=0 \quad \text{... (iii)}$$

At $x=-2$

So, $6(2)^2+2a(2)+b=0$

$$24+4a+b=0 \quad \text{... (iv)}$$

By solving Eqs. (iii) and (iv), we get

$$a=-3,\ b=-12$$

Hence, $a=-3$, $b=-12$, $c=0$

172. *(b)*

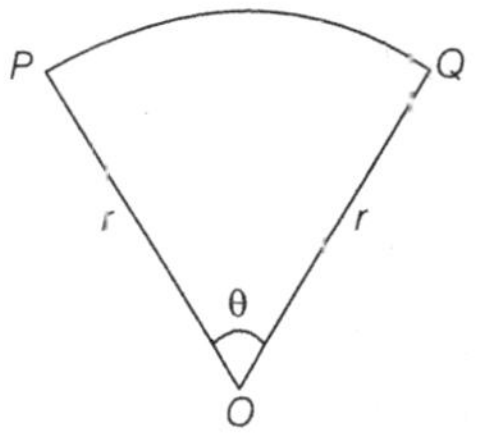

Perimeter of sector $=2r+r\theta$

$$\Rightarrow \quad 60=2r+r\theta \text{ (given)}$$
$$\Rightarrow \quad \theta=\frac{60-2r}{r}$$

Now, area of sector,

$$(A)=\frac{\pi r^2\theta}{360^\circ}=\frac{\pi r^2(60-2r)}{360\, r}$$
$$=\frac{\pi r}{180}(30-r)$$
$$\frac{dA}{dr}=\frac{\pi}{180}(30-2r)$$

For maximum area $\frac{dA}{dr}=0$

$\Rightarrow 30-2r=0$

$\Rightarrow 2r=30 \Rightarrow r=15$

and $\frac{d^2A}{dr^2}=\frac{\pi}{180^\circ}(-2)=-\frac{\pi}{90}<0$

Hence, it is maximum at $r=15$ m

173. *(a)* Given,equation of curve is

$$y=x^2-x+4$$

Slope of tangent at $P(1, 4)$ is

$$\frac{dy}{dx}=2x-1 \Rightarrow \left(\frac{dy}{dx}\right)_{(1,4)}=2-1=1$$

So, equation of tangent is

$$y-4=1(x-1)$$
$$\Rightarrow \quad y-x=3 \quad \text{... (i)}$$

and equation of normal at point $P(1, 4)$ is

$$y - 4 = -1(x - 1)$$

$$x + y = 5 \quad \ldots \text{(ii)}$$

Since, the tangent cuts X-axis at A.

Therefore, coordinates of A are $(-3, 0)$

and the normal cuts X-axis at B and coordinates of B are $(5, 0)$.

Therefore, area of ΔPAB

$$= \frac{1}{2}\begin{vmatrix} 1 & 4 & 1 \\ -3 & 0 & 1 \\ 5 & 0 & 1 \end{vmatrix}$$

$$= \frac{1}{2}[1(0) - 4(-3 - 5) + 1(0)]$$

$$= \frac{1}{2}|32| = 16 \text{ sq. units}$$

174. *(d)* $\int \frac{x^3 + 3x^2 + 3x + 1}{(x+1)^5}\, dx$

$$= \int \frac{(x+1)^3}{(x+1)^5}\, dx = \int \frac{dx}{(x+1)^2}$$

$$= -\frac{1}{x+1} + c$$

175. *(c)* Let $I = \int \frac{\operatorname{cosec} x}{\cos^2\left(1 + \log \tan \frac{x}{2}\right)}\, dx$

Put $\quad 1 + \log \tan \frac{x}{2} = t$

$$\Rightarrow \quad \frac{1}{\tan \frac{x}{2}} \cdot \sec^2 \frac{x}{2} \cdot \frac{dx}{2} = dt$$

$$\Rightarrow \quad \frac{dx}{2 \sin \frac{x}{2} \cos \frac{x}{2}} = dt \Rightarrow \frac{dx}{\sin x} = dt$$

$$\Rightarrow \quad \operatorname{cosec} x\, dx = dt$$

So, $I = \int \frac{dt}{\cos^2 t} = \int \sec^2 t\, dt = \tan t + c$

$$= \tan\left(1 + \log \tan \frac{x}{2}\right) + c$$

176. *(b)* Let $I = \int \frac{dx}{x\sqrt{(x^3)^2 - 16}}$

Put $x^3 = t \Rightarrow 3x^2 dx = dt$

So, $\quad I = \frac{1}{3}\int \frac{dt}{x^3\sqrt{(x^3)^2 - 16}}$

$$= \frac{1}{3}\int \frac{dt}{t(\sqrt{t^2 - 16}}$$

$$= \frac{1}{3 \times 4} \sec^{-1}\left(\frac{t}{4}\right) + c$$

$$= \frac{1}{12} \sec^{-1}\left(\frac{x^3}{4}\right) + c$$

177. *(d)* $I_1 = \int_0^{\pi/2} x \sin x\, dx$

$$= [-x \cos x + \int \cos x]_0^{\pi/2}$$

$$= [-x \cos x + \sin x]_0^{\pi/2}$$

$$= 0 + \sin \frac{\pi}{2} - 0 = 1$$

Similarly, $I_2 = \int_0^{\pi/2} x \cos x\, dx$

$$= [x \sin x - \int \sin x]_0^{\pi/2}$$

$$= [x \sin x + \cos x]_0^{\pi/2}$$

$$= \frac{\pi}{2} \sin \frac{\pi}{2} - 1 = \frac{\pi}{2} - 1$$

Hence, $I_1 + I_2 = 1 + \frac{\pi}{2} - 1 = \frac{\pi}{2}$

178. *(b)* Given that, $f(x) = 4x^2 - 3x + 1$

$$g(x) = \frac{f(-x) - f(x)}{x^2 + 3}$$

Therefore,

$$g(x) = \frac{(4x^2 + 3x + 1) - (4x^2 - 3x + 1)}{x^2 + 3} = \frac{6x}{x^2 + 3}$$

Now, $g(-x) = -\frac{6x}{x^2 + 3} = g(x)$

which is an odd function.

Thus, $\int_{-2}^{2} g(x)\, dx = 0$

179. *(a)* Required area

$$= \int_0^2 [(x + 2) - (x^2 - x + 2)]\, dx$$

$$= \int_0^2 [x + 2 - x^2 + x - 2]\, dx = \int_0^2 (-x^2 + 2x)\, dx$$

$$= \left[-\frac{x^3}{3} + x^2\right]_0^2$$

$$= -\frac{8}{3} + 4 - (0) = \frac{-8 + 12}{3} = \frac{4}{3}$$

180. *(d)* Given, differential equation is

$$e^{-x}(y + 1)\, dy + (\cos^2 x - \sin 2x) y\, dx = 0$$

$$\Rightarrow \left(\frac{y + 1}{y}\right) dy + e^x(\cos^2 x - \sin 2x) dx = 0$$

$$\Rightarrow \left(1 + \frac{1}{y}\right) dy + (e^x \cos^2 x - e^x \sin 2x)\, dx = 0$$

$$\Rightarrow d(y + \log y) + d(e^x \cos^2 x) = 0$$

On integrating above equation, we get

$$y + \log y + e^x \cos^2 x = c$$

At $y(0) = 1$

$$\Rightarrow 1 + 0 + e^0 \cdot 1 = c \Rightarrow c = 2$$

Hence, required solution is

$$y + \log y + e^x \cos^2 x = 2$$

COMEDK

Solved Paper 2015

Instructions

- There are 180 questions in all. The number of questions in each section is as given below.

Sections	No. of Questions
Section I : Physics	1-60
Section II : Chemistry	61-120
Section III : Mathematics	121-180

- All the questions are Multiple Choice Questions having four options out of which **ONLY ONE** is correct.
- Candidates will be awarded 1 mark for each correct answer. There will be no negative marking for incorrect answer.
- Time allotted to complete this paper is 3 hrs.

PHYSICS

1. A uniform circular disc of mass 400 g and radius 4.0 cm is rotated about one of its diameter at an angular speed of 10 rot/s. The kinetic energy of the disc is

a. 3.2×10^{-5} J *b.* 1.6×10^{-3} J
c. 3.2×10^{-3} J *d.* 6.4×10^{-4} J

2. Several lamps of 50 W and 100 V rating are available. How many of them can be connected in parallel across a battery of a 120 V of internal resistance 10 Ω, so that all bulbs glow in full power?

a. 2 *b.* 4 *c.* 6 *d.* 8

3. A stone weight 100 N on the surface of the earth. The ratio of its weight at a height of half the radius of the earth to a depth of half the radius of the earth will be approximately

a. 3.6 *b.* 2.2 *c.* 1.8 *d.* 0.9

4. The gravitational field strength at the surface of a certain planet is g. Which of the following is the gravitational field strength at the surface of a planet with twice the radius and twice the mass?

a. $g/2$ *b.* g *c.* $2g$ *d.* $4g$

5. A crane with a steel cable of length 11 m and radius 2.0 cm is employed to lift a block of concrete of mass 40 tons in a building site. If the Young's modulus of steel is 2.0×10^{11} Pa, what will be roughly the increase in the length of the cable while lifting the block? (Take, $g = 10\ \text{ms}^{-2}$)

a. 0.75 cm *b.* 1.25 cm
c. 1.75 cm *d.* 2.50 cm

6. I and V are respectively the current and voltage in a metal wire of resistance R. The I-V graph for the two different temperatures T_1 and T_2 given, then

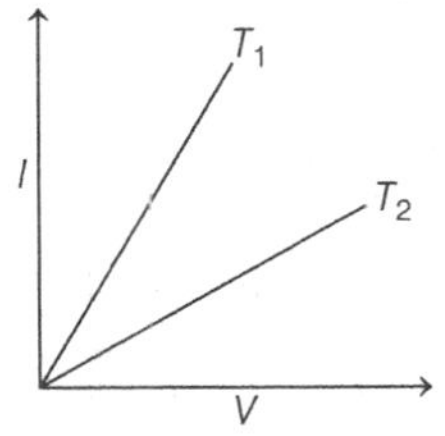

a. $T_1 = T_2$ *b.* $T_1 > T_2$
c. $T_1 < T_2$ *d.* $T_1 = 2T_2$

7. A charged particle moves in a uniform magnetic field. The velocity of the particle at some instant makes an acute angle with the magnetic field. The path of the particle will be

a. a straight line
b. a circle
c. a helix with uniform pitch
d. a helix with non-uniform pitch

8. A certain length of insulated wire can be bent to form either a single circular loop (case I) or a double loop of smaller radius (case II). When the same steady current is passed through the wire, the ratio of the magnetic field at the centre in (case I) to that in (case II) is

a. 1 *b.* 2 *c.* 1/2 *d.* 1/4

9. Inside a cyclotron, a charged particle is subjected to both an electric field and a magnetic field. It gains kinetic energy due to the

a. electric field *b.* magnetic field
c. Both (a) and (b) *d.* None of these

10. The graph showing the variation of the magnetic field strength B with distance r from a long current carrying conductor is

a.
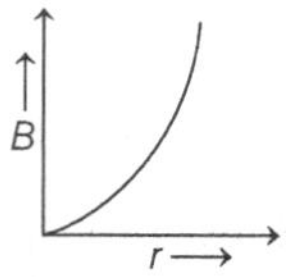

b.
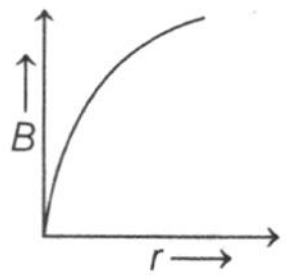

c.
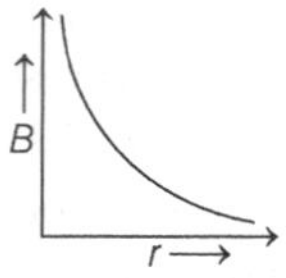

d.
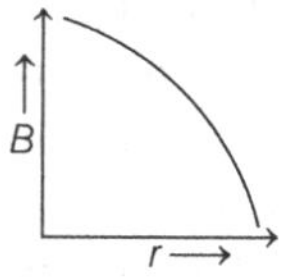

11. The temperature at which centigrade and Fahrenheit scales give the same reading, is

a. – 40° *b.* 40° *c.* – 30° *d.* 30°

12. The correct definition of Meissner effect is

a. the phenomenon of perfect paramagnetism in superconductors
b. the phenomenon of perfect diamagnetism in superconductors
c. the phenomenon of perfect diamagnetism in semiconductors
d. the phenomenon of perfect ferromagnetism in metals

13. A jet plane is travelling west at 450 m/s. If the horizontal component of earth's magnetic field is 4×10^{-4} T and angle of dip is 30°, then the vertical component is

a. 3×10^{-4} T *b.* 4×10^{-4} T
c. 2.3×10^{-4} T *d.* 12.308×10^{-4} T

14. A bicycle generator creates 1.5 V at 15 km/h. The emf generated at 10 km/h is

a. 1.5 V *b.* 2 V
c. 0.5 V *d.* 1 V

15. The instantaneous voltage of a 50 Hz generator giving peak voltage as 300 V. The generator equation for this voltage is

a. $V = 50 \sin 300\pi t$ *b.* $V = 300 \sin 100\pi t$
c. $V = 6 \sin 100\pi t$ *d.* $V = 50 \sin 100\pi t$

16. A transformer is used to light a 100 W, 110 V lamp from a 220 V supply. If the supply current is 0.6 A, then the efficiency of the transformer is

a. 66% *b.* 76%
c. 86% *d.* 96%

17. If instantaneous current is given by $i = 4\cos(\omega t + \phi)$, then the rms value of current is

a. $2\sqrt{2}$ A *b.* 4 A
c. $4\sqrt{2}$ A *d.* zero

18. If the surface is a perfect reflector, then the change in momentum of the wave after falling on the surface is

a. p *b.* $2p$
c. $\frac{p}{2}$ *d.* $-2p$

19. A person sitting firmly over a rotating stool has his arms stretched. If he folds his arms, his angular momentum about the axis of the rotation

a. increases *b.* decreases
c. remains unchanged *d.* doubles

20. The temperature of two bodies A and B are 727°C and 327°C respectively,the ratio $H_A : H_B$ of the rates of heat radiated by them is

a. 727 : 327 *b.* 5 : 3
c. 25 : 9 *d.* 625 : 81

21. The refractive index and the permeability of a medium are respectively 1.5 and 5×10^{-7} Hm^{-1}. The relative permittivity of the medium is nearly

a. 25 *b.* 15 *c.* 6 *d.* 10

22. All lights are switched off, except for a bright point-light source kept at the bottom of a swimming pool filled with clear water of refractive index 4/3. As a result, only a circular patch of 6 m diameter of the water surface is visible to spectators standing around the swimming pool. Which of the following gives the nearest value of the depth of the pool?

a. 1.6 m *b.* 2.0 m
c. 2.6 m *d.* 3.0 m

23. An equiangular glass prism of refractive index 1.6 is kept fully immersed in water of refractive index 4/3, for a certain ray of monochromatic light. What is the closest value for the angle of minimum deviation of the light ray in this setup? (Take, $\sin 37° = 0.6$)

a. 10° *b.* 14°
c. 18° *d.* 22°

24. A concave mirror gives an image three times as large as its object placed at a distance of 20 cm from it. For the image to be real, the focal length should be

a. 10 cm *b.* 15 cm
c. 20 cm *d.* 30 cm

25. Two coherent monochromatic light beams of intensities I and $4I$ are superimposed. The maximum and minimum possible resulting intensities are

a. $5I$ and 0 *b.* $5I$ and $3I$
c. $9I$ and I *d.* $9I$ and $3I$

26. The momentum of electrons having a wavelength 2Å (given, $h = 6.626 \times 10^{-34}$ J-s, $m = 9.1 \times 10^{-35}$ kg) is

a. 6.313×10^{-24} kg-m s^{-1}
b. 3.313×10^{-24} kg-m s^{-1}
c. 9.313×10^{-25} kg-m s^{-1}
d. 12.313×10^{-24} kg-m s^{-1}

27. The photoelectric current of voltage in a certain experiment is 1.5 V. What is the maximum kinetic energy of photoelectrons emitted?

a. 24×10^{-19} J *b.* -24×10^{-19} J
c. 2.4×10^{-19} J *d.* 2.04×10^{-19} J

28. The best waves for emission of electrons from a surface are

a. microwaves *b.* ultraviolet rays
c. infrared rays *d.* X-rays

29. The shortest wavelengths of Paschen, Balmer and Lyman series are in the ratio

a. 9 : 1 : 4 *b.* 1 : 4 : 9
c. 9 : 4 : 1 *d.* 1 : 9 : 4

30. A sample of a radioactive element whose half-life is 30 s contains a million nuclei at a certain instant of time. How many nuclei will be left after 10 s?

a. 3.33×10^5 *b.* 3.78×10^5
c. 1.11×10^5 *d.* 1.26×10^5

31. A nuclear fission is said to be critical when multiplication factor or k

a. $k = 1$ *b.* $k > 1$ *c.* $k < 1$ *d.* $k = 0$

32. In case of a *p-n* junction diode at high value of reverse bias, the current rises sharply. The value of reverse bias is known as

a. cut-in *b.* zener voltage
c. inverse voltage *d.* critical voltage

33. The truth table of a logic gate is given below

Input		Output
A	B	Y
0	0	1
0	1	1
1	0	1
1	1	0

The logic gate is

a. OR gate *b.* AND gate
c. NOR gate *d.* NAND gate

34. In a semiconductor diode, the reverse biased current is due to drift of the free electrons and holes caused by

a. thermal expansion only
b. impurity atoms only
c. Both (a) and (b)
d. Neither (a) nor (b)

35. A TV tower is 120 m high. How much more height is to be added to it, if its coverage range is to become double?

a. 120 m *b.* 240 m
c. 360 m *d.* 480 m

36. A message signal of frequency 10 kHz and peak value of 10 V is used to moderate a carrier of frequency 1 MHz and peak voltage 20 V. The modulation index and side bands produced are

a. 0.4 and 1200 kHz, 990 kHz
b. 0.5 and 1010 kHz, 990 kHz
c. 0.2 and 1010 kHz, 1000 kHz
d. 0.5 and 1500 kHz, 1000 kHz

37. Vector A has a magnitude of 10 units and makes an angle of 30° with the positive X-axis. Vector B has a magnitude of 20 units and makes an angle of 30° with the negative X-axis. What is the magnitude of the resultant between these two vectors?

a. $20\sqrt{3}$ *b.* 35 *c.* $15\sqrt{3}$ *d.* $10\sqrt{3}$

38. A uniform chain of length L is lying partly on a table, the remaining part hanging down from the edge of the table. If the coefficient of friction between the chain and the table is 0.5, what is the minimum length of the chain that should lie on the table, to prevent the chain from slipping down to the ground?

a. $L/3$ *b.* $L/2$
c. $2L/3$ *d.* $3L/4$

39. A bomb of mass 18 kg at rest explodes into two pieces of masses 6 kg and 12 kg. The velocity of 12 kg mass is 4 m/s. The kinetic energy of the other mass is

a. 288 J *b.* 192 J
c. 96 J *d.* 144 J

40. A soap bubble of radius r is blown up to form a bubble of radius $3r$ under isothermal conditions. If σ is the surface tension of soap solution, then the energy spent in blowing is

a. $3\pi\sigma r^2$ *b.* $6\pi\sigma r^2$
c. $12\pi\sigma r^2$ *d.* $64\pi\sigma r^2$

41. The diagram shows a barrel of weight 1.0×10^3 N on a frictionless slope inclined at 30° to the horizontal.

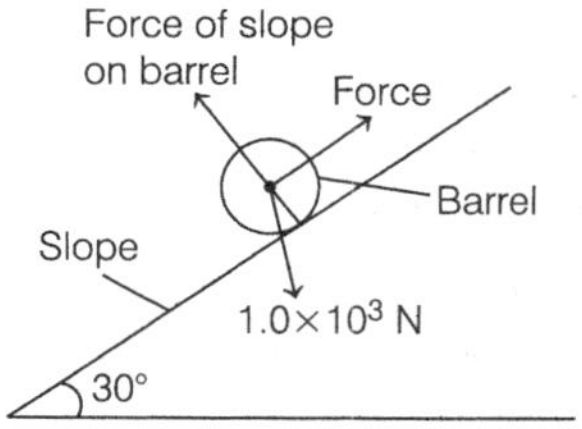

The force is parallel to the slope. What is the work done in moving the barrel a distance of 5.0 m up the slope?

a. 2.5×10^3 J *b.* 4.3×10^3 J
c. 5.0×10^3 J *d.* 1.0×10^3 J

42. A 2 kg mass lying on a table is displaced in the horizontal direction through 50 cm. The work done by the normal reaction will be

a. 10 J *b.* 0
c. 100 erg *d.* 100 J

43. The dimensions of four wires of the same material are given below. In which wire the increase in length will be maximum when the same tension is applied?

a. Length 100 cm, diameter 1 mm
b. Length 200 cm, diameter 2 mm
c. Length 300 cm, diameter 3 mm
d. Length 50 cm, diameter 0.5 mm

44. Under a constant pressure head, the rate of flow of orderly volume flow of liquid through a capillary tube is V. If the length of the capillary is doubled and the diameter of the bore is halved, then the rate of flow would become

a. $V/4$ *b.* $V/8$ *c.* $16V$ *d.* $V/32$

45. A ball is dropped from the top of the building 100 m high. Simultaneously, another ball is thrown upwards from the bottom of the building with such a velocity that the balls collide exactly mid-way. What is the speed in ms^{-1} with which the second ball is thrown? (Take, $g = 10\ ms^{-2}$)

a. 31.6 *b.* 27.8
c. 22.4 *d.* 19.6

46. In an isochoric process

a. work done is constant
b. volume changes, work done remains same
c. volume remains constant and no work is done by the system
d. Both volume and work done changes

47. The average energy of molecules in a sample of oxygen gas at 300 K is 6.21×10^{-21} J. The corresponding values at 600 K are

a. 12.12×10^{-21} J *b.* 8.78×10^{-21} J
c. 6.21×10^{-21} J *d.* 12.42×10^{-21} J

48. A mass M is suspended from a light spring. An additional mass m added displaces the spring further by a distance X. Now, the combined mass will oscillate on the spring with period

a. $T = 2\pi\sqrt{\dfrac{mg}{X(M+m)}}$ *b.* $T = 2\pi\sqrt{\dfrac{(M+m)X}{mg}}$
c. $T = \dfrac{\pi}{2}\sqrt{\dfrac{mg}{X(M+m)}}$ *d.* $T = 2\pi\sqrt{\dfrac{(M+m)}{mg}}$

49. A 10 kg collar is attached to a spring (spring constant 600 N/m), it slides without friction over a horizontal rod. The collar is displaced from its equilibrium position by 20 cm and released. What is the speed of the oscillation?

a. $\sqrt{60} \times 0.2$ m/s *b.* 60×0.2 m/s
c. 60×2 m/s *d.* 6×0.2 m/s

50. A body of mass 1 kg starting from origin with initial velocity of $3\hat{\mathbf{i}} + 4\hat{\mathbf{j}}\ ms^{-1}$. If a constant force of $2\hat{\mathbf{i}} - 3\hat{\mathbf{j}}$ acts on it, find the coordinate of point it reaches in 3 s.

a. (18, −1.5) *b.* (9, 1.5)
c. (18, 1.5) *d.* (9, −1.5)

COMEDK 2015

51. A steel wire has a length of 90 cm which is under a constant tension of 100 N. The speed of the transverse waves that can be produced in the wire will be (take, the mass of the steel wire to be 6×10^{-3} kg)

a. 50 m/s *b.* 50 cm/s
c. $1/3\sqrt{6}$ m/s *d.* $50\sqrt{6}$m/s

52. The number of electrons in 1 C of charges is

a. 6.25×10^{18} *b.* 6.25×10^{16}
c. 6.25×10^{10} *d.* 6.25×10^{12}

53. An electric dipole consists of two opposite charges, each of magnitude 1.0 μC separated by a distance of 2.0 cm. The dipole is placed in an external field of 10^5 NC^{-1}. The maximum torque on the dipole is

a. 0.2×10^{-3} N-m *b.* 1×10^{-3} N-m
c. 2×10^{-3} N-m *d.* 4×10^{-3}N-m

54. Two small charged spheres *A* and *B* have charges 10 μC and 40 μC respectively and are held at separation of 90 cm from each other. At what distance from *A*, electric field intensity would be zero?

a. 22.5 cm *b.* 18 cm *c.* 30 cm *d.* 36 cm

55. A charge *q* is placed at the centre of a cube. The electric flux passing through the cube is

a. $\frac{1}{3}\frac{q}{\varepsilon_0}$ *b.* $\frac{1}{6}\frac{q}{\varepsilon_0}$ *c.* $\frac{q}{\varepsilon_0}$ *d.* $\frac{1}{4}\frac{q}{\varepsilon_0}$

56. A parallel plated capacitor has area 2 m^2 separated by 3 dielectric slabs. Their relative permittivity is 2, 3, 6 and thickness is 0.4 mm, 0.6 mm, 1.2 mm, respectively. The capacitance is

a. 5×10^{-8} F *b.* 11×10^{-8} F
c. 2.95×10^{-8} F *d.* 10×10^{-8}F

57. A particle *A* has charge $+q$ and particle *B* has charge $+4q$, each of them having the same mass *m*. When allowed to fall from rest through the same electrical potential difference, then the ratio of their speeds will become

a. 2 : 1 *b.* 1 : 2
c. 1 : 4 *d.* 4 : 1

58. A body accelerates from rest with a uniform acceleration *a* for a time *t*. The uncertainty in *a* is 8% and the uncertainty in *t* is 4%. The uncertainty in the speed is

a. 32% *b.* 12%
c. 8% *d.* 2%

59. A parallel plate capacitor has a capacity *C*. The separation between the plates is doubled and a dielectric medium is inserted between the plates. If the capacity is 3*C*, then the dielectric constant of the medium will be

a. 1.5 *b.* 3 *c.* 6 *d.* 12

60. Two resistances *A* and *B* have colour codes orange, blue, white and brown, red, green, respectively. Then, ratio of their resistances $A : B$ is

a. 3 : 1 *b.* 1 : 3
c. $1 : 3 \times 10^4$ *d.* $3 \times 10^4 : 1$

COMEDK 2015

CHEMISTRY

61. 20 mL of acetic acid reacts with 20 mL of ethyl alcohol to form ethyl acetate. The density of acid and alcohol are 1 g/mL and 0.7 g/mL respectively. The limiting reagent in this reaction is

a. acetic acid
b. ethyl alcohol
c. acetic acid and ethyl alcohol
d. ester

62. The mass of oxygen gas which occupies 5.6 L at STP would be

a. the gram atomic mass of oxygen
b. one-fourth of the gram atomic mass of oxygen
c. double the gram atomic mass of oxygen
d. half of the gram atomic mass of oxygen

63. Energy associated with the first orbit of He^+ is

a. 8.72×10^{-18} J *b.* 0.872×10^{-18} J
c. -0.872×10^{-18} J *d.* -8.72×10^{-18} J

64. Pick the incorrect statement among those given below.

a. Multiple covalent bonds are shorter, than single covalent bonds between same set of atoms.
b. Bond strength varies inversely with bond length.
c. Bond order of isoelectronic species will be same.
d. Bond enthalpy increases with increasing bond length.

65. For one mole of NaCl(s) the lattice enthalpy is

$Na(s) + 1/2\ Cl_2(g) \xrightarrow{+108.4\ kJ/mol} Na(g) + 1/2\ Cl_2(g)$

$\xrightarrow{+495.6\ kJ/mol} Na^+(g) + 1/2\ Cl_2(g)$

$\xrightarrow{121\ kJ/mol} Na^+(g) + Cl(g)$

$\xrightarrow{-348.6\ kJ/mol} Na^+(g) + Cl^-(g)$

$\xrightarrow{H^o\ lattice} NaCl\ (s)$

$\xrightarrow{-411.2\ kJ/mol} Na(s) + 1/2\ Cl_2(g)$

a. – 788 kJ/mol b. + 878 kJ/mol
c. + 788 kJ/mol d. – 878 kJ/mol

66. An endothermic reaction is found to have +ve entropy change. The reaction will be
a. possible at high temperature
b. possible only at low temperature
c. not possible at any temperature
d. possible at any temperature

67. For an adiabatic change in a system, the condition which is applicable will be
a. $w = 0$ b. $q = -w$
c. $q = w$ d. $q = 0$

68. Which of the following equations give ionic product of water?
I. $NH_3(aq) + H_2O \rightleftharpoons NH_4^+(aq) + OH^-(aq)$
II. $NH_4^+(aq) + H_2O \rightleftharpoons H_3O^+ + NH_3(g)$
III. $NH_2^-(aq) + H_2O \rightleftharpoons NH_3(g) + OH^-(aq)$
IV. $NH_3(g) + OH^-(aq) \rightleftharpoons NH_2^-(aq) + H_2O$
a. II and III b. III and IV
c. I and II d. III and I

69. The number of H^+ ions present in 1 mL of a solution whose pH is 13
a. 6.022×10^{10} b. 6.022×10^{7}
c. 6.022×10^{20} d. 6.022×10^{23}

70. Strongest reducing agent among the following is
I. $Na^+ + e^- \longrightarrow Na(s)$ $E° = -2.71$ V
II. $Al^{3+} + 3e^- \longrightarrow Al(s)$ $E° = -1.66$ V
III. $F_2(g) + 2e^- \longrightarrow 2F^-$ $E° = +2.87$ V
IV. $2H_2O + 2e^- \longrightarrow H_2(g) + 2OH^-(aq)$; $E° = -0.83$ V
a. only IV b. only III
c. only II d. only I

71. Choose the correct statement applicable for the reaction: $2H_2O + 2F_2 \longrightarrow 4HF + O_2$
a. water is oxidised to O_2.
b. F_2 is oxidised to HF.
c. water is reduced to HF.
d. F_2 acts as reducing agent in the reaction.

72. Decomposition of hydrogen peroxide can be prevented by adding
a. NaOH b. MnO_2
c. urea d. oxalic acid

73. Mg is an important component of
a. haemoglobin b. chlorophyll
c. ATP d. florigen

74. $Pb_3O_4 + 4HNO_3 \longrightarrow 2Pb(NO_3)_2 + PbO_2 + 2H_2O$

Which is true about the lead ions in Pb_3O_4?
a. Pb^{2+} reacts with HNO_3 to give lead nitrate.
b. Pb^{4+} reacts with HNO_3 to give lead nitrate.
c. Pb^{2+} reacts with HNO_3 to give PbO_2.
d. Pb^{4+} reacts with HNO_3 to give PbO_2.

75. Which of the following chemicals does not liberate hydrogen gas on reaction with aluminium metal?
a. Dil. sulphuric acid
b. Aqueous sodium hydroxide
c. Dil. hydrochloric acid
d. Conc. nitric acid

76. The decreasing order of reactivity towards electrophilic substitution of the following compounds is

Cl NO_2 CH_3

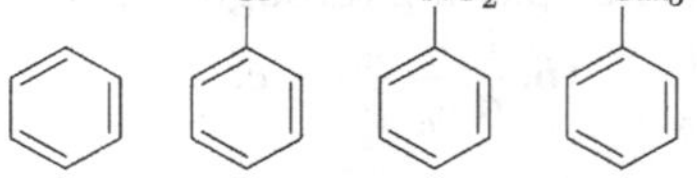

1 2 3 4

a. 1 > 3 > 4 > 2 b. 4 > 1 > 3 > 2
c. 4 > 1 > 2 > 3 d. 1 > 4 > 3 > 2

77. An organic compound weighing 0.15 g gave on Carius estimation, 0.12 g of AgBr.

The percentage of Br in the compound will be close to (Atomic mass of Ag = 108, Br = 80)
a. 46% b. 34.1%
c. 3.41% d. 4.6%

78. Identify the correct IUPAC name of the following compound.

$CH_3CH_2CH_2CH_2CN$

a. Butyl cyanide b. Butanenitrile
c. Pentanenitrile d. Pentyl cyanide

79. Identify the main product in the following reaction.

$C(CH_3)_3OH \xrightarrow[358K]{20\%\ H_3PO_4} ?$

a. $(CH_3)_2C = CH_2$ b. $(CH_3)_2CHOH$
c. $CH_3CH = CHCH_3$ d. $CH_3CH_2CH = CH_2$

80. BOD is a measure of
a. ozone depletion in the stratosphere due to too many free radicals.
b. suspended particulate matter in the air causing lung problems.
c. pesticides which are non-biodegradable in the soil and water.
d. organic material present in water needing dissolved oxygen to break them down depleting oxygen content in water.

81. If same type of atoms are packed in hexagonal close packing and cubic close packing separately, then
a. density of hcp will be greater than ccp
b. density of hcp will be smaller than ccp
c. density of hcp will be equal to ccp
d. density of hcp and ccp will depend upon the temperature of the system

82. Silicon doped with arsenic is
a. *p*-type semiconductor
b. *n*-type semiconductor
c. intrinsic semiconductor
d. insulator

83. Which of the following compounds have the same value of van't Hoff's factor (*i*) as that of $Al_2(SO_4)_3$?
a. $K_4[Fe(CN)_6]$ *b.* NaCl
c. $Al(NO_3)_3$ *d.* Na_2SO_4

84. The standard electrode potential for Daniell cell is 1.1 V. What is the standard Gibbs energy for the reaction ?
a. 212.3 kJ mol^{-1} *b.* –212.3 kJ mol^{-1}
c. 106.15 kJ mol^{-1} *d.* –106.15kJ mol^{-1}

85. The cathode reaction in the dry cell will be
a. $Zn(s) \longrightarrow Zn^{2+} + 2e^-$
b. $MnO_2 + NH_4^+ + e^- \longrightarrow MnO(OH) + NH_3$
c. $Zn(Hg) + 2OH^- \longrightarrow ZnO(s) + H_2O + 2e^-$
d. $MnO(OH) + NH_3 \longrightarrow MnO_2 + NH_4^+ + 2e^-$

86. λ_m° for NH_4Cl, NaOH and NaCl are 130, 248 and 126.5 Ω^{-1} cm^2 mol^{-1} respectively. The λ_m° of NH_4OH will be
a. 251.5 *b.* 244.5 *c.* 130 *d.* 504.5

87. In a chemical reaction i.e., $A + 2B \longrightarrow$ products, when concentration of *A* is doubled, rate of the reaction increases 4 times and when concentration of *B* alone is doubled rate continues to be the same. The order of the reaction is
a. 1 *b.* 2 *c.* 3 *d.* 4

88. Zeolites are shape selective structures because of
a. high adsorption capacity
b. three dimensional network of atoms
c. presence of aluminosilicates
d. honey comb like structure

89. Sulphur sol is a type of
a. emulsion
b. multimolecular colloid
c. lyophilic colloid
d. macromolecular colloid

90. The magnetite ore is
a. ferrous oxide *b.* ferric oxide
c. ferric hydroxide *d.* ferrous-ferric oxide

91. In the metallurgy of aluminium, when the fused matrix is electrolysed, the overall reduction reaction is
a. $Al_2O_3 + 3C \longrightarrow 2Al + 3CO$
b. $Al_2O_3 \longrightarrow 2Al^{3+} + 3O_2$
c. $2Al_2O_3 + 3C \longrightarrow 4Al + 3CO_2$
d. $Al_2O_3 + 2\,CO \longrightarrow 2Al + 2CO_2$

92. Carbon monoxide forms volatile compound with
a. Ni *b.* Cu
c. Al *d.* Si

93. Which of the following reactions does not produce PH_3?
a. White phosphorus with water
b. White phosphorus with conc. NaOH
c. Metal phosphide with dil. HCl
d. Metal phosphides with water

94. The decreasing order of stability of oxides of halogen is
a. fluorine > chlorine > iodine > bromine
b. fluorine > chlorine > bromine > iodine
c. iodine > bromine > chlorine > fluorine
d. iodine > chlorine > bromine > fluorine

95. N_2 does not show property of catenation because
a. it has no *d*-orbitals in the valence shell
b. interelectronic repulsion between non-bonding electrons is greater
c. N≡N has high bond enthalpy
d. nitrogen has very high ionisation enthalpy

96. Hybridised state of bromine in bromine pentafluoride is
a. sp^3d *b.* d^2sp^3
c. dsp^3 *d.* sp^3d^2

97. An element belonging to chalcogen group is

a. carbon *b.* phosphorus
c. chlorine *d.* sulphur

98. More number of oxidation state are exhibited by the actinoids, than by lanthanoids. The main reason for this is

a. greater metallic character of lanthanoids than that of their corresponding actinoids
b. more active nature of actinoids
c. more energy difference between $5f$ and $6d$-orbitals, than that between $4f$ and $5d$-orbitals
d. lesser energy difference between $5f$ and $6d$-orbitals, than that between $4f$ and $5d$-orbitals

99. A transition elements with atomic number 24 will have its magnetic moment

a. 5.92 BM
b. 6.93 BM
c. it will be diamagnetic
d. it will be more than 8 BM

100. In tetrahedral permanganate ion π-bonding type between metal and oxygen is

a. $p\pi$-$p\pi$ *b.* $d\pi$-$p\pi$ *c.* $d\pi$-$d\pi$ *d.* $d\pi$-s

101. Which of the following pairs has the same size?

a. Fe^{2+}, Ni^{2+} *b.* Zr^{4+}, Ti^{4+}
c. Zr^{4+}, Hf^{4+} *d.* Zn^{2+}, Hf^{4+}

102. $[Ti(H_2O)_6]^{2+}$ is a $3d^2$ system, the value of crystal field stabilisation energy decreases by

a. $4\times10^{-1}\Delta_o$ *b.* $4.0\Delta_o$
c. $8.0\Delta_o$ *d.* $8\times10^{-1}\Delta_o$

103. Among the complexes of Ni listed below, the following is the only correct statement about the given compounds.

I. $[Ni(CO)_4]$ II. $[Ni(CN)_4]^{2-}$
III. $[NiCl_4]^{2-}$

a. all of them have tetrahedral geometry.
b. I and III are tetrahedral and II has square planar geometry.
c. I and II are tetrahedral and III is square planar.
d. all of them have square planar geometry.

104. The formula for sodium trioxalatoaluminate (III) is

a. $Na_4[Al(C_2O_4)_3]$ *b.* $Na_3[Al(C_2O_4)]_3$
c. $Na_3[Al(C_2O_4)_3]$ *d.* $Na_2[Al(C_2O_4)_3]$

105. Which one of the following coordination entity is chiral?

a. *trans*-$[CrCl_2(ox)_2]^{3-}$
b. *cis*-$[Co(NH_3)_4Cl_2]^+$
c. *cis*-$[CrCl_2(ox)_2]^{3-}$
d. *trans*-$[Co(NH_3)_4Cl_2]^+$

106. Which of the following compounds is responsible for depletion of ozone layer?

a. Freon *b.* Chloroform
c. DDT *d.* Iodoform

107. Ethanol, when warmed with iodine and sodium carbonate gives a yellow coloured crystalline solid, which is used in preparation of antiseptic ointments. The yellow coloured crystalline substance is

a. chloroform *b.* iodoform
c. carbon tetrachloride *d.* dichloromethane

108. Consider the acid strength of the carboxylic acids.

I. PhCOOH II. *o*-$NO_2C_6H_4COOH$
III. *p*-$NO_2C_6H_4COOH$ IV. *m*-$NO_2C_6H_4COOH$

a. I > II > III > IV *b.* IV > III > II > I
c. II > III > IV > I *d.* II > IV > III > I

109. Which of the following is the correct sequence of relative acidic strength?

a. $FCH_2COOH > ClCH_2COOH > BrCH_2COOH$
b. $ClCH_2COOH > BrCH_2COOH > FCH_2COOH$
c. $BrCH_2COOH > ClCH_2COOH > FCH_2COOH$
d. $ClCH_2COOH > FCH_2COOH > BrCH_2COOH$

110. A mixture of methylamine and dimethyl amine is given to you. The reagents used to separate the components of the mixture are

a. $CHCl_3$ and HCl *b.* $C_6H_5SO_2Cl$ and KOH
c. $C_6H_5SO_2Cl$ and HCl *d.* $CHCl_3$ and KOH

111. Gabriel phthalimide synthesis is used for the preparation of

a. secondary amines *b.* amides
c. primary amines *d.* tertiary amines

112. The correct increasing order of basic strength of following amines,

$C_2H_5NH_2$, NH_3, $(C_2H_5)_2NH$, $C_6H_5NH_2$ in gaseous state is

a. $(C_2H_5)_2NH < C_2H_5NH_2 < NH_3 < C_6H_5NH_2$
b. $C_6H_5NH_2 < (C_2H_5)_2NH < C_2H_5NH_2 < NH_3$
c. $C_6H_5NH_2 < NH_3 < C_2H_5NH_2 < (C_2H_5)_2NH$
d. $(C_2H_5)_2NH < C_2H_5NH_2 < C_6H_5NH_2 < NH_3$

113. The sequence of bases on RNA molecule synthesise on the GCATA strand of DNA is

a. CGUAU *b.* CGTAT
c. TACGC *d.* AYCGC

114. α-helix and β-pleated structures of proteins are classified as

a. primary structure *b.* secondary structure
c. tertiary structure *d.* quaternary structure

115. Which statement is not true for describing enzymes?
a. They are polypeptides.
b. There are glycosidic linkages between the molecules.
c. They are specific for a particular reaction.
d. They catalyse biological reactions.

116. Which of the following are monosaccharides?
a. Glucose and maltose
b. Glucose and sucrose
c. Glucose and ribose
d. None of the above

117. Nylon-6, 6 is an example of a polymer formed by
a. chain growth polymerisation
b. crossed linked polymerisation
c. addition polymerisation
d. step growth polymerisation

118. Which of the following will form a biodegradable polymer?
a. Glycine and aminocaproic acid.
b. Ethylene glycol and phthalic acid.
c. Hexamethylenediamine and adipic acid.
d. 1, 3-butadiene and acrylonitrile.

119. Detergents can be made biodegradable and pollution free by
a. using cyclic hydrocarbon chain
b. shortening the hydrocarbon chain
c. using unbranched hydrocarbon chain
d. hydrocarbons with more branching

120. Sodium rosinate is generally added in the soap because it
a. prevents rapid drying of soap
b. produces rich lather
c. gives antiseptic property
d. acts as a perfume

MATHEMATICS

121. If two sets A and B have 99 elements in common, then the number of elements common to the sets $A \times B$ and $B \times A$ is
a. 2^{99} *b.* 99^2
c. 100 d. 18

122. If $f(x) = e^x$ and $g(x) = \log e^x$, then which of the following is true?
a. $f\{g(x)\} \neq g\{f(x)\}$
b. $f\{g(x)\} = g\{f(x)\}$
c. $f\{g(x)\} + g\{f(x)\} = 0$
d. $f\{g(x)\} - g\{f(x)\} = 1$

123. The number of bijective functions from the set A to itself, if A contains 108 elements is
a. 108 *b.* $(108)!$ *c.* $(108)^2$ d. 2^{108}

124. If a class of 175 students the following data shows the number of students opting one or more subjects. Mathematics 100, Physics 70, Chemistry 40. Mathematics and Physics 30, Mathematics and Chemistry 28, Physics and Chemistry 23, Mathematics, Physics and Chemistry 18. The number of students who have opted Mathematics alone is
a. 35 *b.* 48
c. 60 d. 22

125. If a set A has 4 elements, then the total number of proper subsets of set A, is
a. 16 *b.* 14
c. 15 *d.* 17

126. If $\tan(x+y) = 33$ and $x = \tan^{-1} 3$, then y is
a. $\frac{3}{10}$ *b.* $\frac{33}{10}$
c. $\tan^{-1}\left(\frac{1}{3}\right)$ *d.* $\tan^{-1}\left(\frac{3}{10}\right)$

127. $\cot^{-1}(21) + \cot^{-1}(13) + \cot^{-1}(-8) =$
a. 0 *b.* $\cot^{-1} 26$
c. π *d.* None of these

128. $\tan\left(\cos^{-1}\left(\frac{1}{5\sqrt{2}}\right) - \sin^{-1}\left(\frac{4}{\sqrt{17}}\right)\right)$ is equal to
a. $\frac{\sqrt{29}}{3}$ *b.* $\frac{29}{3}$ *c.* $\frac{\sqrt{3}}{29}$ *d.* $\frac{3}{29}$

129. The number of solutions of the equation $|\cot x| = \cot x + \frac{1}{\sin x}$, $(0 \le x \le 2\pi)$ is
a. 0 *b.* 1 *c.* 2 *d.* 3

130. $\frac{\sin x - \sin 3x}{\sin^2 x - \cos^2 x}$ is equal to
a. $-2\sin x$ *b.* $\frac{2}{\sin x}$
c. $\frac{1}{\sin x}$ *d.* $2\sin x$

131. In a ΔABC, $\operatorname{cosec} A(\sin B \cos C + \cos B \sin C) =$
a. 0 *b.* 1
c. -1 *d.* None of these

132. Amplitude of the complex number $i\sin\left(\frac{\pi}{19}\right)$ is

a. $\frac{\pi}{19}$ **b.** $-\frac{\pi}{19}$ **c.** $\frac{\pi}{2}$ **d.** $\frac{\pi}{2}-\frac{\pi}{19}$

133. Given, 5 line segments of lengths 2, 3, 4, 5, 6 units. Then, the number of triangles that can be formed by joining these segments is

a. ${}^5C_3-3$ **b.** ${}^5C_3$
c. ${}^5C_3-1$ **d.** ${}^5C_3-2$

134. How many numbers greater than 1000000 be formed from 2, 3, 0, 3, 4, 2, 3 ?

a. 420 **b.** 360 **c.** 400 **d.** 300

135. The expression

$$\frac{1}{\sqrt{(3x+1)}}\left[\left(\frac{1+\sqrt{3x+1}}{2}\right)^7-\left(\frac{1-\sqrt{3x+1}}{2}\right)^7\right] \text{ is}$$

a polynomial in x of degree

a. 7 **b.** 5
c. 4 **d.** 3

136. If in the expansion of $(1+px)^n$, $n\in N$, the coefficient of x and x^2 are 8 and 24, then

a. $n=3, p=2$ **b.** $n=5, p=3$
c. $n=4, p=3$ **d.** $n=4, p=2$

137. $11^3+12^3+13^3+\ldots\ldots+20^3$ is

a. an even integer.
b. an odd integer divisible by 5.
c. multiple of 10.
d. an odd integer but not a multiple of 5.

138. The medians AD and BE of a triangle with vertices $A(0, b)$, $B(0, 0)$ and $C(a, 0)$ are perpendicular to each other, if

a. $a=\frac{b}{2}$ **b.** $b=\frac{a}{2}$
c. $ab=1$ **d.** $a=\pm\sqrt{2}b$

139. Let a and b be non-zero real such that $a\neq b$. Then, the equation of the line passing through the origin and the point of intersection of $\frac{x}{a}+\frac{y}{b}=1$ and $\frac{x}{b}+\frac{y}{a}=1$ is

a. $ax+by=0$ **b.** $bx+ay=0$
c. $y-x=0$ **d.** $x+y=0$

140. A straight lines meets the coordinates axes at A and B, so that the centroid of the $\Delta\, OAB$ is (1, 2). Then, the equation of the line AB is

a. $x+y=6$ **b.** $2x+y=6$
c. $x+2y=6$ **d.** $3x+y=6$

141. The direction ratios of the line which is perpendicular to the lines $\frac{x-7}{2}=\frac{y+17}{-3}=\frac{z-6}{1}$ and $\frac{x+5}{1}=\frac{y+3}{2}=\frac{z-4}{-2}$ are

a. $<4, 5, 7>$ **b.** $<4, -5, 7>$
c. $<4, -5, -7>$ **d.** $<-4, 5, 7>$

142. A line making angles 45° and 60° with the positive directions of the axis of X and Y, makes with the positive direction of Z-axis, an angle of

a. 60° **b.** 120°
c. 60° and 120° **d.** None of these

143. The shortest distance between the lines $\frac{x-3}{3}=\frac{y-8}{-1}=\frac{z-3}{1}$ and $\frac{x+3}{-3}=\frac{y+7}{2}=\frac{z-6}{4}$ is

a. $\sqrt{30}$ **b.** $2\sqrt{30}$ **c.** $5\sqrt{30}$ **d.** $3\sqrt{30}$

144. $\lim_{x\to\infty}\left(\sqrt{a^2x^2+bx+x}-ax\right)=$

a. $\frac{b+1}{2a}$ **b.** $\frac{b}{a}$ **c.** 0 **d.** $\frac{2b}{a}$

145. If $y=|\cos x|+|\sin x|$, then $\frac{dy}{dx}$ at $x=\frac{2\pi}{3}$ is

a. $\frac{1-\sqrt{3}}{2}$ **b.** 0
c. $\frac{1}{2}(\sqrt{3}-1)$ **d.** None of these

146. The slant height of a cone is fixed at 7 cm. If the rate of increase of its height is 0.3 cm/sec, then the rate of increase of its volume when its height is 4 cm is

a. $\frac{\pi}{2}$ cc/sec **b.** π cc/sec
c. $\frac{\pi}{5}$ cc/sec **d.** $\frac{\pi}{10}$ cc/sec

147. A ladders 5 m long is leaning against a wall. The bottom of the ladder is pulled along the ground away from the wall, at the rate of 2m/sec. The speed at which its height on the wall decreases when the foot of the ladder is 4 m away from the wall is

a. $\frac{3}{8}$ m/sec **b.** $\frac{8}{3}$ m/sec
c. $\frac{5}{3}$ m/sec **d.** $\frac{2}{3}$ m/sec

148. The angle between the curve $y^2=4ax$ and $ay=2x^2$ is

a. $\tan^{-1}\frac{3}{4}$ **b.** $\tan^{-1}\frac{3}{5}$
c. $\tan^{-1}\frac{4}{3}$ **d.** $\tan^{-1}\frac{5}{3}$

COMEDK 2015

149. The maximum area in square units of an isosceles triangle inscribed in an ellipses $\frac{x^2}{a^2}+\frac{y^2}{b^2}=1$ with its vertex at one end of the major axis is

a. $\sqrt{3}\,ab$ sq units
b. $\frac{3\sqrt{3}}{4}ab$ sq units
c. $\frac{5\sqrt{3}}{4}ab$ sq units
d. None of these

150. If $f(x+y)=f(x)f(y)$ for all x and y and $f(5)=2$, $f'(0)=3$, then $f'(5)$ is

a. 5
b. 6
c. 0
d. None of these

151. If $f(x)=\log_{x^2}(\log x)$, then $f'(x)$ at $x=e$ is

a. 0
b. 1
c. $\frac{1}{e}$
d. $\frac{1}{2e}$

152. The value of c in Lagrange's mean value theorem for the function $f(x)=\log(\sin x)$ in the interval $\left[\frac{\pi}{6},\frac{5\pi}{6}\right]$ is

a. $\frac{\pi}{4}$
b. $\frac{\pi}{2}$
c. $\frac{2\pi}{3}$
d. None of these

153. $\int_{-1}^{1}(x^{27}\cos x+e^x)dx=$

a. $\frac{2e-1}{e}$
b. $\frac{e+1}{e}$
c. $e-\frac{1}{e}$
d. $\frac{1}{e}$

154. The value of the integral

$$\int_0^{\pi}\frac{x\sin^{2n}x}{\sin^{2n}x+\cos^{2n}x}dx \text{ is}$$

a. π^2
b. $2\pi^2$
c. $\frac{\pi^2}{4}$
d. $\frac{\pi^2}{2}$

155. $\int\frac{x^3-1}{x^3+x}dx=$

a. $x-\log x+\log(x^2+1)-\tan^{-1}x+c$
b. $x-\log x+\frac{1}{2}\log(x^2+1)-\tan^{-1}x+c$
c. $x+\log x+\log(x^2+1)-\tan^{-1}x+c$
d. $x+\log x+\frac{1}{2}\log(x^2+1)-\tan^{-1}x+c$

156. If $\int\frac{\cos 8x+1}{\tan 2x-\cot 2x}dx=a\cos 8x+c$, then $a=$

a. $-\frac{1}{16}$
b. $\frac{1}{8}$
c. $\frac{1}{16}$
d. $-\frac{1}{8}$

157. If $\int_0^{\pi}x f(\sin x)\,dx=A\int_0^{\pi/2}f(\sin x)dx$, then A is equal to

a. 0
b. 2π
c. $\frac{\pi}{4}$
d. π

158. Area bounded by the curve $y=x^3$, the X-axis and the ordinates at $x=-2$ and $x=1$, is

a. -9 sq units
b. $-\frac{15}{4}$ sq units
c. $\frac{15}{4}$ sq units
d. $\frac{17}{4}$ sq units

159. The area in square units bounded by the normal at (1, 2) to the parabola $y^2=4x$, X-axis and the curve is given by

a. $\frac{10}{3}$
b. $\frac{7}{3}$
c. $\frac{4}{3}$
d. None of these

160. Area bounded by the Y-axis, $y=\cos x$, $y=\sin x$, when $0\le x\le\frac{\pi}{2}$ is

a. $\sqrt{2}-1$
b. $2(\sqrt{2}-1)$
c. $(\sqrt{2}+1)$
d. $\sqrt{2}$

161. The area in square units of the region bounded by $y^2=9x$ and $y=3x$ is

a. 2
b. $\frac{1}{4}$
c. $\frac{1}{2}$
d. 1

162. $\int_1^e\log x\,dx=$

a. 1
b. $e-1$
c. $e+1$
d. 0

163. The differential equation of the family of parabolas $y^2=4ax$, where a is parameter, is

a. $\frac{dy}{dx}=\frac{y}{2x}$
b. $\frac{dy}{dx}=-\frac{y}{2x}$
c. $\frac{dy}{dx}=-\frac{2y}{x}$
d. $\frac{dy}{dx}=\frac{2y}{x}$

164. If $\frac{dy}{dx}=\frac{y+x\tan\frac{y}{x}}{x}$, then $\sin\left(\frac{y}{x}\right)=$

a. cx^2
b. cx
c. cx^3
d. $\log x$

165. The general solution of the differential equation $\left(\frac{dy}{dx}\right) + y \cdot g'(x) = g(x) \cdot g'(x)$, where $g(x)$ is a given function of x is

a. $g(x) + \log(1 + y + g(x)) = c$
b. $g(x) + \log(1 + y - g(x)) = c$
c. $g(x) - \log(1 + y - g(x)) = c$
d. $g(x) - \log(1 - y + g(x)) = c$

166. The product of the degree and order of the differential equation $\left(\frac{d^2y}{dx^2}\right)^2 - \left(\frac{dy}{dx}\right)^3 = y^3$ is

a. 4 b. 6
c. 2 d. 3

167. Given, two vectors $\hat{\mathbf{i}} - \hat{\mathbf{j}}$ and $\hat{\mathbf{i}} - 2\hat{\mathbf{j}}$. The unit vector, coplanar with the two given vectors and perpendicular to $(\hat{\mathbf{i}} - \hat{\mathbf{j}})$ is

a. $\frac{1}{\sqrt{2}}(\hat{\mathbf{i}} + \hat{\mathbf{j}})$ b. $\frac{1}{\sqrt{5}}(2\hat{\mathbf{i}} + \hat{\mathbf{j}})$
c. $\pm\frac{1}{\sqrt{2}}(\hat{\mathbf{i}} + \hat{\mathbf{j}})$ d. None of these

168. If **a**, **b**, **c** are three non-zero vectors such that each one of them are perpendicular to the sum of the other two vectors, then the value of $|\mathbf{a} + \mathbf{b} + \mathbf{c}|^2$ is

a. $|\mathbf{a}|^2 + |\mathbf{b}|^2 + |\mathbf{c}|^2$ b. $|\mathbf{a}| + |\mathbf{b}| + |\mathbf{c}|$
c. $2(|\mathbf{a}|^2 + |\mathbf{b}|^2 + |\mathbf{c}|^2)$ d. $\frac{1}{2}(|\mathbf{a}|^2 + |\mathbf{b}|^2 + |\mathbf{c}|^2)$

169. If A and B are 2 matrices such that $AB = A$ and $BA = B$, then B^2 is equal to

a. B b. A
c. zero matrix d. 1

170. If a, b, c are in AP, then the value of the determinant $\begin{vmatrix} x+2 & x+3 & x+2a \\ x+3 & x+4 & x+2b \\ x+4 & x+5 & x+2c \end{vmatrix}$ is

a. 0 b. 1
c. x d. $2x$

171. If $A = \begin{bmatrix} a & 0 & 0 \\ 0 & a & 0 \\ 0 & 0 & a \end{bmatrix}$, then $\det(\text{adj } A)$ is

a. a^{27} b. a^9
c. a^6 d. a^2

172. If $A = \begin{bmatrix} 1 & 0 \\ 1 & 1 \end{bmatrix}$ and $A^8 = aA + bI$, then $(a, b) =$

a. (8, 7) b. (– 7, 8)
c. (8, – 7) d. (– 8, – 7)

173. An urn contains 9 balls, 2 of which are white, 3 blue and 4 black. 3 balls are drawn at random from the urn. The chance that 2 balls will be of the same colour and the third of a different colour is

a. $\frac{45}{84}$ b. $\frac{55}{84}$ c. $\frac{35}{84}$ d. $\frac{25}{84}$

174. 6 boys and 6 girls in a row at random. The probability that all the girls sit together is

a. $\frac{1}{432}$ b. $\frac{12}{431}$
c. $\frac{1}{132}$ d. None of these

175. Three dice are rolled once. The chance of getting a score of 5 is

a. $\frac{5}{216}$ b. $\frac{1}{6}$ c. $\frac{1}{36}$ d. $\frac{1}{7^2}$

176. A bag contains 3 white, 4 black, 2 red balls. If 2 balls are drawn at random, then the probability that both the balls are white is

a. $\frac{1}{18}$ b. $\frac{1}{36}$ c. $\frac{1}{12}$ d. $\frac{1}{24}$

177. The solution of $\frac{6x}{4x-1} < \frac{1}{2}$ is

a. $x < \frac{-1}{8}$ b. $\frac{-1}{8} < x < \frac{1}{4}$
c. $x < \frac{-1}{8}$ and $x > \frac{1}{4}$ d. $x > \frac{1}{8}$

178. If $S^2 = at^2 + 2bt + c$, then acceleration is

a. directly proportional to S.
b. inversely proportional to S.
c. directly proportional to S^2.
d. inversely proportional to S^3.

179. The mean and variance for the data 6, 7, 10, 12, 13, 4, 8, 12 respectively are

a. $8, \sqrt{26.25}$ b. $9, \sqrt{9.25}$
c. 8, 26.25 d. 9, 9.25

180. If the conjugate of $(x + iy)(1 - 2i)$ is $1 + i$, then

a. $x - iy = \frac{1-i}{1-2i}$ b. $x + iy = \frac{1-i}{1-2i}$
c. $x = \frac{1}{5}$ d. $x = -\frac{1}{5}$

ANSWERS

Physics

1. (*)	**2.** (b)	**3.** (d)	**4.** (a)	**5.** (c)	**6.** (c)	**7.** (c)	**8.** (d)	**9.** (a)	**10.** (c)
11. (a)	**12.** (b)	**13.** (c)	**14.** (d)	**15.** (b)	**16.** (b)	**17.** (a)	**18.** (d)	**19.** (c)	**20.** (d)
21. (c)	**22.** (c)	**23.** (b)	**24.** (b)	**25.** (c)	**26.** (b)	**27.** (c)	**28.** (d)	**29.** (c)	**30.** (*)
31. (a)	**32.** (b)	**33.** (d)	**34.** (c)	**35.** (c)	**36.** (b)	**37.** (d)	**38.** (c)	**39.** (b)	**40.** (d)
41. (a)	**42.** (b)	**43.** (d)	**44.** (d)	**45.** (a)	**46.** (c)	**47.** (d)	**48.** (b)	**49.** (a)	**50.** (a)
51. (d)	**52.** (a)	**53.** (c)	**54.** (c)	**55.** (c)	**56.** (c)	**57.** (b)	**58.** (b)	**59.** (c)	**60.** (d)

Chemistry

61. (b)	**62.** (d)	**63.** (d)	**64.** (d)	**65.** (a)	**66.** (a)	**67.** (d)	**68.** (c)	**69.** (b)	**70.** (d)
71. (a)	**72.** (c)	**73.** (b)	**74.** (a)	**75.** (d)	**76.** (c)	**77.** (b)	**78.** (c)	**79.** (a)	**80.** (d)
81. (c)	**82.** (b)	**83.** (a)	**84.** (b)	**85.** (b)	**86.** (a)	**87.** (b)	**88.** (d)	**89.** (b)	**90.** (d)
91. (c)	**92.** (a)	**93.** (a)	**94.** (d)	**95.** (b)	**96.** (d)	**97.** (d)	**98.** (d)	**99.** (b)	**100.** (b)
101. (c)	**102.** (d)	**103.** (b)	**104.** (c)	**105.** (c)	**106.** (a)	**107.** (b)	**108.** (c)	**109.** (a)	**110.** (b)
111. (c)	**112.** (c)	**113.** (a)	**114.** (b)	**115.** (b)	**116.** (c)	**117.** (d)	**118.** (a)	**119.** (c)	**120.** (b)

Mathematics

121. (b)	**122.** (b)	**123.** (b)	**124.** (c)	**125.** (c)	**126.** (d)	**127.** (c)	**128.** (d)	**129.** (b)	**130.** (d)
131. (b)	**132.** (c)	**133.** (a)	**134.** (b)	**135.** (d)	**136.** (d)	**137.** (b)	**138.** (d)	**139.** (c)	**140.** (b)
141. (a)	**142.** (a)	**143.** (d)	**144.** (a)	**145.** (c)	**146.** (d)	**147.** (b)	**148.** (b)	**149.** (b)	**150.** (b)
151. (d)	**152.** (b)	**153.** (c)	**154.** (c)	**155.** (b)	**156.** (c)	**157.** (d)	**158.** (d)	**159.** (a)	**160.** (a)
161. (c)	**162.** (a)	**163.** (a)	**164.** (b)	**165.** (b)	**166.** (a)	**167.** (c)	**168.** (a)	**169.** (a)	**170.** (a)
171. (c)	**172.** (c)	**173.** (b)	**174.** (c)	**175.** (c)	**176.** (c)	**177.** (b)	**178.** (d)	**170.** (d)	**180.** (b)

Note (*) None of the option is correct.

HINTS & SOLUTIONS

Physics

1. *(*)* Given, mass of disc, $M = 400 \text{ g} = 0.4 \text{ kg}$

Radius, $R = 4 \text{ cm} = 4 \times 10^{-2} \text{ m}$

Angular speed, $\omega = 2\pi \times 10$

$= 20\pi \text{ rad/s}$

$\therefore$ Moment of inertia of disc about its diameter

$$I_d = \frac{1}{4} MR^2$$

$\therefore$ Kinetic energy of disc

$$= \frac{1}{2} I_d \omega^2$$

$$= \frac{1}{2} \times \frac{1}{4} MR^2 \times \omega^2 = \frac{1}{8} MR^2 \omega^2$$

$$= \frac{1}{8} \times 0.4 \times (4 \times 10^{-2})^2 \times (20\pi)^2$$

$$= 3.2 \times 10^{-1} \text{ J}$$

Hence, no option is correct.

2. *(b)* According to given condition, let n number of bulbs are connected in parallel as shown below

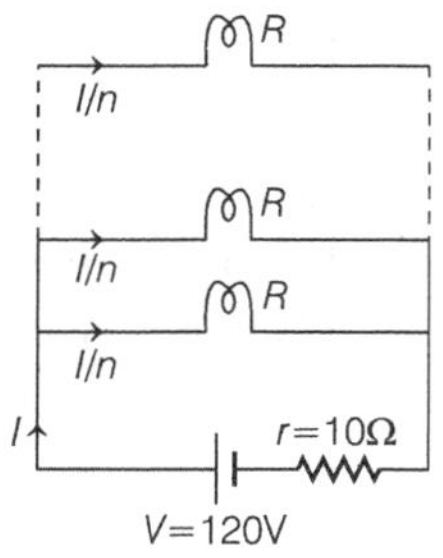

Resistance of each bulb, $R = \frac{V^2}{P}$ $\left[\because P = \frac{V^2}{R}\right]$

$$= \frac{100^2}{50} = 200\ \Omega$$

Using KVL in the lowest loop,

$$120 - 10I - \frac{I}{n} \times 200 = 0$$

$$\Rightarrow \quad 12 - I = \frac{20I}{n} \quad \dots \text{(i)}$$

Power delivered by battery = Sum of power used in bulbs

$$(120 - 10I)I = 50n$$

$$\Rightarrow \quad (12 - I)I = 5n$$

$$\Rightarrow \quad \frac{20I}{n} \cdot I = 5n \quad \text{[from Eq. (i)]}$$

$$\Rightarrow \quad 4I^2 = n^2$$

$$\Rightarrow \quad I = \frac{n}{2} \quad \dots \text{(ii)}$$

From Eqs. (i) and (ii), we get

$$12 - \frac{n}{2} = \frac{20}{n} \times \frac{n}{2} \Rightarrow n = 4$$

3. *(d)* Weight of stone at the surface of the earth, $w = 100 \text{ N}$

At height h from the surface of earth, gravitational acceleration,

$$g_h = \frac{g}{\left(1 + \frac{h}{R}\right)^2}$$

At depth d from the surface of the earth, gravitational acceleration,

$$g_d = g\left(1 - \frac{d}{R}\right)$$

According to question,

$$\frac{\text{Weight at } h = R/2}{\text{Weight at } d = R/2} = \frac{mg_{h\,(\text{at } h = R/2)}}{mg_{d\,(\text{at } h = R/2)}}$$

$$= \frac{\frac{g}{\left(1 + \frac{h}{R}\right)^2} \ (\text{at } h = R/2)}{g\left(1 - \frac{d}{R}\right) \ \text{at}(d = R/2)}$$

$$= \frac{\frac{1}{\left(1 + \frac{R/2}{R}\right)^2}}{1 - \frac{R/2}{R}} = \frac{4/9}{1/2} = \frac{8}{9} = 0.9$$

4. *(a)* At the surface of the planet, gravitational acceleration,

$$g = \frac{GM}{R^2} \quad \dots \text{(i)}$$

where, M = mass of the planet

R = radius of the planet.

When $M' = 2M$ and $R' = 2R$, then

$$g' = \frac{GM'}{R'^2}$$

$$= \frac{G \cdot 2M}{(2R)^2} = \frac{GM}{2R^2} = \frac{1}{2} \cdot g \quad \text{[from Eq. (i)]}$$

$$\Rightarrow \quad g' = \frac{g}{2}$$

5. *(c)* Given, length, $l = 11 \text{ m}$

Radius, $r = 2 \text{ cm}$

$= 2 \times 10^{-2} \text{ m}$

Mass, $m = 40$ tons

$= 4 \times 10^4 \text{ kg}$

Increase in length, $\Delta l = ?$

We know that, Young's modulus,

$$Y = \frac{mgl}{\pi r^2(\Delta l)}$$

$$\Rightarrow \quad \Delta l = \frac{mgl}{\pi r^2 Y}$$

$$= \frac{4 \times 10^4 \times 10 \times 11}{3.14 \times (2 \times 10^{-2})^2 \times 2 \times 10^{11}}$$

$$= 1.75 \times 10^{-2} \text{ m}$$

$$= 1.75 \text{ cm}$$

6. *(c)* From the *I-V* graph,

Slope of the line $= \frac{1}{R}$

$$\Rightarrow \quad R = \frac{1}{\text{slope}}$$

Since, slope of line having temperature T_1 is greater than slope of line having temperature T_2.

Hence, $R_2 > R_1$

Since, on increasing temperature of a conductor, its resistance increases. Hence, $T_2 > T_1$

7. *(c)* When a charged particle moves in uniform magnetic field making an acute angle with the direction of magnetic field, then it moves on helical path with uniform pitch.

8. *(d)* Magnetic field at the centre due to current carrying circular loop having N turns is given as

$$B = \frac{\mu_0 NI}{2r}$$

If l be the length of wire, then for the first case,

$$2\pi r_1 = l$$

$$\Rightarrow \quad r_1 = \frac{l}{2\pi}$$

$\therefore$ Magnetic field, $B_1 = \frac{\mu_0 \cdot 1 \cdot I}{2 \cdot r_1} = \frac{\mu_0 I}{2 \cdot l / 2\pi}$

$$B_1 = \frac{\mu_0 I \pi}{l} \quad \dots \text{(i)}$$

For the second case,

$$2 \times 2\pi r_2 = l$$

$$\Rightarrow \quad r_2 = \frac{l}{4\pi}$$

$$\therefore \quad B_2 = \frac{\mu_0 \cdot 2 \cdot I}{2r_2} = \frac{2\mu_0 I}{2 \cdot \frac{l}{4\pi}}$$

$$\Rightarrow \quad B_2 = \frac{4\mu_0 I\pi}{l} = 4 \times B_1 \quad \text{[from Eq. (i)]}$$

$$\Rightarrow \quad \frac{B_1}{B_2} = \frac{1}{4}$$

9. *(a)* Inside a cyclotron, charged particle gains kinetic energy only due to electric field, because in magnetic field, its kinetic energy remains unchanged.

10. *(c)* Magnetic field strength B due to long straight current carrying conductor at a distance r is given as

$$B = \frac{\mu_0}{2\pi} \cdot \frac{I}{r}$$

$$\Rightarrow \quad B \propto \frac{1}{r}$$

Hence, correct variation of B with r is shown in the graph given in option (c).

11. *(a)* Using relation,

$$\frac{F - 32}{180} = \frac{C}{100} \quad \dots \text{(i)}$$

If $F = C = x$, then substituting value of Eq. (i), we get

$$\Rightarrow \quad \frac{x - 32}{180} = \frac{x}{100} \Rightarrow \frac{x}{5} = \frac{x - 32}{9}$$

$$\Rightarrow \quad 9x = 5x - 160 \Rightarrow 160 = -4x$$

$$\therefore \quad x = -40°$$

This is the required temperature at which centigrade and Fahrenheit scale give same reading.

12. *(b)* Superconductors in the Meissner state exhibit perfect diamagnetism or superdiamagnetism, meaning that the total magnetic field is very close to zero deep inside them.

13. *(c)* Given, $B_H = 4 \times 10^{-4}$ T

Angle of dip, $\delta = 30°$

$B_V = ?$

We know that,

$$\tan \delta = \frac{B_V}{B_H}$$

$$\Rightarrow \quad B_V = B_H \tan \delta$$

$$= 4 \times 10^{-4} \tan 30°$$

$$= \frac{4}{\sqrt{3}} \times 10^{-4}$$

$$= 2.3 \times 10^{-4} \text{ T}$$

14. *(d)* Initial speed of bicycle, $v_1 = 15$ km/h

Emf produced, $e_1 = 1.5$ V

Final speed of bicycle, $v_2 = 10$ km/h

If emf generated at speed v_2 be e_2, then

$$e = Bvl$$

$$\Rightarrow \quad e \propto v$$

$$\Rightarrow \quad \frac{e_2}{e_1} = \frac{v_2}{v_1} = \frac{10}{15}$$

$$\Rightarrow \quad \frac{e_2}{e_1} = \frac{2}{3} \Rightarrow e_2 = \frac{2}{3} e_1 = \frac{2}{3} \times 1.5 = 1 \text{ V}$$

15. *(b)* Given, frequency of AC, $\nu = 50$ Hz

Peak voltage, $V_0 = 300$ V

Generator equation for the voltage is given as

$$V = V_0 \sin \omega t$$

$$= V_0 \sin 2\pi\nu t$$

$$= 300 \sin(2\pi \times 50 \times t)$$

$$= 300 \sin 100\pi t$$

16. *(b)* For a transformer,

Input voltage, $V_1 = 220$ V

Input current, $I_1 = 0.6$ A

Output power, $P_2 = 100$ W

From, input power, $P_1 = V_1 I_1$

$= 220 \times 0.6$

$= 132$ W

We know that, efficiency of transformer,

$$\eta = \frac{P_2}{P_1} = \frac{100}{132} = 0.7576$$

$$= 75.76\% \simeq 76\%$$

17. *(a)* Instantaneous current,

$$i = 4\cos(\omega t + \phi)$$

Comparing with standard equation, $i = i_0 \cos(\omega t + \phi)$, we get

$\therefore$ Peak current, $i_0 = 4$ A

Hence, $i_{rms} = \frac{i_0}{\sqrt{2}}$

$$= \frac{4}{\sqrt{2}} = 2\sqrt{2} \text{ A}$$

18. *(d)* p is the momentum of incident wave.

$\therefore$ Momentum of reflected wave after reflecting from perfect reflector $= -p$

$\therefore$ Change in momentum = Final momentum − Initial momentum

$$= -p - p = -2p$$

19. *(c)* According to conservation of angular momentum, when no external torque is applied on the rotating system, then its angular momentum remains unchanged.

20. *(d)* Given, $T_A = 727°C$ and $T_B = 327°C$

As we know, rate of heat radiated,

$$Q \propto T^4$$

$$\Rightarrow \quad \frac{Q_A}{Q_B} = \frac{H_A}{H_B} = \left(\frac{273 + 727}{273 + 327}\right)^4 = \frac{625}{81}$$

21. *(c)* Given, refractive index of the medium, $n = 1.5$

Permeability of the medium,

$$\mu = 5 \times 10^{-7} \text{ Hm}^{-1}$$

Relative permeability of the medium,

$$\mu_r = \frac{\mu}{\mu_0} = \frac{5 \times 10^{-7}}{4\pi \times 10^{-7}} = \frac{5}{4\pi}$$

We know that, refractive index,

$$n = \sqrt{\varepsilon_r \mu_r}$$

$$n^2 = \varepsilon_r \mu_r$$

$$\Rightarrow \quad \varepsilon_r = \frac{n^2}{\mu_r} = \frac{(1.5)^2}{5/4\pi}$$

$$= \frac{(1.5)^2 \times 4\pi}{5} = 5.7 \simeq 6$$

22. *(c)* For the given situation, the ray diagram is shown below.

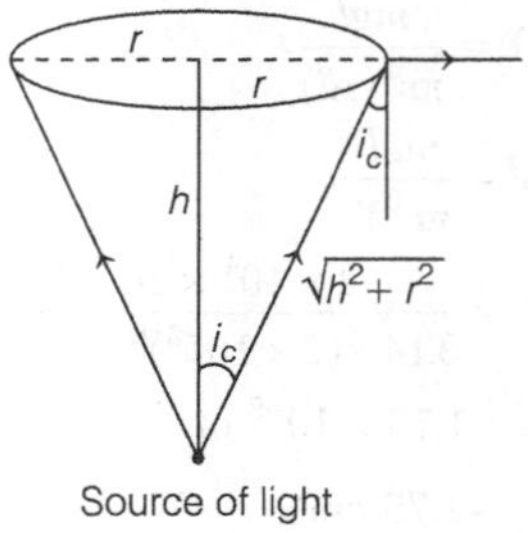

Refractive index of water, $\mu_w = \frac{4}{3}$

$$r = \frac{D}{2} = \frac{6}{2} = 3 \text{ m}$$

The given situation is possible only for the case of total internal reflection. If i_C be the critical angle, then

$$\sin i_C = \frac{1}{\mu_w}$$

$$\Rightarrow \quad \sin i_C = \frac{1}{4/3}$$

$$\Rightarrow \quad \sin i_C = \frac{3}{4}$$

$$\Rightarrow \quad \frac{r}{\sqrt{r^2 + h^2}} = \frac{3}{4} \qquad \left[\because \sin i_C = \frac{r}{\sqrt{r^2 + h^2}}\right]$$

$$\Rightarrow \quad \frac{3}{\sqrt{3^2 + h^2}} = \frac{3}{4}$$

$$\Rightarrow \quad 9 + h^2 = 16$$

$$\Rightarrow \quad h^2 = 7, h = \sqrt{7} = 2.6 \text{ m}$$

23. *(b)* For equiangular glass prism, $A = 60°$

Refractive index of prism, $\mu_p = 1.6$

Refractive index of water, $\mu_w = \frac{4}{3}$

We know that,

$${}^w\mu_p = \frac{\sin\left(\frac{A + \delta_m}{2}\right)}{\sin A/2}$$

$$\frac{\mu_p}{\mu_w} = \frac{\sin\left(\frac{60 + \delta_m}{2}\right)}{\sin 60/2}$$

$$\Rightarrow \quad \frac{1.6}{4/3} = \frac{\sin\left(\frac{60 + \delta_m}{2}\right)}{\sin 30°}$$

$$\Rightarrow \quad \sin\left(\frac{A + \delta_m}{2}\right) = \frac{1.6 \times 3}{4} \times \sin 30°$$

$$\Rightarrow \quad \sin\left(\frac{A + \delta_m}{2}\right) = 0.6$$

$$\Rightarrow \quad \sin\frac{A + \delta_m}{2} = \sin 37° \qquad [\because \sin 37 = 0.6]$$

$\Rightarrow \quad \dfrac{A+\delta_m}{2} = 37°$

$\Rightarrow \quad 60 + \delta_m = 2 \times 37 = 74°$

$\Rightarrow \quad \delta_m = 74 - 60 = 14°$

24. *(b)* Given, size of image formed by concave mirror,

$h_2 = 3h_1$

where, h_1 is the size of object.

$$m = \frac{h_2}{h_1} = \frac{3h_1}{h_1} = 3$$

But for real image, magnification m will be negative.

$\therefore \quad m = -3$

$\Rightarrow \quad -\dfrac{v}{u} = -3$

$\Rightarrow \quad v = 3u$

Here, $\quad u = -20$ cm,

$\therefore \quad v = 3(-20) = -60$ cm

By using mirror formula,

$$\frac{1}{f} = \frac{1}{u} + \frac{1}{v}$$

$$= \frac{1}{-20} + \frac{1}{-60} = -\frac{1}{15}$$

$\Rightarrow \quad f = -15$ cm

25. *(c)* Intensities of two monochromatic sources,

$I_1 = I$ and $I_2 = 4I$

Maximum intensity,

$$I_{\max} = (\sqrt{I_1} + \sqrt{I_2})^2$$

$$= I_1 + I_2 + 2\sqrt{I_1 I_2}$$

$$= I + 4I + 2\sqrt{I}\sqrt{4I} = 9I$$

Minimum intensity,

$$I_{\min} = (\sqrt{I_1} - \sqrt{I_2})^2$$

$$= I_1 + I_2 - 2\sqrt{I_1}\sqrt{I_2}$$

$$= I + 4I - 2\sqrt{I}\sqrt{4I}$$

$$= 5I - 4I = I$$

26. *(b)* Given, $h = 6.626 \times 10^{-34}$ J-s

$m = 9.1 \times 10^{-35}$ kg

Wavelength, $\lambda = 2$ Å

$= 2 \times 10^{-10}$ m

$\therefore$ Momentum of electron is given as

$$p = \frac{h}{\lambda} \qquad \left[\because p = \frac{h}{\lambda}\right]$$

$$= \frac{6.626 \times 10^{-34}}{2 \times 10^{-10}} = 3.313 \times 10^{-24} \text{ kg-ms}^{-1}$$

27. *(c)* Given, $V_0 = 1.5$ V

Maximum kinetic energy of emitted photoelectron,

$$K_{\max} = eV_0$$

$$= 1.6 \times 10^{-19} \times 1.5 = 2.4 \times 10^{-19} \text{ J}$$

28. *(d)* The best waves for emission of electrons from a surface are X-rays because when X-ray photon strikes a metal surface, then produce Compton or photoelectric effect more suitably.

29. *(c)* Wavelength λ of spectral lines in H-atom is given as

$$\frac{1}{\lambda} = R\left(\frac{1}{n_1^2} - \frac{1}{n_2^2}\right) \qquad \dots \text{(i)}$$

For shortest wavelength of Paschen series,

$n_1 = 3$ and $n_2 = \infty$

$\therefore$ From Eq. (i), we get

$$\frac{1}{\lambda_{PS}} = R\left(\frac{1}{3^2} - \frac{1}{\infty}\right) = \frac{R}{9}$$

$$\Rightarrow \quad \lambda_{PS} = \frac{9}{R} \qquad \dots \text{(ii)}$$

For shortest wavelength in Balmer series,

$n_1 = 2, n_2 = \infty$

$\therefore$ From Eq. (i), we get

$$\frac{1}{\lambda_{BS}} = R\left(\frac{1}{2^2} - \frac{1}{\infty}\right) = \frac{R}{4}$$

$$\Rightarrow \quad \lambda_{BS} = \frac{4}{R} \qquad \dots \text{(iii)}$$

For shortest wavelength of Lyman series,

$n_1 = 1$ and $n_2 = \infty$

$\therefore$ From Eq. (i), we get

$$\frac{1}{\lambda_{LS}} = R\left(\frac{1}{1^2} - \frac{1}{\infty}\right) = R$$

$$\Rightarrow \quad \lambda_{LS} = \frac{1}{R}$$

Hence, from Eq. (i), (ii) and (iii), we have

$$\lambda_{PS} : \lambda_{BS} : \lambda_{LS} = \frac{9}{R} : \frac{4}{R} : \frac{1}{R}$$

$$= 9 : 4 : 1$$

30. *(*)* Half-life of radioactive sample,

$T_{1/2} = 30$ s, $N_0 = 10^6$

If N be the remaining number of nuclei after $t = 10$ s, then according to radioactive decay law,

$$N = N_0\left(\frac{1}{2}\right)^n = 10^6\left(\frac{1}{2}\right)^{t/T_{1/2}}$$

$$= 10^6\left(\frac{1}{2}\right)^{\frac{10}{30}} = 10^6\left(\frac{1}{2}\right)^{1/3}$$

$$= 10^6(0.796) = 7.96 \times 10^5$$

31. *(a)* A nuclear fission is said to be critical when multiplication factor k will be equal to unity.

i.e., $\quad k = 1$

32. *(b)* In case of a p-n junction diode at high value of reverse bias voltage, the current rises sharply due to zener breakdown. At zener voltage, zener breakdown occurs and current rises sharply.

33. *(d)* According to given truth table, logic expression of the output Y for the given input A and B is given as

$$Y = \overline{AB}$$

which is the output expression for NAND gate.

34. *(c)* In a semiconductor diode, the reverse biased current is due to drift of the free electrons and holes which are produced by thermal expansion, impurity atoms etc.

35. *(c)* Initial height of TV tower, $h_1 = 120$ m

Coverage range of TV tower is given as

$$d = \sqrt{2Rh}$$

where, R is radius of the earth.

$$\Rightarrow \quad \frac{d_1}{d_2} = \sqrt{\frac{h_1}{h_2}}$$

$$\Rightarrow \quad \frac{d_1}{2d_1} = \sqrt{\frac{120}{h_2}} \qquad [\because d_2 = 2d_1]$$

$$\Rightarrow \quad \frac{1}{4} = \frac{120}{h_2}$$

$$\Rightarrow \quad h_2 = 480 \text{ m}$$

$\therefore$ Height to be added $= h_2 - h_1$

$$= 480 - 120 = 360 \text{ m}$$

36. *(b)* Frequency of message signal, $f_m = 10$ kHz

Carrier frequency, $f_c = 1$ MHz $= 1000$ kHz

Peak value of message signal, $V_m = 10$ V

Peak value of carrier signal, $V_c = 20$ V

$\therefore$ Modulation index, $\mu = \dfrac{V_m}{V_c} = \dfrac{10}{20} = 0.5$

Upper side band frequency,

$$f_{\text{USB}} = f_c + f_m = 1000 + 10 = 1010 \text{ kHz}$$

Lower side band frequency,

$$f_{\text{LSB}} = f_c - f_m = 1000 - 10 = 990 \text{ kHz}$$

37. *(d)* Given, $A = 10$ units

$B = 20$ units

$\theta = 30°$

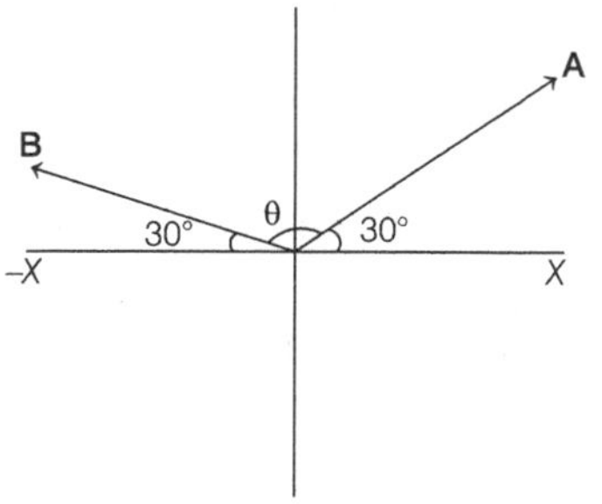

The given situation is shown in the figure. The angle between **A** and **B**,

$$\theta = 180° - 30° - 30° = 120°$$

$\therefore$ Magnitude of the resultant vector,

$$R = \sqrt{A^2 + B^2 + 2AB\cos\theta}$$

$$= \sqrt{10^2 + 20^2 + 2 \times 10 \times 20 \cos 120°}$$

$$= \sqrt{100 + 400 - 200}$$

$$= 10\sqrt{3}$$

38. *(c)* Let length of chain lying the table be y.

Mass per unit length of the chain $= \dfrac{M}{L}$

Mass of the chain lying on the table, $M' = \dfrac{M}{L}.y$

Mass of the length $(L - y)$ of hanging chain $= \dfrac{M}{L}(L - y)$

At equilibrium,

Friction force between table and chain

= Weight of hanging part of the chain

$$\mu\left(\frac{M}{L}y\right)g = \frac{M}{L}(L - y)g$$

$$\Rightarrow \quad \mu y = L - y$$

$$\Rightarrow \quad 0.5y = L - y \qquad [\because \mu = 0.5]$$

$$\Rightarrow \quad y = \frac{2L}{3}$$

39. *(b)* Mass of bomb, $M = 18$ kg

Mass of pieces, $m_1 = 6$ kg, $m_2 = 12$ kg

Velocity of 12 kg mass, $v_2 = 4$ m/s

Let v_1 be the velocity of 6 kg mass.

According to conservation of linear momentum,

$$M \times 0 = m_1v_1 + m_2v_2$$

$$\Rightarrow \quad m_1v_1 = -m_2v_2$$

$$6v_1 = -12 \times 4$$

$$\Rightarrow \quad v_1 = -8 \text{ m/s}$$

Kinetic energy of other (6 kg) mass,

$$K = \frac{1}{2}m_1v_1^2$$

$$= \frac{1}{2} \times 6 \times (-8)^2 = 3 \times 64 = 192 \text{ J}$$

40. *(d)* Surface area of bubble of radius, $r = 4\pi r^2$

Surface area of bubble of radius, $3r = 4\pi(3r)^2 = 36\pi r^2$

Therefore, increase in surface area

$$= 36\pi r^2 - 4\pi r^2 = 32\pi r^2$$

Since, a bubble has two surfaces, the total increase in surface area $= 2 \times 32\pi r^2 = 64\,\pi r^2$

$\therefore$ Energy spent = Work done = Surface tension $\times$ Total increase in surface area $= 64\,\pi\sigma r^2$

41. *(a)* The given situation is shown below

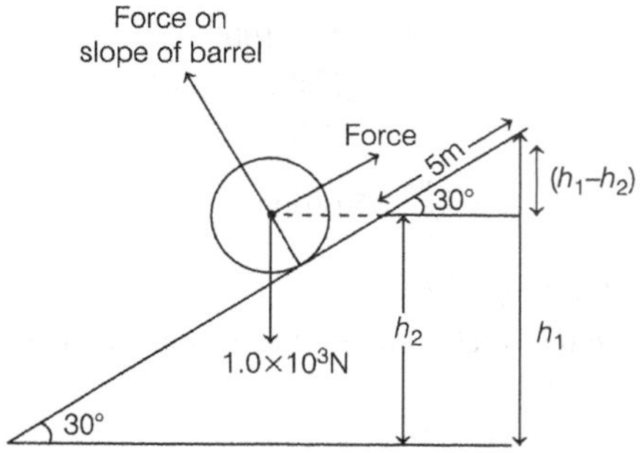

Work done in moving the barrel on the frictionless slope is equal to change in potential energy.

i.e. $W = mg(h_1 - h_2)$ ... (i)

Here, $mg = 1 \times 10^3$ N

From figure, $\sin 30° = \frac{h_1 - h_2}{5}$

$\Rightarrow$ $h_1 - h_2 = 5 \sin 30° = \frac{5}{2} = 2.5$ m

Putting these values in Eq. (i), we get

$$W = 1 \times 10^3 (2.5) = 2.5 \times 10^3 \text{ J}$$

42. *(b)* Since, displacement on the body of mass 2 kg is in the horizontal direction while normal reaction acts on the body in perpendicular to the displacement.

Hence, $\theta = 0$

$\therefore$ Work done, $W = Fs \cos 90° = 0$

43. *(d)* We know that, Young's modulus of elasticity,

$$Y = \frac{FL}{\pi r^2 l} \quad \text{[where, } l \text{ is change in length]}$$

$$\Rightarrow \quad l = \frac{FL}{\pi r^2 Y}$$

$$\Rightarrow \quad l \propto \frac{L}{r^2} \propto \frac{L}{d^2} \quad \text{[where, } d = \text{diameter]}$$

$$\Rightarrow \quad l \propto \frac{L}{d^2}$$

Among the given options, $\frac{L}{d^2}$ is maximum for the values of $L = 50$ cm and $d = 0.5$ mm.

44. *(d)* Given, $V_1 = V, l_1 = l, r_1 = r$

$$l_2 = 2l_1 = 2l$$

$$r_2 = \frac{r_1}{2} = \frac{r}{2}$$

$$V_2 = ?$$

According to Poiseuille's formula, the rate of flow of liquid through a narrow tube is given as

$$V = \frac{\pi p r^4}{8\eta l}$$

$$\Rightarrow \quad V \propto \frac{r^4}{l}$$

$$\Rightarrow \quad \frac{V_2}{V_1} = \left(\frac{r_2}{r_1}\right)^4 \cdot \frac{l_1}{l_2}$$

$$= \left(\frac{r/2}{r}\right)^4 \left(\frac{l}{2l}\right) = \left(\frac{1}{2}\right)^4 \cdot \frac{1}{2} = \frac{1}{32}$$

$$\Rightarrow \quad V_2 = \frac{V_1}{32} = \frac{V}{32}$$

45. *(a)* The given situation is shown in the figure.

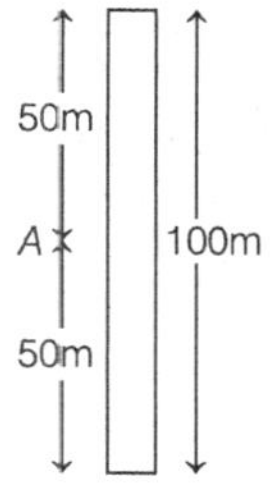

For the first ball, time taken to reach at mid point A,

$$t = \sqrt{\frac{2h}{g}}$$

$$= \sqrt{\frac{2 \times 50}{10}} = \sqrt{10} \text{ s}$$

For the second ball,

$$v = 0, u = ?, a = -g$$

$\therefore$ From equation, $v = u + gt$

$$0 = u - gt_1$$

$$\Rightarrow \quad t_1 = \frac{u}{g}$$

Since, both balls collide at some time,

Hence, $t = t_1$

$$\sqrt{10} = \frac{u}{g}$$

$$\Rightarrow \quad u = 10\sqrt{10} \text{ m/s} = 31.6 \text{ m/s}$$

46. *(c)* In isochoric process, volume of the system remains constant.

i.e. $\Delta V = V_1 - V_2 = V - V = 0 \quad [\because V_1 = V_2 = V]$

Hence, work done, $W = p \times \Delta V = p \times 0 = 0$

47. *(d)* At temperature, $T_1 = 300$ K

Average kinetic energy, $E_1 = 6.21 \times 10^{-21}$ J

$\therefore$ $T_2 = 600$ K, $E_2 = ?$

We know that, average kinetic energy of gas molecule,

$$E \propto T$$

$$\Rightarrow \quad \frac{E_2}{E_1} = \frac{T_2}{T_1} \Rightarrow E_2 = \frac{T_2}{T_1} \times E_1$$

$$= \frac{600}{300} \times 6.21 \times 10^{-21}$$

$$= 2 \times 6.21 \times 10^{-21}$$

$$= 12.42 \times 10^{-21} \text{ J}$$

48. *(b)* At initial condition of spring,

$$Mg = kX_0 \quad \text{... (i)}$$

When mass m is added, then at equilibrium,

$$(M + m)g = k(X + X_0)$$

$$\Rightarrow Mg + mg = kX + kX_0$$
$$\Rightarrow Mg + mg = kX + Mg \quad \text{[from Eq. (i)]}$$
$$\Rightarrow mg = kX$$
$$\Rightarrow k = \frac{mg}{X} \quad \dots \text{(ii)}$$

∴ Time period,

$$T = 2\pi\sqrt{\frac{\text{Total mass of the block}}{\text{Force constant } k}} = 2\pi\sqrt{\frac{M+m}{mg/X}} = 2\pi\sqrt{\frac{(M+m)X}{mg}}$$

49. *(a)* Given, amplitude, $A = 20 \text{ cm} = 0.2 \text{ m}$

Force constant, $k = 600 \text{ Nm}^{-1}$

$$m = 10 \text{ kg}$$

Maximum speed of oscillation,

$$v_{max} = A\omega = A\sqrt{\frac{k}{m}} \quad \left[\because \omega = \sqrt{\frac{k}{m}}\right]$$
$$= 0.2\sqrt{\frac{600}{10}} = 0.2\sqrt{60} \text{ m/s}$$

50. *(a)* Given, initial velocity, $u = 3\hat{\mathbf{i}} + 4\hat{\mathbf{j}}$

Force, $F = 2\hat{\mathbf{i}} - 3\hat{\mathbf{j}}$

Initial velocity along X-axis and Y-axis are $u_x = 3 \text{ ms}^{-1}$ and $u_y = 4 \text{ ms}^{-1}$, respectively.

Similarly, $F_x = 2$ N and $F_y = -3$ N

If acceleration along X and Y-axes are a_x and a_y, then

$$a_x = \frac{F_x}{m} = \frac{2}{1} = 2 \text{ m/s}^2 \quad [\because F = ma]$$
$$a_y = \frac{F_y}{m} = \frac{-3}{1} = -3 \text{ m/s}^2$$
$$s_x = u_x t + \frac{1}{2}a_x t^2 = 3 \times 3 + \frac{1}{2} \times 2 \times 9 = 18 \text{ m}$$
$$s_y = u_y t + \frac{1}{2}a_y t^2 = 4 \times 3 + \frac{1}{2} \times (-3) \times 9$$
$$= 12 - 13.5 = -1.5 \text{ m}$$

So, required x and y-coordinates of point $= (18, -1.5)$

51. *(d)* Given, tension is the wire, $T = 100$ N

Mass of steel wire, $m = 6 \times 10^{-3}$ kg

Length, $l = 90 \text{ cm} = 0.9 \text{ m}$

Mass per unit length of steel wire,

$$\mu = \frac{m}{l} = \frac{6 \times 10^{-3}}{0.9} = \frac{2}{3} \times 10^{-2} \text{ kg-m}^{-1}$$

Speed of transverse wave,

$$v = \sqrt{\frac{T}{\mu}} = \sqrt{\frac{100}{\left(\frac{2}{3}\right) \times 10^{-2}}} = \frac{300}{\sqrt{6}} = 50\sqrt{6} \text{ m/s}$$

52. *(a)* Charge, $q = 1$ C

If n be the total number of electrons in 1 C of charge, then $q = ne$

$$\Rightarrow n = \frac{q}{e} = \frac{1}{1.6 \times 10^{-19}} = 6.25 \times 10^{18} \text{ electrons}$$

53. *(c)* $|q_1| = |q_2| = 1\mu\text{C} = 10^{-6}$ C

$$2l = 2 \text{ cm} = 2 \times 10^{-2} \text{ m}$$
$$E = 10^5 \text{ NC}^{-1}$$

$$\therefore \text{Maximum torque, } \tau_{max} = pE\sin 90° = pE = q(2l)E$$
$$= 10^{-6} \times 2 \times 10^{-2} \times 10^5 = 2 \times 10^{-3} \text{ N-m}$$

54. *(c)* The given situation is shown below,

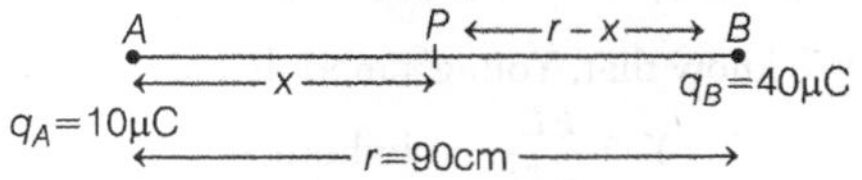

Let electric field at point P at a distance x from A is zero.

At point P, $E_A = E_B$

$$\Rightarrow \frac{1}{4\pi\varepsilon_0}\frac{q_A}{x^2} = \frac{1}{4\pi\varepsilon_0} \cdot \frac{q_B}{(r-x)^2}$$
$$\Rightarrow \frac{10 \times 10^{-6}}{x^2} = \frac{40 \times 10^{-6}}{(r-x)^2}$$
$$\Rightarrow \left(\frac{1}{x}\right)^2 = \left(\frac{2}{r-x}\right)^2$$
$$\Rightarrow \frac{1}{x} = \frac{2}{r-x}$$
$$\Rightarrow 2x = r - x$$
$$\Rightarrow x = \frac{r}{3} = \frac{90}{3} = 30 \text{ cm}$$

55. *(c)* According to Gauss's law, total electric flux passing through the cube,

$$\phi = \frac{\text{total enclosed charge}}{\varepsilon_0} = \frac{q}{\varepsilon_0}$$

56. *(c)* The given situation is shown below,

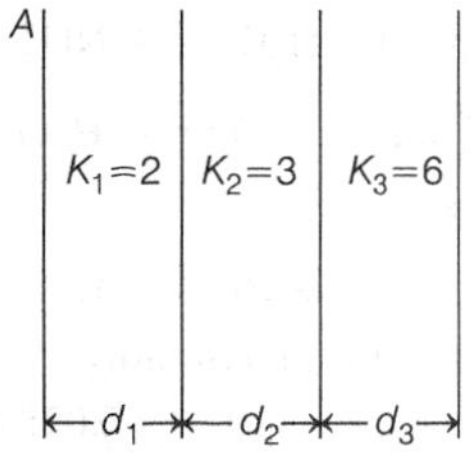

$$d_1 = 0.4\text{ mm} = 4 \times 10^{-4}\text{ m}$$
$$d_2 = 0.6\text{ mm} = 6 \times 10^{-4}\text{ m}$$
$$d_3 = 1.2\text{ mm} = 1.2 \times 10^{-3}\text{ m}$$

The given arrangement will be equal to three capacitors connected in series.

i.e. $C_1 = \dfrac{\varepsilon_0 K_1 A}{d_1}$, $C_2 = \dfrac{\varepsilon_0 K_2 A}{d_2}$

and $C_3 = \dfrac{\varepsilon_0 K_3 A}{d_3}$

Equivalent capacitance is given as,

$$\frac{1}{C_{eq}} = \frac{1}{C_1} + \frac{1}{C_2} + \frac{1}{C_3} = \frac{1}{\varepsilon_0 A}\left(\frac{d_1}{K_1} + \frac{d_2}{K_2} + \frac{d_3}{K_3}\right)$$

$$\frac{1}{C_{eq}} = \frac{1}{\varepsilon_0 A}\left[\frac{4 \times 10^{-4}}{2} + \frac{6 \times 10^{-4}}{3} + \frac{1.2 \times 10^{-3}}{6}\right]$$

$$\Rightarrow \frac{1}{C_{eq}} = \frac{1}{\varepsilon_0 A}[6 \times 10^{-4}]$$

$$C_{eq} = \frac{\varepsilon_0 A}{6 \times 10^{-4}} = \frac{8.85 \times 10^{-12} \times 2}{6 \times 10^{-4}} = 2.95 \times 10^{-8}\text{ F}$$

57. *(b)* Given, $m_1 = m_2 = m$

$$q_1 = q$$
$$q_2 = 4q$$

We know that

$$E = \frac{1}{2}mv^2 = qV$$

$$\Rightarrow \quad v^2 \propto q$$

[For same value of potential difference V]

$$\Rightarrow \quad v \propto \sqrt{q}$$

$$\Rightarrow \quad \frac{v_1}{v_2} = \sqrt{\frac{q_1}{q_2}} = \sqrt{\frac{q}{4q}} = \frac{1}{2}$$

$$\Rightarrow \quad v_1 : v_2 = 1 : 2$$

58. *(b)* Given, uncertainity in acceleration, $\dfrac{\Delta a}{a} \times 100 = 8\%$

Uncertainity in time, $\dfrac{\Delta t}{t} \times 100 = 4\%$

Since, body starts motion from rest, hence by the first equation of motion,

$$v = u + at$$
$$v = 0 + at$$

$$\Rightarrow \quad \frac{\Delta v}{v} = \frac{\Delta a}{a} + \frac{\Delta t}{t}$$

$$\Rightarrow \quad \frac{\Delta v}{v} \times 100 = \frac{\Delta a}{a} \times 100 + \frac{\Delta t}{t} \times 100$$

$$= 8\% + 4\% = 12\%$$

59. *(c)* We know that, capacitance of a parallel plate capacitor,

$$C = \frac{\varepsilon_0 A}{d} \quad \ldots \text{(i)}$$

where, A = area of plate

d = separation between the plates.

When $d' = 2d$, then

$$C' = \frac{\varepsilon_0 AK}{d'}$$

$$\Rightarrow \quad 3C = \frac{\varepsilon_0 AK}{2d} \quad [\because C' = 3C]$$

$$\Rightarrow \quad 3C = \frac{\varepsilon_0 A}{d} \cdot \frac{K}{2}$$

$$\Rightarrow \quad 3C = C \cdot \frac{K}{2} \quad \text{[from Eq. (i)]}$$

$$\Rightarrow \quad 3 = \frac{K}{2}$$

$$\Rightarrow \quad K = 6$$

60. *(d)* Using colour code for carbon resistor, (For A)

Orange	Blue	White
↓	↓	↓
3	6	9

$$\therefore \quad R_A = 36 \times 10^9\,\Omega$$

Similarly, (For B)

Brown	Red	Green
↓	↓	↓
1	2	5

$$\therefore \quad R_B = 12 \times 10^5\,\Omega$$

$$\therefore \quad \frac{R_A}{R_B} = \frac{36 \times 10^9}{12 \times 10^5} = 3 \times 10^4$$

$$\therefore R_A : R_B = 3 \times 10^4 : 1$$

COMEDK 2015

Chemistry

61. *(b)* Mass of 20 mL of acetic acid = $20 \times 1 = 20$ g

Mass of 20 mL of ethyl alcohol = $20 \times 0.7 = 14$ g

For the reaction,

$$\underset{60\text{ g}}{CH_3COOH} + \underset{46\text{ g}}{C_2H_5OH} \xrightarrow[-H_2O]{} CH_3COOC_2H_5$$

60 g of acetic acid requires = 46 g of ethyl alcohol

20 g of acetic acid requires = $\frac{46}{60} \times 20 = 15.3$ g of ethyl alcohol

Therefore, ethyl alcohol is the limiting reagent.

62. *(d)* Mass of oxygen in 22.4 L at STP = 32 g

Mass of oxygen in 5.6 L at STP = $\frac{32}{22.4} \times 5.6 = 8$ g

$= \frac{1}{2} \times$ gram atomic mass of oxygen

Therefore, mass of oxygen gas in 5.6 L at STP would be the half of the gram atomic mass of oxygen.

63. *(d)* For H-like particles,

$$E_n = \frac{-21.78 \times 10^{-19}}{n^2} Z^2 \text{ J}$$

$$= \frac{-21.78 \times 10^{-19}}{1^2} \times (2)^2 \text{ [For helium, } Z = 2, n = 1]$$

$$= -8.72 \times 10^{-18} \text{ J}$$

64. *(d)* Bond enthalpy decreases with increasing bond length as the intermolecular force of attraction decreases with increase in the distance between the constituent particles.

65. *(a)*

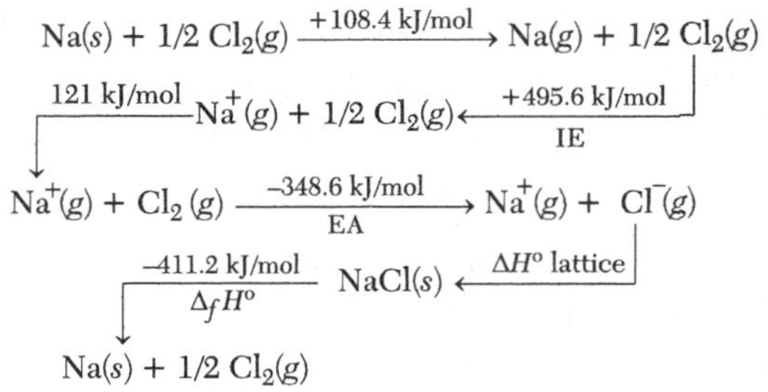

According to Hess law,

$$\Delta_f H^\circ = S + D + \text{IE} + \text{EA} + U$$

$$-411.2 = 108.4 + 121 + 495.6 - 348.6 + U$$

$$U = -787.6 \text{ kJ/mol} \simeq -788 \text{ kJ/mol}$$

66. *(a)* Given, $\Delta S = +$ ve and $\Delta H = +$ ve (For endothermic reaction)

Now, $\Delta G = \Delta H - T\Delta S$

For a reaction to be spontaneous, ΔG should be –ve which is possible only at high temperature i.e., when $T\Delta S > \Delta H$.

67. *(d)* For an adiabatic change in a system, no heat is exchanged between the system and the surroundings i.e., $q = 0$.

68. *(c)* Ionic product of water is given by following reaction,

I. $NH_3(aq) + H_2O \rightleftharpoons NH_4^+ + OH^-(aq)$

II. $NH_4^+(aq) + H_2O \rightleftharpoons H_3O^+ + NH_3(g)$

69. *(b)* pH = 13

$$[H]^+ = 10^{-pH} = 10^{-13} \text{ mol L}^{-1}$$

$\Rightarrow$ 1000 mL solution contains

$$= 10^{-13} \times 6.022 \times 10^{23} \text{ H}^+ \text{ ions}$$

$$= 6.022 \times 10^{10} \text{ H}^+ \text{ ions}$$

1 mL solution contains

$$= \frac{6.022 \times 10^{10}}{1000} = 6.022 \times 10^7 \text{ H}^+ \text{ ions.}$$

70. *(d)* Lower the $E°$ value (more negative), stronger is the reducing agent.

$\therefore Na^+$ is the strongest reducing agent.

71. *(a)* Water is oxidised to O_2 and F_2 is reduced to HF as follows.

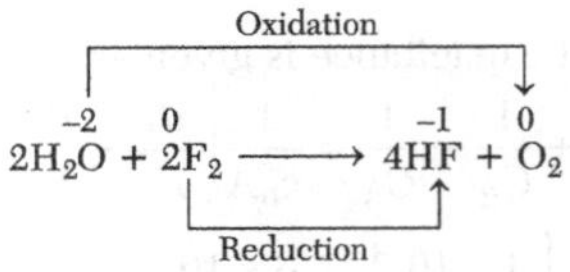

72. *(c)* H_2O_2 decomposes slowly on exposure to light.

$$2H_2O_2(l) \longrightarrow 2H_2O(l) + O_2(g)$$

Its decomposition can be prevented by adding urea as a stabiliser.

73. *(b)* Mg is an important component of chlorophyll which is used in synthesis of food by plants in presence of sunlight.

74. *(a)* Pb_3O_4 is a mixture of PbO_2 + PbO and only PbO i.e., Pb^{2+} reacts with HNO_3 to form $Pb(NO_3)_2$.

75. *(d)* Dil. and conc. HNO_3 has no effect on Al.

Aluminium is rendered passive by nitric acid due to the formation of a thin film of oxide (Al_2O_3) on its surface.

$$2Al + 6HNO_3(\text{conc.}) \longrightarrow Al_2O_3 + 6NO_2 + 3H_2O$$

Aluminium reacts with H_2SO_4 to libreate H_2 gas.

$$2Al + 3H_2SO_4 \longrightarrow Al_2(SO_4)_3 + 3H_2\uparrow$$

Aluminium also reacts with aqueous alkali and liberates dihydrogen.

$$2Al(s) + 2NaOH(aq) + 6H_2O(l) \longrightarrow 2Na[Al(OH)_4](aq) + 3H_2(g)$$

Aluminium dissolves in dil. HCl and liberates dihydrogen.

$$2Al(s) + 6HCl(aq) \longrightarrow 2Al^{3+}(aq) + 6Cl^-(aq) + 3H_2(g)$$

76. *(c)* Due to $+I$-effect of —CH_3 group (4) has higher electron density, than benzene (1). Due to strong $-I$-effect of —Cl group and strong $-I$ and $-M$-effect of

—NO_2 group, both (2) and (3) have lower electron density, than benzene (1).

As $-I$-effect of —Cl group is weaker, than that of —NO_2 (3) has much lower electron density than (2).

Hence, nitrobenzene will have high reactivity towards electrophilic substitution due to lower electron density on benzene ring.

Thus, the overall reactivity order towards electrophilic substitution is 4 > 1 > 2 > 3.

77. *(b)* Percentage of bromine in the compound

$$= \frac{80}{188} \times \frac{\text{Mass of AgBr formed}}{\text{Mass of substance taken}} \times 100$$

$$= \frac{80}{188} \times \frac{0.12}{0.15} \times 100 = 34.04\%$$

78. *(c)* The IUPAC name of compound

$$\overset{5}{C}H_3\overset{4}{C}H_2\overset{3}{C}H_2\overset{2}{C}H_2\overset{1}{C}N$$ is pentane nitrile.

79. *(a)* The major product in the reaction is

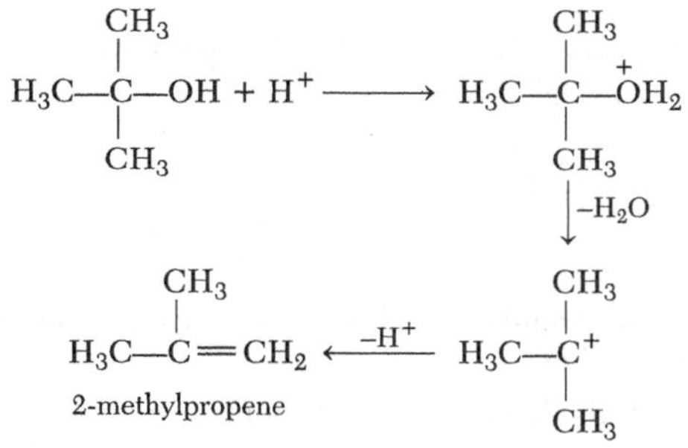

80. *(d)* BOD is a measure of organic material present in water needing dissolved oxygen for decomposition Hence, depleting the oxygen content in water.

81. *(c)* Hexagonal close packing and cubic close packing are equally efficient.

∴Density of both the packings will be same.

82. *(b)* When, Si (having 4 valence electrons) is doped with As (having 5 valence electrons), 4 electrons form covalent bonds, while the fifth electron remains free and increase conductivity. Hence, Si doped with As is *n*-type semiconductor.

83. *(a)* The dissociation of compounds take place as follows:

$$Al_2(SO_4)_3 \longrightarrow 2Al^{3+} + 3SO_4^{2-}, i=5$$

$$K_4[Fe(CN)_6] \longrightarrow 4K^+ + [Fe(CN)_6]^{4-}, i=5$$

$$NaCl \longrightarrow Na^+ + Cl^-, i=2$$

$$Al(NO_3)_3 \longrightarrow Al^{3+} + 3NO_3^-, i=4$$

$$Na_2SO_4 \longrightarrow 2Na^+ + SO_4^{2-}, i=3$$

84. *(b)* Net reaction occuring in a Daniell cell is

$$Zn(s) + Cu^{2+}(aq) \longrightarrow Zn^{2+}(aq) + Cu(s)$$

$$\Delta G = -nFE^\circ = -2 \times 96500 \times 1.1$$

$$= -212300 \text{ J mol}^{-1} = -212.3 \text{ kJ mol}^{-1}$$

85. *(b)* The cathode reaction in dry cell is

$$MnO_2 + NH_4^+ + e^- \longrightarrow MnO(OH) + NH_3$$

86. *(a)* $\lambda^\circ_{m(NH_4OH)} = \lambda^\circ_{m(NH_4Cl)} + \lambda^\circ_{m(NaOH)} - \lambda^\circ_{m(NaCl)}$

$$= 130 + 248 - 126.5 = 251.5\ \Omega^{-1}\text{cm}^2\ \text{mol}^{-1}$$

87. *(b)* Let the order of reaction w.r.t. A is x and w.r.t. B is y.

$$r_1 = k[A]^x[B]^y \quad \ldots\text{(i)}$$

$$r_2 = k[2A]^x[B]^y \quad \ldots\text{(ii)}$$

$$r_3 = k[A]^x[2B]^y \quad \ldots\text{(iii)}$$

$$\frac{r_1}{r_2} = \frac{k[A]^x[B]^y}{k[2A]^x[B]^y} \Rightarrow \frac{1}{4} = \left(\frac{1}{2}\right)^x$$

$$\Rightarrow \left(\frac{1}{2}\right)^2 = \left(\frac{1}{2}\right)^x$$

$$\Rightarrow x = 2$$

Similarly,

$$\frac{r_1}{r_3} = \frac{k[A]^x[B]^y}{k[A]^x[2B]^y} \Rightarrow 1 = \left(\frac{1}{2}\right)^y$$

$$\Rightarrow \left(\frac{1}{2}\right)^0 = \left(\frac{1}{2}\right)^y$$

$$y = 0$$

Hence, the rate of equation is

$$\text{Rate} = k[A]^2[B]^0$$

Order of reaction = 2

88. *(d)* The reactions taking place in zeolites depend upon the size and shape of the reactant and product molecules and upon the pores and cavities of the zeolities. Hence, they are shape-selective catalyst.

89. *(b)* Sulphur sol is a type of multimolecular colloid as it consists of particles containing a thousand or more of S_8 sulphur molecules.

90. *(d)* Chemical formula of magnetite is Fe_3O_4.

The IUPAC name is iron (II, III) oxide and common chemical name is ferrous-ferric oxide.

91. *(c)* The overall reduction reaction of fused matrix is

$$2Al_2O_3 + 3C \longrightarrow 4Al + 3CO_2$$

92. *(a)* Nickel on heating in a stream of carbon monoxide forms a volatile complex, nickel tetracarbonyl.

$$\underset{\text{Impure}}{Ni} + 4CO \xrightarrow{330-350\text{ K}} \underset{\substack{\text{Volatile}\\\text{compound}}}{[Ni(CO)_4]}$$

93. *(a)* White phosphorus (P_4) with water do not produce PH_3, while with NaOH, Ca_3P_2 + HCl and ($Ca_3P_2 + H_2O$) it gives PH_3 as follows :

$$P_4 + 3NaOH + 3H_2O \longrightarrow 3NaH_2PO_2 + PH_3$$

$$Ca_3P_2 + 6HCl \longrightarrow 3CaCl_2 + 2PH_3$$

$$Ca_3P_2 + 6H_2O \longrightarrow 3Ca(OH)_2 + 2PH_3$$

94. *(d)* In oxides of halogen, the bonds are mainly covalent due to small difference in electronegativity between the halogens and oxygen. The bond polarity, however, increases as we move from F to I.

The stability of oxides of iodine is greater than those of chlorine, while bromine oxides are the least stable. Iodine-oxygen bond is stable due to greater polarity of the bond, while the stability of the chlorine-oxygen bond is due to multiple bond formation involving *d*-orbitals of the chlorine atom. Bromine being in between lacks both these characteristics. Thus, the stability of oxides of halogens decreases in the following order

$$I > Cl > Br > F$$

95. *(b)* Nitrogen does not show property of catenation. Since, N—N single bond is very weak due to large interelectronic repulsions between the lone pairs of electrons present on the N-atoms of N—N bond having small bond length.

96. *(d)* Hybridisation = number of σ bond + lone pair + coordinate bond

$$= 5 + 1 + 0 = 6\ (sp^3d^2)$$

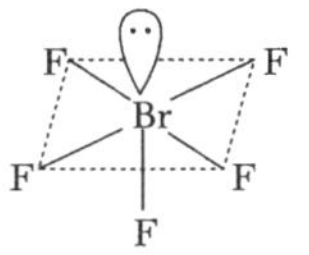

Distarted octahedral
or square pyramidal

97. *(d)* Group 16 elements are called chalcogens.
∴ Sulphur belongs to chalcogen family.

98. *(d)* More number of oxidation state are exhibited by the actinoids, than by lanthanoids. The main reason for this is lesser energy difference between $5f$ and $6d$-orbitals, than that between $4f$ and $5d$-orbitals.

99. *(b)* Outer electronic configuration of the element with atomic number 24 is $3d^5\,4s^1$.

Number of unpaired electrons = 6

$$\mu = \sqrt{n(n+2)}\ \text{BM} = \sqrt{6(6+2)} = \sqrt{48}$$
$$= 6.928 = 6.93\ \text{BM}$$

100. *(b)* The π-bonding type between metal and oxygen is $d\pi$- $p\pi$ bonding. (*d*-orbital of Mn and *p*-orbital of oxygen)

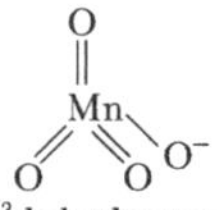

sp^3-hybridisation
(Tetrahedral)

101. *(c)* The similarity in the size of ions of the elements belonging to the same group of the second and third transition series is due to the effect of lanthanoid contraction. Thus, Zr^{4+} and Hf^{4+} has same size.

102. *(d)* For a $3d^2$ system, electrons will go into more stable t_{2g} orbitals and each electron going into a t_{2g} orbital is stabilised by $0.4\Delta_o$ i.e., 2 electrons will be stabilised by $0.8\Delta_o$ or $8\times10^{-1}\Delta_o$.

103. *(b)* $_{28}Ni = 3d^8 4s^2$

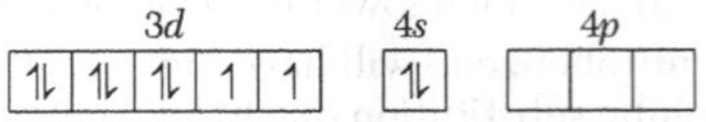

In $[Ni(CO)_4]$, CO is a strong field ligand which causes pairing of electrons.

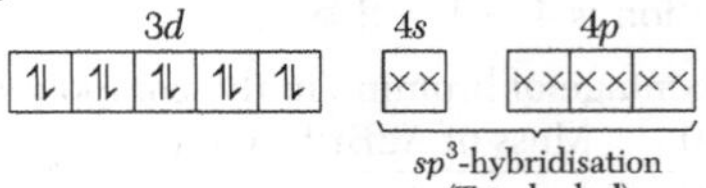

sp^3-hybridisation
(Tetrahedral)

In $[Ni(CN)_4]^{2-}$, CN^- is a strong field ligand which causes pairing of electrons.

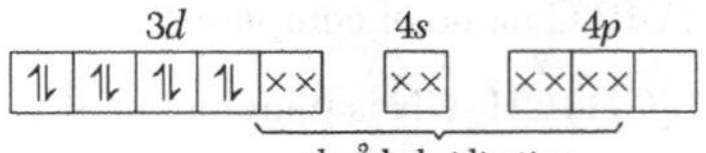

dsp^2-hybridisation
(Square planar)

In $[NiCl_4]^{2-}$, Cl^- is a weak field ligand, so no pairing of electrons takes place.

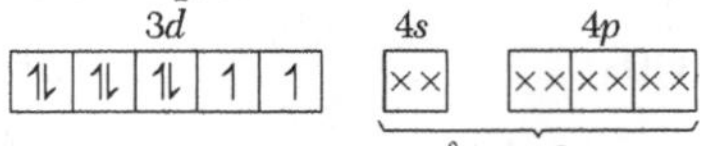

sp^3-hybridisation
(Tetrahedral)

104. *(c)* The formula for sodium trioxalatoaluminate (II) is $Na_3[Al(C_2O_4)_3]$.

105. *(c)* Octahedral complex of general formula $[M(AA)_2a_2]^{n\pm}$ show optical isomerism. *Trans* form of $[M(AA)_2a_2]^{n\pm}$ does not show optical isomerism due to symmetry.

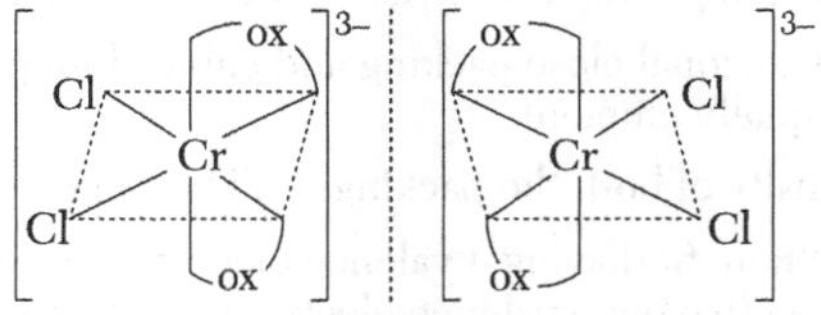

cis-d-isomer Mirror *cis-l*-isomer

cis-$[Co(NH_3)_4Cl_2]^+$ and *trans*-$[Co(NH_3)_4Cl_2]^+$ do not show optical isomerism due to symmetry.

106. *(a)* Freons are chlorofluorocarbons introduced into the atmosphere from aerosol sprays and refrigerating equipments. They have a very long life time and when they reach stratosphere, they undergo photochemical decomposition and destroy ozone by the following sequence of reactions.

$$CF_2Cl_2 \xrightarrow{h\nu} CF_2Cl^{\bullet} + Cl^{\bullet}$$
$$CFCl_3 \xrightarrow{h\nu} CFCl_2^{\bullet} + Cl^{\bullet}$$
$$Cl^{\bullet} + O_3 \longrightarrow ClO^{\bullet} + O_2$$
$$ClO^{\bullet} + [O] \longrightarrow Cl^{\bullet} + O_2$$

107. *(b)* Ethanol gives iodoform test to produce yellow ppt as follows

$$\underset{\text{Ethanol}}{CH_3CH_2OH} + 4I_2 + 3Na_2CO_3 \longrightarrow \underset{\substack{\text{Iodoform}\\\text{(Yellow ppt.)}}}{CHI_3} + HCOONa + 5NaI + 2H_2O + 3CO_2$$

108. *(c)* Due to $-I$ and $-R$-effects of —NO_2 group, nitrobenzoic acids are stronger acids, than benzoic acid
Due to *ortho*-effect, *o*-nitrobenzoic acid is the strongest acid.
In *p*-nitrobenzoic acid both $-R$-effect and $-I$-effect of the —NO_2 group increase the acidity, while in *m*-nitrobenzoic acid only the weaker $-I$-effect increases the acidity.
Hence, the order of acidic strength is
o-nitrobenzoic acid > *p*-nitrobenzoic acid > *m*-nitrobenzoic acid > benzoic acid.

109. *(a)* Acid strength increases as the electronegativity of halogen increases because the anion formed after H^+ ion release, is stabilised by $-I$-effect.
The order of $-I$-effect is F > Cl > Br > I.
∴ Order of acidic strength is as follows :
$FCH_2COOH > ClCH_2COOH > BrCH_2COOH$

110. *(b)* A mixture of methylamine (1° amine) and dimethylamine (2° amine) can KOH be separated with the help of $C_6H_5SO_2Cl$ and (Hinsberg's method).
Methylamine will form N-methylbenzene - sulphonamide, which is soluble in KOH.
Dimethylamine will form
N, N-dimethylbenzenesulphonamide which is insoluble in KOH.

111. *(c)* Gabriel phthalimide synthesis is used for the preparation of pure aliphatic and alkyl primary amines.

112. *(c)* Aniline is less basic than ammonia and aliphatic amines due to delocalisation of lone pair of electrons on the benzene ring.
Aliphatic amines are stronger bases, than ammonia due to $+I$-effect of alkyl group. More the number of alkyl groups stronger is the base.
Hence, basic strength will follow the following order
$(C_2H_5)_2NH > C_2H_5NH_2 > NH_3 > C_6H_5NH_2$

113. *(a)* In RNA molecule, the base uracil (U) appears opposite to base adenine (A), cytosine (C) appears opposite to guanine (G), adenine (A) appears opposite to thymine (T) and guanine (G) appears opposite to cytosine (C).
The sequence of RNA is CGUAU.

114. *(b)* α-helix and β-pleated structures of proteins are classified as secondary structure.

115. *(b)* Glycosidic linkages are present in carbohydrates.

116. *(c)* Glucose and ribose are monosaccharides.

117. *(d)* Nylon-6, 6 is an example of step growth polymerisation as monomers adipic acid and hexamethylenediamine are bifunctional and form bond with the loss of simple molecules. The dimer formed also contains two functional groups, thus undergoes a series of condensations in a stepwise manner.

118. *(a)* Glycine and aminocaproic acid forms nylon-2-nylon-6, which is a biodegradable polymer.

$$\underset{\text{Glycine}}{nH_2N—CH_2—COOH} + \underset{\text{Aminocaproic acid}}{nH_2N—(CH_2)_5—COOH} \xrightarrow{-(n-1)H_2O} \left(\underset{\substack{\|\\O}}{C}—CH_2—NH—\underset{\substack{\|\\O}}{C}—(CH_2)_5—NH \right)_n$$

Nylon-2-nylon-6
(Biodegradable)

119. *(c)* Detergents can be made biodegradable and pollution free by using unbranched hydrocarbon chain.

120. *(b)* Sodium rosinate is generally added in soap because it produces rich lather.

Mathematics

121. *(b)* Since, $n(A \cap B) = 99$

$$n((A \times B) \cap (B \times A)) = n((A \cap B) \times (B \cap A)) = n(A \cap B) \cdot n(B \cap A) = n(A \cap B) \cdot n(A \cap B) = 99 \cdot 99 = (99)^2$$

122. *(b)* We have, $f(x) = e^x$ and $g(x) = \log e^x$
Now, $f(g(x)) = f(\log e^x) = e^{\log e^x} = e^x$
and $g(f(x)) = g(e^x) = \log e^{e^x} = e^x \log e = e^x$
Hence, $f(g(x)) = g(f(x))$.

123. *(b)* Since, number of one-one onto functions from a set A having n elements to itself is $n!$.

124. *(c)* Let M, P and C be the set of students who opted Mathematics, Physics and Chemistry respectively.
Then, $n(M) = 100$, $n(P) = 70$, $n(C) = 40$
$n(M \cap P) = 30$, $n(M \cap C) = 28$, $n(P \cap C) = 23$,
$n(M \cap P \cap C) = 18$
Number of students who opted Mathematics alone

$$= n(M \cap P' \cap C')$$
$$= n(M \cap (P \cup C)')$$
$$= n(M) - n(M \cap (P \cup C))$$
$$= n(M) - n((M \cap P) \cup (M \cap C))$$
$$= n(M) - n(M \cap P) - n(M \cap C) + n(M \cap P \cap C)$$
$$= 100 - 30 - 28 + 18 = 60$$

125. *(c)* $n(A) = 4$ (given)

$\therefore$ Total number of subsets of $A = 2^4 = 16$

$\therefore$ Number of proper subsets $= 16 - 1 = 15$

126. *(d)* We have, $\tan(x + y) = 33$

$$\Rightarrow \frac{\tan x + \tan y}{1 - \tan x \tan y} = 33$$

$$\Rightarrow \frac{3 + \tan y}{1 - 3\tan y} = 33 \quad [\because x = \tan^{-1} 3 \Rightarrow \tan x = 3]$$

$$\Rightarrow 3 + \tan y = 33 - 99\tan y$$

$$\Rightarrow 100\tan y = 30$$

$$\Rightarrow \tan y = \frac{3}{10}$$

$$\Rightarrow y = \tan^{-1}\frac{3}{10}$$

127. *(c)* We have, $\cot^{-1}(21) + \cot^{-1}(13) + \cot^{-1}(-8)$

$$= \tan^{-1}\left(\frac{1}{21}\right) + \tan^{-1}\left(\frac{1}{13}\right) + \cot^{-1}(-8)$$

$$= \tan^{-1}\left(\frac{\frac{1}{21} + \frac{1}{13}}{1 - \frac{1}{21} \times \frac{1}{13}}\right) + \cot^{-1}(-8)$$

$$= \tan^{-1}\left(\frac{34}{272}\right) + (\pi - \cot^{-1} 8)$$

$$[\because \cot^{-1}(-x) = \pi - \cot^{-1} x]$$

$$= \tan^{-1}\left(\frac{1}{8}\right) - \cot^{-1} 8 + \pi$$

$$= \tan^{-1}\left(\frac{1}{8}\right) - \tan^{-1}\left(\frac{1}{8}\right) + \pi = \pi$$

128. *(d)* $\tan\left(\cos^{-1}\left(\frac{1}{5\sqrt{2}}\right) - \sin^{-1}\left(\frac{4}{\sqrt{17}}\right)\right)$

$$= \tan\left(\frac{\pi}{2} - \sin^{-1}\left(\frac{1}{5\sqrt{2}}\right) - \sin^{-1}\left(\frac{4}{\sqrt{17}}\right)\right)$$

$$\left[\because \cos^{-1} x = \frac{\pi}{2} - \sin^{-1} x\right]$$

$$= \tan\left(\frac{\pi}{2} - \left(\sin^{-1}\frac{4}{\sqrt{17}} + \sin^{-1}\frac{1}{5\sqrt{2}}\right)\right)$$

$$= \tan\left(\frac{\pi}{2} - \sin^{-1}\left(\frac{4}{\sqrt{17}} \cdot \sqrt{1 - \frac{1}{50}} + \frac{1}{5\sqrt{2}} \cdot \sqrt{1 - \frac{16}{17}}\right)\right)$$

$$= \tan\left(\frac{\pi}{2} - \sin^{-1}\left(\frac{4}{\sqrt{17}} \cdot \frac{7}{5\sqrt{2}} + \frac{1}{5\sqrt{2}} \cdot \frac{1}{\sqrt{17}}\right)\right)$$

$$= \cot\left(\sin^{-1}\frac{29}{5\sqrt{2} \cdot \sqrt{17}}\right) \quad \left[\because \tan\left(\frac{\pi}{2} - x\right) = \cot x\right]$$

$$= \cot\left(\cot^{-1}\frac{3}{29}\right) = \frac{3}{29}$$

129. *(b)* With the help of group of $\cot x$, we know that

When $x \in \left(0, \frac{\pi}{2}\right] \cup \left(\pi, \frac{3\pi}{2}\right]$, then $\cot x \geq 0$

$$\therefore \quad |\cot x| = \cot x + \frac{1}{\sin x}$$

$$\Rightarrow \cot x = \cot x + \frac{1}{\sin x} \Rightarrow \frac{1}{\sin x} = 0$$

$\Rightarrow$ No solution exist. ...(i)

When $x \in \left(\frac{\pi}{2}, \pi\right) \cup \left(\frac{3\pi}{2}, 2\pi\right)$, then $\cot x < 0$

$$|\cot x| = \cot x + \frac{1}{\sin x}$$

$$\therefore \quad -\cot x = \cot x + \frac{1}{\sin x}$$

$$\Rightarrow \quad -2\cot x = \frac{1}{\sin x}$$

$$\Rightarrow \quad \cos x = \frac{-1}{2} \Rightarrow x = \frac{2\pi}{3} \quad \text{...(ii)}$$

$\therefore$ From Eqs. (i) and (ii), only one solution exists.

130. *(d)* $\frac{\sin x - \sin 3x}{\sin^2 x - \cos^2 x}$

$$= \frac{2\sin\left(\frac{x - 3x}{2}\right)\cos\left(\frac{x + 3x}{2}\right)}{-(\cos^2 x - \sin^2 x)}$$

$$= \frac{2\cos 2x \sin(-x)}{-\cos 2x} = \frac{-2\sin x \cos 2x}{-\cos 2x} = 2\sin x$$

131. *(b)* $\text{cosec}\, A(\sin B \cos C + \cos B \sin C)$

$$= \text{cosec}\, A \sin(B + C)$$

$$= \text{cosec}\, A \sin(180° - A)$$

[$\because$ A, B and C are angles of a triangle]

$$= \frac{1}{\sin A}\sin A = 1$$

132. *(c)* Let $z = i\sin\frac{\pi}{19}$

or $z = 0 + i\sin\frac{\pi}{19}$

Let amplitude of z be θ, then

$$\sin\theta = \frac{\sin\frac{\pi}{19}}{\sqrt{0^2 + \left(\sin\frac{\pi}{19}\right)^2}} \quad \left[\because \sin\theta = \frac{b}{\sqrt{a^2 + b^2}}\right]$$

$$\text{or } \sin\theta = \frac{\sin\frac{\pi}{19}}{\sin\frac{\pi}{19}} = 1 \Rightarrow \theta = \frac{\pi}{2}$$

133. *(a)* To form a triangle, 3 line segments are needed. We can choose 3 line segment from 5 line segments in ${}^5C_3$ ways. We know that in a triangle, sum of two sides is always greater than third side.

So, line segments of length (2, 3, 5), (2, 3, 6) and (2, 4, 6) do not form any triangle.

$\therefore$ Total number of triangles formed $= {}^5C_3 - 3$.

134. *(b)* Since, the number is to be greater than 1000000 it must be of seven digits and should begin with either 2 or 3 or 4.

Number of numbers formed $= \dfrac{6 \times 6!}{2! \times 3!} = 360$

135. *(d)* We have,

$$\frac{1}{\sqrt{(3x+1)}}\left\{\left(\frac{1+\sqrt{3x+1}}{2}\right)^7 - \left(\frac{1-\sqrt{3x+1}}{2}\right)^7\right\}$$

$$= \frac{1}{2^7\sqrt{(3x+1)}}\{(1+\sqrt{(3x+1)})^7 - (1-\sqrt{(3x+1)})^7\} \quad \ldots \text{(i)}$$

Now, $(1+\sqrt{3x+1})^7 - (1-\sqrt{3x+1})^7$

$[{}^7C_0 + {}^7C_1\sqrt{(3x+1)} + {}^7C_2(\sqrt{3x+1})^2 + \ldots + {}^7C_7(\sqrt{3x+1})^7]$

$-[{}^7C_0 - {}^7C_1\sqrt{3x+1} + {}^7C_2(\sqrt{3x+1}))^2 \ldots - {}^7C_7(\sqrt{3x+1})^7]$

$= 2[{}^7C_1(\sqrt{3x+1}) + {}^7C_3(\sqrt{3x+1})^3 + {}^7C_5(\sqrt{3x+1})^5 + {}^7C_7(\sqrt{3x+1})^7]$

$= 2\sqrt{3x+1} \times [7 + 35(3x+1) + 21(3x+1)^2 + (3x+1)^3]$

Now, putting above value in Eq. (i), so the given expression becomes

$$\frac{1}{2^6}[42 + 105x + 21(3x+1)^2 + (3x+1)^3]$$

So, degree of x in given expression is 3.

136. *(d)* We have, $(1+px)^n$

$\therefore \quad T_{r+1} = {}^nC_r(1)^{n-r}(px)^r \Rightarrow T_{r+1} = {}^nC_r p^r x^r$

Coefficient of $x^r = {}^nC_r p^r$

Now, coefficient of $x = {}^nC_1 p = 8$ (put $r = 1$)

$\Rightarrow \quad np = 8 \quad \ldots$ (i)

Also, coefficient of $x^2 = {}^nC_2 p^2 = 24$ (put $r = 2$)

$$\frac{n(n-1)}{2}p^2 = 24$$

$$\Rightarrow \quad \frac{n(n-1)}{2}\left(\frac{8}{n}\right)^2 = 24 \quad \text{(from Eq. (i))}$$

$$\Rightarrow \quad \frac{64(n-1)}{2n} = 24 \Rightarrow 4(n-1) = 3n \Rightarrow n = 4$$

From Eq. (i), we get $p = 2$

137. *(b)* We have,

$11^3 + 12^3 + 13^3 + \ldots + 20^3$

$= (1^3 + 2^3 + \ldots + 10^3 + 11^3 + 12^3 + \ldots + 20^3) - (1^3 + 2^3 + \ldots + 10^3)$

$= \Sigma(20)^3 - \Sigma(10)^3$

$$= \left(\frac{20(20+1)}{2}\right)^2 - \left(\frac{10(10+1)}{2}\right)^2$$

$= (10 \times 21)^2 - (5 \times 11)^2 = (210 - 55)(210 + 55)$

$= 155 \times 265 = 41075 = 5 \times 8215$

138. *(d)* We have, BE and AD are the medians. So, E and D are the mid-points of AC and BC respectively.

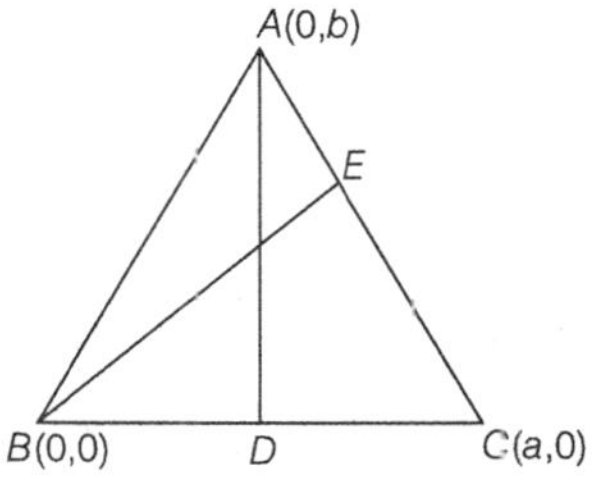

$\therefore$ Coordinates of $E = \left(\dfrac{a}{2}, \dfrac{b}{2}\right)$

and coordinates of $D = \left(\dfrac{a}{2}, 0\right)$

Now, slope of median $BE = m_1 = \dfrac{b}{a}$

Also, slope of median $AD = m_2 = \dfrac{-2b}{a}$

Now, m_1 and m_2 are perpendicular if $m_1 m_2 = -1$

$$\Rightarrow \frac{b}{a} \times \frac{(-2b)}{a} = -1 \Rightarrow 2b^2 = a^2 \Rightarrow a = \pm\sqrt{2}b$$

139. *(c)* Given, equation of lines are

$$\frac{x}{a} + \frac{y}{b} = 1 \quad \ldots \text{(i)}$$

and $$\frac{x}{b} + \frac{y}{a} = 1 \quad \ldots \text{(ii)}$$

$\Rightarrow \quad bx + ay = ab \quad \ldots$ (iii)

and $\quad ax + by = ab \quad \ldots$ (iv)

Solving Eqs. (iii) and (iv), we get

$$(a^2 - b^2)y = a^2b - ab^2 = ab(a-b) \Rightarrow y = \frac{ab}{a+b}$$

Substituting the value of y in Eq. (iii), we get

$$bx + a\left(\frac{ab}{a+b}\right) = ab \Rightarrow bx = ab - \frac{a^2b}{a+b}$$

$$\Rightarrow bx = \frac{ab^2}{a+b} \Rightarrow x = \frac{ab}{a+b}$$

$\therefore$ Point of intersection is $\left(\dfrac{ab}{a+b}, \dfrac{ab}{a+b}\right)$.

Since, equation of the line passing through origin is $y = mx$

$\therefore$ When it passes through $\left(\dfrac{ab}{a+b}, \dfrac{ab}{a+b}\right)$, then we get

$m = 1$

Hence, required equation of line is $y - x = 0$.

140. *(b)* Since, straight line meets the coordinate axes at A and B, so equation of line intercept form is $\frac{x}{a}+\frac{y}{b}=1$.

Let G represents the centroid of ΔOAB. Given that $G=(1, 2)$.

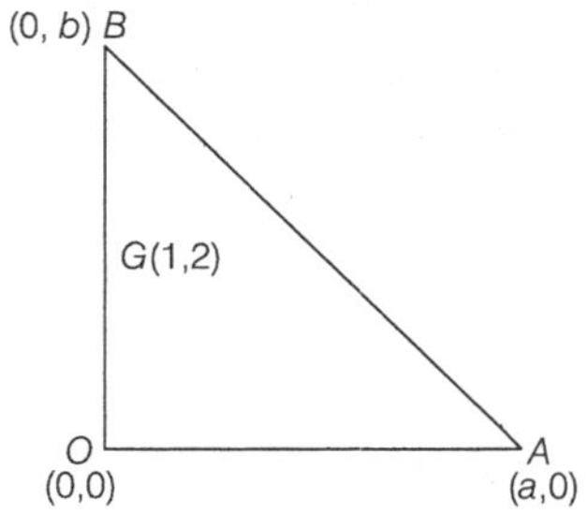

$$\therefore \text{Centroid } G\left(\frac{0+a+0}{3}, \frac{0+0+b}{3}\right)=(1,2) \quad \text{(given)}$$

$$\Rightarrow \frac{a}{3}=1 \Rightarrow a=3, \frac{b}{3}=2 \Rightarrow b=6$$

Hence, required equation of line is

$$\frac{x}{3}+\frac{y}{6}=1 \Rightarrow 2x+y=6$$

141. *(a)* Let DR's of line are $< a, b, c >$, then

$$2a-3b+c=0 \quad \text{and} \quad a+2b-2c=0$$

$$\Rightarrow \frac{a}{6-2}=\frac{b}{1+4}=\frac{c}{4+3} \Rightarrow \frac{a}{4}=\frac{b}{5}=\frac{c}{7}$$

DR's of line are $<4, 5, 7>$.

142. *(a)* Let the line makes an angle x with positive direction of Z-axis. Then, we have

$$\cos^2 45^\circ+\cos^2 60^\circ+\cos^2 x=1$$

$$\Rightarrow \left(\frac{1}{\sqrt{2}}\right)^2+\left(\frac{1}{2}\right)^2+\cos^2 x=1$$

$$\Rightarrow \cos^2 x=1-\frac{1}{2}-\frac{1}{4}$$

$$\Rightarrow \cos^2 x=\frac{1}{4} \Rightarrow \cos x=\frac{1}{2}$$

Neglecting $\cos x=\frac{-1}{2}$, because line is in I-octant)

$$\Rightarrow x=60^\circ$$

143. *(d)* $L_1: \frac{x-3}{3}=\frac{y-8}{-1}=\frac{z-3}{1}$

$L_2: \frac{x+3}{-3}=\frac{y+7}{2}=\frac{z-6}{4}$

Shortest distance between two lines

$$=\left|\frac{\begin{vmatrix} x_2-x_1 & y_2-y_1 & z_2-z_1 \\ a_1 & b_1 & c_1 \\ a_2 & b_2 & c_2 \end{vmatrix}}{\sqrt{(b_1c_2-b_2c_1)^2+(c_1a_2-c_2a_1)^2+(a_1b_2-a_2b_1)^2}}\right|$$

$$=\left|\frac{\begin{vmatrix} -3-3 & -7-8 & 6-3 \\ 3 & -1 & 1 \\ -3 & 2 & 4 \end{vmatrix}}{\sqrt{(-4-2)^2+(-3-12)^2+(6-3)^2}}\right|$$

$$=\left|\frac{\begin{vmatrix} -6 & -15 & 3 \\ 3 & -1 & 1 \\ -3 & 2 & 4 \end{vmatrix}}{\sqrt{(-6)^2+(-15)^2+(3)^2}}\right| \quad \text{On expanding the determinant along } C_3.$$

$$=\frac{3(6-3)-1(-12-45)+4(6+45)}{\sqrt{36+225+9}}$$

$$=\frac{9+57+204}{\sqrt{270}}=\frac{270}{\sqrt{270}}=\sqrt{270}=3\sqrt{30}$$

144. *(a)* We have, $\lim_{x\to\infty}(\sqrt{a^2x^2+bx+x}-ax)$

$$=\lim_{x\to\infty}\left((\sqrt{a^2x^2+bx+x}-ax)\times\frac{(\sqrt{a^2x^2+bx+x}+ax)}{(\sqrt{a^2x^2+bx+x}+ax)}\right)$$

$$=\lim_{x\to\infty}\left(\frac{(a^2x^2+bx+x)-a^2x^2}{x\left\{\sqrt{a^2+\frac{b}{x}+\frac{1}{x}}+a\right\}}\right)$$

$$=\lim_{x\to\infty}\left(\frac{(b+1)x}{x\left\{\sqrt{a^2+\frac{b}{x}+\frac{1}{x}}+a\right\}}\right)=\frac{b+1}{2a}$$

145. *(c)* We have, $y=|\cos x|+|\sin x|$

At $x=\frac{2\pi}{3}$, $\cos x$ is negative and $\sin x$ is positive.

$$\therefore \quad y=-\cos x+\sin x$$

$$\Rightarrow \frac{dy}{dx}=\sin x+\cos x$$

$$\therefore \left.\frac{dy}{dx}\right|_{\text{at } x=2\pi/3}=\sin\left(\frac{2\pi}{3}\right)+\cos\left(\frac{2\pi}{3}\right)$$

$$=\frac{\sqrt{3}}{2}-\frac{1}{2}=\frac{\sqrt{3}-1}{2}$$

146. *(d)* We have, slant height of cone $(l)=7$ cm

$$\Rightarrow l^2=h^2+r^2 \quad \ldots\text{(i)}$$

$$\Rightarrow r^2=7^2-4^2 \quad [\text{when } h=4 \text{ cm}]$$

$$\Rightarrow r^2=33$$

$$\Rightarrow r=\sqrt{33} \text{ cm}$$

Now, differentiating Eq. (i) w.r.t. l, we get

$$0 = 2h\frac{dh}{dt} + 2r\frac{dr}{dt}$$

$$\Rightarrow \quad \frac{dr}{dt} = -\frac{h}{r}\frac{dh}{dt} \quad \ldots \text{(ii)}$$

Volume of the cone, $V = \frac{1}{3}\pi r^2 h$

$$\frac{dV}{dt} = \frac{1}{3}\pi\left[2rh\frac{dr}{dt} + r^2\frac{dh}{dt}\right]$$

$$\Rightarrow \frac{dV}{dt} = \frac{1}{3}\pi\left[2rh\left(\frac{-h}{r}\frac{dh}{dt}\right) + r^2\frac{dh}{dt}\right] \quad \text{(from Eq. (ii))}$$

$$\Rightarrow \frac{dV}{dt} = \frac{1}{3}\pi\left[-2h^2\frac{dh}{dt} + r^2\frac{dh}{dt}\right]$$

$$\Rightarrow \frac{dV}{dt} = \frac{1}{3}\pi\frac{dh}{dt}[-2h^2 + r^2]$$

$$\Rightarrow \left[\frac{dV}{dt}\right]_{h=4} = \frac{1}{3}\pi(0.3)[-2\times 4^2 + (\sqrt{33})^2]$$

$$= \frac{\pi}{10}[1] = \frac{\pi}{10} \text{ cc/sec}$$

147. *(b)* Let AB be the ladder of length 5 m.

We are given, $\frac{dx}{dt} = 2$ m/sec

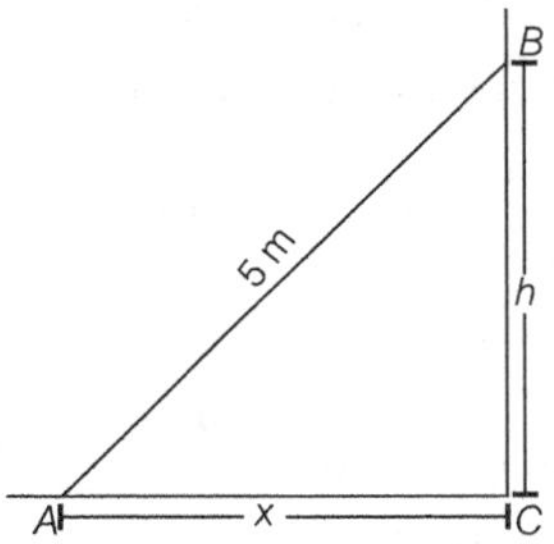

In ΔABC,

$$AB^2 = AC^2 + BC^2$$

$$\Rightarrow \quad (5)^2 = x^2 + h^2 \quad \ldots \text{(i)}$$

Differentiating Eq. (i) w.r.t. t, we get

$$0 = 2x\frac{dx}{dt} + 2h\frac{dh}{dt}$$

$$\Rightarrow \quad \frac{dh}{dt} = \frac{-x}{h}\frac{dx}{dt} \quad \ldots \text{(ii)}$$

Now, from Eq. (i), when $x = 4$

$$h^2 = 25 - 16$$

$$\Rightarrow h^2 = 9 \Rightarrow h = 3 \text{ m}$$

From Eq. (ii), we get $\left[\frac{dh}{dt}\right] = \frac{-4}{3}\times 2 = \frac{-8}{3}$

$\because$ The negative sign shows the height decreases and decreasing rate is $\frac{8}{3}$ m/sec.

148. *(b)* We have, $\quad y^2 = 4ax \quad \ldots$ (i)

and $\quad ay = 2x^2 \quad \ldots$ (ii)

Solving Eqs. (i) and (ii), we get

$$x = a \text{ and } y = 2a$$

Differentiating Eq. (i) w.r.t. x, we get

$$2y\frac{dy}{dx} = 4a$$

Now, $\quad \left[\frac{dy}{dx}\right]_{(a,\,2a)} = \frac{4a}{2(2a)} = 1$

$$\Rightarrow \quad m_1 = 1$$

Now, differentiating Eq. (ii) w.r.t. x, we get

$$a\frac{dy}{dx} = 4x \Rightarrow \left[\frac{dy}{dx}\right]_{(a,\,2a)} = \frac{4a}{a} = 4$$

$$\Rightarrow \quad m_2 = 4$$

$\because$ Angle between curves is equal to angle between their tangents.

$$\tan\theta\left|\frac{m_2 - m_1}{1 + m_1 m_2}\right| \Rightarrow \tan\theta = \left|\frac{4-1}{1+4\times(1)}\right|$$

$$\Rightarrow \tan\theta = \frac{3}{5} \Rightarrow \theta = \tan^{-1}\left(\frac{3}{5}\right)$$

149. *(b)* Let ΔABC be an isosceles triangle inscribed in the ellipse $\frac{x^2}{a^2} + \frac{y^2}{b^2} = 1.$

Let coordinate of A be $(a, 0)$.

Area of ΔABC, $A = \frac{1}{2}\times AD \times BC$

$$= \frac{1}{2}\times(a + x)\times 2y = y(a + x)$$

$$= \sqrt{b^2\left(1 - \frac{x^2}{a^2}\right)}(a + x) = \frac{b}{a}\sqrt{a^2 - x^2}(a + x)$$

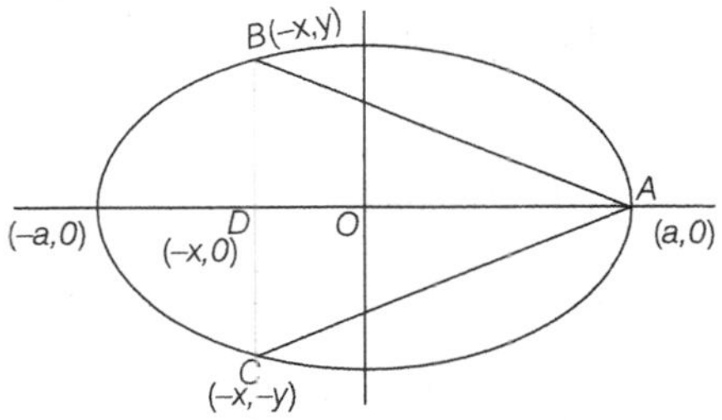

$$\Rightarrow \frac{dA}{dx} = \frac{b}{a}\left[(a + x)\frac{1}{2}\times\frac{-2x}{\sqrt{a^2 - x^2}} + \sqrt{a^2 - x^2}\right]$$

$$= \frac{b}{a}\left[\frac{-x(a + x) + (a^2 - x^2)}{\sqrt{a^2 - x^2}}\right]$$

Put $\frac{dA}{dx} = 0$

$$\Rightarrow \quad 2x^2 + ax - a^2 = 0$$

$$\Rightarrow \quad 2x^2 + 2ax - ax - a^2 = 0$$

$$\Rightarrow \quad (2x - a)(x + a) = 0$$

$$\Rightarrow \quad x = \frac{a}{2}, -a$$

Since, $\frac{d^2A}{dx^2} < 0$, for $x = \frac{a}{2}$

$\therefore$ Maximum area $= \frac{b}{a} \cdot \left(a + \frac{a}{2}\right)\sqrt{a^2 - \frac{a^2}{4}}$

$= \frac{b}{a} \cdot \frac{3}{2}(a) \frac{\sqrt{3}\,a}{2} = \frac{3\sqrt{3}\,ab}{4}$ sq units

150. *(b)* We have, $f(x+y) = f(x)\,f(y)$

Putting $x = y = 0$

$\Rightarrow \quad f(0+0) = f(0)\,f(0)$

$\Rightarrow \quad f(0) = [f(0)]^2$

$\Rightarrow \quad f(0) = 1$

Now, $f'(5) = \lim_{h \to 0} \frac{f(5+h) - f(5)}{h}$

$= \lim_{h \to 0} \frac{f(5)\,f(h) - f(5)}{h} = \lim_{h \to 0} f(5)\left[\frac{f(h) - 1}{h}\right]$

$= f(5) \lim_{h \to 0}\left[\frac{f(h) - f(0)}{h}\right] \qquad [\because f(0) = 1]$

$= 2 \times f'(0) = 2 \times 3 = 6$

151. *(d)* We have, $f(x) = \log_{x^2}(\log x)$

$\Rightarrow \quad f(x) = \frac{1}{2}[\log_x(\log x)] \qquad \left[\because \log_{a^n} b = \frac{1}{n}\log_a b\right]$

$\Rightarrow \quad f(x) = \frac{1}{2}\left[\frac{\log(\log x)}{\log x}\right] \qquad \left(\because \log_a b = \frac{\log b}{\log a}\right)$

$\Rightarrow f'(x) = \frac{1}{2}\left[\frac{\log(x)\frac{d}{dx}[\log(\log(x))] - \log(\log x)\frac{d}{dx}\log x}{(\log x)^2}\right]$

$= \frac{1}{2}\left[\frac{\log(x)\frac{1}{\log x} \times \frac{1}{x} - \left(\log(\log x)\frac{1}{x}\right)}{(\log x)^2}\right]$

$= \frac{1}{2}\left[\frac{\frac{1}{x} - \frac{\log(\log(x))}{x}}{(\log x)^2}\right]$

$\Rightarrow \quad f'(x) = \frac{1}{2}\left[\frac{1 - \log\log(x)}{x(\log x)^2}\right]$

$\Rightarrow \quad f'(e) = \frac{1}{2}\left[\frac{1 - \log\log(e)}{e(\log e)^2}\right] = \frac{1}{2}\left[\frac{1-0}{e}\right] = \frac{1}{2e}$

152. *(b)* $f(x) = \log(\sin(x))$ is continuous in $\left[\frac{\pi}{6}, \frac{5\pi}{6}\right]$ and differentiable in $\left(\frac{\pi}{6}, \frac{5\pi}{6}\right)$ as its derivative

$f'(x) = \frac{1}{\sin x}\cos x = \cot x$

Now, $f\left(\frac{\pi}{6}\right) = \log\left(\sin\left(\frac{\pi}{6}\right)\right) = \log\left(\frac{1}{2}\right)$

$f\left(\frac{5\pi}{6}\right) = \log\sin\left(\frac{5\pi}{6}\right) = \log\sin\left(\pi - \frac{\pi}{6}\right) = \log\left(\frac{1}{2}\right)$

Now, according to Lagrange's mean value theorem, there exists a point $c \in \left(\frac{\pi}{6}, \frac{5\pi}{6}\right)$ such that

$f'(c) = \frac{f\left(\frac{\pi}{6}\right) - f\left(\frac{5\pi}{6}\right)}{\left(\frac{\pi}{6} - \frac{5\pi}{6}\right)} \Rightarrow \cot c = 0 \quad \Rightarrow c = \frac{\pi}{2}$

153. *(c)* Let $\quad I = \int_{-1}^{1}(x^{27}\cos x + e^x)\,dx$

$\Rightarrow \quad I = \int_{-1}^{1} x^{27}\cos x\,dx + \int_{-1}^{1} e^x\,dx$

Since, $f(x) = x^{27}\cos x$ is an odd function.

$\left\{\because \int_{-a}^{a} f(x)\,dx = 0 \text{ if } f(x) \text{ is odd function}\right\}$

So, $\quad I = 0 + [e^x]_{-1}^{1} = e - \frac{1}{e}$

154. *(c)* Let $I = \int_0^{\pi} \frac{x\sin^{2n}x}{\sin^{2n}x + \cos^{2n}x}\,dx \qquad \dots(i)$

$\Rightarrow \quad I = \int_0^{\pi} \frac{(\pi - x)\sin^{2n}(\pi - x)}{\sin^{2n}(\pi - x) + \cos^{2n}(\pi - x)}\,dx$

$= \int_0^{\pi} \frac{(\pi - x)\sin^{2n}x}{\sin^{2n}x + \cos^{2n}x}\,dx \qquad \dots(ii)$

Adding Eqs. (i) and (ii), we get

$2I = \pi\int_0^{\pi} \frac{\sin^{2n}x}{\sin^{2n}x + \cos^{2n}x}\,dx \qquad \dots(iii)$

Let $I_1 = \int_0^{\pi} \frac{\sin^{2n}x}{\sin^{2n}x + \cos^{2n}x}\,dx$

$\Rightarrow \quad I_1 = 2\int_0^{\pi/2} \frac{\sin^{2n}x}{\sin^{2n}x + \cos^{2n}x}\,dx \qquad \dots(iv)$

$\Rightarrow \quad I_1 = 2\int_0^{\pi/2} \frac{\sin^{2n}\left(\frac{\pi}{2} - x\right)}{\sin^{2n}\left(\frac{\pi}{2} - x\right) + \cos^{2n}\left(\frac{\pi}{2} - x\right)}\,dx$

$= 2\int_0^{\pi/2} \frac{\cos^{2n}x}{\cos^{2n}x + \sin^{2n}x}\,dx \qquad \dots(v)$

Adding Eqs. (iv) and (v), we get

$2I_1 = 2\int_0^{\pi/2} 1\,dx = 2.\frac{\pi}{2} = \pi$

$\Rightarrow \quad I_1 = \frac{\pi}{2}$

Substituting the value of I_1 in Eq. (iii), we get

$2I = (\pi)\left(\frac{\pi}{2}\right) \Rightarrow I = \frac{\pi^2}{4}$

155. *(b)* Let

$$I=\int\frac{x^3-1}{x^3+x}\,dx=\int\left(1-\frac{x+1}{x^3+x}\right)dx$$

$$=\int 1dx-\int\frac{x+1}{x(x^2+1)}\,dx=x-\int\frac{x+1}{x(x^2+1)}\,dx\quad\ldots\text{(i)}$$

Now, $\dfrac{x+1}{x(x^2+1)}=\dfrac{A}{x}+\dfrac{Bx+C}{x^2+1}$

(By using partial fractions)

$\Rightarrow x+1=A(x^2+1)+(Bx+C)\,x$

$\Rightarrow x+1=(A+B)x^2+Cx+A$

Comparing coefficients of x^2, x and constant, we get

$A+B=0, C=1, A=1\Rightarrow B=-1$

$\therefore$ From Eq. (i), we get

$$I=x-\int\frac{1}{x}dx-\int\frac{1-x}{x^2+1}\,dx$$

$$=x-\log x-\int\frac{1}{x^2+1}\,dx+\frac{1}{2}\int\frac{2x}{x^2+1}\,dx$$

$$=x-\log x-\tan^{-1}x+\frac{1}{2}\log(x^2+1)+c$$

156. *(c)* $\quad \text{LHS}=\displaystyle\int\frac{\cos 8x+1}{\tan 2x-\cot 2x}\,dx$

$$=\int\frac{2\cos^2 4x}{\left(\dfrac{\sin^2 2x-\cos^2 2x}{\sin 2x\cos 2x}\right)}dx$$

$[\because \cos 2x=2\cos^2 x-1]$

$$=-\int\frac{\cos^2 4x(2\sin 2x\cos 2x)}{(\cos^2 2x-\sin^2 2x)}dx$$

$$=-\int\frac{\cos^2 4x\times\sin 4x}{\cos 4x}\,dx$$

$[\because \sin 2x=2\sin x\cos x]$

$$=-\frac{1}{2}\int 2\sin 4x\cos 4x\,dx$$

$$=-\frac{1}{2}\int\sin 8x\,dx=\frac{1}{2}\times\frac{\cos 8x}{8}+c$$

Now, $\dfrac{1}{2}\dfrac{\cos 8x}{8}+c=a\cos 8x+c$

$\therefore \quad a=\dfrac{1}{16}$

157. *(d)* We have,

$$\int_0^{\pi}x f(\sin x)\,dx=A\int_0^{x/2}f(\sin x)dx$$

Let $\quad I=\displaystyle\int_0^{\pi}x\cdot f(\sin x)\,dx \quad\ldots\text{(i)}$

$\Rightarrow \quad I=\displaystyle\int_0^{\pi}(\pi-x)\,f(\sin(\pi-x))dx$

$\Rightarrow \quad I=\displaystyle\int_0^{\pi}(\pi-x)\,f(\sin x)dx \quad\ldots\text{(ii)}$

Adding Eqs. (i) and (ii), we get

$$2I=\pi\int_0^{\pi}f(\sin x)dx\Rightarrow I=\frac{\pi}{2}\int_0^{\pi}f(\sin x)dx$$

$\Rightarrow \quad I=\dfrac{\pi}{2}\times 2\displaystyle\int_0^{\pi/2}f(\sin x)dx$

$\Rightarrow \quad I=\pi\displaystyle\int_0^{\pi/2}f(\sin x)dx$

$\therefore$ On comparing, we get $A=\pi$

158. *(d)*

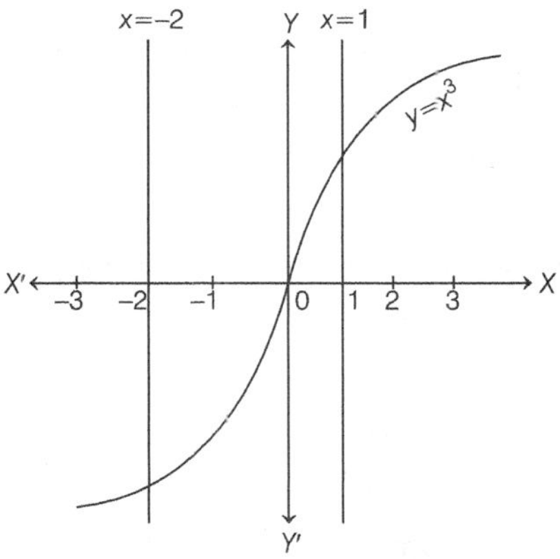

$$\text{Required area}=\left|\int_{-2}^{0}x^3\,dx\right|+\int_0^1 x^3\,dx$$

$$=\left|\left[\frac{x^4}{4}\right]_{-2}^{0}\right|+\left[\frac{x^4}{4}\right]_0^1=\frac{16}{4}+\frac{1}{4}=\frac{17}{4}\text{ sq units}$$

159. *(a)* We have, $y^2=4x$

Differentiating w.r.t. x, we get

$$2y\frac{dy}{dx}=4\Rightarrow\frac{dy}{dx}=\frac{2}{y}$$

$$\left(\frac{dy}{dx}\right)_{(1,\,2)}=\frac{2}{2}=1$$

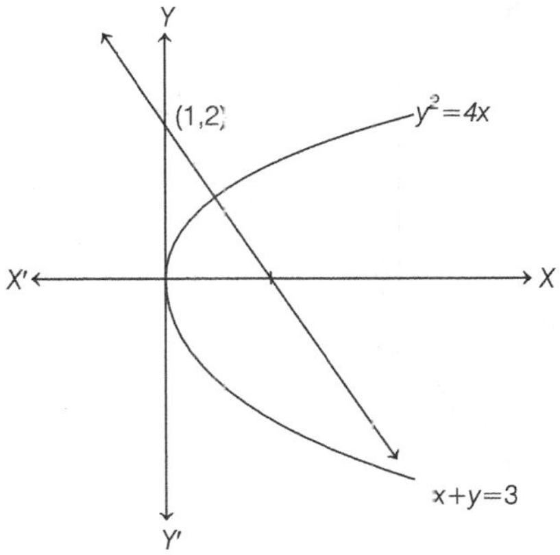

Equation of normal to the curve at (1, 2) is

$$y - y_1 = \frac{1}{\left(-\frac{dy}{dx}\right)}(x - x_1) \Rightarrow (y-2) = -\frac{1}{1}(x-1)$$

$\Rightarrow y - 2 = -x + 1 \Rightarrow x + y = 3$

The line $x + y = 3$ meets the X-axis at $x = 3$

$$\therefore \text{Required area} = \int_0^1 \sqrt{4x}\, dx + \int_1^3 (3-x)\, dx$$

$$= 2\left[\frac{x^{3/2}}{3/2}\right]_0^1 + \left[3x - \frac{x^2}{2}\right]_1^3$$

$$= \frac{4}{3}(1) + \left[9 - \frac{9}{2} - 3 + \frac{1}{2}\right] = \frac{4}{3} + \left(\frac{9}{2} - \frac{5}{2}\right)$$

$$= \frac{4}{3} + \frac{4}{2} = \frac{4}{3} + 2 = \frac{10}{3} \text{ sq units}$$

160. *(a)* $\sin x$ and $\cos x$ intersects each other at $\left(\frac{\pi}{4}, \frac{1}{\sqrt{2}}\right)$

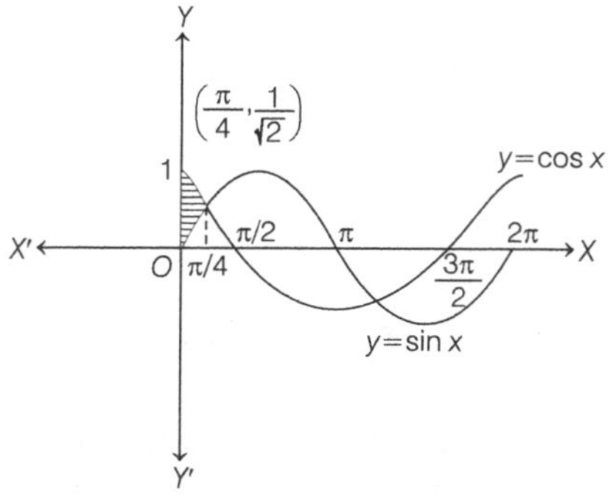

$$\therefore \text{Required area} = \int_0^{\pi/4} \cos x\, dx - \int_0^{\pi/4} \sin x\, dx$$

$$= [\sin x]_0^{\pi/4} - [-\cos x]_0^{\pi/4}$$

$$= \frac{1}{\sqrt{2}} - \left[\frac{-1}{\sqrt{2}} + 1\right] = \frac{2}{\sqrt{2}} - 1 = \sqrt{2} - 1$$

161. *(c)* Intersecting points of $y^2 = 9x$ and $y = 3x$ is (0, 0) and (1, 3).

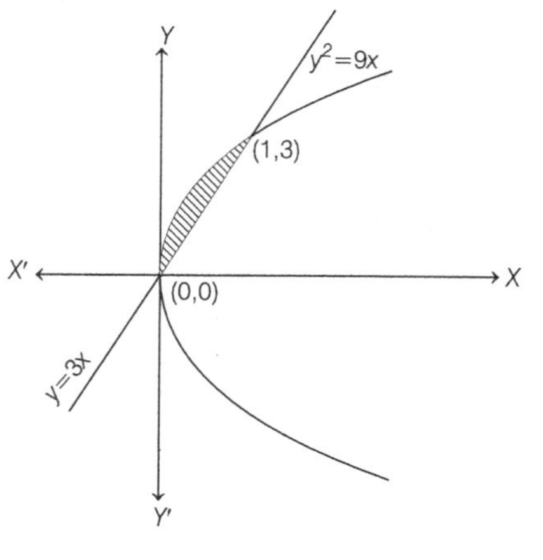

$$\therefore \text{Required area} = \int_0^1 (\sqrt{9x} - 3x)\, dx$$

$$= 3\int_0^1 (\sqrt{x} - x)\, dx = 3\left[\frac{x^{3/2}}{3/2} - \frac{x^2}{2}\right]_0^1$$

$$= 3\left(\frac{2}{3} - \frac{1}{2}\right) = 3\left(\frac{1}{6}\right) = \frac{1}{2} \text{ sq unit}$$

162. *(a)* We have, $\int_1^e \log x\, dx$

$$= [\log x \int 1\, dx]_1^e - \int_1^e \left(\frac{d}{dx}\log x \int 1\, dx\right) dx$$

$$= [\log x \cdot x]_1^e - \int_1^e \frac{1}{x} \cdot x\, dx$$

$$= [e \log e - 1 \log(1)] - \int_1^e 1\, dx$$

$$= e - [x]_1^e = e - [e - 1] = 1$$

163. *(a)* Given, equation of parabola is $y^2 = 4ax$ ... (i)

Differentiating Eq. (i) w.r.t. x, we get

$$2y\frac{dy}{dx} = 4a$$

$$\Rightarrow \quad \frac{dy}{dx} = \frac{2a}{y} \Rightarrow a = \frac{y}{2}\frac{dy}{dx}$$

Substituting the value of a in Eq. (i), we get

$$y^2 = 4 \cdot \frac{y}{2}\frac{dy}{dx} x$$

$$\Rightarrow \quad y^2 = 2xy\frac{dy}{dx} \Rightarrow \frac{dy}{dx} = \frac{y}{2x}$$

164. *(b)* We have, $\frac{dy}{dx} = \frac{y + x\tan\frac{y}{x}}{x}$ ... (i)

Given, differential equation is in homogeneous form.

$\therefore$ Put $y = vx$ in Eq. (i), we get

$$v + x\frac{dv}{dx} = v + \tan v \Rightarrow \frac{1}{\tan v}\, dv = \frac{dx}{x}$$

Taking integration on both sides, we get

$$\log(\sin v) = \log x + \log c$$

$$\Rightarrow \log\frac{\sin v}{x} = \log c \Rightarrow \sin\left(\frac{y}{x}\right) = xc$$

165. *(b)* Given, differential equation is

$$\frac{dy}{dx} + y \cdot g'(x) = g(x) \cdot g'(x)$$

This is in the form of linear differential equation.

So, $\quad \text{IF} = e^{\int g'(x)dx} = e^{g(x)}$

Required solution is

$$y.e^{g(x)} = \int g(x) \cdot g'(x) \cdot e^{g(x)} dx + c'$$

Put $\quad g(x) = t \Rightarrow g'(x)dx = dt$

$$\therefore \quad y.e^{g(x)} = \int te^t dt + c'$$

$\Rightarrow\ y.e^{g(x)} = te^t - e^t + c'$

$\Rightarrow\ y.e^{g(x)} = (g(x)-1)e^{g(x)} + c'$

or $(y - g(x) + 1)e^{g(x)} = c'$

Taking log on both sides, we get

$g(x) + \log(1 + y - g(x)) = c$

Where, $c = \log c'$

166. *(a)* Given, differential equation is $\left(\dfrac{d^2y}{dx^2}\right)^2 - \left(\dfrac{dy}{dx}\right)^3 = y^3$

So, Order = 2 and Degree = 2

$\therefore$ Order × Degree = 2 × 2 = 4

167. *(c)* Let $\mathbf{a} = \hat{\mathbf{i}} - \hat{\mathbf{j}}$ and $\mathbf{b} = \hat{\mathbf{i}} - 2\hat{\mathbf{j}}$

The required vector is along the vector

$$\mathbf{a}\times(\mathbf{a}\times\mathbf{b}) = (\mathbf{a}\cdot\mathbf{b})\mathbf{a} - (\mathbf{a}\cdot\mathbf{a})\,\mathbf{b}$$
$$= 3(\hat{\mathbf{i}} - \hat{\mathbf{j}}) - 2(\hat{\mathbf{i}} - 2\hat{\mathbf{j}})$$
$$= 3\hat{\mathbf{i}} - 3\hat{\mathbf{j}} - 2\hat{\mathbf{i}} + 4\hat{\mathbf{j}} = \hat{\mathbf{i}} + \hat{\mathbf{j}}$$

Hence, required vectors are given by

$$\pm\frac{(\hat{\mathbf{i}} + \hat{\mathbf{j}})}{\sqrt{1+1}} = \pm\,.\frac{1}{\sqrt{2}}(\hat{\mathbf{i}} + \hat{\mathbf{j}})$$

168. *(a)* According to the question,

$\mathbf{a}\cdot(\mathbf{b}+\mathbf{c}) = 0,\ \mathbf{b}\cdot(\mathbf{c}+\mathbf{a}) = 0,\ \mathbf{c}\cdot(\mathbf{a}+\mathbf{b}) = 0$

$\Rightarrow\quad \mathbf{a}\cdot\mathbf{b} + \mathbf{a}\cdot\mathbf{c} = 0 \quad \ldots\text{(i)}$

$\mathbf{b}\cdot\mathbf{c} + \mathbf{b}\cdot\mathbf{a} = 0 \quad \ldots\text{(ii)}$

$\mathbf{c}\cdot\mathbf{a} + \mathbf{c}\cdot\mathbf{b} = 0 \quad \ldots\text{(ii)}$

Adding Eqs. (i), (ii) and (iii), we get

$2(\mathbf{a}.\mathbf{b} + \mathbf{b}.\mathbf{c} + \mathbf{c}.\mathbf{a}) = 0 \quad \ldots\text{(iv)}$

Now, $|\mathbf{a} + \mathbf{b} + \mathbf{c}|^2$

$= |\mathbf{a}|^2 + |\mathbf{b}|^2 + |\mathbf{c}|^2 + 2(\mathbf{a}\cdot\mathbf{b} + \mathbf{b}\cdot\mathbf{c} + \mathbf{c}\cdot\mathbf{a})$

$= |\mathbf{a}|^2 + |\mathbf{b}|^2 + |\mathbf{c}|^2$ [using Eq. (iv)]

169. *(a)* We have, $BA = B$

$\Rightarrow (BA)B = BB \Rightarrow B(AB) = B^2$

$\Rightarrow BA = B^2 \Rightarrow B = B^2$

170. *(a)* Let $\Delta = \begin{vmatrix} x+2 & x+3 & x+2a \\ x+3 & x+4 & x+2b \\ x+4 & x+5 & x+2c \end{vmatrix}$

Applying $R_2 \to 2R_2$, we get

$$\Delta = \frac{1}{2}\begin{vmatrix} x+2 & x+3 & x+2a \\ 2x+6 & 2x+8 & 2x+4b \\ x+4 & x+5 & x+2c \end{vmatrix}$$

Applying $R_2 \to R_2 - (R_1 + R_3)$, we get

$$\Delta = \frac{1}{2}\begin{vmatrix} x+2 & x+3 & x+2a \\ 0 & 0 & 4b-(2a+2c) \\ x+4 & x+5 & x+2c \end{vmatrix}$$

$$\Rightarrow \Delta = \frac{1}{2}\begin{vmatrix} x+2 & x+3 & x+2a \\ 0 & 0 & 0 \\ x+4 & x+5 & x+2c \end{vmatrix} \quad \begin{bmatrix} \because a, b, c \text{ are in AP} \\ \therefore 2b = a + c \end{bmatrix}$$

$\Rightarrow \Delta = 0$

171. *(c)* Since, $A = \begin{bmatrix} a & 0 & 0 \\ 0 & a & 0 \\ 0 & 0 & a \end{bmatrix}$

$\Rightarrow |A| = a\cdot a\cdot a = a^3$

Using formula $|\text{adj } A| = |A|^{n-1}$, we get

$\det(\text{adj } A) = (a^3)^{3-1} = (a^3)^2 = a^6$

172. *(c)* We have, $A = \begin{bmatrix} 1 & 0 \\ 1 & 1 \end{bmatrix}$

$$A^2 = A\cdot A = \begin{bmatrix} 1 & 0 \\ 1 & 1 \end{bmatrix}\begin{bmatrix} 1 & 0 \\ 1 & 1 \end{bmatrix} = \begin{bmatrix} 1 & 0 \\ 2 & 1 \end{bmatrix}$$

$$A^3 = A^2\cdot A = \begin{bmatrix} 1 & 0 \\ 2 & 1 \end{bmatrix}\begin{bmatrix} 1 & 0 \\ 1 & 1 \end{bmatrix} = \begin{bmatrix} 1 & 0 \\ 3 & 1 \end{bmatrix}$$

Similarly, $A^8 = \begin{bmatrix} 1 & 0 \\ 8 & 1 \end{bmatrix}$

Now, $A^8 = aA + bI$

$$\Rightarrow \begin{bmatrix} 1 & 0 \\ 8 & 1 \end{bmatrix} = a\begin{bmatrix} 1 & 0 \\ 1 & 1 \end{bmatrix} + b\begin{bmatrix} 1 & 0 \\ 0 & 1 \end{bmatrix}$$

$$\Rightarrow \begin{bmatrix} 1 & 0 \\ 8 & 1 \end{bmatrix} = \begin{bmatrix} a+b & 0 \\ a & a+b \end{bmatrix}$$

$\therefore a = 8$ and $a + b = 1$

$\Rightarrow b = 1 - 8 = -7$

173. *(b)* Let E_1, E_2 and E_3be the the events such that drawn ball is white, blue and black respectively.

The required probability

$= {}^3P_1P(E_1)P(E_1)P(\overline{E})_1 + {}^3P_1P(E_2)P(E_2)P(\overline{E}_2) + {}^3P_1P(E_3)P(E_3)P(\overline{E}_3)$

$= 3\times\dfrac{2}{9}\times\dfrac{1}{8}\times\dfrac{7}{7} + 3\times\dfrac{3}{9}\times\dfrac{2}{8}\times\dfrac{6}{7} + 3\times\dfrac{4}{9}\times\dfrac{3}{8}\times\dfrac{5}{7}$

$= 3\left[\dfrac{14+36+60}{9\times8\times7}\right] = \dfrac{3\times110}{9\times8\times7} = \dfrac{55}{84}$

174. *(c)* 6 boys and 6 girls sit in a row in 12! ways. Number of ways when all six girls sit together = 7! × 6!

Required probability $= \dfrac{7!\times 6!}{12!} = \dfrac{1}{132}$

175. *(c)* Total number of outcomes = 6 × 6 × 6 = 216

When sum of numbers is 5, then outcomes are (1, 1, 3), (1, 2, 2), (1, 3, 1), (2, 1, 2), (2, 2, 1) and (3, 1, 1).

Required probability $= \dfrac{6}{216} = \dfrac{1}{36}$

176. *(c)* Total number of balls = 9

Probability of drawn two white balls

$$\frac{3}{9}\times\frac{2}{8}=\frac{1}{12}$$

177. *(b)* Given, inequality is

$$\frac{6x}{4x-1}<\frac{1}{2}\Rightarrow\frac{12x}{4x-1}<1$$

$$\Rightarrow \quad \frac{12x}{4x-1}-1<0\Rightarrow\frac{8x+1}{4x-1}<0 \quad \dots\text{(i)}$$

For above inequality Eq. (i), we have two cases either

Case I $8x+1>0, 4x-1<0$

Case II $8x+1<0$, $4x-1>0$

From Case (I), we get $x>\frac{-1}{8}, x<\frac{1}{4}$

$$\therefore \quad x\in\left(-\frac{1}{8},\frac{1}{4}\right) \quad \dots\text{(ii)}$$

From Case (II), $x<\frac{-1}{8}, x>\frac{1}{4}$, both of which can not be true.

$\therefore$ Eq. (ii) represent the solution set of given inequality.

178. *(d)* We have, $S^2=at^2+2bt+c$ ... (i)

Differentiating Eq. (i) w.r.t. t, we get

$$2S\frac{dS}{dt}=2at+2b$$

$$\Rightarrow\frac{dS}{dt}=\left(\frac{at+b}{S}\right) \quad \dots\text{(ii)}$$

Differentiating Eq. (ii) w.r.t. t, we get

$$\frac{d^2S}{dt^2}=\frac{S\frac{d}{dt}(at+b)-(at+b)\frac{dS}{dt}}{S^2}$$

$$\Rightarrow\frac{d^2S}{dt^2}=\frac{aS-(at+b)\frac{(at+b)}{S}}{S^2} \quad \text{[using Eq. (ii)]}$$

$$\Rightarrow\frac{d^2S}{dt^2}=\frac{aS^2-(at+b)^2}{S^3}$$

$$\Rightarrow\frac{d^2S}{dt^2}=\frac{a(at^2+2bt+c)-[(at)^2+b^2+2atb]}{S^3}$$

[using Eq. (i)]

$$\Rightarrow\frac{d^2S}{dt^2}=\frac{a^2t^2+2abt+ac-a^2t^2-b^2-2atb}{S^3}$$

$$\Rightarrow\frac{d^2S}{dt^2}=\frac{ac-b^2}{S^3}$$

$$\Rightarrow \text{Acceleration}=\left(\frac{d^2S}{dt^2}\right)\propto\frac{1}{S^3}$$

179. *(d)* Data is 6, 7, 10, 12, 13, 4, 8, 12

Here, $n=8$

$\therefore$ Mean

$$=\frac{6+7+10+12+13+4+8+12}{8}$$

$$=\frac{72}{8}=9$$

Now, variance $=\frac{1}{n}\Sigma x_i^2-(\bar{x})^2$

$$=\frac{1}{8}[(6)^2+(7)^2+(10)^2+(12)^2+(13)^2+(4)^2+(8)^2+(12)^2]-81$$

$$=\frac{1}{8}[722]-81=90.25-81=9.25$$

180. *(b)* We have, $\overline{(x+iy)(1-2i)}=1+i$

$$\Rightarrow \quad \overline{(x+iy)(1-2i)}=1+i$$

$$\Rightarrow \quad (x-iy)(1+2i)=1+i$$

$$\Rightarrow \quad x-iy=\frac{1+i}{1+2i}$$

$$\Rightarrow \quad \overline{x-iy}=\overline{\left(\frac{1+i}{1+2i}\right)}=\frac{1-i}{1-2i}$$

$$\Rightarrow \quad x+iy=\frac{1-i}{1-2i}$$

COMEDK 2015

COMEDK

Solved Paper 2014

Instructions

- There are 180 questions in all. The number of questions in each section is as given below.

Sections	No. of Questions
Section I : Physics	1-60
Section II : Chemistry	61-120
Section III : Mathematics	121-180

- All the questions are Multiple Choice Questions having four options out of which **ONLY ONE** is correct.
- Candidates will be awarded 1 mark for each correct answer. There will be no negative marking for incorrect answer.
- Time allotted to complete this paper is 3 hrs.

PHYSICS

1. Which of the following statements is not correct regarding conservation laws?

a. A conservation law is a hypothesis based on observations and experiments.
b. Conservation laws do not have a deep connection with symmetries of nature.
c. A conservation law cannot be proved.
d. Conservation of energy, linear momentum, angular momentum are considered to be fundamental laws of Physics.

2. The increase in the height of the tower of height 200 m to get its coverage range tripled is

a. 800 m *b.* 1600 m *c.* 900 m *d.* 700 m

3. The value of g at a height equal to half the radius of the earth from the earth's surface is

a. $\frac{g}{2}$ *b.* $\frac{g}{3}$ *c.* $\frac{4g}{9}$ *d.* $\frac{g}{4}$

4. The maximum and minimum distances of a comet from the sun are 1.4×10^{12} m and 7×10^{10} m. If its velocity nearest to the sun is 6×10^{14} ms^{-1}, what is its velocity in the farthest position?

(Assume the comet to be spherical)

a. 1000 ms^{-1} *b.* 2000 ms^{-1}
c. 3000 ms^{-1} *d.* 4000 ms^{-1}

5. The centre of mass of a system of two bodies of masses M and m, $(M > m)$, separated by a distance d is

a. midway between the bodies
b. closer to the heavier body
c. closer to the lighter body
d. at the centre of the heavier body

6. A pump on the ground floor of a building can pump up water to fill the tank of 30 m^3 in 15 min. If the tank is 40 m above the ground, and the efficiency of the pump is 30%, the power consumed by the pump is ($g = 10$ ms^{-2})

a. 4.4 kW *b.* 44 kW
c. 440 kW *d.* 0.44 kW

7. The resistance of a galvanometer is 2.5 Ω and it requires 50 mA for full scale deflection. The value of shunt resistance required to convert it into an ammeter of range 0 to 5 A is

a. 2.5×10^{-2} Ω *b.* 0.25×10^{-2} Ω

c. 0.025×10^{-2} Ω *d.* 0.0025×10^{-2} Ω

8. Zener diode is used to regulate the voltage supply because, while using a Zener diode

a. voltage remains constant, even when current varies much

b. Both voltage and current remain constant

c. voltage varies much, but current remains constant

d. Both voltage and current vary together

9. In an inelastic collision, which of the following is true?

a. Momentum is conserved but not KE

b. KE is conserved, but not momentum

c. Both momentum and KE are conserved

d. Neither momentum nor KE are conserved

10. If a change in current of 0.01 A in one coil produces a change in magnetic flux of 2×10^{-2} weber in another coil, then the mutual inductance between coils is

a. 0 *b.* 0.5 H *c.* 2 H *d.* 3 H

11. An aeroplane is flying horizontally with a velocity of 360 km h^{-1}. The distance between the tips of the wings of the aeroplane is 50 m. The vertical component of the earth's magnetic field is 4×10^{-4} Wbm^{-2}. The induced emf is

a. 200 V *b.* 20 V *c.* 2V *d.* 0.2 V

12. The inductance in a coil plays the same role as

a. inertia in mechanics

b. energy in mechanics

c. momentum in mechanics

d. force in mechanics

13. The mutual inductance between two coils depends upon

a. the medium between the coils only

b. the separation between the coils only

c. Both the medium and the separation

d. Neither the medium nor the separation

14. The normal magnetic flux passing through a coil changes with time according to the equation $\phi = 6t^2 - 5t + 1$. What is the magnitude of the induced current at $t = 0.253$ s and resistance 10Ω?

a. 1.2 A *b.* 0.8 A

c. 0.6 A *d.* 0.2 A

15. For an electromagnetic wave, which of the following statements is true?

a. Electric field is constant and magnetic field varies.

b. Magnetic field is constant and electric field varies.

c. Both electric and magnetic fields are constant.

d. Both electric and magnetic fields vary.

16. If A is the angle of prism, r angle of refraction, then the condition for minimum deviation is

a. $A = r^2$ *b.* $A = 2r$

c. $A = \frac{r}{2}$ *d.* $A = r$

17. A concave mirror forms an enlarged, erect, virtual image of an object, only when the object is placed

a. at focus

b. between pole and focus

c. at the centre of curvature

d. between focus and centre of curvature

18. A man stands symmetrically between two large plane mirrors fixed to two adjacent walls of a rectangular room. The number of images formed are

a. 4 *b.* 3 *c.* 2 *d.* 6

19. A sinusoidal voltage of peak value 300 V and an angular frequency $\omega = 400$ $rads^{-1}$ is applied to series L-C-R circuit, in which $R = 3\Omega$, $L = 20$ mH and $C = 625$ μF. The peak current in the circuit is

a. $30\sqrt{2}$ A *b.* 60 A

c. 100 A *d.* $60\sqrt{2}$ A

20. A ray of light falls upon a 60° prism ($\mu = \sqrt{2}$) and it suffers minimum deviation. The angle of incidence for this ray must be

a. 30° *b.* 45° *c.* 60° *d.* 75°

21. A source of light of wavelength 5000 Å is placed at one end of a table 2 m long and 5 mm above its flat well polished top. The fringe width of the interference bands seen on a screen located at the end of the table is

a. 2×10^{-5} m *b.* 2×10^{-4} m

c. 2×10^{-3} m *d.* 2×10^{-2} m

22. A screen is placed 2 m away from a narrow slit. It the first minimum lies 5 mm from either side of the central maxima, when plane waves of wavelength 5×10^{-7} m are used, the slit width is

a. 4.8×10^{-4} m *b.* 2×10^{-4} m

c. 5×10^{-4} m *d.* 2.4×10^{-4} m

23. A galaxy moves with respect to the earth, so that sodium line of 589.0 nm is observed at 589.6 nm. The speed of the galaxy is

a. 300 kms^{-1} *b.* 306 kms^{-1}
c. 400 kms^{-1} *d.* 406 kms^{-1}

24. Newton's rings are observed normally in reflected light of wavelength 5000 Å. The diameter of the 10th dark ring is 0.005 m. The radius of curvature of the lens is

a. 1 m *b.* 1.25 m *c.* 2 m *d.* 0.5 m

25. The amount of energy required to separate a hydrogen atom into a proton and an electron is

a. 1.36 eV *b.* 13.6 eV *c.* 0.136 eV *d.* 136 eV

26. The energy equivalent of 1 g of a substance is

a. 4.5×10^{13} J *b.* 9×10^{16} J
c. 9×10^{13} J *d.* 18×10^{13} J

27. Two small drops of mercury, each of radius *r*, coalesce to form a single large drop of radius *R*. The ratio of the total surface energies before and after the change is

a. $1 : 2^{1/3}$ *b.* $2^{1/3} : 1$ *c.* 2 : 1 *d.* 1 : 2

28. Find the energy equivalent of one atomic mass unit in joules and in MeV.

a. 1.66×10^{-10} J, 93.15 MeV
b. 3×10^{-10} J, 9.315 MeV
c. 1.5×10^{-10} J, 931.5 MeV
d. 2.5×10^{-10} J, 931.5 MeV

29. Two amplifiers are connected one after the other in series (cascaded). The first amplifier has a voltage gain of 10 and the second has a voltage gain of 20. If the input signal is 0.01 V, what is the output AC signal?

a. 1.5 V *b.* 2 V *c.* 2.5 V *d.* 3.0 V

30. A transistor works as an amplifier when,

a. emitter-base junction is forward biased and collector-base junction is reverse biased
b. emitter-base junction is reverse biased and collector-base junction is forward biased
c. Both junctions are forward biased
d. Both junctions are reverse biased

31. In a common base circuit, collector base voltage changes by 0.6 V and collector current changes by 0.02 mA. Then, the output resistance is

a. $6 \times 10^4\ \Omega$ *b.* $3 \times 10^4\ \Omega$
c. $9 \times 10^4\ \Omega$ *d.* $18 \times 10^4\ \Omega$

32. A repeater in TV transmission is

a. only a receiver
b. only a transmitter
c. a receiver and a transmitter
d. demodulator

33. The waves suitable for transmission of radio signals are

a. infrared
b. waves longer than infrared
c. waves shorter than infrared
d. X-rays

34. A wire of length 2 m is made from 10 cm^3 of copper. A force *F* is applied so that its length increases by 2 mm. Another wire of length 8 m is made from the same volume of copper. If the force *F* is applied to it, its length will increase by

a. 0.8 cm *b.* 1.6 cm
c. 2.4 cm *d.* 3.2 cm

35. A tennis ball of mass *m* strikes a wall with a velocity *v* and retraces the same path. Calculate the change in momentum.

a. $+4mv$ *b.* $-4mv$ *c.* $+2mv$ *d.* $-2mv$

36. A monkey of mass 40 kg climbs up a rope which can stand a maximum tension of 600 N. The rope will break, when the monkey

a. climbs up with an acceleration 6 ms^{-2}
b. climbs down with an acceleration of 4 ms^{-1}
c. climbs up with uniform speed of 5 ms^{-1}
d. slides down the rope freely under gravity

37. A shell of mass 20 g is fired by a gun of mass 100 kg. If the shell leaves the gun with a speed of 80 ms^{-1}, then the speed of recoil of the gun is

a. 3.2 cms^{-1} *b.* 1.6 cms^{-1}
c. 1 cms^{-1} *d.* 2.4 cms^{-1}

38. Two boys are standing at ends *A* and *B* of a ground where *AB* = 200 m. The boy at *B* starts running in a direction perpendicular to *AB* with a speed of 6 ms^{-1}. The boy at *A* starts simultaneously with a velocity of 10 ms^{-1} and catches the other at time, *t* where the time, *t* is

a. 50 s *b.* 20 s
c. 25 s *d.* 12.5 s

39. A car covers the first half distance between two places at 40 kmph and the other half at 60 kmph. The average speed of the car is

a. 48 kmph *b.* 120 kmph
c. 50 kmph *d.* 24 kmph

40. The dimensions of universal gravitational constant is

a. $[M^2L^3T^{-2}]$ *b.* $[M^{-1}L^3T^{-2}]$
c. $[M^{-2}L^3T^{-2}]$ *d.* $[M^2L^{-3}T^{-2}]$

41. Which two of the following quantities are dimensionally equivalent?
(i) Force
(ii) Pressure
(iii) Young's modulus
(iv) Energy
a. (i) and (ii) *b.* (i) and (iii)
c. (ii) and (iii) *d.* (ii) and (iv)

42. The temperature of an object is 60°C. Its value in Fahrenheit scale is
a. 120°F *b.* 130°F *c.* 140°F *d.* 110°F

43. A pan filled with hot food cools from 94°C to 86°C in 2 min, when the room temperature is 20°C. The time taken for the food to cool from 86°C to 74°C will be
a. 500 s *b.* 420 s *c.* 200 s *d.* 210 s

44. A system containing a ball is oscillating on a frictionless horizontal plane. The position of the mass when its potential energy and its kinetic energy both are equal, is (let A is the amplitude of oscillation)
a. A *b.* $A/\sqrt{2}$ *c.* $A/2$ *d.* $A/\sqrt{3}$

45. The universal gas law $\left(\dfrac{pV}{T} = \text{constant}\right)$ is applicable to
a. isothermal changes only *b.* adiabatic changes only
c. Both (a) and (b) *d.* Neither (a) nor (b)

46. On an average, a human heart is found to beat 72 times a minute. Its frequency and period are
a. 1.2 Hz, 0.83 s *b.* 2.5 Hz, 1.2 s
c. 2 Hz, 1.2 s *d.* 2.5 Hz, 0.83 s

47. A hospital uses an ultrasonic scanner to locate tumors in a tissue. The operating frequency of the scanner is 4.2 MHz. The speed of sound in a tissue is 1.7 km s^{-1}. The wavelength of sound in the tissue is
a. 4×10^{-3} m *b.* 8×10^{-3} m
c. 4×10^{-4} m *d.* 8×10^{-4} m

48. A policeman on duty detects a drop of 15% in the pitch of the horn of a motor car as it crosses him. If the velocity of sound is 330 ms^{-1}, then calculate the speed of the car.
a. 26.7 ms^{-1} *b.* 27.6 ms^{-1}
c. 53.4 ms^{-1} *d.* 54.3 ms^{-1}

49. An electric dipole placed in a non-uniform electric field experiences
a. only torque *b.* only force
c. Both (a) and (b) *d.* Neither (a) nor (b)

50. For a polar molecule, which of the following statements is true?
a. The centre of gravity of electrons and protons coincide.
b. The centre of gravity of electrons and protons do not coincide.
c. The charge distribution is always symmetrical.
d. The dipole moment is always zero.

51. A 10 mF capacitor has been charged to a potential of 100 V. Suddenly if it explodes, the energy given out is
a. 50 J *b.* 10^5 J
c. 50 mJ *d.* 10^3 J

52. The region between the parallel plates of capacitor is filled with parallel layers of air and paper (of dielectric constant 4). The space between the plates is 1 mm and the thickness of paper is 0.75 mm. The ratio of the voltage across air and paper is
a. $\dfrac{1}{2}$ *b.* $\dfrac{3}{4}$ *c.* $\dfrac{4}{3}$ *d.* $\dfrac{1}{3}$

53. Two copper wires, one of length 1 m and the other of length 9 m have the same resistance. The diameters are in the ratio
a. 3 : 1 *b.* 1 : 3
c. 9 : 1 *d.* 1 : 9

54. Which of the following is a correct statement?
a. Heat produced in a conductor varies directly as the current flowing.
b. Heat produced in a conductor varies inversely as the current flowing.
c. Heat produced in a conductor varies directly as the square of the current flowing.
d. Heat produced in a conductor varies inversely as the square of the current flowing.

55. A proton and an α-particle are projected with the same kinetic energy at right angles to a uniform magnetic field. The ratio of the radii of their paths is
a. 2 : 1 *b.* 1 : 2 *c.* 1 : 1 *d.* 2 : 3

56. The magnetic properties of a magnet is lost at its
a. melting point *b.* boiling point
c. Curie point *d.* triple point

57. Electromagnets are made of soft iron because soft iron has
a. low susceptibility and low retentivity
b. high susceptibility and low retentivity
c. high susceptibility and high retentivity
d. low susceptibility and high retentivity

58. Three charges $-q$, $+Q$ and $-q$ are placed at equal distances along a straight line. If the total PE of the system is zero, then the ratio Q/q becomes

a. $\frac{1}{8}$ *b.* $\frac{1}{6}$

c. $\frac{1}{4}$ *d.* $\frac{1}{2}$

59. The equivalent resistance of the circuit between A and B is

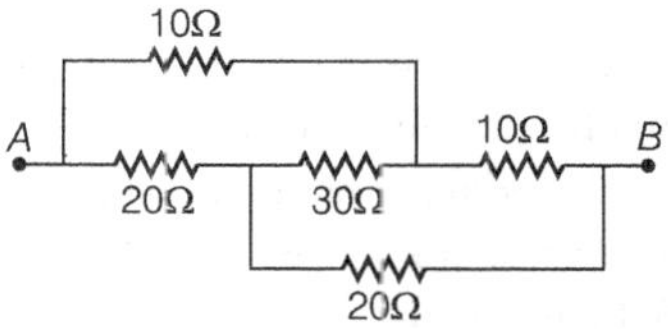

a. 30 Ω *b.* 20 Ω *c.* 10 Ω *d.* 8 Ω

60. The TV signals have a bandwidth of 3.7 MHz. The number of TV channels that can be accommodated with a band of 3700 GHz is

a. 10^4 *b.* 10^5 *c.* 10^6 *d.* 10^7

CHEMISTRY

61. Density of 3 M solution of NaCl is 1.25 g/mL. The mass of the solvent in the solution is

a. 1075.4 g *b.* 10.745 g

c. 10.754 g *d.* 1074.5 g

62. An orbital with $n = 3$, $l = 1$ is designated as

a. 1*s* *b.* 3*s* *c.* 3*p* *d.* 3*d*

63. A 150 watt bulb emits light of wavelength 6600 Å and only 8% of the energy is emitted as light. How many photons are emitted by the bulb per second?

a. 4×10^{19} *b.* 3.24×10^{19}

c. 4.23×10^{20} *d.* 3×10^{20}

64. In the following sets of ions, which one is not isoelectronic with the rest of the species?

O^{2-}, F^-, Na, Mg^{2+}, Al^{3+}, Ne

a. Mg^{2+} *b.* Al^{3+}

c. O^{2-} *d.* Na

65. For all gases, at any given pressure, the graph of volume *vs* temperature (in celsius) is a straight line. This graph is called

a. isomer *b.* isochore

c. isobar *d.* isotherm

66. Atomic numbers of vanadium, chromium, nickel and iron are 23, 24, 28 and 26 respectively. Which one of these is expected to have the highest second ionisation enthalpy?

a. Cr *b.* V *c.* Fe *d.* Ni

67. Which of these represents the correct order of their increasing bond order?

a. $C_2^{2-} < He_2^+ < O_2^+ < O_2^-$

b. $He_2^+ < O_2^- < O_2^+ < C_2^{2-}$

c. $O_2^- < O_2^+ < C_2^{2-} < He_2^+$

d. $O_2^+ < C_2^{2-} < O_2^- < He_2^+$

68. Pick up the incorrect statement.

a. Dipole moment of ammonia is due to orbital dipole and resultant dipole in the same direction.

b. In BF_3 bond dipoles are higher but dipole moment is zero.

c. Dipole moment is a vector quantity.

d. O_2 and H_2 show bond dipole due to polarisation.

69. The mole fraction of dioxygen in a neon-dioxygen mixture is 0.18. If the total pressure of the mixture is 25 bar, the partial pressure of neon in the mixture would be

a. 25.18 bar *b.* 25.82 bar

c. 4.5 bar *d.* 20.5 bar

70. Standard molar enthalpies of formation of $CaCO_3(s)$, $CaO(s)$ and $CO_2(g)$ are -1206.92 kJ mol^{-1}, -635.09 kJ mol^{-1} and -393.51 kJ mol^{-1} respectively. The $\Delta_r H$, for decomposition of $CaCO_3(s)$ is

a. 178.3 kJ mol^{-1} *b.* -178.3 kJ mol^{-1}

c. 1448.5 kJ mol^{-1} *d.* -1448.5 kJ mol^{-1}

71. $\Delta_r G°$ for the conversion of O_2 to ozone,

$\frac{3}{2}O_2(g) \longrightarrow O_3(g)$ at 298 K is

(K_p for this conversion is 1×10^{-29})

a. 16.54 kJ mol^{-1} *b.* 165.4 kJ mol^{-1}

c. 1654 kJ mol^{-1} *d.* 1.654 kJ mol^{-1}

72. In which of the following case, does the reaction go farthest to completion if

a. $K_C = 10^2$ *b.* $K_C = 10$ *c.* $K_C = 10^{-2}$ *d.* $K_C = 1$

73. One mole of PCl_5 is heated in a closed 2 dm^3 vessel. At equilibrium 40% PCl_5 is dissociated. Calculate the equilibrium constant.

a. 0.066 *b.* 0.154 *c.* 0.133 *d.* 0.266

74. The non-existence of PbI_4 and $PbBr_4$ is due to
a. highly oxidising nature of Pb^{4+} ions
b. highly reducing nature of I^- and Br^- ions
c. larger size of Pb^{4+}, Br^- and I^- ions
d. Both (a) and (b)

75. Which of the following species do not show disproportionation reaction?
a. ClO^- *b.* ClO_4^- *c.* ClO_2^- *d.* ClO_3^-

76. Sodium dissolves in liquid NH_3 to give a deep blue solution. This is due to
a. ammoniated Na^+
b. ammoniated Na^-
c. formation of Na^+ / Na^- pair
d. ammoniated electrons

77. Fullerene with formula C_{60} has a structure where every carbon atom is
a. *sp*-hybridised *b.* sp^2-hybridised
c. sp^3-hybridised *d.* not hybridised

78. Maleic acid and fumaric acid are
a. optical isomers
b. geometrical isomers
c. functional isomers
d. positional isomers

79. The IUPAC name of tertiary butyl chloride is
a. 2-chloro-2-methylpropane
b. 3-chlorobutane
c. 4-chlorobutane
d. 1, 2-dichloro-3-methylpropane

80. The compound which on ozonolysis produces a mixture of propanone and ethanal is
a. 2-methyl but-1-ene *b.* 2-pentene
c. 2-pentyne *d.* 2-methyl but-2-ene

81. When 2-bromopentane is heated with alcoholic solution of potassium hydroxide, the major product obtained is
a. pent-1-ene *b.* pent-2-ene
c. pent-1-yne *d.* pent-2-yne

82. Rain water is called acid rain when its pH
a. falls below zero
b. falls below 5.6
c. is above 5.6 but less than 10
d. is above 10

83. Schottky defect in crystals is observed when
a. an ion leaves its normal site and occupies an interstitial site.
b. unequal number of cations and anions are missing from the crystal lattice.
c. equal number of cations and anions are missing from the crystal lattice.
d. there is large difference in size of positive and negative ions.

84. A crystalline solid has A^- ions at the corners and face centres, whereas B^+ ions are at the body centre and edge centres of the unit cell. The simplest formula of the compound will be
a. A_2B *b.* AB_2 *c.* AB_3 *d.* AB

85. The radius of an atom is 300 pm. If it crystallises in a face-centered cubic lattice, the length of the edge of the unit cell is
a. 488.5 pm *b.* 848.5 pm
c. 884.5 pm *d.* 484.5 pm

86. When the concentration is expressed as the number of moles of solute per kilogram of the solvent, it is known as
a. molarity *b.* molality
c. normality *d.* mole fraction

87. van't Hoff factors of equimolal solutions of sodium chloride, barium chloride and glucose in water are
a. 2, 3, 0 respectively *b.* 2, 3, 6 respectively
c. 2, 3, 4 respectively *d.* 2, 3, 1 respectively

88. A one molal solution of sodium chloride in water has the same boiling point as
a. 1 m solution of magnesium sulphate
b. 1 m solution of magnesium chloride
c. 1 m solution of aluminium sulphate
d. 1 m solution of aluminium chloride

89. Vapour pressure of water at 293 K is 17.535 mm Hg. The vapour pressure of water at 293 K containing 25 g of glucose dissolved in 450 g of water is
a. 17.439 mm Hg *b.* 17.535 mm Hg
c. 0.097 mm Hg *d.* 34.973 mm Hg

90. In a electrochemical cell, the reaction will be feasible when
a. $\Delta G = -$ ve, $E = +$ve
b. $\Delta G = +$ ve, $E = -$ve
c. $\Delta G = 0$, $E = -$ve
d. $\Delta G = 0$, $E = 0$

91. The standard emf of the cell $Zn \mid Zn^{2+} \parallel Ag^+ \mid Ag$ is 1.56 V. If the standard reduction potential of Ag is 0.8 V, the standard oxidation potential of Zn is
a. – 0.76 V *b.* + 0.76 V
c. – 2.36 V *d.* + 2.36 V

92. The molar conductivities of NaOH, NaCl and $BaCl_2$ at infinite dilution are 2.481×10^{-2} S m^2 mol^{-1}, 1.265×10^{-2} S m^2 mol^{-1} and 2.800×10^{-2} S m^2 mol^{-1} respectively. The molar conductivity of $Ba(OH)_2$ at infinite dilution will be

a. 5.232×10^{-2} S m^2 mol^{-1}
b. 9.654×10^{-2} S m^2 mol^{-1}
c. 4.016×10^{-2} S m^2 mol^{-1}
d. 1.145×10^{-2} S m^2 mol^{-1}

93. The rate of a chemical reaction doubles for every 10°C rise in temperature. If the temperature increases by 60°C, the rate of reaction increases

a. 20 times *b.* 32 times
c. 64 times *d.* 128 times

94. An endothermic reaction, $A \rightarrow B$ has an activation energy as x kJ/mol. If the energy change of the reaction is y kJ, the activation energy of the reverse reaction is

a. $-x$ *b.* $x - y$
c. $x + y$ *d.* $y - x$

95. $aP + bQ \longrightarrow$ products, when $[P]$ is doubled keeping $[Q]$ constant and rate increases 2 times, when $[P]$ is constant and $[Q]$ is doubled and rate increases four times. The overall order is

a. 1 *b.* 2 *c.* 3 *d.* 2.5

96. Semiconductors of very high purity are obtained by

a. liquation
b. vapour phase refining
c. zone refining
d. electrolysis

97. Sodium cyanide is added as a depressant in the froth floatation process when the ore contains a mixture of ZnS and PbS. This is because

a. $Pb(CN)_2$ gets precipitated without any effect on ZnS
b. ZnS forms soluble complex, while PbS forms froth.
c. PbS forms soluble complex, while ZnS forms froth.
d. $Zn(CN)_2$ gets precipitated without any effect on PbS

98. Solid A reacts with strong $NaOH(aq)$ liberating a foul smelling gas B which spontaneously burn in air giving smoky rings. A and B are respectively.

a. p_{red} and PH_3 *b.* p_{White} and PH_3
c. S and H_2S *d.* p_{white} and H_2S

99. $SO_2 + 2H_2S \longrightarrow 3S + 2H_2O$ This equation represents preparation of sulphur sol by

a. hydrolysis *b.* oxidation
c. reduction *d.* double decomposition

100. Which of the following inert gas compounds is not formed?

a. $XeOF_4$ *b.* XeO_3 *c.* XeF_2 *d.* NeF_2

101. Nitrogen shows maximum covalency of 4 whereas, other heavier elements of the group show higher covalency because,

a. it has higher electronegativity
b. it has smaller size
c. it has only 4-orbitals available in the valence shell
d. it prefers to form multiple bonds with atoms

102. The photographic industry relies on the special light sensitive properties of

a. NaI *b.* NaBr *c.* AgCl *d.* AgBr

103. In acidic medium, potassium permanganate oxidises oxalic acid to

a. oxalate *b.* carbon dioxide
c. acetate *d.* acetic acid

104. The complex $[PtCl_2(en)_2]^{2+}$ ion shows

a. structural isomerism only
b. optical isomerism only
c. geometrical and optical isomerism
d. geometrical isomerism only

105. The complex $[Ag(NH_3)_2][Ag(CN)_2]$ has the IUPAC name

a. diamminesilver (I) dicyanosilver (I)
b. diamminesilver (I) dicyanoargentate (I)
c. dicyanosilver (I) diammineargentate (I)
d. diamminesilver (I) dicyanoargentate (I)

106. Molar conductance of a complex of cobalt is zero. Then its structure would be

a. $[Co(NH_3)]_3Cl_3$ *b.* $[Co(NH_3)Cl]Cl_3$
c. $[Co(NH_3)_3Cl_2]Cl$ *d.* $[Co(NH_3)_3Cl_3]$

107. The reaction, $CH_3CH_2I + KOH(aq) \longrightarrow CH_3CH_2OH - KI$ is classified as

a. electrophilic substitution
b. nucleophilic substitution
c. electrophilic addition
d. nucleophilic addition

108. For S_N1 reaction, the order of reactivity of haloalkanes is

a. tertiary halide < secondary halide < primary halide
b. tertiary halide < secondary halide > primary halide
c. tertiary halide > secondary halide > primary halide
d. tertiary halide > secondary halide < primary halide

109. The major product obtained when chlorobenzene is nitrated with HNO_3 + conc. H_2SO_4 is

a. 1-chloro-4-nitrobenzene
b. 1-chloro-2-nitrobenzene
c. 1-chloro-3-nitrobenzene
d. 1-chloro-1-nitrobenzene

110. The unstable intermediate dichlorocarbene $[:CCl_2]$ is formed during

a. Kolbe's reaction
b. Friedel-Crafts reaction
c. Williamson synthesis
d. Reimer-Tiemann reaction

111. Phenols are highly acidic compared to alcohols due to

a. the higher molecular mass of phenols
b. the stronger hydrogen bonds in phenols
c. alkoxide ion is a strong conjugate base
d. phenoxide ion is resonance stabilised

112. Arrangement of following compounds based on their boiling points in the increasing order.
n-butane, 1-butanol, ethoxyethane and 1-propanol will be

a. 1-propanol > *n*-butane > ethoxyethane > 1-butanol
b. *n*-butane < ethoxyethane < 1-propanol < 1-butanol
c. *n*-butane < 1-propanol < ethoxyethane < 1-butanol
d. 1-propanol < *n*-butane < ethoxyethane < 1-butanol

113. Among 2-chloropropanoic acid, 3-chloro-propanoic acid, 2-2-dichloroacetic acid and propanoic acid the K_a values will be in the order,

a. 2, 2-dichloroacetic acid > 2-chloropropanoic acid > 3-chloropropanoic acid > propanoic acid
b. 3-chloropropanoic acid > 2-chloropropanoic acid > 2, 2-dichloroacetic acid > propanoic acid
c. 2, 2-dichloroacetic acid > 3-chloropropanoic acid > 2-chloropropanoic acid > propanoic acid
d. 2, 2-dichloroacetic acid > propanoic acid > 2-chloropropanoic acid > 3-chloropropanoic acid

114. A reaction between a carbonyl compound and a Grignard reagent is termed as

a. nucleophilic addition
b. electrophilic addition
c. S_N1 reaction
d. S_N2 reaction

115. Ethanal is treated with a primary alcohol in presence of HCl gas. The reaction is known as

a. aldol condensation
b. acetal formation
c. cross aldol condensation
d. Cannizzaro reaction

116. $CH_3—CN \xrightarrow{Na/C_2H_5OH} A \xrightarrow{HNO_2} B \xrightarrow[573\ K]{Cu} C$

here C is

a. $CH_3—CH_2NHOH$
b. $CH_3—CHO$
c. $CH_3CO—NH_2$
d. $CH_3—COOH$

117. In nucleic acids the nucleotides are linked by

a. ester linkage *b.* amide linkage
c. peptide linkage *d.* glycosidic linkage

118. Amino acids exist as zwitter ions at

a. acidic pH *b.* basic pH
c. neutral pH *d.* isoelectric pH

119. Which one of the following is an addition polymer?

a. Terylene *b.* Nylon-6, 6
c. Neoprene *d.* Teflon

120. Among the following compounds, the only one which is not an artificial sweetening agent is

a. aspartame *b.* sucrose
c. sucralose *d.* saccharin

MATHEMATICS

121. Which of the following is an empty set?

a. $\{x|x$ is a real number and $x^2 - 1 = 0\}$

b. $\{x|x$ is a real number and $x^2 + 3 = 0\}$

c. $\{x|x$ is a real number and $x^2 - 9 = 0\}$

d. $\{x|x$ is a real number and $x^2 = x + 2\}$

122. The number of proper subsets of a set having $n+1$ elements is

a. 2^{n+1} *b.* $2^{n+1} - 1$

c. $2^{n+1} - 2$ *d.* 2^{n-2}

123. The domain of the function $y = \sqrt{x-2} + \sqrt{1-x}$ is

a. $x \le 2$ *b.* $x \ge 2$

c. Null set *d.* The set of all numbers

124. If A = {1, 2, 3, 4}, then which one of the following is reflexive?

a. {(1, 1), (2, 3), (3, 3)}

b. {(1, 1), (2, 2), (3, 3), (4, 4)}

c. {(1, 2), (2, 1) (3, 2), (2, 3)}

d. {(1, 2), (1, 3), (1, 4)}

125. If $f(x) = \frac{2x-3}{3x+4}$, then $f^{-1}\left(\frac{-4}{3}\right) =$

a. Zero *b.* $\frac{3}{4}$

c. $-\frac{2}{3}$ *d.* None of these

126. If $f:[0, \infty) \to [2, \infty)$ is given by $f(x) = x + \frac{1}{x}$, then $f^{-1}(x)$ equals

a. $\frac{x + \sqrt{x^2 - 4}}{2}$ *b.* $\frac{x}{1 + x^2}$

c. $\frac{2x - \sqrt{x^2 - 4}}{2}$ *d.* $1 + \sqrt{x^2 - 4}$

127. The value of $\frac{\tan 330° \sec 420° \sin 300°}{\tan 135° \sin 210° \sec 315°}$ is equal to

a. $\frac{1}{\sqrt{2}}$ *b.* $\sqrt{2}$ *c.* $\frac{1}{\sqrt{3}}$ *d.* $\sqrt{3}$

128. If $\sin(120 - A) = \sin(120 - B)$ and $0 < A, B < \pi$ then all values of A and B are given by

a. $A + B = \frac{\pi}{3}$ *b.* $A = B$ or $A + B = \frac{\pi}{3}$

c. $A = B$ *d.* $A + B = 0$

129. If $\cot^{-1}\frac{1}{5} + \cot^{-1}\frac{1}{3} - \cot^{-1}\frac{4}{7} = \cot^{-1} x$, then x is equal to

a. 0 *b.* 3 *c.* $\frac{1}{\sqrt{3}}$ *d.* ∞

130. If $1 + i = (x + iy)(u + iv)$, then $\tan^{-1}\left(\frac{y}{x}\right) + \cot^{-1}\left(\frac{u}{v}\right)$ has the value

a. $n\pi + \frac{\pi}{6}, n \in I$ *b.* $2n\pi + \frac{\pi}{3}, n \in I$

c. $n\pi + \frac{\pi}{4}, n \in I$ *d.* $n\pi - \frac{\pi}{3}, n \in I$

131. For a natural number n, which one is the correct statement?

a. $1^3 + 2^3 + ... + n^3 = (1 + 2 + ... + n)^2$

b. $1^3 + 2^3 + ... + n^3 > (1 + 2 + ... + n)^2$

c. $1^3 + 2^3 + ... + n^3 < (1 + 2 + ... + n)^2$

d. $1^3 + 2^3 + ... + n^3 \ne (1 + 2 + ... + n)^2$

132. If a complex number lies in the III quadrant. Find the quadrant in which its conjugate lies.

a. I quadrant *b.* II quadrant

c. III quadrant *d.* IV quadrant

133. If β satisfies the inequation $x^2 - x - 6 > 0$, then a value exists for

a. $\cos^{-1}(\cos\beta)$ *b.* $\sec(\sec^{-1}\beta)$

c. $\tan(\tan^{-1}\beta)$ *d.* $\sin(\sin^{-1}\beta)$

134. If ${}^{56}P_{r+6} : {}^{54}P_{r+3} = 30800 : 1$, then

a. $r = 41$ *b.* $r = 51$

c. $r = 31$ *d.* None of these

135. If the coefficient of x^5 and x^6 in $\left(2 + \frac{x}{3}\right)^n$ are equal, then n is

a. 51 *b.* 31

c. 41 *d.* None of these

136. The term independent of x in $\left[\sqrt{\left(\frac{x}{3}\right)} + \sqrt{\left(\frac{3}{2x^2}\right)}\right]^{10}$ is

a. $\frac{5}{4}$ *b.* $\frac{7}{4}$

c. $\frac{9}{4}$ *d.* None of these

137. The sum of the series

$$\frac{1^2}{1\cdot 2}+\frac{1^2+2^2}{2\cdot 3}+\frac{1^2+2^2+3^2}{3\cdot 4}+\ldots \text{upto 20}$$

terms is

a. $\frac{205}{3}$ *b.* $\frac{200}{3}$

c. $\frac{220}{3}$ *d.* $\frac{210}{3}$

138. The angle between lines $\sqrt{3}x+y=1$ and $x+\sqrt{3}y=1$ is

a. $\frac{\pi}{6}$ *b.* $\frac{3\pi}{4}$

c. $\frac{5\pi}{2}$ *d.* $\frac{\pi}{3}$

139. If a is a parameter then an equation of a family of lines having the sum of the intercepts on axes equal to 7 is

a. $4x+3y=12a$

b. $3x+4y=7a$

c. $7x+ay=a(7-a)$

d. $ay=(7-a)(a-x)$

140. The equation of the ellipse whose centre is at the origin and the X-axis is major axis, which passes through the points $(-3, 1)$ and $(2, -2)$ is

a. $5x^2+3y^2=32$

b. $3x^2+5y^2=32$

c. $5x^2-3y^2=32$

d. $3x^2+5y^2+32=0$

141. The equation of the lines joining the vertex of the parabola $y^2=6x$ to the point on it which have abscissa 24 are

a. $y\pm 2x=0$ *b.* $2y\pm x=0$

c. $x\pm y=0$ *d.* $2x\pm 3y=0$

142. From a point $P(a, b, c)$ perpendicular PA, PB are drawn to yz and zx planes. Find the equation of the plane OAB, where O is the origin.

a. $bcx+cay+abz=0$

b. $bcx+cay-abz=0$

c. $bcx-cay+abz=0$

d. $-bcx+cay+abz=0$

143. Find the distance of a point $(1, 2, 3)$ from the plane $3y+4z+4=0$.

a. 4.4 *b.* 4 *c.* 4.04 *d.* 4.44

144. AB and CD are two line segments, where $A(2, 3, 0)$, $B(6, 9, 0)$, $C(-6, -9, 0)$. P and Q are mid-point of AB and CD, respectively and L is the mid-point of PQ. Find the distance of L from the plane $3x+4z+25=0$

a. 25 *b.* 15 *c.* 5 *d.* 40

145. Determine the plane through the intersection of the planes $x+2y+3z-4=0$ and $2x+y-z+5=0$ and perpendicular to the plane $5x+3y+6z+8=0$

a. $-51x-15y-50z-173=0$

b. $51x+15y-50z+173=0$

c. $51x-15y+50z-173=0$

d. $51x+50y+15z+173=0$

146. $\lim_{x\to 0}\frac{xa^x-x}{1-\cos x}$ is equal to

a. $\log a$ *b.* $\frac{1}{2}\log a$ *c.* $2\log a$ *d.* $2\log 2$

147. If $y=\tan x$, then $\frac{d^2y}{dx^2}=$

a. $1+y^2$ *b.* $2y(1+y^2)$

c. $y(1+y^2)$ *d.* $2y(1-y^2)$

148. If $y=\tan^{-1}\left(\frac{a-x}{1+ax}\right)$, then $\frac{dy}{dx}=$

a. $\frac{1}{(1+x^2)}$ *b.* $\frac{a}{(1+ax^2)}$

c. $-\frac{1}{(1+x^2)}$ *d.* $\frac{x}{(1+x^2)}$

149. If $f(x)=\begin{cases}[x]+[-x], & x\neq 2\\ K, & x=2\end{cases}$, then $f(x)$ is continuous at $x=2$, provided K is equal to

a. 2 *b.* 1 *c.* -1 *d.* 0

150. The curve $x^2-xy+y^2=27$ has tangents parallel to X-axis at

a. $(-3, -6)$ and $(3, -6)$

b. $(3, 6)$ and $(-3, -6)$

c. $(-3, 6)$ and $(-3, -6)$

d. $(3, -6)$ and $(-3, 6)$

151. The point on the circle $x^2+y^2=2$ at the abscissa and ordinate increase at the same ate is

a. $(-1, -1)$ *b.* $(1, -1)$

c. $(1, 1)$ *d.* $(-1, 4)$

152. A spherical balloon is being inflated at the rate of 35 cm/min. When its radius is 7 cm, its surface area increases at the rate of

a. $10\text{ cm}^2/\text{min}$ *b.* $15\text{ cm}^2/\text{min}$

c. $20\text{ cm}^2/\text{min}$ *d.* $25\text{ cm}^2/\text{min}$

153. $\int e^x(\cos x - \sin x)\,dx$ is equal to

a. $e^x \cos x + C$ **b.** $e^x \sin x + C$
c. $-e^x \cos x + C$ **d.** $-e^x \sin x + C$

154. The solution of $(2x - 10y^3)\dfrac{dy}{dx} + y = 0$ is

a. $xy^2 = 2y^5 + C$ **b.** $yx^2 = 2y^5 + C$
c. $x^2y^2 = 2y^5 + C$ **d.** None of these

155. The solution of
$(x+y)^2\left(x\dfrac{dy}{dx} + y\right) = xy\left(1 + \dfrac{dy}{dx}\right)$ is

a. $\log(xy) = -\dfrac{1}{x+y} + C$

b. $\log\left(\dfrac{x}{y}\right) = -\dfrac{1}{x+y} + C$

c. $\log(xy) = \dfrac{1}{x-y} + C$

d. None of the above

156. Find $\sin\theta$, if θ is the angle between the vectors $3\hat{i} + \hat{j} + 2\hat{k}$ and $\hat{i} + \hat{j} + 2\hat{k}$.

a. $\sqrt{\dfrac{5}{21}}$ **b.** $\dfrac{5}{\sqrt{21}}$ **c.** $\dfrac{4}{\sqrt{21}}$ **d.** $\sqrt{\dfrac{3}{21}}$

157. If **a** and **b** are two vectors of magnitude 2, each inclined at an $\angle 60°$, then angle between **a** and **a** + **b** is

a. 30° **b.** 45° **c.** 60° **d.** 90°

158. If $\begin{bmatrix} -2 & 5 \\ 3 & -1 \end{bmatrix}\begin{bmatrix} x \\ y \end{bmatrix} = \begin{bmatrix} 1 & 2 \\ 3 & 4 \end{bmatrix}\begin{bmatrix} 3 \\ -1 \end{bmatrix}$, then (x, y) is

a. (1, 2) **b.** (− 1, 2) **c.** (1, − 2) **d.** (2, 1)

159. If the product of the matrix $B = \begin{bmatrix} 2 & 6 & 4 \\ 1 & 0 & 1 \\ -1 & 1 & -1 \end{bmatrix}$

with a matrix A has the inverse $C = \begin{bmatrix} -1 & 0 & 1 \\ 1 & 1 & 3 \\ 2 & 0 & 2 \end{bmatrix}$,

then A^{-1} equals

a. $\begin{bmatrix} -3 & -5 & 5 \\ 0 & 9 & 14 \\ 2 & 2 & 9 \end{bmatrix}$ **b.** $\begin{bmatrix} -3 & 5 & 5 \\ 0 & 0 & 9 \\ 2 & 14 & 16 \end{bmatrix}$

c. $\begin{bmatrix} -3 & -5 & -5 \\ 0 & 0 & 2 \\ 2 & 14 & 6 \end{bmatrix}$ **d.** $\begin{bmatrix} -3 & -5 & -5 \\ 0 & 9 & 2 \\ 2 & 14 & 6 \end{bmatrix}$

160. A and B are two matrices such that $AB = B$, $BA = A$, then $A^2 + B^2 =$

a. $2AB$ **b.** $2BA$ **c.** $A + B$ **d.** AB

161. If α, β, γ are the roots of $x^3 + a^2x + b = 0$, then the value of $\begin{vmatrix} \alpha & \beta & \gamma \\ \beta & \gamma & \alpha \\ \gamma & \alpha & \beta \end{vmatrix}$ is

a. $-a^3$ **b.** $a^3 - 3b$ **c.** a^3 **d.** 0

162. The value of $\begin{vmatrix} 4 & 4 & 4 \\ (a+a^{-1})^2 & (b+b^{-1})^2 & (c+c^{-1})^2 \\ (a-a^{-1})^2 & (b-b^{-1})^2 & (c-c^{-1})^2 \end{vmatrix}$ is

a. 0 **b.** $4abc$
c. $4(abc)^{-1}$ **d.** $4[abc + (abc)^{-1}]$

163. Given that, $P(A) = 0.1$, $P(B \mid A) = 0.6$ and $P(B \mid A^C) = 0.3$ what is $P(A \mid B) = ?$

a. $\dfrac{2}{11}$ **b.** $\dfrac{4}{11}$ **c.** $\dfrac{7}{11}$ **d.** $\dfrac{9}{11}$

164. A card is picked at random from a pack of cards. Given that the picked card is a queen, what is the probability that it is a spade?

a. $\dfrac{1}{3}$ **b.** $\dfrac{4}{13}$ **c.** $\dfrac{1}{4}$ **d.** $\dfrac{1}{2}$

165. If the occurrence of an event A implies that occurrence of an event B, the $P(A^C \cap B^C)$ is equal to

a. $P(B^C)$ **b.** $P(A^C)\,P(B^C)$
c. $P(A^C)$ **d.** $1 - P(A \cap B)$

166. A certain item is manufactured by 3 factory F_1, F_2 and F_3 with 30% of item made in F_1, 20% in F_2 and 50% in F_3. It is found that 2% of the items produced by F_1. 3% of the items produced by F_2 and 4% of the items produced by F_3 are defective. Suppose that an items selected at random from the stock is found defective. What is the probability that the item came from F_1?

a. $\dfrac{1}{16}$ **b.** $\dfrac{1}{8}$ **c.** $\dfrac{1}{3}$ **d.** $\dfrac{3}{16}$

167. Ram obtained 60 and 85 in first two unit tests. The minimum marks he should get in the third test to have an average of atleast 55 marks is

a. $x \geq 20$ **b.** $x \leq 20$
c. $x > 20$ **d.** $x < 20$

168. Coefficient of variation of two distributions are 60 and 70, and their standard deviation are 21 and 16 respectively. What are their arithmetic means?

a. 35, 20   *b.* 35, 22.85
c. 30, 22.85   *d.* 30, 20

169. Consider an experiment E in which a box contains 10 identical tickets numbered 1 to 10 and 2 tickets are drawn at random from the box. What is the probability that both the tickets have even number on them?

a. $\frac{4}{9}$ *b.* $\frac{1}{3}$ *c.* $\frac{2}{9}$ *d.* $\frac{1}{9}$

170. Which of the following is not a logical statement?

a. Two non-empty sets have always a non-empty intersection.
b. The real number '*n*' is less than 2.
c. Two individuals are always related.
d. None of the above

171. A mathematical model written to construct a maximum area rectangle out of a thread of length 10 cm is given by maximise lb.
Such that $2(l+b)=10$, $l, b>0$, where l and b are the length and breadth of the rectangle.
This is not a linear programming problem because

a. l and b is always positive.
b. first constraints is an equation.
c. the objective function is no maximise.
d. objective function is not linear.

172. Laksmi wants to buy few bangles and ear drops. Each bangle costs ₹ 5 and each ear drop costs ₹ 10. She should buy atleast 6 bangles and atmost 2 ear drops. If she buys x bangles and y ear drops with minimum expenditure, then the formulation for this linear programming is

a. Maximize $5x+10y$ subject to $x \geq 6$,$y \leq 2$, x, $y \geq 0$.
b. Minimise $5x+10y$ subject to $x \geq 6$, $y \leq 2$, $x, y \geq 0$.
c. Maximise $x+y$ subject to $5x+10y \leq 50$, $x, y \geq 0$.
d. Maximise $6x+2y$ subject to $5x+10y \leq 50$, x, $y \geq 0$.

173. The function $f(x)=\log(x+\sqrt{x^2+1})$ is

a. an even function.
b. an odd function.
c. a periodic function.
d. neither an even nor an odd function.

174. The number of real roots of the equation $x^4+\sqrt{x^4+20}=22$ is

a. 4   *b.* 2   *c.* 0   *d.* 1

175. If the sum of first n natural numbers is $\frac{1}{78}$ times the sum their cubes, then the value of n is

a. 11   *b.* 12   *c.* 13   *d.* 14

176. If a polygon of n sides 275 diagonals, then n is equal to

a. 25   *b.* 35   *c.* 20   *d.* 15

177. 7^9+9^7 is divisible by

a. 128   *b.* 24   *c.* 64   *d.* 72

178. $\begin{vmatrix} 1 & 1 & 1 \\ a & b & c \\ a^2-bc & b^2-ca & c^2-ab \end{vmatrix}$ is equal to

a. 0   *b.* 1
c. abc *d.* $(a-b)(b-c)(c-a)$

179. The number of values of x in $[0, 2\pi]$ satisfying the equation $3\cos 2x-10\cos x+7=0$ is

a. 1   *b.* 2   *c.* 3   *d.* 4

180. $\lim_{x \to -\infty} \frac{2x-1}{\sqrt{x^2+2x+1}}$ is equal to

a. 2   *b.* −2   *c.* 1   *d.* −1

ANSWERS

Physics

1. (b)	**2.** (b)	**3.** (c)	**4.** (*)	**5.** (b)	**6.** (b)	**7.** (a)	**8.** (a)	**9.** (a)	**10.** (c)
11. (c)	**12.** (a)	**13.** (c)	**14.** (d)	**15.** (d)	**16.** (b)	**17.** (b)	**18.** (b)	**19.** (b)	**20.** (b)
21. (b)	**22.** (b)	**23.** (b)	**24.** (b)	**25.** (b)	**26.** (c)	**27.** (b)	**28.** (c)	**29.** (b)	**30.** (a)
31. (b)	**32.** (c)	**33.** (b)	**34.** (d)	**35.** (d)	**36.** (a)	**37.** (b)	**38.** (c)	**39.** (a)	**40.** (b)
41. (c)	**42.** (c)	**43.** (d)	**44.** (b)	**45.** (c)	**46.** (a)	**47.** (c)	**48.** (a)	**49.** (c)	**50.** (b)
51. (a)	**52.** (c)	**53.** (b)	**54.** (c)	**55.** (c)	**56.** (c)	**57.** (b)	**58.** (c)	**59.** (*)	**60.** (c)

Chemistry

61. (d)	**62.** (c)	**63.** (a)	**64.** (d)	**65.** (c)	**66.** (a)	**67.** (b)	**68.** (d)	**69.** (d)	**70.** (a)
71. (b)	**72.** (a)	**73.** (c)	**74.** (d)	**75.** (b)	**76.** (d)	**77.** (b)	**78.** (b)	**79.** (a)	**80.** (d)
81. (b)	**82.** (b)	**83.** (c)	**84.** (d)	**85.** (b)	**86.** (b)	**87.** (d)	**88.** (a)	**89.** (a)	**90.** (a)
91. (b)	**92.** (a)	**93.** (c)	**94.** (b)	**95.** (c)	**96.** (c)	**97.** (b)	**98.** (b)	**99.** (b)	**100.** (d)
101. (c)	**102.** (d)	**103.** (b)	**104.** (c)	**105.** (b,d)	**106.** (d)	**107.** (b)	**108.** (c)	**109.** (a)	**110.** (d)
111. (d)	**112.** (b)	**113.** (a)	**114.** (a)	**115.** (b)	**116.** (b)	**117.** (a)	**118.** (d)	**119.** (c, d)	**120.** (b)

Mathematics

121. (b)	**122.** (b)	**123.** (c)	**124.** (b)	**125.** (d)	**126.** (a)	**127.** (b)	**128.** (b)	**129.** (a)	**130.** (c)
131. (a)	**132.** (b)	**133.** (b)	**134.** (a)	**135.** (c)	**136.** (d)	**137.** (c)	**138.** (a)	**139.** (d)	**140.** (b)
141. (b)	**142.** (b)	**143.** (a)	**144.** (c)	**145.** (b)	**146.** (c)	**147.** (b)	**148.** (c)	**149.** (c)	**150.** (b)
151. (b)	**152.** (a)	**153.** (a)	**154.** (a)	**155.** (a)	**156.** (a)	**157.** (a)	**158.** (d)	**159.** (d)	**160.** (c)
161. (d)	**162.** (a)	**163.** (a)	**164.** (c)	**165.** (a)	**166.** (d)	**167.** (a)	**168.** (b)	**169.** (c)	**170.** (d)
171. (d)	**172.** (b)	**173.** (b)	**174.** (b)	**175.** (b)	**176.** (a)	**177.** (c)	**178.** (a)	**179.** (d)	**180.** (b)

Note (*) None of the option is correct.

HINTS & SOLUTIONS

Physics

1. *(b)* The laws of conservation have a deep connection with symmetries of nature. This is first theorised by Noether. Noether's first theorem states that any differentiable symmetry of the action of a physical system has a corresponding conservation law. This means that conservation laws are observed because of the symmetries of nature.

2. *(b)* Given, height of the tower, $h_1 = 200$ m

   If R be the radius of the earth, then coverage range,

$$d = \sqrt{2Rh} \Rightarrow d \propto \sqrt{h}$$

$$\Rightarrow \quad \frac{d_1}{d_2} = \sqrt{\frac{h_1}{h_2}}$$

Since, $\quad d_2 = 3d_1$

$$\therefore \quad \frac{d_1}{3d_1} = \sqrt{\frac{h_1}{h_2}}$$

$$\Rightarrow \quad \frac{1}{3} = \sqrt{\frac{200}{h_2}}$$

$$\Rightarrow \quad \frac{1}{9} = \frac{200}{h_2}$$

$$\Rightarrow \quad h_2 = 1800 \text{ m}$$

∴ Increase in the height of the tower

= 1800 m − 200 m = 1600 m

3. *(c)* The value of g at height h from the surface of the earth is given as

$$g_h = \frac{g}{\left(1 + \frac{h}{R_e}\right)^2}$$

$$= \frac{g}{\left(1 + \frac{R_e/2}{R_e}\right)^2} \qquad \left(h = \frac{R_e}{2}\right)$$

$$= \frac{g}{\left(1 + \frac{1}{2}\right)^2} = \frac{4g}{9}$$

4. *(*)* The given situation is shown below

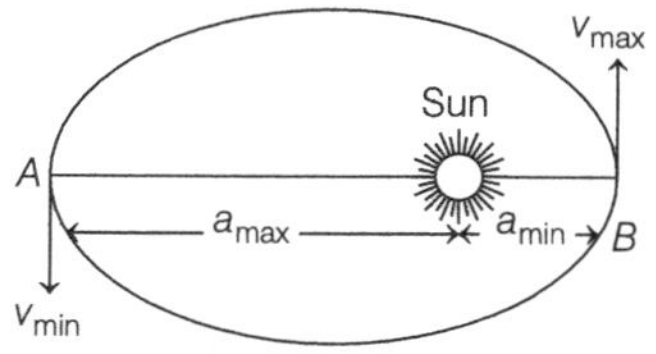

$$a_{max} = 1.4 \times 10^{12} \text{ m}$$

$$a_{min} = 7 \times 10^{10} \text{ m}$$

The velocity of the comet is maximum, when it is nearest to the sun and minimum when it is farthest from the sun.

$$\therefore \quad v_{max} = 6 \times 10^{14} \text{ m/s}$$

Applying the law of conservation of angular momentum at points A and B, we get

$$mv_{min}a_{max} = mv_{max}a_{min} \qquad (\because L = mvr)$$

$$\Rightarrow \quad v_{min} = \frac{v_{max} \times a_{min}}{a_{max}}$$

$$= \frac{6 \times 10^{14} \times 7 \times 10^{10}}{1.4 \times 10^{12}}$$

$$= 3 \times 10^{13} \text{ ms}^{-1}$$

No option is correct.

5. *(b)* The given situation is shown below

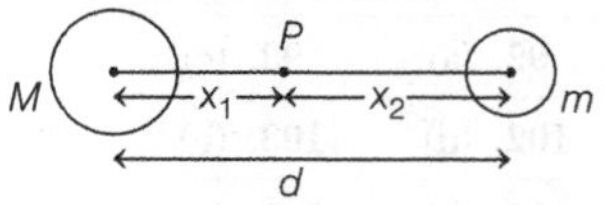

Let P be the location of centre of mass.

If x_1 and x_2 be the distances of the centre of mass P from the two bodies of mass M and $m (M > m)$ respectively, then

$$Mx_1 = mx_2$$

$$\Rightarrow \quad \frac{x_1}{x_2} = \frac{m}{M}$$

Since, $\quad M > m$

$$\therefore \quad \frac{x_1}{x_2} < 1$$

$$\Rightarrow \quad x_1 < x_2$$

Thus, position of centre of mass is closer to the heavier body.

6. *(b)* Volume of water in tank, $V = 30 \text{ m}^3$

   Time taken to fill the tank,

   $t = 15 \text{ min} = 15 \times 60 = 900$ s

   Height of the tank, $h = 40$ m

   ∴ Mass of pumped water, m = Volume × Density of water

$$= 30 \times 10^3 = 3 \times 10^4 \text{ kg}$$

   Work done by the pump to fill the tank,

$$W = mgh$$

$$= 3 \times 10^4 \times 10 \times 40$$

$$= 1.2 \times 10^7 \text{ J}$$

∴ Output power of the pump,

$$P_o = \frac{W}{t} = \frac{1.2 \times 10^7}{900} = \frac{4}{3} \times 10^4 \text{ W}$$

As we know, efficiency $= \dfrac{\text{Output power } (P_o)}{\text{Input power } (P_i)}$

$$\Rightarrow \quad 0.3 = \frac{4/3 \times 10^4}{P_i}$$

$$\Rightarrow \quad P_i = \frac{4 \times 10^4}{3 \times 0.3} = 4.4 \times 10^4 \text{ W} = 44 \text{ kW}$$

7. *(a)* Given, resistance of galvanometer, $R_g = 2.5\ \Omega$

Full scale deflection current,

$$I_g = 50 \text{ mA} = 50 \times 10^{-3} \text{ A}$$
$$= 0.05 \text{ A}$$

Range of galvanometer is (0-5)A

$$\therefore \quad I = 5 \text{ A}$$

If R_s be the shunt resistance, then

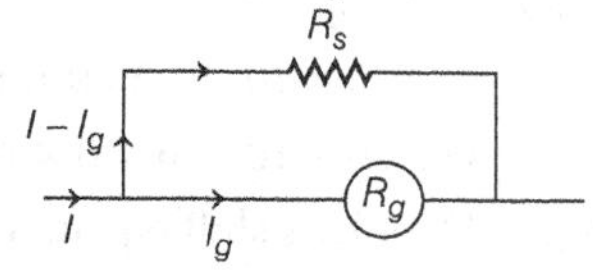

$$(I - I_g)R_s = I_g R_g$$

$$\Rightarrow \quad R_s = \frac{I_g R_g}{I - I_g}$$

$$= \frac{0.05 \times 2.5}{5 - 0.05}$$

$$= 0.025\ \Omega = 2.5 \times 10^{-2}\ \Omega$$

8. *(a)* In a Zener diode, voltage across it remains constant even when current varies much or wide range. This property of the Zener diode is used to regulate the voltage supply.

9. *(a)* In an inelastic collision, momentum is conserved but kinetic energy is not conserved.

10. *(c)* Given, $\Delta I = 0.01$ A

$$\Delta\phi = 2 \times 10^{-2} \text{ Wb}$$

We know that, $\Delta\phi = M\Delta I$

where, M is mutual inductance between the coils.

$$\therefore \quad M = \frac{\Delta\phi}{\Delta I}$$

$$= \frac{2 \times 10^{-2}}{0.01} = 2 \text{ H}$$

11. *(c)* Given, velocity of aeroplane,

$$v = 360 \text{ kmh}^{-1}$$

$$= 360 \times \frac{5}{18} \text{ ms}^{-1} = 100 \text{ ms}^{-1}$$

Distance between the tips of wings,

$$l = 50 \text{ m}$$

Vertical component of earth's magnetic field, $B_V = 4 \times 10^{-4} \text{ Wbm}^{-2}$

$\therefore$ Induced emf, $e = B_V v l$

$$= 4 \times 10^{-4} \times 100 \times 50 = 2 \text{ V}$$

12. *(a)* The inductance in a coil plays the same role as inertia plays in mechanics.

13. *(c)* The mutual inductance between the two coils depends upon the medium and the separation between them both.

14. *(d)* Given, magnetic flux

$$\phi = 6t^2 - 5t + 1,\ R = 10\ \Omega$$

Induced emf,

$$e = -\frac{d\phi}{dt}$$

$$= -\frac{d}{dt}(6t^2 - 5t + 1)$$

$$e = -12t + 5$$

At $t = 0.253$ s, $e = -12 \times 0.253 + 5$

$$= -3.036 + 5 = 1.964 \text{ V}$$

$\therefore$ Induced current, $I = \dfrac{e}{R}$

$$= \frac{1.964}{10} = 0.1964 \text{ A} \simeq 0.2 \text{ A}$$

15. *(d)* In electromagnetic wave, both electric and magnetic fields vary with time.

16. *(b)* For refraction through prism,

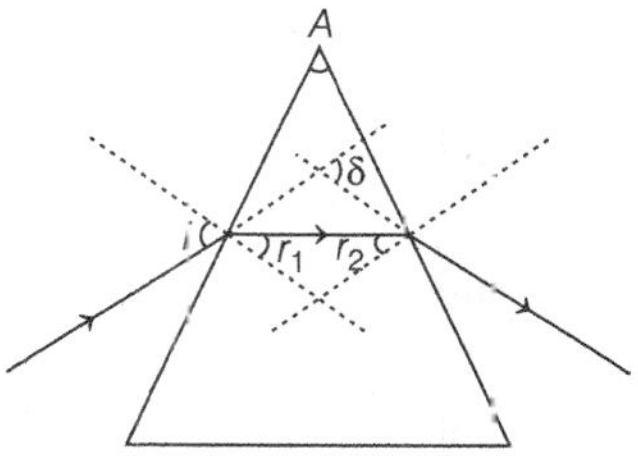

$$A = r_1 + r_2$$

For the case of minimum deviation,

$$r_1 = r_2 = r$$

$$\therefore \quad A = r + r = 2r$$

17. *(b)* Image formed by a concave mirror is erect, enlarged and virtual only when object is placed between pole and focus as shown below,

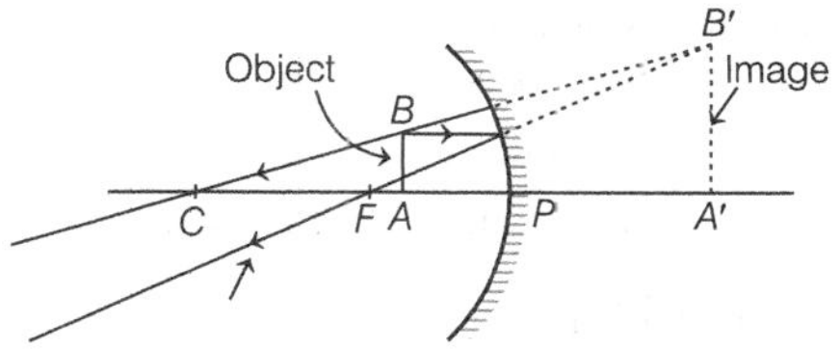

18. *(b)* Number of images when an object is placed symmetrically between plane mirrors inclined at an angle θ, is given as

$$n = \frac{360}{\theta} - 1$$

Here, $\theta = 90°$

$$\therefore \quad n = \frac{360}{90} - 1 = 4 - 1 = 3$$

19. *(b)* Given, $V_m = 300$ V, $\omega = 400$ rads^{-1}

$$R = 3\,\Omega,\ L = 20\text{ mH} = 20 \times 10^{-3}\text{ H}$$

and $$C = 625\,\mu\text{F} = 625 \times 10^{-6}\text{ F}$$

Impedance of the circuit,

$$Z = \sqrt{R^2 + (X_L - X_C)^2}$$

Here, $$X_L = \omega L = 400 \times 20 \times 10^{-3} = 8\Omega$$

and $$X_C = \frac{1}{\omega C} = \frac{1}{400 \times 625 \times 10^{-6}} = 4\ \Omega$$

$$Z = \sqrt{3^2 + (8-4)^2} = \sqrt{25} = 5\Omega$$

$\therefore$ Peak current, $I_m = \frac{V_m}{Z} = \frac{300}{5} = 60$ A

20. *(b)* Given, angle of prism, $A = 60°$

$$\mu = \sqrt{2}$$

We know that,

$$\mu = \frac{\sin\left(\frac{A + \delta_m}{2}\right)}{\sin A/2}$$

$$\Rightarrow \quad \sqrt{2} = \frac{\sin\left(\frac{60° + \delta_m}{2}\right)}{\sin\frac{60}{2}}$$

$$\Rightarrow \quad \sin\left(\frac{60° + \delta_m}{2}\right) = \sqrt{2}\sin 30°$$

$$\Rightarrow \quad \sin\left(\frac{60° + \delta_m}{2}\right) = \frac{1}{\sqrt{2}}$$

$$\Rightarrow \quad \sin\left(\frac{60° + \delta_m}{2}\right) = \sin 45°$$

$$\Rightarrow \quad \frac{60° + \delta_m}{2} = 45°$$

$$\Rightarrow \quad \delta_m = 30°$$

In the case of minimum deviation, angle of incidence,

$$i = \frac{A + \delta_m}{2} = \frac{60° + 30°}{2} = 45°$$

21. *(b)* Given, wavelength of light used,

$$\lambda = 5000\,\text{Å} = 5 \times 10^{-7}\text{ m}$$

$$D = 2\text{ m}$$

$$d = 5\text{ mm} = 5 \times 10^{-3}\text{ m}$$

$\therefore$ Fringe width, $\beta = \frac{D\lambda}{d}$

$$= \frac{2 \times 5 \times 10^{-7}}{5 \times 10^{-3}} = 2 \times 10^{-4}\text{ m}$$

22. *(b)* Given, distance between source and screen, $D = 2$ m

Distance of first minimum from the central maximum, $y = 5\text{ mm} = 5 \times 10^{-3}$ m

Wavelength, $\lambda = 5 \times 10^{-7}$ m

We know that,

$$y_n = \frac{n\lambda D}{d}$$

For first minimum, $n = 1$

$$\therefore \quad y_1 = \frac{\lambda D}{d}$$

$$\Rightarrow \quad d = \frac{\lambda D}{y_1} = \frac{5 \times 10^{-7} \times 2}{5 \times 10^{-3}} = 2 \times 10^{-4}\text{ m}$$

23. *(b)* Given, wavelength of sodium line,

$$\lambda = 589.0\text{ nm} = 5.89 \times 10^{-7}\text{ m}$$

Observed wavelength,

$$\lambda' = 589.6\text{ nm} = 5.896 \times 10^{-7}\text{m}$$

$\therefore$ Change in wavelength,

$$\Delta\lambda = \lambda' - \lambda$$
$$= 5.896 \times 10^{-7} - 5.89 \times 10^{-7}$$
$$= 0.006 \times 10^{-7}\text{ m} = 6 \times 10^{-10}\text{ m}$$

According to Doppler's shift equation,
Speed of galaxy is given as

$$v = \frac{\Delta\lambda}{\lambda} \times c$$

$$= \frac{6 \times 10^{-10}}{5.89 \times 10^{-7}} \times 3 \times 10^8$$

$$= 3.06 \times 10^5\text{ m/s}$$

$$= 306 \times 10^3\text{ m/s} = 306\text{ km/s}$$

24. *(b)* In Newton's ring experiment, diameter of nth dark ring,

$$D_n = 2\sqrt{n\lambda R}$$

$$\Rightarrow \quad R = \frac{D_n^2}{4n\lambda} \quad \ldots \text{(i)}$$

Given, $n = 10$, $D_{10} = 0.005$ m

$$\lambda = 5000\,\text{Å} = 5 \times 10^{-7}\text{ m}$$

$\therefore$ Putting these values in Eq. (i), we get

$$R = \frac{(0.005)^2}{4 \times 10 \times 5 \times 10^{-7}} = 1.25\text{ m}$$

25. *(b)* The amount of energy required to separate a hydrogen atom into a proton and an electron is equal to its ionisation energy which is equal to 13.6 eV.

26. *(c)* Given, $m = 1\text{ g} = 10^{-3}$ kg

According to Einstein's mass-energy equation,

$$E = mc^2 = 10^{-3} \times (3 \times 10^8)^2 = 9 \times 10^{13}\text{ J}$$

27. *(b)* As, radius of bigger drop, $R = n^{1/3}\,r = 2^{1/3}r$

$$\Rightarrow R^2 = 2^{2/3}\,r^2 \Rightarrow \frac{r^2}{R^2} \text{ or } 2^{-2/3}$$

$$\frac{\text{Initial surface energy}}{\text{Final surface energy}} = \frac{2(4\pi r^2 T)}{(4\,\pi R^2 T)} = 2\left(\frac{r^2}{R^2}\right)$$

$$= 2 \times 2^{-2/3} = 2^{1/3} \text{ or } 2^{1/3} : 1$$

28. *(c)* Given, mass is equivalent to 1 amu, i.e. $m = 1$ amu

$$= 1.6605 \times 10^{-27} \text{ kg}$$

According to Einstein's mass-energy equivalent equation,

$$E = mc^2$$
$$= 1.6605 \times 10^{-27} \times (3 \times 10^8)^2$$
$$= 1.49 \times 10^{-10} \text{ J}$$
$$= \frac{1.49 \times 10^{-10}}{1.6 \times 10^{-19}} \text{ eV}$$
$$= 931.5 \times 10^6 \text{ eV}$$
$$= 931.5 \text{ MeV}$$

29. *(b)* Voltage gain of first amplifier,

$$A_1 = 10$$

Voltage gain of second amplifier,

$$A_2 = 20$$

Input signal voltage,

$$V_i = 0.01 \text{ V}$$

Total voltage gain, when two amplifiers are connected in series (cascaded), is given as

$$A = A_1 A_2 = 10 \times 20 = 200$$

We know that, voltage gain

$$A = \frac{\text{output voltage } (V_o)}{\text{input voltage } (V_i)}$$

$$\Rightarrow \quad 200 = \frac{V_o}{0.01}$$

$$\Rightarrow \quad V_o = 200 \times 0.01 = 2 \text{ V}$$

30. *(a)* A transistor works as an amplifier, when emitter-base junction is in forward biased and collector-base junction is in reverse biased.

31. *(b)* In common base circuit, change in collector base voltage,

$$V_{CB} = 0.6 \text{ V}$$
$$\Delta I_C = 0.02 \text{ mA} = 2 \times 10^{-5} \text{ A}$$

$\therefore$ Output resistance,

$$R_{\text{out}} = \frac{\Delta V_{CB}}{\Delta I_C} = \frac{0.6}{2 \times 10^{-5}} = 3 \times 10^4 \ \Omega$$

32. *(c)* Repeater is used between a receiver and a transmitter to extend transmission of radiowaves in communication system, so that signal can cover longer distances or be received on the other side of an obstruction.

33. *(b)* The waves suitable for transmission of radio signals are radiowaves. Radiowaves are a type of electromagnetic radiation with wavelengths in the electromagnetic spectrum longer than infrared radiation.

34. *(d)* Given, change in length of wire, $l_1 = 2$ mm, $l_2 = ?$, length of wire, $L_1 = 2$ m and length of another wire, $L_2 = 8$ m

Change in length, $l = \frac{FL}{AY} = \frac{FL^2}{(A \cdot L)Y} = \frac{FL^2}{VY}$

$[\because V = A \cdot L]$

where, Y is Young's modulus.

$\therefore \quad l \propto L^2 \quad$ (as V, Y and F are constants)

$$\frac{l_2}{l_1} = \left(\frac{L_2}{L_1}\right)^2 = \left(\frac{8}{2}\right)^2 = 16$$

$$\Rightarrow \quad l_2 = 16 l_1 = 16 \times 2 \text{ mm}$$
$$= 32 \text{ mm} = 3.2 \text{ cm}$$

35. *(d)* The given situation is shown below

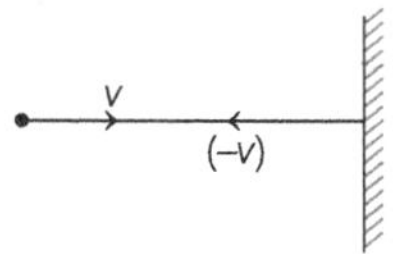

Change in momentum,

$$\Delta p = p_f - p_i = m(-v) - (mv) = -mv - mv = -2mv$$

36. *(a)* Mass of the monkey, $m = 40$ kg

Maximum tension that the rope can bear, $T_{\max} = 600$ N

In option (a), acceleration of monkey, $a = 6 \text{ m/s}^2$ (upward)

$\therefore$ By equation of motion,

$$T - mg = ma$$
$$\Rightarrow \quad T = m(g + a)$$
$$= 40(10 + 6) = 640 \text{ N}$$

Since, $T > T_{\max}$, hence in this case, rope will break. Therefore, option (a) is correct.

In option (b), acceleration of monkey, $a = 4 \text{ m/s}^2$ (downward)

$\therefore$ By equation of motion,

$$T = m(g - a) = 40(10 - 4) = 240 \text{ N}$$

Since, $T < T_{\max}$, then the rope will not break.

In option (c), monkey climbs up with uniform speed, $v = 5$ m/s

$\therefore$ Acceleration, $a = 0 \text{ m/s}^2$

Hence, by equation of motion, $T = mg$

$$= 40 \times 10 = 400 \text{ N}$$

Since, $T < T_{\max}$, hence rope will not break.

In option (d), acceleration, $a = g$

$\therefore \quad T = m(g - a) = m(g - g) = 0$ N.

Since, $T < T_{\max}$, the rope will not break.

Therefore, only option (a) is correct.

37. *(b)* Given, mass of shell, $m_s = 20 \text{ g} = 0.02$ kg

Mass of gun, $m_g = 100$ kg

Speed of shell, $v_s = 80$ m/s

Let v_g be the speed of the recoil of gun, then according to law of conservation of linear momentum.

Total initial momentum = Total final momentum

$$\Rightarrow \quad 0 = m_s v_s + m_g v_g$$
$$\Rightarrow \quad 0 = 0.02 \times 80 + 100 v_g$$
$$\Rightarrow \quad 0 = 1.6 + 100 v_g$$

$$\Rightarrow \quad v_g = \frac{-1.6}{100}$$

$$= -1.6 \times 10^{-2} \text{ m/s} = -1.6 \text{ cm/s}$$

Negative sign indicates that gun moves in opposite direction to that of shell.

$\therefore$ Speed of recoil of gun = 1.6 cm/s

38. *(c)* The given situation is shown below

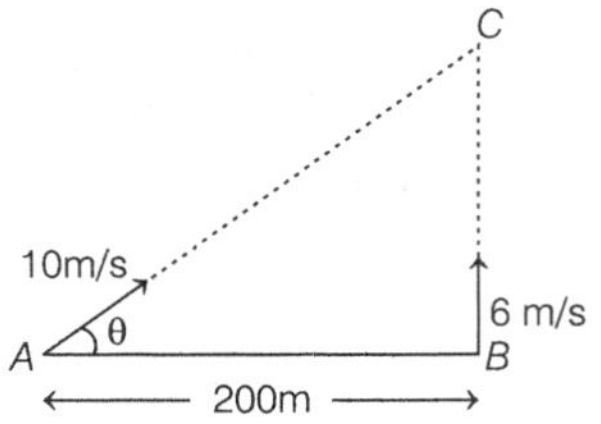

$$v_A = 10 \text{ m/s}$$

$$v_B = 6 \text{ m/s}$$

The two boys meet at point C after a time t.

Horizontal component of velocity of v_A.

$$v_{AB} = v_A \cos\theta = 10\cos\theta$$

$$= 10\left(\frac{\sqrt{10^2 - 6^2}}{10}\right)$$

$$= 8 \text{ m/s}$$

$$\therefore \quad t = \frac{AB}{v_{AB}} = \frac{200}{8} = 25 \text{ s}$$

39. *(a)* The given situation is shown below

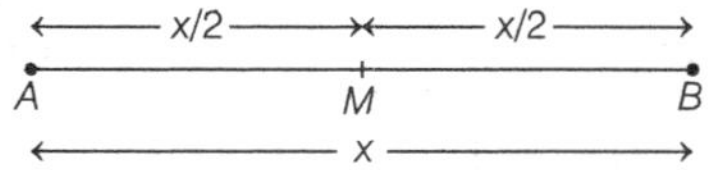

Let the distance between the two places is x km.

$$\therefore \quad AM = MB = \frac{x}{2} \text{ km}$$

Time taken by the car to cover first half (AM) with the speed of 40 km/h is given as

$$t_1 = \frac{AM}{40} = \frac{x/2}{40} = \frac{x}{80} \text{ h}$$

Similarly, time taken by the car to cover second half (MB) with the speed of 60 km/h is given as

$$t_2 = \frac{MB}{60} = \frac{x/2}{60} = \frac{x}{120} \text{ h}$$

$\therefore$ Average speed of car,

$$v_{\text{avg}} = \frac{\text{Total distance travelled}}{\text{Total time taken}}$$

$$= \frac{x}{\frac{x}{80} + \frac{x}{120}} = \frac{x}{\frac{5x}{240}}$$

$$= \frac{240}{5} = 48 \text{ km/h}$$

40. *(b)* According to Newton's law of gravitation,

$$F = \frac{Gm_1m_2}{r^2}$$

where, F = force between two objects of masses m_1 and m_2 and r = distance between m_1 and m_2.

$$\therefore \quad G = \frac{Fr^2}{m_1m_2}$$

$$\Rightarrow \quad [G] = \frac{[F][r^2]}{[m_1][m_2]} = \frac{[MLT^{-2}][L^2]}{[M][M]} = [M^{-1}L^3T^{-2}]$$

41. *(c)* We know that,

Force = Mass × Acceleration

$$\Rightarrow \quad F = m \times a$$

$$\Rightarrow \quad [F] = [m][a] = [M][LT^{-2}] = [MLT^{-2}]$$

$$\text{Pressure } (p) = \frac{\text{Force}(F)}{\text{Area}(A)}$$

$$\Rightarrow \quad [p] = \frac{[F]}{[A]} = \frac{[MLT^{-2}]}{[L^2]} = [ML^{-1}T^{-2}]$$

$$\text{Young's modulus, } Y = \frac{\text{Stress}}{\text{Strain}}$$

$$\Rightarrow \quad [Y] = \frac{[\text{Stress}]}{[\text{Strain}]} = \frac{[F/A]}{[\text{Strain}]}$$

$$= \frac{[ML^{-1}T^{-2}]}{[M^0L^0T^0]}$$

$$= [ML^{-1}T^{-2}]$$

Energy = Work done = Force × Displacement

$$\Rightarrow \quad [\text{Energy}] = [\text{Force}] \times [\text{Displacement}]$$

$$= [MLT^{-2}][L] = [ML^2T^{-2}]$$

Hence, we see that dimensions of pressure and Young's modulus is same.

42. *(c)* Temperature of object in °C,

$$T_C = 60°\text{C}$$

Temperature of object in Fahrenheit scale, $T_F = ?$

We know that,

$$\frac{T_C}{5} = \frac{T_F - 32}{9}$$

$$\Rightarrow \quad \frac{60}{5} = \frac{T_F - 32}{9}$$

$$\Rightarrow \quad 12 = \frac{T_F - 32}{9}$$

$$\Rightarrow \quad T_F = 108 + 32 = 140°\text{F}$$

43. *(d)* According to Newton's law of cooling,

$$\frac{T_1 - T_2}{t} = K\left(\frac{T_1 + T_2}{2} - T_s\right) \quad \ldots \text{(i)}$$

where, T_s is the temperature of surrounding.

For the first case, $T_1 = 94°\text{C}$, $T_2 = 86°\text{C}$

$$t = 2 \text{ min} = 120 \text{ s}, T_s = 20°\text{C}$$

$\therefore$ Putting these values in Eq. (i), we get

$$\frac{94 - 86}{120} = K\left(\frac{94 + 86}{2} - 20\right)$$

$$\Rightarrow \quad K = \frac{8}{120 \times 70} \quad \ldots \text{(ii)}$$

For the second case, $T_1 = 86°C, T_2 = 74°C$

$\therefore$ From Eq. (i), we get

$$\frac{86-74}{t} = K\left(\frac{86+74}{2} - 20\right)$$

$$\Rightarrow \quad \frac{12}{t} = \frac{8}{120 \times 70}(60)$$

$$\Rightarrow \quad t = 210 \text{ s}$$

44. *(b)* Kinetic energy of the system in SHM,

$$KE = \frac{1}{2}m\omega^2(A^2 - x^2)$$

Potential energy of the system in SHM, $PE = \frac{1}{2}m\omega^2 x^2$

According to question, PE = KE

$$\frac{1}{2}m\omega^2 x^2 = \frac{1}{2}m\omega^2(A^2 - x^2)$$

$$\Rightarrow \quad x^2 = A^2 - x^2$$

$$\Rightarrow \quad 2x^2 = A^2 \Rightarrow x = \frac{A}{\sqrt{2}}$$

45. *(c)* The universal gas law, $\frac{pV}{T}$ = constant is applicable to both isothermal and adiabatic changes.

46. *(a)* Frequency of human heart,

$$f = \frac{72}{60}\text{ Hz} = \frac{6}{5}\text{ Hz} = 1.2 \text{ Hz}$$

Time period, $T = \frac{1}{f} = \frac{1}{1.2} = 0.83$ s

47. *(c)* Given, frequency, $f = 4.2 \text{ MHz} = 4.2 \times 10^6$ Hz

Velocity of sound, $v = 1.7 \text{ kms}^{-1} = 1.7 \times 10^3 \text{ ms}^{-1}$

The wavelength of sound in the tissue is given as

$$\lambda = \frac{v}{f} \qquad (\because v = f\lambda)$$

$$= \frac{1.7 \times 10^3}{4.2 \times 10^6} = 4 \times 10^{-4} \text{ m}$$

48. *(a)* Given, velocity of sound, $v = 330$ m/s

Let frequency of horn be f and speed of the car be v_c. The frequency of the horn of the car heard by the policeman before it crosses him is given as

$$f' = f\left(\frac{v}{v - v_c}\right) \qquad \dots \text{(i)}$$

and after it crosses him is given as

$$f'' = f\left(\frac{v}{v + v_c}\right) \qquad \dots \text{(ii)}$$

From Eqs. (i) and (ii), we get

$$\frac{f''}{f'} = \frac{v - v_c}{v + v_c} = \frac{330 - v_c}{330 + v_c}$$

$$\Rightarrow \quad \frac{f''}{f'} = \frac{330 - v_c}{330 + v_c} \qquad \dots \text{(iii)}$$

Since, $f'' = f' - 15\%$ of $f' = 0.85 f'$

$\therefore$ From Eq. (iii), we get

$$\frac{0.85 f'}{f'} = \frac{330 - v_c}{330 + v_c}$$

$$\Rightarrow \quad 0.85 = \frac{330 - v_c}{330 + v_c} \Rightarrow v_c = 26.7 \text{ ms}^{-1}$$

49. *(c)* When an electric dipole is placed in a non-uniform electric field, then it experiences both force and torque. Since, forces on the charges are not linear in non-uniform electric field, so the dipole will also experience a non-zero torque along with a net force.

50. *(b)* In a polar molecule, the centre of gravity of electrons and protons do not coincide.

51. *(a)* Given, capacitance, $C = 10 \text{ mF} = 10^{-2}$ F

Potential, $V = 100$ V

When capacitor explodes, then its whole stored potential energy is given out in the form of heat and lightning.

$$\therefore \quad E_{out} = \frac{1}{2}CV^2 = \frac{1}{2} \times 10^{-2} \times (100)^2 = 50\text{J}$$

52. *(c)* The given situation is shown below

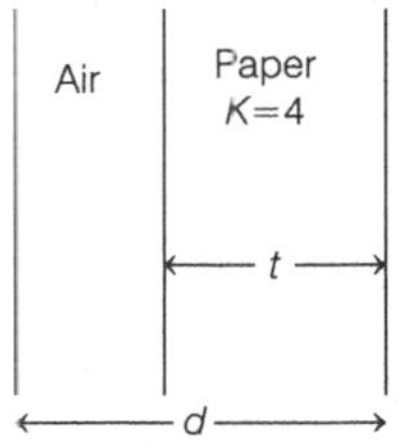

$$d = 1 \text{ mm}$$

Thickness of paper, $t = 0.75$ mm

According to diagram, it is clear that given capacitor is equivalent to a two capacitors connected in series. In series combination, charge on each capacitor is same.

Hence, $Q_{air} = Q_{paper}$

$$\Rightarrow \quad C_{air}V_{air} = C_{paper}V_{paper}$$

$$\frac{V_{air}}{V_{paper}} = \frac{C_{paper}}{C_{air}} = \frac{\frac{\varepsilon_0 KA}{t}}{\frac{\varepsilon_0 A}{d - t}}$$

$$= \frac{K(d-t)}{t} = \frac{4(1 - 0.75)}{0.75} = \frac{4}{3}$$

53. *(b)* For first copper wire,

$$l_1 = 1 \text{ m}$$

For second copper wire, $l_2 = 9$ m

We have to find, diameter ratio of two wires, i.e. $\frac{d_1}{d_2} = ?$

Since, both copper wires have same resistances.

i.e. $\qquad R_1 = R_2$

COMEDK 2014

$$\Rightarrow \quad \rho \cdot \frac{l_1}{A_1} = \rho \cdot \frac{l_2}{A_2} \qquad \left(R = \rho . \frac{l}{A} \right)$$

$$\Rightarrow \quad \frac{l_1}{\left(\frac{\pi d_1^2}{4}\right)} = \frac{l_2}{\left(\frac{\pi d_2^2}{4}\right)}$$

$$\Rightarrow \quad \frac{l_1}{d_1^2} = \frac{l_2}{d_2^2}$$

$$\Rightarrow \quad \frac{d_1}{d_2} = \sqrt{\frac{l_1}{l_2}} = \sqrt{\frac{1}{9}} = \frac{1}{3} \text{ or } 1:3$$

54. *(c)* Heat produced in a conductor is given as

$$H = i^2 Rt$$

$$\Rightarrow \quad H \propto i^2$$

where, i = current, R = resistance and t = time.

55. *(c)* Radius of circular path of a charged particle in uniform magnetic field, when it enters perpendicular direction of magnetic field.

$$r = \frac{mv}{Bq} \qquad \ldots \text{(i)}$$

where, m = mass, v = velocity and q = charge.

We know that, kinetic energy,

$$K = \frac{1}{2} mv^2$$

$$\Rightarrow \quad v = \sqrt{\frac{2K}{m}} \qquad \ldots \text{(ii)}$$

From Eqs. (i) and (ii), we get

$$r = \frac{m}{Bq} \cdot \sqrt{\frac{2K}{m}}$$

$$r = \frac{\sqrt{2Km}}{Bq}$$

For the same value of kinetic energy,

$$r \propto \frac{\sqrt{m}}{q}$$

$$\Rightarrow \quad \frac{r_p}{r_\alpha} = \sqrt{\frac{m_p}{m_\alpha}} \cdot \frac{q_\alpha}{q_p} = \sqrt{\frac{m_p}{4m_p}} \cdot \left(\frac{2q_p}{q_p}\right) = \frac{1}{1} \text{ or } 1:1$$

56. *(c)* The magnetic properties of a magnet is lost at its Curie point because above this temperature. Magnetic domains to be disrupted permanently.

57. *(b)* Electromagnets are made of soft iron because soft iron has a very high value of susceptibility and low retentitivity.

58. *(c)* The given situation is shown below

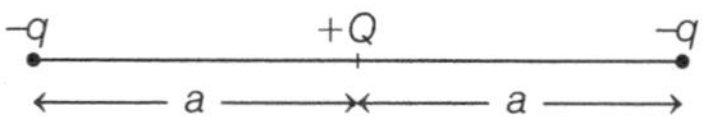

Total potential energy of the system = 0

$$\Rightarrow \frac{1}{4\pi\varepsilon_0}\left[\frac{(-q)Q}{a} + \frac{(+Q)(-q)}{a} + \frac{(-q)(-q)}{2a}\right] = 0$$

$$\Rightarrow \quad -\frac{qQ}{a} - \frac{qQ}{a} + \frac{q^2}{2a} = 0 \Rightarrow \frac{2qQ}{a} = \frac{q^2}{2a}$$

$$\Rightarrow \quad 2Q = \frac{q}{2} \Rightarrow \frac{Q}{q} = \frac{1}{4}$$

59. *(*)* The given circuit diagram is redrawn as

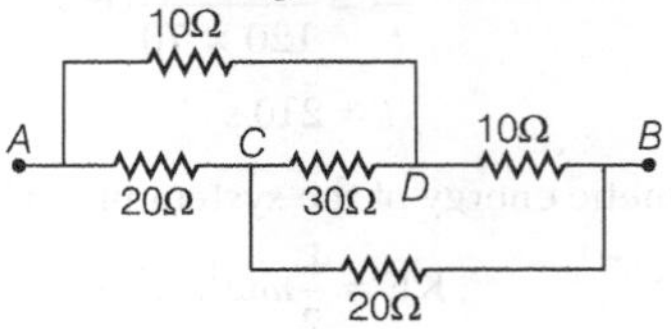

⇓

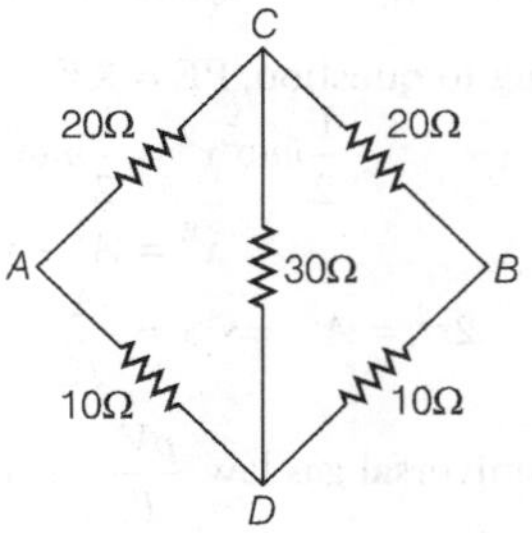

Since,

$$\frac{R_{AC}}{R_{AD}} = \frac{R_{BC}}{R_{DB}}$$

Given circuit is balanced Wheatstone bridge, hence 30 Ω resistance is useless.

Therefore,

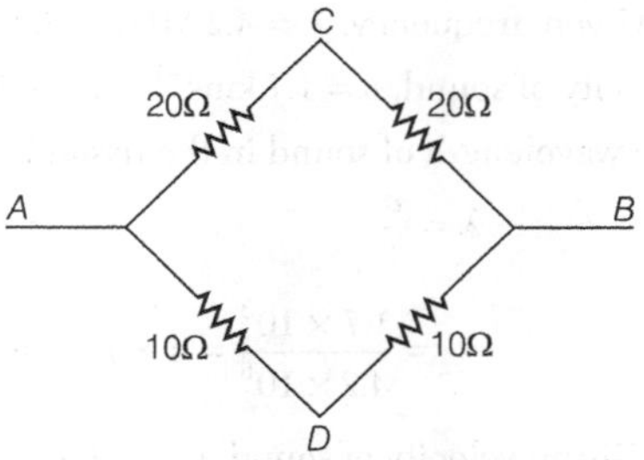

$$\therefore \quad R_{AB} = (20 + 20) \,||\, (10 + 10)$$

$$= 40||20 = \frac{40 \times 20}{40 + 20}$$

$$= \frac{800}{60} = \frac{40}{3} \,\Omega = 13.33\,\Omega$$

60. *(c)* Bandwidth of each TV channel = 3.7 MHz

$$= 3.7 \times 10^6 \text{ Hz}$$

Total bandwidth available

$$= 3700 \text{ GHz} = 3.7 \times 10^{12} \text{ Hz}$$

Number of TV channels

$$= \frac{\text{Total bandwidth available}}{\text{Bandwidth of one channel}}$$

$$= \frac{3.7 \times 10^{12}}{3.7 \times 10^6} = 10^6$$

Chemistry

61. (*d*) $d = 1.25$ g/mL, conc. of solution = 3 M

= 3 moles in one litre of the solution.

Molar mass of NaCl = $23 + 35.5 = 58.5$ g mol^{-1}

Volume of solution = 1 L = 1000 mL

Mass of solution = $d \times V$

$= 1.25 \text{ g mL}^{-1} \times 1000 \text{ mL} = 1250 \text{ g}$

Mass of solute (NaCl) = $n \times$ molar mass

$= 3 \times 58.5 = 175.5$ g

Mass of solvent = mass of solution − mass of solute

$= 1250 - 175.5 = 1074.5$ g

62. (*c*) For 3*p*-orbital, $n = 3$ and $l = 1$.

63. (*a*) Power of the bulb = 150 W = 150 J s^{-1}

As only 8% of the energy is emitted as light so, the total energy emitted per second

$$= \frac{150 \text{ J} \times 8}{100} = 12 \text{ J}$$

Energy of one photon, $E = h\nu = \frac{hc}{\lambda}$

$$= \frac{(6.626 \times 10^{-34} \text{ Js}) \times (3 \times 10^8 \text{ ms}^{-1})}{6600 \times 10^{-10} \text{ m}}$$

$= 3.0118 \times 10^{-19}$ J

∴ Number of photons emitted per second

$$= \frac{12 \text{ J}}{3.0118 \times 10^{-19} \text{ J}} = 3.98 \times 10^{19} \approx 4.0 \times 10^{19}$$

64. (*d*) $O^{2-}(10e^-)$, $F^-(10e^-)$, $Na(11e^-)$, $Mg^{2+}(10e^-)$, $Al^{3+}(10e^-)$ and $Ne(10e^-)$

Thus, Na is not isoelectronic with the rest of the species.

65. (*c*) The graph of volume *vs* temperature at constant pressure is called isobar.

66. (*a*) Second ionisation enthalpy of Cr is highest because after the removal of 1st electron, Cr acquires a stable half-filled d^5 configuration thus, removal of 2nd electron is very difficult.

67. (*b*) $He_2^+ = \sigma 1s^2, \sigma^* 1s^1$

Bond order $= \frac{1}{2}(N_b - N_a)$

N_b is number of bonding electrons

N_a is number of anti-bonding electrons

$$= \frac{1}{2}(2-1) = \frac{1}{2} = 0.5$$

$C_2^{2-} = \sigma 1s^2, \sigma^* 1s^2, \sigma 2s^2, \sigma^* 2s^2, (\pi 2p_x^2 = \pi 2p_y^2), \sigma 2p_z^2$

$$BO = \frac{1}{2}(10-4) = \frac{6}{2} = 3.0$$

$O_2^+ = \sigma 1s^2, \sigma^* 1s^2, \sigma 2s^2, \sigma^* 2s^2, \sigma 2p_z^2, (\pi 2p_x^2 = \pi 2p_y^2), \pi^* 2p_x^1$

$$BO = \frac{1}{2}(10-5) = \frac{5}{2} = 2.5$$

$O_2^- = \sigma 1s^2, \sigma^* 1s^2, \sigma 2s^2, \sigma^* 2s^2, \sigma 2p_z^2, (\pi 2p_x^2 = \pi 2p_y^2), (\pi^* 2p_x^2 = \pi^* 2p_y^1)$

$$BO = \frac{1}{2}(10-7) = \frac{3}{2} = 1.5$$

Thus, the correct order of increasing bond order is $He_2^+ < O_2^- < O_2^+ < C_2^{2-}$.

68. (*d*) O_2 and H_2 do not show bond dipole as they are homoatomic molecules, hence, they are non-polar.

69. (*d*) Given, $p_{total} = 25$ bar, $\chi_{O_2} = 0.18$

Using the relation; $\chi_{O_2} + \chi_{Ne} = 1$

$\chi_{Ne} = 1 - 0.18 = 0.82$

$p_{Ne} = \chi_{Ne} \times p_{tota} = 0.82 \times 25 = 20.5$ bar

70. (*a*) $CaCO_3(s) \longrightarrow CaO(s) + CO_2(g)$

$\Delta_r H° = \Delta_f H°(CaO) + \Delta_f H°(CO_2) - \Delta_f H°(CaCO_3)$

$= -635.09 + (-393.51) - (-1206.92)$

$= 178.3$ kJ mol^{-1}.

71. (*b*) $\Delta_r G° = -2.303\, RT \log K_p$

$= -2.303 \times 8.314 \times 298 \times \log(1 \times 10^{-29})$

$= 165469.6$ J mol^{-1} = 165.47 kJ mol^{-1}

72. (*a*) Equilibrium constant, $K_C = \frac{[\text{Products}]}{[\text{Reactants}]}$

Higher value of K_C, indicates higher concentration of products which means the reaction goes more towards the completion.

73. (*c*)

	PCl_5	$\rightleftharpoons$ PCl_3	+ Cl_2
Initial conc.	$\frac{1}{2} = 0.5$	0	0
Equili. conc.	$\frac{1-0.4}{2} = \frac{0.6}{2}$	$\frac{0.4}{2}$	$\frac{0.4}{2}$

$$K_C = \frac{[PCl_3][Cl_2]}{[PCl_5]} = \frac{\frac{0.4}{2} \times \frac{0.4}{2}}{\frac{0.6}{2}} = \frac{(0.4)^2}{2 \times 0.6} = 0.133$$

74. (*d*) The non-existence of PbI_4 and $PbBr_4$ is probably due to the strong oxidising power of Pb^{4+} ions and strong reducing power of I^- and Br^- ions.

75. (*b*) ClO_4^- does not show disproportionate because in this oxoanion chlorine is present in its highest oxidation state (+7). The disproportionation reactions for the other three oxoanions of chlorine are as follows :

$$3\overset{+1}{Cl}O^- \longrightarrow 2\overset{-1}{Cl}^- + \overset{+5}{Cl}O_3^-$$

$$6\overset{+3}{Cl}O_2^- \xrightarrow{h\nu} 4\overset{+5}{Cl}O_3^- + 2\overset{-1}{Cl}^-$$

$$4\overset{+5}{Cl}O_3^- \longrightarrow \overset{-1}{Cl}^- + 3\overset{+7}{Cl}O_4^-$$

76. *(d)* $Na + (x+y)NH_3 \longrightarrow [Na(NH_3)_x]^+ + [e(NH_3)_y]^-$.

The deep blue colour of the solution is due to the ammoniated electron which absorbs energy in the visible region of light and thus, imparts blue colour to the solution.

77. *(b)* In fullerene with formula C_{60}, all the carbon atoms are equal and they undergo sp^2 hybridisation.

78. *(b)* Maleic acid and fumaric acid both are geometrical isomers.

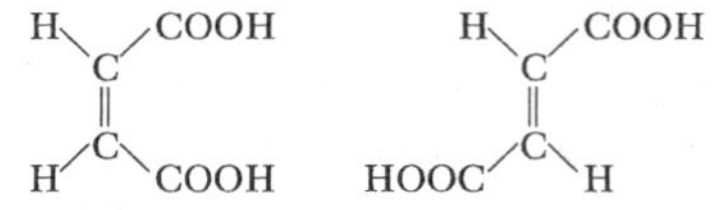

Maleic acid *cis*-butenedioic acid — Fumaric acid *trans*-butenedioic acid

79. *(a)* IUPAC name of tertiary butyl chloride is 2-chloro-2-methylpropane.

80. *(d)* 2-methyl but-2-ene on ozonolysis produce mixture of ethanal and propanone.

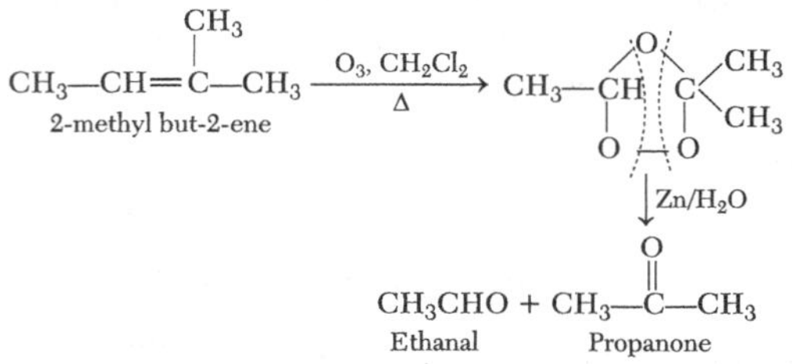

81. *(b)* According to Saytzeff rule, in dehydrohalogenation reactions, the preferred product is that alkene which has the greater number of alkyl groups attached to the doubly bonded carbon atoms. Thus, 2-bromopentane gives pent-2-ene as the major product.

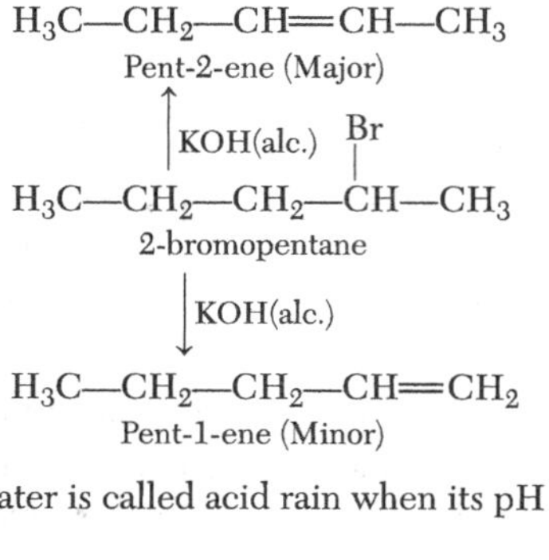

82. *(b)* Rain water is called acid rain when its pH falls below 5.6.

83. *(c)* The number of missing cations and anions are equal in Schottky defect to maintain electrical neutrality.

84. *(d)* Number of A^- ions $= \underset{\text{(At corners)}}{\frac{1}{8} \times 8} + \underset{\text{(At face centres)}}{\frac{1}{2} \times 6} = 4$

Number of B^+ ions $= \underset{\text{(At body centre)}}{1} + \underset{\text{(At edge centres)}}{12 \times \frac{1}{4}} = 4$

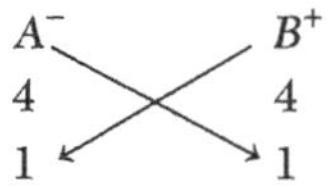

The simplest formula of the compound is *AB*.

85. *(b)* For fcc, $a = 2\sqrt{2}r$

$= 2 \times 1.414 \times 300 \text{ pm} = 848.5 \text{ pm}$

86. *(b)* When the concentration is expressed as the number of moles of solute per kilogram of solvent, it is known as molality.

87. *(d)* $NaCl(aq) \longrightarrow Na^+(aq) + Cl^-(aq)$

van't Hoff factor, $i = 2$

$BaCl_2(aq) \longrightarrow Ba^{2+}(aq) + 2Cl^-(aq)$, $i = 3$

Glucose does not undergo dissociation or association hence, $i = 1$

88. *(a)* $\Delta T_b = iK_b m$

Two solutions having same molality and same van't Hoff factors will have same elevation in boiling points (ΔT_b) and thus, have same boiling points (T_b).

For NaCl, $i = 2$; $MgSO_4$, $i = 2$; $MgCl_2$, $i = 3$;

$Al_2(SO_4)_3$, $i = 5$ and $AlCl_3$, $i = 4$.

Thus, one molal solution of sodium chloride in water has the same boiling point as one molal solution of $MgSO_4$.

89. *(a)* $\frac{p^\circ - p_s}{p^\circ} = \frac{w_2 \times M_1}{w_1 \times M_2}$

$$\frac{17.535 - p_s}{17.535} = \frac{25 \times 18}{450 \times 180} = 5.55 \times 10^{-3}$$

$$17.535 - p_s = 5.55 \times 10^{-3} \times 17.535$$

$$p_s = 17.535(1 - 0.00555)$$

$$p_s = 17.535 \times 0.99445$$

$$p_s = 17.437 \text{ mm Hg.}$$

90. *(a)* In a electrochemical cell, the reaction will be feasible when, ΔG is – ve which is possible only when *E* is +ve as $\Delta G = -nFE$.

91. *(b)* For the cell, $Zn \mid Zn^{2+} \parallel Ag^+ \mid Ag$

$$E^\circ_{cell} = E^\circ_{cathode} - E^\circ_{anode}$$

$$1.56 \text{ V} = E^\circ_{Ag^+/Ag} - E^\circ_{Zn^{2+}/Zn}$$

$$1.56 \text{ V} = 0.8 \text{ V} - E^\circ_{Zn^{2+}/Zn}$$

$$E^\circ_{Zn^{2+}/Zn} = -0.76 \text{ V}$$

$$\therefore \quad E^\circ_{Zn/Zn^{2+}} = -E^\circ_{Zn^{2+}/Zn}$$

$$= -(-0.76) = +0.76 \text{ V}$$

92. *(a)* $\Lambda^\circ_m[Ba(OH)_2]$

$= \Lambda^\circ_m(BaCl_2) + 2\Lambda^\circ_m(NaOH) - 2\Lambda^\circ_m(NaCl)$

$= (2.8 + 2 \times 2.481 - 2 \times 1.265) \times 10^{-2} \text{ S m}^2\text{mol}^{-1}$

$= (2.8 + 4.962 - 2.53) \times 10^{-2} \text{ S m}^2 \text{ mol}^{-1}$

$= 5.232 \times 10^{-2} \text{ S m}^2\text{mol}^{-1}$

93. *(c)* For every 10°C rise in temperature, the rate of a chemical reaction doubles thus, for 60°C rise in temperature the rate of reaction increases by 2^n.

where, $n = \frac{\Delta T}{10} = \frac{60}{10} = 6$

$\therefore \quad r_1 = 2^n r = 2^6 r \Rightarrow r_1 = 64r$

So, when the temperature increases by 60°C, then the rate of reaction increases by 64 times.

94. *(b)* Consider the following graph,

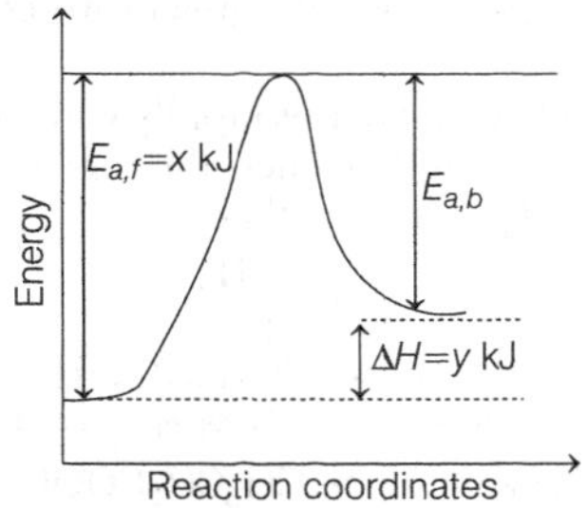

From the above graph

$$x = y + E_{a,b}$$
$$E_{a,b} = x - y \text{ kJ}$$

95. *(c)* For a reaction,

$$aP + bQ \rightarrow \text{Products}$$
$$r = k[P]^a[Q]^b \quad \dots \text{(i)}$$
$$2r = k[2P]^a[Q]^b \quad \dots \text{(ii)}$$
$$4r = k[P]^a[2Q]^b \quad \dots \text{(iii)}$$

On dividing Eqs. (ii) by (i), we get

$$2 = 2^a \Rightarrow a = 1$$

On dividing Eqs. (iii) by (i), we get

$$4 = 2^b \Rightarrow b = 2$$

$\therefore$ Overall order $= a + b = 1 + 2 = 3$.

96. *(c)* Semiconductor of very high purity are obtained by zone refining. Zone refining method is very useful for producing semiconductors and other metals of very high purity, e.g., Ge, Si, B, Ga and In.

97. *(b)* NaCN forms a soluble complex with ZnS thus, it selectively prevents ZnS from coming to the froth but allows PbS to come with the froth.

$$4NaCN + ZnS \longrightarrow \underset{\text{[Soluble complex]}}{Na_2[Zn(CN)_4]} + Na_2S$$

98. *(b)* $\underset{\substack{\text{White}\\\text{phosphorus}\\(A)}}{P_4(s)} + 3NaOH(aq) + 3H_2O(l) \longrightarrow \underset{\substack{\text{Phosphine}\\(B)}}{PH_3(g)} + 3NaH_2PO_2(aq)$

Phosphine has unpleasant odour like that of garlic or rotten fish. It burns in air to give clouds of P_4O_{10} which act as smoke screens.

99. *(b)* The reaction,

$SO_2 + 2H_2S \xrightarrow{\text{Oxidation}} 3S\text{ (sol.)} + 2H_2O$, represent the preparation of sulphur sol by oxidation.

100. *(d)* NeF_2 does not form inert gas compound due to high ionisation enthalpy because of small size.

101. *(c)* Covalency of nitrogen is restricted to four due to absence of *d*-orbitals in its valence shell. Only four orbitals (one 2*s* and three 2*p*-orbitals) are available in its valence shell.

102. *(d)* The photographic industry relies on the special light sensitive properties of AgBr.

103. *(b)* In acidic medium, oxalic acid is oxidised to CO_2 (carbon dioxide) by $KMnO_4$.

$$5(COOH)_2 + 2KMnO_4 + 3H_2SO_4 \longrightarrow K_2SO_4 + 2MnSO_4 + 10\,CO_2 + 8H_2O$$

104. *(c)* $[PtCl_2(en)_2]^{2+}$ complex forms geometrical isomers (*cis* and *trans*). *Trans*-isomer does not show optical isomerism, since it is symmetrical while *cis*-isomer shows optical isomerism as it is unsymmetrical.

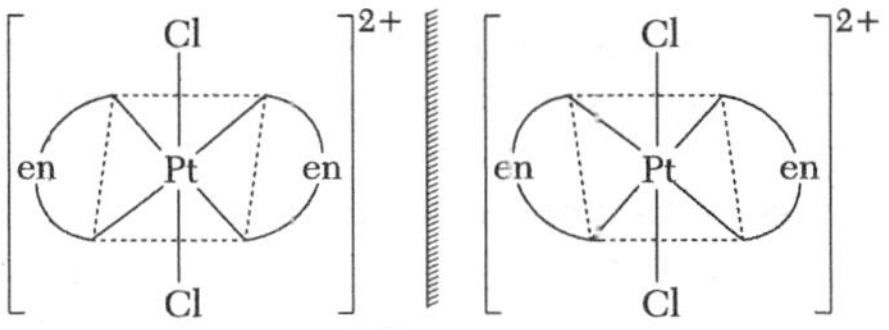

trans-$[PtCl_2(en)_2]^{2+}$ isomer–optically inactive
(Superimposable mirror images)

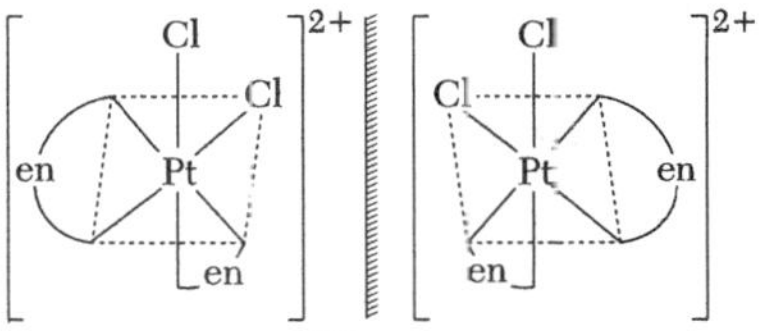

cis-$[PtCl_2(en)_2]^{2+}$ isomer–optically inactive
(Non-superimposable mirror images)

105. *(b, d)* Both options are same. The IUPAC name of complex $[Ag(NH_3)_2]^+ [Ag(CN)_2]^-$ is diamminesilver (I) dicyanoargentate (I).

106. *(d)* Molar conductance of $[Co(NH_3)_3Cl_3]$ is zero as it does not ionise in solution.

107. *(b)* Alkyl halides are hydrolysed to corresponding alcohols by boiling with aqueous alkali solution (NaOH or KOH).

$$CH_3CH_2I + KOH \longrightarrow CH_3CH_2OH + KI$$

This is nucleophilic substitution reaction in which the attacking nucleophile is OH^-.

108. *(c)* S_N1 reaction is two steps reaction in which carbocation is formed as an intermediate in step I (rate determining step). Greater the stability of carbocation, greater will be its ease of formation from alkylhalide and faster will be the rate of reaction.

Stability of carbocation follows the order :

Tertiary > Secondary > Primary

due to decreasing +*I*-effect.

Thus, the order of reactivity of haloalkanes towards S_N1 reaction is
tertiary halide > secondary halide > primary halide.

109. *(a)* The given reaction takes place as follows :

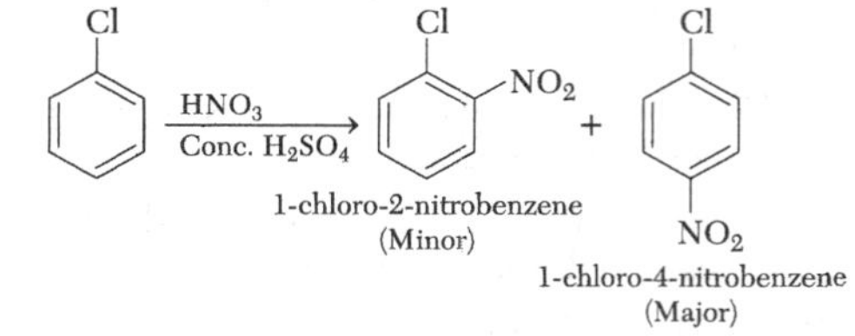

Chlorine is a *o*, *p*-directing and deactivating group.
Chlorine is deactivating because of its –*I*-effect. As inductive effect is distance dependent so, electron density is lower at *ortho* position than *para* position. Thus, the nitration occurs at *para* position.

110. *(d)* The unstable intermediate [$:CCl_2$] is formed in Reimer-Tiemann reaction which is an electrophilic substitution reaction and occurs through the following steps.

(i) **Generation of electrophile**

$$HO^- + CHCl_3 \rightleftharpoons H_2O + CCl_3^- \longrightarrow :CCl_2 + Cl^-$$

Dichlorocarbene (Electrophile)

(ii) **Electrophilic substitution**

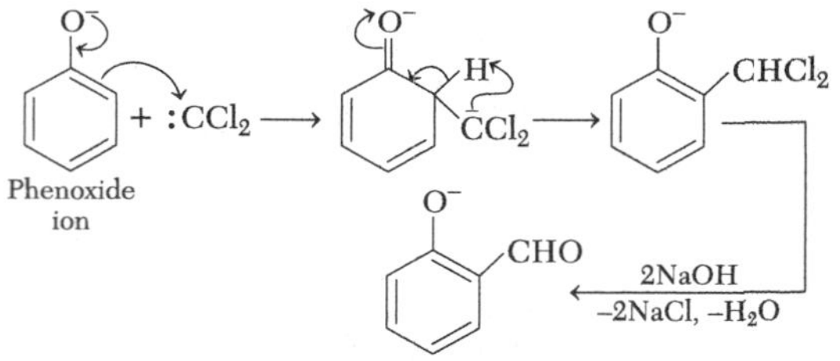

111. *(d)* Phenols are highly acidic compared to alcohols due to formation of phenoxide ion which is stabilised by resonance.

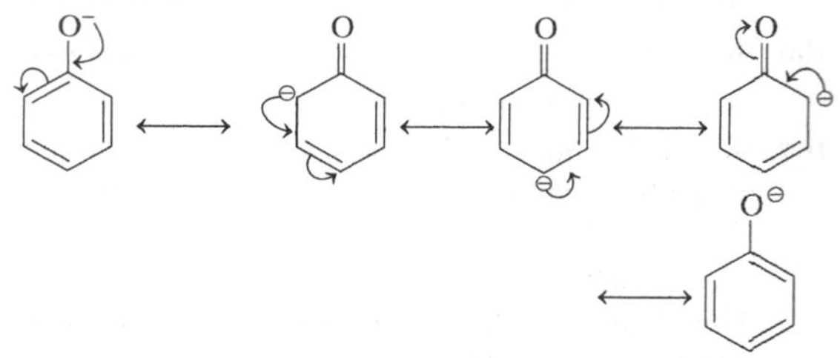

112. *(b)* Boiling point increases with increase in molecular mass so, 1-butanol has higher boiling point than 1-propanol.

Unlike alcohols, ethers do not form hydrogen bonds thus, they have lower boiling points than the corresponding alcohols.

Due to weak dipole-dipole interactions, the boiling points of lower ethers are only slightly higher than those of the *n*-alkanes having comparable molecular masses.

Thus, the increasing order of boiling points is
n-butane <ethoxyethane < 1-propanol < 1-butanol.

113. *(a)* Acidic strength $\propto k_a$ values

Due to – *I*-effect of electron withdrawing —Cl group, chloropropanoic acid is stronger acid than propanoic acid. Further, greater the number of electron withdrawing substitutents, greater would be the acidic strength.

Inductive effect decreases rapidly with distance and so, is the acidic strength. Hence, the correct order of acidic strength (or k_a values) will be

$$Cl_2CHCOOH > ClCH(CH_3)COOH >$$
2,2-dichloroacetic acid, 2-chloropropanoic acid

$$ClCH_2CH_2COOH > CH_3CH_2COOH$$
3-chloropropanoic acid, Propanoic acid

114. *(a)* Addition of Grignard reagents to carbonyl compounds is an example of nucleophilic addition reactions.

115. *(b)* The given reaction is known as acetal formation reaction.

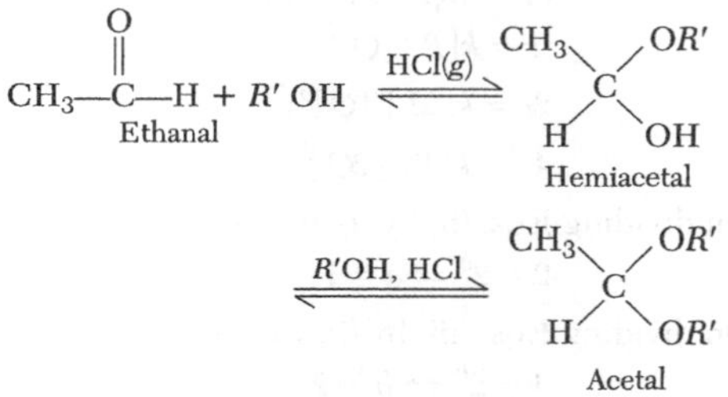

116. *(b)* The complete reaction takes place as follows :

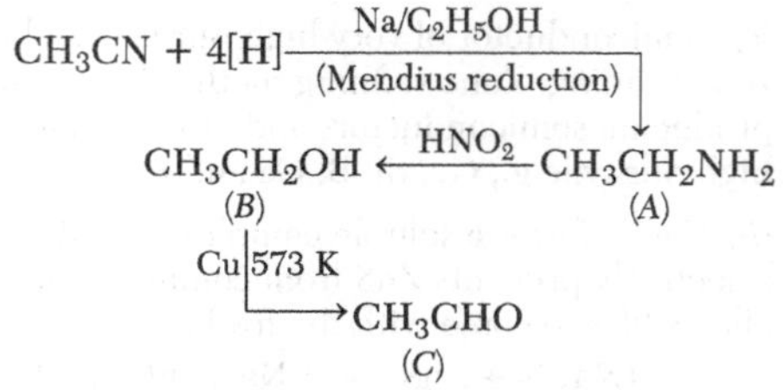

117. *(a)* In nucleic acids the nucleotides are joined together by phosphodiester linkage between 5′ and 3′ carbon atoms of the pentose sugar.

118. *(d)* Amino acids exists as Zwitter ions at isoelectric pH.

119. *(c, d)* Neoprene and teflon are formed by addition polymerisation, while terylene and nylon-6,6 are formed by condensation polymerisation.

120. *(b)* Sucrose is natural sweetener while aspartame, sucralose and saccharin are artificial sweeteners.

Mathematics

121. *(b)* In option (b), $x^2 + 3 = 0$

$\Rightarrow \quad x = \sqrt{-3} \in C$

$\Rightarrow$ x is not a real number.

$\Rightarrow$ It is an empty set.

122. *(b)* If a set having n elements then its number of subsets $= 2^n$

$\therefore$ Numbers of proper susbets of a set having $(n+1)$ elements $= 2^{n+1} - 1$.

123. *(c)* Given, function is

$y = \sqrt{x-2} + \sqrt{1-x}$

Since, $x - 2 \geq 0$ and $1 - x \geq 0$

$\Rightarrow \quad x \geq 2 \quad \ldots \text{(i)}$

$\Rightarrow \quad x \leq 1 \quad \ldots \text{(ii)}$

$\therefore$ From Eqs. (i) and (ii), $x = \phi$

124. *(b)* Given, $A = [1, 2, 3, 4]$

Let R be a reflexive relation on A, then for each $x \in A$, $(a, a) \in R$

$\therefore$ Option (b) is true.

125. *(d)* $f(x) = \dfrac{2x-3}{3x+4}$

Let $f(x) = y = \dfrac{2x-3}{3x+4}$

On cross multiplication, we get

$3xy + 4y = 2x - 3$

$\Rightarrow x(3y - 2) = -3 - 4y$

$$\Rightarrow \quad x = \frac{-3-4y}{3y-2} \Rightarrow x = f^{-1}(y) = \frac{-3-4y}{3y-2}$$

Put $y = -\dfrac{4}{3}$, we get

$$f^{-1}\left(-\frac{4}{3}\right) = \frac{-3-4\times\left(-\dfrac{4}{3}\right)}{3\left(-\dfrac{4}{3}\right)-2}$$

$$= \frac{-3+\dfrac{16}{3}}{-4-2} = \frac{7}{3\times(-6)} = -\frac{7}{18}$$

126. *(a)* Let $f(x) = y = x + \dfrac{1}{x}$

or $xy = x^2 + 1$ or $x^2 - xy + 1 = 0$

Since, $x \in [0, \infty)$

$\therefore \quad D \geq 0 \Rightarrow y^2 - 4 \geq 0 \Rightarrow y \in [2, \infty)$

$$\therefore \quad x = \frac{y \pm \sqrt{y^2-4}}{2}$$

i.e. $$x = \frac{y-\sqrt{y^2-4}}{2} \text{ or } x = \frac{y-\sqrt{y^2-4}}{2}$$

$$\Rightarrow \quad f^{-1}(y) = \frac{y+\sqrt{y^2-4}}{2}$$

or $$f^{-1}(y) = \frac{y-\sqrt{y^2-4}}{2}$$

Replace by x,

$$f^{-1}(x) = \frac{x+\sqrt{x^2-4}}{2}$$

or $$f^{-1}(x) = \frac{x-\sqrt{x^2-4}}{2}$$

127. *(b)* We have, $\dfrac{\tan 330° \sec 420° \sin 300°}{\tan 135° \sin 210° \sec 315°}$

$$= \frac{\tan(360-30)° \sec(360+60)° \sin(360-60)°}{\tan(180-45)° \sin(180+30)° \sec(360-45)°}$$

$$= \frac{-\tan 30° \times \sec 60° \times (-\sin 60°)}{(-\tan 45°)(-\sin 30°)\sec 45°}$$

[$\tan(2\pi - \theta) = -\tan\theta$, $\sec(2\pi \pm \theta) = \sec\theta$, $\sin(2\pi - \theta) = -\sin\theta$, $\sin(\pi + \theta) = -\sin\theta$, $\tan(\pi - \theta) = -\tan\theta$]

$$= \frac{1\times 2\times\sqrt{3}\times 2}{\sqrt{3}\times 2\times 1\times\sqrt{2}} = \sqrt{2}$$

128. *(b)* Given, equation is

$\sin(120 - A) = \sin(120 - B)$

Since, sine is positive in II quadrant.

$\therefore$ Either $120 - A = 120 - B$

$\Rightarrow \quad A = B$

or $\quad 120 - A = 180 - (120 - B)$

$\Rightarrow \quad 120 - A = 60 + B \Rightarrow A + B = \dfrac{\pi}{3}$

129. *(a)* Given, equation is

$$\cot^{-1}\frac{1}{5} + \cot^{-1}\frac{1}{3} - \cot^{-1}\frac{4}{7} = \cot^{-1}x$$

$$\Rightarrow \tan^{-1}5 + \left(\tan^{-1}3 - \tan^{-1}\frac{7}{4}\right) = \tan^{-1}\frac{1}{x}$$

$$\Rightarrow \tan^{-1}5 + \tan^{-1}\left(\frac{3-\dfrac{7}{4}}{1+3\times\dfrac{7}{4}}\right) = \tan^{-1}\frac{1}{x}$$

$$\Rightarrow \tan^{-1}5 + \tan^{-1}\left(\frac{1}{5}\right) = \tan^{-1}\frac{1}{x}$$

$$\Rightarrow \tan^{-1}5 + \cot^{-1}5 = \tan^{-1}\frac{1}{x}$$

$$\Rightarrow \tan^{-1}\frac{1}{x} = \frac{\pi}{2} \qquad \left[\tan^{-1}\theta + \cot^{-1}\theta = \frac{\pi}{2}\right]$$

$$\Rightarrow \frac{1}{x} = \tan\frac{\pi}{2} = \infty \Rightarrow x = 0$$

130. *(c)* Given, equation is

$$1 + i = (x + iy)(u + iv)$$

$$\Rightarrow 1 + i = (xu - yv) + i(xv + yu)$$

Comparing real and imaginary parts, we get

$$xu - yv = 1 \quad \ldots (i)$$

$$xv + yu = 1 \quad \ldots (ii)$$

Multiply Eq. (i) by u and Eq. (ii) by v and then adding, we get

$$x(u^2 + v^2) = u + v \Rightarrow x = \frac{u+v}{u^2+v^2}$$

From Eq. (i)

$$y = \frac{xu - 1}{v} = \frac{u - v}{u^2 + v^2}$$

(Substituting the value of x)

Now, $\tan^{-1}(y/x) + \cot^{-1}(u/v)$

$$\tan^{-1}\left(\frac{u-v}{u+v}\right) + \cot^{-1}(u/v)$$

$$= \tan^{-1}\left(\frac{1 - \frac{v}{u}}{1 + \frac{v}{u}}\right) + \cot^{-1}(u/v)$$

$$= \tan^{-1}(1) - \tan^{-1}\left(\frac{v}{u}\right) + \tan^{-1}\left(\frac{v}{u}\right)$$

$$= n\pi + \pi/4, n \in I$$

131. *(a)* $1^3 + 2^3 + \ldots. + n^3$

$$= \left(\frac{n(n+1)}{2}\right)^2 = (1 + 2 + \ldots. + n)^2$$

132. *(b)* Let $z = a + ib$

Then, in third quadrant $a < 0, b < 0$.

Its conjugate $\bar{z} = \overline{a + ib} = a - ib = a + (-ib)$

$= a + ik$, where $k = -b$

$\Rightarrow \quad a < 0, k > 0$

$\Rightarrow \quad \bar{z}$ lies in II quadrant.

133. *(b)* Since, β satisfy the inequation

$$x^2 - x - 6 > 0$$

$$\Rightarrow \beta^2 - \beta - 6 > 0$$

$$\Rightarrow (\beta - 3)(\beta + 2) > 0$$

$$\Rightarrow \beta > 3, \beta < -2$$

134. *(a)* Given, ${}^{56}P_{r+6} : {}^{54}P_{r+3} = 30800 : 1$

$$\Rightarrow \frac{{}^{56}P_{r+6}}{{}^{54}P_{r+3}} = \frac{30800}{1}$$

$$\Rightarrow \frac{56! \times (51 - r)!}{(50 - r)! \times 54!} = \frac{30800}{1}$$

$$\Rightarrow 56 \times 55 \times (51 - r) = 30800$$

$$\Rightarrow 51 - r = 10 \Rightarrow r = 41$$

135. *(c)* Given, expansion is $\left(2 + \frac{x}{3}\right)^n$

Let t_{r+1} be general term.

Then, $t_{r+1} = {}^nC_r 2^{n-r}\left(\frac{x}{3}\right)^r = {}^nC_r 2^{n-r} \cdot 3^{-r} x^r$

Since, coefficient of x^5 and x^6 are equal.

$$\therefore \quad {}^nC_6 2^{n-6} 3^{-6} = {}^nC_5 2^{n-5} 3^{-5}$$

$$\Rightarrow \frac{{}^nC_6}{{}^nC_5} = 2 \times 3 \Rightarrow \frac{n! \times 5! \times (n-5)!}{(n-6)! \times 6! \times n!} = 6$$

$$\Rightarrow \frac{n-5}{6} = 6 \Rightarrow n - 5 = 36 \Rightarrow n = 41$$

136. *(d)* Given, expansion is $\left[\sqrt{\left(\frac{x}{3}\right)} + \sqrt{\left(\frac{3}{2x^2}\right)}\right]^{10}$

Let t_{r+1} be general term, then

$$t_{r+1} = {}^{10}C_r \left(\sqrt{\frac{x}{3}}\right)^{10-r} \left(\sqrt{\frac{3}{2x^2}}\right)^r$$

$$= {}^{10}C_r \frac{x^{\frac{10-r}{2}}}{3^{\frac{10-r}{2}}} \cdot \frac{3^{r/2}}{2^{r/2} \cdot x^r} = {}^{10}C_r x^{5 - \frac{r}{2} - r} \cdot \frac{3^{r-5}}{2^{r/2}}$$

For the term independent of x.

Puts $5 - \frac{r}{2} - r = 0$

$$\Rightarrow 5 - \frac{3}{2}r = 0 \Rightarrow \frac{3}{2}r = 5 \Rightarrow r = \frac{10}{3}$$

Fractional value of r is not possible. So, no term is independent of x.

137. *(c)* Let

$$S = \frac{1^2}{1 \cdot 2} + \frac{1^2 + 2^2}{2 \cdot 3} + \frac{1^2 + 2^2 + 3^2}{3 \cdot 4} + \ldots.$$

upto 20 terms

Let t_n be nth terms of series.

Then, $t_n = \dfrac{1^2 + 2^2 + 3^2 + \ldots. + n^2}{n.(n+1)}$

$$= \frac{\Sigma n^2}{n(n+1)} = \frac{n(n+1)(2n+1)}{6.n(n+1)} = \frac{2n+1}{6}$$

Taking summation on both sides

$$\sum_{n=1}^{20} t_n = \frac{2}{6}\sum_{n=1}^{20} n + \frac{1}{6}\sum_{n=1}^{20} 1$$

$$= \frac{1}{3} \times \left(\frac{20(20+1)}{2}\right) + \frac{1}{6} \times 20$$

$$= \frac{1}{3}\left(\frac{20 \times 21}{2}\right) + \left(\frac{10}{3}\right) = \frac{210}{3} + \frac{10}{3} = \frac{220}{3}$$

138. *(a)* Given, equations of lines are

$$\sqrt{3}x + y = 1 \quad \ldots (i)$$

and $\quad x + \sqrt{3}y = 1 \quad \ldots (ii)$

COMEDK 2014

Let m_1 and m_2 be slopes of Eqs. (i) and (ii), then

$$m_1 = -\sqrt{3}, m_2 = -\frac{1}{\sqrt{3}}$$

Let θ be angle between them, then

$$\tan\theta = \left|\frac{m_1 - m_2}{1 + m_1 m_2}\right| = \left|\frac{-\sqrt{3} + \frac{1}{\sqrt{3}}}{1 + \sqrt{3}\cdot\frac{1}{\sqrt{3}}}\right| = \left|\frac{-3+1}{2\sqrt{3}}\right| = \frac{1}{\sqrt{3}}$$

$\Rightarrow \quad \theta = \frac{\pi}{6}$

139. *(d)* Since, equation of family of lines is $\frac{x}{a} + \frac{y}{b} = 1$ ... (i)

Sum of intercepts $= a + b = 7$ (given)

$\Rightarrow \quad b = 7 - a$

Substitute $b = 7 - a$ in Eq. (i), we get

$$\frac{x}{a} + \frac{y}{7-a} = 1$$

$\Rightarrow (7-a)x + ay = a(7-a) \Rightarrow ay = (7-a)(a-x)$

140. *(b)* Let equation of ellipse be $\frac{x^2}{a^2} + \frac{y^2}{b^2} = 1$

Since it passes through the points $(-3, 1)$ and $(2, -2)$

$\therefore \quad \frac{(-3)^2}{a^2} + \frac{(1)^2}{b^2} = 1$ and $\frac{(2)^2}{a^2} + \frac{(-2)^2}{b^2} = 1$

$\Rightarrow \quad \frac{9}{a^2} + \frac{1}{b^2} = 1$ ... (i)

$\Rightarrow \quad \frac{4}{a^2} + \frac{4}{b^2} = 1$ ...(ii)

Multiply by 4 in Eq. (i) and subtracting Eq. (i) from Eq. (ii),

$$3a^2 = 32 \Rightarrow a^2 = \frac{32}{3}$$

Substituting in Eq. (i), gives

$$\frac{9 \times 3}{32} + \frac{1}{b^2} = 1$$

$\Rightarrow \quad \frac{1}{b^2} = 1 - \frac{27}{32} = \frac{5}{32} \Rightarrow b^2 = \frac{32}{5}$

$\therefore$ Required equation is

$$\frac{3x^2}{32} + \frac{5y^2}{32} = 1 \text{ or } 3x^2 + 5y^2 = 32$$

141. *(b)* Given, equation of parabola is $y^2 = 6x$

Substitute $x = 24$

$y^2 = 6 \times 24$

$y = \pm\sqrt{6 \times 24} = \pm\sqrt{6 \times 6 \times 4} = \pm(6 \times 2) = \pm 12$

$\therefore$ Point on the parabola is $(24, 12)$, $(24, -12)$ vertex of given parabola is $(0, 0)$.

$\therefore$ Equation of lines passing through $(0, 0)$ and $(24, 12)$, $(24, -12)$ is

$$y = \frac{12}{24}x, \; y = \frac{-12}{24}x$$

$\Rightarrow \quad 2y - x = 0, 2y + x = 0$

$\Rightarrow \quad 2y \pm x = 0$ are required equations of lines.

142. *(b)* $P(a, b, c)$ and PA and PB are perpendicular to YZ and ZX planes. Hence, coordinate of A and B are $(0, b, c)$ and $(a, 0, c)$ respectively.

Equation of plane passing through $(C, 0, 0)$, $(0, b, c)$ and $(a, 0, c)$ is $\begin{vmatrix} x & y & z \\ 0 & b & c \\ a & 0 & c \end{vmatrix} = 0$

$\Rightarrow \quad x(bc - 0) - y(0 - ac) + z(0 - ab) = 0$

$\Rightarrow \quad bcx + acy - abz = 0$

143. *(a)* Perpendicular distance of point $(1, 2, 3)$ from plane $3y + 4z + 4 = 0$

$$= \left|\frac{3(2) + 4(3) + 4}{\sqrt{(3)^2 + (4)^2}}\right| = \left|\frac{6+16}{5}\right| = \left|\frac{22}{5}\right| = 4.4$$

144. *(c)*

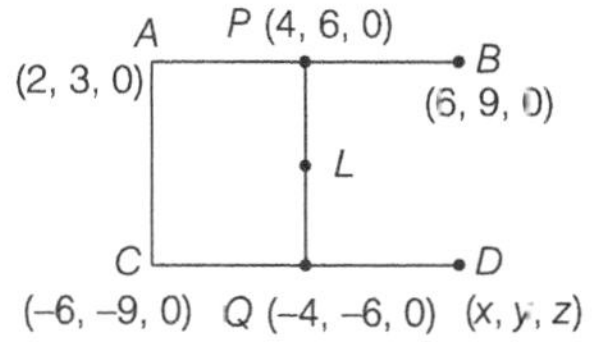

Let coordinate of D is (x, y, z).

Using mid-point formula,

$$Q = \left(\frac{x-6}{2}, \frac{y-9}{2}, \frac{z+0}{2}\right)$$

Also, $\quad P = \left(\frac{2-6}{2}, \frac{3+9}{2}, \frac{0+0}{2}\right) = (4, 6, 0)$

Since, $AC \parallel PQ$

$\therefore$ D.R'.s of line AC = D.R' s of line PQ

$\Rightarrow (-8, -12, 0) = \left(\frac{x-14}{2}, \frac{y-21}{2}, \frac{z}{2}\right)$

$\Rightarrow x = -2, y = -3, z = 0$

$\Rightarrow D(-2, -3, 0) \Rightarrow Q(-4, -6, 0)$

If L is mid-point of PQ, then

$$L\left(\frac{4-4}{2}, \frac{6-6}{2}, 0\right) = (0, 0, 0)$$

$\therefore$ Perpendicular distance of $L(0, 0, 0)$ from the plane $3x + 4z + 25 = 0$ is

$$\left|\frac{3(0) + 4(0) + 25}{\sqrt{(3)^2 + (4)^2}}\right| = \left|\frac{25}{\sqrt{25}}\right| = \sqrt{25} = 5$$

145. *(b)* Equation of plane through the intersection of planes $x + 2y + 3z - 4 = 0$ and $2x + y - z + 5 = 0$ is

$(x + 2y + 3z - 4) + k(2x + y - z + 5) = 0$

or $(1 + 2k)x + (2 + k)y + (3 - k)z + (5k - 4) = 0$ ... (i)

D.R.' s of normal of plane (i) are

$= \langle (1 + 2k), (2 + k), (3 - k) \rangle$

Given, $5x + 3y + 6z + 8 = 0$ ... (ii)

D.R.'s of plane (ii) are $<5, 3, 6>$.
Since Eq. (i) is Perpendicular to the plane (ii),

$\therefore \quad 5(1+2k)+(2+k)3+6(3-k)=0$

$\Rightarrow \quad 5+10k+6+3k+18-6k=0$

$\Rightarrow 7k+29=0 \Rightarrow k=\dfrac{-29}{7}$

$\therefore$ Required equation of plane is

$$(x-2y+3z-4)+\left(-\frac{29}{7}\right)(2x+y-z+5)=0$$

$\Rightarrow 7x+14y+21z-28-58x-29y+29z-145=0$

$\Rightarrow -51x-15y+50z-173=0$

$\Rightarrow 51x+15y-50z+173=0$

146. *(c)* $\lim\limits_{x\to 0}\dfrac{xa^x-x}{1-\cos x}=\lim\limits_{x\to 0}\dfrac{x(a^x-1)}{2\sin^2\frac{x}{2}}$

$[\because \cos 2\theta = 1-2\sin^2\theta]$

$$=\lim_{x\to 0}\frac{a^x-1}{\left(\dfrac{\sin\frac{x}{2}}{\frac{x}{2}}\right)^2}\times\frac{2}{x}$$

$$=\frac{\lim\limits_{x\to 0}2\left(\dfrac{a^x-1}{x}\right)}{\left[\lim\limits_{x\to 0}\dfrac{\sin\frac{x}{2}}{\frac{x}{2}}\right]^2}=2\log a$$

147. *(b)* Given, $y=\tan x$

Differentiating w.r.t. x both sides,

$$\frac{dy}{dx}=\sec^2 x$$

Taking again derivative w.r.t. x,

$$\frac{d^2y}{dx^2}=2\sec x\cdot\sec x\tan x$$
$$=2\sec^2 x\tan x=2\tan x(1+\tan^2 x)$$
$$=2y(1+y^2)$$

148. *(c)* Given, $y=\tan^{-1}\left(\dfrac{a-x}{1+ax}\right)$

$\Rightarrow \quad y=\tan^{-1}a-\tan^{-1}x$

Taking derivative w.r.t. x on both sides, we get

$$\frac{dy}{dx}=-\frac{1}{1+x^2}$$

149. *(c)* $f(x)=\begin{cases}[x]+[-x], & x\neq 2\\ K, & x=2\end{cases}$

Since, $f(x)$ is continuous at $x=2$

$\therefore \lim\limits_{x\to 2^-}f(x)=\lim\limits_{x\to 2^+}f(x)=f(2)$

Now, $\lim\limits_{x\to 2^-}f(x)=\lim\limits_{x\to 2^-}[x]+[-x]$

$=1+(-2)=-1$

$\lim\limits_{x\to 2^+}f(x)=\lim\limits_{x\to 2^+}[x]+[-x]=2-3=-1$

$\Rightarrow \quad K=-1$

150. *(b)* Given, equation of curve is

$$x^2-xy+y^2=27 \quad \ldots \text{(i)}$$

Taking derivative w.r.t. x on both sides

$$2x-\frac{x\,dy}{dx}-y+2y\frac{dy}{dx}=0$$

$\Rightarrow \quad \dfrac{dy}{dx}(2y-x)=y-2x \Rightarrow \dfrac{dy}{dx}=\dfrac{y-2x}{2y-x}$

Since, curve has tangent parallel to X-axis.

$\therefore$ Slope of tangent $=0$

$\Rightarrow \quad \dfrac{dy}{dx}=0\Rightarrow\dfrac{y-2x}{2y-x}=0$

$\Rightarrow \quad y=2x \quad \ldots \text{(ii)}$

Now, solving Eqs. (i) and (ii), we get

$$x^2-2x^2+4x^2=27\Rightarrow 3x^2=27\Rightarrow x=\pm 3$$

For $x=3$, $y=6$ and $x=-3$, $y=-6$

$\therefore$ Points are $(3, 6)$ and $(-3, -6)$.

151. *(b)* Given, equation of circle is

$$x^2+y^2=2 \quad \ldots \text{(i)}$$

Taking derivative w.r.t. 't' on both sides.

$$2x\frac{dx}{dt}+2y\frac{dy}{dt}=0\Rightarrow x\frac{dx}{dt}+y\frac{dy}{dt}=0$$

If abscissa and ordinate increase at the same rate, we have

$$\frac{dx}{dt}=\frac{dy}{dt}$$

$$x\frac{dx}{dt}+y\frac{dx}{dt}=0\Rightarrow\frac{dx}{dt}(x+y)=0$$

Since, $\quad \dfrac{dx}{dt}\neq 0$

$\Rightarrow \quad x+y=0\Rightarrow x=-y \quad \ldots \text{(ii)}$

Solving Eqs. (i) and (ii), we get

$$x^2+(-x)^2=2\Rightarrow x=\pm 1$$

For $x=1$, $y=-1$ and $x=-1$, $y=1$

Required point are $(1,-1)$ and $(-1, 1)$.

152. *(a)* Given, $\dfrac{dV}{dt}=35$

where, V is volume of spherical balloon.

Also, $V=\dfrac{4}{3}\pi r^3$

$\Rightarrow \quad \dfrac{d}{dt}\left(\dfrac{4}{3}\pi r^3\right)=35\Rightarrow\dfrac{4}{3}\pi\times 3r^2\dfrac{dr}{dt}=35$

$\Rightarrow \quad \dfrac{dr}{dt}=\dfrac{35\times 3}{4\pi\times 3r^2}$

Let S be surface area of sphere, then $S = 4\pi r^2$

Taking derivative w.r.t. r

$$\frac{dS}{dt} = 8\pi \times r\frac{dr}{dt} = 8\pi \times r \times \frac{35\times 3}{4\pi \times 3r^2}$$

Substitute, $r = 7$

$$\frac{dS}{dt} = \frac{2\times 35\times 3}{3\times 7} = 10 \text{ cm}^2\text{/min}$$

153. *(a)* Let $I = \int e^x(\cos x - \sin x)\,dx$

$$= \int e^x \cos x\,dx - \int e^x \sin x\,dx$$

$$= \int e^x \cos x\,dx - [e^x(-\cos x) - \int e^x(-\cos x)\,dx]$$

$$= \int e^x \cos x\,dx + e^x \cos x - \int e^x \cos x\,dx$$

$$= e^x \cos x + C$$

154. *(a)* Given, differential equation is

$$(2x - 10y^3)\frac{dy}{dx} + y = 0 \Rightarrow \frac{dy}{dx} = \frac{-y}{2x - 10y^3}$$

$$\Rightarrow \quad \frac{dx}{dy} = \frac{2x - 10y^3}{-y} = \frac{-2x}{y} + 10y^2$$

$$\Rightarrow \quad \frac{dx}{dy} + \frac{2}{y}x = 10y^2$$

Compare with linear differential equation

$$\frac{dx}{dy} + Px = Q \Rightarrow \text{IF} = e^{\int \frac{2}{y}dy} = e^{\log y^2} = y^2$$

$\therefore$ Required solution is $x.\,y^2 = \int 10y^2 \cdot y^2 dy + C$

i.e. $\quad xy^2 = 2y^5 + C$

155. *(a)* Given, differential equation is

$$\Rightarrow \quad (xy)^{-1}\left(x\frac{dy}{dx} + y\right) = (x+y)^{-2}\left(1 + \frac{dy}{dx}\right)$$

$$\Rightarrow \int (xy)^{-1}\left(x\frac{dy}{dx} + y\right)dx = \int (x+y)^{-2}\left(1 + \frac{dy}{dx}\right)dx \quad \ldots\text{(i)}$$

Using integral,

$$\int (f(x))^n f'(x)dx = \frac{(f(x))^{n+1}}{n+1}$$

and $\quad \int \frac{f'(x)}{f(x)}dx = \log(f(x)) + C$

From Eq. (i) $\quad \log(xy) = \frac{(x+y)^{-1}}{-1} + C$

$$\Rightarrow \quad \log(xy) = \frac{-1}{x+y} + C$$

156. *(a)* Let $\mathbf{a} = 3\mathbf{i} + \mathbf{j} + 2\mathbf{k}$ and $\mathbf{b} = \mathbf{i} + \mathbf{j} + 2\mathbf{k}$

$$\mathbf{a}\times\mathbf{b} = \begin{vmatrix} \mathbf{i} & \mathbf{j} & \mathbf{k} \\ 3 & 1 & 2 \\ 1 & 1 & 2 \end{vmatrix}$$

$$= \mathbf{i}(2-2) - \mathbf{j}(6-2) + \mathbf{k}(3-1) = -4\mathbf{j} + 2\mathbf{k}$$

$$|\mathbf{a}\times\mathbf{b}| = \sqrt{(-4)^2 + (2)^2} = \sqrt{16+4} = \sqrt{20}$$

Since, $|\mathbf{a}\times\mathbf{b}| = |\mathbf{a}||\mathbf{b}|\sin\theta$,

If θ is angle between **a** and **b**.

$$\sqrt{20} = \sqrt{9+1+4}\sqrt{1+1+4}\sin\theta$$

$$\Rightarrow \sin\theta = \frac{\sqrt{20}}{\sqrt{6}\sqrt{14}}$$

$$\Rightarrow \sin\theta = \sqrt{\frac{20}{6\times 14}} = \sqrt{\frac{5}{21}}$$

157. *(a)* Let θ be angle between **a** and **b** then $\theta = 60°$ (given)

Since, $|\mathbf{a}+\mathbf{b}|^2 = |\mathbf{a}|^2 + |\mathbf{b}|^2 + 2\mathbf{a}\cdot\mathbf{b}$

$$= 4 + 4 + (2\times 2\times 2\times \cos 60°)$$

$$= 8 + 8\cos 60° = 8 + 4 = 12$$

$$\Rightarrow \quad |\mathbf{a}+\mathbf{b}| = \sqrt{12} = 2\sqrt{3}$$

Now, $\mathbf{a}\cdot(\mathbf{a}+\mathbf{b}) = |\mathbf{a}||\mathbf{a}+\mathbf{b}|\cos x$

where x is angle between **a** and **a** + **b**.

$$\Rightarrow \quad \mathbf{a}\cdot\mathbf{a} + \mathbf{a}\cdot\mathbf{b} = 4\sqrt{3}\cos x$$

$$\Rightarrow \quad 4 + 2\times 2\cos 60° = 4\sqrt{3}\cos x$$

$$\Rightarrow \quad 6 = 4\sqrt{3}\cos x$$

$$\Rightarrow \quad \cos x = \frac{\sqrt{3}}{2} = \cos\frac{\pi}{6} \Rightarrow x = 30°$$

158. *(d)* $\begin{bmatrix} -2 & 5 \\ 3 & -1 \end{bmatrix}_{2x\times 2}\begin{bmatrix} x \\ y \end{bmatrix}_{2\times 1} = \begin{bmatrix} 1 & 2 \\ 3 & 4 \end{bmatrix}_{2\times 2}\begin{bmatrix} 3 \\ -1 \end{bmatrix}_{2\times 1}$

$$\Rightarrow \quad \begin{bmatrix} -2x + 5y \\ 3x - y \end{bmatrix} = \begin{bmatrix} 1 \\ 5 \end{bmatrix}$$

$$\Rightarrow \quad -2x + 5y = 1,\ 3x - y = 5$$

or $\quad y = 3x - 5 \quad \ldots$(i)

$$\Rightarrow \quad -2x + 5(3x-5) = 1$$

$$\Rightarrow \quad -2x + 15x - 25 = 1$$

$$\Rightarrow \quad 13x = 26 \Rightarrow x = 2$$

Substituting $x = 2$ in Eq. (i), we get

$$y = 6 - 5 = 1$$

Hence, $(x, y) = (2, 1)$

159. *(d)* $(BA)^{-1} = C$ (given)

or $\quad A^{-1}B^{-1} = C$

$$\text{or } A^{-1}\begin{bmatrix} 2 & 6 & 4 \\ 1 & 0 & 1 \\ -1 & 1 & -1 \end{bmatrix}^{-1} = \begin{bmatrix} -1 & 0 & 1 \\ 1 & 1 & 3 \\ 2 & 0 & 2 \end{bmatrix}$$

Multiply by B on both sides, we get

$$A^{-1}(B^{-1}B) = \begin{bmatrix} -1 & 0 & 1 \\ 1 & 1 & 3 \\ 2 & 0 & 2 \end{bmatrix}\begin{bmatrix} 2 & 6 & 4 \\ 1 & 0 & 1 \\ -1 & 1 & -1 \end{bmatrix}$$

$$\text{or} \quad A^{-1} = \begin{bmatrix} -3 & -5 & -5 \\ 0 & 9 & 2 \\ 2 & 14 & 6 \end{bmatrix}_{3\times 3}$$

160. *(c)* Given, $AB = B$

Multiply by A on both sides

$$ABA = BA \quad \ldots \text{(i)}$$

Also, $BA = A$

Multiply by B on both sides

$$BAB = AB \quad \ldots \text{(ii)}$$

Adding Eqs. (i) and (ii), we get

$$ABA + BAB = BA + AB$$

$$\Rightarrow \quad A(BA) + B(AB) = BA + AB$$

$$\Rightarrow \quad AA + BB = A + B$$

$$\Rightarrow \quad A^2 + B^2 = A + B$$

161. *(d)* Given, equation is $x^3 + a^2x + b = 0$

Since, α, β, γ are its roots.

$\therefore$ Sum of roots $= \alpha + \beta + \gamma = 0 \quad \ldots \text{(i)}$

Now, $\begin{vmatrix} \alpha & \beta & \gamma \\ \beta & \gamma & \alpha \\ \gamma & \alpha & \beta \end{vmatrix}$

Using operation $C_1 \to C_1 + C_2 + C_3$, we get

$$\begin{vmatrix} (\alpha+\beta+\gamma) & \beta & \gamma \\ (\alpha+\beta+\gamma) & \gamma & \alpha \\ (\alpha+\beta+\gamma) & \alpha & \beta \end{vmatrix} = \begin{vmatrix} 0 & \beta & \gamma \\ 0 & \gamma & \alpha \\ 0 & \alpha & \beta \end{vmatrix} = 0 \quad \text{[Using Eq. (i)]}$$

162. *(a)* Given determinant is

$$\begin{vmatrix} 4 & 4 & 4 \\ (a+a^{-1})^2 & (b+b^{-1})^2 & (c+c^{-1})^2 \\ (a-a^{-1})^2 & (b-b^{-1})^2 & (c-c^{-1})^2 \end{vmatrix}$$

Using operation $R_2 \to R_2 - R_3$, we get

$$\begin{vmatrix} 4 & 4 & 4 \\ 4aa^{-1} & 4bb^{-1} & 4cc^{-1} \\ (a-a^{-1})^2 & (b-b^{-1})^2 & (c-c^{-1})^2 \end{vmatrix}$$

$$= \begin{vmatrix} 4 & 4 & 4 \\ 4 & 4 & 4 \\ (a-a^{-1})^2 & (b-b^{-1})^2 & (c-c^{-1})^2 \end{vmatrix} = 0$$

[R_1 and R_2 are identical rows]

163. *(a)* Given, $P(B|A) = 0.6$

$$\Rightarrow \quad \frac{P(B \cap A)}{P(A)} = 0.6$$

$$\Rightarrow \quad P(B \cap A) = 0.6 \times 0.1 = 0.06$$

Also, $\quad P(B|A^C) = 0.3$

$$\Rightarrow \quad \frac{P(B \cap A^C)}{P(A^C)} = 0.3$$

$$\Rightarrow \quad \frac{P(B) - P(B \cap A)}{1 - P(A)} = 0.3$$

$$\Rightarrow \quad \frac{P(B) - 0.06}{0.9} = 0.3$$

$$\Rightarrow \quad P(B) = 0.33$$

Now, $P(A|B) = \dfrac{P(A \cap B)}{P(B)} = \dfrac{0.06}{0.33} = \dfrac{2}{11}$

164. *(c)* Let A be the event that a card is queen and B be the event that it is a spade.

Now, $P(B|A) = \dfrac{P(B \cap A)}{P(A)} = \dfrac{1/52}{4/52} = \dfrac{1}{4}$

165. *(a)* $P(A^C \cap B^C) = P((A \cup B)^C) = 1 - P(A \cup B)$

Since, probability of occurrence of an event A implies the occurrence of event B,

$\therefore A \subset B \Rightarrow A \cup B = B$

$\Rightarrow P(A^C \cap B^C) = 1 - P(B) = P(B^C)$

166. *(d)* Let events T_1, T_2, T_3 be the following

T_1 : The item is manufactured by factory F_1.

T_2 : The item is manufactured by factory F_2.

T_3 : : The item is manufactured by factory F_3 .

Clearly, T_1, T_2, T_3 are mutually exclusive and exhaustive events.

$$P(T_1) = 30\% = 0.3, P(T_2) = 20\% = 0.2$$

$$P(T_3) = 50\% = 0.5$$

Let E be the event that item is defective.

Now, $\quad P(E|T_1) = 2\% = 0.02$

$\quad P(E|T_2) = 3\% = 0.03$

$\quad P(E|T_3) = 4\% = 0.04$

Hence, by Bayes' theorem, we have

$$P(T_1|E) = \frac{P(T_1)\,P(E|T_1)}{P(T_1)P(E|T_1) + P(T_2)(P(E|T_2) + P(T_3)P(E|T_3)}$$

$$= \frac{0.3 \times 0.02}{0.3 \times 0.02 + 0.2 \times 0.03 + 0.5 \times 0.04}$$

$$= \frac{0.006}{0.006 + 0.006 + 0.20} = \frac{0.006}{0.032} = \frac{6}{32} = \frac{3}{16}$$

167. *(a)* To get an average of atleast 55 marks,

We have,

$$\frac{60 + 85 + x}{3} \geq 55$$

$$\Rightarrow \quad 145 + x \geq 165$$

$$\Rightarrow \quad x \geq 165 - 145$$

$$\Rightarrow \quad x \geq 20$$

168. *(b)* Coefficient of variation $= \dfrac{\sigma}{\bar{x}} \times 100$

For first distribution, $60 = \dfrac{21}{\bar{x}} \times 100$

$$\bar{x} = \frac{21 \times 100}{60} = 35$$

For second distribution, $70 = \dfrac{16}{\bar{x}} \times 100$

$$\bar{x} = \frac{16 \times 100}{70} = 22.85$$

Hence, required means are 35, 22.85.

169. *(c)* Required probability $= \frac{5}{10} \times \frac{4}{9} = \frac{2}{9}$

170. *(d)* Two non-empty sets have always non-empty intersection $\rightarrow$ logical

The real number n is less 2 $\rightarrow$ logical

Two individuals are always related $\rightarrow$ logical

171. *(d)* Objective function is not linear.

172. *(b)* Minimise $5x + 10y$

Subject to $x \geq 6$

$y \leq 2$

$x, y \geq 0$

173. *(b)* Given,

$$f(x) = \log(x + \sqrt{x^2 + 1})$$

$$\therefore \quad f(x) + f(-x) = \log(x + \sqrt{x^2 + 1}) + \log(-x + \sqrt{x^2 + 1}) = \log(1) = 0$$

$$\Rightarrow \quad f(-x) = -f(x)$$

Hence, $f(x)$ is an odd function.

174. *(b)* Given, $x^4 + \sqrt{x^4 + 20} = 22$

Add both sides 20, we get

$$x^4 + 20 + \sqrt{x^4 + 20} = 22 + 20$$

Let $\sqrt{x^4 + 20} = y$

$$\therefore \quad y^2 + y - 42 = 0$$

$$\Rightarrow \quad (y - 6)(y + 7) = 0$$

$$\Rightarrow \quad y = 6 \qquad [\because y \neq -7]$$

$$\Rightarrow \sqrt{x^4 + 20} = 6 \Rightarrow x^4 + 20 = 36$$

$$\Rightarrow \quad x^4 = 16 \Rightarrow x = \pm 2$$

Hence, the number of real roots of the equation is 2.

175. *(b)* Since, $\Sigma n = \frac{1}{78} \Sigma n^3$

$$\Rightarrow \quad \frac{n(n+1)}{2} = \frac{1}{78} \times \frac{n^2(n+1)^2}{4}$$

$$\Rightarrow \quad n^2 + n - 156 = 0$$

$$\Rightarrow \quad (n + 13)(n - 12) = 0$$

$$\Rightarrow \quad n = 12 \qquad [\because n \neq -13]$$

176. *(a)* A polygon of n sides has number of diagonals

$$= \frac{n(n-3)}{2} = 275 \qquad \text{[given]}$$

$$\Rightarrow \quad n^2 - 3n - 550 = 0$$

$$\Rightarrow \quad (n - 25)(n + 22) = 0$$

$$\therefore \quad n = 25 \qquad [\because n \neq -22]$$

177. *(c)* Now, $7^9 = (8 - 1)^9 = -1(1 - 8)^9$

$$= -1 + {}^9C_1 8 - {}^9C_2 8^2 + \dots + {}^9C_9 8^9$$

and $\quad 9^7 = (1 + 8)^7 = 1 + {}^7C_1 8 + {}^7C_2 8^2 + {}^7C_3 8^3 + \dots + {}^7C_7 8^7$

$$\therefore \; 7^9 + 9^7 = 8({}^9C_1 + {}^7C_1) + 8^2({}^7C_2 - {}^9C_2) + \dots$$

$$= 8(9 + 7) + 8^2(21 - 36) + \dots$$

$$= 64 \times 2 + 64(-15) + \dots$$

Hence, it is divisible by 64.

178. *(a)* Let $\Delta = \begin{vmatrix} 1 & 1 & 1 \\ a & b & c \\ a^2 - bc & b^2 - ca & c^2 - ab \end{vmatrix}$

On applying $C_3 \rightarrow C_3 - C_2$ and $C_2 \rightarrow C_2 - C_1$, we get

$$\Delta = \begin{vmatrix} 1 & 0 & 0 \\ a & b - a & c - b \\ a^2 - bc & (b^2 - a^2) + c(b - a) & (c^2 - b^2) + a(c - b) \end{vmatrix}$$

$$= 1[(b - a)(c - b)(c + b + a) - (c - b)(b - a)(b + a + c)] = 0$$

179. *(d)* Given, $3\cos 2x - 10\cos x + 7 = 0$

$$\Rightarrow \quad 6\cos^2 x - 10\cos x + 4 = 0 \qquad [\because \cos 2x = 2\cos^2 x - 1]$$

$$\Rightarrow 2(3\cos x - 2)(\cos x - 1) = 0$$

$$\Rightarrow \quad \cos x = 1 \text{ or } \cos x = \frac{2}{3}$$

Hence, $\cos x$ is positive in Ist and IVth quadrants.

Hence, the total number of solutions is 4.

180. *(b)* $\lim_{x \to -\infty} \frac{2x - 1}{\sqrt{x^2 + 2x + 1}}$

$$= \lim_{y \to \infty} \frac{-2 - \frac{1}{y}}{\sqrt{1 - \frac{2}{y} + \frac{1}{y^2}}} \qquad [\text{put } x = -y,\; x \rightarrow -\infty]$$

$$= -\frac{2}{1} = -2$$

COMEDK

Solved Paper 2013

Instructions

- There are 180 questions in all. The number of questions in each section is as given below.

Sections	No. of Questions
Section I : Physics	1-60
Section II : Chemistry	61-120
Section III : Mathematics	121-180

- All the questions are Multiple Choice Questions having four options out of which **ONLY ONE** is correct.
- Candidates will be awarded 1 mark for each correct answer. There will be no negative marking for incorrect answer.
- Time allotted to complete this paper is 3 hrs.

PHYSICS

1. The difference between the apparent frequency of a source of sound as perceived by the observer during its approach and recession is 2% of the frequency of the source. If the speed of sound in air is 300 ms^{-1}, then the velocity of the source is

a. 1.5 ms^{-1} ***b.*** 12 ms^{-1} ***c.*** 6 ms^{-1} ***d.*** 3 ms^{-1}

2. Three long straight wires A, B and C are carrying currents as shown in figure, then the resultant force on B is directed

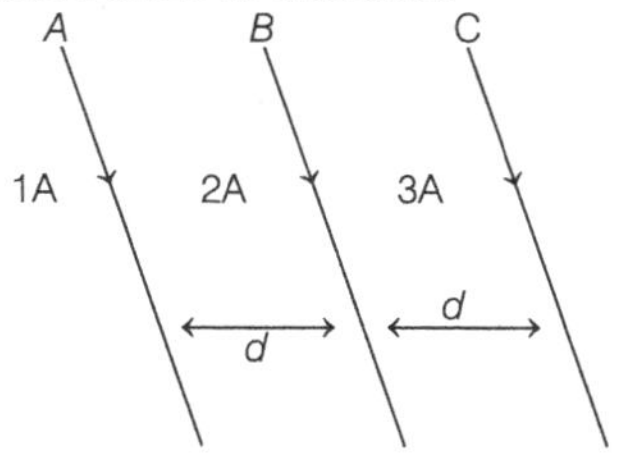

a. perpendicular to the plane of paper and outward

b. perpendicular to the plane of paper and inward

c. towards A

d. towards C

3. Curie-Weiss law is obeyed by iron

a. at Curie temperature only

b. at all temperatures

c. below Curie temperature

d. above Curie temperature

4. A magnet N-S is suspended from a spring and when it oscillates, the magnet moves in and out of the coil C. The coil is connected to a galvanometer G, then as the magnet oscillates

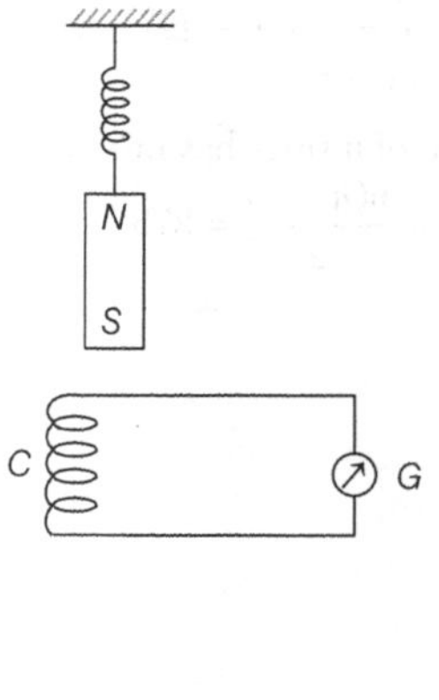

a. G shows no deflection
b. G shows deflection to the left and right but the amplitude steadily decreases
c. G shows deflection to the left and right with constant amplitude
d. G shows deflection on one side

5. The dimensional formula for inductance is
a. $[ML^2T^{-2}A^{-2}]$ *b.* $[ML^2TA^{-2}]$
c. $[ML^2T^{-1}A^{-2}]$ *d.* $[ML^2T^{-2}A^{-1}]$

6. The maximum current that can be measured by a galvanometer of resistance 40 Ω, is 10 mA. It is converted into a voltmeter that can read upto 50 V. The resistance to be connected in series with the galvanometer (in Ω) is
a. 2010 *b.* 4050 *c.* 5040 *d.* 4960

7. The spectrum obtained from the chromosphere of the sun at the time of total solar eclipse is
a. line emission spectrum
b. band emission spectrum
c. continuous emission spectrum
d. line absorption spectrum

8. Heavy water is
a. compound of deuterium and oxygen
b. water at 4°C
c. water, in which soap does not lather
d. compound of heavy oxygen and heavy hydrogen

9. The nuclear reactor at Kaiga is a
a. research reactor *b.* fusion reactor
c. breeder reactor *d.* power reactor

10. When a body moves in a circular path, no work is done by the force since
a. force and displacement are perpendicular to each other
b. the force is always away from the centre
c. there is no displacement
d. there is no net force

11. A bullet moving with a speed of 100 ms^{-1} can just penetrate two planks of equal thickness, then the number of such planks penetrated by the same bullet when the speed is doubled will be
a. 6 *b.* 10 *c.* 4 *d.* 8

12. Two bodies of masses 1 kg and 2 kg have equal momentum, then the ratio of their kinetic energies is
a. 2 : 1 *b.* 3 : 1
c. 1: 3 *d.* 1 : 1

13. Absorption coefficient of an open window is
a. 1 *b.* 0.25 *c.* zero *d.* 0.5

14. The loudness and pitch of a sound note depend on
a. intensity and velocity
b. frequency and velocity
c. intensity and frequency
d. frequency and number of harmonics

15. In Melde's experiment in the transverse mode, the frequency of the tuning fork and the frequency of the waves in the string are in the ratio
a. 2 : 1 *b.* 4 : 1
c. 1 : 1 *d.* 1 : 2

16. An electron is accelerated through a potential difference of 45.5 V. The velocity acquired by it is (in ms^{-1})
a. 10^6 *b.* zero
c. 4×10^6 *d.* 4×10^4

17. An unknown resistance R_1 is connected in series with a resistance of 10 Ω. This combination is connected to one gap of a meter bridge, while a resistance R_2 is connected in the other gap. The balance point is at 50 cm. Now, when the 10 Ω resistance is removed, the balance point shifts to 40 cm. The value of R_1 (in Ω) is
a. 20 *b.* 10
c. 60 *d.* 40

18. In the circuit shown, the internal resistance of the cell is negligible. The steady state current in the 2 Ω resistor is

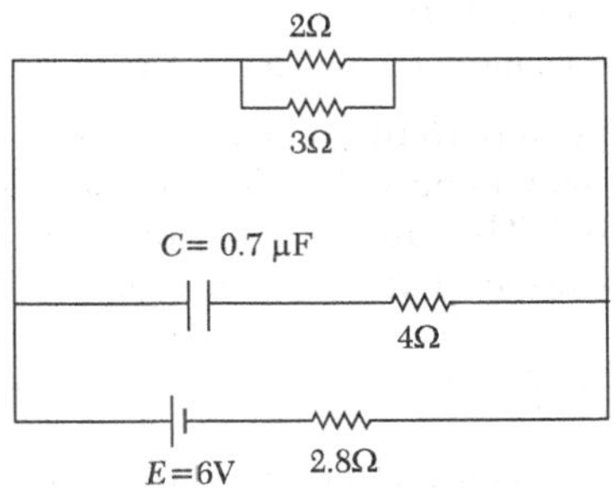

a. 0.6 A *b.* 1.2 A
c. 0.9 A *d.* 1.5 A

19. A rectangular coil of 300 turns has an average area of 25 cm × 10 cm. The coil rotates with a speed of 50 cps in uniform magnetic field of strength 4×10^{-2} T about an axis perpendicular to the field. The peak value of the induced emf (in V) is
a. 300 π *b.* 3000 π *c.* 3 π *d.* 30 π

COMEDK 2013

20. In an *L-C-R* circuit, the potential difference between the terminals of the inductance is 60 V, between the terminals of the capacitor is 30 V and that between the terminals of resistance is 40 V. The supply voltage will be equal to

a. 130 V *b.* 10 V
c. 50 V *d.* 70 V

21. A vertical circular coil of radius 0.1 m and having 10 turns carries a steady current. When the plane of the coil is normal to the magnetic meridian, a neutral point is observed at the centre of the coil. If $B_H = 0.314 \times 10^{-4}$ T, the current in the coil is

a. 0.5 A *b.* 0.25 A
c. 2 A *d.* 1 A

22. A thread is tied slightly loose to a wire frame as shown in figure and the frame is dipped into a soap solution and taken out. The frame is completely covered with the film. When the portion *A* is punctured with a pin, the thread

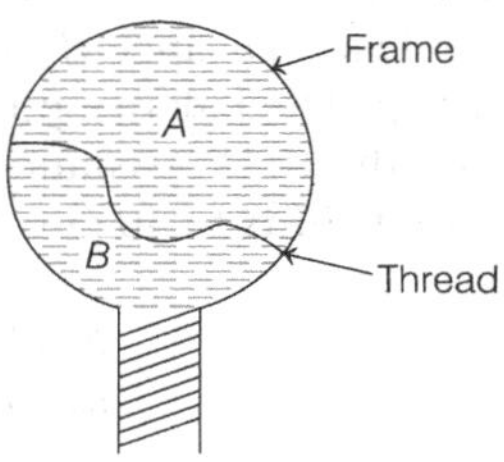

a. becomes concave towards *A*
b. becomes convex towards 5*A*
c. Either (a) or (b) depending on the size of *A* with respect to *B*
d. remains in the initial position

23. Oxygen is 16 times heavier than hydrogen. Equal volumes of hydrogen and oxygen are mixed. The ratio of speed of sound in the mixture to that in hydrogen is

a. $\sqrt{8}$ *b.* $\sqrt{2/17}$
c. $\sqrt{1/8}$ *d.* $\sqrt{32/17}$

24. If two waves of the same frequency and amplitude respectively on superposition produce a resultant disturbance of the same amplitude, the waves differ in phase by

a. π *b.* zero *c.* $\pi/3$ *d.* $2\pi/3$

25. A man, standing between two cliffs, claps his hands and starts hearing a series of echoes at intervals of one second. If the speed of sound in air is 340 ms^{-1}, then the distance between the cliffs is

a. 680 m *b.* 1700 m *c.* 340 m *d.* 1620 m

26. A beam of light of wavelength 600 nm from a source falls on a single slit 1 mm wide and the resulting diffraction pattern is observed on a screen 2 m away. The distance between the first dark fringes on either side of the central bright fringe is

a. 2.4 cm *b.* 2.4 mm
c. 1.2 mm *d.* 1.2 cm

27. The pair of quantities having same dimensions is

a. impulse and surface tension
b. angular momentum and work
c. work and torque
d. Young's modulus and energy

28. The displacement *x* (in m) of a particle of mass *m* (in kg) moving in one dimension under the action of a force, is related to time *t* (in s) by $t = \sqrt{x} + 3$. The displacement of the particle when its velocity is zero, will be

a. 4 m *b.* 0 *c.* 6 m *d.* 2 m

29. Vectors **A**, **B** and **C** are such that $\mathbf{A} \cdot \mathbf{B} = 0$ and $\mathbf{A} \cdot \mathbf{C} = 0$, then the vector parallel to **A** is

a. $\mathbf{A} \times \mathbf{B}$ *b.* $\mathbf{B} + \mathbf{C}$
c. $\mathbf{B} \times \mathbf{C}$ *d.* **B** and **C**

30. The primary of a transformer when connected to a DC battery of 10 V draws a current of 1 mA. The number of turns of the primary and secondary windings are 50 and 100, respectively. The voltage in the secondary and the current drawn by the circuit in the secondary are respectively

a. 20 V and 2.0 mA *b.* 10 V and 0.5 mA
c. 0 and 0 *d.* 20 V and 0.5 mA

31. One coolie takes 1 min to raise a suitcase through a height of 2 m but the second coolie takes 30 s to raise the same suitcase to the same height. The powers of two coolies are in the ratio.

a. 1 : 3 *b.* 2 : 1 *c.* 3 : 1 *d.* 1 : 2

32. An electric dipole of dipole moment *p* is aligned parallel to a uniform electric field *E*. The energy required to rotate the dipole by 90° is

a. p^2E *b.* pE *c.* infinity *d.* pE^2

33. A car is moving in a circular horizontal track of radius 10 m with a constant speed of 10 m/s. A bob is suspended from the roof of the car by a light wire of length 1.0 m. The angle made by the wire with the vertical is

a. $\frac{\pi}{3}$ *b.* $\frac{\pi}{6}$ *c.* $\frac{\pi}{4}$ *d.* 0°

34. The radius of a planet is twice the radius of earth. Both have almost equal average mass-densities. v_p and v_e are escape velocities of the planet and the earth, respectively, then

a. $v_p = 1.5\, v_e$ *b.* $v_p = 2v_e$
c. $v_e = 3v_p$ *d.* $v_e = 1.5v_p$

35. If the ratio of diameters, lengths and Young's modulus of steel and copper wires shown in the figure are p, q and s respectively, then the corresponding ratio of increase in their lengths would be

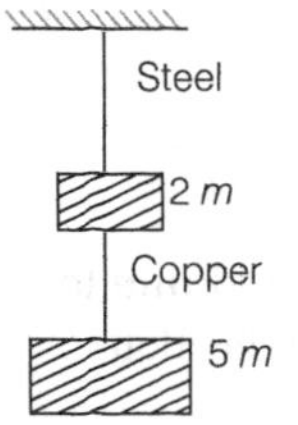

a. $\frac{5q}{7sp^2}$ *b.* $\frac{7q}{5sp^2}$
c. $\frac{2q}{5sp}$ *d.* $\frac{7q}{5sp}$

36. Which of the following relations does not give the equation of an adiabatic process, where terms have their usual meaning?

a. $p^{1-\gamma}T^{\gamma}$ = constant *b.* pV^{γ} = constant
c. $TV^{\gamma-1}$ = constant *d.* $p^{\gamma}T^{1-\gamma}$ = constant

37. A particle of mass m is kept at rest at a height $3R$ from the surface of earth, where R is radius of earth and M is mass of earth. The minimum speed with which it should be projected, so that it does not return back, is (g is acceleration due to gravity on the surface of earth)

a. $\left(\frac{GM}{2R}\right)^{1/2}$ *b.* $\left(\frac{gR}{4}\right)^{1/2}$
c. $\left(\frac{2g}{R}\right)^{1/2}$ *d.* $\left(\frac{GM}{R}\right)^{1/2}$

38. H-polaroid is prepared by

a. orienting herapathite crystal in the same direction in nitrocellulose
b. using thin tourmaline crystals
c. stretching polyvinyl alcohol and then heated with dehydrating agent
d. stretching polyvinyl alcohol and then impregnating with iodine

39. SI unit of permittivity is

a. $C^2m^2N^2$ *b.* $C^2m^{-2}N^{-1}$
c. $C^2m^2N^{-1}$ *d.* $C^{-1}m^2N^{-2}$

40. A spherical drop of capacitance 1 μF is broken into eight drops of equal radius, then the capacitance of each small drop is

a. $\frac{1}{2}$ μF *b.* $\frac{1}{4}$ μF *c.* $\frac{1}{8}$ μF *d.* 8 μF

41. Two equal forces (P each) act at a point inclined to each other at an angle of 120°. The magnitude of their resultant is

a. $P/2$ *b.* $P/4$ *c.* P *d.* $2P$

42. Threshold wavelength for photoelectric emission from a metal surface is 5200 Å. Photoelectrons will be emitted, when this surface is illuminated with monochromatic radiation from

a. 1 W IR lamp *b.* 50 W UV lamp
c. 50 W IR lamp *d.* 10 W IR lamp

43. In Young's double slit experiment, if monochromatic light used is replaced by white light, then

a. no fringes are observed
b. only central fringe is white, all other fringes are coloured
c. all bright fringes become white
d. all bright fringes have colours between violet and red

44. Which state of triply ionised Beryllium (Be^{+++}) has the same orbital radius as that of the ground state of hydrogen ?

a. $n = 3$ *b.* $n = 4$ *c.* $n = 1$ *d.* $n = 2$

45. If M is the atomic mass and A is the mass number, packing fraction is given by

a. $\frac{M}{M-A}$ *b.* $\frac{M-A}{A}$
c. $\frac{A}{M-A}$ *d.* $\frac{A-M}{A}$

46. A count rate meter shows a count of 240 per min from a given radioactive source. One hour later, the meter shows a count rate of 30 per min. The half-life of the source is

a. 80 min *b.* 120 min
c. 20 min *d.* 30 min

47. Two conductors of the same material have their diameters in the ratio 1 : 2 and their lengths in the ratio 2 : 1. If the temperature difference between their ends is the same, then the ratio of amounts of heat conducted per second through them will be

a. 4 : 1 *b.* 1 : 4 *c.* 8 : 1 *d.* 1 : 8

48. Blowing air with open mouth is an example of

a. isobaric process *b.* isochoric process
c. isothermal process *d.* adiabatic process

49. Sound waves in air are always longitudinal because
a. of the inherent characteristics of sound waves in air
b. air does not have a modulus of rigidity
c. air is a mixture of several gases
d. density of air is very small

50. An uncharged sphere of metal is placed inside a charged parallel plate capacitor. The lines of force will look like

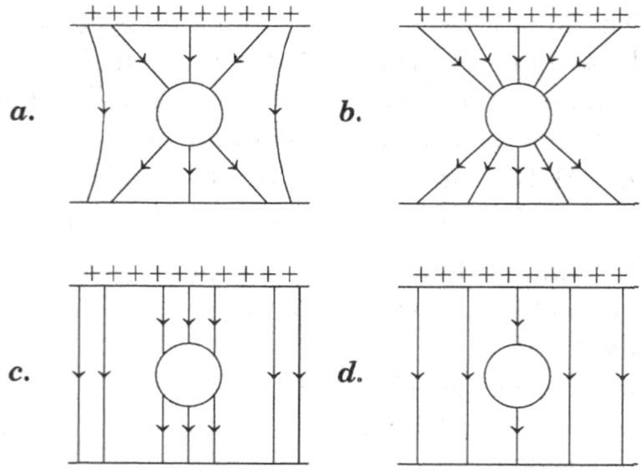

51. A current flows in a conductor from East to West. The direction of the magnetic field at a point above the conductor is
a. towards East *b.* towards West
c. towards North *d.* towards South

52. A bar magnet is equivalent to
a. toroid carrying current
b. straight conductor carrying current
c. solenoid carrying current
d. circular coil carrying current

53. Excitation energy of a hydrogen like ion in its first excitation state is 40.8 eV. Energy needed to remove the electron from the ion in ground state is
a. 40.8 eV *b.* 27.2 eV
c. 54.4 eV *d.* 13.6 eV

54. The refractive index of a particular material is 1.67 for blue light, 1.65 for yellow light and 1.63 for red light. The dispersive power of the material is
a. 0.031 *b.* 1.60
c. 0.0615 *d.* 0.024

55. An ideal gas heat engine operates in a Carnot's cycle between 227°C and 127°C. It absorbs 6×10^4 J at high temperature. The amount of heat converted into work is
a. 1.6×10^4 J *b.* 1.2×10^4 J
c. 4.8×10^4 J *d.* 3.5×10^4 J

56. Which one of the following graphs represents the behaviour of an ideal gas ?

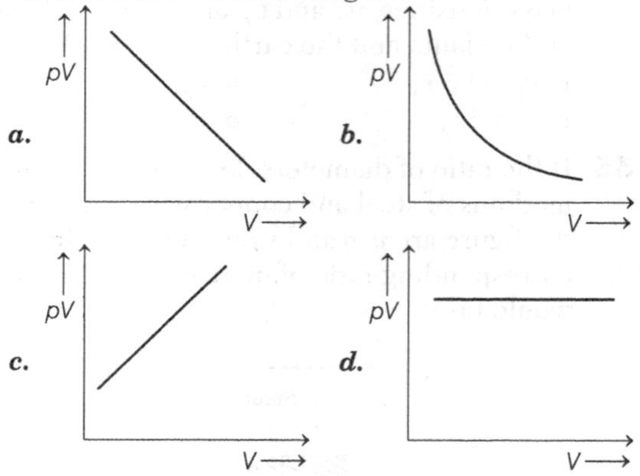

57. Rainbow is formed due to
a. total internal reflection
b. scattering
c. refraction
d. dispersion and total internal reflection

58. A beam of parallel rays is brought to focus by a plano-convex lens. A thin concave lens of the same focal length is joined to the first lens. The effect of this is
a. the focus shifts to infinity
b. the focal point shifts towards the lens by a small distance
c. the focal point shifts away from the lens by a small distance
d. the focus remains undisturbed

59. When a body is earth connected, electrons from the earth flow into the body. This means the body is
a. charged negatively
b. an insulator
c. uncharged
d. charged positively

60. Effective capacitance between A and B in the figure shown is (all capacitances are in μF)

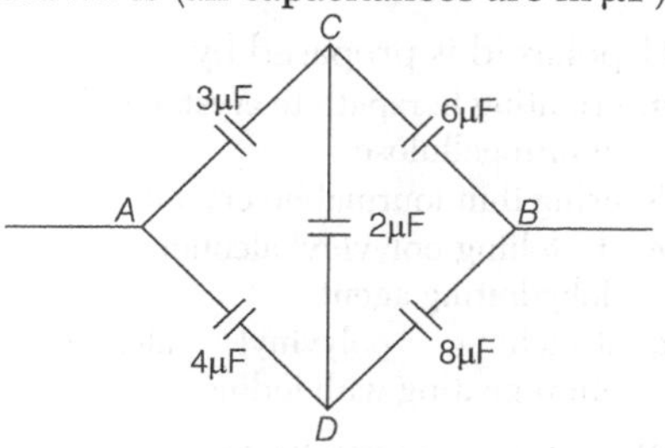

a. $\frac{3}{14}$ μF *b.* $\frac{14}{3}$ μF
c. 21 μF *d.* 23 μF

CHEMISTRY

61. A colourless crystalline salt *X* is soluble in dilute HCl. On adding NaOH solution, it gives a white precipitate which is insoluble in excess of NaOH. *X* is

a. $Al_2(SO_4)_3$ *b.* $ZnSO_4$
c. $MgSO_4$ *d.* $SnCl_2$

62. Which metal is used to make alloy steel for armour plates, safes and helmets ?

a. Al *b.* Mn *c.* Cr *d.* Pb

63. Iodoform test is not answered by

a. C_2H_5OH *b.* CH_3OH
c. CH_3COCH_3 *d.* $CH_3—CH(OH)—CH_3$

64. A gaseous carbon compound is soluble in dilute HCl. The solution on treating with $NaNO_2$ gives off nitrogen leaving behind a solution, which smells of wood spirit. The carbon compound is

a. HCHO *b.* CO
c. $C_2H_5NH_2$ *d.* CH_3NH_2

65. Which of the following statements is incorrect regarding benzyl chloride ?

a. It gives white precipitate with alcoholic $AgNO_3$.
b. It is an aromatic compound with substitution in the side chain.
c. It undergoes nucleophilic substitution reaction.
d. It is less reactive than vinyl chloride.

66. Enthalpy of formation of HF and HCl are – 161 kJ and – 92 kJ respectively. Which of the following statements is incorrect?

a. HCl is more stable than HF.
b. HF and HCl are exothermic compounds.
c. The affinity of fluorine to hydrogen is greater than the affinity of chlorine to hydrogen.
d. HF is more stable than HCl.

67. Heat liberated with 100 mL of 1 N NaOH is neutralised by 300 mL of 1 N HCl

a. 11.56 kJ *b.* 5.73 kJ
c. 22.92 kJ *d.* 17.19 kJ

68. For a reaction $A + B \longrightarrow C + D$, if concentration of *A* is doubled without altering that of *B*, rate doubles. If concentration of *B* is increased nine-times without altering that of *A*, rate triples. Order of the reaction is

a. 2 *b.* 1 *c.* $1\frac{1}{2}$ *d.* $1\frac{1}{3}$

69. In Goldschmidt aluminothermic process, thermite contains

a. 3 parts of Al_2O_3 and 4 parts of Al
b. 3 parts of Fe_2O_3 and 2 parts of Al
c. 3 parts of Fe_2O_3 and 1 part of Al
d. 1 part of Fe_2O_3 and 1 part of Al

70. The structure of orthophosphoric acid is

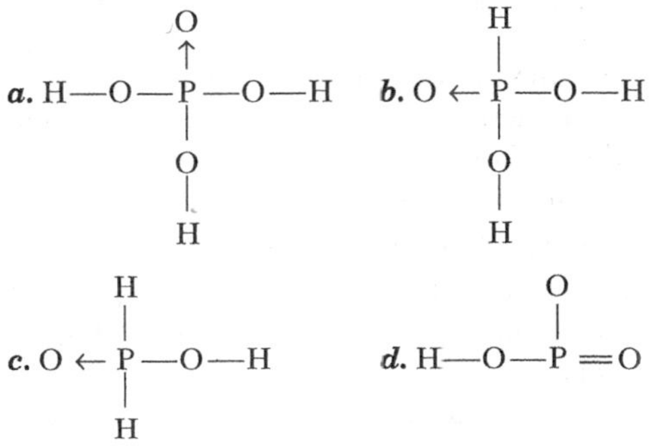

71. A galvanic cell is constructed using the redox reaction,

$$\frac{1}{2}H_2(g) + AgCl(s) \rightleftharpoons H^+(aq) + Cl^-(aq) + Ag(s)$$

it is represented as

a. Pt| $H_2(g)$ | HCl(*sol*) || $AgNO_3(sol)$ | Ag
b. Ag| AgCl(*s*) | KCl (*sol*) || HCl(*sol*), $H_2(g)$ | Pt
c. Pt | $H_2(g)$ | KCl(*sol*) || AgCl(*s*) | Ag
d. Pt| $H_2(g)$, HCl(*sol*) || AgCl(*s*) | Ag

72. Same amount of electric current is passed through solutions of $AgNO_3$ and HCl. If 1.08 g of silver is obtained in the first case, the amount of hydrogen liberated at STP in the second case is

a. 224 cm^3 *b.* 1.008 g
c. 112 cm^3 *d.* 22400 cm^3

73. The flame colours of metal ions are due to

a. Frenkel defect
b. Schottky defect
c. metal deficiency defect
d. metal excess defect

74. The order of reactivities of methyl halides in the formation of Grignard reagent is

a. $CH_3I > CH_3Br > CH_3Cl$
b. $CH_3Cl > CH_3Br > CH_3I$
c. $CH_3Br > CH_3Cl > CH_3I$
d. $CH_3Br > CH_3I > CH_3Cl$

75. The reaction of an organic compound with ammonia followed by nitration of the product gives a powerful explosive, called RDX. The organic compound is

a. phenol *b.* toluene
c. glycerine *d.* formaldehyde

76. A signature, written in carbon pencil weighs 1 mg. What is the number of carbon atoms present in the signature?

a. 5.02×10^{23} *b.* 5.02×10^{20}
c. 6.02×10^{20} *d.* 0.502×10^{20}

77. NH_3 and HCl gas are introduced simultaneously from the two ends of a long tube. A white ring of NH_4Cl appears first

a. nearer to the HCl end *b.* at the centre of the tube
c. throughout the tube *d.* nearer to the NH_3 end

78. A gas formed by the action of alcoholic KOH on ethyl iodide, decolourises alkaline $KMnO_4$. The gas is

a. C_2H_6 *b.* CH_4 *c.* C_2H_2 *d.* C_2H_4

79. Which of the following is not a characteristic of chemisorption?

a. ΔH is of the order of 400 kJ
b. Adsorption is irreversible
c. Adsorption may be multimolecular layer
d. Adsorption is specific

80. The concentration of electrolyte required to coagulate a given amount of As_2S_3 sol is minimum in the case of

a. magnesium nitrate *b.* potassium nitrate
c. potassium sulphate *d.* aluminium nitrate

81. Identify the organic compound which, on heating with strong solution of NaOH, partly converted into an acid salt and partly into alcohol

a. benzyl alcohol *b.* acetaldehyde
c. acetone *d.* benzaldehyde

82. The process by which synthesis of protein takes place based on the genetic information present in *m*-RNA is called

a. translation *b.* transcription
c. replication *d.* messenger hypothesis

83. The enthalpies of formation of Al_2O_3 and Cr_2O_3 are − 1596 kJ and − 1134 kJ respectively. ΔH for the reaction,

$2Al + Cr_2O_3 \longrightarrow 2Cr + Al_2O_3$ is

a. − 2730 kJ *b.* − 462 kJ
c. − 1365 kJ *d.* +2730 kJ

84. The gaseous reaction

$A + B \rightleftharpoons 2C + D + Q$ is most favoured at

a. low temperature and high pressure
b. high temperature and high pressure
c. high temperature and low pressure
d. low temperature and low pressure

85. Temperature coefficient of a reaction is 2. When temperature is increased from 30° C to 100°C, rate of the reaction increases by

a. 128 times *b.* 100 times
c. 500 times *d.* 250 times

86. The volume of water to be added to $\frac{N}{2}$ HCl to prepare 500 cm^3 of $\frac{N}{10}$ solution is

a. 450 cm^3 *b.* 100 cm^3
c. 45 cm^3 *d.* 400 cm^3

87. The equivalent weight of a certain trivalent element is 20. Molecular weight of its oxide is

a. 152 *b.* 56
c. 168 *d.* 68

88. Identify the reaction that doesn't take place during the smelting process of copper extraction

a. $2FeS + 3O_2 \longrightarrow 2FeO + 2SO_2 \uparrow$
b. $Cu_2O + FeS \longrightarrow Cu_2S + FeO$
c. $2Cu_2S + 3O_2 \longrightarrow 2Cu_2O + 2SO_2 \uparrow$
d. $FeO + SiO_2 \longrightarrow FeSiO_3$

89. Pick out the complex compound in which the central metal atom obeys EAN rule strictly.

a. $K_4[Fe(CN)_6]$
b. $K_3[Fe(CN)_6]$
c. $[Cr(H_2O)_6]Cl_3$
d. $[Cu(NH_3)_4]SO_4$

90. In a reversible reaction, the catalyst

a. increases the activation energy of the backward reaction
b. increases the activation energy of the forward reaction
c. decreases the activation energy of both, forward and backward reaction
d. decreases the activation energy of forward reaction

91. Solubility product of a salt *AB* is 1×10^{-8} in a solution in which concentration of *A* is 10^{-3} M. The salt will precipitate when the concentration of *B* becomes more than

a. 10^{-4} M *b.* 10^{-7} M
c. 10^{-6} M *d.* 10^{-5} M

92. The standard reduction potentials of Zn and Ag in water at 298 K are,

$$Zn^{2+} + 2e^- \rightleftharpoons Zn, \quad E° = -0.76\ V$$

and $$Ag^+ + e^- \rightleftharpoons Ag; \quad E° = +0.80\ V.$$

Which of the following reactions take place?

a. $Zn^{2+}(aq) + 2Ag(s) \longrightarrow 2Ag^+(aq) + Zn(s)$
b. $Zn(s) + 2Ag^+(aq) \longrightarrow Zn^{2+}(aq) + 2Ag(s)$
c. $Zn^{2+}(aq) + Ag^+(aq) \longrightarrow Zn(s) + Ag(s)$
d. $Zn(s) + Ag(s) \longrightarrow Zn^{2+}(aq) + Ag^+(aq)$

93. The ratio of cationic radius to anionic radius in an ionic crystal is greater than 0.732. Its coordination number is

a. 6 *b.* 8
c. 1 *d.* 4

94. Dacron is obtained by the condensation polymerisation of

a. dimethyl terephthalate and ethylene glycol
b. terephthalic acid and formaldehyde
c. phenol and phthalic acid
d. phenol and formaldehyde

95. 4-chloro-3, 5-dimethyl phenol is called

a. chloramphenicol *b.* paracetamol
c. barbital *d.* dettol

96. The percentage *s*-character of the hybrid orbitals in methane, ethene and ethyne are respectively

a. 25, 33, 50 *b.* 25, 50, 75
c. 50, 75, 100 *d.* 10, 20, 40

97. In the manufacture of sulphuric acid by contact process, Tyndall box is used to

a. filter dust particles
b. remove impurities
c. convert SO_2 to SO_3
d. test the presence of dust particles

98. The pH value of gastric juice in human stomach is about 1.8 and in the small intestine it is about 7.8. The pK_a value of aspirin is 3.5. Aspirin will be

a. completely ionised in the small intestine and in the stomach
b. unionised in the small intestine and in the stomach
c. ionised in the small intestine and almost unionised in the stomach
d. ionised in the stomach and almost unionised in the small intestine

99. The number of α and β-particles emitted during the transformation of $_{90}Th^{232}$ to $_{82}Pb^{208}$ are respectively

a. 4, 2 *b.* 2, 2 *c.* 8, 6 *d.* 6, 4

100. When chlorine is passed through warm benzene in presence of the sunlight, the product obtained is

a. benzotrichloride *b.* chlorobenzene
c. gammexane *d.* DDT

101. Ethyl benzoate reacts with PCl_5 to give

a. $C_2H_5Cl + C_6H_5COCl + POCl_3 + HCl$
b. $C_2H_5Cl + C_6H_5COCl + POCl_3$
c. $CH_3COCl + C_6H_5COCl + POCl_3$
d. $C_2H_5Cl + C_6H_5COOH + POCl_3$

102. Pick out the statement which is not relevant in the discussion of colloids

a. sodium aluminium silicate is used in the softening of hard water.
b. potash alum is used in shaving rounds and as a styptic in medicine.
c. artificial rain is caused by throwing electrified sand on the clouds from an aeroplane.
d. deltas are formed at a place where the river pours its water into the sea.

103. A wooden box excavated from Indus valley had an activity of 1.18×10^{13} disintegration per minute per g of carbon. What is the approximate age of this civilisation?

a. 4000 years *b.* 5700 years
c. 8100 years *d.* 6000 years

104. For a reaction, if $K_p > K_C$, the forward reaction is favoured by

a. low pressure *b.* high pressure
c. high temperature *d.* low temperature

105. In a lime kiln, to get higher yield of CO_2, the measure that can be taken is

a. to remove CaO
b. to add more $CaCO_3$
c. to maintain high temperature
d. to pump out CO_2

106. What is the volume of '20 volume H_2O_2' required to get 5000 cm^3 of oxygen at STP?

a. 250 cm^3 *b.* 50 cm^3 *c.* 100 cm^3 *d.* 125 cm^3

107. The IUPAC name of $(CH_3)_3C—CH=CH_2$ is

a. 1, 1, 1-trimethyl-2-propene
b. 3, 3, 3-trimethyl-2-propene
c. 2, 2-dimethyl-3-butene
d. 3, 3-dimethyl-1-butene

108. Railway wagon axles are made by heating iron rods embedded in charcoal powder.
This process is known as

a. tempering *b.* case-hardening
c. sherardising *d.* annealing

109. Thomas slag is

a. $CaSiO_3$ *b.* $Ca_3(PO_4)_2$
c. $MnSiO_3$ *d.* $CaCO_3$

110. Urea is preferred to ammonium sulphate as a nitrogenous fertiliser because

a. it is more soluble in water
b. it is cheaper than ammonium sulphate
c. it is quite stable
d. it does not cause acidity in the soil

111. Two gas cylinders having same capacity have been filled with 44 g of H_2 and 44 g of CO_2 respectively. If the pressure in CO_2 cylinder is 1 atmosphere at a particular temperature. The pressure in the hydrogen cylinder at the same temperature is

a. 2 atm *b.* 1 atm
c. 22 atm *d.* 44 atm

112. Angular momentum of an electron in the *n*th orbit of hydrogen atom is given by

a. $\frac{nh}{2\pi}$ *b.* nh *c.* $\frac{2\pi}{nh}$ *d.* $\frac{\pi}{2nh}$

113. The element with atomic number 36 belongs to .... block in the periodic table.

a. *p* *b.* *s* *c.* *f* *d.* *d*

114. The function of $AlCl_3$ in Friedel-Craft's reaction is

a. to absorb HCl
b. to absorb water
c. to produce nucleophile
d. to produce electrophile

115. An important reaction of acetone is auto-condensation in presence of concentrated sulphuric acid to give the aromatic compound ..... .

a. mesitylene *b.* mesityl oxide
c. trioxane *d.* phorone

116. Kinetic energy of one mole of an ideal gas at 300 K in kJ is

a. 3.74 *b.* 348
c. 34.8 *d.* 3.48

117. The tripeptide hormone present in most living cells is

a. glutathione *b.* glutamine
c. oxytocin *d.* ptyalin

118. Phenol $\xrightarrow{NaNO_2/H_2SO_4} B \xrightarrow{H_2O} C \xrightarrow{NaOH} D$

name of the reaction is

a. Liebermann's reaction
b. Phthalein fusion test
c. Reimer-Tiemann reaction
d. Schotten-Baumann reaction

119. Energy is stored in our body in the form of

a. ATP *b.* ADP
c. fats *d.* carbohydrates

120. An organic compound answers Molisch's test as well as Benedict's test, but it does not answer Scliwanoff's test. Most probably, it is

a. sucrose *b.* protein
c. fructose *d.* maltose

MATHEMATICS

121. $\sim p \wedge q$ is logically equivalent to

a. $p \to q$ *b.* $q \to p$
c. $\sim(p \to q)$ *d.* $\sim(q \to p)$

122. Which of the following is the inverse of the proposition : "If a number is a prime, then it is odd"?

a. If a number is not a prime, then it is odd
b. If a number is not a prime, then it is not odd
c. If a number is not odd, then it is not a prime
d. If a number is odd, then it is a prime

123. What must be the matrix *X* if

$$2X + \begin{bmatrix} 1 & 2 \\ 3 & 4 \end{bmatrix} = \begin{bmatrix} 3 & 8 \\ 7 & 2 \end{bmatrix}?$$

a. $\begin{bmatrix} 1 & 3 \\ 2 & -1 \end{bmatrix}$ *b.* $\begin{bmatrix} 1 & -3 \\ 2 & -1 \end{bmatrix}$

c. $\begin{bmatrix} 2 & 6 \\ 4 & -2 \end{bmatrix}$ *d.* $\begin{bmatrix} 2 & -6 \\ 4 & -2 \end{bmatrix}$

124. The value of $\begin{vmatrix} 1 & 1 & 1 \\ bc & ca & ab \\ b+c & c+a & a+b \end{vmatrix}$ is

a. 1
b. 0
c. $(a-b)(b-c)(c-a)$
d. $(a+b)(b+c)(c+a)$

125. The value of $\begin{vmatrix} 441 & 442 & 443 \\ 445 & 446 & 447 \\ 449 & 450 & 451 \end{vmatrix}$ is

a. $441 \times 446 \times 4510$ *b.* 0
c. -1 *d.* 1

125. The value of $\begin{vmatrix} 441 & 442 & 443 \\ 445 & 446 & 447 \\ 449 & 450 & 451 \end{vmatrix}$ is

a. $441 \times 446 \times 4510$ *b.* 0 *c.* -1 *d.* 1

126. $(\mathbf{a} \cdot \hat{\mathbf{i}})\hat{\mathbf{i}} + (\mathbf{a} \cdot \hat{\mathbf{j}})\hat{\mathbf{j}} + (\mathbf{a} \cdot \hat{\mathbf{k}})\hat{\mathbf{k}}$ is equal to

a. a *b.* 2a *c.* 3a *d.* 0

127. Inverse of the matrix $\begin{bmatrix} \cos 2\theta & -\sin 2\theta \\ \sin 2\theta & \cos 2\theta \end{bmatrix}$ is

a. $\begin{bmatrix} \cos 2\theta & -\sin 2\theta \\ \sin 2\theta & \cos 2\theta \end{bmatrix}$ *b.* $\begin{bmatrix} \cos 2\theta & \sin 2\theta \\ \sin 2\theta & -\cos 2\theta \end{bmatrix}$

c. $\begin{bmatrix} \cos 2\theta & \sin 2\theta \\ \sin 2\theta & \cos 2\theta \end{bmatrix}$ *d.* $\begin{bmatrix} \cos 2\theta & \sin 2\theta \\ -\sin 2\theta & \cos 2\theta \end{bmatrix}$

128. If $|\mathbf{a}| = 3$, $|\mathbf{b}| = 4$, then a value of λ for which $\mathbf{a} + \lambda\mathbf{b}$ is perpendicular to $\mathbf{a} - \lambda\,\mathbf{b}$ is

a. $\frac{9}{16}$ *b.* $\frac{3}{4}$ *c.* $\frac{3}{2}$ *d.* $\frac{4}{3}$

129. The projection of $\mathbf{a} = 2\hat{\mathbf{i}} + 3\hat{\mathbf{j}} - 2\hat{\mathbf{k}}$ on $\mathbf{b} = \hat{\mathbf{i}} + 2\hat{\mathbf{j}} + 3\hat{\mathbf{k}}$ is

a. $\frac{1}{\sqrt{14}}$ *b.* $\frac{2}{\sqrt{14}}$ *c.* $\sqrt{14}$ *d.* $\frac{-2}{\sqrt{14}}$

130. In the group (1, 2, 3, 4, 5, 6) under multiplication 7, $2^{-1} \times 4$ is equal to

a. 1 *b.* 4 *c.* 2 *d.* 3

131. The maximum of the function $3\cos x - 4\sin x$ is

a. 2 *b.* 3 *c.* 4 *d.* 5

132. If the distance 'S' metres traversed by a particle in t seconds is given by $S = t^3 - 3t^2$, then the velocity of the particle when the acceleration is zero, in m/sec is

a. 3 *b.* -2 *c.* -3 *d.* 2

133. For the curve $y^n = a^{n-1}x$ if the subnormal at any point is a constant, then n is equal to

a. 1 *b.* 2 *c.* -2 *d.* -1

134. If $x = A\cos 4t + B\sin 4t$, then $\frac{d^2x}{dt^2}$ is equal to

a. $-16x$ *b.* $16x$ *c.* x *d.* $-x$

135. If tangent to the curve $x = at^2$, $y = 2at$ is perpendicular to X-axis, then its point of contact is

a. (a, a) *b.* $(0, a)$ *c.* $(0, 0)$ *d.* $(a, 0)$

136. The general solution of the differential equation $\frac{dy}{dx} + \frac{1 + \cos 2y}{1 - \cos 2y} = 0$ is given by

a. $\tan y + \cot x = c$ *b.* $\tan y - \cot x = c$

c. $\tan x - \cot y = c$ *d.* $\tan x + \cot x = c$

137. The degree of the differential equation $\left(1 + \left(\frac{dy}{dx}\right)^2\right)^{3/4} = \left(\frac{d^2y}{dx^2}\right)^{1/3}$ is

a. 2 *b.* 4 *c.* 9 *d.* 1

138. The area enclosed between the curves $y = x^3$ and $y = \sqrt{x}$ is, (in square units)

a. $\frac{5}{3}$ *b.* $\frac{5}{4}$ *c.* $\frac{5}{12}$ *d.* $\frac{12}{5}$

139. $\int_0^{\pi/8} \cos^3 4\theta \, d\theta$ is equal to

a. $\frac{5}{3}$ *b.* $\frac{5}{4}$ *c.* $\frac{1}{3}$ *d.* $\frac{1}{6}$

140. $\int_0^{\pi/2} \frac{\cos x - \sin x}{1 + \cos x \sin x} dx$ is equal to

a. 0 *b.* $\frac{\pi}{2}$ *c.* $\frac{\pi}{4}$ *d.* $\frac{\pi}{6}$

141. If $ax^2 - y^2 + 4x - y = 0$ represents a pair of lines, then a is equal to

a. -16 *b.* 16 *c.* 4 *d.* -4

142. What is the equation of the locus of a point which moves such that 4 times its distance from the X-axis is the square of its distance from the origin?

a. $x^2 + y^2 - 4y = 0$

b. $x^2 + y^2 - 4|y| = 0$

c. $x^2 + y^2 - 4x = 0$

d. $x^2 + y^2 - 4|x| = 0$

143. Equation of the straight line making equal intercepts on the axes and passing through the point (2, 4) is

a. $4x - y - 4 = 0$

b. $2x + y - 8 = 0$

c. $x + y - 6 = 0$

d. $x + 2y - 10 = 0$

144. If the area of the triangle with vertices $(x, 0)$, (1, 1) and (0, 2) is 4 sq units, then the value of x is

a. -2 *b.* -4 *c.* -6 *d.* 8

145. $\lim_{a \to \pi/2} \frac{\frac{\pi}{2} - \theta}{\cot \theta} =$

a. 0 *b.* − 1 *c.* 1 *d.* ∞

146. The co-axial system of circles given by $x^2 + y^2 + 2gx + c = 0$ for $c < 0$ represents

a. intersecting circles
b. non-intersecting circles
c. touching circles
d. touching or non-intersecting circles

147. The radius of the circle passing through the point (6, 2) and two of whose diameters are $x + y = 6$ and $x + 2y = 4$ is

a. 4 *b.* 6 *c.* 20 *d.* $\sqrt{20}$

148. If (0, 6) and (0, 3) are respectively the vertex and focus of a parabola, then its equation is

a. $x^2 + 12y = 72$ *b.* $x^2 - 12y = 72$
c. $y^2 - 12x = 72$ *d.* $y^2 + 12x = 72$

149. For the ellipse $25x^2 + 9y^2 - 150x - 90y + 225 = 0$ the eccentricity e is equal to

a. $\frac{2}{5}$ *b.* $\frac{3}{5}$ *c.* $\frac{4}{5}$ *d.* $\frac{1}{5}$

150. If the foci of the ellipse $\frac{x^2}{16} + \frac{y^2}{b^2} = 1$ and the hyperbola $\frac{x^2}{144} - \frac{y^2}{81} = \frac{1}{25}$ coincide then the value of b^2 is

a. 1 *b.* 7 *c.* 5 *d.* 9

151. The differential coefficient is $f(\sin x)$ with respect to x where $f(x) + \log x$ is

a. $\tan x$ *b.* $\cot x$ *c.* $f(\cos x)$ *d.* $\frac{1}{x}$

152. If $f(x) = \begin{cases} \frac{1 - \cos x}{x} & x \neq 0 \\ k & x = 0 \end{cases}$ is continuous at $x = 0$, then the value of k is

a. 0 *b.* $\frac{1}{2}$ *c.* $\frac{1}{4}$ *d.* $-\frac{1}{2}$

153. If $\omega = \frac{-1 + \sqrt{3}i}{2}$ then $(3 + \omega + 3\omega^2)^4$ is

a. 16 *b.* − 16 *c.* 16 ω *d.* 16 ω^2

154. If $y = \tan^{-1}(\sec x - \tan x)$, then $\frac{dy}{dx}$ is equal to

a. 2 *b.* − 2 *c.* $\frac{1}{2}$ *d.* $-\frac{1}{2}$

155. If $x + \frac{1}{x} = 2 \cos \alpha$, then $x^n + \frac{1}{x^n}$ is equal to

a. $2^n \cos \alpha$ *b.* $2^n \cos n\alpha$
c. $2i\sin n\alpha$ *d.* $2\cos n\alpha$

156. $\int_{-1}^{1} |1 - x| \, dx$ is equal to

a. − 2 *b.* 0 *c.* 2 *d.* 4

157. $\int \frac{dx}{x(x^7 + 1)}$ is equal to

a. $\log\left(\frac{x^7}{x^7 + 1}\right) + c$
b. $\frac{1}{7}\log\left(\frac{x^7}{x^7 + 1}\right) + c$
c. $\log\left(\frac{x^7 + 1}{x^7}\right) + c$
d. $\frac{1}{7}\log\left(\frac{x^7 + 1}{x^7}\right) + c$

158. $\int \sqrt{x} e^{\sqrt{x}} dx$ is equal to

a. $2\sqrt{x} - e^{\sqrt{x}} - 4\sqrt{x e^{\sqrt{x}}} + c$
b. $(2x - 4\sqrt{x} + 4)e^{\sqrt{x}} + c$
c. $(2x + 4\sqrt{x} + 4)\, e^{\sqrt{x}} + c$
d. $(1 - 4\sqrt{x})\, e^{\sqrt{x}} + c$

159. $\int \frac{dx}{x^2 + 2x + 2}$ is equal to

a. $\sin^{-1}(x + 1) + c$ *b.* $\sinh^{-1}(x + 1) + c$
c. $\tanh^{-1}(x + 1) + c$ *d.* $\tan^{-1}(x + 1) + c$

160. If a tangent to the curve $y = 6x - x^2$ is parallel to the line $4x - 2y - 1 = 0$, then the point of tangency on the curve is

a. (2, 8) *b.* (8, 2)
c. (6, 1) *d.* (4, 2)

161. 0.5737373 … is equal to

a. $\frac{284}{497}$ *b.* $\frac{284}{495}$ *c.* $\frac{568}{999}$ *d.* $\frac{567}{990}$

162. The number of solutions for the equation $x^2 - 5|x| + 6 = 0$ is

a. 4 *b.* 3 *c.* 2 *d.* 1

163. How many numbers of 6-digits can be formed from the digits of the number 112233 ?

a. 30 *b.* 60 *c.* 90 *d.* 120

164. The last digit in 7^{300} is

a. 7 *b.* 9 *c.* 1 *d.* 3

165. If $\frac{\log x}{a-b}=\frac{\log y}{b-c}=\frac{\log z}{c-a}$, then xyz is equal to

a. 0 *b.* 1
c. – 1 *d.* 2

166. The smallest positive integer n for which $(1+i)^{2n}=(1-i)^{2n}$ is

a. 1 *b.* 2
c. 3 *d.* 4

167. If $\cos^{-1}p+\cos^{-1}q+\cos^{-1}r=\pi$, then $p^2+q^2+r^2+2pqr$ is equal to

a. 3 *b.* 1
c. 2 *d.* – 1

168. If $\sin^{-1}\frac{x}{5}+\operatorname{cosec}^{-1}\frac{5}{4}=\frac{\pi}{2}$, then x is equal to

a. 1 *b.* 4
c. 3 *d.* 5

169. If $0\le x\le\pi$ and $81^{\sin^2 x}+81^{\cos^2 x}=30$, then x is equal to

a. $\frac{\pi}{6}$ *b.* $\frac{\pi}{2}$
c. $\frac{\pi}{4}$ *d.* $\frac{3\pi}{4}$

170. The equation of the director circle of the hyperbola $\frac{x^2}{16}-\frac{y^2}{4}=1$ is given by

a. $x^2+y^2=16$ *b.* $x^2+y^2=4$
c. $x^2+y^2=20$ *d.* $x^2+y^2=12$

171. If Q_1 is the set of all relations other than 1 with the binary operation * defined by $a*b=a+b-ab$ for all a, b in Q_1, then the identity in Q_1 with respect to * is

a. 1 *b.* 0
c. – 1 *d.* 2

172. The circle $x^2+y^2-8x+4y+4=0$ touches

a. X-axis
b. Y-axis
c. both axes
d. neither X-axis nor Y-axis.

173. Which of the following is true ?

a. The set of all fourth roots of unity is a multiplicative group
b. The set of all cube roots of unity is an additive group
c. $(ab)^{-1}=a^{-1}b^{-1}$ for all a, b in any group G
d. If $(ab)^2=a^2b^2$ for all a, b in any group G, then the group G is non-abelian

174. The set of all integral multiples of 5 is a subgroup of

a. The set of all rational numbers under multiplication
b. The set of all integers under multiplication
c. The set of all non-zero rational numbers under multiplication
d. The set of all integers under addition

175. The value of k so that $x^2+y^2+kx+4y+2=0$ and $2(x^2+y^2)-4x-3y+k=0$ cut orthogonally is

a. $\frac{10}{3}$ *b.* $-\frac{8}{3}$ *c.* $-\frac{10}{3}$ *d.* $\frac{8}{3}$

176. $\lim_{x\to\infty}\left(1-\frac{4}{x-1}\right)^{3x-1}$ is equal to

a. e^{12} *b.* e^{-12} *c.* e^4 *d.* e^3

177. If $A+B+C=180^\circ$, then $\Sigma\tan\frac{A}{2}\tan\frac{B}{2}$ is equal to

a. 0 *b.* 1 *c.* 2 *d.* 3

178. In a ΔABC if $b=2$, $B=30^\circ$ then the area of the circumcircle of ΔABC in square units is

a. π *b.* 2π *c.* 4π *d.* 6π

179. If $\sin x+\sin^2 x=1$, then $\cos^{12}x+3\cos^{10}x+3\cos^8 x+\cos^6 x$ is equal to

a. 1 *b.* 2
c. 3 *d.* 0

180. If R denotes the set of all real number, then the function $f:R\to R$ defined $f(x)=|x|$ is

a. one-one only
b. onto only
c. both one-one and onto
d. neither one-one nor onto

ANSWERS

Physics

1. (d)	**2.** (d)	**3.** (d)	**4.** (b)	**5.** (a)	**6.** (d)	**7.** (d)	**8.** (a)	**9.** (d)	**10.** (a)
11. (d)	**12.** (a)	**13.** (a)	**14.** (c)	**15.** (c)	**16.** (c)	**17.** (a)	**18.** (c)	**19.** (d)	**20.** (c)
21. (a)	**22.** (a)	**23.** (b)	**24.** (d)	**25.** (c)	**26.** (b)	**27.** (c)	**28.** (b)	**29.** (c)	**30.** (c)
31. (d)	**32.** (b)	**33.** (c)	**34.** (b)	**35.** (b)	**36.** (d)	**37.** (a)	**38.** (d)	**39.** (b)	**40.** (a)
41. (c)	**42.** (b)	**43.** (b)	**44.** (d)	**45.** (b)	**46.** (c)	**47.** (d)	**48.** (a)	**49.** (b)	**50.** (a)
51. (c)	**52.** (c)	**53.** (c)	**54.** (c)	**55.** (b)	**56.** (d)	**57.** (d)	**58.** (a)	**59.** (d)	**60.** (b)

Chemistry

61. (c)	**62.** (b)	**63.** (b)	**64.** (d)	**65.** (d)	**66.** (a)	**67.** (b)	**68.** (c)	**69.** (c)	**70.** (a)
71. (d)	**72.** (c)	**73.** (d)	**74.** (a)	**75.** (d)	**76.** (d)	**77.** (a)	**78.** (d)	**79.** (c)	**80.** (d)
81. (d)	**82.** (a)	**83.** (b)	**84.** (d)	**85.** (a)	**86.** (b)	**87.** (c)	**88.** (a)	**89.** (a)	**90.** (c)
91. (d)	**92.** (b)	**93.** (b)	**94.** (a)	**95.** (d)	**96.** (a)	**97.** (d)	**98.** (d)	**99.** (d)	**100.** (c)
101. (b)	**102.** (a)	**103.** (c)	**104.** (a)	**105.** (d)	**106.** (a)	**107.** (d)	**108.** (b)	**109.** (b)	**110.** (d)
111. (c)	**112.** (a)	**113.** (a)	**114.** (d)	**115.** (a)	**116.** (a)	**117.** (a)	**118.** (a)	**119.** (a)	**120.** (d)

Mathematics

121. (d)	**122.** (b)	**123.** (a)	**124.** (c)	**125.** (b)	**126.** (a)	**127.** (d)	**128.** (b)	**129.** (b)	**130.** (c)
131. (d)	**132.** (c)	**133.** (b)	**134.** (a)	**135.** (c)	**136.** (b)	**137.** (b)	**138.** (c)	**139.** (d)	**140.** (a)
141. (b)	**142.** (b)	**143.** (c)	**144.** (c)	**145.** (c)	**146.** (a)	**147.** (d)	**148.** (a)	**149.** (c)	**150.** (b)
151. (b)	**152.** (a)	**153.** (c)	**154.** (d)	**155.** (d)	**156.** (c)	**157.** (b)	**158.** (b)	**159.** (d)	**160.** (a)
161. (b)	**162.** (a)	**163.** (c)	**164.** (c)	**165.** (b)	**166.** (b)	**167.** (b)	**168.** (c)	**169.** (a)	**170.** (d)
171. (b)	**172.** (b)	**173.** (a)	**174.** (d)	**175.** (c)	**176.** (b)	**177.** (b)	**178.** (c)	**179.** (a)	**180.** (d)

HINTS & SOLUTIONS

Physics

1. *(d)* If frequency of source be f_s, then

$$f_{\text{approach}} - f_{\text{recession}} = \frac{2}{100} \times f_o$$

$$\Rightarrow \quad f_s\left(\frac{v + v_s}{v}\right) - f_s\left(\frac{v - v_s}{v}\right) = \frac{f_s}{50}$$

$$\Rightarrow \quad \frac{2v_s}{v} = \frac{1}{50} \Rightarrow \frac{2v_s}{300} = \frac{1}{50}$$

$$\Rightarrow \quad v_s = \frac{300}{2 \times 50} = 3 \text{ ms}^{-1}$$

2. *(d)* The magnetic force between two current carrying wires for current in same direction is attractive.

Thus, force on B due to the magnetic field produced due to wire A is

$$F_A = B_A I_B l = \frac{\mu_0 \times I_A}{2\pi d} \times I_B \times l$$

$$= \frac{\mu_0 \times 1 \times 2 \times l}{2\pi d} = \frac{2\mu_0 l}{2\pi d}, \text{ towards } A \quad \ldots\text{(i)}$$

Similarly, force due to field of wire C,

$$F_C = B_C I_B l = \frac{\mu_0 I_C I_B l}{2\pi d} = \frac{\mu_0 \times 3 \times 2 \times l}{2\pi d}$$

$$\Rightarrow \quad F_C = \frac{6\mu_0 l}{2\pi d}, \text{ towards } C \quad \ldots\text{(ii)}$$

From Eqs. (i) and (ii) we get

$$F_C > F_A$$

∴ The resultant force on B is directed towards C.

3. *(d)* Ferromagnetic materials like iron obeys Curie-Weiss law above its Curie temperature. According to Curie-Weiss law, magnetic susceptiblity (χ) of ferromagnetic material is related with temperature T as

$$\chi = \frac{C}{T - T_C}$$

where, C = Curie constant

and T_C = Curie temperature.

4. *(b)* As the magnet oscillates about its mean position performing SHM, the magnetic flux of the coil changes and emf is induced in it. So, the galvanometer shows deflection to the left and right for both in and out motion. But due to eddy currents, the velocity of magnet decreases So, the amplitude of deflection also decreases steadily.

5. *(a)* As we know, magnetic flux, $\phi = LI$

$$\Rightarrow \quad L = \frac{\phi}{I} = \frac{BA}{I}$$

$$\therefore \text{ Dimensions of } [\text{L}] = \frac{[\text{B}][\text{A}]}{[\text{I}]}$$

$$= \frac{[\text{ML}^0\text{T}^{-2}\text{A}^{-1}][\text{L}^2]}{[\text{A}]} = [\text{ML}^2\text{T}^{-2}\text{A}^{-2}]$$

6. *(d)* Given, $G = 40\,\Omega$, $I_g = 10\,\text{mA} = 10 \times 10^{-3}$ A

$$V = 50 \text{ V}$$

Let R be the resistance connected in series with the galvanometer to convert into voltmeter, then

$$V = I_g(G + R)$$

$$\Rightarrow \quad 50 = 10 \times 10^{-3}(40 + R)$$

$$\Rightarrow \quad \frac{50}{10 \times 10^{-3}} = 40 + R$$

$$\Rightarrow \quad R = 5000 - 40 = 4960\,\Omega$$

7. *(d)* Chromosphere is the outer region of the sun just above the photosphere. The photosphere emits continuous spectrum that passes through the chromosphere after some absorption. These absorption lines are observed in solar spectrum.

During a total solar eclipse, when the light from photosphere is cut-off, the chromosphere is visible to us. Hence, the line absorption spectrum with continuous background is seen during a total solar eclipse.

8. *(a)* Heavy water (D_2O) contains heavy hydrogen or deuterium and oxygen.

9. *(d)* The nuclear reactor at Kaiga is a power reactor and named as Kaiga Atomic Power Station.

It is used for electricity and power generation.

10. *(a)* In a circular path, the centripetal force acts towards the centre of circle and the displacement is along the tangent to the circle. Hence, $\theta = 90°$

∴ Work done $W = \mathbf{F} \cdot \mathbf{s} = Fs\cos\theta$

$$= Fs\cos 90° = 0$$

11. *(d)* Given, $u_1 = 100 \text{ ms}^{-1}$

$\Rightarrow u_2 = 2 \times u_1 = 2 \times 100 = 200 \text{ ms}^{-1}$

Using equation of motion,

$$v^2 = u^2 - 2as \qquad (\because \text{ acceleration is negative})$$

As, final velocity, $v = 0$

$$\Rightarrow \quad u^2 = 2as \text{ or } s = \frac{u^2}{2a} \Rightarrow s \propto u^2$$

$$\therefore \quad \frac{s_1}{s_2} = \frac{u_1^2}{u_2^2} = \frac{(100)^2}{(200)^2} = \frac{1}{4}$$

$$\Rightarrow \quad s_2 = 4s_1 = 4 \times 2 \text{ planks} = 8 \text{ planks}$$

12. *(a)* Given, $m_1 = 1$ kg, $m_2 = 2$ kg

The kinetic energy is related to momentum of body by the formula given as

$$K = \frac{p^2}{2m}$$

$$\therefore \quad \frac{K_1}{K_2} = \frac{m_2}{m_1} = \frac{2}{1} \qquad (\because \text{ momentum is same})$$

13. *(a)* An open window is like a perfectly black body that absorbs completely the quantity being transferred, so its absorption coefficient is unity or 1.

14. *(c)* The loudness depends on the amplitude of sound wave, thus it depends on its intensity.

The pitch of a sound describes how low or high a note is produced by the instrument. Thus, it depends on the frequency of sound source.

15. *(c)* In Melde's experiment, the change in frequency is produced when the tension in the string is increased. So, a resonance is required between tuning fork and the frequency of waves produced. For this, the frequencies of both should be same or their ratio be 1 : 1.

16. *(c)* As we know,

Kinetic energy of electron = Energy acquired due to potential (V_0)

$$\Rightarrow \quad \frac{1}{2}m_e v^2 = eV_0$$

$$\Rightarrow \quad v = \sqrt{\frac{2eV_0}{m_e}}$$

$$= \sqrt{\frac{2\times 1.6\times 10^{-19}\times 45.5}{9.1\times 10^{-31}}}$$

$$= \sqrt{16\times 10^{12}} = 4\times 10^6 \text{ ms}^{-1}$$

17. *(a)* In first case, $P = R_1 + 10$, $Q = R_2$, $l = 50$ cm

For balanced condition,

$$\frac{P}{Q} = \frac{l}{100 - l}$$

$$\Rightarrow \quad \frac{R_1 + 10}{R_2} = \frac{50}{50}$$

$$\Rightarrow \quad R_1 + 10 = R_2 \quad \ldots\text{(i)}$$

Similarly, for second case,

$$P = R_1, Q = R_2, l = 40 \text{ cm}$$

$$\Rightarrow \quad \frac{R_1}{R_2} = \frac{40}{100 - 40} = \frac{40}{60}$$

$$\Rightarrow \quad R_2 = \frac{3}{2}R_1 \quad \ldots\text{(ii)}$$

Putting value of R_2 from Eq. (ii) in Eq (i), we get

$$R_1 + 10 = \frac{3}{2}R_1$$

$$\Rightarrow \quad R_1 = 2\times 10 = 20\,\Omega$$

18. *(c)* 2Ω and $3\,\Omega$ resistors are in parallel, so their equivalent resistance,

$$R_{eq} = \frac{2\times 3}{2+3} = \frac{6}{5} = 1.2\Omega$$

As capacitor blocks DC at steady state, so the resistor $4\,\Omega$ is ineffective.

The R_{eq} and 2.8Ω are in series, so total resistance of circuit,

$$R_T = 1.2 + 2.8 = 4\,\Omega$$

Current in circuit, $I = \dfrac{V}{R_T} = \dfrac{6}{4} = 1.5$ A

Potential across the combination of 2Ω and $3\,\Omega$ resistors $\quad V' = 1.5\times 1.2 = 1.8$ V

$\therefore$ The steady state current in 2Ω resistor is

$$I' = \frac{V'}{2} = \frac{1.8}{2} = 0.9 \text{ A}$$

19. *(d)* Peak value of emf is induced, when longer side of rectangular coil moves perpendicular to the field.

Given, $\quad f = 50$ cps,

$$A = 25\times 10\times 10^{-4}\text{ m}^2$$

$$= 250\times 10^{-4}\text{ m}^2$$

$$B = 4\times 10^{-2}\text{ T, and } N = 300$$

Peak value of induced emf, $e_0 = NAB\omega$

$$= 300\times 250\times 10^{-4}\times 4\times 10^{-2}\times 2\pi\times 50$$

$$= 30\pi \text{ V}$$

20. *(c)* Given, $V_R = 40$ V, $V_L = 60$ V, $V_C = 30$ V

For an *L-C-R* circuit, the supply voltage

$$V = \sqrt{V_R^2 + (V_L - V_C)^2}$$

$$= \sqrt{40^2 + (60-30)^2}$$

$$= \sqrt{40^2 + 30^2}$$

$$= \sqrt{1600 + 900} = \sqrt{2500} = 50\text{V}$$

21. *(a)* Given, $R = 0.1$ m, $N = 10$, $B_H = 0.314\times 10^{-4}$ T

For neutral point, the magnetic field at the centre of coil carrying current is equal to the horizontal component of earth's field.

i.e. $$B_H = \frac{\mu_0 NI}{2R}$$

$$\Rightarrow \quad I = \frac{2B_H R}{\mu_0 N}$$

$$= \frac{2\times 0.314\times 10^{-4}\times 0.1}{4\pi\times 10^{-7}\times 10}$$

$$= \frac{0.314\times 10^{-4}}{2\times 3.14\times 10^{-7}\times 100} = 0.5 \text{ A}$$

22. *(a)* When portion *A* is punctured, the soap solution comes out of the hole. So, due to surface tension, the solution in part *B* tries to pull it toward itself. Thus, the thread becomes concave towards *A*.

23. *(b)* Velocity of sound in a gas is given by

$$v = \sqrt{\frac{\gamma RT}{M}}$$

where, γ = specific heat ratio

and M = molecular mass of gas.

For hydrogen, $$v_H = \sqrt{\frac{\gamma RT}{M_1}} \quad \ldots\text{(i)}$$

For mixture of gases, molecular mass,

$$M_{\text{mix}} = \frac{n_1 M_1 + n_2 M_2}{n_1 + n_2}$$

Here, $\quad n_1 = n_2 \quad$ (for equal volumes)

COMEDK 2013

and $M_2 = 16M_1$ (given)

$$M_{mix} = \frac{M_1 + 16M_1}{2} = \frac{17M_1}{2}$$

$\therefore$ Velocity of sound, $v_{mix} = \sqrt{\frac{\gamma RT}{M_{mix}}}$ ...(ii)

Dividing Eq. (ii) by Eq. (i) we get

$$\frac{v_{mix}}{v_H} = \sqrt{\frac{\gamma RT}{M_{mix}}} \times \sqrt{\frac{M_1}{\gamma RT}}$$

$$= \sqrt{\frac{M_1}{M_{mix}}} = \sqrt{\frac{2}{17}}$$

24. *(d)* The resultant amplitude after super position of two wave differing in phase by ϕ is given by

$$A_R^2 = A_1^2 + A_2^2 + 2A_1A_2\cos\phi$$

Here, $A_1 = A_2 = A_R = A$

$\Rightarrow$ $A^2 = 2A^2 + 2A^2\cos\phi$

$\Rightarrow$ $\cos\phi = -\frac{1}{2}$

$\Rightarrow$ $\phi = \pi - \frac{\pi}{3} = \frac{2\pi}{3}$

25. *(c)* Let x be the distance between a cliff and man, then time taken by the echo,

$t = \frac{2x}{v} = 1$ (given)

$\Rightarrow$ $x = \frac{v}{2} = \frac{340}{2} = 170$ m

$\therefore$ Distance between two cliffs

$= 2x = 2 \times 170 = 340$ m

26. *(b)* Given $\lambda = 600$ nm $= 600 \times 10^{-9}$ m

$D = 2$m, $d = 1$ mm $= 1 \times 10^{-3}$ m

The distance of first dark fringe from central bright fringe,

$$y = \frac{D\lambda}{d}$$

$$= \frac{2 \times 600 \times 10^{-9}}{1 \times 10^{-3}} = 1.2 \text{ mm}$$

$\therefore$ Distance between first dark fringe on either side of central bright fringe $= 2y = 1.2 \times 2 = 2.4$ mm

27. *(c)* Impulse = Force × Time

$= [MLT^{-2}][T] = [MLT^{-1}]$

Surface tension $= \frac{\text{Force}}{\text{Length}}$

$$= \frac{[MLT^{-2}]}{[L]} = [ML^0T^{-2}]$$

Angular momentum

= Moment of intertia × Angular velocity

$= [ML^2][T^{-1}] = [ML^2T^{-1}]$

Work = Force × Distance $= [MLT^{-2}][L] = [ML^2T^{-2}]$

Torque = Force × Distance $= [ML^2T^{-2}]$

Energy $= [ML^2T^{-2}]$

Young's modulus $= \frac{\frac{\text{Force}}{\text{Area}}}{\frac{\Delta L}{L}}$

$$= \frac{[MLT^{-2}] \times [L]}{[L^2] \times [L]} = [ML^{-1}T^{-2}]$$

$\therefore$ Work and torque have same dimensions.

28. *(b)* Given, $t = \sqrt{x} + 3$

$\Rightarrow$ $\sqrt{x} = t - 3$

or $x = (t-3)^2$

Velocity, $v = \frac{dx}{dt} = \frac{d}{dt}(t-3)^2 = 2(t-3)$

When velocity of particle is zero, then

$2(t-3) = 0$

$\Rightarrow$ $t = 3$ s

At $t = 3$ s, $x = (3-3)^2 = 0$

29. *(c)* As per Boolean expressions,

$\mathbf{A} \times (\mathbf{B} \times \mathbf{C}) = (\mathbf{A} \cdot \mathbf{C})\mathbf{B} - (\mathbf{A} \cdot \mathbf{B})\mathbf{C} = 0 - 0 = 0$

$\therefore$ $(\mathbf{B} \times \mathbf{C})$ is parallel to $\mathbf{A}$.

30. *(c)* A transformer does not work on DC supply because mutual induction does not take place due to constant value of current. So, $V_S = 0$ and $I_S = 0$.

31. *(d)* Here, work done $= mgh$

As, m and h is same, so work done will be same in both cases.

Power, $P = \frac{\text{Work done }(W)}{\text{Time taken }(t)}$

$\Rightarrow$ $\frac{P_1}{P_2} = \frac{t_2}{t_1} = \frac{30}{60} = \frac{1}{2}$ or 1 : 2

32. *(b)* Given $\theta_1 = 0°$, $\theta_2 = 90°$

The energy required to rotate the dipole from angle θ_1 to θ_2 is equal to work done.

i.e., $E = W = -pE(\cos\theta_2 - \cos\theta_1)$

$= -pE(\cos 90° - \cos 0°)$

$= -pE(0 - 1) = pE$

33. *(c)* Given, $r = 10$ m, $v = 10$ m/s

If θ be the angle made by the wire with the vertical, then

$$\tan\theta = \frac{v^2}{rg}$$

$$= \frac{(10)^2}{(10)(10)} = 1$$

$\Rightarrow$ $\theta = 45°$ or $\frac{\pi}{4}$

34. *(b)* The escape velocity of earth,

$$v_e = \sqrt{\frac{2GM_e}{R_e}} = R_e\sqrt{\frac{8}{3}\pi G\rho_e}$$

Similarly for a planet,

$$v_p = R_p\sqrt{\frac{8}{3}\pi G\rho_p}$$

$\therefore \quad \dfrac{v_e}{v_p} = \dfrac{R_e}{R_p}\sqrt{\dfrac{\rho_e}{\rho_p}}$

Here, $R_p = 2R_e, \rho_e = \rho_p \Rightarrow \dfrac{v_e}{v_p} = \dfrac{1}{2}$ or $v_p = 2v_e$

35. *(b)* Young's modulus, $Y = \dfrac{FL}{A\Delta L} = \dfrac{4FL}{\pi D^2 \Delta L}$

$\Rightarrow \quad \Delta L = \dfrac{4FL}{\pi D^2 Y}$

The ratio of increase in length of steel and copper is

$$\frac{\Delta L_s}{\Delta L_c} = \frac{F_s L_s}{D_s^2 Y_s} \times \frac{D_c^2 Y_c}{F_c L_c} = \frac{F_s}{F_c} \times \frac{L_s}{L_c} \times \left(\frac{D_c}{D_s}\right)^2 \times \frac{Y_c}{Y_s}$$

Force on steel wire, $F_s = (2m + 5m)g = 7\,mg$

Force on copper wire, $F_c = 5\,mg$

$\Rightarrow \quad \dfrac{F_s}{F_c} = \dfrac{7}{5}$

Also, $\dfrac{D_s}{D_c} = p, \dfrac{L_s}{L_c} = q, \dfrac{Y_s}{Y_c} = s$

$\therefore \quad \dfrac{\Delta L_s}{\Delta L_c} = \dfrac{7}{5} \times q \times \dfrac{1}{p^2} \times \dfrac{1}{s} = \dfrac{7q}{5sp^2}$

36. *(d)* For adiabatic process,

$$pV^\gamma = \text{constant}$$

For an ideal gas, $pV = nRT$ or $p = \dfrac{nRT}{V}$

$\Rightarrow \quad \dfrac{nRT}{V} V^\gamma = \text{constant}$

$\Rightarrow \quad TV^{\gamma - 1} = \text{constant}$

Again, from ideal gas equation,

$$V = \frac{nRT}{p}$$

$\Rightarrow \quad p\left(\dfrac{nRT}{p}\right)^\gamma = \text{constant}$

$\Rightarrow \quad p^{1-\gamma} T^\gamma = \text{constant}$

Hence, relation shown in option (d) is not for adiabatic process.

37. *(a)* The escape velocity from earth's surface is given by

$$v_e = \sqrt{\frac{2GM}{R+h}}$$

Given, $h = 3R$

$\Rightarrow \quad v_e = \sqrt{\dfrac{2GM}{4R}} = \sqrt{\dfrac{GM}{2R}}$

38. *(d)* H-polaroid is prepared by stretching a thin sheet of polyvinyl alcohol and then impregnating with iodine. In this process, the molecules are oriented in the direction of applied strain.

39. *(b)* From Coulomb's law, force between two charges,

$$F = \frac{1}{4\pi\varepsilon_0} \frac{q_1 q_2}{r^2}$$

$\Rightarrow \quad \varepsilon_0 = \dfrac{q_1 q_2}{4\pi r^2 F}$

$\therefore$ Unit of $\varepsilon_0 = \dfrac{\text{C}\cdot\text{C}}{\text{m}^2\text{N}} = \dfrac{\text{C}^2}{\text{m}^2\text{N}} = \text{C}^2\text{m}^{-2}\text{N}^{-1}$

40. *(a)* As, the volume remains constant, so

$$\frac{4}{3}\pi R^3 = 8\left(\frac{4}{3}\pi r^3\right)$$

$\Rightarrow \quad R = 2r$ or $r = \dfrac{R}{2}$

Capacitance of spherical capacitor,

$$C = 4\pi\varepsilon_0 R$$

$\Rightarrow \quad C \propto R$

$\therefore \quad \dfrac{C_1}{C_2} = \dfrac{R}{r} = \dfrac{2r}{r} = 2 \Rightarrow C_2 = \dfrac{C_1}{2} = \dfrac{1}{2}\mu\text{F}$

41. *(c)* The magnitude of resultant of two forces is given by

$$R = \sqrt{A^2 + B^2 + 2AB\cos\theta}$$

Given, $A = B = P$ and $\theta = 120°$

$\therefore \quad R = \sqrt{P^2 + P^2 + 2P^2 \cos 120°}$

$= \sqrt{2P^2\left(1 - \dfrac{1}{2}\right)} = P$

42. *(b)* Given, $\lambda_0 = 5200\text{Å} = 5200 \times 10^{-10}$ m

$\therefore$ Threshold frequency, $f_0 = \dfrac{c}{\lambda_0} = \dfrac{3 \times 10^8}{5200 \times 10^{-10}}$

$= 5.76 \times 10^{14}$ Hz

It lies in the frequency range of UV-rays, so 50 W UV lamp is used for this emission.

43. *(b)* When the monochromatic light in Young's double slit experiment is replaced by white light, a white central bright fringe is observed as all wavelengths of light have zero phase difference at centre while at all other points, it is different for different colours. So different colour fringes are observed on both sides.

44. *(d)* The radius in Bohr's atomic model is given by

$$r = 0.53\frac{n^2}{Z}\text{Å}$$

For Be^{3+}, $Z_{Be} = 4$, $n_{Be} = ?$

For H, $Z_H = 1$, $n_H = 1$

As per question,

$$r_{Be} = r_H$$

$\Rightarrow \quad \dfrac{n_{Be}^2}{Z_{Be}} = \dfrac{n_H^2}{Z_H}$

$\Rightarrow \quad n_{Be} = \sqrt{n_H^2\left(\dfrac{Z_{Be}}{Z_H}\right)} = \sqrt{1 \times \dfrac{4}{1}} = 2$

45. *(b)* Packing fraction is the ratio of mass defect to the number of nucleons. Mass defect is the difference in the actual isotopic mass (M) and mass number (A).

$\therefore$ Packing fraction $= \dfrac{M - A}{A}$

where, A is mass number or number of nucleons.

COMEDK 2013

46. *(c)* In radioactive decay, the decay rate is proportional to the amount of substance. So, for change of count rate from 240 per min to 30 per min, let N be the number of half-life passed in one hour. Then,

$$\frac{240}{2^N} = 30$$

$$\Rightarrow \quad 2^N = 8$$

$$\Rightarrow \quad N = 3$$

Half-life, $t_{1/2} = \frac{1\text{h}}{3} = \frac{60}{3}\text{ min} = 20\text{ min}$

47. *(d)* The rate of heat conduction is given by

$$H = \frac{d\theta}{dt} = \frac{kA}{l}\Delta T$$

Here, ΔT is same for both conductors, so ratio of heat conduction,

$$\frac{H_1}{H_2} = \frac{A_1}{l_1} \times \frac{l_2}{A_2}$$

$$= \frac{d_1^2}{l_1} \times \frac{l_2}{d_2^2} \qquad \left(\because A = \frac{\pi d^2}{4}\right)$$

$$= \left(\frac{d_1}{d_2}\right)^2 \cdot \frac{l_2}{l_1}$$

$$= \left(\frac{1}{2}\right)^2 \times \frac{1}{2} = \frac{1}{8}$$

48. *(a)* The air blown by mouth has same pressure as that of atmosphere, so it is an example of isobaric process.

49. *(b)* Longitudinal waves in air travels in the form as compression and rarefaction that changes its elastic properties. The air is a completely elastic medium, which does not have a modulus of rigidity. So, sound waves travel in it as a longitudinal wave.

50. *(a)* When an uncharged metal sphere is placed between two charged parallel plate capacitor, negative charge is induced on its upper side and on equal positive charge on its lower side. So, the lines of force enters the sphere normally as shown in figure of option (a).

51. *(c)* According to right hand rule, the thumb points in the direction of current, i.e. from East to West, then the curled fingers at a point above the conductor will point in the direction of magnetic field, i.e towards North.

52. *(c)* A bar magnet is equivalent to a solenoid carrying current as both produces similar magnetic field around them.

53. *(c)* The energy of nth state in hydrogen like atom,

$$E_n = -\frac{13.6Z^2}{n^2}\text{eV}$$

The energy of first excitation,

$$E_2 - E_1 = \frac{-13.6 \times Z^2}{(2)^2} + \frac{13.6 \times Z^2}{(1)^2} = 40.8 \quad \text{(given)}$$

$$\Rightarrow \quad Z^2 = \frac{40.8 \times 4}{13.6 \times 3} = 4$$

or $\quad Z = 2$

$\therefore$ Energy needed to remove an electron from the ion in ground state, $E = -(E_1) = -\left[\frac{-13.6 \times (2)^2}{(1)^2}\right] = 54.4\text{ eV}$

54. *(c)* Given, $\mu_b = 1.67, \mu_y = 1.65, \mu_r = 1.63$

Dispersive power of material $= \frac{\mu_b - \mu_r}{\mu_y - 1}$

$$= \frac{1.67 - 1.63}{1.65 - 1} = \frac{0.04}{0.65} = 0.0615$$

55. *(b)* Given, $T_1 = 227°\text{C} = 227 + 273 = 500\text{K}$

$T_2 = 127°\text{C} = 127 + 273 = 400\text{K}$

Heat input, $H_i = 6 \times 10^4$ J

Efficiency of Carnot engine,

$$\eta = 1 - \frac{T_2}{T_1}$$

$$= 1 - \frac{400}{500} = \frac{1}{5}$$

Also, efficiency,

$$\eta = \frac{\text{Work output}}{\text{Heat input}} = \frac{W}{6 \times 10^4}$$

$$\Rightarrow \quad W = \eta \times 6 \times 10^4 = \frac{1}{5} \times 6 \times 10^4$$

$$= 1.2 \times 10^4 \text{ J}$$

56. *(d)* For an ideal gas, $pV = nRT$

At constant temperature, pV = constant.

So, pV does not vary with V and pV- V graph is a straight line parallel to V- axis as shown in option (d).

57. *(d)* The rainbow is formed in the sky after rain shower, due to tiny droplets of water which act as optical medium. When sunlight falls on them, it is totally internally reflected inside them and when comes out it got dispersed in its constituent colours. Thus, a rainbow is formed due to dispersion and total internal reflection.

58. *(a)* The focal length of the combination is given by

$$\frac{1}{F} = \frac{1}{f_1} + \frac{1}{f_2}$$

f_1 = focal length of plano-convex lens $= f$

f_2 = focal length of concave lens $= -f$

$$\therefore \quad \frac{1}{F} = \frac{1}{f} + \frac{1}{-f} = 0$$

$$\Rightarrow \quad F = \infty$$

Hence, focus shifts to infinity.

59. *(d)* Earth is a good conductor. So, when a body is earthed, electrons flow from earth to the body. It means, the body must be deficient of electrons i.e. it is positively charged.

60. *(b)* As it is a balanced Wheatstone bridge, so C and D are same potential and the capacitor 2μF is ineffective.

The 3μF and 6μF in upper portion are in series, so equivalent capacitance,

$$C_1 = \frac{3 \times 6}{3+6} = \frac{18}{9} = 2\mu F$$

Similarly, $C_2 = \frac{4 \times 8}{4+8} = \frac{32}{12} = \frac{8}{3}\mu F$

C_1 and C_2 are in parallel, so their equivalent capacitance

$$C = C_1 + C_2 = 2 + \frac{8}{3} = \frac{14}{3}\mu F$$

Chemistry

61. *(c)* $MgSO_4$ is soluble in HCl and gives $MgCl_2$ and H_2SO_4.

$$\underset{(X)}{MgSO_4(s)} + 2HCl(aq) \longrightarrow MgCl_2 + H_2SO_4(aq)$$

On adding NaOH to $MgCl_2$, it gives white ppt. of $Mg(OH)_2$.

$$MgCl_2(aq) + \underset{\text{Excess}}{2NaOH(aq)} \longrightarrow \underset{\text{White ppt.}}{Mg(OH)_2(s)} + NaCl$$

62. *(b)* Mn is used to make alloy steel for armour plates, safes and helmets as Mn increases harden-ability by lowering transformation points and causing transformation to be sluggish.

63. *(b)* Iodoform test is given by compounds having ,

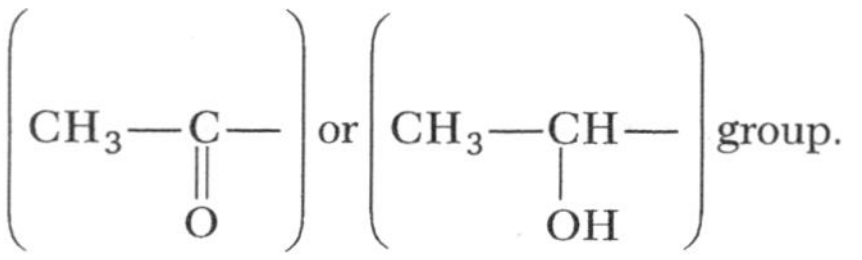

Thus, compound CH_3OH do not contain these groups. Hence, it do not give iodoform test.

64. *(d)* The gaseous carbon compound, methyl amine (CH_3NH_2) is soluble in dil. HCl and forms soluble hydrogen chloride salt solution.

This solution on treating with $NaNO_2$ gives nitrogen leaving behind a methanol solution with wood spirit smell.

65. *(d)* Benzyl chloride is more reactive than vinyl chloride as benzyl carbocation is stabilised by resonance. While, in vinyl chloride due to partial double bond character became of resonance, the C—Cl bond strength increases. Hence, reactivity of vinyl chloride decreases.

66. *(a)* As enthalpy of formation of HF is more negative, than that of HCl and HF is more stable than HCl. The bond strength of hydrogen with halogen decrease down the group due to increases in size.

67. *(b)* Equivalent of NaOH neutralised by HCl

$$= 100 \times 1 \times 10^{-3} = 0.1 \text{ mol}$$

$\therefore$ Heat released $= 57.3 \times 0.1 = 5.73$ kJ

68. *(c)* If $[A]$ double's then, $r_1 = 2r$

If $[B]$ increased 9 times then, $r_2 = 3r$

$\therefore$ Order w.r.t. A is 1 and order w.r.t B is $\frac{1}{2}$.

$\therefore$ Order of reaction $= 1 + \frac{1}{2} = 1\frac{1}{2}$.

69. *(c)* In Goldschmidt aluminothermic process, thermite contains 3 parts of Fe_2O_3 and 1 part of aluminium (Al).

$$Fe_2O_3 + 2Al \longrightarrow Al_2O_3 + 2Fe + \text{Heat}$$

70. *(a)* The structure of orthophosphoric acid is

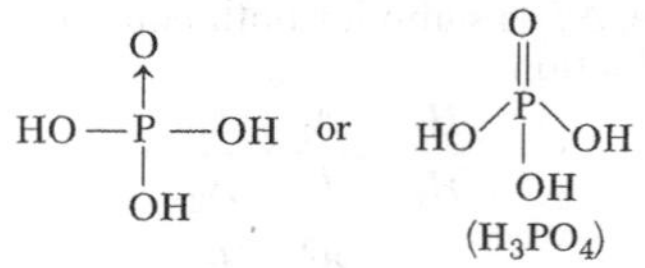

(H_3PO_4)

71. *(d)* At anode, oxidation occurs of H_2(gas), while at cathode reduction of AgCl take place.

$\therefore$ The cell notation is

Pt | $H_2(g)$, HCl(*sol*) || AgCl (*s*) | Ag

72. *(c)* If current is same then,

E_{wt} of Ag $= E_{wt}$ of H_2

$$\frac{1.08}{108} = \frac{x}{1}$$

$\therefore$ Mass of H_2, $x = 10^{-2}$ g

2g of H_2 at STP occupy 22400 cm^3

$\therefore$ 10^{-2} g of H_2 at STP occupy

$$= \frac{22400}{2} \times 10^{-2} \text{ cm}^3 = 112 \text{ cm}^3$$

73. *(d)* The flame colours of metal ions are due to metal excess defect. The free electrons can be exited to higher energy levels giving absorption spectra and as a consequence their compounds are coloured.

74. *(a)* The order of reaction of methyl halides increases from fluorine to iodine due to decrease in C—X bond strength.

$\therefore$ The order of reactivities of methyl halides in formation of Grignard reagent is

$$CH_3I > CH_3Br > CH_3Cl$$

75. *(d)* Formaldehyde on reaction with ammonia gives urotropine which on nitration gives RDX.

Formaldehyde + NH_3 $\longrightarrow$ Urotropine

$\downarrow$ Nitration

Cyclo trimethylene-tri nitramine (RDX)

76. *(d)* Number of carbon atoms

$$= \frac{\text{mass}}{\text{molar mass}} \times 6.023 \times 10^{23}$$

$$= \frac{10^{-3}}{12} \times 6.023 \times 10^{23}$$

$$= 5.02 \times 10^{19} = 0.502 \times 10^{20}$$

77. *(a)* Distance travelled by gas is directly proportional to rate of diffusion

$$\therefore \quad r_{NH_3}(l_1) \propto \frac{1}{\sqrt{M_{NH_3}}} \propto \frac{1}{\sqrt{17}}$$

$$r_{HCl}(l_2) \propto \frac{1}{\sqrt{M_{HCl}}} \propto \frac{1}{\sqrt{36.5}}$$

$$\because \quad r_{NH_3} > r_{HCl}$$

$\therefore$ Length travelled by NH_3 is greater than HCl.

Hence, white ring of NH_4Cl is formed nearer to HCl end.

78. *(d)* By the action of alc. KOH on ethyl iodide, ethylene gas is formed by elimination reaction. Ethylene decolourises alkaline $KMnO_4$.

$$\underset{\text{Ethyl iodide}}{C_2H_5—I} \xrightarrow{\text{alc. KOH}} \underset{\text{Ethylene}}{C_2H_4}$$

$$\underset{\text{Ethylene}}{CH_2 = CH_2} + KMnO_4 \text{ (alk.)} \longrightarrow \underset{\text{Colourless}}{(CH_2OH)_2}$$

79. *(c)* Chemisorption is highly specific and will not form if there is no possibility of chemical bonding between adsorbent and adsorbate.

$\therefore$ Chemisorption doesn't form multimolecular layer and hence, option (c) is incorrect.

80. *(d)* The concentration of electrolyte required to coagulate a given amount of As_2S_3 sol is minimum in case of aluminium nitrate.

As_2S_3 is negatively charge sol. In aluminium nitrate, the charge on Al cation is + 3 which is maximum among given cations. Hence, its coagulating power is maximum.

81. *(d)* Benzaldehyde lacks α-H atom. On heating with strong NaOH solution, it undergoes Cannizzaro reaction to produce benzoic acid and benzyl alcohol. Benzoic acid forms sodium salt with NaOH.

$$\underset{\text{Benzaldehyde}}{2C_6H_5CHO} \xrightarrow{\text{NaOH}} \underset{\text{Sodium salt of benzoic acid}}{C_6H_5COONa} + \underset{\text{Benzyl alcohol}}{C_6H_5CH_2OH}$$

82. *(a)* The process by which synthesis of protein takes place based on the genetic information present in *m*-RNA is called translation.

83. *(b)* $\Delta H_{\text{Reaction}} = (\Delta H_f)_{\text{Product}} - (\Delta H_f)_{\text{Reactant}}$

$$= -1596 - (-1134) = -462 \text{ kJ}$$

84. *(d)* For the reaction

$$A + B \rightleftharpoons 2C + D + Q$$

As the reaction is exothermic, low temperature favours formed direction according to Le-Chatelier's principle.

Also $\Delta n_{(g)} = (2 + 1) - (1 + 1) = 1$

$\because \quad \Delta n_g = +\text{ve}$

(low pressure favours forward direction)

$\therefore$ Low pressure and temperature favours formed direction for the reaction.

85. *(a)* For every 10°C rise in temperature, rate increase by 2 times i.e.,

$$r_1 = 2^n r$$

where, $$n = \frac{\Delta t}{10} = \frac{100 - 30}{10} = 7$$

$$\therefore \quad r_1 = 2^7 r \Rightarrow r_1 = 128r$$

86. *(b)* Moles of HCl $= \frac{1}{2} \times V$ $\quad \left\{\frac{N}{2}\text{ HCl}\right\}$

For preparing $\frac{N}{10}$ solution,

$$\frac{1}{10} = \frac{\frac{1}{2} \times V}{500}$$

$$\therefore \quad V = \frac{1000}{10} = 100 \text{ cm}^3$$

87. *(c)* Equivalent weight $= \frac{\text{molecular weight}}{\text{valence factor}}$

$\therefore$ Molecular weight $= 20 \times 3 = 60$

It's oxide is M_2O_3 and molecular weight

$$= 2 \times 60 + 16 \times 3 = 120 + 48 = 168$$

88. *(a)* The reaction that doesn't take place during the smelting process of extraction is

$$2FeS + 3O_2 \longrightarrow 2FeO + 2SO_2 \uparrow$$

This reaction occurs during roasting, which comes before smelting.

89. *(a)* In $K_4[Fe(CN)_6]$, the central metal atom obeys EAN rule.

EAN $= Z - X + Y = 26 - 2 + 12 = 36$

where,

Z = atomic number

X = number of electrons lost, while forming metal ion.

Y = number of electron donated by ligands.

90. *(c)* In a reversible reaction, the catalyst decreases the activation energy of both, forward and backward reaction.

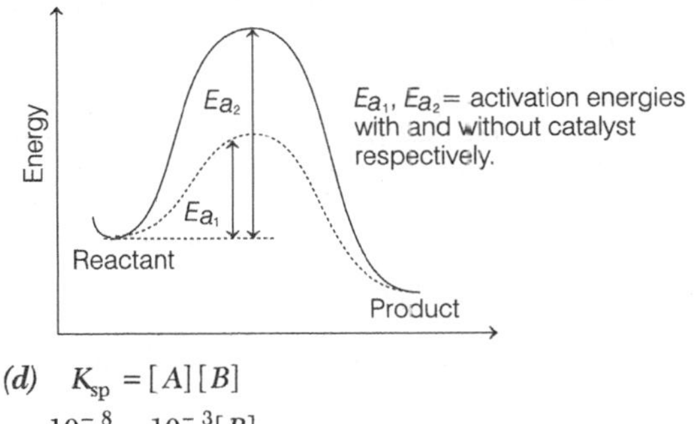

91. *(d)* $K_{sp} = [A][B]$

$$10^{-8} = 10^{-3}[B]$$

$$[B] = 10^{-5} \text{ M}$$

$\therefore$ Salt will precipitate when $[B] > 10^{-5}$

92. *(b)* For reaction to be spontaneous, $E^{\circ}_{cell} > 0$

For option (b),

$E^{\circ}_{cell} = (E^{\circ}_{red})_{Cathode} - (E^{\circ}_{red})_{Anode}$

$= 0.80 - (-0.76) = 1.56$ V

$\therefore$ It will be spontaneous reaction

$\because E^{\circ}_{cell} > 0$.

93. *(b)* When the radius ratio is between 0.732 - 1.000, the coordination number is 8 and arrangement is body centered cubic (bcc) packing.

94. *(a)* Dacron is obtained by the condensation polymerisation of ethylene glycol and terephthalic acid.

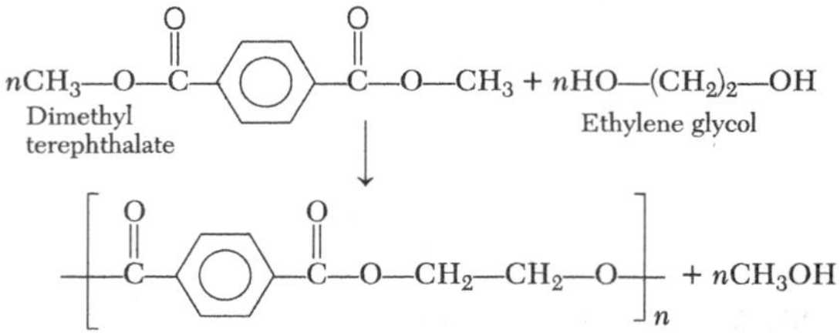

95. *(d)* 4-chloro-3, 5-dimethyl phenol is called dettol. It is a well known antiseptic. It's structure is

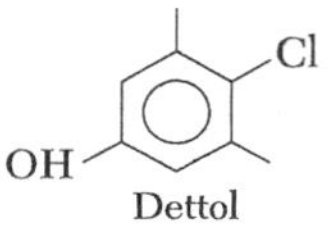

Dettol

96. *(a)*

	Methane	Ethene	Ethyne
Hydrocarbon	CH_4	C_2H_4	C_2H_2
Hybridisation	sp^3	sp^2	sp
% s-character	25	33	50

97. *(d)* In the manufacture of sulphuric acid by contact process, Tyndall box is used to test the presence of dust particles.

98. *(d)* Aspirin is an acidic compound. It will not dissociate in acidic medium i.e., small intestine in order to react with base but will dissociate in basic medium.

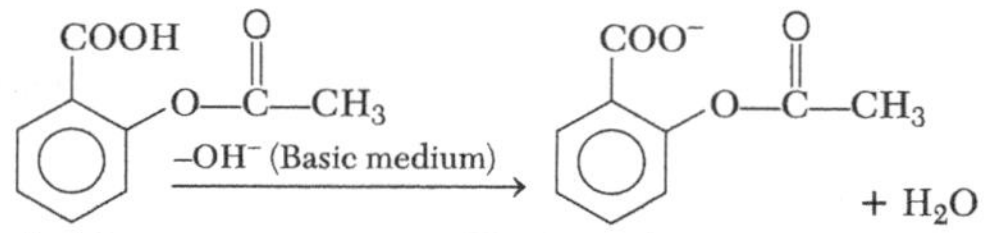

Aspirin Dissociate of aspirin

99. *(d)* $^{232}_{90}Th \longrightarrow ^{208}_{82}Pb + n\alpha + m\beta$

Number of α-particles, $n = \dfrac{232 - 208}{4} = 6$

Now, for charge balanced

$$90 = 82 + 2n - m$$
$$m = 4$$

Number of β-particles, $m = 4$

100. *(c)* When chlorine is passed through warm benzene in presence of sunlight, the product obtained is gammexane.

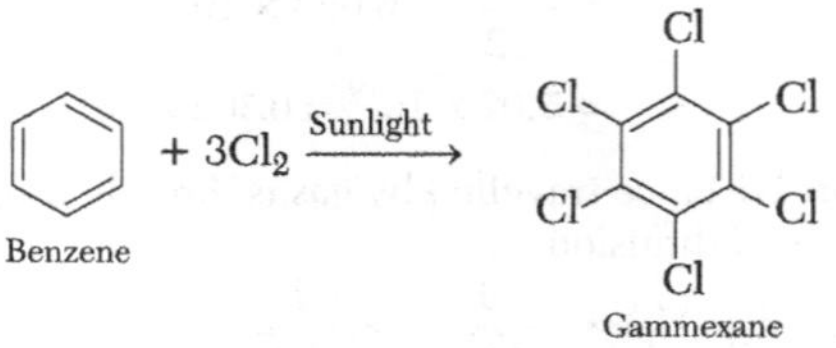

101. *(b)* Ethyl benzoate reacts with PCl_5 to give C_2H_5Cl, C_6H_5COCl and $POCl_3$.

$\underset{\text{Ethyl benzoate}}{C_6H_5COOCH_2CH_3} + PCl_5 \longrightarrow$

$\underset{\text{Ethyl chloride}}{C_2H_5Cl} + \underset{\text{Benzoate chloride}}{C_6H_5COCl} + \underset{\text{Phosphorus oxychloride}}{POCl_3}$

102. *(a)* The statement that, sodium aluminium silicate is used in softening of hard water is not relevant with colloids.

It is a substitution reaction of calcium salts with zeolite.

103. *(c)* $\dfrac{dN}{dt} = \lambda N$

$$\frac{dN}{dt} = \frac{1}{T}\,\frac{6.023 \times 10^{23}}{12} \qquad \left\{\because \lambda = \frac{1}{T}\right\}$$

$$T = \frac{6.023 \times 10^{23}}{12 \times 1.18 \times 10^{13}} \qquad \left\{\frac{dN}{dt} = 1.18 \times 10^{13}\right\}$$

$= 42530 \times 10^6$ min

$= \dfrac{4253 \times 10^6}{60 \times 24 \times 365}$ years

$= 8092$ years

≈ 8100 years

104. *(a)* $K_p = K_C(RT)^{\Delta n}$

If Δn is positive than $K_p > K_C$ also,

gaseous moles of product > moles of reactant.

$\therefore$ Forward reaction is favoured by low pressure, according to Le-Chatelier's principle.

105. *(d)* In a lime kiln, to get higher yield of CO_2, the measure that can be taken is to pump out CO_2. This will reduce the pressure of CO_2 and reaction will shift in forward direction.

$$CaCO_3 \xrightarrow{\text{Heat}} CaO + CO_2$$

106. *(a)* 20 volume of H_2O_2 means that, 1 L of H_2O_2 on decomposition gives 20 L of oxygen.

$\therefore$ 5 L of oxygen will be obtained from

$= \dfrac{5}{20} \times 1 = 0.250$ L of H_2O_2

or $= 250$ cm^3 of 20 volume H_2O_2.

107. *(d)* The IUPAC name of

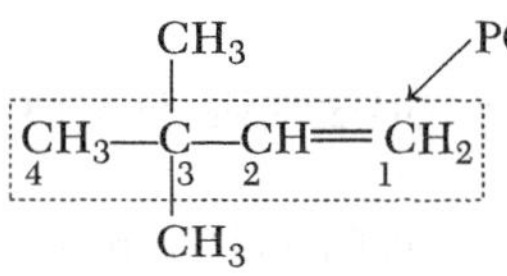

is 3, 3-dimethyl-1-butene.

108. *(b)* The process of hardening of iron rods of railway wagon axles embedded in charcoal powder is known as case-hardening. In this process surface of iron rods get hardened by depositing a layer of steel on its surface.

109. *(b)* Thomas slag is tetracalcium phosphorus nonaoxide. It's molecular formula is $Ca_3(PO_4)_2$.

110. *(d)* Urea is preferred to ammonium sulphate as a nitrogenous fertiliser because it does not cause acidity in the soil.

111. *(c)* Pressure in the cylinder is directly proportional to the number of moles of gases.

$$44 \text{ g of } H_2 \text{ has} = \frac{44}{2} = 22 \text{ moles of } H_2$$

$$44 \text{ g of } CO_2 \text{ has} = \frac{44}{44} = 1 \text{ mole of } H_2$$

$$\therefore \text{ Pressure of } H_2 (p_{H_2}) = \frac{22}{1} \times 1 = 22 \text{ atm.}$$

112. *(a)* According to Bohr's model, angular momentum of nth orbit of hydrogen atom is mvr_n or $\frac{nh}{2\pi}$.

113. *(a)* Electronic configuration of atomic number 36

$$= 1s^2, 2s^2, 2p^6, 3s^2\ 3p^6\ 3d^{10} 4s^2\ 4p^6$$

As the last electrons is filled in p-orbital, so it belongs to p-block in periodic table.

114. *(d)* The function of $AlCl_3$ in Friedel-Craft's reaction is to produce electrophile.

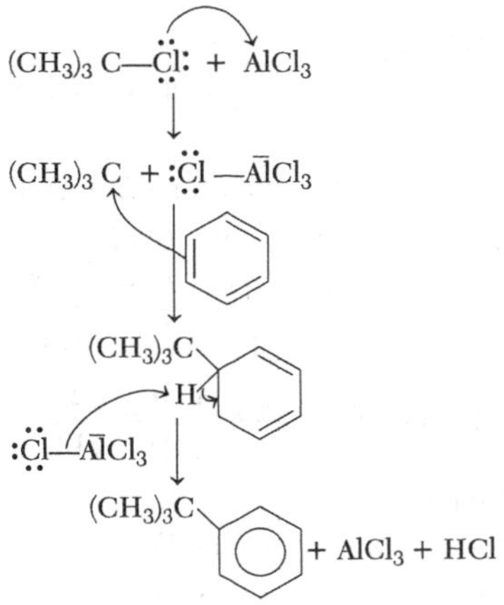

115. *(a)* An important reaction of acetone is auto-condensation in presence of concentrated sulphuric acid to give the aromatic compound mesitylene.

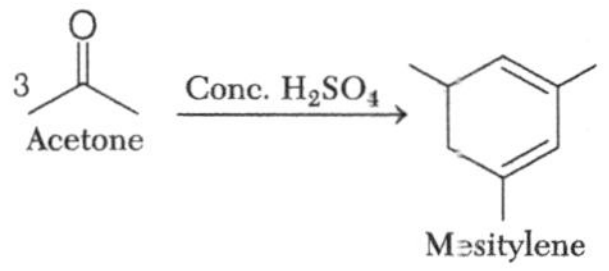

116. *(a)* Kinetic energy $= \frac{3}{2}RT$

$$= \frac{3}{2} \times 8.314 \times 300$$

$$= 3741.3 \text{ J} = 3.74 \text{ kJ}$$

117. *(a)* The tripeptide hormone present in most living cell is glutathione.

The three amino acids present are glutamic acid, cysteine and glycine.

118. *(a)* The given reaction is Liebermann's reaction. It is test for phenol.

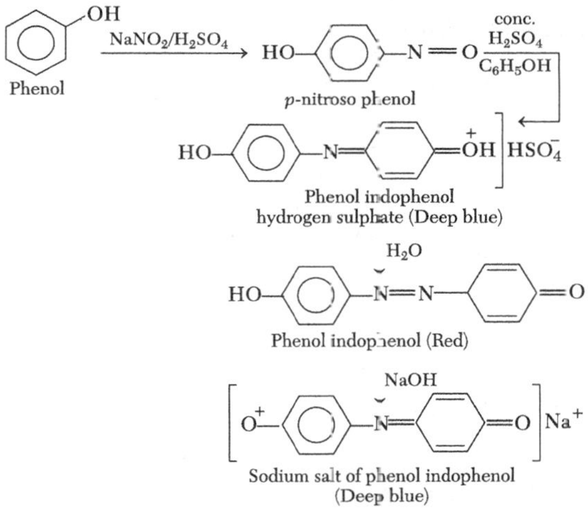

119. *(a)* Energy is stored in our body in the form of ATP (Adeniotriphosphate). The stored energy is released by the breakdown of ATP. The released energy is used by muscles and other parts of body.

120. *(d)* Molisch's test is used to detect all kinds of carbohydrates. The Benedict test identifies reducing sugars (mono saccharides and some disaccharides) which have free ketone or aldehyde functional group.

Scliwanoff's test is used for detection of fructose or keto group in sugar solution. Therefore, give negative test for maltose.

Hence, organic compound is maltose.

COMEDK 2013

Mathematics

121. *(d)*

p	q	$\sim p$	$\sim p \wedge q$	$p \to q$	$q \to p$	$\sim(p \to q)$	$\sim(q \to p)$
T	T	F	F	T	T	F	F
T	F	F	F	F	T	T	F
F	T	T	T	T	F	F	T
F	F	T	F	T	T	F	F

From table,

$\sim p \wedge q \cong \sim (q \to p)$

122. *(b)* Let p : A number is a prime.

q : A number is odd.

The given proposition is $p \to q$

Now, inverse of $(p \to q)$ is $\sim p \to \sim q$

Therefore, the inverse of the given proposition is 'If a number is not a prime, then it is not odd.'

123. *(a)* We have,

$$2X + \begin{bmatrix} 1 & 2 \\ 3 & 4 \end{bmatrix} = \begin{bmatrix} 3 & 8 \\ 7 & 2 \end{bmatrix}$$

$$\Rightarrow \quad 2X = \begin{bmatrix} 3 & 8 \\ 7 & 2 \end{bmatrix} - \begin{bmatrix} 1 & 2 \\ 3 & 4 \end{bmatrix}$$

$$\Rightarrow \quad 2X = \begin{bmatrix} 2 & 6 \\ 4 & -2 \end{bmatrix}$$

$$\Rightarrow \quad X = \frac{1}{2}\begin{bmatrix} 2 & 6 \\ 4 & -2 \end{bmatrix} = \begin{bmatrix} 1 & 3 \\ 2 & -1 \end{bmatrix}$$

124. *(c)* We have, $\begin{vmatrix} 1 & 1 & 1 \\ bc & ca & ab \\ b+c & c+a & a+b \end{vmatrix}$

On applying $C_1 \to C_1 - C_2, C_2 \to C_2 - C_3$, we get

$$\begin{vmatrix} 0 & 0 & 1 \\ -c(a-b) & -a(b-c) & ab \\ -(a-b) & -(b-c) & a+b \end{vmatrix}$$

Taking common $(a-b), (b-c)$ from C_1, C_2 respectively, we get

$$(a-b)(b-c)\begin{vmatrix} 0 & 0 & 1 \\ -c & -a & ab \\ -1 & -1 & a+b \end{vmatrix}$$

On expanding along R_1, we get

$(a-b)(b-c) \cdot 1 (c-a)$

$= (a-b)(b-c)(c-a)$

125. *(b)* We have,

$$\begin{vmatrix} 441 & 442 & 443 \\ 445 & 446 & 447 \\ 449 & 450 & 451 \end{vmatrix}$$

On applying, $C_1 \to C_1 - C_2, C_2 \to C_2 - C_3$, we get

$$\begin{vmatrix} -1 & -1 & 443 \\ -1 & -1 & 447 \\ -1 & -1 & 451 \end{vmatrix} = 0 \quad [\because C_1 \text{ and } C_2 \text{ are identical}]$$

126. *(a)* Let $\mathbf{a} = x\hat{\mathbf{i}} + y\hat{\mathbf{j}} + z\hat{\mathbf{k}}$, then

$(\mathbf{a} \cdot \hat{\mathbf{i}}) + (\mathbf{a} \cdot \hat{\mathbf{j}})\hat{\mathbf{j}} + (\mathbf{a} \cdot \hat{\mathbf{k}})\hat{\mathbf{k}}$

$= [(x\hat{\mathbf{i}} + y\hat{\mathbf{j}} + z\hat{\mathbf{k}} \cdot \hat{\mathbf{i}}] \cdot \hat{\mathbf{i}} + [(x\hat{\mathbf{i}} + y\hat{\mathbf{j}} + z\hat{\mathbf{k}}).\hat{\mathbf{j}}]\hat{\mathbf{j}} +$

$[(x\hat{\mathbf{i}} + y\hat{\mathbf{j}} + z\hat{\mathbf{k}}) \cdot \hat{\mathbf{k}}]\,\hat{\mathbf{k}}$

$= (x)\hat{\mathbf{i}} + (y)\hat{\mathbf{j}} + (z)\hat{\mathbf{k}} = x\hat{\mathbf{i}} + y\hat{\mathbf{i}} + \hat{\mathbf{k}} = \mathbf{a}$

127. *(d)* Let $A = \begin{bmatrix} \cos 2\theta & -\sin 2\theta \\ \sin 2\theta & \cos 2\theta \end{bmatrix}$

Now, $|A| = \begin{vmatrix} \cos 2\theta & -\sin 2\theta \\ \sin 2\theta & \cos 2\theta \end{vmatrix}$

$= \cos^2 2\theta - (-\sin^2 2\theta)$

$= \cos^2 2\theta + \sin^2 2\theta = 1$

Again, $A^{-1} = \dfrac{1}{|A|}\begin{vmatrix} \cos 2\theta & \sin 2\theta \\ -\sin 2\theta & \cos 2\theta \end{vmatrix}$

$$\left[\because \begin{bmatrix} a & b \\ c & d \end{bmatrix}^{-1} = \frac{1}{ad-bc}\begin{bmatrix} d & -b \\ -c & a \end{bmatrix}\right]$$

$$= \begin{bmatrix} \cos 2\theta & \sin 2\theta \\ -\sin 2\theta & \cos 2\theta \end{bmatrix}$$

128. *(b)* Since, $(\mathbf{a} + \lambda\mathbf{b}) \perp (\mathbf{a} - \lambda\mathbf{b})$, then

$(\mathbf{a} + \lambda\mathbf{b}) \cdot (\mathbf{a} - \lambda\mathbf{b}) = 0$

$\Rightarrow \quad |\mathbf{a}|^2 - \lambda^2|\mathbf{b}|^2 = 0 \Rightarrow |\mathbf{a}^2| = \lambda^2|\mathbf{b}|^2$

$\Rightarrow \quad \lambda = \dfrac{|\mathbf{a}|}{|\mathbf{b}|} = \dfrac{3}{4}$

129. *(b)* We have,

$\mathbf{a} = 2\hat{\mathbf{i}} + 3\hat{\mathbf{j}} - 2\hat{\mathbf{k}}, \mathbf{b} = \hat{\mathbf{i}} + 2\hat{\mathbf{j}} + 3\hat{\mathbf{k}}$

Now,

$\mathbf{a} \cdot \mathbf{b} = (2\hat{\mathbf{i}} + 3\hat{\mathbf{j}} - 2\hat{\mathbf{k}}) \cdot (\hat{\mathbf{i}} + 2\hat{\mathbf{j}} + 3\hat{\mathbf{k}})$

$= 2 + 6 - 6 = 2$

and $\quad |\mathbf{b}| = \sqrt{(1)^2 + (2)^2 + (3)^2}$

$= \sqrt{1 + 4 + 9} = \sqrt{14}$

$\therefore$ Projection of $\mathbf{a}$ on $\mathbf{b} = \dfrac{\mathbf{a} \cdot \mathbf{b}}{|\mathbf{b}|} = \dfrac{2}{\sqrt{14}}$

130. *(c)* We have,

$2 \times 4 = 1 (\text{mod } 7)$

Hence, $\quad 2^{-1} = 4 (\text{mod } 7)$

Now, $\quad 2^{-1} \times 4 = 4 \times 4 = 16$

Now, $\quad 16 = (2 \times 7) + 2$

$\therefore \quad 16 = 2 (\text{mod } 7)$

$\Rightarrow \quad 2^{-1} \times 4 = 2 (\text{mod } 7)$

131. *(d)* We know that,

$$a\sin x + b\cos x \le \sqrt{a^2 + b^2}$$

$\therefore\ 3\cos x - 4\sin x \le \sqrt{(-4)^2 + (3)^2} = \sqrt{16 + 9} = 5$

$\therefore$ Maximum value is 5.

132. *(c)* We have,

$$S = t^3 - 3t^2$$

$\Rightarrow \dfrac{dS}{dt} = 3t^2 - 6t$ and $\dfrac{d^2S}{dt^2} = 6t - 6$

Now, acceleration, $\dfrac{d^2S}{dt^2} = 0$

$\Rightarrow\ 6t - 6 = 0$

$\Rightarrow\ t = 1$

$\therefore$ Velocity $= \left.\dfrac{dS}{dt}\right|_{t=1}$

$= 3(1)^2 - 6(1) = 3 - 6 = -3$ m/sec

133. *(b)* We have,

$$y^n = a^{n-1}x$$

$\Rightarrow\ n \cdot y^{n-1}\dfrac{dy}{dx} = a^{n-1}$

$\Rightarrow\ y^{n-1}\dfrac{dy}{dx} = \dfrac{1}{n}a^{n-1}$

$\Rightarrow\ \dfrac{dy}{dx} = \dfrac{1}{n}a^{n-1}\,y^{1-n}$

$\therefore$ Length of the subnormal $= \left|y\dfrac{dy}{dx}\right|$

$= \left|y \times \dfrac{1}{n}\,a^{n-1}\,y^{1-n}\right|$

$= \left|\dfrac{1}{n}\,a^{n-1}\,y^{2-n}\right|$

Since, length of subnormal is constant.

$\therefore\ 2 - n = 0$

$\Rightarrow\ n = 2$

134. *(a)* We have,

$$x = A\cos 4t + B\sin 4t$$

$\Rightarrow \dfrac{dx}{dt} = A(-\sin 4t \cdot 4) + B(\cos 4t \cdot 4)$

$= -4A\sin 4t + 4B\cos 4t$

Again,

$\dfrac{d^2x}{dt^2} = -4A(\cos 4t \cdot 4) + 4B(-\sin 4t \cdot 4)$

$= -16A\cos 4t - 16B\sin 4t$

$= -16[A\cos 4t + B\sin 4t] = -16x$

135. *(c)* We have,

$$x = at^2,\ y = 2at$$

Now, $\dfrac{dx}{dt} = 2at,\ \dfrac{dy}{dt} = 2a$

$\therefore\ \dfrac{dy}{dx} = \dfrac{dy/dt}{dx/dt} = \dfrac{2a}{2at} = \dfrac{1}{t}$

Since, tangent is perpendicular to X-axis, then

$$\frac{dy}{dx} = \frac{1}{0}$$

$\Rightarrow\ \dfrac{1}{t} = \dfrac{1}{0} \Rightarrow t = 0$

$\therefore\ x = at^2 = 0$ and $y = 2at = 0$

So, required point is (0, 0).

136. *(b)* We have,

$$\frac{dy}{dx} + \frac{1 + \cos 2y}{1 - \cos 2x} = 0$$

$\Rightarrow\ \dfrac{dy}{dx} = -\left(\dfrac{1 + \cos 2y}{1 - \cos 2x}\right)$

$\Rightarrow\ \dfrac{dy}{dx} = -\dfrac{2\cos^2 y}{2\sin^2 x}$

$\Rightarrow\ \sec^2 y\,dy = -\operatorname{cosec}^2 x\,dx$

$\Rightarrow \int \sec^2 y\,dy + \int \operatorname{cosec}^2 x\,dx = 0$

$\Rightarrow\ \tan y - \cot x = c$

137. *(b)* We have,

$$\left(1 + \left(\frac{dy}{dx}\right)^2\right)^{3/4} = \left(\frac{d^2y}{dx^2}\right)^{1/3}$$

$\Rightarrow\ \left(1 + \left(\dfrac{dy}{dx}\right)^2\right)^9 = \left(\dfrac{d^2y}{dx^3}\right)^4$

$\therefore$ Degree = 4

138. *(c)*

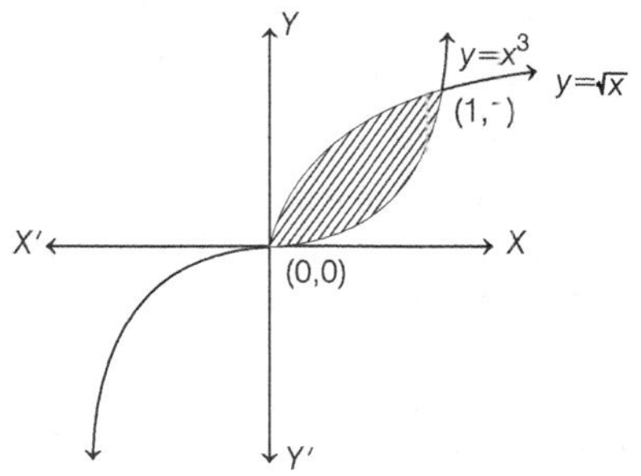

Required area $= \displaystyle\int_0^1 (\sqrt{x} - x^3)\,dx$

$= \left[\dfrac{2x^{3/2}}{3} - \dfrac{x^4}{4}\right]_0^1$

$= \dfrac{2}{3} - \dfrac{1}{4} = \dfrac{5}{12}$

139. *(d)* Let

$$I = \int_0^{\pi/8} \cos^3 4\theta\,d\theta = \int_0^{\pi/8} \frac{\cos 12\theta + 3\cos 4\theta}{4}\,d\theta$$

$= \dfrac{1}{4}\left[\dfrac{\sin 12\theta}{12} + \dfrac{3\sin 4\theta}{4}\right]_0^{\pi/8} = \dfrac{1}{4}\left[\dfrac{1}{12}\sin\dfrac{3\pi}{2} + \dfrac{3}{4}\sin\dfrac{\pi}{2}\right]$

$= \dfrac{1}{4}\left[-\dfrac{1}{12} + \dfrac{3}{4}\right] = \dfrac{1}{4}\left(\dfrac{-1 + 9}{12}\right) = \dfrac{8}{4 \times 12} = \dfrac{1}{6}$

140. *(a)* Let $I = \int_0^{\pi/2} \frac{\cos x - \sin x}{1 + \cos x \sin x}\, dx$ ... (i)

$$= \int_0^{\pi/2} \frac{\cos\left(\frac{\pi}{2} - x\right) - \sin\left(\frac{\pi}{2} - x\right)}{1 + \cos\left(\frac{\pi}{2} - x\right)\sin\left(\frac{\pi}{2} - x\right)}\, dx$$

$$\left[\because \int_0^a f(x)\,dx = \int_0^a f(a-x)\,dx\right]$$

$\therefore \quad I = \int_0^{\pi/2} \frac{\sin x - \cos x}{1 + \sin x \cos x}\, dx$ ... (ii)

On adding Eqs. (i) and (ii), we get

$$2I = 0 \Rightarrow I = 0$$

141. *(b)* $ax^2 - y^2 + 4x - y = 0$ represents a pair of straight line, if

$$\begin{vmatrix} a & 0 & 2 \\ 0 & -1 & -1/2 \\ 2 & -1/2 & 0 \end{vmatrix} = 0$$

$$\Rightarrow \quad a\left(0 - \frac{1}{4}\right) + 2(0 + 2) = 0$$

$$\Rightarrow \quad -\frac{a}{4} + 4 = 0$$

$$\Rightarrow \quad a = 16$$

142. *(b)* Let the required point be $P(x, y)$. Then,

$$4|y| = (\sqrt{(x-0)^2 + (y-0)^2})^2$$

$$\Rightarrow \quad 4|y| = x^2 + y^2$$

$$\Rightarrow x^2 + y^2 - 4|y| = 0$$

143. *(c)* Let the equation of line be

$$x + y = a \qquad [\because a = b]$$

Now, given line passes through (2, 4), then

$$2 + 4 = a$$

$$\Rightarrow \quad a = 6$$

$\therefore$ Equation of line is $x + y - 6 = 0$

144. *(c)* We have,

$$\frac{1}{2}\begin{vmatrix} x & 0 & 1 \\ 1 & 1 & 1 \\ 0 & 2 & 1 \end{vmatrix} = \pm 4$$

$$\Rightarrow \quad x(1-2) + 1(2-0) = \pm 8$$

$$\Rightarrow \quad -x + 2 = \pm 8$$

$$\Rightarrow \quad x = 2 \pm 8 \Rightarrow x = 10, -6$$

145. *(c)* We have,

$$\lim_{\theta \to \frac{\pi}{2}} \frac{\frac{\pi}{2} - \theta}{\cot\theta} = \lim_{\theta \to \frac{\pi}{2}} \frac{-1}{-\operatorname{cosec}^2\theta} \quad \text{[using L' Hospital Rule]}$$

$$\Rightarrow \lim_{\theta \to \frac{\pi}{2}} \sin^2\theta = \sin^2\frac{\pi}{2} = 1$$

146. *(a)* The equation $x^2 + y^2 + 2gx + c = 0$ represents co-axial system of circle having centre at $(-g, 0)$ and radius $= \sqrt{g^2 - c}$.

As $c < 0$, radius is always greater than 0. So, it has imaginary limiting points which show that circles are intersecting.

147. *(d)* We have, diameters of circle are

$$x + y = 6 \text{ and } x + 2y = 4$$

On solving above equations, we get

$$x = 8 \text{ and } y = -2$$

$\therefore$ Centre of circle is $(8, -2)$.

Since, circle passes through $(6, 2)$.

$$\therefore \text{Radius} = \sqrt{(8-6)^2 + (-2-2)^2} = \sqrt{4 + 16} = \sqrt{20}$$

148. *(a)* The vertex and focus of the parabola are (0, 6) and (0, 3) respectively.

Clearly, axis is Y-axis.

$\therefore$ Latusrectum = 4 (Distance between vertex and focus)

$$= 4\sqrt{(0-0)^2 + (6-3)^2} = 12$$

Also, the vertex is on the right hand side of the focus, so the parabola opens downward.

Hence, equation of the parabola is

$$(x - 0)^2 = -12(y - 6)$$

$$\Rightarrow \quad x^2 = -12y + 72$$

$$\Rightarrow \quad x^2 + 12y = 72$$

149. *(c)* We have,

$$25x^2 + 9y^2 - 150x - 90y + 225 = 0$$

$$\Rightarrow 25(x^2 - 6x) + 9(y^2 - 10y) + 225 = 0$$

$$\Rightarrow 25[(x-3)^2 - 9] + 9[(y-5)^2 - 25] + 225 = 0$$

$$\Rightarrow 25(x-3)^2 - 225 + 9(y-5)^2 - 225 + 225 = 0$$

$$\Rightarrow \quad 25(x-3)^2 + 9(y-5)^2 = 225$$

$$\Rightarrow \quad \frac{(x-3)^2}{9} + \frac{(y-5)^2}{25} = 1$$

On comparing with $\frac{(x-h)^2}{a^2} + \frac{(y-k)^2}{b^2} = 1$, we have

$$a = 3, b = 5$$

$$\therefore \text{Eccentricity, } e = \sqrt{1 - \frac{a^2}{b^2}} = \sqrt{1 - \frac{9}{25}} = \frac{4}{5}$$

150. *(b)* The equation of the ellipse is $\frac{x^2}{16} + \frac{y^2}{b^2} = 1$ and equation of the hyperbola is $\frac{x^2}{144} - \frac{y^2}{81} = \frac{1}{25}$ or

$$\frac{x^2}{\left(\frac{12}{5}\right)^2} - \frac{y}{\left(\frac{9}{5}\right)^2} = 1$$

$\therefore$ Eccentricity of ellipse, $e = \sqrt{1 - \frac{b^2}{16}}$

and eccentricity of hyperbola,

$$e' = \sqrt{1 + \frac{\left(\frac{9}{5}\right)^2}{\left(\frac{12}{5}\right)^2}} = \sqrt{1 + \frac{81}{144}} = \frac{15}{12}$$

Since, foci of ellipse and hyperbola coincide.

$\therefore \quad 4e = \frac{12}{5}e'$

$\Rightarrow \quad e = \frac{3}{5}e'$

$\Rightarrow \quad \sqrt{1 - \frac{b^2}{16}} = \frac{3}{5} \times \frac{15}{12}$

$\Rightarrow \quad 1 - \frac{b^2}{16} = \left(\frac{3}{4}\right)^2 \Rightarrow b^2 = 7$

151. *(b)* We have,

$f(x) = \log x$

$\therefore \quad f(\sin x) = \log \sin x$

On differentiating both sides w.r.t. x, we get

$\frac{d}{dx} f(\sin x) = \frac{1}{\sin x} . \cos x = \cot x$

152. *(a)* We have,

$$f(x) = \begin{cases} \frac{1 - \cos x}{x}, & x \neq 0 \\ k, & x = 0 \end{cases}$$

Since, $f(x)$ is continuous at $x = 0$

$\therefore \quad f(0) = \lim_{x \to 0} f(x)$

$\Rightarrow \quad k = \lim_{x \to 0} \frac{1 - \cos x}{x}$

$\Rightarrow \quad k = \lim_{x \to 0} \frac{2\sin^2 (x/2)}{x}$

$\Rightarrow \quad k = \lim_{x \to 0} \frac{\sin(x/2)}{(x/2)} \times \sin(x/2)$

$\Rightarrow \quad k = 1 \times 0$

$\Rightarrow \quad k = 0$

153. *(c)* We have,

$(3 + \omega + 3\omega^2)^4$

$= (3 + 3\omega + 3\omega^2 - 2\omega)^4$

$= [3(1 + \omega + \omega^2) - 2\omega]^4$

$= (3 \times 0 - 2\omega)^4$

$[\because 1 + \omega + \omega^2 = 0 \text{ or } \omega^3 = 1]$

$= (-2\omega)^4 = 16\omega^4$

$= 16\omega \quad [\because \omega^4 = \omega^3 \cdot \omega = \omega]$

154. *(d)* We have,

$y = \tan^{-1}(\sec x - \tan x)$

$y = \tan^{-1}\left[\frac{1 - \sin x}{\cos x}\right]$

$= \tan^{-1}\left[\frac{1 - \cos\left(\frac{\pi}{2} - x\right)}{\sin\left(\frac{\pi}{2} - x\right)}\right]$

$= \tan^{-1}\left[\frac{2\sin^2\left(\frac{\pi}{4} - \frac{x}{2}\right)}{2\sin\left(\frac{\pi}{4} - \frac{x}{2}\right)\cos\left(\frac{\pi}{4} - \frac{x}{2}\right)}\right]$

$= \tan^{-1}\left\{\tan\left(\frac{\pi}{4} - \frac{x}{2}\right)\right\} = \frac{\pi}{4} - \frac{x}{2}$

$\therefore \quad \frac{dy}{dx} = -\frac{1}{2}$

155. *(d)* We have,

$x + \frac{1}{x} = 2\cos\alpha$

$\Rightarrow \quad x^2 + 1 = 2x\cos\alpha$

$\Rightarrow \quad x^2 - (2\cos\alpha)x + 1 = 0$

$\Rightarrow \quad x = \frac{2\cos\alpha \pm \sqrt{4\cos^2\alpha - 4}}{2}$

$= \frac{2\cos\alpha \pm \sqrt{-4\sin^2\alpha}}{2}$

$= \frac{2\cos\alpha \pm 2(\sin\alpha)i}{2} = \cos\alpha \pm (\sin\alpha)i$

Now, $\quad x^n = (\cos\alpha \pm (\sin\alpha)i)^n = \cos n\alpha \pm i\sin n\alpha$

and $\quad \frac{1}{x^n} = (\cos\alpha \pm (\sin\alpha)i)^{-n} = \cos n\alpha \mp i\sin n\alpha$

$\therefore x^n + \frac{1}{x^n} = (\cos n\alpha \pm i\sin n\alpha) + (\cos n\alpha \mp i\sin n\alpha)$

$= 2\cos n\alpha$

156. *(c)* Let $I = \int_{-1}^{1} |1 - x|\, dx$

$= \int_{-1}^{1} (1 - x)\, dx \quad \left[\because |x| = \begin{cases} -x, & x < 0 \\ x, & x \geq 0 \end{cases}\right]$

$= \left[x - \frac{x^2}{2}\right]_{-1}^{1} = \left(1 - \frac{1}{2}\right) - \left(-1 - \frac{1}{2}\right) = \frac{1}{2} + \frac{3}{2} = 2$

157. *(b)* Let $I = \int \frac{1}{x(x^7 + 1)}\, dx$

$= \int \frac{x^6}{x^7(x^7 + 1)}\, dx$

Put $\quad x^7 = t \Rightarrow 7x^6\, dx = dt$

$\therefore \quad I = \frac{1}{7}\int \frac{dt}{t(t+1)} = \frac{1}{7}\int\left(\frac{1}{t} - \frac{1}{t+1}\right) dt$

$= \frac{1}{7}[\log t - \log(t + 1)] + c$

$= \frac{1}{7}\log\left(\frac{t}{t+1}\right) + c = \frac{1}{7}\log\left(\frac{x^7}{x^7 + 1}\right) + c$

COMEDK 2013

158. *(b)* Let $I = \int \sqrt{x}\, e^{\sqrt{x}}\, dx$

Put $\sqrt{x} = t \Rightarrow x = t^2 \Rightarrow dx = 2t\, dt$

$\therefore I = 2\int \underset{\text{I}}{t^2} \underset{\text{II}}{e^t}\, dt$

$= 2[t^2e^t - \int e^t \cdot 2t\, dt]$

$= 2[t^2e^t - 2\int \underset{\text{I}}{t}\underset{\text{II}}{e^t} dt]$

$= 2[t^2e^t - 2(te^t - \int e^t \cdot 1\, dt)]$

$= 2[t^2e^t - 2te^t + 2e^t] + c$

$= (2t^2 - 4t + 4)e^t + c$

$= (2x - 4\sqrt{x} + 4)\, e^{\sqrt{x}} + c$

159. *(d)* Let $I = \int \frac{dx}{x^2 + 2x + 2}$

$= \int \frac{dx}{(x+1)^2 + 1} = \tan^{-1}(x+1) + c$

160. *(a)* Let $P(x_1, y_1)$ be the required point. The given curve is

$$y = 6x - x^2$$

$$\Rightarrow \frac{dy}{dx} = 6 - 2x$$

$$\Rightarrow \left(\frac{dy}{dx}\right)_{(x_1, y_1)} = 6 - 2x_1$$

Since, the tangent at (x_1, y_1) is parallel to the line $4x - 2y - 1 = 0$.

$\therefore$ Slope of the tangent at (x_1, y_1) = Slope of the line $4x - 2y - 1 = 0$

$$\Rightarrow \left(\frac{dy}{dx}\right)_{(x_1, y_1)} = 2$$

$$\Rightarrow 6 - 2x_1 = 2 \Rightarrow x_1 = 2$$

$$\therefore y_1 = 6x_1 - x_1^2 = 6 \times 2 - 2^2 = 8$$

Thus, required point is (2, 8).

161. *(b)* Let $x = 0.5737373....$

$\Rightarrow 10x = 5.737373....$

$\Rightarrow 1000x = 573.7373....$

$\Rightarrow 1000x - 10x = 573 - 5$

$\Rightarrow 990x = 568$

$\Rightarrow x = \frac{568}{990}$

$\Rightarrow x = \frac{284}{495}$

162. *(a)* We have,

$x^2 - 5|x| + 6 = 0$

$|x|^2 - 5|x| + 6 = 0 \qquad [\because x^2 = |x|^2]$

$(|x| - 3)(|x| - 2) = 0$

$|x| = 3, 2$

$\Rightarrow x = \pm 3, \pm 2$

$\therefore$ Number of solution is 4.

163. *(c)* Required number of 6-digits number

$= \frac{6!}{2!\,2!\,2!} = \frac{720}{8} = 90$

164. *(c)* We have,

$7^1 = 7$

$7^2 = 49$

$7^3 = 343$

$7^4 = 2401$

and so on.

Thus, the last digit repeat itself in multiple of 4.

Since, 300 is divisible by 4, the units digit of 7^{300} would be 1.

165. *(b)* Let

$$\frac{\log x}{a - b} = \frac{\log y}{b - c} = \frac{\log z}{c - a} = k$$

$\Rightarrow \log x = k(a - b),$

$\log y = k(b - c)$

and $\log z = k(c - a)$

Now, $\log x + \log y + \log z =$

$k(a - b + b - c + c - a)$

$\Rightarrow \log(xyz) = 0$

$\Rightarrow xyz = 1$

166. *(b)* We have,

$(1 + i)^{2n} = (1 - i)^{2n}$

$\Rightarrow \left(\frac{1+i}{1-i}\right)^{2n} = 1$

$\Rightarrow \left(\frac{1+i}{1-i} \times \frac{1+i}{1+i}\right)^{2n} = 1$

$\Rightarrow \left(\frac{1 + i^2 + 2i}{1 - i^2}\right)^{2n} = 1$

$\Rightarrow \left(\frac{1 - 1 + 2i}{1 + 1}\right)^{2n} = 1$

$\Rightarrow i^{2n} = 1$

$\Rightarrow 2n = 4 \qquad [\because i^4 = 1]$

$\Rightarrow n = 2$

167. *(b)* We have,

$= \cos^{-1} p + \cos^{-1} q + \cos^{-1} r = \pi$

$\Rightarrow \cos^{-1} p + \cos^{-1} q = \pi - \cos^{-1} r$

$\Rightarrow \cos^{-1}(pq - \sqrt{1 - p^2}\sqrt{1 - q^2}) = \pi - \cos^{-1} r$

$\Rightarrow pq - \sqrt{1 - p^2}\sqrt{1 - q^2} = \cos(\pi - \cos^{-1} r)$

$\Rightarrow pq - \sqrt{1 - p^2}\sqrt{1 - q^2} = -\cos(\cos^{-1} r)$

$\Rightarrow pq - \sqrt{1 - p^2}\sqrt{1 - q^2} = -r$

$\Rightarrow pq + r = \sqrt{1 - p^2}\sqrt{1 - q^2}$

$\Rightarrow (pq + r)^2 = (1 - p^2)(1 - q^2)$

$\Rightarrow p^2q^2 + r^2 + 2pqr = 1 - p^2 - q^2 + p^2q^2$

$\Rightarrow p^2 + q^2 + r^2 + 2pqr = 1$

168. *(c)* We have,

$$\sin^{-1}\frac{x}{5} + \text{cosec}^{-1}\frac{5}{4} = \frac{\pi}{2}$$

$$\Rightarrow \sin^{-1}\frac{x}{5} + \sin^{-1}\frac{4}{5} = \frac{\pi}{2}$$

$$\Rightarrow \sin^{-1}\frac{x}{5} + \cos^{-1}\frac{3}{5} = \frac{\pi}{2}$$

$$\Rightarrow \sin^{-1}\frac{x}{5} = \frac{\pi}{2} - \cos^{-1}\frac{3}{5}$$

$$\Rightarrow \sin^{-1}\frac{x}{5} = \sin^{-1}\frac{3}{5}$$

$$\Rightarrow \frac{x}{5} = \frac{3}{5}$$

$$\Rightarrow x = 3$$

169. *(a)* We have,

$$81^{\sin^2 x} + 81^{\cos^2 x} = 30$$

$$\Rightarrow 81^{\sin^2 x} + 81^{\cos^2 x} = 3 + 27$$

$$= 81^{\sin^2 x} + 81^{\cos^2 x}$$

$$= (81)^{\frac{1}{4}} + (81)^{\frac{3}{4}}$$

$$\Rightarrow \sin^2 x = \frac{1}{4} \text{ and } \cos^2 x = \frac{3}{4}$$

$$\Rightarrow \sin x = \frac{\pm 1}{2} \text{ and } \cos x = \frac{\pm\sqrt{3}}{2}$$

Since, $0 < x < \pi$

$$\Rightarrow \sin x = \frac{1}{2} \text{ and } \cos x = \frac{\sqrt{3}}{2}$$

$$\Rightarrow x = \frac{\pi}{6}$$

170. *(d)* Equation of director circle of hyperbola,

$$\frac{x^2}{a^2} - \frac{y^2}{b^2} = 1 \text{ is } x^2 + y^2 = a^2 - b^2$$

Hence, director circle of $\frac{x^2}{16} - \frac{y^2}{4} = 1$ is

$$x^2 + y^2 = 16 - 4 \Rightarrow x^2 + y^2 = 12$$

171. *(b)* Let e be the identity element, then

$$a * e = a$$

$$\Rightarrow a + e - ae = a$$

$$\Rightarrow e(1 - a) = 0$$

$$\Rightarrow e = 0 \qquad [a \neq 1]$$

172. *(b)* We have, $x^2 + y^2 - 8x + 4y + 4 = 0$

$$\Rightarrow (x^2 - 8x + 16) + (y^2 + 4y + 4) = 16$$

$$\Rightarrow (x - 4)^2 + (y + 2)^2 = 4^2$$

$\therefore$ Centre is $(4, -2)$ and radius is 4.

Hence, given circle touches Y-axis.

173. *(a)* (a) Set of all fourth roots of unity is

$a = \{1, -1, i, -i\}$

Now, $1 \times (-1) = -1 \in G$

$1 \times i = i \in G$

$1 \times (-i) = -i \in G$

$(-1) \times i = -i \in G$

$(-1) \times (-i) = i \in G$

$i \times (-i) = -i^2 = 1 \in G$

So, it is true.

(b) Set of all cube root of unit is

$$H = \{1, w, w^2\}$$

Now, $1 + w = -w^2 \notin H$

So, it is false.

(c) It is not true, as this is possible only, when a is an abelian group, i.e. $ab = ba$

(d) We have,

$$(ab)^2 = a^2b^2$$

$$\Rightarrow (ab)(ab) = (aa)(bb)$$

$$\Rightarrow (b)(a) = (a)(b) \Rightarrow ba = ab$$

$\Rightarrow a$ is an abelian group.

So, it is false.

174. *(d)* Let H consist of the integral multiple of 5, i.e.

$$H = \{5x : x \in I\}$$

This H is the non-empty subset of I.

Now, let $a = 5r$ and $b = 5s$ any two elements of H, where r and s are some integers.

We have, $a + b = 5r + 5s = 5(r + s) \in H$.

$(r + s)$ comes out to be the some integer.

$\therefore a \in H, b \in H \Rightarrow (a + b) \in H$

Hence, H is a subgroup of set of all integers under addition.

175. *(c)* Given, circles can be written as

$$x^2 + y^2 + kx + 4y + 2 = 0$$

and $x^2 + y^2 - 2x - \frac{3}{2}y + \frac{k}{2} = 0$

Since, both circles are orthogonal, then

$$2g_1g_2 + 2f_1f_2 = c_1 + c_2$$

$$\Rightarrow -k - 3 = 2 + \frac{k}{2}$$

$$\frac{3k}{2} = -5$$

$$\Rightarrow k = -\frac{10}{3}$$

176. *(b)* $\lim_{x \to \infty}\left(1 - \frac{4}{x - 1}\right)^{3x - 1}$ $[1^\infty \text{ form}]$

$$= e^{\lim_{x \to \infty}\left(\frac{-4}{x - 1}\right)(3x - 1)}$$

$$= e^{\lim_{x \to \infty} -\frac{12x + 4}{x - 1}} = e^{-12}$$

177. *(b)* We have,

$$A + B + C = \pi$$

$$\Rightarrow \quad A + B = \pi - C$$

$$\Rightarrow \quad \frac{A}{2} + \frac{B}{2} = \frac{\pi}{2} - \frac{C}{2}$$

$$\Rightarrow \quad \tan\left(\frac{A}{2} + \frac{B}{2}\right) = \tan\left(\frac{\pi}{2} - \frac{C}{2}\right)$$

$$\Rightarrow \quad \frac{\tan\frac{A}{2} + \tan\frac{B}{2}}{1 - \tan\frac{A}{2}\tan\frac{B}{2}} = \cot\frac{C}{2}$$

$$\Rightarrow \quad \frac{\tan\frac{A}{2} + \tan\frac{B}{2}}{1 - \tan\frac{A}{2}\tan\frac{B}{2}} = \frac{1}{\tan\frac{C}{2}}$$

$$\Rightarrow \quad \tan\frac{C}{2}\tan\frac{A}{2} + \tan\frac{B}{2}\tan\frac{C}{2}$$

$$= 1 - \tan\frac{A}{2}\tan\frac{B}{2}$$

$$\Rightarrow \quad \tan\frac{A}{2}\tan\frac{B}{2} + \tan\frac{B}{2}\tan\frac{C}{2} + \tan\frac{C}{2}\tan\frac{A}{2} = 1$$

$$\Rightarrow \quad \Sigma\tan\frac{A}{2}\tan\frac{B}{2} = 1$$

178. *(c)* We have,

$$\frac{b}{\sin B} = 2R$$

$$\Rightarrow \quad R = \frac{B}{2\sin B} = \frac{2}{2 \times \sin 30^\circ} = 2$$

$\therefore$ Area of circumcircle $= \pi R^2$

$$= \pi(2)^2 = 4\pi$$

179. *(a)* We have,

$$\sin x + \sin^2 x = 1$$

$$\Rightarrow \quad \sin x = 1 - \sin^2 x$$

$$\Rightarrow \quad \sin x = \cos^2 x$$

Now, $\cos^{12} x + 3\cos^{10} x + 3\cos^8 x + \cos^6 x$

$$= \sin^6 x + 3\sin^5 x + 3\sin^4 x + \sin^3 x$$

$$= \sin^3 x[\sin^3 x + 3\sin^2 x + 3\sin x + 1]$$

$$= \sin^3 x(\sin x + 1)^3$$

$$= (\sin^2 x + \sin x)^3$$

$$= (1)^3 = 1$$

180. *(d)* We have,

$$f(x) = |x|$$

Now, $f(1) = |1| = 1$

and $f(-1) = |-1| = 1$

$\therefore$ $f(1) = f(-1)$ but $1 \neq -1$

So, $f(x)$ is not one-one.

Again, $|x| \geq 0, \forall\ x \in R$

So, range of $f(x) = [0, \infty]$

$\therefore$ Range $\neq$ Co-domain

So, $f(x)$ is not onto.

COMEDK 2013

COMEDK

Solved Paper 2012

Instructions

- There are 180 questions in all. The number of questions in each section is as given below.

Sections	No. of Questions
Section I : Physics	1-60
Section II : Chemistry	61-120
Section III : Mathematics	121-180

- All the questions are Multiple Choice Questions having four options out of which **ONLY ONE** is correct.
- Candidates will be awarded 1 mark for each correct answer. There will be no negative marking for incorrect answer.
- Time allotted to complete this paper is 3 hrs.

PHYSICS

1. The number of neutrons in ${}_{92}U^{235}$ nucleus is

a. 327 *b.* 235
c. 143 *d.* 92

2. Reverse saturation current of a diode

a. is independent of temperature
b. increases with increase in temperature
c. decreases with increase in temperature
d. may increase or decrease with increase in temperature depending on the semiconductor

3. A radioactive sample has a half-life of 10 min. If 64 nuclei are contained in the sample the number of nuclei that would decay after, 50 min is

a. 2 *b.* 5
c. 59 *d.* 62

4. The carrier of electromagnetic interaction is

a. gluon *b.* photon
c. meson *d.* graviton

5. The output of NOT gate when its input is 0

a. is 1 *b.* is 0
c. can be 0 or 1 *d.* is 0 and 1

6. LCD stands for

a. Light Carrying Diode
b. Liquid Crystal Display
c. Long Crystal Display
d. Light Crystal Display

7. Which of the following statement is false?

a. Sound and light waves exhibit interference.
b. Sound and light waves exhibit diffraction.
c. Light wave exhibits polarisation, while sound wave does not.
d. Sound wave exhibits polarisation, while light wave does not.

8. The correct relation between S, θ, L and C for an optically active solution is

a. $S = \theta LC$ *b.* $\theta = SLC$
c. $L = \theta SC$ *d.* $C = \theta LS$

9. An inductor and a resistor are connected to an AC supply of 50 V and 50 Hz If the voltage across the resistor is 40 V, then the voltage across the inductor will be

a. 10 V *b.* 20 V
c. 30 V *d.* 60 V

10. A 10μF capacitor is charged to 10 V and disconnected from the battery. If another uncharged 10μF capacitor is connected across it in parallel, then the voltage across the combination will be

a. 5V *b.* 10V *c.* 20V *d.* Zero

11. When two light nuclei fuse to form a relatively heavier nucleus, then the specific binding energy of the product nucleus is

a. lower than that of the reacting nuclei
b. equal to that of the reacting nuclei
c. greater than that of the reacting nuclei
d. equal to exactly half of either of the reacting nuclei

12. Two point charges $Q_1 = 2\,\mu C$ and $Q_2 = 1\,\mu C$ are placed as shown. The coordinates of the point P are (2 cm, 1 cm). The electric intensity vector at P subtends an angle θ with the positive X-axis. The value of θ is given by

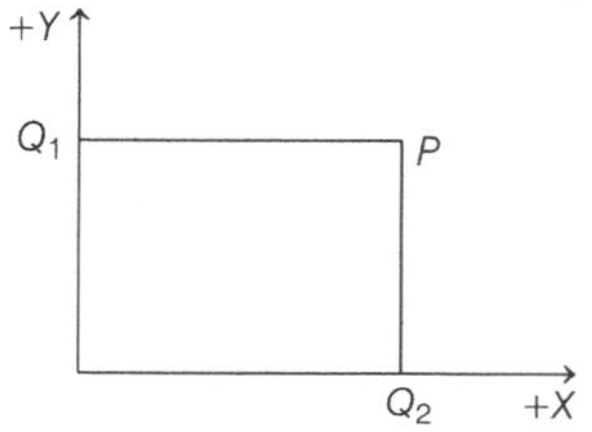

a. $\tan\theta = 1$ *b.* $\tan\theta = 2$
c. $\tan\theta = 3$ *d.* $\tan\theta = 4$

13. The direction of the force on a current carrying conductor held perpendicular to an uniform magnetic field is given by

a. Fleming's right hand rule
b. Ampere's swimming rule
c. Maxwell's right hand cork screw rule
d. Fleming's left hand rule

14. A convex lens of focal length F is placed in contact with a concave lens of focal length F. The equivalent focal length of the combination is

a. infinity *b.* $F/2$ *c.* $2F$ *d.* zero

15. If $x = at + bt^2$, where x is measured in metre and t in second, then the dimension of (b/a) is

a. $[LT^{-2}]$ *b.* $[LT^{-1}]$ *c.* $[T]$ *d.* $[T^{-1}]$

16. A particle is moving eastward with a velocity $5\ ms^{-1}$. In 10 s the velocity changes to $5\ ms^{-1}$ northwards. The average acceleration in this time is

a. $\frac{1}{\sqrt{2}}\ ms^{-2}$, towards North-West
b. $\frac{1}{2}\ ms^{-2}$, towards North-West
c. $\frac{1}{\sqrt{2}}\ ms^{-2}$, towards North-East
d. $\frac{1}{2}\ ms^{-2}$, towards North-East

17. A mass of 0.1 kg is hung at the 20 cm mark from a 1m rod weighing 0.25 kg pivoted at its centre. The rod will not topple if

a. No other mass is attached to the rod
b. 0.15 kg is hung at 80 cm mark
c. 0.15 kg is hung at 70 cm mark
d. 0.10 kg is hung at 70 cm mark

18. Which of the following cannot be explained on the basis of Bernoulli's principle?

a. Lift on an aircraft's wing
b. Ink filler
c. Swing of a cricket ball
d. Atomizer

19. The layer in the Earth's atmosphere which reflects radio waves from the Earth, thus helping radio communication is

a. stratosphere *b.* mesosphere
c. troposphere *d.* ionosphere

20. The reaction of the floor on an object placed on the floor of an elevator is maximum when elevator

a. is stationary
b. accelerates upwards
c. cable snaps and it falls freely towards the Earth
d. accelerates downwards

21. A particle is projected at an angle of 30° with the horizontal with a momentum p. At the highest point its momentum is

a. $\frac{\sqrt{3}}{4}p$ *b.* $\frac{2}{\sqrt{3}}p$
c. p *d.* $\frac{1}{2}p$

22. A block of mass 0.1 kg is held against a wall by applying a horizontal force of 5 N on it. If μ_s between the wall and the block is 0.5, the magnitude of the frictional force acting on the block is

a. 0.98 N *b.* 0.49 N
c. 4.9 N *d.* 2.5 N

23. A ring rolls down an inclined plane. The ratio of the rotational kinetic energy to translational kinetic energy is

a. 1 : 3 *b.* 1 : 1
c. 3 : 1 *d.* 2 : 1

COMEDK 2012

24. If 120 J of work is done in 2 min by a water pump, then the power of the pump is

a. 14.4 kW *b.* 240 W *c.* 60 W *d.* 1 W

25. Assuming, $g_{(\text{Moon})} = \left(\frac{1}{6}\right) g_{\text{Earth}}$ and $D_{(\text{Moon})} = \left(\frac{1}{4}\right) D_{\text{Earth}}$, where g and D are the acceleration due to gravity and diameter respectively, the escape velocity from the Moon is

a. $\frac{11.2}{24}$ kms^{-1} *b.* $11.2 \times \sqrt{24}$ kms^{-1}

c. $\frac{11.2}{\sqrt{24}}$ kms^{-1} *d.* 11.2×24 kms^{-1}

26. The work done in taking an ideal gas through one cycle of operation as shown in the indicator diagram below

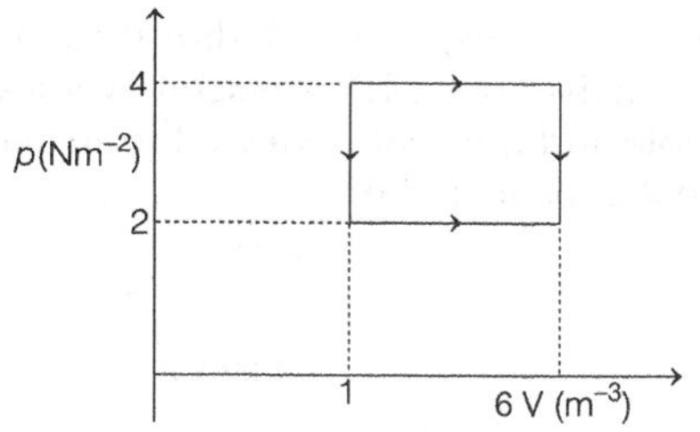

a. 10^{-5} J *b.* 10^{-3} J

c. 10^{-2} J *d.* 10 J

27. The ratio of speed of sound in hydrogen to that in oxygen at the same temperature is

a. 1 : 4 *b.* 4 : 1 *c.* 1 : 1 *d.* 16 : 1

28. A black body at a temperature T radiates energy at the rate of E Wm^{-2}. If the temperature is decreased by $T/2$, then the energy radiated will be

a. $E/4$ *b.* $E/16$ *c.* $E/8$ *d.* $E/32$

29. A particle executes simple harmonic motion with amplitude A. The distance moved by the particle in one oscillation is

a. zero *b.* A *c.* $2A$ *d.* $4A$

30. A capacitor of 10 μF is connected to a 10 V cell. The maximum charge on the capacitor will be

a. 1 μC *b.* 10 μC

c. 100 μC *d.* 1000 μC

31. A wire of uniform cross-section has a resistance R. It is cut into ten equal parts. The parts are connected in parallel between two points A and B. The effective resistance between A and B will be

a. 0.01 R *b.* 0.1 R *c.* R *d.* 10 R

32. Wires made of iron and silicon are cooled from 50°C to 30°C, then

a. resistance of both wires decreases
b. resistance of both wires increases
c. resistance of iron increases and that of silicon decreases
d. resistance of iron decreases and that of silicon increases

33. In a meter bridge a copper coil is connected in the right gap and a resistance of 10 Ω in the left gap. The balance point is obtained at 0.2 m. The resistance of the coil is

a. 40 Ω *b.* 5 Ω *c.* 20 Ω *d.* 2.5 Ω

34. Two identical concentric coils X and Y carrying currents in the ratio 1 : 2 are arranged in mutually perpendicular planes. If the magnetic field due to coil X is B, then the net field at their common centre is

a. B *b.* $2B$ *c.* $3B$ *d.* $\sqrt{5}B$

35. Which of the following is based on mechanical effect of electric current?

a. AC dynamo *b.* DC dynamo
c. AC or DC motor *d.* Electric geyser

36. According to Faraday's law of electromagnetic induction an emf is induced in a coil, if

a. electric flux links with the coil
b. magnetic flux links with the coil
c. magnetic flux linked with the coil changes
d. electric flux linked with the coil changes

37. The current in a coil changes from 1 mA to 5 mA in 4 milli second. If the coefficient of self-induction of the coil is 10 mH, then the magnitude of the self-induced emf is

a. 10 mV *b.* 5 mV *c.* 2.5 mV *d.* 1 mV

38. The graph of kinetic energy of photoelectron *versus* frequency of incident radiation is shown for two metals M and N. We may definitely conclude

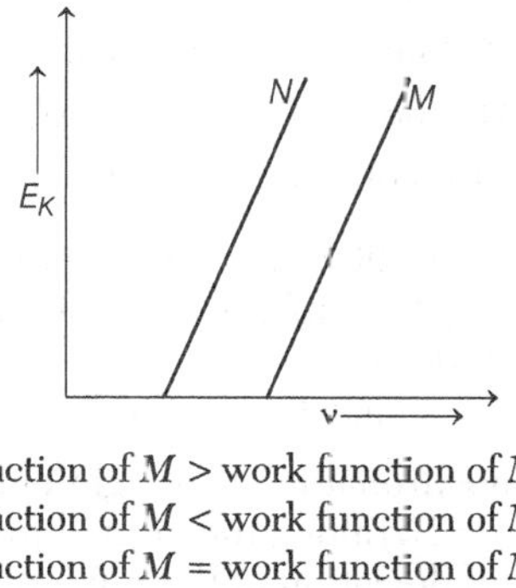

a. work function of M > work function of N
b. work function of M < work function of N
c. work function of M = work function of N
d. at the threshold frequency of M the kinetic energy of the photoelectron emitted by M is more than that emitted by N

COMEDK 2012

39. Choose the wrong statement.
a. Alpha particles can be scattered by Gold nucleus.
b. X-ray can be diffracted by crystals.
c. UV-radiation can cause photoelectric effect.
d. Electrons cannot be diffracted by crystals.

40. In the case of the Bohr atom model if E_K and U are the kinetic and potential energies of an electron in an orbit, then
a. $E_K + U = 0$ *b.* $E_K - U = 0$
c. $2E_K + U = 0$ *d.* $E_K + 2U = 0$

41. The ratio of the magnetic fields at the centre of a circular coil carrying current to that at a point whose distance is half of the radius of the coil is
a. $2\sqrt{5} : 8$ *b.* $5\sqrt{5} : 8$
c. $5\sqrt{5} : 4$ *d.* $2\sqrt{5} : 4$

42. The difference between the wavelengths of the stokes line and anti-stokes lines in the Raman spectrum of H-Br molecule is 100Å. If the wavelength of the anti-stokes line is 5000 Å, then the wavelength of the incident radiation is
a. 5050 Å *b.* 4950 Å *c.* 5100 Å *d.* 4900 Å

43. Optical pumping means transferring electrons
a. from ground state to metastable state
b. from metastable state to a higher excited state
c. from a state higher than the metastable state to the metastable state
d. from a state lower than the metastable state to a state higher than the metastable state

44. An open pipe immersed in water to half its length. The ratio of the fundamental frequency of the pipe before and after immersion in water is
a. 1 : 2 *b.* 1 : 1 *c.* 1 : 3 *d.* 1 : 4

45. Assuming, $R = 8.3\ \text{J mol}^{-1}\ \text{K}^{-1}$ and $\gamma = 1.4$ the values of C_p and C_V of a gas are
a. $29.05\ \text{J mol}^{-1}\ \text{K}^{-1}, 20.75\ \text{J mol}^{-1}\ \text{K}^{-1}$
b. $20.75\ \text{J mol}^{-1}\ \text{K}^{-1}, 29.05\ \text{J mol}^{-1}\ \text{K}^{-1}$
c. $16.60\ \text{J mol}^{-1}\ \text{K}^{-1}, 8.300\ \text{J mol}^{-1}\ \text{K}^{-1}$
d. $8.300\ \text{J mol}^{-1}\ \text{K}^{-1}, 16.60\ \text{J mol}^{-1}\ \text{K}^{-1}$

46. A star *A* is 100 times brighter than star *B*. Then, $m_B - m_A$ the difference in their apparent magnitudes is
a. 100 *b.* 0.01 *c.* 5 *d.* 0.2

47. A monochromatic ray of light enters into a glass slab $(n = 1.5)$ along the normal to the surface. The angle of deviation of the refracted ray is
a. 90° *b.* 45° *c.* 30° *d.* 0°

48. A ray of light passing from glass to water is incident on the glass-water interface at 65°. If the critical angle for the pair of media is 63°.
a. The ray will emerge into water with a deviation of 2° from the normal
b. The ray will be refracted into water with a deviation of 2°
c. The ray will be totally internally reflected back into glass with a deviation of 50°
d. The ray will be totally internally reflected back into glass with a deviation of 2°

49. An equilateral prism is kept in the minimum deviation position. If the angle of incidence of a monochromatic ray at a refracting face is 49° 30′, then the angle of minimum deviation of the ray will be
a. 39° *b.* 49°30′
c. 40°30′ *d.* 51°

50. A glass hemisphere of radius 0.1 cm and refractive index 1.5 is placed over a spot on a table and the spot is viewed from above. The spot appears to be

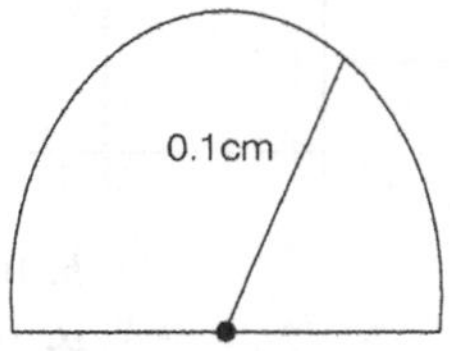

a. 0.1 m above the top surface of the hemisphere
b. 0.1 m below the top surface of the hemisphere
c. 0.033 m above the top surface of the hemisphere
d. exactly on the top surface of the hemisphere

51. Photoelectric effect and Raman effect can be explained on the basis of
a. Newton's corpuscular theory of light
b. Huygens wave theory of light
c. Maxwell's electromagnetic theory of light
d. Planck's quantum theory of light

52. In an interference pattern the ratio of the intensity of light at the bright fringe to that at the dark fringe is 9 : 1. Then, the ratio of the amplitudes of the two interfering waves
a. 3 : 1 *b.* 2 : 1 *c.* 1 : 4 *d.* 5 : 4

53. Diffraction effects are more easily detected in the case of sound waves than light waves because
a. sound waves are longitudinal
b. sound waves have smaller wavelength
c. sound waves have larger wavelength
d. sound waves are transverse

54. If θ is the polarising angle for a medium in which the speed of light is v, then according to Brewster's law

a. $\theta = \sin^{-1}(c/v)$

b. $\theta = \tan^{-1}(c/v)$

c. $\theta = \cos^{-1}(c/v)$

d. $\theta = \sin^{-1}(v/c)$

55. Two polaroid A and B are kept with their transmission axes at an angle θ with respect to one another. If the transmitted intensity of light $I_t = 0.75\ I_0$, where I_0 is the intensity of light incident on the system, then θ is

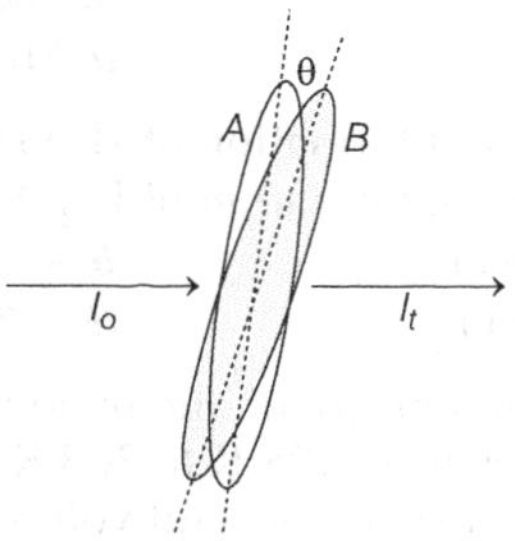

a. 30° *b.* 45° *c.* 60° *d.* 90°

56. The electric force between two point charges separated by a certain distance in air is F. The distance at which they should be placed in a medium of relative permittivity k, so that the force remains the same, is

a. d *b.* $\frac{d}{k}$ *c.* kd *d.* $\frac{d}{\sqrt{k}}$

57. A positively charged particle is released from rest in a region of uniform electric field. The particle will move

a. with constant speed

b. with constant velocity

c. with constant acceleration

d. with variable acceleration

58. Two charges q and $-2q$ are separated by a distance d. If the electric intensity at the site of q is E, then the electric field at the site of $-2q$ is

a. E *b.* $E/2$

c. $-2E$ *d.* $-E/2$

59. Choose the correct statement.

a. A p-type semiconductor is positively charged.

b. The Boolean expression $1 \cdot 0 = 0$.

c. The majority carrier in n-type semiconductor is hole.

d. A transistor cannot be used as a switch.

60. "Plum pudding" model of an atom was proposed by

a. C.V. Raman *b.* N. Bohr

c. E. Rutherford *d.* J.J. Thomson

CHEMISTRY

61. Which of the following is not a protein?

a. Wool *b.* Cellulose

c. Hair *d.* Nail

62. Which of the following is not true for the adsorption of a gas on a solid?

a. Increase in temperature favors adsorption

b. Enthalpy change is negative

c. Adsorption is more specific

d. Entropy change is negative

63. Peptisation is a process in which

a. precipitate becomes true solution

b. true solution becomes a suspension

c. a colloid gets coagulated

d. a suspension gets converted into a colloid

64. The mole fraction of benzene in a solution containing 39% by mass in an organic solvent of molecular mass 122 is

a. 0.5 *b.* 0.6

c. 0.4 *d.* 0.35

65. $Zn(s) + Cl_2\ (1\ atm) \longrightarrow Zn^{2+} + 2Cl^-; E° = 2.0\ V$

To increase the emf of the above cell

a. $[Zn^{2+}]$ should be increased

b. $[Zn^{2+}]$ should be decreased

c. $[Cl^-]$ should be increased

d. partial pressure of Cl_2 should be decreased

66. Two ions A^+ and B^- have radii 104 and 200 pm respectively, in a cubic close packed crystal of compound AB. The coordination number of A^+ is

a. 4 *b.* 8

c. 6 *d.* 3

67. The mass of a non-volatile solute of molar mass 60 g mol^{-1} that should be dissolved in 126 g of water to reduce its vapour pressure to 99% will be

a. 2.8 g *b.* 5.6 g

c. 8.4 g *d.* 4.2 g

68. The pH of boiling water is 6.4. This implies that boiling water is

a. slightly basic *b.* slightly acidic
c. neutral *d.* amphoteric

69. The spin only magnetic moment of Ni^{2+} (in BM) in aqueous solution will be

a. 1.73 *b.* 2.84 *c.* 3.42 *d.* 2.25

70. An organic compound which produces a bluish green flame when heated on a copper wire is

a. benzaldehyde *b.* aniline
c. chlorobenzene *d.* benzoic acid

71. Phenol can be distinguished from ethyl alcohol using

a. Na *b.* $AlCl_3$
c. NaOH *d.* $FeCl_3$

72. The time required for 100% completion of zero order reaction is

a. $\frac{a}{k}$ *b.* $\frac{a}{2k}$ *c.* $\frac{2a}{k}$ *d.* $\frac{k}{a}$

73. The EAN of central metal atom in $[Co(NH_3)_6]Cl_3$ is [Atomic number of Co = 27]

a. 34 *b.* 35 *c.* 36 *d.* 32

74. The alcohol obtained during the hydrolysis of ground nut oil is

a. glycol *b.* butan-1-ol
c. pentan-2-ol *d.* propane 1, 2, 3-triol

75. Which one of the following ores is concentrated by froth floatation process?

a. Magnesite *b.* Magnetite
c. Galena *d.* Malachite

76. Which of the following electron transitions in the H-atom will release the largest amount of energy?

a. $n = 3$ to $n = 2$ *b.* $n = 2$ to $n = 1$
c. $n = 5$ to $n = 2$ *d.* $n = 6$ to $n = 2$

77. An electron having spin quantum number of $s = \frac{-1}{2}$ and magnetic quantum number, $m = +3$ can be present in

a. both s-orbital and p-orbital
b. only p-orbital
c. only f-orbital
d. both d-orbital and f-orbital

78. The atomic number of the element with highest ionisation energy among the following is

a. Z = 16 *b.* Z = 14
c. Z = 13 *d.* Z = 15

79. Number of atoms in 560 cm^3 of oxygen at STP is

a. $\frac{1}{20} \times 6.022 \times 10^{23}$ *b.* $\frac{1}{40} \times 6.022 \times 10^{23}$
c. $\frac{1}{16} \times 6.022 \times 10^{23}$ *d.* $\frac{1}{32} \times 6.022 \times 10^{23}$

80. The volume of CO_2 (in cm^3) liberated at STP, when 1.06 g of anhydrous sodium carbonate is treated with excess of dilute HCl is [atomic mass of Na = 23]

a. 112 *b.* 224 *c.* 56 *d.* 2240

81. The oxidation number of oxygen is – 1 in

a. NO_2 *b.* PbO_2
c. Na_2O_2 *d.* MnO_2

82. The heat of formation of $H_2O(l)$ is – 286 kJ. The heat of formation of $H_2O(g)$ is likely to be

a. – 286 kJ *b.* + 286 kJ
c. – 341 kJ *d.* – 242.8 kJ

83. The temperature of one mole of an ideal gas increases from 298 K to 308 K, when it absorbs 200 J of heat at constant volume. The change in the internal energy of the gas is

a. 200 J *b.* 140 J
c. – 200 J *c.* – 140 J

84. 100 mL of $\frac{N}{5}$ HCl was added to 1 g of pure $CaCO_3$. What would remain after the reaction?

a. 0.5 g of $CaCO_3$
b. Neither $CaCO_3$ nor HCl
c. 50 mL of HCl
d. 25 mL of HCl

85. The RMS velocity of CH_4, He and SO_2 are in the ratio of

a. 16 : 4 : 64 *b.* 2 : 1 : 4
c. 2 : 4 : 1 *d.* 1 : 4 : 2

86. A negative catalyst will

a. lower the activation energy of the reaction
b. does not alter the activation energy of the reaction
c. provide a new and easy path to the reaction
d. increases the activation energy of the reaction

87. The number of σ and π-bonds in pent-2-yne is

a. 12 and 2 *b.* 11 and 2
c. 13 and 2 *d.* 12 and 3

88. In Lassaigne's test for nitrogen in an organic compound, the blue colouration is due to the formation of

a. ferro-ferriccyanide *b.* ferric-ferrocyanide
c. potassium ferrocyanide *d.* potassium ferrocyanide

89. The organic compound obtained during the addition of HBr to propene in the presence of peroxide catalyst is
a. 2-bromopropane *b.* 2-bromopropene
c. 1-bromopropane *d.* 1-bromopropene

90. On passing H_2S into a solution containing both Zn^{2+} and Cu^{2+} in acidic medium, only CuS gets precipitated. This is because
a. K_{sp} of CuS < K_{sp} of ZnS
b. K_{sp} of CuS = K_{sp} of ZnS
c. K_{sp} of CuS > K_{sp} of ZnS
d. CuS is more stable than ZnS

91. The volume of H_2 obtained at STP, when Mg obtained by passing a current of 0.5 A through molten $MgCl_2$ for 32.2 min is treated with excess of dilute HCl is approximately [Equivalent mass of Mg = 12]
a. 56 cm^3 *b.* 28 cm^3
c. 5.6 cm^3 *d.* 112 cm^3

92. Markownikoff's rule is applicable to
a. C_3H_6 + HBr *b.* C_2H_4 + HCl
c. C_3H_6 + Cl_2 *d.* C_2H_4 + HBr

93. The reaction of ethene is the presence of H^+ can be example for
a. − *I*-effect *b.* + *E*-effect
c. − *E*-effect *d.* + *I*-effect

94. $CH_3—CN \xrightarrow{\text{Dil. HCl}} A \xrightarrow{\text{LiAlH}_4} B \xrightarrow{\text{PCl}_5} C \xrightarrow{\text{Alc. KOH}} D$. The product *D* in the above sequence of reactions is
a. acetaldehyde *b.* ethyne
c. ethene *d.* acetyl chloride

95. An organic compound is optically active if, it
a. is planar
b. is super imposable on its mirror image
c. contains chiral centres
d. is non-super imposable on its mirror image

96. Identify the electrophile in the following.
a. $R—NH_2$ *b.* NH_3
c. $AlCl_3$ *d.* CN_6

97. The ionisation constant of phenol is more than that of ethanol because
a. phenoxide ion is a stronger base than ethoxide ion
b. phenoxide ion is stabilised by resonance
c. ethoxide ion is stabilised by resonance
d. phenoxide ion is aromatic while ethoxide ion is aliphatic

98. The product *C* in the following sequence of chemical reaction is

$$CH_3—COOH \xrightarrow{Ca(OH)_2} A \xrightarrow{\text{Heat}} B \xrightarrow{NH_2OH} C$$

a. acetaldoxime *b.* formaldoxime
c. ethane nitrile *d.* acetoxime

99. Which of the following statements is not true?
a. Acetic acid is stronger than chloro acetic acid.
b. Formic acid is the strongest of all aliphatic monocarboxylic acids.
c. Benzoic acid is stronger acid than acetic acid.
d. Propanoic acid is weaker than acetic acid.

100. Maximum number of molecules of methyl iodide that can react with one molecule of methyl amine is
a. 4 *b.* 3 *c.* 2 *d.* 1

101. The amine which will not liberate nitrogen with nitrous acid is
a. ethyl amine *b.* methyl amine
c. dimethyl amine *d.* 2-amino propane

102. Which of the following is aromatic?
a. Lysine *b.* Proline
c. Serine *d.* Tyrosine

103. The mass of hydrogen in gram required to completely saturate 1 mole of triolein is
a. 6 *b.* 3
c. 2 *d.* 9

104. $CH_3—CH_2—OH \xrightarrow{A} CH_3—CH_2—Cl \xrightarrow{B} CH_2 = CH_2$. *A* and *B* in this sequence of reactions are
a. KOH (*aq*) and PCl_5 *b.* PCl_5 and KOH (*aq*)
c. Cl_2 and KOH (*alc*) *d.* PCl_5 and KOH (*alc*)

105. The enthalpy of neutralisation of HCl and NaOH is *x* kJ. The heat evolved, when 500 mL of 2N HCl is mixed with 250 mL of 4 N NaOH will be
a. x *b.* $\frac{x}{2}$ *c.* $\frac{x}{4}$ *d.* $\frac{2x}{3}$

106. $A + B \rightleftharpoons C + D$

The initial concentrations of *A* and *B* are equal. At equilibrium, the concentration of *C* is twice that of *A*. The equilibrium constant of the reaction is
a. $\frac{9}{4}$ *b.* 4 *c.* $\frac{1}{9}$ *d.* $\frac{4}{9}$

107. The dissociation of lime stone in the slag zone of the blast furnace is
a. exothermic accompanied by increase in entropy
b. endothermic accompanied by decrease in entropy
c. endothermic accompanied by increase in entropy
d. exothermic with no change in entropy

108. Which of the following is not true for concentrated H_2SO_4?
a. Sulphonating agent *b.* Oxidising agent
c. Dehydrating agent *d.* Deliquescent in nature

109. Which of the following noble gases has the highest van der Waals' force of attraction?
a. Ar *b.* Ne *c.* Xe *d.* He

110. Which one of the following metal ions is coloured?
a. Ti^+ *b.* Cu^+ *c.* V^{4+} *d.* Zn^{2+}

111. Coordination number of nickel in $[Ni(C_2O_4)_3]^{4-}$ is
a. 3 *b.* 12 *c.* 6 *d.* 4

112. IUPAC name of $[CrCl_2(NH_3)_4]NO_3$ is
a. tetraamminedichlorochromium (I) nitrate
b. dichlorotetraamminechromium (III) nitrate
c. tetraamminedichlorochromium (IV) nitrate
d. tetraamminedichlorochromium (III) nitrate

113. Decomposition of NH_3 on the surface of platinum has a rate constant of 2.5×10^{-4} mol dm^{-3}s^{-1} at 350 K. The order of the reaction is
a. 0 *b.* 1 *c.* 1/2 *d.* 2

114. The rate equation of a gaseous reaction is given by $r = k[A][B]$. If the volume of the reaction vessel is suddenly reduced to 1/2 of the initial volume, the reaction rate relating to the original rate will be
a. $\frac{1}{4}$ *b.* 4 *c.* $\frac{1}{2}$ *d.* 2

115. The reduction potential of an electrode can be increased by
a. increasing the area of the electrode
b. decreasing the temperature
c. increasing the temperature
d. decreasing the concentration of metal ions

116. An electric current is passed through silver and water voltameters connected in series. The cathode of the silver voltameter weighed 0.054 g more at the end of electrolysis. The volume of O_2 evolved at the anode of water voltameter is
a. 5.6 cm^3 *b.* 11.2 cm^3
c. 22.4 cm^3 *d.* 2.8 cm^3

117. The pH of a mixture of 10 mL of 0.1 M H_2SO_4. 5 mL of 0.2 N HCl and 5 mL of 0.1 M $Ca(OH)_2$ is
a. 1 *b.* 0.5 *c.* 0 *d.* 1.5

118. The conjugate acid of NH_2^- is
a. NH_4^+ *b.* NH_3 *c.* NH_2OH *d.* NH^-

119. Phenyl isocyanide is formed when chloroform is treated with alcoholic potassium hydroxide and
a. benzaldehyde *b.* aniline
c. phenol *d.* nitrobenzene

120. Which of the following does not undergo aldol condensation reaction?
a. CH_3—CHO *b.* $ClCH_2$—CHO
c. C_6H_5—CHO *d.* $CHCl_2$—CHO

MATHEMATICS

121. If the area of the circle $7x^2 + 7y^2 - 7x + 14y + k - 0$ is 12π sq units, then the value of k is
a. $\frac{-43}{4}$ *b.* $\frac{-301}{4}$ *c.* -16 *d.* ± 4

122. A man running a race-course notes that the sum of the distances from the two flag posts from him is always 10 m and the distance between the flag posts is 8 m. The equations of the path traced by the man is given by
a. $\frac{x^2}{9} + \frac{y^2}{25} = 1$ *b.* $\frac{x^2}{9} + \frac{y^2}{16} = 1$
c. $\frac{x^2}{25} + \frac{y^2}{9} = 1$ *d.* $\frac{x^2}{16} + \frac{y^2}{25} = 1$

123. The number of common tangents to the circles $x^2 + y^2 - 2x - 4y + 1 = 0$ and $x^2 + y^2 - 12x - 16y + 91 = 0$ is
a. 1 *b.* 2 *c.* 3 *d.* 4

124. Equation of the chord of the circle $x^2 + y^2 + 4x - 6y - 9 = 0$ bisected at (0, 1) is
a. $y - 1 = x$ *b.* $y + 1 = x$
c. $y + 1 = 2x$ *d.* $y - 1 = 3x$

125. The angle between two asymptotes of the hyperbola $\frac{x^2}{25}-\frac{y^2}{16}=1$ is

a. $\tan^{-1}\frac{4}{5}$ *b.* $2\tan^{-1}\frac{4}{5}$
c. $2\tan^{-1}\frac{5}{4}$ *d.* $\pi-2\tan^{-1}\frac{4}{5}$

126. The parametric equation of a parabola is $x=t^2+1,\ y=2t+1$. The cartesian equation of its directrix is

a. $y=0$ *b.* $x=-1$
c. $x=0$ *d.* $x-1=0$

127. If $|\mathbf{a}\times\mathbf{b}|=5$ and $|\mathbf{a}\cdot\mathbf{b}|=3$, then $|\mathbf{a}|^2\,|\mathbf{b}|^2$ is equal to

a. 16 *b.* 31 *c.* 25 *d.* 34

128. The direction cosines of the vector $2\hat{\mathbf{i}}+\hat{\mathbf{j}}-2\hat{\mathbf{k}}$ is equal to

a. $\frac{2}{3},\frac{1}{3},-\frac{2}{3}$ *b.* $\frac{2}{3},\frac{1}{3},\frac{2}{3}$
c. $\frac{1}{3},\frac{2}{3},-\frac{2}{3}$ *d.* $\frac{2}{3},\frac{2}{3},\frac{1}{3}$

129. If 1, ω, ω^2 are the cube roots of unity, then $(3+3\omega^2+5\omega)^6-(2+6\omega^2+2\omega)^3$ is equal to

a. 32 *b.* 64 *c.* 0 *d.* -1

130. If $\int_{\log 2}^{x}\frac{dy}{\sqrt{e^y-1}}=\frac{\pi}{6}$, then x is equal to

a. $\log_e 4$ *d.* $\log_e 2$ *c.* 4 *d.* 2

131. $\int_{-8}^{8}(\sin^{93}x+x^{295})dx=$

a. 1 *b.* -1 *c.* 0 *d.* $\frac{8}{3}$

132. Area of the ellipse $\frac{x^2}{25}+\frac{y^2}{16}=1$ is given by

a. 25 π sq units *b.* 20 π sq units
c. 4 π sq units *d.* 5 π units

133. The order of the differential equation

$$\left[1+\left(\frac{dy}{dx}\right)^5\right]^{\frac{2}{3}}=\frac{d^3y}{dx^3}$$

a. 2 *b.* 1 *c.* 3 *d.* $\frac{2}{3}$

134. The solution of $\frac{dy}{dx}-1=e^{x-y}$ is

a. $e^{x-y}+x=c$ *b.* $e^{-(x-y)}+x=c$
c. $e^{-(x-y)}=x+c$ *d.* $e^{x-y}=x+c$

135. If $\sin^{-1}\left(\frac{2p}{1+p^2}\right)-\cos^{-1}\left(\frac{1-q^2}{1+q^2}\right)=\tan^{-1}\left(\frac{2x}{1+x^2}\right)$, then the value of x is equal to

a. $\frac{p+q}{1+pq}$ *b.* $\frac{p-q}{1-pq}$
c. $\frac{p-q}{pq-1}$ *d.* $\frac{p-q}{1+pq}$

136. The unit vector in the direction of the vector $\mathbf{a}+2\mathbf{b}-\mathbf{c}$ is equal to

a. $\frac{\mathbf{a}+2\mathbf{b}-\mathbf{c}}{\sqrt{6}}$ *b.* $\frac{\mathbf{a}+2\mathbf{b}-\mathbf{c}}{2}$
c. $\frac{\mathbf{a}+2\mathbf{b}-\mathbf{c}}{4}$ *d.* $\frac{\mathbf{a}+2\mathbf{b}-\mathbf{c}}{6}$

137. Identify the false statement.

a. A non-empty subset H of group G is a subgroup of G if and only if for every a, $b\in H\to a*b^{-1}\in H$
b. The intersection of two subgroups of a group G is again a subgroup.
c. A group of order three is not abelian
d. If in a group F, $(ab)^2=a^2b^2,\forall\, a,b\in G$ then G is abelian

138. If $y=\tan^{-1}\left(\frac{1}{1+x+x^2}\right)+\tan^{-1}\left(\frac{1}{x^2+3x+3}\right)+\tan^{-1}\left(\frac{1}{x^2+5x+7}\right)+\ldots+$ upto n terms then, $\frac{dy}{dx}$ at $x=0$ and $n=1$ is equal to

a. $\frac{1}{2}$ *b.* $-\frac{1}{2}$
c. 0 *d.* $\frac{1}{3}$

139. If $\cot\alpha\cot\beta=2$, then $\frac{\cos(\alpha+\beta)}{\cos(\alpha-\beta)}$ is equal to

a. 3 *b.* $\frac{2}{3}$
c. $\frac{1}{3}$ *d.* $\tan\alpha\tan\beta$

140. If ω is a cube root of unity, then the value of determinant $\begin{vmatrix}1+\omega & \omega^2 & \omega\\ \omega^2+\omega & -\omega & \omega^2\\ 1+\omega^2 & \omega & \omega^2\end{vmatrix}$ is equal to

a. $1+\omega$ *b.* $1-\omega$
c. 0 *d.* ω^2

141. If the tangent to the curve $2y^3 = ax^2 + x^3$ at the point (a, a) cuts off intercepts α and β on the coordinate axes, where $\alpha^2 + \beta^2 = 61$, then the value of a is equal to

a. 25 *b.* 36
c. $\pm$ 30 *d.* $\pm$ 40

142. Length of the subtangent at (a, a) on the curve $y^2 = \dfrac{x^2}{2a + x}$ is equal to

a. $\frac{18}{5}$ *b.* $\frac{18a}{5}$
c. $-\frac{18a^2}{5}$ *d.* $\frac{18a^2}{5}$

143. The function $f(x) = 5 + 36x + 3x^2 - 2x^3$ is increasing in the interval

a. $(-2, 3)$ *b.* $(2, 3)$
c. $[2, 3)$ *d.* $(2, 3]$

144. Divide 20 into two parts such that the product of one part and the cube of the other is maximum. The two parts are

a. (12, 8) *b.* (15, 5)
c. (10, 10) *d.* (2, 18)

145. The number of positive divisors of 4896 is

a. 32 *b.* 34
c. 36 *d.* 38

146. The last digit of $583! + 7^{291}$ is

a. 1 *b.* 2
c. 0 *d.* 3

147. $\int x^x (1 + \log x)\, dx =$

a. $x^x + C$ *b.* $x^{-x} + x$
c. $x \log x + x$ *d.* $\log x + x$

148. If $\int \frac{xe^x}{(1+x)^2} dx = e^x f(x) + c$, then $f(x)$ is equal to

a. $\frac{1}{(1+x)^2}$ *b.* $\frac{x}{(1+x)}$
c. $\frac{1}{1+x}$ *d.* $\frac{x}{(1+x)^2}$

149. $\int_0^{\pi/2} \frac{\sin 2t}{\sin^4 t + \cos^4 t} dt =$

a. π *b.* $\frac{\pi}{3}$ *c.* $\frac{\pi}{4}$ *d.* $\frac{\pi}{2}$

150. If $4^{\log_9 3} + 9^{\log_2 4} = 10^{\log_x 83}$, then x is equal to

a. 10 *b.* 4
c. -10 *d.* -4

151. If $p = 3^{\frac{1}{3}} \cdot 3^{\frac{2}{9}} \cdot 3^{\frac{3}{27}} \ldots \infty$, then $p^{\frac{4}{3}} =$

a. $3^{\frac{1}{4}}$ *b.* 3
c. 9 *d.* $3^{\frac{3}{4}}$

152. If α, β, γ are the roots of the equation $x^3 - 3x^2 + 2x - 1 = 0$, then the value of $(1-\alpha)(1-\beta)(1-\gamma)$ is

a. 1 *b.* 2
c. -1 *d.* -2

153. The middle term in the expansion of $(1 + x)^{2n}$ is

a. $\frac{1 \cdot 3 \cdot 5 \ldots (2n-1)}{n} x^n$
b. $\frac{1 \cdot 3 \cdot 5 \ldots (2n-1)}{n!} 2^{n-1} x^n$
c. $\frac{1 \cdot 3 \cdot 5 \ldots (2n)}{n!} x^n$
d. $\frac{1 \cdot 3 \cdot 5 \ldots (2n-1)}{n!} 2^n x^n$

154. If $p \rightarrow (\sim q \vee r)$ is false, then the truth values of p, q and r are

a. T, T, F *b.* T, F, T
c. F, T, T *d.* F, F, T

155. If $\frac{2}{9!} + \frac{2}{3!7!} + \frac{1}{5!5!} = \frac{2^a}{b!}$, where $a, b \in N$, then the ordered pair (a, b) is

a. (10, 9) *b.* (10, 7)
c. (9, 10) *d.* (5, 10)

156. $\tan 10° \tan 20° \tan 30° \tan 40° \tan 50° \tan 60° \tan 70° \tan 80° =$

a. 0 *b.* -1 *c.* $\frac{1}{\sqrt{3}}$ *d.* 1

157. If $\tan\theta = \frac{m}{n}$, then $n \cos 2\theta + m \sin 2\theta$ is equal to

a. n *b.* n^2
c. $\frac{n}{m}$ *d.* $\frac{m^2}{n^2}$

158. If $\frac{b+c}{11} = \frac{c+a}{12} = \frac{a+b}{13}$, then $\cos A$ is equal to

a. $\frac{5}{7}$ *b.* $\frac{1}{5}$ *c.* $\frac{2}{5}$ *d.* $\frac{1}{7}$

159. If $a = \cos 2\alpha + i \sin 2\alpha$, $b = \cos 2\beta + i \sin 2\beta$, then $\sqrt{\frac{a}{b}} + \sqrt{\frac{b}{a}} =$

a. $2 i \sin(\alpha - \beta)$ *b.* $2 i \sin(\alpha + \beta)$
c. $2 \cos(\alpha + \beta)$ *d.* $2 \cos(\alpha - \beta)$

160. If $y = \log\left[\tan\left(\frac{\pi}{4} + \frac{x}{2}\right)\right]$, then $\frac{dy}{dx} =$

a. $\sec x$ *b.* $\sin x$
c. $\operatorname{cosec} x$ *d.* $\sec\frac{x}{2}$

161. If $y = \sin^2\left(\tan^{-1}\sqrt{\frac{1-x^2}{1+x^2}}\right)$, then $\frac{dy}{dx} =$

a. x *b.* $-x$
c. 1 *d.* -1

162. If $\sqrt{\frac{x}{y}} + \sqrt{\frac{y}{x}} = \sqrt{a}$, then $y.\frac{dx}{dy} =$

a. $\frac{x}{y}$ *b.* $\frac{y}{x}$
c. x *d.* 0

163. If $x = \frac{1-t}{1+t}$, $y = \frac{2t}{1+t}$, then $\frac{d^2y}{dx^2} =$

a. $\frac{2t}{(1+t)^2}$ *b.* $\frac{1}{(1+t)^4}$
c. $\frac{2t}{(1+t)^2}$ *d.* 0

164. In the group $G = \{1, 5, 7, 11\}$ under $\otimes_{12}$ the value of $7 \otimes_{12} 11^{-1}$ is equal to

a. 5 *b.* 7
c. 11 *d.* 1

165. Which of the following is a subgroup of the group $G = \{1, 2, 3, 4, 5, 6\}$ under $\otimes 7$?

a. $\{2, 6, 1\}$ *b.* $\{1, 2, 4\}$
c. $\{5, 4, 2\}$ *d.* $\{2, 3, 1\}$

166. If $A = \begin{bmatrix} 3 & -3 & 4 \\ 2 & -3 & 4 \\ 0 & -1 & 1 \end{bmatrix}$, $B = (\text{adj } A)$ and $C = 5A$, then $\frac{|C|}{|\text{adj } B|}$ is equal to

a. 25 *b.* -1 *c.* 5 *d.* -5

167. If $A = \begin{bmatrix} 1 & 1 & 1 \\ 1 & 2 & 3 \\ 1 & 3 & 4 \end{bmatrix}$, $B = \begin{bmatrix} 7 \\ 16 \\ 22 \end{bmatrix}$, $X = \begin{bmatrix} x \\ y \\ z \end{bmatrix}$ and $AX = B$, then z is equal to

a. 1 *b.* -1 *c.* -3 *d.* 3

168. If $A = \begin{bmatrix} 1 & \log_b a \\ \log_a b & 1 \end{bmatrix}$, then $|A|$ is equal to

a. 0 *b.* $\log_a b$ *c.* -1 *d.* $\log_b a$

169. If a vertex of traingle is (3, 3) and the mid-points of two sides through this vertex are $\left(2, \frac{3}{2}\right)$ and $\left(4, \frac{3}{2}\right)$, then the centroid of the triangle is given by

a. (1, 3) *b.* (3, 0) *c.* (3, 1) *d.* (0, 3)

170. The image of the point (2, 4) on the line $x + y - 10 = 0$ is

a. (4, 8) *b.* (6, 5)
c. (6, 8) *d.* (0, 10)

171. If the sum of the slopes of the lines given by $x^2 - 4pxy + 8y^2 = 0$ is three times their product, then p has the value

a. $\frac{1}{4}$ *b.* 4 *c.* 3 *d.* $\frac{3}{4}$

172. $\lim_{x \to 0}\left(\frac{1+5x^2}{1+3x^2}\right)^{\frac{1}{x^2}} =$

a. e^2 *b.* e *c.* $\frac{1}{e}$ *d.* $\frac{5}{3}$

173. If $f(x) = \begin{cases} \dfrac{e^x - 1}{4x} & \text{for } x \neq 0 \\ \dfrac{k+x}{4} & \text{for } x = 0 \end{cases}$ is continuous at $x = 0$, then $k =$

a. 5 *b.* 3 *c.* 2 *d.* 0

174. The non-adjacent vertex in the graph is

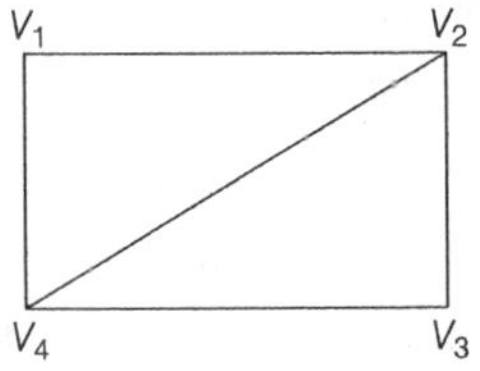

a. V_1V_2 *b.* V_4V_3 *c.* V_2V_4 *d.* V_1V_3

175. $\sin\left[2\cos^{-1}\cot\left(2\tan^{-1}\frac{1}{2}\right)\right]$ is equal to

a. $\frac{3\sqrt{7}}{8}$ *b.* $\frac{5\sqrt{7}}{8}$ *c.* $\frac{5\sqrt{7}}{2}$ *d.* $\frac{3\sqrt{7}}{2}$

176. The multiplicative inverse of $\frac{3+4i}{4-5i}$ is

a. $\left(\frac{-8}{25}, \frac{31}{25}\right)$ *b.* $\left(\frac{-8}{25}, \frac{-31}{25}\right)$
c. $\left(\frac{8}{25}, \frac{-31}{25}\right)$ *d.* $\left(\frac{-8}{25}, \frac{31}{5}\right)$

177. The general solution of
$\tan x - \sin x = 1 - \tan x \cdot \sin x$

a. $x = n\pi + \frac{\pi}{4}$ and or $x = n\pi + (-1)^n\left(\frac{-\pi}{2}\right)$

b. $x = \frac{n\pi}{4} - \frac{\pi}{4}$ and or $x = n\pi + (-1)^n\left(-\frac{\pi}{2}\right)$

c. $x = n\pi + \frac{\pi}{4}$

d. $x = n\pi + \frac{\pi}{6}$ and or $\pi = n\pi + (-1)^n\left(-\frac{\pi}{2}\right)$

178. The angle between the circles
$x^2 + y^2 + 4x + 2y + 1 = 0$ and
$x^2 + y^2 - 2x + 6y - 6 = 0$ is

a. $\frac{\pi}{6}$ *b.* $\frac{\pi}{3}$ *c.* $\frac{\pi}{2}$ *d.* $\cos^{-1}\left(\frac{7}{16}\right)$

179. If $|\mathbf{a}| = 2, |\mathbf{b}| = 7$ and $\mathbf{a} \times \mathbf{b} = 3\hat{\mathbf{i}} + 2\hat{\mathbf{j}} + 6\hat{\mathbf{k}}$, then the angle between **a** and **b** is

a. $\frac{\pi}{3}$ *b.* $\frac{\pi}{6}$ *c.* $\frac{\pi}{2}$ *d.* $\frac{\pi}{4}$

180. The domain of the function
$f(x) = \log(1 - x) + \sqrt{x^2 - 1}$

a. $(-\infty, -1)$
b. $(-\infty, -1]$
c. $(-\infty, 2]$
d. $(-\infty, 0)$

ANSWERS

COMEDK 2012

Physics

1. (c)	2. (b)	3. (d)	4. (b)	5. (a)	6. (b)	7. (d)	8. (b)	9. (c)	10. (a)
11. (c)	12. (b)	13. (d)	14. (a)	15. (d)	16. (a)	17. (c)	18. (b)	19. (d)	20. (b)
21. (*)	22. (a)	23. (b)	24. (d)	25. (c)	26. (d)	27. (b)	28. (b)	29. (d)	30. (c)
31. (a)	32. (d)	33. (a)	34. (d)	35. (c)	36. (c)	37. (a)	38. (a)	39. (d)	40. (c)
41. (b)	42. (a)	43. (d)	44. (b)	45. (a)	46. (c)	47. (d)	48. (c)	49. (a)	50. (*)
51. (d)	52. (b)	53. (c)	54. (b)	55. (a)	56. (d)	57. (c)	58. (b)	59. (b)	60. (d)

Chemistry

61. (b)	62. (a)	63. (d)	64. (b)	65. (b)	66. (c)	67. (d)	68. (c)	69. (b)	70. (c)
71. (d)	72. (a)	73. (c)	74. (d)	75. (c)	76. (b)	77. (c)	78. (d)	79. (a)	80. (b)
81. (c)	82. (d)	83. (a)	84. (b)	85. (c)	86. (d)	87. (a)	88. (b)	89. (c)	90. (a)
91. (d)	92. (a)	93. (b)	94. (c)	95. (d)	96. (c)	97. (b)	98. (d)	99. (a)	100. (a)
101. (c)	102. (d)	103. (a)	104. (d)	105. (a)	106. (b)	107. (c)	108. (a)	109. (c)	110. (c)
111. (c)	112. (d)	113. (b)	114. (b)	115. (b)	116. (d)	117. (a)	118. (b)	119. (b)	120. (c)

Mathematics

121. (b)	122. (c)	123. (d)	124. (a)	125. (b)	126. (c)	127. (d)	128. (a)	129. (c)	130. (a)
131. (c)	132. (b)	133. (c)	134. (c)	135. (d)	136. (a)	137. (c)	138. (b)	139. (c)	140. (*)
141. (c)	142. (d)	143. (a)	144. (b)	145. (c)	146. (d)	147. (a)	148. (c)	149. (d)	150. (a)
151. (b)	152. (c)	153. (d)	154. (a)	155. (c)	156. (d)	157. (a)	158. (b)	159. (d)	160. (a)
161. (b)	162. (c)	163. (d)	164. (a)	165. (b)	166. (*)	167. (d)	168. (a)	169. (c)	170. (c)
171. (d)	172. (a)	173. (b)	174. (d)	175. (a)	176. (b)	177. (a)	178. (d)	179. (b)	180. (b)

Note (*) None of the option is correct.

HINTS & SOLUTIONS

Physics

1. *(c)* The atomic mass or mass number of an atom $_ZX^A$ is given by

$$A = Z + N$$

where, A = mass number, Z = atomic number
and N = number of neutrons.
For, $_{92}U^{235}$, $A = 235$ and $Z = 92$

$$N = A - Z = 235 - 92 = 143$$

2. *(b)* With the rise of temperature, the density of minority charge carriers increases due to breaking of some covalent bonding in a semiconductor in reverse biased condition. So, the reverse saturation current increases.

3. *(d)* Given, $t_{1/2} = 10$ min, $N_0 = 64$, $t = 50$ min

The number of half-lives in 50 min,

$$n = \frac{t}{t_{1/2}} = \frac{50}{10} = 5$$

In 5 half-lives, number of nuclei left undecayed,

$$N = N_0\left(\frac{1}{2}\right)^n = 64 \times \left(\frac{1}{2}\right)^5 = \frac{64}{32} = 2$$

$\therefore$ Number of nuclei decayed $= N_0 - N = 64 - 2 = 62$

4. *(b)* Photons of different energies carries the electromagnetic spectrum of all rays. They have no mass and travels at the speed of light.

5. *(a)* The NOT gate is also called invertor as it reverses the input in its output i.e.,

Input (A)	Output ($Y = \overline{A}$)
1	0
0	1

6. *(b)* LCD stands for Liquid Crystal Display. It is a special thin flat panel display or other electronically modulated optical device that uses the light modulating properties of liquid crystals combined with polarisers. Liquid crystal do not emit light directly, instead using a backlight or reflector to produce images in colour or monochromatic.

7. *(d)* Polarisation is the property of wave to oscillates in more than one orientation. The sound waves always oscillates in the direction of wave propagation, so polarisation is not possible in them. While light can be polarised.

8. *(b)* For an optically active solution, the angle through which a plane polarised light is rotated, is given as

$$\theta = SLC$$

where, S = correction factor, L = path length
and C = concentration of solution.

9. *(c)* Given, $V_S = 50$ V, $V_R = 40$ V

For an L-R circuit,

$$V_S = \sqrt{V_R^2 + V_L^2}$$

$$\Rightarrow \quad V_L = \sqrt{V_S^2 - V_R^2} = \sqrt{50^2 - 40^2} = \sqrt{2500 - 1600} = \sqrt{900} = 30 \text{ V}$$

10. *(a)* Common potential difference for a parallel combination of capacitors, is

$$V_C = \frac{V_1C_1 + V_2C_2}{C_1 + C_2}$$

Given, $V_2 = 0, V_1 = 10$ V,
$C_1 = C_2 = 10\mu\text{F} = 10 \times 10^{-6}$ F

$$\therefore \quad V_C = \frac{10 \times 10 \times 10^{-6}}{(10 + 10) \times 10^{-6}} = \frac{100}{20} = 5 \text{ V}$$

11. *(c)* In fusion of two lighter nuclei to form a relatively heavier nucleus, energy is released. So, the binding energy of the stable product nucleus must be greater than that of the reacting nuclei.

12. *(b)* Given, $Q_1 = 2\mu\text{C} = 2 \times 10^{-6}$C
$Q_2 = 1\mu\text{C} = 1 \times 10^{-6}$C

The electric field intensity at a point P due to a point charge is given by

$$E = \frac{1}{4\pi\varepsilon_0}\frac{Q}{r^2}$$

$$\Rightarrow \quad E \propto \frac{Q}{r^2}$$

$\therefore$ Ratio of electric fields due to Q_1 and Q_2 at point P is

$$\frac{E_1}{E_2} = \frac{Q_1}{r_1^2} \times \frac{r_2^2}{Q_2} = \frac{2 \times 10^{-6}}{(2 \times 10^{-2})^2} \times \frac{(1 \times 10^{-2})^2}{1 \times 10^{-6}} = \frac{1}{2}$$

Here, E_1 is along X-axis and E_2 is along Y-axis. So, the resultant field E have angle θ with X-axis as

$$\tan\theta = \frac{E_2}{E_1} = 2$$

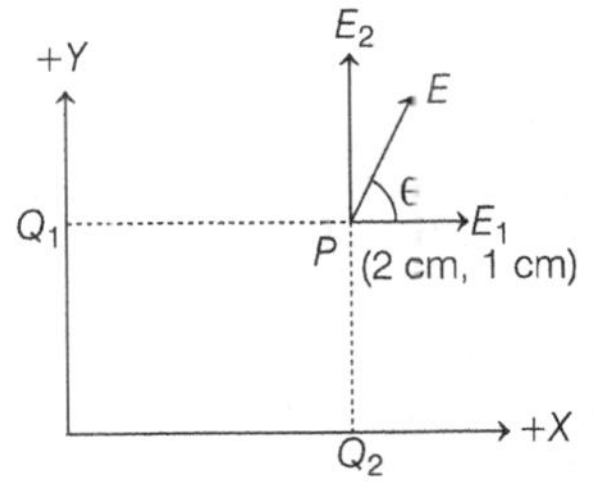

COMEDK 2012

13. *(d)* The direction of force on a current carrying conductor held perpendicular to an uniform magnetic field is given by Fleming's left hand rule.

It states that "If we hold the thumb, forefinger and middle finger of the left hand perpendicular to each other such that the fore finger points in the direction of magnetic field, the middle finger points in the direction of current, then the thumb shows the direction of force on the conductor."

14. *(a)* Given, $f_1 = F$ and $f_2 = -F$

The equivalent focal length of combination of two lenses is

$$\frac{1}{f} = \frac{1}{f_1} + \frac{1}{f_2} = \frac{1}{F} + \frac{1}{-F} = 0$$

or $$f = \frac{1}{0} = \infty \quad \text{(infinity)}$$

15. *(d)* Given, $x = at + bt^2$

Here, x is measured in metre (m) and t is in second (s). So, for dimensional consistency of equation,

Dimensions of $a = [a] = \frac{[x]}{[t]} = \frac{[\text{L}]}{[\text{T}]} = [\text{LT}^{-1}]$

Similarly, for b, $[b] = \frac{[x]}{[t^2]} = \frac{[\text{L}]}{[\text{T}^2]} = [\text{LT}^{-2}]$

$\therefore$ Dimensions of $\left[\frac{b}{a}\right] = \frac{[\text{LT}^{-2}]}{[\text{LT}^{-1}]} = [\text{T}^{-1}]$

16. *(a)* Given, $u = 5\text{ ms}^{-1}$, Eastwards

$v = 5\text{ ms}^{-1}$, Northwards

and $\Delta t = 10$ s

Change in velocity $|\Delta v| = \sqrt{u^2 + v^2}$

$= \sqrt{5^2 + 5^2} = 5\sqrt{2}\text{ ms}^{-1}$

Direction of Δv,

$$\tan\theta = \frac{v}{u} = \frac{-5}{5} = -1$$

(taking eastward direction positive)

$\Rightarrow \quad \theta = 135°$

$\therefore$ Average acceleration,

$$a_{\text{avg}} = \frac{\Delta v}{\Delta t} = \frac{5\sqrt{2}}{10} = \frac{1}{\sqrt{2}}\text{ms}^{-2}, \text{ towards North-West}$$

17. *(c)* Given, $m = 0.1$ kg

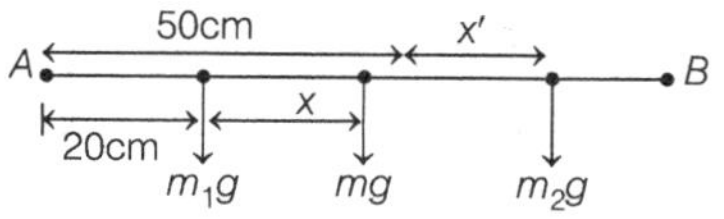

Let x be the position of mass of 0.1 kg from its centre and x' be the position of second mass m_2 that must be suspended to the other end to prevent the rod from toppling. So,

$$x = 50 - 20 = 30\text{ cm} = 0.3\text{ m}$$

The rod will not topple if net torque on it is zero. So, balancing the moments about its centre, we get

$$m_1 gx = m_2 gx'$$

$\Rightarrow \quad m_2 x = 0.1 \times 0.3 = 0.03$ kg-m

From options, it is possible only in case of (c).

$m_2 = 0.15$ kg

$$x' = \frac{0.03}{0.15} = 0.2\text{ m} = 20\text{ cm}$$

$\therefore$ The second mass of 0.15 kg should be hanged at $(50 + 20 =)$ 70 cm mark.

18. *(b)* Ink filler works on the principle of both surface tension and pump. Vacuum in the pen pulls the ink in the bottle to the pen. This ink travels in the pen tip through small openings due to surface tension.

19. *(d)* Ionosphere is the ionised part of Earth's atmosphere, which reflects the radiowaves due to total internal reflection towards earth, thus it helps in radio communication.

20. *(b)* The reaction of the floor on an object placed on the floor of an elevator is maximum, when the elevator accelerates upwards. In this case, normal reaction on it is

$$N = m(g + a)$$

where, m = mass of object,

g = gravitational acceleration

and a = acceleration of elevator.

21. *(*)* Let m be the mass of particle and u be its initial velocity, then

Initial momentum, $p = mu$ ...(i)

At highest point,

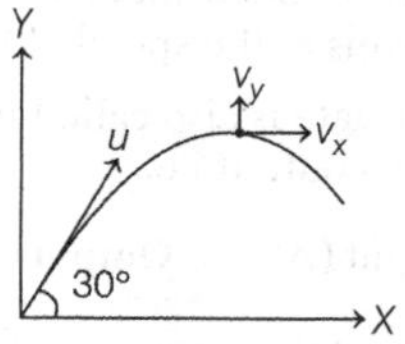

$$v_x = u\cos\theta = u\cos 30° = \frac{\sqrt{3}}{2}u$$

$$v_y = 0$$

$\therefore$ Momentum at highest point is

$$p' = mv_x = mu\left(\frac{\sqrt{3}}{2}\right)$$

$$= \frac{\sqrt{3}}{2}p \quad \text{[using Eq. (i)]}$$

22. *(a)* Since, the block is at rest, the upward frictional force is equal to the weight or gravitational pull of the Earth i.e.,

$$F_S = w = mg = 0.1 \times 9.8 = 0.98\text{ N}$$

23. *(b)* The rotational kinetic energy of a ring is

$$K_R = \frac{1}{2}I\omega^2$$

For a ring, $I = MR^2$ and $\omega = \frac{v}{R}$

$$\therefore \quad K_R = \frac{1}{2}(MR^2)\times\left(\frac{v}{R}\right)^2 = \frac{1}{2}Mv^2$$

Also, translational kinetic energy, $K_T = \frac{1}{2}Mv^2$

$\therefore K_R = K_T$ or $K_R : K_T = 1:1$

24. *(d)* Given, work done, $W = 120$ J

Time, $t = 2$ min $= 2\times 60 = 120$ s

$\therefore$ Power $= \frac{\text{Work done}}{\text{Time}} = \frac{W}{t} = \frac{120}{120} = 1$ W

25. *(c)* As we know, escape velocity, $v_e = \sqrt{2gR}$

Let v_m be escape velocity from moon and v_e be the escape velocity from Earth. Then,

$$\frac{v_m}{v_e} = \sqrt{\frac{2\times g_m \times R_m}{2\times g_e \times R_e}}$$

$$= \sqrt{\frac{g_m \times D_m}{g_e \times D_e}} \quad (\because D = 2R)$$

$$= \sqrt{\frac{\frac{g_e}{6}\times\frac{D_e}{4}}{g_e D_e}} = \frac{1}{\sqrt{24}}$$

$$\therefore \quad v_m = \frac{v_e}{\sqrt{24}} = \frac{11.2}{\sqrt{24}} \text{ km/s} \quad (\because v_e = 11.2 \text{ km/s})$$

26. *(d)* As work done in a cycle is equal to the area enclosed by the cycle.

$\therefore$ Work done, $W = \Delta p \times \Delta V$

$= (4-2)\times(6-1) = 10$ J

27. *(b)* Speed of sound in a gas, $v = \sqrt{\frac{RT}{M}}$

Both, hydrogen and oxygen gas are diatomic. At same temperature,

$$v \propto \frac{1}{\sqrt{M}}$$

$$\therefore \quad \frac{v_H}{v_O} = \sqrt{\frac{M_O}{M_H}} = \sqrt{\frac{32}{2}} = \sqrt{16} = 4 \text{ or } 4:1$$

28. *(b)* According to Stefan's law,

Energy radiated $E \propto T^4$

$$\therefore \quad \frac{E'}{E} = \frac{T'}{T} = \frac{\left(\frac{T}{2}\right)^4}{T^4} = \frac{1}{2^4} = \frac{1}{16}$$

or $\quad E' = \frac{E}{16}$

29. *(d)* The motion of particle in one oscillation is shown below

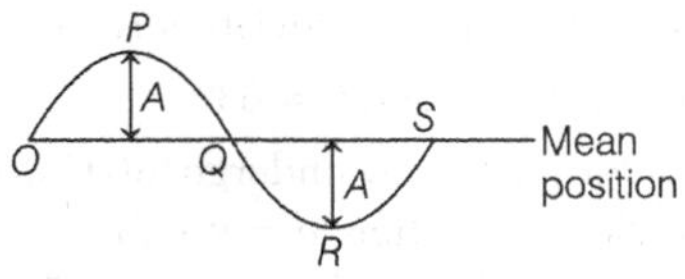

In moving from $O \to P$ distance moved is A. Similarly, for $P \to Q$, $Q \to R$ and $R \to S$, distance moved is A in each case.

$\therefore$ Total distance moved in one oscillation $= 4A$

30. *(c)* Given, $C = 10\mu F = 10\times 10^{-6}$ F

$V = 10$ V

Change, $q = C \times V = 10\times 10^{-6}\times 10$

$= 10^{-4}$ C

$= 100\times 10^{6}$ C

$= 100\,\mu$C

31. *(a)* When a wire of resistance R is cut into 10 equal parts, then resistance of each part,

$$R' = \frac{R}{10} = 0.1R$$

Equivalent resistance of parallel combination of resistors, is

$$R_{eq} = \frac{R'}{10} = \frac{0.1R}{10} = 0.01R$$

32. *(d)* The conductors have positive temperature coefficient, while semiconductors have negative temperature coefficient. So, when iron and silicon wires are cooled from 50°C to 30°C, the resistance of iron decreases, while that of silicon increases.

33. *(a)* Given, $P = 10\,\Omega$, $l = 0.2$ m

In balanced condition of meterbridge,

$$\frac{P}{Q} = \frac{l}{(1-l)}$$

$$\Rightarrow \quad \frac{10}{Q} = \frac{0.2}{1-0.2} = \frac{0.2}{0.8}$$

$$\Rightarrow \quad Q = 40\,\Omega$$

34. *(d)* As two coils are mutually perpendicular, so the field produced by them will also be perpendicular to each other as shown

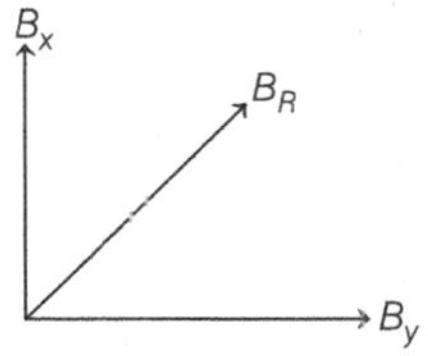

The two coils are identical, so magnetic field,

$$B \propto I$$

or $\quad \frac{B_x}{B_y} = \frac{I_x}{I_y} = \frac{1}{2}$

$\Rightarrow \quad B_y = 2B_x$

$\therefore \quad B_x = B$, then $B_y = 2B$

$\therefore$ Resultant field, $B_R = \sqrt{B_x^2 + B_y^2}$

$= \sqrt{B^2 + (2B)^2}$

$= \sqrt{5}B$

35. *(c)* AC or DC motor is an electrical device which is used to convert an electrical energy into mechanical energy.

36. *(c)* According to the Faraday's law of electromagnetic induction, whenever the magnetic flux linked with a coil changes continuously with time, an emf is induced in the coil.

Its magnitude is equal to the rate of change of magnetic flux i.e.,

$$e = N\frac{d\phi}{dt}$$

where, N is the number of turns in the coil.

37. *(a)* Given, $I_1 = 1\,\text{mA} = 1\times10^{-3}\,\text{A}$

$$I_2 = 5\,\text{mA} = 5\times10^{-3}\,\text{A}$$
$$t = 4\,\text{ms} = 4\times10^{-3}\,\text{s}$$
$$L = 10\,\text{mH} = 10\times10^{-3}\,\text{H}$$

$\therefore$ Self-induced emf, $|e| = L\frac{dI}{dt}$

$$= 10\times10^{-3}\times\frac{(5-1)\times10^{-3}}{4\times10^{-3}} = 10\,\text{mV}$$

38. *(a)* Work function of a metal,

$$W = h\nu_0$$

where, h = Planck's constant

ν_0 = threshold frequency.

As, the threshold frequency of metal M is more than that of metal N, so work function of M is more than that of N, while their kinetic energies are equal.

39. *(d)* Electron wave is used in place of X-rays to study crystals of larger dimensions in electron crystallography. So, they can be diffracted.

40. *(c)* According to Bohr's atomic model,

Kinetic energy K or $E_K = \frac{U}{2}$

where, U = potential energy.

which is negative.

$$\therefore \quad 2E_K + U = 0$$

41. *(b)* The magnetic field due to a circular coil carrying current at its axis is

$$B_x = \frac{\mu_0}{4\pi}\cdot\frac{2\pi N i r^2}{(x^2+r^2)^{3/2}} \quad \ldots\text{(i)}$$

At centre of coil, $B_c = \frac{\mu_0}{4\pi}\frac{2\pi N i}{r}$ ...(ii)

From Eqs. (i) and (ii), we get

$$\frac{B_c}{B_x} = \frac{(x^2+r^2)^{3/2}}{r\times r^2}$$

At, $x = \frac{r}{2}$, $\frac{B_c}{B_x} = \frac{\left(\frac{r^2}{4}+r^2\right)^{3/2}}{r^3} = \frac{\left(\frac{5}{4}\right)^{3/2} r^3}{r^3} = \frac{5\sqrt{5}}{8}$

or $5\sqrt{5} : 8$

42. *(a)* Stokes lines are the radiation of certain wavelengths present in the line spectra, that is associated with the phenomena of fluorescence and the Raman effect. Anti-stokes lines are produced due to already excited atoms or molecules. These lines are symmetrical about the main lines and the wavelength of anti-stokes lines is less than the main line. So, if the difference between wavelengths of stokes line and corresponding anti-stokes line is 100Å, then the difference between anti-stokes line and main line is 50 Å. Therefore, wavelength of incident radiation is 5050 Å.

43. *(d)* Optical pumping is a process in which light is used to raise electrons from a lower energy state in an atom than the metastable state to a higher energy state than the metastable state.

44. *(b)* Let L_o be the length of air column in pipe. After immersion,

$$L_c = \frac{L_o}{2}$$

Fundamental frequency in open pipe, $f_o = \frac{v}{2L_o}$

Fundamental frequency in closed pipe, $f_c = \frac{v}{4L_c}$

$$\therefore \quad \frac{f_o}{f_c} = \frac{\frac{v}{2L_o}}{\frac{v}{4L_c}} = 2\left(\frac{L_c}{L_o}\right) = 2\left(\frac{L_o}{2L_o}\right) = 1:1$$

45. *(a)* Given, $\gamma = 1.4 = \frac{C_p}{C_V}$

$\Rightarrow \quad C_p = 1.4C_V$

Also, $R = C_p - C_V = 8.3$ (given)

$\Rightarrow \quad 1.4C_V - C_V = 8.3$

or $C_V = \frac{8.3}{0.4} = 20.75\,\text{Jmol}^{-1}\text{K}^{-1}$

$$C_p = 1.4C_V = 1.4\times20.75 = 29.05\,\text{Jmol}^{-1}\text{K}^{-1}$$

46. *(c)* Given, $\frac{I_A}{I_B} = 100$

Using magnitude equation,

$$m_B - m_A = -2.5\log\left(\frac{I_B}{I_A}\right)$$
$$= -2.5\log\left(\frac{1}{100}\right) = -2.5\times -2 = 5$$

47. *(d)* When a ray of light enters a glass slab along the normal to the surface, it passes straight without deviation. So, angle of deviation is zero (0°).

48. *(c)* Given, $i = 65°$ and $i_c = 63°$

Since, $i > i_c$, so the ray undergo total internal reflection. The angle of deviation, $d = \pi - 2i$

$$= 180° - 2(65°) = 180° - 130° = 50°$$

49. *(a)* Given, $i = 49°30'$, $A = 60°$ (equilateral prism)
At minimum deviation position, angle of deviation is
$D = 2i - A = 2(49°30') - 60° = 99° - 60° = 39°$

50. (*) Here, $R = -0.1$ cm, $\mu_g = 1.5$

$\therefore \quad u = -0.1$ cm

From refraction formula,

$$\frac{\mu_a - \mu_g}{R} = \frac{\mu_a}{v} - \frac{\mu_g}{u}$$

$$\Rightarrow \frac{1-1.5}{-0.1} = \frac{1}{v} - \frac{1.5}{(-0.1)} \qquad (\because \mu_a = 1)$$

$$\Rightarrow 5 = \frac{1}{v} + 15$$

$$\Rightarrow v = -\frac{1}{10} = -0.1 \text{ cm}$$

Here, negative sign shows that the image will be seen on the same size as that of object.
$\therefore$ The spot appears to be 0.1 cm below the top surface or exactly at the original position.

51. *(d)* Photoelectric effect and Raman effect can be explained on the basis of Planck's quantum theory of light. These verify the particle nature of light.

52. *(b)* Given, $\frac{I_{max}}{I_{min}} = 9$

Since, intensity $\propto$ (amplitude)^2

$$\therefore \frac{A_{max}}{A_{min}} = \frac{a_1 + a_2}{a_1 - a_2} = \sqrt{\frac{9}{1}} = \frac{3}{1}$$

$$\Rightarrow a_1 + a_2 = 3a_1 - 3a_2$$

$$\Rightarrow 2a_1 = 4a_2$$

$$\therefore a_1 : a_2 = 2 : 1$$

53. *(c)* Since, sound waves have higher wavelength, which are comparable to the dimension of interfering objects. So, diffraction effect can easily be detected in sound waves than light waves.

54. *(b)* According to Brewster's law,

$$\mu = \tan\theta_p$$

where, μ = refractive index $= \frac{c}{v}$

and θ_p = polarising angle $= \theta$

$$\therefore \theta = \tan^{-1}\mu = \tan^{-1}\left(\frac{c}{v}\right)$$

55. *(a)* For two polaroids placed at an axis making angle θ with each other, then according to law of malus, the intensity of transmitted light is

$$I_t = I_0 \cos^2\theta$$

Here, $I_t = 0.75 I_0$

$$\Rightarrow 0.75 I_0 = I_0 \cos^2\theta$$

$$\Rightarrow \cos^2\theta = 0.75 = \frac{3}{4}$$

$$\Rightarrow \theta = \cos^{-1}\sqrt{\frac{3}{4}} = \cos^{-1}\left(\frac{\sqrt{3}}{2}\right)$$

$$\therefore \theta = 30°$$

56. *(d)* Let d be the distance in air between two point charges and d_m be the distance between them in medium.
According to question,

$$F = F_m$$

$$\Rightarrow \frac{1}{4\pi\varepsilon_0}\frac{q_1q_2}{d^2} = \frac{1}{4\pi\varepsilon_0 k}\frac{q_1q_2}{d_m^2}$$

$$\Rightarrow d^2 = kd_m^2$$

$$\Rightarrow d_m = \frac{d}{\sqrt{k}}$$

57. *(c)* The force on a charged particle in an electric field is

$$F = qE$$

Also, $F = ma$

$$\Rightarrow a = \frac{F}{m} = \frac{qE}{m}$$

As q and m are constant for a positively charged particle and the electric field is also uniform. So, the particle move with constant acceleration.

58. *(b)* Electric field intensity at a point due to a charge q is given by

$$E = \frac{F}{q}$$

As, the force between the charges is mutual, so the electric field intensity due to charge $-2q$ is

$$E' = \frac{F}{|-2q|} = \frac{1}{2}\frac{F}{q} = \frac{E}{2}$$

59. *(b)* As per Boolean postulates,

$$1 \cdot A = A$$

$$\Rightarrow 1 \cdot 1 = 1 \text{ and } 1 \cdot 0 = 0$$

p-type semiconductor is electrically neutral. The majority charge carriers in n-type semiconductor are electrons.
A transistor can be used as a switch.

60. *(d)* J. J. Thomson gave the first ideal regarding structure of atom. According to him, "an atom is a solid sphere in which entire positive charge is distributed and negative charge or electrons are embedded like seeds in watermelon."
It is also called plum pudding model of an atom.

Chemistry

61. *(b)* Cellulose is not a protein. It is a carbohydrate consisting of 3,000 or more glucose unit, while wool, hair and nails are proteins.

62. *(a)* Adsorption of a gas on a solid is exothermic process as during this process condensation of gas take place.

According to Le-Chatelier principle, increase in temperature favors desorption.

Option (a) is not a true statement.

63. *(d)* Peptisation is a method of preparation of colloids in which a suspension gets converted into a colloid on stirring with a peptising agent.

64. *(b)* Given, 39% by mass of organic solvent in benzene

$\therefore$ 39 g of organic solvent in 100 g solution.

or

39 g of organic solvent in $100 - 39 = 61$ g benzene.

Now, molar mass of organic solvent = 122 g/mol

Molar mass of benzene $(C_6H_6) = 12 \times 6 + 6 = 78$ g/mol

$\therefore$ Moles of benzene $(n_B) = \dfrac{61}{78}$

Moles of organic solvent $(n_O) = \dfrac{39}{122}$

$$\text{Mole fraction of benzene} = \frac{n_B}{n_B + n_O} = \frac{\frac{61}{78}}{\frac{61}{78} + \frac{39}{122}} = 0.6$$

65. *(b)* According to Nernst equation for a cell

$$Zn(s) + Cl_2(1atm) \longrightarrow Zn^{2+} + 2Cl^-; \quad E^\circ = 2\,V$$

$$E = E^\circ - \frac{0.059}{2}\log\frac{[Zn^{2+}]}{[Cl^-]^2}$$

$\therefore$ As $[Zn^{2+}]$ decreases E_{emf} of cell increases.

66. *(c)* $r^+_{A^+} = 104$ pm

$r^-_{B^-} = 200$ pm

$$\text{Radius ratio } \frac{r^+_{A^+}}{r^-_{B^-}} = \frac{104}{200} = 0.52$$

$\because$ It lies between (0.414 to 0.732).

$\therefore$ Coordination number of A^+ is 6.

67. *(d)* Given, molar mass of solute, $\mu_2 = 60$ g/mol

Mass of water $(W_1) = 126$ g

Molar mass of water $(M_1) = 18$ g/mol

$p_{\text{Solution}}(p_s) = 0.99p^\circ$

Relative lowering of vapour pressure

$$\frac{p^\circ - p_s}{p^\circ} = \frac{W_2}{M_2}\frac{M_1}{W_1}$$

$$\frac{p^\circ - 0.99p^\circ}{p^\circ} = \frac{W_2 \times 18}{60 \times 126} = \frac{0.1p^\circ}{p^\circ} = \frac{W_2 \times 18}{60 \times 126}$$

$$\Rightarrow \quad W_2 = \frac{60 \times 126}{18 \times 100} = 4.2\text{ g}$$

68. *(c)* The pH of boiling water is 6.4. This implies that boiling water is neutral. When water is boiled, then concentration of hydrogen ion and hydroxide ion increases with same extent.

69. *(b)* Electronic configuration of Ni = [Ar] $3d^8\ 4s^2$

$Ni^{2+} = [Ar]3d^8$

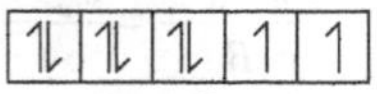

$\therefore$ Number of unpaired electrons = 2

$\therefore$ Magnetic moment $(\mu) = \sqrt{n(n+2)}$

$= \sqrt{2(2+2)} = \sqrt{8} = 2.84.$

70. *(c)* An organic compound containing halogen produces a bluish green flame when heated on a copper wire. This test is called Beilstein's test.

$\therefore$ Chlorobenzene will produce bluish green flame when heated on copper wire.

71. *(d)* Phenol can be distinguished from ethyl alcohol using $FeCl_3$ because phenol gives voilet colour compound with $FeCl_3$. While, alcohol do not give voilet colour.

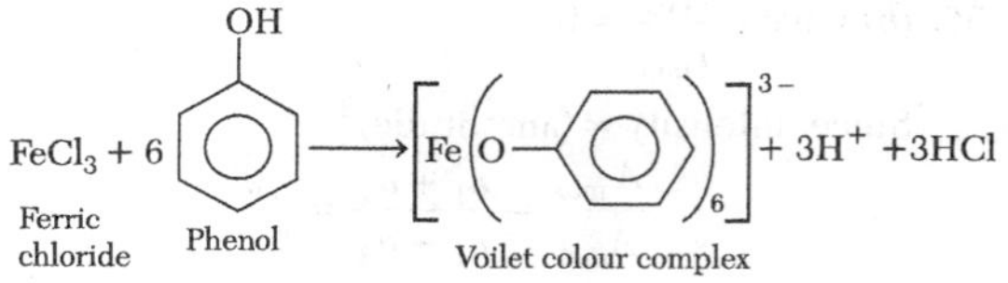

72. *(a)* For zero order of reaction,

$$\text{Rate, } \frac{-dx}{dt} = k$$

$$\therefore \quad dt = \frac{-dx}{k}$$

On integration,

$$\int_0^T dt = -\int_a^0 \frac{dx}{k}$$

$$T = \frac{a}{k}$$

73. *(c)* EAN of central atom in $[Co(NH_3)_6]Cl_3$

$= Z - (ON) + 2 \times (CN)$

where, Z = atomic number

ON = oxidation number

CN = coordination number

ON of Co $\Rightarrow x + 6 \times 0 - 3 = 0$

$\therefore \quad x = 3$

CN = 6

$\therefore \quad EAN = 27 - 3 + 2 \times 6 = 36$

74. *(d)* The alcohol obtained during the hydrolysis of ground nut oil is propane 1, 2, 3- triol.

It's structure is

$$HO—CH_2—\underset{\underset{OH}{|}}{CH}—CH_2—OH$$

75. *(c)* Froth floatation method is used to concentrate sulphide ores.
Galena is sulphide ore with formula PbS.
$\therefore$ Galena is concentrated by froth floatation process.

76. *(b)* The energy for electron transition is

$$E = -13.6Z^2\left[\frac{1}{n_2^2} - \frac{1}{n_1^2}\right]$$

$$\therefore \quad E \propto \left(\frac{1}{n_2^2} - \frac{1}{n_1^2}\right)$$

For $n = 2$ to $n = 1$ value of E is highest.
$E_2 = 13.6 \times (0.75) = 10.2$
For $n = 6$ to $n = 2$

$$E = -13.6\left(\frac{1}{36} - \frac{1}{4}\right)$$

$$= 13.6 \times \frac{8}{36} = 3.02$$

It is less than E_2.
$\therefore$ For electron transition $n = 2$ to $n = 1$, energy released is maximum.

77. *(c)* Magnetic quantum number, $m = +3$
As $m = +l$ to $-l$
$\therefore$ $l = 3$ for f-orbital.

78. *(d)* The electronic configuration is
(a) $Z = 16 : 1s^2 2s^2 2p^6 3s^2 3p^4$
(b) $Z = 14 : 1s^2 2s^2 2p^6 3s^2 3p^2$
(c) $Z = 13 : 1s^2 2s^2 2p^6 3s^2 3p^1$
(d) $Z = 15 : 1s^2 2s^2 2p^6 3s^2 3p^3$
$\because$ For $Z = 15$, p-orbital has stable half-filled configuration.
$\therefore$ It will have highest ionisation energy.

79. *(a)* Moles of oxygen $= \dfrac{\text{volume (in cm}^3)}{22400 \text{ cm}^3} = \dfrac{560}{22400}$ mol

1 molecule of oxygen = 2 atoms of oxygen
$\therefore$ Number of atoms of oxygen

$$= 6.022 \times 10^{23} \times \frac{560}{22400} \times 2$$

$$= \frac{1}{20} \times 6.022 \times 10^{23}$$

80. *(b)*

$$\underset{\substack{1 \text{ mol} \\ = 1.06 \text{ g}}}{Na_2CO_3} + \underset{\text{(dil.)}}{2HCl \text{ (dil.)}} \longrightarrow 2NaCl + \underset{\substack{1 \text{ mol} \\ = 22400 \text{ cm}^3}}{CO_2} + H_2O$$

1.06 g Na_2CO_3 gives $= 22400 \text{ cm}^3$ of CO_2

$$\therefore 1.06 \text{ g gives} = \frac{1.06 \times 22400}{106} = 224 \text{cm}^3 \text{ of } CO_2$$

81. *(c)* General oxidation state of oxygen is (−2). But in peroxide, it's oxidation state is (−1).
$\therefore$ The oxidation number of oxygen is −1 in Na_2O_2.

$$2 \times 1 + 2x = 0$$
$$x = -1$$

82. *(d)* The heat of formation of $H_2O(g)$ will be less than the heat of formation of $H_2O(l)$, as heat of condensation is not included in formation of H_2O in gases state i.e.

$$H_2(g) + \frac{1}{2}O_2(g) \xrightarrow{\Delta H_1} H_2O(g) \xrightarrow{\Delta H_2} H_2O(l)$$

$\therefore$ $|\Delta H_{f(H_2O)_l}| = |\Delta H_1 + \Delta H_2| = 286$ kJ
But $|\Delta H_{f(H_2O)_g}| = |\Delta H_1| < 286$ kJ
$\therefore$ $\Delta H_{f(H_2O)_g} = -242.8$ kJ

83. *(a)* According to first law of thermodynamics
$\Delta Q + \Delta W = \Delta U$
$\Delta W = 0$, then $\Delta Q = \Delta U$ {$\because$ Volume is constant}
$\Delta Q = 200$ J
$\Delta U = 200$ J

84. *(b)* Number of moles of $CaCO_3 = \dfrac{W}{M} = \dfrac{1}{100}$
$= 0.01$ mol
$\therefore$ Molar mass of $CaCO_3 = 100 \text{ g mol}^{-1}$
100 mL of $\dfrac{N}{5}$ HCl $= \dfrac{100}{1000} \times \dfrac{1}{5} = 0.02$ mol
The reaction is

$$\underset{1 \text{ mole}}{CaCO_3} + \underset{2 \text{ moles}}{2HCl} \longrightarrow CaCl_2 + CO_2 + H_2O$$

$\therefore$ 0.01 mole of $CaCO_3$ reacts with 0.02 mole of HCl.
$\therefore$ Both are completely consumed in the given reaction.

85. *(c)* $v_{rms} = \sqrt{\dfrac{3RT}{M}}$

$v_{rms} \propto \dfrac{1}{\sqrt{M}}$, where M = molecular mass

$\Rightarrow v_{rms(CH_4)} : v_{rms(He)} : v_{rms(SO_2)}$

$\Rightarrow \dfrac{1}{\sqrt{16}} : \dfrac{1}{\sqrt{4}} : \dfrac{1}{\sqrt{64}} \Rightarrow \dfrac{1}{4} : \dfrac{1}{2} : \dfrac{1}{8}$

$\Rightarrow 2 : 4 : 1$

86. *(d)* A negative catalyst will increases the activation energy of the reaction.

87. *(a)* Pent-2-yne is

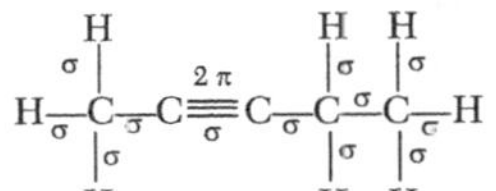

$\therefore$ σ-bonds = 12 and π-bonds = 2

88. *(b)* The blue colouration is due to formation of ferric ferrocyanide, $Fe_4[Fe(CN)_6]_3$ in Lassaigne's test for nitrogen.

89. *(c)* The addition of HBr to propene in presence of peroxide follows Kharash effect.

$$\underset{\text{Propene}}{CH_3—CH=CH_2} + HBr \xrightarrow{\text{Peroxide}} \underset{\text{1-bromopropane}}{CH_3—CH_2—CH_2—Br}$$

90. *(a)* On passing H_2S into a solution containing Zn^{2+} and Cu^{2+} ions, ZnS and CuS are formed.
The solubility product of CuS is less than that of ZnS.
∴ CuS get precipitated.

91. *(d)* $I = 0.5$ A

$$t = 32.2 \times 60 = 1932.0 \text{ s}$$

$$\therefore \text{ Mg obtained} = ZIt = \frac{12}{96500} \times 0.5 \times 1932.0 = 0.12012 \text{ g}$$

$$Mg + 2HCl \longrightarrow MgCl_2 + H_2\uparrow$$

24g of Mg gives = 22400 cm^3 of H_2

$$0.12012 \text{ g Mg gives} = \frac{22400}{24} \times 0.12012 = 112 \text{ cm}^3$$

92. *(a)* According to Markownikoff's rule, addition of HBr to alkene take place such that a stable carbocation is formed.
It is applicable to propene.

93. *(b)* The reaction of ethene in the presence of H^+ is an example of $+E$-effect as complete transfer of multiple bonded electron take place towards attacking reagent.

$$H_2C{=}CH_2 + H^+ \longrightarrow H_3C{-}\overset{+}{C}H_2$$

94. *(c)* The complete reaction is as follows

$$\underset{}{CH_3CN} \xrightarrow{\text{Dil. HCl}} \underset{(A)}{CH_3COOH} \xrightarrow{LiAlH_4} \underset{(B)}{CH_3CH_2OH} \xrightarrow{PCl_5} \underset{(C)}{CH_3CH_2Cl} \xrightarrow{\text{alc. KOH}} \underset{\text{Ethene }(D)}{CH_2{=}CH_2}$$

95. *(d)* An organic compound is optically active if, it is non-super imposable on its mirror image.

96. *(c)* $AlCl_3$ is an example of Lewis acid. It is an electron acceptor.
Hence, it is an example of electrophile.

97. *(b)* Ionisation constant (K_a) of phenol is more than that of ethanol because phenol is more acidic than alcohol. On ionisation, phenol gives phenoxide ion which is stabilised due to resonance.

98. *(d)* The complete reaction is as follows

$$CH_3COOH \xrightarrow{Ca(OH)_2} \underset{(A)}{(CH_3COO)_2Ca} \xrightarrow{\Delta} \underset{(B)}{CH_3COCH_3} \xrightarrow{NH_2OH} \underset{\text{Acetoxime }(C)}{CH_3{-}\underset{\underset{CH_3}{|}}{C}{=}N{-}OH}$$

99. *(a)* Statement (a) is incorrect and can be corrected as, chloro acetic acid is stronger than acetic acid due to $-I$-effect of chloro group which leads to stabilisation of carboxylate ion.

100. *(a)* The reaction of methyl iodide and methyl amine is as follows

$$\underset{\text{Methyl amine (1° amine)}}{CH_3NH_2} \xrightarrow{CH_3I} \underset{\text{2° amine}}{(CH_3)_2NH} \xrightarrow{CH_3I} \underset{\text{3° amine}}{(CH_3)_3N} \xrightarrow{CH_3I} (CH_3)_4N^+I^-$$

∴ 4 molecules of methyl iodide can react with one molecule of methyl amine.

101. *(c)* Only aliphatic primary amines react with nitrous acid to give alcohols with the evolution of N_2 gas.

$$R{-}NH_2 + HONO \xrightarrow{273-278\,K} R{-}OH + N_2 + H_2O$$

∵ Dimethyl amine is a secondary amine, it will not give N_2 gas.

102. *(d)* Tyrosine is aromatic in nature. It's structure is

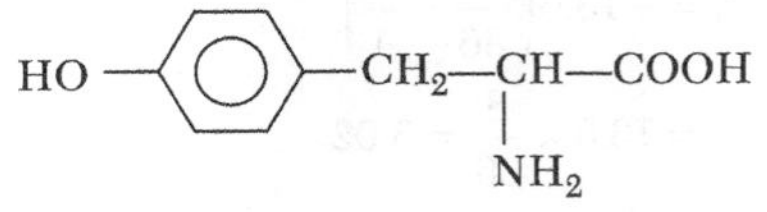

103. *(a)* One mole of triolein contain three double bonds. Hence, during hydrogenation, it adds three moles of hydrogen.
One mole of hydrogen = 2g.
∴ Three moles of hydrogen = 6 g.

104. *(d)* The reaction is as follows,

$$CH_3{-}CH_2{-}OH \xrightarrow{PCl_5\,(A)} CH_3CH_2Cl \xrightarrow{\text{alc. KOH }(B)} CH_2{=}CH_2$$

∴ $A = PCl_5$ and B = alc. KOH.

105. *(a)* Number of gram equivalent of HCl

$$= N_1V_1 = 2 \times \frac{500}{1000} = 1$$

No. of gram equivalent of NaOH

$$= N_2V_2 = 4 \times \frac{250}{1000} = 1$$

∵ Both NaOH and HCl are one gram equivalents.
∴ Heat evolved during reaction is equal to enthalpy of neutralisation i.e. x kJ.

106. *(b)*

	A	+	B	⇌	C	+	D
Initially	x		x		0		0
At equilibrium	y		y		$2y$		$2y$

Equilibrium constant

$$k = \frac{[C][D]}{[A][B]} = \frac{2y \times 2y}{y \times y} = 4$$

107. *(c)* Dissociation of lime stone is an endothermic reaction. Hence, entropy increases in this reaction.

$$\underset{\text{Lime stone}}{CaCO_3(s)} \xrightarrow{\Delta} CaO(s) + CO_2(g);\ \Delta H = +Q \text{ kJ}$$

108. *(a)* Sulphuric acid (H_2SO_4) is hygroscopic in nature, it absorbs atmospheric moisture without changing physical state. It is not deliquescent in nature.
∴ Option (a) is not true.

109. *(c)* van der Waals' force of attraction increase with increase in atomic mass. On going down the group atomic mass increases.

$\therefore$ Xe has the highest van der Waals' force of attraction.

110. *(c)* Atomic number of V is 23.

Electronic configuration of $V = [Ar]4s^2 3d^3$

$$V^{4+} = [Ar]3d^1$$

$\because$ It contains one unpaired electron, hence it is coloured. While Ti^+, Cu^+ and Zn^{2+} do not have unpaired electron.

111. *(c)* Oxalate $(C_2O_4^{2-})$ is an example of bidendate ligand. Three oxalate ligands form six coordinate bond around Ni^{2+} ion. Hence, coordination number is 6.

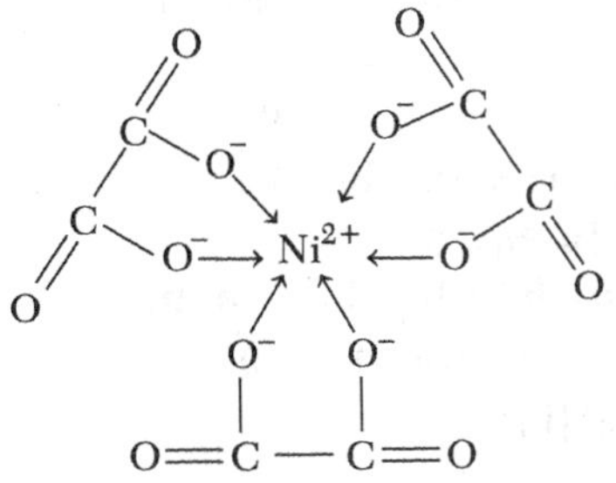

112. *(d)* Oxidation number of Cr in $[CrCl_2(NH_3)_4]NO_3$

$\Rightarrow x + 2\times(-1) + 0 + (-1) = 0$

$x = 3$

IUPAC name of $[CrCl_2(NH_3)_4]NO_3$ is tetraamminedichlorochromium (III) nitrate.

113. *(b)* Unit of rate constant of nth order

$$(k) = \left(\frac{\text{mol}}{\text{dm}^3}\right)^{1-n} s^{-1}$$

for zero order $(n) = 0$

$\therefore \quad k = \text{mol dm}^{-3}\ s^{-1}$

$\therefore$ The order of reaction is 1st.

114. *(b)* The concentration of gaseous $\propto \dfrac{1}{\text{volume}}$

$\therefore$ If volume of vessel is reduced of initial volume to half then concentration increases to two-times.

$\therefore \quad [A'] = 2[A]$

$[B'] = 2[B]$

Initially, $\quad r = k[A][B]$

After reduction of volume, $r_1 = k_2[A']2[B']$

$r_1 = 4k[A'][B'] \quad (k_2 = k)$

$r_1 = 4r$

$\therefore$ Rate increases to 4 times of original rate.

115. *(b)* The reduction potential of an electrode can be increased by increase in $[M^{n+}]$ or decrease in temperature.

$$M^{n+} + ne^- \longrightarrow M \qquad \text{(Reduction)}$$

$$E = E^\circ - \frac{RT}{nF}\ln\frac{[M]}{[M^{n+}]}$$

116. *(d)* According to Faraday second law,

$$\frac{W_{Ag}}{W_{O_2}} = \frac{E_{Ag}}{E_{O_2}}$$

$$\frac{0.054}{W_{O_2}} = \frac{108}{8}$$

$$W_{O_2} = \frac{0.054}{108}\times 8 = 4\times 10^{-3}\ g$$

$\therefore$ 32 g of oxygen (O_2) at STP liberates 22400 cm^3.

$\therefore$ 4×10^{-3} g of oxygen will liberate

$$= \frac{4\times10^{-3}\times 22400}{32} = 2.8 cm^3$$

117. *(a)* Millimoles of $H^+ = N_1V_1 + N_2V_2$

$10\times 0.1\times 2 + 5\times 0.2 = 2 + 1 = 3$

Millimoles of $OH^- = N_3V_3$

$= 0.1\times 5\times 2 = 1$

$\therefore$ After neutralisation millimoles of H^+ left

$= 3 - 1 = 2$

$\therefore$ Concentration of H^+

$$= \frac{\text{moles of } H^+}{\text{volumes of solution}}$$

$$= \frac{2}{10+5+5} = \frac{2}{20} = 01$$

$\therefore \quad pH = -\log[H^+] = -\log(10^{-1}) = 1$

118. *(b)* Conjugate acid NH_3 is obtained by addition of H^+ ion to the base NH_2^- is

$$\underset{\text{Base}}{NH_2^-} + H^+ \longrightarrow \underset{\text{Conjugate acid}}{NH_3}$$

119. *(b)* Phenyl isocyanide is obtained from the carbylamine reaction as follows :

$$\underset{\text{Aniline}}{C_6H_5NH_2} + \underset{\text{Chloroform}}{CHCl_3} + \underset{\text{Potassium hydroxide}}{3KOH} \longrightarrow \underset{\text{Phenyl isocyanide}}{C_6H_5NC} + 3KCl + 3H_2O$$

120. *(c)* Aldol condensation is a characteristic reaction of aldehyde having α-hydrogen atom.

Benzaldehyde do not contain any α-hydrogen atom.

$\therefore$ It do not undergoes aldol condensation reaction.

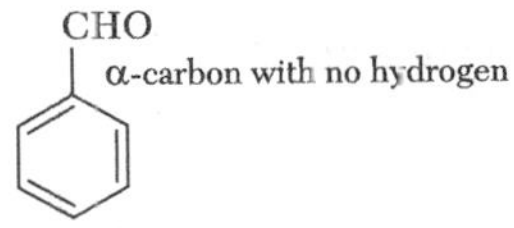

Benzaldehyde

Mathematics

121. *(b)* We have,

$$7x^2 + 7y^2 - 7x + 14y + k = 0$$

$$x^2 + y^2 - x + 2y + \frac{k}{7} = 0$$

Here, $C \equiv \left(\frac{1}{2}, -1\right)$

and $r = \sqrt{\frac{1}{4} + 1 - \frac{k}{7}}$

$$r = \sqrt{\frac{5}{4} - \frac{k}{7}}$$

Given that, Area = 12π sq. unit

$\Rightarrow$ $12\pi = \pi\left(\frac{5}{4} - \frac{k}{7}\right)$

$\Rightarrow$ $12 = \frac{5}{4} - \frac{k}{7} \Rightarrow 12 = \frac{35 - 4k}{28}$

$\Rightarrow$ $336 = 35 - 4k$

$\Rightarrow$ $4k = -301 \Rightarrow k = -\frac{301}{4}$

122. *(c)* Given that, $SP + S'P = 10$

$\Rightarrow$ $2a = 10 \Rightarrow a = 5$

and $2ae = 8$

$ae = 4$

$\because$ $b^2 = a^2(1 - e^2)$

$= a^2 - (ae)^2$

$= 25 - 16 = 9$

Hence, required equation is

$$\frac{x^2}{25} + \frac{y^2}{9} = 1$$

123. *(d)* We have,

$$x^2 + y^2 - 2x - 4y + 1 = 0$$

and $x^2 + y^2 - 12x - 16y + 91 = 0$

Here, $C_1 \equiv (1, 2)$ and $r_1 = \sqrt{1 + 4 - 1} = 2$

and $C_2 \equiv (6, 8)$ and $r_2 = \sqrt{36 + 64 - 91} = 3$

Now, $C_1C_2 = \sqrt{25 + 36} = \sqrt{61}$

Here, $r_1 + r_2 = 5 < \sqrt{61}$

So, circle are far apart.

Hence, number of common tangents is 4.

124. *(a)* Given, equation of circle is

$$x^2 + y^2 + 4x - 6y - 9 = 0$$

Here, $T = S_1$

$x(0) + y(1) + 2(x + 0) - 3(y + 1) - 9 = 0 + 1 + 0 - 6 - 9$

$\Rightarrow y + 2x - 3y - 3 - 9 = 1 - 15$

$\Rightarrow$ $2x - 2y - 12 = 1 - 15$

$\Rightarrow$ $2x - 2y + 2 = 0$

$\Rightarrow$ $x - y + 1 = 0$

125. *(b)* Given, equation of hyperbola is $\frac{x^2}{25} - \frac{y^2}{16} = 1$

Here, $a^2 = 25 \Rightarrow a = 5$

$b^2 = 16 \Rightarrow b = 4$

Now, $\theta = 2\tan^{-1}\left(\frac{b}{a}\right) = 2\tan^{-1}\left(\frac{4}{5}\right)$

126. *(c)* Given that, $x = t^2 + 1 \Rightarrow x - 1 = t^2$

and $y = 2t + 1 \Rightarrow y - 1 = 2t$

Now, $(y - 1)^2 = 4t^2 = 4(x - 1)$

$(y - 1)^2 = 4(x - 1)$

So, $x - 1 = -1$

$\Rightarrow$ $x = 0$

127. *(d)* We have, $|\mathbf{a} \times \mathbf{b}| = 5$

and $|\mathbf{a} \cdot \mathbf{b}| = 3$

$\because$ $|\mathbf{a} \times \mathbf{b}|^2 = |\mathbf{a}|^2 |\mathbf{b}|^2 - (\mathbf{a} \cdot \mathbf{b})^2$

$\Rightarrow$ $25 = |\mathbf{a}|^2 |\mathbf{b}|^2 - 9$

$\Rightarrow |\mathbf{a}|^2 |\mathbf{b}|^2 = 34$

128. *(a)* Let $\mathbf{a} = 2\hat{\mathbf{i}} + \hat{\mathbf{j}} - 2\hat{\mathbf{k}}$

So, $|\mathbf{a}| = \sqrt{4 + 1 + 4} = \sqrt{9} = 3$

So, direction cosines of vector are $\frac{2}{3}, \frac{1}{3}, -\frac{2}{3}$.

129. *(c)* We have,

$(3 + 3\omega^2 + 5\omega)^6 - (2 + 6\omega^2 + 2\omega)^3$

$= [3(1 + \omega^2) + 5\omega]^6 - [2(1 + \omega) + 6\omega^2]^3$

$= [3(-\omega) + 5\omega]^6 - [2(-\omega^2) + 6\omega^2]^3$

$= (2\omega)^6 - (4\omega^2)^3$

$= 2^6\omega^6 - 64\omega^6$

$= 64 - 64 = 0$

130. *(a)* We have,

$$\int_{\log 2}^{x} \frac{1}{\sqrt{e^y - 1}}\, dy = \frac{\pi}{6}$$

Let $\sqrt{e^y - 1} = t$

$\Rightarrow$ $e^y - 1 = t^2$

$\Rightarrow$ $e^y = 1 + t^2$

$\Rightarrow$ $e^y dy = 2t\, dt$

$\Rightarrow$ $(1 + t^2)\, dy = 2t\, dt$

$\Rightarrow$ $dy = \frac{2t}{(1 + t^2)}\, dt$

Now, $\int_1^{\sqrt{e^{x-1}}} \frac{2t}{(1 + t^2) \times t}\, dt = \frac{\pi}{6}$

$$\Rightarrow \int_1^{\sqrt{e^x-1}} \frac{dt}{1+t^2} = \frac{\pi}{12}$$

$$\Rightarrow [\tan^{-1} t]_1^{\sqrt{e^x-1}} = \frac{\pi}{12}$$

$$\Rightarrow \tan^{-1}\sqrt{e^x-1} - \frac{\pi}{4} = \frac{\pi}{12}$$

$$\Rightarrow \tan^{-1}\sqrt{e^x-1} = \frac{\pi}{3}$$

$$\Rightarrow \tan(\tan^{-1}\sqrt{e^x-1}) = \tan\left(\frac{\pi}{3}\right)$$

$$\Rightarrow \sqrt{e^x-1} = \sqrt{3}$$

$$\Rightarrow e^x - 1 = 3 \Rightarrow e^x = 4$$

$$\Rightarrow x = \log 4$$

131. *(c)* Since, $(\sin^{93} x + x^{295})$ is a odd function.

So, $\int_{-8}^{8}(\sin^{93} x + x^{295})\, dx = 0$

132. *(b)* We have,

$$\frac{x^2}{25} + \frac{y^2}{16} = 1$$

Here, $a^2 = 25 \Rightarrow a = 5$

$b^2 = 16 \Rightarrow b = 4$

So, required area $= \pi ab$

$= \pi(5)(4)$

$= 20\pi$ sq units

133. *(c)* Given, differential equation is

$$\left[1 + \left(\frac{dy}{dx}\right)^5\right]^{\frac{2}{3}} = \frac{d^3y}{dx^3}$$

Here, highest derivative is $\frac{d^3y}{dx^3}$.

So, order = 3

134. *(c)* Given, differential equation is

$$\frac{dy}{dx} - 1 = e^{x-y}$$

Put $x - y = t$

$$\Rightarrow 1 - \frac{dy}{dx} = \frac{dt}{dx}$$

So, given equation becomes,

$$-\frac{dt}{dx} = e^t$$

$$-e^{-t}dt = dx$$

Integrating both sides, we get

$$e^{-t} = x + c$$

$$e^{-(x-y)} = x + c$$

135. *(d)* We have,

$$\sin^{-1}\left(\frac{2p}{1+p^2}\right) - \cos^{-1}\left(\frac{1-q^2}{1+q^2}\right) = \tan^{-1}\left(\frac{2x}{1+x^2}\right)$$

$$\Rightarrow 2\tan^{-1} p - 2\tan^{-1} q = 2\tan^{-1} x$$

$$\Rightarrow 2(\tan^{-1} p - \tan^{-1} q) = 2\tan^{-1} x$$

$$\Rightarrow \tan^{-1} p - \tan^{-1} q = \tan^{-1} x$$

$$\Rightarrow \tan^{-1}\left(\frac{p-q}{1+pq}\right) = \tan^{-1} x$$

$$\Rightarrow x = \frac{p-q}{1+pq}$$

136. *(a)* Given that, $\mathbf{a} + 2\mathbf{b} - \mathbf{c}$

So, required unit vector $= \frac{\mathbf{a} + 2\mathbf{b} - \mathbf{c}}{\sqrt{1+4+1}} = \frac{\mathbf{a} + 2\mathbf{b} - \mathbf{c}}{\sqrt{6}}$

137. *(c)* It is a false option because every group of order 3 is abelian because it is closed as well.

138. *(b)* We have,

$$y = \tan^{-1}\left(\frac{1}{1+x(x+1)}\right) + \tan^{-1}\left(\frac{1}{1+(x+1)(x+2)}\right) + \tan^{-1}\left(\frac{1}{1+(x+2)(x+3)}\right) + \ldots + \tan^{-1}\left(\frac{1}{1+(x+n-1)(x+n)}\right)$$

When $n = 1$, then

$$y = \tan^{-1}\left(\frac{1}{1+x(x+1)}\right)$$

$$= \tan^{-1}\left(\frac{(x+1)-x}{1+x(x+1)}\right)$$

$$y = \tan^{-1}(x+1) - \tan^{-1} x$$

$$\frac{dy}{dx} = \frac{1}{1+(x+1)^2} - \frac{1}{1+x^2}$$

$$\left.\frac{dy}{dx}\right|_{x=0} = \frac{1}{1+(0+1)^2} - \frac{1}{1+(0)^2}$$

$$= \frac{1}{1+1} - \frac{1}{1} = \frac{1}{2} - 1 = -\frac{1}{2}$$

139. *(c)* We have,

$\cot\alpha \cot\beta = 2$

Now, $\frac{\cos(\alpha+\beta)}{\cos(\alpha-\beta)} = \frac{\cos\alpha\cos\beta - \sin\alpha\sin\beta}{\cos\alpha\cos\beta + \sin\alpha\sin\beta}$

$$= \frac{\cot\alpha\cot\beta - 1}{\cot\alpha\cot\beta + 1} = \frac{2-1}{2+1} = \frac{1}{3}$$

140. *(*)* We have, $\begin{vmatrix} 1+\omega & \omega^2 & \omega \\ \omega^2+\omega & -\omega & \omega^2 \\ 1+\omega^2 & \omega & \omega^2 \end{vmatrix}$

$$= \begin{vmatrix} 1+\omega+\omega^2 & \omega^2 & \omega \\ \omega^2 & -\omega & \omega^2 \\ 1+\omega+\omega^2 & \omega & \omega^2 \end{vmatrix} \quad (C_1 \to C_1 + C_2)$$

$$= \begin{vmatrix} 0 & \omega^2 & \omega \\ \omega^2 & -\omega & \omega^2 \\ 0 & \omega & \omega^2 \end{vmatrix}$$

$= 0 - \omega^2(\omega^4 - 0) + \omega(\omega^3 - 0)$

$= -\omega^6 + \omega^4$

$= -1 + \omega \quad [\because \omega^3 = 1]$

$= \omega - 1$

141. *(c)* Given, equation of curve is

$2y^3 = ax^2 + x^3$

$\Rightarrow \quad 6y^2 \dfrac{dy}{dx} = 2ax + 3x^2$

$\Rightarrow \quad \dfrac{dy}{dx} = \dfrac{2ax + 3x^2}{6y^2}$

$\Rightarrow \quad \left.\dfrac{dy}{dx}\right|_{(a,\, a)} = \dfrac{2a^2 + 3a^2}{6a^2} = \dfrac{5a^2}{6a^2} = \dfrac{5}{6}$

So, x-intercept $= -\dfrac{a}{5} = \alpha$

and y-intercept $= \dfrac{a}{6} = \beta$

$\because \quad \alpha^2 + \beta^2 = 61$

$\Rightarrow \quad \dfrac{a^2}{25} + \dfrac{a^2}{36} = 61$

$\Rightarrow \quad \dfrac{61a^2}{36 \times 25} = 61$

$\Rightarrow \quad a^2 = 36 \times 25$

$\Rightarrow \quad a = \pm 6 \times 5 = \pm 30$

142. *(d)* $y^2 = \dfrac{x^2}{2a + x}$

$2y\dfrac{dy}{dx} = \dfrac{2x}{2a+x} - \dfrac{x^2}{(2a+x)^2}$

At (a, a), $\left(\dfrac{dy}{dx}\right)_{(a,\, a)} = \dfrac{5}{18a}$

Length of subtangent at $(x_1, y_1) = \dfrac{y_1}{\left(\dfrac{dy}{dx}\right)_{(x_1, y_1)}}$

$\therefore$ Length of subtangent at $(a, a) = \dfrac{a}{\left(\dfrac{dy}{dx}\right)_{(a,\, a)}} = \dfrac{18a^2}{5}$

143. *(a)* Given, $f(x) = 5 + 36x + 3x^2 - 2x^3$

$\Rightarrow \quad f'(x) = 36 + 6x - 6x^2$

$= -6(x^2 - x - 6)$

$= -6(x^2 - 3x + 2x - 6)$

$= -6(x - 3)(x + 2)$

For increasing function, $f'(x) > 0$

$\Rightarrow \quad (x - 3)(x + 2) < 0$

$\Rightarrow \quad x < 3$ and $x > -2$

$\Rightarrow \quad -2 < x < 3$

Hence, function $f(x)$ is increasing in $(-2, 3)$ interval.

144. *(b)* According to question,

$x + y = 20 \quad \ldots \text{(i)}$

and $\quad p = xy^3 = (20 - y)y^3 \quad$ [by Eq. (i)]

$p = 20y^3 - y^4$

$\Rightarrow \quad \dfrac{dp}{dy} = 60y^2 - 4y^3$

$\Rightarrow \quad \dfrac{d^2p}{dy^2} = 120y - 12y^2$

Now, $\quad \dfrac{dp}{dy} = 0 \Rightarrow 60y^2 - 4y^3 = 0$

$\Rightarrow \quad 60y^2 = 4y^3$

$\Rightarrow \quad 4y = 60 \Rightarrow y = 15$

$\therefore \quad x = 5$

Hence, two parts are (15, 5).

145. *(c)* We have, $4896 = 2^5 \times 3^2 \times 17^1$

So, $T(a) = (1 + 5)(1 + 2)(1 + 1) = 36$

146. *(d)* We have, $583! \equiv 0 \pmod{10}$

and $\quad 7^2 = -1 \pmod{10}$

So, $(7^2)^{145} \cdot 7^1 = (-1)^{145} \cdot 7^1 \pmod{10}$

$\Rightarrow \quad 7^{291} = -7 \pmod{10} \equiv 3 \pmod{10}$

So, $583! + 7^{291} = 3 \pmod{10}$

Hence, last digit is 3.

147. *(a)* We have, $I = \int x^x(1 + \log x)dx$

Let $\quad x^x = t$

$\Rightarrow \quad \dfrac{dt}{dx} = x^x \log x + x^x$

$\Rightarrow \quad \dfrac{dt}{dx} = x^x(1 + \log x)$

$\Rightarrow \quad dt = x^x(1 + \log x)\, dx$

Now, $\quad I = \int dt$

$= t + C = x^x + C$

148. *(c)* We have, $I = \int \dfrac{xe^x}{(1+x)^2} dx$

$= \int \dfrac{(x + 1 - 1)}{(x+1)^2} e^x \, dx$

$$= \int \left[\frac{1}{x+1} - \frac{1}{(x+1)^2} \right] e^x \, dx$$

$$= e^x \frac{1}{(1+x)} + C$$

On comparing, we get

$$f(x) = \frac{1}{1+x}$$

149. *(d)* We have,

$$I = \int_0^{\pi/2} \frac{\sin 2t}{\sin^4 t + \cos^4 t} dt$$

$$= \int_0^{\pi/2} \frac{2\sin t \cos t}{\sin^4 t + \cos^4 t} dt$$

$$= \int_0^{\pi/2} \frac{2\tan t \sec^2 t}{(\tan^2 t)^2 + 1} dt$$

Put $\tan^2 t = x$

$(2\tan t \sec^2 t)\, dt = dx$

$$\therefore \quad I = \int_0^{\infty} \frac{1}{1+x^2} dx = [\tan^{-1} x]_0^{\infty} = \frac{\pi}{2}$$

150. *(a)* We have,

$$4^{\log_9 3} + 9^{\log_2 4} = 10^{\log_x 83}$$

$$\Rightarrow 4^{\frac{1}{2}\log_3 3} + 9^{2\log_2 2} = 10^{\log_x 83}$$

$$\Rightarrow 2 + 81 = 10^{\log_x 83}$$

$$\Rightarrow 83 = 10^{\log_x 83}$$

$$\Rightarrow \log_{10} 83 = \log_x 83$$

$$\Rightarrow x = 10$$

151. *(b)* We have,

$$p = 3^{\frac{1}{3}} . 3^{\frac{2}{9}} . 3^{\frac{3}{27}}$$

$$= 3^{\frac{1}{3}\left[1 + \frac{2}{3} + \frac{3}{9} + \dots \infty\right]}$$

$$= 3^{\frac{1}{3}\left[\frac{a}{1-r} + \frac{ar}{(1-r)^2}\right]}$$

$$= 3^{\frac{1}{3}\left[\frac{1}{1-\frac{1}{3}} + \frac{1 . \frac{1}{3}}{\left(1-\frac{1}{3}\right)^2}\right]}$$

$$= 3^{\frac{1}{3}\left[\frac{3}{2} + \frac{3}{4}\right]}$$

$$= 3^{\frac{1}{3}\left[\frac{12+6}{8}\right]} = 3^{\frac{1}{3}\left(\frac{18}{8}\right)} = 3^{\frac{3}{4}}$$

Now, $p^{4/3} = \left(3^{\frac{3}{4}}\right)^{\frac{4}{3}}$

$$= 3^{\frac{3}{4} \times \frac{4}{3}} = 3^1 = 3$$

152. *(c)* We have,

$$x^3 - 3x^2 + 2x - 1$$

So, $\alpha + \beta + \gamma = 3$

$\alpha\beta + \beta\gamma + \gamma\alpha = 2$

$\alpha\beta\gamma = 1$

Now, $(1-\alpha)(1-\beta)(1-\gamma)$

$= 1 - (\alpha + \beta + \gamma) + (\alpha\beta + \beta\gamma + \gamma\alpha) - \alpha\beta\gamma$

$= 1 - 3 + 2 - 1 = -1$

153. *(d)* The middle term in the expansion of $(1+x)^{2n}$ is $\left(\frac{2n}{2} + 1\right)$th term i.e. $(n+1)$ th term.

$$= \frac{(2n)!}{n!\,n!} x^n$$

$$= \frac{2n(2n-1)(2n-2)....3\cdot2\cdot1}{\{n(n-1)(n-2)\dots3\cdot2\cdot1\}^2} x^n$$

$$= \frac{(2n(2n-2)(2n-4)\dots4.2\}\ \{(2n-1)(2n-3)\dots(3\cdot1)\}}{\{n(n-1)(n-2)\dots3\cdot2\cdot1\}^2} x^n$$

$$= \frac{2^n\{n(n-1)(n-2)\dots3\cdot2\cdot1\}\ \{((2n-1)(2n-3)\dots3\cdot1\}}{\{n(n-1)(n-2)\dots3\cdot2\cdot1\}^2} x^n$$

$$= \frac{2^n\{(2n-1)(2n-3)\dots3\cdot1\}}{\{n(n-1)(n-2)\dots3\cdot2\cdot1\}} x^n$$

$$= \frac{(2n-1)(2n-3)\dots3\cdot1}{n!} x^n 2^n$$

154. *(a)* Given that, $p \rightarrow (\sim q \vee r)$ is false.

$\Rightarrow (\sim q \vee r)$ is false and p is true.

$\Rightarrow q$ is true, r is false and p is true.

155. *(c)* We have,

$$\frac{2}{9!} + \frac{2}{3!7!} + \frac{1}{5!5!} = \frac{2^a}{b!}$$

$$\Rightarrow \frac{1}{9!}\left[2 + \frac{2\cdot8\cdot9}{3!} + \frac{6\cdot7\cdot8\cdot9}{5!}\right] = \frac{2^a}{b!}$$

$$\Rightarrow \frac{1}{9!}\left[2 + 24 + \frac{126}{5}\right] = \frac{2^a}{b!}$$

$$\Rightarrow \frac{1}{9!}\left[26 + \frac{126}{5}\right] = \frac{2^a}{b!}$$

$$\Rightarrow \frac{1}{9!}\left[\frac{256}{5}\right] = \frac{2^a}{b!}$$

$$\Rightarrow \frac{1}{9!}\frac{256 \times 2}{5 \times 2} = \frac{512}{10!} = \frac{2^9}{10!} = \frac{2^a}{b!} \Rightarrow a = 9 \text{ and } b = 10$$

156. *(d)* $\tan 10° \tan 20° \tan 30° \tan 40° \tan 50$

$\tan 60° \tan 70° \tan 80°$

$$= \tan 10° \tan 20° \left(\frac{1}{\sqrt{3}}\right) \tan 40° \tan(90° - 40°)$$

$(\sqrt{3}) \tan(90° - 20°) \tan(90° - 10°)$

$= \tan 10° \tan 20° \tan 40° \cot 40° \cot 20° \cot 10°$

$= 1$

157. *(a)* We have, $\tan\theta = \dfrac{m}{n}$

Now, $n\cos 2\theta + m\sin 2\theta$

$$= n\left[\frac{1-\tan^2\theta}{1+\tan^2\theta}\right] + m\left[\frac{2\tan\theta}{1+\tan^2\theta}\right]$$

$$= n\left[\frac{1-\frac{m^2}{n^2}}{1+\frac{m^2}{n^2}}\right] + m\left[\frac{2\frac{m}{n}}{1+\frac{m^2}{n^2}}\right]$$

$$= n\left[\frac{n^2-m^2}{n^2+m^2}\right] + \left[\frac{\frac{2m^2}{n}\times n^2}{n^2+m^2}\right]$$

$$= n\left(\frac{n^2-m^2}{m^2+n^2}\right) + \frac{2m^2n}{n^2+m^2} = \frac{n(n^2-m^2)+2m^2n}{(m^2+n^2)}$$

$$= \frac{n[n^2-m^2+2m^2]}{(m^2+n^2)} = \frac{n(n^2+m^2)}{(m^2+n^2)} = n$$

158. *(b)* Let $\dfrac{b+c}{11} = \dfrac{c+a}{12} = \dfrac{a+b}{13} = k$

$\Rightarrow b+c = 11k,\ c+a = 12k,\ a+b = 13k$

Now, $2(a+b+c) = 36k$

$a+b+c = 18k$

So, $a = 7k$

$b = 6k$

and $c = 5k$

Now, $\cos A = \dfrac{b^2+c^2-a^2}{2bc}$

$$= \frac{36k^2+25k^2-49k^2}{2(30k^2)} = \frac{12k^2}{60k^2} = \frac{1}{5}$$

159. *(d)* We have, $a = \cos 2\alpha + i\sin 2\alpha$

and $b = \cos 2\beta + i\sin 2\beta$

$$\frac{a}{b} = \frac{Cis\ 2\alpha}{Cis\ 2\beta} = Cis(2\alpha - 2\beta)$$

So, $\sqrt{\dfrac{a}{b}} = Cis(\alpha-\beta) = \cos(\alpha-\beta) + i\sin(\alpha-\beta)$

and $\sqrt{\dfrac{b}{a}} = \cos(\alpha-\beta) - i\sin(\alpha-\beta)$

Now, $\sqrt{\dfrac{a}{b}} + \sqrt{\dfrac{b}{a}} = \cos(\alpha-\beta) + i\sin(\alpha-\beta)$

$+ \cos(\alpha-\beta) - i\sin(\alpha-\beta) = 2\cos(\alpha-\beta)$

160. *(a)* We have,

$$y = \log\left[\tan\left(\frac{\pi}{4}+\frac{x}{2}\right)\right]$$

So, $\dfrac{dy}{dx} = \dfrac{1}{\tan\left(\frac{\pi}{4}+\frac{x}{2}\right)}\cdot\sec^2\left(\dfrac{\pi}{4}+\dfrac{x}{2}\right)\cdot\dfrac{1}{2}$

$$= \frac{1}{2\sin\left(\frac{\pi}{4}+\frac{x}{2}\right)\cos\left(\frac{\pi}{4}+\frac{x}{2}\right)}$$

$$= \frac{1}{\sin\left[2\left(\frac{\pi}{4}+\frac{x}{2}\right)\right]} = \frac{1}{\cos x} = \sec x$$

161. *(b)* We have, $y = \sin^2\left[\tan^{-1}\sqrt{\dfrac{1-x^2}{1+x^2}}\right]$

Put $x^2 = \cos\theta$

So, $y = \sin^2\left[\tan^{-1}\sqrt{\dfrac{1-\cos\theta}{1+\cos\theta}}\right]$

$$= \sin^2\left[\tan^{-1}\left(\tan\frac{\theta}{2}\right)\right]$$

$$= \sin^2\frac{\theta}{2} = \frac{1-\cos\theta}{2} = \frac{1-x^2}{2}$$

$$\frac{dy}{dx} = \frac{-2x}{2} = -x$$

162. *(c)* We have,

$$\sqrt{\frac{x}{y}} + \sqrt{\frac{y}{x}} = \sqrt{a}$$

$$\left(\sqrt{\frac{x}{y}} + \sqrt{\frac{y}{x}}\right)^2 = a$$

$$\frac{x}{y} + \frac{y}{x} + 2 = a$$

Differentiating both sides w.r.t. x,

$$\frac{y - x\frac{dy}{dx}}{y^2} + \frac{x\frac{dy}{dx} - y}{x^2} = 0$$

$$\Rightarrow \frac{y - x\frac{dy}{dx}}{y^2} = -\frac{\left(x\frac{dy}{dx} - y\right)}{x^2}$$

$$\Rightarrow xy^2\frac{dy}{dx} - y^3 = -x^2y + x^3\frac{dy}{dx}$$

$$\Rightarrow \frac{dy}{dx}(xy^2 - x^3) = -x^2y + y^3$$

$$\Rightarrow \frac{dy}{dx} = \frac{y(y^2-x^2)}{x(y^2-x^2)}$$

$$\Rightarrow \frac{dy}{dx} = \frac{y}{x}$$

Now, $y\cdot\dfrac{dx}{dy} = y\cdot\dfrac{x}{y} = x$

163. *(d)* We have, $x = \dfrac{1-t}{1+t}$

$$\frac{dx}{dt} = \frac{-(1+t)-(1-t)}{(1+t)^2} = \frac{-2}{1+t^2} \text{ and } y = \frac{2t}{1+t}$$

$$\frac{dy}{dt}=\frac{(1+t)2-2t}{(1+t)^2}=\frac{2}{(1+t)^2}$$

Now, $\frac{dy}{dx}=\frac{dy/dt}{dx/dt}=-1$

and $\frac{d^2y}{dx^2}=0$

164. *(a)* Clearly, $11^{-1}=11$ $[\because 11\otimes_{12}11=1]$

So, $7\otimes_{12}11^{-1}=7\otimes_{12}11=5$

165. *(b)* Option (c) cannot be subgroup as identity '1' is not present.

Option (d) cannot be a subgroup of $2\otimes_7 3=6 \notin \{1,2,3\}$.

Option (a) cannot be a subgroup as $2\otimes_7 6=5 \notin \{2,6,1\}$.

So, option (b) is a subgroup.

166. *(*)* We have,

$$A=\begin{bmatrix}3&-3&4\\2&-3&4\\0&-1&1\end{bmatrix}$$

Now, $|A|=\begin{vmatrix}3&-3&4\\2&-3&4\\0&-1&1\end{vmatrix}$

$=3(-3+4)+3(2-0)+4(-2-0)$
$=3+6-8=1$

Now, $\frac{|C|}{|\text{adj } B|}=\frac{|5A|}{|B|^{3-1}}=\frac{5^3|A|}{|B|^2}=\frac{5^3|A|}{|\text{adj } A|^2}$

$=\frac{5^3|A|}{(|A|^2)^2}=\frac{5^3|A|}{|A|^4}=\frac{5^3}{|A|^3}$

$=\frac{5^3}{1^3}=5^3$

167. *(d)* We have, $A=\begin{bmatrix}1&1&1\\1&2&3\\1&3&4\end{bmatrix}$, $B=\begin{bmatrix}7\\16\\22\end{bmatrix}$

$X=\begin{bmatrix}x\\y\\z\end{bmatrix}$

Now, $AX=B$

$x+y+z=7$ ...(i)
$x+2y+3z=16$ ...(ii)
$x+3y+4z=22$ ...(iii)

Subtracting Eq. (i) from Eq. (ii), we get

$y+2z=9$ ...(iv)

Subtracting Eq. (iii) from Eq. (ii), we get

$y+z=6$ ...(v)

Subtracting Eq. (v) from Eq. (iv), we get

$z=3$

168. *(a)* We have, $A=\begin{bmatrix}1&\log_b a\\\log_a b&1\end{bmatrix}$

Now, $|A|=\begin{vmatrix}1&\log_b a\\\log_a b&1\end{vmatrix}$

$=1-\log_a b\log_b a$

$=1-\log_a b\times\frac{1}{\log_a b}\quad\left\{\because \log_b a=\frac{1}{\log_a b}\right\}$

$=1-1=0$

169. *(c)* Let the vertices of ΔABC are $A(3,3)$, $B(x_1,y_1)$ and $C(x_2,y_2)$.

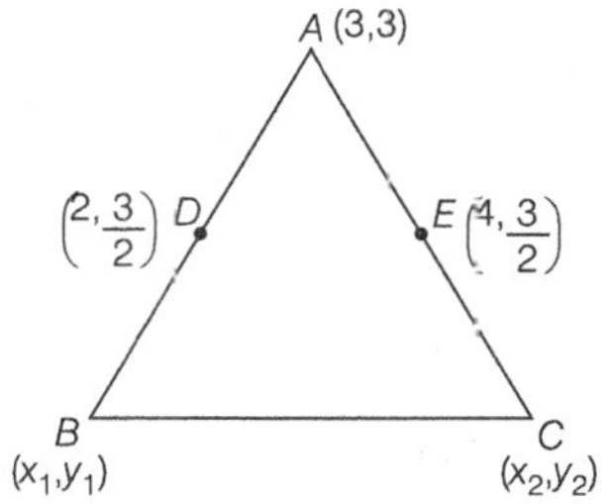

Now, $\frac{x_1+3}{2}=2$ and $\frac{y_1+3}{2}=\frac{3}{2}$

$x_1+3=4$ and $y_1+3=3$

$x_1=1$ and $y_1=0$

So, $B\equiv(1,0)$

and $\frac{x_2+3}{2}=4$ and $\frac{y_2+3}{2}=\frac{3}{2}$

$x_2+3=8$ and $y_2+3=3$

$x_2=5$ and $y_2=0$

So, $C\equiv(5,0)$

Hence, centroid $=\left(\frac{3+1+5}{3},\frac{3+0+0}{3}\right)$

$=\left(\frac{9}{3},\frac{3}{3}\right)=(3,1)$

170. *(c)* Let the image of point $(2,4)=(h,k)$, then

$$\frac{h-x_1}{a}=\frac{k-y_1}{b}=\frac{-2(ax_1+by_1+c)}{a^2+b^2}$$

$$\frac{h-2}{1}=\frac{k-4}{1}=\frac{-2(2+4-10)}{1^2+1^2}$$

$$\frac{h-2}{1}=\frac{k-4}{1}=\frac{-2(-4)}{2}$$

$$\frac{h-2}{1}=\frac{k-4}{1}=4$$

$h-2=4$ and $k-4=4$

$h=6$ and $k=8$

So, $(h,k)=(6,8)$

171. *(d)* Given, equation of line is $x^2-4pxy+8y^2=0$

On comparing with $ax^2+2hxy+by^2=0$

$\Rightarrow$ $a=1, b=8, 2h=-4p$

COMEDK 2012

Given that, $m_1 + m_2 = 3m_1m_2$

$$\Rightarrow \quad -\frac{2h}{b} = \frac{3a}{b}$$

$$\Rightarrow \quad -2h = 3a$$

$$\Rightarrow \quad 4p = 3a$$

$$\Rightarrow \quad p = \frac{3a}{4}$$

$$\Rightarrow \quad p = \frac{3}{4} \qquad [\because a = 1]$$

172. *(a)* $\lim_{x \to 0} \left(\frac{1 + 5x^2}{1 + 3x^2}\right)^{\frac{1}{x^2}}$

$$= \lim_{x \to 0} \frac{(1 + 5x^2)^{\frac{1}{5x^2}.5}}{(1 + 3x^2)^{\frac{1}{3x^2}.3}} = \frac{e^5}{e^3} = e^{5-3} = e^2$$

173. *(b)* $\because f(x)$ is continuous at $x = 0$

So, $\lim_{x \to 0} f(x) = f(0)$

$$\Rightarrow \quad \lim_{x \to 0} \frac{e^{3x-1}}{4x} = \frac{k + 0}{4}$$

$$\Rightarrow \quad \frac{1}{4} \lim_{x \to 0} 3\left(\frac{e^{3x} - 1}{3x}\right) = \frac{k}{4}$$

$$\Rightarrow \quad 3 \lim_{x \to 0} \frac{e^{3x} - 1}{3x} = k \Rightarrow 3 \times 1 = k \Rightarrow k = 3$$

174. *(d)* Non-adjacent vertex are not connected through edge.

$\therefore$ V_1V_3 is correct option.

175. *(a)* $\sin\left[2\cos^{-1}\left\{\cot\left(\tan^{-1}\frac{1}{1 - \frac{1}{4}}\right)\right\}\right]$

$$= \sin\left[2\cos^{-1}\left\{\cot\left(\tan^{-1}\frac{4}{3}\right)\right\}\right]$$

$$= \sin\left[2\cos^{-1}\frac{3}{4}\right] = \sin 2\theta$$

$$\left[\text{where, } \cos\theta = \frac{3}{4} \text{ and } \theta = \cos^{-1}\frac{3}{4}\right]$$

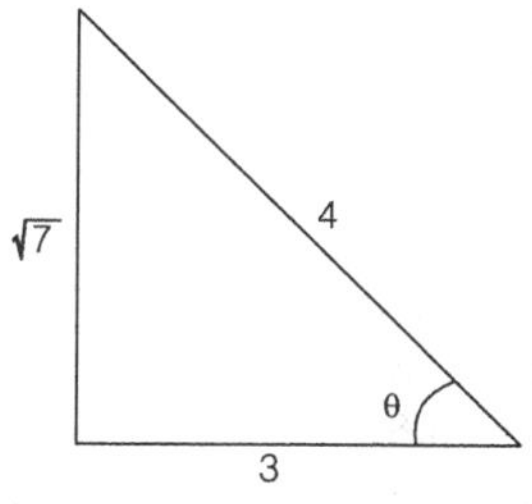

$$= 2\sin\theta\cos\theta = 2\frac{\sqrt{7}}{4}.\frac{3}{4} = \frac{3\sqrt{7}}{8}$$

176. *(b)* $\frac{3 + 4i}{4 - 5i}$

Now, multiplicative inverse is

$$\frac{4 - 5i}{3 + 4i} \times \frac{3 - 4i}{3 - 4i}$$

$$= \frac{(4 - 5i)(3 - 4i)}{9 + 16}$$

$$= \frac{12 - 16i - 15i + 20i^2}{25} = \frac{-8 - 31i}{25} = \left(-\frac{8}{25}, -\frac{31}{25}\right)$$

177. *(a)* $\tan x - \sin x = 1 - \tan x \sin x$

$$\Rightarrow \tan x + \tan x \sin x = 1 + \sin x$$

$$\tan x(1 + \sin x) - (1 + \sin x) = 0$$

$$(1 + \sin x)(\tan x - 1) = 0$$

$$\Rightarrow \quad \tan x - 1 = 0 \quad \text{or} \quad 1 + \sin x = 0$$

$$\tan x = 1 = \tan\frac{\pi}{4} \quad \text{or} \quad \sin x = -1 = \sin\left(-\frac{\pi}{2}\right)$$

$$x = n\pi + \frac{\pi}{4} \quad \text{or} \quad x = n\pi + (-1)^n\left(-\frac{\pi}{2}\right)$$

178. *(d)* Let θ be the angle of intersection of two given circles having centres $(-g, -f) = (-2, -1)$ and $(-g_1, -f_1) = (1, -3)$ respectively, then

$$\cos\theta = \left|\frac{-2gg_1 - 2ff_1 + c + c_1}{2\sqrt{g^2 + f^2 - c}\sqrt{g_1^2 + f_1^2 - c_1}}\right|$$

$$= \left|\frac{-2(2)(-1) - 2(1)(3) + 1 - 6}{2\sqrt{4 + 1 - 1}\sqrt{1 + 9 + 6}}\right|$$

$$= \left|\frac{4 - 6 - 5}{2(2)(4)}\right| = \left(\frac{7}{6}\right)$$

$$\theta = \cos^{-1}\left(\frac{7}{16}\right)$$

179. *(b)* We have, $|\mathbf{a}| = 2, |\mathbf{b}| = 7$

and $\quad \mathbf{a} \times \mathbf{b} = 3\hat{\mathbf{i}} + 2\hat{\mathbf{j}} + 6\hat{\mathbf{k}}$

So, $\quad |\mathbf{a} \times \mathbf{b}| = \sqrt{9 + 4 + 36} = \sqrt{49} = 7$

Since, $|\mathbf{a} \times \mathbf{b}| = |\mathbf{a}||\mathbf{b}|\sin\theta\,|\hat{\mathbf{n}}|$

$$\Rightarrow \quad 7 = (2)(7)\sin\theta \cdot 1 \; [\because |\hat{\mathbf{n}}| = 1]$$

$$\Rightarrow \quad \sin\theta = \frac{1}{2} \Rightarrow \sin\theta = \sin\frac{\pi}{6} \Rightarrow \quad \theta = \frac{\pi}{6}$$

180. *(b)* We have, $f(x) = \log(1 - x) + \sqrt{x^2 - 1}$

$\log(1 - x)$ is defined if $1 - x > 0 \Rightarrow x < 1$

$$\Rightarrow \quad x \in (-\infty, -1) \qquad \ldots \text{(i)}$$

and $\sqrt{x^2 - 1}$ is defined if $x^2 - 1 \geq 0$

$$\Rightarrow \quad x^2 \geq 1$$

$$\Rightarrow \quad x \geq 1 \text{ or } x \leq -1 \qquad \ldots \text{(ii)}$$

By Eqs. (i) and (ii), required domain is $(-\infty, -1]$.

COMEDK

MOCK TESTS 1-5

COMEDK

Mock Test 1

Instructions

- There are 180 questions in all. The number of questions in each section is as given below.

Sections	No. of Questions
Section I : Physics	1–60
Section II : Chemistry	61–120
Section III : Mathematics	121–180

- All the questions are Multiple Choice Questions having four options out of which **ONLY ONE** is correct.
- Candidates will be awarded 1 mark for each correct answer. There will be no negative marking for incorrect answer.
- Time allotted to complete this paper is 3 hrs.

PHYSICS

1. Hydrogen atom from excited state comes to the ground state by emitting a photon of wavelength λ. If R is the Rydberg constant, then the principal quantum number n of the excited state is

a. $\sqrt{\dfrac{\lambda R}{\lambda R-1}}$ *b.* $\sqrt{\dfrac{\lambda}{\lambda R-1}}$

c. $\sqrt{\dfrac{\lambda R^2}{\lambda R-1}}$ *d.* $\sqrt{\dfrac{\lambda R}{\lambda-1}}$

2. A car accelerates from rest at constant rate for first 10 s and covers a distance x. It covers a distance y in next 10 s at the same acceleration. Which of the following is true?

a. $x = 3y$ *b.* $y = 3x$

c. $x = y$ *d.* $y = 2x$

3. Tritium having a half-life of 12.5 yr, undergo β-decay. Fraction of sample remaining undecayed after 25 yr will be

a. $\dfrac{1}{8}$ *b.* $\dfrac{1}{2}$ *c.* $\dfrac{1}{4}$ *d.* $\dfrac{1}{16}$

4. The period of oscillation of a simple pendulum is $T = 2\pi\sqrt{L/g}$. Measured value of L is 20.0 cm known to 1mm accuracy and time for 100 oscillations of the pendulum is found to be 90 s using a wrist watch of resolution.The accuracy in the determination of g is

a. 2% *b.* 3% *c.* 1% *d.* 5%

5. The plot of the number N of decayed nuclei *versus* activity R of a radioactive sample is correctly depicted in graph

a.

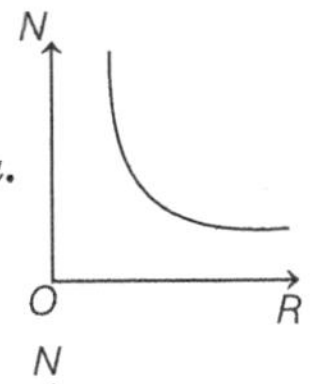

b.

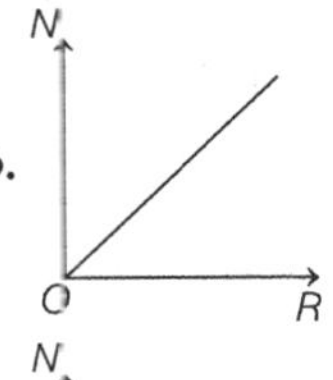

c.

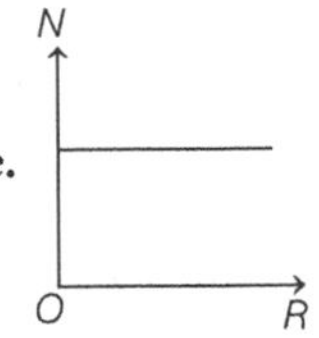

d.

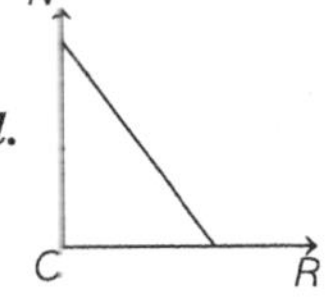

6. If $F = 6\pi\eta^a r^b v^c$,
where, F = viscous force, η = coefficient of viscosity, r = radius of spherical body, v = terminal velocity of the body.
The values of a, b and c are

a. $a = 1, b = 2, c = 1$ b. $a = 1, b = 1, c = 1$
c. $a = 2, b = 1, c = 1$ d. $a = 2, b = 1, c = 2$

7. A body which is initially at rest at a height R above the surface of the earth of radius, R, falls freely towards the earth, then its velocity on reaching the surface of earth is

a. $\sqrt{2gR}$ b. $\sqrt{gR}$ c. $\sqrt{\frac{3}{2}gR}$ d. $\sqrt{4gR}$

8. A sample of gas expands from volume V_1 to V_2. The amount of work done by the gas is greatest when the expansion is

a. adiabatic b. isobaric
c. isothermal d. equal in all three cases

9. A particle executing SHM has a maximum speed of 30 cm s^{-1} and a maximum acceleration of 60 cm s^{-2}. The period of oscillation is

a. π s b. $\frac{\pi}{2}$ s c. 2π s d. $\frac{\pi}{t}$ s

10. The current i and voltage V graph for a given metallic wire at two different temperatures T_1 and T_2 are shown in the figure. It is concluded that

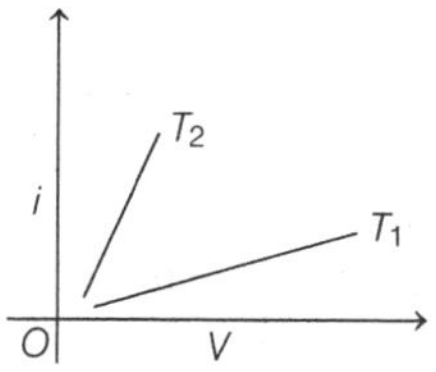

a. $T_1 > T_2$ b. $T_1 < T_2$
c. $T_1 = T_2$ d. $T_1 = 2T_2$

11. In case of a simple pendulum, time period *versus* length is depicted by

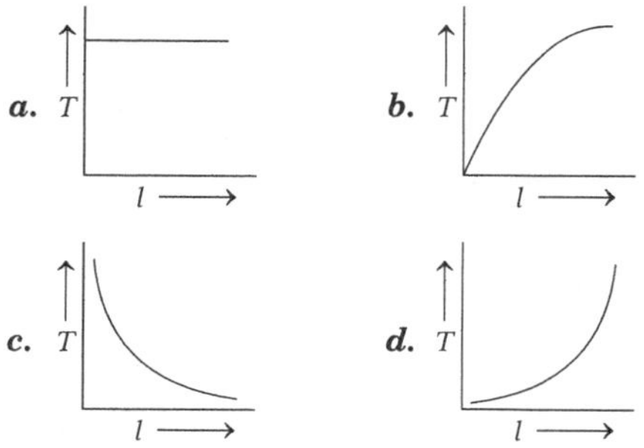

12. A carbon resistor of (47 ± 4.7) kΩ is to be marked with rings of different colours for its identification. The colour code sequence will be

a. Yellow - Green - Violet - Gold
b. Yellow - Violet - Orange - Silver
c. Violet - Yellow - Orange - Silver
d. Green - Orange - Violet - Gold

13. A load suspended by a massless spring produces an extension of x cm in equilibrium. When it is cut into two unequal parts, the same load produces an extension of 7.5 cm when suspended by the larger part of length 60 cm. When it is suspended by the smaller part, the extension is 5.0 cm. Then,

a. $x = 12.5$ cm
b. $x = 3.0$ cm
c. the length of the original spring is 90 cm
d. the length of the original spring is 80 cm

14. A parallel plate air capacitor has a capacitance 18 μF. If the distance between the plates is tripled and a dielectric medium is introduced, the capacitance becomes 72 μF. The dielectric constant of the medium is

a. 4 b. 9
c. 12 d. 2

15. A metal block is experiencing an atmospheric pressure of 10^5 Nm^{-2}. When the same block is placed in a vacuum chamber, the fractional change in its volume (the bulk modulus of metal is 1.25×10^{11} Nm^{-2})

a. 4×10^{-7}
b. 2×10^{-7}
c. 8×10^{-7}
d. 1×10^{-7}

16. Three equipotential surfaces are shown in the figure

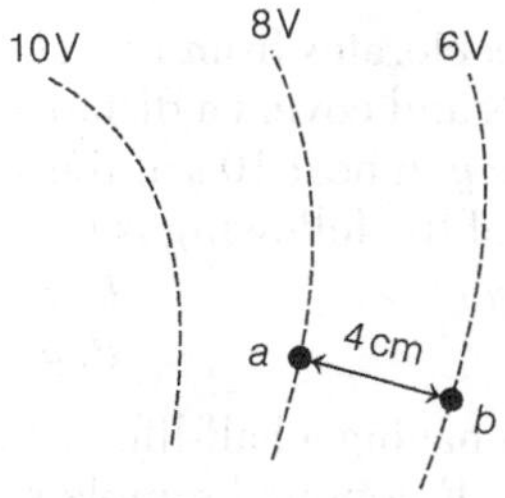

Which of the following option correctly represents the corresponding field lines?

a. 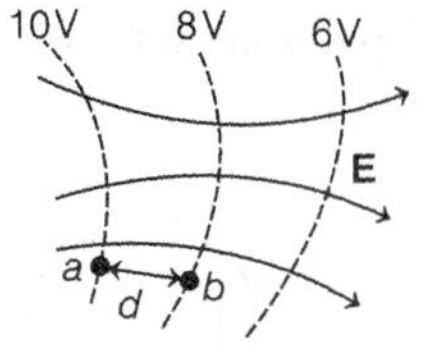

b. 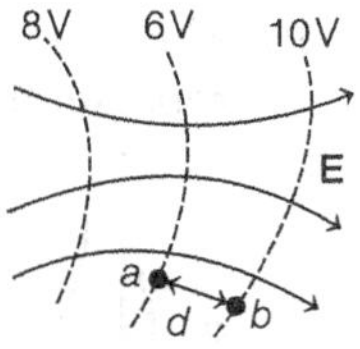

c. 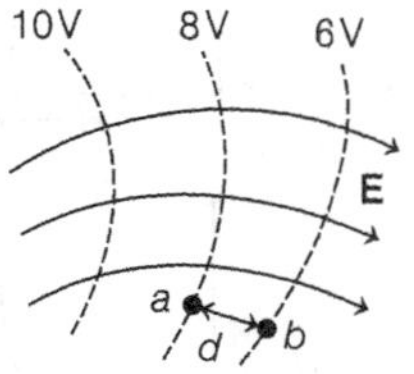

d. None of these

17. A hole is made at the bottom of the tank filled with water (density $= 1000\ \text{kgm}^{-3}$). If the total pressure at the bottom of the tank is three atmospheres (1 atmosphere $= 10^5\ \text{Nm}^{-2}$), then the velocity of efflux is nearest to

a. $\sqrt{400}\ \text{ms}^{-1}$ *b.* $\sqrt{200}\ \text{ms}^{-1}$
c. $\sqrt{600}\ \text{ms}^{-1}$ *d.* $\sqrt{500}\ \text{ms}^{-1}$

18. If same charge q is placed inside a sphere and cube having radius 1m and side 2m, respectively. What will be the ratio of flux passing through them?

a. 1 : 1 *b.* 1 : 8 *c.* 8 : 1 *d.* 1 : 2

19. A uniform metallic rod rotates about its perpendicular bisector with constant angular speed. If it is heated uniformly to raise its temperature slightly

a. its speed of rotation increases
b. its speed of rotation decreases
c. its speed of rotation remains same
d. its speed increases because its moment of inertia increases

20. The ratio of the forces between two small spheres with constant charge (i) in air (ii) in a medium of dielectric constant K is

a. $1 : K$ *b.* $K : 1$ *c.* $1 : K^2$ *d.* $K^2 : 1$

21. At what temperature is the root mean square velocity of the gaseous hydrogen molecules equal to that of oxygen molecules at 47°C?

a. 20 K *b.* 80 K
c. – 73 K *d.* 3 K

22. Distance of 5th dark fringe from centre is 4 mm. If $D = 2$ m and $\lambda = 600$ nm, then distance between slits is

a. 1.35 mm *b.* 2.00 mm
c. 3.25 mm *d.* 10.35 mm

23. A body cools from 50°C to 40°C in 5 min. The surrounding temperature is 20°C. In what further time (in minute) will it cool to 30°C?

a. 5 *b.* $\frac{15}{2}$
c. $\frac{25}{3}$ *d.* 10

24. The electric field of an electromagnetic wave in free space is given by $\mathbf{E} = 10\cos(10^7 t + kx)\mathbf{j}$ Vm^{-1}, where t and x are in seconds and metres, respectively. It can be inferred that,

a. the wavelength λ is 188.4m
b. the wave number k is 0.33 radm^{-1}
c. the wave amplitude is 20Vm^{-1}
d. None of the above

25. A straight wire carrying a current of 12 A is bent into a semi-circular loop of radius 2.0 cm. What will be magnetic field at the centre of the semi-circular loop?

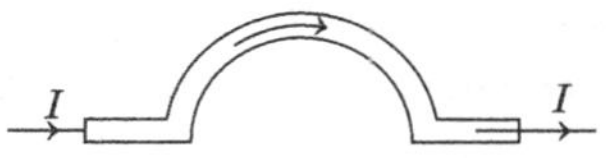

a. $\mathbf{B} = 1.9 \times 10^{-4}$ T, ⊙
b. $\mathbf{B} = 1.9 \times 10^{4}$ T, ⊙
c. $\mathbf{B} = 1.9 \times 10^{-4}$ T, ⊗
d. $\mathbf{B} = 1.9 \times 10^{4}$ T, ⊗

26. If the critical angle for light going from medium A to B is θ. Then, find the speed of light in medium B, if speed of light is v in medium A.

a. $v(1 - \cos\theta)$ *b.* $\frac{v}{\cos\theta}$
c. $\frac{v}{\sin\theta}$ *d.* $v(1 - \sin\theta)$

27. A toroid of core of inner radius 0.25 m and outer radius 0.26 m around which 3500 turns of a wire are wound. If the current in the wire is 11 A, then magnetic field inside the core of the toroid is

a. 3×10^{2} T *b.* 3×10^{-2} T
c. 3×10^{-7} T *d.* 3×10^{7} T

28. In an electromagnetic wave in free space, the root mean square value of the electric field is $E_{rms} = 6$ V/m. The peak value of the magnetic field is

a. 1.41×10^{-8} T *b.* 2.83×10^{-8} T
c. 0.70×10^{-8} T *d.* 4.23×10^{-8} T

29. The Young's double slit experiment is performed with blue and green light of wavelengths 4360 Å and 5460 Å, respectively. If x is the distance of 4th maximum from the central one, then

a. $x(\text{blue}) = x\ (\text{green})$ *b.* $x\ (\text{blue}) > x\ (\text{green})$
c. $x(\text{blue}) < x\ (\text{green})$ *d.* $\frac{x(\text{blue})}{x(\text{green})} = \frac{5460}{4360}$

30. Three bodies having masses 5 kg, 4 kg and 2 kg is moving at the speed of 5 m/s, 4 m/s and 2 m/s respectively along X-axis. The magnitude of velocity of CM is

a. 1.0 m/s *b.* 4 m/s
c. 0.9 m/s *d.* 1.3 m/s

31. A concave lens of glass of refractive index 1.5 has both surfaces of same radius of curvature R. On immersing it in a medium of refractive index 1.75, it will behave as a

a. convergent lens of focal length 3.5 R
b. convergent lens of focal length 3.0 R
c. divergent lens of focal length 3.5 R
d. divergent lens of focal length 3.0 R

32. Three particles each of mass m gram situated at the vertices of an equilateral triangle ABC of side l cm (as shown in the figure).

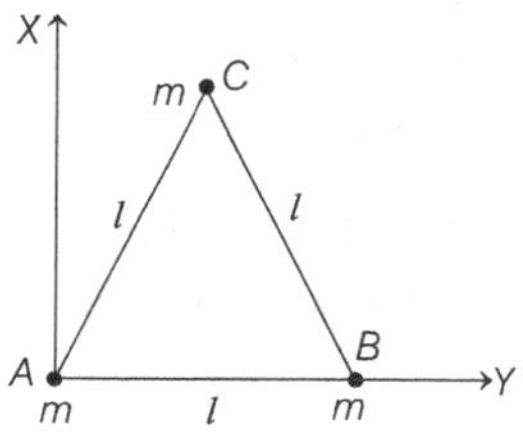

The moment of inertia of the system about a line AX perpendicular to AB and in the plane of ABC (in gcm ^{2}) units will be

a. $\left(\frac{3}{4}\right)ml^2$ *b.* $2ml^2$
c. $\left(\frac{5}{4}\right)ml^2$ *d.* $\left(\frac{3}{2}\right)ml^2$

33. At a certain place, horizontal component is $\sqrt{3}$ times the vertical component. The angle of dip at this place is

a. zero *b.* $\pi/3$
c. $\pi/6$ *d.* None of these

34. A particle moves along the X-axis from $x = 0$ to $x = 5$ m under the influence of a force given by $F = 7 - 2x + 3x^2$. The work done in the process is

a. 70 J *b.* 270 J *c.* 35 J *d.* 135 J

35. The M-H curve for a paramagnetic material is represented by figure.

a. 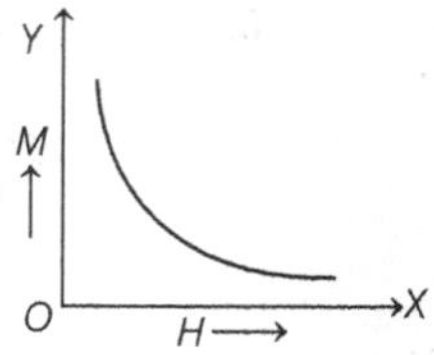

b. 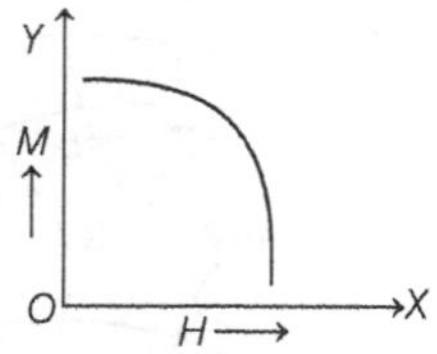

c. 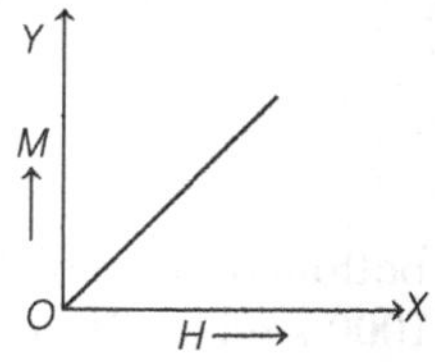

d. 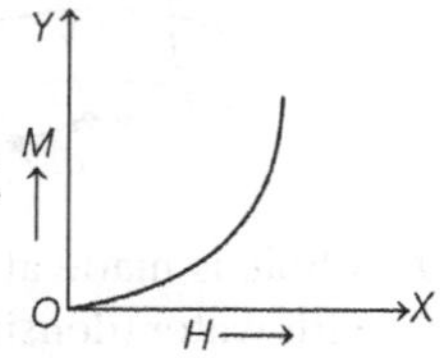

36. The momentum of a body is increased by 20%. The percentage increase in kinetic energy is

a. 54% *b.* 44% *c.* 100% *d.* 50%

37. Figure shows a series L-C-R circuit, connected to a variable frequency source of 200 V with $C = 80\ \mu\text{F}$, $L = 5$ H and $R = 40\ \Omega$. The source frequency which drives the circuit at resonance is

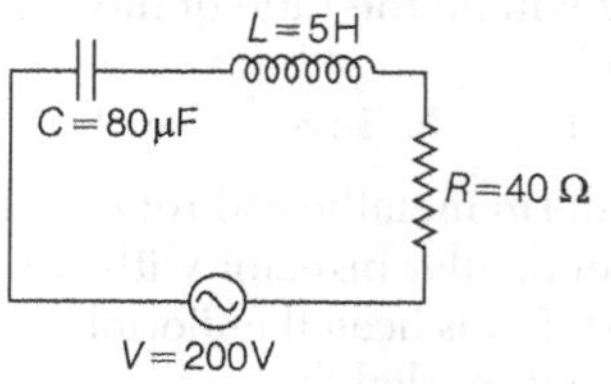

a. 25 Hz *b.* $\frac{25}{\pi}$ Hz
c. 50 Hz *d.* $\frac{50}{\pi}$ Hz

38. A cyclist riding the bicycle at a speed of $14\sqrt{3}$ m/s takes a turn a circular road of radius $20\sqrt{3}$ m without skidding. What is his inclination to the vertical?

a. 30° *b.* 90°
c. 48° *d.* 60°

39. In an AC-circuit, the instantaneous values of emf and current are $\varepsilon = 200 \sin 314t$ V and $I = \sin(314t + \pi/3)$ A. The average power consumed is

a. 200 W *b.* 100 W
c. 50 W *d.* 25 W

40. If the radius of curvature of the path of two particle of same masses are in the ratio 1 : 2, then in order to have constant centripetal force, their velocity should be in the ratio of

a. 1 : 4 *b.* 4 : 1 *c.* 4 : 2 *d.* $1 : \sqrt{2}$

41. Two parallel rails of a railway track insulated from each other and with the ground are connected to a millivoltmeter. The distance between the rails is 1 m. A train is travelling with a velocity of 72 kmh^{-1} along the track. The reading of the millivoltmeter (in mV) is (vertical component of the earth's magnetic induction is 2×10^{-5} T)

a. 1.44 *b.* 0.72
c. 0.4 *d.* 0.2

42. The mass of a lift is 2000 kg. When the tension in the supporting cable is 28000 N, then its acceleration is

a. 30 ms^{-2}, downwards *b.* 4 ms^{-2}, upwards
c. 4 ms^{-2}, downwards *d.* 14 ms^{-2}, upwards

43. An $\angle AOB$ made of a conducting wire moves along its bisector through a magnetic field B as suggested by figure.

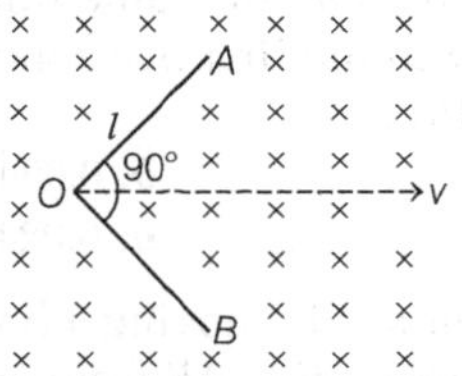

Find the emf induced between A and B, if the magnetic field is perpendicular to the plane of the paper. (where, $AO = BO = l$)

a. $\frac{Bvl}{\sqrt{2}}$ *b.* Bv
c. $\sqrt{2}Blv$ *d.* Blv

44. An explosion breaks a rock into three parts in a horizontal plane. Two of them go off at right angles to each other. The first part of mass 1 kg moves with a speed of 12 ms^{-1} and the second part of mass 2 kg moves with 8 ms^{-1} speed. If the third part flies off with 4 ms^{-1} speed, then its mass is

a. 3 kg *b.* 5 kg
c. 7 kg *d.*17 kg

45. Light of wavelengths λ_A and λ_B falls on two identical metal plates A and B, respectively. The maximum kinetic energy of photoelectrons is K_A and K_B respectively, then which one of the following relations is true? (Take, $\lambda_A = 2\lambda_B$)

a. $K_A < \frac{K_B}{2}$ *b.* $2K_A = K_B$
c. $K_A = 2K_B$ *d.* $K_A > 2K_B$

46. A ball is rolled off along the edge of the table with horizontal with velocity 4 m/s. It hits the ground after time 0.4 s. Which of the following statement is wrong.
($g = 10\ m/s^2$)

a. The height of table is 0.8 m.
b. It hits the ground at an angle of 60° with the vertical.
c. It covers a horizontal distance 1.6 m from the table.
d. It hits the ground with vertical velocity 4 m/s.

47. An hydrogen atom and Li^+ ion are both in the second excited state. If L_H and L_{Li} are their respective electronic angular momentums and E_H and E_{Li} their respective energies, then

a. $L_H > L_{Li}$ and $|E_H|>|E_{Li}|$
b. $L_H = L_{Li}$ and $|E_H|<|E_{Li}|$
c. $L_H = L_{Li}$ and $|E_H|>|E_{Li}|$
d. $L_H > L_{Li}$ and $|E_H|<|E_{Li}|$

48. A particle starting from the origin $O(0, 0)$ moves in a straight line in the XY-plane. Its coordinates at a later time are $(\sqrt{3}, 3)$. The path of the particle makes with the X-axis an angle of

a. 30° *b.* 45° *c.* 60° *d.* 0°

49. Three semiconductors are arranged in the decreasing order of their energy gap as follows. The correct arrangement is

a. tin, germanium, silicon
b. tin, silicon, germanium
c. silicon, germanium, tin
d. silicon, tin, germanium

50. The following figure shows a logic gate circuit with two inputs A and B, and the output C. The voltage waveform of A, B and C are as shown below

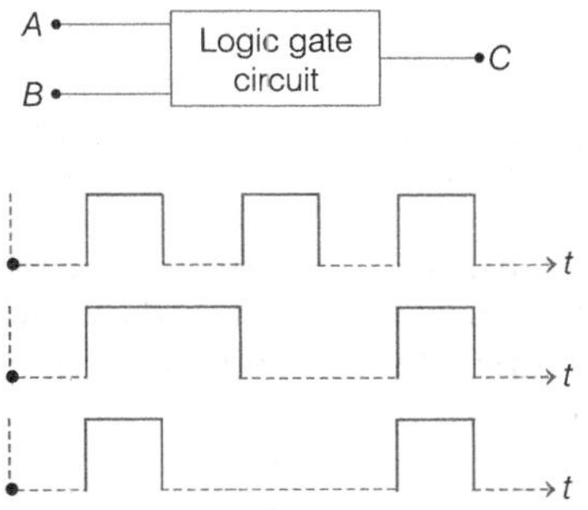

The logic circuit gate is

a. AND gate *b.* NAND gate
c. NOR gate *d.* OR gate

MOCK TEST 1

51. The correct curve between the height or depression h of liquid in a capillary tube and its radius r is

a.
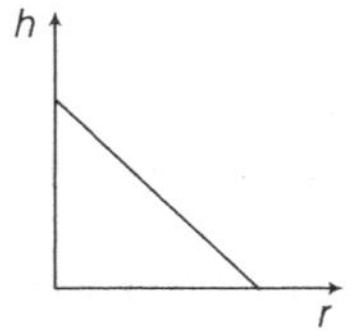

b.
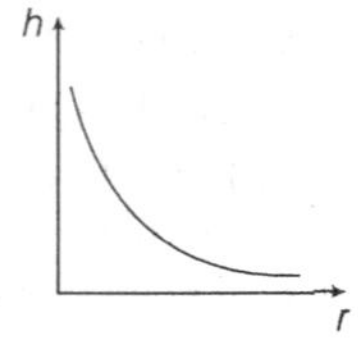

c.
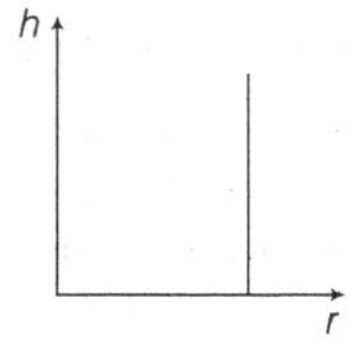

d.
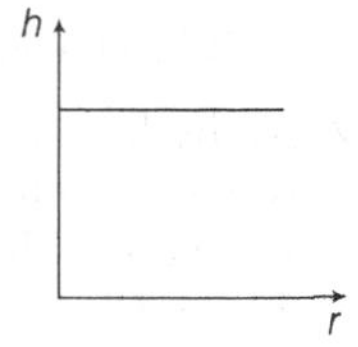

52. Two charges of equal magnitude q are placed in air at a distance $2a$ apart and third charge $-2q$ is placed at mid-point. The potential energy of the system is (ε_0 = permittivity of free space)

a. $-\frac{q^2}{8\pi\varepsilon_0 a}$ *b.* $-\frac{3q^2}{8\pi\varepsilon_0 a}$

c. $-\frac{5q^2}{8\pi\varepsilon_0 a}$ *d.* $-\frac{7q^2}{8\pi\varepsilon_0 a}$

53. Variation of photoelectric current with collector plate potential for different intensities I_1 and I_2 (such that $I_1 > I_2$) at a fixed frequency is

a.
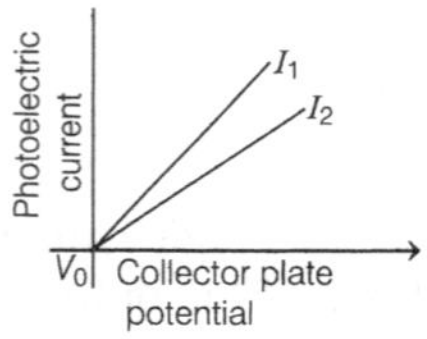

b.
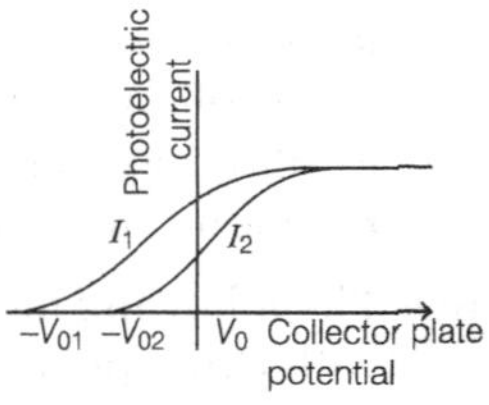

c.
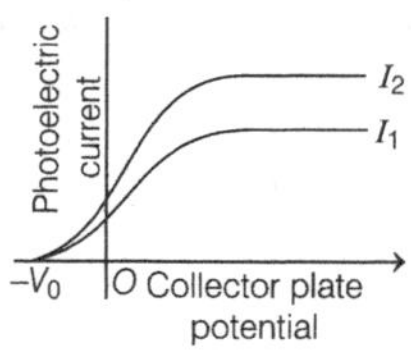

d.
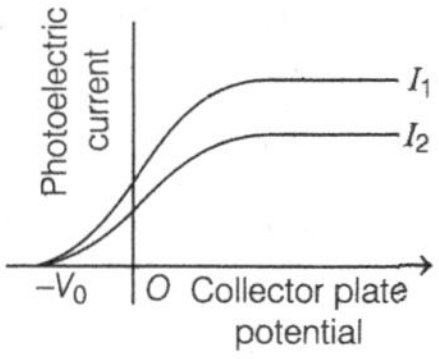

54. A particle starts its motion from rest such that its velocity remains constant. If the distance covered in first 10 s is s_1 and that covered in the first 20 s is s_2, then

a. $s_2 = 2s_1$ *b.* $s_2 = 3s_1$

c. $s_2 = 4s_1$ *d.* $s_2 = s_1$

55. 3 moles of an ideal monoatomic gas performs a cycle as shown in figure. The gas temperatures $T_A = 400$ K, $T_B = 800$ K, $T_C = 2400$ K, $T_D = 1200$ K, work done by the gas is

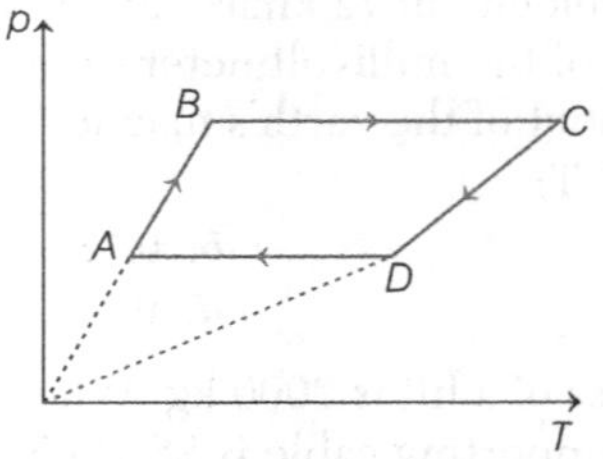

a. 10 kJ *b.* 24 kJ *c.* 30 kJ *d.* 40 kJ

56. In the experiment for the determination of the speed of sound in air using the resonance column method, the length of the air column that resonates in the fundamental mode, with a tuning fork is 0.1 m. When this length is changed to 0.35 m, the same tuning fork resonates with the first overtone. Calculate the end correction.

a. 0.012 m *b.* 0.025 m

c. 0.05 m *d.* 0.024 m

57. Energy required in moving a body of mass m from a distance $2R$ to $4R$ from centre of earth of mass M is

a. $\frac{GMm}{12R^2}$ *b.* $\frac{GMm}{3R^2}$ *c.* $\frac{GMm}{8R}$ *d.* $\frac{GMm}{4R}$

58. One mole of ideal monoatomic gas ($\gamma = 5/3$) is mixed with one mole of diatomic gas ($\gamma = 7/5$). What is γ for the mixture? (γ denotes the ratio of specific heat at constant pressure, to that at constant volume)

a. 3/2 *b.* 23/15 *c.* 35/23 *d.* 4/3

59. The wavelength is 120 cm when the source is stationary. If the source is moving with relative velocity of 60 ms^{-1} towards the observer, then the wavelength of the sound wave reaching to the observer will be

(velocity of sound, $v = 330\ \text{ms}^{-1}$)

a. 98 cm *b.* 140 cm

c. 120 cm *d.* 1440 cm

60. The minimum length of antenna required to transmit a radio signal of frequency 20 MHz is

a. 5 m *b.* 7.5 m

c. 2 m *d.* 3.75 m

CHEMISTRY

61. The increasing order of the density of alkali metals is

a. Li< K< Na< Rb< Cs
b. Li < Na < K < Rb < Cs
c. Cs < Rb < Na < K < Li
d. Cs < Rb < K < Na < Li

62. What will be the final concentration of solution when 2.0 L of 3.0 M sugar solution and 3.0 L of 2.5 M sugar solutions are mixed? If the solution is now diluted to 10 L, what molarity will it have?

a. 5.5 M and 2.7 M *b.* 5.5 M and 1.35 M
c. 2.7 M and 1.35 M *d.* 3.5 M and 2.5 M

63. Consider the following addition reaction,

$$CH_3\underset{\displaystyle CH_3}{\underset{|}{C}}HCH{=}CH_2 + HBr \longrightarrow$$

Select the incorrect statement about this reaction.

a. It follows electrophilic addition mechanism
b. Most stable intermediate is the carbocation, i.e. $CH_3\underset{\displaystyle CH_3}{\underset{|}{C}}H\overset{\oplus}{C}HCH_3$
c. Final product is $(CH_3)_2\underset{\displaystyle Br}{\underset{|}{C}}CH_2CH_3$
d. In presence of benzoyl peroxide, final product is $(CH_3)_2CHCH_2CH_2Br$

64. Identify the wrong statement in the following.

a. Amongst isoelectronic species, smaller the positive charge on the cation, smaller is the ionic radius
b. Amongst isoelectronic species, greater the negative charge on the anion, larger is the ionic radius
c. Atomic radius of the elements increases as one moves down the periodic table
d. Atomic radius of the elements decreases as one moves across from left to right in the 2nd period of the periodic table

65. Haemoglobin contains 0.33% of iron by weight. The molecular weight of haemoglobin is approximately 67200. The number of iron atoms (atomic. weight of Fe is 56) present in one molecule of haemoglobin are

a. 1 *b.* 6
c. 4 *d.* 2

66. Which of the following will not show geometrical isomerism?

a. 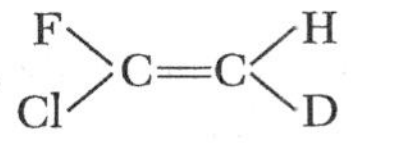
b. 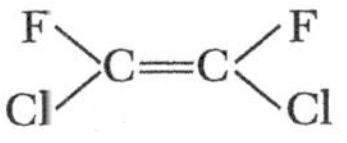
c. 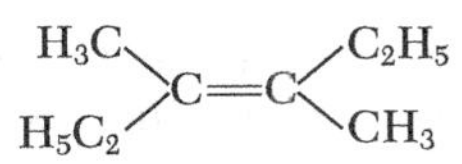
d. 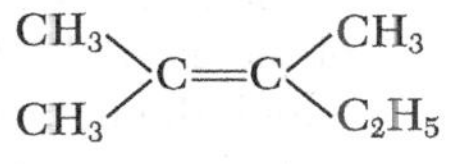

67. If the quantum number l could have the value of n also then Fe(26) would have unpaired electrons

a. 2 *b.* 3 *c.* 4 *d.* 5

68. 800 g of a 40% solution by weight was cooled. 100 g of solute precipitated. The percentage composition of remaining solution is

a. 31.4% *b.* 55.6% *c.* 67.8% *d.* 69.6%

69. The rubber used for manufacturing types is vulcanised with

a. 3% S
b. 7% S
c. 1% S
d. All of these can be used

70. Which ion has the largest radius?

a. Se^{2-} *b.* F^- *c.* O^{2-} *d.* Rb^+

71. 2.9 g of an ideal gas at 368 K occupied the same volume an 0.184 g of H_2 at 290 K. Under isobaric condition. Thus, number of mole of ideal gas taken

a. 0.40 *b.* 0.0725
c. 13.8 *d.* 0.029

72. Total vapour pressure of mixture of 1 mole of volatile component A (p°_A = 100 mm Hg) and 3 moles of volatile component B (p°_B = 60 mm Hg) is 75 mm. For such case

a. there is positive deviation from Raoult's law
b. boiling point has been lowered
c. force of attraction between A and B is smaller than that between A and A or between B and B
d. All the above statements are correct

73. The alkane is not obtained from

a. hydroxylation of ethyne
b. $C_2H_5OH \xrightarrow[150^\circ C]{HI/Red\ P}$
c. butanone $\xrightarrow[Reflux]{Zn\text{-}Hg/HCl}$
d. electrolysis of sodium propanoate solution

74. The value of K_p for the reaction, $2H_2S\,(g) \rightleftharpoons 2H_2(g) + S_2(g)$ is 1.2×10^{-2} at 1065°C. The value for K_C is

a. $< 1.2 \times 10^{-2}$ *b.* $> 1.2 \times 10^{-2}$
c. 1.2×10^{-2} *d.* 0.12×10^{-2}

75. A quantity of gas is confined in a chamber of constant volume. When the chamber is immersed in a bath of melting ice, the pressure of the gas is 1000 Torr. Final temperature at which the pressure barometer indicates an absolute pressure of 400 Torr, is

a. 109 K *b.* 273 K *c.* 373 K *d.* 0 K

76. Which of the following compounds will react with sodium hydroxide solution in water?

a. C_6H_5OH *b.* $C_6H_5CH_2OH$
c. $(CH_3)_3CHO$ *d.* C_2H_5OH

77. Consider the following compounds.

1. $Na_2S_2O_3$ 2. $Na_2S_4O_6$
3. $CaOCl_2$

Among these compounds identify those that have different oxidation states for same type of atoms.

a. Both 1 and 3 *b.* Both 2 and 3
c. Both 1 and 2 *d.* 1, 2 and 3

78. In the complete combustion of C_2H_6, 54 g of H_2O is formed and 370 kcal of heat is evolved. Hence, heat of combustion of C_2H_6 is

a. 370 kcal mol^{-1} *b.* – 370 kcal mol^{-1}
c. – 6.61 kcal mol^{-1} *d.* 6.61 kcal mol^{-1}

79. HI cleaves ether *A* forming

A : 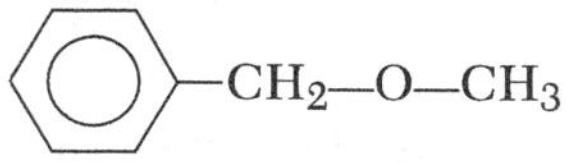

a. 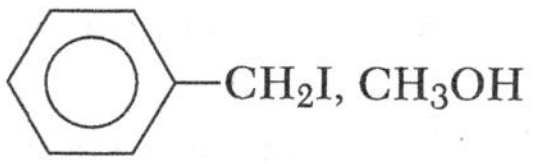

b. 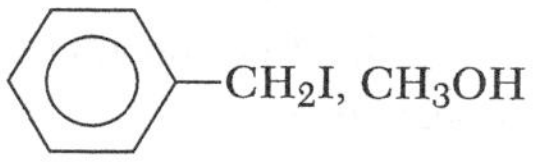

c. 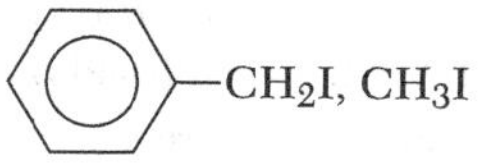

d. 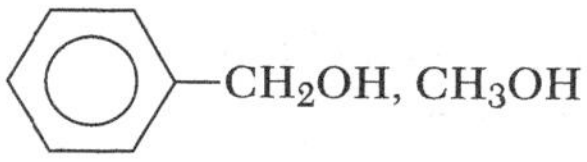

80. The slag obtained during the extraction of copper from copper pyrites is composed of

a. Cu_2S *b.* $CuSiO_3$
c. $FeSiO_3$ *d.* SiO_2

81. The following compound can exhibit

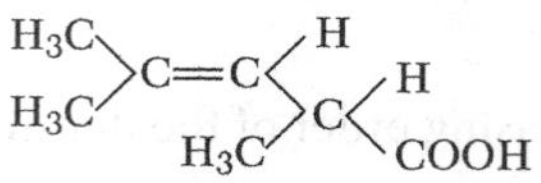

a. geometrical isomerism
b. geometrical and optical isomerism
c. optical isomerism
d. tautomerism

82. $TiCl_4$ is a

a. Bronsted-Lowry acid *b.* Bronsted-Lowry base
c. Lewis acid *d.* Lewis base

83. The reaction of cyanamide, $NH_2CN(s)$ with dioxygen was carried out in a bomb calorimeter, and $\Delta E°$ was found to be –742.7 kJ mol^{-1} at 298 K. Thus, enthalpy change for the reaction at 298 K is

$$NH_2CN\,(g) + 1.5O_2(g) \longrightarrow N_2(g) + CO_2(g) + H_2O(l)$$

a. –741.5 kJ mol^{-1} *b.* –740.4 kJ mol^{-1}
c. –742.7 kJ mol^{-1} *d.* +742.7 kJ mol^{-1}

84. IUPAC name of the following compound is

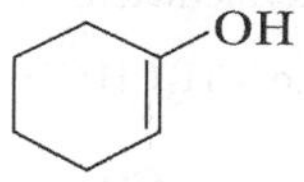

a. 1-cyclohexenol *b.* 2-cyclohexenol
c. 1-cyclohexen-1-ol *d.* 1-cyclohexen-2-ol

85. In the complex $[Pt(O_2)(en)_2(Br)]^{2+}$, coordination number and oxidation number of platinum are

a. 4, 3 *b.* 4, 5 *c.* 4, 6 *d.* 6, 4

86. The number of P—O—P bonds in cyclic metaphosphoric acid is

a. zero *b.* two *c.* three *d.* four

87. Which is hydrolysed at the fastest rate?

a. 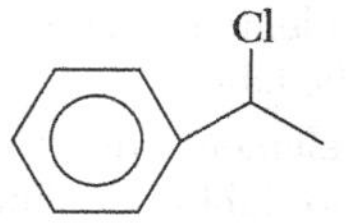

b. 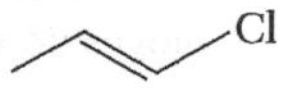

c. 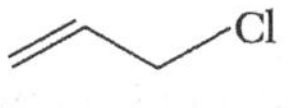

d. 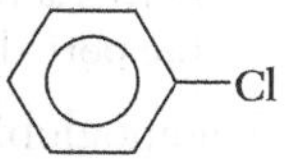

88. In 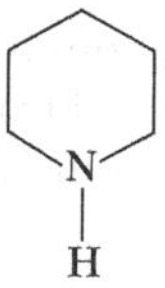

hybrid state of N-atom is

a. sp^2 *b.* sp^3 *c.* sp^3d^2 *d.* sp

MOCK TEST 1

89. For the following equilibrium
$N_2O_4 \rightleftharpoons 2NO_2; K_C = 0.67$.
If we start with 3 moles of NO_2 and 1 mole of N_2O_4 in 1 L flask, then NO_2 present at equilibrium is
a. 1.5 mol *b.* 2.0 mol *c.* 0.5 mol *d.* 1.0 mol

90. Out of following resonance stabilised compounds are

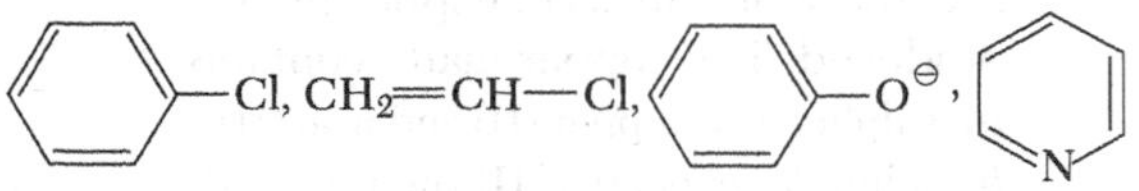

I II III IV

a. Both I and II *b.* I, III and IV
c. I, II, III and IV *d.* II, III and IV

91. Which of the following have identical bond order?
I. CN^- II. O_2^- III. NO^+ IV. CN^+
Choose the correct option.
a. Both I and III *b.* Both II and IV
c. I, II and III *d.* Both I and IV

92. In the electrolysis of aqueous sodium chloride solution which of the half-cell reaction will occur at anode?
a. $Na^+(aq) + e^- \longrightarrow Na(s); E^\ominus_{cell} = -2.71$ V
b. $2H_2O(l) \longrightarrow O_2(g) + 4H^+(aq) + 4e^-$; $E^\ominus_{cell} = -1.23$ V
c. $H^+(aq) + e^- \longrightarrow \frac{1}{2}H_2(g); E^\ominus_{cell} = 0.00$ V
d. $Cl^-(aq) \longrightarrow \frac{1}{2}Cl_2(g) + e^-; E^\ominus_{cell} = 1.36$ V

93. Biochemical oxygen demand (BOD) is a measure of organic material present in water. BOD value less than 5 ppm indicates a water sample to be
a. rich in dissolved oxygen
b. poor in dissolved oxygen
c. highly polluted
d. not suitable for aquatic life

94. Among the following species
$NF_3, NO_3^-, BF_3, H_3O^+, N_3H$
identify the iso-structural pairs.
a. $[NF_3, NO_3^-]$ and $[BF_3, H_3O^+]$
b. $[NF_3, N_3H]$ and $[NO_3^-, BF_3]$
c. $[NF_3, H_3O^+]$ and $[NO_3^-, BF_3]$
d. $[NF_3, H_3O^+]$ and $[N_3H, BF_3]$

95. Relative decrease in vapour pressure of an aqueous NaCl is 0.167. Number of moles of NaCl present in 180 g of H_2O is
a. 2 mol *b.* 1 mol *c.* 3 mol *d.* 4 mol

96. σ-complex formed in the chlorination of benzene is

a. 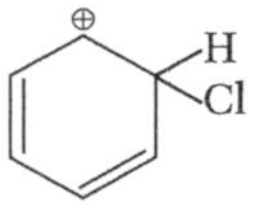

b. 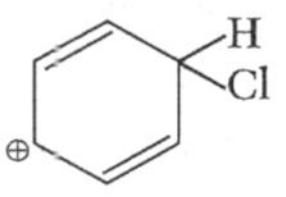

c. 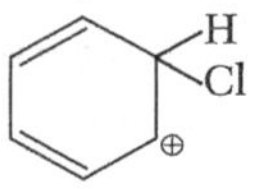

d. All of these

97. $K_2Cr_2O_7 / H^+$ changes to green by
a. Fe^{2+} *b.* SO_2
c. Both Fe^{2+} and SO_2 *d.* CO_2

98. Ice crystallises in a hexagonal lattice having volume of the unit cell as 132×10^{-24} cm^3. If density is 0.92 g cm^{-3} at a given temperature, then number of H_2O molecules per unit cell is
a. 1 *b.* 2 *c.* 3 *d.* 4

99. Which reaction is not expected to occur?
a. $[(CH_3)_2CH]$ CuLi $\xrightarrow{C_2H_5—Br}$
b. $(C_2H_5)_2$—CuLi $\xrightarrow{(CH_3)_3C—Br}$
c. Both (a) and (b)
d. None of the above

100. Which of the following methods would you use to extinguish a fire of Li, Na or K metals?
a. Water *b.* Nitrogen
c. Carbon dioxide *d.* Asbestos blanket

101. Each rubidium halide crystallising in the NaCl type lattice has a unit cell length 0.30 Å greater than that for corresponding potassium salt ($r_{K^+} = 1.33$ Å) of the same halogen. Hence, ionic radius of Rb^+ is
a. 1.18 Å *b.* 1.48 Å *c.* 1.63 Å *d.* 1.03 Å

102. Addition of which of the following reagents to alkene is stereospecific.
I. Br_2
II. $KMnO_4$
III. $BH_3 \cdot THF / H_2O_2 \cdot NaOH$
Select the correct reagents.
a. Both I and II *b.* Both II and III
c. Both I and III *d.* I, II and III

MOCK TEST 1

103. The total number of possible isomers for the complex compound $[Cu^{II}(NH_3)_4][Pt^{II}Cl_4]$

a. 3 *b.* 6
c. 5 *d.* 4

104. What is X in the following reaction?

$$^{226}_{88}Ra \longrightarrow ^{222}_{86}Rn + X$$

a. ^1_1H *b.* ^2_1H
c. ^4_2He *d.* ^3_1H

105. Which statement about aspirin is not true?

a. Aspirin belongs to narcotic analgesics.
b. It is effective in relieving pain.
c. It has antiblood clotting action.
d. It is a neurologically active drug.

106. An olefin on ozonolysis yields a mixture of acetone and methyl ethyl ketone. The possible structure of the olefin is

a. $CH_3C(CH_3){=}C(CH_3)CH_3$ *b.* $C_2H_5C(C_2H_5){=}CH_2$
c. $CH_3C(CH_3){=}C(CH_3)CH_2CH_3$ *d.* $CH_3CH{=}CHCH_3$

107. In a first order reaction, $A \longrightarrow P$, the ratio of $a/(a-x)$ was found to be 8 after 60 min. If the concentration is 0.1 M then the rate of reaction is

a. 2.226×10^{-3} mol L^{-1} min^{-1}
b. 3.466×10^{-3} mol L^{-1} min^{-1}
c. 4.455×10^{-3} mol L^{-1} min^{-1}
d. 5.532×10^{-3} mol L^{-1} min^{-1}

108. In which of the following case benzene is formed?

a. Sodium benzoate is heated with sodalime
b. Calcium benzoate is heated
c. Mixture of calcium benzoate and calcium acetate is heated
d. In all the above cases

109. CH_3CH_2OH on reaction with bleaching powder forms

a. $CHCl_3$ *b.* CCl_3CHO
c. CH_2ClCHO *d.* CCl_4

110. Which of the following elements do not show the properties characteristic of *d*-block elements?

a. Cu, Ag, Au
b. Zn, Hg, Cd
c. Sc, Ti, V
d. Fe, Co, Ni

111. Glycogen is a branched chain polymer of α-D-glucose units in which chain is formed by C_1-C_4 glycosidic linkage, whereas branching occurs by the formation of C_1-C_6 glycosidic linkage. Structure of glycogen is similar to

a. amylose *b.* amylopectin
c. cellulose *d.* glucose

112. When copper ore is mixed with silica in a reverberatory furnace, copper matte is produced. The copper matte contains

a. sulphides of copper (II) and iron (II)
b. sulphides of copper (II) and iron (III)
c. sulphides of copper (I) and iron (II)
d. sulphides of copper (I) and iron (III)

113. For the gas-phase decomposition,

$$PCl_5(g) \rightleftharpoons PCl_3(g) + Cl_2(g)$$

a. $\Delta H < 0, \Delta S < 0$ *b.* $\Delta H > 0, \Delta S > 0$
c. $\Delta H > 0, \Delta S < 0$ *d.* $\Delta H < 0, \Delta S > 0$

114. $[AgI]\,I^-$ colloidal sol can be coagulated by the addition of a suitable cation. 1 mol of $[AgI]\,I^-$ requires mol of $AgNO_3$, $Pb(NO_3)_2$ and $Fe(NO_3)_3$ as

a. 1, 1, 1 *b.* 1, 2, 3 *c.* $1, \frac{1}{2}, \frac{1}{3}$ *d.* 6, 3, 2

115. Which of the following oxides is acidic in nature ?

a. B_2O_3 *b.* Al_2O_3
c. Ga_2O_3 *d.* In_2O_3

116. Identify the strongest and weakest bases among the following and choose the correct code that are given below of these compounds.

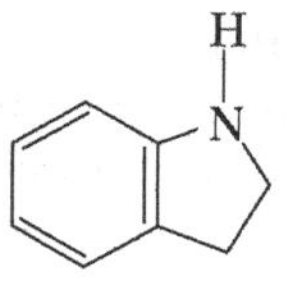
I

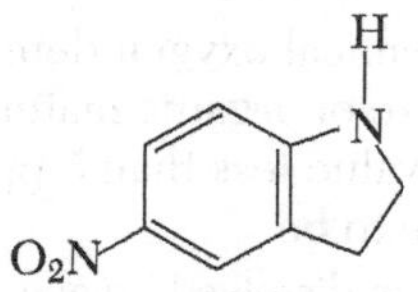
II

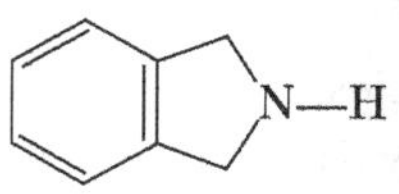
III

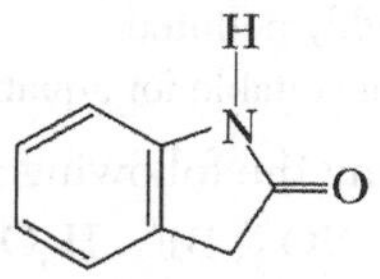
IV

	Strongest	Weakest
a.	IV	I
b.	IV	II
c.	I	IV
d.	III	IV

117. Which of the following enhances leathering property of soap?
a. Sodium carbonate *b.* Sodium rosinate
c. Sodium stearate *d.* Trisodium phosphate

118. Which of the following metals does not liberate hydrogen gas when dil. HCl is added to it?
a. Ag *b.* Zn *c.* Mg *d.* Sn

119. Graph between $\log\left(\frac{x}{m}\right)$ and $\log p$ is a straight line at angle 45° with intercept OA as shown below. Hence, $\left(\frac{x}{m}\right)$ at a pressure of 0.2 atm is

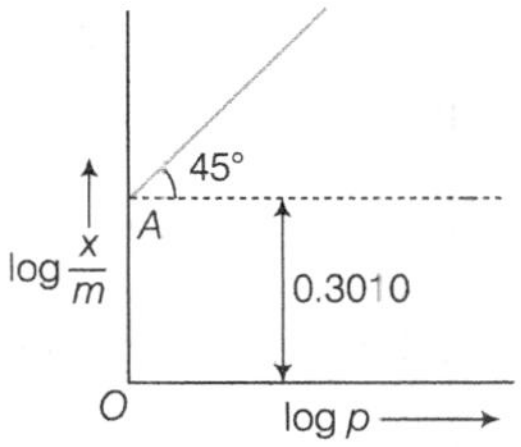

a. 0.2 *b.* 0.4 *c.* 0.6 *d.* 0.8

120. The number of electrons involved in the reduction of one nitrate ion into hydrazine is
a. 7 *b.* 5 *c.* 8 *d.* 4

MATHEMATICS

121. Let $A = R - \{3\}$ and $B = R - \{1\}$. Consider the function $f : A \to B$ defined by $f(x) = \left(\frac{x-2}{x-3}\right)$.
Then, f is
a. injective *b.* bijective
c. surjective *d.* many-one

122. Let $f : N \to S$ be a function defined as $f(x) = 4x^2 + 12x + 15$, where $S \subset R$ is the range of f. Then, inverse of f is
a. $f^{-1}(y) = \frac{\sqrt{y+6} - 3}{2}, y \geq 6$
b. $f^{-1}(y) = \frac{\sqrt{y-6} + 3}{2}, y \geq 6$
c. $f^{-1}(y) = \frac{\sqrt{y-6} - 3}{2}, y \geq 6$
d. $f^{-1}(y) = \frac{\sqrt{y+6} + 3}{2}, y \geq 6$

123. If the function $f : [1, \infty) \to [1, \infty)$ is defined by $f(x) = 2^{x(x-1)}$ is invertible, then $f^{-1}(x)$ is
a. $\left(\frac{1}{2}\right)^{x(x-1)}$ *b.* $\frac{1}{2}(1 + \sqrt{1 + 4\log_2 x})$
c. $\frac{1}{2}(1 - \sqrt{1 + 4\log_2 x})$ *d.* not defined

124. If $\frac{\sin(x+y)}{\sin(x-y)} = \frac{a+b}{a-b}$, then $\frac{\tan x}{\tan y}$ is equal to
a. $\frac{a}{b}$ *b.* $\frac{b}{a}$
c. $2a$ *d.* $2b$

125. The value of
$\cos^4 \frac{\pi}{8} + \cos^4 \frac{3\pi}{8} + \cos^4 \frac{5\pi}{8} + \cos^4 \frac{7\pi}{8}$ is
a. $\frac{1}{\sqrt{2}}$ *b.* $\frac{3}{2}$ *c.* $\frac{1}{2}$ *d.* 0

126. If $\tan \alpha = \frac{m}{m+1}$ and $\tan \beta = \frac{1}{2m+1}$, then $\alpha + \beta$ is equal to
a. $\frac{\pi}{2}$ *b.* $\frac{\pi}{3}$ *c.* $\frac{\pi}{6}$ *d.* $\frac{\pi}{4}$

127. The number of solutions of equation $\tan x + \sec x = 2\cos x$ lying in the interval $[0, 2\pi]$ is
a. 0 *b.* 1 *c.* 2 *d.* 3

128. If for real values of x, $\cos\theta = x + \frac{1}{x}$, then
a. θ is an acute angle
b. θ is right angle
c. θ is an obtuse angle
d. No value of θ is possible

129. The value of tan 22°30′ is
a. 0 *b.* $\frac{1}{\sqrt{2}}$ *c.* $\frac{1}{\sqrt{2}+1}$ *d.* $\frac{1}{\sqrt{2}-1}$

130. The value of the function
$\tan \frac{1}{2}\left[\sin^{-1}\frac{2x}{1+x^2} + \cos^{-1}\frac{1-y^2}{1+y^2}\right]$,
$|x| < 1$, $y > 0$ and $xy < 1$ is
a. $x - y$ *b.* $\frac{x-y}{1+xy}$ *c.* $x + y$ *d.* $\frac{x+y}{1-xy}$

131. If $10^n + 3 \cdot 4^{n+2} + k$ is divisible by 9, for all $n \in N$, then the least positive integral value of k is

a. 5 *b.* 3 *c.* 7 *d.* 1

132. The value of $\sum_{n=1}^{13} (i^n + i^{n+1})$, where $n \in N$ is

a. 0 *b.* i *c.* $i+1$ *d.* $i-1$

133. If the real part of $\frac{\bar{z}+2}{\bar{z}-1}$ is 4, then the locus of the point representing z in the complex plane is a

a. circle *b.* parabola
c. ellipse *d.* hyperbola

134. $\sin x + i\cos 2x$ and $\cos x - i\sin 2x$ are conjugate to each other for

a. $x = n\pi$ *b.* $x = \left(n + \frac{1}{2}\right)\frac{\pi}{2}$
c. $x = 0$ *d.* No value of x

135. A real value of x satisfies the equation $\left(\frac{3-4ix}{3+4ix}\right) = \alpha - i\beta\,(\alpha, \beta \in R)$, if $\alpha^2 + \beta^2$ is equal to

a. 1 *b.* -1 *c.* 2 *d.* -2

136. The total number of words formed by 2 vowels and 3 consonants taken from 4 vowels and 5 consonants is

a. 60 *b.* 120 *c.* 7200 *d.* 720

137. Everybody in a room shakes hands with everybody else. If the total number of hand shakes is 66, then the total number of persons in the room is

a. 11 *b.* 12 *c.* 13 *d.* 14

138. The number of ways in which we can choose a committee from four men and six women, so that the committee includes atleast two men and exactly twice as many women as men is

a. 94 *b.* 126
c. 128 *d.* None of these

139. If the integers $r > 1$, $n > 2$ and coefficients of $(3r)$th and $(r+2)$nd terms in the Binomial expansion of $(1+x)^{2n}$ are equal, then

a. $n = 2r$ *b.* $n = 3r$
c. $n = 2r + 1$ *d.* None of these

140. If the seventh term from the beginning and the end in the expansion of $\left(\sqrt[3]{2} + \frac{1}{\sqrt[3]{3}}\right)^n$ are equal, then n equals

a. 10 *b.* 11 *c.* 12 *d.* 13

141. If x, $2y$ and $3z$ are in AP where the distinct numbers x, y and z are in GP, then the common ratio of the GP is

a. 3 *b.* $\frac{1}{3}$
c. 2 *d.* $\frac{1}{2}$

142. Let S_n denotes the sum of the cubes of the first n natural numbers and s_n denotes the sum of the first n natural numbers, then $\sum_{r=1}^{n} \frac{S_r}{s_4}$ equals

a. $\frac{n(n+1)(n+2)}{6}$ *b.* $\frac{n(n+1)}{2}$
c. $\frac{n^2+3n+2}{2}$ *d.* None of the above

143. The tangent of angle between the lines whose intercepts on the axes are $(a, -b)$ and $(b, -a)$ respectively, is

a. $\frac{a^2-b^2}{ab}$ *b.* $\frac{b^2-a^2}{2}$
c. $\frac{b^2-a^2}{2ab}$ *d.* None of these

144. The distance of the point of intersection of the lines $2x - 3y + 5 = 0$ and $3x + 4y = 0$ from the line $5x - 2y = 0$ is

a. $\frac{130}{17\sqrt{29}}$ *b.* $\frac{13}{7\sqrt{29}}$
c. $\frac{130}{7}$ *d.* None of these

145. The equation of the lines which pass through the point $(3, -2)$ and are inclined at 60° to the line $\sqrt{3}x + y = 1$ is

a. $y + 2 = 0$, $\sqrt{3}x - y - 2 - 3\sqrt{3} = 0$
b. $x - 2 = 0$, $\sqrt{3}x - y + 2 + 3\sqrt{3} = 0$
c. $\sqrt{3}x - y - 2 - 3\sqrt{3} = 0$
d. None of the above

146. Equation of a circle which passes through (3, 6) and touches the axes is

a. $x^2 + y^2 + 6x + 6y + 3 = 0$
b. $x^2 + y^2 - 6x - 6y - 9 = 0$
c. $x^2 + y^2 - 6x - 6y + 9 = 0$
d. None of the above

147. The equation of a circle with origin as centre and passing through the vertices of an equilateral triangle whose median is of length $3a$ is

a. $x^2 + y^2 = 9a^2$ *b.* $x^2 + y^2 = 16a^2$
c. $x^2 + y^2 = 4a^2$ *d.* $x^2 + y^2 = a^2$

148. If the vertex of the parabola is the point $(-3, 0)$ and the directrix is the line $x + 5 = 0$, then its equation is

a. $y^2 = 8(x+3)$ *b.* $x^2 = 8(y+3)$
c. $y^2 = -8(x+3)$ *d.* $y^2 = 8(x+5)$

149. If the line $y = mx + 1$ is tangent to the parabola $y^2 = 4x$, then the value of m is

a. 0 *b.* 1 *c.* 2 *d.* 3

150. If equation of the ellipse whose focus is $(1, -1)$, then directrix the line $x - y - 3 = 0$ and eccentricity $\frac{1}{2}$ is

a. $7x^2 + 2xy + 7y^2 - 10x + 10y + 7 = 0$
b. $7x^2 + 2xy + 7y^2 + 7 = 0$
c. $7x^2 + 2xy + 7y^2 + 10x - 10y - 7 = 0$
d. None of the above

151. If the eccentricity of an ellipse is $\frac{5}{8}$ and the distance between its foci is 10, then the latusrectum of the ellipse is

a. 39 *b.* $\frac{39}{4}$ *c.* $\frac{39}{2}$ *d.* $\frac{39}{8}$

152. The eccentricity of the hyperbola whose latusrectum is 8 and conjugate axis is equal to half of the distance between the foci is

a. $\frac{4}{3}$ *b.* $\frac{4}{\sqrt{3}}$
c. $\frac{2}{\sqrt{3}}$ *d.* None of these

153. The coordinates of a point on the line $\frac{x+2}{3} = \frac{y+1}{2} = \frac{z-3}{2}$ at a distance of $\frac{6}{\sqrt{2}}$ from the point $(1, 2, 3)$ is

a. (56, 43, 111) *b.* $\left(\frac{56}{17}, \frac{43}{17}, \frac{111}{17}\right)$
c. (2, 1, 3) *d.* (−2, −1, −3)

154. $\lim_{x \to 0} \left(\sin mx \cot \frac{x}{\sqrt{3}} \right) = 2$, then m is equal to

a. $2\sqrt{3}$ *b.* $\frac{2\sqrt{3}}{5}$ *c.* $\frac{2\sqrt{3}}{3}$ *d.* $\frac{2\sqrt{3}}{7}$

155. If $f(x) = \begin{cases} \dfrac{\sin^3(\sqrt{x}) \log(1+3x)}{(\tan^{-1}\sqrt{x})^2 (e^{5\sqrt{x}} - 1)x}, & x \neq 0 \\ a, & x = 0 \end{cases}$

is continuous in [0, 1], then

a. $a = 0$ *b.* $a = \frac{3}{5}$ *c.* $a = 2$ *d.* $a = \frac{5}{3}$

156. If $f(x) = \frac{x^n - a^n}{x - a}$ for some constant a, then $f'(a)$ is equal to

a. 1 *b.* 0
c. $\frac{1}{2}$ *d.* Does not exist

157. $\frac{d}{dx}\left[\log\left\{e^x \left(\frac{x-2}{x+2}\right)\right\}^{3/4}\right]$ is equal to

a. 1 *b.* $\frac{x^2+1}{x^2-4}$
c. $\frac{x^2-1}{x^2-4}$ *d.* $e^x \frac{x^2-1}{x^2-4}$

158. If $\cos\frac{x}{2}\cos\frac{x}{2^2}\cos\frac{x}{2^3}\ldots\cos\frac{x}{2^n} = f(x)$,

then $\frac{1}{2}\tan\frac{x}{2} + \frac{1}{2^2}\tan\frac{x}{2^2} + \ldots + \frac{1}{2^n}\tan\frac{x}{2^n}$ is equal to

a. $\frac{f'(x)}{f(x)}$ *b.* $\frac{f(x)}{f'(x)}$ *c.* $\frac{-f'(x)}{f(x)}$ *d.* 0

159. If $y = |\sin x|^{|x|}$, then the value of $\frac{dy}{dx}$ at $x = -\frac{\pi}{6}$ is

a. $\frac{2^{-\frac{\pi}{6}}}{6}[6\log 2 - \sqrt{3}\pi]$ *b.* $\frac{2^{\frac{\pi}{6}}}{6}[6\log 2 + \sqrt{3}\pi]$
c. $\frac{2^{-\frac{\pi}{6}}}{6}[6\log 2 + \sqrt{3}\pi]$ *d.* None of the above

160. Let $f''(x) = -f(x)$, where $f(x)$ is a continuous double differentiable function and $g(x) = f'(x)$.

If $F(x) = \left[f\left(\frac{x}{2}\right)\right]^2 + \left[g\left(\frac{x}{2}\right)\right]^2$ and $F(5) = 5$, then $F(10)$ is

a. 0 *b.* 5 *c.* 10 *d.* 25

161. The function f given by $f(x) = 2x^2 - 3x$, is

a. strictly increasing in the interval $\left(\frac{3}{4}, \infty\right)$
b. strictly decreasing in the interval $\left(-\infty, \frac{3}{4}\right)$
c. Both (a) and (b) are true
d. Both (a) and (b) are false

162. The least value of a, such that the function f given by $f(x) = x^2 + ax + 1$ is strictly increasing on (1, 2), is

a. −1 *b.* −2 *c.* 0 *d.* 1

163. If $\frac{d}{dx}\{f(x)\} = \frac{1}{1+x^2}$, then $\frac{d}{dx}\{f(x^3)\}$ is equal to

a. $\frac{3x}{1+x^3}$ *b.* $\frac{3x^2}{1+x^6}$

c. $\frac{-6x^5}{(1+x^6)^2}$ *d.* $\frac{-6x^5}{1+x^6}$

164. $\int \frac{[10x^9 + 10^x \log_e 10]\,dx}{x^{10}+10^x}$ equals

a. $10^x - x^{10} + C$ *b.* $10^x + x^{10} + C$

c. $(10^x - x^{10})^{-1} + C$ *d.* $\log|10^x + x^{10}| + C$

165. $\int \frac{dx}{\sin^2 x \cos^2 x}$ equals

a. $\tan x + \cot x + C$ *b.* $\tan x - \cot x + C$

c. $\tan x \cot x + C$ *d.* $\tan x - \cot 2x + C$

166. $\int \frac{\sqrt{x}}{\sqrt{a^3 - x^3}}\,dx$ is equal to

a. $\frac{1}{3}\sin^{-1}\sqrt{\frac{x^3}{a^3}} + C$ *b.* $\frac{2}{3}\sin^{-1}\sqrt{\frac{x^3}{a^3}} + C$

c. $\frac{2}{3}\sin^{-1}\sqrt{\frac{x}{a}} + C$ *d.* None of the above

167. $\int \frac{dx}{x(x^2+1)}$ is equal to

a. $\log|x| - \frac{1}{2}\log(x^2+1) + C$

b. $\log|x| + \frac{1}{2}\log(x^2+1) + C$

c. $-\log|x| + \frac{1}{2}\log(x^2+1) + C$

d. $\frac{1}{2}\log|x| + \log(x^2+1) + C$

168. $\int \frac{x + \sin x}{1 + \cos x}\,dx$ is equal to

a. $\log|1 + \cos x| + C$

b. $\log|x + \sin x| + C$

c. $x - \tan x/2 + C$

d. $x \tan\left(\frac{x}{2}\right) + C$

169. Limit of

$$\int_0^x \left[\frac{1}{\sqrt{1+t^2}} - \frac{1}{1+t}\right] dt \text{ as } x \to \infty \text{ is}$$

a. $\log_2 e$ *b.* $\log_e 2$

c. $\log_2\left(\frac{1}{e}\right)$ *d.* $\log_{1/e} 2$

170. The area bounded by $y = -x^2 + 2x + 3$ and $y = 0$ is

a. 32 sq units *b.* $\frac{32}{3}$ sq units

c. $\frac{1}{32}$ sq unit *d.* $\frac{1}{3}$ sq unit

171. The function $y = \sqrt{a^2 - x^2}$, $x \in (-a, a)$ is the solution of the differential equation

a. $x + y\frac{dy}{dx} = 0\ (y \neq 0)$ *b.* $y + x\frac{dy}{dx} = 0\ (x \neq 0)$

c. $x - y\frac{dy}{dx} = 0\ (y \neq 0)$ *d.* $y - x\frac{dy}{dx} = 0\ (x \neq 0)$

172. The differential equation of the family of circles with fixed radius 5 units and centre on the line $y = 2$ is

a. $(x-2)^2 y'^2 = 25 - (y-2)^2$

b. $(x-2)(y')^2 = 25 - (y-2)^2$

c. $(y-2)(y')^2 = 25 - (y-2)^2$

d. $(y-2)^2 (y')^2 = 25 - (y-2)^2$

173. If **a** is a vector of magnitude 50, collinear with the vector $\mathbf{b} = 6\mathbf{i} - 8\mathbf{j} - \frac{15}{2}\mathbf{k}$ and makes an acute angle with the positive direction of Z-axis, then **a** is equal to

a. $-24\mathbf{i} + 32\mathbf{j} + 30\mathbf{k}$ *b.* $24\mathbf{i} - 32\mathbf{j} - 30\mathbf{k}$

c. $-12\mathbf{i} + 16\mathbf{j} - 15\mathbf{k}$ *d.* $12\mathbf{i} - 16\mathbf{j} - 15\mathbf{k}$

174. If $2\mathbf{a} + 3\mathbf{b} - 5\mathbf{c} = 0$, then the ratio in which **c** divides **AB** is

a. 3 : 2 internally *b.* 3 : 2 externally

c. 2 : 3 internally *d.* 2 : 3 externally

175. Let $A = \begin{bmatrix} 1 & -1 & 1 \\ 2 & 1 & -3 \\ 1 & 1 & 1 \end{bmatrix}$ and $10B = \begin{bmatrix} 4 & 2 & 2 \\ -5 & 0 & \alpha \\ 1 & -2 & 3 \end{bmatrix}$.

If B is the inverse of matrix A, then α is equal to

a. -2 *b.* 1 *c.* 2 *d.* 5

176. If A is a square matrix such that $A^2 = I$, then $(A-I)^3 + (A+I)^3 - 7A$ is equal to

a. A *b.* $I - A$

c. $I + A$ *d.* $3A$

177. If $\Delta = \begin{vmatrix} b^2c^2 & bc & b+c \\ c^2a^2 & ca & c+a \\ a^2b^2 & ab & a+b \end{vmatrix}$, then Δ is equal to

a. abc *b.* a^2b^2 *c.* 0 *d.* $-ab$

178. Given that, A and B are two events such that $P(B)=\frac{3}{5}$, $P(A/B)=\frac{1}{2}$ and $P(A\cup B)=\frac{4}{5}$. Then, $P(A)$ is equal to

a. $\frac{3}{10}$ *b.* $\frac{1}{5}$

c. $\frac{1}{2}$ *d.* $\frac{3}{5}$

179. The negation of the statement "72 is divisible by 2 and 3" is

a. 72 is not divisible by 2 or 72 is not divisible by 3
b. 72 is not divisible by 2 and 72 is not divisible by 3
c. 72 is divisible by 2 and 72 is not divisible by 3
d. 72 is not divisible by 2 and 72 is divisible by 3

180. The maximum value of $Z=4x+3y$, if the feasible region for an LPP is shown in following figure, is

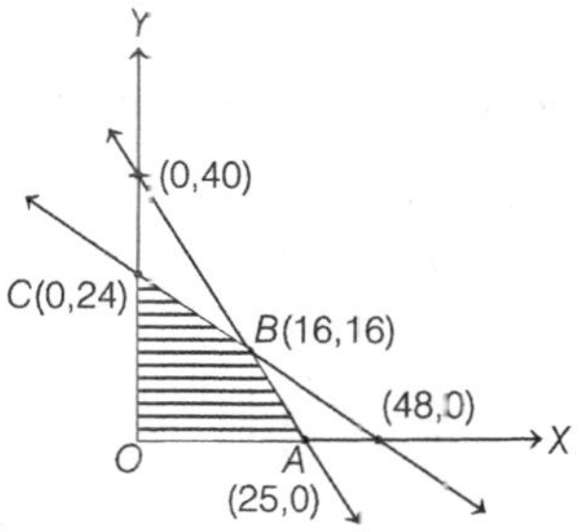

a. 112 *b.* 100 *c.* 72 *d.* 110

ANSWERS

Physics

1. (a)	**2.** (b)	**3.** (c)	**4.** (b)	**5.** (d)	**6.** (b)	**7.** (b)	**8.** (b)	**9.** (a)	**10.** (a)
11. (b)	**12.** (b)	**13.** (a)	**14.** (c)	**15.** (c)	**16.** (c)	**17.** (a)	**18.** (a)	**19.** (b)	**20.** (b)
21. (a)	**22.** (a)	**23.** (c)	**24.** (a)	**25.** (c)	**26.** (c)	**27.** (b)	**28.** (b)	**29.** (c)	**30.** (b)
31. (a)	**32.** (c)	**33.** (c)	**34.** (d)	**35.** (c)	**36.** (b)	**37.** (b)	**38.** (d)	**39.** (c)	**40.** (d)
41. (c)	**42.** (b)	**43.** (c)	**44.** (b)	**45.** (a)	**46.** (b)	**47.** (b)	**48.** (c)	**49.** (c)	**50.** (a)
51. (b)	**52.** (d)	**53.** (d)	**54.** (c)	**55.** (b)	**56.** (b)	**57.** (d)	**58.** (a)	**59.** (a)	**60.** (d)

Chemistry

61. (a)	**62.** (c)	**63.** (b)	**64.** (a)	**65.** (c)	**66.** (d)	**67.** (a)	**68.** (a)	**69.** (b)	**70.** (a)
71. (b)	**72.** (d)	**73.** (a)	**74.** (a)	**75.** (a)	**76.** (a)	**77.** (d)	**78.** (b)	**79.** (b)	**80.** (c)
81. (c)	**82.** (c)	**83.** (a)	**84.** (c)	**85.** (d)	**86.** (c)	**87.** (a)	**88.** (b)	**89.** (b)	**90.** (c)
91. (a)	**92.** (d)	**93.** (a)	**94.** (c)	**95.** (b)	**96.** (d)	**97.** (c)	**98.** (d)	**99.** (a)	**100.** (d)
101. (b)	**102.** (d)	**103.** (a)	**104.** (c)	**105.** (a)	**106.** (c)	**107.** (b)	**108.** (a)	**109.** (a)	**110.** (b)
111. (b)	**112.** (a)	**113.** (b)	**114.** (c)	**115.** (a)	**116.** (d)	**117.** (b)	**118.** (a)	**119.** (b)	**120.** (a)

Mathematics

121. (b)	**122.** (c)	**123.** (b)	**124.** (a)	**125.** (b)	**126.** (d)	**127.** (c)	**128.** (d)	**129.** (c)	**130.** (d)
131. (a)	**132.** (d)	**133.** (a)	**134.** (d)	**135.** (a)	**136.** (c)	**137.** (b)	**138.** (a)	**139.** (a)	**140.** (c)
141. (b)	**142.** (a)	**143.** (c)	**144.** (a)	**145.** (a)	**146.** (c)	**147.** (c)	**148.** (a)	**149.** (b)	**150.** (a)
151. (b)	**152.** (c)	**153.** (b)	**154.** (c)	**155.** (b)	**156.** (d)	**157.** (c)	**158.** (c)	**159.** (a)	**160.** (b)
161. (c)	**162.** (b)	**163.** (b)	**164.** (d)	**165.** (b)	**166.** (b)	**167.** (a)	**168.** (d)	**169.** (b)	**170.** (b)
171. (a)	**172.** (d)	**173.** (a)	**174.** (a)	**175.** (d)	**176.** (a)	**177.** (c)	**178.** (c)	**179.** (a)	**180.** (a)

HINTS & SOLUTIONS

Physics

1. *(a)* According to Rydberg's formula, $\frac{1}{\lambda} = R\left(\frac{1}{n_f^2} - \frac{1}{n_i^2}\right)$

Here, $n_f = 1$, $n_i = n$

$$\frac{1}{\lambda} = R\left(\frac{1}{1^2} - \frac{1}{n^2}\right)$$

$$\frac{1}{\lambda} = R\left(1 - \frac{1}{n^2}\right) \quad \text{...(i)}$$

$$\Rightarrow \quad \frac{R}{n^2} = R - \frac{1}{\lambda} \Rightarrow n = \sqrt{\frac{\lambda R}{\lambda R - 1}}$$

2. *(b)* From equation of motion, we have

$$s = ut + \frac{1}{2}at^2$$

where, u is initial velocity, t is time and a is acceleration.

Since, car accelerates from rest $u = 0$, $t = 10$s

$$\therefore s = 0 + \frac{1}{2} \times a \times (10)^2 = 50a \Rightarrow a = \frac{s}{50} \quad \text{...(i)}$$

Also, $v = u + at$

where, v is final velocity.

$\therefore$ Velocity after 10 s is

$$v = 0 + a \times 10$$

$$= 10a = 10 \times \frac{s}{50} \quad \text{...(ii)}$$

In the next 10 s, car moves with constant acceleration and with initial velocity v.

$$\therefore \quad s' = vt + \frac{1}{2}at^2$$

$$s' = \frac{s}{50} \times 10 \times 10 + \frac{1}{2} \times \frac{s}{50} \times 100 = 3s$$

Given, $s = x$ and $s' = y$

$\therefore \quad y = 3x$

3. *(c)* Fraction of radioactive substance remains undecayed $= \frac{N}{N_0} = \left(\frac{1}{2}\right)^n$

where, $n = t / T_{1/2}$

$$\Rightarrow \quad N = N_0 \left(\frac{1}{2}\right)^{\frac{t}{T_{1/2}}}$$

Given, $T_{1/2} = 12.5$ yr, $t = 25$ yr

$$\Rightarrow \quad N = N_0\left(\frac{1}{2}\right)^{\left(\frac{25}{12.5}\right)}$$

$$N = N_0\left(\frac{1}{2}\right)^2$$

$$\frac{N}{N_0} = \frac{1}{4}$$

Thus, fraction of sample (N / N_0) remaining undecayed after 25 yr will be $\frac{1}{4}$.

4. *(b)* Given, time period, $T = 2\pi\sqrt{\frac{L}{g}}$

Thus, changes can be expressed as $= \frac{2\Delta T}{T} = \pm\frac{\Delta L}{L} \pm \frac{\Delta g}{g}$

According to the question, we can write

$$\frac{\Delta L}{L} = \frac{0.1 \text{ cm}}{20.0 \text{ cm}} = \frac{1}{200}$$

Again, time period, $T = \frac{90}{100}$ s and

$$\Delta T = \frac{1}{200} \text{s} \Rightarrow \frac{\Delta T}{T} = \frac{1}{90}$$

$$\therefore \quad \frac{\Delta g}{g} = \frac{\Delta L}{L} + \frac{2\Delta T}{T}$$

or

$$\frac{\Delta g}{g} \times 100\% = \left(\frac{\Delta L}{L}\right) \times 100\% + \left(\frac{2\Delta T}{T}\right) \times 100\%$$

$$= \left(\frac{1}{200} \times 100\right)\% + 2 \times \frac{1}{90} \times 100\%$$

$$= 2.72\% = 3\%$$

Thus, accuracy in the determination of g is approximately 3 %.

5. *(d)* We know that,

Number of undecayed nuclei, $N = N_0 e^{-\lambda t}$

where, N_0 = number of nuclei at $t = 0$

and decay rate, $R = R_0 e^{-\lambda t}$

where, $R_0 = \lambda N_0$ is the decay rate at $t = 0$.

$$\Rightarrow \quad R = \lambda N_0 e^{-\lambda t}$$

$\therefore$ Number of decayed nuclei,

$$N_{\text{decayed}} = N_0 - N = N_0 - N_0 e^{-\lambda t}$$

$$= N_0 - \frac{R}{\lambda}$$

This represents equation of a straight line with negative slope. So, graph between N and R is correctly depicted in option (d).

6. *(b)* According to homogeneity principle,

$$[F] = [6\pi\eta^a r^b v^c]$$

or $[MLT^{-2}] = [ML^{-1}T^{-1}]^a \, [L]^b [LT^{-1}]^c$

or $[MLT^{-2}] = [\, M^a \, L^{-a+b+c} T^{-a-c}]$

Equating the coefficients and powers, we get

$\therefore \quad a = 1, -a + b + c = 1$

and $\quad -a - c = -2$

After solving $a = 1$, $b = 1$, $c = 1$

7. *(b)* Increase in kinetic energy = Decrease in potential energy

$$\therefore \quad \frac{1}{2}mv^2 = \frac{mgR}{1+R/R} = \frac{mgR}{2} \quad \left(\Delta U = \frac{mgh}{1+h/R} \right)$$

$$\Rightarrow \quad \frac{1}{2}mv^2 = \frac{mgR}{2} \Rightarrow v = \sqrt{gR}$$

8. *(b)* The p-V diagram for isobaric, isothermal and adiabatic process of an ideal gas is shown in graph below.

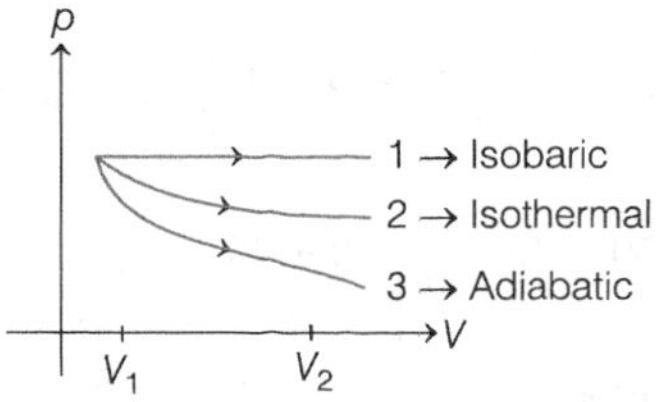

In thermodynamics, for same change in volume, the work done is maximum for the curve having maximum area enclosed (isobaric) with the volume axis.

9. *(a)* Let equation of a SHM is represented by

$$y = a \sin \omega t$$

$$v = \frac{dy}{dt} = a\,\omega \cos \omega t$$

$$\Rightarrow \quad v_{max} = a\omega = 30 \quad \text{...(i)}$$

$$\text{Acceleration, } a = \frac{dy^2}{dt^2} = -a\omega^2 \sin \omega t$$

$$a_{max} = \omega^2 a = 60 \quad \text{...(ii)}$$

From Eqs. (i) and (ii), we get

$$\omega(\omega a) = 60 \Rightarrow \omega(30) = 60 \Rightarrow \omega = 2 \text{ rad s}^{-1}$$

$$\Rightarrow \quad \frac{2\pi}{T} = 2 \text{ rad s}^{-1} \Rightarrow T = \pi \text{ s}$$

10. *(a)* From i-V graph, we find that

$$(\text{Slope})_2 > (\text{Slope})_1$$

$$\Rightarrow \quad \frac{1}{R_2} > \frac{1}{R_1} \quad \left[\frac{i}{V} = \frac{1}{R} \right]$$

$$\Rightarrow \quad R_1 > R_2$$

As R_1 and R_2 are directly proportional to the T_1 and T_2, respectively.

$$\Rightarrow \quad T_1 > T_2$$

11. *(b)* $T = 2\pi \sqrt{\frac{l}{g}}$ or $T^2 \propto l$

i.e. T-l graph is a parabola.

12. *(b)* Given, $R = (47 \pm 4.7)\ \text{k}\Omega = 47 \times 10^3 \Omega \pm 10\%\ \Omega$

As per the colour code for carbon resistors, the colour assigned to numbers are as

4 → Yellow
7 → Violet
10^3 → Orange
10% → Silver

Hence, the bands of colour on carbon resistor in sequence are, yellow violet, orange and silver.

13. *(a)* Elongation of the wire, $\Delta l = \frac{Fl}{AY}$ (can also be applied for a spring)

$$\therefore \quad \Delta l \propto l$$

$$\frac{7.5}{5.0} = \frac{60}{l_2}$$

$$\Rightarrow \quad l_2 = 40 \text{ cm}$$

∴ Length of original spring is (60 + 40) cm = 100 cm

$$\text{Now,} \quad \frac{x}{7.5} = \frac{100}{60}$$

$$\therefore \quad x = 12.5 \text{ cm}$$

14. *(c)* Initially, $C_0 = \frac{\varepsilon_0 A}{d} = 18\mu\text{F}$ ...(i)

When $d' = 3d$ and a dielectric medium is introduced,

$$C = \frac{K\varepsilon_0 A}{3d} = 72\mu\text{F} \quad \text{...(ii)}$$

On dividing Eq. (ii) by Eq. (i), we get

$$\frac{K}{3} = \frac{72}{18} = 4$$

∴ Dielectric constant, $K = 12$

15. *(c)* As, $B = \frac{-\Delta p}{\Delta V / V}$

$$\therefore \quad \frac{\Delta V}{V} = \frac{\Delta p}{B} = \frac{10^5}{1.25 \times 10^{11}} = 8 \times 10^{-7}$$

16. *(c)* The field lines are perpendicular to the equipotential surfaces. So, in the given figure, this condition, is correctly depicted in option (c) only.

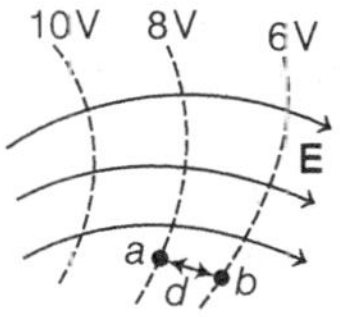

17. *(a)* Neglecting gravitational head, difference in pressure energy per unit volume = difference in kinetic energy per unit volume

$$\therefore \quad (3p_0 - p_0) = \frac{1}{2}\rho v^2 \text{ or } v = 2\sqrt{\frac{p_0}{\rho}} = 2\sqrt{\frac{10^5}{10^3}}$$

[where, p_0 = atmospheric pressure = 10^5 N/m^2]

$$= 20 \text{ ms}^{-1} \text{ or } \sqrt{400} \text{ ms}^{-1}$$

18. *(a)* According to Gauss's law, electric flux passing through a closed surface is equal to $\frac{1}{\varepsilon_0}$ times the charge q enclosed by the surface,

$$\text{i.e.} \quad \phi = \frac{q}{\varepsilon_0}$$

Since, cube and sphere both enclose same charge, therefore flux passing through cube and sphere is same, i.e. $\phi_{sphere} = \phi_{cube}$

$\therefore \quad \phi_{sphere} : \phi_{cube} = 1:1$

19. *(b)* As the rod is heated, it expands. No external torque is acting on the system, so angular momentum should be conserved.

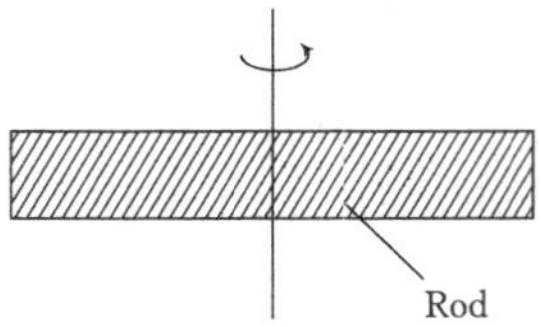

L = angular momentum,

$= I\omega = \text{constant} \Rightarrow I_1\omega_1 = I_2\omega_2$

Due to expansion of the rod, $I_2 > I_1$

$$\Rightarrow \quad \frac{\omega_2}{\omega_1} = \frac{I_1}{I_2} < 1 \quad \Rightarrow \quad \omega_2 < \omega_1$$

So, angular velocity (speed of rotation) decreases.

20. *(b)* Relative permittivity ε_r is also called dielectric constant K.

The force between charges in air is

$$F_{air} = \frac{1}{4\pi\varepsilon_0} \cdot \frac{q_1 q_2}{r^2} \quad \ldots(i)$$

The force between charges in a medium of dielectric constant K,

$$F_{medium} = \frac{1}{4\pi\varepsilon_0 K} \cdot \frac{q_1 q_2}{r^2} \quad \ldots(ii)$$

On dividing Eq. (i) by Eq. (ii), we get

$$\Rightarrow \quad \frac{F_{air}}{F_{medium}} = \frac{\frac{1}{4\pi\varepsilon_0} \cdot \frac{q_1 q_2}{r^2}}{\frac{1}{4\pi\varepsilon_0 K} \cdot \frac{q_1 q_2}{r^2}} = \frac{K}{1}$$

So, the ratio of the forces between two small spheres is $K : 1$.

21. *(a)* Since, $v_{rms} = \sqrt{\frac{3RT}{M}}$

$$\Rightarrow \quad T = \frac{Mv_{rms}^2}{3R}$$

$$\Rightarrow \quad T \propto M \qquad (\because v_{rms} \text{ and } R = \text{constant})$$

$$\Rightarrow \quad \frac{T_{H_2}}{T_{O_2}} = \frac{M_{H_2}}{M_{O_2}} \Rightarrow \frac{T_{H_2}}{(273+47)} = \frac{2}{32}$$

$$\Rightarrow \quad T_{H_2} = \frac{2}{32} \times T_{O_2} = \frac{2}{32} \times 320 = 20 \text{ K}$$

$$[\; T_{O_2} = 47 + 273 = 320 \text{ K}]$$

22. *(a)* Given, distance between source and screen, $D = 2\,\text{m}$

Distance of 5th dark fringe from centre $= 4\text{mm} = 4 \times 10^{-3}\text{m}$

Wavelength, $\lambda = 600 \text{ nm} = 6 \times 10^{-7}$ m

Distance of 5th dark fringe from centre

$$= \beta + \beta + \beta + \beta + \frac{\beta}{2} = \frac{9\beta}{2}$$

where, β = fringe width.

$$\frac{9B}{2} = 4 \times 10^{-3}$$

$$\Rightarrow \quad \frac{9}{2} \cdot \frac{D\lambda}{d} = 4 \times 10^{-3}$$

$$\Rightarrow \quad d = \frac{9D\lambda}{8 \times 10^{-3}} = \frac{9 \times 2 \times 6 \times 10^{-7}}{8 \times 10^{-3}}$$

$$= 1.35 \times 10^{-3} \text{ m} = 1.35 \text{ mm}$$

23. *(c)* Applying, $\frac{T_1 - T_2}{t} = \alpha\left[\frac{T_1 - T_2}{2} - T_0\right]$ two times, we have

$$\text{or} \quad \frac{50 - 40}{5} = \alpha\left[\frac{50 + 40}{2} - 20\right] \quad \ldots(i)$$

$$\text{and} \quad \frac{40 - 30}{t} = \alpha\left[\frac{40 + 30}{2} - 20\right] \quad \ldots(ii)$$

Solving these two equations, we get

$$t = \frac{25}{3} \text{ min}$$

24. *(a)* Given, $\mathbf{E} = 10\cos(10^7 t + kx)\mathbf{j}\text{Vm}^{-1}$

Comparing with the general equation

$E = E_0 \cos(\omega t + kx)$, we get

Amplitude of wave = 10 Vm^{-1}

and angular frequency, $\omega = 10^7$

$$c = \frac{\omega}{k} \quad \Rightarrow \quad 3 \times 10^8 = \frac{10^7}{k}$$

$$\Rightarrow \quad k = \frac{1}{30} = 0.033 \text{ rad m}^{-1} \qquad \left[\; k = \frac{2\pi}{\lambda}\right]$$

$$\Rightarrow \quad \frac{2\pi}{\lambda} = \frac{1}{30} \Rightarrow \lambda = 2\pi \times 30 = 188.4 \text{ m}$$

25. *(c)* Given, current, $I = 12\,\text{A}$

Radius, $R = 2 \text{ cm} = 2 \times 10^{-2}$ m

Magnetic field at the centre of current carrying circular loop,

$$B_c = \frac{\mu_0 I}{2R} = \frac{\mu_0}{2\pi} \cdot \frac{\pi I}{R}$$

Magnetic field at the centre of semi-circular loop,

$$B = \frac{B_c}{2} = \frac{\mu_0}{4\pi} \frac{\pi I}{R}$$

$$= 10^{-7} \times \frac{3.14 \times 12}{2 \times 10^{-2}}$$

$$= 1.9 \times 10^{-4} \text{ T}$$

Thus, **B** is 1.9×10^{-4} T normal to the plane of the paper going into it, i.e. ⊗.

26. *(c)* We know that, $\sin\theta = \frac{n_2}{n_1}$

As, refractive index of a medium, $n = \frac{c}{v}$, where c and v are the speed of light in vacuum and medium, respectively.

$\Rightarrow \quad \sin\theta = \frac{v}{v'}$

Here, v is speed in medium A and v' is speed in medium B,

$\Rightarrow \quad v' = \frac{v}{\sin\theta}$

27. *(b)* Given, inner radius of toroid = 0.25 m
Outer radius of toroid = 0.26 m
Number of turns = 3500
and current = 11 A

$\therefore$ Mean radius, $r_m = \frac{0.25 + 0.26}{2} = 25.5 \times 10^{-2}$ m

Number of turns in unit length,

$$n = \frac{N}{2\pi r_m} = \frac{3500}{2\pi \times 25.5 \times 10^{-2}}$$

Magnetic field of a toroid,

$$B = \mu_0 nI = 4\pi \times 10^{-7} \times \frac{3500}{2p \times 25.5 \times 10^{-2}} \times 11$$

$$= 3 \times 10^{-2}\ \text{T}$$

28. *(b)* Given, root mean square value of electric field,

$$E_{rms} = 6\ \text{V/m}$$

We know that, peak value of electric field,

$$E_0 = \sqrt{2}\, E_{rms} \Rightarrow E_0 = \sqrt{2} \times 6\ \text{V/m}$$

Also, we know that, $c = \frac{E_0}{B_0}$

where, c = speed of light in vacuum
and B_0 = peak value of magnetic field.

$$\Rightarrow \quad B_0 = \frac{E_0}{c} = \frac{\sqrt{2} \times 6}{3 \times 10^8} = \frac{8.48}{3} \times 10^{-8} = 2.83 \times 10^{-8}\ \text{T}$$

Thus, peak value of magnetic field B_0 is 2.83×10^{-8} T.

29. *(c)* Given, wavelength of blue light, $\lambda_{blue} = 4360$Å
and wavelength of green light, $\lambda_{green} = 5460$ Å
Position of nth maximum from central maxima is

$$x_n = \frac{n\lambda D}{d} \Rightarrow x_n \propto \lambda$$

As, $\quad \lambda_{blue} < \lambda_{green}$ (given)

So, $\quad x(\text{blue}) < x\ (\text{green})$

30. *(b)* $v_{CM} = \frac{m_1 v_1 + m_2 v_2 + m_3 v_3}{m_1 + m_2 + m_3}$

$$= \frac{5 \times 5 + 4 \times 4 + 2 \times 2}{5 + 4 + 2} = \frac{45}{11}$$

$$= 4.09 \simeq 4\ \text{m/s}$$

31. *(a)* Given, for concave lens of glass, $n_g = 1.5$
Refractive index of the medium, $n_m = 1.75$
Applying lens Maker's formula,

$$\frac{1}{f} = ({}^m n_g - 1)\left(\frac{1}{R_1} - \frac{1}{R_2}\right)$$

$$= \left(\frac{n_g}{n_m} - 1\right)\left(\frac{1}{R_1} - \frac{1}{R_2}\right)$$

$$= \left(\frac{1.5}{1.75} - 1\right)\left(\frac{1}{-R} - \frac{1}{+R}\right)$$

$$\Rightarrow \quad \frac{1}{f} = \frac{(1.5 - 1.75)}{1.75} \times \left(-\frac{2}{R}\right)$$

$$\Rightarrow \quad f = \frac{1.75}{0.25 \times 2} R = \frac{7}{2} R = (+\ 3.5\ R)$$

Since, f is positive, so it behaves as convergent lens of focal length (+ 3.5 R).

32. *(c)* Moment of inertia of the system about AX is given by

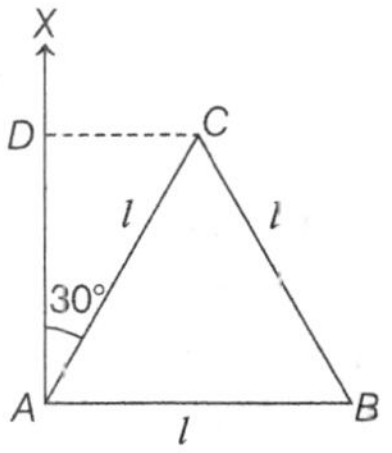

$$= m_A r_A^2 + m_B r_B^2 + m_C r_C^2$$

$$= m(0)^2 + m(l)^2 + m(l\sin 30°)^2$$

$$= ml^2 + \frac{ml^2}{4} = \frac{5}{4} ml^2$$

33. *(c)* Given that, $H_E = \sqrt{3} V_E$, where H_E = horizontal component of earth's magnetic field and V_E = vertical component of earth's magnetic field.

$$\text{Angle of dip, } \tan\delta = \frac{V_E}{H_E}$$

$$\tan\delta = \frac{V_E}{H_E} = \frac{V_E}{\sqrt{3} V_E} = \frac{1}{\sqrt{3}} = \tan 30°$$

$\therefore$ Angle of dip, $\delta = 30° = \pi/6$ rad

34. *(d)* Work done, $dW = F \cdot dx$

$$\Rightarrow \quad W = \int_0^5 (7 - 2x + 3x^2)\, dx$$

$$= [\,7x - x^2 + x^3\,]_0^5$$

$$\therefore \quad = 7 \times 5 - (5)^2 + (5)^3 = 135\ \text{J}$$

35. *(c)* In a paramagnetic material, $M = C\frac{B}{T} = C\frac{\mu H}{T}$

$[\because B = \mu H]$

Hence, $\quad M \propto H$

Therefore, the graph between H and M is a straight line represented by in figure

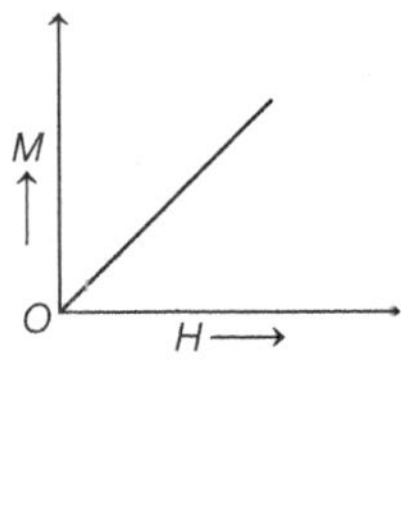

36. *(b)* Increase in KE $= \dfrac{p^2}{2m}$

New momentum $= p + 20\%$ of $p = p + \dfrac{p}{5} = \dfrac{6p}{5}$

$$KE_f = \frac{\left(\frac{6}{5}p\right)^2}{2m} = \frac{36}{25}\frac{p^2}{2m}$$

$$\Delta KE = \frac{36}{25}\cdot\frac{p^2}{2m} - \frac{p^2}{2m} = \frac{11p^2}{25 \times 2m}$$

$$\text{Percentage increase} = \frac{\Delta KE}{KE} \times 100 = \frac{\frac{11p^2}{25 \times 2m}}{\frac{p^2}{2m}} \times 100$$

$$= \frac{11}{25} \times 100 = 44\%$$

37. *(b)* Given, $C = 80\mu F = 80 \times 10^{-6} F$, $L = 5$ H and $R = 40\ \Omega$

At resonance, source frequency, $\nu = \dfrac{1}{2\pi\sqrt{LC}}$

$$\therefore \quad \nu = \frac{1}{2 \times \pi \times \sqrt{5 \times 80 \times 10^{-6}}}$$

$$= \frac{1}{2 \times \pi \sqrt{(400 \times 10^{-6})}} = \frac{1}{2 \times \pi \times 2 \times 10^{-2}}$$

$$= \frac{100}{\pi \times 4} = \frac{25}{\pi} \text{ Hz}$$

38. *(d)* Given, $v = 14\sqrt{3}$ m/s, $r = 20\sqrt{3}$

$$\text{Angle, } \theta = \tan^{-1}\left(\frac{v^2}{rg}\right)$$

$$= \tan^{-1}\left(\frac{(14\sqrt{3})^2}{20\sqrt{3} \times 9.8}\right)$$

$$= \tan^{-1}(\sqrt{3})$$

$$\Rightarrow \quad \theta = 60^\circ$$

39. *(c)* Given, $\varepsilon = 200 \sin 314t$ and $I = \sin(314t + \pi/3)$

$$\therefore \quad \phi = \frac{\pi}{3}, \varepsilon_m = 200 \text{ V}, I_m = 1 \text{ A}$$

$$V_{rms} = \frac{\varepsilon_m}{\sqrt{2}} = \frac{200}{\sqrt{2}}$$

$$i_{rms} = \frac{I_m}{\sqrt{2}} = \frac{1}{\sqrt{2}}$$

$\therefore$ Average power consumed is

$$P = V_{rms}\, i_{rms} \cos\phi = \frac{200}{\sqrt{2}}\frac{1}{\sqrt{2}} \cos \pi/3$$

$$= \frac{200}{2} \times \frac{1}{2} = 50 \text{ W}$$

40. *(d)* The centripetal force, $F = \dfrac{mv^2}{r}$

$$r = \frac{mv^2}{F}$$

$$\therefore \quad r \propto v^2$$

or $\quad v \propto \sqrt{r}$ [If m and F are constant.]

$$\frac{v_1}{v_2} = \sqrt{\frac{r_1}{r_2}} = \sqrt{\frac{1}{2}} = \frac{1}{\sqrt{2}} \Rightarrow v_1 : v_2 = 1 : \sqrt{2}$$

41. *(c)* Given, v = velocity of train $= 72 \times \dfrac{5}{18} = 20 \text{ ms}^{-1}$

l = distance between the rails = 1 m

B = vertical component of earth's magnetic field $= 2 \times 10^{-5}$ T

$\therefore$ Induced emf, $\varepsilon = Bvl = 2 \times 10^{-5} \times 20 \times 1$

$$= 40 \times 10^{-5} \text{ V}$$
$$= 40 \times 10^{-2} \text{ mV} = 0.4 \text{ mV}$$

42. *(b)* Here, lift is accelerating upward at the rate of a.

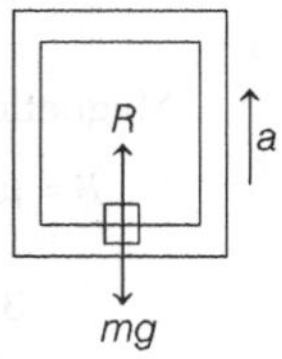

Hence, equation of motion is written as

$R - mg = ma$

$28000 - 20000 = 2000a$

$$\Rightarrow a = \frac{8000}{2000} = 4\text{ms}^{-2}, \text{ upwards}$$

43. *(c)* The emf induced between A and B as shown below is given by

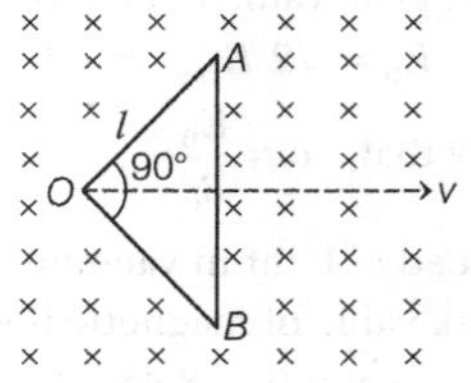

$$\varepsilon = Bv(AB)$$

In ΔAOB, $AB = \sqrt{AO^2 + BO^2} = \sqrt{l^2 + l^2} = \sqrt{2}l$

$$\therefore \quad \varepsilon = Bv(\sqrt{2}l) = \sqrt{2}Bvl$$

44. *(b)* Momentum is conserved before and after collision. We have,

$$\mathbf{p}_1 + \mathbf{p}_2 + \mathbf{p}_3 = 0 \qquad [\ p = mv]$$

$$\therefore \quad 1 \times 12\mathbf{i} + 2 \times 8\mathbf{j} + \mathbf{p}_3 = 0$$

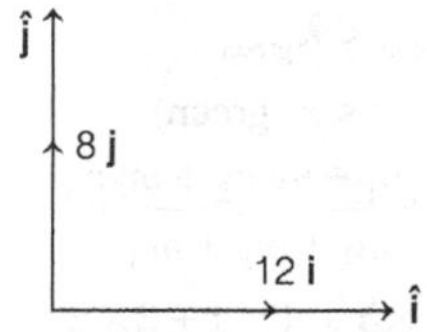

$$\Rightarrow \quad 12\mathbf{i} + 16\mathbf{j} + \mathbf{p}_3 = 0$$

$$\Rightarrow \quad \mathbf{p}_3 = -(12\mathbf{i} + 16\mathbf{j})$$

$$\therefore \quad p_3 = \sqrt{(12)^2 + (16)^2}$$

$$= \sqrt{144 + 256} = 20 \text{ kg-m/s}$$

Now, $\quad p_3 = m_3 v_3$

$$\Rightarrow \quad m_3 = \frac{p_3}{v_3} = \frac{20}{4} = 5 \text{ kg}$$

45. *(a)* Let the work function for both the metal plates A and B, being identical is ϕ.

According to Einstein photoelectric equation, for metal plate A,

$$K_A = \frac{hc}{\lambda_A} - \phi$$

$$\Rightarrow \quad 2K_A = \frac{2hc}{\lambda_A} - 2\phi$$

$$\text{or} \quad 2K_A + \phi = \frac{2hc}{\lambda_A} - \phi \quad \ldots\text{(i)}$$

It is given that, wavelength of metal B is half of metal A, i.e. $\lambda_B = \frac{\lambda_A}{2}$, therefore

$$K_B = \frac{hc}{\lambda_B} - \phi = \frac{2hc}{\lambda_A} - \phi$$

$$\Rightarrow \quad 2K_A + \phi = K_B \quad [\text{ using Eq. (i)}]$$

Thus, the relation between K_A and K_B can be expressed as

$$\Rightarrow \quad K_A < \frac{K_B}{2}$$

46. *(b)* Height of table,

$$h = \frac{1}{2}gt^2 = \frac{1}{2} \times 10 \times (0.4)^2 = 0.8\,\text{m}$$

Horizontal distance covered $= u_x t$

$= 4 \times 0.4 = 1.6$ m

Vertical velocity on reaching ground,

$$v_y = u_y + a_y t = 0 + 10 \times 0.4 = 4\text{ m/s}$$

Horizontal velocity on reaching ground,

$$v_c = v_x = 4\text{ m/s}$$

If θ is the angle at which the ball hits the ground with the vertical, then

$$\tan\theta = \frac{v_x}{v_y} = \frac{4}{4} = 1 \Rightarrow \theta = 45°$$

47. *(b)* Angular momentum of an electron, $L = \frac{nh}{2\pi}$

As, in 2nd excited state, $n = 3$, for both H and Li^+.

$$\Rightarrow \quad L_H = L_{Li}$$

$$\text{Energy,} \quad E_n = \frac{-Z^2\,(13.6)}{n^2} \Rightarrow E_n \propto Z^2$$

$$\text{As,} \quad Z_H = 1 \text{ and } Z_{Li^+} = 3$$

$$\therefore \quad |E_{Li}| > |E_H|$$

48. *(c)* Draw the situation as shown. OA represents the path of the particle starting from origin $O(0, 0)$. Draw a perpendicular from point A to X-axis.

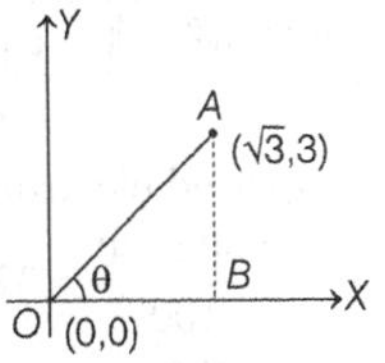

Let path of the particle makes an angle θ with the X-axis, then

$$\tan\theta = \text{slope of line } OA$$

$$= \frac{AB}{OB} = \frac{3}{\sqrt{3}} = \sqrt{3} \text{ or } \theta = 60°$$

49. *(c)* Energy gap E_g for silicon, germanium and tin respectively is as follows $(E_g)_{Si} = 1.1$ eV

$(E_g)_{Ge} = 0.72$ eV and $(E_g)_{Sn} \approx 0$ eV

Thus, $(E_g)_{Si} > (E_g)_{Ge} > (E_g)_{Sn}$

50. *(a)* The Boolean expression which satisfies the output of this logic gate is $C = A \cdot B$, which is for AND gate.

51. *(b)* $h = \frac{2T\cos\theta}{rdg}$

$$\therefore \quad h \propto \frac{1}{r}.$$

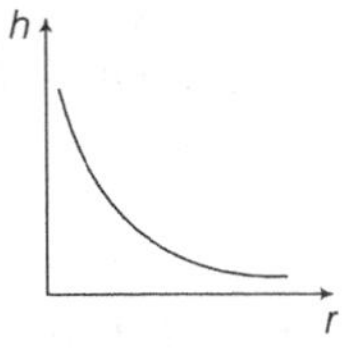

52. *(d)* Here, potential energy of the system,

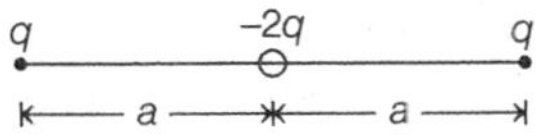

$$U = \frac{1}{4\pi\varepsilon_0}\left[\frac{q_1q_2}{r_{12}} + \frac{q_1q_3}{r_{13}} + \frac{q_2q_3}{r_{23}}\right]$$

$$= \frac{1}{4\pi\varepsilon_0}\left[\frac{qq}{2a} + \frac{q(-2q)}{a} + \frac{q(-2q)}{a}\right]$$

$$= \frac{1}{4\pi\varepsilon_0}\left[\frac{q^2}{2a} + \frac{-2q^2}{a} - \frac{2q^2}{a}\right]$$

$$= \frac{1}{4\pi\varepsilon_0}\left[\frac{-4q^2}{a} + \frac{q^2}{2a}\right] = \frac{-7q^2}{8\pi\varepsilon_0 a}$$

53. *(d)* Variation of photoelectric current with collector plate potential for different intensities is shown correctly below as

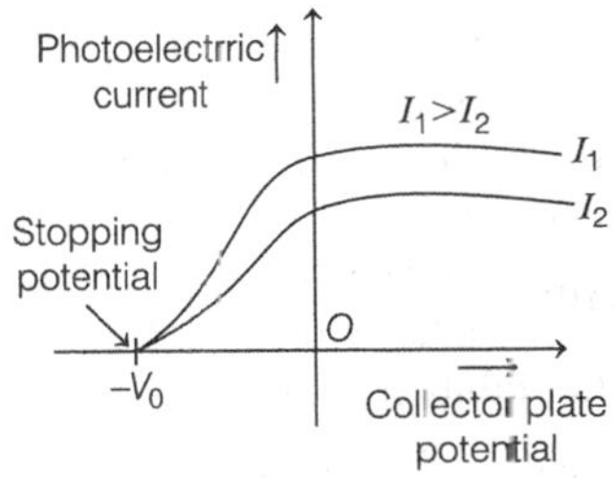

Here for greater intensity I_1, more photoelectrons are emitted and hence saturation current is more. Thus, graph corresponding to I_1 will be above than that of I_2. Since, the stopping potential is independent of intensity, hence the graphs converge at same value of stopping potential V_0 for both the intensities I_1 and I_2.

54. *(c)* We know that, from second equation of motion,

$$s = ut + \frac{1}{2}at^2 \quad \ldots\text{(i)}$$

Given, distance, $s = s_1$ in first 10 s.

Distance, $s = s_2$ in first 20 s and $u = 0$

So, $s_1 = \frac{1}{2}a(t_1)^2$ ...(ii)

$s_2 = \frac{1}{2}a(t_2)^2$ ...(iii)

From Eqn. (ii) and (iii), we get

$$\frac{s_1}{s_2} = \left(\frac{t_1}{t_2}\right)^2 = \left(\frac{10}{20}\right)^2 = \frac{1}{4} \Rightarrow s_2 = 4s_1$$

55. *(b)* $W_{BC} = 3R(T_C - T_B) \Rightarrow W_{AB} = W_{CD} = 0$

Because, the processes are isochoric,

$W_{DA} = 3R(T_A - T_D)$

∴ Total work done

$$W_{BC} + W_{DA} = 3R(T_A + T_C - T_B - T_D) = 3R(400 + 2400 - 800 - 1200) = 2400R = 24 \text{ kJ}$$

56. *(b)* Let x be the end correction, then according to question.

$$\frac{v}{4(l_1 + x)} = \frac{3v}{4(l_2 + x)}$$

[Since, $l_1 = 0.1$ m, $l_2 = 0.35$ m]

$\Rightarrow$ $x = 0.025$ m

57. *(d)* Change in potential energy in displacing a body from r_1 to r_2 is given by

$$\Delta U = GMm\left[\frac{1}{r_1} - \frac{1}{r_2}\right] = GMm\left(\frac{1}{2R} - \frac{1}{4R}\right) = \frac{GMm}{4R}$$

58. *(a)*
$$\gamma_{mix} = \frac{\frac{\mu_1\gamma_1}{\gamma_1 - 1} + \frac{\mu_2\gamma_2}{\gamma_2 - 1}}{\frac{\mu_1}{\gamma_1 - 1} + \frac{\mu_2}{\gamma_2 - 1}} = \frac{\frac{1 \times \frac{5}{3}}{\left(\frac{5}{3} - 1\right)} + \frac{1 \times \frac{7}{5}}{\left(\frac{7}{5} - 1\right)}}{\frac{1}{\left(\frac{5}{3} - 1\right)} + \frac{1}{\left(\frac{7}{5} - 1\right)}} = \frac{3}{2}$$

59. *(a)* $f' = f\left(\frac{v}{v - v_s}\right)$

$$\Rightarrow \lambda' = \lambda\left(\frac{v - v_s}{v}\right) \Rightarrow \lambda' = 120\left(\frac{330 - 60}{330}\right) = 98 \text{ cm}$$

60. *(d)* $v = 20$ MHz $= 20 \times 10^6$ Hz

Wavelength of antenna is,

$$\lambda = \frac{c}{v} = \frac{3 \times 10^8}{20 \times 10^6} = 15 \text{ m}$$

The minimum length of antenna

$$= \frac{\lambda}{4} = \frac{15}{4} = 3.75 \text{ m}$$

Chemistry

61. *(a)* On moving downward in a group, density increases but the density of K is somewhat lesser than Na. Thus, the order of density is Li < K < Na < Rb < Cs.

Densities are

Li — 0.53 g/cc Na — 0.97 g/cc

K — 0.86 g/cc Rb — 1.53 g/cc

Cs — 1.90 g/cc

62. *(c)* Moles of solute in solution-I = 2 × 3 = 6

Moles of solute in solution-II = 3 × 2.5 = 7.5

Total moles of solute after mixing = 6 + 7.5 = 13.5

Total volume = 2 + 3 = 5 L

$$\therefore \text{ Molarity} = \frac{\text{total moles}}{\text{total volume}} = \frac{13.5}{5} = 2.7 \text{ M}$$

Volume after dilution = 10 L

$$\therefore \text{ Now, molarity after dilution} = \frac{13.5}{10} = 1.35 \text{ M}$$

63. *(b)*

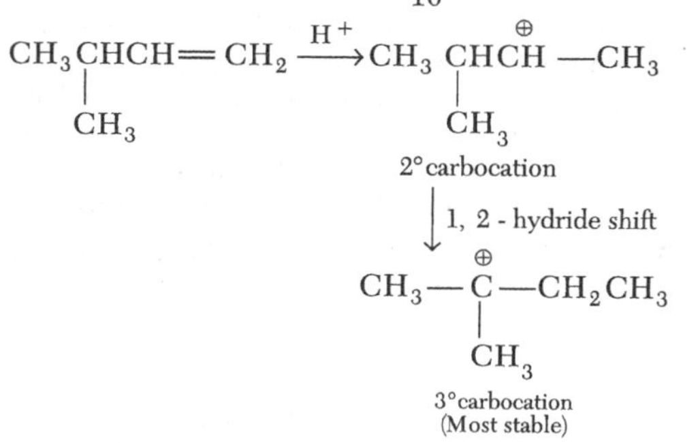

64. *(a)* Atomic radius of the elements decreases across a period from left to right due to increase in effective nuclear charge. On moving down a group, since number of shells increases, so atomic radius increases. Amongst isoelectronic species, ionic radius increases with increase in negative charge and decreases with positive charge.

65. *(c)* 100 g haemoglobin contains = 0.33 g Fe

$$\therefore 67200 \text{ g haemoglobin contains} = \frac{0.33 \times 67200}{100} \text{ g Fe} = 221.76 \text{ g Fe}$$

$$\therefore \text{ Number of Fe atoms} = \frac{221.76}{56} \approx 4$$

66. *(d)* In option (d), a carbon with double bond has two same functional groups (CH_3) attached. The rotation around carbon will not produce a new compound. Hence, geometrical isomerism is not possible.

67. *(a)* Electronic configuration of Fe (26) is

$1s^2, 1p^6, 2s^2, 2p^6, 3d^8, 3s^2$ [⇅ | ⇅ | ⇅ | ↑ | ↑] $3d^8$ [⇅] $3s^2$

∴ There are two unpaired electrons present.

68. *(a)* Solute present $= \frac{800 \times 40}{100} = 320$ g

Solvent = 800 − 320 = 480 g

Solute precipitated = 100 g

Solute remained in solution = 220 g

Total weight of solution after precipitation

$= 480\text{ g} + 220\text{ g} = 700\text{ g}$

700 g solution has solute = 220 g

100 g solution has solute $= \frac{220}{700} \times 100 = 31.4\%$

69. *(b)* Rubber vulcanised with 3 - 10% sulphur is more rigid and hence used for manufacturing tyres. While the rubber vulcanised with 1 - 3% sulphur is soft and stretchy, so used to make rubber band.

70. *(a)* Being isoelectronic to Rb^+, greater the nuclear charge, smaller the size, hence Se^{2-} has the largest radius (on move down a group, radii increase).

71. *(b)*

$$(pV)_X = nRT = \frac{2.9}{m} R \times 3.68$$

$$(pV)_{H_2} = nRT = \frac{0.184}{2} R \times 290$$

$$(pV)_X = (pV)_{H_2} \qquad \text{(given)}$$

$$\therefore \quad \frac{2.9}{M} \times 368 = \frac{0.184}{2} \times 290$$

where M is the molar mass of ideal gas.

$$\therefore \quad \left(\frac{2.9}{M}\right) = \text{moles of } X = \frac{0.184 \times 290}{2 \times 368} = 0.0725$$

72. *(d)* According to Raoult's law,

$$p = p_A^\circ \chi_A + p_B^\circ \chi_B = \frac{100}{4} + \frac{60 \times 3}{4}$$

$= 70\text{ mm} < 75\text{ mm}$ (experimental)

Thus, there is positive deviation. This mixture is more volatile due to decrease in bp. Thus, (b) is true; also force of attraction is decreased, thus (c) is true.

73. *(a)* Hydroxylation of ethyne

$$HC{\equiv}CH + H_2O \xrightarrow{H^+} CH_2{=}CH{-}OH$$

$\downarrow$ Tautomerisation

$$CH_3-CHO$$

74. *(a)* Δn_g = moles of gaseous products − moles of gaseous reactants

$= 3 - 2 = 1$

$$K_p = K_C (RT)^{\Delta n_g}$$

$$K_C = \frac{K_p}{RT} = \frac{1.2 \times 10^{-2}}{0.0821 \times 1338} = 1.09 \times 10^{-4} < 1.2 \times 10^{-2}$$

75. *(a)* Initial temperature (of melting ice) = 0°C = 273 K

At constant volume, $p \propto T$

$$\therefore \quad T_2 = \frac{p_2 T_1}{p_1} = \frac{400 \times 273}{1000} = 109.2\text{ K} \approx 109\text{ K}$$

76. *(a)* Phenol is more acidic in nature because by the loss of one proton, it gives phenoxide ion. This phenoxide ion is resonance stabilised. As phenoxide ion is a stable intermediate so, the tendency to give proton is more in phenol than the others. Phenols being more acidic than alcohol dissolves in NaOH.

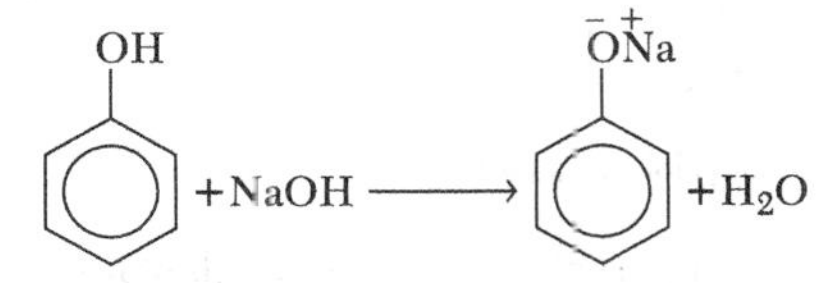

77. *(d)* For $Na_2S_2O_3$, oxidation number of S = − 2, + 6

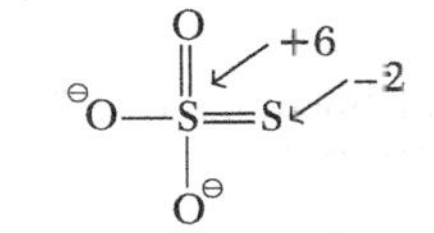

For $Na_2S_4O_6$, oxidation number of S = 0, + 5

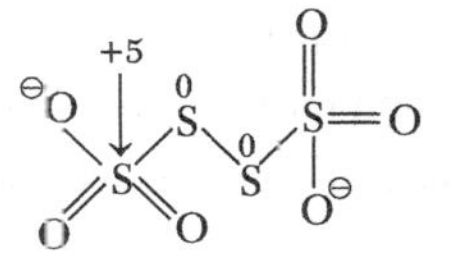

For $CaOCl_2$, oxidation number of chlorine (ClO^-, Cl^-) = −1, + 1

78. *(b)* $\underset{\text{1 mole}}{C_2H_6} + 3.5O_2 \longrightarrow 2CO_2 + \underset{\text{3 moles = 54 g}}{3H_2O}$

Since, 54 g of H_2O is formed by 1 mole combustion of C_2H_6. As combustion reaction is exothermic reaction so, sign of heat of combustion is negative.

∴ Heat of combustion of C_2H_6 = − 370 kcal mol^{-1}

79. *(b)*

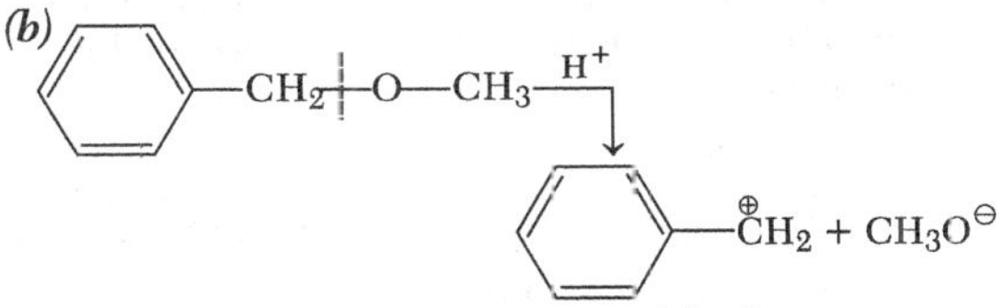

Resonance stabilised carbocation

Thus, products are 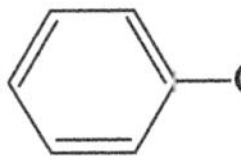 $-CH_2I$ and CH_3OH.

80. *(c)* Iron is an impurity in copper pyrites, so slag is

$$FeO + SiO_2 \longrightarrow \underset{\substack{\text{Slag} \\ \text{(Ferrous silicate)}}}{FeSiO_3}$$

81. *(c)*

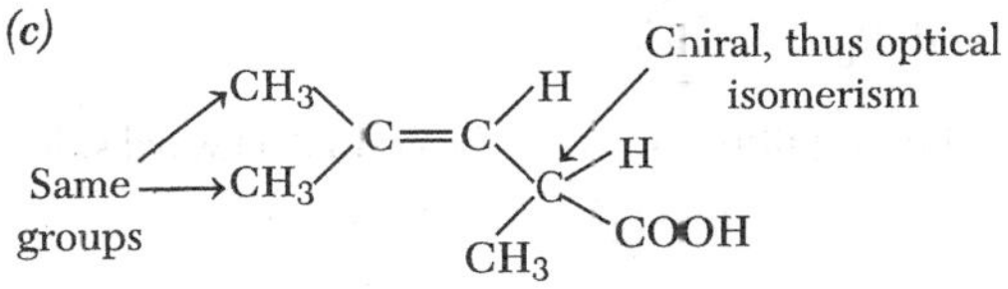

82. *(c)* $TiCl_4$ has electron deficient Ti, thus accepts electron-pair from electron-rich species (Lewis base). Thus, $TiCl_4$ is a Lewis acid.

83. *(a)* $\Delta n_g = 2 - 1.5 = 0.5$

$$\therefore \quad \Delta H^\circ = \Delta E^\circ + \Delta n_g RT$$

$$= -742.7 + 0.5 \times 8.314 \times 10^{-3} \times 298$$

$$= -741.5\text{ kJ mol}^{-1}$$

MOCK TEST 1

84. *(c)*

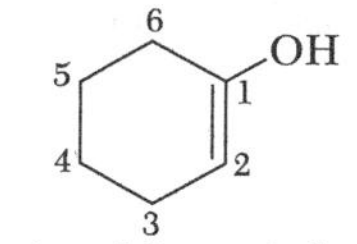

1-cyclohexen-1-ol

85. *(d)* O_2^- (superoxide) — monodentate

en — bidentate

Br — monodentate

Thus, coordination number of Pt = 6

$$[Pt(O_2)\ (en)_2\ (Br)]^{2+}$$
$$\downarrow \quad \downarrow \quad \downarrow \quad \downarrow$$
$$x-1 \quad +0 \quad -1 \quad =2$$
$$\therefore \quad x=+4$$

Thus, oxidation number of Pt = + 4 .

86. *(c)* Cyclic metaphosphoric acid is $(HPO_3)_3$.

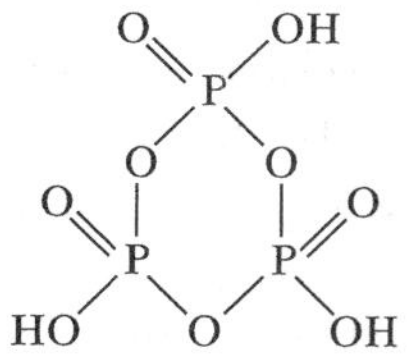

Thus, number of P—O—P bonds in cyclic metaphosphoric acid are three.

87. *(a)* Benzylic chloride is hydrolysed at fastest rate due to stabilisation of intermediate carbocation by conjugation.

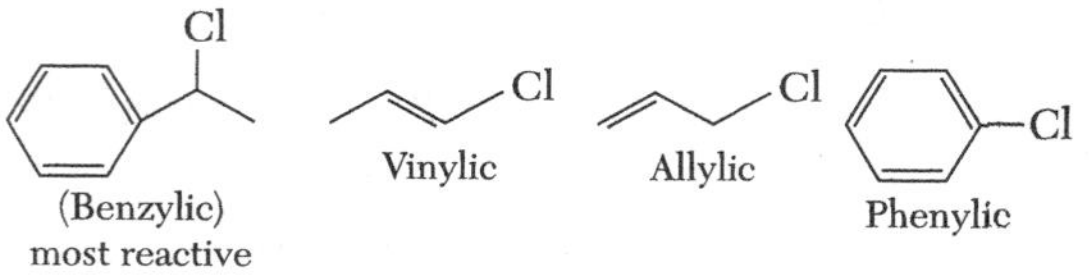

88. *(b)* In

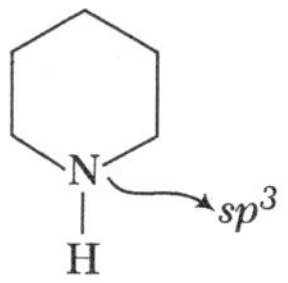

N-atom is sp^3-hybridised.

89. *(b)* $N_2O_4(g) \rightleftharpoons 2NO_2(g);\ Q = \dfrac{[NO_2]^2}{[N_2O_4]} = 9 > K_C$

and $K_C = \dfrac{(3-2x)^2}{1+x}$

Thus, equilibrium is displaced in backward side.

$$\underset{\substack{3 \\ (3-2x)}}{2NO_2(g)} \rightleftharpoons \underset{\substack{1 \\ (1+x)}}{N_2O_4(g)}$$

$$K_C' = \frac{1}{K_C} = \frac{1}{0.67} \Rightarrow \frac{(1+x)}{(3-2x)^2} = 1.5$$

Only permissible value of x that satisfies above equation is $x = 0.5$

Thus, NO_2 at equilibrium $= 3 - 2x = 2$ moles

90. *(c)* All are resonance stabilised.

I.

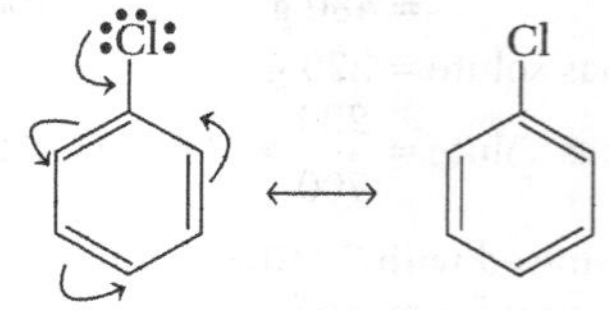

II. $CH_2{=}CH{-}\ddot{Cl}: \longleftrightarrow \overset{\ominus}{C}H_2{-}CH{=}\overset{\oplus}{Cl}$

III.

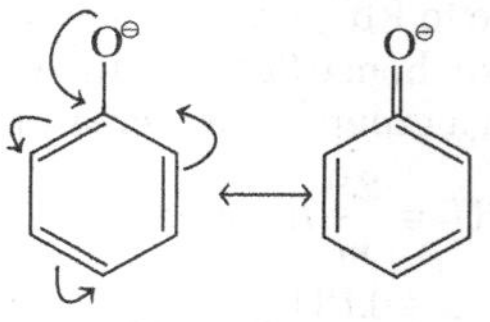

IV.

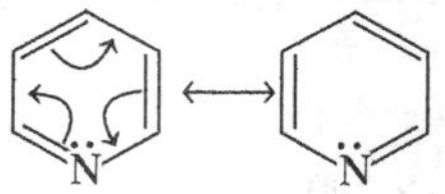

91. *(a)*

		Electrons	Bond order
I.	CN^-	14	3
II.	O_2^-	17	1.5
III.	NO^+	14	3
IV.	CN^+	12	2

Here, I and III have identical bond order.

92. *(d)* In case of electrolysis of aqueous NaCl oxidation reaction occurs at anode as follows:

$$Cl^-\ (aq) \longrightarrow \frac{1}{2}Cl_2(g) + e^-; \qquad E^\circ_{cell} = 1.36\ V$$

$$2H_2O\ (l) \longrightarrow O_2(g) + 4H^+(aq)\ + 4e^-;\ E^\circ_{cell} = -1.23\ V$$

But due to lower E°_{cell} value, water get oxidised in preference of Cl^- *(aq)*. However, the actual reaction taking place in the concentrated solution of NaCl is (d) and not (b) i.e. Cl_2 is produced but O_2 not.

This unexpected result is explained on the basis of the concept of 'overvoltage', i.e. water needs greater voltage for oxidation to O_2 (as it is kinetically slow process) than that needed for oxidation of Cl^- ions to Cl_2. Thus, the correct option is (d) not (b).

93. *(a)* The total amount of oxygen consumed by microorganisms (bacteria) in decomposing organic matter present in certain volume of a sample of water is called biochemical oxygen demand (BOD) of the water.

Water considered to be pure if it has BOD less than 5 ppm, whereas highly polluted water has BOD more than 17 ppm.Thus, water having BOD less than 5 ppm is rich in dissolved oxygen.

94. *(c)*

	Lone pair	Hybridisation
NF_3	1	sp^3
NO_3^-	0	sp^2
BF_3	0	sp^2
H_3O^+	1	sp^3
N_3H	0	N_x sp
	1	N_z sp^2
	1	N_y sp

$$H—\ddot{N}_z=\ddot{N}_x\equiv \ddot{N}_y$$

Thus, NO_3^-, BF_3 and NF_3, H_3O^+ are iso-structural pairs.

95. *(b)* $\frac{\Delta p}{p^\circ} = \frac{n_2 i}{n_2 i + n_1}$

n_2 = moles of solute (NaCl)

n_1 = moles of solvent (H_2O) = 10

$i = 2$

For NaCl,

$\therefore \quad 0.167 = \frac{2n_2}{2n_2 + 10}$

$n_2 = 1$ mol

96. *(d)*

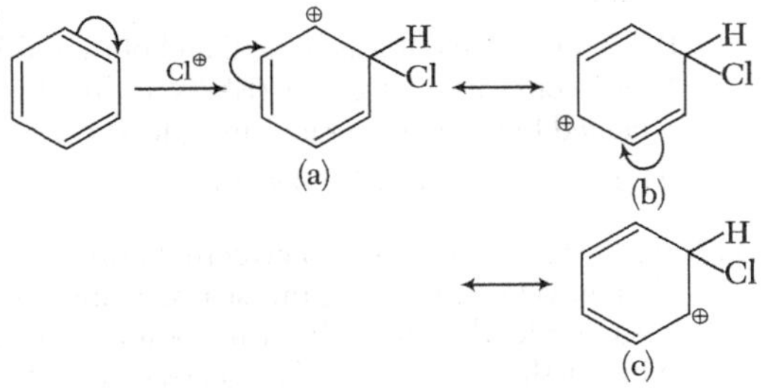

97. *(c)* $Cr_2O_7^{2-} + SO_2 + H^+ \longrightarrow \underset{\text{Green}}{Cr^{3+}} + SO_4^{2-}$

$\xrightarrow{Fe^{2+} + H^+} \underset{\text{Green}}{Cr^{3+}} + Fe^{3+}$

Both SO_2 and Fe^{2+} reduce $Cr_2O_7^{2-}$ to Cr^{3+} (green).

98. *(d)* Density, $d = \frac{MZ}{N_0 a^3}$

where,

M = molar mass = 18 g mol^{-1}

N_0 = Avogadro's number = 6.02×10^{23}

Volume, $a^3 = 132 \times 10^{-24}$ cm^3

$\therefore \quad 0.92 = \frac{18 \times Z}{6.02 \times 10^{23} \times 132 \times 10^{-24}}$

$\therefore \quad Z = 4$

99. *(a)* It is Corey-House synthesis of alkane. Gilmann reagent $[(CH_3)_2CH]$ CuLi should react with RX such that RX is MeX or 1° or 2° cycloalkyl halide for good yield.

100. *(d)*

(a) Water reacts with alkali metals.

(b) N_2 forms nitrides with Li.

(c) CO_2 reacts with Na_2O_2 or KO_2 formed and releases O_2 which helps to spreed fire.

Thus, asbestos is the best.

101. *(b)* There is increase in 0.30 Å unit length. This is due to two atoms at the corners.

Thus, $r_{Rb^+} = 1.33 \text{ Å} + \frac{0.30 \text{ Å}}{2} = 1.48 \text{ Å}$

102. *(d)* A reaction is stereospecific when each of the two specific stereoisomers of a starting material yields a particular stereoisomer as a product.

Br_2 gives anti-addition but $KMnO_4$ and BH_3.THF gives *syn*-addition.

103. *(a)* $[\overset{II}{Pt}(NH_3)_4][\overset{II}{Cu}Cl_4]$;

$[\overset{II}{Pt}(NH_3)_3Cl][\overset{II}{Cu}(NH_3)Cl_3]$

$[\overset{II}{Cu}(NH_3)_3Cl][\overset{II}{Pt}(NH_3)Cl_3]$

Thus, there are three possible isomers for the complex

$[\overset{II}{Cu}(NH_3)_4][\overset{II}{Pt}Cl_4]$

104. *(c)* ${}^{226}_{88}Ra \longrightarrow {}^{222}_{86}Rn + {}^{b}_{a}X$

$86 + a = 88$, thus $a = 2$

$222 + b = 226$, thus $b = 4$

Thus, ${}^{b}_{a}X$ is ${}^{4}_{2}He$.

105. *(a)* Aspirin inhibits the synthesis of compound known as prostaglandins which stimulate inflammation in the tissues and cause pain.

So, it is effective in relieving pain. Beside this, aspirin has many other effects such as reducing fever (antipyretic) and preventing blood platelet coagulation.

Because of this anti-blood clotting action, it is widely used to prevent heart attacks. It does not make a person addictive as it is non-narcotic drug.

106. *(c)* Olefin $\xrightarrow{O_3/Zn}$

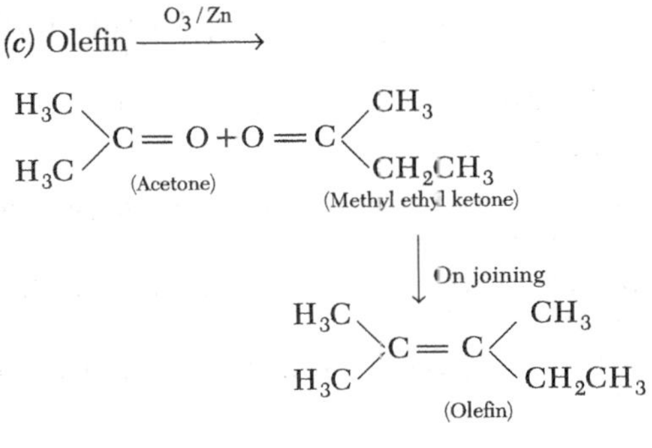

107. *(b)* $k = \frac{2.303}{t}\log\left(\frac{a}{a-x}\right)$

$$= \frac{2.303}{60}\log 8 = 0.03466\ \text{min}^{-1}$$

$$\left(\frac{dx}{dt}\right) = k[A] = 0.03466 \times 0.1$$

$$= 3.466 \times 10^{-3}\ \text{mol L}^{-1}\ \text{min}^{-1}.$$

108. *(a)*

(a) 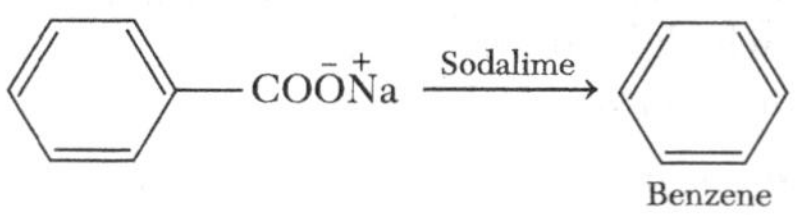

Benzene

(b) $(C_6H_5COO)_2Ca \xrightarrow{\Delta} C_6H_5COC_6H_5 + CaCO_3$

(c) $(C_6H_5COO)_2Ca + (CH_3COO)_2Ca \xrightarrow{\Delta}$

$$2C_6H_5COCH_3 + 2CaCO_3$$

109. *(a)* Ethanol on reaction with bleaching powder $(CaOCl_2)$ gives $CHCl_3$ as follow:

$$CaOCl_2 + H_2O \longrightarrow Ca(OH)_2 + Cl_2$$
$$Cl_2 + H_2O \longrightarrow 2HCl + [O]$$
$$CH_3CH_2OH + [O] \longrightarrow CH_3CHO + H_2O$$
$$CH_3CHO + 3Cl_2 \longrightarrow \underset{\text{Chloral}}{CCl_3CHO} + 3HCl$$
$$2CCl_3CHO + Ca(OH)_2 \longrightarrow (HCOO)_2Ca + 2CHCl_3$$

110. *(b)* Transition metals have incompletely filled *d* subshell in their ground state or in their oxidation state but Zn, Cd and Hg don't have this characteristic.

111. *(b)* Glycogen is a branched chain polymer of α-D-glucose units in which chain is formed by $C_1—C_4$ glycosidic linkage, whereas branching occurs by the formation of $C_1—C_6$ glycosidic linkage. Structure of glycogen can be shown below similar to the structure of amylopectin.

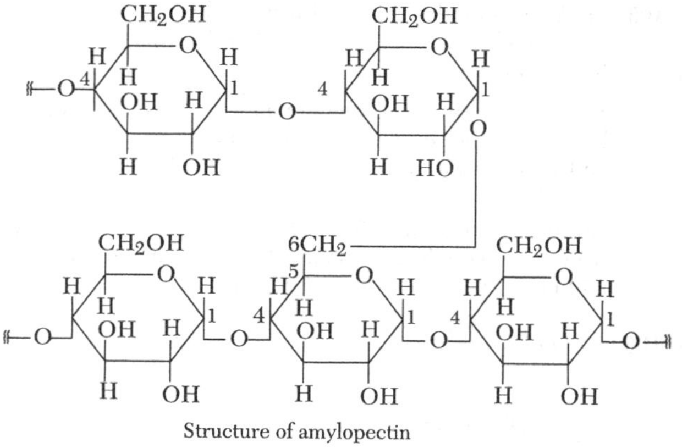

Structure of amylopectin

Glycogen is also known as animal starch present in liver, muscles and brain.

112. *(a)* Matte is CuS + FeS i.e. sulphide of copper (II) and iron (II).

113. *(b)* The given reaction is endothermic reaction thus, $\Delta H > 0$.

Also number of moles of gaseous substances increases, hence randomness increases.

Thus, $\Delta S > 0$.

114. *(c)* Negatively charged colloidal sol is formed, when $AgNO_3$ is completely precipitated as AgI and extra KI is adsorbed on AgI.

$$Ag^+ + I^- \longrightarrow AgI$$
$$AgI + I^- \longrightarrow [AgI]I^-$$

Thus, $[Ag^+] < [I^-]$

$$\underset{\substack{3\text{ moles}\\1\text{ mole}}}{3[AgI]I^-} + \underset{\substack{1\text{ mole}\\\frac{1}{3}\text{ mole}}}{Fe^{3+}} \longrightarrow 3AgI + FeI_3$$

Thus, 1 mole of $[AgI]I^-$ is coagulated by the addition of 1 mole of $AgNO_3$ or 1/2 mole $Pb(NO_3)_2$ or 1/3 mole of $Fe(NO_3)_3$.

115. *(a)* The acidic nature of oxides changes from acidic to basic through amphoteric on moving down the group.

$$\underset{\substack{\text{More acidic,}\\\text{less basic}}}{B_2O_3},\ \underset{\text{Amphoteric}}{Al_2O_3, Ga_2O_3},\ \underset{\text{Basic}}{In_2O_3, Tl_2O_3}$$

116. *(d)* I. 2° aromatic

II. 2° aromatic but less basic than I due to $—NO_2$ (EWG).

III. 2° aliphatic is most basic due to + *I*-effect of alkyl group.

IV. 2° aromatic but less basic than both I and II due to adjacent carbonyl group. (EWG) is directly attached to benzene nucleus thus, least basic.

Thus, order is $\underset{\text{Least}}{IV} < II < I < \underset{\text{Most}}{III}$

117. *(b)* Shaving soaps contain glycerol to prevent rapid drying. While preparing this soaps, a gum called rosin is added to them. It forms sodium rosinate which lathers well. Laundary soaps contain fillers, like sodium rosinate, sodium silicate, borax and sodium carbonate.

Trisodium polyphosphate is an important filler added to detergent powders and liquid detergents.

118. *(a)* The metals, present below hydrogen in the electrochemical series, cannot liberate hydrogen from the dilute acids.

Among the given metals only Ag is present below hydrogen in electrochemical series, so it does not evolve hydrogen with dil. HCl.

$$Ag + \text{dil. HCl} \longrightarrow \text{No reaction}$$

119. *(b)* $\frac{x}{m} = Kp^{1/n}$

Taking log on both sides

$$\log\frac{x}{m} = \log K + \frac{1}{n}\log p$$

On comparing with $y = mx + c$

Slope, $\frac{1}{n} = \tan 45° = 1$

and $\log K = 0.3010 \Rightarrow K = 2$

$\therefore \log \frac{x}{m} = \log 2 + 1 \times \log 0.2$

$= \log 2 + \log 0.2 = \log 0.4$

$\therefore \frac{x}{m} = 0.4$

120. (*a*) The balanced ionic equation is

$$2NO_3^- + 16H^+ + 14e^- \longrightarrow N_2H_4 + 6H_2O$$

Two nitrate ions when reduced involves 14 electrons, one nitrate ion will involve $\frac{14}{2} = 7$ electrons.

Mathematics

121. (*b*) Here, $A = R - \{3\}$, $B = R - \{1\}$

and $f : A \to B$ is defined as $f(x) = \left(\frac{x-2}{x-3}\right)$

Let $x, y \in A$ such that $f(x) = f(y)$

$\Rightarrow \frac{x-2}{x-3} = \frac{y-2}{y-3}$

$\Rightarrow (x-2)(y-3) = (y-2)(x-3)$

$\Rightarrow xy - 3x - 2y + 6 = xy - 3y - 2x + 6$

$\Rightarrow -3x - 2y = -3y - 2x$

$\Rightarrow 3x - 2x = 3y - 2y \Rightarrow x = y$

Therefore, f is one-one. Let $y \in B = R - \{1\}$. Then, $y \neq 1$

The function f is onto, if there exists $x \in A$ such that $f(x) = y$.

Now, $f(x) = y$

$\Rightarrow \frac{x-2}{x-3} = y$

$\Rightarrow x - 2 = xy - 3y$

$\Rightarrow x(1-y) = -3y + 2$

$\Rightarrow x = \frac{2-3y}{1-y} \in A \left(y \neq 1 \text{ and } \frac{2-3y}{1-y} \neq 3 \right)$

Thus, for any $y \in B$, there exists $\frac{2-3y}{1-y} \in A$ such that

$$f\left(\frac{2-3y}{1-y}\right) = \frac{\left(\frac{2-3y}{1-y}\right) - 2}{\left(\frac{2-3y}{1-y}\right) - 3}$$

$$= \frac{2 - 3y - 2 + 2y}{2 - 3y - 3 + 3y} = \frac{-y}{-1} = y$$

Therefore, f is onto. Hence, function f is one-one and onto.

122. (*c*) Let y be an arbitrary element of range f. Then, $y = 4x^2 + 12x + 15$, for some x in N, which implies that $y = (2x+3)^2 + 6$. This gives $x = \frac{((\sqrt{y-6}) - 3)}{2}$, $sy \geq 6$.

Let us define $g : S \to N$ by $g(y) = \frac{((\sqrt{y-6}) - 3)}{2}$.

Now, $gof(x) = g(f(x)) = g(4x^2 + 12x + 15)$

$= g((2x+3)^2 + 6)$

$= \frac{((\sqrt{(2x+3)^2 + 6 - 6}) - 3)}{2}$

$= \frac{(2x + 3 - 3)}{2} = x$

and $fog(y) = f\left(\frac{((\sqrt{y-6}) - 3)}{2}\right)$

$= \left(\frac{2((\sqrt{y-6}) - 3)}{2} + 3\right)^2 + 6$

$= ((\sqrt{y-6}) - 3 + 3)^2 + 6$

$= (\sqrt{y-6})^2 + 6$

$= y - 6 + 6 = y$

Hence, $gof = I_N$ and $fog = I_S$. This implies that f is invertible with $f^{-1} = g$.

123. (*b*) Let $y = f(x) \Rightarrow f^{-1}(y) = x$. The given function is

$$f(x) = 2^{x(x-1)}$$

$\Rightarrow x(x-1) = \log_2 f(x)$

$\Rightarrow x^2 - x - \log_2 f(x) = 0$

$\Rightarrow x = \frac{1 \pm \sqrt{1 + 4\log_2 f(x)}}{2}$

$\Rightarrow x = \frac{1 + \sqrt{1 + 4\log_2 f(x)}}{2}$

(x lies in the interval $[1, \infty)$)

$\therefore f^{-1}(y) = \frac{1 + \sqrt{1 + 4\log_2 y}}{2}$ [$y = f(x)$]

$\therefore f^{-1}(x) = \frac{1 + \sqrt{1 + 4\log_2 x}}{2}$ (replacing y by x)

124. (*a*) Given that, $\frac{\sin(x+y)}{\sin(x-y)} = \frac{a+b}{a-b}$

Using componendo and dividendo,

$$\frac{\sin(x+y) + [\sin(x-y)]}{\sin(x+y) - \sin(x-y)} = \frac{a+b+a-b}{a+b-a+b}$$

$$\Rightarrow \frac{2\sin\left(\frac{x+y+x-y}{2}\right)\cdot\cos\left(\frac{x+y-x+y}{2}\right)}{2\cos\left(\frac{x+y+x-y}{2}\right)\cdot\sin\left(\frac{x+y-x+y}{2}\right)} = \frac{2a}{2b}$$

$$\left[\begin{array}{l}\sin x + \sin y = 2\sin\frac{x+y}{2}\cdot\cos\frac{x-y}{2} \text{ and} \\ \sin x - \sin y = 2\cos\frac{x+y}{2}\cdot\sin\frac{x-y}{2}\end{array}\right]$$

$$\Rightarrow \frac{\sin x\cdot\cos y}{\cos x\cdot\sin y} = \frac{a}{b} \Rightarrow \frac{\tan x}{\tan y} = \frac{a}{b}$$

125. *(b)* Given expression,

$$\cos^4\frac{\pi}{8} + \cos^4\frac{3\pi}{8} + \cos^4\frac{5\pi}{8} + \cos^4\frac{7\pi}{8}$$

$$= \cos^4\frac{\pi}{8} + \cos^4\frac{3\pi}{8} + \cos^4\left(\pi - \frac{3\pi}{8}\right) + \cos^4\left(\pi - \frac{\pi}{8}\right)$$

$$= \cos^4\frac{\pi}{8} + \cos^4\frac{3\pi}{8} + \cos^4\frac{3\pi}{8} + \cos^4\frac{\pi}{8}$$

$$= 2\left[\cos^4\frac{\pi}{8} + \cos^4\frac{3\pi}{8}\right]$$

$$= 2\left[\cos^4\frac{\pi}{8} + \cos^4\left(\frac{\pi}{2} - \frac{\pi}{8}\right)\right] = 2\left[\cos^4\frac{\pi}{8} + \sin^4\frac{\pi}{8}\right]$$

$$= 2\left[\left(\cos^2\frac{\pi}{8} + \sin^2\frac{\pi}{8}\right)^2 - 2\cos^2\frac{\pi}{8}\cdot\sin^2\frac{\pi}{8}\right]$$

$$= 2\left[1 - 2\cos^2\frac{\pi}{8}\cdot\sin^2\frac{\pi}{8}\right]$$

$$= 2 - \left(2\sin\frac{\pi}{8}\cdot\cos\frac{\pi}{8}\right)^2 = 2 - \left(\sin\frac{2\pi}{8}\right)^2$$

$$= 2 - \left(\frac{1}{\sqrt{2}}\right)^2 = 2 - \frac{1}{2} = \frac{3}{2}$$

126. *(d)* Given that, $\tan\alpha = \dfrac{m}{m+1}$ and $\tan\beta = \dfrac{1}{2m+1}$

Now, $\tan(\alpha+\beta) = \dfrac{\tan\alpha + \tan\beta}{1 - \tan\alpha\cdot\tan\beta}$

$$\Rightarrow \tan(\alpha+\beta) = \frac{\frac{m}{m+1} + \frac{1}{2m+1}}{1 - \left(\frac{m}{m+1}\right)\left(\frac{1}{2m+1}\right)}$$

$$\Rightarrow \tan(\alpha+\beta) = \frac{m(2m+1) + m + 1}{(m+1)(2m+1) - m}$$

$$\Rightarrow \tan(\alpha+\beta) = \frac{2m^2 + m + m + 1}{2m^2 + 2m + m + 1 - m}$$

$$\Rightarrow \tan(\alpha+\beta) = \frac{2m^2 + 2m + 1}{2m^2 + 2m + 1}$$

$$\Rightarrow \tan(\alpha+\beta) = 1$$

$$\therefore \alpha + \beta = \frac{\pi}{4}$$

127. *(c)* Given equation, $\tan x + \sec x = 2\cos x$

$$\Rightarrow \frac{\sin x}{\cos x} + \frac{1}{\cos x} = 2\cos x$$

$$\Rightarrow 1 + \sin x = 2\cos^2 x$$

$$\Rightarrow 1 + \sin x = 2(1 - \sin^2 x)$$

$$\Rightarrow 1 + \sin x = 2 - 2\sin^2 x$$

$$\Rightarrow 2\sin^2 x + \sin x - 1 = 0$$

$$\Rightarrow 2\sin^2 x + 2\sin x - \sin x - 1 = 0$$

$$\Rightarrow 2\sin x(\sin x + 1) - 1(\sin x + 1) = 0$$

$$\Rightarrow (\sin x + 1)(2\sin x - 1) = 0$$

$$\Rightarrow \sin x + 1 = 0 \text{ or } (2\sin x - 1) = 0$$

$$\Rightarrow \sin x = -1, \sin x = \frac{1}{2}$$

$$\therefore x = \frac{3\pi}{2}, x = \frac{\pi}{6}$$

Hence, only two solutions possible.

128. *(d)* Here, $\cos\theta = x + \dfrac{1}{x}$

$$\Rightarrow \cos\theta = \frac{x^2+1}{x}$$

$$x^2 - x\cos\theta + 1 = 0$$

For real value of x, $(-\cos\theta)^2 - 4\times1\times1 \geq 0$ [$\because$ Discriminant $(D) \geq 0$]

$$\cos^2\theta \geq 4$$

$$\cos\theta \in (-\infty, -2) \cup [2, \infty)$$

which is not possible. [$\because -1 \leq \cos\theta \leq 1$]

129. *(c)* Let $\theta = 45°$

We know that, $\tan\dfrac{\theta}{2} = \dfrac{\sin\frac{\theta}{2}}{\cos\frac{\theta}{2}} = \dfrac{2\sin\frac{\theta}{2}\cdot\cos\frac{\theta}{2}}{2\cos^2\frac{\theta}{2}}$

$$\Rightarrow \tan\frac{\theta}{2} = \frac{\sin\theta}{1+\cos\theta}$$

$$\therefore \tan 22°30' = \frac{\sin 45°}{1+\cos 45°} \quad [\because \theta = 45°]$$

$$= \frac{\frac{1}{\sqrt{2}}}{1+\frac{1}{\sqrt{2}}} = \frac{1}{\sqrt{2}+1}$$

130. *(d)* We have,

$$\tan\frac{1}{2}\left[\sin^{-1}\frac{2x}{1+x^2} + \cos^{-1}\frac{1-y^2}{1+y^2}\right]$$

$$\left[\begin{array}{l}\because 2\tan^{-1}x = \sin^{-1}\left(\frac{2x}{1+x^2}\right) \\ \text{and } 2\tan^{-1}y = \cos^{-1}\left(\frac{1-y^2}{1+y^2}\right)\end{array}\right]$$

$$= \tan\left(\frac{1}{2}(2\tan^{-1}x + 2\tan^{-1}y)\right)$$

$$= \tan\left[\frac{1}{2} \times 2(\tan^{-1}x + \tan^{-1}y)\right]$$

$$= \tan(\tan^{-1}x + \tan^{-1}y)$$

$$= \tan\left[\tan^{-1}\left(\frac{x+y}{1-xy}\right)\right] = \frac{x+y}{1-xy}$$

$$\left(\because \tan^{-1}x + \tan^{-1}y = \tan^{-1}\frac{x+y}{1-xy}\right)$$

131. *(a)* Let $P(n): 10^n + 3 \cdot 4^{n+2} + k$ is divisible by 9, for all $n \in N$.

For $n = 1$, the given statement is also true

$10^1 + 3 \cdot 4^{1+2} + k$ is divisible by 9.

$$= 10 + 3 \cdot 64 + k = 10 + 192 + k = 202 + k$$

If $(202 + k)$ is divisible by 9, then the least value of k must be 5.

$202 + 5 = 207$ is divisible by 9

$$\Rightarrow \frac{207}{9} = 23$$

Hence, the least value of k is 5.

132. *(d)* Given that, $\sum_{n=1}^{13} (i^n + i^{n+1}), n \in N$

$$= (i + i^2 + i^3 + i^4 + i^5 + i^6 + i^7 + i^8 + i^9 + i^{10} + i^{11} + i^{12} + i^{13}) + (i^2 + i^3 + i^4 + i^5 + i^6 + i^7 + i^8 + i^9 + i^{10} + i^{11} + i^{12} + i^{13} + i^{14})$$

$$= (i + 2i^2 + 2i^3 + 2i^4 + 2i^5 + 2i^6 + 2i^7 + 2i^8 + 2i^9 + 2i^{10} + 2i^{11} + 2i^{12} + 2i^{13} + i^{14})$$

$$= i - 2 - 2i + 2 + 2i + 2(i^4)i^2 + 2(i)^4 i^3 + 2(i^2)^4 + 2(i^2)^4 i + 2(i^2)^5 + 2(i^4)^2 \cdot i^3 + 2(i^4)^3 + 2(i^4)^3 i (i^2)^7$$

$$= i - 2 - 2i + 2 + 2i - 2 - 2i + 2 + 2i - 2 - 2i + 2 + 2i - 1$$

$$= -1 + i$$

Alternate method

$$\sum_{n=1}^{13} (i^n + i^{n+1}), n \in N = \sum_{n=1}^{13} i^n (1 + i)$$

$$= (1+i)[i + i^2 + i^3 + i^4 + i^5 + i^6 + i^7 + i^8 + i^9 + i^{10} + i^{11} + i^{12} + i^{13}]$$

$$= (1+i)[i^{13}] \qquad \left[\because i^n + i^{n+1} + i^{n+2} + i^{n+3} = 0, \sum_{n=1}^{12} i^n = 0\right]$$

$$= (1+i)i \qquad [\because (i^4)^3 \cdot i = i]$$

$$= (i^2 + i) = i - 1$$

133. *(a)* Let $z = x + iy$

$$\text{Now, } \frac{\bar{z}+2}{\bar{z}-1} = \frac{x - iy + 2}{x - iy - 1}$$

$$= \frac{[(x+2) - iy][(x-1) + iy]}{[(x-1) - iy][(x-1) + iy]}$$

$$= \frac{(x-1)(x+2) - iy(x-1) + iy(x+2) + y^2}{(x-1)^2 + y^2}$$

$$= \frac{(x-1)(x+2) + y^2 + i[(x+2)y - (x-1)y]}{(x-1)^2 + y^2}$$

$$[\because -i^2 = 1]$$

Taking real part, $\dfrac{(x-1)(x+2) + y^2}{(x-1)^2 + y^2} = 4$

$$\Rightarrow x^2 - x + 2x - 2 + y^2 = 4(x^2 - 2x + 1 + y^2)$$

$\Rightarrow 3x^2 + 3y^2 - 9x + 6 = 0$, which represents a circle.

Hence, z lies on the circle.

134. *(d)* Let $z = \sin x + i\cos 2x$

and $\quad \bar{z} = \sin x - i\cos 2x \qquad$ ...(i)

Given that, $\bar{z} = \cos x - i\sin 2x \qquad$ ...(ii)

$\therefore \sin x - i\cos 2x = \cos x - i\sin 2x$

$\Rightarrow \quad \sin x = \cos x$ and $\cos 2x = \sin 2x$

$\Rightarrow \quad \tan x = 1$ and $\tan 2x = 1$

$\Rightarrow \quad \tan x = \tan\dfrac{\pi}{4}$

and $\quad \tan 2x = \tan\dfrac{\pi}{4}$

$\Rightarrow \quad x = n\pi + \dfrac{\pi}{4}$ and $2x = n\pi + \dfrac{\pi}{4}$

For $n = 0, 1, 2, 3, \ldots$

$x = \dfrac{\pi}{4}, \dfrac{5\pi}{4}, \dfrac{9\pi}{4}, \ldots$ and $x = \dfrac{\pi}{8}, \dfrac{5\pi}{8}, \dfrac{9\pi}{8}, \ldots$

No value of x coincide.

135. *(a)* Given equation,

$$\left(\frac{3 - 4ix}{3 + 4ix}\right) = \alpha - i\beta \ (\alpha, \beta \in R)$$

$$\Rightarrow \left[\frac{3 - 4ix}{3 + 4ix}\right] = \alpha - i\beta$$

$$\text{Now, } (\alpha - i\beta) = \frac{(3 - 4ix)(3 - 4ix)}{(3 + 4ix)(3 - 4ix)}$$

$$= \frac{9 + 16i^2x^2 - 24ix}{9 - 16i^2x^2}$$

$$\Rightarrow \alpha - i\beta = \frac{9 - 16x^2 - 24ix}{9 + 16x^2}$$

$$\Rightarrow \alpha - i\beta = \frac{9 - 16x^2}{9 + 16x^2} - \frac{i24x}{9 + 16x^2} \qquad \text{...(i)}$$

$$\therefore \alpha + i\beta = \frac{9 - 16x^2}{9 + 16x^2} + \frac{i24x}{9 + 16x^2} \qquad \text{...(ii)}$$

$$\text{So, } (\alpha - i\beta)(\alpha + i\beta) = \left(\frac{9 - 16x^2}{9 + 16x^2}\right)^2 - \left(\frac{i24x}{9 + 16x^2}\right)^2$$

$$\therefore \alpha^2 + \beta^2 = \frac{81 + 256x^4 - 288x^2 + 576x^2}{(9 + 16x^2)^2}$$

$$= \frac{81 + 256x^4 + 288x^2}{(9 + 16x^2)^2}$$

$$= \frac{(9 + 16x^2)^2}{(9+16x^2)^2} = 1$$

136. *(c)* Given that, total number of vowels = 4 and total number of consonants = 5

Total number of words formed by 2 vowels and 3 consonants

$$= {}^4C_2 \times {}^5C_3 = \frac{4!}{2!2!} \times \frac{5!}{3!2!}$$

$$= \frac{4 \times 3!}{2!2!} \times \frac{5 \times 4 \times 3 \times 2!}{3! \times 2!} = \frac{4 \times 5 \times 4 \times 3}{4}$$

$$= 5 \times 4 \times 3 = 60$$

Arrangement of these words is 5! *i.e.*, 120.

So, total number of words = $60 \times 120 = 7200$

137. *(b)* Let the total number of persons in the room is n.

We know that, two persons form 1 hand shaken.

$\therefore$ Required number of hand shakes = ${}^nC_2$

$$= \frac{n!}{2!(n-2)!} = \frac{n(n-1)}{2}$$

According to the question, $\frac{n(n-1)}{2} = 66$

$\Rightarrow \quad n(n-1) = 132$

$\Rightarrow \quad n^2 - n - 132 = 0$

$\Rightarrow \quad (n-12)(n+11) = 0$

$\Rightarrow \quad n = 12, -11$ [inadmissible]

$\therefore \quad n = 12$

138. *(a)* Number of men = 4

and number of women = 6

It is given that committee includes two men and exactly twice as many women as men.

Thus, possible selection is given in following table

Men	Women
2	4
3	6

Required number of committee formed

$$= {}^4C_2 \times {}^6C_4 + {}^4C_3 \times {}^6C_6$$

$$= 6 \times 15 + 4 \times 1 = 94$$

139. *(a)* Given that, $r > 1, n > 2$ and the coefficients of $(3r)$th and $(r+2)$th term are equal in the expansion of $(1+x)^{2n}$.

Then, $T_{3r} = T_{3r-1+1} = {}^{2n}C_{3r-1}\, x^{3r-1}$

and $T_{r+2} = T_{r+1+1} = {}^{2n}C_{r+1}\, x^{r+1}$

Given, ${}^{2n}C_{3r-1} = {}^{2n}C_{r+1}$

$[\because {}^nC_x = {}^nC_y \Rightarrow x + y = n]$

$\Rightarrow \quad 3r - 1 + r + 1 = 2n$

$\Rightarrow \quad 4r = 2n$

$\Rightarrow \quad n = \frac{4r}{2}$

$\therefore \quad n = 2r$

140. *(c)* Given expansion is $\left(\sqrt[3]{2} + \frac{1}{\sqrt[3]{3}}\right)^n$.

$\therefore \quad T_7 = T_{6+1} = {}^nC_6(\sqrt[3]{2})^{n-6}\left(\frac{1}{\sqrt[3]{3}}\right)^6 \quad$ ...(i)

Since, T_7 from end is same as the T_7 from beginning of $\left(\frac{1}{\sqrt[3]{3}} + \sqrt[3]{2}\right)^n$.

Then, $\quad T_7 = T_{6+1} = {}^nC_6\left(\frac{1}{\sqrt[3]{3}}\right)^{n-6}(\sqrt[3]{2})^6 \quad$ ...(ii)

Given that, ${}^nC_6(2)^{\frac{n-6}{3}}(3)^{-6/3} = {}^nC_6(3)^{-\frac{(n-6)}{3}}\, 2^{6/3}$

$\Rightarrow \quad (2)^{\frac{n-12}{3}} = \left(\frac{1}{3^{1/3}}\right)^{n-12}$

which is true, when $\frac{n-12}{3} = 0$.

$\Rightarrow \quad n - 12 = 0$

$\Rightarrow \quad n = 12$

141. *(b)* Given, x, $2y$ and $3z$ are in AP.

Then, $\quad 2y = \frac{x+3z}{2}$

$\Rightarrow \quad y = \frac{x+3z}{4}$

$\Rightarrow \quad 4y = x + 3z \quad$ ...(i)

and x, y, z are in GP.

Then, $\quad \frac{y}{x} = \frac{z}{y} = \lambda$

$\Rightarrow y = x\lambda$ and $z = \lambda y = \lambda^2 x$

On substituting these values in Eq. (i), we get

$$4(x\lambda) = x + 3(\lambda^2 x)$$

$\Rightarrow \quad 4\lambda x = x + 3\lambda^2 x \Rightarrow 4\lambda = 1 + 3\lambda^2$

$\Rightarrow \quad 3\lambda^2 - 4\lambda + 1 = 0 \Rightarrow (3\lambda - 1)(\lambda - 1) = 0$

$\therefore \quad \lambda = \frac{1}{3}, \lambda = 1$

142. *(a)* $\sum_{r=1}^{n} \frac{S_r}{s_r} = \frac{S_1}{s_1} + \frac{S_2}{s_2} + \frac{S_3}{s_3} + \quad + \frac{S_n}{s_n}$

Let T_n be the nth term of the above series.

$$\therefore \quad T_n = \frac{S_n}{s_n} = \frac{\left[\frac{n(n+1)}{2}\right]^2}{\frac{n(n+1)}{2}}$$

$$= \frac{n(n+1)}{2} = \frac{1}{2}[n^2 + n]$$

$\therefore$ Sum of the above series = ΣT_n

MOCK TEST 1

$= \frac{1}{2}[\Sigma n^2 + \Sigma n]$

$= \frac{1}{2}\left[\frac{n(n+1)(2n+1)}{6} + \frac{n(n+1)}{2}\right]$

$= \frac{1}{2} \cdot \frac{n(n+1)}{2}\left[\frac{(2n+1)}{3} + 1\right]$

$= \frac{1}{4} n(n+1)\left[\frac{2n+1+3}{3}\right]$

$= \frac{1}{4 \times 3} n(n+1)(2n+4)$

$= \frac{1}{12} n(n+1)(2n+4)$

$= \frac{1}{6} n(n+1)(n+2)$

143. *(c)* Since, intercepts on the axes are $a, -b$ then equation of the line is $\frac{x}{a} - \frac{y}{b} = 1$.

$\Rightarrow \quad \frac{y}{b} = \frac{x}{a} - 1$

$\Rightarrow \quad y = \frac{bx}{a} - b$

So, the slope of this line *i.e.*, $m_1 = \frac{b}{a}$.

Also, for intercepts on the axes as $b, -a$, then equation of the line is

$\frac{x}{b} - \frac{y}{a} = 1$

$\Rightarrow \quad \frac{y}{a} = \frac{x}{b} - 1$

$\Rightarrow \quad y = \frac{a}{b} x - a$

and slope of this line *i.e.*, $m_2 = \frac{a}{b}$

$\therefore \tan\theta = \frac{\frac{b}{a} - \frac{a}{b}}{1 + \frac{a}{b} \cdot \frac{b}{a}} = \frac{\frac{b^2 - a^2}{ab}}{2} = \frac{b^2 - a^2}{2ab}$

144. *(a)* Given equation of lines

$2x - 3y + 5 = 0 \quad \ldots(i)$

and $\quad 3x + 4y = 0 \quad \ldots(ii)$

From Eq. (ii), put the value of $x = \frac{-4y}{3}$ in Eq. (i), we get

$2\left(\frac{-4y}{3}\right) - 3y + 5 = 0$

$\Rightarrow \quad -8y - 9y + 15 = 0$

$\Rightarrow \quad y = \frac{15}{17}$

From Eq. (ii), $3x + 4 \cdot \frac{15}{17} = 0$

$\Rightarrow \quad x = \frac{-60}{17 \cdot 3} = \frac{-20}{17}$

So, the point of intersection is $\left(\frac{-20}{17}, \frac{15}{17}\right)$.

$\therefore$ Required distance from the line $5x - 2y = 0$ is,

$d = \frac{\left|-5 \times \frac{20}{17} - 2\left(\frac{15}{17}\right)\right|}{\sqrt{25+4}} = \frac{\left|\frac{-100}{17} - \frac{30}{17}\right|}{\sqrt{29}} = \frac{130}{17\sqrt{29}}$

[$\because$ distance of a point $p(x_1, y_1)$ from the line $ax + by + c = 0$ is $d = \frac{|ax_1 + by_1 + c|}{\sqrt{a^2 + b^2}}$]

145. *(a)* So, the given point A is $(3, -2)$.

So, the equation of line $\sqrt{3}x + y = 1$.

$\Rightarrow \quad y = -\sqrt{3}x + 1$

$\therefore$ Slope, $m_1 = -\sqrt{3}$

Let slope of the required line be m_2.

$\therefore \quad \tan\theta = \left|\frac{-\sqrt{3} - m_2}{1 - \sqrt{3}m_2}\right| \quad \left[\because \tan\theta = \left|\frac{m_1 - m_2}{1 + m_1 m_2}\right|\right]$

$\Rightarrow \tan 60° = \pm\left(\frac{-\sqrt{3} - m_2}{1 - \sqrt{3}m_2}\right) \quad \ldots(i)$

$\Rightarrow \quad \sqrt{3} = \left(\frac{-\sqrt{3} - m_2}{1 - \sqrt{3}m_2}\right) \quad$ [taking positive sign]

$\Rightarrow \quad \sqrt{3} - 3m_2 = -\sqrt{3} - m_2$

$\Rightarrow \quad 2\sqrt{3} = 2m_2$

$\Rightarrow \quad m_2 = \sqrt{3}$

$\therefore$ Equation of line passing through $(3, -2)$ is

$y + 2 = \sqrt{3}(x - 3)$

$y - \sqrt{3}x + 2 + 3\sqrt{3} = 0$

$\Rightarrow \sqrt{3}x - y - 2 - 3\sqrt{3} = 0 \quad \ldots(i)$

[taking negative sign from Eq. (i)]

$\Rightarrow \quad \sqrt{3} - 3m_2 = \sqrt{3} + m_2$

$\Rightarrow \quad m_2 = 0$

$\therefore$ The equation of line is

$y + 2 = 0(x - 3)$

$\Rightarrow \quad y + 2 = 0 \quad \ldots(iii)$

So, the required equation of lines are

$\sqrt{3}x - y - 2 - 3\sqrt{3} = 0$ and $y + 2 = 0$.

146. *(c)* Let centre of the circle be (a, a), then equation of the circle is $(x - a)^2 + (y - a)^2 = a^2$.

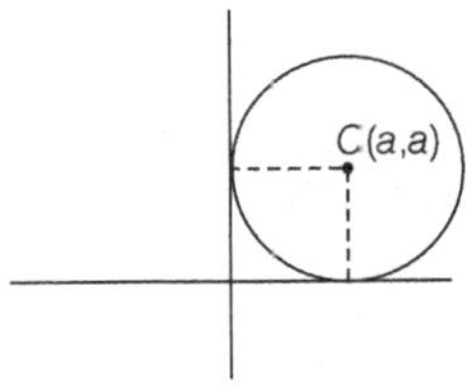

Since, the point (3, 6) lies on this circle, then

$$(3-a)^2+(6-a)^2=a^2$$
$$\Rightarrow \quad a^2+9-6a+36-12a+a^2=a^2$$
$$\Rightarrow \quad a^2-18a+45=0$$
$$\Rightarrow \quad a^2-15a-3a+45=0$$
$$\Rightarrow \quad a(a-15)-3(a-15)=0$$
$$\Rightarrow \quad (a-3)(a-15)=0$$
$$\Rightarrow \quad a=3, a=15$$

So, the equation of circle is

$$(x-3)^2+(y-3)^2=9$$
$$\Rightarrow \quad x^2-6x+9+y^2-6y+9=9$$
$$\Rightarrow \quad x^2+y^2-6x-6y+9=0$$

147. *(c)* Given that, length of the median $AD = 3a$

Radius of the circle $= \frac{3}{2} \times$ Length of median

$$= \frac{2}{3} \times 3a = 2a$$

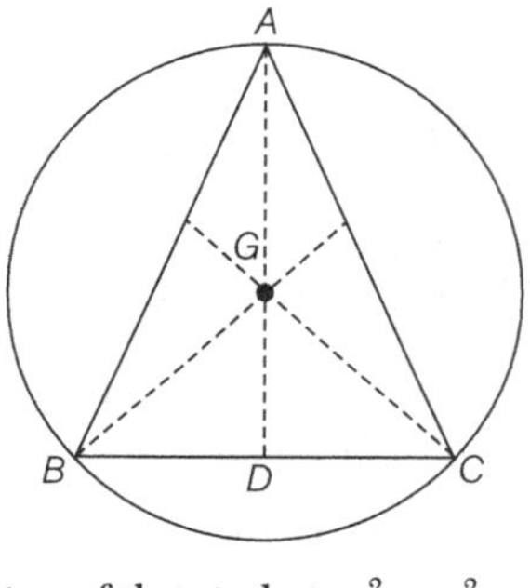

So, the equation of the circle is $x^2+y^2=4a^2$.

148. *(a)* Here, vertex $=(-3, 0)$

and directrix, $x+5=0$

Let us draw the graph with the help of above information.

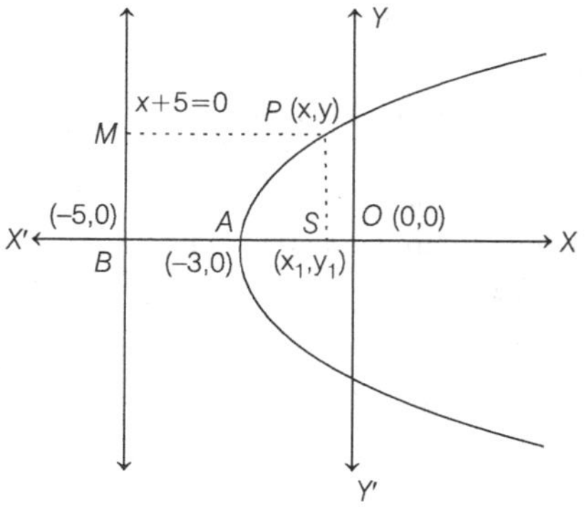

Since, axis of the parabola is a line perpendicular to directrix and A is the mid-point of BS.

Then, $-3 = \frac{x_1-5}{2}$

$$\Rightarrow \quad -6 = x_1 - 5 \Rightarrow x_1 = -1,$$

$$0 = \frac{0+y_1}{2} \Rightarrow y_1 = 0$$

$$\therefore \quad S=(-1, 0)$$
$$PM = PS$$
$$\Rightarrow \quad |x+5| = \sqrt{(x+1)^2+y^2}$$
$$\Rightarrow \quad x^2+2x+1+y^2 = x^2+10x+25$$
$$\Rightarrow \quad y^2 = 8x+24$$
$$\Rightarrow \quad y^2 = 8(x+3)$$

149. *(b)* Given that, line $y = mx+1$ is tangent to the parabola $y^2 = 4x$.

$$\therefore \quad y = mx+1 \quad \text{...(i)}$$
$$\text{and} \quad y^2 = 4x \quad \text{...(ii)}$$

From Eqs. (i) and (ii),

$$m^2x^2+2mx+1=4x$$
$$\Rightarrow \quad m^2x^2+2mx-4x+1=0$$
$$\Rightarrow \quad m^2x^2+x(2m-4)+1=0$$

For real values of m discriminant $= 0$

$$(2m-4)^2-4m^2 \times 1 = 0$$
$$\Rightarrow \quad 4m^2+16-16m-4m^2=0$$
$$\Rightarrow \quad 16m = 16$$
$$\therefore \quad m = 1$$

150. *(a)* Given that, focus of the ellipse is $(1, -1)$ and the equation of directrix is $x-y-3=0$ and $e = \frac{1}{2}$

Let $P(x, y)$ and $F(1, -1)$.

$$\therefore \quad \frac{PF}{\text{Distance of } P \text{ from } (x-y-3=0)} = \frac{1}{2}$$
$$\Rightarrow \quad \frac{\sqrt{(x-1)^2+(y+1)^2}}{\frac{|x-y-3|}{\sqrt{2}}} = \frac{1}{2}$$
$$\Rightarrow \quad \frac{2[x^2-2x+1+y^2+2y+1]}{(x-y-3)^2} = \frac{1}{4}$$
$$\Rightarrow \quad 8x^2-16x+16+8y^2+16y = x^2+y^2+9-2xy+6y-6x$$
$$\Rightarrow \quad 7x^2+7y^2+2xy-10x+10y+7=0$$

151. *(b)* Given that, eccentricity $= \frac{5}{8}$, *i.e.*, $e = \frac{5}{8}$

Let equation of the ellipse be $\frac{x^2}{a^2}+\frac{y^2}{b^2}=1$,

Since the foci of this ellipse is $(\pm ae, 0)$.

$\therefore$ Distance between foci $= \sqrt{(ae+ae)^2}$

$$\Rightarrow \quad 2\sqrt{a^2e^2} = 10$$

[distance between its foci = 10]

$$\Rightarrow \quad \sqrt{a^2e^2} = 5$$
$$\Rightarrow \quad a^2e^2 = 25$$

MOCK TEST 1

$$\Rightarrow \quad a^2 = \frac{25 \times 64}{25}$$

$$\therefore \quad a = 8$$

We know that,

$$b^2 = a^2(1 - e^2)$$

$$\Rightarrow \quad b^2 = 64\left(1 - \frac{25}{64}\right)$$

$$\Rightarrow \quad b^2 = 64\left(\frac{64 - 25}{64}\right)$$

$$b^2 = 39$$

∴ Length of latusrectum of ellipse

$$= \frac{2b^2}{a} = 2\left(\frac{39}{8}\right) = \frac{39}{4}$$

152. *(c)* Length of latusrectum of the hyperbola *i.e.*,

$$8 = \frac{2b^2}{a} \Rightarrow b^2 = 4a \quad \text{...(i)}$$

∴ Distance between the foci = $2ae$

Since, transverse axis be a and conjugate axis be b.

$$\therefore \quad \frac{1}{2}(2ae) = 2b$$

$$\Rightarrow \quad ae = 2b \quad \text{...(ii)}$$

$$b^2 = a^2(e^2 - 1) \quad \text{...(iii)}$$

From Eqs. (i) and (ii),

$$4a = \frac{a^2e^2}{4}$$

$$\Rightarrow \quad 16a = a^2e^2$$

$$\Rightarrow \quad 16 = ae^2 \Rightarrow a = \frac{16}{e^2}$$

Eq. (iii), $4a = a^2(e^2 - 1)$

$$\Rightarrow \quad \frac{4}{a} = e^2 - 1$$

$$\Rightarrow \quad \frac{4e^2}{16} = e^2 - 1$$

$$\Rightarrow \quad e^2\left(1 - \frac{4}{16}\right) = 1$$

$$\Rightarrow \quad e^2\left(\frac{12}{16}\right) = 1$$

$$\Rightarrow \quad e^2 = \left(\frac{16}{12}\right)$$

$$\Rightarrow \quad e^2 = \frac{4}{3} \Rightarrow e = \frac{2}{\sqrt{3}}$$

153. *(b)* Given equation of line is

$$\frac{x+2}{3} = \frac{y+1}{2} = \frac{z-3}{2} = \lambda \quad \text{(let)}$$

$$\Rightarrow x = 3\lambda - 2,\ y = 2\lambda - 1,\ z = 2\lambda + 3 \quad \text{...(i)}$$

∴ Coordinates of any point on the line are $(3\lambda - 2, 2\lambda - 1, 2\lambda + 3)$.

The distance between this point and (1, 2, 3) is $\frac{6}{\sqrt{2}}$

$$\therefore \quad \sqrt{(3\lambda - 2 - 1)^2 + (2\lambda - 1 - 2)^2 + (2\lambda + 3 - 3)^2} = \frac{6}{\sqrt{2}}$$

$$\Rightarrow (3\lambda - 3)^2 + (2\lambda - 3)^2 + (2\lambda)^2 = \frac{36}{2}$$

(squaring on both sides)

$$\Rightarrow 9\lambda^2 + 9 - 18\lambda + 4\lambda^2 + 9 - 12\lambda + 4\lambda^2 = 18$$

$$\Rightarrow \quad 17\lambda^2 - 30\lambda = 0$$

$$\Rightarrow \quad \lambda(17\lambda - 30) = 0$$

$$\Rightarrow \quad \lambda = 0, \frac{30}{17}$$

Substituting the values of λ in Eq. (i), we get the required point $(-2, -1, 3)$ or $\left(\frac{56}{17}, \frac{43}{17}, \frac{111}{17}\right)$.

154. *(c)* Given, $\lim_{x \to 0}\left(\sin mx \cot \frac{x}{\sqrt{3}}\right) = 2$

$$\Rightarrow \lim_{x \to 0} \frac{\sin mx}{mx} \cdot mx \cdot \frac{1}{\tan \frac{x}{\sqrt{3}}} = 2$$

$$\Rightarrow \lim_{x \to 0} \frac{\sin mx}{mx} \cdot mx \cdot \frac{\frac{x}{\sqrt{3}}}{\tan \frac{x}{\sqrt{3}}} \cdot \frac{1}{\frac{x}{\sqrt{3}}} = 2$$

$$\Rightarrow \lim_{x \to 0} \frac{\sin mx}{mx} \cdot \lim_{x \to 0} \frac{\frac{x}{\sqrt{3}}}{\tan \frac{x}{\sqrt{3}}} \cdot \lim_{x \to 0} \frac{mx}{\frac{x}{\sqrt{3}}} = 2$$

$$\Rightarrow \quad \sqrt{3}m = 2$$

$$\therefore \quad m = \frac{2\sqrt{3}}{3}$$

155. *(b)* We have,

$$f(x) = \begin{cases} \dfrac{\sin^3(\sqrt{x})\log(1 + 3x)}{(\tan^{-1}\sqrt{x})^2(e^{5\sqrt{x}} - 1)x}, & x \neq 0 \\ a, & x = 0 \end{cases}$$

For continuity in [0, 1], $f(0) = \lim_{x \to 0} f(x)$

$$\therefore \quad \lim_{x \to 0} \frac{\sin^3 \sqrt{x} \log(1 + 3x)}{x(\tan^{-1}\sqrt{x})^2(e^{5\sqrt{x}} - 1)} = a$$

$$\left[\lim_{x \to 0} \frac{e^x - 1}{x} = 1\right.$$

$$\lim_{x \to 0} \frac{\sin x}{x} = 1$$

$$\lim_{x \to 0} \frac{\tan^2 x}{x} = 1$$

$$\left.\lim_{x \to 0} \frac{\log(1 + x)}{x} = 1\right]$$

MOCK TEST 1

$$\Rightarrow \lim_{x \to 0}\left[\frac{3}{5}\frac{\sin^3\sqrt{x}}{(\sqrt{x})^3}\cdot\frac{(\sqrt{x})^2}{(\tan^{-1}\sqrt{x})^2}\times \frac{\log(1+3x)}{3x}\cdot\frac{5\sqrt{x}}{(e^{5\sqrt{x}}-1)}\right] = a$$

$$\Rightarrow a = \frac{3}{5}$$

156. *(d)* Given, $f(x) = \dfrac{x^n - a^n}{x - a}$

$$\therefore \quad f'(x) = \frac{(x-a)nx^{n-1} - (x^n - a^n)(1)}{(x-a)^2}$$

[by quotient rule]

$$\Rightarrow \quad f'(x) = \frac{nx^{n-1}(x-a) - x^n + a^n}{(x-a)^2}$$

Now, $f'(a) = \dfrac{na^{n-1}(0) - a^n + a^n}{(x-a)^2}$

$$\Rightarrow \quad f'(a) = \frac{0}{0}$$

So, $f'(a)$ does not exist,
Since, $f(x)$ is not defined at $x = a$.
Hence, $f'(x)$ at $x = a$ does not exist.

157. *(c)* Let $y = \left[\log\left\{e^x\left(\dfrac{x-2}{x+2}\right)^{3/4}\right\}\right]$

$$= \log e^x + \log\left(\frac{x-2}{x+2}\right)^{3/4}$$

$$\Rightarrow \quad y = x + \frac{3}{4}[\log(x-2) - \log(x+2)]$$

On differentiating w.r.t. x, we get

$$\frac{dy}{dx} = \frac{d}{dx}\left[x + \frac{3}{4}\{\log(x-2) - \log(x+2)\}\right]$$

$$= 1 + \frac{3}{4}\left[\frac{1}{x-2} - \frac{1}{x+2}\right] = 1 + \frac{3}{x^2-4} \Rightarrow \frac{dy}{dx} = \frac{x^2-1}{x^2-4}$$

158. *(c)* $f(x) = \cos\dfrac{x}{2}\cos\dfrac{x}{2^2}\cos\dfrac{x}{2^3} \quad \cos\dfrac{x}{2^n}$

Taking log on both sides, we get

$$\log f(x) = \log\cos\frac{x}{2} + \log\cos\frac{x}{2^2} + \quad \log\cos\frac{x}{2^n}$$

On differentiating w.r.t. x, we get

$$\frac{f'(x)}{f(x)} = -\left(\frac{1}{2}\tan\frac{x}{2} + \frac{1}{2^2}\tan\left(\frac{x}{2^2}\right) + \quad + \frac{1}{2^n}\tan\frac{x}{2^n}\right)$$

$$\Rightarrow -\frac{f'(x)}{f(x)} = \frac{1}{2}\tan\frac{x}{2} + \frac{1}{2^2}\tan\frac{x}{2^2} + \quad + \frac{1}{2^n}\tan\frac{x}{2^n}$$

159. *(a)* Given, $y = |\sin x|^{|x|}$

In the neighbourhood of $-\dfrac{\pi}{6}$, $|x|$ and $|\sin x|$ both are negative

i.e., $y = (-\sin x)^{(-x)}$

Now, $y|_{\text{at } x = \frac{-\pi}{6}} = \left\{-\sin\left(-\dfrac{\pi}{6}\right)\right\}^{-(-\pi/6)}$

$$= \left(\frac{1}{2}\right)^{\pi/6}$$

Taking log on both sides, we get
$\log y = (-x)\cdot\log(-\sin x)$
On differentiating w.r.t. x, we get

$$\frac{1}{y}\frac{dy}{dx} = (-x)\left(\frac{1}{-\sin x}\right)\cdot(-\cos x) + \log(-\sin x)\cdot(-1)$$

$$= -x\cot x - \log(-\sin x)$$

$$= -[x\cot x + \log(-\sin x)]$$

$$\Rightarrow \frac{dy}{dx} = -y[x\cot x + \log(-\sin x)]$$

$$= \frac{(2)^{\frac{-\pi}{6}}[6\log 2 - \sqrt{3}\pi]}{6}$$

$$\Rightarrow \quad \left.\frac{dy}{dx}\right|_{x=-\pi/6}$$

160. *(b)* Given, $\dfrac{d}{dx}(f'(x)) = -f(x)$

$\Rightarrow \qquad g'(x) = -f(x) \qquad [\;g(x) = f'(x)$, given]

Also given that

$$F(x) = \left\{f\left(\frac{x}{2}\right)\right\}^2 + \left\{g\left(\frac{x}{2}\right)\right\}^2$$

$$\Rightarrow \quad F'(x) = 2\left\{f\left(\frac{x}{2}\right)\right\}f'\left(\frac{x}{2}\right)\cdot\frac{1}{2} + 2\left\{g\left(\frac{x}{2}\right)\right\}g'\left(\frac{x}{2}\right)\cdot\frac{1}{2}$$

$$= f\left(\frac{x}{2}\right)g\left(\frac{x}{2}\right) + g\left(\frac{x}{2}\right)\left(-f\left(\frac{x}{2}\right)\right) = 0$$

Hence, $F(x)$ is a constant.
Therefore, $F(10) = 5$

161. *(c)* Given, $f(x) = 2x^2 - 3x$

Differentiating w.r.t. x, $f'(x) = 4x - 3$

On putting $f'(x) = 0$, we get $4x - 3 = 0$

$\Rightarrow x = 3/4$

The point $x = 3/4$ divides the real line into two disjoint intervals namely

$\left(-\infty, \dfrac{3}{4}\right)$ and $\left(\dfrac{3}{4}, \infty\right)$.

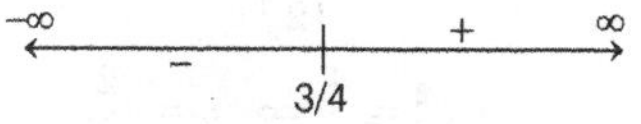

Intervals	Sign of $f'(x)$	Nature of $f(x)$
$\left(-\infty, \dfrac{3}{4}\right)$	(–) negative ($x < 3/4$)	Strictly decreasing
$\left(\dfrac{3}{4}, \infty\right)$	(+) positive ($x > 3/4$)	Strictly increasing

Hence, $f(x)$ is strictly increasing on $\left(\frac{3}{4}, \infty\right)$ and strictly decreasing on $\left(-\infty, \frac{3}{4}\right)$.

162. *(b)* We find $f'(x)$, then for $1 < x < 2$, put $f'(x) > 0$ and find the required least value of a.

Given, $f(x) = x^2 + ax + 1 \Rightarrow f'(x) = 2x + a$

In interval (1, 2), $1 < x < 2 \Rightarrow 2 < 2x < 4$

$\Rightarrow (2 + a) < (2x + a) < (4 + a)$

Since, $f(x)$ is strictly increasing function, then

$(2 + a) > 0$ [for this $f'(x) > 0$ and $(2x + a) > (2 + a)$]

$\therefore \quad (2 + a) > 0 \Rightarrow a > -2$.

Hence, the least value of $a = -2$.

163. *(b)* We have, $\frac{d}{dx}\{f(x)\} = \frac{1}{1 + x^2}$

On integrating both sides, we get

$$f(x) = \tan^{-1} x + C \qquad \left(\int \frac{1}{1 + x^2} dx = \tan^{-1} x\right)$$

Now $\frac{d}{dx} f(x^3) = \frac{d}{dx}(\tan^{-1} x^3 + C)$

$$= \frac{1}{1 + (x^3)^2} \cdot 3x^2 + 0 \qquad \left(\frac{d}{dx} \tan^{-1} x = \frac{1}{1 + x^2}\right)$$

$$= \frac{3x^2}{1 + x^6}$$

164. *(d)* $\int \left(\frac{10x^9 + 10^x \log_e 10}{x^{10} + 10^x}\right) dx$

Let $x^{10} + 10^x = t$

$\Rightarrow (10x^9 + 10^x \log_e 10)\, dx = dt$

$\Rightarrow dx = \frac{dt}{10x^9 + 10^x \log_e 10}$

$$\therefore \int \left(\frac{10x^9 + 10^x \log_e 10}{x^{10} + 10^x}\right) dx = \int \frac{10x^9 + 10^x \log_e 10}{t} \times \frac{dt}{10x^9 + 10^x \log_e 10}$$

$$= \int \frac{dt}{t} = \log|t| + C = \log|10^x + x^{10}| + C$$

165. *(b)* $\int \frac{dx}{\sin^2 x \cos^2 x} = \int \frac{\sin^2 x + \cos^2 x}{\sin^2 x \cdot \cos^2 x} dx$

$(\sin^2 x + \cos^2 x = 1)$

$$= \int \frac{\sin^2 x}{\sin^2 x \cdot \cos^2 x} dx + \int \frac{\cos^2 x}{\sin^2 x \cdot \cos^2 x} dx$$

$$= \int \frac{1}{\cos^2 x} dx + \int \frac{1}{\sin^2 x} dx$$

$$= \int \sec^2 x\, dx + \int \operatorname{cosec}^2 x\, dx$$

$$= \tan x - \cot x + C$$

166. *(b)* We have, $I = \int \frac{\sqrt{x}}{\sqrt{a^3 - x^3}} dx$

$$I = \int \frac{\sqrt{x}}{\sqrt{(a^{3/2})^2 - \left(x^{\frac{3}{2}}\right)^2}} dx$$

Put, $x^{\frac{3}{2}} = t$

$\Rightarrow \frac{3}{2} x^{\frac{1}{2}} dx = dt$

$\Rightarrow \sqrt{x}\, dx = \frac{2}{3} dt$

$$\therefore \quad I = \frac{2}{3} \int \frac{dt}{\sqrt{\left(a^{\frac{3}{2}}\right)^2 - t^2}}$$

$$= \frac{2}{3} \sin^{-1}\left(\frac{t}{a^{\frac{3}{2}}}\right) + C$$

$$= \frac{2}{3} \sin^{-1}\left(\frac{x^{\frac{3}{2}}}{a^{\frac{3}{2}}}\right) + C$$

$$= \frac{2}{3} \sin^{-1} \sqrt{\frac{x^3}{a^3}} + C$$

167. *(a)* Let $\frac{1}{x(x^2 + 1)} = \frac{A}{x} + \frac{Bx + C}{x^2 + 1}$

$\Rightarrow 1 = A(x^2 + 1) + (Bx + C)x$

On equating the coefficients of x^2, x and constant term on both sides, we get

$A + B = 0, C = 0$ and $A = 1$

On solving these equations, we get

$A = 1, B = -1$ and $C = 0$

$$\therefore \quad \frac{1}{x(x^2 + 1)} = \frac{1}{x} + \frac{-x}{x^2 + 1}$$

$$\therefore \quad \int \frac{1}{x(x^2 + 1)} dx = \int \left\{\frac{1}{x} - \frac{x}{x^2 + 1} dx\right\}$$

$$= \log|x| - \frac{1}{2}\log(x^2 + 1) + C$$

$\left[x^2 + 1 = t \Rightarrow 2x dx = dt \Rightarrow x dx = \frac{dt}{2},\right.$

$\left.\therefore \int \frac{x}{x^2 + 1} dx = \int \frac{1}{t} \frac{dt}{2} = \frac{1}{2} \log t = \frac{1}{2} \log(x^2 + 1)\right]$

168. *(d)* Let $I = \int \frac{x + \sin x}{1 + \cos x} dx = \int \frac{x + 2\sin(x/2) \cdot \cos(x/2)}{1 + 2\cos^2(x/2) - 1} dx$

$$\Rightarrow \int \frac{x}{2\cos^2(x/2)} dx + \int \frac{2\sin(x/2)\cos(x/2)}{2\cos^2(x/2)} dx$$

$$= \frac{1}{2}\int x\sec^2\frac{x}{2}\,dx + \int \tan\frac{x}{2}\,dx$$
I II
$$= \frac{1}{2}\left[x\int \sec^2\frac{x}{2}\,dx - \int\left[\frac{d}{dx}(x)\int \sec^2\frac{x}{2}\,dx\right]dx\right] + \int \tan\frac{x}{2}\,dx$$
$$= \frac{1}{2}\left[x\tan\frac{x}{2}\cdot 2 - 2\int \tan\frac{x}{2}\,dx\right] + \int \tan\frac{x}{2}\,dx$$
$$= x\tan\frac{x}{2} - \int \tan\frac{x}{2}\,dx + \int \tan\frac{x}{2}\,dx = x\tan\frac{x}{2} + C$$

169. *(b)* Let
$$f(x) = \int_0^x \left[\frac{1}{\sqrt{1+t^2}} - \frac{1}{1+t}\right]dt$$
$$= \int \log|t + \sqrt{1+t^2}| - \log|1+t|)]_0^x$$
$$= \left[\log\left|\frac{t+\sqrt{1+t^2}}{1+t}\right|\right]_0^x = \log\left|\frac{x+\sqrt{1+x^2}}{1+x}\right|$$
$$\lim_{x\to\infty} f(x) = \lim_{x\to\infty}\log\left(\frac{\sqrt{1+x^2}+x}{1+x}\right)$$
$$= \log\lim_{x\to\infty}\left(\frac{\sqrt{\frac{1}{x^2}+1}+1}{\frac{1}{x}+1}\right)$$
$$= \log_e 2 \qquad \left[\because \lim_{x\to\infty}\frac{1}{x} = 0\right]$$

170. *(b)* Intersection points of given curves with X-axis are $(-1, 0)$ and $(3, 0)$.

$\therefore$ Required area $= \int_{-1}^{3}(-x^2 + 2x + 3)\,dx$

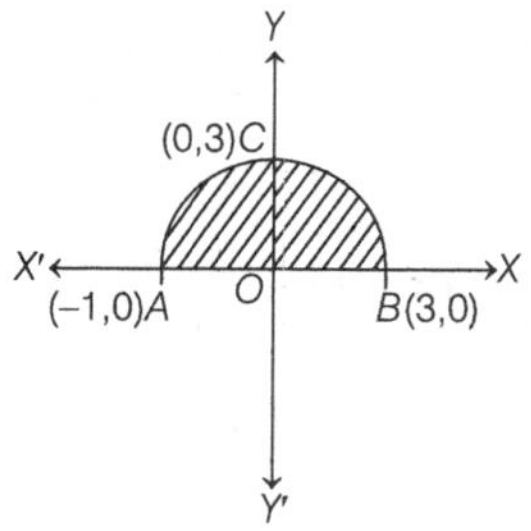

$$= \left[-\frac{x^3}{3} + \frac{2x^2}{2} + 3x\right]_{-1}^{3}$$
$$= \left[-9 + 9 + 9 - \left(\frac{1}{3} + 1 - 3\right)\right]$$
$$= \frac{32}{3}\text{ sq units}$$

171. *(a)* Consider, $y = \sqrt{a^2 - x^2}$

On differentiating both sides w.r.t. x, we get
$$\frac{dy}{dx} = y' = \frac{d}{dx}\sqrt{a^2 - x^2}$$
$$\Rightarrow \quad y' = \frac{1}{2}(a^2 - x^2)^{\frac{1}{2}-1}\frac{d}{dx}(a^2 - x^2)$$
$$\Rightarrow \quad y' = \frac{1}{2\sqrt{a^2 - x^2}}(-2x) = \frac{-x}{\sqrt{a^2 - x^2}}$$
On substituting the value of y' in equation $x + y\dfrac{dy}{dx} = 0$, we get
$$\text{LHS} = x + yy' = x + \sqrt{a^2 - x^2} \times \frac{-x}{\sqrt{a^2 - x^2}}$$
$$= x - x = 0 \qquad (\because y = \sqrt{a^2 - x^2})$$
$$\Rightarrow \quad x + yy' = 0$$
$\therefore y = \sqrt{a^2 - x^2}$ is a solution of the differential equation $x + y\dfrac{dy}{dx} = 0$.

172. *(d)* The equation of family of circles with centre on $y = 2$ and of radius 5 is
$$(x - \alpha)^2 + (y - 2)^2 = 5^2 \qquad \text{...(i)}$$
$$\Rightarrow \quad x^2 + \alpha^2 - 2\alpha x + y^2 + 4 - 4y = 25$$
On differentiating w.r.t. x, we get
$$2x - 2\alpha + 2y\frac{dy}{dx} - 4\frac{dy}{dx} = 0$$
$$\Rightarrow \quad \alpha = x + \frac{dy}{dx}(y - 2)$$
On putting the value of α in Eq. (i), we get
$$\left(x - x - \frac{dy}{dx}(y-2)\right)^2 + (y-2)^2 = 5^2$$
$$\Rightarrow \left(\frac{dy}{dx}\right)^2 (y-2)^2 = 25 - (y-2)^2$$
$$\Rightarrow y'^2(y-2)^2 = 25 - (y-2)^2$$

173. *(a)* Since, $\mathbf{a} = m\mathbf{b}$ for some scalar m *i.e.*,
$$\mathbf{a} = m\left(6\mathbf{i} - 8\mathbf{j} - \frac{15}{2}\mathbf{k}\right)$$
$$\Rightarrow \quad |\mathbf{a}| = |m|\sqrt{36 + 64 + \frac{225}{4}}$$
$$\Rightarrow \quad 50 = \frac{25}{2}|m|$$
$$\Rightarrow \quad |m| = 4 \Rightarrow m = \pm 4$$
Since, $\mathbf{a}$ makes an acute angle with the positive direction of Z-axis, so its z-component must be positive and hence, m must be -4.
$$\therefore \mathbf{a} = -4\left(6\mathbf{i} - 8\mathbf{j} - \frac{15}{2}\mathbf{k}\right) = -24\mathbf{i} + 32\mathbf{j} + 30\mathbf{k}$$

174. (a) Given, $2\mathbf{a} + 3\mathbf{b} - 5\mathbf{c} = 0$

$$\Rightarrow \quad \frac{2\mathbf{a} + 3\mathbf{b}}{5} = \mathbf{c}$$

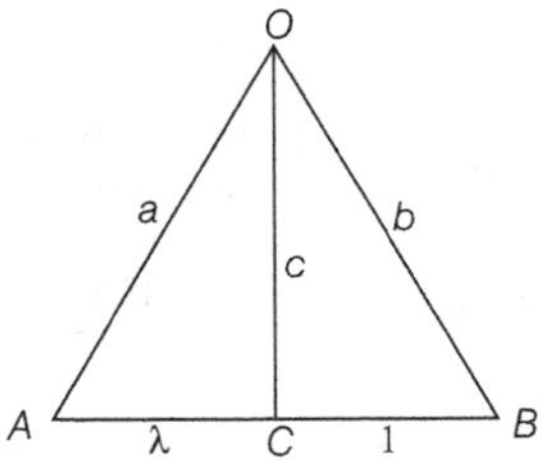

$$\Rightarrow \quad \frac{2\mathbf{a} + 3\mathbf{b}}{2+3} = \mathbf{c}$$

$$\Rightarrow \quad \frac{\mathbf{a} + \frac{3}{2}\mathbf{b}}{1 + \frac{3}{2}} = \mathbf{c} \quad \ldots\text{(i)}$$

Let **c** divides **AB** in the ratio $\lambda : 1$

Then, $$\mathbf{c} = \frac{\mathbf{a} + \lambda\mathbf{b}}{1+\lambda} \quad \ldots\text{(ii)}$$

On comparing Eqs. (i) and (ii), we get $\lambda = \frac{3}{2}$

$\therefore$ Required ratio is 3 : 2 internally.

175. (d) Since, B is the inverse of matrix A, *i.e.*, $B = A^{-1}$.

$$\therefore \quad 10A^{-1} = \begin{bmatrix} 4 & 2 & 2 \\ -5 & 0 & \alpha \\ 1 & -2 & 3 \end{bmatrix}$$

$$\Rightarrow 10A^{-1}A = \begin{bmatrix} 4 & 2 & 2 \\ -5 & 0 & \alpha \\ 1 & -2 & 3 \end{bmatrix} A$$

$$\Rightarrow 10I = \begin{bmatrix} 4 & 2 & 2 \\ -5 & 0 & \alpha \\ 1 & -2 & 3 \end{bmatrix} \begin{bmatrix} 1 & -1 & 1 \\ 2 & 1 & -3 \\ 1 & 1 & 1 \end{bmatrix} \quad (\because A^{-1}A = I)$$

$$\Rightarrow \begin{bmatrix} 10 & 0 & 0 \\ 0 & 10 & 0 \\ 0 & 0 & 10 \end{bmatrix} = \begin{bmatrix} 10 & 0 & 0 \\ -5+\alpha & 5+\alpha & -5+\alpha \\ 0 & 0 & 10 \end{bmatrix}$$

On equating the corresponding elements, we get

$-5 + \alpha = 0$ and $5 + \alpha = 10$

$\Rightarrow \quad \alpha = 5$

176. (a) Given that, $A^2 = I$

Consider, $(A - I)^3 + (A + I)^3 - 7A$

$= A^3 - I^3 - 3A^2I + 3AI^2 + A^3 + I^3 + 3A^2I + 3AI^2 - 7A$

$$\left[\begin{array}{l} (a+b)^3 = a^3 + b^3 + 3a^2b + 3ab^2 \\ \text{and } (a-b)^3 = a^3 - b^3 - 3a^2b + 3ab^2 \end{array}\right]$$

$= 2A^3 + 6AI^2 - 7A = 2A^2 \cdot A + 6AI - 7A$

$(\because A^3 = A^2 \cdot A$ and $I^2 = I)$

$= 2I \cdot A + 6A - 7A \quad (\because A^2 = I)$

$= 2A + 6A - 7A = 8A - 7A = A$

177. (c) We have, $$\Delta = \begin{vmatrix} b^2c^2 & bc & b+c \\ c^2a^2 & ca & c+a \\ a^2b^2 & ab & a+b \end{vmatrix}$$

Applying $R_1 \to aR_1$, $R_2 \to bR_2$ and $R_3 \to cR_3$, we get

$$\Delta = \frac{1}{abc}\begin{vmatrix} a\,b^2c^2 & abc & ab+ac \\ b\,c^2a^2 & abc & bc+ba \\ c\,a^2b^2 & abc & ac+bc \end{vmatrix}$$

$$\Delta = \frac{(abc)^2}{abc}\begin{vmatrix} bc & 1 & ab+ac \\ ca & 1 & bc+ba \\ ab & 1 & ac+bc \end{vmatrix}$$

taking out abc common from C_1 and C_2)

Applying $C_3 \to C_3 + C_1$, we get

$$\Delta = abc\begin{vmatrix} bc & 1 & ab+bc+ac \\ ca & 1 & ab+bc+ac \\ ab & 1 & ab+bc+ac \end{vmatrix}$$

$$= (abc)(ab+bc+ac)\begin{vmatrix} bc & 1 & 1 \\ ca & 1 & 1 \\ ab & 1 & 1 \end{vmatrix}$$

(taking out $ab + bc + ac$ common from C_3)

$\Delta = (abc)(ab + bc + ac) \cdot 0$ ($\because C_2$ and C_3 are identical)

$\therefore \quad \Delta = 0$

178. (c) Let $P(A) = x$

Given that,

$$P(B) = \frac{3}{5},\ P\left(\frac{A}{B}\right) = \frac{1}{2} \text{ and } P(A \cup B) = \frac{4}{5}$$

$$P\left(\frac{A}{B}\right) = \frac{P(A \cap B)}{P(B)}$$

$$\therefore \quad \frac{1}{2} = \frac{P(A \cap B)}{\frac{3}{5}}$$

$\Rightarrow \quad P(A \cap B) = \dfrac{1 \times 3}{2 \times 5}$

$\Rightarrow \quad P(A \cap B) = \dfrac{3}{10}$.

$P(A \cup B) = P(A) + P(B) - P(A \cap B)$

$\dfrac{4}{5} = x + \dfrac{3}{5} - \dfrac{3}{10}$

$\Rightarrow \quad x = \dfrac{4}{5} - \dfrac{3}{5} + \dfrac{3}{10} = \dfrac{8 - 6 + 3}{10} = \dfrac{5}{10} = \dfrac{1}{2}$

179. *(a)* Let p : 72 is divisible by 2 and 3.

Let q : 72 is divisible by 2.

r : 72 is divisible by 3.

$\sim q$: 72 is not divisible by 2.

$\sim r$: 72 is not divisible by 3.

$\sim (q \wedge r) : \sim q \vee \sim r$

$\Rightarrow$ 72 is not divisible by 2 or 72 is not divisible by 3.

180. *(a)* The feasible region is bounded. Therefore, maximum of Z must occur at the corner points of the feasible region.

Corner Point	Value of Z
$O(0, 0)$	$4(0) + 3(0) = 0$
$A(25, 0)$	$4(25) + 3(0) = 100$
$B(16, 16)$	$4(16) + 3(16) = 112$ ← Maximum
$C(0, 24)$	$4(0) + 3(24) = 72$

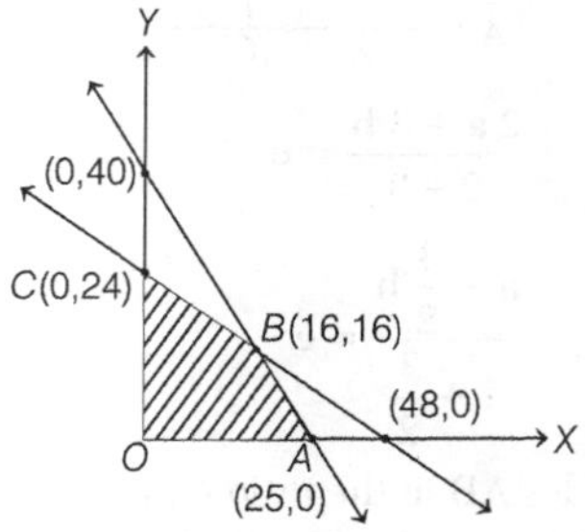

Hence, the maximum value of Z is 112.

COMEDK

Mock Test 2

Instructions

- There are 180 questions in all. The number of questions in each section is as given below.

Sections	No. of Questions
Section I : Physics	1-60
Section II : Chemistry	61-120
Section III : Mathematics	121-180

- All the questions are Multiple Choice Questions having four options out of which **ONLY ONE** is correct.
- Candidates will be awarded 1 mark for each correct answer. There will be no negative marking for incorrect answer.
- Time allotted to complete this paper is 3 hrs.

PHYSICS

1. A helicopter rises vertically with a speed of 100 ms^{-1}. If helicopter has length 10 m and horizontal component of earth's magnetic field is $5\times 10^{-3}\text{ Wb m}^{-2}$, then the induced emf between the tip of nose and tail of helicopter is

a. 50 V *b.* 0.5 V *c.* 5 V *d.* 25 V

2. A stone is thrown at an angle θ with the horizontal reaches a maximum height H. Then the time of flight of stone will be

a. $\sqrt{\frac{2H}{g}}$ *b.* $2\sqrt{\frac{2H}{g}}$

c. $\frac{2\sqrt{2H\sin\theta}}{g}$ *d.* $\frac{\sqrt{2H\sin\theta}}{g}$

3. The resistance R_t of a conductor varies with temperature t as shown in figure. If the variation is represented by $R_t = R_0(1+\alpha t+\beta t^2)$. Then,

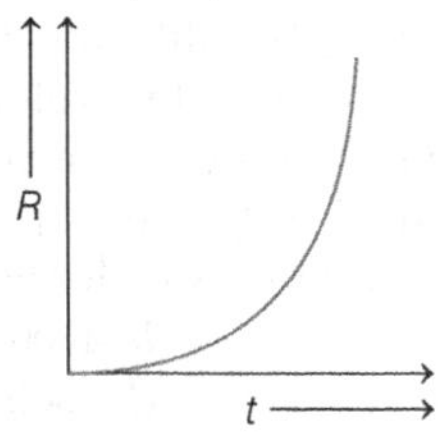

a. α and β both are negative

b. α is positive but β is negative

c. α and β both are positive

d. α is negative but β is positive

4. Charge passing through a conductor of cross-section area $A = 0.3\text{ m}^2$ is given by $q = (3t^2+5t+2)\text{ C}$, where t is in second. What is the value of drift velocity at $t = 2\text{s}$? (Take, $n = 2\times 10^{25}/\text{m}^3$)

a. 0.77×10^{-5} m/s *b.* 1.77×10^{-5} m/s

c. 2.08×10^{5} m/s *d.* 0.57×10^{5} m/s

5. What is the magnetic field at the centre of arc in the figure below?

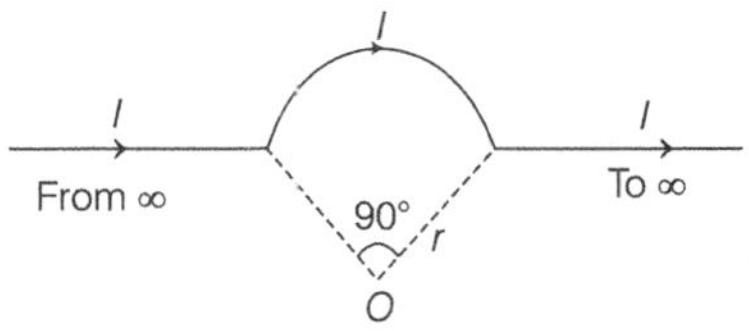

a. $\frac{\mu_0}{4\pi}\frac{2I}{r}[\sqrt{2}+\pi]$ *b.* $\frac{\mu_0}{4\pi}\frac{2I}{r}\left[\sqrt{2}+\frac{\pi}{4}\right]$

c. $\frac{\mu_0}{4\pi}\frac{I}{r}[\sqrt{2}+\pi]$ *d.* $\frac{\mu_0}{4\pi}\frac{I}{r}\left[\sqrt{2}+\frac{\pi}{4}\right]$

6. A black body at 227°C radiates heat at a rate of 7 cal/cm^{2}s. At a temperature of 727°C, the rate of heat radiated in the same units will be

a. 112 *b.* 105 *c.* 101 *d.* 89

7. An electric kettle has two heating coils. When one of the coils is connected to an AC source, the water in the kettle boils in 10 min. When the other coil is used the water boils in 40 min. If both the coils are connected in parallel, the time taken by the same quantity of water to boil will be

a. 8 min *b.* 4 min *c.* 25 min *d.* 15 min

8. The length of a simple pendulum executing SHM is increased by 21%. The percentage increase in the time period of the pendulum of increased length is

a. 10% *b.* 11% *c.* 21% *d.* 42%

9. A particle executes SHM between $x = -A$ and $x = +A$. The time taken for it to go from 0 to $A/2$ is T_1 and to go from $A/2$ to A is T_2. Then,

a. $T_1 < T_2$ *b.* $T_1 > T_2$
c. $T_1 = T_2$ *d.* $T_1 = 2T_2$

10. A particle is executing SHM with an amplitude of 4 cm. At the mean position the velocity of the particle is 10 cm s^{-1}. The distance of the particle from the mean position when its speed becomes 5 cm s^{-1} is

a. $\sqrt{3}$ cm *b.* $\sqrt{5}$ cm *c.* $2\sqrt{3}$ cm *d.* $2\sqrt{5}$ cm

11. A column of air at 88°C and a tuning fork produce 6 beats/s when sounded together. When temperature is 16°C, then two produce only one beat per second. What is the frequency of tuning fork?

a. 53.9 Hz *b.* 97.7 Hz *c.* 41.5 Hz *d.* 87.7 Hz

12. The magnetic field due to a straight conductor of uniform cross-section of radius *a* and carrying a steady current is represented by

a.
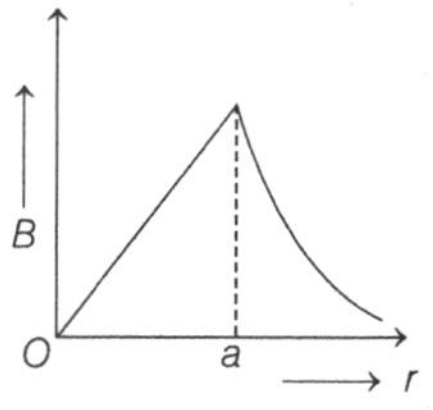

b.
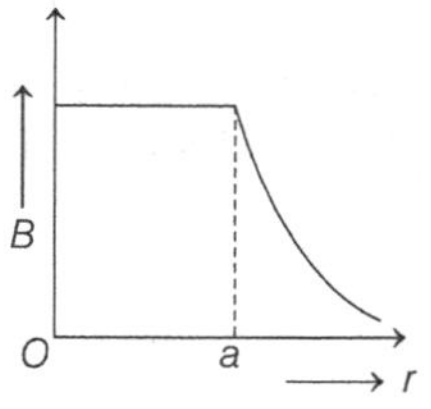

c.
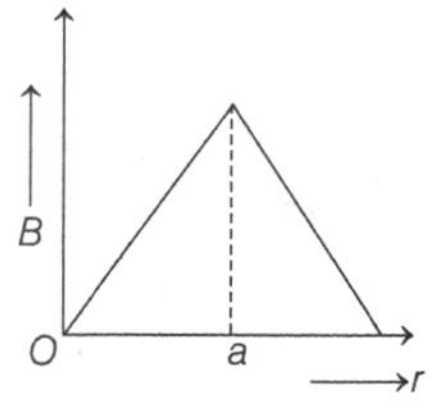

d.
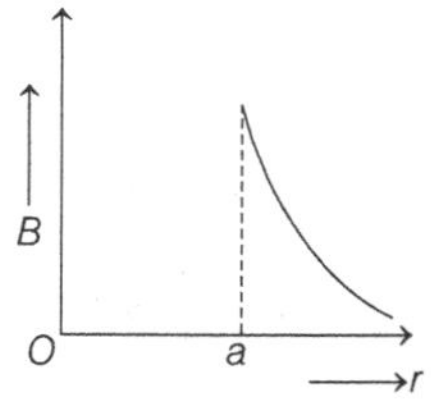

13. A thermodynamic system is taken through the cycle *PQRSP*. The net work done by the system is

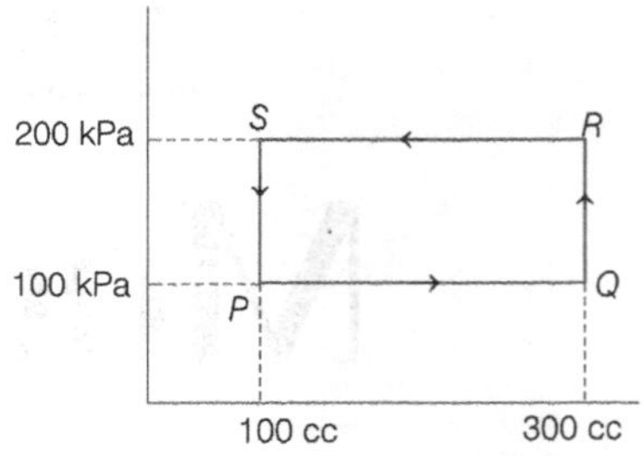

a. 6×10^6 J *b.* -2×10^6 J
c. -6×10^6 J *d.* 2×10^6 J

14. An EM wave is propagating in a medium with a velocity $\mathbf{v} = v\hat{\mathbf{i}}$. The instantaneous oscillating electric field of this EM wave is along $+Y$-axis. Then, the direction of oscillating magnetic field of EM wave will be along

a. $-y$-direction
b. $+z$-direction
c. $-z$-direction
d. $-x$-direction

15. Which of the following processes is reversible?

a. Transfer of heat by radiation
b. Electrical heating of a nichrome wire
c. Transfer of heat by conduction
d. Isothermal compression

16. A ray of light is incident at the glass-water interface at an angle (as shown below) and it emerges finally parallel to the surface of water, then the value of n_g would be

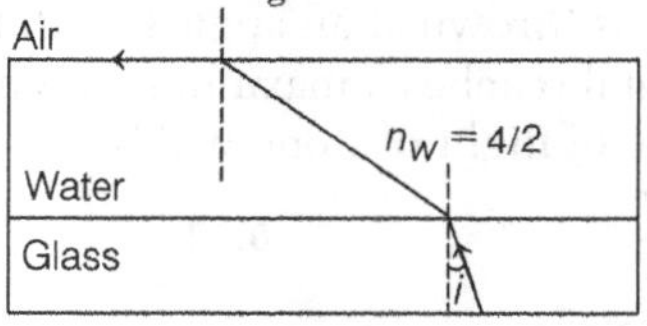

a. $(4/3) \sin i$ *b.* $1/\sin i$
c. $4/3$ *d.* 1

17. For what value of m_a will the total power per cycle be maximum in the modulated wave?

a. 0 *b.* 1
c. 1/2 *d.* greater than 1

18. The Young's double slit experiment is performed with light of wavelength 6000 Å, where in 16 fringes occupy a certain region on the screen. If 24 fringes occupy the same region with another light of wavelength λ, then λ is

a. 6000 Å *b.* 4500 Å
c. 5000 Å *d.* 4000 Å

19. An iron block is on a boat which floats in a pond. The block is thrown into the water. The level of water in the pond will be

a. equal to the earlier level
b. less than the earlier level
c. more than the earlier level
d. depends on how large the block is

20. In a photoelectric effect experiment, the threshold wavelength of light is 380 nm. If the wavelength of incident light is 260 nm, the maximum kinetic energy of emitted electrons will be

$$\left[\text{Given, } E\,(\text{in eV}) = \frac{1237}{\lambda(\text{in nm})}\right]$$

a. 15.1 eV *b.* 3.0 eV *c.* 1.5 eV *d.* 4.5 eV

21. The graph shows the behaviour of a length of wire in the region for which the substance obeys Hooke's law. P and Q represent.

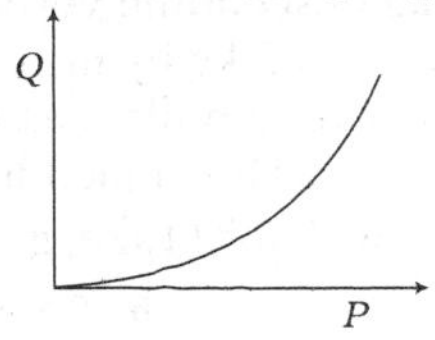

a. P = applied force, Q = extension
b. P = extension, Q = applied force
c. P = extension, Q = stored elastic energy
d. P = stored elastic energy, Q = extension

22. Radiation of wavelength λ is incident on a photocell. The fastest emitted electron has speed v. If the wavelength is changed to $\frac{3\lambda}{4}$, then the speed of the fastest emitted electron will be

a. $> v\left(\frac{4}{3}\right)^{1/2}$ *b.* $< v\left(\frac{4}{3}\right)^{1/2}$

c. $= v\left(\frac{4}{3}\right)^{1/2}$ *d.* $= v\left(\frac{3}{4}\right)^{1/2}$

23. Two wires of same diameter of the same material having the length l and $2\,l$. If the force F is applied on each, then the ratio of the work done in the two wires will be

a. 1 : 2 *b.* 1 : 4 *c.* 2 : 1 *d.* 1 : 1

24. A point source of light is used in an experiment on photoelectric effect. Which of the following curves best represents the variation of photoelectric current i with distance x of the source from the emitter?

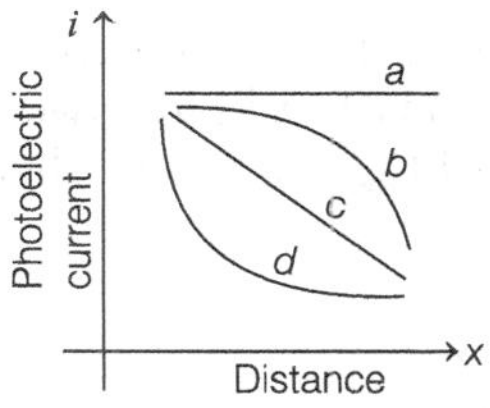

a. a *b.* b *c.* c *d.* d

25. A body is projected vertically upwards from the surface of earth with a velocity equal to half the escape velocity. If R be the radius of earth, maximum height attained by the body from the surface of earth is

a. $\frac{R}{6}$ *b.* $\frac{R}{3}$ *c.* $\frac{2R}{3}$ *d.* R

26. If the binding energy of the electron in a hydrogen atom is 13.6 eV, then energy required to remove electron from first excited state of Li^{2+} is

a. 122.4 eV *b.* 30.6 eV
c. 13.6 eV *d.* 3.4 eV

27. A satellite is moving in a circular orbit round the earth with a diameter of orbit $2R$. At a certain point a rocket fixed to the satellite is fired such that it increases the velocity of the satellite tangentially. The resulting orbit of the satellite would be

a. same as before
b. circular orbit with diameter greater than $2R$
c. elliptical orbit with minimum distance from the earth equal to R
d. elliptical orbit with maximum distance from the earth equal to R

28. Transition from state $n = 4$ to $n = 3$ in a hydrogen like atom results in a UV-radiation. IR radiation will be obtained in the transition, when

a. $2 \to 1$ *b.* $3 \to 2$
c. $1 \to 2$ *d.* $5 \to 4$

29. A thin uniform circular disc of mass M and radius R is rotating in a horizontal plane about an axis passing through its centre and perpendicular to its plane with an angular velocity ω. Another disc of same dimensions but of mass $\frac{1}{4}M$ is placed gently on the first disc co-axially. The angular velocity of the system is

a. $\frac{2}{3}\omega$ *b.* $\frac{4}{5}\omega$ *c.* $\frac{3}{4}\omega$ *d.* $\frac{1}{3}\omega$

MOCK TEST 2

30. If a nucleus with mass number $A = 240$ with $E_{bn} = 7.6$ MeV breaks into two fragments of $A = 120$ and $E_{bn} = 8.5$ MeV, then released energy is around

a. 216 MeV
b. 200 MeV
c. 100 MeV
d. Cannot be estimated from given data

31. A rigid body rotates with an angular momentum L. If its rotational kinetic energy is made 4 times, its angular momentum will become

a. $4L$ *b.* $16L$ *c.* $\sqrt{2}\,L$ *d.* $2L$

32. A mixture consists of two radioactive materials A_1 and A_2 with half-lives of 20 s and 10 s, respectively. Initially, the mixture has 40 g of A_1 and 160 g of A_2. The amount of the two in the mixture will become equal after

a. 60 s *b.* 80 s *c.* 20 s *d.* 40 s

33. An engine exerts a force $\mathbf{F} = (20\mathbf{i} - 3\mathbf{j} + 5\mathbf{k})$ N and moves with velocity $\mathbf{v} = (6\mathbf{i} + 20\mathbf{j} - 3\mathbf{k})$ ms^{-1}. The power of the engine (in watt) is

a. 45 *b.* 75 *c.* 20 *d.* 10

34. The electrical resistance to the diffusion current in a *p-n* junction because of depletion layer, is large due to the presence of

a. strong electric field
b. large number of charge carriers
c. electrons as charge carriers
d. holes as charge carriers

35. A body moves from rest with a constant acceleration. Which one of the following graphs represents the variation of its kinetic energy K with the distance travelled x?

a.
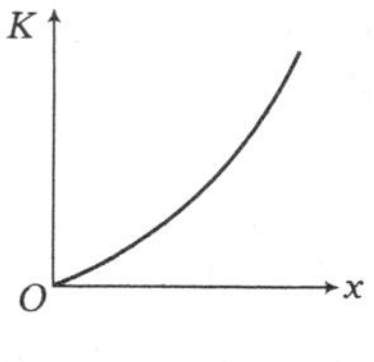

b.
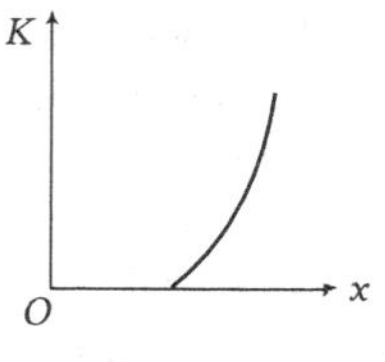

c.
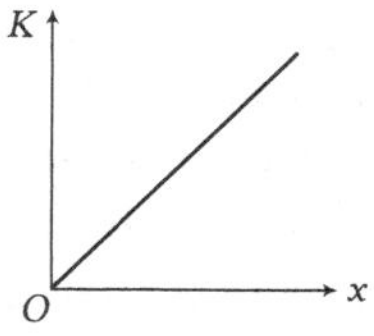

d.
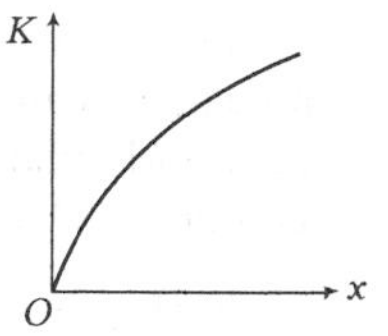

36. The angle of dip at a certain place where the horizontal and vertical components of the earth's magnetic field are equal is

a. 30° *b.* 90° *c.* 60° *d.* 45°

37. Two blocks of mass 5 kg and 3 kg are attached to the ends of a string passing over a smooth pulley fixed to the ceiling of an elevator. A man inside the elevator accelerated upwards, finds the acceleration of the blocks to be $\frac{9}{32}g$. The acceleration of the elevator is

a. $\frac{g}{3}$ *b.* $\frac{g}{4}$
c. $\frac{g}{8}$ *d.* $\frac{g}{6}$

38. The relative permeability of a substance X is slightly less than unity and that of substance Y is slightly more than unity, then

a. X is paramagnetic and Y is ferromagnetic
b. X is diamagnetic and Y is ferromagnetic
c. X and Y both are paramagnetic
d. X is diamagnetic and Y is paramagnetic

39. A mass of 3 kg descending vertically downwards supports a mass of 2 kg by means of a light string passing over a pulley. At the end of 5 s the string breaks . How much high from now the 2 kg mass will go? (Take, $g = 9.8$ ms^{-2})

a. 4.9 m *b.* 9.8 m
c. 19.6 m *d.* 2.45 m

40. A circular coil expands radially in a region of magnetic field and no electromotive force is produced in the coil. This can be because

a. the magnetic field is constant
b. the magnetic field is not in the same plane as the circular coil and it may or may not vary
c. the magnetic field has a perpendicular (to the plane of the coil) component whose magnitude is decreasing suitably
d. there is a constant magnetic field in the perpendicular (to the plane of the coil) direction

41. For a given velocity, a projectile has the same range R for two angles of projection. If t_1 and t_2 are the time of flight in the two cases, then $t_1 = t_2$ is equal to

a. $\frac{2R}{g}$ *b.* $\frac{R}{g}$
c. $\frac{4R}{g}$ *d.* $\frac{R}{2g}$

42. The graphs shown below, depict the variation of current I_m *versus* angular frequency ω for four different *L-C-R* circuits. The graph which has maximum quality factor is

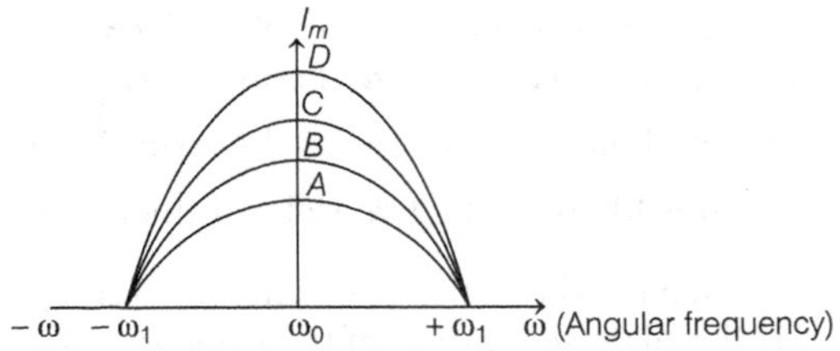

a. A *b.* B *c.* C *d.* D

43. A particle moves along a straight line OX. At a time t (in seconds) the distance $x = 40 + 12t - t^3$. How long would the particle travel before coming to rest?

a. 24 m *b.* 40 m *c.* 56 m *d.* 16 m

44. In a series L-C-R AC circuit, the voltage across each of the components, L, C and R is 20 V. The voltage across the L-C combination will be

a. 50 V *b.* $50\sqrt{2}$ V
c. 100 V *d.* Zero

45. At a metro station, a girl walks up a stationary escalator in time t_1. If she remains stationary on the escalator, then the escalator take her up in time t_2. The time taken by her to walk up on the moving escalator will be

a. $\frac{(t_1 + t_2)}{2}$ *b.* $\frac{t_1 t_2}{(t_2 - t_1)}$
c. $\frac{t_1 t_2}{(t_2 + t_1)}$ *d.* $t_1 - t_2$

46. Young's double slit experiment is performed with sodium (yellow) light of wavelength 589.3 nm and the interference pattern is observed on a screen 100 cm away. The 10th bright fringe has its centre at a distance of 12 mm from the central maximum. The separation between the slits is

a. 0.49 mm *b.* 0.6 mm
c. 0.7 mm *d.* 0.53 mm

47. Which of the following diagrams does not represents a streamline flow?

a. 

b. 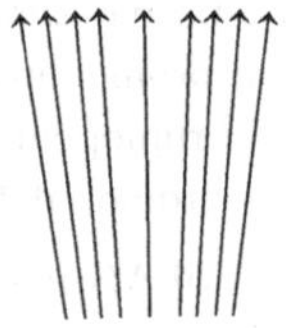

c. 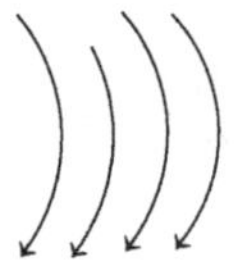

d. 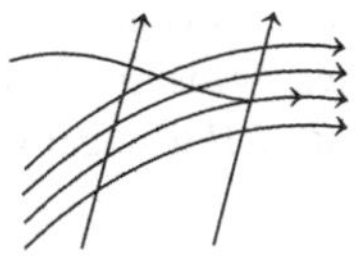

48. A lens is made of flint glass (refractive index = 1.5). When the lens is immersed in a liquid of refractive index 1.25, the focal length

a. increases by a factor of 1.25
b. increases by a factor of 2.5
c. increases by a factor of 1.2
d. decreases by a factor of 1.2

49. A parallel plate capacitor is charged to 100×10^{-6} C. Due to radiations, falling from a radiating source, the plate loses charge at the rate of 2×10^{-7} Cs^{-1}. The magnitude of displacement current is

a. 10^{-6} A *b.* 10^{-4} A
c. 2×10^{-7} A *d.* 2×10^{-7} mCs^{-1}

50. A proper combination of 3 NOT and 1 AND gates is shown. If $A = 0$, $B = 1$ and $C = 1$, then the output of this combination is

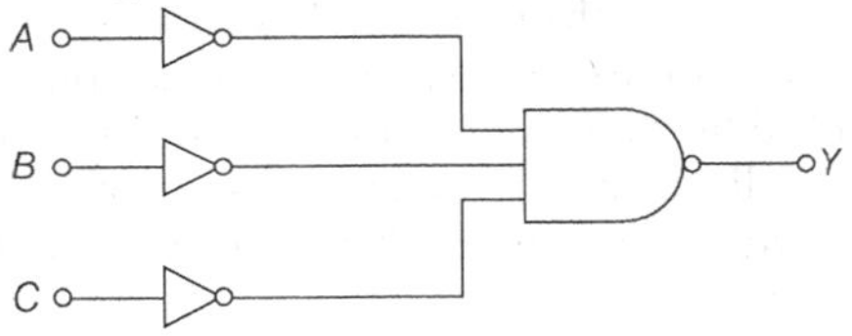

a. 1 *b.* zero
c. not predictable *d.* None of these

51. In the given circuit, all diodes are ideal. The current through battery is

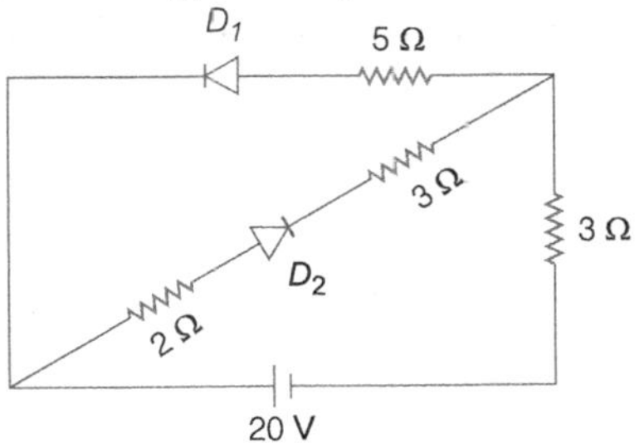

a. 2.5 A *b.* 1 A
c. 3 A *d.* 4 A

52. A physical quantity Q is calculated according to the expression

$$Q = \frac{A^3 B^3}{C\sqrt{D}}$$

If percentage errors in A, B, C, D are 2%, 1%, 3% and 4%, respectively. What is the percentage error in Q?

a. ± 8% *b.* ± 10%
c. ± 14% *d.* ± 12%

53. In Young's double slit experiment the fringe width is 1×10^{-4} m. If the distance between the slit and screen is doubled and distance between the two slit is reduced to half and wavelength is changed from 6.4×10^{-7} m to 4.0×10^{-7} m, then the value of new fringe width will be

a. 0.15×10^{-4} m *b.* 2.0×10^{-4} m

c. 1.25×10^{-4} m *d.* 2.5×10^{-4} m

54. Which of the following pairs of physical quantities does not have same dimensional formula?

a. Work and torque

b. Angular momentum and Planck's constant

c. Tension and surface tension

d. Impulse and linear momentum

55. In Young's double slit experiment, the slits are 2 mm apart and are illuminated by photons of two wavelengths $\lambda_1 = 12000$ Å and $\lambda_2 = 10000$ Å. At what minimum distance from the common central bright fringe on the screen, 2 m from the slit, will a bright fringe from one interference pattern coincide with a bright fringe from the other?

a. 8 mm *b.* 6 mm *c.* 4 mm *d.* 3 mm

56. In the figure, proton moves a distance d in a uniform electric field E as shown in the figure. Does the electric field do a positive or negative work on the proton? Does the electric potential energy of the proton increase or decrease?

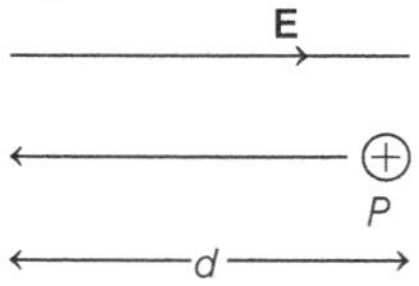

a. Negative, increase *b.* Positive, decrease

c. Negative, decrease *d.* Positive, increase

57. A parallel plate capacitor has the space between its plates filled by the two slabs of thickness $\frac{d}{2}$ each, having dielectric constants K_1 and K_2 and d is the plate separation of the capacitor. The capacity of the capacitor is

a. $\frac{2\varepsilon_0 d}{A}\left(\frac{K_1 + K_2}{K_1 K_2}\right)$ *b.* $\frac{2\varepsilon_0 A}{d}\left(\frac{K_1 K_2}{K_1 + K_2}\right)$

c. $\frac{2\varepsilon_0 d}{A}(K_1 + K_2)$ *d.* $\frac{2\varepsilon_0 A}{d}\left(\frac{K_1 + K_2}{K_1 K_2}\right)$

58. Two point charges placed at a certain distance r in air exert a force F on each other. Then, the distance r' at which these charges will exert the same force in a medium of dielectric constant K is given by

a. r *b.* r/K

c. $r/\sqrt{K}$ *d.* $r\sqrt{K}$

59. Eight dipoles of charges of magnitude e each are placed inside a cube. The total electric flux coming out of the cube will be

a. $\frac{8e}{\varepsilon_0}$ *b.* $\frac{16e}{\varepsilon_0}$ *c.* $\frac{e}{\varepsilon_0}$ *d.* Zero

60. A black body radiates power P and maximum energy is radiated by it around a wavelength λ_0. The temperature of the black body is now changed such that it radiates maximum energy around the wavelength $3\lambda_0/4$. The power radiated by it now is

a. $\frac{256}{81}P$ *b.* $\frac{27}{64}P$ *c.* $\frac{64}{27}P$ *d.* $\frac{81}{256}P$

CHEMISTRY

61. The entropy change involved in the isothermal reversible expansion of 2 moles of an ideal gas from a volume of $10\ dm^3$ to $100\ dm^3$ at 27°C is

a. 38.3 J mol^{-1} K^{-1}

b. 35.8 J mol^{-1} K^{-1}

c. 32.3 J mol^{-1} K^{-1}

d. 42.3 J mol^{-1} K^{-1}

62. $CrCl_3 \cdot 4H_2O$ will exist as

a. $[Cr(H_2O)_3Cl_3] \cdot H_2O$ *b.* $[Cr(H_2O)_4Cl_2]Cl$

c. Both (a) and (b) *d.* None of these

63. Which of the following is an allylic halide?

a. 3-bromo-2-methylpropene

b. 3-bromobut-1-ene

c. 3-bromopent-2-ene

d. 4-bromobut-1-ene

64. Sign of ΔG is positive at low temperature when

a. ΔH is positive and ΔS is positive

b. ΔH is negative and ΔS is negative

c. ΔH is negative but ΔS is positive

d. ΔH is negative and ΔS is zero

65. Which one of the following salts (high spin for paramagnetic samples) will have the strongest attraction to a magnetic field?

a. $MnSO_4$ *b.* $CoSO_4$
c. $CuSO_4$ *d.* $ZnSO_4$

66. Under basic conditions which one suffers elimination the most?

a. $(CH_3)_3CCl$ *b.* $(H_3C)_2CHCH_2Cl$
c. $CH_3CH_2CH(Cl)CH_3$ *d.* $CH_3CH_2CH_2CH_2Cl$

67. For the reaction, $H_2O\,(s) \rightleftharpoons H_2O\,(l)$ at 0°C and normal pressure

a. $\Delta H > T\Delta S$ *b.* $\Delta H = T\Delta S$
c. $\Delta H = \Delta G$ *d.* $\Delta H < T\Delta S$

68. $CH_2{=}CHCH_2CH{=}CH_2 \xrightarrow{NBS} A$. *A* is

a. $CH_2{=}CHCH(Br)CH{=}CH_2$
b. $CH_2{=}CHCH{=}CHCH_2Br$
c. $CH_2{=}CHCH_2CH{=}CHBr$
d. $CH_2{=}CHCH_2C(Br){=}CH_2$

69. In the following reaction,

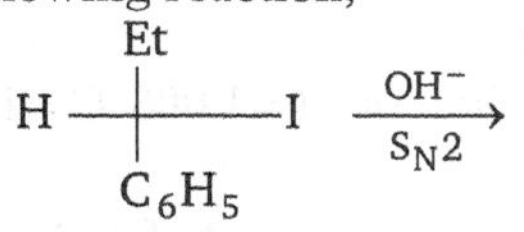

product formed

a. retains configuration
b. inverts configuration
c. is a racemic mixture
d. is a *meso* compound

70. Which of the following phosphorus is the most reactive?

a. Red phosphorus
b. White phosphorus
c. Scarlet phosphorus
d. Violet phosphorus

71. The paramagnetic behaviour of B_2 is due to the presence of

a. 2 unpaired electrons in π_bMO
b. 2 unpaired electrons in $\overset{*}{\pi}$MO
c. 2 unpaired electrons in $\overset{*}{\sigma}$MO
d. 2 unpaired electrons in σ_bMO

72. Out of $H_2S_2O_3, H_2S_4O_6, H_2SO_5$ and $H_2S_2O_8$, peroxy acids are

a. $H_2S_2O_3, H_2S_4O_6$ *b.* $H_2S_4O_6, H_2SO_5$
c. $H_2SO_5, H_2S_2O_8$ *d.* $H_2S_2O_3, H_2S_2O_8$

73. The hybridisation of atomic orbitals of N in NO_2^+, NO_3^- and NH_4^+ respectively are

a. sp, sp^2, sp^3 *b.* sp, sp^3, sp^2
c. sp^2, sp, sp^3 *d.* sp^2, sp^3, sp

74. Zeigler-Natta catalyst is

a. $ZnCl_2$ *b.* $AlR_3 + TiCl_4$
c. Cu /ZnO - Cr_2O_3 *d.* Pt

75. The process of converting hydrated into anhydrous alumina is called

a. roasting *b.* smelting
c. dressing *d.* calcination

76. All the following molecules are linear except one

a. SO_2 *b.* CO_2 *c.* HCN *d.* NO

77. When initial concentration of a reactant is doubled in a reaction, its half-life period is not affected. The order of the reaction is

a. zero
b. first
c. second
d. more than zero but less than first

78. 100 mL of a colloidal solution is completely precipitated by addition of 5 mL of 1 M NaCl solution. What is the coagulation value of NaCl?

a. 50 *b.* 5
c. 0.005 *d.* None of these

79. During electrolysis of acidified nature, O_2 gas is formed at the anode. To produce O_2 gas at the anode at the rate of 0.224 cc per second at STP, current passed is

a. 0.224 A *b.* 2.24 A
c. 9.64 A *d.* 3.86 A

80. The electron affinities of N, O, S and Cl are such that

a. N < O < S < Cl *b.* O < N < Cl < S
c. O = Cl < N = S *d.* O < S < Cl < N

81. The vapour pressure of pure liquid solvent *A* is 0.80 atm. When a non-volatile substance *B* is added to the solvent, its vapour pressure drops to 0.60 atm. Mole fraction of the component *B* in the solution is

a. 0.50 *b.* 0.25
c. 0.75 *d.* 0.40

82. The newly discovered element with atomic number 117 would be placed in

a. alkali metals
b. alkaline earth metals
c. halogens
d. noble gases

83. The number of octahedral void(s) per atom present in a cubic closed packed structure is

a. 1 *b.* 3 *c.* 2 *d.* 4

84. Mole fraction of glycine molecule in 0.140 molal aqueous solution is

a. 1.4×10^{-1} *b.* 8.6×10^{-1}
c. 2.51×10^{-3} *d.* 9.9748×10^{-1}

85. The correct decreasing order of ionic radius is

a. $C^{4-} > N^{3-} > O^{2-} > F^-$
b. $F^- > O^{2-} > N^{3-} > C^{4-}$
c. $O^{2-} > F^- > C^{4-} > N^{3-}$
d. $N^{3-} > O^{2-} > F^- > C^{4-}$

86. Which of the following compound possesses the C—H bond with the lowest bond dissociation energy?

a. Toluene
b. Benzene
c. *n*-pentane
d. 2, 2-dimethylpropane

87. Which one of the following defects in the crystal lowers its density?

a. *F*-centres *b.* Interstitial defect
c. Frenkel defect *d.* Schottky defect

88. Which of the following enzymes is present in animals like cow, buffaloes, etc. to digest compound like paper, cloth etc.

a. Ureaze *b.* Cellulase
c. Silicons *d.* Sucrose

89.

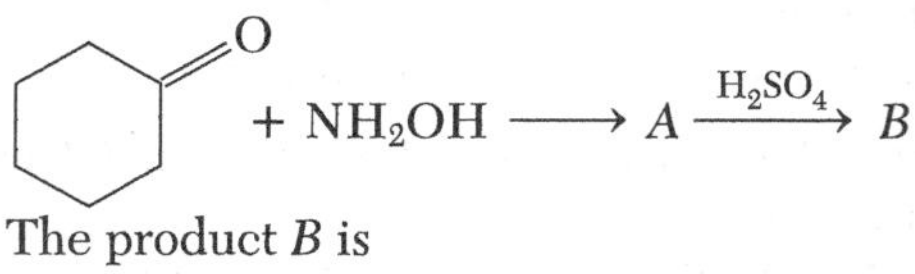

The product *B* is

a.
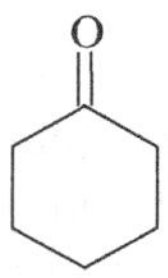

b.
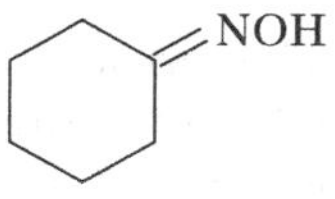

c.
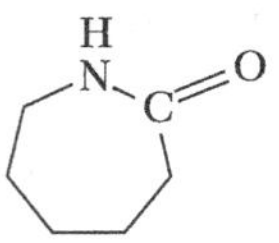

d.
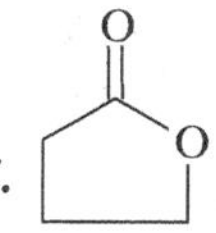

90. Aldol condensation reaction is not given by

a. $C_6H_5CH_2CHO$ *b.* C_6H_5CHO
c. CH_3CHO *d.* CH_3COCH_3

91. The atomic number of an element is 17. The number of orbitals containing electron pairs in its valence shell are

a. 2 *b.* 3 *c.* 4 *d.* 5

92. Identify (*Y*) in the series

$$CH \equiv CH \xrightarrow{O_3/NaOH} (X) \xrightarrow{Zn/CH_3COOH} (Y)$$

a. CH_3OH
b. $CH_2COOH—CH_2COOH$
c. CH_3CH_2COOH
d. $CH_2OH—CH_2OH$

93. Excess nitrate in drinking water causes

a. methemoglobinemia *b.* kidney damage
c. liver damage *d.* leucoderma

94. Which does not contain conjugate system?

a. $CH_2=CH—COOH$ *b.* $CH_2=CHCHO$
c. $CH_3CH=CH_2$ *d.*
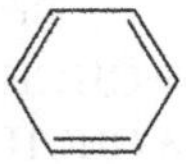

95. A carbon compound contains 12.8% of carbon, 2.1% of hydrogen and 85.1% of bromine. The molecular weight of the compound is 187.9. Calculate the molecular formula of the compound.
(Atomic weight of H = 1.008, C = 12.0 and Br = 79.9)

a. CH_3Br *b.* CH_2Br_2I
c. $C_2H_4Br_2$ *d.* $C_2H_3Br_3$

96. Which is hydrated to maximum extent?

a. *cis* $CH_3CH=CHCH_3$
b. *trans* $CH_3CH=CHCH_3$
c. *trans*
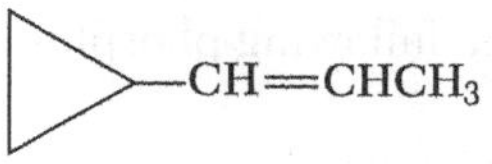

d.
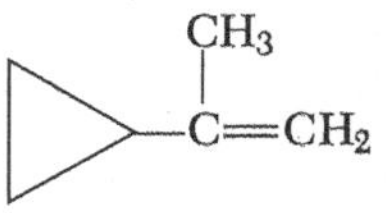

97. Stability of hydrides of carbon family is in order

a. $CH_4 > SiH_4 > GeH_4 > SnH_4 > PbH_4$
b. $CH_4 < SiH_4 < GeH_4 < SnH_4 < PbH_4$
c. $CH_4 > SnH_4 > GeH_4 > SiH_4 > PbH_4$
d. None of the above

98. Total number of optical isomers of

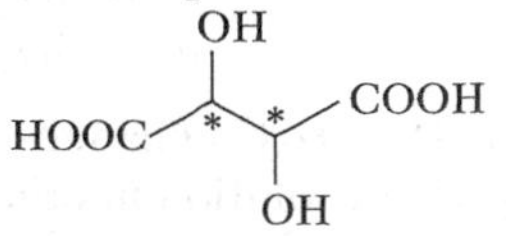

a. 2 *b.* 3 *c.* 4 *d.* 5

99. A mixture of NaCl and Na_2CO_3 is given. On heating 12 g of the mixture with dil. HCl, 2.24 g of CO_2 is evolved. The amounts of NaCl in mixture is

a. 6.6 g *b.* 5.8 g *c.* 6.8 g *d.* 7.2 g

100. Water gas is produced by

a. passing steam over red hot coke
b. passing steam and air over red hot coke
c. burning coke in excess of air
d. burning coke in limited supply of air

101. 6.0 g urea is decomposed by 2 M NaOH. Volume of 2M NaOH required is

a. 50 mL *b.* 100 mL
c. 150 mL *d.* 40 mL

102. Which of the metal carbonates is decomposed on heating?

a. $MgCO_3$ *b.* Na_2CO_3
c. K_2CO_3 *d.* Rb_2CO_3

103. Decarboxylation will not take place by heating of

a. methyl malonic acid *b.* succinic acid
c. acetoacetic acid *d.* In all cases

104. 2 moles of an ideal gas are expanded isothermally and reversibly from 1 L to 10 L at 300 K. What is the work done?

a. 4.98 kJ *b.* 11.47 kJ
c. –11.47 kJ *d.* 0 kJ

105. The base pair of bases in DNA are held together by

a. ionic bonds *b.* H-bond
c. phosphate group *d.* deoxyribose group

106. pH of the solution after NaCl solution is electrolysed will

a. remain constant *b.* increase
c. decrease *d.* cannot be determined

107. The heating of phenyl-methyl ethers with HI produces

a. benzene *b.* ethyl chlorides
c. iodobenzene *d.* phenol

108. Equanil is

a. artificial sweetener *b.* tranquiliser
c. antihistamine *d.* antifertility drug

109. The reaction $C_6H_4CH{=}CHCHO$ with $NaBH_4$ yields

a. $C_6H_5CH_2CH_2CH_2OH$ *b.* $C_6H_5CH{=}CHCH_2OH$
c. $C_6H_5CH_2CH_2CHO$ *d.* $C_6H_5CH_2CHOHCH_3$

110. In the reaction,

$$Ag_2O + H_2O_2 \longrightarrow 2Ag + H_2O + O_2$$

H_2O_2 acts as

a. reducing agent *b.* oxidising agent
c. bleaching agent *d.* None of these

111. Which one of the following ethers is the most unreactive to cleavage with HBr?

a. $C_6H_5OCH_2C_6H_5$
b. $H_2C=CHCH_2OCH_2CH=CH_2$
c. $C_6H_5OC_6H_5$
d. $(CH_3)_3COC(CH_3)_3$

112. In the reaction, $H_2(g) + Cl_2(g) \rightleftharpoons 2HCl(g)$

a. $K_p \neq K_C$ *b.* $K_p = K_C$ *c.* $K_p > K_C$ *d.* $K_p < K_C$

113.

Which is true about C—O bond lengths?

a. $x = y$ *b.* $x > y$
c. $x < y$ *d.* is not predictable

114. Pyridine is less basic than triethylamine because

a. pyridine has aromatic character
b. nitrogen in pyridine is sp^2-hybridised
c. pyridine is a cyclic system
d. in pyridine, lone pair of nitrogen is delocalised

115. Distribution of molecules with velocity is represented by the curve as shown, velocity at point *A* is

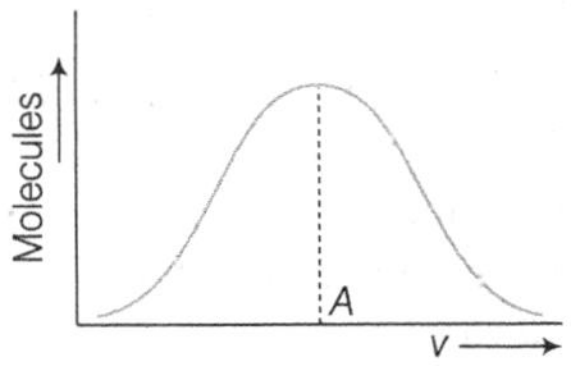

a. $\sqrt{\frac{3RT}{M}}$ *b.* $\sqrt{\frac{2RT}{M}}$ *c.* $\sqrt{\frac{8RT}{\pi M}}$ *d.* $\sqrt{\frac{RT}{M}}$

116. Xenon fluoride acts as fluoride acceptor with

a. RbF *b.* CsF
c. Both (a) and (b) *d.* None of these

117. Ni^{2+}, in traces, can be tested using

a. sodium nitroprusside
b. dimethyl glyoxime
c. ammonium sulphocyanide
d. potassium ferrocyanide

118. Equal masses of methane and oxygen are mixed in an empty container at 25°C. The fraction of the total pressure exerted by oxygen is

a. $\frac{2}{3}$ *b.* $\frac{1}{3} \times \frac{273}{298}$ *c.* $\frac{1}{3}$ *d.* $\frac{1}{2}$

119. Which one of the following oxoacid of chlorine is the least oxidising in nature?

a. HClO *b.* $HClO_2$
c. $HClO_3$ *d.* $HClO_4$

120. In acidic medium H_2O_2 changes $K_2Cr_2O_7$ to CrO_5 (deep violet solution in ether) having two peroxy linkage. Oxidation number of Cr in CrO_5 is

a. +10 *b.* −10 *c.* +4 *d.* +6

MATHEMATICS

121. Which of the following function is one-one?

a. $f(x) = \sin x, x \in [-\pi, \pi)$

b. $f(x) = \sin x, x \in \left[-\frac{3\pi}{2}, -\frac{\pi}{4}\right]$

c. $f(x) = \cos x, x \in \left[-\frac{\pi}{2}, \frac{\pi}{2}\right]$

d. $f(x) = \cos x, x \in \left[\pi, \frac{3\pi}{2}\right)$

122. If $f : B \to A$ is defined by $f(x) = \frac{3x+4}{5x-7}$ and $g : A \to B$ is defined by $g(x) = \frac{7x+4}{5x-3}$, where $A = R - \left\{\frac{3}{5}\right\}$ and $B = R - \left\{\frac{7}{5}\right\}$ and I_A is an identity function on A and I_B is identity function on B, then

a. $fog = I_A$ and $gof = I_A$ *b.* $fog = I_A$ and $gof = I_B$
c. $fog = I_B$ and $gof = I_B$ *d.* $fog = I_B$ and $gof = I_A$

123. Consider the binary operations $* : R \times R \to R$ and $o : R \times R \to R$ defined as $a * b = |a - b|$ and $aob = a \; \forall \; a, b \in R$. Then, which of the following is correct?

a. $*$ is not commutative and not associative
b. o is associative and commutative
c. $a * (boc) \neq (a * b) \, o \, (a * c)$
d. o is not distributive over $*$

124. If $\cos(\theta + \phi) = m \cos(\theta - \phi)$, then $\frac{1-m}{1+m} \cot\phi$ is equal to

a. $\sin\theta$ *b.* $\sin\phi$ *c.* $\tan\theta$ *d.* $\tan\phi$

125. If $a\cos 2\theta + b\sin 2\theta = c$ has α and β as its roots, then $\tan\alpha + \tan$ is equal to

a. $\frac{2b}{a+c}$ *b.* $\frac{2a}{b+c}$
c. $\frac{2c}{a+b}$ *d.* 0

126. The general of the equation

$$\sin x - 3\sin 2x + \sin 3x = \cos x - 3\cos 2x + \cos 3x \text{ is}$$

a. $n\pi + \frac{\pi}{4}$ *b.* $\frac{n\pi}{2} + \frac{\pi}{8}$
c. $n\pi + \frac{\pi}{8}$ *d.* $\frac{n\pi}{2} + \frac{\pi}{4}$

127. The value of $\cos 12° + \cos 84° + \cos 156° + \cos 132°$ is

a. $\frac{1}{2}$ *b.* 1
c. $-\frac{1}{2}$ *d.* $\frac{1}{8}$

128. The value of $\tan^{-1}\left[2\cos\left(2\sin^{-1}\frac{1}{2}\right)\right]$ is

a. π *b.* $\frac{\pi}{2}$ *c.* $\frac{\pi}{4}$ *d.* $\frac{\pi}{3}$

129. The value of x for which $\sin\left(\sin^{-1}\frac{1}{5} + \cos^{-1}x\right) = 1$, is

a. $\frac{2}{5}$ *b.* $\frac{1}{5}$ *c.* $-\frac{1}{5}$ *d.* −1

130. The greatest and least value of $(\sin^{-1}x)^2 + (\cos^{-1}x)^2$ are respectively

a. $\frac{5\pi^2}{4}$ and $\frac{\pi^2}{8}$ *b.* $\frac{\pi}{2}$ and $-\frac{\pi}{2}$
c. $\frac{\pi^2}{4}$ and $-\frac{\pi^2}{4}$ *d.* $\frac{\pi^2}{4}$ and 0

131. For all $n \in N$, $3 \cdot 5^{2n+1} + 2^{3n+1}$ is divisible by

a. 19 *b.* 17
c. 23 *d.* Both (b) and (c)

132. If $|z + 1| = z + 2(1 + i)$, then the value of z is

a. $\frac{1}{2} - 2i$ *b.* $\frac{1}{2} + 2i$
c. $1 - 2i$ *d.* $1 + 2i$

MOCK TEST 2

133. The real value of α for which the expression $\dfrac{1-i\sin\alpha}{1+2i\sin\alpha}$ is purely real is

a. $(n+1)\dfrac{\pi}{2}$ *b.* $(2n+1)\dfrac{\pi}{2}$

c. $n\pi$ *d.* None of the above

where, $n \in N$.

134. If $\left(\dfrac{1+i}{1-i}\right)^x = 1$, then

a. $x = 2n+1$ *b.* $x = 4n$

c. $x = 2n$ *d.* $x = 4n+1$

where, $n \in N$.

135. Which of the following is correct for any two complex numbers z_1 and z_2?

a. $|z_1 z_2| = |z_1||z_2|$

b. $\arg(z_1 z_2) = \arg(z_1)\cdot\arg(z_2)$

c. $|z_1+z_2| = |z_1| + |z_2|$

d. $|z_1+z_2| \geq |z_1| - |z_2|$

136. If a convex polygon has 44 diagonals, then the number of its sides is

a. 8 *b.* 11 *c.* 3 *d.* 7

137. If a five-digit number divisible by 3 is to be formed using the numbers 0, 1, 2, 3, 4 and 5 without repetitions, then the total number of ways this can be done is

a. 216 *b.* 600 *c.* 240 *d.* 3125

138. The number of words which can be formed out of the letters of the word 'ARTICLE', so that vowels occupy the even place is

a. 1440 *b.* 144

c. 7! *d.* ${}^4C_4 \times {}^3C_3$

139. The two successive terms in the expansion of $(1+x)^{24}$ whose coefficients are in the ratio 1 : 4 are

a. 3rd and 4th *b.* 4th and 5th

c. 5th and 6th *d.* 6th and 7th

140. If the middle term of $\left(\dfrac{1}{x} + x\sin x\right)^{10}$ is equal to $7\dfrac{7}{8}$, then the value of x is

a. $2n\pi + \dfrac{\pi}{6}$ *b.* $n\pi + \dfrac{\pi}{6}$

c. $n\pi + (-1)^n\dfrac{\pi}{6}$ *d.* $n\pi + (-1)^n\dfrac{\pi}{3}$

141. If in an AP, $S_n = q\,n^2$ and $S_m = qm^2$, where S_r denotes the sum of r terms of the AP, then S_q is equal to

a. $\dfrac{q^3}{2}$ *b.* mnq

c. q^3 *d.* $(m+n)\,q^2$

142. The minimum value of $4^x + 4^{1-x}$, $x \in R$ is

a. 2 *b.* 4 *c.* 1 *d.* 0

143. If the line $\dfrac{x}{a} + \dfrac{y}{b} = 1$ passes through the points (2, –3) and (4, –5), then (a, b) is

a. (1, 1) *b.* (–1, 1)

c. (1, –1) *d.* (–1, –1)

144. The equations of the lines passing through the point (1, 0) and at a distance $\sqrt{3}/2$ from the origin, are

a. $\sqrt{3}x + y - \sqrt{3} = 0$, $\sqrt{3}x - y - \sqrt{3} = 0$

b. $\sqrt{3}x + y + \sqrt{3} = 0$, $\sqrt{3}x - y + \sqrt{3} = 0$

c. $x + \sqrt{3}y - \sqrt{3} = 0$, $x - \sqrt{3}y - \sqrt{3} = 0$

d. None of the above

145. The coordinates of the foot of perpendiculars from the point (2, 3) on the line $y = 3x + 4$ is given by

a. $\left(\dfrac{37}{10}, \dfrac{-1}{10}\right)$ *b.* $\left(-\dfrac{1}{10}, \dfrac{37}{10}\right)$

c. $\left(\dfrac{10}{37}, -10\right)$ *d.* $\left(\dfrac{2}{3}, -\dfrac{1}{3}\right)$

146. The equation of a circle which touches both the axes and the line $3x - 4y + 8 = 0$ and lies in the third quadrant is

a. $x^2 + y^2 + 4x + 4y + 2 = 0$

b. $x^2 + y^2 + 8x + 8y + 4 = 0$

c. $x^2 + y^2 + 4x + 4y + 4 = 0$

d. $x^2 + y^2 + 8x + 8y + 2 = 0$

147. If one end of a diameter of the circle $x^2 + y^2 - 4x - 6y + 11 = 0$ is (3, 4), then the coordinates of the other end of the diameter is

a. (1, –2) *b.* (1, 2) *c.* (2, 1) *d.* (1, 5)

148. If the focus of a parabola is (0, – 3) and its directrix is $y = 3$, then its equation is

a. $x^2 = -12y$ *b.* $x^2 = 12y$

c. $y^2 = -12x$ *d.* $y^2 = 12x$

149. If the parabola $y^2 = 4ax$ passes through the point (3, 2), then the length of its latusrectum is

a. $\dfrac{2}{3}$ *b.* $\dfrac{4}{3}$

c. $\dfrac{1}{3}$ *d.* 4

150. If e is eccentricity of the ellipse $\frac{x^2}{a^2}+\frac{y^2}{b^2}=1$ (where, $a< b$), then

a. $b^2=a^2(1-e^2)$
b. $a^2=b^2(1-e^2)$
c. $a^2=b^2(e^2-1)$
d. $b^2=a^2(e^2-1)$

151. An ellipse is described by using an endless string which is passed over two pins.
If the axes are 6 cm and 4 cm, the length of the string is

a. $2\sqrt{5}$
b. $\sqrt{5}$
c. $6+2\sqrt{5}$
d. $2+2\sqrt{5}$

152. The distance between the foci of a hyperbola is 16 and its eccentricity is $\sqrt{2}$. Its equation is

a. $x^2-y^2=32$
b. $\frac{x^2}{4}-\frac{y^2}{9}=1$
c. $2x-3y^2=7$
d. None of the above

153. The value of p, so that the lines
$\frac{1-x}{3}=\frac{7y-14}{2p}=\frac{z-3}{2}$
and $\frac{7-7x}{3p}=\frac{y-5}{1}=\frac{6-z}{5}$ are at right angle, is

a. $\frac{10}{11}$
b. $\frac{70}{11}$
c. $\frac{10}{7}$
d. $\frac{70}{9}$

154. The value of $f(0)$, so that the function
$f(x)=\frac{\sqrt{a^2-ax+x^2}-\sqrt{a^2+ax+x^2}}{\sqrt{a+x}-\sqrt{a-x}}$ becomes continuous for all x, is given by

a. $a^{3/2}$
b. $a^{1/2}$
c. $-a^{1/2}$
d. $-a^{3/2}$

155. A function $f:R\to R$ satisfies the equation $f(x+y)=f(x)f(y)$ for all $x, y\in R, f(x)\neq 0$. Suppose that the function is differentiable at $x=0$ and $f'(0)=2$. Then,

a. $f'(x)=f(x)$
b. $f'(x)=2f(x)$
c. $2f'(x)=f(x)$
d. None of the above

156. If $f(x)=x^{100}+x^{99}+\quad +x+1$, then $f'(1)$ is equal to

a. 5050
b. 5049
c. 5051
d. 50051

157. Let $f(x)=2^{2x-1}$ and $\phi(x)=-2^x+2x\log 2$.
If $f'(x)>\phi'(x)$, then

a. $0<x<1$
b. $0\le x<1$
c. $x>0$
d. $x\ge 0$

158. The derivative of $\sqrt{\frac{(x-3)(x^2+4)}{3x^2+4x+5}}$ with respect to x is

a. $\frac{1}{2}\sqrt{\frac{(x-3)(x^2+4)}{3x^2+4x+5}}\left[\frac{1}{x-3}+\frac{2x}{x^2+4}-\frac{6x+4}{3x^2+4x+5}\right]$
b. $\frac{1}{2}\sqrt{\frac{(x-3)(x^2+4)}{3x^2+4x+5}}\left[\frac{1}{x-3}-\frac{2x}{x^2+4}+\frac{6x+4}{3x^2+4x+5}\right]$
c. $\frac{1}{2}\sqrt{\frac{(x-3)(x^2+4)}{3x^2+4x+5}}\left[\frac{1}{x-3}-\frac{2x}{x^2+4}-\frac{6x+4}{3x^2+4x+5}\right]$
d. None of the above

159. If $f(x)=\cos x\cdot\cos 2x\cdot\cos 4x\cdot\cos 8x\cdot\cos 16x$, then the value of $f'\left(\frac{\pi}{4}\right)$ is

a. 1
b. $\sqrt{2}$
c. $\frac{1}{\sqrt{2}}$
d. 0

160. The derivative of $(e^{\sec^2 x}+3\cos^{-1}x)$ is valid in

a. $[1,1]-\{0\}$
b. $(-1,1)$
c. $(-1,1)-\{0\}$
d. None of these

161. For $0<\theta<\frac{\pi}{2}$, the value of θ, if it increases twice as fast as its sine, is

a. $\frac{\pi}{2}$
b. $\frac{\pi}{3}$
c. $\frac{\pi}{6}$
d. None of these

162. The radius of a cylinder is increasing at the rate of 3m/s and its altitude is decreasing at the rate of 4m/s. The rate of change of volume when radius is 4m and altitude is 6m, is

a. $20\pi\ m^3/s$
b. $40\pi\ m^3/s$
c. $60\pi\ m^3/s$
d. None of these

163. If $\int\frac{3e^x-5e^{-x}}{4e^x+5e^{-x}}dx=ax+b\log|4e^x+5e^{-x}|+C$, then

a. $a=\frac{-1}{8}, b=\frac{-7}{8}$
b. $a=\frac{1}{8}, b=\frac{7}{8}$
c. $a=\frac{-1}{8}, b=\frac{7}{8}$
d. $a=\frac{1}{8}, b=\frac{-7}{8}$

164. Let $f(x)=\dfrac{\sin^2 \pi x}{1+\pi^x}$. Then, $\int [f(x)+f(-x)]\,dx$ is equal to

a. 0 **b.** $x+C$

c. $\dfrac{x}{2}-\dfrac{\sin 2\pi x}{4\pi}+C$ **d.** $\dfrac{x}{2}-\dfrac{\cos \pi x}{2\pi}+C$

165. The integral value of $\dfrac{1}{\sqrt{7-6x-x^2}}$ is

a. $\log\left[2x+\sqrt{7-6x-x^2}\right]+C$

b. $\dfrac{1}{2}\log\left|\dfrac{x+3}{x-3}\right|+C$

c. $\sin^{-1}\left(\dfrac{x+3}{4}\right)+C$

d. None of the above

166. The value of $\int \dfrac{e^x}{(1+e^x)(2+e^x)}\,dx$ is

a. $\log\left(\dfrac{1+e^x}{1+2e^x}\right)+C$ **b.** $\log\left(\dfrac{1+e^x}{2+e^x}\right)+C$

c. $\log\left(\dfrac{2+e^x}{1+e^x}\right)+C$ **d.** None of the above

167. If $\int_2^e\left(\dfrac{1}{\log x}-\dfrac{1}{(\log x)^2}\right)dx=a+\dfrac{b}{\log 2}$, then

a. $a=e, b=-2$ **b.** $a=e, b=2$

c. $a=-e, b=2$ **d.** None of the above

168. The value of $\int_0^a \dfrac{\sqrt{x}}{\sqrt{x}+\sqrt{a-x}}\,dx$ is

a. $\dfrac{3a}{2}$ **b.** a **c.** $\dfrac{a}{2}$ **d.** $2a$

169. The area (in sq units) bounded by the curves $y=\sqrt{x}$, $2y-x+3=0$ and X-axis lying in the first quadrant is

a. 9 **b.** 36

c. 18 **d.** $\dfrac{27}{4}$

170. $y=2e^{2x}-e^{-x}$ is the solution of the differential equation

a. $y''+y'+2y=0$

b. $y''-y'+2y=0$

c. $y''+y'=0$

d. $y''-y'-2y=0$

171. The particular solution of the differential equation $\log\left(\dfrac{dy}{dx}\right)=3x+4y$ given that $y=0$ when $x=0$, is

a. $4e^{3x}+3e^{-4y}-7=0$

b. $3e^{3x}+4e^{4y}+7=0$

c. $4e^{3x}-3e^{4y}-7=0$

d. $3e^{3x}+4e^{4y}-7=0$

172. If the position vectors of A, B and C are respectively $2\mathbf{i}-\mathbf{j}+\mathbf{k}$, $\mathbf{i}-3\mathbf{j}-5\mathbf{k}$ and $3\mathbf{i}-4\mathbf{j}-4\mathbf{k}$, then the value of $\cos^2 A$ is equal to

a. 0 **b.** $\dfrac{6}{41}$

c. $\dfrac{35}{41}$ **d.** 1

173. Let $ABCD$ be the parallelogram whose sides AB and AD are represented by the vectors $2\mathbf{i}+4\mathbf{j}-5\mathbf{k}$ and $\mathbf{i}+2\mathbf{j}+3\mathbf{k}$ respectively. Then, if $\mathbf{a}$ is a unit vector parallel to $\mathbf{AC}$, then $\mathbf{a}$ is equal to

a. $(3\mathbf{i}-6\mathbf{j}-2\mathbf{k})/3$

b. $(3\mathbf{i}+6\mathbf{j}+2\mathbf{k})/3$

c. $(3\mathbf{i}-6\mathbf{j}-3\mathbf{k})/7$

d. $(3\mathbf{i}+6\mathbf{j}-2\mathbf{k})/7$

174. If $F(x)=\begin{bmatrix}\cos x & -\sin x & 0\\ \sin x & \cos x & 0\\ 0 & 0 & 1\end{bmatrix}$, then $F(x)\cdot F(y)$ is equal to

a. $F(xy)$ **b.** $F(x)+F(y)$

c. $F(x+y)$ **d.** $F(x-y)$

175. If $A=\begin{bmatrix}0 & 2y & z\\ x & y & -z\\ x & -y & z\end{bmatrix}$ satisfies the equation $A'A=I$, then the values of x, y and z are

a. $x=\pm\dfrac{1}{\sqrt{3}}, y=+\dfrac{1}{\sqrt{6}}, z=\pm\dfrac{1}{\sqrt{2}}$

b. $x=\pm\dfrac{1}{\sqrt{2}}, y=\pm\dfrac{1}{\sqrt{3}}, z=\pm\dfrac{1}{\sqrt{6}}$

c. $x=\pm\dfrac{1}{\sqrt{6}}, y=\pm\dfrac{1}{\sqrt{6}}, z=\pm\dfrac{1}{\sqrt{2}}$

d. $x=\pm\dfrac{1}{\sqrt{2}}, y=\pm\dfrac{1}{\sqrt{6}}, z=\pm\dfrac{1}{\sqrt{3}}$

176. If $\begin{vmatrix}x+1 & x+2 & x+a\\ x+2 & x+3 & x+b\\ x+3 & x+4 & x+c\end{vmatrix}=0$, then a, b, c are

a. in GP **b.** in HP

c. equal **d.** in AP

177. Let A and B be two events such that

$P(A) = \frac{3}{8}$, $P(B) = \frac{5}{8}$ and $P(A \cup B) = \frac{3}{4}$.

Then, $P(A/B) \cdot P(A^{-1}/B)$ is equal to

a. $\frac{2}{5}$ *b.* $\frac{3}{8}$ *c.* $\frac{3}{20}$ *d.* $\frac{6}{25}$

178. The contrapositive of the statement "If 7 is greater than 5, then 8 is greater than 6" is

a. If 8 is greater than 6, then 7 is greater than 5
b. If 8 is not greater than 6, then 7 is greater than 5
c. If 8 is not greater than 6, then 7 is not greater than 5
d. If 8 is greater than 6, then 7 is not greater than 5

179. The maximum and minimum values of the objective function

$Z = 3x - 4y$

subject to the constraints

$x - 2y \leq 0$

$-3x + y \leq 4$

$x - y \leq 6$

$x, y \geq 0$

are respectively

a. 12, 10
b. 10, 12
c. 12, does not exist
d. 5, 12

180. Solution of $\frac{|x-2|-1}{|x-2|-2} \leq 0$ is

a. [0, 1] *b.* [3, 4]
c. $(0, 1] \cup (3, 4)$ *d.* $(0, 1] \cup [3, 4)$

MOCK TEST 2

ANSWERS

Physics

1. (c)	2. (b)	3. (c)	4. (b)	5. (b)	6. (a)	7. (a)	8. (a)	9. (a)	10. (c)
11. (c)	12. (a)	13. (b)	14. (b)	15. (d)	16. (b)	17. (b)	18. (d)	19. (b)	20. (c)
21. (c)	22. (a)	23. (a)	24. (d)	25. (b)	26. (b)	27. (c)	28. (d)	29. (b)	30. (a)
31. (d)	32. (d)	33. (a)	34. (a)	35. (c)	36. (d)	37. (c)	38. (d)	39. (a)	40. (c)
41. (a)	42. (d)	43. (c)	44. (d)	45. (c)	46. (a)	47. (d)	48. (b)	49. (c)	50. (a)
51. (a)	52. (c)	53. (d)	54. (c)	55. (b)	56. (a)	57. (b)	58. (c)	59. (d)	60. (a)

Chemistry

61. (a)	62. (c)	63. (b)	64. (a)	65. (a)	66. (a)	67. (b)	68. (b)	69. (b)	70. (b)
71. (a)	72. (c)	73. (a)	74. (b)	75. (d)	76. (a)	77. (b)	78. (a)	79. (d)	80. (a)
81. (b)	82. (c)	83. (a)	84. (c)	85. (a)	86. (a)	87. (d)	88. (b)	89. (c)	90. (b)
91. (b)	92. (d)	93. (a)	94. (c)	95. (c)	96. (d)	97. (a)	98. (b)	99. (a)	100. (a)
101. (b)	102. (a)	103. (a)	104. (c)	105. (b)	106. (b)	107. (d)	108. (b)	109. (b)	110. (a)
111. (c)	112. (b)	113. (c)	114. (b)	115. (b)	116. (c)	117. (b)	118. (c)	119. (d)	120. (d)

Mathematics

121. (d)	122. (b)	123. (d)	124. (c)	125. (c)	126. (b)	127. (c)	128. (c)	129. (b)	130. (a)
131. (d)	132. (a)	133. (c)	134. (b)	135. (a)	136. (b)	137. (a)	138. (b)	139. (c)	140. (c)
141. (c)	142. (b)	143. (d)	144. (a)	145. (b)	146. (c)	147. (b)	148. (a)	149. (b)	150. (b)
151. (c)	152. (a)	153. (b)	154. (c)	155. (b)	156. (a)	157. (c)	158. (a)	159. (b)	160. (b)
161. (b)	162. (d)	163. (c)	164. (c)	165. (c)	166. (b)	167. (a)	168. (c)	169. (a)	170. (d)
171. (a)	172. (c)	173. (d)	174. (c)	175. (d)	176. (d)	177. (d)	178. (c)	179. (c)	180. (d)

HINTS & SOLUTIONS

Physics

1. *(c)* Given, $B_H = 5 \times 10^{-3}$ Wbm^{-2}

$l = 10$ m and $v = 100$ ms^{-1}

The induced emf between tip of nose and tail of helicopter is given by

$$\varepsilon = B_H v l = 5 \times 10^{-3} \times 100 \times 10 = 5 \text{ V}$$

2. *(b)* We know that, $H = \dfrac{u^2 \sin^2 \theta}{2g}$ ...(i)

and $T = \dfrac{2u \sin \theta}{g} \Rightarrow T^2 = \dfrac{4u^2 \sin^2 \theta}{g^2}$ ...(ii)

From Eqs. (i) and (ii), we get

$\therefore \quad \dfrac{T^2}{H} = \dfrac{8}{g} \Rightarrow T = \sqrt{\dfrac{8H}{g}} = 2\sqrt{\dfrac{2H}{g}}$

3. *(c)* Graph indicates that resistance increases with increase in temperature, so α and β both are positive.

4. *(b)* Given, $A = 0.3 \text{ m}^2$, $n = 2 \times 10^{25}/\text{m}^3$,

and $q = (3t^2 + 5t + 2)$ C

$\therefore I = \dfrac{dq}{dt} = \dfrac{d}{dt}(3t^2 + 5t + 2) = 6t + 5$

At $t = 25$, $I = 6 \times 2 + 5 = 17$

$\therefore$ Drift velocity, $v_d = \dfrac{I}{neA}$

$$= \frac{17}{2 \times 10^{25} \times 1.6 \times 10^{-19} \times 0.3}$$

$$= \frac{17}{0.96 \times 10^{-6}} = 1.77 \times 10^{-5} \text{ m/s}$$

5. *(b)* The given situation is shown below

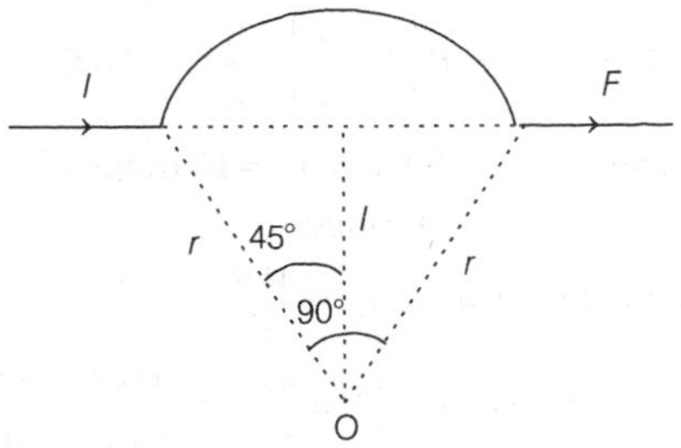

Here, $\cos 45° = \dfrac{l}{r}$

$\Rightarrow \quad l = \dfrac{r}{\sqrt{2}}$

Hence, B = magnetic field due to straight wire + magnetic field due to curved wire

$$= B_1 + B_2 = \frac{\mu_0}{4\pi} \frac{2I}{r/\sqrt{2}} + \frac{\mu_0}{4\pi} \frac{2\pi I}{r}\left(\frac{1}{4}\right)$$

$$= \frac{\mu_0}{4\pi} \frac{2I}{r}\left[\sqrt{2} + \frac{\pi}{4}\right]$$

6. *(a)* According to Stefan's law, $E = \sigma T^4$

$\therefore \quad 7 = \sigma(227 + 273)^4 = \sigma \times (500)^4$

and $\quad x = \sigma(727 + 273)^4 = \sigma \times (1000)^4$

Hence, $\quad \dfrac{x}{7} = \dfrac{(1000)^4}{(500)^4} = 16$

$\Rightarrow \quad x = 16 \times 7 = 112 \text{ cal/cm}^2\text{s}$

7. *(a)* $\quad H = \dfrac{V^2}{R} t \Rightarrow \dfrac{H}{V^2} = \dfrac{t}{R} = \text{constant}$

$\therefore \quad t \propto R$

$$R_p = \frac{R_1 R_2}{R_1 + R_2}$$

$\therefore \quad t_p = \dfrac{t_1 t_2}{t_1 + t_2} = \dfrac{10 \times 40}{10 + 40} = 8 \text{ min}$

8. *(a)* Time period of a simple pendulum is given by

$$= 2\pi\sqrt{\frac{l}{g}} \quad \text{...(i)}$$

21% increase $l \Rightarrow l' = l + \dfrac{21}{100} l = \dfrac{121}{100} l$

Therefore, $T' = 2\pi\sqrt{\dfrac{l'}{g}} = 2\pi\sqrt{\dfrac{121/100l}{g}}$

$= \dfrac{11}{10} T$ [Using Eq. (i)]

Hence, percentage increase in the time period,

$$= \frac{T' - T}{T} \times 100\% = \frac{\frac{11}{10}T - T}{T} \times 100\% = 10\%$$

9. *(a)* Let the equation of SHM be, $y = A \sin \omega t$

Then, in the first case, $\dfrac{A}{2} = A \sin \omega T_1$

i.e. $\quad \omega T_1 = \sin^{-1} \dfrac{1}{2} = \dfrac{\pi}{6}$

Therefore, $T_1 = \dfrac{\pi}{6\omega}$

Also, $T_2 = \dfrac{T}{4} - T_1 = \dfrac{2\pi}{4\omega} - \dfrac{\pi}{6\omega} = \dfrac{\pi}{3\omega}$

Therefore, $\quad T_1 < T_2$

10. *(c)* Here, $v = \omega[A^2 - y^2]^{1/2}$

or $v^2 = \omega^2 [A^2 - y^2]$

Also $v_{max} = \omega A$

i.e. $10 = \omega \times 4$

$\Rightarrow \omega = 2.5$

Putting, $v = 5 \text{ cms}^{-1}$, $\omega = 2.5$ and $A = 4$ cm

$$(5)^2 = (2.5)^2[(4)^2 - (y)^2]$$

$$\Rightarrow \frac{25}{2.5 \times 2.5} = (4)^2 - (y)^2$$

$$\Rightarrow y^2 = 16 - 4 = 12$$

$$\Rightarrow y = 2\sqrt{3} \text{ cm}$$

11. *(c)* We know that, $\nu \propto v$ and $v \propto \sqrt{T}$

Therefore, $\frac{\nu_{88}}{\nu_{16}} = \frac{v_{88}}{v_{16}} = \sqrt{\frac{273 + 88}{273 + 16}} = \frac{19}{17}$

As $\nu_{16} < \nu_{88}$, hence frequency of tuning fork ν is less than the frequency of air column.

Therefore, $\nu_{88} = \nu + 6$ and $\nu_{16} = \nu + 1$

$$\therefore \frac{\nu + 6}{\nu + 1} = \frac{19}{17}$$

On solving, we get

$$\nu = 41.5 \text{ Hz}$$

12. *(a)* The magnetic field at a point outside the straight conductor is given by

$$B = \frac{\mu_0 I}{2\pi r}$$

It means $B \propto \frac{1}{r}$ [if, $r > a$][hyperbola]

The magnetic field at a point inside the conductor is

$$B = \frac{\mu_0 I \times r}{2\pi a^2}$$

or $B \propto r$ [if, $r < a$] [straight line]

13. *(b)* Work done = area enclosed in indicator diagram *PQRSP*

$$= \Delta p \, \Delta V = (p_P - p_S)(V_Q - V_P)$$

$$= (100 \times 10^3 \times 10^5 - 200 \times 10^3 \times 10^5)$$

$$(300 \times 10^{-6} - 100 \times 10^{-6})$$

$$= 10^{10}(1 - 2) \times 10^{-4}(3 - 1) = -2 \times 10^6 \text{ J}$$

14. *(b)* Here, given that velocity of EM wave, $\mathbf{v} = v\mathbf{i}$ and instantaneous oscillating electric field, $\mathbf{E} = E\mathbf{j}$

As we already know that, during the propagation of EM waves through a medium oscillating electric and magnetic field vectors are mutually perpendicular to each other and the direction of propagation of the wave $(\mathbf{E} \times \mathbf{B})$.

i.e. $\mathbf{E} \times \mathbf{B} = \mathbf{v}$

$\Rightarrow (E\mathbf{j}) \times \mathbf{B} = v\mathbf{i}$ ...(i)

As we know that, from vector algebra,

$\mathbf{j} \times \mathbf{k} = \mathbf{i}$ ...(ii)

Comparing Eqs. (i) and (ii), we get

$$\mathbf{B} = B\mathbf{k}$$

where, B be the magnitude of magnetic field.

Thus, we can say that the direction of oscillating magnetic field of the EM wave will be along $+z$-direction.

15. *(d)* Isothermal compresion is reversible.

16. *(b)* The given ray of light is as shown below

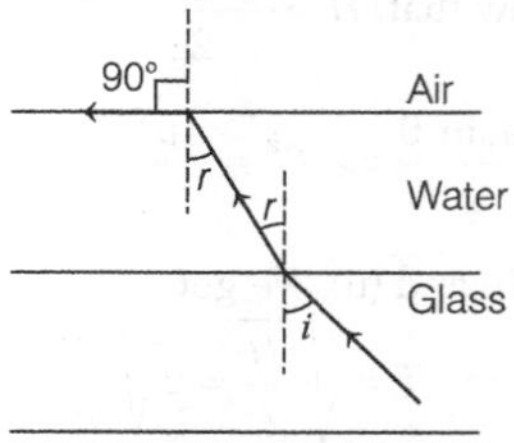

For glass-water interface, applying Snell's law

$\frac{\sin i}{\sin r} = \frac{n_w}{n_g} \Rightarrow n_g = \frac{n_w \sin r}{\sin i}$ ...(i)

For water-air interface, angle of incidence in water = r

Again, $\frac{\sin r}{\sin 90°} = \frac{n_a}{n_w} = \frac{1}{n_w}$

$\Rightarrow \sin r = \frac{1}{n_w}$ ...(ii)

From Eqs. (i) and (ii), we get

$$n_g = \frac{(n_w) \times \left(\frac{1}{n_w}\right)}{\sin i} \Rightarrow n_g = \frac{1}{\sin i}$$

17. *(b)* Since, $P = P_c\left[1 + \frac{m_a^2}{2}\right]$

Power will be maximum for 100% modulation i.e. $m_a = 1$

Therefore, $P_{max} = P_c\left[1 + \frac{1}{2}\right] = \frac{3}{2}P_c = 1.5P_c$

18. *(d)* Given, $\lambda_1 = 6000$ Å, $n_1 = 16$ fringes

and $n_2 = 24$ fringes

Position of nth fringe, $x_n = \frac{nD\lambda}{d}$

Now, for two fringes, $\frac{\lambda_1}{\lambda_2} = \frac{n_2}{n_1} \Rightarrow \frac{6000}{\lambda_2} = \frac{24}{16}$

$$\Rightarrow \lambda_2 = \frac{6000 \times 16}{24} = \frac{96000}{24} = 4000 \text{ Å}$$

19. *(b)* When iron block was floating, it displaces V_1 volume of water such that weight of this V_1 volume of water is equal to weight of block. But since density of iron is more than density of water, this volume V_1 will be greater than volume V_2 of iron block. When iron block sinks in the pond, it displaces water of volume equal to its own volume V_2.

Since $V_1 > V_2$ displaced volume in first case was more than displaced volume in second case. Hence, level will fall.

20. *(c)* Given, threshold wavelength, $\lambda_0 = 380$ nm

Wavelength of incident light, $\lambda = 260$ nm

Using Einstein's relation of photoelectric effect,

$$(KE)_{max} = eV_0 = h\nu - h\nu_0 \quad \text{...(i)}$$

But $$h\nu = E = \frac{1237}{\lambda(\text{nm})} \text{ eV} \quad \text{(given)}$$

$$\therefore \quad E_0 = \frac{1237}{\lambda_0(\text{nm})} \text{ eV} \quad \text{...(ii)}$$

From Eqs. (i) and (ii), we get

$$(KE)_{max} = E - E_0 \left(\frac{1237}{\lambda} - \frac{1237}{\lambda_0}\right) \text{eV}$$

$$= 1237\left[\frac{1}{\lambda} - \frac{1}{\lambda_0}\right] \text{eV} (\lambda \text{ in nm}) \quad \text{... (iii)}$$

By putting values of λ and λ_0 in Eq. (iii), we get

$$(KE)_{max} = 1237\left(\frac{1}{260} - \frac{1}{380}\right) \text{eV}$$

$$= 1237 \times \left[\frac{380 - 260}{380 \times 260}\right] \text{eV}$$

$$\Rightarrow \quad (KE)_{max} = 1.5 \text{ eV}$$

21. *(c)* Graph between applied force and extension will be straight line because in elastic range,

Applied force $\propto$ extension

But the graph given is parabolic in nature.

So, it will be between extension and stored elastic energy.

As, $U = 1/2kx^2$ or $U \propto x^2$

22. *(a)* If the wavelength of radiation λ is incident on a photocell, then according to Einstein's photoelectric emission of light,

$$E = (KE)_{max} + \phi \text{ or } \frac{hc}{\lambda} = (KE)_{max} + \phi \quad \text{... (i)}$$

Similarly, if the wavelength of radiation is changed to $\frac{3\lambda}{4}$, then

$$\frac{hc}{\left(\frac{3\lambda}{4}\right)} = (KE)'_{max} + \phi$$

$$\Rightarrow \quad \frac{4}{3}\left(\frac{hc}{\lambda}\right) = (KE)'_{max} + \phi \quad \text{...(ii)}$$

Substituting the value of $\left(\frac{hc}{\lambda}\right)$ from Eq. (i) in the above Eq. (ii), we get

$$\frac{4}{3}[(KE)_{max} + \phi] = (KE)'_{max} + \phi$$

$$\frac{4}{3}(KE)_{max} + \frac{4}{3}\phi - \phi = (KE)'_{max}$$

$$\frac{4}{3}(KE)_{max} + \frac{\phi}{3} = (KE)'_{max} \quad \text{...(iii)}$$

If v and v' are the maximum speed of emitted electron when the wavelength of light is λ and $\frac{3\lambda}{4}$ respectively, so Eq. (iii) can be written as

$$\frac{1}{2}mv'^2 = \frac{4}{3}\left(\frac{1}{2}mv^2\right) + \frac{\phi}{3}$$

i.e. $$v' > v\left(\frac{4}{3}\right)^{1/2}$$

23. *(a)* Work done, $W = \frac{1}{2}Fl$

$\therefore$ Work done $W \propto l$ (F is constant)

$$\therefore \quad \frac{W_1}{W_2} = \frac{l_1}{l_2} = \frac{l}{2l} = \frac{1}{2}$$

24. *(d)* As the distance of source from the surface increases, intensity of radiation decreases.

Intensity, $I \propto \frac{1}{(\text{distance } x)^2}$ and

Photoelectric current $(i) \propto$ intensity (I)

Thus, the variation of i *versus* x is correctly depicted by the curve d in the given figure.

25. *(b)* Applying conservation of mechanical energy,

$$\frac{1}{2}m\left(\frac{v_e}{2}\right)^2 = \frac{mgh}{1 + \frac{h}{R}} \quad \text{or} \quad \frac{v_e^2}{8} = \frac{gh}{1 + \frac{h}{R}}$$

or $$\frac{2gR}{8} = \frac{gh}{1 + h/R} \quad \text{...(i) } [\because v_e = \sqrt{2gR}]$$

On solving Eq. (i), we get

$$h = \frac{R}{3}$$

26. *(b)* Energy of electron in first excited state of hydrogen

$$E_n = -\frac{13.6}{n^2} = -\frac{13.6}{2^2}$$

$$= -3.40 \text{ eV} \quad (n = 2 \text{ in first excitation})$$

So, for doubly ionised lithium ($Z = 3$), energy will be

$$E_n = (E_H)Z^2 = -3.40 \times 9 = -30.6 \text{ eV}$$

$\therefore$ Energy required to remove electron = ionisation energy $= -E_n = 30.6$ eV

27. *(c)* The initial position will become the perigee (nearest) position. So, the resulting orbit of the satellite will become elliptical orbit with minimum distance from the earth equal to R.

28. *(d)* As, $\lambda_{IR} > \lambda_{UV}$

Also, wavelength of emitted radiation, $\lambda \propto \frac{1}{\Delta E}$

$$\Rightarrow \quad \lambda \propto n^2 \quad [\because E \propto 1/n^2]$$

As, for UV-radiation, the transition is from $n = 4$ to $n = 3$, so for IR (infrared) radiation, the transition will be from $5 \rightarrow 4$.

29. *(b)* We have, $I_1\omega_1 = I_2\omega_2$ or $\omega_2 = \frac{I_1}{I_2}\omega_1$

$$= \frac{(1/2\,MR^2)}{(1/2\,MR^2) + (1/2)(1/4\,MR^2)}\,\omega = \frac{4}{5}\,\omega$$

30. *(a)* Given,

E_{bn} for $A = 240$ nucleus is about 7.6 MeV.

E_{bn} for the two $A = 120$ fragment nuclei is about 8.5 MeV.

So, gain in binding energy of nucleon is about

$$= 8.5 - 7.6 = 0.9 \text{ MeV}.$$

Hence, the total gain in binding energy is

$$240 \times 0.9 = 216 \text{ MeV}.$$

31. *(d)* Angular momentum, $L = \sqrt{2KI}$

(Just like $p = \sqrt{2Km}$)

K is made 4 times. Hence, L will become 2 times as

$$L \propto \sqrt{K}.$$

32. *(d)* For 40 g of A_1,

$$40\text{ g} \xrightarrow[\text{half-life}]{20\text{s}} 20\text{ g} \xrightarrow{20\text{s}} 10\text{ g}$$

For 160 g of A_2,

$$160\text{ g} \xrightarrow[\text{half-life}]{10\text{s}} 80\text{ g} \xrightarrow{10\text{s}} 40\text{ g} \xrightarrow{10\text{s}} 20\text{ g} \xrightarrow{10\text{s}} 10\text{ g}$$

So, after 40s, the amount of the two radioactive materials A_1 and A_2 in the mixture will become equal.

33. *(a)* Power of the engine,

$$P = \mathbf{F}\cdot\mathbf{v} = (20\mathbf{i} - 3\mathbf{j} + 5\mathbf{k})\cdot(6\mathbf{i} + 20\mathbf{j} - 3\mathbf{k})$$

$$= 120 - 60 - 15 = 45 \text{ W}$$

34. *(a)* Depletion region is the space-charge region on the either side of the junction together. One to the positive space charge region on n-side and negative space charge region on p-side, due to which an electric field directed from the positive charge towards negative charge develops.

This field give rise to drift current which is opposite to diffusion current.

Due to this only, the resistance to the diffusion current by this region is large because of the presence of strong electric field.

35. *(c)* From work-energy theorem,

Work done = change in kinetic energy

$\Rightarrow \quad F\cdot x = \Delta K$

$\therefore \quad$ (as F = constant because a = constant)

$\Rightarrow \quad \Delta K \propto x$

Therefore ΔK-x graph is a straight line passing through origin.

36. *(d)* Given that, $V_E = H_E$

Angle of dip, $\tan\delta = \frac{V_E}{H_E} = \frac{H_E}{H_E} = 1 = \tan 45°$

Angle of dip, $\delta = 45°$

37. *(c)* Let acceleration of lift is a upwards. Then, with respect to lift

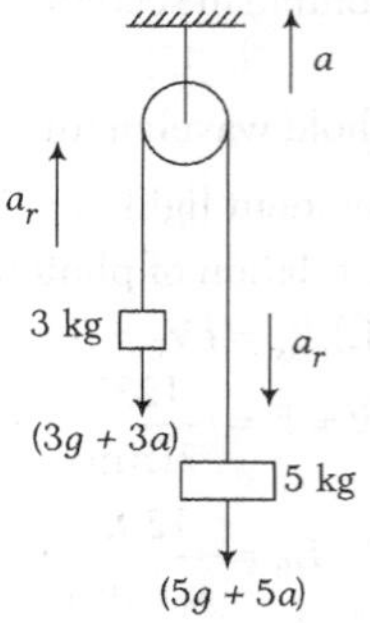

$$a_r = \frac{\text{Net pulling force}}{\text{Total mass}}$$

$$= \frac{(5g + 5a) - (3g + 3a)}{8}$$

$$\Rightarrow \quad \frac{9}{32}g = \frac{(g + a)}{4}$$

$$\therefore \quad a = \frac{g}{8}$$

38. *(d)* For substance X, $\mu_r < 1$ then it must be diamagnetic. Similarly, $\mu_r > 1$ for substance Y, then it must be paramagnetic.

39. *(a)* Acceleration of system before breaking the string was

$$a = \frac{\text{Net pulling force}}{\text{Total mass}} = \frac{3g - 2g}{5} = \frac{g}{5}$$

After 5 s velocity of system, $v = at = \frac{g}{5} \times 5 = g \text{ ms}^{-2}$

Now, $h = \frac{v^2}{2g} = \frac{g^2}{2g} = \frac{g}{2} = 4.9 \text{ m}$

40. *(c)* A circular coil expands radially in a region of magnetic field only, if (i) the magnetic field is in the same plane as the circular coil or (ii) the magnetic field has a perpendicular (to the plane of the coil) component whose magnitude is decreasing suitably in such a way that the cross-product of magnetic field and surface area of plane of coil remain constant at every instant.

Then, no electro-motive, force is produced in the coil.

41. *(a)* $R = \frac{u^2 \sin 2\theta}{g}$ at angles θ and $(90° - \theta)$

Now, $t_1 = \frac{2u\sin\theta}{g}$

and $t_2 = \frac{2u\sin(90° - \theta)}{g} = \frac{2u\cos\theta}{g}$

$$\therefore \quad t_1 t_2 = \frac{2}{g}\cdot\frac{u^2\cdot 2\sin\theta\cos\theta}{g} = \frac{2}{g}\left[\frac{u^2\sin 2\theta}{g}\right] = \frac{2R}{g}$$

42. *(d)* As the resonance peak is sharper for circuit D, so it has maximum Q-factor or quality factor.

43. *(c)* Distance travelled by the particle is

$$x = 40 + 12t - t^3$$

We know that, speed is defined as the rate of change of distance i.e.,

$$v = \frac{dx}{dt}$$

$$\therefore \quad v = \frac{d}{dt}(40 + 12t - t^3) = 0 + 12 - 3t^2$$

But final velocity, $v = 0$

$$\therefore 12 - 3t^2 = 0 \Rightarrow t^2 = \frac{12}{3} = 4 \Rightarrow t = 2\text{s}$$

Hence, distance travelled by the particle before coming to rest is given by $x = 40 + 12(2) - (2)^3 = 40 + 24 - 8 = 56$ m

44. *(d)* Given, $V_L = V_C = V_R = 20$ V

Net voltage across *L-C* combination $= V_L - V_C = 0$ V

45. *(c)* In this question, we have to find net velocity with respect to the earth that will be equal to velocity of the girl plus velocity of escalator.

Let displacement is *L*, then velocity of girl $v_g = \frac{L}{t_1}$

velocity of escalator, $v_e = \frac{L}{t_2}$

Net velocity of the girl $= v_g + v_e = \frac{L}{t_1} + \frac{L}{t_2}$

If t is total time taken in covering distance L, then

$$\frac{L}{t} = \frac{L}{t_1} + \frac{L}{t_2} \Rightarrow t = \frac{t_1 t_2}{t_1 + t_2}$$

46. *(a)* Given, wavelength, $\lambda = 589.3 \text{ nm} = 589.3 \times 10^{-9}$ m

Distance of screen, $D = 100$ cm $= 1$ m

Position of 10th bright fringe, $x = 12 \text{ mm} = 12 \times 10^{-3}$ m

Position of 10th bright fringe $= \frac{10\lambda D}{d}$

$$\Rightarrow \frac{10\lambda D}{d} = 12\text{ mm} \Rightarrow d = \frac{10\lambda D}{12 \times 10^{-3}}$$

$\therefore$ The separation between the slits,

$$d = \frac{10 \times 589.3 \times 10^{-9} \times 1}{12 \times 10^{-3}} = 4.9 \times 10^{-4} \text{ m} = 0.49 \text{ mm}$$

47. *(d)* In a streamline flow at any given point, the velocity of each passing fluid particles remains constant. If we consider a cross-sectional area, then a point on the area cannot have a different velocities at the same time, hence two streamlines of flow cannot cross each other.

48. *(b)* When lens is in air,

From lens Maker's formula,

$$\frac{1}{f_1} = ({}^a n_g - 1)\left(\frac{1}{R_1} - \frac{1}{R_2}\right) \quad \ldots\text{(i)}$$

When lens is immersed in liquid,

$$\frac{1}{f_2} = ({}^l n_g - 1)\left(\frac{1}{R_1} - \frac{1}{R_2}\right) \quad \ldots\text{(ii)}$$

On dividing Eq. (i) by Eq. (ii), we get

$$\frac{f_2}{f_1} = \frac{({}^a n_g - 1)}{({}^l n_g - 1)}$$

$$\Rightarrow \frac{f_2}{f_1} = \frac{(1.5 - 1)}{\left(\frac{1.5}{1.25} - 1\right)} \qquad \left({}^l n_g = \frac{n_g}{n_l} \text{ and } n_l = 1.25\right)$$

$$\Rightarrow \frac{f_2}{f_1} = \frac{0.5 \times 1.25}{0.25} = 2.5 \text{ or } f_2 = 2.5 f_1$$

Hence, focal length increases by a factor of 2.5 when immersed in liquid.

49. *(c)* Given, rate of loss of charge is $2 \times 10^{-7}\text{Cs}^{-1}$.

Magnitude of displacement current is given by

$$i_d = i_C = \left|\frac{dq}{dt}\right| = 2 \times 10^{-7} \text{ Cs}^{-1} = 2 \times 10^{-7} \text{ A}$$

$\therefore$ Displacement current is 2×10^{-7} A.

50. *(a)* The simplified circuit is shown in figure below.

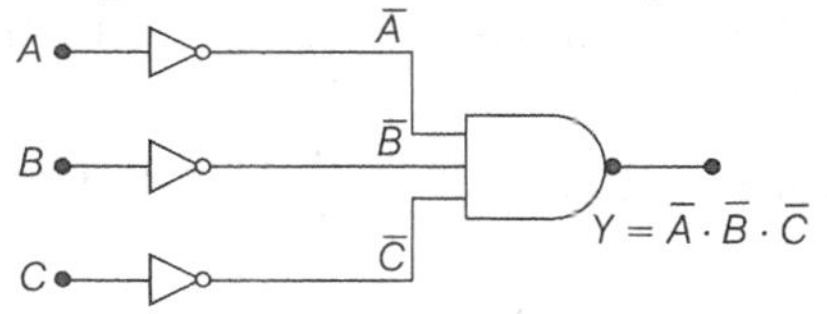

So, output $Y = \overline{\bar{A} \cdot \bar{B} \cdot \bar{C}} = \bar{\bar{A}} + \bar{\bar{B}} + \bar{\bar{C}} = A + B + C$

If $\quad A = 0, B = 1, C = 1$

$\therefore \quad Y = 0 + 1 + 1 = 1$

51. *(a)* Since, D_1 is in reverse biased, so current through 5 Ω resistance is zero but D_2 is forward biased, so D_2 behaves as a resistor of zero resistance. The equivalent circuit is

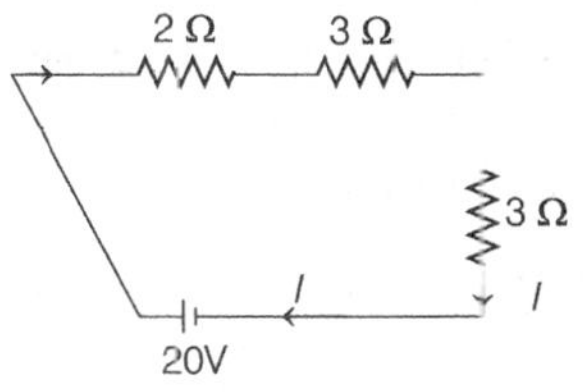

$$I = \frac{20}{8} \Rightarrow I = 2.5 \text{ A}$$

52. *(c)* Given, in question, $Q = \frac{A^3 B^3}{C\sqrt{D}}$

$$\frac{\Delta Q}{Q} = 3\left(\frac{\Delta A}{A}\right) + 3\left(\frac{\Delta B}{B}\right) + \left(\frac{\Delta C}{C}\right) + \frac{1}{2}\left(\frac{\Delta D}{D}\right)$$

Given that, $\frac{\Delta A}{A} \times 100 = 2, \frac{\Delta B}{B} \times 100 = 1$

$$\frac{\Delta C}{C} \times 100 = 3, \frac{\Delta D}{D} \times 100 = 4$$

$$\therefore \frac{\Delta Q}{Q} \times 100 = (3\times 2) + (3\times 1) + (3) + \frac{1}{2}\times (4)$$
$$= \pm 14\%$$

53. *(d)* Given, wavelengths, $\lambda_1 = 6.4 \times 10^{-7}$ m

$\lambda_2 = 4.0 \times 10^{-7}$ m

Now, in YDSE fringe width, $\beta = \frac{\lambda D}{d}$

$$\therefore \frac{\beta_2}{\beta_1} = \frac{\lambda_2}{\lambda_1}\frac{D_2}{D_1}\frac{d_1}{d_2}$$

$$\Rightarrow \beta_2 = \frac{\beta_1 \times \lambda_2 \times 2D_1 \times d_1}{\lambda_1 \times D_1 \times d_1/2} \quad \left[\because \text{Given } D_2 = 2D_1 \text{ and } d_2 = d_1/2\right]$$

$$\Rightarrow \beta_2 = \beta_1 \times \frac{\lambda_2}{\lambda_1} \times 4 = 1\times 10^{-4} \times \frac{4.0\times 10^{-7}}{6.4\times 10^{-7}} \times 4 \quad [\beta_1 = 1\times 10^{-4}\text{ m}]$$

$$\Rightarrow \beta_2 = 2.5\times 10^{-4}\text{ m}$$

54. *(c)* (a) Work = Force × Distance = $[MLT^{-2}][L] = [ML^2T^{-2}]$

Torque = force × distance = $[ML^2T^{-2}]$

(b) Angular momentum = $mvr = [M][LT^{-1}][L] = [ML^2T^{-1}]$

Planck's constant = $\frac{E}{v} = \frac{[ML^2T^{-2}]}{[T^{-1}]} = [ML^2T^{-1}]$

(c) Tension = Force = $[MLT^{-2}]$

Surface tension = $\frac{\text{Force}}{\text{Length}} = \frac{[MLT^{-2}]}{[L]} = [ML^0T^{-2}]$

(d) Impulse = Force × Time = $[MLT^{-2}][T] = [MLT^{-1}]$

Momentum = Mass × Velocity = $[M][LT^{-1}] = [MLT^{-1}]$

55. *(b)* Given, wavelengths,

$\lambda_1 = 12000$ Å and $\lambda_2 = 10000$ Å,

Distance of screen, $D = 2$ m

and distance between slits, $d = 2\text{ mm} = 2\times 10^{-3}$ m

We have, $\frac{\lambda_1}{\lambda_2} = \frac{12000}{10000} = \frac{6}{5} = \frac{n_2}{n_1}$ $[n_1\lambda_1 = n_2\lambda_2]$

As, $x = \frac{n_1\lambda_1 D}{d} = \frac{5\times 12000\times 10^{-10}\times 2}{2\times 10^{-3}}$ $[n_1 = 5]$

$= 5\times 1.2\times 10^4 \times 10^{-10}\times 10^3 = 6$ mm

56. *(a)* Since, the proton is moving against the direction of electric field, so work is done on the proton against electric field. It implies that electric field does negative work on the proton.

Again, proton is moving in electric field from low potential region to high potential region, hence its potential energy increases.

57. *(b)* Here, due the insertion of two slabs between the capacitor plates, two new capacitors are formed whose new capacitances are

Capacitance, $C_1 = \frac{K_1\varepsilon_0 A}{d/2} = \frac{2K_1\varepsilon_0 A}{d}$ and $C_2 = \frac{2K_2\varepsilon_0 A}{d}$

$$\therefore \frac{1}{C_s} = \frac{1}{C_1} + \frac{1}{C_2} = \frac{d}{2K_1\varepsilon_0 A} + \frac{d}{2K_2\varepsilon_0 A} = \frac{d}{2\varepsilon_0 A}\left(\frac{K_1+K_2}{K_1K_2}\right)$$

$$\therefore \text{Capacity, } C_s = \frac{2\varepsilon_0 A}{d}\left(\frac{K_1K_2}{K_1+K_2}\right)$$

58. *(c)* Force exerted between two point charges in air

$$F = \frac{q_1q_2}{4\pi\varepsilon_0 r^2}$$

So, force exerted between two point charges in a medium of dielectric constant K is $F' = \frac{q_1q_2}{4\pi\varepsilon_0 K(r')^2}$

where, r' is the distance.

Given, $F = F'$

$$\Rightarrow \frac{q_1q_2}{4\pi\varepsilon_0 r^2} = \frac{q_1q_2}{4\pi\varepsilon_0 K(r')^2}$$

$$\Rightarrow \frac{1}{r^2} = \frac{1}{K(r')^2}$$

$$\Rightarrow r^2 = K(r')^2 \Rightarrow r = \sqrt{K}\,r'$$

$$\therefore r' = \frac{r}{\sqrt{K}}$$

59. *(d)* Net charges of one dipole $= -e + e = 0$

Net charge of 8 dipoles $= 8\times 0 = 0$

$\therefore$ Net charge inside cube, $q = 0$

By Gauss's law,

Total flux emerging from surface, $\phi = \frac{q}{\varepsilon_0} = \frac{0}{\varepsilon_0} = 0$

60. *(a)* According to Wien's law,

$\lambda_m T = \text{constant}$

or $T \propto \frac{1}{\lambda_m}$

λ_m has become $\frac{3}{4}$ times.

$\therefore$ Temperature will have become $\frac{4}{3}$ times.

Now, according to Stefan's law, power $P \propto T^4$. Therefore, new power will be

$$P' = \left(\frac{4}{3}\right)^4 P = \frac{256}{81}P$$

MOCK TEST 2

Chemistry

61. *(a)* $\Delta S = 2.303\, nR \log \frac{V_2}{V_1}$

$= 2.303 \times 2 \times 8.3143 \log \frac{100}{10} = 38.3 \text{ J mol}^{-1} \text{ K}^{-1}$

62. *(c)* Coordination number of Cr = 6 and oxidation number = 3

Thus, $CrCl_3 \cdot 4H_2O$ exist as $[Cr(H_2O)_4\ Cl_2]\,Cl$ and $[Cr(H_2O)_3\ Cl_3] \cdot H_2O$.

63. *(b)* 3-bromobut-1-ene is an allylic halide.

$CH_2 = CH - CH(Br) - CH_3$

64. *(a)* $\Delta G = \Delta H - T\Delta S$

Given, $\Delta G = 0$ at low temperature

$\therefore \quad \Delta H - T\Delta S > 0$

$\Delta H > T\Delta S$

(a) At $\Delta H = +ve$, $\Delta S = +ve$

As temperature is low so, $\Delta H > T\Delta S$

So, $\Delta G = +ve$

(b) At $\Delta H = -ve$, $\Delta S = -ve$

As temperature is low so, $\Delta H > T\Delta S$

So, $\Delta G = \Delta H - T\Delta S$

$\therefore \quad \Delta G = -ve$

(c) At $\Delta H = -ve$, $\Delta S = +ve$

$\Delta G = \Delta H - T\Delta S;\ \Delta H = -ve$

(d) At $\Delta H = -ve$, $\Delta S = 0$

$\Delta G = \Delta H - T\Delta S = \Delta H$

$\therefore \quad \Delta G = -ve$

Thus, option (a) is correct.

65. *(a)* Mn^{2+} has five unpaired electrons. So, $MnSO_4$ has highest spin thus, it have strongest attraction to a magnetic field.

66. *(a)* Tertiary alkyl halides undergo fast elimination reaction due to the steric hindrance.

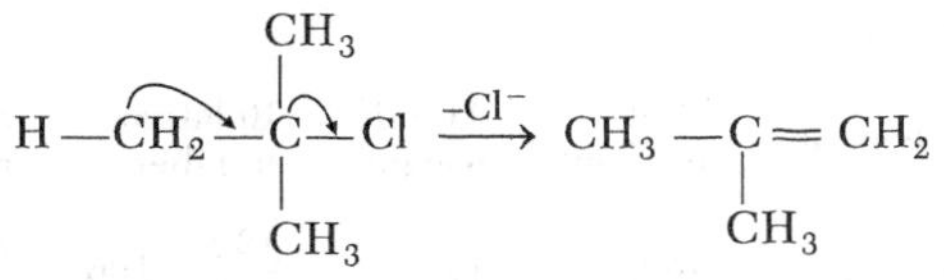

67. *(b)* $H_2O\,(s) \rightleftharpoons H_2O\,(l)$

We know that, $\Delta G = \Delta H - T\Delta S$

At equilibrium, $\Delta G = 0$

Therefore, $\Delta H = T\Delta S$

68. *(b)* Conjugation increases stability.

$CH_2 = CH\dot{C}HCH = CH_2$

$\longleftrightarrow CH_2 = CHCH = CH\dot{C}H_2$

$CH_2 = CHCH = CH\dot{C}H_2$

$\xrightarrow{NBS} CH_2 = CHCH = CHCH_2Br$

69. *(b)* S_N2 reaction takes place by nucleophilic attack on the backside resulting in the formation of inverted product.

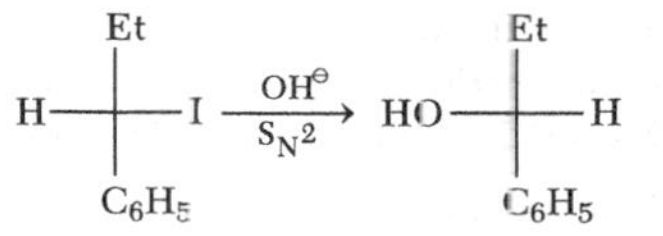

70. *(b)* Due to strain, white phosphorus is most reactive.

71. *(a)* $B_2 = 5 + 5 = 10e^-$

$= \sigma 1s^2, \overset{*}{\sigma} 1s^2, \sigma 2s^2, \overset{*}{\sigma} 2s^2, \pi 2p_x^1 \approx \pi 2p_y^1$

Due to the presence of 2 unpaired electrons π_bMO, B_2 shows paramagnetic behaviour.

72. *(c)* $H_2SO_5 + H_2O \longrightarrow H_2SO_4 + H_2O_2$

$H_2S_2O_8 + 2H_2O \longrightarrow 2H_2SO_4 + H_2O_2$

Both have peroxy linkages. so, they are peroxy acids.

73. *(a)* The hybridisation of given elements are as follows :

NO_2^+ $\quad O = \overset{\oplus}{N} = O \quad sp$

NO_3^- 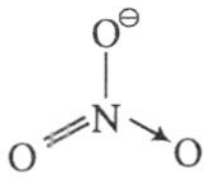 sp^2

NH_4^+ 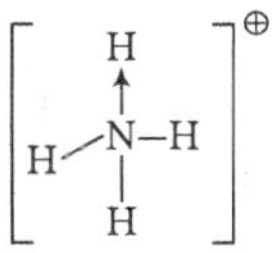 sp^3

74. *(b)* $TiCl_4$ and AlR_3 [R = propyl, ethyl] represents Ziegler-Natta catalyst which acts as a catalyst in polymerisation of ethene.

75. *(d)* Calcination is used for hydrated oxide ores or carbonate ore to convert them into oxides (anhydrous).

76. *(a)* SO_2 has sp^2-hybridisation with angle 119°(bent shape).

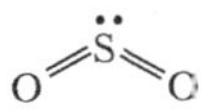

77. *(b)* For a first order reaction

$t_{1/2} = \frac{0.693}{k}$

i.e. half-life period is independent of initial concentration of a reactant. So, doubling the initial concentration does not affect the half-life of the reaction.

78. *(a)* Coagulating value is expressed in millimol L^{-1}.

$\therefore$ Millimol of NaCl $= 5 \times 1 = 5$

Colloidal sol = 100 mL = 0.1 L

$\therefore$ Coagulating value $= \frac{5}{0.1} = 50$

79. *(d)* At STP, 22400 cc of $O_2 = 32$ g

So, 0.224 cc of $O_2 = 3.2 \times 10^{-4}$ g

$$Z = \frac{32}{4 \times 96500}$$

$$i = \frac{w}{Zt} = \frac{3.2 \times 10^{-4} \times 96500 \times 4}{32 \times 1} = 3.86 \text{ A}$$

80. *(a)* N < O < S < Cl

As we move along a period, electron affinity increases. Also as we move down a group it increases, so the order is N < O < S < Cl. Hence, the correct option is (a).

81. *(b)* By Raoult's law,

relative decrease in vapour pressure = mole fraction of solute *B*

$$\chi_B = \frac{p_A^\circ - p}{p_A}$$

Where p_A° and p are the vapour pressures of pure solvent and solution respectively.

$$\chi_B = \frac{0.80 - 0.60}{0.80} = 0.25$$

82. *(c)* The element with atomic number 117 (86 + 19 + 17) will be placed in the 17th group of periodic table i.e. halogens.

83. *(a)* Number of octahedral voids = number of atoms in the close packed structure.

Since, number of atom in one ccp unit = 1

So, number of octahedral void = 1

0.140 m aq. glycine solution means that 0.140 mol of glycine are present in 1 kg or 1000 g of water.

84. *(c)* Moles of glycine = 0.140

$$\text{moles of } H_2O = \frac{1000}{18} = 55.56$$

Total moles = 0.14 + 55.56 = 55.70

$$X_{\text{glycine}} = \frac{n_{(\text{glycine})}}{n_{(\text{total})}} = \frac{0.14}{55.70} = 2.51 \times 10^{-3}.$$

85. *(a)* Size $\propto \frac{1}{Z}$ for isoelectronic anion

Size :	C^{4-} >	N^{3-} >	O^{2-} >	F^-
Atomic number, Z :	6	7	8	9

86. *(a)* Toluene possess the C—H bond with lowest bond dissociation energy as the free radical formed is most stable after dissociation of C—H bond.

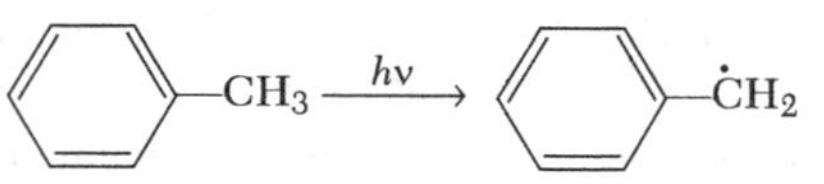

Benzyl free radical (most stable)

87. *(d)* Schottky defect lowers the density of a crystal. It is the vacancy defect in the ionic solids. This defect arises when equal number of cations and anions are missing from the lattice and thus, electrical neutrality is maintained, e.g., CsCl, NaCl, KCl, AgBr in which cations and anions are of almost same size.

88. *(b)* Chemically paper and cloth consists of cellulose. In plant eating animals digestion of cellulose takes place in presence of enzyme cellulase.

89. *(c)*

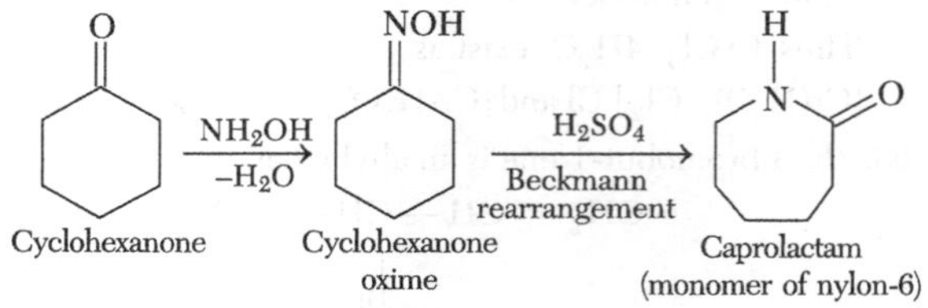

90. *(b)* C_6H_5CHO has no H at α-carbon, thus it do not give aldol condensation reaction.

91. *(b)* Atomic number = 17

Electronic configuration = $1s^2 2s^2 2p^6 3s^2 3p^5$

Valence shell 3s [⥮] 3p [⥮ | ⥮ | 1] (p_x p_y p_z)

Orbitals which containing electron pairs are $3s$, $3p_x$, $3p_y$.

So, the total orbitals are three.

92. *(d)* The given reaction takes place as follows :

$$CH\equiv CH \xrightarrow{O_3/NaOH} CHO-CHO \xrightarrow[\text{Reduction}]{Zn/CH_3COOH} CH_2OH-CH_2OH$$

93. *(a)* Excess of nitrate in drinking water causes methemoglobinemia.

94. *(c)* As $H-\overset{H}{\underset{H}{C}}-\overset{H}{C}=\overset{H}{C}-H$ does not contains any alternative double bond.

95. *(c)*

Element	% of element	Atomic weight	Relative number	Simple ratio
Carbon	12.8	12	$\frac{12.8}{12} = 1.06$	$\frac{1.06}{1.06} = 1$
Hydrogen	2.10	1	$\frac{2.10}{1} = 2.10$	$\frac{2.10}{1.06} = 2$
Bromine	85.1	80	$\frac{85.1}{80} = 1.06$	$\frac{1.06}{1.06} = 1$

Hence, the empirical formula becomes CH_2Br.

Empirical weight of $CH_2Br = 12 + 2 + 80 = 94$

As we know that,

$$\text{Multiple } (n) = \frac{\text{molecular weight}}{\text{empirical weight}} = \frac{187.9}{94} = 2$$

Molecular formula = (Empirical formula)$_n$

$$= (CH_2Br)_2 = C_2H_4Br_2$$

96. *(d)* Most stable 3° carbocation is formed

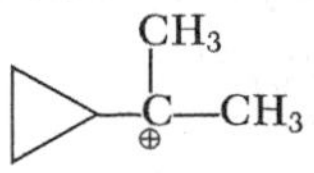

Thus, this is hydrated to maximum extent.

97. *(a)* As we go down the group in periodic table, ionic nature increases but covalent nature decreases. Thus, stability decreases so, CH_4 is most stable.

$$CH_4 > SiH_4 > GeH_4 > SnH_4 > PbH_4$$

Also due to inert pair effect stability of +4 state decreases down the group.

98. *(b)*

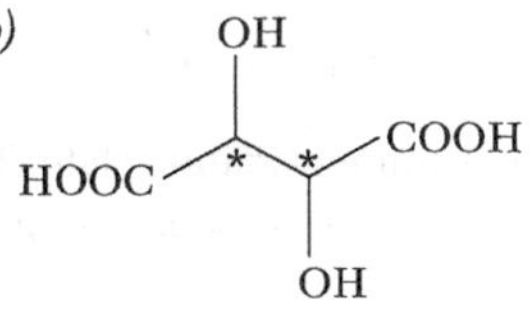

Number of asymmetric C-atoms = 2

Number of optically active isomers

$$= 2^{n-1} = 2^{2-1} = 2^1 = 2$$

Number of optically active *meso* form

$$= 2^{(n-2)/2} = 2^0 = 1$$

Number of optically active racemic form $= \frac{2}{2} = 1$

Total optical isomers = 2 + 1 = 3

99. *(a)* CO_2 is form Na_2CO_3 only.

$$\underset{\substack{106g \\ ?}}{Na_2CO_3} + 2HCl \longrightarrow 2NaCl + \underset{\substack{44g \\ 2.24\,g}}{CO_2} + H_2O$$

44 g CO_2 is formed by = 106 g of Na_2CO_3

$\therefore$ 2.24 g CO_2 is formed by $= \frac{106}{44} \times 2.24$g of Na_2CO_3

$$= 5.4\text{g}$$

Thus, mass of NaCl = 12 − 5.4 = 6.6 g

100. *(a)* Water gas is produced by passing steam over red hot coke.

The reaction involved is

$$H_2O(g) + C(s) \longrightarrow CO(g) + H_2(g) \; [\Delta H = 131 \text{ kJ/mol}]$$

101. *(b)* $CO(NH_2)_2 + 2NaOH \longrightarrow Na_2CO_3 + 2NH_3$

1 mole urea reacts with 2 moles NaOH.

Molar mass of $[CO(NH_2)_2]$ = 60.0 g/mol (6.0 g urea) 0.1 mole required = 0.2 mole of NaOH

1000 mL NaOH solution contains 2 moles of NaOH.

Volume that contains 0.2 mole NaOH

$$= \frac{0.2}{2.0} \times 1000 \text{ mL} = 100 \text{ mL}$$

102. *(a)* The carbonates of alkali metals (i.e. Na_2CO_3, K_2CO_3, Rb_2CO_3) are stable up to 1000°C, whereas carbonates of alkaline earth metals decomposes on heating to form corresponding metal oxide and CO_2.

$$MgCO_3 \xrightarrow{\Delta} MgO + CO_2$$

103. *(a)* Decarboxylation takes place if there are two —COOH groups attached to same carbon (*gem*-position) or there is keto group at β-position or (C = C) at β, γ-position w.r.t. COOH groups.

$\therefore$ In methylmalonic acid

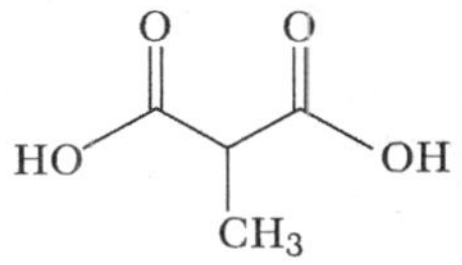

decarboxylation does not take place.

104. *(c)* For isothermal reversible process,

$$W = -2.303\, nRT \log \frac{V_2}{V_1}$$

Where W is workdone, n = 2 moles (no. of moles of gas), R = gas constant, T = 300 K (temperature), V_2 and V_1 are final and initial volume.

$$W = -2.303 \times 2 \times 8.314 \times 300 \log \frac{10}{1}$$

$$W = -11478 \text{ J}$$

$$W = -11.48 \text{ kJ} \approx -11.47 \text{ kJ}$$

Sign of workdone for an isothermal reversible process is negative.

105. *(b)* The pair of bases are held with each other by H-bond.

106. *(b)* During electrolysis of NaCl(*aq*) solution,

$$2H^+ + 2e^- \longrightarrow H_2$$

The hydrogen ion concentration decreases and the pH of the solution increases.

107. *(d)* The given reaction takes place as follows :

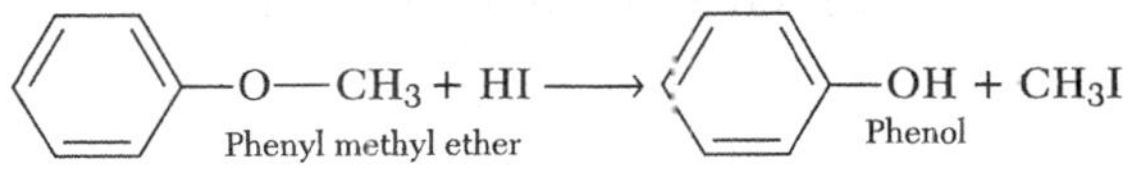

108. *(b)* Equanil is a tranquiliser.

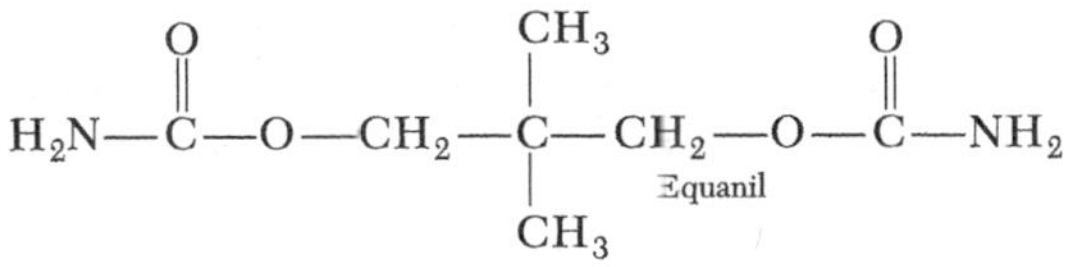

MOCK TEST 2

109. *(b)*

$$C_6H_4CH{=}CHCHO \xrightarrow{NaBH_4} C_6H_5CH{=}CHCH_2OH$$

—CHO is reduced to —CH_2OH.

110. *(a)* Decrease in ON (reduction)

$$\overset{+1}{Ag_2}O + H_2\overset{-1}{O_2} \longrightarrow 2\overset{0}{Ag} + H_2O + \overset{0}{O_2}$$

Increase in ON (oxidation)

The oxidation number of O in H_2O_2 increases. Hence, H_2O_2 acts as a reducing agent as it is undergoing oxidation.

111. *(c)* Due to the delocalisation of one pair of electrons of O-atom with phenyl ring in both side makes it very stable.

112. *(b)* $H_2(g) + Cl_2(g) \rightleftharpoons 2HCl(g); K_p = K_C(RT)^{\Delta n}$

Δn_g = number of moles of gaseous products − number of moles of gaseous reactants $= 2 - 2 = 0$

$K_p = K_C(RT)^0$ or $K_p = K_C$.

113. *(c)* There is also double bond character in (C—O) bond of phenol due to resonance. There is no resonance in alcohol.

114. *(b)* Pyridine is less basic than triethylamine due to presence of sp^2-hybridised nitrogen. So, electrons are tightly attracted to nitrogen atom and thus, not easily available to give.

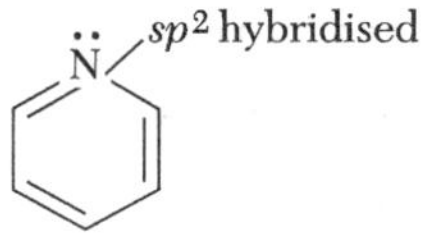

115. *(b)* Distribution of molecules is maximum at most probable velocity.

From kinetic gas equation,

$$v = \sqrt{\frac{2RT}{M}}$$

116. *(c)* $RbF + XeF_6 \longrightarrow [Rb]^+[XeF_7]^-$

$CsF + XeF_6 \longrightarrow [Cs]^+[XeF_7]^-$

117. *(b)* Ni^{2+} can be tested by dimethyl glyoxime (DMG).

$$Ni^{2+} + 2DMG \longrightarrow \underset{\text{Cherry red ppt.}}{[Ni(DMG)_2]^{2+}}$$

118. *(c)* Suppose the equal mass of methane and oxygen $= w = 1$ g.

Mole fraction of oxygen $(\chi_{O_2}) = \dfrac{w/32}{w/32 + w/16}$

$$= \frac{1/32}{3/32} = \frac{1}{3}$$

Let the total pressure $= p$

Pressure exerted by oxygen (partial pressure)

$$= \chi_{O_2} \times p_{\text{total}} = p \times \frac{1}{3}.$$

119. *(d)* $HClO_4$ has Cl in maximum oxidation state. Thus, is not further oxidised. Hence, it is least oxidising in nature.

120. *(d)*

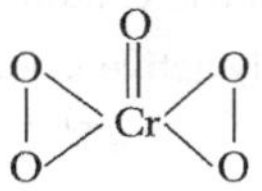

Oxidation number of oxygen in peroxide = −1

So, $x + 4(-1) + 1(-2) = 0$

$x - 4 - 2 = 0$

$x = +6$

Mathematics

121. *(d)* Any function $f(x)$ will be a one-one function, if the line parallel to X-axis (*i.e.*, horizontal line) cuts the graph of $f(x)$ only at one point. Otherwise, it is said to be many-one function.

Now, consider the graph of $\sin x$ and $\cos x$ as follows

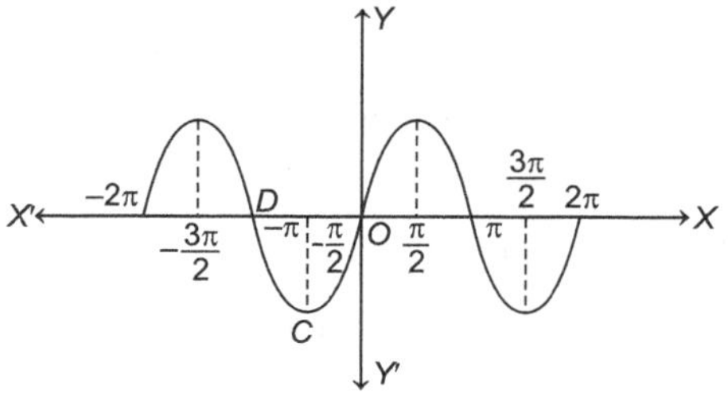

Graph of sin *x*

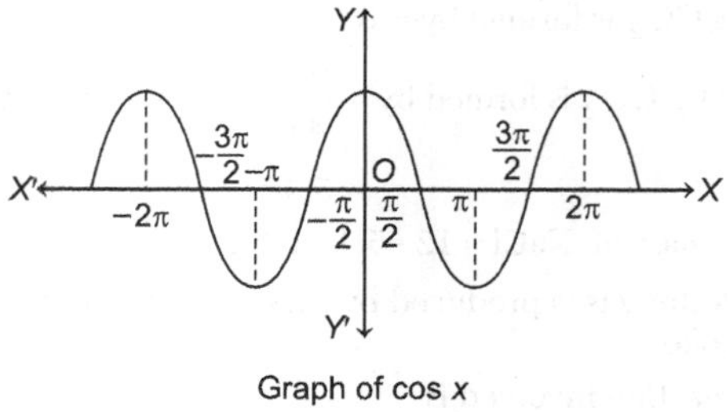

Graph of cos *x*

Now, in the graph of $\sin x$, if we draw the horizontal line, it will cut the $\sin x$ at two points in the intervals

$$[-\pi, \pi] \text{ and } \left[\frac{-3\pi}{2}, \frac{-\pi}{4}\right]$$

Also, in the graph of $\cos x$, if we draw the horizontal line, it will cut the $\cos x$ at two points in the interval

$\left[\frac{-\pi}{2}, \frac{\pi}{2}\right]$ but in the interval $\left[\pi, \frac{3\pi}{2}\right]$, it will cut the $\cos x$ at only one point.

$\therefore$ The function $f(x) = \cos x,\ x \in \left[\pi, \frac{3\pi}{2}\right)$ is one-one.

122. (*b*) We have,

$$gof(x) = g\left(\frac{3x+4}{5x-7}\right) = \frac{7\left(\frac{(3x+4)}{(5x-7)}\right)+4}{5\left(\frac{(3x+4)}{(5x-7)}\right)-3}$$

$$= \frac{21x+28+20x-28}{15x+20-15x+21} = \frac{41x}{41} = x$$

Similarly, $fog(x) = f\left(\frac{7x+4}{5x-3}\right)$

$$= \frac{3\left(\frac{(7x+4)}{(5x-3)}\right)+4}{5\left(\frac{(7x+4)}{(5x-3)}\right)-7}$$

$$= \frac{21x+12+20x-12}{35x+20-35x+21} = \frac{41x}{41} = x$$

Thus, $gof(x) = x,\ \forall\ x \in B$ and $fog(x) = x,\ \forall\ x \in A$, which implies that $gof = I_B$ and $fog = I_A$.

123. (*d*) Given that, $* : R \times R \to R$

and $o : R \times R \to R$ defined as

$$a * b = |a - b| \text{ and } aob = a,\ \forall\ a, b \in R.$$

For $a, b \in R$, we have

$$a * b = |a - b|,$$
$$b * a = |b - a| = |-(a-b)| = |a - b|$$

Therefore, $a * b = b * a$

Thus, the operation $*$ is commutative.

It can be observed that,

$$(1 * 2) * 3 = (|1-2|) * 3 = 1 * 3 = |1-3| = 2$$
$$1 * (2 * 3) = 1 * (|2-3|) = 1 * 1 = |1-1| = 0$$
$$\therefore \quad (1 * 2) * 3 \neq 1 * (2 * 3) \quad (\text{where, } 1, 2, 3 \in R)$$

Therefore, the operation $*$ is not associative.

Now, consider the operation o. It can be observed that $1o2 = 1$ and $2o1 = 2$

Therefore, the $1o2 \neq 2o1$ where $1, 2 \in R$.

Thus, the operation o is not commutative.

Let $a, b, c \in R$. Then, we have

$$(aob)\,oc = aoc = a,$$
$$ao(boc) = aob = a$$
$$\Rightarrow \quad (aob)\,oc = ao(boc)$$

Therefore, the operation o is associative.

Now, let $a, b, c \in R$, then we have

$$a * (boc) = a * b = |a - b|$$
$$(a * b)o(a * c) = (|a - b|)$$
$$(|a-b|)o(|a-c|) = |a - b|$$

Hence, $a * (boc) = (a * b)\,o(a * c)$

Now, $1o(2 * 3) = 1o(|2-3|) = 1o1 = 1$

$$(1o2) * (1o3) = 1 * 1 = |1 - 1| = 0$$

Therefore, $1o(2 * 3) \neq (1o2) * (1o3)$

where $1, 2, 3, \in R$.

Therefore, the operation o does not distribute over $*$.

124. (*c*) Given that,

$$\cos(\theta + \phi) = m\cos(\theta - \phi)$$

$$\Rightarrow \quad \frac{\cos(\theta+\phi)}{\cos(\theta-\phi)} = \frac{m}{1}$$

Using componendo and dividendo rule,

$$\frac{\cos(\theta-\phi) - \cos(\theta+\phi)}{\cos(\theta-\phi)+\cos(\theta+\phi)} = \frac{1-m}{1+m}$$

$$\Rightarrow \quad \frac{-2\sin\left(\frac{\theta-\phi+\theta+\phi}{2}\right).\sin\left(\frac{\theta-\phi-\theta-\phi}{2}\right)}{2\cos\left(\frac{\theta-\phi+\theta+\phi}{2}\right)\cdot\cos\left(\frac{\theta-\phi-\theta-\phi}{2}\right)} = \frac{1-m}{1+m}$$

$$\Rightarrow \quad \frac{\sin\theta\cdot\sin\phi}{\cos\theta\cdot\cos\phi} = \frac{1-m}{1+m} \quad \left[\begin{array}{l}\sin(-\theta) = -\sin\theta \\ \text{and } \cos(-\theta) = \cos\theta\end{array}\right]$$

$$\Rightarrow \quad \tan\theta\cdot\tan\phi = \frac{1-m}{1+m}$$

$$\Rightarrow \quad \tan\theta = \left(\frac{1-m}{1+m}\right)\cot\phi$$

125. (*c*) Given that, $a\cos 2\theta + b\sin 2\theta = c$

$$\Rightarrow a\left(\frac{1-\tan^2\theta}{1+\tan^2\theta}\right) + b\left(\frac{2\tan\theta}{1+\tan^2\theta}\right) = c$$

$$\left[\sin 2\theta = \frac{2\tan\theta}{1+\tan^2\theta} \text{ and } \cos 2\theta = \frac{1-\tan^2\theta}{1+\tan^2\theta}\right]$$

$$\Rightarrow a(1-\tan^2\theta) + 2b\tan\theta = c(1+\tan^2\theta)$$
$$\Rightarrow a - a\tan^2\theta + 2b\tan\theta = c + c\tan^2\theta$$
$$\Rightarrow (a+c)\tan^2\theta - 2b\tan\theta + c - a = 0$$

Since, this equation has $\tan\alpha$ and $\tan\beta$ as its roots.

$$\tan\alpha + \tan\beta = \frac{-(-2b)}{a+c} = \frac{2b}{a+c}$$

126. (*b*) Given equation,

$\sin x - 3\sin 2x + \sin 3x = \cos x - 3\cos 2x + \cos 3x$

$$\Rightarrow 2\sin\left(\frac{x+3x}{2}\right)\cdot\cos\left(\frac{3x-x}{2}\right) - 3\sin 2x$$
$$= 2\cos\left(\frac{3x+x}{2}\right)\cdot\cos\left(\frac{3x-x}{2}\right) - 3\cos 2x$$

$\Rightarrow 2\sin 2x \cos x - 3\sin 2x = 2\cos 2x \cdot \cos x - 3\cos 2x$

$\Rightarrow \sin 2x(2\cos x - 3) = \cos 2x(2\cos x - 3)$

$\Rightarrow \frac{\sin 2x}{\cos 2x} = 1$

$\Rightarrow \tan 2x = 1$

$\Rightarrow \tan 2x = \tan\frac{\pi}{4}$

$\Rightarrow \quad 2x = n\pi + \frac{\pi}{4}$

$\therefore \quad x = \frac{n\pi}{2} + \frac{\pi}{8}$

127. (*c*) Given expression,

$$\cos 12° + \cos 84° + \cos 156° + \cos 132°$$
$$= \cos 12° + \cos 156° + \cos 84° + \cos 132°$$
$$= 2\cos\left(\frac{12° + 156°}{2}\right)\cdot\cos\left(\frac{12° - 156°}{2}\right) + 2\cos\left(\frac{84° + 132°}{2}\right)\cdot\cos\left(\frac{84° - 132°}{2}\right)$$
$$= 2\cos 84° \cos 72° + 2\cos 108° \cdot \cos 24°$$
$$= 2\cos 84° \cos(90° - 18°) + 2\cos(90° + 18°)\cdot\cos 24°$$
$$= 2\cos 84° \sin 18° - 2\sin 18° \cos 24°$$
$$= 2\sin 18°(\cos 84° - \cos 24°)$$
$$= 2\sin 18° \cdot 2\sin\left(\frac{84° + 24°}{2}\right)\cdot\sin\left(\frac{24° - 84°}{2}\right)$$
$$= -4\sin 18° \sin 54° \sin 30°$$
$$= -4\left(\frac{\sqrt{5} - 1}{4}\right)\left(\frac{1}{2}\right)\cdot\cos 30°$$
$$= -(\sqrt{5} - 1)\left(\frac{\sqrt{5} + 1}{4}\right)\left(\frac{1}{2}\right)$$
$$= -\left(\frac{5 - 1}{8}\right) = \frac{-4}{8} = \frac{-1}{2}$$

128. (*c*) We have,

$$\tan^{-1}\left[2\cos\left(2\sin^{-1}\frac{1}{2}\right)\right]$$
$$= \tan^{-1}\left[2\cos\left\{2\sin^{-1}\left(\sin\frac{\pi}{6}\right)\right\}\right] \qquad \left(\sin\frac{\pi}{6} = \frac{1}{2}\right)$$
$$= \tan^{-1}\left[2\cos\left(2 \times \frac{\pi}{6}\right)\right]$$
$$= \tan^{-1}\left[2\cos\frac{\pi}{3}\right]$$
$$= \tan^{-1}\left[2 \times \frac{1}{2}\right] = \tan^{-1}(1) \qquad \left(\cos\frac{\pi}{3} = \frac{1}{2}\right)$$
$$= \tan^{-1}\left(\tan\frac{\pi}{4}\right) = \frac{\pi}{4} \qquad \left(\tan\frac{\pi}{4} = 1\right)$$

129. (*b*) Given, $\sin\left(\sin^{-1}\frac{1}{5} + \cos^{-1}x\right) = 1$

$\Rightarrow \sin^{-1}\frac{1}{5} + \cos^{-1}x = \sin^{-1}1 \quad (\sin\theta = x \Rightarrow \theta = \sin^{-1}x)$

$\Rightarrow \sin^{-1}\frac{1}{5} + \cos^{-1}x = \sin^{-1}\left(\sin\frac{\pi}{2}\right) \quad \left[\sin\left(\frac{\pi}{2}\right) = 1\right]$

$\Rightarrow \sin^{-1}\frac{1}{5} + \cos^{-1}x = \frac{\pi}{2}$

$\Rightarrow \sin^{-1}\frac{1}{5} = \frac{\pi}{2} - \cos^{-1}x$

$\Rightarrow \sin^{-1}\frac{1}{5} = \sin^{-1}x \qquad \left(\sin^{-1}x + \cos^{-1}x = \frac{\pi}{2}\right)$

$\Rightarrow \quad \frac{1}{5} = x$

130. (*a*) We have, $(\sin^{-1}x)^2 + (\cos^{-1}x)^2$

$$= (\sin^{-1}x + \cos^{-1}x)^2 - 2\sin^{-1}x\cos^{-1}x$$
$$= \frac{\pi^2}{4} - 2\sin^{-1}x\left(\frac{\pi}{2} - \sin^{-1}x\right)$$
$$= \frac{\pi^2}{4} - \pi\sin^{-1}x + 2(\sin^{-1}x)^2$$
$$= 2\left[(\sin^{-1}x)^2 - \frac{\pi}{2}\sin^{-1}x + \frac{\pi^2}{8}\right]$$
$$= 2\left[\left(\sin^{-1}x - \frac{\pi}{4}\right)^2 + \frac{\pi^2}{16}\right]$$

Thus, the least value is $2\left(\frac{\pi^2}{16}\right)$ *i.e.*, $\frac{\pi^2}{8}$

and the greatest value is

$$2\left[\left(\frac{-\pi}{2} - \frac{\pi}{4}\right)^2 + \frac{\pi^2}{16}\right], \text{ i.e., } \frac{5\pi^2}{4}.$$

131. (*d*) Given that, $3\cdot 5^{2n+1} + 2^{3n+1}$

For $n = 1$, $3\cdot 5^{2(1)+1} + 2^{3(1)+1}$

$$= 3\cdot 5^3 + 2^4 = 3 \times 125 + 16 = 375 + 16 = 391$$

Now, $391 = 17 \times 23$

which is divisible by both 17 and 23.

132. (*a*) Given that,

$$|z + 1| = z + 2(1 + i) \qquad \text{...(i)}$$
$$z = x + iy$$

Then, $|x + iy + 1| = x + iy + 2(1 + i)$

$\Rightarrow |x + 1 + iy| = (x + 2) + i(y + 2)$

$\Rightarrow \sqrt{(x + 1)^2 + y^2} = (x + 2) + i(y + 2)$

On squaring both sides, we get

$(x + 1)^2 + y^2 = (x + 2)^2 + i^2(y + 2)^2 + 2i(x + 2)(y + 2)$

$\Rightarrow x^2 + 2x + 1 + y^2$

$$= x^2 + 4x + 4 - y^2 - 4y - 4 + 2i(x + 2)(y + 2)$$

MOCK TEST 2

$\Rightarrow x^2 + y^2 + 2x + 1 = x^2 - y^2 + 4x - 4y$
$+2i(x+2)(y+2)$

On comparing real and imaginary parts, we get

$x^2 + y^2 + 2x + 1 = x^2 - y^2 + 4x - 4y$ ...(ii)

and $2(x+2)(y+2) = 0$

$\Rightarrow x+2=0$ or $y+2=0$

$x=-2$ or $y=-2$ ...(iii)

For $x=-2$,

$2y^2 + 4 + 4y + 1 = 0$ [using Eq. (ii)]

$\Rightarrow \quad 2y^2 + 4y + 5 = 0$

$D = 16 - 4 \times 2 \times 5 < 0$

$\therefore$ Discriminant, $D = b^2 - 4ac < 0$

$\Rightarrow 2y^2 + 4y + 5$ has no real roots.

For $y=-2$,

$2(-2)^2 - 2x + 4(-2) + 1 = 0$ [using Eq. (ii)]

$\Rightarrow 8 - 2x - 8 + 1 = 0$

$\Rightarrow \quad x = 1/2$

$\therefore \quad z = x + iy = \frac{1}{2} - 2i$

133. (c) Given expression,

$$z = \frac{1 - i\sin\alpha}{1 + 2i\sin\alpha} \quad \text{[let]}$$

$$= \frac{(1 - i\sin\alpha)(1 - 2i\sin\alpha)}{(1 + 2i\sin\alpha)(1 - 2i\sin\alpha)}$$

$$= \frac{1 - i\sin\alpha - 2i\sin\alpha + 2i^2\sin^2\alpha}{1 - 4i^2\sin^2\alpha}$$

$$= \frac{1 - 3i\sin\alpha - 2\sin^2\alpha}{1 + 4\sin^2\alpha}$$

$$= \frac{1 - 2\sin^2\alpha}{1 + 4\sin^2\alpha} - \frac{3i\sin\alpha}{1 + 4\sin^2\alpha}$$

It is given that z is a purely real.

$$\therefore \quad \frac{-3\sin\alpha}{1 + 4\sin^2\alpha} = 0$$

$\Rightarrow \quad -3\sin\alpha = 0 \Rightarrow \sin\alpha = 0$

$\alpha = n\pi$

134. (b) Given that, $\left(\frac{1+i}{1-i}\right)^x = 1$

$$\Rightarrow \left[\frac{(1+i)(1+i)}{(1-i)(1+i)}\right]^x = 1$$

$$\Rightarrow \left[\frac{1 + 2i + i^2}{1 - i^2}\right]^x = 1$$

$$\Rightarrow \left[\frac{2i}{1+1}\right]^x = 1$$

$$\Rightarrow \left[\frac{2i}{2}\right]^x = 1$$

$\Rightarrow \quad i^x = 1$

$\Rightarrow \quad i^x = (i^{4n}) \quad [\because i^{4n} = 1, n \in N]$

$\Rightarrow \quad x = 4n$

135. (a) Let $z_1 = r_1(\cos\theta_1 + i\sin\theta_1)$

$\Rightarrow \quad |z_1| = r_1$ ...(i)

and $z_2 = r_2(\cos\theta_2 + i\sin\theta_2)$

$\Rightarrow |z_2| = r_2$ ...(ii)

Now, $z_1 z_2 = r_1 r_2[\cos\theta_1\cos\theta_2 + i\sin\theta_1 \cos\theta_2 + i\cos\theta_1\sin\theta_2 + i^2\sin\theta_1\sin\theta_2]$

$= r_1 r_2[\cos(\theta_1 + \theta_2) + i\sin(\theta_1 + \theta_2)]$

$\Rightarrow \quad |z_1 z_2| = r_1 r_2$

$\therefore \quad |z_1 z_2| = |z_1||z_2|$ [using Eqs. (i) and (ii)]

136. (b) Let the convex polygon has n sides.

$\therefore$ Number of diagonals = ${}^nC_2 - n$

According to the question,

$${}^nC_2 - n = 44$$

$$\frac{n!}{2!(n-2)!} - n = 44$$

$$\Rightarrow \frac{n(n-1)}{2} - n = 44 \Rightarrow n\left[\frac{(n-1)}{2} - 1\right] = 44$$

$$\Rightarrow n\left(\frac{n-1-2}{2}\right) = 44$$

$\Rightarrow \quad n(n-3) = 44 \times 2$

$\Rightarrow \quad n(n-3) = 88$

$\Rightarrow \quad n^2 - 3n - 88 = 0$

$\Rightarrow (n-11)(n+8) = 0$

$\Rightarrow \quad n = 11, -8 \quad [\because n \neq -8]$

$\therefore \quad n = 11$

137. (a) We know that, a number is divisible by 3, when sum of digits in the number must be divisible by 3.

So, if we consider the digits 0, 1, 2, 4, 5, then $(0+1+2+4+5) = 12$

We see that, sum is divisible by 3. Therefore, five-digit numbers using the digit

0, 1, 2, 4, 5 = 4 × 4 × 3 × 2 × 1 = 96

4	4	3	2	1

and if we consider the digit 1, 2, 3, 4, 5, then

$(1+2+3+4+5=15)$

This sum is also divisible by 3.

So, five-digit number can be formed using the digit 1, 2, 3, 4, 5 in 5! ways.

Total number of ways = 96 + 5! = 96 + 120 = 216

MOCK TEST 2

138. (*b*) Total number of letters in the word article is 7, out of which A, E, I are vowels and R, T, C, L are consonants.

Since, it is given that vowels occupy even place, therefore the arrangement of vowel, consonant can be understood with the help of following diagram.

1	2	3	4	5	6	7

Now, vowels can be placed at 2, 4 and 6th position.

Therefore, number of arrangement

$$= {}^3P_3 = 3! = 6 \text{ ways}$$

and consonants can be placed at 1, 3, 5 and 7th position.

Therefore, number of arrangement

$$= {}^4P_4 = 4! = 24$$

$\therefore$ Total number of words $= 6 \times 24 = 144$

139. (*c*) Let two successive terms in the expansion of $(1 + x)^{24}$ are $(r + 1)$th and $(r + 2)$th terms.

$$\therefore \quad T_{r+1} = {}^{24}C_r\, x^r$$

and $$T_{r+2} = {}^{24}C_{r+1}\, x^{r+1}$$

Given that,

$$\frac{{}^{24}C_r}{{}^{24}C_{r+1}} = \frac{1}{4}$$

$$\Rightarrow \frac{\dfrac{(24)!}{r!(24-r)!}}{\dfrac{(24)!}{(r+1)!(24-r-1)!}} = \frac{1}{4}$$

$$\Rightarrow \frac{(r+1)\, r!(23-r)!}{r!(24-r)(23-r)!} = \frac{1}{4}$$

$$\Rightarrow \frac{r+1}{24-r} = \frac{1}{4}$$

$$\Rightarrow 4r + 4 = 24 - r$$

$$\Rightarrow 5r = 20$$

$$\Rightarrow r = 4$$

$\therefore T_{4+1} = T_5$ and $T_{4+2} = T_6$

Hence, 5th and 6th terms.

140. (*c*) Given expansion is $\left(\dfrac{1}{x} + x\sin x\right)^{10}$.

Since, $n = 10$ is even, so this expansion has only one middle term *i.e.*, 6th term.

$$\therefore \quad T_6 = T_{5+1} = {}^{10}C_5\left(\frac{1}{x}\right)^{10-5}(x\sin x)^5$$

$$\Rightarrow \frac{63}{8} = {}^{10}C_5\, x^{-5}x^5\sin^5 x$$

$$\Rightarrow \frac{63}{8} = \frac{10\cdot 9\cdot 8\cdot 7\cdot 6\cdot 5!}{5\cdot 4\cdot 3\cdot 2\cdot 1\cdot 5!}\sin^5 x$$

$$\Rightarrow \frac{63}{8} = 2\cdot 9\cdot 2\cdot 7\cdot \sin^5 x$$

$$\Rightarrow \sin^5 x = \frac{1}{32} \Rightarrow \sin^5 x = \left(\frac{1}{2}\right)^5$$

$$\Rightarrow \sin x = \frac{1}{2} = \sin\left(\frac{\pi}{6}\right)$$

$$\therefore x = n\pi + (-1)^n\, \pi/6$$

141. (*c*) Given, $S_n = qn^2$ and $S_m = qm^2$

$\therefore S_1 = q,\ S_2 = 4q,\ S_3 = 9q$ and $S_4 = 16q$

Now, $T_1 = q$

$\therefore T_2 = S_2 - S_1 = 4q - q = 3q$

$T_3 = S_3 - S_2 = 9q - 4q = 5q$

$T_4 = S_4 - S_3 = 16q - 9q = 7q$

So, the series is $q, 3q, 5q, 7q, \ldots$

Here, $a = q$

and $d = 3q - q = 2q$

$$\therefore \quad S_q = \frac{q}{2}[2\times q + (q-1)\, 2q]$$

$$= \frac{q}{2}\times[2q + 2q^2 - 2q]$$

$$= \frac{q}{2}\times 2q^2 = q^3$$

142. (*b*) We know that, AM $\geq$ GM

$$\Rightarrow \frac{4^x + 4^{1-x}}{2} \geq \sqrt{4^x\cdot 4^{1-x}}$$

$$\Rightarrow 4^x + 4^{1-x} \geq 2\sqrt{4}$$

$$\Rightarrow 4^x + 4^{1-x} \geq 2\cdot 2$$

$$\Rightarrow 4^x + 4^{1-x} \geq 4$$

143. (*d*) Given line is

$$\frac{x}{a} + \frac{y}{b} = 1 \quad \ldots\text{(i)}$$

Since, the points (2, –3) and (4, –5) lie on this line.

$$\therefore \quad \frac{2}{a} - \frac{3}{b} = 1 \quad \ldots\text{(ii)}$$

and $$\frac{4}{a} - \frac{5}{b} = 1 \quad \ldots\text{(iii)}$$

On multiplying by 2 in Eq. (ii) and then subtracting Eq. (iii) from Eq. (ii), we get

$$-\frac{6}{b} + \frac{5}{b} = 1$$

$$\Rightarrow \frac{-1}{b} = 1$$

$$\therefore \quad b = -1$$

On putting $b = -1$ in Eq. (ii), we get

$$\frac{2}{a} + 3 = 1$$

$$\Rightarrow \frac{2}{a} = -2$$

$$\Rightarrow a = -1$$

$$\therefore \quad (a, b) = (-1, -1)$$

144. (*a*) Let slope of the line be m.

Equation of line passing through (1, 0) is

$$y - 0 = m(x-1)$$

$$\Rightarrow \quad y - mx + m = 0 \quad \ldots(\text{i})$$

Since, the distance from origin is $\frac{\sqrt{3}}{2}$.

Then, $\frac{\sqrt{3}}{2} = \frac{0-0+m}{\sqrt{1+m^2}}$

$$\Rightarrow \frac{\sqrt{3}}{2} = \frac{m}{\sqrt{1+m^2}} \Rightarrow \frac{3}{4} = \frac{m^2}{1+m^2}$$

$$\Rightarrow 3 + 3m^2 = 4m^2$$

$$\Rightarrow \quad m^2 = 3 \Rightarrow m = \pm\sqrt{3}$$

So, the first equation of line is

$$y = \sqrt{3}(x-1)$$

$$\Rightarrow \sqrt{3}x - y - \sqrt{3} = 0$$

and the second equation of line is

$$y = -\sqrt{3}(x-1)$$

$$\Rightarrow \sqrt{3}x + y - \sqrt{3} = 0$$

145. (*b*) Given, equation of the line is

$$y = 3x + 4 \quad \ldots(\text{i})$$

$\therefore$ Slope of this line, $m_1 = 3$

So, the slope of line OP is $-\frac{1}{3}$. $[\because OP \perp AB]$

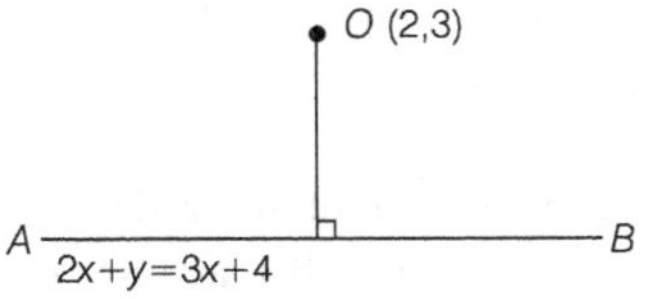

$\therefore$ Equation of line OP is

$$y - 3 = -\frac{1}{3}(x-2)$$

$$\Rightarrow \quad 3y - 9 = -x + 2$$

$$\Rightarrow \quad x + 3y - 11 = 0 \quad \ldots(\text{ii})$$

Using the value of y from Eq. (i) in Eq. (ii), we get

$$x + 3(3x+4) - 11 = 0$$

$$\Rightarrow \quad x + 9x + 12 - 11 = 0$$

$$\Rightarrow \quad 10x + 1 = 0 \Rightarrow x = -\frac{1}{10}$$

Put $x = \frac{-1}{10}$ in Eq. (i), we get

$$y = \frac{-3}{10} + 4 = \frac{-3+40}{10} = \frac{37}{10}$$

So, the foot of perpendicular is $\left(-\frac{1}{10}, \frac{37}{10}\right)$.

146. (*c*)

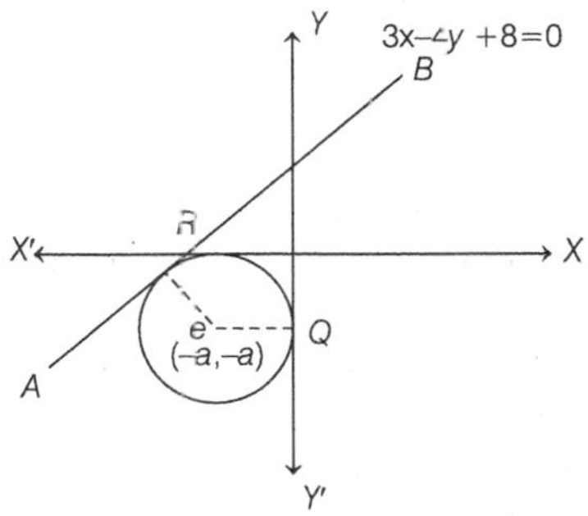

Let a be the radius of the circle. Then, the coordinates of the circle are $(-a, -a)$. Now, perpendicular distance from C to the line AB = Radius of the circle

$$d = \left|\frac{-3a + 4a + 8}{\sqrt{9+16}}\right| = \left|\frac{a+8}{5}\right|$$

$$a = \pm\left(\frac{a+8}{5}\right)$$

Taking positive sign, $a = \frac{a+8}{5}$

$$\Rightarrow \quad 5a = a + 8$$

$$\Rightarrow \quad 4a = 8 \Rightarrow a = 2$$

Taking negative sign, $a = \frac{-a-8}{5}$

$$\Rightarrow \quad 5a = -a - 8$$

$$\Rightarrow \quad 6a = -8 \Rightarrow a = -4/3$$

But $a \neq -4/3$

$\therefore a = 2$

So, the equation of circle is

$$(x+2)^2 + (y+2)^2 = 2^2 \quad [\because a = 2]$$

$$\Rightarrow \quad x^2 + 4x + 4 + y^2 + 4y + 4 = 4$$

$$\Rightarrow \quad x^2 + y^2 + 4x + 4y + 4 = 0$$

147. (*b*) Given equation of the circle is

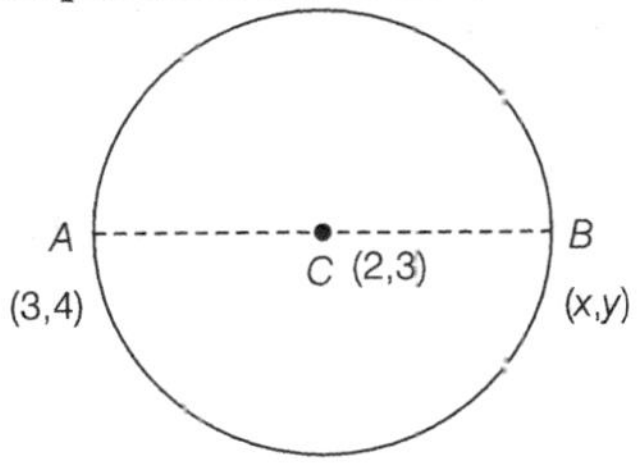

$$x^2 + y^2 - 4x - 6y + 11 = 0$$

$$\therefore \quad 2g = -4 \text{ and } 2f = -6$$

So, the centre of the circle is $(-g, -f)$, i.e. (2, 3).

Since, the mid-point of AB is (2, 3).

Then, $\quad 2 = \frac{3 + x_1}{2}$

$\Rightarrow \quad 4 = 3 + x_1$

$\therefore \quad x_1 = 1$

and $\quad 3 = \dfrac{4 + y_1}{2}$

$\Rightarrow \quad 6 = 4 + y_1 \quad \Rightarrow y_1 = 2$

So, the coordinates of other end of the diameter will be (1, 2).

148. (*a*) Given that, focus of parabola at $F(0, -3)$ and equation of directrix is $y = 3$.

Let any point on the parabola is $P(x, y)$.

Then, $PF = |y - 3|$

$\Rightarrow \sqrt{(x-0)^2 + (y+3)^2} = |y - 3|$

$\Rightarrow x^2 + y^2 + 6y + 9 = y^2 - 6y + 9$

$\Rightarrow x^2 + 12y = 0 \Rightarrow x^2 = -12y$

149. (*b*) Given that, parabola is

$$y^2 = 4ax \quad \text{... (i)}$$

$\therefore$ Length of latusrectum $= 4a$

Since, the parabola passes through the point (3, 2).

Then, $\quad 4 = 4a(3)$

$\Rightarrow \quad a = 1/3$

$\therefore \quad 4a = 4/3$

150. (*b*) Given that,

$$\frac{x^2}{a^2} + \frac{y^2}{b^2} = 1, \; a < b$$

We know that,

$$e = \sqrt{1 - \frac{a^2}{b^2}}$$

$\Rightarrow \quad e^2 = \dfrac{(b^2 - a^2)}{b^2}$

$\Rightarrow \quad b^2e^2 = b^2 - a^2$

$\Rightarrow \quad a^2 = b^2(1 - e^2)$

151. (*c*) Let equation of the ellipse be

$$\frac{x^2}{a^2} + \frac{y^2}{b^2} = 1.$$

$\therefore \quad 2a = 6$ and $2b = 4 \Rightarrow a = 3$ and $b = 2$

We know that,

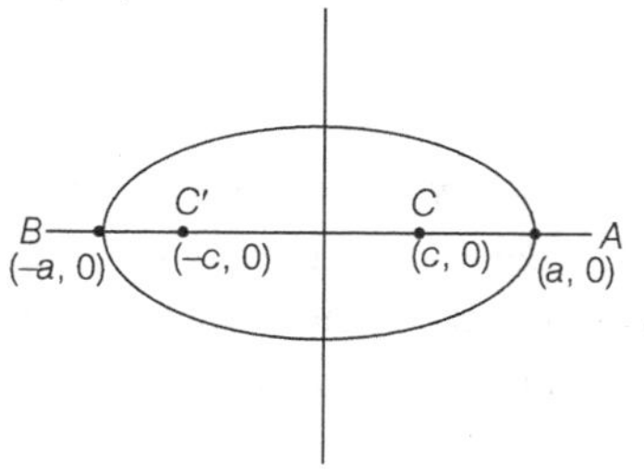

$c^2 = a^2 - b^2 = (3)^2 - (2)^2$ where $c = ae$

$= 9 - 4 = 5 \Rightarrow c = \sqrt{5}$

$\therefore$ Length of string $= AC' + C'C + AC$

$= a + c + 2c + a - c$

$= 2a + 2c = 6 + 2\sqrt{5}$

152. (*a*) Given that, distance between the foci of hyperbola *i.e.*, $2ae = 16$

$\Rightarrow \quad ae = 8 \quad \text{...(i)}$

and $\quad e = \sqrt{2} \quad \text{...(ii)}$

Now, $\quad \sqrt{2}\,a = 8$

$\Rightarrow \quad a = 4\sqrt{2}$

$b^2 = a^2(e^2 - 1)$

$\Rightarrow \quad b^2 = 32(2 - 1)$

$\Rightarrow \quad b^2 = 32$

$\therefore \quad \dfrac{x^2}{32} - \dfrac{y^2}{32} = 1$

$\Rightarrow \quad x^2 - y^2 = 32$

153. (*b*) Equation of the given lines can be written as standard form

$$\frac{x-1}{-3} = \frac{y-2}{\frac{2p}{7}} = \frac{z-3}{2}$$

and

$$\frac{x-1}{-\frac{3p}{7}} = \frac{y-5}{1} = \frac{z-6}{-5}$$

Direction ratios of these lines are respectively $-3, \dfrac{2p}{7}, 2$ and $\dfrac{-3p}{7}, 1, -5$.

Two lines with direction ratios $\langle a_1, b_1, c_1 \rangle$ and $\langle a_2, b_2, c_2 \rangle$ are perpendicular to each other, if $a_1a_2 + b_1b_2 + c_1c_2 = 0$.

$\therefore (-3)\left(\dfrac{-3p}{7}\right) + \left(\dfrac{2p}{7}\right)(1) + (2)(-5) = 0$

$\Rightarrow \quad \dfrac{9p}{7} + \dfrac{2p}{7} - 10 = 0$

$\Rightarrow \quad \dfrac{11p}{7} = 10$

$\Rightarrow \quad p = \dfrac{70}{11}$

Thus, the value of p is $\dfrac{70}{11}$.

154. (*c*) $f(x) = \dfrac{\sqrt{a^2 - ax + x^2} - \sqrt{a^2 + ax + x^2}}{\sqrt{a + x} - \sqrt{a - x}}$

$\times \dfrac{\sqrt{a^2 - ax + x^2} + \sqrt{a^2 + ax + x^2}}{\sqrt{a^2 - ax + x^2} + \sqrt{a^2 + ax + x^2}} \times \dfrac{\sqrt{a + x} + \sqrt{a - x}}{\sqrt{a + x} + \sqrt{a - x}}$

$f(x)$ is continuous $\Rightarrow \lim_{x \to 0} f(x) = f(0)$

MOCK TEST 2

$$\therefore f(0)=\lim_{x\to 0}\frac{-2ax(\sqrt{a+x}+\sqrt{a-x})}{2x(\sqrt{a^2-ax+x^2}+\sqrt{a^2+ax+x^2})}$$

$$=\frac{-a(2\sqrt{a})}{a+a}=-\sqrt{a}$$

155. (b) $f'(x)=\lim_{h\to 0}\frac{f(x+h)-f(x)}{h}$

$$f'(x)=\lim_{h\to 0}\frac{f(x)\cdot f(h)-f(x)}{h}$$

$[\because f(x+y)=f(x)f(y)]$

$$f'(x)=\lim_{h\to 0}\frac{f(x)[f(h)-1]}{h} \quad \ldots(\text{i})$$

and $f(x+y)=f(x)f(y)\ \forall x, y\in R$ (given)

$f(0+0)=f(0)\,f(0)$

$f(0)=\{f(0)\}^2$

$\Rightarrow \{f(0)\}^2-f(0)=0$

$\Rightarrow f(0)[f(0)-1]=0$

$f(0)\neq 0$

$\Rightarrow f(0)=1$ $[\because f(x)\neq 0]$

Now, $f'(0)=\lim_{x\to 0}\frac{f(x+0)-f(0)}{x-0}$

$$2=\lim_{x\to 0}\frac{f(x)\cdot f(0)-f(0)}{x-0}$$

$$2=\lim_{x\to 0}\frac{f(0)[f(x)-1]}{x-0} \quad [\because f(0)=1]$$

$$2=\lim_{h\to 0}\frac{f(0+h)-1}{h}$$

$$2=\lim_{h\to 0}\frac{f(0)\cdot f(h)-1}{h} \quad [\because f(0)=1]$$

$$2=\lim_{h\to 0}\frac{f(h)-1}{h} \quad \ldots(\text{ii})$$

From Eqs. (i) and (ii), we have

$f'(x)=2f(x)$

156. (a) Given,

$f(x)=x^{100}+x^{99}+\ldots+x+1$

$\therefore f'(x)=100x^{99}+99x^{98}+\ldots+1+0$

$=100x^{99}+99x^{98}+\ldots+1$

Now, $f'(1)=100+99+\ldots+1$

$$=\frac{100}{2}[2\times 100+(100-1)(-1)]$$

$$=50[200-99]\left[\because S_n=\frac{n}{2}\{2a+(n-1)\,d\}\right]$$

$=50\times 101=5050$

157. (c) Since, $f'(x)>\phi'(x)$

$\Rightarrow 2^{2x-1}(2\log 2)>-2^x\log 2+2\log 2$

$\Rightarrow 2^{2x}>-2^x+2$

$\Rightarrow 2^{2x}+2^x-2>0$

$\Rightarrow (2^x-1)(2^x+2)>0$

$\Rightarrow 2^x-1>0$ $(\because 2^x+2>0$ for all $x)$

$\Rightarrow 2^x>1$

$\therefore x>0$

158. (a) Let $y=\sqrt{\frac{(x-3)(x^2+4)}{(3x^2+4x+5)}}$

Taking log on both sides, we have

$$\log y=\frac{1}{2}[\log(x-3)+\log(x^2+4)-\log(3x^2+4x+5)]$$

Now, differentiating both sides w.r.t. x, we get

$$\frac{1}{y}\cdot\frac{dy}{dx}=\frac{1}{2}\left[\frac{1}{x-3}+\frac{2x}{x^2+4}-\frac{6x+4}{3x^2+4x+5}\right]$$

or
$$\frac{dy}{dx}=\frac{y}{2}\left[\frac{1}{x-3}+\frac{2x}{x^2+4}-\frac{6x+4}{3x^2+4x+5}\right]$$

$$=\frac{1}{2}\sqrt{\frac{(x-3)(x^2+4)}{3x^2+4x+5}}\left[\frac{1}{(x-3)}+\frac{2x}{x^2+4}-\frac{6x+4}{3x^2+4x+5}\right]$$

159. (b) Since, we know that

$$\cos A\cos 2A\cos 2^2A\ldots\cos 2^{n-1}A=\frac{\sin(2^nA)}{2^n\sin A}$$

$$\therefore \cos x\cos 2x\cos 4x\cos 8x\cos 16x=\frac{\sin 32x}{32\sin x}$$

$$\Rightarrow f(x)=\frac{1}{32}\cdot\frac{\sin 32x}{\sin x}$$

$$\therefore f'(x)=\frac{1}{32}\times\frac{\sin x(32\cos 32x)-\sin 32x\cos x}{\sin^2 x}$$

$$\Rightarrow f'\left(\frac{\pi}{4}\right)=\frac{1}{\sin\frac{\pi}{4}}=\sqrt{2}$$

160. (b) Let $y=e^{\sec^2 x}+3\cos^{-1}x$

This is defined at every real number in $[-1, 1]$. Therefore,

$$\frac{dy}{dx}=e^{\sec^2 x}\cdot\frac{d}{dx}(\sec^2 x)+3\left(-\frac{1}{\sqrt{1-x^2}}\right)$$

$$=e^{\sec^2 x}\cdot\left(2\sec x\frac{d}{dx}(\sec x)\right)+3\left(-\frac{1}{\sqrt{1-x^2}}\right)$$

MOCK TEST 2

$$= 2\sec x(\sec x \tan x)\, e^{\sec^2 x} + 3\left(-\frac{1}{\sqrt{1-x^2}}\right)$$

$$= 2\sec^2 x \tan x\, e^{\sec^2 x} + 3\left(-\frac{1}{\sqrt{1-x^2}}\right)$$

Observe that the derivative of the given function is valid only in $(-1, 1)$.

161. (*b*) Since, θ increases twice as fast as its sine.

$\therefore \quad \theta = 2\sin\theta$

On differentiating both sides w.r.t. t, we have

$$\frac{d\theta}{dt} = 2\cos\theta \frac{d\theta}{dt} \quad \left[\because \frac{d}{d\theta}(\sin\theta) = \cos\theta\right]$$

$\Rightarrow \quad 1 = 2\cos\theta$

$\Rightarrow \quad \cos\theta = \frac{1}{2} = \cos\left(\frac{\pi}{3}\right) \quad (\because 0 < \theta < \pi/2)$

$\Rightarrow \quad \theta = \frac{\pi}{3}$

$\therefore$ Required angle is $\frac{\pi}{3}$.

162. (*d*) Let h and r be the height and radius of cylinder.

Given that, $\frac{dr}{dt} = 3$ m/s, $\frac{dh}{dt} = -4$ m/s

Let volume of cylinder, $V = \pi r^2 h$

$$\Rightarrow \quad \frac{dV}{dt} = \pi\left[r^2 \frac{dh}{dt} + h \cdot 2r\frac{dr}{dt}\right]$$

At $r = 4$ m and $h = 6$ m

$$\therefore \quad \frac{dV}{dt} = \pi[-64 + 144] = 80\,\pi\, \text{m}^3/\text{s}$$

163. (*c*) We have,

$$\int \frac{3e^x - 5e^{-x}}{4e^x + 5e^{-x}} dx = ax + b\log|4e^x + 5e^{-x}| + C$$

On differentiating both sides, we get

$$\frac{3e^x - 5e^{-x}}{4e^x + 5e^{-x}} = a + b\frac{(4e^x - 5e^{-x})}{4e^x + 5e^{-x}}$$

$$\therefore 3e^x - 5e^{-x} = a(4e^x + 5e^{-x}) + b(4e^x - 5e^{-x})$$

Comparing coefficients on both sides, we get

$$3 = 4a + 4b \quad \text{...(i)}$$

$$-5 = 5a - 5b \quad \text{...(ii)}$$

On solving Eqs. (i) and (ii), we get

$$a = -\frac{1}{8} \text{ and } b = \frac{7}{8}$$

164. (*c*) $f(x) + f(-x) = \frac{\sin^2 \pi x}{1+\pi^x} + \frac{\sin^2(-\pi x)}{1+\pi^{-x}}$

$$= \frac{\sin^2 \pi x}{1+\pi^x} + \frac{(\sin^2 \pi x)\,\pi^x}{\pi^x + 1}$$

$$= \sin^2 \pi x = \frac{1-\cos 2\pi x}{2}$$

$$\therefore \int [f(x) + f(-x)]\, dx = \int\left[\frac{1-\cos 2\pi x}{2}\right] dx$$

$$= \frac{1}{2}x - \frac{\sin 2\pi x}{4\pi} + C$$

165. (*c*) Let

$$I = \int \frac{1}{\sqrt{7-6x-x^2}} dx = \int \frac{1}{\sqrt{7-(x^2+6x)}} dx$$

$$= \int \frac{1}{\sqrt{7-[x^2 + 2\times 3x + (3)^2 - (3)^2]}} dx$$

$$= \int \frac{1}{\sqrt{7-[x^2 + 6x + 3^2 - 9]}} dx$$

$$= \int \frac{1}{\sqrt{7-[(x+3)^2 - 9]}} dx = \int \frac{1}{\sqrt{4^2 - (x+3)^2}} dx$$

Let $x + 3 = t \Rightarrow dx = dt$

$$\therefore I = \int \frac{1}{\sqrt{4^2 - t^2}} dt = \sin^{-1}\left(\frac{t}{4}\right) + C$$

$$\left[\because \int \frac{dx}{\sqrt{a^2 - x^2}} = \sin^{-1}\left(\frac{x}{a}\right)\right]$$

$$= \sin^{-1}\left(\frac{x+3}{4}\right) + C \quad [\because t = x+3]$$

166. (*b*) We have, $I = \int \frac{e^x}{(2+e^x)(e^x+1)} dx$

Put, $e^x = t \Rightarrow e^x dx = dt$

$$\therefore I = \int \frac{dt}{(2+t)(t+1)} = \int\left[\frac{1}{1+t} - \frac{1}{t+2}\right] dt$$

$$\left[\begin{aligned} &\because \frac{1}{(1+t)(t+2)} = \frac{A}{t+1} + \frac{B}{t+2} \\ &\Rightarrow 1 = (A+B)\,t + 2A + B \\ &\Rightarrow A + B = 0 \text{ and } 2A + B = 1 \\ &\Rightarrow A = 1 \text{ and } B = -1 \end{aligned}\right]$$

$$= \log|1+t| - \log|t+2| + C$$

$$= \log\left|\frac{1+t}{t+2}\right| + C$$

$$= \log\left(\frac{1+e^x}{2+e^x}\right) + C$$

167. (*a*) Given,

$$\int_2^e \left(\frac{1}{\log x} - \frac{1}{(\log x)^2}\right) dx = a + \frac{b}{\log 2}$$

Put $\log x = z \Rightarrow x = e^z$

$\Rightarrow \quad dx = e^z dz$

MOCK TEST 2

$$\therefore \int_2^e \left(\frac{1}{\log x} - \frac{1}{(\log x)^2}\right) dx = \int_{\log 2}^1 \left(\frac{1}{z} - \frac{1}{z^2}\right) e^z dz$$

$$= \int_{\log 2}^1 e^z \left(\frac{1}{z} + d\left(\frac{1}{z}\right)\right) dz = \left[e^z \cdot \frac{1}{z}\right]_{\log 2}^1 = e - \frac{2}{\log 2}$$

$$[\quad \int e^x (f(x) + f'(x)) dx = e^x \cdot f(x)]$$

$\therefore a = e$ and $b = -2$

168. (*c*) Let $I = \int_0^a \frac{\sqrt{x}}{\sqrt{x} + \sqrt{a-x}} dx$ ...(i)

$$I = \int_0^a \frac{\sqrt{a-x}}{\sqrt{a-x} + \sqrt{a-(a-x)}} dx$$

$$\left[\quad \int_0^a f(x) dx = \int_0^a f(a-x) dx\right]$$

$$= \int_0^a \frac{\sqrt{a-x}}{\sqrt{a-x} + \sqrt{x}} dx \quad \text{...(ii)}$$

On adding Eqs. (i) and (ii), we get

$$2I = \int_0^a \frac{\sqrt{x} + \sqrt{a-x}}{\sqrt{a-x} + \sqrt{x}} dx$$

$$\Rightarrow \quad 2I = \int_0^a 1\, dx = [x]_0^a = a - 0 = a \quad \Rightarrow I = \frac{a}{2}$$

169. (*a*) Given curves are

$$y = \sqrt{x} \quad \text{...(i)}$$

and $\quad 2y - x + 3 = 0$ ...(ii)

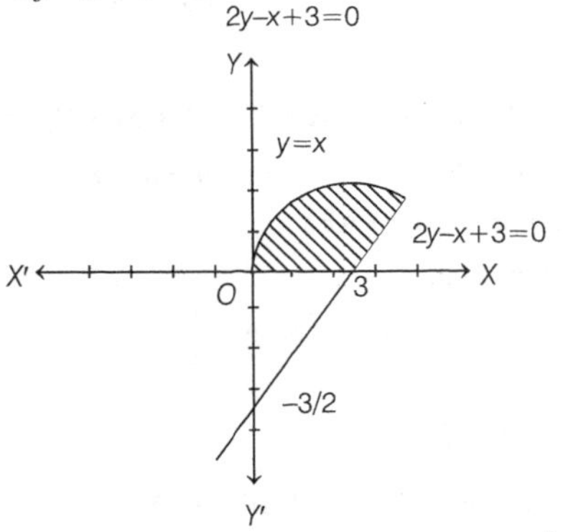

On solving Eqs. (i) and (ii), we get

$$2\sqrt{x} - (\sqrt{x})^2 + 3 = 0 \Rightarrow (\sqrt{x})^2 - 2\sqrt{x} - 3 = 0$$

$$\Rightarrow (\sqrt{x} - 3)(\sqrt{x} + 1) = 0$$

$$\Rightarrow \sqrt{x} = 3 \qquad (\quad \sqrt{x} = -1 \text{ is not possible})$$

$$\therefore \quad y = 3$$

$$\therefore \text{Required area} = \int_0^3 (x_2 - x_1) dy$$

$$= \int_0^3 \{(2y + 3) - y^2\} dy$$

$$= \left[y^2 + 3y - \frac{y^3}{3}\right]_0^3 = 9 + 9 - 9 = 9$$

170. (*d*) Given,

$$y = 2e^{2x} - e^{-x}$$

$$\Rightarrow \quad y' = 4e^{2x} + e^{-x}$$

Þ $\quad y'' = 8e^{2x} - e^{-x}$

$$\Rightarrow y'' = 4e^{2x} + e^{-x} + 4e^{2x} - 2e^{-x}$$

$$\Rightarrow y'' = y' + 2(2e^{2x} - e^{-x})$$

$$\Rightarrow y'' = y' + 2y$$

$$\Rightarrow y'' - y' - 2y = 0$$

171. (*a*) The given differential equation can be written as

$$\frac{dy}{dx} = e^{(3x + 4y)}$$

or $\quad \frac{dy}{dx} = e^{3x} \cdot e^{4y}$ ...(i)

On separating the variables, we get

$$\frac{dy}{e^{4y}} = e^{3x} dx$$

Therefore, $\int e^{-4y} dy = \int e^{3x} dx$

$$\Rightarrow \quad \frac{e^{-4y}}{-4} = \frac{e^{3x}}{3} + C$$

or $\quad 4e^{3x} + 3e^{-4y} + 12C = 0$ ...(ii)

On substituting $x = 0$ and $y = 0$ in Eq. (ii), we get

$$4 + 3 + 12C = 0$$

or $\quad C = \frac{-7}{12}$

On substituting the value of C in Eq. (ii), we get

$$4e^{3x} + 3e^{-4y} - 7 = 0$$

which is a particular solution of the given differential equation.

172. (*c*) Let

$\mathbf{OA} = 2\mathbf{i} - \mathbf{j} + \mathbf{k}$, $\mathbf{OB} = \mathbf{i} - 3\mathbf{j} - 5\mathbf{k}$

and $\quad \mathbf{OC} = 3\mathbf{i} - 4\mathbf{j} - 4\mathbf{k}$

$\therefore \quad a = |\mathbf{OA}| = \sqrt{6}$,

$b = |\mathbf{OB}| = \sqrt{35}$

and $\quad c = |\mathbf{OC}| = \sqrt{41}$

$$\therefore \quad \cos A = \frac{b^2 + c^2 - a^2}{2bc}$$

$$= \frac{(\sqrt{35})^2 + (\sqrt{41})^2 - (\sqrt{6})^2}{2\sqrt{35} \times \sqrt{41}}$$

$$\Rightarrow \quad \cos A = \sqrt{\frac{35}{41}}$$

$$\Rightarrow \quad \cos^2 A = \frac{35}{41}$$

173. (*d*) Let $\mathbf{R}_1 = 2\mathbf{i} + 4\mathbf{j} - 5\mathbf{k}$

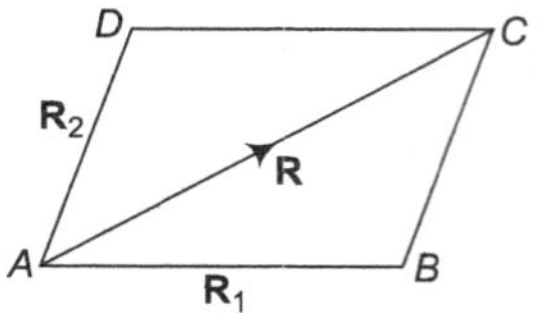

and $\mathbf{R}_2 = \mathbf{i} + 2\mathbf{j} + 3\mathbf{k}$

$\therefore \mathbf{R}$ (along $\mathbf{AC}$) $= \mathbf{R}_1 + \mathbf{R}_2$

$= 3\mathbf{i} + 6\mathbf{j} - 2\mathbf{k}$

$\therefore$ $\mathbf{a}$ (unit vector along AC) $= \dfrac{\mathbf{R}}{|\mathbf{R}|}$

$$= \frac{3\mathbf{i} + 6\mathbf{j} - 2\mathbf{k}}{\sqrt{9 + 36 + 4}} = \frac{1}{7}(3\mathbf{i} + 6\mathbf{j} - 2\mathbf{k})$$

174. (*c*) $F(x)\,F(y) = \begin{bmatrix} \cos x & -\sin x & 0 \\ \sin x & \cos x & 0 \\ 0 & 0 & 1 \end{bmatrix} \begin{bmatrix} \cos y & -\sin y & 0 \\ \sin y & \cos y & 0 \\ 0 & 0 & 1 \end{bmatrix}$

$$= \begin{bmatrix} \cos x \cos y - \sin x \sin y & -\sin y \cos x - \sin x \cos y & 0 \\ \sin x \cos y + \cos x \sin y & -\sin x \sin y + \cos x \cos y & 0 \\ 0 & 0 & 1 \end{bmatrix}$$

$$= \begin{bmatrix} \cos(x+y) & -\sin(x+y) & 0 \\ \sin(x+y) & \cos(x+y) & 0 \\ 0 & 0 & 1 \end{bmatrix}$$

$$\begin{bmatrix} \cos(A+B) = \cos A \cos B - \sin A \sin B \\ \sin(A+B) = \sin A \cos B + \sin B \cos A \end{bmatrix}$$

Now, replacing x by $(x + y)$ in $F(x)$,

$$F(x+y) = \begin{bmatrix} \cos(x+y) & -\sin(x+y) & 0 \\ \sin(x+y) & \cos(x+y) & 0 \\ 0 & 0 & 1 \end{bmatrix}$$

$\therefore \quad F(x)\,F(y) = F(x + y)$

175. (*d*) Given, $\quad A'\,A = I$

$$\therefore \begin{bmatrix} 0 & 2y & z \\ x & y & -z \\ x & -y & z \end{bmatrix}' \begin{bmatrix} 0 & 2y & z \\ x & y & -z \\ x & -y & z \end{bmatrix} = I$$

$$\Rightarrow \begin{bmatrix} 0 & x & x \\ 2y & y & -y \\ z & -z & z \end{bmatrix} \begin{bmatrix} 0 & 2y & z \\ x & y & -z \\ x & -y & z \end{bmatrix} = \begin{bmatrix} 1 & 0 & 0 \\ 0 & 1 & 0 \\ 0 & 0 & 1 \end{bmatrix}$$

$$\Rightarrow \begin{bmatrix} 0 + x^2 + x^2 & 0 + xy - xy & 0 - xz + xz \\ 0 + yx - yx & 4y^2 + y^2 + y^2 & 2yz - yz - yz \\ 0 - zx + zx & 2yz - yz - yz & z^2 + z^2 + z^2 \end{bmatrix} = \begin{bmatrix} 1 & 0 & 0 \\ 0 & 1 & 0 \\ 0 & 0 & 1 \end{bmatrix}$$

$$\Rightarrow \begin{bmatrix} 2x^2 & 0 & 0 \\ 0 & 6y^2 & 0 \\ 0 & 0 & 3z^2 \end{bmatrix} = \begin{bmatrix} 1 & 0 & 0 \\ 0 & 1 & 0 \\ 0 & 0 & 1 \end{bmatrix}$$

On comparing the corresponding elements, we have

$2x^2 = 1,\ 6y^2 = 1,\ 3z^2 = 1$

$\Rightarrow x^2 = \dfrac{1}{2},\ y^2 = \dfrac{1}{6},\ z^2 = \dfrac{1}{3}$

$\Rightarrow \ x = \pm\dfrac{1}{\sqrt{2}},\ y = \pm\dfrac{1}{\sqrt{6}},\ z = \pm\dfrac{1}{\sqrt{3}}$

176. (*d*) Given,

$$\begin{vmatrix} x+1 & x+2 & x+a \\ x+2 & x+3 & x+b \\ x+3 & x+4 & x+c \end{vmatrix} = 0$$

Applying $R_1 \to R_1 + R_3 - 2R_2$, we get

$$\begin{vmatrix} 0 & 0 & a + c - 2b \\ x+2 & x+3 & x+b \\ x+3 & x+4 & x+c \end{vmatrix} = 0$$

$\Rightarrow (a + c - 2b)[x^2 + 6x + 8 - (x^2 + 6x + 9)] = 0$

$\Rightarrow (a + c - 2b)(-1) = 0 \ \Rightarrow 2b = a + c$

Thus, a, b, c are in AP.

177. (*d*) Given that,

$$P(A) = \frac{3}{8},\ P(B) = \frac{5}{8}$$

and $P(A \cup B) = \dfrac{3}{4}$

$\therefore \quad P(A \cap B) = P(A) + P(B) - P(A \cup B)$

$$= \frac{3}{8} + \frac{5}{8} - \frac{3}{4}$$

$$= 1 - \frac{3}{4} = \frac{4-3}{4} = \frac{1}{4}$$

Now, $P\left(\dfrac{A}{B}\right) = \dfrac{P(A \cap B)}{P(B)} = \dfrac{\frac{1}{4}}{\frac{5}{8}} = \dfrac{2}{5}$

$$P\left(\frac{A'}{B}\right) = \frac{P(A' \cap B)}{P(B)}$$

$$= \frac{P(B) - P(A \cap B)}{P(B)}$$

$$= \frac{\frac{5}{8}-\frac{1}{4}}{\frac{5}{8}} = \frac{\frac{5-2}{8}}{\frac{5}{8}} = \frac{\frac{3}{8}}{\frac{5}{8}} = \frac{3}{5}$$

$$\therefore P\left(\frac{A}{B}\right)\cdot P\left(\frac{A'}{B}\right) = \frac{3}{5}\times\frac{2}{5} = \frac{6}{25}$$

178. *(c)* Let p : 7 is greater than 5

and q : 8 is greater than 6.

$\therefore p \rightarrow q$

$\sim p$: 7 is not greater than 5.

$\sim q$: 8 is not greater than 6.

$(\sim q) \rightarrow (\sim p)$ *i.e.*, If 8 is not greater than 6, then 7 is not greater than 5.

179. *(c)* The given LPP is

Maximise and minimise $Z = 3x - 4y$

Subject to the constraints are

$$x - 2y \le 0$$
$$-3x + y \le 4$$
$$x - y \le 6$$
$$x, y \ge 0$$

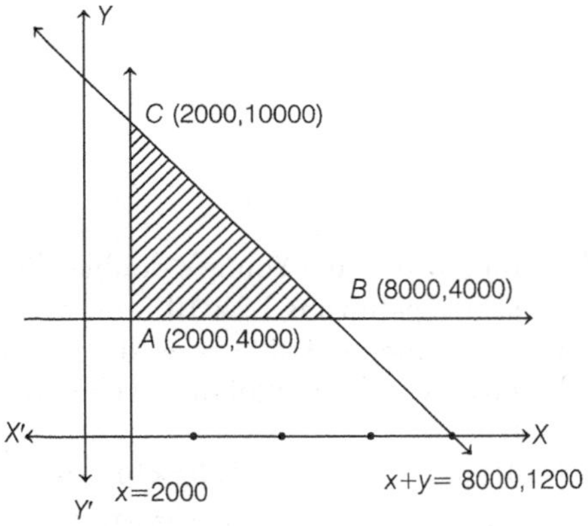

The shaded region is the feasible region which is unbounded.

The feasible unbounded region is AOB and the corner points are $O(0,0)$, A (0,4), B (12, 6). The values of Z at these corner points are given by

Corner point	Corresponding value of
$O(0, 0)$	0
$A(0, 4)$	−16
$B(12, 6)$	12

$\therefore$The maximum value of Z is 12 at (12, 6). Also, to check for the minimum value of Z, we draw the graph of $3x - 4y = -16$.

Since, the open half plane $3x - 4y < -16$ cuts the feasible region at the point (0, 4) and has common area with feasible region.

$\therefore$The given LPP has no minimum solution.

180. *(d)* Let $|x-2| = y$

$$\frac{y-1}{y-2} \le 0$$

$\Rightarrow \quad y - 1 = 0$ and $y - 2 = 0$

$\Rightarrow \quad y = 1$ and $y = 2$

$-\infty \quad +2 \quad -2 \quad + \quad +\infty$

$\Rightarrow 1 \le y < 2$

$\Rightarrow 1 \le |x-2| < 2$

$\Rightarrow 1 \le |x-2|$ and $|x-2| < 2$

$\Rightarrow x - 2 \le -1$

$\Rightarrow x - 2 \ge 1$

and $-2 < x - 2 < 2$

$\Rightarrow x \le 1$ or $x \ge 3$ and $0 < x < 4$

$\Rightarrow x \in (0, 1] \cup [3, 4)$

COMEDK

Mock Test 3

Instructions

- There are 180 questions in all. The number of questions in each section is as given below.

Sections	No. of Questions
Section I : Physics	1-60
Section II : Chemistry	61-120
Section III : Mathematics	121-180

- All the questions are Multiple Choice Questions having four options out of which **ONLY ONE** is correct.
- Candidates will be awarded 1 mark for each correct answer. There will be no negative marking for incorrect answer.
- Time allotted to complete this paper is 3 hrs.

PHYSICS

1. The displacement-time graph of a particle executing SHM is shown in figure. Which of the following statements is false?

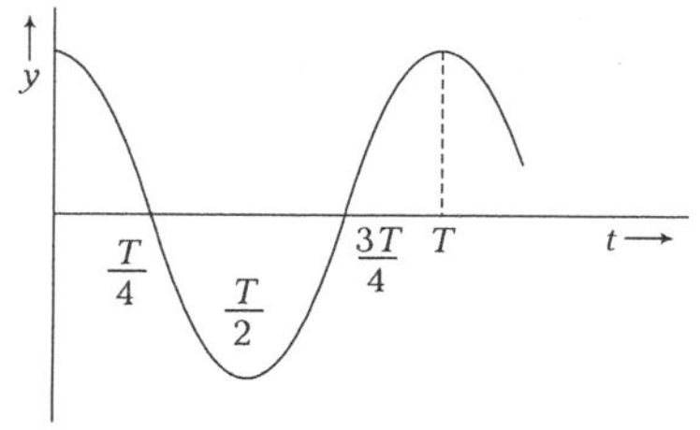

a. The acceleration is maximum at $t = T$.

b. The force is zero at $t = \frac{3T}{4}$.

c. The potential energy equals the total oscillation energy at $t = \frac{T}{2}$.

d. None of the above

2. The flux linked with a coil at any instant t given by $\phi = 10t^2 - 50t + 250$

Then, induced emf at $t = 3$ s is

a. −10 V *b.* 10 V *c.* 190 V *d.* −190 V

3. The fringe width in a Young's double slit interference pattern is 3.2×10^{-4} m, when red light of wavelength 5600Å is used. How much will it change, if blue light of wavelength 4200Å is used?

a. 8×10^{-4} m *b.* 0.8×10^{-4} m

c. 4.2×10^{-4} m *d.* 0.45×10^{-4} m

4. A vehicle needs an engine of 7500 W to keep it moving with a constant velocity of 20 ms^{-1} on a horizontal surface. The force resisting the motion is

a. 375 dyne *b.* 375 N

c. 150000 dyne *d.* 150000 N

5. The cell has an emf of 2V and the internal resistance of this cell is $0.1\,\Omega$, it is connected to resistance of $3.9\,\Omega$, the voltage across the cell will be

a. 1.95 V *b.* 1.5 V *c.* 2 V *d.* 1.8 V

6. In Young's double slit experiment, the slit width and the distance of slits from the screen both are doubled. The fringe width will

a. increases *b.* decreases

c. remain unchanged *d.* None of the above

7. The counting rate observed from a radioactive source at $t = 0$, was 1600 count/s and at $t = 8$ s, it was 100 count/s. The counting rate observed at $t = 6$ s was

a. 400 *b.* 300
c. 200 *d.* 150

8. Two disc of the same material and thickness have radii 0.2 m and 0.6 m. Their moment of inertia about their axes will be in the ratio

a. 1 : 81 *b.* 1 : 27 *c.* 1 : 91 *d.* 1 : 3

9. A solenoid of length 0.5 m has a radius of 1 cm and is made up of 500 turns. It carries a current of 5A. What is the magnetic field inside the solenoid?

a. 6.28×10^{-3} T *b.* 6.28×10^{3} T
c. 6.28×10^{-5} T *d.* 6.28×10^{5} T

10. Hydrogen $({}_1H^1)$, deuterium $({}_1H^2)$, singly ionised helium $({}_2He^4)^+$ and doubly ionised lithium $({}_3Li^8)^{2+}$ all have one electron around the nucleus. Consider an electron transition from $n = 2$ to $n = 1$. If the wavelengths of emitted radiation are $\lambda_1, \lambda_2, \lambda_3$ and λ_4, respectively for four elements, then approximately which one of the following is correct?

a. $4\lambda_1 = 2\lambda_2 = 2\lambda_3 = \lambda_4$
b. $\lambda_1 = 2\lambda_2 = 2\lambda_3 = \lambda_4$
c. $\lambda_1 = \lambda_2 = 4\lambda_3 = 9\lambda_4$
d. $\lambda_1 = 2\lambda_2 = 3\lambda_3 = 4\lambda_4$

11. A 4 kg block A is placed on the top of 8 kg block B which rests on a smooth table.

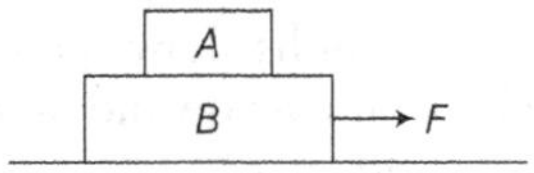

A just slips on B when a force of 12 N is applied on A. Then, the maximum horizontal force F applied on B to make both A and B move together, is

a. 12 N *b.* 24 N
c. 36 N *d.* 48 N

12. A solid cylinder has mass M, length L and radius R. The moment of inertia of this cylinder about a generator is

a. $M\left(\frac{L^2}{12} + \frac{R^2}{4}\right)$ *b.* $\frac{ML^2}{4}$
c. $\frac{1}{2}MR^2$ *d.* $\frac{3}{2}MR^2$

13. In a mixture of H—He$^+$ gas (He$^+$ is singly ionised He atom), H-atoms and He$^+$ ions are excited to their respective first excited states. Subsequently, H atoms transfer their total excitation energy to He$^+$ ions (by collisions). The quantum number n of the state finally populated in He$^+$ ions is

a. 2 *b.* 3
c. 4 *d.* 5

14. The displacement (x)-time (t) graph of a particle is shown in figure. Which of the following is correct?

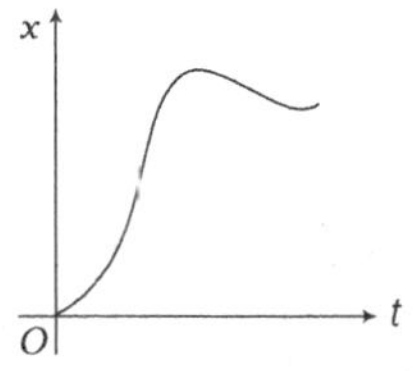

a. Particle starts with zero velocity and variable acceleration
b. Particle starts with non-zero velocity and variable acceleration
c. Particle starts with zero velocity and uniform acceleration
d. Particle starts with non-zero velocity and uniform acceleration

15. A student plot a graph while performing an experiment on photoelectric effect using an evacuated glass tube, for light radiation of same intensity at various frequencies as shown below

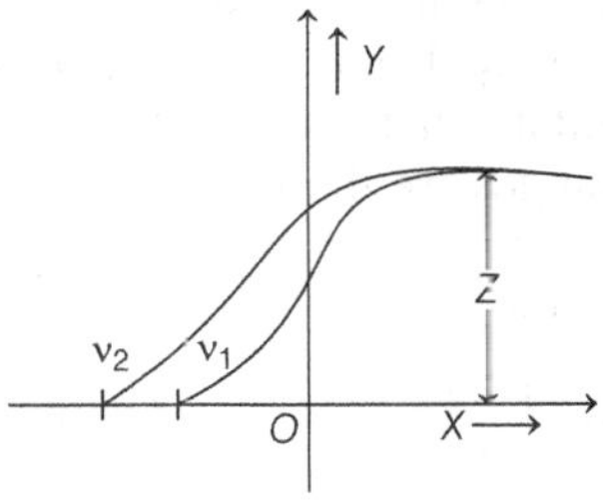

Here,

a. X → Photoelectric current; Y → Retarding potential; Z → Stopping potential
b. X → Retarding plate potential; Y → Photocurrent; Z → Stopping potential
c. X → Collector plate potential; Y → Photocurrent; Z → Saturation current
d. X → Retarding plate potential; Y → Photocurrent; Z → Saturation current

MOCK TEST 3

16. A block of mass m is kept on an inclined plane of a lift moving down with acceleration of $2\ ms^{-2}$. What should be the coefficient of friction to let the block move down with constant velocity relative to lift?

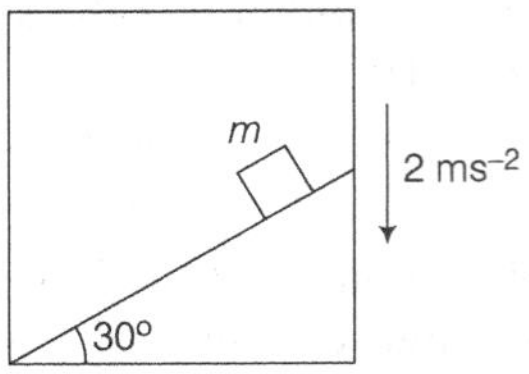

a. $\mu = \frac{1}{\sqrt{3}}$ *b.* $\mu = 0.4$

c. $\mu = 0.8$ *d.* $\mu = \frac{\sqrt{3}}{2}$

17. The magnetic susceptibility of a material of a rod is 499. Permeability of vacuum is $4\pi \times 10^{-7}\ Hm^{-1}$. Absolute permeability of the material of the rod (in Hm^{-1}) is

a. $\pi \times 10^{-4}$ *b.* $2\pi \times 10^{-4}$

c. $3\pi \times 10^{-4}$ *d.* $4\pi \times 10^{-4}$

18. If two drops of same radius are falling through air with a velocity of $5\ cm\ s^{-1}$. If the two drops coalescence to form one drop, then the terminal velocity of the drop is

a. $2.5\ cms^{-1}$ *b.* $10\ cms^{-1}$

c. $5\sqrt{2}\ cms^{-1}$ *d.* $5 \times 4^{1/3}\ cms^{-1}$

19. Two projectiles A and B are thrown from the same point with velocities v and $v/2$, respectively. If B is thrown at an angle 45° with horizontal, what is the inclination of A when their ranges are the same?

a. $\sin^{-1}\left(\frac{1}{4}\right)$ *b.* $\frac{1}{2}\sin^{-1}\left(\frac{1}{4}\right)$

c. $2\sin^{-1}\left(\frac{1}{4}\right)$ *d.* $\frac{1}{2}\sin^{-1}\left(\frac{1}{8}\right)$

20. A metallic surface is irradiated by a monochromatic light of frequency ν_1 and stopping potential is found to be V_1. If the light of frequency ν_2 irradiates the surface. The stopping potential will be

a. $V_1 + \frac{h}{e}(\nu_1 + \nu_2)$

b. $V_1 - \frac{h}{e}(\nu_1 - \nu_2)$

c. $V_1 + \frac{e}{h}(\nu_2 - \nu_1)$

d. $V_1 - \frac{h}{e}(\nu_1 + \nu_2)$

21. The work done when n smaller equal size spherical drops combine to form a bigger size single spherical drop of water is proportional to

a. $(n^{-2/3} - 1)$ *b.* $(n^{-1/3} - 1)$

c. $(n^{1/3} - 1)$ *d.* $(n^{4/3} - 1)$

22. A ball is thrown up with a certain velocity at an angle θ to the horizontal. The kinetic energy KE of the ball varies with height h as

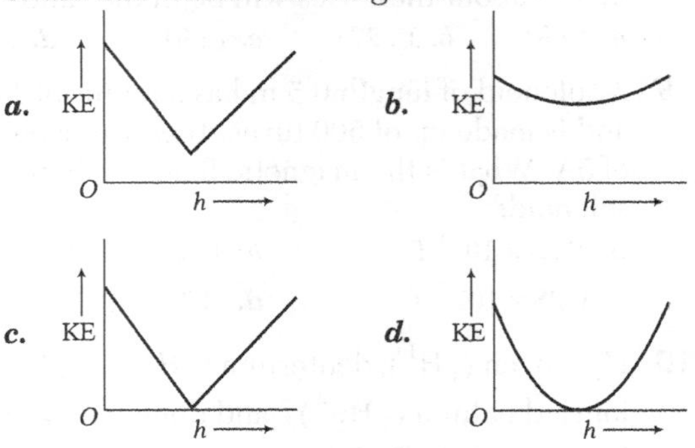

23. The temperature of a wire of length 1 m and area of cross-section $1\ cm^2$ is increased from 0°C to 100°C. If the rod is not allowed to increase in length, then the force required will be ($\alpha = 10^{-5}$ /°C and $Y = 10^{11}\ Nm^{-2}$)

a. 10^3 N *b.* 10^4 N

c. 10^5 N *d.* 10^9 N

24. An ideal gas at 27°C is compressed adiabatically to 8/27 of its original volume. The rise in temperature is (take, $\gamma = 5/3$)

a. 475°C *b.* 150°C

c. 275°C *d.* 402°C

25. Which of these graphs shows potential difference between p-side and n-side of a p-n junction in equilibrium?

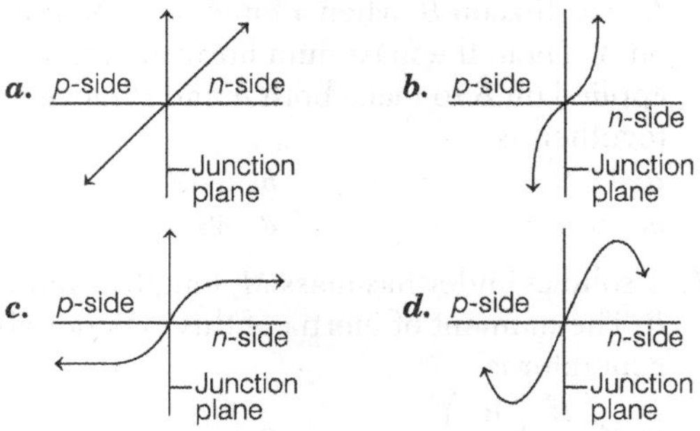

26. The figure shows as logic circuit with two inputs A and B and the output C. The voltge waveforms across A, B and C are as given. The logic circuit gate is

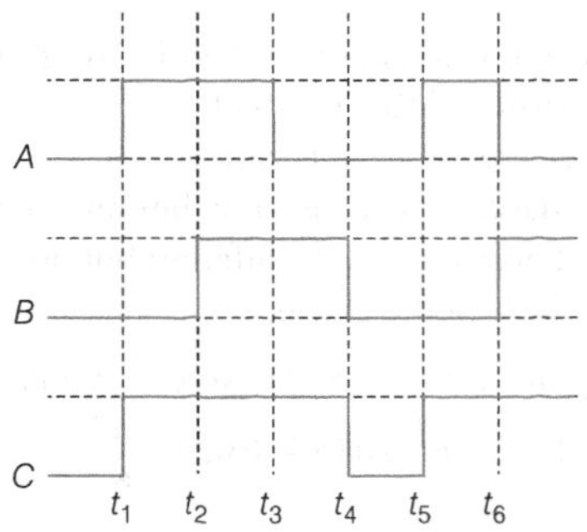

a. OR gate *b.* NOR gate
c. AND gate *d.* NAND gate

27. The magnetic field at the centre of a circular current carrying-conductor of radius r is B_c. The magnetic field on its axis at a distance r from the centre is B_a. The value of $B_c : B_a$ will be

a. $1:\sqrt{2}$ *b.* $1:2\sqrt{2}$ *c.* $2\sqrt{2}:1$ *d.* $\sqrt{2}:1$

28. Mark out the correct statement(s).

a. Total work done by internal forces on a system is always zero.
b. Total work done by internal forces on a system may sometimes be zero.
c. Total work done by friction can never be zero.
d. Total work done by friction is always zero.

29. A what depth below the surface of the earth, the value of g is the same as that at a height of 5 km?

a. 5 km *b.* 2.5 km *c.* 10 km *d.* 6 km

30. If temperature of a metallic wire increases keeping constant electric field, then current density through wire will be

a. increases *b.* decreases
c. remains same *d.* None of these

31. A second pendulum is moved to moon where acceleration due to gravity is 1/6 times that of the earth, the length of the second pendulum on moon would be

a. 6 times *b.* 12 times *c.* $\frac{1}{6}$ times *d.* $\frac{1}{12}$ times

32. Two satellites of earth, S_1 and S_2 are moving in the same orbit. The mass of S_1 is four times the mass of S_2. Which one of the following statements is true?

a. The time period of S_1 is four times that of S_2.
b. The potential energies of earth and satellite in the two cases are equal.
c. S_1 and S_2 are moving with the same speed.
d. The kinetic energies of the two satellites are equal.

33. For two charges q_1 and q_2: if force between them for some separation in air is F, then force between them in a medium of permittivity ε will be

a. $\frac{\varepsilon_0}{\varepsilon}F$ *b.* $\frac{\varepsilon}{\varepsilon_0}F$
c. $\varepsilon\varepsilon_0 F$ *d.* $\frac{F}{\varepsilon_0\varepsilon}$

34. A boat which has a speed of 5 kmh^{-1} in still water crosses a river of width 1 km along the shortest path in 15 min. The velocity of the river (in kmh^{-1}) is

a. 1 *b.* 3
c. 4 *d.* $\sqrt{41}$

35. A sphere encloses an electric dipole with charge $\pm 3\times 10^{-6}$ C. What is the total electric flux across the sphere?

a. -3×10^{-6} N-m^2/C
b. Zero
c. 3×10^{6} N-m^2/C
d. 6×10^{-6} N-m^2/C

36. Volume *versus* temperature graphs for a given mass of an ideal gas are shown in figure. At two different values of constant pressure. What can be inferred about relation between p_1 and p_2?

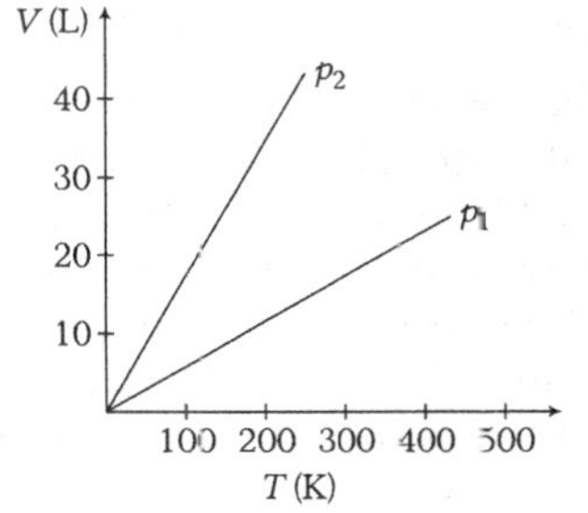

a. $p_1 > p_2$ *b.* $p_1 = p_2$
c. $p_1 < p_2$ *d.* Data is insufficient

37. The ratio of the speed of sound in nitrogen gas to that in helium gas, at 300 K is

a. $\sqrt{\left(\frac{2}{7}\right)}$ *b.* $\sqrt{\left(\frac{1}{7}\right)}$
c. $\frac{\sqrt{3}}{5}$ *d.* $\frac{\sqrt{6}}{5}$

38. For a uniform electric field **E**, along the X-axis, the equipotential surfaces are plane

a. perpendicular to Z-axis
b. parallel to the YZ-plane
c. perpendicular to YZ-plane
d. perpendicular to Y-axis

39. Two sources of sound A and B produces the wave of 350 Hz, in the same phase. The particle P is vibrating under the influence of these two waves, if the amplitudes at the point P produces by the two waves is 0.3 mm and 0.4 mm, then the resultant amplitude of the point P will be when $AP - BP = 25$ cm and the velocity of sound is 350 ms^{-1}.

a. 0.7 mm *b.* 0.1 mm
c. 0.2 mm *d.* 0.5 mm

40. A student measured the length of a rod and wrote it as 3.50 cm.Which instrument did he use to measure it?

a. A meter scale.
b. A vernier caliper, where the 10 divisions in vernier scale matches with 9 divisions in main scale and main scale has 10 divisions in 1 cm.
c. A screw gauge having 100 divisions in the circular scale and pitch as 1 mm.
d. A screw gauge having 50 divisions in the circular scale and pitch as 1 mm.

41. A gang capacitor is formed by interlocking nine plates with each other. The distance between the consecutive plates is 0.885 cm and the overlapping area of the plate is 5 cm^2. The capacity of the unit is

a. 1.06 pF *b.* 4 pF
c. 6.36 pF *d.* 12.72 pF

42. A wall has two layers A and B each made of different materials. The layer A is 10 cm thick and B is 20 cm thick. The thermal conductivity of A is thrice that of B. Under thermal equilibrium, temperature difference across the wall is 35°C. The difference of temperature across the layer A is

a. 20°C *b.* 10°C
c. 15°C *d.* 5°C

43. Resistance of a given wire is obtained by measuring the current flowing in it and the voltage difference applied across it. If the percentage errors in the measurement of the current and the voltage difference are 3% each, then error in the value of resistance of the wire is

a. 6% *b.* zero
c. 1% *d.* 3%

44. Across each of two capacitors of capacitance $1\,\mu\text{F}$ and a potential difference of 10 V is applied. Then, positive plate of one is connected to the negative plate of the other and negative plate of one is connected to the positive plate of the other. After contact,

a. charge on each is zero
b. charge on each is same but non-zero
c. charge on each is different but non-zero
d. None of the above

45. Equation of a progressive wave is given by

$$y = 0.2 \cos \pi \left(0.04\, t + 0.02x - \frac{\pi}{6}\right)$$

The distance is expressed in cm and time in second. What will be the minimum distance between two particles having the phase difference of $\frac{\pi}{2}$?

a. 4 cm *b.* 8 cm *c.* 25 cm *d.* 12.5 cm

46. The angle of a prism is A. One of its refracting surfaces is silvered. Light rays falling at an angle of incidence $2A$ on the first surface returns back through the same path after suffering reflection at the silvered surface. The refractive index μ of the prism is

a. $2 \sin A$ *b.* $2 \cos A$
c. $\frac{1}{2} \cos A$ *d.* $\tan A$

47. An EM wave of maximum frequency 300 kHz and critical frequency 100 kHz is to be transmitted to a height equal to 150 km. Calculate the skip distance.

a. 624 km *b.* 849 km
c. 636 km *d.* 942 km

48. The condition under which a microwave oven heats up a food item containing water molecules most efficiently is

a. the frequency of the microwave must match the resonant frequency of the water molecules
b. the frequency of the microwave has no relation with natural frequency of water molecules
c. microwave are heat waves, so always produce heating
d. infrared waves produce heating in a microwave oven

49. A simple telescope, consisting of an objective of focal length 60 cm and a single eye lens of focal length 5 cm is focused on a distant object in such a way that parallel rays emerge from the eye lens. If the object subtends an angle of 2° at the objective, then the angular width of the image is

a. 10° *b.* 24°
c. 50° *d.* (1/6)°

50. The combination of the gates shown in the figure below produces

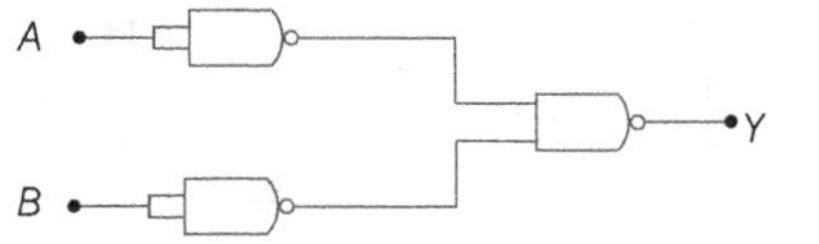

a. NOR gate *b.* OR gate
c. AND gate *d.* XOR gate

51. In an apparatus, the electric field was found to oscillate with an amplitude of 18 Vm^{-1}. The magnitude of the oscillating magnetic field will be

a. 4×10^{-6} T *b.* 6×10^{-8} T
c. 9×10^{-9} T *d.* 11×10^{-11} T

52. The spectrum of a black body at two temperatures 27°C and 327°C is shown in the figure. Let A_1 and A_2 be the areas under the two curves respectively. The value of A_2/A_1 is

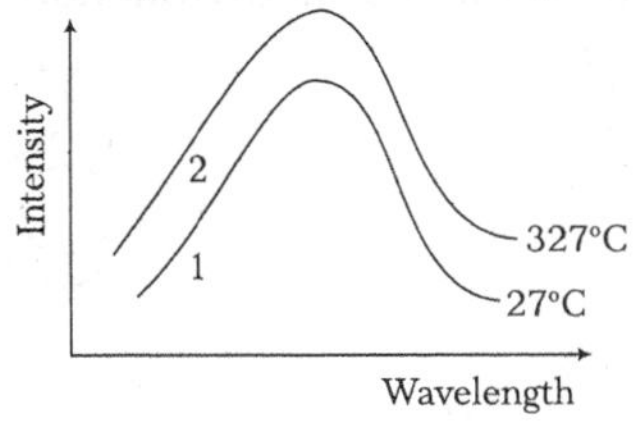

a. 1 : 16 *b.* 4 : 1 *c.* 2 : 1 *d.* 16 : 1

53. One mole of an ideal gas at an initial temperature of T K does 6 R J of work adiabatically. If the ratio of specific heats of this gas at constant pressure and at constant volume is 5/3, the final temperature of gas will be

a. $(T+2.4)$ K *b.* $(T-2.4)$ K
c. $(T+4)$ K *d.* $(T-4)$ K

54. An AC-circuit contains a resistance R, capacitance C and inductance L in series with a source of emf $E=E_0 \sin(\omega t+\phi)$. The current through the circuit is maximum, when

a. $R=L=C$ *b.* $\omega L=\dfrac{1}{\omega C}$
c. $\omega^2=LC$ *d.* $\omega=RLC$

55. What is the modulation index in AM if amplitude of an audio signal is equal to one half of the amplitude of carrier?

a. 1 *b.* 0
c. 0.5 *d.* greater than 1

56. The temperature of a wire is doubled. The Young's modulus of elasticity

a. will also double
b. will become four times
c. will remain same
d. will decrease

57. An AC ammeter is used to measure current in a circuit. When a given direct current passes through the circuit, the AC ammeter reads 3 A. When another alternating current passes through the circuit, the AC ammeter reads 4A. Then, the reading of this ammeter, if DC and AC flow through the circuit simultaneously, is

a. 3 A *b.* 4 A
c. 7 A *d.* 5 A

58. The displacement of a body along X-axis depends on time as $\sqrt{x}=t+1$. Then, the velocity of body

a. increases with time
b. decreases with time
c. independent of time
d. None of the above

59. The correct value of the dip angle at a place is 45°. The dip circle is rotated through 45° out of the magnetic meridian. The apparent angle of dip will be

a. $\tan^{-1}(\sqrt{2})$ *b.* $\tan^{-1}\left(\dfrac{1}{\sqrt{2}}\right)$
c. $\tan^{-1}(2)$ *d.* $\tan^{-1}\left(\dfrac{1}{2}\right)$

60. As a result of change in the magnetic flux linked to the closed loop shown in the figure, an emf V(volt) is induced in the loop. The work done (joules) in taking a charge q (coulomb) once along the loop is

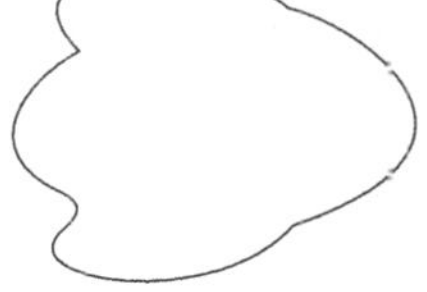

a. qV *b.* Zero
c. $2qV$ *d.* $\dfrac{qV}{2}$

MOCK TEST 3

CHEMISTRY

61. Hydrolysis of sucrose gives,

Sucrose + $H_2O \rightleftharpoons$ Glucose + Fructose

Equilibrium constant (K_C) for the reaction is 2×10^{13} at 300 K. The value of $\Delta G°$ at 300 K is

a. 3.52×10^5 J mol^{-1} *b.* 5.12×10^5 J mol^{-1}
c. 7.64×10^4 J mol^{-1} *d.* -7.64×10^4 J mol^{-1}

62. The temperature at which 10% aqueous solution (w / V) of glucose exhibits the osmotic pressure of 16.4 atm is ($R = 0.082$ dm^3 atm K^{-1}mol^{-1}).

a. 200 K *b.* 180 K *c.* 90 K *d.* 360 K

63. 1.1 mole of *A* is mixed with 2.2 mole of *B* and the mixture is kept in a 1 L flask till the equilibrium, $A + 2B \rightleftharpoons 2C + D$ is reached. At equilibrium, 0.2 mole of *C* is formed. The equilibrium constant would be

a. 0.002 *b.* 0.004 *c.* 0.001 *d.* 0.003

64. At 300 K two pure liquids *A* and *B* have 150 mm Hg and 100 mm Hg vapour pressures, respectively. In an equimolar liquid mixture of *A* and *B*, the mole fraction of *B* in the vapour mixture at this temperature is

a. 0.6 *b.* 0.5 *c.* 0.8 *d.* 0.4

65. Dihydrogen is obtained as a byproduct in the manufacture of

a. sodium hydroxide and bromine by electrolysis
b. potassium hydroxide and bromine by electrolysis
c. sodium hydroxide and chlorine by electrolysis
d. potassium hydroxide and chlorine by electrolysis

66. Which of the following product is formed in the given reaction?

$$R{-}CONH_2 \xrightarrow[\text{(ii) } H_2O]{\text{(i) } LiAlH_4}$$

a. RNH_2 *b.* RCH_2NH_2
c. $RCH_2CH_2NH_2$ *d.* RCN

67. When carbon monoxide reacts with water, product obtained is

a. carbonic acid *b.* carbon dioxide
c. hydrogen *d.* Both (b) and (c)

68. What is *A* in the following reaction?

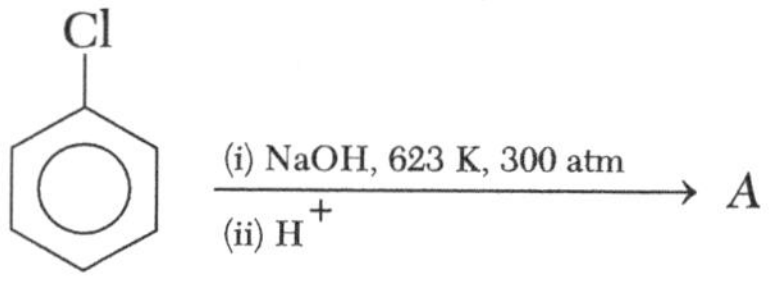

a.
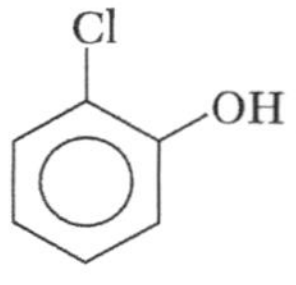

b.

c.
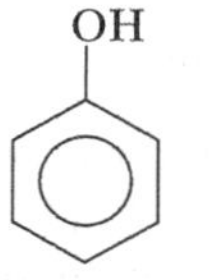

d.

69. The radius of the second Bohr orbit in terms of the Bohr radius, a_0, in Li^{2+} is

a. $\frac{2a_0}{3}$ *b.* $\frac{4a_0}{3}$ *c.* $\frac{4a_0}{9}$ *d.* $\frac{2a_0}{9}$

70. What is the major product(s) formed by the mononitration of 3-methylphenol?

a.
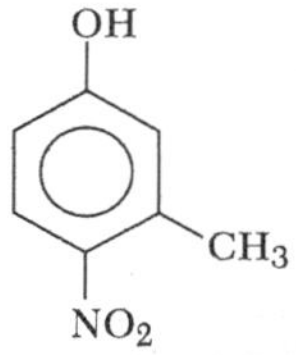

b.
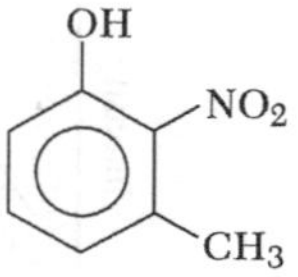

c.
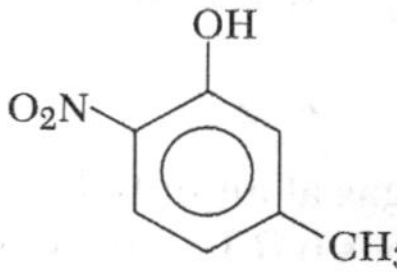

d. Both (a) and (c)

71. Which of the following compounds does not contain all the carbon atoms in the same hybridisation state?

a. H—C≡C—C≡C—H
b. HC≡CH
c. CH_2=C=CH_2
d. CH_2=CH—CH=CH_2

72. On ozonolysis, which of the following compound will give 5-keto-2-methyl hexanal?

a.
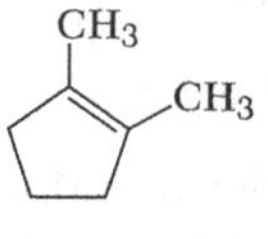

b.
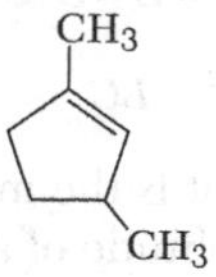

c.
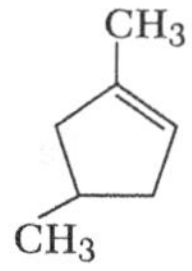

d.
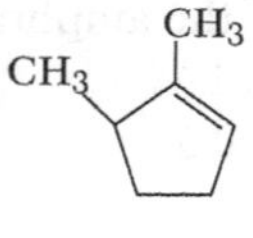

73. If Z is a compressibility factor, van der Waals' equation at low pressure can be written as

a. $Z = 1 + \frac{RT}{pb}$ *b.* $Z = 1 - \frac{a}{VRT}$
c. $Z = 1 - \frac{pb}{RT}$ *d.* $Z = 1 + \frac{pb}{RT}$

74. Receptors are selective in nature because it binds to

a. all types of chemical messengers
b. a particular type of chemical messenger
c. cell membrane
d. All of the above

75. The change in the energy of system, if 500 cal of heat energy are added to a system and system does 350 cal of work on the surroundings will be

a. –150 cal *b.* +150 cal
c. + 850 cal *d.* –850 cal

76. If 10^{-4} dm^3 of water is introduced into a 1.0 dm^3 flask at 300 K, how many moles of water are in the vapour phase when equilibrium is established? (Given, vapour pressure of H_2O at 300 K is 3170 Pa, $R = 8.314$ JK^{-1} mol^{-1}).

a. 5.56×10^{-3} mol *b.* 1.53×10^{-2} mol
c. 4.46×10^{-2} mol *d.* 1.27×10^{-3} mol

77. A solid having density of 9×10^3 kg m^{-3} forms face centred cubic crystals of edge length $200\sqrt{2}$ pm. What is the molar mass of the solid? [Avogadro constant $= 6 \times 10^{23}$ mol^{-1}, $\pi = 3$]

a. 0.03050 kg mol^{-1} *b.* 0.4320 kg mol^{-1}
c. 0.0432 kg mol^{-1} *d.* 0.0216 kg mol^{-1}

78. Which of the following compound is synthesised by Kolbe and Berthelot respectively that shows that organic compounds could be synthesised from inorganic sources in a laboratory?

a. Ethane, methane *b.* Methane, ethane
c. Methane, acetic acid *d.* Acetic acid, methane

79. When pressure is low, the fraction of the surface covered during adsorption follows

a. zero order kinetics
b. first order kinetics
c. second order kinetics
d. fractional order kinetics

80. Which of the following pairs of ions are isoelectronic and isostructural?

a. CO_3^{2-}, SO_3^{2-} *b.* ClO_3^-, CO_3^{2-}
c. SO_3^{2-}, NO_3^- *d.* ClO_3^-, SO_3^{2-}

81. $E^\circ_{cell} = 1.1$ V for Daniell cell. Which of the following expressions are correct description of state of equilibrium in this cell?

a. $1.1 = K_C$ *b.* $\frac{2.303RT}{2F} \log K_C = 1.1$
c. $\log K_C = \frac{3.4}{0.059}$ *d.* $\log K_C = 1.1$

82. Silica is added to the copper pyrites ore, when taken in reverberatory furnace for extraction of Cu. This is because

a. it removes the impurity of iron oxide as slag
b. it reacts with Cu_2O to form slag
c. it reduces Cu_2O to Cu
d. it helps in separation of Cu from Fe

83. Magnesium reacts with acids producing hydrogen and corresponding magnesium salts. In such reaction, Mg undergoes

a. reduction *b.* oxidation
c. redox reaction *d.* simple dissolution

84. If the intermolecular distance between two adjacent copper atoms in solid copper is 256 pm, then the metallic radius of copper is

a. 128 pm *b.* 12.37 Å *c.* 74 pm *d.* 74 Å

85. If 6.3 g of $NaHCO_3$ are added to 15.0 g CH_3COOH solution, the residue is found to weigh 18.0 g. What will be the mass of CO_2 released in the reaction?

a. 4.5 g *b.* 3.3 g *c.* 2.6 g *d.* 2.8 g

86. Lyophobic colloids are not stable because

a. they coagulate by heating them or with the addition of electrolytes
b. they coagulate by freezing them or with the addition of electrolytes
c. they do not coagulate by freezing them with the electrolytes
d. they do not coagulate by heating them with the electrolytes

87. 8 g of NaOH is dissolved in 18 g of H_2O. Mole fraction of NaOH in solution and molality (in mol kg^{-1}) of the solution respectively are

a. 0.2, 11.11 *b.* 0.167, 22.20
c. 0.2, 22.20 *d.* 0.167, 11.11

88. A compound $C_3H_8O_3$ has two primary alcoholic groups and one secondary alcoholic group.

The IUPAC name of this compound is

a. propane-1, 2-diol *b.* propane-1, 3-diol
c. propane-1, 2, 3-triol *d.* 2-methylethane-1-ol

89. Which of the following alkyl halides has maximum density?

a. C_3H_7I *b.* C_2H_5I
c. CH_3Br *d.* CH_3I

90. Which of the following types of element show variable valency?

a. Transition elements *b.* *s*-block elements
c. Actinoids *d.* Both (a) and (c)

91. According to molecular orbital theory, which of the following is true with respect to Li_2^+ and Li_2^-?

a. Both are unstable
b. Li_2^+ is unstable and Li_2^- is stable
c. Both are stable
d. Li_2^+ is stable and Li_2^- is unstable

92. Select the strongest acid among the following compounds.

a. $FCH_2CH_2CH_2OH$
b. $H_3CCH_2CH—CH_2OH$ (F on CH)
c. $CH_3CH_2CF_2CH_2OH$
d. $CH_3CHCH_2CH_2OH$ (F on CH)

93. Which among the following compounds possesses antipyretic properties?

a. 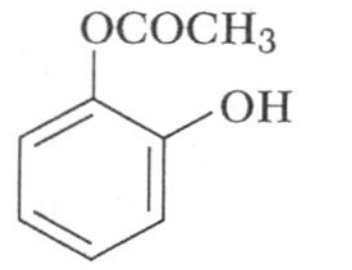

b. 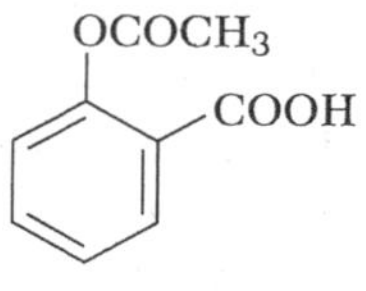

c. 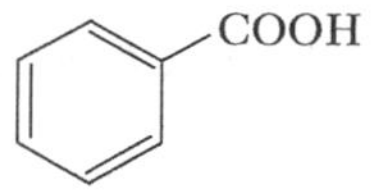

d. 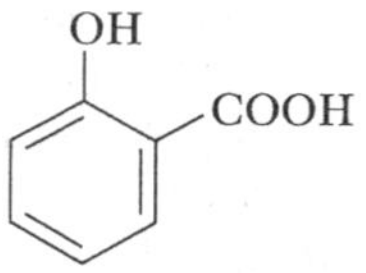

94. Deviation of O—O bond length in ozone molecule from the normal bond length seems as

a. single bond length increases, while double bond length decreases
b. single bond length decreases, while double bond length increases
c. single bond length increases, while double bond length remains same
d. single bond length remains same, while double bond length increases

95. A cubic solid is made up of two elements *A* and *B*. Atoms of element *B* are present at the corners of the cube and atoms *A* at the body centre. Predict the formula of the compound.

a. AB_2 *b.* AB
c. A_2B *d.* None of these

96. The melting of ice

a. is the phase transformation
b. takes place at constant pressure and temperature
c. take place at 373 K
d. Both (a) and (b)

97. *s*-block elements are reactive metals. As we go down the group, the reactivity.

a. increase
b. decrease
c. remains same
d. None of the above

98. Alkali metals dissolve in liquid ammonia and produces

a. deep blue solution
b. a solution which are conducting in nature
c. red coloured solution
d. Both (a) and (b)

99. On passing vapours of phenol over heated zinc, dust it gets reduced to

a. toluene *b.* aniline
c. benzene *d.* phenol

100. The standard enthalpy of formation of $NH_3(g)$ is -81.9 kJ mol^{-1}. The amount of heat required to decompose 26 g of NH_3 (g) into its elements, is

a. 122.9 *b.* 143.8
c. 164.7 *d.* 105.6

101. What is the IUPAC name of the following compound?

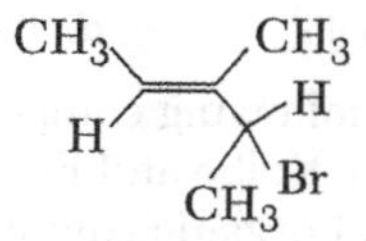

a. 3-bromo-3-methyl-1,2-dimethylprop-1-ene
b. 3-bromo-1,2-dimethylbut-1-ene
c. 2-bromo-3-methylpent-3-ene
d. 4-bromo-3-methylpent-2-ene

102. The alcohols that give best yield of dialkylether on being heated with a trace of sulphuric acid?

a. Pentan-2-ol *b.* 2-methyl butan-2-ol
c. Pentan-1-ol *d.* Propen-2-ol

103. The compound in which the C-atoms form a closed chain are termed as

a. aliphatic hydrocarbons
b. cycloalkanes
c. alkanes
d. alkenes

104. Consider the following.

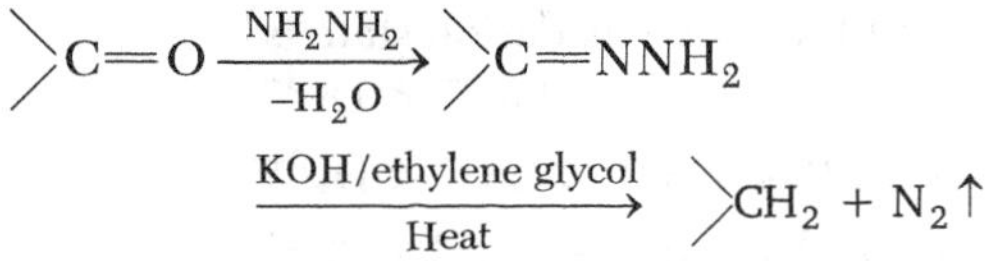

The above reaction is known as,

a. Wolff-Kishner reduction
b. Clemmensen's reduction
c. Both (a) and (b)
d. None of the above

105. Consider the following mechanism :

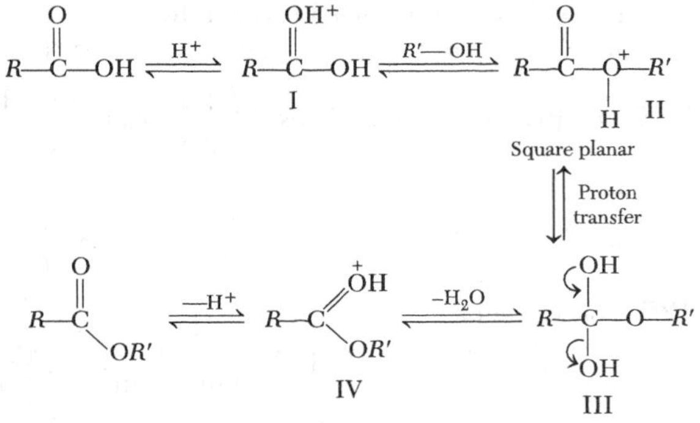

The incorrect structure is

a. I *b.* II *c.* III *d.* IV

106. Consider the following isomers

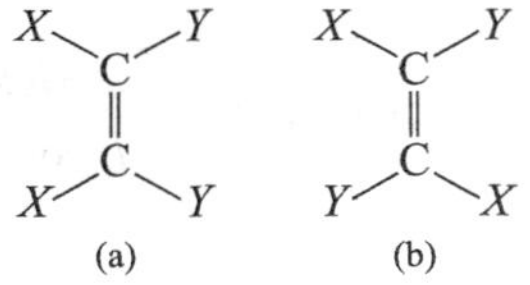

The type of isomers (a) and (b) are

a. chain isomers *b.* functional isomers
c. geometrical isomers *d.* positional isomers

107. The stability of the halides of group 16 elements decreases in the order

a. $Br^- > I^- > Cl^- > F^-$ *b.* $F^- > I^- > Cl^- > Br^-$
c. $F^- > Cl^- > Br^- > I^-$ *d.* $I^- > Cl^- > Br^- > F^-$

108. In an automobile engine, (at high temperature) when fossil fuel is burnt, N_2 and O_2 combine to yield

a. NO *b.* NO_2
c. HNO_3 *d.* Both (a) and (b)

109. The rate constant of the reaction, $A \rightarrow B$ is 0.6×10^{-3} mole per litre per second. If the concentration of A is 5 M, then concentration of B after 20 min is

a. 1.08 M *b.* 3.60 M *c.* 0.36 M *d.* 0.72 M

110. The first noble gas compound obtained was

a. $Xe^+PtF_6^-$ *b.* XeF_4
c. XeF_2 *d.* $XeOF_4$

111. The filling of $4f$-orbital before $5d$-orbital results in a regular decrease in atomic radii called

a. lanthanoid contraction
b. shielding effect
c. actinoid contraction
d. None of the above

112. In which of the following, oxidation state of phosphorus is + 3?

a. Orthophosphoric acid
b. Pyrophosphoric acid
c. Orthophosphorus acid
d. Cyclometaphosphoric acid

113. Which among the following will be named as dibromido *bis* (ethylenediammine) chromium (III) bromide ?

a. $[Cr(en)_3]Br_3$ *b.* $[Cr(en)_2Br_2]Br$
c. $[Cr(en)Br_4]^-$ *d.* $[Cr(en)Br_2]Br$

114. Arrange the following acids in the correct increasing order of their acidic strength

HCl, HBr, HI and HF

a. HI < HBr < HCl < HF
b. HF < HCl < HBr < HI
c. HCl < HBr < HI < HF
d. HBr < HI < HF < HCl

115. Which of the following amino acids is not optically active?

a. Lysine *b.* Glycine
c. Leucine *d.* Glutamine

116. Teflon is manufactured by heating

a. tetrafluoroethane
b. tetrafluoromethylene
c. tetrafluoroethene
d. tetrafluoromethane

117. Acidified potassium dichromate oxidises

a. iodides to iodine
b. sulphides to sulphur
c. tin (IV) to tin (II)
d. Both (a) and (b)

118. If 1 mL of water contains 20 drops then number of molecules in a drop of water is

a. 6.023×10^{23} molecules
b. 1.376×10^{26} molecules
c. 1.62×10^{21} molecules
d. 4.346×10^{20} molecules

119. The primary and secondary valencies of chromium in the complex ion, dichlorodioxalato chromium (III) respectively are

a. 3 and 4
b. 4 and 3
c. 6 and 3
d. 3 and 6

120. The correct order of ionic radii of Ce, Pm, Gd and Dy in +3 oxidation state is

a. $Ce^{3+} < Gd^{3+} < Pm^{3+} < Dy^{3+}$
b. $Ce^{3+} < Pm^{3+} < Gd^{3+} < Dy^{3+}$
c. $Dy^{3+} < Gd^{3+} < Pm^{3+} < Ce^{3+}$
d. $Pm^{3+} < Ce^{3+} < Dy^{3+} < Gd^{3+}$

MATHEMATICS

121. The function $f : R \to R$ defined by $f(x) = \frac{x}{x^2 + 1}$, $\forall x \in R$ is

a. one-one
b. onto
c. both one-one and onto
d. neither one-one nor onto

122. Let $f : R - \left\{-\frac{4}{3}\right\} \to R$ be a function defined as $f(x) = \frac{4x}{3x + 4}$. The inverse of f is the map g : range $f \to R - \left\{-\frac{4}{3}\right\}$ given by

a. $g(y) = \frac{3y}{3 - 4y}$
b. $g(y) = \frac{4y}{4 - 3y}$
c. $g(y) = \frac{4y}{3 - 4y}$
d. $g(y) = \frac{3y}{4 - 3y}$

123. Let $f : R \to R$ be defined as $f(x) = 10x + 7$. Then, the function $g : R \to R$ such that $fog = gof = I_R$ is

a. $\frac{y + 7}{10}$
b. $\frac{7 - y}{10}$
c. $\frac{y - 7}{10}$
d. $10y - 7$

124. If $\tan\alpha = \frac{1}{7}$ and $\tan\beta = \frac{1}{3}$, then $\cos 2\alpha$ is equal to

a. $\sin 2\beta$
b. $\sin 4\beta$
c. $\sin 3\beta$
d. $\cos 2\beta$

125. If $m \sin\theta = n \sin(\theta + 2\alpha)$, then $\tan(\theta + \alpha)\cot\alpha$

a. $\frac{m + n}{m - n}$
b. $\frac{m - n}{m + n}$
c. $\frac{m + n}{mn}$
d. $\frac{m - n}{2m}$

126. If $2\sin^2\theta = 3\cos\theta$, where $0 \le \theta \le 2\pi$, then the value of θ is/are

a. $\frac{\pi}{3}$
b. $\frac{6\pi}{6}$
c. $\frac{\pi}{3}, \frac{5\pi}{3}$
d. $\frac{\pi}{3}, \frac{5\pi}{6}, \frac{2\pi}{3}$

127. If $x = \sec\phi - \tan\phi$ and $y = \operatorname{cosec}\phi + \cot\phi$, then show that $xy + x - y + 1$ is equal to

a. 0
b. 1
c. 2
d. 3

128. The principal value of $\cos^{-1}\left(\frac{1}{2}\right) - 2\sin^{-1}\left(-\frac{1}{2}\right)$ is

a. $\frac{\pi}{3}$
b. $\frac{-\pi}{3}$
c. $\frac{2\pi}{3}$
d. $\frac{\pi}{6}$

129. The value of $\tan^{-1}\left(\frac{-1}{\sqrt{3}}\right) + \cot^{-1}\left(\frac{1}{\sqrt{3}}\right) + \tan^{-1}\left(\sin\left(-\frac{\pi}{2}\right)\right)$ is

a. $\frac{\pi}{6}$
b. $\frac{\pi}{12}$
c. $-\frac{\pi}{12}$
d. $\frac{\pi}{3}$

130. The simplest form of $\tan^{-1}\left[\frac{a\cos x - b\sin x}{b\cos x + a\sin x}\right]$, if $\frac{a}{b}\tan x > -1$ is

a. $\tan^{-1}\frac{a}{b}$
b. $\tan^{-1}\frac{a}{b} + x$
c. $\tan^{-1}\frac{a}{b} - x$
d. $-x$

131. If $x^n - 1$ is divisible by $x - k$, then the least positive integral value of k is

a. 1
b. 2
c. 3
d. 4

132. Solve the equation $|z| = z + 1 + 2i$.

a. $z = \frac{3}{2} - 2i$
b. $z = 3 - 2i$
c. $z = \frac{3}{2} + 2i$
d. $z = 3 + 2i$

133. If $\frac{z - 1}{z + 1}$ is a purely imaginary number $(z \neq -1)$, then the value of $|z|$

a. 1
b. 2
c. 3
d. 4

134. The point represented by the complex number $(2-i)$ is rotated about origin through an angle $\frac{\pi}{2}$ in the clockwise direction, the new position of point is

a. $1+2i$ *b.* $-1-2i$
c. $2+i$ *d.* $-1+2i$

135. For a positive integer n, then the value of $(1-i)^n\left(1-\frac{1}{i}\right)^n$.

a. 2 *b.* 2^n *c.* 3^n *d.* $(-1)^n$

136. The number of integers greater than 7000 that can be formed with the digits 3, 5, 7, 8 and 9 where no digits are repeated is

a. 72 *b.* 120 *c.* 182 *d.* 192

137. The number of 5-digit telephone numbers having atleast one of their digits repeated is

a. 90000 *b.* 10000
c. 30240 *d.* 69760

138. The number of different words that can be formed from the letters of the word 'INTERMEDIATE' such that two vowels never come together is ....

a. 15120 *b.* 13120
c. 151200 *d.* 131200

139. The total number of terms in the expansion of $(x+a)^{100}+(x-a)^{100}$ after simplification is

a. 50 *b.* 202
c. 51 *d.* None of these

140. The coefficient of x^n in the expansion of $(1+x)^{2n}$ and $(1+x)^{2n-1}$ are in the ratio

a. 1 : 2 *b.* 1 : 3
c. 3 : 1 *d.* 2 : 1

141. Let S_n denote the sum of the first n terms of an AP, if $S_{2n}=3S_n$, then $S_{3n}:S_n$ is equal to

a. 4 *b.* 6 *c.* 8 *d.* 10

142. If t_n denotes the nth term of the series $2+3+6+11+18+\ldots$, then t_{50} is

a. 49^2-1 *b.* 49^2
c. 50^2+1 *d.* 49^2+2

143. A line passes through (2, 2) and is perpendicular to the line $3x+y=3$. Its y-intercept is

a. $\frac{1}{3}$ *b.* $\frac{2}{3}$
c. 1 *d.* $\frac{4}{3}$

144. The ratio in which the line $3x+4y+2=0$ divides the distance between the lines $3x+4y+5=0$ and $3x+4y-5=0$ is

a. 1 : 2 *b.* 3 : 7 *c.* 2 : 3 *d.* 2 : 5

145. One vertex of the equilateral triangle with centroid at the origin and one side as $x+y-2=0$ is

a. $(-1,-1)$ *b.* $(2, 2)$
c. $(-2,-2)$ *d.* $(2,-2)$

146. If the line $y=\sqrt{3}x+k$ touches the circle $x^2+y^2=16$, then find the value of k.

a. ±2 *b.* ±3 *c.* ±4 *d.* ±8

147. The equation of a circle concentric with the circle $x^2+y^2-6x+12y+15=0$ and has double of its area is

a. $x^2+y^2-6x+12y-15=0$
b. $x^2+y^2-6x+12y+15=0$
c. $x^2+y^2+6x-12y+15=0$
d. $x^2+y^2+6x-12y-15=0$

148. The focus of a parabolic mirror as shown in figure is at a distance of 5cm from its vertex. If the mirror is 45 cm deep, then the distance AB is

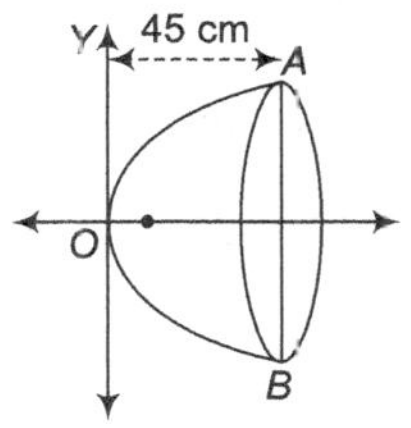

a. 20 cm *b.* 40 cm
c. 60 cm *d.* 80 cm

149. The equations of the lines joining the vertex of the parabola $y^2=6x$ to the points on it which have abscissa 24, are

a. $y\pm 2x=0$ *b.* $2y\pm x=0$
c. $x\pm y=0$ *d.* None of these

150. If the eccentricity of an ellipse be $1/\sqrt{2}$, then its latusrectum is equal to its

a. minor axis *b.* semi-minor axis
c. major axis *d.* semi-major axis

151. If the distance between a focus and corresponding directrix of an ellipse be 8 and the eccentricity be 1/2, then length of the minor axis is

a. 3 *b.* $4\sqrt{2}$
c. 6 *d.* None of these

152. The equation of the hyperbola whose conjugate axis is 5 and the distance between the foci is 13, is

a. $25x^2 - 144y^2 = 900$ b. $144x^2 - 25y^2 = 900$
c. $144x^2 + 25y^2 = 900$ d. $25x^2 + 144y^2 = 900$

153. The locus of the point of intersection of the lines $\sqrt{3}x - y - 4\sqrt{3}k = 0$ and $\sqrt{3}kx + ky - 4\sqrt{3} = 0$ for different value of k, is

a. circle b. parabola
c. hyperbola d. ellipse

154. The equation of the plane through the intersection of the planes $3x - y + 2z - 4 = 0$ and $x + y + z - 2 = 0$ and through the point $(2, 2, 1)$ is

a. $7x - 5y + 4z - 8 = 0$
b. $11x - y + 8z - 8 = 0$
c. $11x - y + 8z - 12 = 0$
d. $7x - 5y + 4z - 12 = 0$

155. If the function

$$f(x) = \begin{cases} x + a^2\sqrt{2}\sin x & , 0 \le x \le \frac{\pi}{4} \\ x\cot x + b & , \frac{\pi}{4} \le x \le \frac{\pi}{2} \\ b\sin 2x - a\cos 2x & , \frac{\pi}{2} < x \le \pi \end{cases}$$

is continuous in the interval $[0, \pi]$, then the values of (a, b) are

I. $(-1, -1)$ II. $(0, 0)$
III. $(-1, 1)$ IV. $(1, 1)$

a. I and II are correct b. II and IV are correct
c. III and IV are correct d. None of these

156. If $f: (-1, 1) \to R$ be a differentiable function with $f(0) = -1$ and $f'(0) = 1$. Let $g(x) = [f(2f(x) + 2)]^2$. Then, $g'(0)$ is equal to

a. 4 b. −4 c. 0 d. −2

157. If $y = \log_2 [\log_2 (x)]$, then $\frac{dy}{dx}$ is equal to

a. $\frac{\log_2 e}{\log_e x}$ b. $\frac{\log_2 e}{x \log_x 2}$
c. $\frac{\log_2 x}{\log_e 2}$ d. $\frac{\log_2 e}{x \log_e x}$

158. If $f(x) = (1 + x)(1 + x^2)(1 + x^4)(1 + x^8)$, then $f'(1)$ is

a. 130 b. 120
c. 110 d. None of these

159. If $f(x) = 1 + nx + \frac{n(n-1)}{2}x^2 + \frac{n(n-1)(n-2)}{6}x^3 + \quad + x^n$, then $f''(1)$ is equal to

a. $n(n-1)\, 2^{n-1}$ b. $(n-1)\, 2^{n-1}$
c. $n(n-1)\, 2^{n-2}$ d. $n(n-1)\, 2^n$

160. If $y = \log(1 + x) - \frac{2x}{2 + x}$ is an increasing function of x throughout

a. $x < -1$ as its domain b. $x > -1$ as its domain
c. $x = -1$ d. $x > 2$ as its domain

161. $f(x) = \left(\frac{e^{2x} - 1}{e^{2x} + 1}\right)$ is

a. a decreasing function b. an increasing function
c. Both (a) and (b) are true d. None of these

162. The distance between the origin and the normal to the curve $y = e^{2x} + x^2$ at $x = 0$ is

a. 2 b. $\frac{\sqrt{3}}{2}$ c. $\frac{\sqrt{5}}{2}$ d. $\frac{2}{\sqrt{5}}$

163. If sum of two numbers is 24 and their product is as large as possible, then one of the number is

a. 23 b. 20
c. 18 d. None of these

164. $\int \frac{e^x(1 + x)}{\cos^2(e^x x)} dx$ equals

a. $-\cot(ex^x) + C$ b. $\tan(xe^x) + C$
c. $\tan(e^x) + C$ d. $\cot(e^x) + C$

165. The value of $\int \frac{x^2 - 1}{x^4 + x^2 + 1} dx$ is equal to

a. $\frac{1}{2}\log\left|\frac{x^2 + x + 1}{x^2 - x + 1}\right| + C$ b. $2\log\left|\frac{x^2 + x + 1}{x^2 - x + 1}\right| + C$
c. $\frac{1}{2}\log\left|\frac{x^2 - x + 1}{x^2 + x + 1}\right| + C$ d. None of these

166. If $\int \frac{2x^2 + 3}{(x^2 - 1)(x^2 + 4)} dx = a \log\left(\frac{x - 1}{x + 1}\right) + b\tan^{-1}\left(\frac{x}{2}\right) + C$, then the value of a and b are

a. $1, -1$ b. $-1, 1$
c. $\frac{1}{2}, \frac{-1}{2}$ d. $\frac{1}{2}, \frac{1}{2}$

MOCK TEST 3

167. $\int_0^{2/3} \frac{dx}{4+9x^2}$ is equal to

a. $\frac{\pi}{6}$ *b.* $\frac{\pi}{12}$ *c.* $\frac{\pi}{24}$ *d.* $\frac{\pi}{4}$

168. The value of $\int_{-\pi/2}^{\pi/2} (x^3 + x\cos x + \tan 5x + 1)\,dx$ is

a. 0 *b.* 2 *c.* π *d.* 1

169. $\int \frac{x^3}{\sqrt{1-x^8}}\,dx$ is equal to

a. $\frac{1}{4}\sin^{-1}(x^4)+C$ *b.* $4\sin^{-1}(x^4)+C$

c. $\frac{1}{4}\sin^{-1}(x^2)+C$ *d.* $4\sin^{-1}(x^2)+C$

170. The area of the region enclosed by the curves $y=x$, $x=e$, $y=\frac{1}{x}$ and the positive X-axis is

a. 1 sq unit *b.* $\frac{3}{2}$ sq units

c. $\frac{5}{2}$ sq units *d.* $\frac{1}{2}$ sq unit

171. The differential equation obtained by eliminating the arbitrary constants a and b from $xy = ae^x + be^{-x}$ is

a. $x\frac{d^2y}{dx^2}+2\frac{dy}{dx}-xy=0$ *b.* $\frac{d^2y}{dx^2}+2y\frac{dy}{dx}-xy=0$

c. $x\frac{d^2y}{dx^2}+2\frac{dy}{dx}+xy=0$ *d.* $\frac{d^2y}{dx^2}+\frac{dy}{dx}-2y=0$

172. The solution of differential equation $\cos y\frac{dy}{dx}=e^{x+\sin y}+x^2e^{\sin y}$ is

a. $e^x - e^{-\sin y}+\frac{x^3}{3}=C$ *b.* $e^{-x}-e^{-\sin y}+\frac{x^3}{3}=C$

c. $e^x + e^{-\sin y}+\frac{x^3}{3}=C$ *d.* $e^x - e^{\sin y}-\frac{x^3}{3}=C$

173. The ratio in which $\mathbf{i}+2\mathbf{j}+3\mathbf{k}$ divides the join of $-2\mathbf{i}+3\mathbf{j}+5\mathbf{k}$ and $7\mathbf{i}-\mathbf{k}$ is

a. 1 : 2 *b.* 1 : 4 *c.* 2 : 3 *d.* 3 : 4

174. The position vectors of the points A and B with respect to O are $2\mathbf{i}+2\mathbf{j}+\mathbf{k}$ and $2\mathbf{i}+4\mathbf{j}+4\mathbf{k}$. The length of the internal bisector of $\angle BOA$ of ΔAOB is

a. $\frac{\sqrt{136}}{9}$ *b.* $\frac{\sqrt{136}}{3}$

c. $\frac{20}{3}$ *d.* $\frac{\sqrt{217}}{9}$

175. If $A=\begin{bmatrix}6&8&5\\4&2&3\\9&7&1\end{bmatrix}$ is the sum of a symmetric matrix B and skew-symmetric matrix C, then B is equal to

a. $\begin{bmatrix}6&6&7\\6&2&5\\7&5&1\end{bmatrix}$ *b.* $\begin{bmatrix}0&2&-2\\-2&5&-2\\2&2&0\end{bmatrix}$

c. $\begin{bmatrix}6&6&7\\-6&2&-5\\-7&5&1\end{bmatrix}$ *d.* $\begin{bmatrix}0&6&-2\\2&0&-2\\-2&-2&0\end{bmatrix}$

176. If $\Delta=\begin{vmatrix}1&x&x^2\\1&y&y^2\\1&z&z^2\end{vmatrix}$ and $\Delta_1=\begin{vmatrix}1&1&1\\yz&zx&xy\\x&y&z\end{vmatrix}$, then

a. $\Delta+\Delta_1=1$ *b.* $\Delta-\Delta_1=0$

c. $\Delta+\Delta_1=0$ *d.* $\Delta-\Delta_1=1$

177. Let $A=\begin{bmatrix}5&5\alpha&\alpha\\0&\alpha&5\alpha\\0&0&5\end{bmatrix}$. If $|A^2|=25$, then $|\alpha|$ equal

a. 5^2 *b.* 1 *c.* $\frac{1}{5}$ *d.* 5

178. If A and B are two events such that $P(A/B)=p$, $P(A)=p$, $P(B)=\frac{1}{3}$ and $P(A\cup B)=\frac{5}{9}$, then p is equals to

a. $\frac{1}{2}$ *b.* $\frac{2}{3}$ *c.* $\frac{1}{3}$ *d.* $\frac{2}{5}$

179. The negation of the statement "Plants take in CO_2 and give out O_2" is

a. Plants do not take in CO_2 and dc not given out O_2

b. Plants do not take in CO_2 or do not give out O_2

c. Plants take is CO_2 and do not give out O_2

d. Plants take in CO_2 or do not give out O_2

180. A manufacturer of electronic circuits has a stock of 200 resistors, 120 transistors and 150 capacitors and is required to produce two types of circuits A and B. Type A requires 20 resistors, 10 transistors and 10 capacitors. Type B requires 10 resistors, 20 transistors and 30 capacitors. If the profit on type A circuit is ₹ 50 and that on type B circuit is ₹ 60, then which of the following constraint does not hold for the given problem?

a. $2x+y\le 20$ *b.* $x+2y\ge 12$

c. $x+3y\le 15$ *d.* All of these

ANSWERS

Physics

1. (d)	**2.** (a)	**3.** (b)	**4.** (b)	**5.** (a)	**6.** (c)	**7.** (c)	**8.** (a)	**9.** (a)	**10.** (c)
11. (b)	**12.** (d)	**13.** (c)	**14.** (a)	**15.** (c)	**16.** (a)	**17.** (b)	**18.** (d)	**19.** (b)	**20.** (b)
21. (c)	**22.** (a)	**23.** (b)	**24.** (d)	**25.** (c)	**26.** (a)	**27.** (c)	**28.** (b)	**29.** (c)	**30.** (b)
31. (c)	**32.** (c)	**33.** (a)	**34.** (b)	**35.** (b)	**36.** (a)	**37.** (c)	**38.** (b)	**39.** (d)	**40.** (b)
41. (b)	**42.** (d)	**43.** (a)	**44.** (a)	**45.** (c)	**46.** (b)	**47.** (b)	**48.** (a)	**49.** (b)	**50.** (b)
51. (b)	**52.** (d)	**53.** (d)	**54.** (b)	**55.** (c)	**56.** (d)	**57.** (d)	**58.** (a)	**59.** (a)	**60.** (a)

Chemistry

61. (d)	**62.** (d)	**63.** (c)	**64.** (d)	**65.** (c)	**66.** (b)	**67.** (d)	**68.** (c)	**69.** (b)	**70.** (d)
71. (c)	**72.** (b)	**73.** (b)	**74.** (b)	**75.** (b)	**76.** (d)	**77.** (a)	**78.** (d)	**79.** (b)	**80.** (d)
81. (b)	**82.** (a)	**83.** (b)	**84.** (a)	**85.** (b)	**86.** (a)	**87.** (d)	**88.** (c)	**89.** (d)	**90.** (d)
91. (d)	**92.** (c)	**93.** (b)	**94.** (b)	**95.** (b)	**96.** (d)	**97.** (a)	**98.** (d)	**99.** (c)	**100.** (a)
101. (d)	**102.** (c)	**103.** (b)	**104.** (a)	**105.** (b)	**106.** (c)	**107.** (c)	**108.** (d)	**109.** (d)	**110.** (a)
111. (a)	**112.** (c)	**113.** (b)	**114.** (b)	**115.** (b)	**116.** (c)	**117.** (d)	**118.** (c)	**119.** (d)	**120.** (c)

Mathematics

121. (d)	**122.** (b)	**123.** (c)	**124.** (b)	**125.** (a)	**126.** (c)	**127.** (a)	**128.** (c)	**129.** (c)	**130.** (c)
131. (a)	**132.** (a)	**133.** (a)	**134.** (b)	**135.** (b)	**136.** (d)	**137.** (d)	**138.** (c)	**139.** (c)	**140.** (d)
141. (b)	**142.** (d)	**143.** (d)	**144.** (b)	**145.** (c)	**146.** (d)	**147.** (a)	**148.** (c)	**149.** (b)	**150.** (d)
151. (d)	**152.** (a)	**153.** (c)	**154.** (a)	**155.** (b)	**156.** (b)	**157.** (d)	**158.** (b)	**159.** (c)	**160.** (b)
161. (b)	**162.** (d)	**163.** (d)	**164.** (b)	**165.** (c)	**166.** (d)	**167.** (c)	**168.** (c)	**169.** (a)	**170.** (b)
171. (a)	**172.** (c)	**173.** (a)	**174.** (b)	**175.** (a)	**176.** (c)	**177.** (c)	**178.** (c)	**179.** (b)	**180.** (b)

HINTS & SOLUTIONS

Physics

1. *(d)* Acceleration is maximum when displacement is maximum.

i.e. at $t = T$

Force is zero when displacement is zero.

i.e. at $t = \frac{T}{4}, \frac{3T}{4}$

Potential energy is maximum, when displacement is maximum.

i.e. at $t = \frac{T}{2}, T$

2. *(a)* Here, $\phi = 10t^2 - 50t + 250$

$$\therefore \quad e = \frac{-d\phi}{dt} = \frac{-d}{dt}(10t^2 - 50t + 250) = -(20t - 50)$$

At $\quad t = 3\text{s}, e = -(20 \times 3 - 50) = -10 \text{ V}$

3. *(b)* Wavelengths, $\lambda_1 = 5600 \text{ Å}$ and $\lambda_2 = 4200 \text{ Å}$

Now, $\quad \frac{\beta_2}{\beta_1} = \frac{\lambda_2}{\lambda_1} = \frac{4200}{5600} \quad [\beta \propto \lambda]$

or $\quad \beta_2 = \frac{6}{8} \times \beta_1 = \frac{6}{8} \times 3.2 \times 10^{-4}$

$$= 2.4 \times 10^{-4} \text{ m}$$

Decrease in fringe width, $\Delta\beta = \beta_1 - \beta_2$

$$= (3.2 - 2.4) \times 10^{-4}$$

$$= 0.8 \times 10^{-4} \text{ m}$$

4. *(b)* Power required to move the vehicle,

$$P = \mathbf{F} \cdot \mathbf{v} \Rightarrow F = \frac{P}{v} = \frac{7500}{20} = 375 \text{ N}$$

5. *(a)* The situation can be drawn as

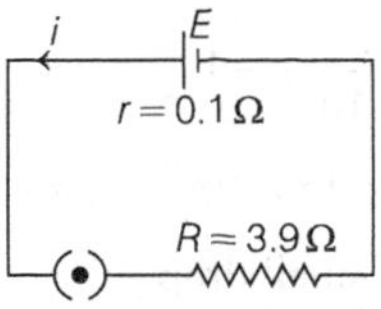

$$\therefore \quad V = E - ir$$

where, r is the internal resistance of cell.

Also, $\quad$ current, $i = \frac{E}{R + r}$

$$\Rightarrow \quad V = E - \left(\frac{E}{R + r}\right)r$$

Putting numerical values, we have

$E = 2 \text{ V}, \ r = 0.1\Omega$ and $R = 3.9\Omega$

$$\Rightarrow V = 2 - \left(\frac{2}{3.9 + 0.1}\right) \times 0.1 \Rightarrow V = 1.95 \text{ V}$$

6. *(c)* As we know, fringe width, $\beta_1 = \frac{\lambda D}{d}$

According to question, $\beta_2 = \lambda\left(\frac{2D}{2d}\right) = \frac{\lambda D}{d}$

[slit width and distance of screen both are doubled]

$$\Rightarrow \quad \beta_1 = \beta_2$$

7. *(c)* Given, $N_0 = 1600$ count/s

$N = 100$ count/s, at $t = 8$s

Number of nuclei left undecayed after n half-lives,

$$N = N_0\left(\frac{1}{2}\right)^n \Rightarrow 100 = 1600\left(\frac{1}{2}\right)^n$$

$$\Rightarrow \quad \left(\frac{1}{2}\right)^n = \frac{1}{16} \Rightarrow \left(\frac{1}{2}\right)^n = \left(\frac{1}{2}\right)^4$$

$$n = 4 \text{ half-lives}$$

Four half-lives equivalent to 8s, so 6 s is equals to three half-lives.

Counting rate observed after 6 s will be,

$$= N_0\left(\frac{1}{2}\right)^3 = \frac{1600}{8} = 200$$

8. *(a)* $I = \frac{1}{2}MR^2 = \frac{1}{2}(V \times \rho)R^2 = \frac{1}{2}(\pi R^2 t \times \rho) \times R^2$

$$\Rightarrow \quad I \propto R^4$$

$$\therefore \quad \frac{I_1}{I_2} = \left(\frac{R_1}{R_2}\right)^4 = \left(\frac{0.2}{0.6}\right)^4 = \frac{1}{81}$$

9. *(a)* Given, length, $l = 0.5$ m, radius, $r = 1$ cm $= 0.01$ m and current, $I = 5$ A.

The number of turns per unit length is

$$n = \frac{500}{0.5} = 1000 \text{ turns m}^{-1}$$

$$l/r = 50$$

i.e. $\quad l >> r.$

Hence, we can use the long solenoid formula.

Magnetic field, $B = \mu_0 nI$

$$= 4\pi \times 10^{-7} \times 10^3 \times 5$$

$$= 6.28 \times 10^{-3} \text{ T}$$

10. *(c)* For transition from $n = 2$ to $n = 1$, using Rydberg's formula, we get

$$\frac{1}{\lambda} = R(Z)^2\left(\frac{1}{1^2} - \frac{1}{2^2}\right)$$

For $\ _1\text{H}^1, \frac{1}{\lambda_1} = R(1)^2\left(\frac{3}{4}\right)$

For ${}_1H^2$, $\frac{1}{\lambda_2} = R(1)^2\left(\frac{3}{4}\right)$

For ${}_2He^4$, $\frac{1}{\lambda_3} = R(2)^2\left(\frac{3}{4}\right)$

For, ${}_3Li^8$, $\frac{1}{\lambda_4} = R(3)^2\left(\frac{3}{4}\right)$

$\Rightarrow \frac{1}{\lambda_1} = \frac{1}{\lambda_2} = \frac{1}{4\lambda_3} = \frac{1}{9\lambda_4}$

$\therefore \lambda_1 = \lambda_2 = 4\lambda_3 = 9\lambda_4$

11. (*b*) When force is applied on *A*, acceleration produced will be

$$\frac{F_A}{m_A + m_B} = \frac{\mu m_A g}{m_B} \quad \ldots \text{(i)}$$

When force is applied on *B*, acceleration produced will be

$$\frac{F_B}{m_A + m_B} = \frac{\mu m_A g}{m_A} \quad \ldots \text{(ii)}$$

Dividing these two equations, we get

$$\frac{F_B}{F_A} = \frac{m_B}{m_A}$$

$$\therefore \quad F_B = \frac{m_B}{m_A} \cdot F_A = \frac{8}{4} \times 12 = 24 \text{ N}$$

12. (*d*) Generator axis of a cylinder in a line lying on it's surface and parallel to axis of cylinder. By parallel axis theorem,

$$I = \frac{MR^2}{2} + MR^2 = \frac{3}{2}MR^2$$

13. (*c*) Energy of electron, $E_n = \frac{-13.6}{n^2}Z^2$

In first excited state, $E_{H_2} = \frac{-13.6(1)^2}{(2)^2} = -3.4 \text{ eV}$

and $E_{He} = \frac{-13.6(2)^2}{(2)^2} = -13.6 \text{ eV}$

H_2 atom gives excitation energy $(13.6 - 3.4 = 10.2 \text{ eV})$ to helium atom.

Now, energy of He ion $= -13.6 + 10.2 = -3.4$ eV

Again, $E = \frac{-13.6}{n^2} \times Z^2 \Rightarrow n = \sqrt{\frac{13.6 \times 4}{3.4}} = 4$

14. (*a*) From the given *x*-*t* graph, it is clear that

At $t = 0, \frac{dx}{dt} = 0$

$\therefore$ Velocity $v = \frac{dx}{dt} = 0$, at $t = 0$

As time passes $\frac{dx}{dt}$ increases.

$\therefore$ Velocity and hence acceleration changes.

15. (*c*) For incident radiation at same intensity and at varying frequencies, the given graph represents the variation of photocurrent with collector plate potential. This can be as shown in graph below

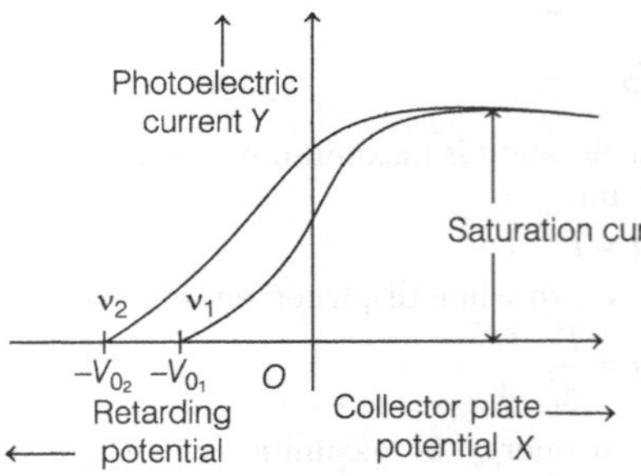

Thus, X = collector plate potential,

Y = photocurrent and Z = saturation current.

16. (*a*) If the block is sliding with constant velocity, then

$$mg\sin\theta = \mu N + ma\sin\theta \quad \ldots \text{(i)}$$

and $N + ma\cos\theta = mg\cos\theta$

$$\Rightarrow \quad N = m(g-a)\cos\theta \quad \ldots \text{(ii)}$$

From Eqs. (i) and (ii), we get

$m(g-a)\sin\theta = \mu m(g-a)\cos\theta$

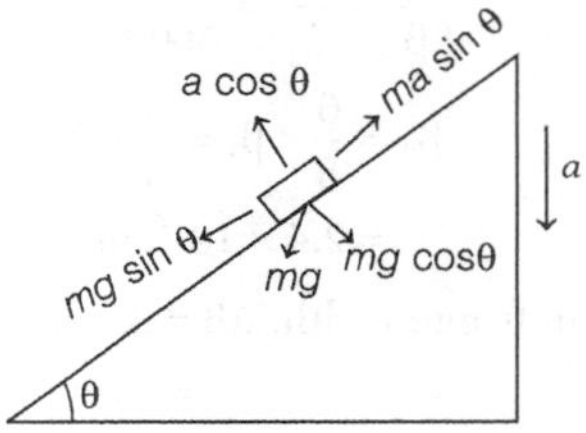

$\Rightarrow \mu = \tan\theta = \tan 30° = \frac{1}{\sqrt{3}}$

17. (*b*) Magnetic susceptibility, $\chi = \mu_r - 1$

or $\chi = \frac{\mu}{\mu_0} - 1$

or $499 = \frac{\mu}{4\pi \times 10^{-7}} - 1$

or $\mu = 500 \times 4\pi \times 10^{-7} = 2\pi \times 10^{-4} \text{ Hm}^{-1}$

18. (*d*) Let r = radius of small drop

R = radius of big drop

Then, volume of 2 small drops = Volume of 1 big drop

i.e. $\frac{4}{3}\pi R^3 = 2 \times \frac{4}{3}\pi r^3$

$\Rightarrow R = 2^{1/3}r$

Now, $\frac{v_1}{v_2} = \frac{r^2}{R^2} = \frac{r^2}{(2^{1/3}r)^2}$

Therefore, $v_2 = 5 \times 4^{1/3} \text{ cms}^{-1}$

19. (*b*) Given, $R_A = R_B$

$$\Rightarrow \frac{v^2 \sin 2\theta}{g} = \frac{(v/2)^2 \sin(2 \times 45°)}{g}$$

$\Rightarrow \quad \sin 2\theta = \frac{1}{4}$ or $\theta = \frac{1}{2}\sin^{-1}\left(\frac{1}{4}\right)$

$\therefore \quad \theta = \frac{1}{2}\sin^{-1}\left(\frac{1}{4}\right)$

20. (*b*) Maximum kinetic energy of a photoelectron emitted from a metallic surface,

$$K_{max} = \frac{1}{2}mv^2 = eV_0 \quad \text{...(i)}$$

where, V_0 is the stopping potential.

Given, frequency of incident light $= \nu_1$ and stopping potential $= V_1$, then according to Einstein's photoelectric equation,

$$K_{max} = h\nu_1 + \phi_0$$

$$\Rightarrow \quad h\nu_1 = \phi_0 + eV_1 \quad \text{[using Eq. (i)] ... (ii)}$$

Similarly, if light of frequency ν_2 irradiates the surface, then

$$h\nu_2 = \phi_0 + eV_2 \quad \text{...(iii)}$$

From Eqs. (ii) and (iii), we get

$$\therefore \quad h(\nu_1 - \nu_2) = e(V_1 - V_2)$$

$$\frac{h}{e}(\nu_1 - \nu_2) = V_1 - V_2$$

$\therefore$ Stopping potential will be $V_2 = V_1 - \frac{h}{e}(\nu_1 - \nu_2)$

21. (*c*) Here, $R = n^{1/3}r \Rightarrow r = n^{-1/3}R$

and $W = (4\pi r^2 \times n - 4\pi R^2)T$

$= (4\pi R^2 n^{1/3} - 4\pi R^2)T$

$= 4\pi R^2 (n^{1/3} - 1)T$

$W \propto (n^{1/3} - 1)$

22. (*a*) $K = K_0 - mgh$, Here $K =$ kinetic energy at height h, $K_0 =$ initial kinetic energy. Variation of K with h is linear. At highest point kinetic energy is not zero.

23. (*b*) $F =$ Force developed

$$F = YA\alpha(\Delta\theta) = 10^{11} \times 10^{-4} \times 10^{-5} \times 100 = 10^4 \text{ N}$$

24. (*d*) We know that, $pV^\gamma =$ constant [using, $pV = RT$]

$TV^{\gamma-1} =$ constant

$T_1V_1^{\gamma-1} = T_2V_2^{\gamma-1}$

$T_1 = \left(\frac{V_2}{V_1}\right)^{\gamma-1} \cdot T_2$

$300 = \left(\frac{8}{27}\right)^{2/3} T_2$

$\Rightarrow \quad T_2 = 675 \text{ K} = 402°\text{C}$

25. (*c*) In a *p*-*n* junction, the loss of electrons from the *n*-region and the gain of electrons by the *p*-region causes a difference of potential across the junction of the two regions. The polarity of this potential is such as to oppose further flow of carriers, so that a condition of equilibrium exists. Since, the *n*-side has lost electrons and *p*-side has acquired electrons. So, the potential of *n*-side is thus positive to that *p*-side.

So, the potential across the junction is correctly depicted in option (c).

26. (*a*) From the given wavefroms, the following truth table can be made

Time interval	Input		Output
	A	B	
$0 - t_1$	0	0	0
$t_1 - t_2$	1	0	1
$t_2 - t_3$	1	1	1
$t_3 - t_4$	0	1	1
$t_4 - t_5$	0	0	0
$t_5 - t_6$	1	0	1

The truth table is required to OR gate.

So, logic circuit gate is OR gate.

27. (*c*) Magnetic field at the centre of a current-carrying conductor,

$$B_c = \frac{\mu_0 I}{2r} \quad \text{...(i)}$$

Magnetic field at axial point due to a current-carrying conductor at distance of r,

$$B_a = \frac{\mu_0 I r^2}{2(r^2 + d^2)^{3/2}}$$

$$\Rightarrow \quad B_a = \frac{\mu_0 I r^2}{2(2r^2)^{3/2}} \quad (d = r)\text{...(ii)}$$

Now, $\frac{B_c}{B_a} = \frac{\mu_0 I}{2r} \times \frac{2(2r^2)^{3/2}}{\mu_0 I r^2} = 2\sqrt{2}$

$B_c : B_a = 2\sqrt{2} : 1$

28. (*b*) Work done by friction may be positive, negative and zero. Work done by conservative internal forces may be zero in a round trip but it is non-zero for non-conservative internal forces.

29. (*c*) Acceleration due to gravity at depth d below the surface of earth,

$$g_d = g\left(1 - \frac{d}{R}\right) \quad \text{...(i)}$$

Acceleration due to gravity at height h from the surface of the earth,

$$g_h = g\left(1 - \frac{2h}{R}\right) \quad \text{...(ii)}$$

Here, $g_h = g_d$

$\therefore \quad g\left(1 - \frac{2h}{R}\right) = g\left(1 - \frac{d}{R}\right) \Rightarrow \frac{2h}{R} = \frac{d}{R}$

$\therefore \quad d = 2h$

Thus, $d = 2 \times 5 = 10$ km

30. (*b*) We know that, current density,

$$J = nev_d \quad \ldots(i)$$

But drift velocity, $v_d = \dfrac{eE\tau}{m}$ ...(ii)

From Eqs. (i) and (ii), we get

$$J = ne \cdot \frac{eE\tau}{m}$$

$$J = \frac{ne^2E\tau}{m} \Rightarrow J \propto \tau$$

Since, on increasing temperature, relaxation time (τ) decreases, therefore current density through wire decreases.

31. (*c*) For second's pendulum at the surface of earth

$$2 = 2\pi\sqrt{\frac{l_e}{g_e}} \quad \ldots(i)$$

$$\left[\because T = 2\pi\sqrt{\frac{l}{g}} \text{ and for second pendulum, } T = 2\text{s}\right]$$

For second's pendulum at the surface of moon

$$2 = 2\pi\sqrt{\frac{l_m}{g_m}} \quad \ldots(ii)$$

From Eqs. (i) and (ii), we get

$$\frac{l_e}{g_e} = \frac{l_m}{g_m} \Rightarrow l_m = \left(\frac{g_m}{g_e}\right)l_e$$

As, $g_m = \dfrac{1}{6}g_e \Rightarrow l_m = \dfrac{l_e}{6} = \dfrac{1}{6}$ times $\quad (\because l_e = 1\text{ m})$

32. (*c*) Orbital velocity of satellite is $v_0 = \sqrt{gR}$ which is independent of mass of satellite.
Option (c) is correct.

33. (*a*) Force in air, $F = \dfrac{1}{4\pi\varepsilon_0} \cdot \dfrac{q_1q_2}{r^2}$

where, ε_0 is the permittivity of free space

and force in medium, $F_m = \dfrac{1}{4\pi\varepsilon_0\varepsilon_r} \cdot \dfrac{q_1q_2}{r^2}$

where, ε_r is relative permittivity.

$$F_{\text{medium}} = \frac{\varepsilon_0}{\varepsilon} \cdot \frac{1}{4\pi\varepsilon_0} \frac{q_1q_2}{r^2} \quad \left(\because \frac{\varepsilon}{\varepsilon_0} = \varepsilon_r\right)$$

$$\Rightarrow \quad F_{\text{medium}} = \frac{\varepsilon_0}{\varepsilon}F$$

34. (*b*) According to the given condition,

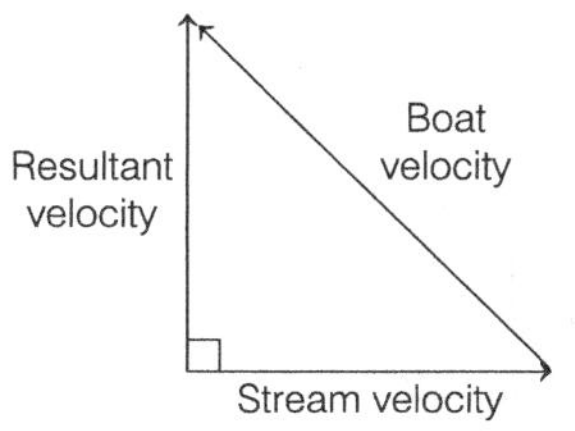

Resultant velocity of boat $= \dfrac{1\text{ km}}{0.25\text{ h}} = 4\text{ kmh}^{-1}$

Also, (velocity of river)^2 + (resultant velocity)^2 = (velocity of boat)^2

$\therefore$ Velocity of river $= \sqrt{(5)^2 - (4)^2} = 3\text{ kmh}^{-1}$

35. (*b*) When a sphere encloses an electric dipole, the situation is as shown

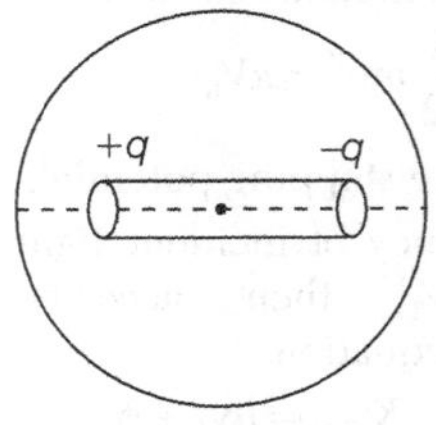

Given, $\quad q = \pm 3 \times 10^{-6}$ C

Thus, according to Gauss's law, the net electric flux across the closed surface is equal to $1/\varepsilon_0$ times the net charge enclosed by it, i.e.

$$\phi_E = \frac{q_{\text{enclosed}}}{\varepsilon_0} = \frac{q_+ + q_-}{\varepsilon_0} = \frac{+3\times10^{-6} - 3\times10^{-6}}{\varepsilon_0} = 0$$

Hence, electric flux across the sphere is zero.

36. (*a*) We know for an ideal gas,

$$pV = nRT \Rightarrow V = \left(\frac{nR}{p}\right)T$$

Slope of the *V*-*T* graph, $m = \dfrac{dV}{dT} = \dfrac{nR}{p}$

[m = slope of *V*-*t* graph]

$$\Rightarrow \quad m \propto \frac{1}{p} \quad [\because nR = \text{constant}]$$

$$\Rightarrow \quad p \propto \frac{1}{m}$$

Hence, $\dfrac{p_1}{p_2} = \dfrac{m_2}{m_1} > 1$

Where, p = pressure, V = volume
n = number of moles of gases,
R = gas constant
T = temperature

where, m_1 is slope of the graph corresponding to p_1 and similarly m_2 is slope corresponding to p_2.

$$\Rightarrow \quad p_2 < p_1 \text{ or } p_1 > p_2$$

37. (*c*) Speed of sound in a gas $v = \sqrt{\dfrac{\gamma RT}{M}}$

$$\frac{v_{N_2}}{v_{He}} = \sqrt{\frac{\gamma_{N_2}}{\gamma_{He}} \times \frac{M_{He}}{M_{N_2}}} = \sqrt{\frac{(7/5)}{(5/3)} \times \frac{4}{28}} = \frac{\sqrt{3}}{5}$$

38. (*b*) For a uniform electric field **E** say, along the *X*-axis, the equipotential surfaces are planes perpendicular to the *X*-axis, i.e. planes parallel to the *YZ*-plane.

39. *(d)* $\therefore \lambda = \frac{v}{f} = \frac{350}{350} = 1\text{m} = 100 \text{ cm}$

Also, path difference (Δx) between the waves at the point of observation is $AP - BP = 25$ cm. Hence,

$$\Rightarrow \quad \Delta\phi = \frac{2\pi}{\lambda}(\Delta x) = \frac{2\pi}{1} \times \left(\frac{25}{100}\right) = \frac{\pi}{2}$$

$$\therefore \quad A = \sqrt{(a_1)^2 + (a_2)^2 + 2a_1a_2 \cos\Delta\phi}$$

$$\Rightarrow \quad A = \sqrt{(a_1)^2 + (a_2)^2} \quad [\cos\Delta\phi = \cos\pi/2 = 0]$$

$$= \sqrt{(0.3)^2 + (0.4)^2} = 0.5 \text{ mm}$$

40. *(b)* If student measures 3.50 cm, it means that there is an uncertainly of order 0.01cm.

For vernier scale with 1 MSD = 1 mm and 9 MSD = 10 VSD

LC of vernier caliper = 1 MSD − 1VSD

$$= \frac{1}{10}\left(1 - \frac{9}{10}\right) = \frac{1}{100} \text{cm}$$

41. *(b)* According to the question, the given arrangement of nine plates is equivalent to the parallel combination of 8 capacitors.

The capacity of each capacitor,

$$C = \frac{\varepsilon_0 A}{d} = \frac{8.854 \times 10^{-12} \times 5 \times 10^{-4}}{0.885 \times 10^{-2}} = 0.5 \text{ pF}$$

Hence, the capacity of the unit of 8 capacitors

$$= 8C = 8 \times 0.5 = 4\text{pF}$$

42. *(d)* $R_A = \frac{10}{3KA} \qquad \left(R = \frac{l}{KA}\right)$

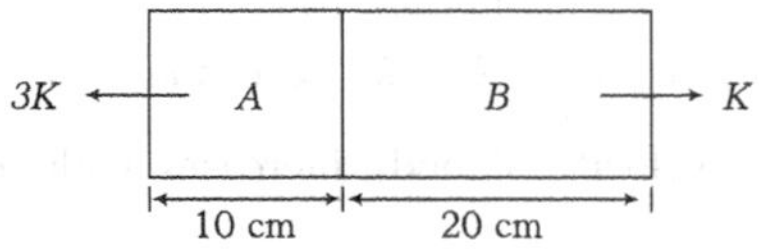

$$R_B = \frac{20}{KA} \Rightarrow \frac{R_A}{R_B} = \frac{1}{6}$$

So let $R_A = R$, then $R_B = 6R$

$$\text{Heat current, } H = \frac{\text{Temperature difference}}{\text{Total resistance}}$$

$$= \frac{35}{7R} = \frac{5}{R}$$

Now, temperature difference across A

$$= H \times R_A = \frac{5}{R} \times R = 5°\text{C}$$

43. *(a)* From Ohm's law, $R = \frac{V}{I}$

$\Rightarrow \ln R = \ln V - \ln I$

$$\Rightarrow \frac{\Delta R}{R} = \frac{\Delta V}{V} + \frac{\Delta I}{I} = 3\% + 3\% = 6\%$$

44. *(a)* Each capacitor will have equal charges. When they are joined as described, they will be in parallel combination. The positive charge will cancel out negative charge of each other.

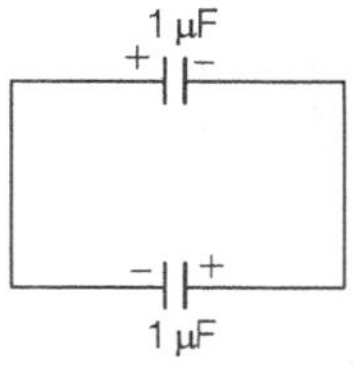

So, net charge in each capacitor will be zero.

45. *(c)* On comparing with $y = a \cos(\omega t + kx - \phi)$, we get

$$k = \frac{2\pi}{\lambda} = 0.02\pi \Rightarrow \lambda = 100 \text{ cm} \Rightarrow \Delta\phi = \frac{\pi}{2}$$

Hence, path difference between them,

$$\Delta x = \frac{\lambda}{2\pi} \times \Delta\phi = \frac{\lambda}{2\pi} \times \frac{\pi}{2} = \frac{\lambda}{4} = \frac{100}{4} = 25 \text{ cm}$$

46. *(b)* According to question, diagram is shown below,

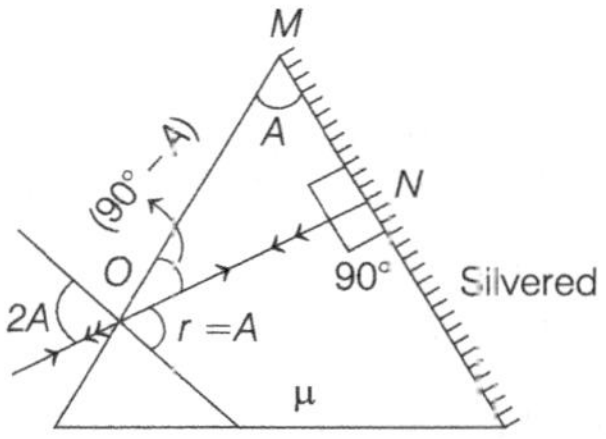

So, $\angle MON = 90° - A$

and $\quad \angle r = 90° - (90° - A) \Rightarrow \angle r = A$

By Snell's law, $\frac{\sin i}{\sin r} = \mu \Rightarrow \frac{\sin(2A)}{\sin(A)} = \mu$

$$\Rightarrow \frac{2\sin A \cos A}{\sin A} = \mu \Rightarrow \mu = 2\cos A$$

47. *(b)* $\therefore D_{\text{skip}} = 2h\sqrt{\left(\frac{\nu}{\nu_c}\right)^2 - 1} = 2 \times 150\sqrt{\left(\frac{300 \times 10^3}{100 \times 10^3}\right)^2 - 1}$

$$= 2 \times 150 \times 2\sqrt{2} = 300 \times 2 \times 1.414$$

$$= 2.828 \times 300 = 848.4 \simeq 849 \text{ km}$$

48. *(a)* It is an electromagnetic wave. The frequency of the microwave oven must match the resonant frequency of the water molecules.

49. *(b)* It is a case of normal adjustment.

Hence, $M = f_o/f_e$

Also, $\quad M = \beta/\alpha$

Therefore, $\frac{\beta}{\alpha} = \frac{f_o}{f_e}$

Here, $f_o = 60 \text{ cm}, f_e = 5 \text{ cm}, \alpha = 2°$

Hence, $\beta = 24°$.

50. *(b)* $Y = \overline{\overline{A} \cdot \overline{B}} = \overline{\overline{A}} + \overline{\overline{B}} = A + B$

Thus, the combination of the gates produces OR gate.

51. *(b)* $\therefore B_0 = \frac{E_0}{c} = \frac{18}{3\times 10^8} = 6\times 10^{-8}$ T

52. *(d)* Area $\propto$ Total energy radiated $\propto T^4$

$$\Rightarrow \frac{A_2}{A_1} = \left(\frac{T_2}{T_1}\right)^4 = \left(\frac{273+327}{273+27}\right)^4$$

$$= \left(\frac{600}{300}\right)^4 = \frac{16}{1} \text{ or } 16:1$$

53. *(d)* Work done in an adiabatic process,

$$W = \frac{nR}{\gamma - 1}(T_i - T_f) \quad \ldots\text{(i)}$$

Here, $W = 6R$ J, $n = 1$ mol,

$R = 8.31\ \text{Jmol}^{-1}\text{K}^{-1}, \gamma = \frac{5}{3}, T_i = T$ K

Substituting given values in Eq. (i), we get

$$\therefore \quad 6R = \frac{R}{\left(\frac{5}{3} - 1\right)}(T - T_f)$$

$$\Rightarrow \quad 6R = \frac{3R}{2}(T - T_f)$$

$$\Rightarrow \quad T - T_f = 4$$

$$\therefore \quad T_f = (T - 4)\text{ K}$$

54. *(b)* When $X_L = X_C$, i.e. $\omega L = 1/\omega C$. The circuit is in resonance. Impedance is equal to resistance alone. i.e. impedance has minimum value.

Hence, due to the minimum value of Z, I will be maximum.

55. *(c)* Here, $E_m = \frac{1}{2}E_c$

Therefore,

$$E_{\max} = E_c + E_m = E_c + \frac{1}{2}E_c = 1.5\ E_c$$

$$E_{\min} = E_c - E_m = E_c - \frac{1}{2}E_c = 0.5\ E_c$$

Also, $m_a = \frac{E_{\max} + E_{\min}}{E_{\max} + E_{\min}} = \frac{1.5\ E_c - 0.5 E_c}{1.5\ E_c + 0.5\ E_c}$

$$m_a = \frac{E_c}{2.0 E_c} = 0.5$$

56. *(d)* We know that with increase in temperature length of a wire changes as

$$L_t = L_o(1 + \alpha\Delta T)$$

where, ΔT is change in the temperature, L_o is original length, α is coefficient of linear expansion and L_t is length at temperature T.

Now we can write, $\Delta L = L_t - L_o = L_o\,\alpha\Delta T$

Young's modulus $(Y) =$

$$\frac{\text{Stress}}{\text{Strain}} = \frac{FL_o}{A\times\Delta L} = \frac{FL_o}{AL_o\,\alpha\Delta T} \propto \frac{1}{\Delta T}$$

As, $\quad Y \propto \frac{1}{\Delta T}$

When temperature increases ΔT increases, hence Y decreases.

57. *(d)* Quantity of heat liberated in the ammeter of resistance R

(i) due to direct current of 3 A

$$= \left((3)^2\frac{R}{J}\right)$$

(ii) due to alternating current of 4 A

$$= \left[(4)^2\frac{R}{J}\right]$$

Total heat produced per second

$$= \frac{(3)^2R}{J} + \frac{(4)^2R}{J} = \frac{25R}{J}$$

Let the equivalent alternating current be I virtual ampere, then

$$\frac{I^2R}{J} = \frac{25R}{J} \text{ or } I = 5\text{ A}$$

58. *(a)* $\sqrt{x} = t + 1$

Squaring both sides, we get $x = (t+1)^2 = t^2 + 2t + 1$

Differentiating it w.r.t. time t, we get

$$\frac{dx}{dt} = 2t + 2$$

Velocity, $v = \frac{dx}{dt} = 2t + 2 \Rightarrow v \propto t$

Hence, velocity of body increases with increase of time.

59. *(a)* $\tan\delta = \frac{V}{H} = 45°$. Hence, $V = H$

When rotated through $45°$ out of magnetic meridian, the vertical component remains unchanged, but the horizontal component changes to $H\cos 45° = H/\sqrt{2}$.

Hence, $\tan\delta' = \frac{V}{H/\sqrt{2}} = \sqrt{2} \Rightarrow \delta' = \tan^{-1}\sqrt{2}$

60. *(a)* $\therefore$ Induced emf

$$= \frac{\text{Work done in taking a charge } q \text{ once along the loop}}{\text{Charge } q}$$

i.e. $\quad V = \frac{W}{q} \Rightarrow W = Vq$

MOCK TEST 3

Chemistry

61. *(d)* Sucrose + $H_2O \rightleftharpoons$ Glucose + Fructose

We know that, $R = 8.314 \text{ J mol}^{-1}\text{K}^{-1}$

Given, $T = 300$ K; $K_C = 2 \times 10^{13}$

$$\Delta G° = -RT \ln K_C \text{ or } -2.303\, RT \log K_C$$

$$\therefore \quad \Delta G° = -2.303 \times 8.314 \text{ J mol}^{-1}\text{ K}^{-1} \times 300 \text{ K} \times \log(2 \times 10^{13})$$

$$\Rightarrow \quad \Delta G° = -7.64 \times 10^4 \text{ J mol}^{-1}.$$

62. *(d)* We know that, osmotic pressure,

$$\pi = CRT = \frac{w \times R \times T}{M \times V}$$

$$\Rightarrow \quad 16.4 = \frac{10 \times 1000}{180 \times 100} \times 0.082 \times T$$

$$\therefore \quad T = \frac{16.4 \times 180}{0.082 \times 100} = 360 \text{ K}$$

63. *(c)*

	A	+ 2B	$\rightleftharpoons$ 2C	+ D
Initial moles	1.1	2.2	0	0
Moles at equil.	1.0	2.0	0.2	0.1

Equilibrium constant for the reaction, $K = \frac{[C]^2[D]}{[A][B]^2}$

$$\therefore \quad K = \frac{[0.2/V]^2[0.1/V]}{[1/V][2/V]^2} = 0.001$$

64. *(d)* In equimolar liquid mixture,

$$\chi_A = 0.5, \chi_B = 0.5$$
$$p = p_A^{\circ}\chi_A + p_B^{\circ}\chi_B$$

So, $p = 0.5 \times 150 + 0.5 \times 100 = 125$

Now, let Y_B be the mole fraction of vapour B then

$$Y_B = \frac{\chi_B p^{\circ}_B}{p} = \frac{0.5 \times 100}{125} = 0.4$$

65. *(c)* Dihydrogen is obtained as a byproduct in the manufacture of sodium hydroxide and chlorine by electrolysis of brine solution.

During electrolysis, the reactions that take place are as follows

At anode $2Cl^-(aq) \longrightarrow Cl_2(g) + 2e^-$

At cathode $2H_2O(l) + 2e^- \longrightarrow H_2(g) + 2OH^-(aq)$

The overall reaction is

$$2Na^+(aq) + 2Cl^-(aq) + 2H_2O(l)$$
$$\downarrow$$
$$Cl_2(g) + H_2(g) + 2Na^+(aq) + 2OH^-(aq)$$

66. *(b)* The amide on reduction with $LiAlH_4$ yields amine.

$$\underset{\text{Alkyl amide}}{R-CONH_2} \xrightarrow[\text{(ii) } H_2O]{\text{(i) } LiAlH_4} \underset{\text{Alkyl amine}}{RCH_2NH_2}$$

67. *(d)* The reaction of CO with H_2O is as follows :

$$CO + H_2O \longrightarrow CO_2 + H_2$$

So, the products obtained are carbon dioxide and hydrogen.

68. *(c)* The product (A) formed is phenol. Chlorobenzene on reaction with sodium hydroxide (NaOH) at temperature (623 K) and pressure (300 atm) gives phenol.

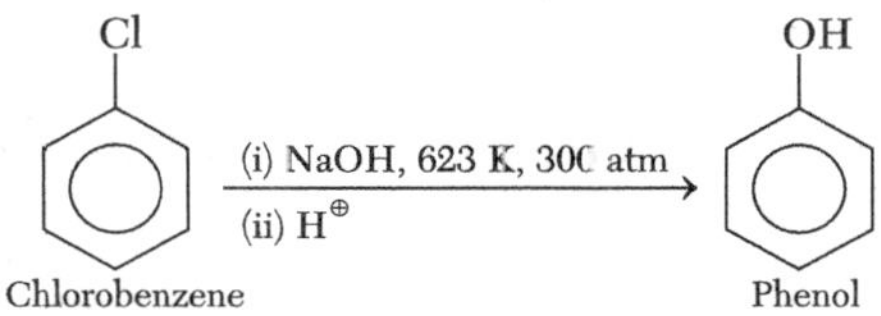

Chlorobenzene Phenol

69. *(b)* According to Bohr model, radius of orbit

$$r_n = \frac{a_0 \times n^2}{Z},$$

where a_0 = Bohr radius

(Radius of 1st orbit of H-atom)

For, Li^{2+}, $Z = 3$ and $n = 2$

$$\therefore \quad r = \frac{2^2 \times a_0}{3} = \frac{4a_0}{3}$$

70. *(d)* Since, —OH and —CH_3 groups are *ortho* and *para*-directing. The major product obtained in the given reaction are as follows

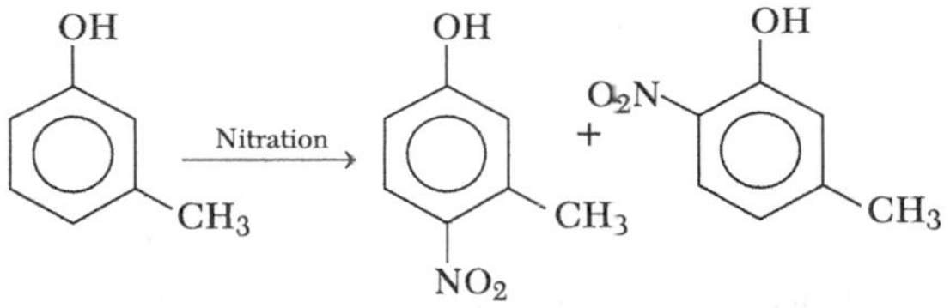

3-methyl phenol 3-methyl-4-nitrophenol 3-methyl-6-nitrophenol

71. *(c)* Hybridisation of carbon atoms in different compounds is shown below

(a) $\underset{sp}{CH}\equiv\underset{sp}{C}-\underset{sp}{C}\equiv\underset{sp}{CH}$

(b) $H-\underset{sp}{C}\equiv\underset{sp}{C}-H$

(c) $\underset{sp^2}{CH_2}=\underset{sp}{C}=\underset{sp^2}{CH_2}$

(d) $\underset{sp^2}{CH_2}=\underset{sp^2}{CH}-\underset{sp^2}{CH}=\underset{sp^2}{CH_2}$

In options (a), (b) and (d), all carbon atoms are in same hybridisation state, i.e. in sp, sp and sp^2 -hybridisation respectively. Only option (c) does not contain all the carbon atom in same hybridisation.

72. *(b)* The ozonolysis reaction of the given compounds are as follows :

(a) 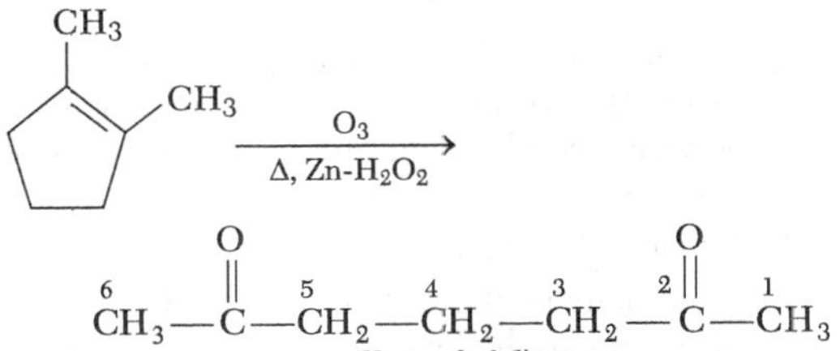

Heptan -2, 6-dione

(b) 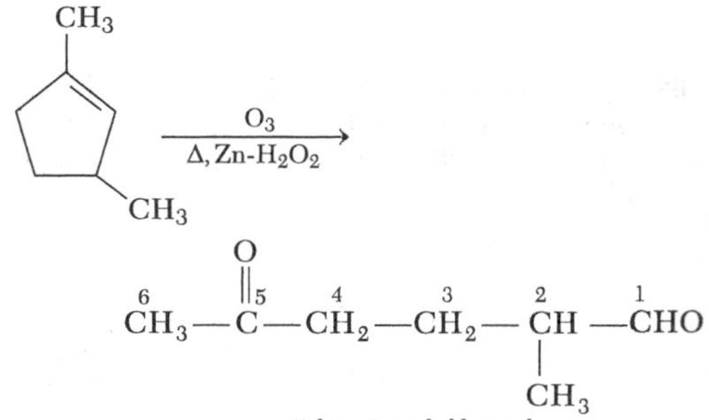

5-keto-2-methyl hexanal

(c) 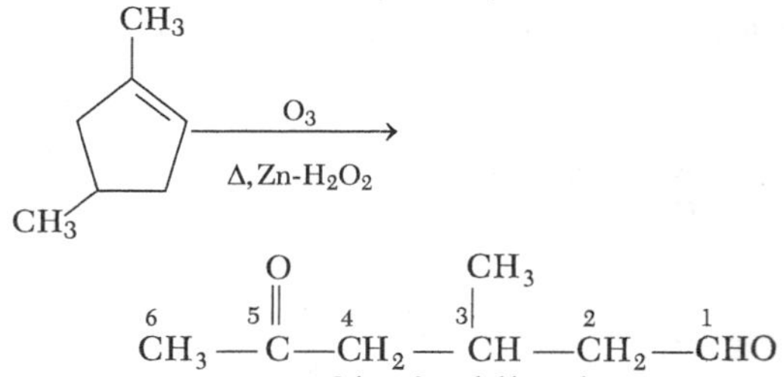

5-keto-3-methyl hexanal

(d) 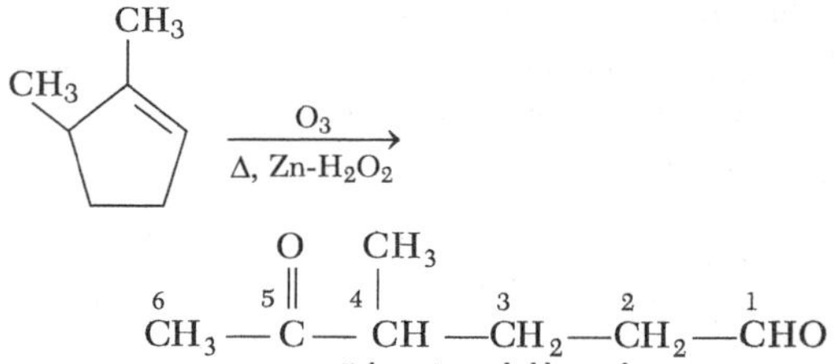

5-keto-4-methyl hexanal

Thus, compound given in option (b) gives 5-keto-2-methyl hexanal.

73. *(b)* van der Waals' equation is given by

$$\left(p+\frac{a}{V^2}\right)(V-b)=RT$$

At low pressure, V decreases. Thus, a/V^2 increases. However, V is still large enough in comparison to 'b'. Hence, 'b' can be neglected. Thus, van der Waals' equation becomes

$$\left(p+\frac{a}{V^2}\right)V=RT \Rightarrow pV+\frac{a}{V}=RT$$

$$\Rightarrow \quad pV=RT-\frac{a}{V} \Rightarrow \frac{pV}{RT}=1-\frac{a}{VRT}$$

$$Z=1-\frac{a}{VRT} \qquad \left[\frac{pV}{RT}=Z\right]$$

74. *(b)* Receptors are selective in nature as they bind to a particular type of chemical messenger. This is because, their binding sites have different shape, structure and amino acid composition.

75. *(b)* Heat absorbed, $q=500$ cal

Work done by the system, $W=-350$ cal

According to the first law of thermodynamics,

$\Delta E=q+W=500+(-350)=+150$ cal

76. *(d)* According to ideal gas equation,

$$pV=nRT$$

or $$n=\frac{pV}{RT}=\frac{3170\times10^{-3}}{8.134\times300}=1.27\times10^{-3}\text{ mol}$$

77. *(a)* Density of a crystal

$$d=\frac{M\times Z}{N_A\times a^3} \Rightarrow M=\frac{d\times N_A\times a^3}{Z}$$

Given, $d=9\times10^3$ kg m^{-3}

$M=$ molar mass of the solid

$Z=4$ (for fcc crystal)

$N_A=$ Avogadro's constant $=6\times10^{23}$ mol^{-1}

$a=$ edge length of the unit cell $=200\sqrt{2}$ pm $=200\sqrt{2}\times10^{-12}$ m

On substituting all the given values, we get

$$=\frac{(9\times10^3)\times(6\times10^{23})\times(200\sqrt{2}\times10^{-12})^3}{4}$$

$$=0.0305\text{ kg mol}^{-1}.$$

78. *(d)* The synthesis of acetic acid by Kolbe (1845) and that of methane by Berthelot (1856) showed that organic compounds could be synthesised from inorganic sources in a laboratory.

79. *(b)* At low pressure, curve is almost straight line, i.e.

$$\frac{x}{m}\propto p \text{ or } \frac{x}{m}=kp$$

Hence, it follows first order kinetics.

80. *(d)* ClO_3^- and SO_3^{2-} ions are isoelectronic and isostructural. Structural formula of given options is as follows

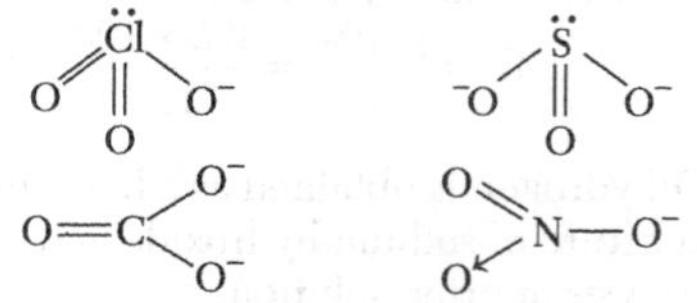

Number of electrons

$CO_3^{2-}=4+18+2=24$, $SO_3^{2-}=6+18+2=26$

$ClO_3^-=7+18+1=26$, $NO_3^-=5+18+1=24$

Hence, ClO_3^- and SO_3^{2-} are isoelectronic as both have same number of electrons and are isostructural as both are pyramidal in shape.

81. *(b)* At state of equilibrium,

$$\Delta G=-RT\ln K$$

$$-nFE^\circ=-RT\,2.303\log K_C$$

$$E^\circ=\frac{+RT2.303\log K_C}{+2F} \quad (n=2,\text{ for Daniell cell})$$

At equilibrium, $E^\circ_{cell}=1.1$

$$\therefore \quad \frac{2.303\,RT}{2F}\log K_C=1.1$$

$$\Rightarrow \quad \log K_C=\frac{2.2}{0.059} \quad \text{[on solving]}$$

82. *(a)* Silica is added to the copper pyrites ore when taken in reverberatory furnace for extraction of copper because silica removes the impurity of FeO present in the copper pyrites as slag ($FeSiO_3$).

83. *(b)* The given reaction is as follows :

$$\overset{0}{Mg}(s) + H_2SO_4(l) \longrightarrow H_2(g) + \overset{+2}{Mg}SO_4(s)$$

Loss of e^- (oxidation takes place)

Thus, oxidation of Mg to $MgSO_4$ takes place.

84. *(a)* Internuclear distance between Cu-atoms in solid copper = 256 pm.

Metallic radius $= \frac{1}{2} \times$ length between two atoms

$$= \frac{1}{2} \times 256 = 128 \text{ pm}$$

85. *(b)* According to law of conservation of mass,

mass of reactants = mass of products

$\therefore\ 6.3 + 15.0 = 18.0 + x$ or $x = 21.3 - 18.0 = 3.3$ g

86. *(a)* Lyophobic colloids are readily precipitated (or coagulated) on addition of small amounts of electrolytes or by heating, hence they are not stable.

87. *(d)* Mole fraction of solute

$$= \frac{\text{number of moles of solute}}{\text{number of moles of solute + number of moles of solvent}}$$

$$\chi_{\text{Solute}} = \frac{n_{\text{Solute}}}{n_{\text{Solute}} + n_{\text{Solvent}}} = \frac{\frac{w_{\text{Solute}}}{Mw_{\text{Solute}}}}{\frac{w_{\text{Solute}}}{Mw_{\text{Solute}}} + \frac{w_{\text{Solvent}}}{Mw_{\text{Solvent}}}}$$

Given, $w_{\text{Solute}} = w_{\text{NaOH}} = 8\text{ g}$

$Mw_{\text{Solute}} = Mw_{\text{NaOH}} = 40 \text{ g mol}^{-1}$

$w_{\text{Solvent}} = w_{H_2O} = 18\text{ g}$

$Mw_{\text{Solvent}} = 18 \text{ g mol}^{-1}$

$$\therefore \quad \chi_{\text{Solute}} = \chi_{\text{NaOH}} = \frac{8/40}{8/40 + 18/18}$$

$$= \frac{0.2}{0.2+1} = \frac{0.2}{1.2} = 0.167$$

$$\text{Now, molality } (m) = \frac{\text{moles of solute}}{\text{mass of solvent (in kg)}}$$

$$= \frac{\frac{w_{\text{Solute}}}{Mw_{\text{Solute}}}}{w_{\text{Solvent}} \text{ (in g)}} \times 100 = \frac{8/40}{18} \times 1000 = \frac{0.2}{18} \times 1000$$

$= 11.11 \text{ mol kg}^{-1}$

88. *(c)* The IUPAC name of the compound $C_3H_8O_3$ that has two primary alcoholic groups and one secondary alcoholic group is propane-1,2,3-triol.

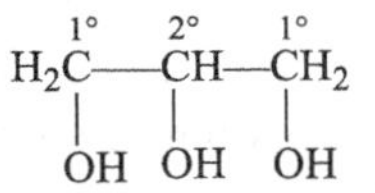

Propane-1, 2, 3-triol

89. *(d)* CH_3I has maximum density because of smallest hydrocarbon part (i.e. CH_3) and contain heaviest halogen (i.e. I).

90. *(d)* Both transition elements and actinoids shows variable valency because the energy of outermost subshell and inner shell is very close.

So, possibility to loss electrons from any of the subshall increases.

91. *(d)* Considering molecular orbital theory (MOT), the electronic configuration of

$$Li_2^+ (Z = 5) = \sigma 1s^2, \sigma^* 1s^2, \sigma 2s^1$$

$$\text{Bond order (BO)} = \frac{N_b - N_a}{2} = \frac{3-2}{2} = \frac{1}{2}$$

The electronic configuration of

$Li_2^- (Z = 7) = \sigma 1s^2, \sigma^* 1s^2, \sigma 2s^2, \sigma^* 2s^1$

$$\text{Bond order (BO)} = \frac{N_b - N_a}{2} = \frac{4-3}{2} = \frac{1}{2}$$

For the species having the same value of BO, the species having lesser number of antibonding electrons $[N_a]$ will be more stable.

Here, N_a of Li_2^+ (2) < N_a of Li_2^- (3)

So, their order of stability will be $Li_2^+ > Li_2^-$.

92. *(c)* $CH_3CH_2CF_2CH_2OH$ is the strongest acid among the given compounds due to more + *I*-effect of two fluorine atoms.

93. *(b)* Aspirin (*o*-acetyl salicylic acid) possesses antipyretic properties.

It's structure is shown below

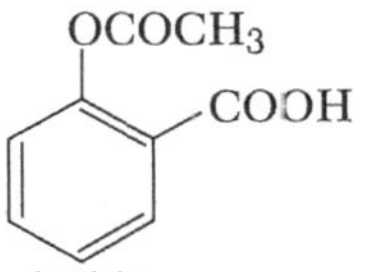

Aspirin

94. *(b)* Deviation of O—O bond length in ozone molecule from the normal bond length seems as single bond length decreases, while double bond length increases from the normal bond length. It is due to resonance.

95. *(b)* As atoms *B* are present at the 8 corners of the cube,

$\therefore$ Number of *B* atoms per unit cell $= 8 \times \frac{1}{8} = 1$

As atom *A* in present at the body centre,

$\therefore$ Number of *A* atoms per unit cell = 1

$\therefore$ Ratio of atoms $A : B = 1 : 1$

Thus, the formula of the compound is *AB*.

96. *(d)* Phase transformations involve the energy changes e.g., ice, requires heat for melting. Normally, this melting takes place at constant pressure and during phase change, temperature remains constant (at 273 K).

97. *(a)* *s*-block elements are reactive metals because they lose the outermost electrons readily to form +1 or +2 ion. The reactivity increases as we go down the group because ionisation enthalpy decreases down the group.

98. *(d)* Alkali metals dissolve in liquid ammonia giving deep blue solutions which are of conducting nature.

$$M + (x+y)\,NH_3 \longrightarrow [M(NH_3)_x]^+ + [e(NH_3)_y]^-$$

Here, M indicate the alkali metals and NH_3 is ammonia.

99. *(c)* The complete reaction is given as follows :

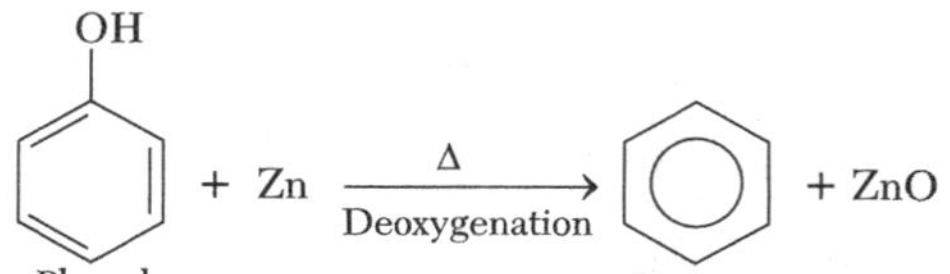

Phenol Benzene

Benzene is formed as the final product.

100. *(a)* Given, $\Delta H_f^\circ [NH_3(g)] = 81.9$ kJ mol^{-1},

Mass of $NH_3 = 26$ g

$$\text{Number of moles of } NH_3 = \frac{\text{Mass}}{\text{Molecular mass}} = \frac{26}{17} = 1.53$$

Now, heat of decomposition for 1.5 moles of NH_3

$= \text{number of moles} \times \text{standard enthalpy}$

$= 1.5 \times 81.9 = 122.9$ kJ

101. *(d)* While, naming the compound, alkene gets priority over functional group (—Br) and numbering starts from alkene side. Hence, IUPAC name is 4-bromo-3-methyl pent-2-ene.

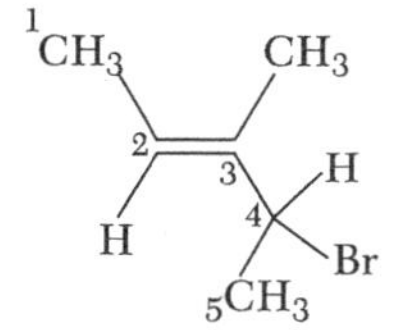

102. *(c)* Pentan-1-ol gives best yield of dialkylether on being heated with a trace of sulphuric acid. It is a primary alcohol and readily undergoes substitution reaction to give ether.

103. *(b)* If carbon atoms form a closed chain in the compound then the compound is known as cycloalkanes.

104. *(a)* The reaction shown below is Wolff-Kishner reduction :

$$>C{=}O \xrightarrow[-H_2O]{H_2NNH_2} >C{=}NNH_2 \xrightarrow[\text{Heat}]{\text{KOH/ethylene glycol}} >CH_2 + N_2\uparrow$$

In this reaction, the carbonyl group of aldehydes and ketones is reduced to —CH_2 group on treatment with hydrazine followed by heating with sodium or potassium hydroxide in high boiling solvent such as ethylene glycol.

105. *(b)* In the given mechanism, structure (II) is incorrect. The correct structure (II) is as follows :

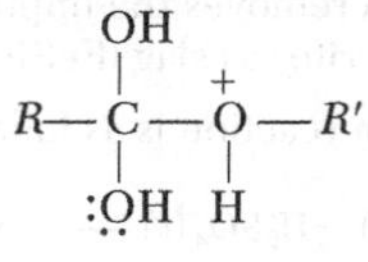

It is a tetrahedral intermediate.

106. *(c)* The type of isomerism exhibited by given isomers (a) and (b) is geometrical isomerism and they (both) are geometrical isomers. In these molecules, the restricted rotation of atoms or groups around the doubly bonded carbon atoms gives rise to different geometries of the compounds.

107. *(c)* Elements of group 16 form a large number of halides of the type EX_6, EX_4 and EX_2 where E is an element of these group 16 and X is a halogen. The stability of these halides decreases in the order :

$$F^- > Cl^- > Br^- > I^-$$

108. *(d)* In an automobile engine (at high temperature) when fossil fuel is burnt, N_2 and O_2 combine to yield nitric oxide (NO) and nitrogen dioxide (NO_2). Reactions involved are as follows :

$$N_2(g) + O_2(g) \xrightarrow{1483\text{ K}} 2NO(g)$$

$$2NO(g) + O_2(g) \longrightarrow 2NO_2(g)$$

109. *(d)* For a zero order reaction, unit of rate constant is (mol L^{-1} s^{-1}).

Hence, we can easily calculate the concentration of B after 20 min by the following formula,

$$X = kt = 0.6 \times 10^{-3} \times 20 \times 60 = 0.72\text{ M}$$

110. *(a)* The first noble gas compound obtained by mixing PtF_6 and xenon, $Xe^+PtF_6^-$.

111. *(a)* The filling of 4*f*-orbital before 5 *d*-orbital results in a regular decrease in atomic radii called lanthanoid contraction which essentially compensates for the expected increase in atomic size with increasing atomic number.

112. *(c)* The structure and oxidation state of oxoacids of phosphorus are as follows

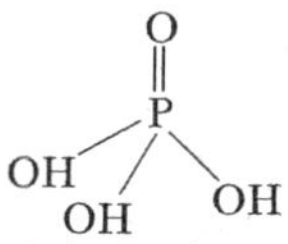

Orthophosphoric acid (H_3PO_4) (O.S. = + 5)

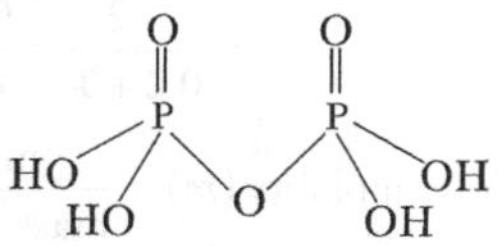

Pyrophosphoric acid ($H_4P_2O_7$) (O.S. = + 5)

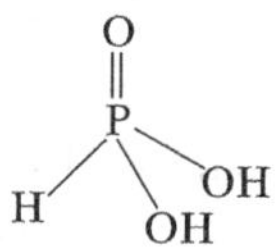

Orthophosphorus acid (H_3PO_3) (O.S. = + 3)

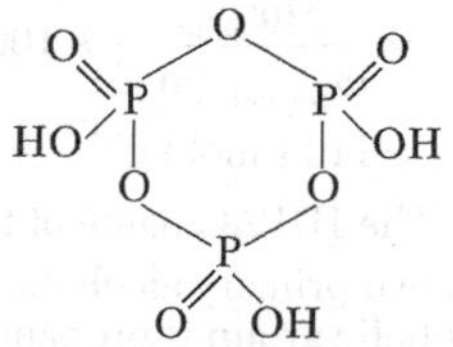

Cyclometaphosphoric acid $(HPO_3)_3$ (O.S. = + 5)

Thus, in orthophosphorus acid, oxidation state of phosphorus is +3.

113. *(b)* Two Br, two (en) and one Cr are parts of the complex. Charge on the complex is +1.

$$\left.\begin{aligned}2\,(Br) &= -2\\ 2\,(en) &= 0\\ 1\,(Cr) &= +3\end{aligned}\right\} = +1$$

Thus, complex ion is $[Cr(en)_2Br_2]^+$

Since, anion is bromide, thus complex dibromido *bis* (ethylenediamine) chromium (III) bromide is written as $[Cr(en)_2Br_2]$ Br.

114. *(b)* On moving down the group, H—*X* bond length increases. So, correct increasing order of their acidic strength is HF < HCl < HBr < HI.

115. *(b)* Glycine (Gly) is not optically active amino acid. It does have a chiral carbon due to the presence of two identical groups

The structure is as follows :

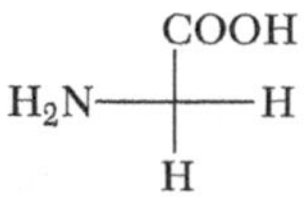

Glycine

116. *(c)* Teflon is manufactured by heating tetrafluoroethene. Reaction is as follows :

$$\underset{\text{Tetrafluoroethene}}{nCF_2 = CF_2} \xrightarrow[\text{High pressure}]{\text{Catalyst}} \underset{\text{Teflon}}{\left(CF_2 - CF_2 \right)_n}$$

117. *(d)* Acidified potassium dichromate oxidises iodides to iodine, sulphides to sulphur, tin(II) to tin(IV), iron(II) salts to iron (III).

118. *(c)* Density of water = 1 g/mL

$\therefore$ 1000 mL = 1000 g

Number of moles of water in 1000 g $(n) = w/m$

$$n = \frac{1000}{18} = 55.56 \text{ moles}$$

$\therefore$ Number of moles in 1 mL of water $(n) = \dfrac{55.56}{1000}$

$= 0.0556$ moles

1 mL of H_2O contain 20 drops.

$\therefore$ Number of moles of H_2O in one drop $= \dfrac{0.0556}{20}$

$= 0.0027$

$$n = \frac{N}{N_A} = \frac{N}{6.023 \times 10^{23}}$$

$$N = n \times N_A = 0.002 \times 6.023 \times 10^{23}$$

$$N = 0.0162 \times 10^{23} = 1.62 \times 10^{21} \text{ molecules}$$

119. *(d)* The primary and secondary valencies of chromium in the complex ion, dichlorodioxalato chromium (III) $[CrCl_2(C_2O_4)_2]^{3-}$ or $[CrCl_2(ox)_2]^{3-}$ are 3 and 6 respectively.

120. *(c)* On going left to right along the period, size decreases.

$\therefore$ Correct order of size is as follows :

$$Dy^{3+} < Gd^{3+} < Pm^{3+} < Ce^{3+}$$

Mathematics

121. *(d)* The given function is $f(x) = \dfrac{x}{x^2+1}$, $\forall\, x \in R$

For $x_1, x_2 \in R$, consider

$$f(x_1) = f(x_2)$$

$$\Rightarrow \quad \frac{x_1}{x_1^2+1} = \frac{x_2}{x_2^2+1}$$

$$\Rightarrow \quad x_1x_2^2 + x_1 = x_2x_1^2 + x_2$$

$$\Rightarrow \quad x_1x_2(x_2 - x_1) = x_2 - x_1$$

$$\Rightarrow \quad (x_2 - x_1)(x_1x_2 - 1) = 0$$

$$\Rightarrow \quad x_1 = x_2 \quad \text{or} \quad x_1x_2 = 1$$

We note that there are points x_1 and x_2 with $x_1 \neq x_2$ and $f(x_1) = f(x_2)$, for instance, if we take $x_1 = 2$ and $x_2 = \dfrac{1}{2}$, then we have $f(x_1) = \dfrac{2}{5}$ and $f(x_2) = \dfrac{2}{5}$ but $2 \neq \dfrac{1}{2}$. Hence, f is not one-one. Also, f is not onto. As, if f is onto, then for $1 \in R$ there exists $x \in R$ such that $f(x) = 1$ which gives $\dfrac{x}{x^2+1} = 1$. But there is no such x in the domain R, since the equation $x^2 - x + 1 = 0$ does not give any real value of x.

122. *(b)* Given that, $f : R - \left\{-\dfrac{4}{3}\right\} \to R$ is defined as

$$f(x) = \frac{4x}{3x+4}$$

Let y be an arbitrary element of range of f.

Then, there exists $x \in R - \left\{-\dfrac{4}{3}\right\}$ such that

$$y = f(x) \Rightarrow y = \frac{4x}{3x+4}$$

$$\Rightarrow 3xy + 4y = 4x \Rightarrow x(4 - 3y) = 4y \Rightarrow x = \frac{4y}{4-3y}$$

Let us define g: range of $f \to R - \left\{-\dfrac{4}{3}\right\}$ as

$$g(y) = \frac{4y}{4-3y}.$$

Now, $(gof)(x) = g(f(x)) = g\left(\dfrac{4x}{3x+4}\right)$

$$= \frac{4\left(\dfrac{4x}{3x+4}\right)}{4 - 3\left(\dfrac{4x}{3x+4}\right)} = \frac{16x}{12x + 16 - 12x} = \frac{16x}{16} = x$$

and $(fog)(y) = f(g(y)) = f\left(\dfrac{4y}{4-3y}\right)$

$$= \frac{4\left(\dfrac{4y}{4-3y}\right)}{3\left(\dfrac{4y}{4-3y}\right)+4} = \frac{16y}{12y+16-12y} = \frac{16y}{16} = y$$

Therefore, $gof = I_{R-\left\{-\frac{4}{3}\right\}}$ and $fog = I_{\text{Range } f}$

Thus, g is the inverse of f *i.e.*, $f^{-1} = g$.

Hence, the inverse of f is the map g: range of $f \to R - \left\{-\dfrac{4}{3}\right\}$, which is given by $g(y) = \dfrac{4y}{4-3y}$.

123. *(c)* It is given that $f: R \to R$ defined as $f(x) = 10x + 7$.

For one-one,

Let $f(x) = f(y)$, where $x, y \in R$

$\Rightarrow \quad 10x + 7 = 10y + 7 \Rightarrow x = y$

Therefore, f is a one-one function.

For onto,

For $y \in R$, let $y = 10x + 7$

$\Rightarrow \quad x = \dfrac{y-7}{10} \in R$

Therefore, for any $y \in R$, there exists

$x = \dfrac{y-7}{10} \in R$ such that

$$f(x) = f\left(\frac{y-7}{10}\right) = 10\left(\frac{y-7}{10}\right) + 7$$

$$= y - 7 + 7 = y$$

Therefore, f is onto. Now, since f is one-one and onto. Therefore, f is an invertible function.

Let us define $g: R \to R$ as $g(y) = \dfrac{y-7}{10}$

Now, we have $gof(x) = g(f(x)) = g(10x+7)$

$$= \frac{(10x+7)-7}{10} = \frac{10x}{10} = x$$

and $\quad fog(y) = f(g(y)) = f\left(\dfrac{y-7}{10}\right)$

$$= 10\left(\frac{y-7}{10}\right) + 7 = y - 7 + 7 = y$$

$\therefore \quad gof = I_R$ and $fog = I_R$

Hence, the required function $g: R \to R$ is defined as $g(y) = \dfrac{y-7}{10}$.

124. *(b)* Given that, $\tan\alpha = \dfrac{1}{7}$ and $\tan\beta = \dfrac{1}{3}$

$$\cos 2\alpha = \frac{1-\frac{1}{49}}{1+\frac{1}{49}} = \frac{\frac{48}{49}}{\frac{50}{49}} \qquad \left\{\cos 2\alpha = \frac{1-\tan^2\alpha}{1+\tan^2\alpha}\right\}$$

$$= \frac{48}{50} = \frac{24}{25}$$

$\Rightarrow \quad \cos 2\alpha = \dfrac{24}{25}$ ...(i)

We know that, $\sin 4\beta = \dfrac{2\tan 2\beta}{1+\tan^2 2\beta}$ ...(ii)

and $\tan 2\beta = \dfrac{2\tan\beta}{1-\tan^2\beta} = \dfrac{2\times\frac{1}{3}}{1-\frac{1}{9}} = \dfrac{\frac{2}{3}}{\frac{8}{9}} = \dfrac{2\times 9}{3\times 8} = \dfrac{3}{4}$

From Eq. (ii),

$$\sin 4\beta = \frac{2\times\frac{3}{4}}{1+\frac{9}{16}} = \frac{\frac{6}{4}}{\frac{25}{16}} = \frac{6\times 16}{4\times 25}$$

$\Rightarrow \quad \sin 4\beta = \dfrac{24}{25}$

$\Rightarrow \quad \sin 4\beta = \cos 2\alpha$

$\therefore \quad \cos 2\alpha = \sin 4\beta$

125. *(a)* Given that, $m\sin\theta = n\sin(\theta + 2\alpha)$

$\therefore \quad \dfrac{\sin(\theta+2\alpha)}{\sin\theta} = \dfrac{m}{n}$

Using componendo and dividendo, we get

$$\frac{\sin(\theta+2\alpha)+\sin\theta}{\sin(\theta+2\alpha)-\sin\theta} = \frac{m+n}{m-n}$$

$$\Rightarrow \frac{2\sin\left(\frac{\theta+2\alpha+\theta}{2}\right)\cdot\cos\left(\frac{\theta+2\alpha-\theta}{2}\right)}{2\cos\left(\frac{\theta+2\alpha+\theta}{2}\right)\cdot\sin\left(\frac{\theta+2\alpha-\theta}{2}\right)} = \frac{m+n}{m-n}$$

$\left[\because \sin x + \sin y = 2\sin\dfrac{x+y}{2}\cdot\cos\dfrac{x-y}{2}\right.$ and $\left.\sin x - \sin y = 2\cos\dfrac{x+y}{2}\sin\cdot\dfrac{x-y}{2}\right]$

$$\Rightarrow \frac{\sin(\theta+\alpha)\cdot\cos\alpha}{\cos(\theta+\alpha)\cdot\sin\alpha} = \frac{m+n}{m-n}$$

$$\Rightarrow \tan(\theta+\alpha)\cdot\cot\alpha = \frac{m+n}{m-n}$$

126. *(c)* Given that,

$2\sin^2\theta = 3\cos\theta$

$\Rightarrow \quad 2 - 2\cos^2\theta = 3\cos\theta$

$\Rightarrow \quad 2\cos^2\theta + 4\cos\theta - \cos\theta - 2 = 0$

$\Rightarrow \quad 2\cos\theta(\cos\theta + 2) - 1(\cos\theta + 2) = 0$

$\Rightarrow \quad (\cos\theta + 2)(2\cos\theta - 1) = 0$

$\Rightarrow \quad \cos\theta = -2$ is not possible $\quad [\because -1 \le \cos\theta \le 1]$

$2\cos\theta = 1$

$\Rightarrow \quad \cos\theta = \dfrac{1}{2} \Rightarrow \cos\theta = \cos\dfrac{\pi}{3}$

MOCK TEST 3

$\therefore \quad \theta = \frac{\pi}{3}$

Also, $\cos\theta = \cos\left(2\pi - \frac{\pi}{3}\right)$

$\Rightarrow \quad \cos\theta = \cos\frac{5\pi}{3}$

$\therefore \quad \theta = \frac{5\pi}{3}$

So, the values of θ are $\frac{\pi}{3}$ and $\frac{5\pi}{3}$.

127. (a) Given that, $x = \sec\phi - \tan\phi$ ...(i)

and $y = \text{cosec}\,\phi + \cot\phi$ ...(ii)

Now, $1 \cdot xy = (\sec\phi - \tan\phi)(\text{cosec}\,\phi + \cot\phi)$

$\Rightarrow xy = \sec\phi \cdot \text{cosec}\,\phi - \text{cosec}\,\phi \cdot \tan\phi + \sec\phi \cdot \cot\phi - \tan\phi \cdot \cot\phi$

$\Rightarrow xy = \sec\phi \cdot \text{cosec}\,\phi - \frac{1}{\cos\phi} + \frac{1}{\sin\phi} - 1$

$\Rightarrow 1 + xy = \sec\phi\,\text{cosec}\,\phi - \sec\phi + \text{cosec}\,\phi$ ...(iii)

From Eqs. (i) and (ii), we get

$x - y = \sec\phi - \tan\phi - \text{cosec}\,\phi - \cot\phi$

$\Rightarrow x - y = \sec\phi - \text{cosec}\,\phi - \frac{\sin\phi}{\cos\phi} - \frac{\cos\phi}{\sin\phi}$

$\Rightarrow x - y = \sec\phi - \text{cosec}\,\phi - \left(\frac{\sin^2\phi + \cos^2\phi}{\sin\phi \cdot \cos\phi}\right)$

$\Rightarrow x - y = \sec\phi - \text{cosec}\,\phi - \frac{1}{\sin\phi \cdot \cos\phi}$

$\Rightarrow x - y = \sec\phi - \text{cosec}\,\phi - \text{cosec}\,\phi \cdot \sec\phi$

$\Rightarrow x - y = -(\sec\phi \cdot \text{cosec}\,\phi - \sec\phi + \text{cosec}\,\phi)$

$\Rightarrow x - y = -(xy + 1)$ [from Eq. (iii)]

$\Rightarrow xy + x - y + 1 = 0$

128. (c) Given, $\cos^{-1}\left(\frac{1}{2}\right) - 2\sin^{-1}\left(\frac{-1}{2}\right)$

$= \cos^{-1}\left(\cos\frac{\pi}{3}\right) - 2\sin^{-1}\left(-\sin\frac{\pi}{6}\right)$

$= \cos^{-1}\left(\cos\frac{\pi}{3}\right) - 2\sin^{-1}\left(\sin\left(\frac{-\pi}{6}\right)\right)$

[$\sin(-x) = -\sin x$]

$= \frac{\pi}{3} - 2\left(\frac{-\pi}{6}\right) \quad \{\cos^{-1}(\cos x) = x, x \in [0, \pi]$,

and $\sin^{-1}(\sin x) = x, x \in \left[-\frac{\pi}{2}, \frac{\pi}{2}\right]\} = \frac{\pi}{3} + \frac{\pi}{3} = \frac{2\pi}{3}$

129. (c) Given,

$\tan^{-1}\left(-\frac{1}{\sqrt{3}}\right) + \cot^{-1}\left(\frac{1}{\sqrt{3}}\right) + \tan^{-1}\left[\sin\left(\frac{-\pi}{2}\right)\right]$

$= \tan^{-1}\left(-\frac{1}{\sqrt{3}}\right) + \cot^{-1}\left(\frac{1}{\sqrt{3}}\right) + \tan^{-1}\left(-\sin\frac{\pi}{2}\right)$

[$\sin(-\theta) = -\sin\theta$]

$= \frac{-\pi}{6} + \frac{\pi}{3} - \tan^{-1}\left(\sin\frac{\pi}{2}\right)$ [$\tan^{-1}(-x) = -\tan^{-1}x$]

$= \frac{\pi}{6} - \tan^{-1}(1) = \frac{\pi}{6} - \frac{\pi}{4} = -\frac{\pi}{12}$

130. (c) We have,

$\tan^{-1}\left[\frac{a\cos x - b\sin x}{b\cos x + a\sin x}\right] = \tan^{-1}\left[\frac{\frac{a\cos x - b\sin x}{b\cos x}}{\frac{b\cos x + a\sin x}{b\cos x}}\right]$

$= \tan^{-1}\left[\frac{\frac{a}{b} - \tan x}{1 + \frac{a}{b}\tan x}\right]$

$= \tan^{-1}\frac{a}{b} - \tan^{-1}(\tan x)$

$= \tan^{-1}\frac{a}{b} - x$

131. (a) Let $P(n): x^n - 1$ is divisible by $(x - k)$.

For $n = 1$, $x^1 - 1$ is divisible by $(x - k)$.

Since, if $x - 1$ is divisible by $x - k$. Then, the least positive integral value of k is 1.

132. (a) The given equation is $|z| = z + 1 + 2i$ ...(i)

Let $z = x + iy$

From Eq. (i), $|x + iy| = x + iy + 1 + 2i$

$\Rightarrow \sqrt{x^2 + y^2} = x + iy + 1 + 2i$

[$|z| = \sqrt{x^2 + y^2}$]

$\Rightarrow \sqrt{x^2 + y^2} = (x + 1) + i(y + 2)$

On squaring both sides, we get

$x^2 + y^2 = (x + 1)^2 + i^2(y + 2)^2 + 2i(x + 1)(y + 2)$

$\Rightarrow x^2 + y^2 = x^2 + 2x + 1 - y^2 - 4y - 4 + 2i(x + 1)(y + 2)$

On comparing real and imaginary parts,

$x^2 + y^2 = x^2 + 2x + 1 - y^2 - 4y - 4$

i.e., $2y^2 = 2x - 4y - 3$ ...(ii)

and $2(x + 1)(y + 2) = 0$

$(x + 1) = 0$ or $(y + 2) = 0$

$\Rightarrow x = -1$ or $y = -2$

For $x = -1$, $2y^2 = -2 - 4y - 3$

$2y^2 + 4y + 5 = 0$ [using Eq. (ii)]

$\Rightarrow y = \frac{-4 \pm \sqrt{16 - 2 \times 4 \times 5}}{4}$

$\Rightarrow y = \frac{-4 \pm \sqrt{-24}}{4} \notin R$

For $y = -2$, $2(-2)^2 = 2x - 4(-2) - 3$ [using Eq. (ii)]

$\Rightarrow 8 = 2x + 8 - 3 \Rightarrow 2x = 3 \Rightarrow x = 3/2$

$\therefore z = x + iy = 3/2 - 2i$

133. (a) Let $z = x + iy$

$$\frac{z-1}{z+1} = \frac{x+iy-1}{x+iy+1}, z \neq -1$$

$$= \frac{x-1+iy}{x+1+iy} = \frac{(x-1+iy)(x+1-iy)}{(x+1+iy)(x+1-iy)}$$

$$= \frac{(x^2-1)+iy(x+1)-iy(x-1)-i^2y^2}{(x+1)^2-(iy)^2}$$

$$\Rightarrow \quad \frac{z-1}{z+1} = \frac{(x^2-1)+y^2+i[y(x+1)-y(x-1)]}{(x+1)^2+y^2}$$

Given that, $\frac{z-1}{z+1}$ is a purely imaginary numbers.

Then, $\frac{(x^2-1)+y^2}{(x+1)^2+y^2} = 0$

$\Rightarrow \quad x^2-1+y^2 = 0 \Rightarrow x^2+y^2 = 1$

$\Rightarrow \quad \sqrt{x^2+y^2} = \sqrt{1} \Rightarrow |z| = 1 \; [\because |z| = \sqrt{x^2+y^2}]$

134. (b) Given that, $z = 2 - i$

It is rotated about origin through an angle $\frac{\pi}{2}$ in the clockwise direction.

$\therefore$ New position $= ze^{-i\pi/2} = (2-i)\,e^{-i\pi/2}$

$$= (2-i)\left[\cos\left(\frac{-\pi}{2}\right) + i\sin\left(\frac{-\pi}{2}\right)\right] = (2-i)[0-i]$$

$$= -2i - 1 = -1 - 2i$$

135. (b) Given expression $= (1-i)^n\left(1-\frac{1}{i}\right)^n$

$$= (1-i)^n(i-1)^n \cdot i^{-n} = (1-i)^n(1-i)^n(-1)^n \cdot i^{-n}$$

$$= [(1-i)^2]^n(-1)^n \cdot i^{-n} = (1+i^2-2i)^n(-1)^n i^{-n}$$

$$[\because i^2 = -1]$$

$$= (1-1-2i)^n(-1)^n i^{-n} = (-2)^n \cdot i^n(-1)^n i^{-n}$$

$$= (-1)^{2n} \cdot 2^n = 2^n$$

136. (d) Here, we have to find the number of integers greater than 7000 with the digits 3, 5, 7, 8 and 9. So, with these digits, we can make maximum five-digit number because repeatition is not allowed.

Now, all the five-digit numbers are greater than 7000.

Number of ways of forming 5-digit number

$$= 5 \times 4 \times 3 \times 2 \times 1 = 120$$

and all the four-digit numbers greater than 7000 can be formed in following manner.

Thousand place can be filled in 3 ways. Hundred place can be filled in 4 ways. Tenth place can be filled in 3 ways. Units place can be filled in 2 ways.

Thus, we have total number of 4-digit number

$$= 3 \times 4 \times 3 \times 2 = 72$$

$\therefore$ Total number of integers $= 120 + 72 = 192$

137. (d) If all the digits repeated, then number of 5 digit telephone numbers can be formed in 10^5 ways and if no digit repeated, then 5-digit telephone numbers can be formed in ${}^{10}P_5$ ways.

$\therefore$ Required number of ways $= 10^5 - {}^{10}P_5$

$$= 100000 - \frac{10!}{5!}$$

$$= 100000 - 10 \times 9 \times 8 \times 7 \times 6$$

$$= 100000 - 30240 = 69760$$

138. (c) Total number of letters in the word 'INTERMEDIATE' = 12

out of which 6 are consonants and 6 are vowels. The arrangement of these 12 alphabets in which two vowels never come together can be understand with the help of follow manner.

V	C	V	C	V	C	V	C	V	C	V	C	V

6 consonants out of which 2 are alike can be placed in $\frac{6!}{2!}$ ways and 6 vowels, out of which 3 E's alike and 2 I's are alike can be arranged at seven place in ${}^7P_6 \times \frac{1}{3!} \times \frac{1}{2!}$ ways.

$\therefore$Total number of words $= \frac{6!}{2!} \times {}^7P_6 \times \frac{1}{3!} \times \frac{1}{2!} = 151200$

139. (c) Here, $(x+a)^{100} + (x-a)^{100}$

Total number of terms is 102 in the expansion of $(x+a)^{100} + (x-a)^{100}$

50 terms of $(x+a)^{100}$ cancel out 50 terms of $(x-a)^{100}$.

51 terms of $(x+a)^{100}$ get added to the 51 terms of $(x-a)^{100}$.

Alternate Method

$$(x+a)^{100} + (x-a)^{100}$$

$$= {}^{100}C_0\,x^{100} + {}^{100}C_1\,x^{99}a + \ldots + {}^{100}C_{100}\,a^{100}$$

$$+ {}^{100}C_0\,x^{100} - {}^{100}C_1\,x^{99}a + \ldots + {}^{100}C_{100}\,a^{100}$$

$$= 2[\underbrace{{}^{100}C_0\,x^{100} + {}^{100}C_2\,x^{98}a^2 + \ldots + {}^{100}C_{100}\,a^{100}}_{\text{51 terms}}]$$

140. (d) Coefficient of x^n in the expansion of $(1+x)^{2n}$ $= {}^{2n}C_n$

and coefficient of x^n in the expansion of $(1+x)^{2n-1}$ $= {}^{2n-1}C_n$

$$\frac{{}^{2n}C_n}{{}^{2n-1}C_n} = \frac{\frac{(2n)!}{n!n!}}{\frac{(2n-1)!}{n!(n-1)!}} = \frac{(2n)!\,n!\,(n-1)!}{n!\,n!\,(2n-1)!}$$

$$= \frac{2n\,(2n-1)!\,n!\,(n-1)!}{n!\,n(n-1)!\,(2n-1)!} = \frac{2n}{n} = \frac{2}{1} = 2:1$$

141. *(b)* Let first term be a and common difference be d.

Then, $$S_n = \frac{n}{2}[2a + (n-1)d] \quad \text{...(i)}$$

$$\therefore \quad S_{2n} = \frac{2n}{2}[2a + (2n-1)d]$$

$$S_{2n} = n[2a + (2n-1)d] \quad \text{...(ii)}$$

$$S_{3n} = \frac{3n}{2}[2a + (3n-1)d] \quad \text{...(iii)}$$

According to the question, $S_{2n} = 3S_n$

$$n[2a + (2n-1)d] = 3\frac{n}{2}[2a + (n-1)d]$$

$$\Rightarrow \quad 4a + (4n-2)d = 6a + (3n-3)d$$

$$\Rightarrow \quad -2a + (4n - 2 - 3n + 3)d = 0$$

$$\Rightarrow \quad -2a + (n+1)d = 0$$

$$\Rightarrow \quad d = \frac{2a}{n+1} \quad \text{...(iv)}$$

Now,

$$\frac{S_{3n}}{S_n} = \frac{\frac{3n}{2}[2a + (3n-1)d]}{\frac{n}{2}[2a + (n-1)d]} = \frac{6a + (9n-3)\frac{2a}{n+1}}{2a + (n-1)\frac{2a}{n+1}}$$

$$= \frac{6an + 6a + 18an - 6a}{2an + 2a + 2an - 2a} = \frac{24an}{4an}$$

$$\Rightarrow \quad \frac{S_{3n}}{S_n} = 6$$

142. *(d)* Let S_n be sum of the series

$2 + 3 + 6 + 11 + 18 + \quad + t_{50}$.

$\therefore \quad S_n = 2 + 3 + 6 + 11 + 18 + \quad + t_{50}$ ...(i)

and $S_n = 0 + 2 + 3 + 6 + 11 + 18 + \quad + t_{49} + t_{50}$ ...(ii)

On subtracting Eq. (ii) from Eq. (i), we get

$$0 = 2 + 1 + 3 + 5 + 7 + \quad - t_{50}$$

$$\Rightarrow \quad t_{50} = 2 + [1 + 3 + 5 + 7 + \quad \text{upto 49 terms}]$$

$$\therefore \quad t_{50} = 2 + [1 + 3 + 5 + 7 + \quad \text{upto 49 terms}]$$

$$= 2 + \frac{49}{2}[2 \times 1 + 48 \times 2]$$

$$= 2 + \frac{49}{2} \times [2 + 96]$$

$$= 2 + [49 + 49 \times 48]$$

$$= 2 + 49 \times 49 = 2 + (49)^2$$

143. *(d)* Given line is $y = 3 - 3x$.

$$\therefore \quad m = -3$$

Then, slope of the required line $= -\frac{1}{m} = -\frac{1}{3} = \frac{1}{3}$

Equation of the required line is passing through (2, 2) is

$$y - 2 = \frac{1}{3}(x - 2)$$

$$\Rightarrow \quad 3y - 6 = x - 2$$

$$\Rightarrow \quad x - 3y + 4 = 0$$

For y-intercept, put $x = 0$, $0 - 3y + 4 = 0$

$$\Rightarrow \quad y = \frac{4}{3}$$

144. *(b)* Let point $A(x_1, y_1)$ lies on the line $3x + 4y + 5 = 0$, then $3x_1 + 4y_1 + 5 = 0$

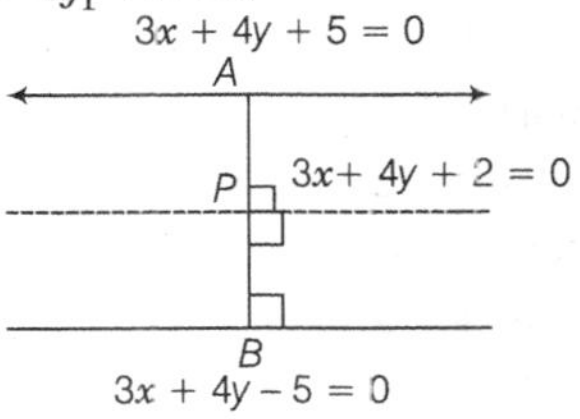

Now, perpendicular distance from A to the line

$3x + 4y + 2 = 0$

$$\Rightarrow \frac{|3x_1 + 4y_1 + 2|}{\sqrt{9+16}} = \frac{|-5-2|}{\sqrt{9+16}} = \left|\frac{-7}{5}\right| = \frac{7}{5}$$

Let point $B(x_2, y_2)$ lies on the line $3x + 4y - 5 = 0$ *i.e.,* $3x_2 + 4y_2 - 5 = 0$.

Now, perpendicular distance from B to the line $3x + 4y + 2 = 0$,

$$\frac{|3x_2 + 4y_2 + 2|}{\sqrt{9+16}} = \frac{|+5-2|}{\sqrt{9+16}} = \frac{3}{5}$$

Hence, the required ratio is $\frac{3}{5} : \frac{7}{5}$, *i.e.* 3 : 7.

145. *(c)* Let ABC be the equilateral triangle with vertex $A(h, k)$.

Let the coordinates of D are (α, β).

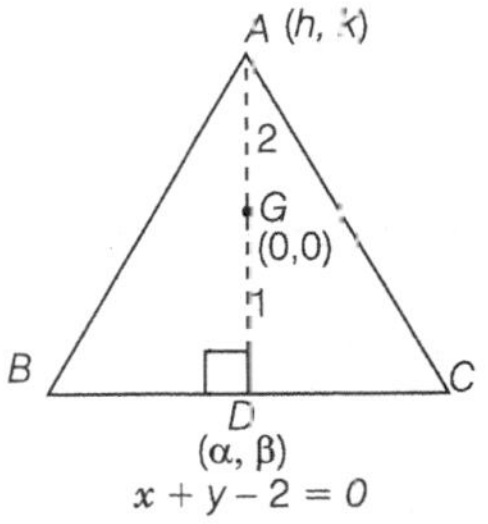

We know that, centroid G divides AD in 2 : 1

$$\therefore \quad 0 = \frac{2\alpha + h}{3} \text{ and } 0 = \frac{2\beta + k}{3}$$

$$\Rightarrow \quad 2\alpha = -h \text{ and } 2\beta = -k \quad \text{...(i)}$$

Also, $D(\alpha, \beta)$ lies on the line $x + y - 2 = 0$.

$$\therefore \quad \alpha + \beta - 2 = 0 \quad \text{...(ii)}$$

Since, the slope of line BC *i.e.,* $m_{BC} = -1$

and slope of the line AG *i.e.,* $m_{AG} = \frac{k-0}{h-0} = \frac{k}{h}$

$$AD \perp BC$$

$\Rightarrow \quad (-1)\cdot\left(\frac{k}{h}\right)=-1$

$\Rightarrow \quad h=k$ ...(iii)

From Eqs. (i) and (iii),

$$2\alpha=-h \text{ and } 2\beta=-h$$

$\therefore \quad \alpha=\beta$

From Eq. (ii), $2\alpha-2=0 \Rightarrow \alpha=1$

If $\alpha=1$, then $\beta=1$

From Eq. (i), $h=-2, k=-2$

So, the vertex A is $(-2,-2)$.

146. *(d)* Given equation of circle,

$$x^2+y^2=16$$

$\therefore$ Radius $=4$ and centre $=(0,0)$

Now, perpendicular from (0, 0) to line $\{y=\sqrt{3}x+k\}$ = Radius of the circle

$$\left|\frac{0-0+k}{\sqrt{3+1}}\right|=4 \quad \text{...(i)}$$

{ Since the distance from the point (m, n) to the line $Ax+By+C=0$ is $d=\left|\frac{Am+Bn+C}{\sqrt{A^2+B^2}}\right|$}

Eq. (i) $\quad \pm\frac{k}{2}=4$

$\therefore \quad k=\pm 8$

147. *(a)* Given equation of the circle is

$$x^2+y^2-6x+12y+15=0 \quad \text{...(i)}$$

On comparing with $x^2+y^2+2gx+2fy+c=0$

$\therefore \quad 2g=-6 \Rightarrow g=-3$

$2f=12 \Rightarrow f=6$

and $\quad c=15$

$\therefore$ Centre $=(-g,-f)=(3,-6)$

So, the centre of the required circle will be (3, – 6).
[since, the circles are concentric]

Radius of the given circle

$$=\sqrt{g^2+f^2-c}$$
$$=\sqrt{9+36-15}=\sqrt{30}$$

Let radius of the required circle $=r_1$

$\therefore$ 2 × Area of the given circle = Area of the required circle

$\Rightarrow \quad 2[\pi(\sqrt{30})^2]=\pi r_1^2$

$\Rightarrow \quad 60=r_1^2 \Rightarrow r_1=\sqrt{60}$

$\therefore \quad \sqrt{g^2+f^2-c}=\sqrt{60}$

$\Rightarrow \quad 9+36-c=60$

$\Rightarrow \quad c=-15$

So, the required equation of circle is $x^2+y^2-6x+12y-15=0$.

148. *(c)* Since, the distance from the focus to the vertex is 5cm. We have, $a=5$. If the origin is taken at the vertex and the axis of the mirror lies along the positive X-axis, the equation of the parabolic section is

$$y^2=4(5)x=20x$$

Note that $x=45$. Thus, $y^2=900$

Therefore, $\quad y=\pm 30$

Hence, $\quad AB=2y=2\times 30=60$ cm.

149. *(b)* Let P and Q be points on the parabola $y^2=6x$ and OP, OQ be the lines joining the vertex O to the points P and Q whose abscissa are 24.

Thus, $\quad y^2=6\times 24=144$ or $y=\pm 12$

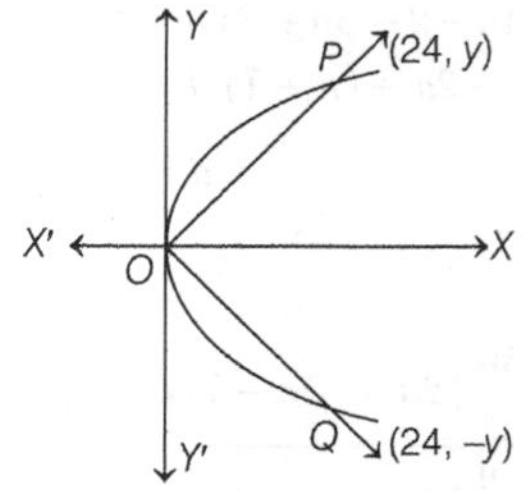

Therefore, the coordinates of the points P and Q are (24, 12) and (24, – 12) respectively. Hence, the lines are

$$y=\pm\frac{12}{24}x \Rightarrow 2y=\pm x$$

150. *(d)* Given that, $e=\frac{1}{\sqrt{2}}$,

latusrectum $=\frac{2b^2}{a}=\frac{2a^2}{a}\left(1-\frac{1}{2}\right)=a$

$[\ b^2=a^2(1-e^2)]$

i.e., semi-major axis.

151. *(d)* Given that, $\frac{a}{e}-ae=8$

Also, $\quad e=\frac{1}{2}$

$\Rightarrow \quad a=\frac{8e}{1-e^2}=\frac{8(4)}{2(3)}=\frac{16}{3} \quad [\ b^2=a^2(1-e^2)]$

$\therefore \quad b=\frac{16}{3}\sqrt{\left(1-\frac{1}{4}\right)}=\frac{16}{3}\frac{\sqrt{3}}{2}=\frac{8\sqrt{3}}{3}$

Hence, the length of minor axis is $\frac{16\sqrt{3}}{3}$.

152. *(a)* Conjugate axis is 5 and distance between foci $=13$
$\Rightarrow 2b=5$ and $2ae=13$.

Now, also we know for hyperbola

$$b^2=a^2(e^2-1) \Rightarrow \frac{25}{4}=\frac{(13)^2}{4e^2}(e^2-1)$$

$\Rightarrow \quad \frac{25}{4}=\frac{169}{4}-\frac{169}{4e^2}$ or $e^2=\frac{169}{144} \Rightarrow e=\frac{13}{12}$

$\therefore \quad a = \dfrac{13}{2e}$

$\Rightarrow \quad a = 6, b = \dfrac{5}{2}$ or hyperbola is $\dfrac{x^2}{36} - \dfrac{y^2}{\frac{25}{4}} = 1$

$\Rightarrow \quad 25x^2 - 144y^2 = 900$

153. *(c)* Multiplying both, we get $3x^2 - y^2 = 48$

or $\quad \dfrac{x^2}{\left(\frac{48}{3}\right)} - \dfrac{y^2}{48} = 1$, which is a hyperbola.

154. *(a)* The equation of any plane through the intersection of the planes

$$3x - y + 2z - 4 = 0$$

and $\quad x + y + z - 2 = 0$ is

$(3x - y + 2z - 4) + \lambda(x + y + z - 2) = 0 \quad \ldots(i)$

The plane passes through the point (2, 2, 1). Therefore, this point will satisfy Eq. (i).

$\therefore \quad (3 \times 2 - 2 + 2 \times 1 - 4) + \lambda(2 + 2 + 1 - 2) = 0$

$\Rightarrow \quad (6 - 4) + 3\lambda = 0 \Rightarrow 2 + 3\lambda = 0$

$\Rightarrow \quad \lambda = \dfrac{-2}{3}$

Substituting this value of λ in Eq. (i), we obtain the required plane as

$$(3x - y + 2z - 4) - \frac{2}{3}(x + y + z - 2) = 0$$

$\Rightarrow \; 9x - 3y + 6z - 12 - 2x - 2y - 2z + 4 = 0$

$\Rightarrow \quad 7x - 5y + 4z - 8 = 0$

This is the required equation of the plane.

155. *(b)* At $x = \dfrac{\pi}{4}$

$$\text{LHL} = \lim_{x \to \frac{\pi}{4}^-} f(x) = \lim_{x \to \frac{\pi}{4}^-} (x + a^2\sqrt{2}\sin x) = a^2 + \frac{\pi}{4}$$

$$\text{RHL} = \lim_{x \to \frac{\pi}{4}^+} f(x) = \lim_{x \to \frac{\pi}{4}^+} (x\cot x + b) = b + \frac{\pi}{4}$$

Since, $f(x)$ is continuous at $x = \dfrac{\pi}{4}$

$\therefore \quad a^2 + \dfrac{\pi}{4} = b + \dfrac{\pi}{4}$

$\therefore \quad a^2 = b \quad \ldots(i)$

At $\quad x = \dfrac{\pi}{2}$

$$\text{LHL} = \lim_{x \to \frac{\pi}{2}^-} f(x) = \lim_{x \to \frac{\pi}{2}^-} (x\cot x + b) = b$$

$$\text{RHL} = \lim_{x \to \frac{\pi}{2}^+} f(x) = \lim_{x \to \frac{\pi}{2}^+} (b\sin 2x - a\cos 2x) = a$$

$f(x)$ is continuous at $x = \dfrac{\pi}{2}$

$\therefore \quad a = b \quad \ldots(ii)$

Solving Eqs. (i) and (ii), we get

$$a^2 - a = 0 \Rightarrow a = 0, 1$$

when $a = 0, b = 0$ and when $a = 1, b = 1$

156. *(b)* Given, $g(x) = [f(2f(x) + 2]^2$

$\therefore g'(x) = 2f(2f(x) + 2) \cdot f'(2f(x) + 2) \cdot 2f'(x)$

$= 4f(2f(x) + 2)f'(2f(x) + 2)f'(x)$

$g'(0) = 4f(2f(0) + 2)f'(2f(0) + 2)f'(0)$

$= 4f(0)f'(0)f'(0) [\; f(0) = -1$ and $f'(0) = -1]$

$= -4$

$\therefore g'(0) = 4f(0)f'(0)f'(0) = -4$

157. *(d)* Given, $y = \log_2 [\log_2(x)]$

$$= \frac{\log_e(\log_2 x)}{\log_e 2} = \frac{\log\left[\frac{\log_e x}{\log_e 2}\right]}{\log_e 2}$$

$$\Rightarrow \quad y = \frac{\log(\log_e x) - \log_e(\log_e 2)}{\log_e 2}$$

On differentiating w.r.t. x, we get

$$\frac{dy}{dx} = \frac{1}{\log_e 2}\left[\frac{1}{x\log_e x} - 0\right] = \frac{\log_2 e}{x\log_e x}$$

158. *(b)* Given, $f(x) = (1 - x)(1 + x^2)(1 - x^4)(1 + x^8)$

Taking log on both sides, we get

$$\log(f(x)) = \log\{(1 + x)(1 + x^2)(1 + x^4)(1 + x^8)\}$$

$$\Rightarrow \log(f(x)) = \log(1 + x) + \log(1 + x^2) + \log(1 + x^4) + \log(1 + x^8)$$

On differentiating both sides w.r.t. x, we get

$$\frac{d}{dx}\log(f(x)) = \frac{d}{dx}\log(1 + x) + \frac{d}{dx}\log(1 + x^2) + \frac{d}{dx}\log(1 + x^4) + \frac{d}{dx}\log(1 + x^8)$$

$$\frac{1}{f(x)} f'(x) = \frac{1}{1 + x}(0 + 1) + \frac{1}{1 + x^2}(0 + 2x) + \frac{1}{1 + x^4}(0 + 4x^3) + \frac{1}{1 + x^8}(0 + 8x^7)$$

$$\Rightarrow \; f'(x) = f(x)\left\{\frac{1}{1 + x} + \frac{2x}{1 + x^2} + \frac{4x^3}{1 + x^4} + \frac{8x^7}{1 + x^8}\right\}$$

$$= (1 + x)(1 + x^2)(1 + x^4)(1 + x^8)\left\{\frac{1}{1 + x} + \frac{2x}{1 + x^2} + \frac{4x^3}{1 + x^4} + \frac{8x^7}{1 + x^8}\right\}$$

$$\therefore \; f'(1) = (1 + 1)(1 + 1)(1 + 1)(1 + 1)\left\{\frac{1}{1 + 1} + \frac{2}{1 + 1} + \frac{4}{1 + 1} + \frac{8}{1 + 1}\right\}$$

$$= 2^4\left\{\frac{1}{2} + 1 + 2 + 4\right\} = 16\left(\frac{15}{2}\right) = 120$$

159. *(c)* Given,

$$f(x) = 1 + nx + \frac{n(n-1)}{2!}x^2 + \frac{n(n-1)(n-2)}{3!}x^3 + \ldots + x^n$$

$$\Rightarrow \quad f(x) = (1+x)^n$$

$$f'(x) = n(1+x)^{n-1}$$

$$f''(x) = n(n-1)(1+x)^{n-2}$$

$$f''(1) = n(n-1)\,2^{n-2}$$

160. *(b)* Given, $y = \log(1+x) - \frac{2x}{(2+x)}$.

On differentiating, we get

$$\frac{dy}{dx} = \frac{d}{dx}\left[\log(1+x) - \frac{2x}{2+x}\right]$$

$$= \frac{1}{1+x} - \frac{(2+x)\frac{d}{dx}(2x) - 2x\frac{d}{dx}(2+x)}{(2+x)^2}$$

$$= \frac{1}{1+x} - \frac{4+2x-2x}{(2+x)^2} = \frac{1}{1+x} - \frac{4}{(2+x)^2}$$

$$= \frac{(2+x)^2 - 4(1+x)}{(1+x)(2+x)^2} = \frac{4+x^2+4x-4-4x}{(1+x)(2+x)^2}$$

$$= \frac{x^2}{(1+x)(2+x)^2}$$

When, $x \in (-1, \infty)$, then $\frac{x^2}{(2+x)^2} > 0$ and $(1+x) > 0$

$\therefore y' > 0$ when $x > -1$.

Hence, y is an increasing function throughout $(x > -1)$ as its domain.

161. *(b)* Given, $f(x) = \frac{e^{2x}-1}{e^{2x}+1}$

$$\therefore \quad f(-x) = \frac{e^{-2x}-1}{e^{-2x}+1} = \frac{1-e^{2x}}{1+e^{2x}} = -f(x)$$

$\therefore f(x)$ is an odd function.

Now, $\quad f'(x) = \frac{4e^{2x}}{(1+e^{2x})^2} > 0, \ \forall\, x \in R$

$\Rightarrow f(x)$ is an increasing function.

162. *(d)* Given curve is $y = e^{2x} + x^2$

at $\quad x = 0, y = 1$

Now, $\quad \frac{dy}{dx} = 2e^{2x} + 2x$

$$\Rightarrow \quad \left.\frac{dy}{dx}\right|_{(0,1)} = 2 + 0 = 2$$

Slope of normal at $(0, 1) = -\frac{1}{2+0} = -\frac{1}{2}$

$\therefore$ Equation of normal is $y - 1 = -\frac{1}{2}(x - 0)$

$$\Rightarrow \quad 2y - 2 = -x$$

$$\Rightarrow \quad x + 2y - 2 = 0$$

$\therefore$ Required distance $= \left|\frac{0+0-2}{\sqrt{1+4}}\right| = \frac{2}{\sqrt{5}}$

163. *(d)* Let one number be x. Then, the other number is $(24 - x)$.

(sum of the two numbers is 24)

Let y denotes the product of the two numbers.

Thus, we have

$$y = x(24 - x) = 24x - x^2$$

On differentiating twice w.r.t. x, we get

$$\frac{dy}{dx} = 24 - 2x \quad \text{and} \quad \frac{d^2y}{dx^2} = -2$$

Now, put $\frac{dy}{dx} = 0$

$$\Rightarrow \quad 24 - 2x = 0 \Rightarrow x = 12$$

At $x = 12$, $\frac{d^2y}{dx^2} = -2 < 0$

By second derivative test, $x = 12$ is the point of local maxima of y. Thus, the product of the numbers is maximum when the numbers are 12 and $24 - 12 = 12$. Hence, the numbers are 12 and 12.

164. *(b)* $\int \frac{e^x(1+x)}{\cos^2(e^x x)}dx$

Let $\quad xe^x = t$

$$\Rightarrow \quad (xe^x + e^x) = \frac{dt}{dx} \Rightarrow dx = \frac{dt}{e^x(x+1)}$$

$$\therefore \int \frac{e^x(1+x)}{\cos^2(e^x x)}dx = \int \frac{e^x(1+x)}{\cos^2 t} \times \frac{dt}{e^x(1+x)}$$

$$= \int \frac{1}{\cos^2 t}dt = \int \sec^2 t\, dt$$

$$= \tan t + C = \tan(xe^x) + C$$

165. *(c)* Let $I = \int \frac{x^2-1}{x^4+x^2+1}dx$

On dividing numerator and denominator by x^2, we get

$$I = \int \frac{1 - \frac{1}{x^2}}{x^2 + 1 + \frac{1}{x^2}}dx$$

$$I = \int \frac{1 - \frac{1}{x^2}}{\left(x + \frac{1}{x}\right)^2 - 1}dx$$

Let $t = x + \frac{1}{x}$

$$\Rightarrow \quad \left(1 - \frac{1}{x^2}\right)dx = dt$$

MOCK TEST 3

$\therefore \quad I = \int \frac{dt}{t^2 - 1}$

$\Rightarrow \quad I = \frac{1}{2(1)} \log \left| \frac{t-1}{t+1} \right| + C$

$\Rightarrow \quad I = \frac{1}{2} \log \left| \frac{x + \frac{1}{x} - 1}{x + \frac{1}{x} + 1} \right| + C$

$\Rightarrow \quad I = \frac{1}{2} \log \left| \frac{x^2 - x + 1}{x^2 + x + 1} \right| + C$

166. *(d)* We have, $I = \int \frac{2x^2 + 3}{(x^2 - 1)(x^2 + 4)} dx$ put $x^2 = t$

Let $\quad \frac{2t + 3}{(t-1)(t+4)} = \frac{A}{t-1} + \frac{B}{t+4} \quad \ldots \text{(i)}$

$\Rightarrow \quad 2t + 3 = A(t + 4) + B(t - 1)$

$\Rightarrow \quad 2t + 3 = (A + B)\,t + 4A - B$

On comparing the coefficients of t and constant term on both the sides, we get

$A + B = 2 \quad \text{and} \quad 4A - B = 3$

On solving the above equations, we get

$A = 1 \quad \text{and} \quad B = 1$

On putting the values of A and B in Eq. (i), we get

$\frac{2t+3}{(t-1)(t+4)} = \frac{1}{t-1} + \frac{1}{t+4}$

$\therefore \quad I = \int \frac{dt}{x^2 - 1} + \int \frac{dt}{x^2 + 4} \quad (\text{Put } t = x^2)$

$= \frac{1}{2} \log \left| \frac{x-1}{x+1} \right| + \frac{1}{2} \tan^{-1} \frac{x}{2} + C$

But, $\quad I = a \log \left| \frac{x-1}{x+1} \right| + b \tan^{-1} \frac{x}{2} + C$

$\therefore \quad a = \frac{1}{2}, b = \frac{1}{2}$

167. *(c)* $\int_0^{2/3} \frac{1}{4 + 9x^2} dx = \frac{1}{9} \int_0^{2/3} \frac{1}{\frac{4}{9} + x^2} dx$

$= \frac{1}{9} \int_0^{2/3} \frac{1}{\left(\frac{2}{3}\right)^2 + x^2} dx$

$= \frac{1}{9} \cdot \frac{1}{2/3} \left[\tan^{-1} \left(\frac{x}{2/3} \right) \right]_0^{2/3}$

$\left(\int \frac{dx}{a^2 + x^2} = \frac{1}{a} \tan^{-1} \frac{x}{a} \right)$

$= \frac{1}{6} \left[\tan^{-1} \left(\frac{3x}{2} \right) \right]_0^{2/3}$

$= \frac{1}{6} \left[\tan^{-1} \left(\frac{3}{2} \cdot \frac{2}{3} \right) - \tan^{-1} 0 \right]$

$= \frac{1}{6} (\tan^{-1} 1 - 0)$

$= \frac{1}{6} \cdot \frac{\pi}{4} = \frac{\pi}{24}$

168. *(c)* Let $I = \int_{-\pi/2}^{\pi/2} (x^3 + x \cos x + \tan^5 x + 1)\, dx$

$\Rightarrow \quad I = \int_{-\pi/2}^{\pi/2} x^3 dx + \int_{-\pi/2}^{\pi/2} x \cos x \, dx + \int_{-\pi/2}^{\pi/2} \tan^5 x \, dx + \int_{-\pi/2}^{\pi/2} 1 \, dx$

We know that,

$$\int_{-a}^{a} f(x) dx = \begin{cases} 2\int_0^a f(x) dx, & \text{if } f(x) \text{ is even} \\ 0, & \text{if } f(x) \text{ is odd} \end{cases}$$

$\therefore \quad I = 0 + 0 + 0 + 2\int_0^{\pi/2} 1 \, dx.$

[x^3, $x \cos x$ and $\tan^5(x)$ are odd functions]

$\therefore \quad I = 2[x]_0^{\pi/2} = \frac{2\pi}{2} = \pi$

169. *(a)* Let $I = \int \frac{x^3}{\sqrt{1 - x^8}} dx$

Put $x^4 = t \Rightarrow 4x^3 dx = dt$

$\Rightarrow \quad dx = \frac{dt}{4x^3}$

$\therefore \quad I = \int \frac{x^3}{\sqrt{1 - t^2}} \frac{dt}{4x^3} = \frac{1}{4} \int \frac{1}{\sqrt{1 - t^2}} dt = \frac{1}{4} \sin^{-1} t + C$

$\left[\int \frac{dx}{\sqrt{a^2 - x^2}} = \sin^{-1} \left(\frac{x}{a} \right) \right]$

$= \frac{1}{4} \sin^{-1}(x^4) + C$

170. *(b)* Given, $y = x$, $x = e$ and $y = \frac{1}{x}$, $x \geq 0$

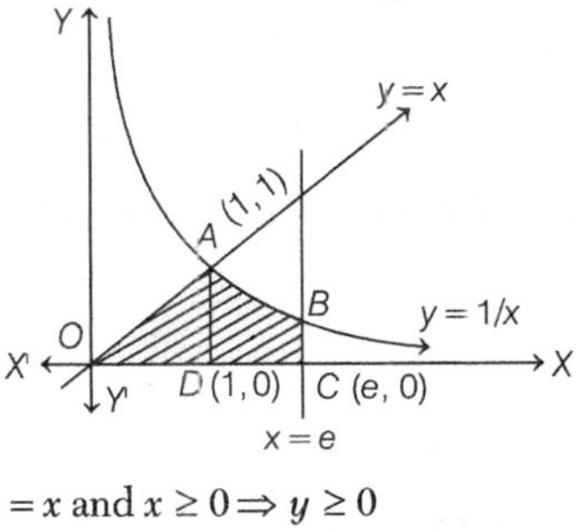

Since, $y = x$ and $x \geq 0 \Rightarrow y \geq 0$

$\therefore$ Area to be calculated in first quadrant shown in figure.

$\therefore$ Area = Area of ΔODA + Area of $ABCD$

$= \frac{1}{2}(1 \times 1) + \int_1^e \frac{1}{x} dx = \frac{1}{2} + [\log|x|]_1^e$

MOCK TEST 3

$$= \frac{1}{2} + [\log|x|]_1^e$$

$$= \frac{1}{2} + 1 = \frac{3}{2} \text{ sq units}$$

171. *(a)* The given function is

$$xy = ae^x + be^{-x} \quad \text{...(i)}$$

On differentiating Eq. (i) w.r.t. x, we get

$$x\frac{dy}{dx} + y = ae^x - be^{-x}$$

Again, differentiating w.r.t. x, we get

$$x\frac{d^2y}{dx^2} + \frac{dy}{dx} + \frac{dy}{dx} = ae^x + be^{-x}$$

$$\Rightarrow \quad x\frac{d^2y}{dx^2} + 2\frac{dy}{dx} - xy = 0 \quad \text{[Using Eq. (i)]}$$

172. *(c)* Given, $\cos y \dfrac{dy}{dx} = e^{x + \sin y} + x^2 e^{\sin y}$

$$\Rightarrow \cos y \, dy = e^{\sin y}(e^x + x^2)\, dx$$

$$\Rightarrow \int \frac{\cos y}{e^{\sin y}} dy = \int (e^x + x^2)\, dx$$

Put $\sin y = t$ in LHS

$$\Rightarrow \cos y \, dy = dt$$

$$\int \frac{dt}{e^t} = \int (e^x + x^2)\, dx$$

$$\Rightarrow \quad -e^{-t} = e^x + \frac{x^3}{3} + C$$

$$\Rightarrow \quad e^x + e^{-\sin y} + \frac{x^3}{3} = C'$$

173. *(a)* Let the line joining the points with position vectors $-2\mathbf{i} + 3\mathbf{j} + 5\mathbf{k}$ and $7\mathbf{i} - \mathbf{k}$ be divided in the ratio $\lambda : 1$ by $\mathbf{i} + 2\mathbf{j} + 3\mathbf{k}$.

$$\therefore \frac{\lambda(7\mathbf{i} - \mathbf{k}) + (-2\mathbf{i} + 3\mathbf{j} + 5\mathbf{k})}{\lambda + 1} = \mathbf{i} + 2\mathbf{j} + 3\mathbf{k}$$

$$\Rightarrow (7\lambda - 2)\mathbf{i} + 3\mathbf{j} + (5 - \lambda)\mathbf{k} = (\lambda + 1)\mathbf{i} + 2(\lambda + 1)\mathbf{j} + 3(\lambda + 1)\mathbf{k}$$

On equating the coefficient of $\mathbf{i}$, we get

$$7\lambda - 2 = \lambda + 1$$

$$\Rightarrow \quad \lambda = \frac{1}{2}$$

Hence, required ratio $= \lambda : 1 = 1 : 2$

174. *(b)* $|\mathbf{OA}| = \sqrt{4 + 4 + 1} = 3$

and $|\mathbf{OB}| = \sqrt{4 + 16 + 16} = 6$

$$|\mathbf{OA}| = 2\mathbf{i} + 2\mathbf{j} + \mathbf{k}$$

$$|\mathbf{OB}| = 2\mathbf{i} + 4\mathbf{j} + 4\mathbf{k}$$

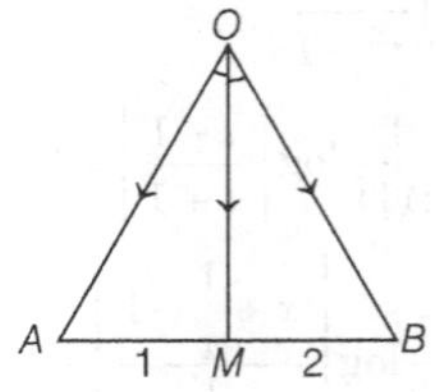

We know, $\dfrac{AM}{MB} = \dfrac{|\mathbf{OA}|}{|\mathbf{OB}|} = \dfrac{3}{6} = \dfrac{1}{2}$

$\therefore$ Postion vector of $M = \dfrac{2\,\mathbf{OA} + \mathbf{OB}}{2 + 1}$

$$= \frac{2(2\mathbf{i} + 2\mathbf{j} + \mathbf{k}) + 1(2\mathbf{i} + 4\mathbf{j} + 4\mathbf{k})}{3}$$

$$= \frac{6\mathbf{i} + 8\mathbf{j} + 6\mathbf{k}}{3}$$

$\therefore$ Length of bisector $|\mathbf{OM}| = \sqrt{\dfrac{1}{9}(36 + 64 + 36)}$

$$= \frac{\sqrt{136}}{3} \text{ units}$$

$\therefore$ Required length of a vector is $\dfrac{\sqrt{136}}{3}$.

175. *(a)* We have, $A = \begin{bmatrix} 6 & 8 & 5 \\ 4 & 2 & 3 \\ 9 & 7 & 1 \end{bmatrix} \Rightarrow A' = \begin{bmatrix} 6 & 4 & 9 \\ 8 & 2 & 7 \\ 5 & 3 & 1 \end{bmatrix}$

$$A = \left(\frac{A + A'}{2}\right) + \left(\frac{A - A'}{2}\right)$$

Here, $\dfrac{A + A'}{2}$ is the symmetric part of A and $\dfrac{A - A'}{2}$ is the skew-symmetric part of A.

$\therefore$ We have, symmetric matrix, $B = \dfrac{A + A'}{2}$

$$= \frac{1}{2}\left\{\begin{bmatrix} 6 & 8 & 5 \\ 4 & 2 & 3 \\ 9 & 7 & 1 \end{bmatrix} + \begin{bmatrix} 6 & 4 & 9 \\ 8 & 2 & 7 \\ 5 & 3 & 1 \end{bmatrix}\right\}$$

$$= \frac{1}{2}\begin{bmatrix} 12 & 12 & 14 \\ 12 & 4 & 10 \\ 14 & 10 & 2 \end{bmatrix} = \begin{bmatrix} 6 & 6 & 7 \\ 6 & 2 & 5 \\ 7 & 5 & 1 \end{bmatrix}$$

176. *(c)* We have, $\Delta_1 = \begin{vmatrix} 1 & 1 & 1 \\ yz & zx & xy \\ x & y & z \end{vmatrix}$

By interchanging rows and columns, we get

$$\Delta_1 = \begin{vmatrix} 1 & yz & x \\ 1 & zx & y \\ 1 & xy & z \end{vmatrix} = \frac{1}{xyz}\begin{vmatrix} x & xyz & x^2 \\ y & xyz & y^2 \\ z & xyz & z^2 \end{vmatrix} = \frac{xyz}{xyz} \cdot \begin{vmatrix} x & 1 & x^2 \\ y & 1 & y^2 \\ z & 1 & z^2 \end{vmatrix}$$

$$=(-1)\begin{vmatrix}1 & x & x^2\\ 1 & y & y^2\\ 1 & z & z^2\end{vmatrix} = -\Delta \text{ (interchanging } C_1 \text{ and } C_2)$$

$$\Rightarrow \quad \Delta_1 + \Delta = 0$$

177. *(c)* Since, $A = \begin{bmatrix}5 & 5\alpha & \alpha\\ 0 & \alpha & 5\alpha\\ 0 & 0 & 5\end{bmatrix}$

$$\therefore \quad A^2 = \begin{bmatrix}5 & 5\alpha & \alpha\\ 0 & \alpha & 5\alpha\\ 0 & 0 & 5\end{bmatrix}\begin{bmatrix}5 & 5\alpha & \alpha\\ 0 & \alpha & 5\alpha\\ 0 & 0 & 5\end{bmatrix}$$

$$= \begin{bmatrix}25 & 25\alpha + 5\alpha^2 & 10\alpha + 25\alpha^2\\ 0 & \alpha^2 & 5\alpha^2 + 25\alpha\\ 0 & 0 & 25\end{bmatrix}$$

$$\Rightarrow \quad |A^2| = \begin{vmatrix}25 & 25\alpha + 5\alpha^2 & 10\alpha + 25\alpha^2\\ 0 & \alpha^2 & 5\alpha^2 + 25\alpha\\ 0 & 0 & 25\end{vmatrix}$$

Expanding along R_3,

$$25\begin{vmatrix}25 & 25\alpha + 5\alpha^2\\ 0 & \alpha^2\end{vmatrix} = 625\alpha^2$$

$$\Rightarrow \quad 25 = 625\alpha^2 \qquad \text{(given)}$$

$$\Rightarrow \quad |\alpha| = 1/5$$

178. *(c)* Given that, $P(A \cup B) = \frac{5}{9}$, $P(A) = p$ and $P(B) = \frac{1}{3}$

We know that, $P(A \cap B) = P(A) + P(B) - P(A \cup B)$

$$= p + \frac{1}{3} - \frac{5}{9}$$

$$= p + \frac{3-5}{9}$$

$$= p + \left(\frac{-2}{9}\right) = p - \frac{2}{9}$$

Now, $P\left(\frac{A}{B}\right) = \frac{P(A \cap B)}{P(B)} = p$ (given)

$$\Rightarrow \quad \frac{p - \frac{2}{9}}{\frac{1}{3}} = p \Rightarrow \frac{9p-2}{3} = p$$

$$\Rightarrow \quad 9p - 2 = 3p$$

$$\Rightarrow \quad 6p = 2$$

$$\Rightarrow \quad p = \frac{1}{3}$$

179. *(b)* Let p : Plants take in CO_2 and give out O_2.

Let q : Plants take in CO_2.

r : Plants give out O_2.

$\sim q$: Plants do not take in CO_2.

$\sim r$: Plants do not give out O_2.

$\sim(q \wedge r)$: Plants do not take in CO_2 or do not give out O_2.

180. *(b)* Let the manufacturer produces x units of type A circuits and y units of type B circuits.

Given that, x units of type A circuits require 20 resistors and y units of type B circuits require 10 resistors and since a manufacturer of electronic circuit has a stock of 200 resistors.

We have, $20x + 10y \le 200 \Rightarrow 2x + y \le 20$

Similarly, for 120 transistors, we have

$$10x + 20y \le 120 \Rightarrow x + 2y \le 12$$

and for 150 capacitors, we have

$$10x + 30y \le 150 \Rightarrow x + 3y \le 15$$

Clearly, x and y are non-negative integers

$\therefore \quad x \ge 0, y \ge 0$

Thus, the constraints of the LPP are

$$2x + y \le 20$$
$$x + 2y \le 12$$
$$x + 3y \le 15$$
$$x \ge 0, y \ge 0.$$

COMEDK

Mock Test 4

Instructions

- There are 180 questions in all. The number of questions in each section is as given below.

Sections	No. of Questions
Section I : Physics	1-60
Section II : Chemistry	61-120
Section III : Mathematics	121-180

- All the questions are Multiple Choice Questions having four options out of which **ONLY ONE** is correct.
- Candidates will be awarded 1 mark for each correct answer. There will be no negative marking for incorrect answer.
- Time allotted to complete this paper is 3 hrs.

PHYSICS

1. Aerofoils are so designed that the speed of air

a. on top side is more than on lower side

b. on top side is less than on lower side

c. is same on both sides

d. is turbulent

2. The quantity having same dimension as that of Planck's constant is

a. work *b.* linear momentum

c. angular momentum *d.* impulse

3. On bombarding U^{235} by slow neutron, 200 MeV energy is released. If the power output of atomic reactor is 1.6 MW, then the rate of fission will be

a. $5 \times 10^{22}\ s^{-1}$ *b.* $5 \times 10^{16}\ s^{-1}$

c. $8 \times 10^{16}\ s^{-1}$ *d.* $20 \times 10^{16}\ s^{-1}$

4. The numbers 5.355 and 5.345 on rounding off to 3 significant figures will give

a. 5.35 and 5.34 *b.* 5.36 and 5.35

c. 5.35 and 5.35 *d.* 5.36 and 5.34

5. In a Young's experiment, two coherent sources are placed 0.90 mm apart and the fringes are observed one metre away. If it produces the second dark fringe at a distance of 1 mm from the central fringe, then wavelength of monochromatic light used would be

a. 60×10^{4} cm *b.* 10×10^{-4} cm

c. 10×10^{-5} cm *d.* 6×10^{-5} cm

6. A particle moves in *XY*-plane according to the equation $x = 4t^2 + 5t + 16$ and $y = 5t$

The acceleration of the particle is

a. 8 *b.* 13

c. 14 *d.* 16

7. A hollow double concave lens is made of very thin transparent material. It can be filled with air or either of two liquids L_1 or L_2 having refractive indices n_{L_1} and n_{L_2}, respectively (such that $n_{L_1} > n_{L_2} > 1$). The lens will diverge a parallel beam of light, if it is filled with

a. air and placed in air

b. air and immersed in L_1

c. L_1 and immersed in L_2

d. L_2 and immersed in L_1

8. The Young's double slit experiment is performed with blue and with green light of wavelengths 4360 Å and 5460 Å, respectively. If x is the distance of 4th maxima from the central one, then

a. $x_{blue} = x_{green}$
b. $x_{blue} > x_{green}$
c. $x_{blue} < x_{green}$
d. x_{blue} / x_{green}

9. A stone of mass 2 kg is projected upwards with KE of 98 J. The height at which the KE of the body becomes half its original value, is given by (take, $g = 9.8\,\text{ms}^{-2}$)

a. 5 m *b.* 2.5 m *c.* 1.5 m *d.* 0.5 m

10. Assuming the earth to be a sphere of uniform mass density, how much would body weight half way down to the centre of earth, if it weighed 250 N on the surface?

a. 150 N *b.* 175 N *c.* 125 N *d.* 200 N

11. Two capacitors C_1 and C_2 are charged to 120 V and 200 V, respectively. It is found that by connecting them together, then the potential on each one can be made zero. Then,

a. $5C_1 = 3C_2$ *b.* $3C_1 = 5C_2$
c. $3C_1 + 5C_2 = 0$ *d.* $9C_1 = 4C_2$

12. Two small identical electrical dipoles AB and CD, each of dipole moment p are kept at an angle of 120° as shown in the figure. If this system is subjected to electric field (**E**) directed along direction which makes $\theta°$ with XY-plane. Then, the magnitude and direction of the torque acting on this is

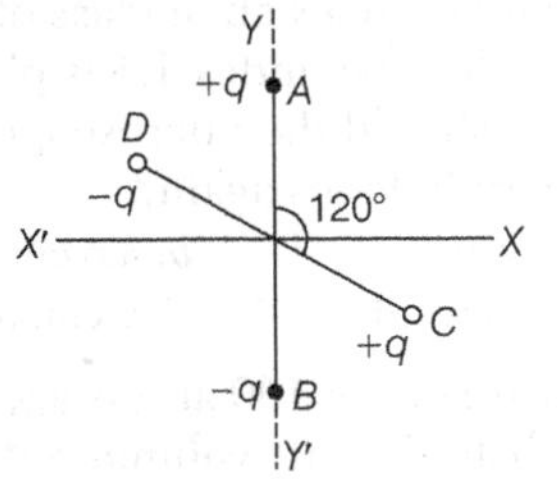

a. $pE\sin\theta$, along Z-axis
b. $2pE\sin\theta$, along Z-axis
c. $\frac{\sqrt{3}}{2} pE\sin\theta$, along Z-axis
d. $\frac{1}{2} pE\sin\theta$, along Z-axis

13. A rectangular film of liquid is extended from (4 cm × 2 cm) to (5 cm × 4 cm). If the workdone is 3×10^{-4} J. The value of the surface tension of the liquid is

a. 0.250 N/m *b.* 0.125 N/m
c. 0.2 N/m *d.* 8.0 N/m

14. Suppose the spheres A and B with charge 6.5×10^{-7} C have identical sizes and distance between centres is 50 cm. A third sphere of the same size but uncharged is brought in contact with the first, then brought in contact with the second and finally removed from both. What is the new force of repulsion between A and B?

a. 5.7×10^{-3} N *b.* 1.5×10^{-2} N
c. 0.24 N *d.* 0.24×10^{-2} N

15. Two blocks of masses 2 m and m are in equilibrium as shown in the figure . Now, the string between the blocks is suddenly broken. The accelerations of the blocks A and B respectively, at that instant are

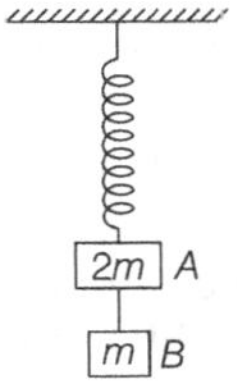

a. g and g *b.* g and $\frac{g}{2}$
c. $\frac{g}{2}$ and g *d.* $\frac{g}{2}$ and $\frac{g}{2}$

16. The number of electrons moving per second through the filament of a lamp of 100 W, operating at 200 V is

a. 3.1×10^{18} *b.* 3.1×10^{19}
c. 4.8×10^{18} *d.* 4.8×10^{19}

17. The range of a projectile when launched at angle θ is same as when launched at angle 2θ. What is the value of θ ?

a. 15° *b.* 30°
c. 45° *d.* 60°

18. An electric bulb is marked 100 W, 230 V. If the supply voltage drops to 115 V, what is the heat and light energy produced by the bulb in 20 min?

a. 20000 J *b.* 25000 J
c. 30000 J *d.* 35000 J

19. The arc's BC (radius = b) and AD (radius = a) of loop are joined by the straight wires AB and CD. A steady current I is flowing in the loop. Angle made by AB and CD at the origin is 30°. Another straight thin wire with steady current I, flowing out of plane of the paper is kept at the origin.

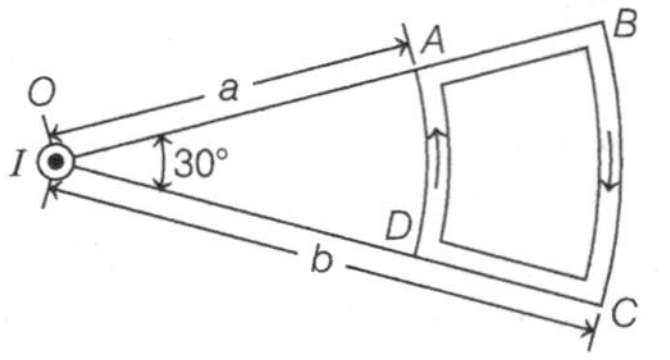

The magnitude of the magnetic field B due to loop $ABCD$ at the origin O is

a. zero

b. $\frac{\mu_0 I (a-b)}{24\, ab}$

c. $\frac{\mu_0 I}{4\pi}\left(\frac{a-b}{ab}\right)$

d. $\frac{\mu_0 I}{4\pi}\left[2(a-b)+\frac{\pi}{3}(a+b)\right]$

20. Two blocks are in contact on a frictionless table. One has mass m and the other $2m$. A force F is applied on $2m$ as shown in the figure. Now the same force F is applied from the right on m. In the two cases the ratio of force of contact between the two blocks will be

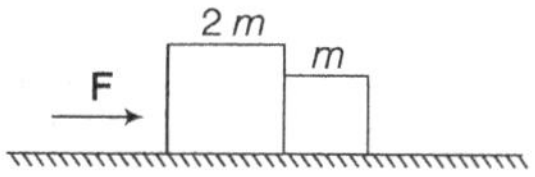

a. 1 : 1 *b.* 1: 2 *c.* 2 : 1 *d.* 1 : 3

21. Two toroids 1 and 2 have total number of turns 200 and 100 respectively with average radii 40 cm and 20 cm, respectively. If they carry same current i, the ratio of the magnetic fields along the two loops is

a. 1 : 1 *b.* 4 : 1 *c.* 2 : 1 *d.* 1 : 2

22. If a body of mass 200 g falls from a height 200 m and its total potential energy is converted into kinetic energy, at the point of contact of the body with the surface, then decrease in potential energy of the body at the contact is (Take, $g = 10\ ms^{-2}$)

a. 900 J *b.* 600 J *c.* 400 J *d.* 200 J

23. The height at which the weight of a body becomes 1/16th, its weight on the surface of the earth (radius R), is

a. 5 R *b.* 15 R *c.* 3 R *d.* 4 R

24. A block of ice at −10°C is slowly heated and converted to steam at 100°C. Which of the following curves represent the phenomenon qualitatively?

a.

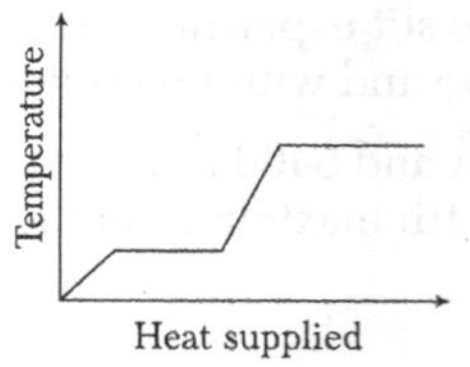

b.

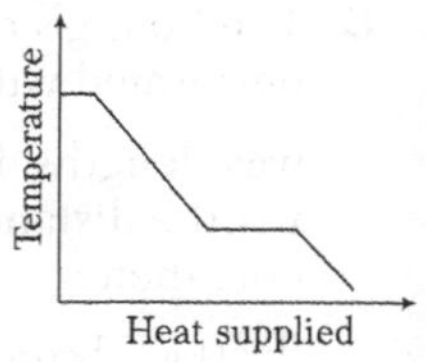

c.

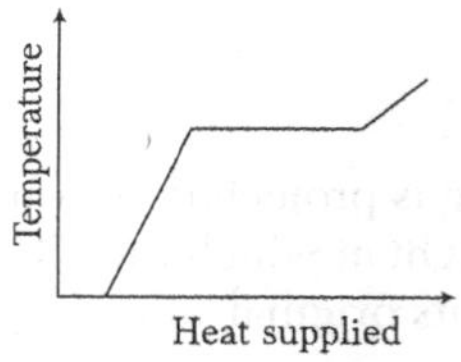

d.

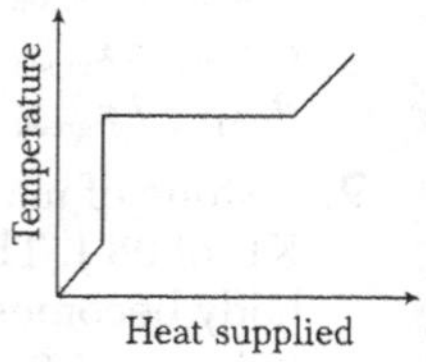

25. An electromagnetic wave going through vacuum is described by
$E = E_0 \sin(kx - \omega t)$; $B = B_0 \sin(kx - \omega t)$. Which of the following equations is true ?

a. $E_0 k = B_0 \omega$ *b.* $E_0 \omega = B_0 k$

c. $E_0 B_0 = \omega k$ *d.* None of these

26. For a normal eye, the cornea of eye provides a converging power of 40 D and the least converging power of the eye lens behind the cornea is 20 D. Using this information, the distance between the retina and the cornea-eye lens can be estimated to be

a. 5 cm *b.* 2.5 m

c. 1.67 cm *d.* 1.5 cm

27. Work done in converting one gram of ice at − 10°C into steam at 100°C is

a. 3045 J *b.* 6056 J

c. 721 J *d.* 616 J

28. A microscope is focussed on a mark on a piece of paper and then a slab of glass of thickness 3 cm and refractive index 1.5 is placed over the mark. How should the microscope be moved to get the mark in focus again?

a. 1 cm, upward *b.* 4.5 cm, downward

c. 1 cm, downward *d.* 2 cm, upward

29. When a pressure of 100 atm is applied on a spherical ball, then its volume reduces to 0.01%. The bulk modulus of the material of the rubber (in dyne cm^{-2}) is

a. 10×10^{12} *b.* 100×10^{12}

c. 1×10^{12} *d.* 20×10^{12}

30. The decreasing order of wavelength of infrared, microwave, ultraviolet and gamma rays is

a. gamma rays, ultraviolet, infrared, microwaves
b. microwaves, gamma rays, infrared, ultraviolet
c. infrared, microwave, ultraviolet, gamma rays
d. microwave, infrared, ultraviolet, gamma rays

31. A steel wire of length 80 cm and area of cross-section 10^{-5} m^2 is joined with an aluminium wire of length 60 cm and area of cross-section 3×10^{-5} m^2. The composite string is stretched by a tension 100 N. What is minimum frequency of tuning fork, which can produce standing wave in it with node at the joint?

(Given, $\rho_{\text{Steel}} = 7800$ kg m^{-3}, $\rho_{\text{Al}} = 2600$ kg m^{-3})

a. 87.5 Hz *b.* 97.8 Hz
c. 67.9 Hz *d.* 89.5 Hz

32. Two waves represented by the following equations are travelling in the same medium

$$y_1 = 5 \sin 2\pi(75\,t - 0.25x)$$
$$y_2 = 10 \sin 2\pi(150\,t - 0.50x)$$

The intensity ratio $\frac{I_1}{I_2}$ of the two waves is

a. 1 : 2 *b.* 1 : 4
c. 1 : 8 *d.* 1 : 16

33. The time period of a simple pendulum inside a stationary lift is $\sqrt{5}$ s. What will be the time period when the lift moves upward with an acceleration $\frac{g}{4}$?

a. $\sqrt{5}$ s *b.* $2\sqrt{5}$ s
c. $(2+\sqrt{5})$ s *d.* 2 s

34. An inductor of reactance 1 Ω and a resistor of 2 Ω are connected in series to the terminals of a 6 V (rms) AC source. The power dissipated in the circuit is

a. 8 W *b.* 12 W
c. 14.4 W *d.* 18 W

35. What is the output Y in the following circuit, when all the three inputs A, B, C are first 0 and then 1?

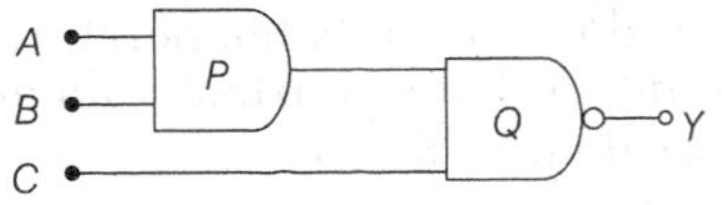

a. 0, 1 *b.* 0, 0 *c.* 1, 0 *d.* 1, 1

36. A square of side L metres lies in the XY-plane in a region, where the magnetic field is given by $B = B_0(2\mathbf{i} + 3\mathbf{j} + 4\mathbf{k})$ T, where B_0 is constant. The magnitude of flux passing through the square is

a. $(2\,B_0\,L^2)$ Wb *b.* $(3\,B_0\,L^2)$ Wb
c. $(4\,B_0\,L^2)$ Wb *d.* $(\sqrt{29}\,B_0\,L^2)$ Wb

37. A transmitter transmits at a wavelength of 300 m. A condenser of capacitance 2.4 μF is being used. The value of the inductance for the resonant circuit is approximately

a. 10^{-4} H *b.* 10^{-6} H
c. 10^{-8} H *d.* 10^{-10} H

38. A car starts moving along a line, first with acceleration $a = 5$ ms^{-2} starting from rest, then uniformly and finally decelerating at the same rate a and comes to rest. The total time of motion is 25 s. The average speed during the time is 20 ms^{-1}. How long does particle move uniformly?

a. 10 s *b.* 12 s *c.* 20 s *d.* 15 s

39. The magnetic flux linked with a coil varies with time as $\phi = (3t^2 + 4t + 9)$ Wb. What is the induced emf at, $t = 2$ s?

a. 3 V *b.* 4 V *c.* 9 V *d.* 16 V

40. Ten moles of an ideal gas at constant temperature 600 K is compressed from 100 L to 10 L. The work done in the process is

a. 4.11×10^4 J *b.* -4.11×10^4 J
c. 11.4×10^4 J *d.* -11.4×10^4 J

41. The magnetic susceptibility is negative for

a. paramagnetic material only
b. ferromagnetic material only
c. paramagnetic and ferromagnetic materials
d. diamagnetic material only

42. Two wires A and B are of the same material. Their lengths are in the ratio 1 : 2 and the diameter are in the ratio 2 : 1. If they are pulled by the same force, their increase in length will be in the ratio

a. 2 : 1 *b.* 1 : 4
c. 1 : 8 *d.* 8 : 1

43. The variation of magnetic susceptibility (χ) with absolute temperature T for a ferromagnetic is given in figure, by

a.
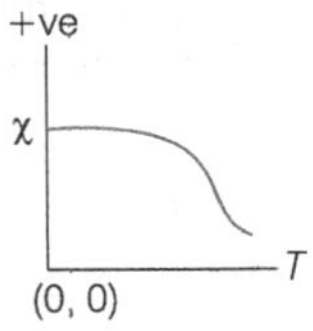

b.
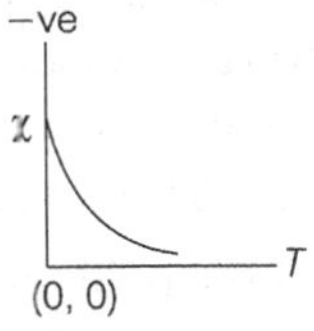

c.
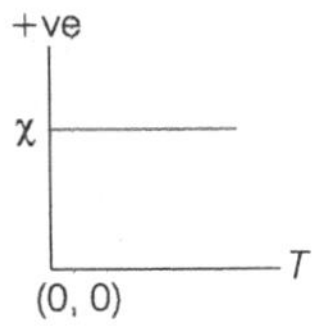

d.
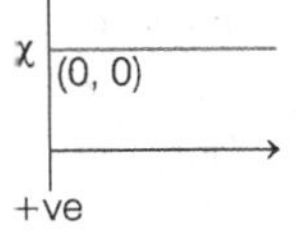

44. A linear harmonic oscillator of force constant 2×10^6 Nm^{-1} and amplitude 0.01 m has a total mechanical energy of 160 J. Its
a. maximum potential energy is 160 J
b. maximum potential energy is 100 J
c. minimum potential energy is zero
d. minimum potential energy is 100 J

45. Two bodies of masses 1 kg and 3 kg have position vectors $\mathbf{i} + 2\,\mathbf{j} + \mathbf{k}$ and $-3\,\mathbf{i} - 2\,\mathbf{j} + \mathbf{k}$, respectively. The centre of mass of this system has a position vector

a. $-2\mathbf{i} + 2\mathbf{k}$ *b.* $-2\,\mathbf{i} - \mathbf{j} + \mathbf{k}$
c. $2\mathbf{i} - \mathbf{j} - 2\,\mathbf{k}$ *d.* $-\mathbf{i} + \mathbf{j} + \mathbf{k}$

46. The velocity of a body depends on time according to the equation $v = \frac{t^2}{10} + 20$.
The body is undergoing
a. uniform acceleration
b. uniform retardation
c. non-uniform acceleration
d. zero acceleration

47. A *T* shaped object with dimensions shown in the figure, is lying on a smooth floor. A force **F** is applied at the point *P* parallel to *AB*, such that the object has only the translational motion without rotation. Find the location of *P* with respect to *C*.

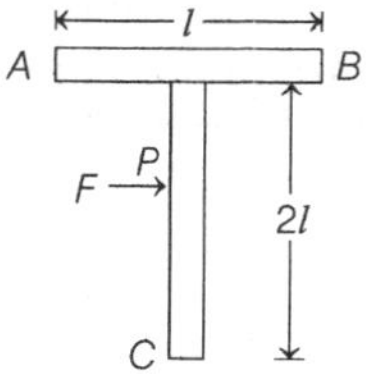

a. $\frac{4}{3}l$ *b.* l *c.* $\frac{2}{3}l$ *d.* $\frac{3}{2}l$

48. The TV transmission tower in Delhi has a height of 240 m. The distance up to which the broadcast can be received (taking the radius of the earth to be 6.4×10^6 m) is
a. 100 km *b.* 60 km *c.* 55 km *d.* 50 km

49. Three point charges $+q_1$, $-2q$ and $-2q$ are placed at the vertices of an equilateral triangle of side *a*. The work done by some external force to increase their separation to 2*a* will be

a. $\frac{1}{4\pi\varepsilon_0}\frac{2q^2}{a}$ *b.* $\frac{1}{4\pi\varepsilon_0}\frac{q^2}{2a}$
c. $\frac{1}{4\pi\varepsilon_0}\frac{q}{a^2}$ *d.* Zero

50. In an experiment on photoelectric effect, the slope of the cut-off voltage *versus* frequency of incident light is found to be 4.12×10^{-15} V-s. Calculate the value of Planck's constant.
a. 6.0×10^{-34} Js *b.* 0.63×10^{-34} Js
c. 6.59×10^{-34} Js *d.* zero

51. What is the work done in moving a $2\,\mu C$ point charge from corner *A* to corner *B* of a square *ABCD* in figure, when a $10\,\mu C$ charge exists at the centre of the square?

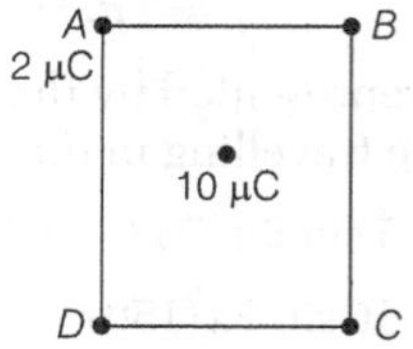

a. Zero *b.* 5 *c.* 2 *d.* 20

52. A typical *p*-*n* junction solar cell is as shown in the figure below

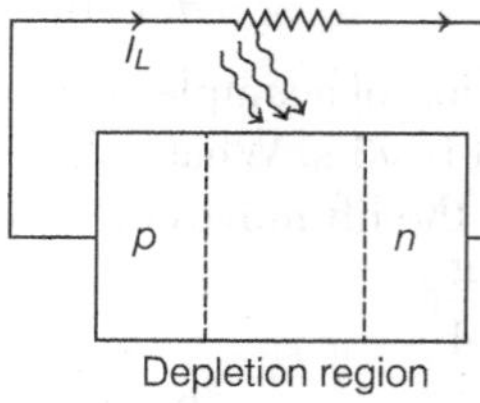

The generation of emf by it, is due to
a. generation of electrons and holes due to light
b. separation of electrons and holes due *E* electric field of depletion region
c. collection of electrons at *n*-side and holes at *p*-side
d. All of the above

53. 40 cal of heat is needed to raise the temperature of 1 mole of an ideal monoatomic gas from 20°C to 30°C at a constant pressure. The amount of heat required to raised its temperature over the same interval of a constant volume. ($R = 2$ cal $mol^{-1}K^{-2}$) is
a. 20 cal *b.* 40 cal *c.* 60 cal *d.* 80 cal

54. The ratio of the nuclear radii of the gold isotope $^{197}_{79}Au$ and silver isotope $^{107}_{47}Ag$, is
a. 1.23 *b.* 0.216 *c.* 2.13 *d.* 3.46

55. Two molecules of a gas have speeds of 9×10^6 m/s and 1×10^6 m / s, respectively. What is the root mean square speed of these molecules?
a. $\sqrt{39} \times 10^6$ m/s *b.* 6×10^6 m/s
c. $\sqrt{41} \times 10^6$ m/s *d.* 8×10^6 m/s

56. Consider the binding energy of ${}_{17}Cl^{35}$ and ${}_{15}P^{31}$ are 287.67 MeV and 262.48 MeV, respectively. Then,

a. ${}_{17}Cl^{35}$ is more stable than ${}_{15}P^{31}$
b. ${}_{15}P^{31}$ is more stable than ${}_{17}Cl^{35}$
c. Stability of both the elements is equivalent
d. cannot be estimated from the given data

57. Which of the following statements is correct for any thermodynamic system?

a. The internal energy changes in all processes.
b. Internal energy and entropy are state functions.
c. The change in entropy can never be zero.
d. The work done in an adiabatic process is always zero.

58. In a common emitter amplifier circuit using an *n-p-n* transistor, the phase difference between the input and the output voltages will be

a. 90° *b.* 135° *c.* 180° *d.* 45°

59. If h is Planck's constant, the momentum of a photon of wavelength 1 Å is

a. $10^{10}h$ *b.* h *c.* $10^{2}h$ *d.* $10^{-12}h$

60. If radius of first Bohr orbit is r, then the radius of second Bohr's orbit will be

a. $2r$ *b.* $8r$
c. $4r$ *d.* $2\sqrt{2}r$

CHEMISTRY

61. The partial pressure of carbon monoxide from the following data will be

$$CaCO_3(s) \overset{\Delta}{\rightleftharpoons} CaO(s) + CO_2\uparrow; K_{p_1} = 8\times10^{-2}$$

$$CO_2(g) + C(s) \rightleftharpoons 2CO(g); K_{p_2} = 2$$

a. 0.2 atm *b.* 0.6 atm
c. 0.8 atm *d.* 0.4 atm

62. The internal energy change when a system goes from state A to B is 40 kJ/mol. If the system goes from A to B by a reversible path and returns to state A by an irreversible path, what would be the net change in internal energy?

a. 40 kJ *b.* > 40 kJ *c.* < 40 kJ *d.* Zero

63. The third ionisation enthalpy is minimum form

a. Mn *b.* Ni *c.* Co *d.* Fe

64. Reverse osmosis is a process,

a. in which applied pressure to the solution side, is larger than the osmotic pressure
b. in which solvent moves from solution of higher concentration to solution of lower concentration
c. which is used for desalination of sea water
d. All of the above

65. Orbital having 3 angular nodes and 3 total nodes is

a. $5p$ *b.* $3d$ *c.* $4f$ *d.* $6d$

66. The correct order of the basic strength of amines in aqueous medium is

a. $C_2H_5NH_2 > (C_2H_5)_2NH > (C_2H_5)_3N$
b. $C_2H_5NH_2 > (C_2H_5)_3N > (C_2H_5)_2NH$
c. $(C_2H_5)_2NH > (C_2H_5)_3N > C_2H_5NH_2$
d. $(C_2H_5)_2NH > C_2H_5NH_2 > (C_2H_5)_3N$

67. 0.03% of carbon dioxide present in the atmosphere can be removed by

a. conversion of CO_2 to glucose
b. photosynthesis
c. chemical change of CO_2 to carbohydrate
d. All of the above

68. Calculate the bond enthalpy of Xe—F bond as given in the equation

$$XeF_4(g) \longrightarrow Xe^+(g) + F^-(g) + F_2(g) + F(g);$$

[Given, $\Delta_r H = 292$ kcal mol^{-1}
Ionisation energy of Xe = 279 kcal/mol
Bond energy (F—F) = 38 kcal/mol
Electron affinity of F = 85 kcal/mol]

a. 8.5 kcal/mol *b.* 34 kcal/mol
c. 24 kcal/mol *d.* None of these

69. In a crystalline solid, having formula XY_2O_4, oxide ions are arranged in cubic close packed lattice, while cations X are present in tetrahedral voids and cations Y are present in octahedral voids. The percentage of tetrahedral voids occupied by X is

a. 12.5% *b.* 25%
c. 50% *d.* 75%

70. The vapour pressure of pure $CHCl_3$ and CH_2Cl_2 are 200 and 41.5 atm respectively. The weight of $CHCl_3$ and CH_2Cl_2 are respectively 11.9 g and 17 g.
The vapour pressure of solution will be

a. 80.5 atm *b.* 79.5 atm
c. 94.3 atm *d.* 105.5 atm

71. At 25°C and 760 mm of Hg pressure, a gas occupies 600 mL volume. What will be its pressure at a height where temperature is 10°C and volume of the gas is 640 mL?

a. 677 mm Hg *b.* 600 mm Hg
c. 700 mm Hg *d.* 752 mm Hg

72. Consider the reaction given below.

 $+ RX \xrightarrow{\text{Anhyd. AlCl}_3} A + \text{HCl}$, here, *A* is

a. methylbenzene *b.* toluene
c. alkylbenzene *d.* ethylbenzene

73. The structure of protein which refers to the shape in which a long polypeptide chain can exist is

a. primary structure
b. secondary structure
c. tertiary structure
d. quaternary structure

74. Select the by-product formed in the reaction,

$$ROH + PCl_5 \longrightarrow RCl + A$$

Here, *A* is

a. $POCl_3 + HCl$
b. H_3PO_3 + no other by-product
c. $H_3PO_3 + HCl$
d. $POCl_3$ + no other by-product

75. The value of $\Delta G°$ for the phosphorylation of glucose in glycolysis is 13.8 kJ/mol. The value of K_C at 298 K is

a. 7.72×10^{-4} *b.* 5.62×10^{-4}
c. 4.81×10^{-3} *d.* 3.81×10^{-3}

76. The value of Z for real gases below Boyle's temperature initially

a. increases
b. decreases
c. remain same
d. increases then decreases

77. Consider the following reaction,

$$H_2(g) + X_2(g) \longrightarrow 2HX(g)$$

where, X = F, Cl, Br and I.

The order of reactivity of X_2 towards hydrogen is

a. $F_2 > Cl_2 > Br_2 > I_2$
b. $Cl_2 > Br_2 > F_2 > I_2$
c. $I_2 > Br_2 > Cl_2 > F_2$
d. $I_2 > Cl_2 > F_2 > Br_2$

78. Boron behaves anomalously with respect to its other group members, because boron has comparatively

a. small size
b. large charge to radius ratio
c. high electronegativity
d. All of the above

79. Which hydrogen in given compound is easily replaceable during bromination reaction in presence of light?

$$\underset{\delta}{CH_3}—\underset{\gamma}{CH_2}—\underset{\beta}{CH}=\underset{\alpha}{CH_2}$$

a. β-hydrogen *b.* δ-hydrogen
c. γ-hydrogen *d.* α-hydrogen

80. Which of the following type of reaction is represented by the given equation ?

$$3MnO_4^{2-} + 4H^+ \longrightarrow 2MnO_4^- + MnO_2 + 2H_2O$$

a. Reduction in acidic medium
b. Oxidation in acidic medium
c. Disproportionation in acidic medium
d. Reduction

81. The type of hybridisation and number of lone pair(s) of electrons of Xe in $XeOF_4$, respectively, are

a. sp^3d^2 and 1 *b.* sp^3d and 2
c. sp^3d and 1 *d.* sp^3d^2 and 2

82. Which type of compound is shown by the following structure?

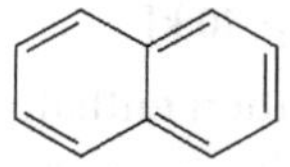

Naphthalene

a. Alicyclic compound
b. Benzenoid aromatic compound
c. Non-benzenoid aromatic compound
d. Acyclic compound

83. In the cyanide extraction process of silver from argentite ore, the oxidising and reducing agents used are

a. O_2 and CO respectively
b. O_2 and Zn dust respectively
c. HNO_3 and Zn dust respectively
d. HNO_3 and CO respectively

84. Which of the following would undergo S_N2 reaction faster?

a.  *b.* 

c.  *d.* 

85. The correct order of electronegativity of carbon in ethane, ethene and ethyne is
a. ethane < ethene < ethyne
b. ethyne < ethene < ethane
c. ethene < ethyne < ethane
d. ethene < ethane < ethyne

86. Which of the following is correct?
a. $SO_3^{2-} \rightarrow$ Tetrahedral *b.* $NO_2^- \rightarrow$ Trigonal planar
c. $ClO_4^- \rightarrow$ Tetrahedral *d.* $NH_3 \rightarrow$ Trigonal planar

87. Carbon monoxide is a highly poisonous gas for human beings because
a. it binds to haemoglobin to form stable compound
b. it is carcinogenic in nature
c. it induces the chance of heart attack
d. it affects nervous system fatally

88. In the reaction, $2KClO_3 \longrightarrow 2KCl + 3O_2$, the elements which have been oxidised and reduced respectively are
a. chlorine and oxygen *b.* oxygen and chlorine
c. potassium and oxygen *d.* oxygen and potassium

89. The equivalent weight of an element is 4. Its chloride has a vapour density 59.25. Then the valency of the element is
a. 4 *b.* 3 *c.* 2 *d.* 1

90. Given below are the half-cell reactions,
$$Mn^{2+} + 2e^- \longrightarrow Mn;\ E° = -1.18\ V$$
$$2[Mn^{3+} + e^- \longrightarrow Mn^{2+}];\ E° = +1.51\ V$$
The $E°$ for $3\ Mn^{2+} \longrightarrow Mn + 2Mn^{3+}$ will be
a. –2.69 V, the reaction will not occur
b. –2.69 V, the reaction will occur
c. –0.33 V, the reaction will not occur
d. –0.33 V, the reaction will occur

91. Lithium halides have some covalent characters. It is because of
a. the high polarisation capacity of Li^+
b. the low polarisation capacity of Li^+
c. the high melting point of LiX
d. None of the above

92. Which of the following has minimum bond length?
a. O_2 *b.* O_2^+ *c.* O_2^- *d.* O_2^{2-}

93. Which one of the following polymers is prepared by condensation polymerisation?
a. Teflon *b.* Natural rubber
c. Styrene *d.* Nylon-6,6

94. Which of the following molecule has net dipole moment zero?
a. HF *b.* H_2O
c. BF_3 *d.* $CHCl_3$

95. Which of the following pairs have same radii?
a. Am and Cm *b.* U and Np
c. Bk and Cm *d.* Pu and Th

96. $[Co(NH_3)_5SO_4]Br$ and $[Co(NH_3)_5Br]SO_4$ are
a. linkage isomers
b. coordination isomers
c. ionisation isomers
d. solvate isomers

97. $KMnO_4$ reacts with oxalic acid according to the equation,
$$2MnO_4^- + 5C_2O_4^{2-} + 16H^+ \longrightarrow 2Mn^{2+} + 10CO_2 + 8H_2O$$
Here, 20 mL of 0.1 M $KMnO_4$ is equivalent to
a. 20 mL of 0.5 M $H_2C_2O_4$
b. 50 mL of 0.1 M $H_2C_2O_4$
c. 50 mL of 0.01 M $H_2C_2O_4$
d. 20 mL of 0.1 M $H_2C_2O_4$

98. The noble gases exhibit very low chemical reactivity due to
a. unavailability of valence electrons
b. stable configuration
c. availability of large number of valence electrons
d. None of the above

99. In the given equation,
$$4Fe(s) + 3O_2(g) \longrightarrow 2Fe_2O_3(s)$$
The entropy change is $-549.4\ JK^{-1}\ mol^{-1}$ at 298 K. ($\Delta_r H° = -1648 \times 10^3\ J\ mol^{-1}$). The above reaction is
a. spontaneous
b. non-spontaneous
c. non-spontaneous at 500 K
d. None of the above

100. Iodination of alkanes is always carried out in the presence of some oxidising agents like HIO_3. This is because
a. it is a very fast process
b. it is a reversible reaction
c. I—I bond is very weak
d. All of the above

101. The first ionisation potential of Na is 5.1 eV. The value of electron gain enthalpy of Na^+ will be
a. –2.55 eV *b.* –5.1 eV
c. –10.2 eV *d.* +2.55 eV

MOCK TEST 4

102. A unit cell contains atoms (A) at all the corners and atoms (B) at alternate faces and all edge centres. Atoms (C) are present at face centres left from (B) and one at each body diagonal at distance of 1/4th of body diagonal from corner. Formula of the compound is

a. $A_3B_8C_7$ *b.* AB_4C_6
c. $A_6B_4C_8$ *d.* $A_2B_9C_{11}$

103. Which of the following structures are the components of an antiseptic?

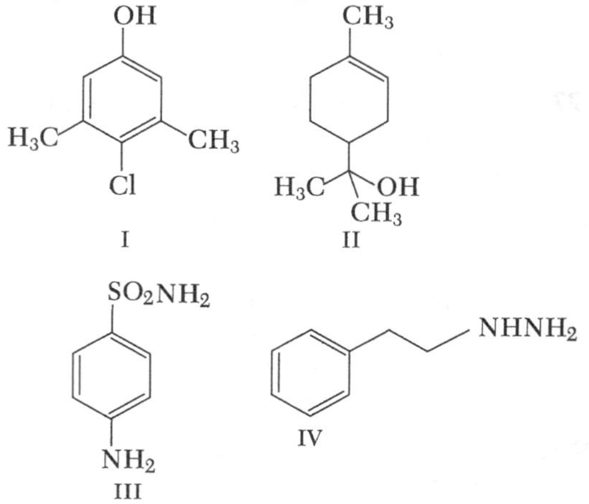

a. I and III *b.* I and II
c. II and IV *d.* II and III

104. Among the properties (A) reducing, (B) oxidising, (C) complexing, the set of properties shown by CN^- ion towards metal species is

a. B and C *b.* A and C
c. A, B and C *d.* A and B

105. Consider the following structures :

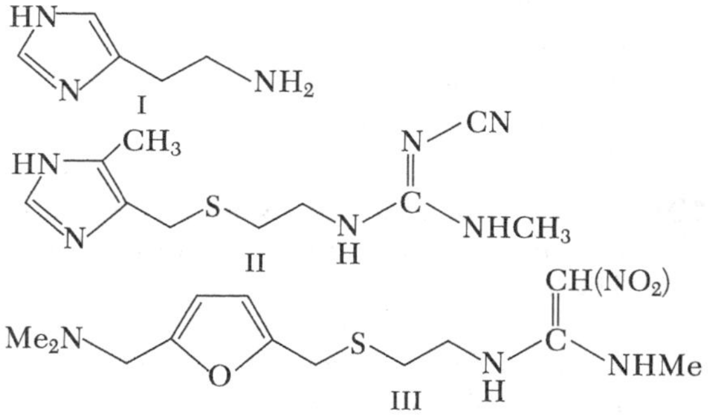

In the above structures I, II and III are :

I II III

a. Histamine; Cimetidine; Ranitidine
b. Histamine; Ranitidine; Cimetidine
c. Cimetidine; Ranitidine; Histamine
d. Cimetidine; Histamine; Ranitidine

106. Conversion of oxygen into ozone is non-spontaneous at

a. low temperature
b. all temperature
c. high temperature
d. room temperature

107. In Freundlich adsorption isotherm, the value of $\frac{1}{n}$ is

a. between 0 and 1 in all cases
b. between 2 and 4 in all cases
c. 1 in case of physical adsorption
d. 1 in case of chemisorption

108. Which of the following resonating structures is incorrect?

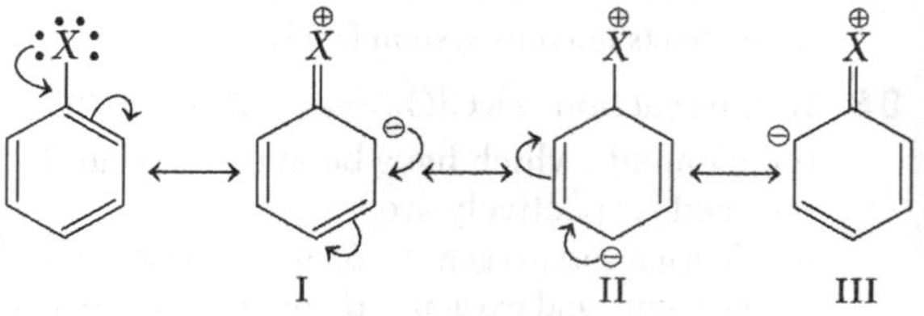

a. Only I *b.* Only II
c. Only III *d.* None of these

109. A first order reaction has a rate constant of $2.303 \times 10^{-3}\ s^{-1}$. The time required for 40 g of this reactant to reduce to 10 g will be [Given that $\log_{10} 2 = 0.3010$]

a. 230.3 s *b.* 301 s
c. 2000 s *d.* 602 s

110. The major product of the following reaction is

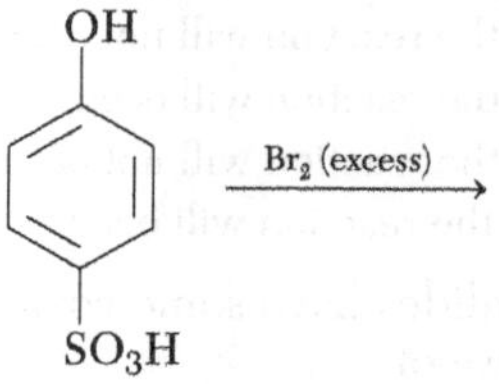

a.

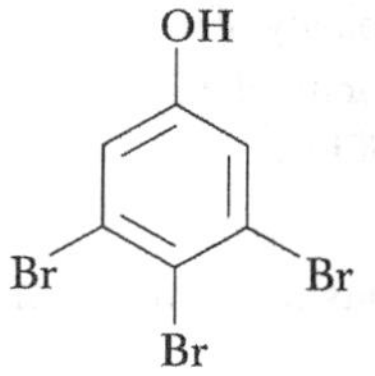

b.

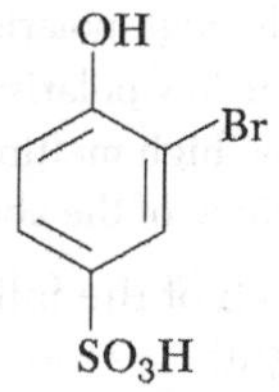

c.

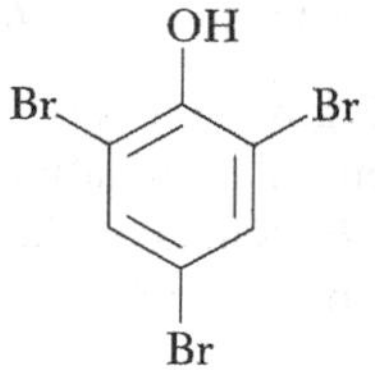

d.

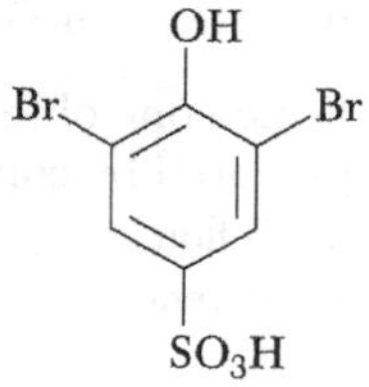

MOCK TEST 4

111. Chlorine reacts with

a. metals and non-metals to form chlorides
b. compounds containing hydrogen to form HCl
c. hydrocarbons and give substitution products with saturated hydrocarbons
d. All of the above

112. Aromatic carboxylic acids do not undergo Friedel-Craft's reaction because

a. carboxyl group acts as an activating and *meta*-directing group
b. carboxyl group act as a deactivating and *ortho* and *para*-directing group
c. carboxyl group act as an activating and *ortho*-directing group
d. carboxyl group acts as deactivating and the catalyst

113. Alkenes react with water in the presence of acid as catalyst to form alcohols.

$$CH_3CH{=}CH_2 + H_2O \overset{H^+}{\rightleftharpoons} CH_3{-}\underset{\displaystyle OH}{\underset{|}{CH}}{-}CH_3$$

The reaction takes place in accordance with

a. Hofmann elimination rule
b. Saytzeff rule
c. Markownikoff's rule
d. anti-Markownikoff's addition

114. The potential difference between the fixed layer and diffused layer of opposite charges in the colloidal system is known as

a. *Zeta* potential
b. gravitational potential
c. standard potential
d. ionic potential

115. Which of the following substrates give the same product on the reduction with DIBAL-H?

a. $CH_3-(CH_2)_9-CN$ and $CH_3(CH_2)_9-COOH$
b. $CH_3-(CH_2)_9-CN$ and $CH_3(CH_2)_9-COOC_2H_5$
c. $CH_3-(CH_2)_9-COOH$ and $CH_3(CH_2)_9-CHO$
d. $CH_3(CH_2)_9-COOH$ and $CH_3(CH_2)_9COOC_2H_5$

116. PCl_5 is prepared by the action of excess of Cl_2 on

a. P_4 *b.* PCl_3 *c.* P *d.* $POCl_3$

117. Which of the following compounds produces an orange-red precipitate with 2, 4-DNP reagent?

a. Acetamide *b.* Dimethyl ether
c. Butanone *d.* Propylbutanoate

118. The order of reactivity of hydrogen halides with ether is as follows :

a. HBr > HI > HCl *b.* HCl > HBr > HI
c. HI > HBr > HCl *d.* HCl > HI > HBr

119. Zinc sulphate contains 22.65% zinc and 43.9% water of crystallisation. If the law of constant proportions is true then the weight of zinc required to produce 20 g of the zinc sulphate crystals will be

a. 45.3 g *b.* 4.53 g
c. 0.453 g *d.* 453 g

120. The reaction of alcohol/phenol with acid chloride is carried out in the presence of pyridine in order to

a. neutralise HCl which is formed during the reaction
b. shift the equilibrium to right hand side
c. Both (a) and (b)
d. None of the above

MATHEMATICS

121. Let $A = \{1, 2, 3, \quad , n\}$ and $B = \{a, b\}$. Then, the number of surjections from A into B is

a. ${}^nP_2$ *b.* $2^n - 2$
c. $2^n - 1$ *d.* None of the above

122. Let $A = N \times N$ and $*$ be the binary operation on A defined by $(a, b) * (c, d) = (a + c, b + d)$. Then,

a. $*$ is commutative only
b. $*$ is associative and identity element for $*$ does not exist
c. $*$ is associative only
d. identity element for $*$ in A exists

123. Let $f : R \to R$ be given by $f(x) = \tan x$. Then, $f^{-1}(1)$ is

a. $\frac{\pi}{4}$ *b.* $\left\{n\pi + \frac{\pi}{4} : n \in Z\right\}$
c. Does not exist *d.* None of these

124. If $\cot\theta + \tan\theta = 2\operatorname{cosec}\theta$, then the general value of θ is

a. $n\pi \pm \frac{\pi}{3}$ *b.* $n\pi \pm \frac{\pi}{6}$
c. $2n\pi \pm \frac{\pi}{3}$ *d.* $2n\pi \pm \frac{\pi}{6}$

125. If A lies in the second quadrant and $3\tan A + 4 = 0$, then the value of $2\cot A - 5\cos A + \sin A$ is

a. $\frac{-53}{10}$ b. $\frac{23}{10}$ c. $\frac{37}{10}$ d. $\frac{7}{10}$

126. If $\tan\theta = \frac{a}{b}$, then $b\cos 2\theta + a\sin 2\theta$ is equal to

a. a b. b

c. $\frac{a}{b}$ d. None of these

127. If $\frac{\pi}{2} \le x \le \frac{3\pi}{2}$, then $\sin^{-1}(\sin x)$ is equal to

a. x b. $-x$

c. $\pi + x$ d. $\pi - x$

128. If $\sin(\cot^{-1}(x+1)) = \cos(\tan^{-1} x)$, then the value of x is

a. $-\frac{1}{2}$ b. $\frac{1}{2}$ c. 0 d. $\frac{9}{4}$

129. The value of $\tan^{-1}\frac{\sqrt{1+x^2}+\sqrt{1-x^2}}{\sqrt{1+x^2}-\sqrt{1-x^2}}$ is equal to

a. $\frac{\pi}{4} + \cos^{-1} x^2$ b. $\frac{\pi}{2} + \frac{1}{2}\cos^{-1} x^2$

c. $\frac{\pi}{4} + \frac{1}{2}\cos^{-1} x^2$ d. $\cos^{-1} x^2$

130. The value of $\tan\left(\frac{\pi}{4} + \frac{1}{2}\cos^{-1}\frac{a}{b}\right) + \tan\left(\frac{\pi}{4} - \frac{1}{2}\cos^{-1}\frac{a}{b}\right)$ is

a. $\frac{a}{b}$ b. $\frac{b}{a}$

c. $\frac{2a}{b}$ d. $\frac{2b}{a}$

131. If $P(n): 2n < n!, n \in N$, then $P(n)$ is true for all $n \ge$

a. 1 b. 2 c. 3 d. 4

132. If $z = x + iy$ lies in the third quadrant, then $\frac{\bar{z}}{z}$ also lies in the third quadrant, if

a. $x > y > 0$ b. $x < y < 0$

c. $y < x < 0$ d. $y > x > 0$

133. The complex number z which satisfies the condition $\left|\frac{i+z}{i-z}\right| = 1$ lies on

a. circle $x^2 + y^2 = 1$ b. the X-axis

c. the Y-axis d. the line $x + y = 1$

134. $|z_1 + z_2| = |z_1| + |z_2|$ is possible, if

a. $z_2 = \bar{z}_1$ b. $z_2 = \frac{1}{z_1}$

c. $\arg(z_1) = \arg(z_2)$ d. $|z_1| = |z_2|$

135. The real value of θ for which the expression $\frac{1 + i\cos\theta}{1 - 2i\cos\theta}$ is a real number is

a. $n\pi + \frac{\pi}{4}$ b. $n\pi + (-1)^n \frac{\pi}{4}$

c. $2n\pi \pm \frac{\pi}{2}$ d. None of these

136. The sum of the digits in unit place of all the numbers formed with the help of 3, 4, 5 and 6 taken all at a time is

a. 432 b. 108 c. 36 d. 18

137. In a football championship, 153 matches were played. Every two teams played one match with each other. The number of teams, participating in the championship is

a. 17 b. 18 c. 19 d. 20

138. The total number of ways in which six '+' and four '–' signs can be arranged in a line such that no two signs '–' occur together, is

a. 35 b. 36 c. 40 d. 46

139. If A and B are coefficient of x^n in the expansions of $(1+x)^{2n}$ and $(1+x)^{2n-1}$ respectively, then $\frac{A}{B}$ equals

a. 1 b. 2 c. $\frac{1}{2}$ d. $\frac{1}{n}$

140. The coefficient of $a^{-6}b^4$ in the expansion of $\left(\frac{1}{a} - \frac{2b}{3}\right)^{10}$ is

a. $\frac{1120}{27}$ b. $\frac{1420}{27}$

c. $\frac{1520}{27}$ d. $\frac{1720}{27}$

141. If the sum of n terms of an AP is given by $S_n = 3n + 2n^2$, then the common difference of the AP is

a. 3 b. 2 c. 6 d. 4

142. The lengths of three unequal edges of a rectangular solid block are in GP. If the volume of the block is 216 cm^3 and the total surface area is 252 cm^2, then the length of the longest edge is

a. 12 cm b. 6 cm c. 18 cm d. 3 cm

MOCK TEST 4

143. The equation of the straight line passing through the point (3, 2) and perpendicular to the line $y = x$ is

a. $x - y = 5$ *b.* $x + y = 5$
c. $x + y = 1$ *d.* $x - y = 1$

144. If the coordinates of the middle point of the portion of a line intercepted between the coordinate axes is (3, 2), then the equation of the line will be

a. $2x + 3y = 12$ *b.* $3x + 2y = 12$
c. $4x - 3y = 6$ *d.* $5x - 2y = 10$

145. Equations of diagonals of the square formed by the lines $x = 0$, $y = 0$, $x = 1$ and $y = 1$ are

a. $y = x, y + x = 1$
b. $y = x, x + y = 2$
c. $2y = x, y + x = \frac{1}{3}$
d. $y = 2x, y + 2x = 1$

146. The point (4, 1) undergoes the following two successive transformations

(i) Reflection about the line $y = x$
(ii) Translation through a distance 2 units along the positive X-axis.

Then, the final coordinates of the point are

a. (4, 3) *b.* (3, 4)
c. (1, 4) *d.* $\left(\frac{7}{2}, \frac{7}{2}\right)$

147. The area of the circle centred at (1, 2) and passing through the point(4, 6) is

a. 5π *b.* 10π
c. 25π *d.* None of these

148. Equation of the circle with centre on the Y-axis and passing through the origin and the point (2, 3) is

a. $x^2 + y^2 + 13y = 0$
b. $3x^2 + 3y^2 + 13x + 3 = 0$
c. $6x^2 + 6y^2 - 13y = 0$
d. $x^2 + y^2 + 13x + 3 = 0$

149. A beam is supported at its ends by supports which are 12 m apart. Since, the load is concentrated at its centre, there is deflection of 3 cm at the centre and the deflected beam is in the shape of a parabola.

The distance between deflection of 1cm and the centre is

a. $2\sqrt{6}$ m *b.* $3\sqrt{6}$ m
c. $4\sqrt{6}$ m *d.* $5\sqrt{6}$ m

150. The locus of a variable point whose distance from $(-2, 0)$ is $\frac{2}{3}$ times its distance from the line $x = -\frac{9}{2}$, is

a. ellipse *b.* parabola
c. hyperbola *d.* None of these

151. The equation $\frac{x^2}{2-r} + \frac{y^2}{r-5} + 1 = 0$ represents an ellipse, if

a. $r > 2$
b. $2 < r < 5$
c. $r > 5$
d. None of the above

152. The equations of the transverse and conjugate axes of the hyperbola $16x^2 - y^2 + 64x + 4y + 44 = 0$, are respectively

a. $x = 2, y + 2 = 0$ *b.* $x = 2, y = 2$
c. $y = 2, x + 2 = 0$ *d.* None of these

153. The distance between the directrices of the hyperbola $x = 8 \sec \theta$ and $y = 8 \tan \theta$, is

a. $16\sqrt{2}$ *b.* $\sqrt{2}$
c. $8\sqrt{2}$ *d.* $4\sqrt{2}$

154. If a plane cuts off intercepts -6, 3 and 4 from the coordinate axes X, Y and Z respectively, then the length of the perpendicular from the origin to the plane is

a. $\frac{1}{\sqrt{61}}$ *b.* $\frac{13}{\sqrt{61}}$
c. $\frac{12}{\sqrt{29}}$ *d.* $\frac{5}{\sqrt{41}}$

155. If $f(x) = 1 - x + x^2 - x^3 + \quad - x^{99} + x^{100}$, then $f'(1)$ is equal to

a. 150 *b.* -50
c. -150 *d.* 50

156. The function $f(x) = \begin{cases} x[x], & \text{if } 0 \le x < 2 \\ (x-1)x, & \text{if } 2 \le x < 3 \end{cases}$ is

a. differentiable at $x = 2$
b. not differentiable at $x = 2$
c. continuous at $x = 2$
d. None of the above

157. If $y = (1 + x)(1 + x^2)(1 + x^4) \ldots (1 + x^{2^n})$, then the value of $\frac{dy}{dx}$ at $x = 0$ is

a. 0 *b.* -1
c. 1 *d.* None of these

158. The function given by $f(x) = x^3 - 3x^2 + 3x - 100$ is

a. increasing on R **b.** decreasing on R
c. strictly decreasing on R **d.** None of these

159. The angle between the curves $y = a^x$ and $y = b^x$ is equal to

a. $\tan^{-1}\left(\left|\frac{a-b}{1+ab}\right|\right)$

b. $\tan^{-1}\left(\left|\frac{a+b}{1-ab}\right|\right)$

c. $\tan^{-1}\left(\left|\frac{\log b + \log a}{1 + \log a \log b}\right|\right)$

d. $\tan^{-1}\left(\left|\frac{\log a - \log b}{1 + \log a \log b}\right|\right)$

160. The point on the curve $x^2 = 2y$ which is nearest to the point (0, 5) is

a. $(2\sqrt{2}, 4)$ **b.** $(2\sqrt{2}, 0)$
c. (0, 0) **d.** (2, 2)

161. If a and b are positive numbers such that $a > b$, then the minimum value of

$a\sec\theta - b\tan\theta, \left(0 < \theta < \frac{\pi}{2}\right)$ is

a. $\sqrt{a^2 - b^2}$ **b.** $\sqrt{a^2 + b^2}$
c. $\frac{1}{\sqrt{a^2 - b^2}}$ **d.** $\frac{1}{\sqrt{a^2 + b^2}}$

162. If $y = a\log x + bx^2 + x$ has its extremum at $x = -1$ and $x = 2$, then

a. $a = 2, b = \frac{1}{2}$ **b.** $a = 2, b = \frac{-1}{2}$
c. $a = \frac{-1}{2}, b = 2$ **d.** $a = \frac{1}{2}, b = 2$

163. $\int e^x \left(\frac{1-x}{1+x^2}\right)^2 dx$ is equal to

a. $\frac{e^x}{1+x^2} + C$ **b.** $\frac{-e^x}{1+x^2} + C$
c. $\frac{e^x}{(1+x^2)^2} + C$ **d.** $\frac{-e^x}{(1+x^2)^2} + C$

164. The value of the integral $\int_0^{\pi/2} \frac{\sin x}{1 + \cos^2 x} dx$ is

a. $\frac{\pi}{2}$ **b.** $\frac{\pi}{6}$ **c.** $\frac{\pi}{4}$ **d.** 0

165. $\int_0^1 x(1-x)^n \, dx$ is equal to

a. $\frac{1}{(n+1)} + \frac{1}{(n+2)}$ **b.** $\frac{1}{(n+1)(n+2)}$
c. $(n+1)(n+2)$ **d.** $\frac{(n+1)}{(n+2)}$

166. $\int_{-3\pi/2}^{-\pi/2} [(x+\pi)^3 + \cos^2(x)] \, dx$ is equal to

a. $\left(\frac{\pi^4}{32}\right) + \frac{\pi}{2}$ **b.** $\frac{\pi}{2}$
c. $\frac{\pi}{4} - 1$ **d.** $\frac{\pi^4}{32}$

167. The value of $\int f'(ax+b)[f(ax+b)]^n \, dx$ is

a. $\frac{[f(ax+b)]^{n+1}}{n+1} + C$

b. $\frac{\frac{1}{a}[f(ax+b)]^{n+1}}{n+1} + C$

c. $\frac{a[f(ax+b)]^{n+1}}{n+1} + C$

d. None of the above

168. $\int \frac{\cos 2x}{(\sin x + \cos x)^2} dx$ is equal to

a. $\frac{-1}{\sin x + \cos x} + C$

b. $\log|\sin x + \cos x| + C$

c. $\log|\sin x - \cos x| + C$

d. $\frac{1}{(\sin x + \cos x)^2}$

169. Smaller area enclosed (in sq units) by the circle $x^2 + y^2 = 4$ and the line $x + y = 2$ is

a. $2(\pi - 2)$ **b.** $\pi - 2$
c. $2\pi - 1$ **d.** $2(\pi + 2)$

170. The function $xy = \log y + C$ is the solution of the differential equation

a. $y' = \frac{y^2}{1 - xy} \; (xy \neq 1)$ **b.** $y' = \frac{-y^2}{1 - xy} \; (x, y \neq 1)$
c. $y' = \frac{y^2}{1 + xy} \; (xy \neq -1)$ **d.** None of the above

171. The equation of a curve whose tangent at any point on it different from origin has slope $y + \frac{y}{x}$, is

a. $y = e^x$ **b.** $y = kx \cdot e^x$
c. $y = kx$ **d.** $y = x \cdot e^{x^2}$

172. If $y(t)$ is a solution of $(1+t)\frac{dy}{dt}-ty=-1$ and $y(0)=-1$, then $y(1)$ is equal to

a. $-\frac{1}{2}$ *b.* $e+\frac{1}{2}$

c. $e-\frac{1}{2}$ *d.* $\frac{1}{2}$

173. If *ABCDEF* is a regular hexagon with $\mathbf{AB}=\mathbf{a}$ and $\mathbf{BC}=\mathbf{b}$, then $\mathbf{CE}$ is equal to

a. $\mathbf{b}-\mathbf{a}$ *b.* $-\mathbf{b}$

c. $\mathbf{b}-2\mathbf{a}$ *d.* None of these

174. Let **a**, **b** and **c** be three non-zero vectors such that no two of these are collinear. If the vector $\mathbf{a}+2\mathbf{b}$ is collinear with **c** and $\mathbf{b}+3\mathbf{c}$ is collinear with **a** (λ being some non-zero scalar), then $\mathbf{a}+2\mathbf{b}+6\mathbf{c}$ equals

a. $\lambda\mathbf{a}$ *b.* $\lambda\mathbf{b}$

c. $\lambda\mathbf{c}$ *d.* 0

175. If $A=\begin{bmatrix}0 & 2\\ 3 & -4\end{bmatrix}$ and $kA=\begin{bmatrix}0 & 3a\\ 2b & 24\end{bmatrix}$, then the values of *k*, *a*, *b* are respectively

a. $-6, -12, -18$

b. $-6, 4, 9$

c. $-6, -4, -9$

d. $-6, 12, 18$

176. If *A* is a skew-symmetric matrix of odd order *n*, then

a. $|A|=0$

b. $|A|=-1$

c. $|A|=|A'|$

d. None of these

177. In a ΔABC, if

$$\begin{vmatrix}1 & 1 & 1\\ 1+\sin A & 1+\sin B & 1+\sin C\\ \sin A+\sin^2 A & \sin B+\sin^2 B & \sin C+\sin^2 C\end{vmatrix}$$

$=0$, then ΔABC is a/an

a. equilateral triangle *b.* isosceles triangle

c. right angled triangle *d.* None of the above

178. Three persons *A*, *B* and *C*, fire at a target in turn, starting with *A*. Their probability of hitting the target are 0.4, 0.3 and 0.2 respectively. The probability of two hits is

a. 0.024 *b.* 0.188

c. 0.336 *d.* 0.452

179. The converse of the statement "If $x>y$, then $x+a>y+a$" is

a. If $x<y$, then $x+a<y+a$

b. If $x+a>y+a$, then $x>y$

c. If $x<y$, then $x+a<y+a$

d. If $x>y$, then $x+a<y+a$

180. Anil wants to invest atmost ₹ 12000 in bonds *A* and *B*. According to the rules, he has to invest atleast ₹ 2000 in bond *A* and atleast ₹ 4000 in bond *B*. If the rate of interest in bond *A* is 8% per annum and on bond *B* is 10% per annum, then to maximise the interest, the investment in bond *A* and *B* are respectively

a. ₹ 10000 and ₹ 2000

b. ₹ 2000 and ₹ 10000

c. ₹ 6000 and ₹ 6000

d. None of the above

ANSWERS

Physics

1. (a)	2. (c)	3. (b)	4. (d)	5. (d)	6. (a)	7. (d)	8. (c)	9. (b)	10. (c)
11. (b)	12. (a)	13. (b)	14. (a)	15. (c)	16. (a)	17. (b)	18. (c)	19. (b)	20. (b)
21. (a)	22. (c)	23. (c)	24. (a)	25. (a)	26. (c)	27. (a)	28. (a)	29. (c)	30. (d)
31. (d)	32. (b)	33. (d)	34. (c)	35. (c)	36. (c)	37. (c)	38. (d)	39. (d)	40. (d)
41. (d)	42. (c)	43. (a)	44. (a)	45. (b)	46. (c)	47. (a)	48. (c)	49. (d)	50. (c)
51. (a)	52. (d)	53. (a)	54. (a)	55. (c)	56. (b)	57. (b)	58. (c)	59. (a)	60. (c)

Chemistry

61. (d)	62. (d)	63. (d)	64. (d)	65. (c)	66. (c)	67. (d)	68. (b)	69. (a)	70. (c)
71. (a)	72. (c)	73. (b)	74. (a)	75. (d)	76. (b)	77. (a)	78. (d)	79. (c)	80. (c)
81. (a)	82. (b)	83. (b)	84. (d)	85. (a)	86. (c)	87. (a)	88. (b)	89. (b)	90. (a)
91. (a)	92. (b)	93. (d)	94. (c)	95. (b)	96. (c)	97. (b)	98. (b)	99. (a)	100. (b)
101. (b)	102. (d)	103. (b)	104. (b)	105. (a)	106. (b)	107. (a)	108. (b)	109. (d)	110. (c)
111. (d)	112. (b)	113. (c)	114. (a)	115. (b)	116. (a)	117. (c)	118. (c)	119. (b)	120. (c)

Mathematics

121. (b)	122. (b)	123. (b)	124. (c)	125. (b)	126. (b)	127. (d)	128. (a)	129. (c)	130. (d)
131. (d)	132. (b)	133. (b)	134. (c)	135. (c)	136. (b)	137. (b)	138. (a)	139. (b)	140. (a)
141. (d)	142. (a)	143. (b)	144. (a)	145. (a)	146. (b)	147. (c)	148. (*)	149. (a)	150. (a)
151. (b)	152. (c)	153. (c)	154. (c)	155. (d)	156. (b)	157. (c)	158. (a)	159. (d)	160. (a)
161. (a)	162. (b)	163. (a)	164. (c)	165. (b)	166. (b)	167. (b)	168. (b)	169. (b)	170. (a)
171. (b)	172. (a)	173. (c)	174. (d)	175. (c)	176. (a)	177. (b)	178. (b)	179. (b)	180. (b)

HINTS & SOLUTIONS

Physics

1. *(a)* The aerofoils are so designed that,

$$p_{\text{top side}} < p_{\text{lower side}}$$

so that the aerofoils get a lifting force in upward direction.

According to Bernoulli's theorem, where the pressure is large, the velocity will be minimum or *vice-versa*.

Thus, $$v_{\text{top side}} > v_{\text{lower side}}$$

2. *(c)* Planck's constant, $h = \dfrac{E}{\nu}$

So, dimension of h is $= \left[\dfrac{ML^2T^{-2}}{T^{-1}}\right] = [ML^2T^{-1}]$

Angular momentum, $L = mvr$

Dimension of L is $= [M]\,[LT^{-1}]\,[L] = [ML^2T^{-1}]$

Work, W = Force × Displacement

$\therefore$ Dimensions of $W = [MLT^{-2}] \times [L] = [ML^2T^{-2}]$

Linear momentum, p = Mass × Velocity

Dimensions of $p = [M][LT^{-1}] = [MLT^{-1}]$

Impulse, $I = \dfrac{\text{Force}}{\text{Time}}$

The dimensions of $I = \dfrac{[MLT^{-2}]}{[T]} = [MLT^{-3}]$

Hence, only angular momentum has same dimensions as that of Planck's constant.

3. *(b)* Energy released on bombarding U^{235} by neutron

$= 200\,\text{MeV}$

$= 200 \times 10^6 \times 1.6 \times 10^{-19}\ \text{J}$

Power output of atomic reactor = 1.6 MW

$$= 1.6 \times 10^6 \text{ W}$$

$$\therefore \text{ Rate of fission } = \frac{1.6 \times 10^6}{200 \times 10^6 \times 1.6 \times 10^{-19}} = 5 \times 10^{16} \text{ s}^{-1}$$

4. *(d)* The number 5.355 rounded off to three significant figures becomes 5.36, since preceding digit of 5 is odd, hence it is raised by 1.

On other hand, the number 5.345 rounded off to three significant figures becomes 5.34. Since, the preceding digit of 5 is even.

5. *(d)* Distance of nth dark fringe from central fringe,

$$x_n = \frac{(2n-1)\lambda D}{2d}$$

For second dark fringe, $n = 2$

$$\therefore \quad x_2 = \frac{(2 \times 2 - 1)\lambda D}{2d} = \frac{3\lambda D}{2d}$$

$$\Rightarrow \quad 1 \times 10^{-3} = \frac{3 \times \lambda \times 1}{2 \times 0.9 \times 10^{-3}} \Rightarrow \lambda = 6 \times 10^{-5} \text{ cm}$$

6. *(a)* Acceleration of the particle is given as

$$a = \sqrt{a_x^2 + a_y^2}$$

$$\text{Here, } a_x = \frac{d^2x}{dt^2} = \frac{d}{dt}\cdot\frac{dx}{dt} = \frac{d}{dt}\left[\frac{d}{dt}\cdot(4t^2 + 5t + 16)\right]$$

$$= \frac{d}{dt}(8t + 5) = 8$$

$$\text{and} \quad a_y = d^2y/dt^2 = \frac{d}{dt}\cdot\frac{dy}{dt} = \frac{d}{dt}\left[\frac{d}{dt}\cdot 5t\right] = \frac{d}{dt}\cdot 5 = 0$$

$$\Rightarrow \quad a = \sqrt{a_x^2 + a_y^2} = \sqrt{(8)^2 + 0} = 8$$

7. *(d)* For the given concave lens to behave as a diverging lens its focal length f must be negative. As in the lens Maker's formula given as follows :

$$\frac{1}{f} = ({}^1n_2 - 1)\left(\frac{1}{R_1} - \frac{1}{R_2}\right)$$

where, ${}^1n_2$ is the refractive index of the medium 2 (i.e. the medium inside the thin lens) with respect to the refractive index of medium 1 (i.e. the medium outside of the lens) the expression $\left(\frac{1}{R_1} - \frac{1}{R_2}\right)$ is negative.

So, $({}^1n_2 - 1) > 0 \Rightarrow \frac{n_2}{n_1} > 1$ or $n_2 > n_1$

Thus, if the lens is filled with L_2 having refractive index n_{L_2} and placed in L_1 having refractive index n_{L_1}, the above condition will be satisfied and it will diverge a parallel beam of light.

8. *(c)* Distance of nth maxima, $x = n\lambda\frac{D}{d} \Rightarrow x \propto \lambda$

As, $\lambda_b < \lambda_g$;

$\therefore x_{\text{blue}} < x_{\text{green}}$

9. *(b)* According to conservation of energy, at this height (h).

$$\text{PE} = \frac{\text{KE}}{2}$$

$$\Rightarrow \quad mgh = \frac{98}{2}$$

$$\therefore mgh = \frac{98}{2} \text{ or } 2 \times 9.8 \times h = 49 \text{ or } h = 2.5 \text{ m}$$

10. *(c)* Weight of the body at earth's surface,

$$W = mg = 250 \text{ N} \quad \ldots\text{(i)}$$

Acceleration due to gravity at depth h from earth's surface

$$g' = g\left(1 - \frac{h}{R_e}\right)$$

Here, $h = R_e/2$

$$\therefore \quad g' = g\left(1 - \frac{R_e/2}{R_e}\right) = g\left(1 - \frac{1}{2}\right) \Rightarrow g' = \frac{g}{2}$$

$\therefore$ Weight of the body at depth h,

$$W' = mg = \frac{mg}{2}$$

Using Eq. (i), we get

$$W' = \frac{250}{2} = 125 \text{ N}$$

So, weight of the body will be 125 N.

11. *(b)* Two capacitors are given as below

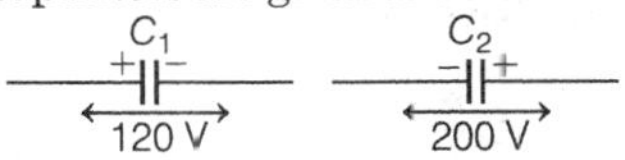

For potential to be made zero after connection, the charge on both capacitors should be equal.

$$\therefore \quad q_1 = q_2$$

$$C_1V_1 = C_2V_2 \Rightarrow 120\,C_1 = 200\,C_2$$

$$\Rightarrow \quad 3C_1 = 5C_2$$

12. *(a)* Given, dipole moment of dipoles AB and $CD = p$

Angle, $\theta = 120°$

If p_1 and p_2 are the dipole moments of AB and CD, then net dipole moment,

$$p_{\text{net}} = \sqrt{p_1^2 + p_2^2 + 2p_1p_2\cos\theta}$$

$$= \sqrt{p^2 + p^2 + 2p^2\cos 120°} \quad [\,p_1 = p_2 = p]$$

$$= \sqrt{p^2 + p^2 - p^2} = p \quad \left[\cos 120° = -\frac{1}{2}\right]$$

When this system is subjected to electric field E at an angle θ,

$$\tau = p_{\text{net}}E\sin\theta$$

$\Rightarrow \tau = pE\sin\theta = \mathbf{p} \times \mathbf{E}$ and it is along positive Z-axis, because τ acts perpendicular to plane containing **p** and **E**, i.e. perpendicular to XY-plane.

13. (*b*) Increase in surface energy

= Work done in area × Surface tension

Increase in surface area,

$$\Delta A = (5 \times 4 - 4 \times 2) \times 2$$
$$= (20 - 8) \times 2 = 24 \text{ cm}^2 = 24 \times 10^{-4} \text{ m}^2$$

So, work done, $W = T \cdot \Delta A$

$$3 \times 10^{-4} = T \times 24 \times 10^{-4}$$
$$T = \frac{1}{8} = 0.125 \text{ N/m}$$

14. (*a*) When *A* and *C* are touched, charge is distributed equally on them as shown below

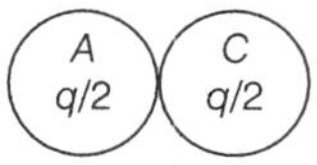

i.e. $q_A = q_C = \dfrac{q}{2}$

When *C* is touched with *B*, total charge of *B* and *C*

$$= q + q/2 = \frac{3q}{2}$$

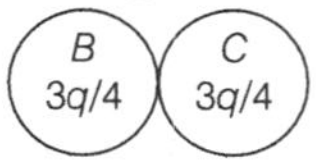

When *B* and *C* are separated, then charge is equally shared between them, i.e. $q_B = q_C = \dfrac{3q}{4}$

So, finally we have following situation

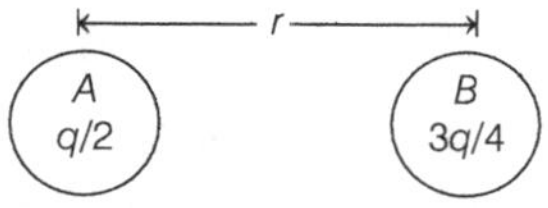

Given, $q_A = q_B = 6.5 \times 10^{-7}$ C and $r = 50 \times 10^{-2}$ m

∴ New force of repulsion between *A* and *B* is

$$F = \frac{9 \times 10^9 \times q_A q_B}{r^2} = \frac{9 \times 10^9 \times \frac{1}{2} \times \frac{3}{4} \times (6.5 \times 10^{-7})^2}{(0.5)^2}$$
$$= 5.7 \times 10^{-3} \text{ N}$$

15. (*c*) For the equilibrium condition of mass $A(2m)$

$$F_s = T + 2mg$$

where, F_s = Restoring force in the string

$$F_s = mg + 2mg$$
$$F_s = 3\,mg$$
$$\therefore \quad T = mg$$

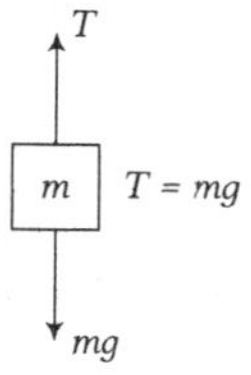

When the string breaks, *T* will suddenly disappear.

For *B*, $F_s - 2mg = 2ma$

$$3mg - 2mg = 2ma \qquad [F_s = 3mg]$$
$$a = g/2$$

16. (*a*) Given, $P = 100$ W and $V = 200$ V

As, power, $P = Vi$

$$\Rightarrow \quad i = \frac{P}{V} = \frac{100}{200} = 0.5 \text{ A}$$

Charge passing through the lamp in 1s,

$$q = i \times t = 0.5 \times 1 = 0.5 \text{ C} \qquad (\because t = 1 \text{ s})$$

Therefore, number of electrons moving through the filament per second,

$$n = q/e = \frac{0.5}{1.6 \times 10^{-19}} = 3.1 \times 10^{18}$$

17. (*b*) Range of projectile launched at an angle θ is same as the range of projectile launched at angle 2θ.

$$\Rightarrow \quad \frac{u^2 \sin 2(2\theta)}{g} = \frac{u^2 \sin 2\theta}{g} \Rightarrow \sin 2(2\theta) = \sin 2\theta$$
$$\Rightarrow 2\sin 2\theta \cos 2\theta = 2\sin\theta\cos\theta$$
$$4\sin\theta\cos\theta\cos 2\theta = 2\sin\theta\cos\theta$$
$$\Rightarrow 4\cos 2\theta = 2 \Rightarrow \cos 2\theta = \frac{1}{2}$$
$$\Rightarrow \quad \cos 2\theta = \cos 60° \Rightarrow 2\theta = 60°$$
$$\Rightarrow \quad \theta = 30°$$

18. (*c*) Resistance of bulb, $R = \dfrac{V^2}{P} = \dfrac{(230)^2}{100} = 529\ \Omega$

When the voltage drops to 115 V, heat and light energy produced by the bulb in 20 min is given by

$$W = \frac{V^2}{R} t = \frac{(115)^2}{529} \times 20 \times 60 = 30000 \text{ J}$$

19. (*b*) Consider the figure given below

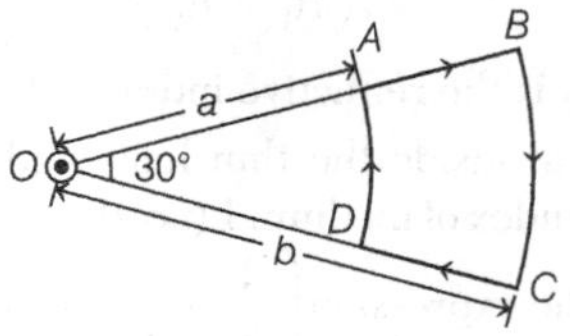

The magnetic field at the centre of an arc subtended at an angle θ is given by $B = \dfrac{\mu_0 I}{2R} \times \dfrac{\theta}{2\pi}$

where, *I* is current and *R* is radius.

Now, magnetic field due to wire *AB* and *CD* is

$$B_{AB} = B_{CD} = 0 \quad [\because \theta = 0° \text{ for } AB \text{ and } CD]$$

and due to arc *BC*,

$$B_{BC} = \frac{\mu_0 I}{2b} \times \left(\frac{\pi}{6}\right) \times \frac{1}{2\pi}, \text{ downward}$$
$$\left[\theta = \frac{\pi}{6}, R = b\right]$$

Similarly due to arc DA,

$$B_{DA} = \frac{\mu_0 I}{2a} \times \left(\frac{\pi}{6}\right) \times \frac{1}{2\pi}, \text{ upward} \quad \left[\theta = \frac{\pi}{6}, R = a\right]$$

$\therefore$ Net magnetic field at O,

$$B = B_{AB} + B_{BC} + B_{CD} + B_{DA}$$

$$\Rightarrow \quad B = 0 + \frac{\mu_0 I}{4b} \times \left(\frac{\pi}{6\pi}\right) + 0 - \frac{\mu_0 I}{4a} \times \left(\frac{\pi}{6\pi}\right)$$

$$= \frac{\mu_0 I}{24b} - \frac{\mu_0 I}{24a} = \frac{\mu_0 I}{24\,ab}(a - b)$$

20. *(b)* Acceleration in both the cases will be same.

$$N_1 = ma \text{ but } N_2 = (2m)a$$

$$\therefore \quad \frac{N_1}{N_2} = \frac{1}{2}$$

21. *(a)* The magnetic field within the turns of toroid is

$$B = \frac{\mu_0 NI}{2\pi r}$$

where, N = number of turns, I = current in loops

and r = radius of each turn.

Given, $N_1 = 200, N_2 = 100, r_1 = 40$ cm, $r_2 = 20$ cm

and current I is same, then

$$\frac{B_1}{B_2} = \frac{\mu_0 N_1 I}{2\pi r_1} \times \frac{2\pi r_2}{\mu_0 N_2 I}$$

Substituting the given values in the above relation, we get

$$\frac{B_1}{B_2} = \left(\frac{N_1}{N_2}\right)\left(\frac{r_2}{r_1}\right)$$

$$= \left(\frac{200}{100}\right)\left(\frac{20}{40}\right) = 2 \times \frac{1}{2} = 1$$

$\therefore \quad B_1 : B_2 = 1 : 1$

The ratio of their magnetic fields along the two loops is 1 : 1.

22. *(c)* Mass of the body, $m = 200 \text{ g} = 200 \times 10^{-3}$ kg

Height of the body, $h = 200$ m

Potential energy, $U = mgh = 200 \times 10^{-3} \times 10 \times 200$

$= 400$ J

23. *(c)* According to the question,

$$\frac{GMm}{(R+h)^2} = \frac{1}{16}\frac{GMm}{R^2}$$

where, m = mass of the body

and $\frac{GM}{R^2}$ = gravitational acceleration.

$$\frac{1}{(R+h)^2} = \frac{1}{16R^2}$$

or $\quad \frac{R}{R+h} = \frac{1}{4}$ or $\frac{R+h}{R} = 4$

$$h = 3R$$

24. *(a)* Temperature first increases from −10°C to 0°C. Then, remains constant at 0°C till whole ice is melted. Then, it increases from 0°C to 100°C. Again, it remains constant at 100°C till whole water converts into steam.

25. *(a)* We know $E_0 = cB_0$, where c is the velocity of light.

$$\therefore \quad c = \nu\lambda = \frac{\omega}{2\pi}\lambda = \frac{\omega}{k}$$

Thus, $\quad E_0 = \frac{\omega}{k} B_0$

or $\quad E_0 k = B_0\,\omega$

26. *(c)* Given, $P_1 = 40$ D and $P_2 = 20$ D

We have, $P_{eff} = 40 + 20 = 60$ D

$$\therefore \quad f = \frac{100}{P_{eff}} = \frac{100}{60} = 1.67 \text{ cm}$$

27. *(a)* Ice (−10°C) converts into steam as follows

(c_i = specific heat of ice, c_w = specific heat of water)

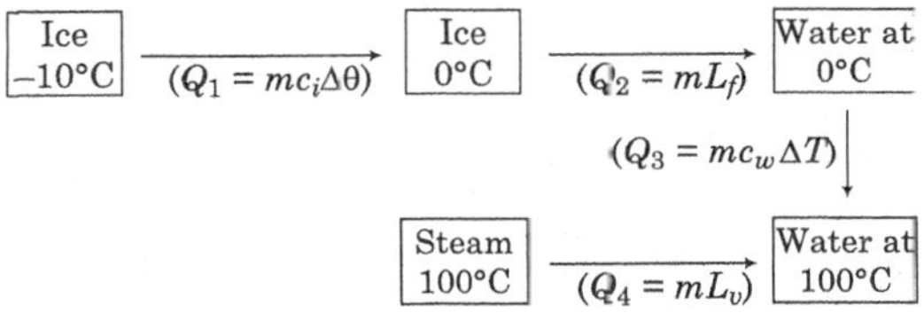

Total heat required, $Q = Q_1 + Q_2 + Q_3 + Q_4$

$$\Rightarrow Q = 1 \times 0.5(10) + 1 \times 80 + 1 \times 1 \times (100 - 0) + 1 \times 540 = 725 \text{ cal}$$

Hence, work done, $W = JQ = 4.2 \times 725 = 3045$ J

28. *(a)* Apparent depth of mark as seen through a glass slab of thickness x and refractive index μ is

$$= \frac{\text{real depth}}{\text{refractive index}} = \frac{3}{1.5} = 2 \text{ cm}$$

As image appears to be raised by 1 cm, therefore microscope must be moved upward by 1 cm.

29. *(c)* Bulk modulus of the material of the rubber,

$$B = \frac{\Delta p}{\Delta V / V} = \frac{100}{0.01/100} = 10^6 \text{ atm} = 10^{11} \text{ Nm}^{-2}$$

[Since, 1 atm = 10^5 N/m^2]

$$= 10^{12} \text{ dyne cm}^{-2}$$

30. *(d)* Decreasing order of wavelength of various rays is Microwave > Infrared > Ultraviolet > Gamma rays.

31. *(d)* The frequency of the stretched string is given by

$$\nu = \frac{n}{2l}\sqrt{\frac{T}{\mu}}$$

Therefore,

$$\nu_{steel} = \frac{n_1}{2 \times 80 \times 10^{-2}}\sqrt{\frac{100}{7800 \times 10^{-5}}} \quad \ldots(i)$$

and $$\nu_{Al} = \frac{n_2}{2 \times 60 \times 10^{-2}} \sqrt{\frac{100}{3 \times 10^{-5} \times 2600}} \quad \ldots \text{(ii)}$$

On solving Eqs. (i) and (ii), we get

$$\frac{n_1}{n_2} = \frac{4}{3}$$

$$\nu_{steel} = \frac{4}{2 \times 0.8} \sqrt{\frac{100}{7800 \times 10^{-5}}} = 89.5 \text{ Hz}$$

[from Eq. (i)]

In composite string, different harmonics give rise to a common frequency.

$$\therefore \quad \nu_{steel} = \nu_{Al} = 89.5 \text{ Hz}$$

32. *(b)* $\therefore \frac{I_1}{I_2} = \frac{A_1^2}{A_2^2} = \left(\frac{5}{10}\right)^2 = \frac{1}{4}$ or $1 : 4$

33. *(d)* $T = 2\pi \sqrt{\frac{l}{g}}$ and $T' = 2\pi \sqrt{\frac{l}{\left(g + \frac{g}{4}\right)}}$

[For upward motion with acceleration a]

Time period, $T = 2\pi \sqrt{\frac{l}{g + a}}$

or $$T' = \frac{2}{\sqrt{5}} T = 2 \text{ s} \qquad [\, T = \sqrt{5} \text{ s}]$$

34. *(c)* Here, $X_L = 1\,\Omega$, $R = 2\Omega$, $E_V = 6\text{ V}$, $P = ?$

$$\therefore \quad Z = \sqrt{X_L^2 + R^2} = \sqrt{1^2 + 2^2} = \sqrt{5}\,\Omega$$

$$\therefore \quad I_V = \frac{E_V}{Z} = \frac{6}{\sqrt{5}} \text{ A}$$

$$\therefore \quad P = E_V I_V \cos\theta$$

$$= 6 \times \frac{6}{\sqrt{5}} \times \frac{2}{\sqrt{5}}$$

$$= 14.4 \text{ W}$$

35. *(c)* Output of the given circuit is given by

$$y = \overline{(AB)(C)} = \overline{AB} + \overline{C} = \overline{A} + \overline{B} + \overline{C}$$

When $A = B = C = 0$,

$$Y_1 = \overline{0} + \overline{0} + \overline{0} = 1 + 1 + 1 = 1$$

When $A = B = C = 1$,

$$Y_2 = \overline{1} + \overline{1} + \overline{1} = 0 + 0 + 0 = 0$$

36. *(c)* Here, $\mathbf{A} = L^2 \mathbf{k}$

and $\mathbf{B} = B_0 (2\mathbf{i} + 3\mathbf{j} + 4\mathbf{k})$

$\phi = ?$

As, $\phi = \mathbf{B} \cdot \mathbf{A} = B_0 (2\mathbf{i} + 3\mathbf{j} + 4\mathbf{k}) \cdot L^2 \mathbf{k}$

$\therefore \quad \phi = (4 B_0 L^2)$ Wb

37. *(c)* Given, $\lambda = 300$ m, $c = 3 \times 10^8$ m/s

$$\therefore \text{Frequency, } n = \frac{c}{\lambda} = \frac{3 \times 10^8}{300} = 10^6 \text{ Hz}$$

Resonance frequency, $n = \frac{1}{2\pi \sqrt{LC}}$

or $$\sqrt{LC} = \frac{1}{2\pi n} \text{ or } LC = \frac{1}{4\pi^2 n^2}$$

Here, $$C = 2.4 \times 10^{-6} \text{ F}$$

$$\therefore \quad L = \frac{1}{4\pi^2 (10^6)^2 \times 2.4 \times 10^{-6}} = 10^{-8} \text{ H}$$

38. *(d)* Average velocity $= \frac{\text{Total displacement}}{\text{Total time}}$

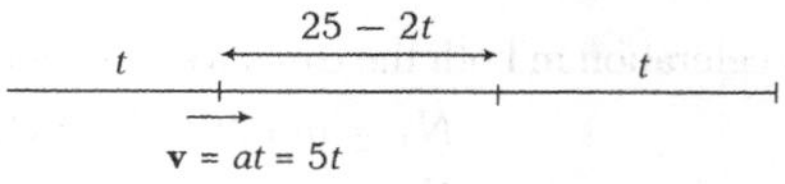

or $$20 = \frac{\frac{1}{2} \times a \times t^2 + (at)(25 - 2t) + \frac{1}{2} \times a \times t^2}{25}$$

Solving this equation with, $a = 5 \text{ ms}^{-2}$ we get,

$$t = 15 \text{ s}$$

Thus, the particle moved uniformly for

$$25 - 2t = 25 - 2 \times 5 = 15 \text{ s.}$$

39. *(d)* Given, $\phi = (3t^2 + 4t + 9)$ Wb

$$\therefore \; e = \frac{d\phi}{dt} = \frac{d(3t^2 + 4t + 9)}{dt} = 6t + 4$$

At $t = 2$, we get

$$e = 6 \times 2 + 4 = 16 \text{ V}$$

40. *(d)* Work done in an isothermal process,

$$W = 2.3026\, nRT \log_{10}\left(\frac{V_2}{V_1}\right)$$

$$= 2.3026 \times 10 \times 8.3 \times 600 \log_{10}\left(\frac{10}{100}\right)$$

$$= -11.4 \times 10^4 \text{ J}$$

41. *(d)* As we know the relation between the magnetic permeability and susceptibility of material, i.e.

$$\mu_r = 1 + \chi_m \quad \ldots \text{(i)}$$

For diamagnetic substances, $\mu_r < 1$

So, according to Eq. (i), the magnetic susceptibility (χ_m) of diamagnetic substance will be negative.

42. *(c)* $Y = \frac{F/A}{\Delta L / L} = \frac{F}{A} \times \frac{L}{\Delta L} = \frac{4F}{\pi d^2} \times \frac{L}{\Delta L} \qquad \left(\because A = \frac{\pi d^2}{4}\right)$

Hence, $$\frac{\Delta L_1}{\Delta L_2} = \frac{F_1}{F_2} \times \frac{d_2^2}{d_1^2} \times \frac{L_1}{L_2} \times \frac{Y_2}{Y_1}$$

$$= \frac{F}{F} \times \left(\frac{1}{2}\right)^2 \times \left(\frac{1}{2}\right) \times \frac{Y}{Y} = \frac{1}{8} \text{ or } 1 : 8$$

43. *(a)* As temperature of a ferromagnetic material is raised, its susceptibility χ remains constant first and then decreases as shown in figure (a).

44. *(a)* $\frac{1}{2}kA^2 = \frac{1}{2} \times 2 \times 10^6 \times (0.01)^2 = 100\,\text{J}$

At mean position, $U = 60$ J and $K = 100$ J
At extreme positions, $U = 160$ J and $K = 0$

45. *(b)* The position vector of centre of mass

$$\mathbf{r} = \frac{m_1\mathbf{r}_1 + m_2\mathbf{r}_2}{m_1 + m_2} = \frac{1(\mathbf{i} + 2\mathbf{j} + \mathbf{k}) + 3(-3\mathbf{i} - 2\mathbf{j} + \mathbf{k})}{1 + 3}$$

$$= \frac{1}{4}(-8\,\mathbf{i} - 4\,\mathbf{j} + 4\,\mathbf{k}) = -2\mathbf{i} - \mathbf{j} + \mathbf{k}$$

46. *(c)* It is given that

$$v = \frac{t^2}{10} + 20$$

Differentiating both sides w.r.t. time, we get

$$\frac{dv}{dt} = \frac{2t}{10} + 0 = \frac{t}{5}$$

$\therefore$ Acceleration, $a = \frac{dv}{dt} = \frac{t}{5} \neq$ constant

Hence, it is a case of non-uniform acceleration.

47. *(a)* Position vector of centre of mass of the system,

$$r_{\text{cm}} = \frac{m_1r_1 + m_2r_2}{m_1 + m_2} = \frac{m2l + 2ml}{m + 2m} = \frac{4ml}{3m} = \frac{4}{3}l$$

48. *(c)* $\therefore d = \sqrt{2Rh} = \sqrt{2 \times 6.4 \times 10^4 \times 240}$ m $= 55$ km

49. *(d)* Work done in increasing the separation from a to $2a$ is

$$W = U_f - U_i \qquad \ldots\text{(i)}$$

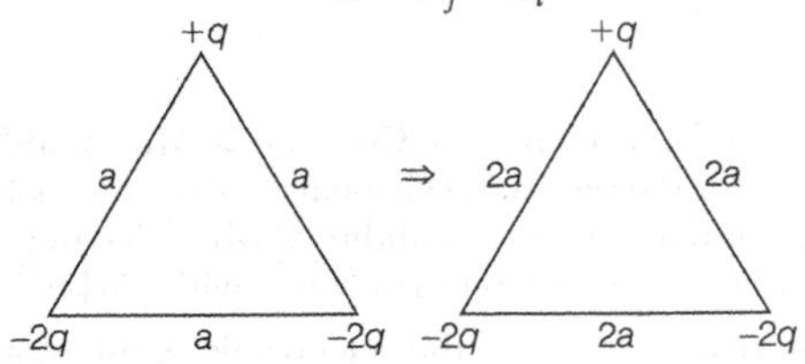

Here,

$$U_i = \frac{1}{4\pi\varepsilon_0}\left[\frac{q(-2q)}{a} + \frac{q(-2q)}{a} + \frac{(-2q)(-2q)}{a}\right]$$

$$= \frac{1}{4\pi\varepsilon_0 a}[-2q^2 - 2q^2 + 4q^2] = 0$$

Similarly,

$$U_f = \frac{1}{4\pi\varepsilon_0(2a)}(-2q^2 - 2q^2 + 4q^2) = 0$$

Hence, from Eq. (i)

$$W = U_f - U_i = 0$$

50. *(c)* The graph of cut-off voltage *versus* frequency of incident light is as shown below

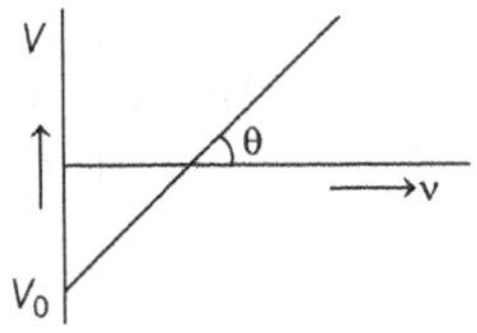

where, slope of graph, $\tan\theta = 4.12 \times 10^{-15}$ V-s
and charge on electron, $e = 1.6 \times 10^{-19}$ C

From graph, we can write $\tan\theta = \frac{\Delta V}{\Delta \nu}$

As we know, for photoelectric effect, $eV = h\nu - \phi$

Differentiating both sides of the above equation, we get

$$\frac{\Delta V}{\Delta \nu} = \frac{h}{e}$$

$$\therefore \quad \frac{h}{e} = 4.12 \times 10^{-15}$$

$$h = 1.6 \times 10^{-19} \times 4.12 \times 10^{-15} = 6.592 \times 10^{-34}$$

$\therefore$ Value of Planck's constant is 6.592×10^{-34} Js.

51. *(a)* As charges at A and B are at equal distance from $10\,\mu$C at the centre. So, potential at A and B due to $10\,\mu$C charge are equal.

$\therefore$ Potential difference, $(V_A - V_B) = 0$

Thus, work done, $W_{AB} = q(V_B - V_A) = 0$.

52. *(d)* The generation of emf by a solar cell, when light falls on, is due to the following three basic processes : generation, separation and collection.

(i) Generation of electron-hole pairs due to light (with $h\nu > E_g$) close to the junction.

(ii) Separation of electrons and holes due to electric field E of the depletion region. Electrons are swept to n-side and holes to p-side.

(iii) The electrons reaching the n-side are collected by the front contact and holes reaching p-side are collected by the back contact.
Thus, p-side becomes positive and n-side becomes negative giving rise to photovoltage.
Hence, all the given options are correct.

53. *(a)* At constant pressure,

$$(\Delta Q)_p = \mu C_p \Delta T$$
$$= 1 \times C_p \times (30 - 20) = 40$$
$$C_p = 4 \text{ cal mol}^{-1}\text{K}^{-1}$$
$$C_V = C_p - R$$
$$= 4 - 2 = 2 \text{ cal mol}^{-1}\text{K}^{-1}$$

Now, $(\Delta Q)_V = \mu C_V \Delta T = 1 \times 2 \times (30 - 20)$
$= 20$ cal

54. *(a)* Given, atomic mass of gold isotopes, $A_1 = 197$

and atomic mass of silver isotope, $A_2 = 107$

As, radius of nucleus, $R = R_0A^{1/3}$

$$\therefore \quad \frac{R_1}{R_2} = \left(\frac{A_1}{A_2}\right)^{1/3}$$

$$= \left(\frac{197}{107}\right)^{1/3} = 1.225 \simeq 1.23$$

The ratio of nuclear radii of the gold isotope $^{197}_{97}\text{Au}$ and silver isotope $^{107}_{47}\text{Ag}$ is 1.23.

55. *(c)* By definition,

$v_{rms} = \sqrt{\frac{v_1^2 + v_2^2}{2}}$, where v_1 and v_2 are the individual velocities of the two particles.

Given, $v_1 = 9 \times 10^6$ m/s

and $v_2 = 1 \times 10^6$ m/s

$$\therefore \quad v_{rms} = \sqrt{\frac{(9 \times 10^6)^2 + (1 \times 10^6)^2}{2}}$$

$$= \sqrt{\frac{81 \times 10^{12} + 1 \times 10^{12}}{2}}$$

$$= \sqrt{\frac{(81+1) \times 10^{12}}{2}} = \sqrt{\frac{82 \times 10^{12}}{2}}$$

$$= \sqrt{41} \times 10^6 \text{ m/s}$$

56. *(b)* Given, E_{bn} of chlorine = 287.67 MeV

and E_{bn} of phosphorus = 262.48 MeV

Binding energy per nucleon of $_{17}Cl^{35}$

$$= \frac{\text{Binding energy}}{\text{Mass number}} = \frac{287.67}{35} = 8.22 \text{ MeV}$$

Similarly,

$$\text{Binding energy per nucleon of } _{15}P^{31} = \frac{262.48}{31} = 8.47 \text{ MeV}$$

Since, BE of $_{15}P^{31}$ is more than BE of $_{17}Cl^{35}$, hence $_{15}P^{31}$ is more stable.

57. *(b)* Internal energy and entropy are definitely state functions as they depend only on the final and initial states. Internal energy does not change in isothermal process. ΔS can be zero for adiabatic process. Work done in adiabatic process may be non-zero.

58. *(c)*

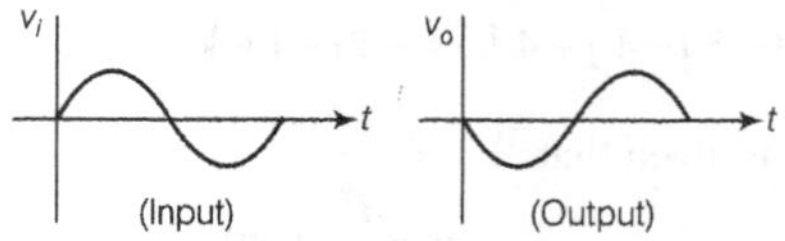

In a CE *n-p-n* transistor amplifier, output is 180° out of phase with input.

59. (a) Momentum of photon, $p = \frac{E}{c} = \frac{h\nu}{c} = \frac{h}{\lambda}$

Given, wavelength, $\lambda = 1$ Å $= 1 \times 10^{-10}$ m

$$\Rightarrow p = \frac{h}{\lambda} = \frac{h}{1 \times 10^{-10}} = 10^{10} h$$

60. *(c)* According to Bohr atomic radius, $r_n \propto n^2$

where, n is principal quantum number.

$$\therefore \quad \frac{r_n}{r_1} = \frac{n^2}{1^2} \Rightarrow r_n = n^2 r \qquad [\because r_1 = r]$$

So, for $n = 2$, $r_2 = 2^2 r = 4r$

Chemistry

61. *(d)* $CaCO_3(s) \overset{\Delta}{\rightleftharpoons} CaO(s) + CO_2\uparrow; K_{p_1} = 8 \times 10^{-2}$

$$CO_2(g) + C(s) \longrightarrow 2CO(g); K_{p_2} = 2$$

Thus, for the reaction,

$$CaCO_3(s) + C(s) \rightleftharpoons CaO(s) + 2CO(g)$$

$$K'_p = K_{p_1} \times K_{p_2} = 8 \times 10^{-2} \times 2 = 16 \times 10^{-2}$$

$$\therefore \quad K'_p = (p_{CO(g)})^2$$

$$\Rightarrow \quad p_{CO} = \sqrt{K'_p} = \sqrt{16 \times 10^{-2}} = 4 \times 10^{-1} = 0.4 \text{ atm}$$

62. *(d)* The net change in internal energy, i.e. $\Delta E = 0$ as it is a cyclic process.

63. *(d)* Fe has minimum value of third ionisation enthalpy. Ground state electronic configuration of Fe is $[Ar]3d^6 4s^2$.

Fe^{2+} has $[Ar]3d^6$ configuration, whereas Fe^{3+} has $[Ar]3d^5$. The latter is a stable configuration and easier to ionise Fe^{2+} to Fe^{3+} than expected.

Hence, possess least value.

Ni has highest value of third ionisation enthalpy due to its greater nuclear charge and smaller size.

Due to the same reason, Co > Fe > Mn should be the order for the remaining elements, but the anomalous order is due to greater stability of Mn^{2+} having $[Ar]3d^5$ configuration than Mn^{3+} with $[Ar]3d^4$.

Whereas, for Co^+, the electronic configuration is $[Ar]3d^7$, Thus, ionisation enthalpy needed to remove third electron is less as compared to that of Mn^{2+}.

64. *(d)* Reverse osmosis is a process in which direction of osmosis is reversed, if a pressure larger than the osmotic pressure is applied to the solution. It is a process in which solvent moves from solution of higher concentration to solution of lower concentration. This method is used in desalination to get salt water from sea water.

65. *(c)* Angular node $(l) = 3$

Total nodes = radial nodes + angular nodes

$$3 = (n - l - 1) + l$$

$$3 = n - 1$$

$$\Rightarrow \quad n = 4$$

$\therefore$ Orbital having 3 angular nodes and 3 total nodes

$$= nl = 4f \qquad [\because l = 3 \text{ for } f\text{- orbital}]$$

66. *(c)* The combined role of the inductive effect, solvation effect and steric hindrance of the alkyl group decides the basic strength of alkylamines in the aqueous medium. In case, the alkyl group is big such as C_2H_5, there will be steric hindrance to H-bonding. The order of basic strength in case of ethyl substituted amines in aqueous solution is as follows :

$$(C_2H_5)_2NH(2°) > (C_2H_5)_3N(3°) > C_2H_5NH_2(1°)$$

67. *(d)* 0.03% of carbon dioxide present in atmosphere can be removed by photosynthesis, which is a process of conversion of atmospheric CO_2 to carbohydrate like glucose. The overall chemical change can be expressed as shown below

$$6CO_2 + 12H_2O \xrightarrow[\text{Chlorophyll}]{h\nu} C_6H_{12}O_6 + 6O_2 + 6H_2O$$

68. *(b)* Given, I.E. of Xe = 279 kcal/mol

B.E. (F—F) = 38 kcal/mol

Electron affinity of F = 85 kcal/mol

$$\Delta_r H = \text{heat supplied} - \text{heat evolved}$$

$$\therefore \quad 292 = (4x + 279) - (38 + 85)$$

$$\Rightarrow \quad x = \frac{292 - 279 + 38 + 85}{4} \Rightarrow x = 34 \text{ kcal mol}^{-1}.$$

69. *(a)* In a cubic close packed lattice of oxide ions, there would be two tetrahedral and one octahedral void per oxide ion. Since, the formula shows the presence of 4 oxide ions, the number of tetrahedral voids is eight and that of octahedral voids is four. Out of the eight tetrahedral voids, one is occupied by *X*.

∴ Percentage of tetrahedral voids occupied

$$= \frac{1}{8} \times 100 = 12.5\%$$

70. *(c)* $p^\circ_{CHCl_3} = 200$ atm, $p^\circ_{CH_2Cl_2} = 41.5$ atm

$$n_{CHCl_3} = \frac{11.9}{11.9} = 0.1$$

$$n_{CH_2Cl_2} = \frac{17}{85} = 0.2$$

$$p_T = p^\circ_A \chi_A = p^\circ_B \chi_B = 200 \times \frac{0.1}{0.3} + 41.5 \times \frac{0.2}{0.3}$$

$$= 94.33 \text{ atm}$$

71. *(a)* $p_1 = 760$ mm Hg, $V_1 = 600$ mL,

$T_1 = 25 + 273 = 298$ K

$V_2 = 640$ mL and $T_2 = 10 + 273 = 283$ K

According to combined gas law, $\frac{p_1V_1}{T_1} = \frac{p_2V_2}{T_2}$

$$\Rightarrow \quad p_2 = \frac{p_1V_1T_2}{T_1V_2}$$

$$\Rightarrow \quad p_2 = \frac{(760 \text{ mm Hg}) \times (600 \text{ mL}) \times (283 \text{ K})}{(298 \text{ K}) \times (640 \text{ mL})}$$

$$= 676.6 \text{ mmHg} \approx 677 \text{ mm Hg}$$

72. *(c)* When benzene is treated with an alkyl halide in the presence of anhydrous aluminium chloride, alkylbenzene is formed.

This reaction is called Friedel-Craft's alkylation reaction as shown below

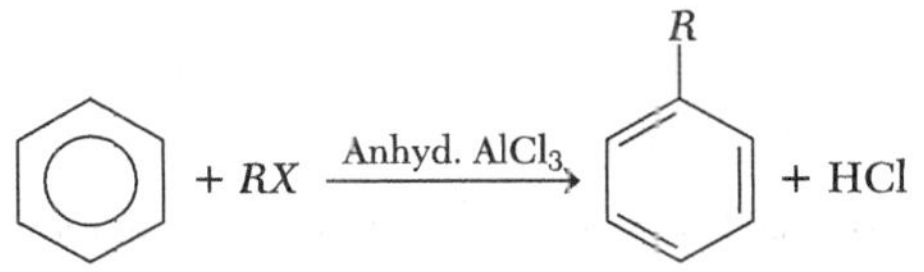

Benzene Alkyl benzene

73. *(b)* The secondary structure of protein refers to the shape in which a long polypeptide chain can exist. These structures arise due to the regular folding of the backbone of the polypeptide chain due to hydrogen bonding between $-\overset{\overset{\displaystyle O}{\|}}{C}-$ and —NH— groups of the peptide bond.

74. *(a)* The by-product (A) formed in the reaction is $POCl_3$ and HCl.

Complete reaction is

$$\underset{\text{Alcohol}}{ROH} + PCl_5 \longrightarrow R\text{—}Cl + \underset{(A)}{POCl_3} + HCl$$

75. *(d)* Given, $\Delta G° = 13.8$ kJ / mol

$$= 13.8 \times 10^3 \text{ J / mol}$$

$$\Delta G° = -RT \ln K_C$$

$$\Rightarrow \quad 13800 = -8.314 \times 298 \times \ln K_C$$

$$\Rightarrow \quad K_C = 3.81 \times 10^{-3}$$

76. *(b)* Below Boyle's temperature, real gases first show decrease in Z value with increasing pressure, which reaches a minimum value.

77. *(a)* Reaction of hydrogen with fluorine occurs even in the dark, while with iodine it requires a catalyst.

Thus, the order of reactivity of X_2 is

$$F_2 > Cl_2 > Br_2 > I_2.$$

78. *(d)* Boron behaves anomalously w.r.t its other group members due to its extremely small size, high electronegativity and also large charge to radius ratio.

79. *(c)* The compound has two allyl hydrogen atoms (γ). When reacts with $Br_2/h\nu$, it readily undergoes allylic free radical substitution and forms 3, 3-dibromobut-1-ene.

$$\underset{\text{But-1-ene}}{\overset{\delta}{CH_3}\text{—}\overset{\gamma}{CH_2}\text{—}\overset{\beta}{CH}=\overset{\alpha}{CH_2}} \xrightarrow[-HBr]{Br_2/h\nu}$$

$$\underset{\text{3-bromo-but-1-ene}}{\underset{\delta}{CH_3}\text{—}\underset{\gamma}{\overset{\overset{\displaystyle Br}{|}}{CH}}\text{—}\underset{\beta}{CH}=\underset{\alpha}{CH_2}} \xrightarrow[-HBr]{Br_2/h\nu} \underset{\text{3, 3-dibromobut-1-ene}}{\underset{\delta}{CH_3}\text{—}\underset{\underset{\displaystyle Br}{|}}{\overset{\overset{\displaystyle Br}{|}}{C_\gamma}}\text{—}\underset{\beta}{CH}=\underset{\alpha}{CH_2}}$$

80. *(c)* Type of reaction which is represented by the given equation is disproportionation reaction in acidic medium. Here, a single species undergoes simultaneous oxidation and reduction.

Reduction

$$3MnO_4^{2-} + 4H^+ \longrightarrow MnO_2 + 2MnO_4^- + 2H_2O$$

Oxidation

81. *(a)* In $XeOF_4$, Xe is sp^3d^2-hybridised. Geometry of the molecule is octahedral, but shape of the molecule is square pyramidal.

According to VSEPR theory, it has one π-bond. Remaining six electron pairs form an octahedron with one position occupied by a lone pair.

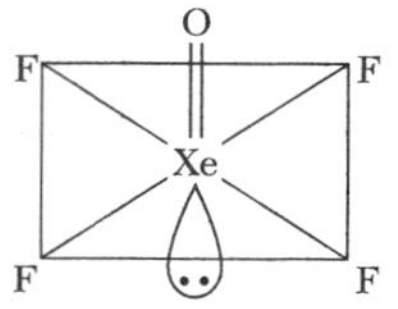

Number of bp = 5
Number of lp = 1

Here, Xe contains one lone pair of electrons.

82. *(b)* The given compound contains benzene nucleus and follow Huckel rule so, naphthalene is a benzenoid aromatic compound.

83. *(b)* The reactions involved in extraction of silver from argentite ore by cyanide process are

$$Ag_2S + CN^- + O_2 \longrightarrow 2[Ag(CN)_2]^- + SO_2 \quad ...(i)$$

$$2[Ag(CN)_2]^- + Zn \longrightarrow [Zn(CN)_4]^{2-} + 2Ag \quad ...(ii)$$

In the reaction (i), sulphide is oxidised to SO_2 by oxygen. In the reaction (ii), silver ion (Ag^+) is reduced to Ag by Zn.

Therefore, O_2 is oxidising agent and Zn is reducing agent.

84. *(d)* Iodobutane (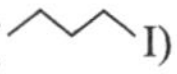) undergoes S_N2 reaction faster because I^- is a good leaving group.

85. *(a)*

Hydrocarbons	Molecular formula	% *s*-character
Ethane	$CH_3—CH_3$	25%
Ethene	$CH_2 = CH_2$	33%
Ethyne	$CH \equiv CH$	50%

As we know that, electronegativity $\propto$ % *s*-character $\propto$ acidic character

Hence, correct order of electronegativity in the given compounds is, ethane < ethene < ethyne.

86. *(c)* Option (c) is correct.

ClO_4^- is tetrahedral. Other options are incorrect.

Corrected forms are as follows :

The structure with hybridisation of given compounds are as follows :

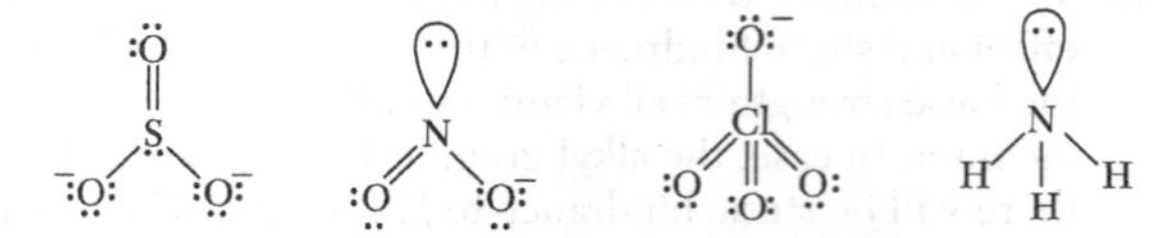

Sulphite ion (SO_3^{2-}) sp^2-trigonal planar; Nitrite ion (NO_2^-) sp^2-bent; Perchlorate ion (ClO_4^-) sp^3-tetrahedral; Ammonia (NH_3) sp^3-pyramidal

87. *(a)* Carbon monoxide (CO) is highly poisonous gas for human being because it binds to haemoglobin to form carboxyhaemoglobin complex, which is about 300 times more stable than the oxygen-haemoglobin complex.

88. *(b)*

$$2K\overset{+1}{}\overset{+5}{Cl}\overset{-2}{O_3} \longrightarrow 2\overset{+1}{K}\overset{-1}{Cl} + 3\overset{0}{O_2}$$

Loss of e^- (oxidation)

Gain of e^- (reduction)

Thus, oxygen is oxidised and chlorine is reduced in the above reaction as loss of e^- in oxygen and gain of e^- in Cl takes place.

89. *(b)* Vapour density $= 59.25$

Molecular mass $= 2\times$ vapour density

$= 2\times 59.25 = 118.50$

$MCl_n = 118.50$

$M + n\times Cl = 118.50$

$4 + n\times Cl = 118.50$

$n \times 35.5 = 114.5 \Rightarrow n = 3$

90. *(a)* If E°_{cell} is positive, reaction is spontaneous, otherwise it is non-spontaneous.

$Mn^{2+} + 2e^- \longrightarrow Mn; E° = -1.18V$

$2Mn^{2+} \longrightarrow 2Mn^{3+} + 2e^-; E° = -1.51$ V

$3Mn^{2+} \longrightarrow Mn + 2Mn^{3+}; E° = E°_{oxi} + E°_{red}$

$= -1.51 + (-1.18) = -2.69V$

Negative E°_{cell} of the reaction indicates that reaction is non-spontaneous.

91. *(a)* Lithium halides are somewhat covalent. It is because of the high polarisation capability of lithium ion. The Li^+ ion is very small in size and hence have high tendency to distorted electron cloud around the negative halide ion. Since, anion with large size can be easily distorted among halides and lithium iodide is the most covalent in nature.

92. *(b)* $O_2(8+8=16) = \sigma 1s^2, \overset{*}{\sigma}1s^2, \sigma 2s^2, \overset{*}{\sigma}2s^2, \sigma 2p_z^2, \pi 2p_x^2 \approx \pi 2p_y^2, \overset{*}{\pi}2p_x^1 \approx \overset{*}{\pi}2p_y^1$

Bond order $= \dfrac{10-6}{2} = 2$

Similarly, $O_2^+ \ (8+8-1=15), BO = \dfrac{10-5}{2} = 2.5$

$\Rightarrow \quad O_2^- (8+8+1=17), \ BO = \dfrac{10-7}{2} = 1.5$

$$\Rightarrow \quad O_2^{2-}(8+8+2=18),\ BO=\frac{10-8}{2}=1$$

$$\therefore \quad \text{Bond order} \propto \frac{1}{\text{bond length}}$$

Thus, O_2^+ has minimum bond length as its bond order is maximum.

93. *(d)* Nylon-6, 6 is prepared by the condensation polymerisation of hexamethylene diamine with adipic acid under high pressure and high temperature. Reaction involved is as follows :

$$\underset{\text{Adipic acid}}{n\text{HOOC(CH}_2)_4\text{COOH}} + \underset{\text{Hexamethylene diamine}}{n\text{H}_2\text{N(CH}_2)_6\text{NH}_2}$$

$$\xrightarrow{\Delta,\ -H_2O} \underset{\text{Nylon-6,6}}{\left[\overset{H}{\overset{|}{N}}-(CH_2)_6-\overset{H}{\overset{|}{N}}-\overset{O}{\overset{\|}{C}}(CH_2)_4-\overset{O}{\overset{\|}{C}} \right]_n}$$

94. *(c)* In BF_3, the dipole moment is zero although the B — F bonds are oriented at an angle of 120° to one another, the three bond moments give a net sum of zero as the resultant of any two is equal and opposite to the third. Structure of BF_3 molecule is as follows :

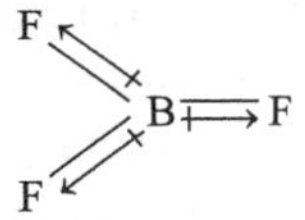

95. *(b)* U and Np have same radii among the given pairs because of lanthanoid contraction.

96. *(c)* $[Co(NH_3)_5SO_4]Br$ and $[Co(NH_3)_5Br]SO_4$ are ionisation isomers, because there is exchange of Br^- and SO_4^{2-} ions.

97. *(b)* $2MnO_4^- + 5C_2O_4^{2-} + 16H^+ \longrightarrow 2Mn^{2+} + 10CO_2 + 8H_2O$

20 mL of 0.1 M $KMnO_4 = 20\times 0.1 = 2$ m mol

$$2 \text{ m mol of } KMnO_4 \equiv 5 \text{ m mol of } C_2O_4^{2-}$$

50 mL of 0.1 M $H_2C_2O_4 = 50\times 0.1 = 5$ m mol

Hence, 20 mL of 0.1 M $KMnO_4 \equiv$ 50 mL of 0.1 M $H_2C_2O_4$.

98. *(b)* The noble gases are completely filled by electrons and it is very difficult to alter this stable electronic configuration, hence they show low chemical reactivity.

99. *(a)* As we know that,

$$\Delta S_{total} = \Delta S_{sys} + \Delta S_{surr}$$

For ΔS_{surr}, we have to consider the heat absorbed by the surroundings which is equal to $-\Delta_r H°$.
At temperature (T), entropy change of the surroundings is

$$\Delta S_{surr} = -\frac{\Delta_r H°}{T} \text{ (at constant pressure)}$$

$$= \frac{-(-1648\times 10^3 \text{ J mol}^{-1})}{298 \text{ K}} = 5530 \text{ JK}^{-1} \text{ mol}^{-1}$$

$$\Delta_r S_{total} = 5530 + (-549.4) = 4980.6 \text{ JK}^{-1} \text{ mol}^{-1}$$

Hence, the above reaction is spontaneous.

100. *(b)* Iodination is very slow and a reversible reaction. It can be carried out in the presence of oxidising agents like HIO_3 or HNO_3 which oxidises the HI formed into I_2 as shown below

$$CH_4 + I_2 \rightleftharpoons CH_3I + HI$$

$$HIO_3 + 5HI \longrightarrow 3I_2 + 3H_2O$$

101. *(b)* $Na \longrightarrow Na^+ + e^-$ [First IE] I.E. = 5.1 eV

$Na^+ + e^- \longrightarrow Na$ [Electron gain enthalpy]

Electron gain enthalpy of Na^+ is reverse of ionisation enthalpy because reaction is reverse, so

$$\Delta H_{eg} = -5.1 \text{ eV}$$

102. *(d)* Number of A atom = 8 (corner) $\times \frac{1}{8}$ (per corner share) = 1

Number of B atoms = 3 (alternate face) $\times \frac{1}{2}$ (face centre share) + 12 (edge) $\times \frac{1}{4}$ (edge centre share)

$$= 1.5 + 3 = 4.5$$

Number of C atoms $= \frac{1}{2} \times 3 + 4 = 5.5$

Formula is $AB_{4.5}C_{5.5}$ or $A_2B_9C_{11}$.

103. *(b)* The names of the given structure are shown below

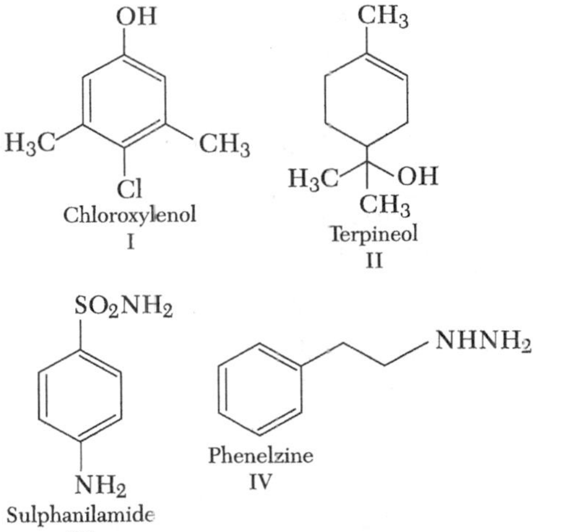

Chloroxylenol I; Terpineol II; Sulphanilamide III; Phenelzine IV

Chloroxylenol and terpineol are components of dettol, which is an antiseptic.

104. *(b)* CN^- is a better complexing agent (C) as well as reducing agent (A).

Thus, properties of (A) and (C) are shown by CN^-.

Property of complexing (C).

$$Ni^{2+} + 4\,CN^- \longrightarrow [Ni(CN)_4]^{2-}$$

Property of reducing (A).

MOCK TEST 4

$$\overset{\text{II}}{Cu}Cl_2 + 5\,KCN \longrightarrow K_3[\overset{\text{I}}{Cu}(CN)_4] + \frac{1}{2}(CN)_2 + 2KCl$$

(CN^- reduces Cu^{2+} to Cu^+)

105. *(a)* The names of the given structures are as follows :
I. Histamine II. Cimetidine III. Ranitidine

106. *(a)* Conversion of oxygen to ozone is a non spontaneous process. Hence, it will not take place at any temperature.

107. *(a)* In Freundlich adsorption isotherm,

$$\frac{x}{m} = kp^{1/n}$$

where, x = amount of adsorbate
m = amount of adsorbent
The value of n is always greater than 1.
So, the value of $1/n$ lies between 0 and 1 in all cases.

108. *(b)* Structure II is incorrect and the correct structure is

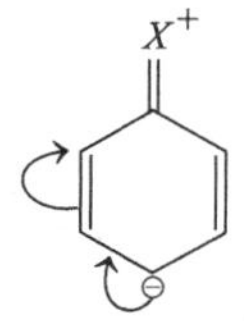

There must be double bond between C and halogen (X) as shown above. Because Cl is an *ortho*/*para*-directing group.

109. *(d)* For first order reaction,

$$t = \frac{2.303}{k}\log\frac{a}{a-x} \quad \ldots(i)$$

Given : $k = 2.303 \times 10^{-3}\ s^{-1}$,
$a = 40$ g, $a - x = 10$ g

On substituting the given values in Eq. (i), we get

$$t = \frac{2.303}{2.303 \times 10^{-3}}\log\frac{40}{10}$$
$$= 10^3 \log 2^2 = 2 \times 10^3 \times \log 2$$
$$= 2 \times 10^3 \times 0.3010 = 602\ s$$

Alternative method

For first order reaction,

$$t_{1/2} = \frac{0.693}{k}$$

$$\Rightarrow \quad t_{1/2}(t_{50\%}) = \frac{0.693}{2.303 \times 10^{-3}} = 301\,s$$

Also, $t_{75\%} = 2t_{50\%}$
$\therefore$ $t_{75\%} = 2 \times 301 = 602$ s

110. *(c)* In phenol, OH group is *ortho* and *para* directing group. Hence, bromination occurs at *para* position to form 2,4,6-tribromophenol.

Since, SO_3 is a good leaving group it, get reduced by bromine.

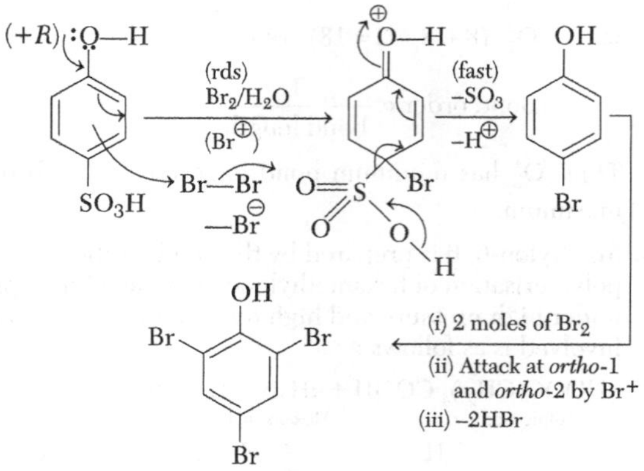

A white ppt. of 2,4,6-tribromophenol

111. *(d)* Chlorine reacts with number of metals and non-metals to form chlorides .

$$2Al + 3Cl_2 \longrightarrow 2AlCl_3$$
$$P_4 + 6Cl_2 \longrightarrow 4PCl_3$$

It has great affinity for hydrogen and reacts with compounds containing hydrogen to form HCl.

$$H_2 + Cl_2 \longrightarrow 2HCl$$
$$H_2S + Cl_2 \longrightarrow 2HCl + S$$

Chlorine reacts with hydrocarbons and gives substitution products with saturated hydrocarbons and addition products with unsaturated hydrocarbons.

$$CH_4 + Cl_2 \xrightarrow{UV} CH_3Cl + HCl$$
$$C_2H_4 + Cl_2 \xrightarrow[\text{temp.}]{\text{Room}} C_2H_4Cl_2$$

112. *(b)* Aromatic carboxylic acids do not undergo Friedel-Craft's reaction because the carboxyl group is deactivating and the catalyst aluminium chloride (Lewis acid) gets bonded to the carboxyl group, which facilitates the reaction at *ortho* and *para*-position.

113. *(c)* Alkenes react with water in the presence of acid as catalyst to form alcohols. In case of unsymmetrical alkenes, the addition reaction takes place in accordance with Markownikoff's rule.

$$\underset{\text{Propene}}{CH_3CH = CH_2} + H_2O \overset{H^\oplus}{\rightleftharpoons} \underset{\text{Propan-2-ol}}{H_3C-\underset{\substack{|\\OH}}{CH}-CH_3}$$

114. *(a)* The potential difference between fixed layer and diffused layer of opposite charges of a colloidal sol is termed as electrokinetic or *zeta* potential.

115. *(b)* Nitrile are selectively reduced by DIBAL-H to imines followed by hydrolysis to aldehyde. Esters are also reduced to aldehydes with DIBAL-H.

$$CH_3-(CH_2)_9-CN \xrightarrow[\text{(ii) } H_2O]{\text{(i) DIBAL-H}} CH_3(CH_2)_9CHO$$

$$CH_3(CH_2)_9 - \underset{\underset{O}{\|}}{C} - OC_2H_5 \xrightarrow[\text{(ii) } H_2O]{\text{(i) DIBAL-H}} CH_3(CH_2)_9CHO$$

116. *(a)* PCl_5 is prepared by the action of Cl_2 on P_4.
The reaction is given as follow :

$$P_4 + 10Cl_2 \longrightarrow 4\,PCl_5$$

117. *(c)* 2, 4-DNP reagent reacts with carbonyl compounds (aldehydes and ketones) to produce orange-red precipitate. Among the given compounds, butanone is a carbonyl compound and, thus can react with 2,4-DNP reagent.

118. *(c)* The order of reactivity of hydrogen halides with ether is HI > HBr > HCl. The cleavage of ethers take place with concentrated HI or HBr at high temperature.

119. *(b)* 100 g crystal has 22.65 g of Zn.
To prepare 20 g zinc sulphate crystals,

$$\text{zinc required} = \frac{22.65}{100} \times 20 = 4.53 \text{ g.}$$

120. *(c)* The reaction of alcohol/phenol with acid chloride is carried out in the presence of a base (pyridine), so as to neutralise HCl which is formed during the reaction.
It shifts the equilibrium to the right hand side.
Thus, both options (a) and (b) are correct.

Mathematics

121. *(b)* Here, $A = \{1, 2, 3, \ldots, n\}$ and $B = \{a, b\}$

Since, every element of domain A has two choices *i.e.*, a or b.

$\therefore$ Number of functions will be 2^n.

Also, there will be a case when all the elements of A will map to a only then, since b is left which do not have pre image in A.

$\therefore$ In such a case, the function from A to B is not onto.

Similarly, when all elements of A will map to b only, then also the function from A to B is not onto.

$\therefore$ Total number of onto functions is $2^n - 2$.

122. *(b)* Given that, $A = N \times N$

and $*$ is a binary operation on A defined by

$$(a,b)*(c,d) = (a + c, b + d)$$

Let $(a,b),(c,d) \in A$

Then, $a,b,c,d \in N$,

we have $(a,b)*(c,d) = (a + c, b + d)$

and

$(c, d)*(a,b) = (c + a, d + b) = (a + c, b + d)$

($\because$ addition is commutative in N)

Therefore, $(a,b)*(c,d) = (c,d)*(a,b)$

Therefore, the operation $*$ is commutative.

Now, let $(a,b),(c,d),(e,f) \in A$

Then, $a,b,c,d,e,f \in N$.

We have, $((a,b)*(c,d))*(e,f) = (a + c, b + d)*(e,f)$
$= (a + c + e, b + d + f)$

and $(a,b)*((c,d)*(e,f)) = (a,b)*(c + e, d + f)$
$= (a + c + e, b + d + f)$

$\therefore$ $((a,b)*(c,d))*(e,f) = (a, b)*((c,d)*(e,f))$

Therefore, the operation $*$ is associative.

An element $e = (e_1, e_2) \in A$ will be an identity element for the operation $*$ if $a * e = a = e * a$, $\forall\, a = (a_1, a_2) \in A$,

i.e., $(a_1 + e_1, a_2 + e_2) = (a_1, a_2) = (e_1 + a_1, e_2 + a_2)$

which is not true for any element in A.

Note that $a + e = a$ for $e = 0$ but 0 does not belong to N.

Therefore, the operation $*$ does not have any identity element.

123. *(b)* The given function $f : R \to R$ is defined as

$$f(x) = \tan x$$

Now, let $f^{-1}(1) = x \Rightarrow 1 = f(x)$

$\Rightarrow \tan x = 1 = \tan \dfrac{\pi}{4}$

$\Rightarrow x = n\pi + \dfrac{\pi}{4}, n \in Z.$

$\Rightarrow f^{-1}(1) = \left\{ n\pi + \dfrac{\pi}{4} : n \in Z \right\}$

124. *(c)* Given that, $\cot\theta + \tan\theta = 2\,\text{cosec}\,\theta$

$\Rightarrow \dfrac{\cos\theta}{\sin\theta} + \dfrac{\sin\theta}{\cos\theta} = \dfrac{2}{\sin\theta}$

$\Rightarrow \dfrac{\cos^2 + \sin^2\theta}{\sin\theta \cdot \cos\theta} = \dfrac{2}{\sin\theta}$

$\Rightarrow \dfrac{1}{\cos\theta} = 2$ $\quad [\because \sin^2\theta + \cos^2\theta = 1]$

$\Rightarrow \cos\theta = \dfrac{1}{2} \Rightarrow \cos\theta = \cos\dfrac{\pi}{3}$

$\therefore \theta = 2n\pi \pm \dfrac{\pi}{3}$

125. *(b)* Given equation, $3\tan A + 4 = 0$

$\Rightarrow 3\tan A = -4$

$\Rightarrow \tan A = \dfrac{-4}{3}$

$\Rightarrow \cot A = \dfrac{-3}{4}$

$\Rightarrow \sec A = \sqrt{1 + \dfrac{16}{9}} = \sqrt{\dfrac{25}{9}} = \pm\dfrac{5}{3}$

$\Rightarrow \sec A = \dfrac{-5}{3}$

[since, A lies in second quadrant]

$$\cos A = \frac{-3}{5}$$

$$\sin A = \sqrt{1 - \frac{9}{25}} = \frac{\sqrt{25-9}}{25} = \pm\frac{4}{5}$$

$$\sin A = \frac{4}{5} \quad \text{[since, } A \text{ lies in second quadrant]}$$

$$\therefore\ 2\cot A - 5\cos A + \sin A = 2\left(\frac{-3}{4}\right) - 5\left(\frac{-3}{5}\right) + \frac{4}{5}$$

$$= \frac{-6}{4} + 3 + \frac{4}{5} = \frac{-30+60+16}{20} = \frac{46}{20} = \frac{23}{10}$$

126. *(b)* Given that, $\tan\theta = \frac{a}{b}$

$$\therefore b\cos 2\theta + a\sin 2\theta = b\left(\frac{1-\tan^2\theta}{1+\tan^2\theta}\right) + a\left(\frac{2\tan\theta}{1+\tan^2\theta}\right)$$

$$= b\left(\frac{1-\frac{a^2}{b^2}}{1+\frac{a^2}{b^2}}\right) + a\left(\frac{\frac{2a}{b}}{1+\frac{a^2}{b^2}}\right)$$

$$= b\left(\frac{b^2-a^2}{b^2+a^2}\right) + \frac{2a^2b}{a^2+b^2}$$

$$= \frac{b}{a^2+b^2}[b^2 - a^2 + 2a^2] = \frac{(a^2+b^2)b}{(a^2+b^2)} = b$$

127. *(d)* $\frac{\pi}{2} \le x \le \frac{3\pi}{2}$

$$\Rightarrow \quad \frac{-3\pi}{2} \le -x \le -\frac{\pi}{2}$$

$$\Rightarrow \quad \pi - \frac{3\pi}{2} \le \pi - x \le \pi - \frac{\pi}{2}$$

$$\frac{-\pi}{2} \le \pi - x \le \frac{\pi}{2}$$

Now, let $\theta = \sin^{-1}(\sin x)$

$$= \sin^{-1}[\sin(\pi - x)]$$

Since, range of $\sin^{-1} x$ is $\left[-\frac{\pi}{2}, \frac{\pi}{2}\right]$

$\therefore\ \theta = \pi - x$

128. *(a)* Let $\cot^{-1}(x+1) = \alpha$ and $\tan^{-1}x = \beta$

$\Rightarrow\ x + 1 = \cot\alpha$ and $x = \tan\beta$

$\Rightarrow \operatorname{cosec}\alpha = \sqrt{1+(x+1)^2}$

and $\sec\beta = \sqrt{1+x^2}$

$$\Rightarrow \quad \sin\alpha = \frac{1}{\sqrt{x^2+2x+2}}$$

$$\text{and} \quad \cos\beta = \frac{1}{\sqrt{1+x^2}}$$

$$\Rightarrow \quad \alpha = \sin^{-1}\frac{1}{\sqrt{x^2+2x+2}}$$

$$\text{and} \quad \beta = \cos^{-1}\left(\frac{1}{\sqrt{1+x^2}}\right)$$

Now, $\sin(\cot^{-1}(x+1)) = \cos(\tan^{-1}x)$

$$\sin\left(\sin^{-1}\frac{1}{\sqrt{x^2+2x+2}}\right) = \cos\left(\cos^{-1}\frac{1}{\sqrt{1+x^2}}\right)$$

$$\Rightarrow \quad \frac{1}{\sqrt{x^2+2x+2}} = \frac{1}{\sqrt{1+x^2}}$$

$$\Rightarrow \quad x^2 + 2x + 2 = 1 + x^2$$

$$\Rightarrow\ 2x = -1 \ \Rightarrow\ x = -\frac{1}{2}$$

129. *(c)* We have, $\tan^{-1}\left(\frac{\sqrt{1+x^2}+\sqrt{1-x^2}}{\sqrt{1+x^2}-\sqrt{1-x^2}}\right)$

Let $x^2 = \cos 2\theta$. Then, we get

Given expression

$$= \tan^{-1}\left(\frac{\sqrt{1+\cos 2\theta}+\sqrt{1-\cos 2\theta}}{\sqrt{1+\cos 2\theta}-\sqrt{1-\cos 2\theta}}\right)$$

$$= \tan^{-1}\left(\frac{\sqrt{2}\cos\theta + \sqrt{2}\sin\theta}{\sqrt{2}\cos\theta - \sqrt{2}\sin\theta}\right)$$

[$1 + \cos 2\theta = 2\cos^2\theta$ and $1 - \cos 2\theta = 2\sin^2\theta$]

$$= \tan^{-1}\left(\frac{\cos\theta + \sin\theta}{\cos\theta - \sin\theta}\right)$$

(divide numerator and denominator inside the bracket by $\cos\theta$)

$$= \tan^{-1}\left(\frac{1+\tan\theta}{1-\tan\theta}\right)$$

$$= \tan^{-1}\left(\frac{\tan\frac{\pi}{4} + \tan\theta}{1 - \left(\tan\frac{\pi}{4}\right)(\tan\theta)}\right) = \tan^{-1}\left[\tan\left(\frac{\pi}{4} + \theta\right)\right]$$

$$\left(\tan(\theta+\phi) = \frac{\tan\theta + \tan\phi}{1 - \tan\theta\tan\phi}\right)$$

$$= \frac{\pi}{4} + \theta = \frac{\pi}{4} + \frac{1}{2}\cos^{-1}x^2$$

$$\left(x^2 = \cos 2\theta \Rightarrow \theta = \frac{1}{2}\cos^{-1}x^2\right)$$

130. *(d)* Given, $\tan\left(\frac{\pi}{4} + \frac{1}{2}\cos^{-1}\frac{a}{b}\right) + \tan\left(\frac{\pi}{4} - \frac{1}{2}\cos^{-1}\frac{a}{b}\right)$

Let $\frac{1}{2}\cos^{-1}\frac{a}{b} = x \ \Rightarrow\ \cos 2x = \frac{a}{b}$

MOCK TEST 4

So, $\tan\left(\frac{\pi}{4}+x\right)+\tan\left(\frac{\pi}{4}-x\right)$

$$=\frac{1+\tan x}{1-\tan x}+\frac{1-\tan x}{1+\tan x}$$

$$=\frac{1+\tan^2 x+2\tan x+1+\tan^2 x-2\tan x}{1-\tan^2 x}$$

$$=\frac{2(1+\tan^2 x)}{1-\tan^2 x}=\frac{2}{\cos 2x}=\frac{2}{\frac{a}{b}}=\frac{2b}{a}$$

131. *(d)* Given that, $P(n): 2n < n!, n \in N$

For $n=1, 2<1!$ [false]

For $n=2, 2\times 2<2! \Rightarrow 4<2$ [false]

For $n=3, 2\times 3<3!$

$6<3!$

$6<3\times 2\times 1$

$(6<6)$ [false]

For $n=4, 2\times 4<4!$

$8<4\times 3\times 2\times 1$

$(8<24)$ [true]

For $n=5, 2\times 5<5!$

$10<5\times 4\times 3\times 2\times 1$

$(10<120)$ [true]

Hence, $P(n)$ is for all $n \geq 4$.

132. *(b)* Given that, $z=x+iy$ lies in third quadrant.

$x<0$ and $y<0$.

Now, $\frac{\bar{z}}{z}=\frac{x-iy}{x+iy}=\frac{(x-iy)(x-iy)}{(x+iy)(x-iy)}$

$$=\frac{x^2-y^2-2ixy}{x^2+y^2}$$

$$\frac{\bar{z}}{z}=\frac{x^2-y^2}{x^2+y^2}-\frac{2ixy}{x^2+y^2}$$

Since, $\frac{\bar{z}}{z}$ also lies in third quadrant.

$\therefore$ $\frac{x^2-y^2}{x^2+y^2}<0$ and $\frac{-2xy}{x^2+y^2}<0$

$x^2-y^2<0$ and $-2xy<0$

$\Rightarrow$ $x^2<y^2$ and $xy>0$

So, $x<y<0$

133. *(b)* Given that, $\left|\frac{i+z}{i-z}\right|=1$

Let $z=x+iy$

$\therefore$ $\left|\frac{x+i(y+1)}{-x-i(y-1)}\right|=1$

$\Rightarrow$ $\frac{x^2+(y+1)^2}{x^2+(y-1)^2}=1$

$\Rightarrow$ $x^2+(y+1)^2=x^2-(y-1)^2$

$\Rightarrow$ $4y=0 \Rightarrow y=0$

So, z lies on X-axis (real axis).

134. *(c)* Given that, $|z_1+z_2|=|z_1|+|z_2|$

$\Rightarrow$ $|r_1(\cos\theta_1+i\sin\theta_1)+r_2(\cos\theta_2+i\sin\theta_2)|$
$=|r_1(\cos\theta_1+i\sin\theta_1)|+|r_2(\cos\theta_2+i\sin\theta_2)|$

$\Rightarrow$ $|(r_1\cos\theta_1+r_2\cos\theta)+i(r_1\sin\theta_1+r_2\sin\theta_2)|$
$=r_1+r_2$

$$\Rightarrow \sqrt{\begin{array}{l} r_1^2\cos^2\theta_1+r_2^2\cos^2\theta_2+2r_1r_2\cos\theta_1\cos\theta_2 \\ +r_1^2\sin^2\theta_1+r_2^2\sin^2\theta_2+2r_1r_2\sin\theta_1\sin\theta_2 \end{array}}=r_1+r_2$$

$$\Rightarrow \sqrt{r_1^2+r_2^2+2r_1r_2[\cos(\theta_1-\theta_2)]}=r_1+r_2$$

On squaring both sides, we get

$r_1^2+r_2^2+2r_1r_2\cos(\theta_1-\theta_2)=r_1^2+r_2^2+2r_1r_2$

$\Rightarrow$ $2r_1r_2[1-\cos(\theta_1-\theta_2)]=0$

$\Rightarrow$ $1-\cos(\theta_1-\theta_2)=0$

$\Rightarrow$ $\cos(\theta_1-\theta_2)=1$

$\Rightarrow$ $\cos(\theta_1-\theta_2)=\cos 0°$

$\Rightarrow$ $\theta_1-\theta_2=0°$

$\Rightarrow$ $\theta_1=\theta_2$

$\therefore$ $\arg(z_1)=\arg(z_2)$

135. *(c)* Given expression $=\frac{1+i\cos\theta}{1-2i\cos\theta}$

$$=\frac{(1+i\cos\theta)(1+2i\cos\theta)}{(1-2i\cos\theta)(1+2i\cos\theta)}$$

$$=\frac{1+i\cos\theta+2i\cos\theta+2i^2\cos^2\theta}{1-4i^2\cos^2\theta}$$

$$=\frac{1+3i\cos\theta-2\cos^2\theta}{1+4\cos^2\theta}$$

For real value of θ, $\frac{3\cos\theta}{1+4\cos^2\theta}=0$

$\Rightarrow$ $3\cos\theta=0$

$\Rightarrow$ $\cos\theta=\cos\frac{\pi}{2}$

$\Rightarrow$ $\theta=2n\pi\pm\frac{\pi}{2}$

136. *(b)* If we fixed 3 at units place.
Total possible number is 3! *i.e.*, 6.

Sum of the digits in unit place of all these numbers
$=3!\times 3$

Similarly, if we fixed 4, 5 and 6 at units place, in each case total possible numbers are 3!.

Required sum of unit digits of all such numbers
$=(3+4+5+6)\times 3!$
$=18\times 3!=18\times 6=108$

137. *(b)* Let the number of team participating in championship be n.

Since, it is given that every two teams played one match with each other.

$\therefore$ Total match played $= {}^nC_2$

According to the question,

$${}^nC_2 = 153$$

$$\Rightarrow \quad \frac{n(n-1)}{2} = 153$$

$$\Rightarrow \quad n^2 - n = 306$$

$$\Rightarrow \quad n^2 - n - 306 = 0$$

$$\Rightarrow \quad (n-18)(n+17) = 0$$

$$\Rightarrow \quad n = 18, -17 \quad \text{[inadmissible]}$$

$$\therefore \quad n = 18$$

138. *(a)* The arrangement can be understand with the help of following figure.

−	+	−	+	−	+	−	+	−	+	−	+	−

Thus, '+' sign can be arranged in 1 way because all are identical.

and 4 negative signs can be arranged at 7 places in ${}^7C_4$ ways.

$$\therefore \quad \text{Total number of ways} = {}^7C_4 \times 1$$

$$= \frac{7!}{4!3!} = \frac{7\times 6\times 5\times 4!}{3!\times 4!}$$

$$= \frac{7\times 6\times 5}{3\times 2\times 1} = 35 \text{ ways}$$

139. *(b)* Since, the coefficient of x^n in the expansion of $(1+x)^{2n}$ is ${}^{2n}C_n$.

$$\therefore \quad A = {}^{2n}C_n$$

Now, the coefficient of x^n in the expansion of $(1+x)^{2n-1}$ is ${}^{2n-1}C_n$.

$$\therefore \quad B = {}^{2n-1}C_n$$

$$\text{Now,} \quad \frac{A}{B} = \frac{{}^{2n}C_n}{{}^{2n-1}C_n} = \frac{2}{1} = 2$$

140. *(a)* Given expression is $\left(\frac{1}{a} - \frac{2b}{3}\right)^{10}$.

Let T_{r+1} has the coefficient of $a^{-6}b^4$.

$$\therefore \quad T_{r+1} = {}^{10}C_r\left(\frac{1}{a}\right)^{10-r}\left(-\frac{2b}{3}\right)^r$$

For coefficient of $a^{-6}b^4$,

$$10 - r = 6 \Rightarrow r = 4$$

Coefficient of $a^{-6}b^4 = {}^{10}C_4(-2/3)^4$

$$\therefore \quad = \frac{10\cdot 9\cdot 8\cdot 7\cdot 6!}{6!\cdot 4\cdot 3\cdot 2\cdot 1}\cdot\frac{2^4}{3^4} = \frac{1120}{27}$$

141. *(d)* Given, $S_n = 3n + 2n^2$

First term of the AP,

$\therefore \quad T_1 = 3\times 1 + 2(1)^2 = 3 + 2 = 5$ and $T_2 = S_2 - S_1$

$$= [3\times 2 + 2\times (2)^2] - [3\times 1 + 2\times (1)^2]$$

$$= 14 - 5 = 9$$

$\therefore$ Common difference $(d) = T_2 - T_1 = 9 - 5 = 4$

142. *(a)* Let the length, breadth and height of rectangular solid block is $\frac{a}{r}$, a and ar respectively.

$$\therefore \quad \text{Volume} = \frac{a}{r}\times a\times ar = 216 \text{ cm}^3$$

$$\Rightarrow \quad a^3 = 216 \Rightarrow a^3 = 6^3$$

$$\therefore \quad a = 6$$

$$\text{Surface area} = 2\left(\frac{a^2}{r} + a^2 r + a^2\right) = 252$$

$$\Rightarrow \quad 2a^2\left(\frac{1}{r} + r + 1\right) = 252$$

$$\Rightarrow \quad 2\times 36\left(\frac{1 + r^2 + r}{r}\right) = 252$$

$$\Rightarrow \quad \frac{1 + r^2 + r}{r} = \frac{252}{2\times 36}$$

$$\Rightarrow \quad 1 + r^2 + r = \frac{126}{36}r \Rightarrow 1 + r^2 + r = \frac{21}{6}r$$

$$\Rightarrow \quad 6 + 6r^2 + 6r = 21r \Rightarrow 6r^2 - 15r + 6 = 0$$

$$\Rightarrow \quad 2r^2 - 5r + 2 = 0 \Rightarrow (2r-1)(r-2) = 0$$

$$\therefore \quad r = \frac{1}{2}, 2$$

For $r = \frac{1}{2}$: Length $= \frac{a}{r} = \frac{6\times 2}{1} = 12$ cm

Breadth $= a = 6$ cm

Height $= ar = 6\times\frac{1}{2} = 3$ cm

For $r = 2$: Length $= \frac{a}{r} = \frac{6}{2} = 3$ cm

Breadth $= a = 6$ cm

Height $= ar = 6\times 2 = 12$ cm

143. *(b)* Since, line passes through the point (3, 2) and perpendicular to the line $y = x$.

Slope $(m) = -1$

[since, line is perpendicular to the line $y = x$]

$\therefore$ Equation of line which passes through (3, 2) is

$$y - 2 = -1(x - 3)$$

$$\Rightarrow \quad y - 2 = -x + 3 \Rightarrow x + y = 5$$

144. *(a)* Since, the coordinates of the middle point are $P(3, 2)$.

$$\therefore \quad 3 = \frac{1 \cdot 0 + 1 \cdot a}{1+1} \Rightarrow 3 = \frac{a}{2} \Rightarrow a = 6$$

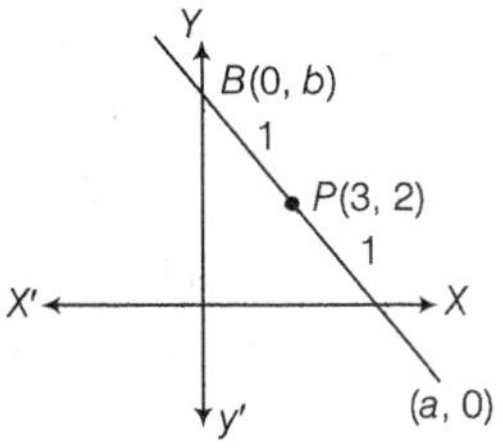

Similarly, $b = 4$

$\therefore$ Equation of the line is $\frac{x}{6} + \frac{y}{4} = 1$

$$\Rightarrow \quad 2x + 3y = 12$$

145. *(a)* Equation of OB is

$$y - 0 = \frac{1-0}{1-0}(x - 0) \Rightarrow y = x$$

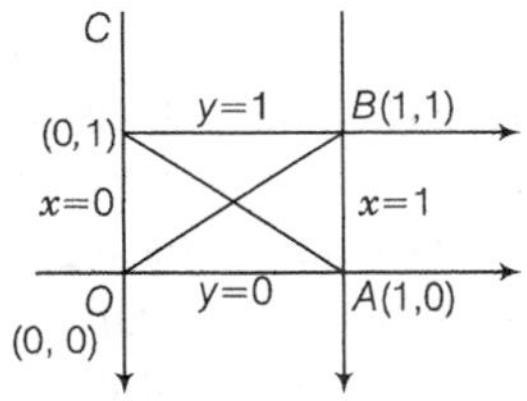

and equation of AC is

$$y - 0 = \frac{1-0}{0-1}(x - 1)$$

$$\Rightarrow \quad y = -x + 1 \Rightarrow x + y - 1 = 0$$

146. *(b)* Let the reflection of $A(4, 1)$ in $y = x$ is $B(h, k)$.

Now, mid-point of AB is $\left(\frac{4+h}{2}, \frac{1+k}{2}\right)$ which lies on $y = x$.

i.e., $\quad \frac{4+h}{2} = \frac{1+k}{2} \Rightarrow h - k = -3 \quad \ldots(i)$

So, the slope of line $y = x$ is 1.

$\therefore \quad$ Slope of $AB = \frac{h-4}{k-1}$

$\Rightarrow \quad 1 \cdot \left(\frac{h-4}{k-1}\right) = -1$

$\Rightarrow \quad h - 4 = 1 - k$

$\Rightarrow \quad h + k = 5 \quad \ldots(ii)$

and $\quad h - k = -3$

$\quad 2h = 2 \Rightarrow h = 1$

On putting $h = 1$ in Eq. (ii), we get

$\quad k = 4$

So, the point is $(1, 4)$.

Hence, after translation the point is $(1 + 2, 4)$ or $(3, 4)$.

147. *(c)* Given that, centre of the circle is $(1, 2)$.

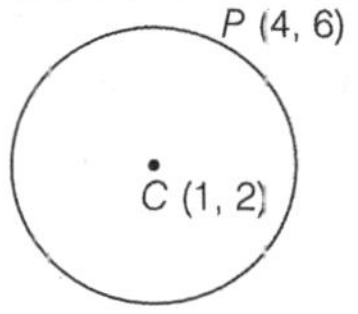

$$CP = \sqrt{9+16} = 5 = \text{Radius of the circle}$$

$\therefore$ Required area $= \pi r^2 = 25\pi$

148. (*) Let general equation of the circle is $x^2 + y^2 + 2gx + 2fy + c = 0$.

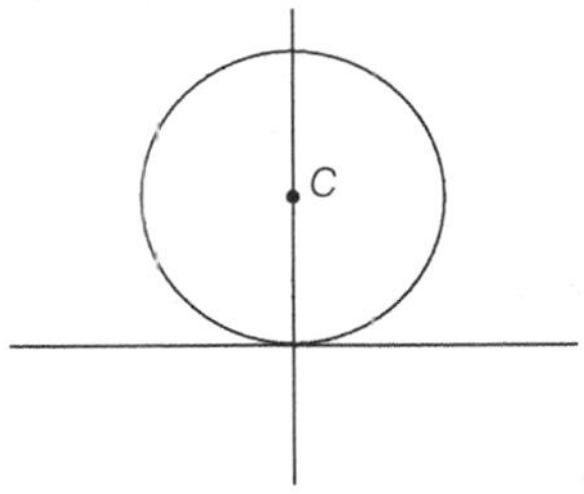

Since the point $(0, 0)$ and $(2, 3)$ lie on it $\Rightarrow c = 0$.

and $\quad 4 + 9 + 4g + 6f = 0$

$\Rightarrow \quad 2g + 3f = -13/2$

Since the centre lie on Y-axis, then $g = 0$.

$\therefore \quad 3f = -13/2$

$\Rightarrow \quad f = -13/6$

So, the equation of circle is

$$x^2 + y^2 - 2\left(\frac{13y}{6}\right) = 0$$

$$\Rightarrow \quad x^2 + y^2 - \frac{13y}{3} = 0$$

$$\Rightarrow \quad 3x^2 + 3y^2 - 13y = 0$$

149. *(a)* Let the vertex be at the lowest point and the axis vertical.

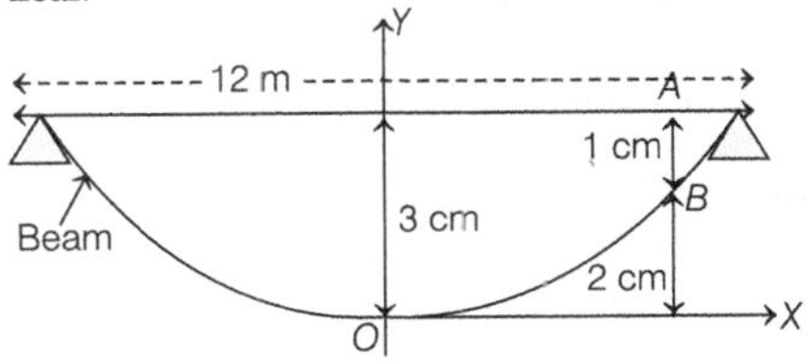

The equation of the parabola takes then form $x^2 = 4ay$.

Since, it passes through $\left(6, \frac{3}{100}\right)$, we have

$(6)^2 = 4a\left(\frac{3}{100}\right)$ i.e., $a = 36 \times \frac{100}{12} = 300$ m.

Let AB be the deflection of the beam which is $\frac{1}{100}$ m.

Coordinates of B are $(x, \frac{2}{100})$.

Therefore, $x^2 = 4 \times 300 \times \frac{2}{100} = 24$

i.e., $x = \sqrt{24} = 2\sqrt{6}$ m

150. *(a)* Let $P(x_1, y_1)$ be any point.

So, $\sqrt{(x_1+2)^2 + y_1^2} = \frac{2}{3}\left(x_1 + \frac{9}{2}\right)$

$\Rightarrow \quad (x_1+2)^2 + y_1^2 = \frac{4}{9}\left(x_1 + \frac{9}{2}\right)^2$

$\Rightarrow \quad 9[x_1^2 + y_1^2 + 4x_1 + 4] = 4\left(x_1^2 + \frac{81}{4} + 9x_1\right)$

$\Rightarrow \quad 5x_1^2 + 9y_1^2 = 45$

$\Rightarrow \quad \frac{x_1^2}{9} + \frac{y_1^2}{5} = 1$

Locus of (x_1, y_1) is $\frac{x^2}{9} + \frac{y^2}{5} = 1$, which is equation of an ellipse.

151. *(b)* $\frac{x^2}{2-r} + \frac{y^2}{r-5} + 1 = 0$

$\Rightarrow \quad \frac{x^2}{r-2} + \frac{y^2}{5-r} = 1$

Hence, $r > 2$ and $r < 5 \Rightarrow 2 < r < 5$.

152. *(c)* The given equation can be written as

$(4x+8)^2 - (y-2)^2 = -44 + 64 - 4$

$\Rightarrow \frac{16(x+2)^2}{16} - \frac{(y-2)^2}{16} = 1$

Transverse and conjugate axes are $y = 2, x = -2$

$\Rightarrow \quad x + 2 = 0$

153. *(c)* Equation of hyperbola is $x = 8\sec\theta$, $y = 8\tan\theta$

$\Rightarrow \quad \frac{x}{8} = \sec\theta, \ \frac{y}{8} = \tan\theta$

$\sec^2\theta - \tan^2\theta = 1 \Rightarrow \frac{x^2}{8^2} - \frac{y^2}{8^2} = 1$

Here, $a = 8, b = 8$

Now, $e = \sqrt{1 + \frac{b^2}{a^2}} = \sqrt{1 + \frac{8^2}{8^2}} = \sqrt{1+1}$

$\Rightarrow \quad e = \sqrt{2}$

$\therefore$Distance between directrices $= \frac{2a}{e} = \frac{2\times 8}{\sqrt{2}} = 8\sqrt{2}$

154. *(c)* Equation of a plane cut-off intercepts -6, 3 and 4 from the coordinate axis is

$\frac{x}{-6} + \frac{y}{3} + \frac{z}{4} = 1 \qquad \left(\frac{x}{a} + \frac{y}{b} + \frac{z}{c} = 1\right)$

$\Rightarrow \quad -2x + 4y + 3z = 12$

$2x - 4y - 3z + 12 = 0$

$\therefore$Length of perpendicular from origin $= \frac{d}{\sqrt{a^2+b^2+c^2}}$

$= \frac{12}{\sqrt{(2)^2 + (-4)^2 + (-3)^2}}$

$= \frac{12}{\sqrt{4+16+9}} = \frac{12}{\sqrt{29}}$

155. *(d)* Given, $f(x) = 1 - x + x^2 - x^3 + \quad - x^{99} + x^{100}$

$f'(x) = 0 - 1 + 2x - 3x^2 + \quad - 99x^{98} + 100x^{99}$

$= -1 + 2x - 3x^2 + \quad - 99x^{98} + 100x^{99}$

$\therefore \ f'(1) = -1 + 2 - 3 + \quad - 99 + 100$

$= (-1 - 3 - 5 - \quad - 99) + (2 + 4 + \quad + 100)$

$\left[S_n = \frac{n}{2}\{2a + (n-1)d\} \right]$

$= -\frac{50}{2}[2\times 1 + (50-1)\,2]$

$+ \frac{50}{2}[2\times 2 + (50-1)2]$

$= -25\,[2 + 49\times 2] + 25[4 + 49\times 2]$

$= -25\,(2+98) + 25\,(4+98)$

$= -25 \times 100 + 25 \times 102$

$= -2500 + 2550 = 50$

156. *(b)* Here, $f(x) = \begin{cases} x[x], & \text{if } 0 \le x < 2 \\ (x-1)x, & \text{if } 2 \le x < 3 \end{cases}$

At $x = 2$

$\text{LHD} = f'(2^-) = \lim_{h\to 0} \frac{f(2-h) - f(2)}{-h}$

$= \lim_{h\to 0} \frac{(2-h)[2-h] - (2-1)\,2}{-h}$

$= \lim_{h\to 0} \frac{(2-h)(1) - 2}{-h} \qquad ([2-h] = 1)$

$= \lim_{h\to 0} \frac{2-h-2}{-h} = \lim_{h\to 0} \frac{-h}{-h} = 1$

$\text{RHD} = f'(2^+) = \lim_{h\to 0} \frac{f(2+h) - f(2)}{h}$

$= \lim_{h\to 0} \frac{(2+h-1)(2+h) - (2-1)(2)}{h}$

$= \lim_{h\to 0} \frac{(h+1)(2+h) - 2}{h}$

$= \lim_{h\to 0} \frac{h^2 + 3h + 2 - 2}{h}$

$= \lim_{h\to 0} \frac{h^2 + 3h}{h} = \lim_{h\to 0} \frac{h(h+3)}{h} = 3$

LHD $\neq$ RHD

$\therefore \quad f(x)$ is not differentiable at $x = 2$.

157. *(c)* Since, $y = (1+x)(1+x^2)(1+x^4)...(1+x^{2^n})$

$\Rightarrow (1-x)\,y = (1-x^2)(1+x^2)(1+x^4)...(1+x^{2^n})$

$= (1-x^4)(1+x^4)...(1+x^{2^n})$

……………

……………

$= (1-x^{2^n})(1+x^{2^n}) \cdot = 1 - x^{2^{n+1}}$

$\therefore \quad y = \dfrac{1-x^{2^{n+1}}}{(1-x)}$

$$\frac{dy}{dx} = \frac{(1-x)(2^{n+1})\cdot(-x^{2^{n+1}-1}) - (1-x^{2^{n+1}})(-1)}{((1-x)^2)}$$

$$\therefore \left(\frac{dy}{dx}\right)_{x=0} = \frac{(1-0)(-2^{n+1}\cdot 0)-(1-0)(-1)}{1} = 1$$

158. *(a)* Given, $f(x) = x^3 - 3x^2 + 3x - 100$

$\Rightarrow \quad f'(x) = 3x^2 - 6x + 3$ (differentiate w.r.t. x)

$= 3(x^2 - 2x + 1) = 3(x-1)^2$

For any $x \in R, (x-1)^2 \ge 0$ since, a perfect square cannot be negative. Then, $f'(x) \ge 0$.

Hence, the given function f is an increasing function on R.

159. *(d)* The point of intersection of given curves is $(0, 1)$.

On differentiating given curves, we get

$$\frac{dy}{dx} = a^x \log a, \ \frac{dy}{dx} = b^x \log b$$

$\Rightarrow \quad m_1 = a^x \log a, \ m_2 = b^x \log b$

At $(0, 1)$, $\quad m_1 = \log a, \ m_2 = \log b$

$$\therefore \quad \tan\theta = \left|\frac{m_1 - m_2}{1 + m_1 m_2}\right| = \left|\frac{\log a - \log b}{1 + \log a \log b}\right|$$

$$\Rightarrow \quad \theta = \tan^{-1}\left|\frac{\log a - \log b}{1 + \log a \log b}\right|$$

160. *(a)* Let d be the distance of the point (x, y) on $x^2 = 2y$ from the point $(0, 5)$, then

$d = \sqrt{(x-0)^2 + (y-5)^2} = \sqrt{x^2 + (y-5)^2}$ ...(i)

$= \sqrt{2y + (y-5)^2}$ (putting $x^2 = 2y$)

$= \sqrt{y^2 - 8y + 25}$

$= \sqrt{y^2 - 8y + 4^2 + 9}$

$= \sqrt{(y-4)^2 + 9}$

d is least when $(y-4)^2 = 0$ i.e., when $y = 4$

When $y = 4$, then $x^2 = 2 \times 4$

$\Rightarrow \quad x = \pm\sqrt{8} = \pm 2\sqrt{2}$

$\therefore$ The points $(2\sqrt{2}, 4)$ and $(-2\sqrt{2}, 4)$ on the given curve are nearest to the point $(0, 5)$. So, (a) is the correct option.

161. *(a)* Let $y = a\sec\theta - b\tan\theta$

$\Rightarrow \quad \dfrac{dy}{d\theta} = a\sec\theta\tan\theta - b\sec^2\theta$

$\Rightarrow \quad \dfrac{dy}{d\theta} = \sec^2\theta(a\sin\theta - b)$

Put $\quad \dfrac{dy}{d\theta} = 0$

$\Rightarrow \quad \sec^2\theta(a\sin\theta - b) = 0$

$\Rightarrow \quad \sin\theta = \dfrac{b}{a}$ $\quad (\because \sec\theta \ne 0)$

Now, $\dfrac{d^2y}{d\theta^2} > 0$, at $\sin\theta = \dfrac{b}{a}$

$\therefore$ Minimum value is

$$y = a.\frac{a}{\sqrt{a^2 - b^2}} - b.\frac{b}{\sqrt{a^2 - b^2}} = \sqrt{a^2 - b^2}$$

162. *(b)* Given, $y = a\log x + bx^2 + x$

$\Rightarrow \quad \dfrac{dy}{dx} = \dfrac{a}{x} + 2bx + 1$

At $\quad x = -1$ and $x = 2$, y has its extreme.

$\therefore \quad -a - 2b + 1 = 0 \Rightarrow a + 2b = 1$ ...(i)

and $\quad \dfrac{a}{2} + 4b + 1 = 0 \Rightarrow a + 8b = -2$ ...(ii)

On solving Eqs. (i) and (ii), we get

$$a = 2, \ b = -\frac{1}{2}$$

163. *(a)* Let $I = \displaystyle\int e^x \left(\frac{1-x}{1+x^2}\right)^2 dx = \int e^x \frac{(1+x^2-2x)}{(1+x^2)^2} dx$

$$= \int e^x \left(\frac{1}{1+x^2} - \frac{2x}{(1+x^2)^2}\right) dx$$

$$= \frac{e^x}{1+x^2} + C$$

[Using $\int e^x[f(x) + f'(x)]\,dx = e^x f(x) + C$]

164. *(c)* Let $I = \displaystyle\int_0^{\pi/2} \frac{\sin x}{1+\cos^2 x} dx$

Put $\quad \cos x = t \Rightarrow -\sin x\,dx = dt \Rightarrow dx = \dfrac{dt}{-\sin x}$

For limit when $x = 0 \Rightarrow t = \cos 0 = 1 \quad (\because t = \cos x)$

and when $\quad x = \dfrac{\pi}{2} \Rightarrow t = \cos\dfrac{\pi}{2} = 0$

$$\therefore \quad I = \int_1^0 \frac{\sin x}{1+t^2}\frac{dt}{(-\sin x)} dx = -\int_1^0 \frac{1}{1+t^2} dt$$

$$= -\left[\frac{1}{1}\tan^{-1}\left(\frac{t}{1}\right)\right]_1^0 \left(\because \int \frac{1}{a^2+x^2} dx = \frac{1}{a}\tan^{-1}\frac{x}{a}\right)$$

MOCK TEST 4

$$= -[\tan^{-1} t]_1^0 = -[\tan^{-1}(0) - \tan^{-1}(1)]$$

$$= -\left(0 - \frac{\pi}{4}\right) = \frac{\pi}{4}$$

165. *(b)* Let $I = \int_0^1 x(1-x)^n\, dx$

$$\Rightarrow \quad I = \int_0^1 (1-x)\{1-(1-x)\}^n\, dx$$

$$\left[\because \int_0^a f(x)dx = \int_0^a f(a-x)dx\right]$$

$$= \int_0^1 (1-x)x^n\, dx = \int_0^1 (x^n - x^{n+1})dx$$

$$= \left[\frac{x^{n+1}}{n+1} - \frac{x^{n+2}}{n+2}\right]_0^1 = \left[\frac{1}{n+1} - \frac{1}{n+2}\right] - 0$$

$$= \frac{(n+2)-(n+1)}{(n+1)(n+2)} = \frac{1}{(n+1)(n+2)}$$

166. *(b)* Let $I = \int_{-3\pi/2}^{-\pi/2} [(x+\pi)^3 + \cos^2 x]dx$ ...(i)

$$I = \int_{-3\pi/2}^{-\pi/2} \left[\left(-\frac{\pi}{2} - \frac{3\pi}{2} - x + \pi\right)^3 + \cos^2\left(-\frac{\pi}{2} - \frac{3\pi}{2} - x\right)\right]dx$$

$$\Rightarrow \quad I = \int_{-3\pi/2}^{-\pi/2} [-(x+\pi)^3 + \cos^2 x]dx \qquad \text{...(ii)}$$

On adding Eqs. (i) and (ii), we get

$$2I = \int_{-3\pi/2}^{-\pi/2} 2\cos^2 x dx$$

$$= \int_{-3\pi/2}^{-\pi/2} (1 + \cos 2x)\, dx$$

$$= \left[x + \frac{\sin 2x}{2}\right]_{-3\pi/2}^{-\pi/2}$$

$$2I = \left\{-\frac{\pi}{2} + \frac{\sin(-\pi)}{2} - \left[\left(\frac{-3\pi}{2}\right) + \frac{\sin(-3\pi)}{2}\right]\right\} = \pi$$

$$\Rightarrow \quad I = \frac{\pi}{2}$$

167. *(b)* Let $I = \int f'(ax+b)\,[f(ax+b)]^n\, dx$

Put $f(ax+b) = t \Rightarrow f'(ax+b)a\, dx = dt$

$$\Rightarrow \quad dx = \frac{dt}{af'(ax+b)}$$

$$\therefore \quad I = \int f'(ax+b)\, t^n \frac{dt}{f'(ax+b)a}$$

$$= \frac{1}{a}\int t^n\, dt = \frac{1}{a}\left(\frac{t^{n+1}}{n+1}\right) + C$$

$$= \frac{1}{a} \cdot \frac{[f(ax+b)]^{n+1}}{n+1} + C$$

168. *(b)* Let $I = \int \frac{\cos 2x}{(\sin x + \cos x)^2} dx = \int \frac{\cos^2 x - \sin^2 x}{(\sin x + \cos x)^2} dx$

$(\because \cos 2x = \cos^2 x - \sin^2 x)$

$$= \int \frac{(\cos x - \sin x)(\cos x + \sin x)}{(\sin x + \cos x)(\sin x + \cos x)} dx$$

$$= \int \frac{\cos x - \sin x}{\sin x + \cos x} dx$$

Put $\sin x + \cos x = t$

$$\Rightarrow \quad (\cos x - \sin x)\, dx = dt$$

$$\therefore \quad I = \int \frac{\cos x - \sin x}{t} \frac{dt}{\cos x - \sin x} = \int \frac{1}{t} dt$$

$$= \log|t| + C = \log|\sin x + \cos x| + C$$

169. *(b)* The smaller area enclosed by the circle $x^2 + y^2 = 4$ and the line $x + y = 2$ is represented by the shaded area *ACBA*.

The intersection points of circle and line are $A(2, 0)$ and $B(0, 2)$.

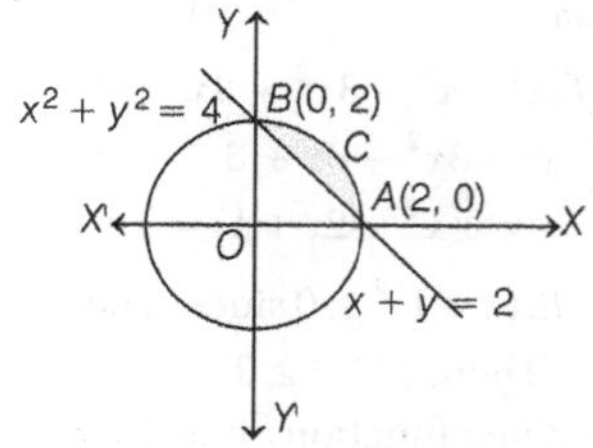

$\therefore$ Required area (shown in shaded region)

$= \text{Area } (OACBO) - \text{Area } (\Delta OAB)$

$$= \int_0^2 \sqrt{4 - x^2}\, dx - \int_0^2 (2 - x)\, dx$$

$(\because x^2 + y^2 = 4 \Rightarrow y = \sqrt{4 - x^2}$ and $x + y = 2$

$\Rightarrow y = 2 - x)$

$$= \left[\frac{x}{2}\sqrt{4 - x^2} + \frac{4}{2}\sin^{-1}\frac{x}{2}\right]_0^2 - \left[2x - \frac{x^2}{2}\right]_0^2$$

$$= \left[\frac{2}{2}\sqrt{4-4} + \frac{4}{2}\sin^{-1}(1) - 0 - \frac{4}{2}\sin^{-1}(0)\right] - [4 - 2]$$

$$\left(\because \int \sqrt{a^2 - x^2}\, dx = \frac{x}{2}\sqrt{a^2 - x^2} + \frac{a^2}{2}\sin^{-1}\frac{x}{a}\right)$$

$$= \left[2 \cdot \frac{\pi}{2}\right] - [4 - 2] = (\pi - 2) \text{ sq units}$$

170. *(a)* Given, $xy = \log y + C$ ...(i)

On differentiating both sides w.r.t. x, we get

$$\frac{d}{dx}(xy) = \frac{d}{dx}(\log y + C)$$

$$\Rightarrow \quad y\frac{d}{dx}x + xy' = \frac{1}{y}y'$$

(using product rule of differentiation in LHS)

$$\Rightarrow \quad xy' + y = \frac{1}{y}y'$$

$$\Rightarrow \quad xy'y + y^2 = y'$$

$\Rightarrow \quad y^2 = y'(1 - xy)$

$\Rightarrow \quad y' = \dfrac{y^2}{1 - xy}$

Hence, $xy = \log y + C$ is a solution of the differential equation $y' = \dfrac{y^2}{1 - xy}, xy \neq 1$

171. *(b)* According to the question,

$$\frac{dy}{dx} = y + \frac{y}{x} = y\left(1 + \frac{1}{x}\right)$$

$$\Rightarrow \quad \frac{dy}{y} = \left(1 + \frac{1}{x}\right) dx$$

On integrating both sides, we get

$$\int \frac{dy}{y} = \int \left(1 + \frac{1}{x}\right) dx$$

$$\Rightarrow \quad \log y = x + \log x + C$$

$$\Rightarrow \quad \log\left(\frac{y}{x}\right) = x + C$$

$$\Rightarrow \quad \frac{y}{x} = e^{x + C} = e^x \cdot e^C$$

$$\Rightarrow \quad \frac{y}{x} = ke^x \Rightarrow y = kx \cdot e^x, \text{ where } k = e^C$$

172. *(a)* Given that, $y(t)$ is the solution of the differential equation

$$(1 + t)\frac{dy}{dt} - ty = 1 \quad \text{and} \quad y(0) = -1$$

Now, the given differential equation can be written as

$$\frac{dy}{dt} - \left(\frac{t}{1 + t}\right) y = \frac{1}{(1 + t)} \quad \text{and} \quad y(0) = -1$$

$$\therefore \quad \text{IF} = e^{\int -\left(\frac{t}{1+t}\right) dt} = e^{-\int \left(1 - \frac{1}{1+t}\right) dt}$$

$$= e^{-t + \log(1 + t)} = e^{-t}(1 + t)$$

$\therefore$ Required solution is

$$ye^{-t}(1 + t) = \int \frac{1}{1 + t} e^{-t}(1 + t)\, dt + C$$

$$= \int e^{-t} dt + C$$

$$\Rightarrow \quad ye^{-t}(1 + t) = -e^{-t} + C$$

Since, $y(0) = -1 \Rightarrow c = 0$

$$\therefore \quad y = -\frac{1}{(1 + t)} \Rightarrow y(1) = -\frac{1}{2}$$

173. *(c)* In ΔABC, $\mathbf{AB} + \mathbf{BC} = \mathbf{AC}$

$\Rightarrow \quad \mathbf{AC} = \mathbf{a} + \mathbf{b}$

AD is parallel to BC and $AD = 2BC$

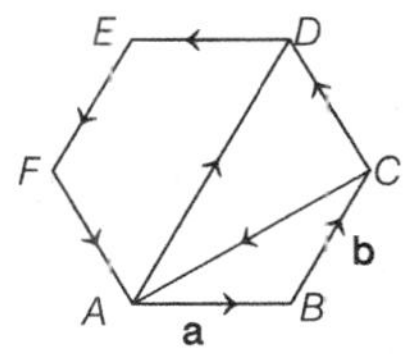

$\therefore \quad \mathbf{AD} = 2\mathbf{b}$

In ΔACD, $\quad \mathbf{AC} + \mathbf{CD} = \mathbf{AD}$

$\Rightarrow \quad \mathbf{CD} = 2\mathbf{b} - (\mathbf{a} + \mathbf{b}) = \mathbf{b} - \mathbf{a}$

Now, $\quad \mathbf{CE} = \mathbf{CD} + \mathbf{DE} = \mathbf{b} - \mathbf{a} - \mathbf{a}$

$= \mathbf{b} - 2\mathbf{a}$

174. *(d)* If $\mathbf{a} + 2\mathbf{b}$ is collinear with $\mathbf{c}$, then

$$\mathbf{a} + 2\mathbf{b} = t\mathbf{c} \quad \ldots(i)$$

Also, if $\mathbf{b} + 3\mathbf{c}$ is collinear with $\mathbf{a}$, then

$$\mathbf{b} + 3\mathbf{c} = \lambda\mathbf{a}$$

$$\Rightarrow \quad \mathbf{b} = \lambda\mathbf{a} - 3\mathbf{c} \quad \ldots(ii)$$

On putting the value of $\mathbf{b}$ in Eq. (i), we get

$$\mathbf{a} + 2(\lambda\mathbf{a} - 3\mathbf{c}) = t\mathbf{c}$$

$$\Rightarrow \quad (\mathbf{a} - 6\mathbf{c}) = t\mathbf{c} - 2\lambda\mathbf{a}$$

On comparing, we get $1 = -2\lambda$ and $-6 = t$

$$\Rightarrow \quad \lambda = -\frac{1}{2} \text{ and } t = -6$$

From Eq. (i),

$$\mathbf{a} + 2\mathbf{b} = -6\mathbf{c}$$

$$\Rightarrow \quad \mathbf{a} + 2\mathbf{b} + 6\mathbf{c} = 0$$

175. *(c)* The given matrix is $A = \begin{bmatrix} 0 & 2 \\ 3 & -4 \end{bmatrix}$.

Now, $$kA = k\begin{bmatrix} 0 & 2 \\ 3 & -4 \end{bmatrix} = \begin{bmatrix} 0 & 2k \\ 3k & -4k \end{bmatrix}$$

Also, it is given that $kA = \begin{bmatrix} 0 & 3a \\ 2b & 24 \end{bmatrix}$

$$\therefore \quad \begin{bmatrix} 0 & 2k \\ 3k & -4k \end{bmatrix} = \begin{bmatrix} 0 & 3a \\ 2b & 24 \end{bmatrix}$$

On equating corresponding elements, we get

$$2k = 3a,\ 3k = 2b \text{ and } -4k = 24$$

$$\Rightarrow \quad k = -6,\ a = -4,\ b = -9$$

176. *(a)* Since, A is a skew-symmetric matrix.

$\therefore \quad A' = -A$

$\Rightarrow \quad |A'| = |-A| \Rightarrow |A'| = (-1)^n |A|$

($|kA| = k^n |A|$, if A is of order n)

$\Rightarrow \quad |A| = (-1)^n |A| (\ |A| = |A'|)$

$\Rightarrow \quad |A| = -|A| \quad$ (n is odd)

$\Rightarrow \quad 2|A| = 0 \Rightarrow |A| = 0$

177. *(b)* $\begin{vmatrix} 1 & 1 & 1 \\ 1+\sin A & 1+\sin B & 1+\sin C \\ \sin A+\sin^2 A & \sin B+\sin^2 B & \sin C+\sin^2 C \end{vmatrix} = 0$

$\Rightarrow \begin{vmatrix} 1 & 1 & 1 \\ 1+\sin A & 1+\sin B & 1+\sin C \\ -\cos^2 A & -\cos^2 B & -\cos^2 C \end{vmatrix} = 0$

(using $R_3 \to R_3 - R_2$)

$\Rightarrow \begin{vmatrix} 1 & 0 & 0 \\ 1+\sin A & \sin B - \sin A & \sin C - \sin B \\ -\cos^2 A & \cos^2 A - \cos^2 B & \cos^2 B - \cos^2 C \end{vmatrix} = 0$

(using $C_3 \to C_3 - C_2$ and $C_2 \to C_2 - C_1$)

By expanding along R_1, we get

$$(\sin B - \sin A)(\sin^2 C - \sin^2 B) - (\sin C - \sin B)(\sin^2 B - \sin^2 A) = 0$$

$\Rightarrow (\sin B - \sin A)(\sin C - \sin B)(\sin C - \sin A) = 0$

$\Rightarrow$ Either $\sin B - \sin A = 0$

or $\sin C - \sin B = 0$ or $\sin C - \sin A = 0$

$\Rightarrow$ Either $A = B$ or $B = C$ or $C = A$

i.e., ΔABC is isosceles.

178. *(b)* Given that,

$P(A) = 0.4,\ P(B) = 0.3,\ = P(C) = 0.2$

$\therefore\ P(\overline{A}) = 1 - P(A) = 1 - 0.4 = 0.6$

$P(\overline{B}) = 1 - P(B) = 1 - 0.3 = 0.7$

$P(\overline{C}) = 1 - P(C) = 1 - 0.2 = 0.8$

Now, P (two hits) $= P(A)\,P(B)\,P(\overline{C}) + P(A)\,P(\overline{B})\,P(C) + P(\overline{A})\,P(B)\,P(C)$

$= 0.4 \times 0.3 \times 0.8 + 0.4 \times 0.7 \times 0.2 + 0.6 \times 0.3 \times 0.2$

$= 0.096 + 0.056 + 0.036 = 0.188$

179. *(b)* Let $p : x > y$

$q : x + a > y + a$

$p \to q$

Converse of the above statement is

$q \to p$

i.e., If $x + a > y + a$, then $x > y$.

180. *(b)* Let the investment in bond A and B are x and y respectively.

Then, our problem is to

Maximise Z = $0.08x + 0.10x$

Subject to constraints are

$x + y \le 12000\ x \ge 2000$

$y \ge 4000,\ y \ge 0$

The graph of the above inequality is given by

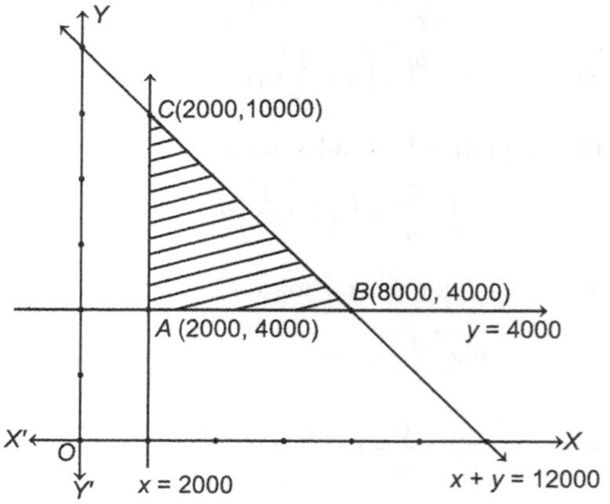

In the above graph shaded region is the feasible bounded region ABC.

Now, the values of Z the the corner points are given by

Corner point	Value of Z
(2000, 4000)	560
(8000, 4000)	1040
(2000, 10000)	1160

From the above table, we see that the maximum value of Z is 1160 which occurs at the point (2000, 10000).

Hence, to maximise the interest ₹ 2000 and ₹ 10000 must be invested in bond A and B, respectively.

COMEDK

Mock Test 5

Instructions

- There are 180 questions in all. The number of questions in each section is as given below.

Sections	No. of Questions
Section I : Physics	1-60
Section II : Chemistry	61-120
Section III : Mathematics	121-180

- All the questions are Multiple Choice Questions having four options out of which **ONLY ONE** is correct.
- Candidates will be awarded 1 mark for each correct answer. There will be no negative marking for incorrect answer.
- Time allotted to complete this paper is 3 hrs.

PHYSICS

1. A galvanometer of resistance $70\,\Omega$ is converted into an ammeter by a shunt resistance $r_s = 0.03\,\Omega$. The value of its resistance will become

a. $0.025\,\Omega$ *b.* $0.022\,\Omega$
c. $0.035\,\Omega$ *d.* $0.030\,\Omega$

2. The horizontal range and maximum height of a projectile are equal. The angle of projection is

a. $\theta = \tan^{-1}\left(\frac{1}{4}\right)$ *b.* $\theta = \tan^{-1}(4)$
c. $\theta = \tan^{-1}(2)$ *d.* $\theta = 45°$

3. The speed of an electron in ground state energy level is $2.6 \times 10^6\ ms^{-1}$, then its speed in third excited state will be

a. $5.6 \times 10^6\ ms^{-1}$ *b.* $6.5 \times 10^5\ ms^{-1}$
c. $5.5 \times 10^5\ ms^{-1}$ *d.* $4.3 \times 10^6\ ms^{-1}$

4. The excess pressure inside an air bubble of radius r just below the surface of water is p_1. The excess pressure inside a drop of the same radius just outside the surface is p_2. If T is the surface tension, then

a. $p_1 = 2p_2$ *b.* $p_1 = p_2$
c. $p_2 = 2p_1$ *d.* $p_2 = 0,\ p_1 \neq 0$

5. Among the four graphs, there is only one graph for which average velocity over the time interval $(0, T)$ can vanish for suitably chosen T. Which one is it?

a.
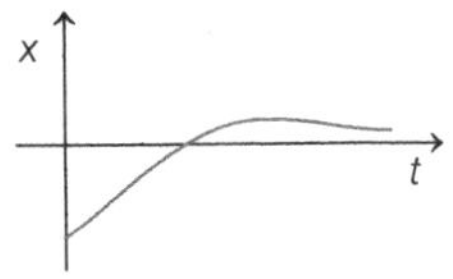

b.
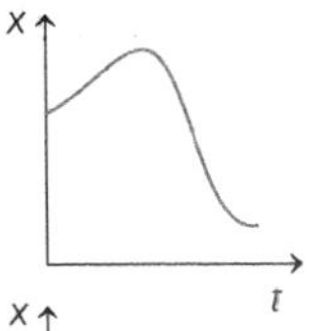

c.
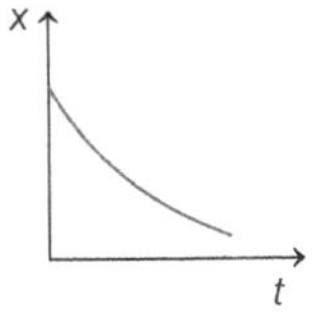

d.
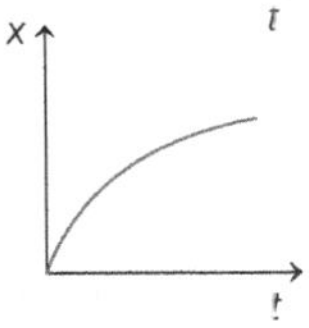

6. A cell can be balanced against 110 cm and 100 cm of potentiometer wire respectively, with and without being short-circuited through a resistance of $10\,\Omega$. Its internal resistance is

a. $1.0\,\Omega$ *b.* $0.5\,\Omega$ *c.* $2.0\,\Omega$ *d.* zero

7. If two vectors are equal in magnitude and their resultant is also equal in magnitude to one of them, then the angle between the two vectors is

a. 60° *b.* 120° *c.* 90° *d.* 0°

8. A particle is moving on a circular path of 10 m radius. At any instant of time, its speed is 5 ms^{-1} and the speed is increasing at a rate of 2 ms^{-2}. The magnitude of net acceleration at this instant is

a. 5 ms^{-2} *b.* 2 ms^{-2} *c.* 3.2 ms^{-2} *d.* 4.3 ms^{-2}

9. Two charges q_1 and q_2 are placed 30 cm apart, as shown in the figure.

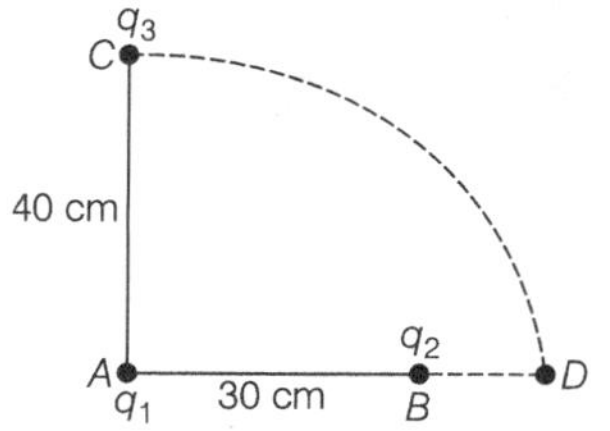

A third charge q_3 is moved along the arc of a circle of radius 40 cm from C to D. The change in the potential energy of the system is $\frac{q_3}{4\pi\varepsilon_0}K$, where K is

a. $8q_2$ *b.* $8q_1$ *c.* $6q_2$ *d.* $6q_1$

10. When 1 m, 1 kg and 1 min are taken as the fundamental units, the magnitude of the force is 36 units. What will be the value of this force in CGS system?

a. 10^5 dyne *b.* 10^3 dyne
c. 10^8 dyne *d.* 10^4 dyne

11. The graph shows the variation of voltage V across the plates of two capacitors A and B *versus* increase of charge Q stored in them. Which of the capacitors has higher capacitance?

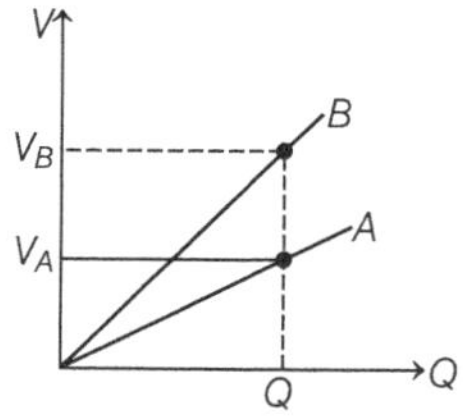

a. Capacitor A
b. Capacitor B
c. Both have same capacitance
d. None of the above

12. If a car is moving in uniform circular motion, then what should be the value of velocity of a car, so that car will not move away from the circle?

a. $v < \sqrt{\mu_s Rg}$ *b.* $v \le \sqrt{\mu_s Rg}$
c. $v < \sqrt{\mu_k Rg}$ *d.* None of these

13. A 1 kW motor is used to pump water from a well 10 m deep. The quantity of water pumped out per second is nearly

a. 1 kg *b.* 10 kg *c.* 100 kg *d.* 1000 kg

14. Two rotating bodies A and B of masses m and $2m$ with moments of inertia I_A and I_B $(I_B > I_A)$ have equal kinetic energy of rotation. If L_A and L_B be their angular momenta respectively, then

a. $L_A > L_B$ *b.* $L_A = \frac{L_B}{2}$
c. $L_A = 2L_B$ *d.* $L_B > L_A$

15. Two strings A and B, made of same materials are stretched by same tension. The radius of string A is double the radius of B. A transverse wave travels on A with speed v_A and on B with speed v_B. The ratio of v_A/v_B is

a. 1/2 *b.* 2
c. 1/4 *d.* 4

16. A radiation of energy E falls normally on a perfectly reflecting surface. The momentum transferred to the surface is

a. $\frac{E}{c}$ *b.* $\frac{2E}{c}$ *c.* Ec *d.* $\frac{E}{c^2}$

17. Suppose that the amplitude of electric field of an electromagnetic wave is $E_0 = 120\ NC^{-1}$ and its frequency is $\nu = 50.0$ MHz. The expressions for E will be (if wave travels along X-axis)

a. $[(120\ NC^{-1})\sin\{(1.05\ radm^{-1})x - (3.14\times 10^8\ rads^{-1})t\}]\mathbf{i}$
b. $[(120\ NC^{-1})\sin\{(1.05\ radm^{-1})x - (3.14\times 10^8\ rads^{-1})t\}]\mathbf{k}$
c. $[(120\ NC^{-1})\ \sin\{(1.05\ rad\ m^{-1})x - (3.14\times 10^8\ rads^{-1})\ t\}]\ \mathbf{j}$
d. $[(120\ NC^{-1})\ \cos\{(1.05\ rad\ m^{-1})x - (3.14\times 10^8\ rads^{-1})\ t\}]\ \mathbf{j}$

18. In Pfund series, ratio of maximum to minimum wavelengths of emitted spectral lines is

a. $\frac{\lambda_{max}}{\lambda_{min}} = \frac{4}{3}$ *b.* $\frac{\lambda_{max}}{\lambda_{min}} = \frac{9}{5}$
c. $\frac{\lambda_{max}}{\lambda_{min}} = \frac{16}{7}$ *d.* $\frac{\lambda_{max}}{\lambda_{min}} = \frac{36}{11}$

19. The force of attraction due to a hollow spherical shell of mass M, radius R and uniform density, on a point mass m situated inside it is

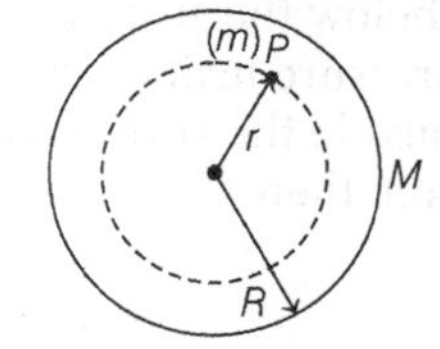

a. $\frac{GmM}{r^2}$ b. $\frac{Gm\,M}{R^2}$

c. zero d. Data insufficient

20. If a particle of charge 10^{-12} C moving along the x-direction with a velocity 10^5 ms^{-1} experiences a force of 10^{-10} N in y-direction due to magnetic field, then the minimum magnetic field is

a. 6.25×10^3 T in z-direction

b. 10^{-15} T in z-direction

c. 6.25×10^{-3} T in z-direction

d. 10^{-3} T in z-direction

21. A hollow cylinder and solid sphere of mass M and radius r are rotating about an axis passing through its centre. If torques of equal magnitude are applied to them, then the ratio of angular accelerations produced is

a. $\frac{2}{5}$ b. $\frac{5}{2}$ c. $\frac{5}{4}$ d. $\frac{4}{5}$

22. A bob of mass m is suspended by a light string of length L. It is imparted a horizontal velocity v_0 at the lowest point A such that it completes a semi-circular trajectory in the vertical plane. The string becomes slack only on reaching the topmost point C as shown in figure.

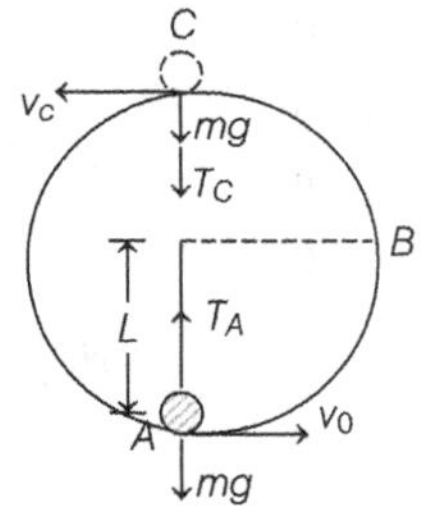

Then, the speed of bob (v_0) at point A is

a. $\sqrt{5gL}$ b. $\sqrt{2gL}$ c. $\sqrt{3gL}$ d. $\sqrt{7gL}$

23. The resistances in the two arms of the meter bridge are 5 Ω and R Ω, respectively. When the resistance R is shunted with an equal resistance, the new balance point is at $1.6\,l_1$. The resistance R is

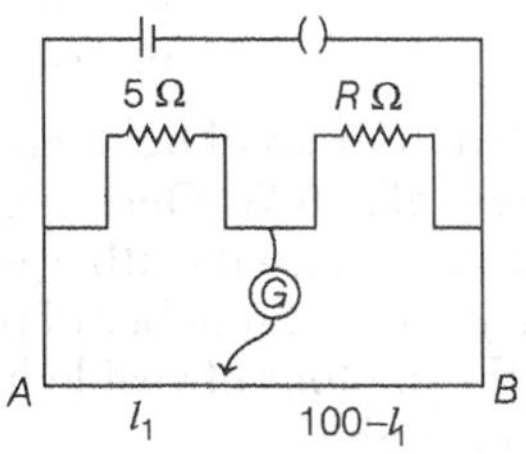

a. 10 Ω b. 15 Ω c. 20 Ω d. 25 Ω

24. Charges q, $2q$, $3q$ and $4q$ are placed at the corners A, B, C and D of a square as shown in the figure. The direction of electric field at the centre of the square is along

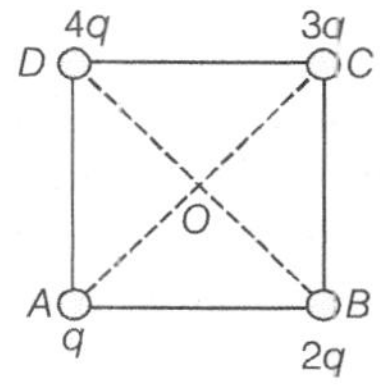

a. AB b. CB c. BD d. AC

25. Two electric dipoles of moment p and $64p$ are placed in opposite direction on a line at a distance of 25 cm. The electric field will be zero at point between the dipoles whose distance from the dipole of moment p is

a. 5 cm b. $\frac{25}{9}$ cm c. 10 cm d. $\frac{4}{13}$ cm

26. LED's are not used for room lighting (although they are used for automobile bulbs and in industrial lighting) because

a. our eyes are not comfortable with very intense light

b. our eyes are not comfortable with monochromatic light

c. LED's are much costlier than bulbs tubelights and CFL's

d. LED manufacture in mass production will be a very polluting process

27. The input resistance of a transistor is 1000 Ω on charging its base current by 10μA, the collector current increases by 2 mA. If a load resistance of 5 kΩ is used in the circuit, the voltage gain of the amplifier is

a. 100 b. 500 c. 1000 d. 1500

28. Which amongst the following is a correct graph of potential energy U of a pair of nucleons as a function of their separation r?

a.
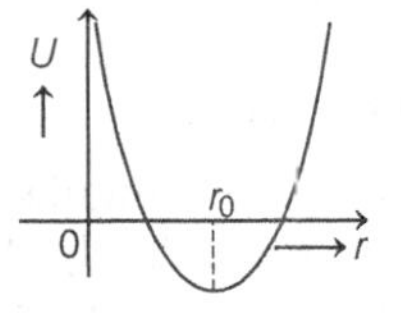

b.
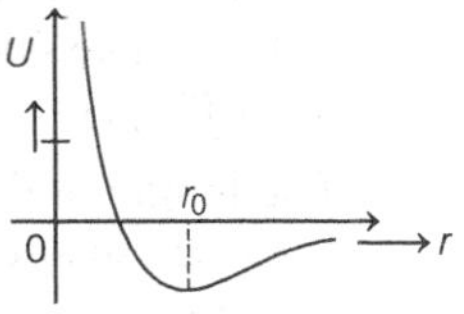

c.
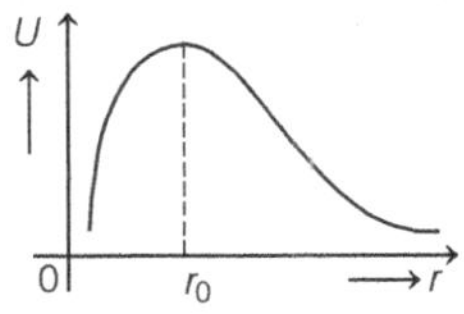

d.
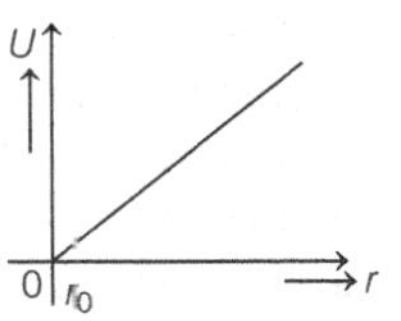

29. If the binding energy per nucleon of deuteron is 2.115 MeV, then its mass defect in atomic mass unit is

a. 0.0024 u *b.* 25.62 u
c. 96.264 u *d.* 0.0045 u

30. In an experiment on photoelectric effect, the frequency ν of incident light is plotted against the stopping potential V_0. The work-function of the photoelectric surface is given by

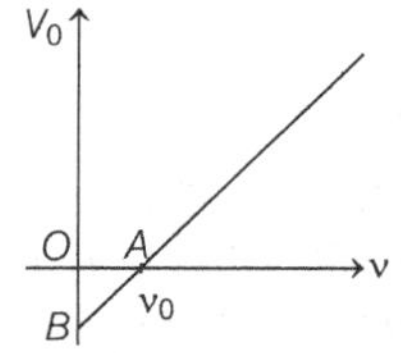

a. $OB \times e$ (in eV)
b. OB (in volts)
c. OA (in eV)
d. the slope of line AB

31. The coefficient of viscosity for hot air is

a. greater than the coefficient of viscosity for cold air
b. smaller than the coefficient of viscosity for cold air
c. same as the coefficient of viscosity for cold air
d. increases or decreases depending on the external pressure

32. A particle moves in a straight line with a constant acceleration. It changes its velocity from 10 ms^{-1} to 20 ms^{-1}, while passing through a distance 135 m in t second. The value of t (in s) is

a. 12 *b.* 9 *c.* 10 *d.* 1.8

33. A double convex lens whose refractive index is 1.33 has both radii of curvature of magnitude 10 cm. If an object is placed at a distance of 5 cm from this lens, then the position of the image formed (in cm) is

a. 7.46 same side of the object
b. 7.46 opposite side of the object
c. 14.45 same side of the object
d. 14.45 opposite side of the object

34. The length and breadth of a rectangular sheet are 16.2 cm and 10.1 cm, respectively. The area of the sheet in appropriate significant figures and error is

a. (164 ± 3) cm^2
b. (163.62 ± 2.6) cm^2
c. (163.6 ± 2.6) cm^2
d. (163.62 ± 3) cm^2

35. A ray of light from a denser medium strikes a rarer medium at an angle of incidence i (see figure).

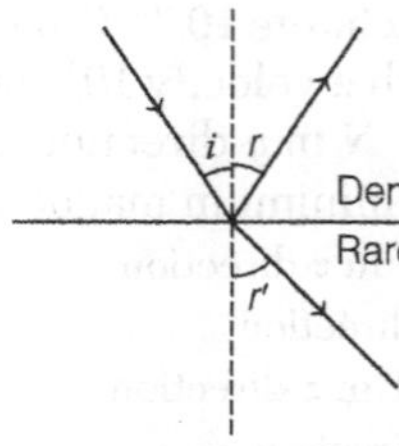

The reflected and refracted rays make an angle of 90° with each other. The angle of reflection and refraction are r and r'. The critical angle is

a. $\sin^{-1}(\tan r)$ *b.* $\sin^{-1}(\cot i)$
c. $\sin^{-1}(\tan r')$ *d.* $\tan^{-1}(\sin i)$

36. In the following circuit, the output Y for all possible inputs A and B is expressed by the truth table

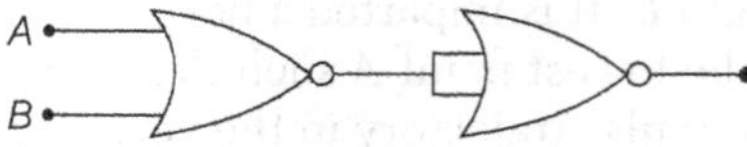

a.

A	B	Y
0	0	0
0	1	0
1	0	0
1	1	0

b.

A	B	Y
0	0	1
0	1	1
1	0	1
1	1	0

c.

A	B	Y
0	0	0
0	1	0
1	0	0
1	1	0

d.

A	B	Y
0	0	0
0	1	1
1	0	1
1	1	1

37. The displacement of an elastic wave is given by the function $y = 3\sin \omega t + 4\cos \omega t$, where y is in cm and t is in second. The resultant amplitude will be

a. 15 cm *b.* 4 cm
c. 5 cm *d.* 3 cm

38. There are two sources of light, each emitting with a power of 200 W. One emits X-rays of wavelength 2 nm and the other visible light of 400 nm. The ratio of number of photons of X-rays to the photons of visible light of the given wavelength is

a. 1 : 100 *b.* 1 : 200
c. 1 : 500 *d.* 1 : 300

39. The expression for displacement of an object in SHM is $x = A\cos\omega t$. The potential energy at $t = T/4$ is

a. $\frac{1}{2}kA^2$ *b.* $\frac{1}{8}kA^2$
c. $\frac{1}{4}kA^2$ *d.* zero

40. Which of the following figures represent the variation of particle's momentum p and the associated de-Broglie wavelength λ?

a.
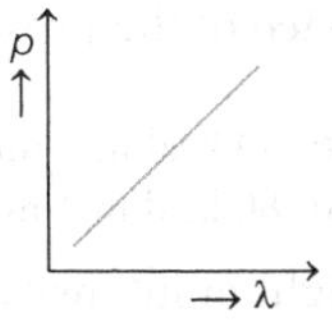

b.
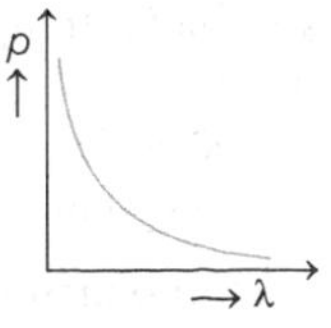

c.
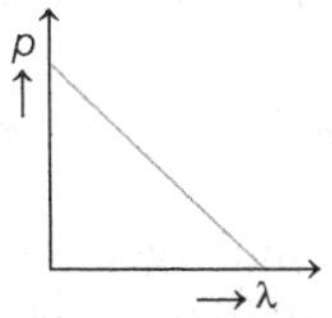

d.
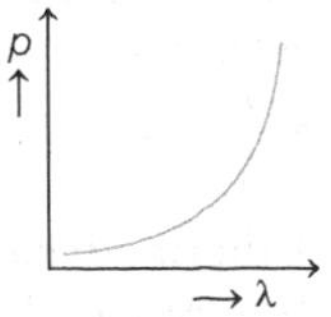

41. Two spring of force constants k_1 and k_2 are connected to a mass m as shown in figure. The frequency of oscillation of the mass is f. If both k_1 and k_2 are made four times their original values, the frequency of oscillation becomes

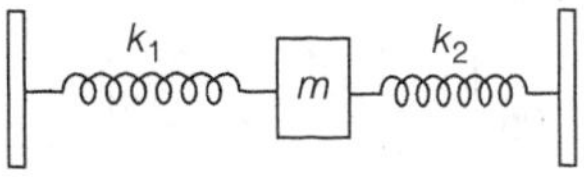

a. $f/2$ *b.* $f/4$
c. $4f$ *d.* $2f$

42. Three solenoid coils of same dimension, same numbers of turns and same numbers of layers of winding are taken. Coil 1 of inductance L_1 was wound using a wire of resistance $11\,\Omega m^{-1}$, coil 2 of inductance L_2 was wound using the similar wire but the direction of winding was reversed in each layer and coil 3 of inductance L_3 was wound using a superconducting wire. The self-inductance of the coils L_1, L_2 and L_3 are such that

a. $L_1 = L_2 = L_3$
b. $L_1 = L_2$, $L_3 = 0$
c. $L_1 = L_3$, $L_2 = 0$
d. $L_1 > L_2 > L_3$

43. It takes 10 min to cool a liquid from 61°C to 59°C. If room temperature is 30°C, then time taken in cooling from 51°C to 49°C is

a. 10 min *b.* 11 min
c. 13 min *d.* 15 min

44. Within the limit of elasticity, which of the following graph obey Hooke's law?

a.
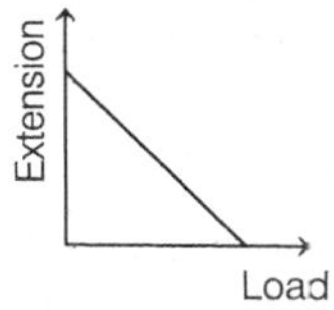

b.
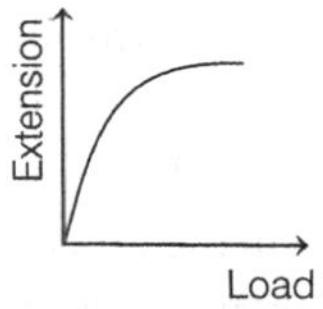

c.
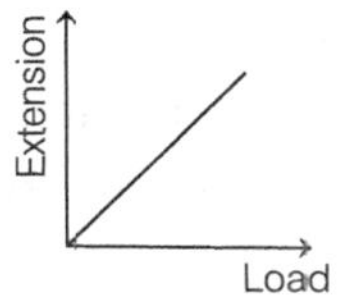

d.
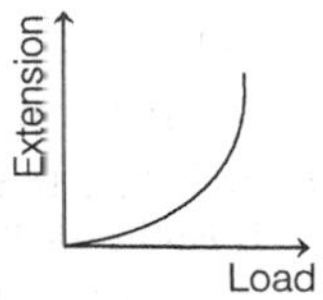

45. If a converging lens of focal length f is placed after the slit and the fringes are obtained on screen placed at the focus of lens in single-slit diffraction. Then, the size of screen is

a. λ/a *b.* $f\lambda/a$ *c.* a/λ *d.* fa/λ

46. In optical communication system operating at 1200 nm, only 2% of the source frequency is available for TV transmission having a bandwidth of 5 MHz. The number of TV channels that can be transmitted is

a. 2 million *b.* 10 million
c. 0.1 million *d.* 1 million

47. Root mean square speed of the molecules of ideal gas is v. If pressure is increased two times at constant temperature, then the rms speed will become

a. $\frac{v}{2}$ *b.* v *c.* $2v$ *d.* $4v$

48. The ratio of resolving powers of an optical microscope for two wavelengths $\lambda_1 = 4000$ Å and $\lambda_2 = 6000$ Å is

a. 8 : 27 *b.* 9 4
c. 3 : 2 *d.* 16 : 81

49. The molar specific heat at constant pressure of an ideal gas is $(7/2)R$. The ratio of specific heat at constant pressure to that at constant volume is

a. 7/5 *b.* 8/7
c. 5/7 *d.* 9/7

50. The diameter of a brass rod is 4 mm and Young's modulus of brass is $9 \times 10^{10}\ Nm^{-2}$. The force required to stretch by 0.1% of its length, is

a. $360\pi N$ *b.* 36 N
c. $144\pi \times 10^3$ N *d.* $36\pi \times 10^5$ N

51. If mass of a planet is 2% of mass of earth. The ratio of gravitational pull of earth on the planet and that of planet on the earth will be

a. 1 : 20 *b.* 2 : 5 *c.* 1 : 1 *d.* 1 : 50

52. A 110 V AC is connected to a transformer of ratio 10. If resistance of secondary coil is 550 Ω, current through secondary coil will be

a. 10 A *b.* 2 A
c. zero *d.* 55 A

53. During an isothermal expansion, a confined ideal gas does –150 J of work against its surroundings. This implies that

a. 300 J of heat has been added to the gas
b. no heat is transferred because the process is isothermal
c. 150 J of heat has been added to the gas
d. 150 J of heat has been removed from the gas

54. What is the magnitude of the equatorial and axial fields due to a bar magnet of length 5.0 cm at a distance of 50 cm from its mid-point ? The magnetic moment of the bar magnet is 0.40 A-m^2.

a. 3.2×10^{-6} T, 6.4×10^{-7} T
b. 4.2×10^{5} T, 6×10^{-7} T
c. 5×10^{-6} T, 3.2×10^{-7} T
d. 3.2×10^{-7} T, 6.4×10^{-7} T

55. A solid ball of density half that of water falls freely under gravity from a height of 19.6 m and then enters water. Neglecting air resistance and viscosity effect in water, the depth upto which the ball will go is (take, $g = 9.8\ \text{m/s}^2$)

a. 19.6 m *b.* 28.4 m
c. 9.8 m *d.* 14.7 m

56. If a magnet is suspended at an angle of 30° to the magnetic meridian, the dip needle makes an angle of 45° with the horizontal. The real dip is

a. $\tan^{-1}(\sqrt{3/2})$ *b.* $\tan^{-1}(\sqrt{3})$
c. $\tan^{-1}(\sqrt{3}/2)$ *d.* $\tan^{-1}(2/\sqrt{3})$

57. The magnetic potential energy stored in a certain inductor is 25 mJ, when the current in the inductor is 60 mA. This inductor is of inductance

a. 1.389 H *b.* 138.88 H
c. 0.138 H *d.* 13.89 H

58. The radiant energy from the sun, incident normally at the surface of the earth is 20 kcal m^{-2} min^{-1}. What would have been the radiant energy, incident normally on the earth, if the sun had a temperature, twice of the present one?

a. 160 kcal m^{-2} min^{-1} *b.* 40 kcal m^{-2} min^{-1}
c. 320 kcal m^{-2} min^{-1} *d.* 80 kcal m^{-2} min^{-1}

59. An unpolarised beam of light of intensity I_0 falls on a polaroid. The intensity of the emergent beam is

a. $\frac{I_0}{2}$ *b.* I_0 *c.* $\frac{I_0}{4}$ *d.* zero

60. A thermodynamics system undergoes cyclic process *ABCDA* as shown in figure. The work done by the system in the cycle is

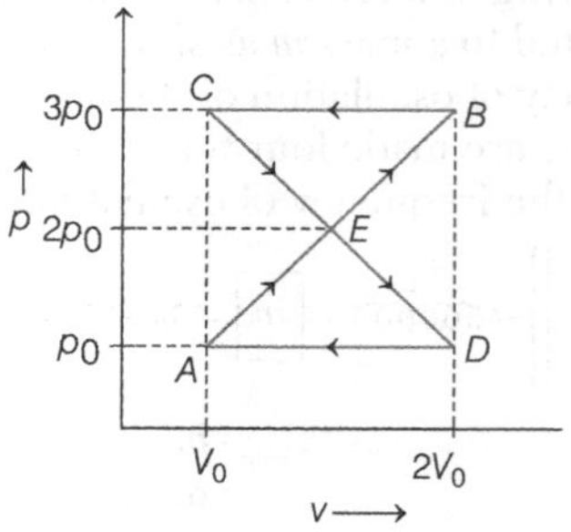

a. p_0V_0 *b.* $2p_0V_0$
c. $\frac{p_0V_0}{2}$ *d.* zero

CHEMISTRY

61. Which one of the following is the weakest acid?

a. HCl *b.* HF
c. H_2SO_4 *d.* HNO_3

62. Two gases *A* and *B* having molar mass 60 and 45 g mol^{-1}, respectively are enclosed in a vessel. The weight of *A* is 0.5 g and that of *B* is 0.2 g. The total pressure of the mixture is 750 mm. The partial pressure of gas *A* and *B* respectively are

a. 260 mm, 490 mm *b.* 190 mm, 560 mm
c. 490 mm, 260 mm *d.* 520 mm, 290 mm

63. Consider two elements *P* and *Q*. If *P* has 2 and *Q* has 6 electrons in their outermost shell, then formula of compound is

a. PQ *b.* P_2Q *c.* P_2Q_3 *d.* PQ_2

64. In nitrobenzene, the *X* attacks on comparatively electron rich *meta*-position resulting in *Y* substitution. Here, *X* and *Y* refer to

a. electrophile, *meta*
b. nucleophile, *meta*
c. deactivating group, *para*
d. activating group, *meta*

65. Which of the following compounds is likely to show both Frenkel and Schottky defects in its crystalline form?

a. AgBr *b.* CsCl *c.* KBr *d.* ZnS

66. If *M* is element of actinoids series, the degree of complex formation decreases in the order

a. $M^{4+} > M^{3+} > MO_2^{2+} > MO_2^{+}$
b. $M^{4+} > MO_2^{2+} > M^{3+} > MO_2^{+}$
c. $MO_2^{+} > MO_2^{2+} > M^{3+} > M^{4+}$
d. $MO_2^{2+} > MO_2^{+} > M^{4+} > M^{3+}$

67. In which pair of ions both the species contain S—S bond?

a. $S_2O_7^{2-}$, $S_2O_3^{2-}$ *b.* $S_4O_6^{2-}$, $S_2O_3^{2-}$
c. $S_2O_7^{2-}$, $S_2O_8^{2-}$ *d.* $S_4O_6^{2-}$, $S_2O_7^{2-}$

68. The major product of the following reaction is

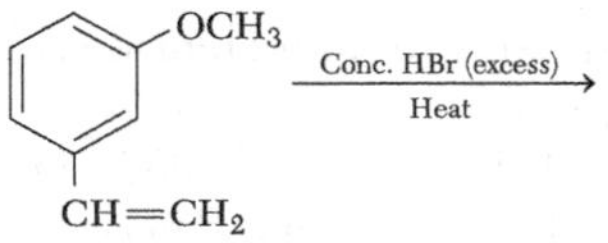

a.  *b.* 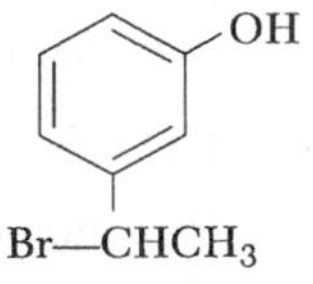

c. 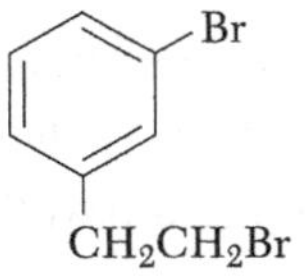 *d.* 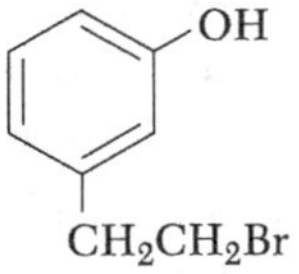

69. $CH_3—CH_2—CH_2—Br \xrightarrow{\text{Alc. KOH}}$

Final product is

a. propene *b.* propanol
c. cyclopropane *d.* propan-1, 2-diol

70. What does *A* point signifies in the figure given below?

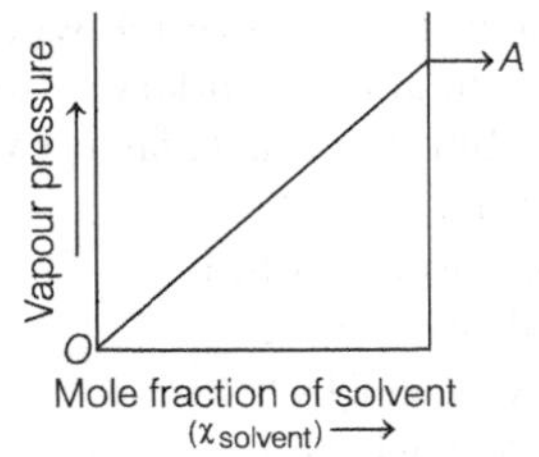

a. Vapour pressure of solute
b. Vapour pressure of pure solvent
c. Vapour pressure of solution
d. None of the above

71. Hydrogenation of vegetable oils using nickel as a catalyst gives edible fat which is

a. coconut oil
b. soyabean oil
c. margarine and vanaspati ghee
d. peanut oil

72. Which of the following effect helps in deciding the stability of *iso*-butylene?

a. Inductive effect
b. Mesomeric effect
c. Hyperconjugative effect
d. Steric effect

73. The compressibility of a gas is less than unity at STP. Therefore

a. $V_m >$ 22.4 L
b. $V_m <$ 22.4 L
c. $V_m =$ 22.4 L
d. $V_m =$ 44.8 L

74. When melamine and formaldehyde polymerise, a resin intermediate is formed. Identify the structure of this intermediate.

a. 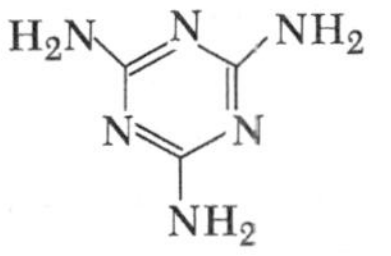 *b.* 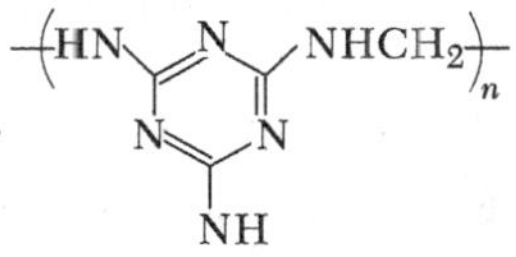

c. 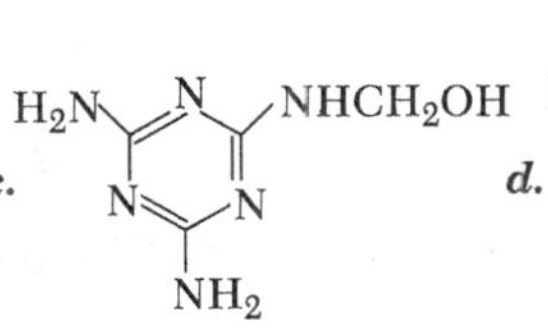 *d.* 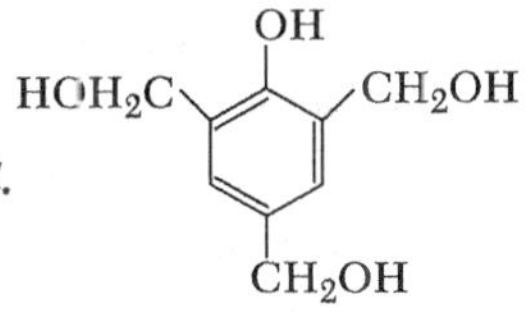

75.

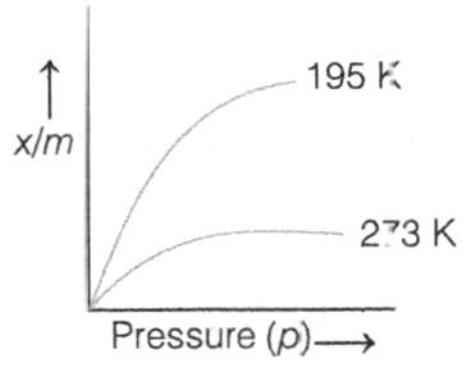

What does the graph of these curves conclude?

a. At constant pressure, physisorption increases with increase in temperature
b. At variable pressure, physisorption increases with increase in temperature
c. At constant pressure, physisorption decreases with increase in temperature
d. At variable pressure, physisorption decreases with increase in temperature

MOCK TEST 5

76. The structure of *iso*-butyl group in an organic compound is

a. 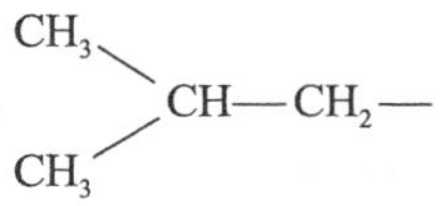

b. $CH_3—CH_2—CH_2—CH_3$

c. $CH_3—CH_2—CH_2—CH_2—$

d. 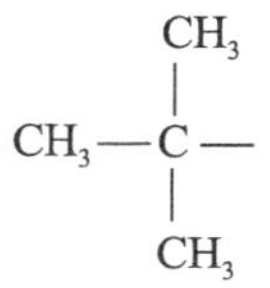

77. Which of the following compounds is not an antacid?

a. Aluminium hydroxide *b.* Cimetidine
c. Phenelzine *d.* Ranitidine

78. A complex compound in which the oxidation number of a metal is zero, is

a. $[Ni(CO)_4]$ *b.* $[Pt(NH_3)_4]Cl_2$
c. $K_3[Fe(CN)_6]$ *d.* $K_4[Fe(CN)_6]$

79. The amorphous form of silica is

a. tridymite *b.* kieselguhr
c. cristobalite *d.* quartz

80. An alkaloid contains 17.28% of nitrogen and its molecular mass is 162. The number of nitrogen atoms present in one molecule of alkaloid is

a. 5 *b.* 4 *c.* 3 *d.* 2

81. The number of orbitals associated with quantum numbers $n = 5, m_s = +\frac{1}{2}$ is

a. 25 *b.* 50 *c.* 15 *d.* 11

82. Which type of activity is not a cause of acid rain?

a. Emission from motor vehicles
b. Generation of electricity in thermal power stations
c. Production of carbon monoxide during combustion of wood
d. Use of fossil fuel in furnaces

83. For the equilibrium,

$2NOCl(g) \rightleftharpoons 2NO(g) + Cl_2(g)$, the value of the equilibrium constant, K_C is 3.75×10^{-6} at 1069 K. The value of K_p for the reaction at this temperature will be

a. 0.133 *b.* 1.242
c. 0.033 *d.* 0.00033

84. The decreasing order of dipole moments of the molecules HF, H_2O, BeF_2, NF_3 is

a. $HF > H_2O > BeF_2 > NF_3$
b. $H_2O > HF > NF_3 > BeF_2$
c. $BeF_2 > NF_3 > HF > H_2O$
d. $NF_3 > BeF_2 > H_2O > HF$

85. In adiabatic conditions, 2 moles of CO_2 gas at 300 K is expanded such that its volume becomes 27 times. Then, the work done is ($C_V = 6$ cal mol^{-1} and $\gamma = 1.33$)

a. 1400 cal *b.* 1000 cal
c. 900 cal *d.* 1200 cal

86. Rate of replacement of hydrogens of alkanes in halogenation process is

a. $1° > 2° > 3°$ *b.* $1° > 3° > 2°$
c. $2° > 1° > 3°$ *d.* $3° > 2° > 1°$

87. When aqueous sodium chloride solution is electrolysed

a. at cathode H^+ is reduced into H_2 instead of Na^+
b. at cathode, Na^+ is reduced to Na
c. Cl^- is oxidised into Cl_2 at cathode
d. Both (b) and (c)

88. The value of $E^\circ_{M^{2+}/M}$ for which of the following transition elements are more negative than expected?

a. Cr, Mn and Zn *b.* Mn, Ni and Zn
c. V, Mn and Cu *d.* Fe, Co and Ni

89. Many aldehydes and ketones are well known for their

a. reactive nature towards *ortho* and *para*-position and shows electrophilic substitution
b. oval shape
c. odour and flavour
d. reactivity towards oxidation and reduction even by weak reagents

90. An unknown alcohol (X) is treated with the "Lucas reagent" to determine whether the alcohol is primary, secondary or tertiary. The type of alcohol that reacts fastest with its mechanism is

a. secondary alcohol by S_N1
b. tertiary alcohol by S_N2
c. secondary alcohol by S_N2
d. tertiary alcohol by S_N1

91. Which one of the following is likely to give a precipitate with $AgNO_3$ solution?

a. $CH_2=CH—Cl$ *b.* CCl_4
c. $CHCl_3$ *d.* $(CH_3)_3CCl$

92. K_f for water is 1.86 K kg mol^{-1}. If your automobile radiator holds 1.0 kg of water, how many grams of ethylene glycol ($C_2H_6O_2$) must you add to get the freezing point of the solution lowered to $-2.8°C$?

a. 72 g *b.* 93 g *c.* 39 g *d.* 27 g

93. An amine (X) react with nitrous acid at low temperatures to form stable diazonium salts. The structure of amine (X) is

a. CH_3NH_2 *b.* $CH_3CH_2NH_2$
c. $CH_3(CH_2)NH_2$ *d.* $C_6H_5NH_2$

94. When O_2 is converted into O_2^{2+}, what will happen?

a. Both paramagnetic character and bond order increase

b. Bond order decreases

c. Paramagnetic character increases

d. Paramagnetic character decreases and bond order increases

95. The major product in the following conversion is

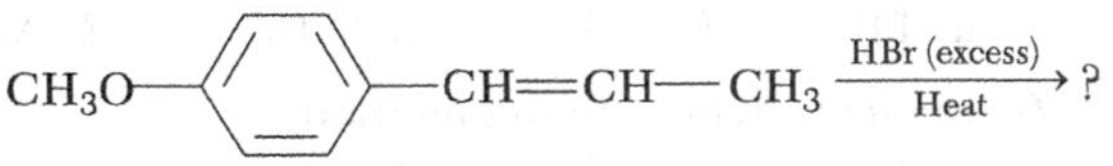

a. 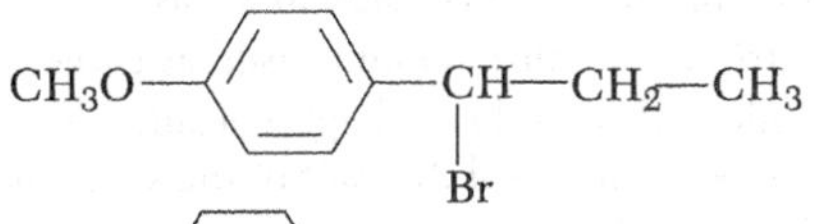

b. 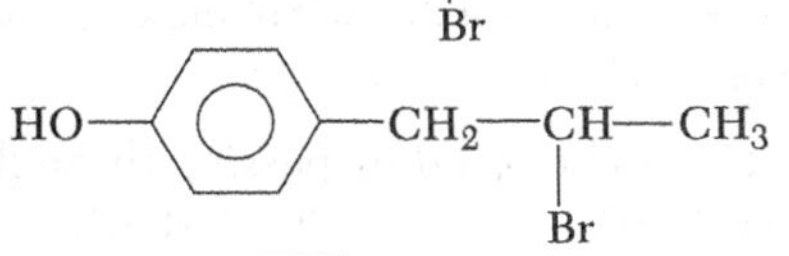

c. 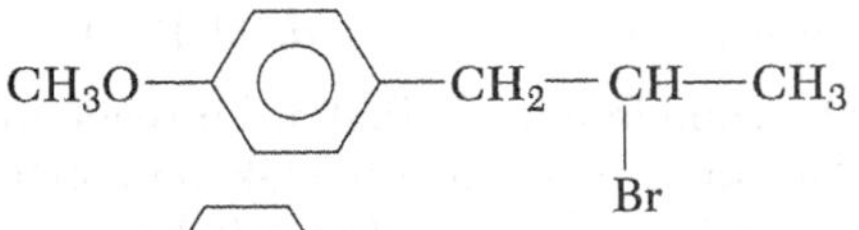

d. 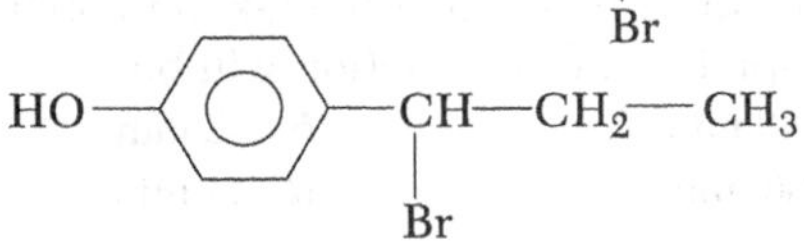

96. For a reaction,
$N_2(g) + 3H_2(g) \longrightarrow 2NH_3(g)$, identify dihydrogen ($H_2$) as a limiting reagent in the following reaction mixtures.

a. 56 g of N_2 + 10 g of H_2
b. 35 g of N_2 + 8 g of H_2
c. 14 g of N_2 + 4 g of H_2
d. 28 g of N_2 + 6 g of H_2

97. $[AlF_6]^{3-}$ exists, while $[BF_6]^{3-}$ does not. Choose the most appropriate reason.

a. Boron is smaller in size
b. Boron cannot expand it valence shell
c. Aluminium shows variable valency
d. Aluminium is more electropositive

98. How many unit cells are present in a cube shaped lattice crystal of NaCl of mass 1.00 g?
[Atomic mass : Na = 23, Cl = 35.5]

a. 2.57×10^{21} *b.* 5.14×10^{21}
c. 1.28×10^{21} *d.* 1.71×10^{21}

99. A gas is found to have the formula $(CO)_x$. Its vapour density is 70. The value of x will be

a. 7 *b.* 4
c. 5 *d.* 6

100. Arrange the following elements in the decreasing order of metallic characters. Si, Be, Mg, Na and P. Select the correct answer.

a. Na > Be > Mg > P > Si
b. Na > Mg > Be > P > Si
c. Na > Be > P > Mg > Si
d. Na > Mg > Be > Si > P

101. For a given reaction, $\Delta H = 35.5$ kJ mol^{-1} and $\Delta S = 83.6$ JK^{-1} mol^{-1}. The reaction is spontaneous at (Assume that ΔH and ΔS do not vary with temperature)

a. $T < 425$ K *b.* $T > 425$ K
c. all the temperatures *d.* $T > 298$ K

102. 2-methylpropan-2-ol is obtained by the reaction of X with water in the presence of conc. H_2SO_4. The compound X is

a. 1-methylpropene
b. 2, 2-dimethylhexane
c. 2-methylpropene
d. 2-methylbutane

103. Which of the following is an anionic detergent?

a. Sodium lauryl sulphate
b. Cetyltrimethyl ammonium bromide
c. Glyceryl oleate
d. Sodium stearate

104. Which of the following is isostructural with $KMnO_4$?

a. K_2SO_4 *b.* K_2MnO_4
c. $KClO_4$ *d.* None of these

105. When the first electron gain enthalpy ($\Delta_{eg}H$) of oxygen is -141 kJ/mol, its second electron gain enthalpy is

a. a positive value
b. a more negative value than the first
c. almost the same as that of the first
d. negative, but less negative than the first

106. Which of the following compounds do not undergo aldol condensation?

a. 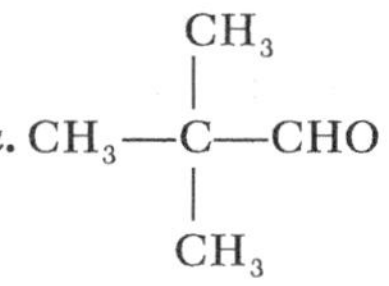   b. CH_3—CHO

c. 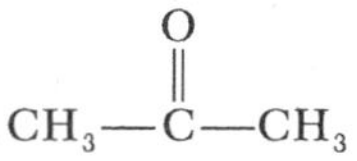   d. CH_3CH_2CHO

107. If the enthalpy change for the transition of liquid water to steam is 30 kJ mol^{-1} at 27°C, the entropy change for the process would be

a. 1.0 J mol^{-1} K^{-1} b. 0.1 J mol^{-1} K^{-1}
c. 100 J mol^{-1} K^{-1} d. 10 J mol^{-1} K^{-1}

108. Consider the following reaction,

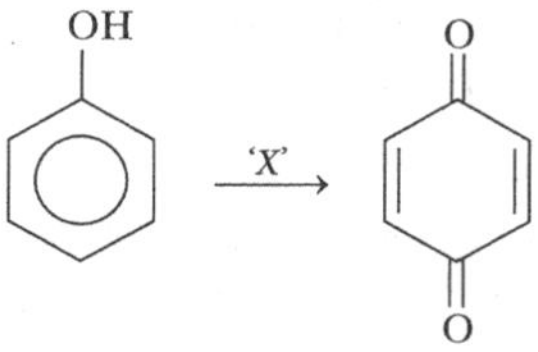

Here, *X* is

a. K_2MnO_4, H_2SO_4 b. $KMnO_4$, H_2SO_4
c. $Na_2Cr_2O_7$, H_2SO_4 d. Na_2CrO_4, HCl

109. Reaction by which benzaldehyde cannot be prepared is

a. 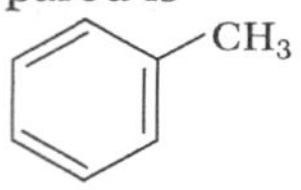 + CrO_2Cl_2 in CS_2 followed by H_3O^+

b.  + CO + HCl in the presence of anhyd. $AlCl_3$

c. 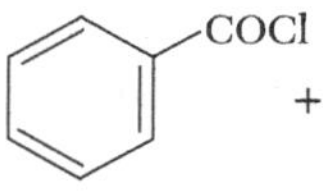 + H_2 in the presence of Pd-$BaSO_4$

d. 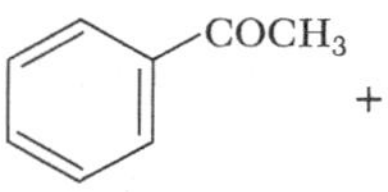 + Zn-Hg and conc. HCl

110. The correct decreasing order of electron releasing tendency of the given elements is

a. Ag > Cu > Zn   b. Zn > Cu > Ag
c. Cu > Ag > Zn   d. Zn > Ag > Cu

111. Which of the following reagent is used to reduce carboxylic acids to primary alcohols?

a. Pd   b. *R*—OH
c. $LiAlH_4$ d. Ni

112. The low solubility of LiF and CsI is due to

a. smaller lattice enthalpy, high hydration enthalpy
b. high lattice enthalpy, smaller hydration enthalpy
c. high lattice enthalpy, high hydration enthalpy
d. low lattice enthalpy, low hydration enthalpy

113. The complex that can show *fac* and *mer*-isomers is

a. $[Pt(NH_3)_2Cl_2]$ b. $[Co(NH_3)_3(NO_2)_3]$
c. $[Co(NH_3)_4Cl_2]^+$ d. $[CoCl_2(en)_2]$

114. Which structure(s) of proteins remain intact during denaturation process?

a. Both secondary and tertiary structures
b. Primary structure only
c. Secondary structure only
d. Tertiary structure only

115. Which of the following hydrides has largest bond angle?

a. PH_3 b. NH_3 c. SbH_3 d. AsH_3

116. In electrolytic refining method,

a. the impure metal is made to act as anode
b. a strip of the pure metal is used as cathode
c. anode and cathode are kept in a suitable electrolytic bath containing soluble salt of the same metal
d. All of the above are true

117. HCl gas can be dried by passing through

a. conc. H_2SO_4 b. dil. H_2SO_4
c. conc. HNO_3 d. dil. HNO_3

118. 99% completion of a first order reaction takes place in 32 min. The time taken in 99.9% completion of the reaction will be

a. 48 min   b. 52 min
c. 56 min   d. 44 min

119. Smoke is precipitated by the

a. Cottrell precipitator   b. colloidal precipitator
c. natural precipitator   d. Planck's precipitator

120. Xenon hexafluoride reacts with silica to form a xenon compound *X*. The oxidation state of xenon in *X* is

a. + 2   b. + 4   c. + 6   d. 0

MATHEMATICS

121. Which of the following functions from Z into Z are bijective?

a. $f(x) = x^3$ *b.* $f(x) = x + 2$

c. $f(x) = 2x + 1$ *d.* $f(x) = x^2 + 1$

122. The identity element for the binary operation $*$ defined on $Q - \{0\}$ as $a * b = \frac{ab}{2}\ \forall\ a, b \in Q - \{0\}$ is

a. 1 *b.* 0

c. 2 *d.* None of these

123. Let $f : N \to R$ be the function defined by $f(x) = \frac{2x-1}{2}$ and $g : Q \to R$ be another function defined by $g(x) = x + 2$. Then, $gof\left(\frac{3}{2}\right)$ is

a. -1 *b.* 1

c. $\frac{7}{2}$ *d.* None of these

124. If $\tan\theta = \frac{\sin\alpha - \cos\alpha}{\sin\alpha + \cos\alpha}$, then $\sin\alpha + \cos\alpha =$

a. $\sqrt{2}\cos\theta$ *b.* $\sqrt{2}\sin\theta$

c. $2\cos\theta$ *d.* $2\sin\theta$

125. If $\sec x \cos 5x + 1 = 0$, where $0 < x \le \frac{\pi}{2}$, then the value of x is

a. $\frac{\pi}{2}$ *b.* $\frac{\pi}{4}$

c. $\frac{\pi}{6}$ *d.* All of these

126. The general solution of the equation $5\cos^2\theta + 7\sin^2\theta - 6$ is

a. $n\pi \pm \frac{\pi}{4}$ *b.* $2n\pi \pm \frac{\pi}{4}$

c. $2n\pi \pm \frac{\pi}{6}$ *d.* $n\pi \pm \frac{\pi}{6}$

127. $\tan^{-1}\sqrt{3} - \cot^{-1}(-\sqrt{3})$ is equal to

a. π *b.* $-\frac{\pi}{2}$ *c.* 0 *d.* $2\sqrt{3}$

128. If $\sin^{-1}\left(\frac{2a}{1+a^2}\right) + \cos^{-1}\left(\frac{1-a^2}{1+a^2}\right) = \tan^{-1}\frac{2x}{1-x^2}$, where $a, x \in]\,0, 1\,[$, then the value of x is

a. 0 *b.* $\frac{a}{2}$ *c.* a *d.* $\frac{2a}{1-a^2}$

129. The number of real solutions of the equation $\tan^{-1}\sqrt{x(x+1)} + \sin^{-1}\sqrt{x^2+x+1} = \frac{\pi}{2}$ is

a. 0 *b.* 1 *c.* 2 *d.* 3

130. Which of the following is true?

a. $\tan^{-1}1 = \tan 1$ *b.* $\tan 1 > \tan^{-1}1$

c. $\tan 1 < \tan^{-1}1$ *d.* None of these

131. The number of subsets of a set containing n distinct elements is.

a. 2^n, for all $n \in N$ *b.* 3^n for all $n \in N$

c. 2^{n+1} for all $n \in N$ *d.* 3^{n-1} for all $n \in N$

132. The value of $(z+3)(\bar{z}+3)$ is equivalent to

a. $|z+3|^2$ *b.* $|z-3|$

c. $z^2 + 3$ *d.* None of these

133. If z is a complex number, then

a. $|z^2| > |z|$ *b.* $|z^2| = |z|^2$

c. $|z^2| < |z|^2$ *d.* $|z^2| \ge |z|^2$

134. The value of arg (x), when $x < 0$ is

a. 0 *b.* $\frac{\pi}{2}$

c. π *d.* None of these

135. If $f(z) = \frac{7-z}{1-z^2}$, where $z = 1 + 2i$, then $|f(z)|$ is equal to

a. $\frac{|z|}{2}$ *b.* $|z$

c. $2|z|$ *d.* None of these

136. The number of ways in which a team of eleven players can be selected from 22 players always including 2 of them and excluding 4 of them is

a. ${}^{16}C_{11}$ *b.* ${}^{16}C_5$

c. ${}^{16}C_9$ *d.* ${}^{20}C_9$

137. The number of triangles that are formed by choosing the vertices from a set of 12 points, seven of which lie on the same line is

a. 105 *b.* 15 *c.* 175 *d.* 185

138. Given 5 different green dyes, four different blue dyes and three different red dyes, the number of combinations of dyes which can be chosen taking atleast one green and one blue dye is

a. 3600 *b.* 3720

c. 3800 *d.* 3300

139. If the coefficients of 2nd, 3rd and the 4th terms in the expansion of $(1+x)^n$ are in AP, then the value of n is

a. 2 *b.* 7 *c.* 11 *d.* 14

140. The position of the term independent of x in the expansion of $\left(\sqrt{\frac{x}{3}}+\frac{3}{2x^2}\right)^{10}$ is

a. Second *b.* Third *c.* Seventh *d.* Tenth

141. If the third term of GP is 4, then the product of its first 5 terms is

a. 4^3 *b.* 4^4
c. 4^5 *d.* None of these

142. If 9 times the 9th term of an AP is equal to 13 times the 13th term, then the 22nd term of the AP is

a. 0 *b.* 22 *c.* 198 *d.* 220

143. The equation of the line passing through the point (1, 2) and perpendicular to the line $x+y+1=0$ is

a. $y-x+1=0$ *b.* $y-x-1=0$
c. $y-x+2=0$ *d.* $y-x-2=0$

144. For specifying a straight line, how many geometrical parameters should be known?

a. 1 *b.* 2
c. 4 *d.* 3

145. A point equidistant from the lines $4x+3y+10=0$, $5x-12y+26=0$ and $7x+24y-50=0$ is

a. (1, −1) *b.* (1, 1)
c. (0, 0) *d.* (0, 1)

146. The lines $2x-3y-5=0$ and $3x-4y=7$ are the diameters of a circle of area $154(=49\pi)$ sq units, then the equation of circle is

a. $x^2+y^2+2x-2y-62=0$
b. $x^2+y^2+2x-2y-47=0$
c. $x^2+y^2-2x+2y-47=0$
d. $x^2+y^2-2x+2y-62=0$

147. The equation of the parabola whose focus is the point (2, 3) and directrix is the line $x-4y+3=0$, is

a. $16x^2+y^2+8xy-74x-78y+212=0$
b. $x^2+16y^2+8xy-74x-78y+212=0$
c. $x^2+16y^2-8xy+74x+78y+212=0$
d. $16x^2+y^2-8xy+74x+78y+212=0$

148. An equilateral triangle is inscribed in the parabola $y^2=4ax$ whose one vertex is at the vertex of the parabola. Then, the length of the side of the triangle is

a. $16a\sqrt{2}$ *b.* $12a\sqrt{3}$
c. $8a\sqrt{3}$ *d.* $10a\sqrt{2}$

149. The length of the latusrectum of the ellipse $3x^2+y^2=12$ is

a. 4 *b.* 3 *c.* 8 *d.* $\frac{4}{\sqrt{3}}$

150. The equation of ellipse whose distance between the foci is equal to 8 and distance between the directrix is 18, is

a. $5x^2-9y^2=180$ *b.* $9x^2-5y^2=180$
c. $x^2+9y^2=180$ *d.* $5x^2+9y^2=180$

151. Equation of the hyperbola with eccentricity $\frac{3}{2}$ and foci at (± 2, 0) is

a. $\frac{x^2}{4}-\frac{y^2}{5}=\frac{4}{9}$ *b.* $\frac{x^2}{9}-\frac{y^2}{9}=\frac{4}{9}$
c. $\frac{x^2}{4}-\frac{y^2}{9}=1$ *d.* None of these

152. The equation of a line passing through the point (−3, 2, −4) and equally inclined to the axes are

a. $x-3=y+2=z-4$
b. $x+3=y-2=z+4$
c. $\frac{x+3}{1}=\frac{y-2}{2}=\frac{z+4}{3}$
d. None of the above

153. The function $f:R-\{0\}\to R$ given by $f(x)=\frac{1}{x}-\frac{2}{e^{2x}-1}$ can be made continuous at $x=0$ by defining $f(0)$ as

a. 2 *b.* −1 *c.* 0 *d.* 1

154. If $f(x)=(x-2)(x-4)(x-6)\dots(x-2n)$, then $f'(2)$ is equal to

a. $(-1)^n 2^{n-1}(n-1)!$ *b.* $(-2)^{n-1}(n-1)!$
c. $(-2)^n n!$ *d.* $(-1)^{n-1}2^n(n-1)!$

155. An edge of a variable cube is increasing at the rate of 10 cm/s. How fast the volume of the cube will increase when the edge is 5 cm long?

a. 750 cm^3/s *b.* 75 cm^3/s
c. 300 cm^3/s *d.* 150 cm^3/s

156. The interval in which $y=x^2e^{-x}$ is increasing, is

a. $(-\infty,\infty)$ *b.* $(-2, 0)$ *c.* $(2,\infty)$ *d.* $(0, 2)$

157. The function $f(x)=\tan^{-1}(\sin x+\cos x)$ is an increasing function in

a. $\left(\frac{\pi}{4},\frac{\pi}{2}\right)$ *b.* $\left(-\frac{\pi}{2},\frac{\pi}{4}\right)$
c. $\left(0,\frac{\pi}{2}\right)$ *d.* $\left(-\frac{\pi}{2},\frac{\pi}{2}\right)$

158. For what value of a, $f(x)=-x^3+4ax^2+2x-5$ is decreasing for all x?

a. (1, 2) *b.* (3, 4) *c.* R *d.* No value of a

159. The function $f(x)=x^3+ax^2+bx+c$, $a^2\le 3b$ has

a. one maximum value
b. one maximum and one minimum value
c. one minimum value
d. no extreme value

160. The greatest value of $\sin^3 x+\cos^3 x$ is

a. 1 *b.* 2 *c.* $\sqrt{2}$ *d.* $\sqrt{3}$

161. On the interval $[0,1]$ the function $x^{25}(1-x)^{75}$ takes its maximum value at the point

a. 0 *b.* $\frac{1}{4}$ *c.* $\frac{1}{2}$ *d.* $\frac{1}{3}$

162. If the function f be given by $f(x)=x^3+\frac{1}{x^3}$, $x\ne 0$, then

a. f is increasing in $(-\infty,-1)\cup(1,\infty)$
b. f is decreasing in $(-1,1)$
c. Both (a) and (b) are true
d. Both (a) and (b) are false

163. If $\int \frac{x^3}{\sqrt{1+x^2}}dx=a(1+x^2)^{3/2}+b\sqrt{1+x^2}+C$, then

a. $a=\frac{1}{3}$, $b=1$ *b.* $a=\frac{-1}{3}$, $b=1$
c. $a=\frac{-1}{3}$, $b=-1$ *d.* $a=\frac{1}{3}$, $b=-1$

164. The value of $\int \frac{3x-1}{\sqrt{x^2+9}}dx$ is equal to

a. $\sqrt{x^2+9}-\log|x+\sqrt{x^2+9}|+C$
b. $\sqrt{x^2+9}+\log|x+\sqrt{x^2+9}|+C$
c. $3\sqrt{x^2+9}-\log|x+\sqrt{x^2+9}|+C$
d. None of the above

165. The value of $\int_0^1 \tan^{-1}\left(\frac{2x-1}{1+x-x^2}\right)dx$ is

a. 1 *b.* 0 *c.* −1 *d.* $\frac{\pi}{4}$

166. $\int \frac{dx}{e^x+e^{-x}}$ is equal to

a. $\tan^{-1}(e^x)+C$
b. $\tan^{-1}(e^{-x})+C$
c. $\log(e^x-e^{-x})+C$
d. $\log(e^x+e^{-x})+C$

167. Area bounded by the curve $y^2=16x$ and the line $y=mx$ is $\frac{2}{3}$, then m is equal to

a. 3 *b.* 4 *c.* 1 *d.* 2

168. The solution of the differential equation $x\left(\frac{dy}{dx}\right)^2+2\sqrt{xy}\frac{dy}{dx}+y=0$ is

a. $x+y=C$ *b.* $\sqrt{x}-\sqrt{y}=\sqrt{C}$
c. $x^2+y^2=C^2$ *d.* $\sqrt{x}+\sqrt{y}=C$

169. If the slope of the tangent to the curve at any point $P(x, y)$ is $\frac{y}{x}-\cos^2\frac{y}{x}$, then the equation of a curve passing through $\left(1,\frac{\pi}{4}\right)$ is

a. $\tan\left(\frac{y}{x}\right)+\log x=1$
b. $\tan\left(\frac{y}{x}\right)+\log y=1$
c. $\tan\left(\frac{x}{y}\right)+\log x=1$
d. $\tan\left(\frac{x}{y}\right)+\log y=1$

170. If $\frac{dy}{dx}=\frac{y+x\tan\frac{y}{x}}{x}$, then $\sin\frac{y}{x}$ is equal to

a. Cx^2 *b.* Cx
c. Cx^3 *d.* Cx^4

171. A unit vector **a** makes an angle $\frac{\pi}{4}$ with Z-axis, if **a** + **i** + **j** is a unit vector, then **a** is equal to

a. $\frac{\mathbf{i}}{2}+\frac{\mathbf{j}}{2}+\frac{\mathbf{k}}{2}$ *b.* $\frac{\mathbf{i}}{2}+\frac{\mathbf{j}}{2}-\frac{\mathbf{k}}{\sqrt{2}}$
c. $-\frac{\mathbf{i}}{2}-\frac{\mathbf{j}}{2}+\frac{\mathbf{k}}{\sqrt{2}}$ *d.* $\frac{\mathbf{i}}{2}-\frac{\mathbf{j}}{2}-\frac{\mathbf{k}}{\sqrt{2}}$

172. For a unit vector **a**, if $(x-\mathbf{a})\cdot(x+\mathbf{a})=12$, then $|\mathbf{x}|$ is equal to

a. $\sqrt{11}$ *b.* $\sqrt{13}$
c. $\sqrt{14}$ *d.* $\sqrt{5}$

173. A unit vector in xy- plane makes an angle of 45° with the vector **i** + **j** and an angle of 60° with the vector 3**i** − 4**j** is

a. $\frac{13}{7}\mathbf{i}+\frac{1}{7}\mathbf{j}$ *b.* $\frac{7}{13}\mathbf{i}+\frac{7}{15}\mathbf{j}$
c. $\frac{13}{14}\mathbf{i}+\frac{1}{14}\mathbf{j}$ *d.* None of these

174. If $2X + 3Y = \begin{bmatrix} 2 & 3 \\ 4 & 0 \end{bmatrix}$ and $3X + 2Y = \begin{bmatrix} 2 & -2 \\ -1 & 5 \end{bmatrix}$.

Then, X and Y are respectively

a. $\begin{bmatrix} -2/5 & 12/5 \\ 11/5 & -3 \end{bmatrix}$ and $\begin{bmatrix} 2/5 & 13/5 \\ 14/5 & 2 \end{bmatrix}$

b. $\begin{bmatrix} -2/5 & -13/5 \\ 14/5 & 2 \end{bmatrix}$ and $\begin{bmatrix} 2/5 & 12/5 \\ 11/5 & 3 \end{bmatrix}$

c. $\begin{bmatrix} 2/5 & 13/5 \\ 14/5 & -2 \end{bmatrix}$ and $\begin{bmatrix} 2/5 & -12/5 \\ -11/5 & 3 \end{bmatrix}$

d. $\begin{bmatrix} 2/5 & -12/5 \\ -11/5 & 3 \end{bmatrix}$ and $\begin{bmatrix} 2/5 & 13/5 \\ 14/5 & -2 \end{bmatrix}$

175. If the value of the determinant $\begin{vmatrix} a & 1 & 1 \\ 1 & b & 1 \\ 1 & 1 & c \end{vmatrix}$ is positive, then

a. $abc > 1$
b. $abc > -8$
c. $abc < -8$
d. $abc > -2$

176. If $x, y \in R$, then the determinant $\begin{vmatrix} \cos x & -\sin x & 1 \\ \sin x & \cos x & 1 \\ \cos(x+y) & -\sin(x+y) & 0 \end{vmatrix}$ lies in the interval

a. $[-\sqrt{2}, \sqrt{2}]$
b. $[-1, 1]$
c. $[-\sqrt{2}, 1]$
d. $[-1, -\sqrt{2}]$

177. There are two bags, one of which contains 3 black and 4 white balls while the other contains 4 black and 3 white balls. A die is thrown. If it shows up 1 or 3, a ball is taken from the Ist bag; but if it shows up any other number, a ball is chosen from the second bag. Then, the probability of choosing a black ball is

a. $\frac{10}{21}$
b. $\frac{1}{21}$
c. $\frac{5}{21}$
d. $\frac{11}{21}$

178. The contrapositive of statement 'If Chandigarh is capital of Punjab, then Chandigarh is in India' is

a. if Chandigarh is not in India, then Chandigarh is not the capital of Punjab
b. if Chandigarh is in India, then Chandigarh is Capital of Punjab
c. if Chandigarh is not capital of Punjab, then Chandigarh is not capital of India
d. if Chandigarh is capital of Punjab, then Chandigarh is not is India

179. Corner points of the feasible region determined by the system of linear constraints are (0, 3), (1, 1) and (3, 0). Let $Z = px + qy$, where $p, q > 0$. Condition on p and q, so that the minimum of Z occurs at (3, 0) and (1, 1), is

a. $p = 2q$
b. $p = \frac{q}{2}$
c. $p = 3q$
d. $p = q$

180. Solve $\frac{1}{|x| - 3} \leq \frac{1}{2}$

a. $x \in (-\infty, -5] \cup (-3, 3) \cup [5, \infty)$
b. $x \in (-\infty, -5] \cup [-3, 3] \cup [5, \infty)$
c. $x \in (-\infty, -5] \cup (-3, 3) \cup [5, \infty)$
d. $x \in (-\infty, -5) \cup [-3, 3] \cup [5, \infty)$

ANSWERS

Physics

1. (d)	2. (b)	3. (b)	4. (b)	5. (b)	6. (a)	7. (b)	8. (c)	9. (a)	10. (b)
11. (a)	12. (b)	13. (b)	14. (d)	15. (a)	16. (b)	17. (c)	18. (d)	19. (c)	20. (d)
21. (a)	22. (a)	23. (b)	24. (b)	25. (a)	26. (b)	27. (c)	28. (b)	29. (d)	30. (a)
31. (a)	32. (b)	33. (a)	34. (a)	35. (a)	36. (d)	37. (c)	38. (b)	39. (d)	40. (b)
41. (d)	42. (b)	43. (d)	44. (c)	45. (b)	46. (d)	47. (b)	48. (c)	49. (a)	50. (a)
51. (c)	52. (b)	53. (c)	54. (d)	55. (a)	56. (c)	57. (d)	58. (c)	59. (a)	60. (d)

Chemistry

61. (b)	62. (c)	63. (a)	64. (a)	65. (a)	66. (b)	67. (b)	68. (b)	69. (a)	70. (b)
71. (c)	72. (c)	73. (b)	74. (c)	75. (c)	76. (a)	77. (c)	78. (a)	79. (b)	80. (d)
81. (a)	82. (c)	83. (c)	84. (b)	85. (d)	86. (d)	87. (a)	88. (b)	89. (c)	90. (d)
91. (d)	92. (b)	93. (d)	94. (d)	95. (d)	96. (a)	97. (b)	98. (a)	99. (c)	100. (d)
101. (b)	102. (c)	103. (a)	104. (c)	105. (a)	106. (a)	107. (c)	108. (c)	109. (d)	110. (b)
111. (c)	112. (b)	113. (b)	114. (b)	115. (b)	116. (d)	117. (a)	118. (a)	119. (a)	120. (c)

Mathematics

121. (b)	122. (c)	123. (d)	124. (a)	125. (d)	126. (a)	127. (b)	128. (d)	129. (c)	130. (b)
131. (a)	132. (a)	133. (b)	134. (c)	135. (a)	136. (c)	137. (d)	138. (b)	139. (b)	140. (b)
141. (c)	142. (a)	143. (b)	144. (b)	145. (c)	146. (c)	147. (a)	148. (c)	149. (d)	150. (d)
151. (a)	152. (b)	153. (d)	154. (b)	155. (a)	156. (d)	157. (b)	158. (d)	159. (d)	160. (a)
161. (b)	162. (c)	163. (d)	164. (c)	165. (b)	166. (a)	167. (b)	168. (d)	169. (a)	170. (b)
171. (c)	172. (b)	173. (c)	174. (d)	175. (b)	176. (a)	177. (d)	178. (a)	179. (b)	180. (a)

HINTS & SOLUTIONS

Physics

1. *(d)* To convert a galvanometer into an ammeter resistance is connected in parallel,

Resistance, $R = \dfrac{R_G r_s}{R_G + r_s}$

Given, $R_G = 70\,\Omega$ and $r_s = 0.03\,\Omega$

$\therefore \quad R = \dfrac{70 \times 0.03}{70 + 0.03} = 0.02998 = 0.030\,\Omega$

2. *(b)* Given, range (R) = maximum height (H)

Also, $R = \dfrac{u^2(2\sin\theta\cos\theta)}{g}$, $H = \dfrac{u^2\sin^2\theta}{2g}$

$\therefore \dfrac{u^2(2\sin\theta\cos\theta)}{g} = \dfrac{u^2\sin^2\theta}{2g}$

$\Rightarrow \quad 2\cos\theta = \dfrac{\sin\theta}{2}$

$\Rightarrow \quad \tan\theta = 4$ or $\theta = \tan^{-1}(4)$

3. *(b)* According to Bohr's model, velocity of electron,

$$v = \frac{2\pi k e^2 Z}{nh} \quad \text{or} \quad v \propto \frac{1}{n}$$

$\therefore \quad \dfrac{v_A}{v_B} = \dfrac{n_B}{n_A}$

$\therefore \quad v_B = v_A \times \dfrac{n_A}{n_B}$

Given, $n_A = 1$, $n_B = 4$ and $v_A = 2.6 \times 10^6\ \text{ms}^{-1}$

$v_B = 2.6 \times 10^6 \times \dfrac{1}{4} = 6.5 \times 10^5\ \text{ms}^{-1}$

4. *(b)* Excess pressure inside an air bubble just below the surface of water, $p_1 = \frac{2T}{r}$, due to only one free surface

and excess pressure inside a drop, $p_2 = \frac{2T}{r}$

$\therefore \quad p_1 = p_2$

The excess pressure inside an air bubble below the surface of water is same as the excess pressure inside a drop of same radius outside the surface of water.

5. *(b)* In graph (b), one value of displacement is obtained at two different time.

Thus, the average displacement of particle is zero. As

$$\text{average velocity} = \frac{\text{Displacement}}{\text{Time}}$$

So, average velocity would be zero.

6. *(a)* In potentiometer experiment, we find internal resistance of a cell.

Let E be the emf of the cell and V the terminal potential difference, then

$$\frac{E}{V} = \frac{l_1}{l_2}$$

where, l_1 and l_2 are lengths of potentiometer wire with and without short-circuited through a resistance.

Given, $l_1 = 110$ cm and $l_2 = 100$ cm, $R = 10\Omega$

So, $\frac{E}{V} = \frac{R+r}{R}$ $\quad [\because E = I(R+r) \text{ and } V = IR]$

$\Rightarrow \quad \frac{R+r}{R} = \frac{l_1}{l_2}$

or $\quad 1 + \frac{r}{R} = \frac{110}{100}$

or $\quad \frac{r}{R} = \frac{10}{100} = \frac{1}{10}$

or $\quad r = \frac{R}{10} = \frac{1}{10} \times 10 = 1.0\,\Omega$

7. *(b)* Given, $R = A = B$ $\quad$ ...(i)

We know that, magnitude of resultant vector is given as

$$R^2 = A^2 + B^2 + 2AB\cos\theta$$

$\therefore \quad R^2 = R^2 + R^2 + 2RR\cos\theta$ $\quad$ [from Eq. (i)]

or $\quad \cos\theta = -\frac{1}{2}$

$\therefore \quad \theta = 120°$

8. *(c)* Given, $r = 10$ m, $v = 5$ ms^{-1} and tangential acceleration, $a_t = 2$ ms^{-2}

Radial acceleration, $a_r = \frac{v^2}{r} = \frac{5 \times 5}{10} = 2.5$ ms^{-2}

Net acceleration, $a = \sqrt{a_r^2 + a_t^2} = \sqrt{(2.5)^2 + 2^2}$

$= \sqrt{10.25} = 3.2$ ms^{-2}

9. *(a)* When charge q_3 is at C, then potential energy of the system is

$$U_C = \frac{1}{4\pi\varepsilon_0}\left[\left(\frac{q_1q_3}{AC} + \frac{q_2q_3}{BC}\right) + \frac{q_1q_2}{AB}\right]$$

$$= \frac{1}{4\pi\varepsilon_0}\left\{\left(\frac{q_1q_3}{0.4} + \frac{q_2q_3}{0.5}\right) + \frac{q_1q_2}{0.3}\right\}$$

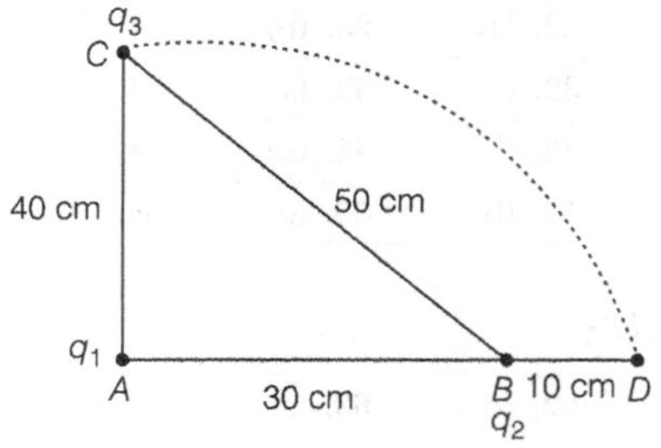

Similarly, when charge q_3 is at D, then potential energy is

$$U_D = \frac{1}{4\pi\varepsilon_0}\left[\left(\frac{q_1q_3}{AC} + \frac{q_2q_3}{BD}\right) + \frac{q_1q_2}{AB}\right]$$

$$= \frac{1}{4\pi\varepsilon_0}\left\{\left(\frac{q_1q_3}{0.4} + \frac{q_2q_3}{0.1}\right) + \frac{q_1q_2}{0.3}\right\}$$

Here, change in potential energy,

$$\Delta U = U_D - U_C$$

$$\frac{q_3}{4\pi\varepsilon_0}K = \frac{1}{4\pi\varepsilon_0}\left(\frac{q_2q_3}{0.1} - \frac{q_2q_3}{0.5}\right)$$

$$\left[\because \Delta U = \frac{q_3K}{4\pi\varepsilon_0}\right]$$

$\Rightarrow \quad K = \left(\frac{q_2}{0.1} - \frac{q_2}{0.5}\right) = 10q_2 - \frac{10q_2}{5}$

$= 10q_2 - 2q_2$

$\Rightarrow \quad K = 8q_2$

10. *(b)* As, dimensional formula of force $= [\text{MLT}^{-2}]$

$n_1 = 36$, $M_1 = 1$ kg, $L_1 = 1$ m, $T_1 = 1$ min $= 60$ s

$n_2 = ?$, $M_2 = 1$ g, $L_2 = 1$ cm, $T_2 = 1$ s

So, conversion of 36 units into CGS system,

i.e. $n_2 = n_1\left[\frac{\text{M}_1}{\text{M}_2}\right]^a\left[\frac{\text{L}_1}{\text{L}_2}\right]^b\left[\frac{\text{T}_1}{\text{T}_2}\right]^c$

$\Rightarrow n_2 = n_1\left[\frac{1\text{ kg}}{1\text{g}}\right]^1\left[\frac{1\text{ m}}{1\text{ cm}}\right]^1\left[\frac{1\text{ min}}{1\text{ s}}\right]^{-2}$

$= 36\left[\frac{1000\text{ g}}{1\text{ g}}\right]\left[\frac{100\text{ cm}}{1\text{ cm}}\right]^1\left[\frac{60\text{ s}}{1\text{ s}}\right]^{-2}$

$= 10^3$ dyne

11. *(a)* From the given graphs, the voltages V_A and V_B of capacitors A and B corresponding to charge Q on each

of the capacitors are $V_A = \frac{Q}{C_A}$ and $V_B = \frac{Q}{C_B}$

or $$\frac{V_B}{V_A} = \frac{Q/C_B}{Q/C_A} = \frac{C_A}{C_B}$$

Since, $V_B > V_A \Rightarrow C_A > C_B$, i.e. the capacitor A has the higher capacitance than B.

12. *(b)* For car of mass M moving in circle of radius R, with velocity v, requires a centripetal force which is obtained from friction force $(\mu_s N)$ between the tyre of car and road, that satisfies the following condition,

$$\frac{mv^2}{R} \le \mu_s mg \quad (\because N = mg)$$

$$v \le \sqrt{\mu_s Rg}$$

Thus, when a car is moving along a circle, then its velocity $v \le \sqrt{\mu_s Rg}$, so that it will not move away from the circle.

13. *(b)* Given, $P = 1\text{ kW} = 1 \times 10^3\text{ W}$ and $h = 10\text{ m}$

As, power, $P = \frac{\text{Work done}}{\text{Time taken}}$

$$\Rightarrow P = \frac{W}{t} = \frac{mgh}{t} \quad [\because W = mgh]$$

$$\Rightarrow \frac{P}{gh} = \frac{m}{t} \Rightarrow \frac{1000}{10 \times 10} = \frac{m}{t}$$

$$\Rightarrow \frac{1000}{100} \times 1 = m \quad (\because t = 1\text{ s})$$

$$\Rightarrow m = 10\text{ kg}$$

So, quantity of water pumped out per second is 10 kg.

14. *(d)* Given, $(\text{KE})_A = (\text{KE})_B$

$$\therefore \frac{1}{2} I_A \omega_A^2 = \frac{1}{2} I_B \omega_B^2$$

$$\frac{I_A \omega_A}{I_B \omega_B} = \frac{\omega_B}{\omega_A} \Rightarrow \frac{L_A}{L_B} = \frac{\omega_B}{\omega_A}$$

Since, $I_B > I_A$

So, according to conservation of angular momentum

$$\omega_B < \omega_A \Rightarrow L_B > L_A \quad [\because L = I\omega]$$

15. *(a)* Given, radius of wire A = 2 (radius of wire B)

i.e. $r_A = 2r_B$

Also, tension $T_B = T_A$

Mass of string A, m_A = volume × density

$$= (\pi r_A^2) l_A \times \rho_A \quad \ldots\text{(i)}$$

and $$m_B = (\pi r_B^2)\, l_B \times \rho_B \quad \ldots\text{(ii)}$$

Dividing Eq. (i) by Eq. (ii), we get

$$\therefore \frac{m_A}{m_B} = \frac{r_A^2\, l_A}{r_B^2\, l_B} \quad (\because \rho_A = \rho_B)$$

$$\Rightarrow \frac{m_A / l_A}{m_B / l_B} = \frac{r_A^2}{r_B^2} \quad \ldots\text{(iii)}$$

Since, linear mass density, $\mu = \frac{m}{l}$

$$\Rightarrow \frac{\mu_A}{\mu_B} = \frac{m_A / l_A}{m_B / l_B} = \left(\frac{r_A}{r_B}\right)^2 \quad \text{[using Eq. (iii)]}$$

We know, speed of transverse wave, $v = \sqrt{\frac{T}{\mu}}$

$$\Rightarrow \frac{v_A}{v_B} = \sqrt{\frac{\mu_B}{\mu_A}} = \frac{r_B}{r_A} = \frac{1}{2} \quad (\because r_A = 2r_B)$$

16. *(b)* Initial momentum of surface, $p_i = \frac{E}{c}$

where, c = velocity of light (constant) and E is energy.

Since, the surface is perfectly reflecting, so the same momentum will be reflected completely.

For perfectly reflecting surface,

final momentum, $p_f = \frac{-E}{c}$ (negative value)

$$\therefore \text{Change in momentum, } \Delta p = p_f - p_i = -\frac{E}{c} - \frac{E}{c} = -\frac{2E}{c}$$

Thus, momentum transferred to the perfectly reflecting surface is

$$\Delta p' = |\Delta p| = \frac{2E}{c}$$

17. *(c)* Given, $E_0 = 120\text{ NC}^{-1}$, $\nu = 50.0\text{ MHz} = 50 \times 10^6\text{ Hz}$

$\therefore$ Angular frequency, $\omega = 2\pi\nu$

$$= (2 \times 3.14\text{ rad})(50 \times 10^6\text{ Hz})$$
$$= 3.14 \times 10^8\text{ rads}^{-1}$$

$$\text{Wave constant, } k = \frac{\omega}{c} = \frac{3.14 \times 10^8\text{ rads}^{-1}}{3 \times 10^8\text{ ms}^{-1}}$$
$$= 1.05\text{ rad m}^{-1}$$

According to the condition, given in the questions, the wave is propagating along X-axis, this means **E** should be along Y-axis and **B** should be along Z-axis.

Clearly, $\mathbf{E} = E_0 \sin(kx - \omega t)\,\mathbf{j}$

$$= [120\text{ NC}^{-1} \sin\{(1.05\text{ rad m}^{-1})x - (3.14 \times 10^8\text{ rads}^{-1})t\}]\,\mathbf{j}$$

18. *(d)* In Pfund series,

$$\frac{1}{\lambda} = R\left(\frac{1}{5^2} - \frac{1}{n^2}\right); \text{ where } n = 6, 7, \ldots$$

For maximum wavelength, $n = 6$

$$\therefore \frac{1}{\lambda_{\text{max}}} = R\left(\frac{1}{5^2} - \frac{1}{6^2}\right) = R\left(\frac{11}{900}\right) \quad \ldots\text{(i)}$$

For minimum wavelength, $n = \infty$.

$$\therefore \frac{1}{\lambda_{\text{min}}} = R\left(\frac{1}{5^2} - \frac{1}{\infty}\right) = \frac{R}{25} \quad \ldots\text{(ii)}$$

From Eqs. (i) and (ii), we get

$$\frac{\lambda_{max}}{\lambda_{min}} = \frac{R/25}{11R/900} = \frac{36}{11}$$

The ratio of maximum to minimum wavelength of emitted spectral lines is 36 : 11.

19. *(c)* Net resultant force at point P inside a hollow spherical shell will be zero because the attractive forces due to various parts of the shell cancel out each other.

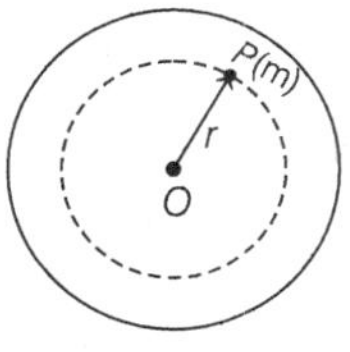

i.e. $|\mathbf{F}_P(\text{net})| = \text{zero}$

20. *(d)* Given, charge, $q = 10^{-12}$ C, velocity, $v = 10^5$ ms^{-1}

Force, $F = 10^{-10}$ N

As we know, force, $F = qvB$

$\therefore$ Magnetic field, $B = \frac{F}{qv} = \frac{10^{-10}}{10^{-12} \times 10^5}$

$$= 10^{-3} \text{ Wb m}^{-2} \text{ or T}$$

So, according to right hand rule, as particle is moving in x-direction and experiences a force in y-direction, then magnetic field is acting along z-direction.

21. *(a)* Moment of inertia of hollow cylinder about its axis of symmetry, $I_1 = MR^2$

Moment of inertia of solid sphere about an axis passing its centre, $I_2 = \frac{2}{5}MR^2$

Let α_1 and α_2 be angular accelerations produced in the cylinder and the sphere respectively, on applying same torque τ in each case. Then,

$$\alpha_1 = \frac{\tau}{I_1} \quad (\text{as } \tau = I\alpha)$$

and $$\alpha_2 = \frac{\tau}{I_2}$$

Their corresponding ratio is

$$\frac{\alpha_1}{\alpha_2} = \frac{I_2}{I_1} = \frac{\frac{2}{5}MR^2}{MR^2} = \frac{2}{5}$$

22. *(a)* The total mechanical energy E of the system is conserved. We take the potential energy of the system to be zero at the lowest point A. Thus, at A,

$$E = \frac{1}{2}mv_0^2 \quad \text{... (i)}$$

The resultant force at A provides the necessary centripetal force.

i.e. $$T_A - mg = \frac{mv_0^2}{L}$$

where, T_A is the tension in the string at A.

At the highest point C, the string becomes slack, as the tension in the string (T_C) becomes zero.

Thus, at C, $$mg = \frac{mv_C^2}{L} \quad \text{... (ii)}$$

and total energy, $E = \frac{1}{2}mv_C^2 + 2mgL$

where, v_C is the speed at C.

$$\Rightarrow \quad v_C^2 = gL \quad \text{...(iii)}$$

From Eqs. (ii) and (iii), we get

$$E = \frac{1}{2}mgL + 2mgL = \frac{5}{2}mgL \quad \text{...(iv)}$$

Equating Eqs. (i) and (iv), we get

$$\frac{5}{2}mgL = \frac{m}{2}v_0^2 \text{ or } v_0 = \sqrt{5gL}$$

23. *(b)* For first case, $\frac{5}{l_1} = \frac{R}{(100 - l_1)}$ ...(i)

Now, by shunting resistance R with an equal resistance R, new resistance in that arm become $R/2$, so

$$\frac{5}{1.6l_1} = \frac{R/2}{(100 - 1.6l_1)} \quad \text{...(ii)}$$

From Eqs. (i) and (ii), we get

$$\frac{1.6}{1} = \frac{(100 - 1.6l_1)}{100 - l_1} \times 2$$

$$\Rightarrow \quad 160 - 1.6l_1 = 200 - 3.2l_1 \Rightarrow 1.6l_1 = 40$$

$$l_1 = \frac{400}{1.6} = 25 \text{ m}$$

From Eq. (i), we get,

$$\frac{5}{25} = \frac{R}{75} \Rightarrow R = 15\,\Omega$$

24. *(b)* Charges at A and C produce net electric field along OA (as $q_C > q_A$). Similarly, charges at B and D produce net electric field along OB (as $q_D > q_B$).

The direction of the fields is as shown in the figure below

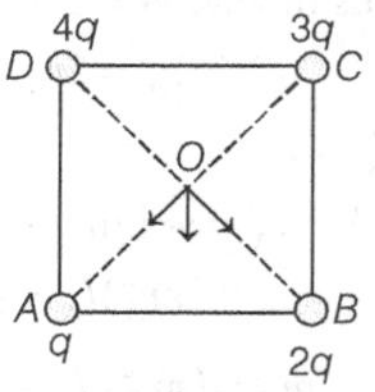

So, the net electric field will be along bisector of angle AOB which parallel to CB.

25. *(a)* Suppose neutral point N lies at a distance x from dipole of moment **p** or at a distance $(25 - x)$ from dipole of moment 64 **p**.

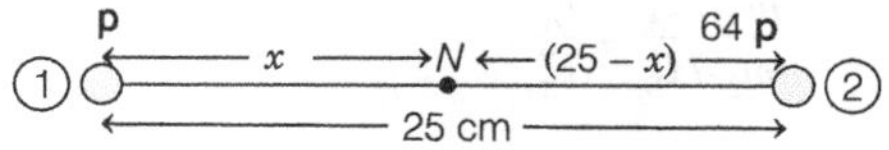

Electric field due to dipole is $E = \frac{2p}{4\pi\varepsilon_0 r^3}$

where, p is dipole moment and r is distance.

$\therefore$ At N, | Electric field due to dipole (1) |

= | Electric field due to dipole (2) |

$$\Rightarrow \frac{1}{4\pi\varepsilon_0} \cdot \frac{2p}{x^3} = \frac{1}{4\pi\varepsilon_0} \cdot \frac{2(64p)}{(25-x)^3}$$

$$\Rightarrow \frac{1}{x^3} = \frac{64}{(25-x)^3} \Rightarrow x = 5 \text{ cm}$$

26. *(b)* Light from an LED lies in the bandwidth 100Å to 500Å or in other words, it is nearly monochromatic light. Since, our eyes are not very comfortable with these types of light. Thus, they are not used for room lighting.

27. *(c)* Current gain, $\beta = \left(\frac{\Delta I_C}{\Delta I_B}\right)_{V_{CE}}$

and voltage gain, $A_V = \frac{\beta \times R_{\text{out}}}{R_{\text{in}}}$

Given, $R_{\text{in}} = 1000\ \Omega$, $\Delta I_B = 10\ \mu\text{A} = 10^{-5}$ A

$R_{\text{out}} = 5\ \text{k}\Omega = 5 \times 10^3 \Omega$

$\Delta I_C = 2\ \text{mA} = 2 \times 10^{-3}$ A

$$\beta = \frac{2 \times 10^{-3}}{10^{-5}} = 200$$

Hence, $A_V = \frac{200 \times 5 \times 10^3}{1000} = 1000$

Thus, voltage gain of the amplifier is 1000.

28. *(b)* Potential energy of a pair of nucleons as a function of their separation is correctly depicted in option (b). For a separation greater than r_0, the force is attractive, so potential energy decreases and for a separation less than r_0, the force is strongly repulsive, so potential energy increases for $r < r_0$.

29. *(d)* Binding energy per nucleon is $E_{\text{bn}} = \frac{E_b}{A}$ ... (i)

For deuteron, atomic mass, $A = 2$ and $E_{\text{bn}} = 2.115$ MeV Substituting these values in Eq. (i), we get

$$2.115 = \frac{E_b}{2}$$

$$E_b = 2 \times 2.115 \text{ MeV}$$

As, $E_b = \Delta mc^2$

$$\Rightarrow \Delta m = \frac{E_b}{c^2}$$

$\therefore$ Mass defect, $\Delta m = \frac{2 \times 2.115\ u}{931.5}$

$= 0.0045$ u

30. *(a)* By Einstein's photoelectric equation, we have

$$eV_0 = h\nu - \phi_0$$

or $V_0 = \frac{h}{e}\nu - \frac{\phi_0}{e}$

Above is a equation of straight line $(y = mx - c)$ with slope $\frac{h}{e}$ and y-intercept $= \frac{\phi_0}{e}$

$\therefore$ Work function, $\phi_0 = e \times y$-intercept (in eV)

As in the given graph y-intercept $= e \times OB$ (in eV)

$= OB$

31. *(a)* For gases, viscosity increases with temperature. Hence, coefficient of viscosity for hot air is greater than coefficient of viscosity for cold air.

32. *(b)* From equation of motion,

$$v^2 = u^2 + 2as$$

$$\Rightarrow a = \frac{v^2 - u^2}{2s}$$

$$= \frac{(20)^2 - (10)^2}{2 \times 135} = \frac{300}{270} = \frac{10}{9} \text{ ms}^{-2}$$

From first equation of motion,

$$v = u + at$$

$$\Rightarrow t = \frac{v-u}{a} = \frac{20-10}{10/9} = \frac{10}{10/9} = 9 \text{ s}$$

33. *(a)* Using lens Maker's formula,

$$\frac{1}{f} = (n-1)\left(\frac{1}{R_1} - \frac{1}{R_2}\right) \quad \ldots \text{(i)}$$

Given, $R_1 = 10$ cm, $R_2 = -10$ cm, $u = -5$ cm

and $n = 1.33$

Substituting the given values in Eq. (i), we get

$$\frac{1}{f} = (1.33 - 1)\left(\frac{1}{10} + \frac{1}{10}\right)$$

$$\frac{1}{f} = 0.33 \times \frac{2}{10} = \frac{0.33}{5} \Rightarrow f = 15.15 \text{ cm}$$

Now, from thin lens formula, $\frac{1}{f} = \frac{1}{v} - \frac{1}{u}$

or image distance, $v = \frac{uf}{u+f} = \frac{-5 \times 15.15}{-5 + 15.15}$

$$= \frac{-75.75}{10.15} = -7.46 \text{ cm}$$

Since, v is – ve hence image will be formed on the same side of the object.

34. *(a)* Here, $l = (16.2 \pm 0.1)$ cm,

$b = (10.1 \pm 0.1)$ cm

$A = l \times b = 16.2 \times 10.1 = 163.62$

Rounding off to one significant figure,

$A = 164 \text{ cm}^2$

MOCK TEST 5

$$\frac{\Delta A}{A}=\left(\frac{\Delta l}{l}+\frac{\Delta b}{b}\right)$$

$$=\frac{0.1}{16.2}+\frac{0.1}{10.1}=\frac{1.01+1.62}{16.2\times 10.1}=2.63\text{ cm}^2$$

Rounding off to one significant figure, $\Delta A = 3\text{cm}^2$

$\therefore\ A=(164\pm 3)\text{cm}^2$

35. *(a)* The given figure is as shown below

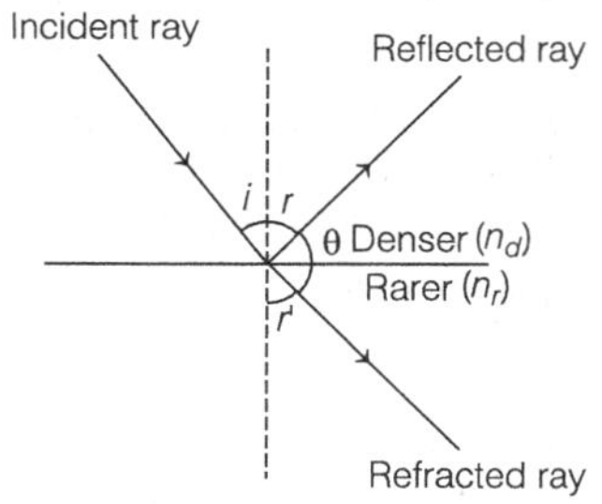

Since, reflected ray and refracted ray make an angle of 90° with each other.

Hence, $\theta = 90°$

So, from figure, $r+\theta+r' = 180°$

$$r + r' = 90° \text{ or } i + r' = 90° \qquad (\ i=r) \quad \ldots\text{(i)}$$

Applying Snell's law, $\dfrac{\sin i}{\sin r'}=\dfrac{n_r}{n_d}$ ...(ii)

Also, critical angle $= i_C = \sin^{-1}\left(\dfrac{n_r}{n_d}\right)$

$\Rightarrow \quad i_C=\sin^{-1}\left(\dfrac{\sin i}{\sin r'}\right)$ [using Eq. (ii)]

As from Eq. (i), $r' = 90° - i$

$\Rightarrow \quad \sin r' = \sin(90° - i) = \cos i$

So, $\quad i_C=\sin^{-1}\left(\dfrac{\sin i}{\cos i}\right)=\sin^{-1}(\tan i)$

or $\quad i_C=\sin^{-1}(\tan r) \qquad (\ i=r)$

36. *(d)* We can simplify the gate circuit as

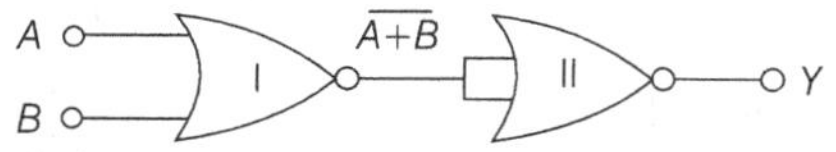

Here, gates I and II are single input NOR gates. The output $\overline{(A+B)}$ of gate I will appear as input of gate II. The final output is

$$Y=\overline{\overline{A+B}}=A+B$$

Hence, its truth table is given as,

A	B	Y
0	0	0
0	1	1
1	0	1
1	1	1

37. *(c)* Given, displacement of an elastic wave,

$$y = 3\sin\omega t + 4\cos\omega t$$

Assume, $\quad 3 = a\cos\phi \quad \ldots\text{(i)}$

$\quad 4 = a\sin\phi \quad \ldots\text{(ii)}$

Squaring and adding Eqs. (i) and (ii), we get

$$a^2\cos^2\phi + a^2\sin^2\phi = 3^2+4^2$$

$$\Rightarrow \quad a^2(\cos^2\phi+\sin^2\phi)=25$$

$$a^2\cdot 1 = 25 \Rightarrow a = 5$$

$$[\quad \sin^2 A + \cos^2 A = 1]$$

Hence, $\quad y = 5\cos\phi\sin\omega t + 5\sin\phi\cos\omega t$

$$=5(\cos\phi\sin\omega t+\sin\phi\cos\omega t)=5\sin(\omega t+\phi)$$

[using the trigonometric identity, $\sin(A+B)=\sin A\cos B+\cos A\sin B$]

Comparing the above equation with the general equation $y = A\sin(\omega t+\phi)$, we get resultant amplitude $= 5$ cm

38. *(b)* Given, $P_1 = P_2 = P = 200$ W, $\lambda_1 = 2$ nm and $\lambda_2 = 400$ nm

Let n_1 and n_2 be the number of photons of X-rays and visible light emitted from the two sources.

As we know,

Power of the source

= Number of photons emitted per second × Energy of one proton

$$\therefore \quad \frac{n_1hc}{\lambda_1}=\frac{n_2hc}{\lambda_2} \text{ or } \frac{n_1}{\lambda_1}=\frac{n_2}{\lambda_2}$$

$$\Rightarrow \quad \frac{n_1}{n_2}=\frac{\lambda_1}{\lambda_2}=\frac{2}{400}=\frac{1}{200}=1:200$$

39. *(d)* Potential energy of an object executing SHM is given by

$$U(x)=\frac{1}{2}kx^2$$

Given, $x = A\cos\omega t$

$$\Rightarrow \quad U(x)=\frac{1}{2}kA^2\cos^2\omega t$$

At $\quad t=\left(\dfrac{T}{4}\right)$

$$U(x)=\frac{1}{2}k^2A^2\cos^2\left(\frac{2\pi}{T}\times\frac{T}{4}\right) \qquad \left(\ \omega=\frac{2\pi}{T}\right)$$

$$=\frac{1}{2}k^2A^2\cos^2\left(\frac{\pi}{2}\right)=0$$

So, PE at $t = T/4$ is zero.

40. *(b)* The de-Broglie wavelength of a particle is given by

$$\lambda = h/p \Rightarrow p\lambda = h$$

This equation is in the form of $yx = c$, which is the equation of a rectangular hyperbola. Hence, the graph given in option (b) is the correct one.

41. *(d)* Since, the given spring with spring constants k_1 and k_2 are in parallel, so the net spring constant of the system is $k_{net} = k_1 + k_2$.
Initially frequency of oscillation,

$$f = \frac{1}{2\pi}\sqrt{\frac{k_{net}}{m}} = \frac{1}{2\pi}\sqrt{\frac{k_1 + k_2}{m}} \quad \ldots(i)$$

Now, when k_1 and k_2 are made by four times their original value, then

$$f' = \frac{1}{2\pi}\sqrt{\frac{k'_1 + k'_2}{m}} = \frac{1}{2\pi}\sqrt{\frac{4k_1 + 4k_2}{m}} = 2f$$

[using Eq. (i)]

Thus, the frequency of oscillation becomes $2f$.

42. *(b)* Solenoids 1 and 2 were wound using the similar wire and same number of turns $\Rightarrow L_1 = L_2$
Solenoid 3 was wound using superconducting wire (means $R = 0$), so infinite current will flow and resistance to the change of current will be zero, hence

$$L_3 = 0$$

So, $L_1 = L_2$ and $L_3 = 0$

43. *(d)* $\frac{\theta_1 - \theta_2}{t} = K\left[\frac{\theta_1 + \theta_2}{2} - \theta_0\right]$

$$\frac{61 - 59}{10} = K\left[\frac{61 + 59}{2} - 30\right] \Rightarrow K = \frac{1}{150}$$

Again, $\frac{51 - 49}{t} = \frac{1}{150}\left[\frac{51 + 49}{2} - 30\right]$

$$t = 15 \text{ min}$$

44. *(c)* According to Hooke's law, within the limit of elasticity, stress is directly proportional to strain.

i.e. Stress $\propto$ Strain

or $\frac{\text{Load}}{\text{Area}} \propto \frac{\text{Extension}}{\text{Original dimension}}$

or Load $\propto$ Extension

Hence, graph given in option (c) obeys Hooke's law.

45. *(b)* If a converging lens of focal length f is placed after the slit and the fringe are obtained on screen, then separation of the central maximum from the first null of the diffraction pattern is λ / a.

If f is the focal length of the lens, then the size of screen will be $f\lambda / a$.

46. *(d)* The frequency optical communication,

$$\nu = \frac{c}{\lambda} \Rightarrow \nu = \frac{3 \times 10^8}{1200 \times 10^{-9}} = 25 \times 10^{13} \text{ Hz}$$

But only 2% of the source frequency is available for TV transmission

$$\nu' = 25 \times 10^{14} \times 2\%$$

$$= 25 \times 10^{14} \times \frac{2}{100} = 5 \times 10^{12} \text{ Hz}$$

Number of channels $= \frac{\nu'}{\text{bandwith}}$

Number of channels $= \frac{5 \times 10^{12}}{5 \times 10^6} = 10^6 = 1$ million

47. *(b)* Root mean square speed,

$$v_{rms} = \sqrt{\frac{3kT}{m}} = \sqrt{\frac{3p}{\rho}}$$

On increasing the pressure by the two times, the density also increases in the same ratio, so that rms speed remains same.

48. *(c)* Given, wavelengths, $\lambda_1 = 4000 Å$ and $\lambda_2 = 6000 Å$

As, resolving power of a microscope, RP $= \frac{1}{\Delta\theta} = \frac{D}{1.22\lambda}$

$$\Rightarrow \quad (\text{RP}) \propto \frac{1}{\lambda(\text{wavelength})}$$

$$\therefore \quad \frac{(\text{RP}_1)}{(\text{RP}_2)} = \frac{\lambda_2}{\lambda_1} = \frac{6000}{4000} = \frac{3}{2}$$

49. *(a)* We have given molar specific heat at constant pressure,

$$C_p = \frac{7}{2}R$$

Mayer's relation, $C_V = C_p - R = \frac{5}{2}R$

Hence, required ratio,

$$\gamma = \frac{C_p}{C_V} = \frac{\left(\frac{7}{2}\right)R}{\left(\frac{5}{2}\right)R} = \frac{7}{5}$$

50. *(a)* Given, diameter of a brass rod, $d = 4$ mm

Radius, $r = 2 \times 10^{-3}$ m

Young's modulus, $Y = 9 \times 10^{10}$ Nm^{-2}

Change in length, $l = 0.1\% L$

$$\Rightarrow \quad \frac{l}{L} = 0.001$$

Young's modulus, $Y = \frac{F}{A} \cdot \frac{L}{l}$

$$\therefore \quad F = YA\frac{l}{L} = 9 \times 10^{10} \times \pi \times (2 \times 10^{-3})^2 \times 0.001$$

$$= 360\ \pi\text{N}$$

51. *(c)* The gravitational forces are mutually equal and opposite, hence the ratio of gravitational pull of the earth on the planet and that of planet on the earth will be 1 : 1.

52. *(b)* Given, $V_p = 110$ V, $k = \frac{N_s}{N_p} = 10$ and $R_s = 550\ \Omega$

$$V_s = V_p \times \frac{N_s}{N_p} = 110 \times 10 = 1100 \text{ V}$$

Current through secondary coil,

i.e. $i_s = \frac{V_s}{R_s} = \frac{1100}{550} = 2\text{A}$

53. *(c)* According to first law of thermodynamics,

$$\Delta Q = \Delta U + \Delta W$$

For isothermal process, $\Delta U = 0$

So, $\Delta Q = -\Delta W$

Given, $\Delta W = -150 J$

So, $\Delta Q = +150$ J

When Q is positive, the heat is added to the gas.

54. *(d)* Given, $m = 0.40 A\text{-}m^2$ and $r = 5.0$ cm $= 0.5$ m

Magnetic field at equatorial line,

$$B_e = \frac{\mu_0 m}{4\pi r^3} = \frac{10^{-7} \times 0.40}{(0.5)^3} = \frac{10^{-7} \times 0.40}{0.125} = 3.2 \times 10^{-7} T$$

Magnetic field at axial line,

$$B_a = \frac{\mu_0 2m}{4\pi r^3} = 6.4 \times 10^{-7} T$$

Hence, the magnetic field at equatorial line and axial line are 3.2×10^{-7} T and 6.4×10^{-7} T, respectively.

55. *(a)* Velocity of ball on reaching the water surface is

$$v = \sqrt{2gh} = \sqrt{2 \times 9.8 \times 19.6} = 19.6 \text{ m/s}$$

If ρ be the density of ball, then density of water 2ρ.

If a is the retardation of the ball in water, then

$$a = \frac{\text{upward thrust} - \text{weight}}{\text{mass}} = \frac{v(2\rho)g - v\rho g}{v\rho}$$

$$\Rightarrow \quad a = g = 9.8 \text{ m/s}^2$$

So, the depth is

$$d = \frac{v^2}{2a} = \frac{19.6 \times 19.6}{2 \times 9.8} = 19.6 \text{ m}$$

56. *(c)* Given, angle of suspension to the magnetic meridian $\alpha = 30°$ and dip angle $\delta' = 45°$.

Hence, $\tan \delta' = \frac{V_E}{H'_E} = \frac{V_E}{H_E \cos \alpha}$

$$\tan \delta' = \frac{\tan \delta}{\cos \alpha} \qquad \left[\because \tan \delta = \frac{V_E}{H_E}\right]$$

$$\Rightarrow \quad \tan \delta = \cos \alpha \tan \delta' = \cos 30° \tan 45° = \frac{\sqrt{3}}{2}$$

$$\delta = \tan^{-1} \frac{\sqrt{3}}{2}$$

$\therefore$ Angle of the real dip is $\tan^{-1}\left(\frac{\sqrt{3}}{2}\right)$

57. *(d)* Given, magnetic potential energy stored in an inductor, $U = 25$ mJ $= 25 \times 10^{-3}$ J

Current in an inductor, $I_0 = 60$ mA $= 60 \times 10^{-3}$ A

As, the expression for energy stored in an inductor is given as

$$U = \frac{1}{2} L I_0^2$$

where, L is the inductance of the inductor.

Substituting the given values in above equation, we get

$$25 \times 10^{-3} = \frac{1}{2} \times L \times (60 \times 10^{-3})^2$$

$$\Rightarrow \quad L = \frac{2 \times 25 \times 10^{-3}}{3600 \times 10^{-6}} = \frac{500}{36} \text{ or } L = 13.89 \text{ H}$$

58. *(c)* We know that,

$$E \propto T^4 \qquad \text{[Stefan's law]}$$

$$\Rightarrow \quad \frac{E_1}{E_2} = \left(\frac{T_1}{T_2}\right)^4 \Rightarrow \frac{20}{E_2} = \left[\frac{T_1}{2T_1}\right]^4$$

$$\Rightarrow \quad E_2 = 320 \text{ kcal m}^{-2} \text{ min}^{-1}$$

59. *(a)* In unpolarised beam, vibrations are probable in all directions in a plane perpendicular to the direction of propagation. Therefore, θ can have any value from 0 to 2π.

$$[\cos^2 \theta]_{av} = \frac{1}{2\pi} \int_0^{2\pi} \cos^2 \theta \, d\theta = \frac{1}{2\pi} \int_0^{2\pi} \left(\frac{1 + \cos 2\theta}{2}\right) d\theta$$

$$= \frac{1}{4\pi}\left([\theta]_0^{2\pi} + \left[\frac{\sin 2\theta}{2}\right]_0^{2\pi}\right) = \frac{1}{4\pi} \times 2\pi = \frac{1}{2}$$

So, using law of Malus, $I = I_0 \cos^2 \theta \Rightarrow I = I_0 \times \frac{1}{2} = \frac{I_0}{2}$

60. *(d)* Work done by the system

W = Area of BCE + Area of ADE

$= -W_0 + W_0 = 0$

Chemistry

61. *(b)* Higher the tendency to give H^+ ion (i.e. to undergo ionisation), stronger will be the acid or *vice-versa.*

HF has poor tendency to give H^+ ion, hence it is the weakest acid among the given.

The order of acidity of given acids is

$$H_2SO_4 > HNO_3 > HCl > HF$$

62. *(c)* Number of moles of A, $n_A = \frac{w_A}{M_A} = \frac{0.50}{60} = 0.0083$

Number of moles of B, $n_B = \frac{w_B}{M_B} = \frac{0.20}{45} = 0.0044$

Total pressure $(p_T) = 750$ mm of Hg

p_A = mole fraction of $A(\chi_A) \times$ total pressure (p_T)

MOCK TEST 5

Mole fraction of A, $\chi_A = \dfrac{n_A}{n_A + n_B}$

$$p_A = \frac{0.0083}{0.0083 + 0.0044} \times 750 = 490 \text{ mm}$$

$$p_B = 750 - 490 = 260 \text{ mm}$$

63. *(a)* Valence electrons in $P = 2$

Valence electrons in $Q = 6$

$$P - 2e^- \longrightarrow P^{2+}$$

$$Q + 2e^- \longrightarrow Q^{2-}$$

$$P^{2+} + Q^{2-} \longrightarrow PQ$$

Since, both show a valency of 2.

So, the formula for the compound will be PQ.

64. *(a)* Nitro group reduces the electron density in the benzene ring due to its strong $-I$-effect.

Nitrobenzene is a resonance hybrid of the following structures

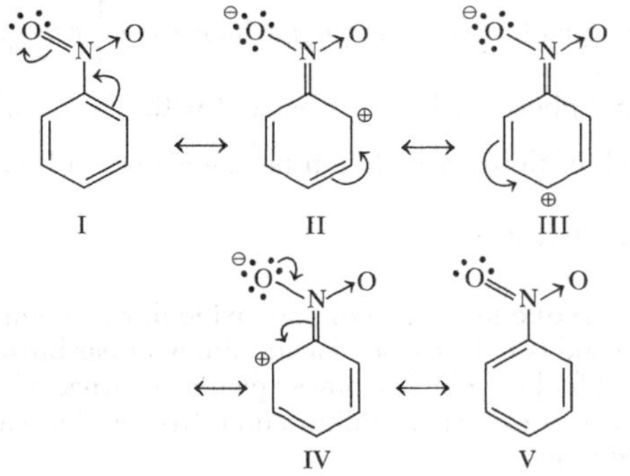

In this case, the overall electron density on benzene ring decreases making further substitution difficult, therefore these groups are also called 'deactivating groups'.

The electron density on *o* and *p*-position is comparatively less than that at *meta*-position. Hence, the electrophile attacks on comparatively electron rich *meta*-position resulting in *meta*-substitution.

65. *(a)* AgBr shows both Schottky and Frenkel defects.

Because the $\frac{r_+}{r_-}$ (radius of cation and radius of anion) ratio in AgBr is not very large or not very small.

(AgCl shows only Schottky defect due to greater value of $\frac{r_+}{r_-}$, whereas AgI shows only Frenkel defect due to smaller value of $\frac{r_+}{r_-}$).

66. *(b)* Higher the charge on the metal ion, smaller is the ionic size and more is the complex forming ability of actinoids. Thus, the degree of complex formation decreases in the order

$$M^{4+} > MO_2^{2+} > M^{3+} > MO_2^{+}$$

67. *(b)* $S_4O_6^{2-}$ and $S_2O_3^{2-}$ have S—S bond. Their structures are given below

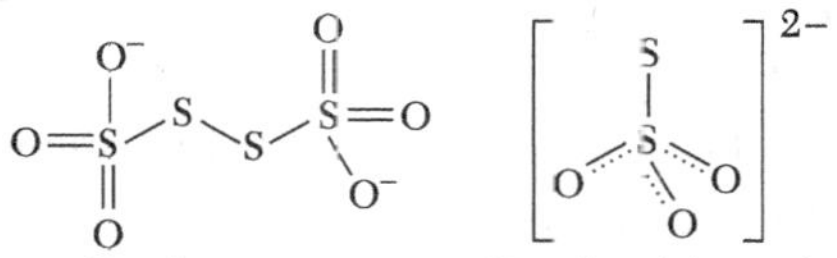

(Tetrathionate ion) ($S_4O_6^{2-}$) (Tetrathiosulphate ion) ($S_2O_3^{2-}$)

68. *(b)* The major product obtained in the reaction is as follows

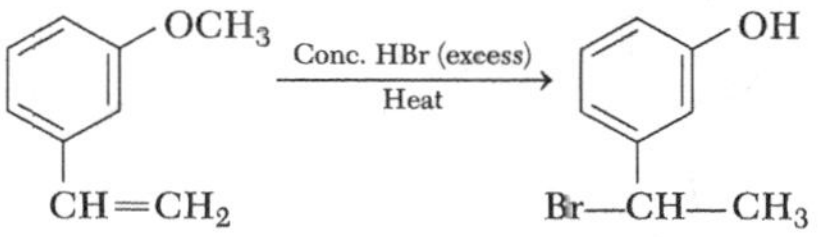

As conc. HBr is in excess. So, reaction will take place at both the substituents.

69. *(a)* When haloalkane containing β-hydrogen atom is heated with alc. KOH solution, then alkene is formed as a result of elimination.

$$\underset{\text{1-bromopropane}}{CH_3CH_2CH_2Br} \xrightarrow{\text{Alc. KOH}} \underset{\text{Propene}}{CH_3CH = CH_2}$$

In this reaction, hydrogen is eliminated from β-carbon and the halogen is lost from α-carbon atom.

As a result, propene is formed as a product.

70. *(b)*

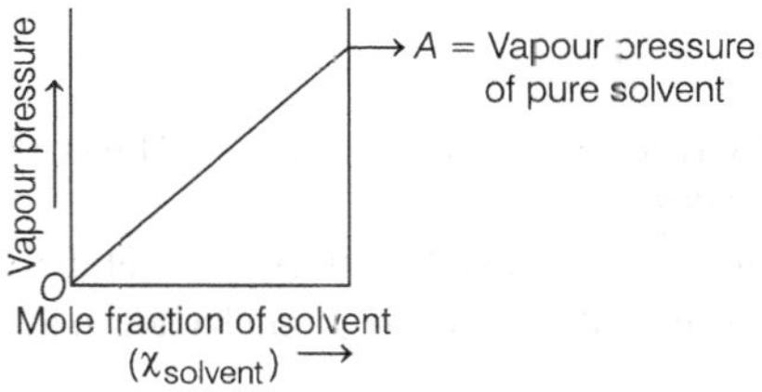

∴ The above given graph is the plot of vapour pressure and mole fraction of the solvent for liquid solutions containing non-volatile solute. In the given graph, the point '*A*' signifies vapour pressure of pure solvent.

71. *(c)* Hydrogenation of vegetable oils using nickel as a catalyst gives edible fats like margarine and vanaspati ghee.

72. *(c)* Hyperconjugative effect helps in deciding the stability of *iso*-butylene. The structures are as follows :

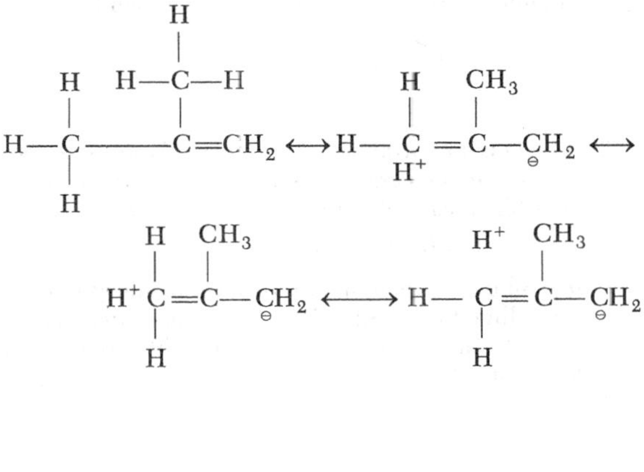

73. *(b)* $Z < 1$

$\Rightarrow \quad \frac{pV}{nRT} < 1 \quad \Rightarrow pV < nRT$

$\Rightarrow \quad [p = 1 \text{ atm}, \; T = 273 \text{ K}, R = 0.0821 \text{ L atm K}^{-1}]$

i.e. $\quad 1 \times V < 1 \times 0.0821 \times 273$

$V < 22.4 \text{ L}$

74. *(c)* When melamine and formaldehyde polymerise, a resin intermediate given in option (c) is formed.

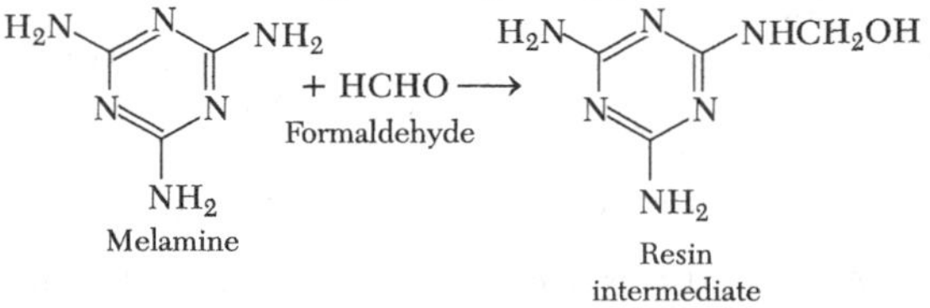

75. *(c)* The graph of these curve concludes that, at a constant pressure, physisorption decreases with increase in temperature, i.e. low temperature is favourable for physical adsorption.

76. *(a)* 'iso' means one methyl group is present at side chain. Hence, the structure of *iso*-butyl group is

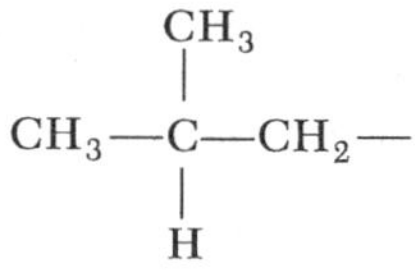

'yl' suffix is used to represent one —H less than the parent hydrocarbon.

77. *(c)* Aluminium hydroxide $[Al(OH)_3]$, cimetidine and ranitidine are antacids, while phenelzine is not.

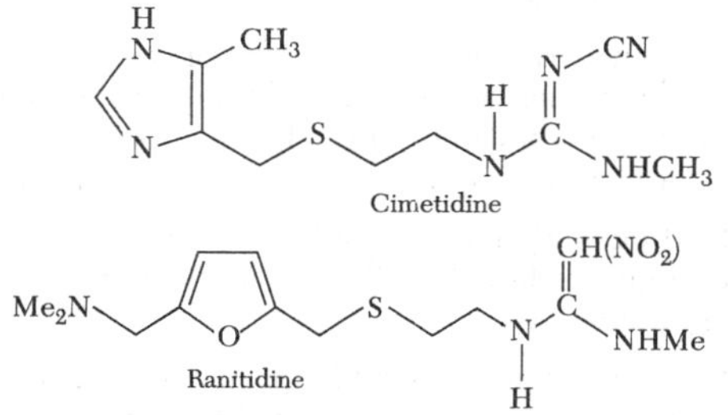

Phenelzine is a tranquiliser, not an antacid.

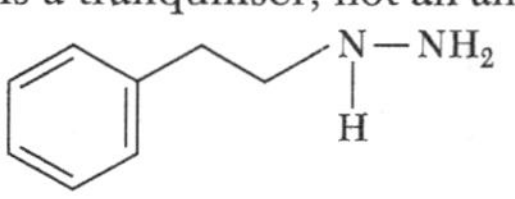

78. *(a)* CO is a neutral ligand, so the oxidation state of metal in metal carbonyl is always zero, which is possible in case of $[Ni(CO)_4]$. $[Ni(CO)_4]$

$x + (0 \times 4) = 0 \Rightarrow x = 0$

79. *(b)* Silica occurs in nature in several amorphous and crystalline forms. Kieselguhr is the amorphous form of silica. Quartz, tridymite and cristobalite are crystalline forms of silica.

80. *(d)* 100 g alkaloid contains nitrogen = 17.28 g

$\therefore$ 162 g alkaloid will contain nitrogen $= \frac{17.28 \times 162}{100}$ g

$= 27.9 \text{ g} \simeq 28 \text{ g}$

Atomic weight of nitrogen = 14

So, number of atoms of nitrogen present in one molecule of alkaloid $= \frac{28}{14} = 2$

81. *(a)* According to quantum mechanical atom model, for each value of n (principal quantum number), there are 'n' different values of l (azimuthal quantum number), i.e. $l = 0, 1, 2, \ldots, (n-1)$ and for each value of l, there are $2l + 1$ different values of m_l (magnetic quantum number), i.e. $m_l = 0, \pm 1, \pm 2 \ldots \pm l$.

$\therefore$Total number of possible combinations of n, l and m_l, for a given value of n is n^2, and each such combination is associated with an orbital. Each orbital can occupy a maximum of two electrons, having a different value of spin quantum number (m_s), which are $+\frac{1}{2}$ or $-\frac{1}{2}$.

$\therefore$ Number of orbitals associated with $n = 5$ is $n^2 = 25$. Each of those orbitals can be associated with $m_s = +\frac{1}{2}$ as well as $m_s = -\frac{1}{2}$.

82. *(c)* Production of carbon monoxide during combustion of wood is not a cause of acid rain, whereas burning of fossil fuel in vehicles, power plants or furnaces produces oxides of sulphur and nitrogen, thus causes acid rain.

83. *(c)* We know that, $K_p = K_C(RT)^{\Delta n_g}$

For the given reaction,

$\Delta n_g = (2 + 1) - 2 = 1$

$\therefore K_p = 3.75 \times 10^{-6} \; (0.0831 \times 1069) \Rightarrow K_p = 0.033$

84. *(b)*

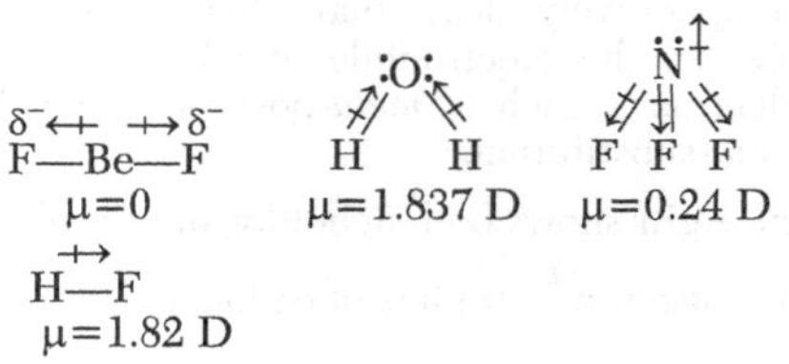

So, the decreasing order of dipole moment is

$\therefore \quad H_2O > HF > NF_3 > BeF_2$

85. *(d)* Given, $T_2 = ?$, $T_1 = 300$ K, $V_2 = 27\,V_1$, $n = 1$ mol

$C_V = 6 \text{ cal mol}^{-1}, \gamma = 1.33.$

In adiabatic conditions,

$$\frac{T_2}{T_1} = \left(\frac{V_1}{V_2}\right)^{\gamma - 1}$$

or, $$\frac{T_2}{T_1} = \left(\frac{1}{27}\right)^{1.33-1} = \left(\frac{1}{27}\right)^{0.33} = \left(\frac{1}{27}\right)^{1/3} = \frac{1}{3}$$

or, $T_2 = 300 \times \frac{1}{3} = 100$ K

Thus, $T_2 < T_1$ and, therefore cooling takes place due to expansion under adiabatic condition.

$$\Delta E = q + W$$
$$\Delta E = W \quad (q = 0 \text{ for adiabatic change})$$
$$\Delta E = -\text{ve because gas expands.}$$
$$\therefore \quad W = -\Delta E = -C_V(T_2 - T_1)$$
$$= -6\,(100 - 300) = 1200 \text{ cal}$$

86. *(d)* In halogenation process, rate of replacement of hydrogens of alkanes is as follows

$$3° > 2° > 1°$$

This is because 3° H is more reactive, than 2° H, which in turn is more reactive, than 1° H.

87. *(a)* When aqueous solution of NaCl is electrolysed, there is a competition between the following reduction reactions at cathode.

$$Na^+ + e^- \longrightarrow Na\,; \quad E°_{cell} = -2.71 \text{ V}$$
$$H^+ + e^- \longrightarrow \frac{1}{2}H_2;\ E°_{cell} = 0.00 \text{ V}$$

The reaction with higher value of $E°$ is preferred and therefore, the second reaction occurs at cathode, i.e. H^+ is reduced instead of Na^+.

88. *(b)* The value of $E°$ for Mn, Ni and Zn are more negative than expected from the trend. The stability of the half-filled d-subshell in Mn^{2+} and the completely filled d^{10}-configuration in Zn^{2+} are related to their $E°$ values, whereas $E°$ for Ni is related to the highest negative $\Delta_{hyd}H°$.

89. *(c)* Many of the aldehydes and ketones are well known for their odour and flavour.

The correct form of all other options are :

(a) Aromatic aldehyde and ketones are *meta*-directive by nature.

(b) They are not of oval shapes.

(d) Aldehydes are only oxidised by mild (or weak) oxidising agents like Tollen's reagent, Fehling solution, etc.

90. *(d)* The reaction of alcohol with Lucas reagent is S_N1 reaction and the rate of reaction is directly proportional to the stability of carbocation formed in the reaction.

Since, 3° R—OH forms 3° carbocation (most stable), hence it will react fastest.

91. *(d)* $(CH_3)_3CCl$ gives a precipitate with $AgNO_3$ solution because it forms stable carbocation. (i.e. tertiary) that readily combines with $AgNO_3$ to give precipitates of AgCl.

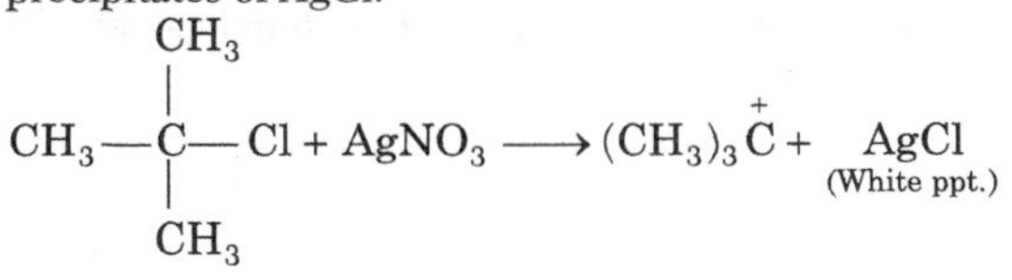

CH_2= CH—Cl forms unstable carbocation. Hence, it does not readily react with $AgNO_3$.

92. *(b)* Coolant glycol $(C_2H_6O_2)$ is a non-electrolyte.

Given, $K_f = 1.86$ K kg mol^{-1}

$w_1 = 1000$ g

$\Delta T_f = (275.8 - 273)$ K $= 2.8$ K

$$\Delta T_f = \frac{1000 \times K_f \times w_2}{M_2 \times w_1}$$

$$\Rightarrow \quad 2.8 = \frac{1000 \times 1.86 \times w_2}{62 \times 1000}$$

$$\therefore \quad w_2 = 93.33 \text{ g} \approx 93 \text{ g}$$

93. *(d)* Structure of amine (X) is C_6H_5—NH_2. Aniline react with nitrous acid at low temperatures (273-278 K) to form benzene diazonium salts. Reaction involved is as follows :

$$\underset{\text{Aniline}}{C_6H_5NH_2} \xrightarrow[273-278\text{ K}]{NaNO_2\ +\ 2HCl} \underset{\text{Benzene diazonium chloride}}{C_6H_5\overset{+}{N_2}\overset{-}{Cl}} + NaCl + 2H_2O$$

94. *(d)* When O_2 is converted into O_2^{2+}, the paramagnetic character decreases and the bond order increases. To get O_2^{2+}, electron is removed from $\pi^* 2p_x$ and $\pi^* 2p_y$. As a result, diamagnetic species is obtain. As two electrons are removed from antibonding orbital, so bond order increases.

95. *(d)* The road map of complete reaction is as follows :

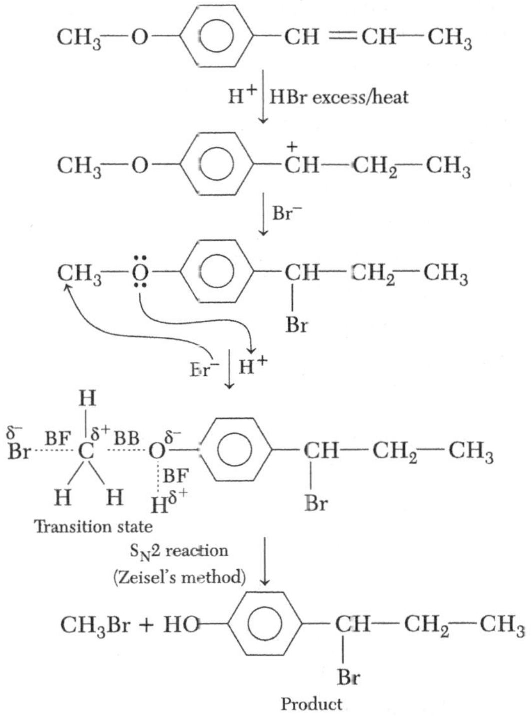

Here BB = Bond breakage, BF = Bond formation

96. *(a)* $N_2(g)+3H_2(g) \longrightarrow 2NH_3(g)$

1 mole of N_2 requires 3 moles of H_2 for formation for ammonia.

$$56 \text{ g of } N_2 = 2 \text{ moles of } N_2$$
$$10 \text{ g of } H_2 = 5 \text{ moles of } H_2$$

Thus, here H_2 acts as limiting reagent.

97. *(b)* The most appropriate reason is that, boron cannot expand its valence shell and its maximum valency is limited to 4, while Al can expand its valence shell and hence, can form $[AlF_6]^{3-}$.

98. *(a)* Mass of one unit cell (m) = volume × density

$$= a^3 \times d = a^3 \times \frac{MZ}{N_A a^3} = \frac{MZ}{N_A}$$

$$m = \frac{58.5 \times 4}{6.02 \times 10^{23}} \text{ g}$$

$\therefore$ Number of unit cells in 1 g $= \frac{1}{m}$

$$= \frac{6.02 \times 10^{23}}{58.5 \times 4} = 2.57 \times 10^{21}$$

99. *(c)* Vapour density = 70

Molecular mass $= 2 \times 70 = 140$

Formula is $[CO]_x$, molecular mass $= 2 \times$ vapour density

Therefore, molecular mass, $(12+16)x = 140$

$\therefore \qquad x = 5$

100. *(d)* Down the group metallic character increases, while in period from left to right metallic character decreases, but non-metallic character increases.

So, the correct order is

$$Na > Mg > Be > Si > P$$

Alkali metals have more metallic character than other groups.

101. *(b)* According to Gibbs-Helmholtz equation,

Gibbs energy $(\Delta G) = \Delta H - T\Delta S$

where, ΔH = enthalpy change

ΔS = entropy change

T = temperature

For a reaction to be spontaneous,

$$\Delta G < 0$$

$\therefore$ Gibbs -Helmholtz equation becomes,

$$\Delta G = \Delta H - T\Delta S < 0$$

or, $\quad \Delta H < T\Delta S$

or, $\quad T > \frac{\Delta H}{\Delta S} = \frac{35.5 \text{ kJ mol}^{-1}}{83.6 \text{ JK}^{-1}\text{mol}^{-1}}$

$$= \frac{35.5 \times 1000 \text{ J mol}^{-1}}{83.6 \text{ J K}^{-1} \text{ mol}^{-1}} = 425 \text{ K}$$

Thus, the reaction is spontaneous at,

$$T > 425 \text{ K}$$

102. *(c)* The reaction is given below

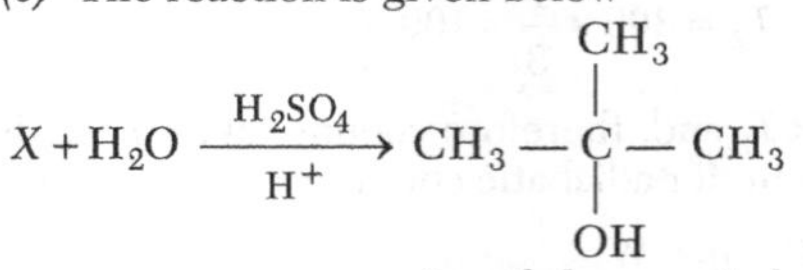

2-methylpropan-2-ol

Formation of 2-methylpropan-2-ol confirms that H^+/OH^- is added to X and as H_2O is removed from this compound. So, X is $CH_3-\underset{\underset{CH_3}{|}}{C}=CH_2$, that is 2-methylpropene.

103. *(a)* Sodium lauryl sulphate

$[(CH_3(CH_2)_{10}CH_2OSO_3^-Na^+)]$ = Anionic detergent

Cetyltrimethyl ammonium bromide

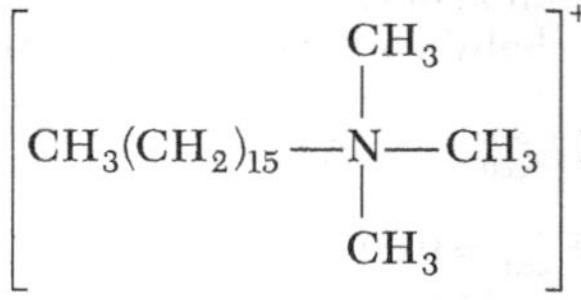

Br^- = cationic detergent

Glyceryl oleate $[(C_{17}H_{32}COO)_3C_3H_5]$ = non-ionic detergent

Sodium stearate $[C_{17}H_{35}COO^-Na^+]$ = anionic soap

104. *(c)* Isostructural compounds are those compounds which have same structure. Potassium permanganate forms a dark purple crystals which are isostructural with $KClO_4$. They both have tetrahedral structure. The structures are as follows :

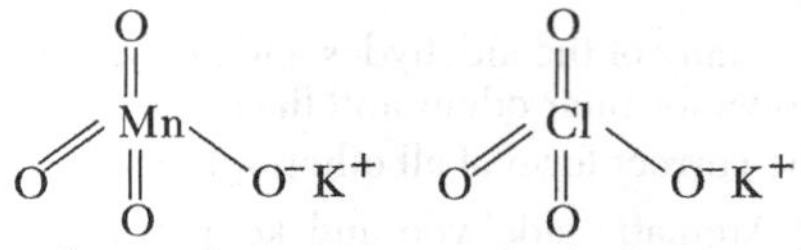

$[KMnO_4]$ $\qquad$ $[KClO_4]$

105. *(a)* As given, the first electron gain enthalpy of oxygen can be shown as,

$O(g) + e^- \longrightarrow O^-(g), \ \Delta_{eg}H_1 = -141$ kJ/mol

The expression of second electron gain enthalpy of oxygen will be,

$$O^-(g) + e^- \longrightarrow O^{2-}(g), \ \Delta_{eg}H_2 = +\text{ ve}$$

$\Delta_{eg}H_2$ of oxygen is positive, i.e. endothermic, because a strong electrostatic repulsion will be observed between highly negative O^- and the incoming electron (e^-). A very high amount of energy will be consumed (endothermic) by the system to overcome the electrostatic repulsion.

106. *(a)* The necessary condition for aldol condensation is the presence of atleast one α-H atom in aldehydes and ketones.

Thus, among the given options, $CH_3—C(CH_3)_2—CHO$ does not undergo aldol condensation as it does not contains any α-hydrogen atom.

107. *(c)* As we know that,

$$\Delta G° = \Delta H° - T\Delta S°$$

Given, $\Delta H_{vap} = 30\ kJ\ mol^{-1}$

$\Delta G° = 0$ at equilibrium,

$$\therefore \quad \Delta S_{vap} = \frac{\Delta H_{vap}}{T} = \frac{30 \times 10^3\ J\ mol^{-1}}{300\ K} = 100\ J\ mol^{-1}\ K^{-1}$$

108. *(c)* In the given reaction *X* is $Na_2Cr_2O_7, H_2SO_4$.

Complete reaction involves the oxidation of phenol to benzoquinone as shown below

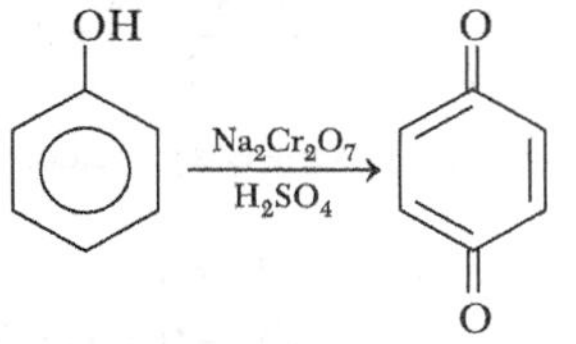

109. *(d)* Reaction (d) will not give benzaldehyde.

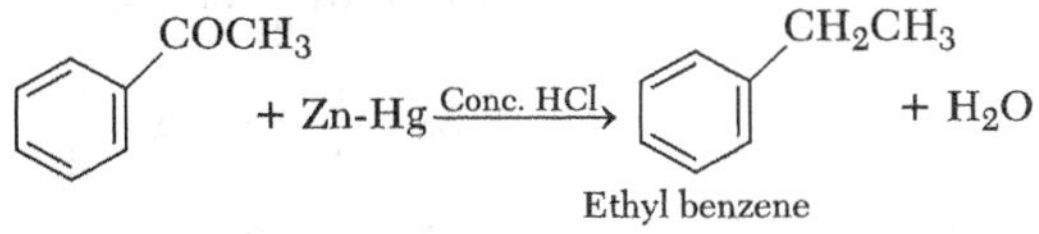

This reaction is known as Clemmensen reduction.

Rest of the reactions will give benzaldehyde.

(a)

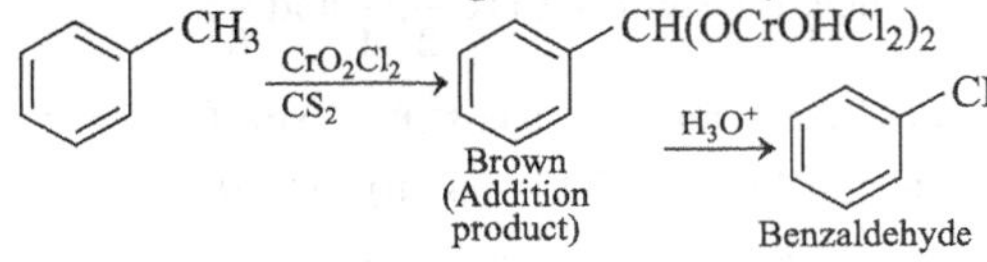

This reaction is known as Etard reaction.

(b)

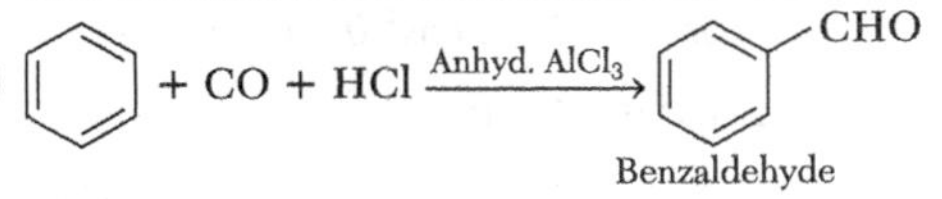

(Gattermann Koch formylation reaction)

(c)

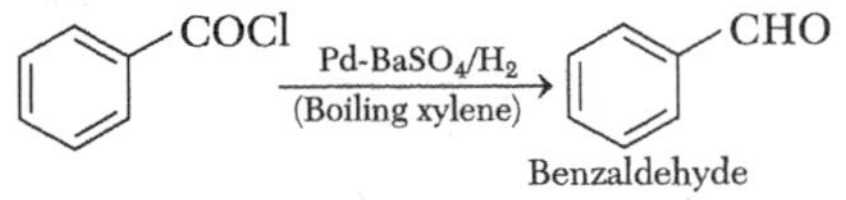

(Rosenmund reaction)

110. *(b)* Zinc releases electrons to copper and copper releases electrons to silver, therefore the electron releasing tendency of the given metals is in the order

$$Zn > Cu > Ag$$

111. *(c)* Carboxylic acids are reduced to primary alcohols in excellent yields by lithium aluminium hydride ($LiAlH_4$), a strong reducing agent.

The reaction is as follows :

$$RCOOH \xrightarrow[\text{(ii) } H_2O]{\text{(i) } LiAlH_4} RCH_2OH$$

112. *(b)* The low solubility of LiF in water is due to its high lattice enthalpy and low solubility of CsI is due to smaller hydration enthalpy of its two ions.

113. *(b)* Octahedral coordination entities of the type $[Ma_3b_3]$ shows geometrical isomers i.e. *fac* and *mer* isomers. Among the given complexes, the complex with general formula $[Ma_3b_3]$ is $[Co(NH_3)_3(NO_2)_3]$. Thus, it can show *fac* and *mer* isomers as follows :

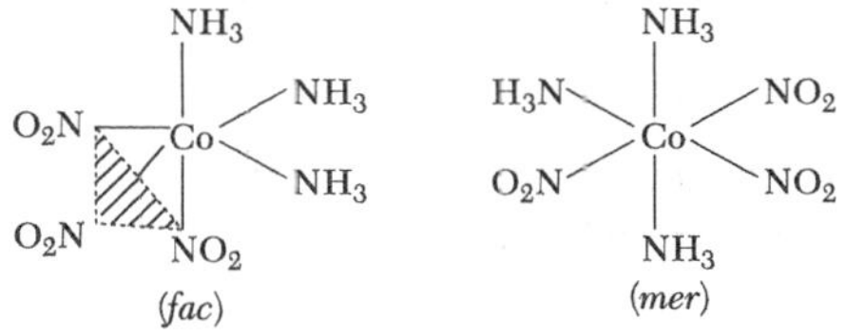

114. *(b)* The loss in biological activity of proteins due to folding of globules and uncoiling of helix is called denaturation of proteins. During denaturation, primary structure remains intact but secondary and tertiary structure are destroyed. e.g., the coagulation of egg white on boiling, curding of milk caused by bacteria due to formation of lactic acid.

115. *(b)* Bond angle gradually decreases down the group as bond pair-lone pair repulsion decreases. Thus, NH_3 has largest bond angle.

116. *(d)* In electrolytic refining method, the impure metal is made to act as anode.

A strip of the same metal in pure form is used as cathode. They are kept in a suitable electrolytic bath containing soluble salt of the same metal.

The more basic metal remains in the solution and the less basic ones go to the anode mud

Anode $\quad M \longrightarrow M^{n+} + ne^-$

Cathode $\quad M^{n+} + ne^- \longrightarrow M$

117. *(a)* HCl gas can be dried by passing through concentrated sulphuric acid (H_2SO_4).

118. *(a)* $k = \frac{2.303}{t}\log\frac{100}{100-x}$

$$k = \frac{2.303}{32}\log\frac{100}{1} \Rightarrow k = 0.144\ min^{-1}$$

$$t = \frac{2.303}{0.144}\log\frac{100}{0.1} \Rightarrow t = 48\ min$$

119. *(a)* Smoke is precipitated by the cottrell smoke precipitator. It neutralises the charge on the carbon particles and neutralises them.

120. *(c)* Xenon hexafluoride reacts with silica to form $XeOF_4$ as follows :

$$2XeF_6 + SiO_2 \longrightarrow 2XeOF_4 + SiF_4$$

The oxidation state of xenon in $XeOF_4$ is + 6 as calculated below

$XeOF_4$

$x + 1(-2) + 4(-1) = 0 \Rightarrow x - 6 = 0 \Rightarrow x = +6$

Mathematics

121. *(b)* The function $f(x) = x + 2$ is one-one as for $x_1, x_2 \in Z$.

Consider, $f(x_1) = f(x_2)$

$\Rightarrow x_1 + 2 = x_2 + 2$

$\Rightarrow x_1 = x_2$

Also, let $y \in$ codomain of $f = Z$ such that

$y = f(x)$

$\Rightarrow y = x + 2$

$\Rightarrow x = y - 2 \in Z$ for all $y \in Z$

$\therefore f$ is onto.

Hence, $f(x) = x + 2$ is bijective.

122. *(c)* The given binary operation $*$ on $Q - \{0\}$ is defined as $a * b = \frac{ab}{2}, \forall\ a, b \in Q - \{0\}$

Now, let e be the identity element for $*$. Then,

$a * e = a = e * a$

$\Rightarrow \frac{ae}{2} = a = \frac{ea}{2}$

$\Rightarrow \frac{ae}{2} = a \Rightarrow e = 2$

123. *(d)* The given function $f : N \to R$ and $g : Q \to R$ are defined by

$$f(x) = \frac{2x - 1}{2} \quad \text{and} \quad g(x) = x + 2$$

Now, $gof\left(\frac{3}{2}\right) = g\left(f\left(\frac{3}{2}\right)\right)$

$$= g\left(\frac{2 \times \frac{3}{2} - 1}{2}\right) = g\left(\frac{3-1}{2}\right) = g\left(\frac{2}{2}\right)$$

$= g(1) = 1 + 2$

$\therefore (gof)\left(\frac{3}{2}\right) = 3$

124. *(a)* Given that, $\tan\theta = \frac{\sin\alpha - \cos\alpha}{\sin\alpha + \cos\alpha}$

$$\Rightarrow \tan\theta = \frac{\cos\alpha(\tan\alpha - 1)}{\cos\alpha(\tan\alpha + 1)}$$

$$\Rightarrow \tan\theta = \frac{\tan\alpha - \tan\frac{\pi}{4}}{1 + \tan\frac{\pi}{4}\cdot\tan\alpha} \quad \left[\tan\frac{\pi}{4} = 1\right]$$

$$\Rightarrow \tan\theta = \tan\left(\alpha - \frac{\pi}{4}\right)$$

$$\Rightarrow \theta = \alpha - \frac{\pi}{4} \Rightarrow \alpha = \theta + \frac{\pi}{4}$$

$$\therefore \sin\alpha + \cos\alpha = \sin\left(\theta + \frac{\pi}{4}\right) + \cos\left(\theta + \frac{\pi}{4}\right)$$

$$= \sin\theta\cdot\cos\frac{\pi}{4} + \cos\theta\cdot\sin\frac{\pi}{4} + \cos\theta\cdot\cos\frac{\pi}{4} - \sin\theta\cdot\sin\frac{\pi}{4}$$

$$= \frac{1}{\sqrt{2}}\sin\theta + \frac{1}{\sqrt{2}}\cos\theta + \frac{1}{\sqrt{2}}\cos\theta - \frac{1}{\sqrt{2}}\sin\theta$$

$$\left[\sin\frac{\pi}{4} = \cos\frac{\pi}{4} = \frac{1}{\sqrt{2}}\right]$$

$$= \frac{2}{\sqrt{2}}\cdot\cos\theta = \sqrt{2}\cos\theta$$

125. *(d)* Given that, $\sec x \cos 5x + 1 = 0$

$$\frac{\cos 5x}{\cos x} + 1 = 0 \Rightarrow \cos 5x + \cos x = 0$$

$$\Rightarrow 2\cos\left(\frac{5x + x}{2}\right)\cdot\cos\left(\frac{5x - x}{2}\right) = 0$$

$$\left[\cos x + \cos y = 2\cos\frac{x+y}{2}\cdot\cos\frac{x-y}{2}\right]$$

$\Rightarrow 2\cos 3x \cdot \cos 2x = 0$

$\Rightarrow \cos 3x = 0$ or $\cos 2x = 0$

$\Rightarrow \cos 3x = \cos\frac{\pi}{2}$ or $\cos 2x = \cos\frac{\pi}{2}$

$\therefore 3x = \frac{\pi}{2} \Rightarrow 2x = \frac{\pi}{2}$

and $x = \frac{\pi}{6} \Rightarrow x = \frac{\pi}{4}$

Hence, the solutions are $\frac{\pi}{2}, \frac{\pi}{4}$ and $\frac{\pi}{6}$.

126. *(a)* Given equation, $5\cos^2\theta + 7\sin^2\theta - 6 = 0$

$\Rightarrow 5\cos^2 + 7(1 - \cos^2\theta) - 6 = 0$

$\Rightarrow 5\cos^2\theta + 7 - 7\cos^2\theta - 6 = 0$

$\Rightarrow 5\cos^2\theta + 7 - 7\cos^2\theta - 6 = 0$

$\Rightarrow -2\cos^2\theta + 1 = 0$

$\Rightarrow 2\cos^2\theta - 1 = 0 \quad \left[\begin{array}{l}\cos^2\theta = \cos^2\alpha \\ \therefore \theta = n\pi \pm \alpha\end{array}\right]$

$\Rightarrow \cos^2\theta = \frac{1}{2}$

$\Rightarrow \cos^2\theta = \cos^2\frac{\pi}{4}$

$\therefore \theta = n\pi \pm \frac{\pi}{4}$

127. *(b)* $\tan^{-1}\sqrt{3} - \cot^{-1}(-\sqrt{3})$

$= \tan^{-1}\sqrt{3} - [\pi - \cot^{-1}\sqrt{3}]$

$[\cot^{-1}(-x) = \pi - \cot^{-1}x]$

$= \tan^{-1}\sqrt{3} - \pi + \cot^{-1}\sqrt{3}$

MOCK TEST 5

$$= \tan^{-1}\sqrt{3} - \pi + \tan^{-1}\frac{1}{\sqrt{3}} \qquad \left(\because \tan^{-1}\frac{1}{x} = \cot^{-1}x\right)$$

$$= \left[\tan^{-1}\sqrt{3} + \tan^{-1}\frac{1}{\sqrt{3}}\right] - \pi$$

$$= \tan^{-1}\frac{\left(\sqrt{3} + \frac{1}{\sqrt{3}}\right)}{1 - \left(\sqrt{3} \times \frac{1}{\sqrt{3}}\right)} - \pi$$

$$\left[\because \tan^{-1}x + \tan^{-1}y = \tan^{-1}\left(\frac{x+y}{1-xy}\right)\right]$$

$$= \tan^{-1}(\infty) - \pi = \frac{\pi}{2} - \pi = -\frac{\pi}{2}$$

128. *(d)* Given,

$$\sin^{-1}\left(\frac{2a}{1+a^2}\right) + \cos^{-1}\left(\frac{1-a^2}{1+a^2}\right) = \tan^{-1}\left(\frac{2x}{1-x^2}\right)$$

$$\Rightarrow \quad 2\tan^{-1}a + 2\tan^{-1}a = \tan^{-1}\left(\frac{2x}{1-x^2}\right)$$

$$\left[\because \sin^{-1}\left(\frac{2x}{1+x^2}\right) = 2\tan^{-1}x \text{ and } \cos^{-1}\left(\frac{1-x^2}{1+x^2}\right) = 2\tan^{-1}x\right]$$

$$\Rightarrow \quad 4\tan^{-1}a = \tan^{-1}\left(\frac{2x}{1-x^2}\right)$$

$$\Rightarrow \quad 2\tan^{-1}\left(\frac{2a}{1-a^2}\right) = \tan^{-1}\left(\frac{2x}{1-x^2}\right)$$

$$\left(\because 2\tan^{-1}x = \tan^{-1}\frac{2x}{1-x^2}\right)$$

$$\Rightarrow \quad 2\tan^{-1}\left(\frac{2a}{1-a^2}\right) = 2\tan^{-1}x$$

On comparing, we get

$$x = \frac{2a}{1-a^2}$$

129. *(c)* $\tan^{-1}\sqrt{x(x+1)} + \sin^{-1}\sqrt{x^2+x+1} = \frac{\pi}{2}$

$$\Rightarrow \quad \tan^{-1}\sqrt{x^2+x} + \sin^{-1}\sqrt{x^2+x+1} = \frac{\pi}{2}$$

This equation holds, if

$$x^2 + x \ge 0 \quad \text{and} \quad 0 \le x^2 + x + 1 \le 1$$

Now, $x^2 + x \ge 0$ and $0 \le x^2 + x + 1 \le 1$

$$\Rightarrow \quad x^2 + x \ge 0 \quad \text{and} \quad x^2 + x + 1 \le 1$$

$$(\because x^2 + x + 1 > 0 \text{ for all } x)$$

$$\Rightarrow \quad x^2 + x \ge 0 \quad \text{and} \quad x^2 + x \le 0$$

$$\Rightarrow \quad x^2 + x = 0 \Rightarrow x = 0, -1$$

Clearly, these two values satisfy the given equation. Hence, $x = 0, -1$ are the solutions of the given equation.

130. *(b)* From figure, we note that $\tan x$ is an increasing function in the interval $\left(-\frac{\pi}{2}, \frac{\pi}{2}\right)$, since $1 > \frac{\pi}{4}$. This gives

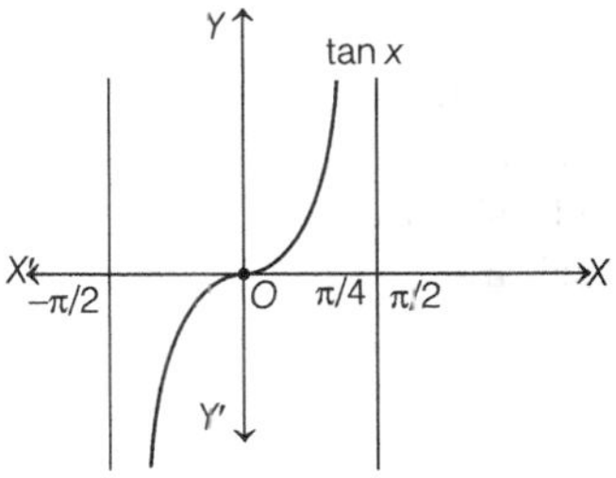

$$\tan 1 > 1 \Rightarrow \tan 1 > 1 > \frac{\pi}{4}$$

$$\Rightarrow \quad \tan 1 > 1 > \tan^{-1}(1)$$

131. *(a)* Let $P(n)$: Number of subset of a set containing n distinct elements is 2^n, for all $n \in N$.

Step I We observe that $P(1)$ is true, for $n = 1$.

Number of subsets of a set contain 1 element is $2^1 = 2$, which is true.

Step II Assume that $P(n)$ is true for $n = k$.

$P(k)$: Number of subsets of a set containing k distinct elements is 2^k, which is true.

Step III To prove $P(k+1)$ is true, we have to show that

$P(k+1)$: Number of subsets of a set containing $(k+1)$ distinct elements is 2^{k+1}.

We know that, with the addition of one element in the set, the number of subsets become double.

$\therefore$ Number of subsets of a set containing $(k+1)$ distinct elements $= 2 \times 2^k = 2^{k+1}$.

So, $P(k+1)$ is true. Hence, $P(n)$ is true.

132. *(a)* Given that, $(z+3)(\bar{z}+3)$

Let $\quad z = x + iy$

$$\Rightarrow \quad (z+3)(\bar{z}+3) = (x + iy + 3)(x + 3 - iy)$$

$$= (x+3)^2 - (iy)^2 = (x-3)^2 + y^2$$

$$= |x + 3 + iy|^2 = |z+3|^2$$

133. *(b)* If z is a complex number, then $z = x + iy$

$$|z| = |x + iy| \quad \text{and} \quad |z|^2 = |x + iy|^2$$

$$\Rightarrow \quad |z|^2 = x^2 + y^2 \qquad \text{...(i)}$$

and $\quad z^2 = (x + iy)^2 = x^2 + i^2y^2 + i2xy$

$$z^2 = x^2 - y^2 + i2xy$$

$$\Rightarrow \quad |z^2| = \sqrt{(x^2 - y^2)^2 + (2xy)^2}$$

$\Rightarrow \quad |z^2| = \sqrt{x^4 + y^4 - 2x^2y^2 + 4x^2y^2}$

$\Rightarrow \quad |z^2| = \sqrt{x^4 + y^4 + 2x^2y^2} = \sqrt{(x^2 + y^2)^2}$

$\Rightarrow \quad |z^2| = x^2 + y^2$ ...(ii)

From Eqs. (i) and (ii),

$$|z|^2 = |z^2|$$

134. *(c)* Let $z = x + 0i$ and $x < 0$

Since, the point $(x, 0)$ represent $z = x + 0i$ lies on the negative side of real axis.

$\therefore$ Principal $\arg(z) = \pi$

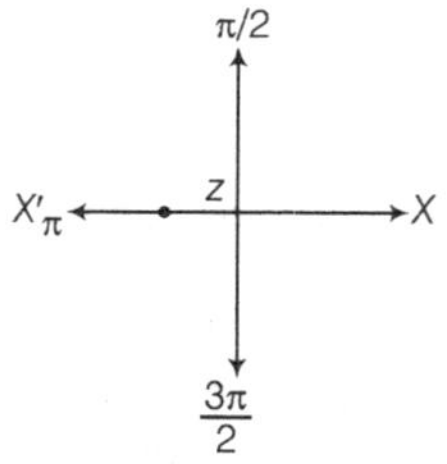

135. *(a)* Let $z = 1 + 2i$ then $|z| = \sqrt{1+4} = \sqrt{5}$

Now, $f(z) = \dfrac{7-z}{1-z^2} = \dfrac{7-1-2i}{1-(1+2i)^2}$

$$= \frac{6-2i}{1-1-4i^2-4i} = \frac{6-2i}{4-4i} = \frac{(3-i)(2+2i)}{(2-2i)(2+2i)}$$

$$= \frac{6-2i+6i-2i^2}{4-4i^2} = \frac{6+4i+2}{4+4} = \frac{8+4i}{8} = 1 + \frac{1}{2}i$$

$f(z) = 1 + \dfrac{1}{2}i$

$\therefore |f(z)| = \sqrt{1 + \dfrac{1}{4}} = \sqrt{\dfrac{4+1}{4}} = \dfrac{\sqrt{5}}{2} = \dfrac{|z|}{2}$

136. *(c)* Total number of players = 22

We have to select a team of 11 players. Selection of 11 players when 2 of them is always included and 4 are never included.

Total number of players = 22 − 2 − 4 = 16

$\therefore$ Required number of selections = ${}^{16}C_9$

137. *(d)* Total number of triangles formed from 12 points taking 3 at a time = ${}^{12}C_3$

But out of 12 points 7 are collinear. So, these 7 points constitute a straight line mean no triangle is formed by joining these 7 points.

$\therefore$ Required number of triangles = ${}^{12}C_3 - {}^{7}C_3$

$= 220 - 35 = 185$

138. *(b)* Possible number of choosing green dyes = 2^5

Possible number of choosing blue dyes = 2^4

Possible number of choosing red dyes = 2^3

If atleast one blue and one green dyes are selected.

Then, total number of selection

$= (2^5 - 1)(2^4 - 1) \times 2^3 = 3720$

139. *(b)* The expansion of $(1 + x)^n$ is

${}^nC_0 + {}^nC_1x + {}^nC_2x^2 + {}^nC_3x^3 + \ldots + {}^nC_nx^n$

$\therefore$ Coefficient of 2nd term = ${}^nC_1$,

Coefficient of 3rd term = ${}^nC_2$

and coefficient of 4th term = ${}^nC_3$.

Given that, ${}^nC_1$, ${}^nC_2$ and ${}^nC_3$ are in AP.

$\therefore \quad 2\,{}^nC_2 = {}^nC_1 + {}^nC_3$

$\Rightarrow \quad 2\left[\dfrac{(n)!}{(n-2)!\,2!}\right] = \dfrac{(n)!}{(n-1)!} + \dfrac{(n)!}{3!(n-3)!}$

$\Rightarrow \quad \dfrac{2 \cdot n(n-1)(n-2)!}{(n-2)!\,2!}$

$$= \frac{n(n-1)!}{(n-1)!} + \frac{n(n-1)(n-2)(n-3)!}{3 \cdot 2 \cdot 1\,(n-3)!}$$

$\Rightarrow \quad n(n-1) = n + \dfrac{n(n-1)(n-2)}{6}$

$\Rightarrow \quad 6n - 6 = 6 + n^2 - 3n + 2$

$\Rightarrow \quad n^2 - 9n + 14 = 0$

$\Rightarrow \quad n^2 - 7n - 2n + 14 = 0$

$\Rightarrow \quad n(n-7) - 2(n-7) = 0$

$\Rightarrow \quad (n-7)(n-2) = 0$

$\therefore \quad n = 2$ or $n = 7$

Since, $n = 2$ is not possible.

$\therefore \quad n = 7$

140. *(b)* Given expansion is $\left(\sqrt{\dfrac{x}{3}} + \dfrac{3}{2x^2}\right)^{10}$.

Let the constant term be T_{r+1}.

Then, $\quad T_{r+1} = {}^{10}C_r \left(\sqrt{\dfrac{x}{3}}\right)^{10-r} \left(\dfrac{3}{2x^2}\right)^r$

$$= {}^{10}C_r \cdot x^{\frac{10-r}{2}} \cdot 3^{\frac{-10+r}{2}} \cdot 3^r \cdot 2^{-r} \cdot x^{-2r}$$

$$= {}^{10}C_r\, x^{\frac{10-5r}{2}}\, 3^{\frac{-10+3r}{2}}\, 2^{-r}$$

For constant term, $10 - 5r = 0 \Rightarrow r = 2$

Hence, third term is independent of x.

141. *(c)* It is given that, $T_3 = 4$

Let a and r the first term and common ratio, respectively.

Then, $\quad ar^2 = 4$ ...(i)

Product of first 5 terms $= a \cdot ar \cdot ar^2 \cdot ar^3 \cdot ar^4$

$= a^5 r^{10} = (ar^2)^5 = (4)^5$ [using Eq. (i)]

142. *(a)* Let first term be a and common difference be d.
According to the question, $9 \cdot T_9 = 13 \cdot T_{13}$

$$9(a + 8d) = 13(a + 12d)$$
$$\Rightarrow 9a + 72d = 13a + 156d$$
$$\Rightarrow (9a - 13a) = 156d - 72d$$
$$\Rightarrow -4a = 84d$$
$$\Rightarrow a = -21d$$
$$\Rightarrow a + 21d = 0 \quad \text{...(i)}$$

$\therefore$ 22nd term *i.e.*, $T_{22} = [a + 21d]$

$$T_{22} = 0$$

143. *(b)* Given point is (1, 2) and slope of the required line is 1.

$$x + y + 1 = 0 \Rightarrow y = -x - 1 \Rightarrow m_1 = -1$$

$\therefore$ Slope of the required line $= \frac{-1}{-1} = 1$

$\therefore$ Equation of required line is

$$y - 2 = 1(x - 1)$$
$$\Rightarrow y - 2 = x - 1$$
$$\Rightarrow y - x - 1 = 0$$

144. *(b)* Equation of straight lines are

$$y = mx + c, \text{ parameter} = 2 \quad \text{...(i)}$$
$$\frac{x}{a} + \frac{y}{b} = 1, \text{ parameter} = 2 \quad \text{...(ii)}$$
$$y - y_1 = m(x - x_1), \text{ parameter} = 2 \quad \text{...(iii)}$$
and $$x\cos w + y\sin w = p, \text{ parameter} = 2 \quad \text{...(iv)}$$

It is clear that from Eqs. (i), (ii), (iii) and (iv), for specifying a straight line clearly two parameters should be known.

145. *(c)* The given equation of lines are

$$4x + 3y + 10 = 0 \quad \text{...(i)}$$
$$\Rightarrow 5x - 12y + 26 = 0 \quad \text{...(ii)}$$
$$\Rightarrow 7x + 24y - 50 = 0 \quad \text{...(iii)}$$

Let the point (h, k) which is equidistant from these lines.

Distance from line (i) $= \frac{|4h + 3k + 10|}{\sqrt{16 + 9}}$

Distance from line (ii) $= \frac{|5h - 12k + 26|}{\sqrt{25 + 144}}$

Distance from the line (iii) $= \frac{|7h + 24k - 50|}{\sqrt{7^2 + 24^2}}$

So, point (h, k) is equidistant from lines (i), (ii) and (iii).

$$\therefore \frac{4h + 3k + 10}{\sqrt{16 + 9}} = \frac{5h - 12k + 26}{\sqrt{25 + 144}} = \frac{7h + 24k - 50}{\sqrt{49 + 576}}$$

$$\Rightarrow \frac{|4h + 3k + 10|}{5} = \frac{|5h - 12k + 26|}{13} = \frac{|7h + 24k - 50|}{25}$$

Clearly, if $h = 0, k = 0$, then $\frac{10}{5} = \frac{26}{13} = \frac{50}{25} = 2$

Hence, the required point is (0, 0).

146. *(c)* The centre of the required circle lies at the intersection of $2x - 3y - 5 = 0$ and $3x - 4y - 7 = 0$. Thus, the coordinates of the centre are $(1, -1)$.

Let r be the radius of the circle. Then, by hypothesis, we have $\pi r^2 = 154 \Rightarrow \frac{22}{7} r^2 = 154 \Rightarrow r = 7$

Hence, the equation of the required circle is

$$(x - 1)^2 + (y + 1)^2 = 7^2$$
$$\Rightarrow x^2 + y^2 - 2x + 2y - 47 = 0$$

147. *(a)* Let $P(x, y)$ be any point on the parabola.
Using the definition of parabola, we have

$$\sqrt{(x - 2)^2 + (y - 3)^2} = \left|\frac{x - 4y + 3}{\sqrt{17}}\right|$$

Squaring, we get $17(x^2 + y^2 - 4x - 6y + 13)$

$$= x^2 + 16y^2 + 9 - 8xy - 24y + 6x$$

or $16x^2 + y^2 + 8xy - 74x - 78y + 212 = 0$

148. *(c)* As shown in the figure APQ denotes the equilateral triangle with its equal side of length l (say).

Here, $AP = l$

So, $AR = l\cos 30° = l\frac{\sqrt{3}}{2}$

Also, $PR = l\sin 30° = \frac{l}{2}$.

Thus, $\left(\frac{l\sqrt{3}}{2}, \frac{l}{2}\right)$ are the coordinates of the point P lying on the parabola $y^2 = 4ax$.

Therefore, $\frac{l^2}{4} = 4a\left(\frac{l\sqrt{3}}{2}\right) \Rightarrow l = 8a\sqrt{3}$

Thus, $8a\sqrt{3}$ is the required length of the side of the equilateral triangle inscribed in the parabola $y^2 = 4ax$

149. *(d)* Given equation of ellipse is

$$3x^2 + y^2 = 12$$
$$\Rightarrow \frac{x^2}{4} + \frac{y^2}{12} = 1$$
$$\therefore a^2 = 4 \Rightarrow a = 2$$
and $$b^2 = 12 \Rightarrow b = 2\sqrt{3}$$
$$b > a$$

$\therefore$ Length of latusrectum $= \frac{2a^2}{b} = \frac{2 \times 4}{2\sqrt{3}} = \frac{4}{\sqrt{3}}$

150. *(d)* According to given condition, $2ae = 8, \frac{2a}{e} = 18$

$$\Rightarrow a = \sqrt{4 \times 9} = 6$$

$\Rightarrow \quad e = \frac{2}{3}, b = 6\sqrt{1 - \frac{4}{9}} = \frac{6}{3}\sqrt{5} = 2\sqrt{5}$

Hence, the required equation is $\frac{x^2}{36} + \frac{y^2}{20} = 1$

i.e., $\quad 5x^2 + 9y^2 = 180$

151. *(a)* Given that, eccentricity of the hyperbola, $e = 3/2$

and $\quad$ foci $=(\pm 2, 0) = (\pm ae, 0)$

$\therefore \quad ae = 2$

$\Rightarrow \quad a \times 3/2 = 2 \Rightarrow a = 4/3$

$b^2 = a^2(e^2 - 1)$

$\Rightarrow \quad b^2 = \frac{16}{9}\left(\frac{9}{4} - 1\right) \Rightarrow b^2 = \frac{16}{9}\left(\frac{5}{4}\right)$

$\Rightarrow \quad b^2 = \frac{20}{9}$

So, the equation of the hyperbola is

$$\frac{x^2}{\frac{16}{9}} - \frac{y^2}{\frac{20}{9}} = 1 \Rightarrow \frac{x^2}{4} - \frac{y^2}{5} = \frac{4}{9}$$

152. *(b)* Since, line equally inclined with the axes.

$\therefore \quad l = m = n \quad \ldots$(i)

The required equation of line is

$$\frac{x - x_1}{l} = \frac{y - y_1}{m} = \frac{z - z_1}{n}$$

$$\frac{x + 3}{l} = \frac{y - 2}{l} = \frac{z + 4}{l} \quad \text{[by Eq. (i)]}$$

$$\Rightarrow \frac{x + 3}{1} = \frac{y - 2}{1} = \frac{z + 4}{1}$$

$\Rightarrow x + 3 = y - 2 = z + 4$

153. *(d)* $\lim_{x \to 0} \frac{e^{2x} - 1 - 2x}{x(e^{2x} - 1)}$

$$= \lim_{x \to 0} \frac{2e^{2x} - 2}{(e^{2x} - 1) + 2xe^{2x}} \quad \text{(using L' Hospital's rule)}$$

$$= \lim_{x \to 0} \frac{4e^{2x}}{4e^{2x} + 4xe^{2x}} = 1$$

(using L' Hospital's rule)

Since, $f(x)$ is continuous at $x = 0$, then

$$\lim_{x \to 0} f(x) = f(0)$$

$\Rightarrow \quad 1 = f(0)$

154. *(b)* $\quad f(x) = (x - 2)(x - 4)(x - 6)\ldots(x - 2n)$

Taking log on both sides of the given equation, we get $\log f(x) = \log(x - 2) + \log(x - 4) + \ldots + \log(x - 2n)$

On differentiating w.r.t. x, we get

$$\frac{1}{f(x)} f'(x) = \frac{1}{x - 2} + \frac{1}{x - 4} + \ldots + \frac{1}{(x - 2n)}$$

$\Rightarrow \quad f'(x) = (x - 4)(x - 6)\ldots(x - 2n)$
$\quad + (x - 2)(x - 6)\ldots(x - 2n)$
$\quad + \ldots + (x - 2)(x - 4)\ldots(x - (2n - 2))$

$\therefore \quad f'(2) = (-2)(-4)\ldots(2 - 2n)$
$\quad = (-2)^{n-1}(1 . 2 \ldots (n - 1)) = (-2)^{n-1}(n - 1)!$

155. *(a)* Let l be the length of an edge and V be the volume of cube at any time t.

$$V = l^3$$

$$\therefore \quad \frac{dV}{dt} = 3l^2 \frac{dl}{dt}$$

$$= 3 \times 5^2 \times 10 \text{ cm}^3/\text{s}$$

$$= 750 \text{ cm}^3/\text{s}$$

156. *(d)* Given, $\quad y = x^2 e^{-x}$

$$\Rightarrow \quad \frac{dy}{dx} = x^2 e^{-x}(-1) + e^{-x}(2x)$$

$$= xe^{-x}(-x + 2) = x(2 - x)e^{-x}$$

For increasing function, $\frac{dy}{dx} > 0 \Rightarrow xe^{-x}(2 - x) > 0$

Case I

$\Rightarrow \quad x > 0$ and $2 - x > 0$

$\Rightarrow \quad x > 0$ and $x < 2$

$\Rightarrow \quad 0 < x < 2$

Case II

$\Rightarrow \quad x < 0$ and $2 - x < 0$

$\Rightarrow \quad x < 0$ and $x > 2$

Hence, there is no value of x exist.

Clearly, it is increasing in (0, 2).

157. *(b)* Since, $f(x) = \tan^{-1}(\sin x + \cos x)$

$$\Rightarrow \quad f'(x) = \frac{1}{1 + (\sin x + \cos x)^2}(\cos x - \sin x)$$

$$= \frac{\sqrt{2}\cos\left(x + \frac{\pi}{4}\right)}{1 + (\sin x + \cos x)^2}$$

For $f(x)$ to be increasing,

$$-\frac{\pi}{2} < x + \frac{\pi}{4} < \frac{\pi}{2} \Rightarrow -\frac{3\pi}{4} < x < \frac{\pi}{4}$$

Hence, option (b) is correct, which lies in the above interval.

158. *(d)* $\quad f(x) = -x^3 + 4ax^2 + 2x - 5$

$\therefore \quad f'(x) = -3x^2 + 8ax + 2$

Since, $f(x)$ is decreasing for all $\forall x$, therefore $f'(x) < 0$

$\Rightarrow \quad -3x^2 + 8ax + 2 < 0$

$\Rightarrow \quad 3x^2 - 8ax - 2 > 0$

Now, $\quad D = (-8a)^2 - 4(3)(-2) < 0$

$\Rightarrow \quad 64a^2 + 24 < 0$

$\Rightarrow \quad a^2 < -\frac{3}{8}$

Hence, no real value of a exist.

159. *(d)* Given, $f(x) = x^3 + ax^2 + bx + c,\ a^2 \le 3b$.

On differentiating w.r.t. x, we get

$$f'(x) = 3x^2 + 2ax + b$$

Put $\quad f'(x) = 0$

$\Rightarrow \quad 3x^2 + 2ax + b = 0$

$$\Rightarrow \quad x = \frac{-2a \pm \sqrt{4a^2 - 12b}}{2 \times 3}$$

$$= \frac{-2a \pm 2\sqrt{a^2 - 3b}}{6}$$

Since, $a^2 \le 3b$,

$\therefore$ x has an imaginary value.

Hence, no extreme value of x exist.

160. *(a)* Let $y = \sin^3 x + \cos^3 x$

$$\frac{dy}{dx} = 3\sin^2 x \cos x - 3\cos^2 x \sin x$$

$$= 3\sin x \cos x(\sin x - \cos x)$$

Put, $\frac{dy}{dx} = 0$, $3\sin x \cos x(\sin x - \cos x) = 0$

$\Rightarrow \quad x = 0, \frac{\pi}{2}$ or $\frac{\pi}{4}$

Now, y has its maximum value at $x = 0$ or $\frac{\pi}{2}$ and $y_{max} = 1$.

161. *(b)* Given, $f(x) = x^{25}(1-x)^{75}$

$$\Rightarrow \quad f'(x) = 25x^{24}(1-x)^{75} - 75x^{25}(1-x)^{74}$$

$$= 25x^{24}(1-x)^{74}(1-4x)$$

Put, $f'(x) = 0 \Rightarrow x = 0, 1, \frac{1}{4}$

If $x < \frac{1}{4}$, then

$$f'(x) = 25x^{24}(1-x)^{74}(1-4x) > 0$$

and if $x > \frac{1}{4}$, then

$$f'(x) = 25x^{24}(1-x)^{74}(1-4x) < 0$$

Thus, $f'(x)$ changes its sign from positive to negative as x passes through $1/4$ from left to right.

Hence, $f(x)$ attains its maximum at $x = 1/4$

162. *(c)* Given, $f(x) = x^3 + \frac{1}{x^3}$

On differentiating w.r.t. x, we get $f'(x) = 3x^2 - \frac{3}{x^4}$

(a) $f(x)$ is increasing, if $f'(x) \ge 0$

$\Rightarrow 3x^2 - \frac{3}{x^4} \ge 0 \Rightarrow x^6 \ge 1 \Rightarrow (x^2)^3 \ge 1$

$\Rightarrow \quad x^2 \ge 1 \Rightarrow x \in (-\infty, -1] \cup [1, \infty)$

Thus, f is increasing in $(-\infty, -1] \cup [1, \infty)$

Hence f is increasing in $(-\infty, -1) \cup (1, \infty)$.

(b) $f(x)$ is decreasing, if $f'(x) \le 0$

$\Rightarrow \quad 3x^2 - \frac{3}{x^4} \le 0$

$\Rightarrow \quad x^6 \le 1 \Rightarrow (x^2)^3 \le 1$

$\Rightarrow \quad x^2 \le 1 \Rightarrow -1 \le x \le 1$ f is decreasing in $-1 < x < 1$.

163. *(d)* Here, $I = \int \frac{x^3}{\sqrt{1+x^2}}dx$

$$= \int \frac{x^2 \cdot x}{\sqrt{1+x^2}}dx$$

Put, $\quad 1 + x^2 = t^2$

$\Rightarrow \quad 2x\,dx = 2t\,dt$

$\Rightarrow \quad x\,dx = t\,dt$

$$I = \int \frac{(t^2-1)\,t}{\sqrt{t^2}}dt$$

$$I = \int \frac{(t^2-1)\,t}{t}dt = \int (t^2-1)\,dt$$

$$I = \frac{t^3}{3} - t + C$$

$$I = \frac{(1+x^2)^{3/2}}{3} - \sqrt{1+x^2} + C$$

Thus, $\frac{(1+x^2)^{3/2}}{3} - \sqrt{1+x^2} + C$

$$= a(1+x^2)^{3/2} + b\sqrt{1+x^2} + C$$

On comparing both sides, we get

$$a = \frac{1}{3} \quad \text{and} \quad b = -1$$

164. *(c)* We have, $I = \int \frac{3x-1}{\sqrt{x^2+9}}dx$

By putting numerator,

$$3x - 1 = A\frac{d}{dx}(x^2+9) + B$$

$$3x - 1 = A(2x) + B$$

$$3x - 1 = 2Ax + B$$

On comparing the coefficients of x and constant term on both sides, we get

$$2A = 3 \text{ and } B = -1$$

$\Rightarrow \quad A = \frac{3}{2}$ and $B = -1$

MOCK TEST 5

$\therefore \quad I = \frac{3}{2}\int \frac{2x}{\sqrt{x^2+9}}\,dx - \int \frac{1}{\sqrt{x^2+9}}\,dx$

$= \frac{3}{2} \times 2\sqrt{x^2+9} - \log|x + \sqrt{x^2+9}| + C$

$\left[\int \frac{f'(x)}{\sqrt{f(x)}}\,dx = 2\sqrt{f(x)} + C\right]$

$= 3\sqrt{x^2+9} - \log|x + \sqrt{x^2+9}| + C$

165. *(b)* Let $I = \int_0^1 \tan^{-1}\left(\frac{2x-1}{1+x-x^2}\right) dx$

$= \int_0^1 \tan^{-1}\left(\frac{x+(x-1)}{1-x(x-1)}\right) dx$

$= \int_0^1 \{\tan^{-1} x + \tan^{-1}(x-1)\}\, dx$

$\left[\tan^{-1} A + \tan^{-1} B = \tan^{-1}\left(\frac{A+B}{1-AB}\right)\right]$

$\Rightarrow \quad I = \int_0^1 \{\tan^{-1} x - \tan^{-1}(1-x)\}\, dx \quad \ldots\text{(i)}$

Also, $I = \int_0^1 \{\tan^{-1}(1-x) - \tan^{-1}(1-(1-x))\}\, dx$

$\left[\int_0^a f(x)\,dx = \int_0^a f(a-x)\,dx\right]$

$\Rightarrow \quad I = \int_0^1 [\tan^{-1}(1-x) - \tan^{-1}(x)]\, dx \quad \ldots\text{(ii)}$

On adding Eqs. (i) and (ii), we get

$2I = 0 \Rightarrow I = 0$

166. *(a)* $I = \int \frac{1}{e^x + e^{-x}}\,dx = \int \frac{1}{e^x + \frac{1}{e^x}}\,dx = \int \frac{e^x}{(e^x)^2+1}\,dx$

Put $e^x = t \Rightarrow e^x dx = dt$ $\quad \left(\int \frac{dx}{1+x^2} = \tan^{-1} x\right)$

$\therefore \quad I = \int \frac{e^x}{t^2+1}\frac{dt}{e^x} = \tan^{-1}(t) + C = \tan^{-1} e^x + C$

167. *(b)* Area $= \int_0^{16/m^2} (\sqrt{16x} - mx)\,dx = \frac{2}{3}$

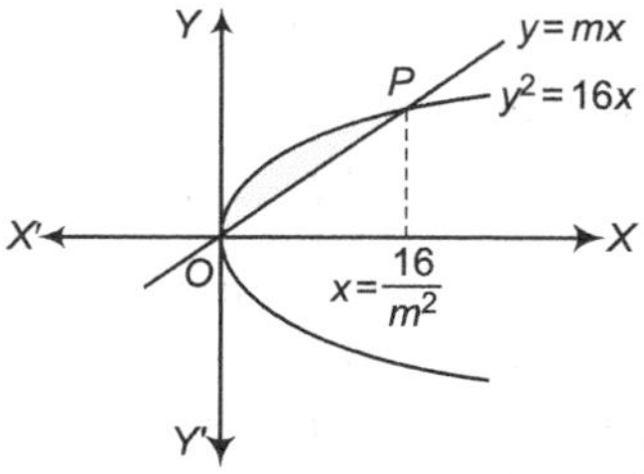

$\Rightarrow \left[4 \cdot \frac{2}{3}x^{3/2} - \frac{mx^2}{2}\right]_0^{16/m^2} = \frac{2}{3}$

$\Rightarrow \frac{1}{m^3}\left[\frac{512}{3} - \frac{256}{2}\right] = \frac{2}{3}$

$\Rightarrow m^3 = \frac{128}{3} \times \frac{3}{2} = 64$

$\therefore \quad m = 4$

168. *(d)* The given differential equation is

$x\left(\frac{dy}{dx}\right)^2 + 2\sqrt{xy}\frac{dy}{dx} + y = 0$

$\Rightarrow \left(\sqrt{x}\frac{dy}{dx} + \sqrt{y}\right)^2 = 0$

$\Rightarrow \sqrt{x}\frac{dy}{dx} + \sqrt{y} = 0$

$\Rightarrow \frac{1}{\sqrt{y}}\,dy + \frac{1}{\sqrt{x}}\,dx = 0$

On integrating both sides, we get

$\int \frac{1}{\sqrt{y}}\,dy + \int \frac{1}{\sqrt{x}}\,dx = 0$

$\Rightarrow 2\sqrt{y} + 2\sqrt{x} = C_1$

$\Rightarrow \sqrt{x} + \sqrt{y} = C \quad \left(\text{where, } C = \frac{C_1}{2}\right)$

169. *(a)* According to the condition,

$\frac{dy}{dx} = \frac{y}{x} - \cos^2\frac{y}{x} \quad \ldots\text{(i)}$

This is a homogeneous differential equation Substituting $y = vx$, we get

$v + x\frac{dv}{dx} = v - \cos^2 v$

$\Rightarrow x\frac{dv}{dx} = -\cos^2 v$

$\Rightarrow \sec^2 v\,dv = -\frac{dx}{x}$

$\Rightarrow \tan v = -\log x + C$

$\Rightarrow \tan\frac{y}{x} + \log x = C \quad \ldots\text{(ii)}$

Substituting $x = 1$, $y = \frac{\pi}{4}$, we get $C = 1$. Thus, we get

$\tan\left(\frac{y}{x}\right) + \log x = 1$

which is the required solution.

170. *(b)* The given differential equation is

$\frac{dy}{dx} = \frac{y + x\tan\frac{y}{x}}{x} \quad \ldots\text{(i)}$

So, put $y = vx$

$\Rightarrow \frac{dy}{dx} = v + x\frac{dv}{dx}$

$\therefore \quad v + x\frac{dv}{dx} = \frac{vx + x\tan\left(\frac{vx}{x}\right)}{x}$

$\Rightarrow \quad x\dfrac{dv}{dx} = v + \tan v - v$

$\Rightarrow \quad \int \cot v \, dv = \int \dfrac{dx}{x}$

$\Rightarrow \quad \log \sin v = \log x + \log C$

$\Rightarrow \quad \sin \dfrac{y}{x} = xC$

171. *(c)* Let $\mathbf{a} = l\mathbf{i} + m\mathbf{j} + n\mathbf{k}$ makes an angle $\dfrac{\pi}{4}$ with Z-axis. Also. $l^2 + m^2 + n^2 = 1$

Here, $n = \cos \dfrac{\pi}{4} = \dfrac{1}{\sqrt{2}}, l^2 + m^2 = \dfrac{1}{2}$ ...(i)

$\therefore \quad \mathbf{a} = l\mathbf{i} + m\mathbf{j} + \dfrac{\mathbf{k}}{\sqrt{2}}$

$\Rightarrow \therefore \quad \mathbf{a} + \mathbf{i} + \mathbf{j} = (l+1)\,\mathbf{i} + (m+1)\,\mathbf{j} + \dfrac{\mathbf{k}}{\sqrt{2}}$

$\Rightarrow \quad |\mathbf{a} + \mathbf{i} + \mathbf{j}| = \sqrt{(l+1)^2 + (m+1)^2 + \left(\dfrac{1}{\sqrt{2}}\right)^2}$

$\Rightarrow \quad 1 = l^2 + m^2 + 2 + 2l + 2m + \dfrac{1}{2}$

$\Rightarrow \quad l + m = -1$ [from Eq. (i)]

$\Rightarrow \quad l^2 + m^2 + 2lm = 1$

$\Rightarrow \quad 2lm = \dfrac{1}{2} \quad \Rightarrow \quad l = m = -\dfrac{1}{2}$

$\left(l = m = \dfrac{1}{2} \text{ is not satisfied the given equation} \right)$

$\therefore \quad \mathbf{a} = -\dfrac{\mathbf{i}}{2} - \dfrac{\mathbf{j}}{2} + \dfrac{\mathbf{k}}{\sqrt{2}}$

172. *(b)* Given, $|\mathbf{a}| = 1$

(It is a unit vector, magnitude of a unit vector is 1.)

and $(\mathbf{x} - \mathbf{a}).(\mathbf{x} + \mathbf{a}) = 12$

$\Rightarrow \mathbf{x}\cdot\mathbf{x} + \mathbf{x}\cdot\mathbf{a} - \mathbf{a}\cdot\mathbf{x} - \mathbf{a}\cdot\mathbf{a} = 12$

($\mathbf{a}\cdot\mathbf{a} = |\mathbf{a}|^2$ and $\mathbf{a}\cdot\mathbf{b} = \mathbf{b}\cdot\mathbf{a}$)

$\Rightarrow \quad |\mathbf{x}|^2 - |\mathbf{a}|^2 = 12$

$\Rightarrow \quad |\mathbf{x}|^2 - 1^2 = 12$

($|\mathbf{a}| = 1$ as a is a unit vector)

$\Rightarrow \quad |\mathbf{x}|^2 = 13$

$\Rightarrow \quad |\mathbf{x}| = \sqrt{13}$

173. *(c)* Let the required unit vector be $\mathbf{r} = a\mathbf{i} + b\mathbf{j}$.

Then, $|\mathbf{r}| = 1$

$\Rightarrow \quad a^2 + b^2 = 1$ ...(i)

Since, **r** makes an angle of 45° with $\mathbf{i} + \mathbf{j}$ and an angle of 60° with $3\mathbf{i} - 4\mathbf{j}$, therefore,

$\cos\dfrac{\pi}{4} = \dfrac{\mathbf{r}\cdot(\mathbf{i} + \mathbf{j})}{|\mathbf{r}||\mathbf{i} + \mathbf{j}|}$

and $\cos\dfrac{\pi}{3} = \dfrac{\mathbf{r}\cdot(3\mathbf{i} - 4\mathbf{j})}{|\mathbf{r}||3\mathbf{i} - 4\mathbf{j}|}$

$\Rightarrow \quad \dfrac{1}{\sqrt{2}} = \dfrac{a+b}{\sqrt{2}}$

and $\dfrac{1}{2} = \dfrac{3a - 4b}{5}$

$\Rightarrow \quad a + b = 1$

and $a - 4b = \dfrac{5}{2}$

$\Rightarrow \quad a = \dfrac{13}{14}, \; b = \dfrac{1}{14} \quad \therefore$

$\mathbf{r} = \dfrac{13}{14}\mathbf{i} + \dfrac{1}{14}\mathbf{j}$

174. *(d)* Given, $2X + 3Y = \begin{bmatrix} 2 & 3 \\ 4 & 0 \end{bmatrix}$ ...(i)

and $3X + 2Y = \begin{bmatrix} 2 & -2 \\ -1 & 5 \end{bmatrix}$ ...(ii)

On multiplying Eq. (i) by 2 and Eq. (ii) by 3 and then subtracting, we get

$2(2X + 3Y) - 3(3x + 2Y) = 2\begin{bmatrix} 2 & 3 \\ 4 & 0 \end{bmatrix} - 3\begin{bmatrix} 2 & -2 \\ -1 & 5 \end{bmatrix}$

$\Rightarrow \quad 4X + 6Y - 9X - 6Y = \begin{bmatrix} 4 & 6 \\ 8 & 0 \end{bmatrix} - \begin{bmatrix} 6 & -6 \\ -3 & 15 \end{bmatrix}$

$\Rightarrow \quad -5X = \begin{bmatrix} 4-6 & 6+6 \\ 8+3 & 0-15 \end{bmatrix} = \begin{bmatrix} -2 & 12 \\ 11 & -15 \end{bmatrix}$

$\Rightarrow \quad X = -\dfrac{1}{5}\begin{bmatrix} -2 & 12 \\ 11 & -15 \end{bmatrix} = \begin{bmatrix} 2/5 & -12/5 \\ -11/5 & 3 \end{bmatrix}$

Then, from Eq. (i), we get

$3Y = \begin{bmatrix} 2 & 3 \\ 4 & 0 \end{bmatrix} - 2X$

$= \begin{bmatrix} 2 & 3 \\ 4 & 0 \end{bmatrix} - 2\begin{bmatrix} 2/5 & -12/5 \\ -11/5 & 3 \end{bmatrix}$

$= \begin{bmatrix} 2 - \dfrac{4}{5} & 3 + \dfrac{24}{5} \\ 4 + \dfrac{22}{5} & 0 - 6 \end{bmatrix} = \begin{bmatrix} 6/5 & 39/5 \\ 42/5 & -6 \end{bmatrix}$

$\therefore \; Y = \dfrac{1}{3}\begin{bmatrix} 6/5 & 39/5 \\ 42/5 & -6 \end{bmatrix} = \begin{bmatrix} 2/5 & 13/5 \\ 14/5 & -2 \end{bmatrix}$

175. *(b)* $\begin{vmatrix} a & 1 & 1 \\ 1 & b & 1 \\ 1 & 1 & c \end{vmatrix} = abc - (a + b + c) + 2$

$\Delta > 0 \Rightarrow abc + 2 > a + b + c$

$\Rightarrow \quad abc + 2 > 3(abc)^{1/3}$

$\left[\text{AM} > \text{GM} \Rightarrow \dfrac{a+b+c}{3} > (abc)^{1/3}\right]$

$\Rightarrow \quad x^3 + 2 > 3x$, where $x = (abc)^{1/3}$

$\Rightarrow \quad x^3 - 3x + 2 > 0$

$\Rightarrow \quad (x-1)^2 (x+2) > 0$

$\Rightarrow \quad x + 2 > 0$

$\{(n-1)^2$ is always positive$\}$

$\Rightarrow \quad x > -2$

$\Rightarrow \quad (abc)^{1/3} > -2$

$\Rightarrow \quad abc > -8$

176. *(a)* The given determinant is

$$\begin{vmatrix} \cos x & -\sin x & 1 \\ \sin x & \cos x & 1 \\ \cos(x+y) & -\sin(x+y) & 0 \end{vmatrix}$$

Applying $R_3 \to R_3 - \cos y\, R_1 + \sin y\, R_2$, we get

$$\Delta = \begin{vmatrix} \cos x & -\sin x & 1 \\ \sin x & \cos x & 1 \\ 0 & 0 & \sin y - \cos y \end{vmatrix}$$

By expanding along R_3, we have

$$\Delta = (\sin y - \cos y)(\cos^2 x + \sin^2 x)$$

$$= (\sin y - \cos y) = \sqrt{2}\left[\frac{1}{\sqrt{2}}\sin y - \frac{1}{\sqrt{2}}\cos y\right]$$

$$= \sqrt{2}\left[\cos\frac{\pi}{4}\sin y - \sin\frac{\pi}{4}\cos y\right] = \sqrt{2}\sin\left(y - \frac{\pi}{4}\right)$$

Hence, $-\sqrt{2} \le \Delta \le \sqrt{2}$.

177. *(d)* Let A : first bag is chosen.

Let B : second bag is chosen.

Let E denote the event of choosing a black ball.

A die is thrown and if it shows up 1 or 3, a ball is taken from the first bag

$\therefore \quad P(A) = \dfrac{2}{6} = \dfrac{1}{3}$

Since, the second bag is chosen when the die shows any of the numbers 2, 4, 5, 6.

Therefore, $\quad P(B) = \dfrac{4}{6} = \dfrac{2}{3}$

Bag I contains 3 black and 4 white balls.

Therefore, $\quad P\left(\dfrac{E}{A}\right) = \dfrac{3}{7}$

Similarly, bag II contains 4 black and 3 white balls.

Therefore, $\quad P\left(\dfrac{E}{B}\right) = \dfrac{4}{7}$

Now, probability of choosing a black ball is given by

$$P(E) = P(A) \times P\left(\frac{E}{A}\right) + P(B) \times P\left(\frac{E}{B}\right)$$

$$= \frac{1}{3} \times \frac{3}{7} + \frac{2}{3} \times \frac{4}{7}$$

$$= \frac{3}{21} + \frac{8}{21} = \frac{11}{21}$$

178. *(a)* Let p : Chandigarh is capital of Punjab.

and q : Chandigarh is in India.

$\sim p$: Chandigarh is not capital of Punjab.

$\sim q$: Chandigarh is not in India.

Contrapositive of the statement $p \to q$ is if$(\sim q)$, then $(\sim p)$.

If Chandigarh is not in India, then Chandigarh is not the capital of Punjab.

179. *(b)* The corner points of the feasible region are (0, 3), (1, 1) and (3, 0).

Also, given that the minimum value of the objective function $Z = px + qy$, $p, q > 0$ occurs at the points (3, 0) and (1, 1)

$\Rightarrow \quad p \cdot 3 + q \cdot 0 = p + q$

$\Rightarrow \quad 3p = p + q$

$\Rightarrow \quad q = 2p$

$\therefore \quad p = \dfrac{q}{2}$

180. *(a)* Given, $\quad \dfrac{1}{|x|-3} \le \dfrac{1}{2}$

$\Rightarrow \quad |x| - 3 \ge 2 \qquad \left[\dfrac{1}{a} < \dfrac{1}{b} \Rightarrow a > b\right]$

$\Rightarrow \quad |x| \ge 5 \qquad$ [adding 3 to both sides]

$\Rightarrow \quad x \le -5$ or $x \ge 5$

$[\because |x| \ge a \Rightarrow x \ge a$ or $x \le -a]$

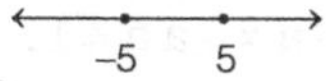

$\Rightarrow \quad x \in (-\infty, -5] \cup [5, \infty) \qquad \ldots$(i)

But $\quad |x| - 3 \ne 0$

Either $\quad |x| - 3 < 0$ or $|x| - 3 > 0$

$\Rightarrow \quad |x| < 3$ or $|x| > 3$

$\Rightarrow \quad -3 < x < 3$ or $x < -3$ or $x > 3 \qquad \ldots$ (ii)

$[\because |x| < a \Rightarrow -a < x < a$ and $|x| > a \Rightarrow x < -a$ or $x > a]$

On combining results of Eqs. (i) and (ii), we get

$x \in (-\infty, -5] \cup (-3, 3) \cup [5, \infty)$